THE
1000
BEST RECIPES

THE
1000
BEST RECIPES

• Triple-tested recipes • Step-by-step photography

bay books

Spicy chicken tarts

Contents

Lasagne

Beef bourguignon

California rolls

Waldorf salad

Garlic prawns

Chocolate fudge pecan pie

You will find the following cookery ratings on the recipes in this book:

A single pot symbol indicates a recipe that is simple and generally straightforward to make— perfect for beginners.

Two symbols indicate the need for just a little more care and a little more time.

Three symbols indicate special recipes that need more investment in time, care and patience— but the results are worth it.

From pantry to table

There's nothing more satisfying than planning your own menu, shopping for fresh ingredients and getting everyone involved in the preparation of the daily meal. Sometimes one course is enough, but often a nibble or light starter before the main meal, or a dessert to follow, is just the touch that everyone looks forward to.

From the selection of recipes in this book, you can plan your week so that you don't have to panic at the end of every busy day.

MENU PLANNING
When planning a menu, be it for a lavish dinner party, a casual Sunday afternoon barbecue or a work-night family meal, it is a good idea to

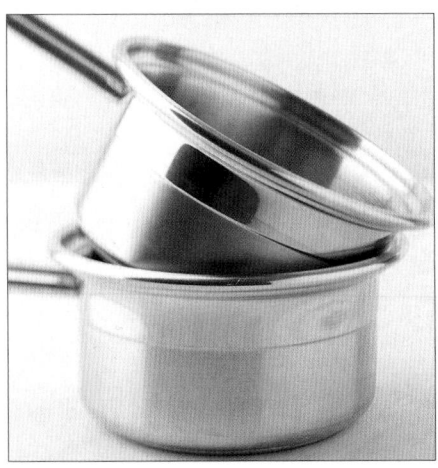

contrast flavours, textures and ingredients throughout the different courses. If you are serving a dessert, make sure it complements the rest of the meal. If the preceding courses are rich and heavy, serve a lighter, more refreshing dessert.

PREPARING AHEAD
Organisation and timing are important. Always read the recipe thoroughly beforehand to identify any steps that can be done in advance. Even spectacular dishes can be prepared in advance, with some components being made the day before. In summer, chilled desserts are ideal options. In the colder months, serve warm desserts that can be made in advance and baked or steamed while the main course is served.

KITCHEN EQUIPMENT
The amount of equipment you need depends on how much and what type of cooking you intend to do. Good-quality equipment lasts a long time and makes the tasks in the kitchen easier, so buy a few pieces at a time as you require them.

PANTRY
Although it is best to shop regularly for meat, seafood and seasonal vegetables, there are many products you will want to have on hand to provide the backbone of your daily cooking. These non-perishable products are common to many recipes or make versatile accompaniments.

PURCHASE & STORAGE TIPS FOR PANTRY GOODS
- Always check the use-by date of products. Try to have a regular clean-out so you know which basic staples need to be restocked.
- Store dry ingredient staples such as baking powder, breadcrumbs, cocoa powder, cornflour, couscous, flour, dried beans, dried fruits, dried herbs and spices, lentils, noodles, nuts, pasta, rice and sugar in airtight containers as weevils can be a problem if you leave them in opened packets.
- Unopened canned products such as tomatoes and beans will last for months provided the cans are not rusty or damaged.
- Most bottles of sauces and condiments should be stored in the refrigerator once they have been opened: check the label.
- Pastes such as tomato and curry can be frozen in ice-cube trays. This allows you to keep them for a longer time and in convenient small portions.
- It is best to buy whole spices and grind them yourself, as needed— they stay fresher than the jars.
- Make sure bottles of oil are kept out of direct light, as they can become rancid. If you keep them in the fridge the oil may thicken and appear cloudy—it will return to normal once it has returned to room temperature.

- Honey, mustards, soy sauce and vinegars are all good to have on hand.

STARTERS
These should complement the rest of the meal and be planned keeping in mind the type of main course being served. Soups are a perfect start to a meal, although the more substantial soups are sufficient for a main course, and are a versatile way of using the freshest ingredients of every category of food. The basis of a good soup is a good-quality stock and the best way to achieve that is to make your own.

STOCKS

A soup or casserole with true depth of flavour has as its base a good-quality stock. The best way to ensure this is to make your own. Stocks take a while to cook but can be quickly prepared and then left to simmer. Before using, all stocks must be skimmed of fat. To remove the fat, the stock can be strained, cooled and refrigerated to allow the fat to congeal on the top. The solidified fat can then easily be removed before the stock is used. If you wish to use the stock immediately, strain the stock, then while it is still hot pass a double thickness of paper towels through it to absorb any fat. To prevent your stocks from becoming cloudy they should not be boiled or stirred during cooking.

MAKING STOCK

Stock should be cooked at simmering point rather than a full boil in order to extract maximum flavour and fragrance from the ingredients and prevent them disintegrating and forming unnecessary scum. All the stocks below will keep in the fridge for 2 days and can be frozen.

CHICKEN STOCK

Place 2 kg (4 lb) chicken bones or a whole boiling chicken in a large stockpot with 2 chopped carrots, 1 chopped leek, 1 chopped onion, 1 chopped celery stick, 1 bay leaf, a few parsley stalks (the leaves make it cloudy), a sprig of thyme and 6 litres of cold water. Bring to the boil, skim off any scum, then reduce the heat and simmer for 2 hours, skimming as necessary. Strain and refrigerate overnight. Makes about 3.5 litres.

Strain the stock, then remove any fat by dragging a sheet of paper towel over the stock's surface.

BEEF OR VEAL STOCK

Preheat the oven to hot 220°C (425°F/Gas 7). Place 2 kg (4 lb) of cut beef bones on an oven tray and roast for 20 minutes. Add 1 quartered onion, 1 chopped carrot, 1 chopped leek and 1 chopped celery stick and roast for another 20 minutes. Transfer the bones and vegetables to a large saucepan or stockpot, discarding any fat left on the roasting tray. Add 2 tablespoons tomato paste, a few parsley stalks, 1 bay leaf and 6 litres of cold water. Bring to the boil, skimming any scum from the surface. Reduce the heat and simmer gently for 3–4 hours, skimming regularly. Strain and refrigerate. Makes about 3 litres.

VEGETABLE STOCK

Chop 1 onion, 4 carrots, 2 parsnips, 4 celery sticks and 2 leeks. Heat 1 tablespoon oil in a heavy-based saucepan or stockpot, add the vegetables and toss to coat in the oil. Cover and cook over medium heat for 5 minutes, without browning. Add 3 litres of water and bring to the boil. Skim the surface, then add 2 bay leaves, 4 unpeeled garlic cloves and a few parsley stalks. Reduce the heat to low and simmer for 1 hour. Strain and refrigerate. Makes 2.5 litres.

FISH STOCK

Place 2 kg (4 lb) chopped and washed white fish bones (such as snapper, cod or whiting), including the heads and tails, into a large heavy-based saucepan. Add 1 diced celery stick, 1 diced onion, 1 diced unpeeled carrot, 1 diced leek and 2 litres of water, and slowly bring to the boil. When boiling, skim the surface then add a sprig of fresh thyme and a bouquet garni. Reduce the heat and simmer gently for 20 minutes, frequently skimming the surface. Fish stock does not improve on additional cooking, in fact this can ruin it by making it bitter and cloudy. Ladle the stock in batches into a sieve lined with damp muslin sitting over a large bowl. To keep the stock clear don't press the solids through the sieve, simply leave the liquid to drain through undisturbed. Cool, then store in the fridge until needed. Makes about 1.5 litres.

FREEZING STOCK

Stock freezes well and will keep for 1–3 months. Freeze it in convenient, measurable portions. To freeze in 1-cup portions, for example, place a plastic bag in a measuring cup and fill with cooled stock. Extract the air from the bag and tightly seal. Once frozen, remove the bag from the cup and label and date it. Another idea is to reduce stock to a concentrated glace, then fill ice-cube trays, freeze them, then store the cubes in a freezer bag and use a few at a time to boost the flavour of sauces. It is important not to season stocks and soups too early, as long cooking or storage concentrates the flavours. Peppercorns added too early can also make a stock cloudy and bitter. It is better to leave seasoning until you are nearly ready to serve.

Pour concentrated stock into ice-cube trays to freeze in convenient portions.

PASTA AND RICE

Pasta and rice feature as the two key staples in the cuisines in much of the Asian world and many Mediterranean countries. They are an increasingly popular substitute as the carbohydrate component of meals in kitchens elsewhere across the world.

TYPES OF PASTA

The choice of pasta shapes, sizes and sauces is almost endless. Now it is possible to choose not only what type of pasta you wish to serve, but also whether to use a dried, fresh or filled pasta to best suit your sauce. A quick, easy and economical meal option, pasta can be served either as a first course as it is in Italy, or as a meal in its own right, accompanied by a simple salad and fresh bread.

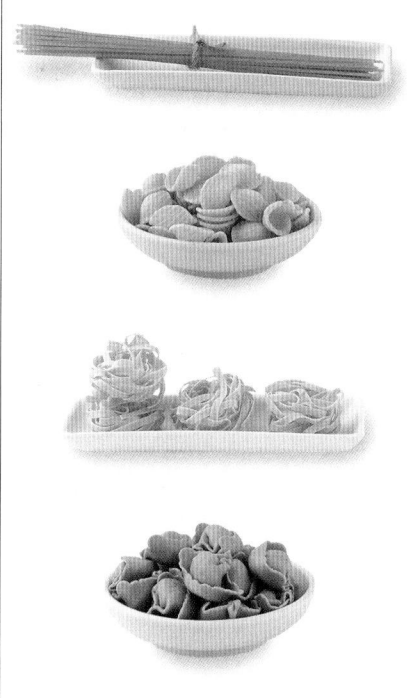

Timing can make all the difference between a good pasta meal and a great one. Having the sauce cooked by the time the pasta is ready is the key. While this is easier when serving slow-cooked dishes such as spaghetti bolognaise, quickly made pasta sauces are best prepared while the pasta cooks. The easiest and cheapest of sauces is one of southern Italy's

most common — a simple bowl of pasta aglio e olio is one of the quickest, most economical yet satisfying meals imaginable. Just-cooked pasta is coated immediately with a dressing of crushed garlic, extra virgin olive oil and plenty of finely chopped fresh flat-leaf parsley.

COOKING PASTA

As a general rule, cook 500 g (1 lb) pasta in 4 litres of boiling water. Use a large saucepan to allow room for expansion and to prevent sticking. Even if you need to cook large amounts of pasta, don't cook more than 1 kg (2 lb) in the same saucepan at one time. Most kitchens are unlikely to have a pan large enough to cope with more than 1 kg (2 lb). Always bring the water to the boil before adding the pasta. Unsalted water will come to the boil faster than salted, so if you wish to add salt do it once the water is boiling. Cooking times vary depending on the type of pasta. Fresh pasta only takes a few minutes to cook but dried pasta can take anything from 8 to 20 minutes, depending on the shape, quantity and brand. It's best to follow the manufacturer's instructions.

IS IT COOKED?

When you think the pasta is ready, the best test is to taste it. It should be just tender, not at all raw or soft and gluggy. This is referred to as al dente, which literally means 'to the tooth' in Italian.

Cooked pasta shouldn't be over-drained as it needs to be a little wet for

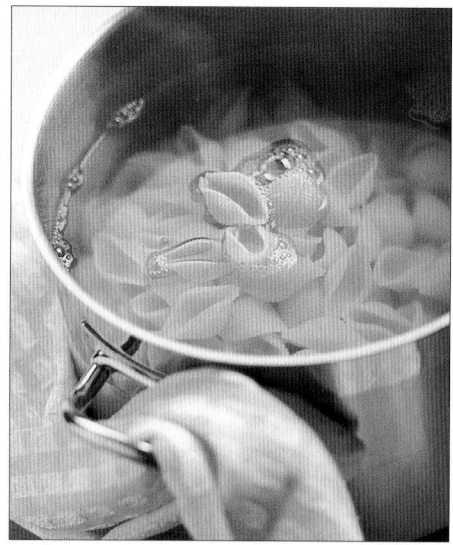

the sauce to coat it well. If you have to leave cooked pasta in the colander even for a few minutes, a little olive oil or butter tossed through hot pasta will prevent it sticking together.

MATCHING PASTA SHAPES AND SAUCES

There is no hard and fast rule as to which pasta shape to have with what sauce but traditionally a chunky pasta goes with a chunky sauce. Thin pastas are best with thin sauces. Smooth, slender spaghetti will not hold a chunky sauce but will suit a sauce of olive oil or a fresh tomato sauce as this allows the strands to stay slippery and separate. Fresh pasta is not necessarily better than dried as they each suit different sauces. If substituting one pasta for another, choose a pasta of a similar shape and size to avoid having too much or not enough sauce.

RICE DISHES

Rice is a cereal grain with a high starch content. It is eaten not only as an accompaniment to other food, such as in a Chinese meal, but also as the main ingredient of many meals, including risotto, paella and the numerous versions of pilafs made in India, Pakistan and Middle Eastern countries like Iran and Turkey. Rice varies in cooking time, so refer to the instructions on the packet.

TYPES OF RICE

Rice is divided into three categories: long-grain, medium-grain and short-grain. Popular long-grain varieties are: basmati, patna (an Indian rice similar to basmati but not as fragrant) and jasmine, a fragrant rice. Long-grain rice is available as brown rice, which is unpolished and has a nutty flavour, or white, which is without husks, bran and germ. Short- and medium-grain rice grains are plumper and are less sticky when cooked. Medium-grain rice is commonly used in Chinese cuisine as the grains cling together, making them easy to eat with chopsticks. Short-grain rice varieties vary from paella rice such as Spanish Calasparra, bahia and bomba rice and Italian arborio or carnaroli for making risotto to sushi rice for making sushi. Short-grain rice is traditionally eaten in Western countries in desserts such as rice pudding. Other varieties are glutinous rice, which comes in black or white, and wild rice.

It is important to use the right type of rice for the style of dish you cook. Use arborio, carnaroli or vialone nano for risotto, as they all have a high starch content which is released as the liquid is gradually added during the cooking process. Some of the liquid evaporates and some is absorbed by the rice. The released starch gives risotto its definitive creamy texture, yet the centre of the grain remains firm to the bite. Long-grain rice such as basmati is used for rice pilafs because of its ability for the grains to stay distinctly separate when cooked. Medium- to short-grain varieties are very popular in Chinese and Japanese cuisines as they absorb water and become plump while at the same time retaining some bite and a fluffy, moist consistency. Southeast Asian cuisines such as those in Thailand prefer to use longer grain rice such as the fragrant jasmine, whose grains remain separate.

COOKING RICE

Rice can be cooked in many ways, including in a rice cooker or in the microwave. However, it is more commonly cooked by the rapid boil method or the absorption method.

Whether you need to rinse rice before cooking depends on the type of rice and the dish being prepared. Rinsing removes any powdered starch slinging to the grains. Most rices these days don't need washing as they have been carefully processed. Some short-grain rices are rinsed before cooking to separate the grains. Rice in sacks may have stones and dust that need removal.

White rice just about trebles in size when cooked, so 1 cup of raw white rice makes 3 cups of cooked rice. Brown rice expands a little less; 1 cup of raw rice makes 2 cups of cooked. Choose the cooking method that suits you best.

ABSORPTION METHOD

Put the rice in a saucepan and rest the tip of your forefinger lightly on the surface of the rice, adding water until it comes up to the first finger joint. Bring to the boil for 1 minute, then cover with a tight-fitting lid, reduce the heat to as low as possible and cook for 10 minutes (or according to packet instructions), or until all the water is absorbed into the rice and dimples form on the surface. Fluff the rice gently with a fork before serving.

FAST-BOILING METHOD

Bring a large saucepan of water to a fast boil. Pour in the rice and cook for 12 minutes (or according to packet instructions), stirring occasionally so it doesn't stick to the base of the pan (brown rice takes about 40 minutes). Drain well.

For the absorption method, rest your fingertip on the rice and add water up to the first finger joint.

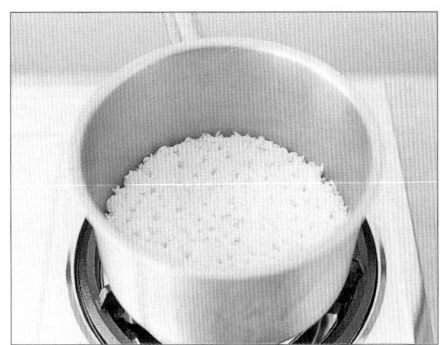

When the rice is cooked, it will have absorbed all the water, and steam holes will appear on top.

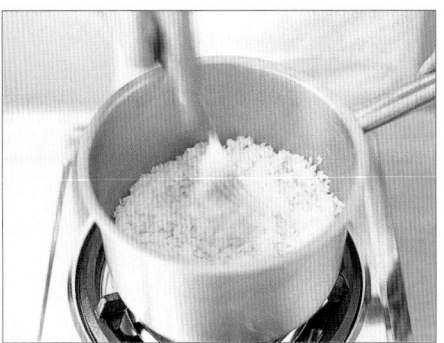

When the rice is cooked, fluff up the grains with a fork just before serving.

CHICKEN

Chicken is the most popular poultry and is a wonderfully versatile base ingredient that suits many different cooking styles.

CUTS OF CHICKEN

Chicken cuts include: double or single breast on the bone, with skin or without; breast fillets; tenderloins (the part just behind the breast); marylands (the whole thigh and leg); thigh cutlets; thigh fillets; wings; and drumsticks.

COOKING CHICKEN

Whichever cut of poultry you are cooking, make sure it is cooked thoroughly, especially when it is on the bone, as undercooked poultry harbours harmful bacteria that can lead to food poisoning.

Flavours that complement chicken include lime, saffron, leek, wine, olive oil, olives, fennel, mushrooms, mustard and cream, and herbs and spices, such as rosemary, parsley, thyme, chilli, coriander and ginger.

WHEN IS IT COOKED?

As it is so important to make sure chicken is cooked thoroughly, check after the specified cooking time.

To test whether roasted poultry is cooked, insert a skewer into the thickest part of the bird (the thigh). If the chicken is cooked, the juices will run clear (not pink). You can also test by twisting or jiggling one of the legs. If it moves easily in its socket, the chicken is cooked. Pan-fried, grilled or barbecued chicken is cooked when the meat is tender enough to fall easily off the bone when tested with a fork. Test fillets for doneness by cutting into the thickest part: if the juices run clear and the flesh is not pink, it's cooked.

MEAT

Meat is a perfect ingredient to incorporate into the diet as there are so many varieties that meals will never seem boring. There are numerous cuts of beef, veal, lamb and pork, each with their own flavour and cooking qualities. It is important to select the best and most appropriate meat for the recipe you intend to cook.

Resting roast meats after cooking and before carving and serving is important as it enhances their tenderness. This allows the juices to flow back from the exterior into the centre of the joint and baste the meat internally. To rest a roast, remove it from the pan, place on a large warmed plate with a lip to catch any juices and cover with foil. Before carving, leave in a warm place for at least 10 minutes. An upturned smaller plate can be placed on the plate so the roast can rest at an angle, as this is extremely effective in conserving the juices.

SEAFOOD

Seafood is divided into three main categories: fish, crustaceans and molluscs. To get the very best out of seafood it is important to match the type with the best cooking method. Seafood should be absolutely fresh when it is bought. It should not be sitting in a pool of water, but on ice which should be changed regularly to prevent thawing. Fresh fish has virtually no smell. When you buy it, it should never smell overly fishy or like ammonia — if it does it is past its best and should be avoided.

COOKING SEAFOOD

Never overcook seafood or it will be dry, tough and rubbery. Remove it from the heat as soon as it is just done — the internal heat will finish the cooking process. Certain types of seafood, such as salmon, trout and oysters, can be eaten raw. If you are serving seafood raw, always make sure it is very fresh and clean, otherwise it may be spoiled by harmful bacteria. Some seafood, such as the more meaty oily fish such as tuna and swordfish, can also be eaten just rare to medium rare, while foods such as delicate scallops only need to be seared on both sides to lightly cook through.

VEGETARIAN

It is now recognised that in many Western countries the diet is slightly imbalanced in that flesh food predominates. Therefore, more people are experimenting with vegetarian food. Whether they want to be strict vegetarians, or just add more vegetarian foods to their day, the recipes in this book will be a good introduction to experimentation with foods and flavours that form part of that cuisine. The recipes include creative ways with grains and pulses and with vegetables and tofu.

VEGETABLES

Fresh vegetables, either cooked or made into delicious salads, can be combined in a limitless variety of ways, all of which are a delicious addition to the table.

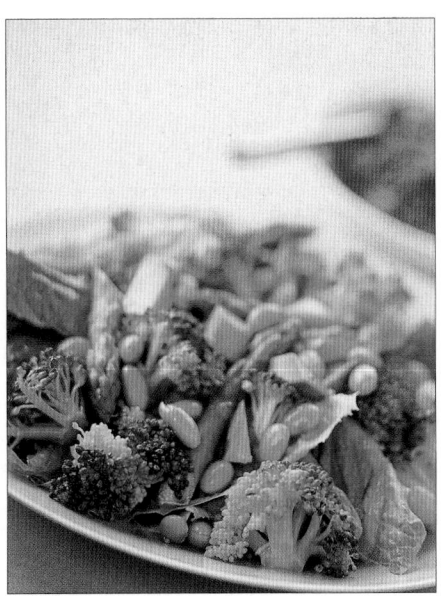

CHOOSING AND STORING

The key to enjoying vegetables is to buy them fresh, when they are in season, and to use them as soon as possible after purchasing, for maximum flavour. Not only is it economical to take advantage of seasonal vegetables, this is the time when they are also abundant and at their best. Buy as small amount of vegetables as is practical for you to buy at one time as most are best not kept for longer than up to a week. Root vegetables and onions will last longer. Fresh leafy green vegetables such as lettuce, rocket, spinach and Asian greens should all be used within 2–3 days of purchase. All vegetables need to be carefully cleaned of pesticides and grit before using.

Most fresh vegetables should be stored in the vegetable drawers of your refrigerator. Wash vegetables immediately before using, not before storing in the refrigerator, as excess moisture will make them rot more quickly. If you wish to wash vegetables before storing, it is recommended that you either pat them dry with paper towels after rinsing, or for leafy vegetables, eliminate excess moisture with a salad spinner. While freezing helps you take advantage of a seasonal glut of produce, most fresh vegetables are not suited to freezing raw. Many such as asparagus, beans, broccoli, carrots, cauliflower, corn, shelled peas and skinned tomatoes can be blanched and frozen for up to 3 months. Cooked vegetables such as purées, soups, sauces and stocks can be frozen, after cooling quickly, for up to 2 months. To defrost, place in the refrigerator. Reheat gently before serving.

DESSERTS

Great meals are remembered for their tempting and luscious desserts. They are a special treat that few can resist. Dessert is the one part of a meal that is purely about pleasure and indulgence rather than sustenance.

ACCOMPANIMENTS

For a change from the expected accompaniments of cream or ice cream, the following ideas can be used to add flair to even the simplest desserts:

Crème fraîche or French soured cream is delicious with fruit desserts.

Mascarpone is a rich, heavy cream cheese served in Italy with pastries, cakes and fruit.

Yoghurt makes an excellent foil for very sweet desserts, or sweeten thick Greek-style yoghurt with honey and serve simply with fresh fruits.

Sorbet or gelato makes a light and refreshing change to ice cream.

Crème anglaise is a thin pouring custard that is perfect served with baked desserts and puddings.

Fruit coulis (puréed fruit with sugar) should be light and not overly sweet, but with a pure taste of fruit. Try berry coulis with rich chocolate cake.

Hors d'oeuvres

CAPSICUM MUFFINS WITH TAPENADE AND MASCARPONE

Preparation time: 20 minutes
Total cooking time: 20 minutes
Makes 24

1 red capsicum
2 cups (250 g/8 oz) plain flour
3 teaspoons baking powder
¾ cup (75 g/2½ oz) grated Parmesan
½ cup (125 ml/4 fl oz) milk
2 eggs, lightly beaten
¼ cup (60 ml/2 fl oz) olive oil
1½ tablespoons olive oil, extra
24 fresh basil leaves
⅓ cup (75 g/2½ oz) mascarpone

TAPENADE
½ cup (80 g/2¾ oz) pitted
    Kalamata olives
1 clove garlic, chopped
2 anchovies (optional)
2 teaspoons drained capers
2 tablespoons olive oil
2 teaspoons lemon juice

1 Cut the capsicum into large flattish pieces. Cook, skin-side-up, under a hot grill until the skin blackens and blisters. Place in a plastic bag and allow to cool. Peel off the skin and finely chop the flesh.
2 Preheat the oven to moderate 180°C (350°F/Gas 4). Lightly grease 24 non-stick mini muffin holes. Sift the flour and baking powder into a bowl, then add the capsicum and Parmesan. Season then make a well in the centre.
3 Pour the combined milk, eggs and oil into the well. Fold gently with a metal spoon until just combined. Do not overmix—the batter should be lumpy. Overmixing will produce tough muffins.
4 Fill each muffin hole with mixture. Bake for 15–20 minutes, or until a skewer comes out clean. Cool slightly. Loosen each muffin with a flat-bladed knife then cool on a wire rack.
5 Meanwhile, to make the tapenade, place the olives, garlic, anchovies and capers in a food processor. Blend until finely chopped, then, while the motor is running, add the oil and lemon juice to form a paste. Season with pepper.
6 Heat the extra oil in a saucepan and fry the basil leaves until they are just crisp. Drain on paper towels.
7 While still warm, cut the tops off the muffins. Spread about ½ teaspoon of mascarpone on each muffin, then add the same amount of tapenade. Put a basil leaf on the top before replacing the muffin 'lids'.

NUTRITION PER MUFFIN
Protein 3.5 g; Fat 7 g; Carbohydrate 10 g;
Dietary Fibre 0.5 g; Cholesterol 23 mg;
485 kJ (115 Cal)

Grill the capsicums until the skin blackens and blisters.

Lightly fold the batter with a metal spoon until just combined.

THAI CHICKEN BALLS

Preparation time: 20 minutes
Total cooking time: 40 minutes
Serves 6

1 kg (2 lb) chicken mince
1 cup (80 g/2¾ oz) fresh breadcrumbs
4 spring onions, sliced
1 tablespoon ground coriander
1 cup (50 g/1¾ oz) chopped coriander
¼ cup (60 ml/2 fl oz) sweet chilli sauce
1–2 tablespoons lemon juice
oil, for frying

1 Preheat the oven to moderately hot 200°C (400°F/Gas 6). Mix the mince and breadcrumbs in a large bowl.
2 Add the spring onion, ground and fresh coriander, chilli sauce and lemon juice, and mix well. Using damp hands, form the mixture into evenly shaped balls that are either small enough to eat with your fingers or large enough to use as burgers.
3 Heat the oil in a deep frying pan, and shallow-fry the chicken balls in batches over high heat until browned all over. Place the chicken balls on a baking tray and bake until cooked

through. (The small chicken balls will take 5 minutes to cook and the larger ones will take 10–15 minutes.) This mixture also makes a delicious filling for sausage rolls.

NUTRITION PER SERVE
Protein 40 g; Fat 8 g; Carbohydrate 10 g;
Dietary Fibre 1 g; Cholesterol 85 mg;
1160 kJ (275 cal)

Mix the spring onion, coriander, chilli sauce and lemon juice into the chicken mixture.

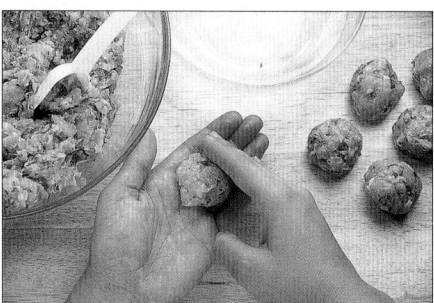
With damp hands, form the mixture into evenly shaped balls.

Fry the chicken balls in oil until they are browned on both sides.

PRAWN SPRING ROLLS

Preparation time: 50 minutes
Total cooking time: 4 minutes
Makes about 18 spring rolls

50 g (1¾ oz) rice vermicelli
2 spring onions
1 Lebanese cucumber, peeled
1 carrot
24 cooked prawns, peeled and
    chopped
2 tablespoons chopped roasted
    unsalted peanuts
2 Chinese mushrooms, soaked,
    chopped finely
½ lettuce, finely shredded
½ cup (25 g/¾ oz) chopped
    fresh mint
50 g (1¾ oz) bean sprouts
375 g (12 oz) rice paper rounds,
    21 cm (8½ inch) diameter

DIPPING SAUCE
2 tablespoons caster sugar
2 tablespoons fish sauce
2 tablespoons lime juice
1 tablespoon rice vinegar or white
    vinegar
1 spring onion, finely chopped
1 small red chilli, seeded and finely
    chopped
1 clove garlic, crushed

1 Put the vermicelli in a bowl, cover with boiling water and leave for 1–2 minutes, or until soft. Rinse under cold water, drain, chop roughly with scissors and put in a bowl.
2 Very finely shred the spring onions, cucumber and carrot into thin 5 cm (2 inch) strips. Blanch the carrot in boiling water for 1 minute, drain and cool. Add the carrot, spring onion and cucumber to the cooled vermicelli with the prawns, peanuts, mushrooms, lettuce, mint and bean sprouts. Toss, using your hands.
3 For each spring roll, soften a rice paper in a bowl of warm water for 10–20 seconds. Lay it on a tea towel and place 3 tablespoons of filling in the centre. Fold in the sides and roll up into a parcel. Seal the edges by brushing with a little water. Place on a serving platter and cover with a damp cloth while you make the rest.

4 To make the dipping sauce, combine the sugar and 2 tablespoons warm water in a small bowl and stir until the sugar dissolves. Add the remaining ingredients and stir well. Serve with the spring rolls.

NUTRITION PER SPRING ROLL
Protein 6 g; Fat 1 g; Carbohydrate 5 g;
Dietary Fibre 1 g; Cholesterol 35 mg;
246 kJ (60 cal)

The spring onion, cucumber and carrot should be cut into short, fine strips.

Soften one sheet of rice paper at a time in a bowl of warm water.

Put the filling in the centre of the rice paper, then roll and fold into a parcel.

CHICKEN CURRY PUFFS

Preparation time: 1 hour 30 minutes
Total cooking time: 35–45 minutes
Makes about 36

2 tablespoons oil
400 g (13 oz) chicken mince
2 cloves garlic, crushed
1 onion, finely chopped
3 coriander roots, finely chopped
2 teaspoons ground turmeric
1½ teaspoons ground cumin
3 teaspoons ground coriander
1 small potato, peeled and
    very finely diced
1 tablespoon chopped fresh coriander
    leaves and stems
3 teaspoons soft brown sugar
½ teaspoon ground black pepper
2 small red chillies, finely chopped
¼ cup (60 ml/2 fl oz) fish sauce
1 tablespoon lime juice
oil, extra, for deep-frying
chilli sauce or satay sauce, to serve

PASTRY
1½ cups (185 g/6 oz) plain flour
½ cup (90 g/3 oz) rice flour
½ teaspoon salt
60 g (2 oz) butter
½ cup (125 ml/4 fl oz) coconut milk

1 Heat the oil in a medium wok or pan. Add the mince and cook over high heat for 3 minutes, or until starting to brown. Break up any lumps of mince as it cooks. Add the crushed garlic, onion, coriander roots, ground turmeric, cumin and coriander, and the potato to the wok. Stir-fry over medium heat for about 5 minutes, or until the mince and potato are tender.

2 Add the fresh coriander, sugar, pepper, chilli, fish sauce and lime juice. Stir until well combined and most of the liquid has evaporated, then remove from the heat and allow to cool.

3 To make the pastry, sift the flours and salt into a medium bowl and rub in the butter until the mixture is fine and crumbly. Make a well in the centre, add the coconut milk and mix with a knife until the mixture forms a dough. Gently knead until the dough is smooth. Cover with plastic wrap and refrigerate for 30 minutes.

4 Divide the dough in half. Roll out one half on a lightly floured surface until it is about 3 mm (⅛ inch) thick and then cut into circles with an 8 cm (3 inch) cutter.

5 Place 2 teaspoons of the filling in the centre of each circle, brush the edges of the pastry lightly with water and fold over to enclose the filling; press the edges to seal. Repeat with the remaining half of the dough, re-rolling the scraps until the dough and the filling are all used.

6 Heat the oil in a large wok or pan. Do not put too much oil in the wok—it should be only half full. Deep-fry the puffs, in batches, until puffed and browned. Remove from oil with a wire mesh drainer, slotted spoon or tongs; drain on paper towels. Serve hot with chilli sauce or satay sauce.

NUTRITION PER SERVE (6)
Protein 3.5 g; Fat 4 g; Carbohydrate 7 g;
Dietary Fibre 0.5 g; Cholesterol 10 mg;
335 kJ (80 cal)

HINT: If time is short, use about eight sheets of ready-rolled puff pastry instead of making the pastry.

Use a spoon or fork to break up any lumps of mince as it cooks.

Stir the ingredients in the wok until well combined and the liquid has evaporated.

Add the coconut milk and mix with a knife until the mixture forms a dough.

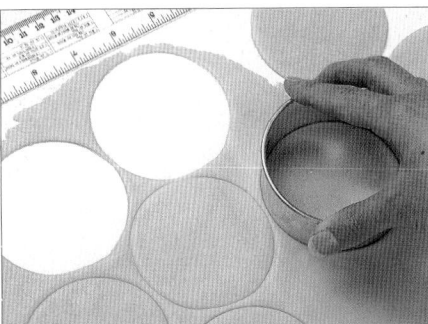

Cut the rolled out dough into circles, using an 8 cm (3 inch) cutter.

Fold the pastry over to enclose the filling and then press the edges to seal.

Add the curry puffs to the hot oil, cooking only a few at a time.

17

SPINACH AND FETA TRIANGLES

Preparation time: 30 minutes
Total cooking time: 40 minutes
Makes 8

1 kg (2 lb) English spinach
¼ cup (60 ml/2 fl oz) olive oil
1 onion, chopped
10 spring onions, sliced
⅓ cup (20 g/¾ oz) chopped fresh
    parsley
1 tablespoon chopped fresh dill
large pinch of ground nutmeg
⅓ cup (35 g/1¼ oz) freshly grated
    Parmesan
150 g (5 oz) crumbled feta cheese
90 g (3 oz) ricotta cheese
4 eggs, lightly beaten
40 g (1¼ oz) butter, melted
1 tablespoon olive oil, extra
12 sheets filo pastry

1 Trim any coarse stems from the spinach. Wash the leaves thoroughly, roughly chop and place in a large pan with just a little water clinging to the leaves. Cover and cook gently over low heat for 5 minutes, or until the leaves have wilted. Drain well and allow to cool slightly before squeezing tightly to remove the excess water.
2 Heat the oil in a heavy-based frying pan. Add the onion and cook over low heat for 10 minutes, or until tender and golden. Add the spring onion and cook for a further 3 minutes. Remove from the heat. Stir in the drained spinach, parsley, dill, nutmeg, Parmesan, feta, ricotta and egg. Season well.
3 Preheat the oven to moderate 180°C (350°F/Gas 4). Grease two baking trays. Combine the melted

butter with the extra oil. Work with three sheets of pastry at a time, keeping the rest covered with a damp tea towel. Brush each sheet with butter mixture and lay them on top of each other. Cut in half lengthways.
4 Spoon 4 tablespoons of the filling on an angle at the end of each strip. Fold the pastry over to enclose the filling and form a triangle. Continue folding the triangle over until your reach the end of the pastry. Put the triangles on the baking trays and brush with the remaining butter mixture. Bake for 20–25 minutes, or until the pastry is golden brown.

NUTRITION PER TRIANGLE
Protein 15 g; Fat 25 g; Carbohydrate 10 g;
Dietary Fibre 4.5 g; Cholesterol 125 mg;
1325 kJ (315 cal)

NOTE: Feta is a salty Greek cheese that should be stored immersed in lightly salted water in the fridge. Rinse and pat dry before using.

VARIATION: If spinach isn't in season you can use silverbeet instead. Use the same quantity and trim the coarse white stems from the leaves.

Brush each sheet of filo pastry with the mixture of butter and oil.

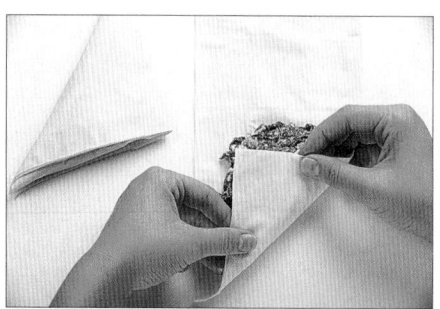

Spoon the filling onto the end of the pastry at an angle. Fold the pastry over it to make a triangle.

Continue folding the triangle parcel until you reach the end of the pastry sheet.

SWEET POTATO AND LENTIL PASTRY POUCHES

Preparation time: 45 minutes
Total cooking time: 55 minutes
Makes 32

2 tablespoons olive oil
1 large leek, finely chopped
2 cloves garlic, crushed
125 g (4 oz) button mushrooms, roughly chopped
2 teaspoons ground cumin
2 teaspoons ground coriander
½ cup (95 g/3 oz) brown or green lentils
½ cup (125 g/4 oz) red lentils
2 cups (500 ml/16 fl oz) vegetable stock
300 g (10 oz) sweet potato, diced
4 tablespoons finely chopped fresh coriander leaves
8 sheets ready-rolled puff pastry
1 egg, lightly beaten
½ leek, extra, cut into thin strips
200 g (6½ oz) plain yoghurt
2 tablespoons grated Lebanese cucumber
½ teaspoon soft brown sugar

1 Preheat the oven to moderately hot 200°C (400°F/Gas 6). Heat the oil in a saucepan over medium heat and cook the leek for 2–3 minutes, or until soft. Add the garlic, mushrooms, cumin and ground coriander and cook for 1 minute, or until fragrant.
2 Add the combined lentils and stock and bring to the boil. Reduce the heat and simmer for 20–25 minutes, or until the lentils are cooked through, stirring occasionally. Add the sweet potato in the last 5 minutes.
3 Transfer to a bowl and stir in the coriander. Season to taste. Cool.

4 Cut the pastry sheets into four even squares. Place 1½ tablespoons of filling into the centre of each square and bring the edges together to form a pouch. Pinch together, then tie each pouch with string. Lightly brush with egg and place on lined baking trays. Bake for 20–25 minutes, or until the pastry is puffed and golden.
5 Soak the leek strips in boiling water

for 30 seconds. Remove the string and re-tie with a piece of blanched leek. Put the yoghurt, cucumber and sugar in a bowl and mix together well. Serve with the pastry pouches.

NUTRITION PER PASTRY POUCH
Protein 5 g; Fat 11 g; Carbohydrate 20 g;
Dietary Fibre 2 g; Cholesterol 17 mg;
835 kJ (200 cal)

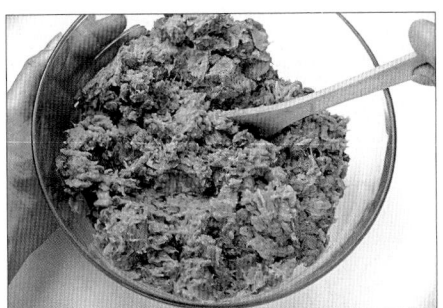

Stir the coriander leaves into the cooked lentils and sweet potato.

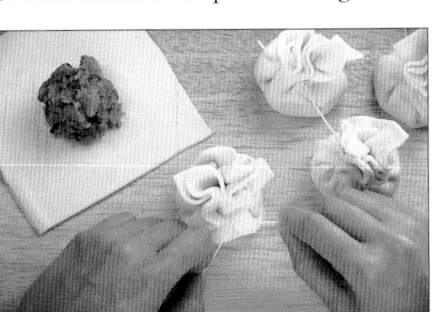

Put the filling in the centre of each square, form a pouch and tie with string.

Blanch the long strips of leek by soaking them for 30 seconds in boiling water.

VEGETABLE SAMOSAS

Preparation time: 35 minutes +
  20 minutes refrigeration
Total cooking time: 30 minutes
Makes 32

4 cups (500 g/1 lb) plain flour
2 tablespoons oil

VEGETABLE FILLING
600 g (1¼ lb) waxy potatoes
185 g (6 oz) cauliflower florets,
  chopped
2 tablespoons vegetable oil
1 onion, chopped
2 cloves garlic, finely chopped
2 tablespoons grated fresh ginger
2 tablespoons mild curry powder
⅔ cup (100 g/3½ oz) frozen peas
2 tablespoons lemon juice
oil, for deep-frying

1 In a food processor, process the flour and 1 teaspoon of salt for 5 seconds. Add the combined oil and 1 cup (250 ml/8 fl oz) of warm water. Process in short bursts until the mixture just comes together. Turn out onto a floured surface and gather into a ball. Cover with plastic wrap and refrigerate for 20 minutes.
2 To make the vegetable filling, chop the potatoes into quarters and cook until tender, then cool and finely dice. Boil or steam the cauliflower until tender, cool and finely dice. Heat the oil in a large frying pan and cook the onion over medium heat for 5 minutes, or until soft. Add the garlic, ginger and curry powder and cook for 2 minutes. Add the potato, cauliflower, peas and lemon juice and mix well. Remove from the heat and cool.

3 Divide the dough into 16 portions. On a lightly floured surface, roll each portion into a 15 cm (6 inch) round, cut the rounds in half and put a tablespoon of the mixture in the middle of each semi-circle. Brush the edge with a little water and fold the pastry over the mixture, pressing the edges to seal.
4 Heat a deep-fat fryer, or fill a deep pan one third full of oil and heat until a cube of bread browns in 15 seconds. Deep-fry the samosas in batches for 1 minute, or until golden. Drain on paper towels and serve hot with mango chutney, sweet chilli sauce or natural yoghurt.

NUTRITION PER SAMOSA
Protein 2.5 g; Fat 3.5 g; Carbohydrate 15 g;
Dietary Fibre 1.5 g; Cholesterol 0 mg;
410 kJ (95 cal)

Process the flour, salt, oil and water until the mixture just comes together.

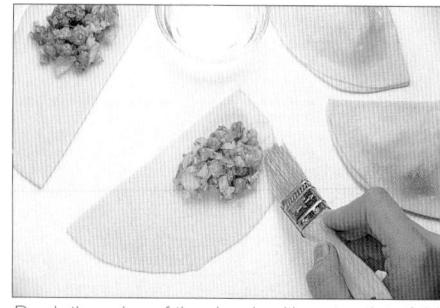

Add the potato, cauliflower, peas and lemon juice to the onion mixture.

Brush the edge of the dough with water, then fold the filling over the top and seal.

BLOODY MARY OYSTER SHOTS

**Preparation time: 10 minutes +
  30 minutes refrigeration**
Total cooking time: Nil
Serves 12

⅓ cup (80 ml/2¾ fl oz) vodka
½ cup (125 ml/4 fl oz) tomato juice
1 tablespoon lemon juice
dash of Worcestershire sauce
2 drops of Tabasco
pinch of celery salt
12 oysters
1 cucumber, peeled, seeded and
  finely julienned

1 Combine the vodka, tomato juice, lemon juice, Worcestershire sauce, Tabasco and celery salt, then refrigerate for 30 minutes, or until chilled. Just before serving, fill each shot glass about two-thirds full. Drop an oyster in each glass, then top with a teaspoon of cucumber. Crack some pepper over each shot glass, then serve.

NUTRITION PER SERVE
Protein 2 g; Fat 0.5 g; Carbohydrate 1 g; Dietary Fibre 0 g; Cholesterol 12 mg; 120 kJ (30 Cal)

NOTE: It is better to use oysters fresh from the shell rather than from a jar as they have a much better, fresher taste.

THINK AHEAD: The tomato mixture can be made a day ahead of time and kept in the fridge. Stir before serving.

VARIATION: If you think your guests are game enough for some fire in their evening, make chilled sake shots—fill each glass two-thirds full of sake, add an oyster, then garnish with cucumber.

Finely shred the peeled and seeded cucumber with a sharp knife.

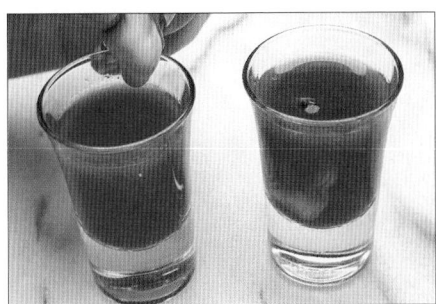
Fill each glass about two-thirds full, then drop in an oyster.

VEGETABLE CHIPS

Preparation time: 20 minutes
Total cooking time: 15 minutes
Serves 6–8

250 g (8 oz) orange sweet potato
250 g (8 oz) beetroot, peeled
250 g (8 oz) potato
oil, for deep-frying

1 Preheat the oven to moderate 180°C (350°F/Gas 4). Run a sharp vegetable peeler along the length of the sweet potato to create ribbons. Cut the beetroot into paper-thin slices with a sharp vegetable peeler or knife. Cut the potato into thin slices, using a mandolin slicer or knife with a crinkle-cut blade (see NOTE).
2 Fill a deep heavy-based saucepan one third full of oil and heat until a cube of bread dropped into the oil browns in 10 seconds. Cook the vegetables in batches for about 30 seconds, or until golden and crispy. You may need to turn them with tongs or a long-handled metal spoon. Drain on paper towels and season with salt.

3 Place all the vegetable chips on a baking tray and keep warm in the oven while cooking the remaining vegetables. Serve with drinks.

NUTRITION PER SERVE (8)
Protein 2 g; Fat 5 g; Carbohydrate 12 g;
Dietary Fibre 2 g; Cholesterol 0 mg;
413 kJ (99 cal)

NOTE: If you don't have a mandolin or crinkle-cut knife at home, simply use a sharp knife to cut fine slices. The cooking time for the chips will remain the same.

Use a sharp vegetable peeler to peel thin strips of sweet potato.

If you have a mandolin, use it for slicing the potatoes very finely.

Deep-fry the vegetables in batches until they are golden and crispy.

BLUE CHEESE AND PORT PATE

Preparation time: 10 minutes +
refrigeration
Total cooking time: Nil
Serves 8

350 g (11 oz) cream cheese, at room
　　temperature
60 g (2 oz) unsalted butter, softened
⅓ cup (80 ml/2¾ fl oz) port
300 g (10 oz) blue cheese, at room
　　temperature, mashed
1 tablespoon snipped fresh chives
45 g (1½ oz) walnut halves

1 Using electric beaters, beat the
cream cheese and butter until smooth,
then stir in the port. Add the blue
cheese and chives and stir until just
combined. Season to taste.
2 Spoon the mixture into a serving
bowl and smooth the surface. Cover
the paté with plastic wrap and
refrigerate until firm.
3 Arrange the walnuts over the top of
the paté, pressing down lightly. Serve
at room temperature with crusty
bread, crackers and celery sticks.

NUTRITION PER SERVE
Protein 12 g; Fat 37 g; Carbohydrate 2.5 g;
Dietary Fibre 0.5 g; Cholesterol 100 mg;
1650 kJ (395 cal)

Stir the blue cheese and chives into the cream
cheese and butter mixture.

Arrange the walnut halves over the surface,
pressing down lightly.

23

SALT AND PEPPER TOFU PUFFS

Preparation time: 15 minutes
Total cooking time: 10 minutes
Serves 4–6

2 x 190 g (6½ oz) packets fried tofu
   puffs
2 cups (250 g/8 oz) cornflour
2 tablespoons salt
1 tablespoon ground white pepper
2 teaspoons caster sugar
4 egg whites, lightly beaten
oil, for deep-frying (see NOTE)
½ cup (125 ml/4 fl oz) sweet chilli sauce
2 tablespoons lemon juice
lemon wedges, to serve

1 Cut the tofu puffs in half and pat
dry with paper towels.
2 Mix the cornflour, salt, pepper and
caster sugar in a large bowl.

3 Dip the tofu into the egg white in
batches, then toss in the cornflour
mixture, shaking off any excess.
4 Fill a deep heavy-based saucepan
or wok one-third full of oil and heat
until a cube of bread dropped into
the oil browns in 15 seconds. Cook
the tofu in batches for 1–2 minutes, or
until crisp. Drain well on paper
towels.
5 Place the sweet chilli sauce and
lemon juice in a bowl and mix

together well. Serve immediately with
the tofu puffs and lemon wedges.

NUTRITION PER SERVE (6)
Protein 55 g; Fat 10 g; Carbohydrate 44 g;
Dietary Fibre 1 g; Cholesterol 0 mg;
1135 kJ (270 cal)

NOTE: It is best to use a good-quality
peanut oil to deep-fry the tofu puffs—
the flavour will be slightly nutty.

Dip the tofu puffs in the egg white, then in the
cornflour, shaking off any excess.

Deep-fry the tofu in batches until crisp, then
remove with a slotted spoon.

PRAWN TOASTS

Preparation time: 20 minutes
Total cooking time: 15 minutes
Makes 36

DIPPING SAUCE
½ cup (125 ml/4 fl oz) tomato sauce
2 cloves garlic, crushed
2 small fresh red chillies, seeded
    and finely chopped
2 tablespoons hoisin sauce
2 teaspoons Worcestershire sauce

350 g (11 oz) raw medium prawns
1 clove garlic
75 g (2½ oz) canned water chestnuts,
    drained
1 tablespoon chopped fresh coriander
2 cm x 2 cm (¾ inch x ¾ inch) piece
    fresh ginger, roughly chopped
2 eggs, separated
¼ teaspoon white pepper
12 slices white bread, crusts removed
1 cup (155 g/5 oz) sesame seeds
oil, for deep-frying

1 To make the dipping sauce, combine all the ingredients in a small bowl.
2 Peel the prawns and gently pull out the dark vein from each prawn back, starting at the head end. Put the prawns in a food processor with the garlic, water chestnuts, coriander, ginger, egg whites, pepper and ¼ teaspoon salt, and process for 20–30 seconds, or until smooth.
3 Brush the top of each slice of bread with lightly beaten egg yolk, then spread evenly with the prawn mixture. Sprinkle generously with sesame seeds. Cut each slice of bread into three even strips.
4 Fill a large heavy-based saucepan or deep-fryer one-third full of oil and

heat to 180°C (350°F), or until a cube of bread dropped into the oil browns in 15 seconds. Deep-fry the toasts in small batches for 10–15 seconds, or until golden and crisp. Start with the prawn mixture facing down, then turn halfway through. Remove the toasts from the oil with tongs or a slotted

spoon and drain on crumpled paper towels. Serve with the dipping sauce.

NUTRITION PER PRAWN TOAST
Protein 3 g; Fat 6.5 g; Carbohydrate 5.5 g;
Dietary Fibre 1 g; Cholesterol 19 mg; 383 kJ
(92 Cal)

Pull the dark vein out of the prawns from the head end.

Use a food processor to blend the prawn mixture until it is smooth.

Brush the bread with egg yolk, then spread with the prawn mixture.

CALIFORNIA ROLLS

Preparation time: 35 minutes +
  15 minutes standing
Total cooking time: 15 minutes
Makes 30

500 g (1 lb) short-grain white rice
¼ cup (60 ml/2 fl oz) rice vinegar
1 tablespoon caster sugar
5 nori sheets
1 large Lebanese cucumber, cut
  lengthways into long batons
1 avocado, thinly sliced
1 tablespoon black sesame seeds,
  toasted
30 g (1 oz) pickled ginger slices
½ cup (125 g/4 oz) mayonnaise
3 teaspoons wasabi paste
2 teaspoons soy sauce

1 Wash the rice under cold running water, tossing, until the water runs clear. Put the rice and 3 cups (750 ml/24 fl oz) water in a saucepan. Bring to the boil over low heat and cook for 5 minutes, or until tunnels form in the rice. Remove from the heat, cover and leave for 15 minutes.
2 Place the vinegar, sugar and 1 teaspoon salt in a small saucepan and stir over low heat until the sugar and salt dissolve.
3 Transfer the rice to a non-metallic bowl and use a wooden spoon to separate the grains. Make a slight well in the centre, slowly stir in the vinegar dressing, then cool a little.
4 Lay a nori sheet, shiny-side-down, on a bamboo mat or flat surface and spread out one-fifth of the rice, leaving a narrow clear border at one end. Arrange one-fifth of the cucumber, avocado, sesame seeds and ginger lengthways over the rice, keeping away from the border. Spread on some of the combined mayonnaise, wasabi and soy sauce and roll to cover the filling. Continue rolling tightly to join the edge, then hold in place for a few seconds. Trim the ends and cut into slices. Serve with wasabi mayonnaise.

NUTRITION PER PIECE
Protein 1.5 g; Fat 3 g; Carbohydrate 15 g;
Dietary Fibre 1 g; Cholesterol 1.5 mg;
380 kJ (90 cal)

Cook the rice until tunnels appear, then cover and leave for 15 minutes.

Slowly pour the vinegar dressing into the rice and stir it through.

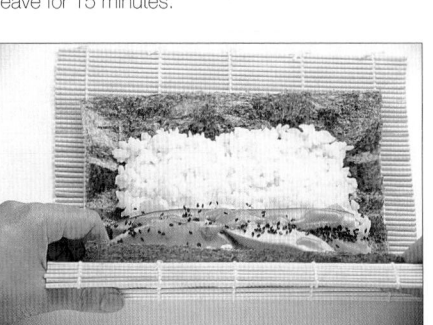

Spread the wasabi mayonnaise mixture over the vegetables and start rolling.

Roll the mat tightly to join the edge, then hold in place for a few seconds.

BEETROOT HUMMUS

Preparation time: 15 minutes
Total cooking time: 40 minutes
Serves 8

500 g (1 lb) beetroot, trimmed
4 tablespoons olive oil
1 large onion, chopped
1 tablespoon ground cumin
400 g (13 oz) can chickpeas, drained
1 tablespoon tahini
⅓ cup (90 g/3 oz) plain yoghurt
3 cloves garlic, crushed
¼ cup (60 ml/2 fl oz) lemon juice
½ cup (125 ml/4 fl oz) vegetable
  stock

1 Scrub the beetroot well. Bring a large saucepan of water to the boil over high heat and cook the beetroot for 35–40 minutes, or until soft and cooked through. Drain and cool slightly before peeling.
2 Meanwhile, heat 1 tablespoon of the oil in a frying pan over medium heat and cook the onion for 2–3 minutes, or until soft. Add the cumin and cook for a further 1 minute, or until fragrant.
3 Chop the beetroot and place in a food processor or blender with the onion mixture, chickpeas, tahini, yoghurt, garlic, lemon juice and stock and process until smooth. With the motor running, add the remaining oil in a thin steady stream. Process until the mixture is thoroughly combined. Serve with Lebanese or Turkish bread.

NUTRITION PER SERVE
Protein 5.5 g; Fat 13 g; Carbohydrate 13 g; Dietary Fibre 5 g; Cholesterol 1.5 mg; 792 kJ (190 cal)

NOTE: Beetroot hummus can be a great accompaniment to a main meal or is delicious as part of a meze platter with bruschetta or crusty bread. Its vivid colour sparks up any table.

VARIATION: You can use 500 g (1 lb) of any vegetable to make the hummus. Try carrot or pumpkin.

Cook the beetroot until soft, then drain and cool slightly before peeling off the skins.

Cook the onion until soft, then add the cumin and cook until fragrant.

Put all the hummus ingredients in a food processor and blend until smooth.

27

GRISSINI

Preparation time: 30 minutes +
1 hour 10 minutes standing
Total cooking time: 20 minutes
Makes 24

7 g (¼ oz) sachet dried yeast
1 teaspoon sugar
4 cups (500 g/1 lb) plain flour
¼ cup (60 ml/2 fl oz) olive oil
¼ cup (15 g/½ oz) chopped basil
4 cloves garlic, crushed
50 g (1¾ oz) Parmesan, grated
2 teaspoons sea salt flakes
2 tablespoons grated Parmesan, extra

1 Put the yeast, sugar and 1¼ cups (315 ml/10 fl oz) warm water in a small bowl and leave in a warm place for about 5–10 minutes, or until frothy. Sift the flour and 1 teaspoon salt into a bowl and stir in the yeast and oil. Add more water if the dough is dry.
2 Gather the dough into a ball and turn out onto a lightly floured surface. Knead for 10 minutes, or until soft and elastic. Divide into two portions and flatten into rectangles. Put the basil and garlic on one portion and the Parmesan on the other. Fold the dough to enclose the fillings, then knead for a few minutes to incorporate evenly.
3 Place the doughs into two lightly oiled bowls and cover with plastic wrap. Leave in a warm place for about 1 hour, or until doubled in volume. Preheat the oven to very hot 230°C (450°F/Gas 8) and lightly grease two large baking trays.
4 Punch down the doughs and knead each again for 1 minute. Divide each piece of dough into 12 portions, and roll each portion into a stick 30 cm (12 inches) long. Place on the baking trays and brush with water. Sprinkle the basil and garlic dough with the sea salt, and the cheese dough with the extra Parmesan. Bake for 15 minutes, or until crisp and golden brown. These can be kept in an airtight container for up to a week.

NUTRITION PER GRISSINI
Protein 3.5 g; Fat 3.5 g; Carbohydrate 16 g;
Dietary Fibre 1 g; Cholesterol 3 mg;
457 kJ (109 cal)

Stir the frothy yeast and oil into the flour and salt until well combined.

Flatten one portion of dough into a rectangle and put the basil and garlic on top.

Punch down the dough with your fist to expel the air and then knead for a minute.

Divide the dough into 12 portions and roll each one into a long stick.

MINI SALMON AND CAMEMBERT QUICHES

Preparation time: 30 minutes
+ 1 hour refrigeration + cooling
Total cooking time: 30 minutes
Makes 24

PASTRY
2 cups (250 g/8 oz) plain flour
150 g (5 oz) butter, chopped
2 egg yolks, lightly beaten
½ teaspoon paprika

FILLING
1 tablespoon olive oil
2 small leeks, finely sliced
75 g (2½ oz) smoked salmon, thinly
    sliced
80 g (2¾ oz) Camembert, chopped
2 eggs, lightly beaten
½ cup (125 ml/4 fl oz) cream
2 teaspoons grated lemon rind
1 teaspoon chopped fresh dill
1 tablespoon finely chopped
    fresh chives, for serving

1 Sift the flour into a large bowl and rub in the butter with your fingertips until the mixture resembles fine breadcrumbs. Make a well, add the egg yolk, paprika and 1 teaspoon water and mix with a flat-bladed knife, using a cutting action, until the mixture comes together in beads. Gently gather together and lift onto a lightly floured work surface. Press together into a ball, wrap in plastic wrap and refrigerate for 30 minutes.
2 Grease two 12-hole patty tins. Divide the pastry into 4 pieces. Roll each between 2 sheets of baking paper to 2 mm (⅛ inch) thick. Cut 24 rounds using a 7 cm (2¾ inch) fluted cutter. Lift the rounds into the patty tins, pressing into shape but being careful not to stretch the pastry. Chill for 30 minutes.
3 Preheat the oven to moderate 180°C (350°F/Gas 4). Bake the pastry for 5 minutes, or until lightly golden. If the pastry has puffed up, press down lightly with a tea towel.
4 For the filling, heat the oil in a frying pan and cook the leek for 2–3 minutes, or until soft. Remove from the pan and cool. Divide the leek, salmon and Camembert pieces among the pastries.

5 Whisk the egg, cream, lemon rind and dill together in a jug, then pour some into each pastry. Bake for 15–20 minutes, or until lightly golden and set. Serve sprinkled with chives.

NUTRITION PER QUICHE
Protein 3.5 g; Fat 10 g; Carbohydrate 9 g;
Dietary Fibre 0.5 g; Cholesterol 59.5 mg;
585 kJ (140 Cal)

NOTE: You can substitute crab meat or small prawns for the salmon.

Cut the rounds and lift into the patty tins, gently pressing into shape.

Bake the pastry rounds for 5 minutes, or until lightly golden.

Pour some of the egg, cream, lemon rind and dill mixture into each pastry case.

SPICED CARROT SOUP SIP

Preparation time: 30 minutes
Total cooking time: 1 hour 10 minutes
Serves 36 (Makes 1.25 litres)

⅓ cup (80 ml/2¾ fl oz) olive oil
2 teaspoons honey
3 teaspoons ground cumin
3 teaspoons coriander seeds, lightly
   crushed
2 cinnamon sticks, broken in half
1.5 kg (3 lb) carrots, cut into even
   chunks (about 3 cm/1¼ inches)
3 cups (750 ml/1½ lb) chicken stock
100 ml (3½ fl oz) cream
¾ cup (185 g/6 oz) sour cream
3 tablespoons fresh coriander leaves

1 Preheat the oven to moderately hot 200°C (400°F/Gas 6). Combine the oil, honey, cumin, coriander seeds, cinnamon sticks, 1 teaspoon salt and plenty of cracked black pepper in a roasting tin. Add the chunks of carrot and mix well to ensure that all the carrot is coated in the spice mixture.
2 Roast for 1 hour, or until the carrot is tender, shaking the pan occasionally during cooking. Remove from the oven, discard the cinnamon sticks with tongs and allow the carrot to cool slightly.
3 Transfer half the carrot chunks, 1½ cups (375 ml/12 fl oz) of the stock and 1 cup (250 ml/8 fl oz) water to a food processor or blender and blend until smooth. Strain through a fine sieve into a clean saucepan. Repeat with the remaining carrots, stock and another 1 cup (250 ml/8 fl oz) water. Bring the soup to a simmer and cook for 10 minutes. Add the cream and season to taste. Ladle into a jug, then pour into shot glasses or espresso cups. Garnish each with ¼ teaspoon sour cream and a coriander leaf.

NUTRITION PER SERVE
Protein 1 g; Fat 5.5 g; Carbohydrate 3 g;
Dietary Fibre 1.5 g; Cholesterol 10.5 mg;
260 kJ (60 Cal)

THINK AHEAD: The soup can be refrigerated for 2 days or frozen before the cream is added for up to 8 weeks.

Stir the carrots into the spice mixture so that they are well coated.

Blend the carrots, stock and water until the mixture is smooth.

MINI BISTEEYA

Preparation time: 30 minutes
Total cooking time: 55 minutes
Makes 24

1 tablespoon olive oil
125 g (4 oz) unsalted butter, melted
1 small onion, finely chopped
2 small chicken breast fillets
    (300 g/10 oz) in total)
2 cloves garlic, crushed
1 large cinnamon stick
¼ teaspoon ground turmeric
1 teaspoon grated fresh ginger
4–5 threads saffron
1 cup (250 ml/8 fl oz) chicken stock
2 eggs, beaten
⅓ cup (55 g/2 oz) sultanas
⅓ cup (50 g/1¾ oz) chopped toasted
    almonds
4 tablespoons chopped fresh
    coriander leaves
9 sheets filo pastry
1 tablespoon icing sugar
2 teaspoons ground cinnamon

1 Lightly grease 24 non-stick mini muffin holes. Preheat the oven to moderate 180°C (350°F/Gas 4) and put a baking tray in the oven to warm.
2 Place the oil and 2 teaspoons of the butter in a large frying pan, add the onion and cook over medium heat for 4–5 minutes, or until just soft, then add the chicken, garlic, cinnamon stick, turmeric, ginger, saffron and stock. Bring to the boil, then reduce the heat to low and poach the chicken for 10 minutes, or until just cooked. Remove the chicken from the pan and allow to cool.
3 Return the pan to the heat and boil until the sauce reduces to ⅓ cup (80 ml/2¾ fl oz). Carefully remove the cinnamon stick and reduce the heat to low. Add the egg to the sauce and cook, stirring constantly with a wooden spoon, for 3–4 minutes, or until the egg is set—the mixture will look curdled, but this is fine. Remove from the heat. Finely shred the chicken, then add to the pan along with the sultanas, toasted almonds and coriander. Season and allow to cool.
4 Keeping the filo covered while you work, take one sheet, brush lightly with the remaining melted butter, cover with another sheet and repeat until you have three buttered sheets. Using a sharp knife, cut 12 squares, each 8 cm (3 inches). Push each of the squares into a muffin hole. Fill each hole with 1 tablespoon of the chicken mixture. Repeat with another 3 sheets and the rest of the filling.
5 Layer three more sheets of filo pastry, buttering each layer as before. Using a 5 cm (2 inch) cutter, cut out 24 rounds. Place a round on top of the chicken mixture, but leave the corners of each pastry base sticking up. Use some of the melted butter to seal the top. Bake on the heated tray for 20 minutes, or until golden. Cool for 5–10 minutes before dusting with the combined icing sugar and cinnamon, then serve.

NUTRITION PER BISTEEYA
Protein 4.5 g; Fat 7.5 g; Carbohydrate 5.5 g;
Dietary Fibre 0.5 g; Cholesterol 38 mg;
442 kJ (106 Cal)

THINK AHEAD: The filling can be made up to 2 days ahead. Assemble up to a day ahead, but cover well with plastic wrap or they will dry out.

Add the egg to the mixture and cook until the egg is set.

Use a teaspoon to put a little of the chicken filling into each of the muffin holes.

SPICY CORN PUFFS

**Preparation time: 25 minutes +
  10 minutes standing**
Total cooking time: 15 minutes
Makes about 36

2 corn cobs
3 tablespoons chopped fresh
  coriander leaves
6 spring onions, finely chopped
1 small fresh red chilli, seeded and
  finely chopped
1 large egg
2 teaspoons ground cumin
½ teaspoon ground coriander
1 cup (125 g/4 oz) plain flour
oil, for deep-frying
sweet chilli sauce, to serve

1 Cut down the side of the corn cobs with a very sharp knife to release the kernels. Roughly chop the kernels, then place them in a large bowl. Holding the cobs over the bowl, scrape down the sides of the cobs with a knife to release all of the corn juice from the cob.
2 Add the fresh coriander, spring onion, chilli, egg, cumin, ground coriander, 1 teaspoon salt and freshly cracked black pepper to taste to the bowl, and stir well. Add the flour and mix well. The texture of the batter will vary depending on how much juice is released from the corn. If the mixture is too dry, add 1 tablespoon water, but no more than that as the batter should be quite thick and dry. Stand for 10 minutes.

3 Fill a large heavy-based saucepan or deep-fryer one-third full of oil and heat to 180°C (350°F), or until a cube of bread dropped in the oil browns in 15 seconds. Drop slightly heaped teaspoons of the corn batter into the oil and cook for about 1½ minutes, or until puffed and golden. Drain on crumpled paper towels and serve immediately with a bowl of the sweet chilli sauce to dip the puffs into.

NUTRITION PER CORN PUFF
Protein 1 g; Fat 3.5 g; Carbohydrate 4.5 g;
Dietary Fibre 0.5 g; Cholesterol 5.5 mg;
225 kJ (55 Cal)

NOTE: The batter should be prepared just before serving, or the corn puffs may fall apart when cooked.

Cut down the sides of the corn cobs to get all the corn kernels.

Mix the flour into the rest of the batter; the batter will be quite dry.

Fry the corn puffs until they puff up and are beautifully golden.

ROAST BEEF ON CROUTES

Preparation time: 20 minutes +
3 hours 15 minutes standing
Total cooking time: 25 minutes
Makes 30

300 g (10 oz) piece beef eye fillet
⅓ cup (80 ml/2¾ fl oz) olive oil
2 cloves garlic, crushed
2 sprigs fresh thyme plus extra
    to garnish
10 slices white bread
1 large clove garlic, peeled, extra

HORSERADISH CREAM
⅓ cup (80 ml/2¾ fl oz) thick cream
1 tablespoon horseradish (see NOTE)
1 teaspoon lemon juice

1 Place the beef in a non-metallic bowl, pour on the combined oil, garlic and thyme and toss to coat well. Cover with plastic wrap and marinate in the refrigerator for about 2–3 hours. Preheat the oven to moderately hot 200°C (400°F/Gas 6).
2 To make the croûtes, cut out three rounds from each slice of bread using a 5 cm (2 inch) fluted cutter. Place the rounds on a baking tray and bake for 5 minutes each side, then rub the whole garlic clove over each side of the rounds and set aside.
3 To make the horseradish cream, put the cream in a small bowl and whisk lightly until thickened. Gently fold in the horseradish and lemon juice, then season with cracked black pepper. Refrigerate until ready to use.
4 Heat a roasting tin in the oven for 5 minutes. Remove the beef from the marinade, reserving the marinade. Generously season the beef on all sides with salt and pepper, then place it in the hot roasting tin and turn it so that all sides of the meat are sealed. Drizzle with 2 tablespoons of the reserved marinade, then roast for 10–12 minutes for rare, or until cooked to your liking. Remove from the oven, cover with foil and rest for 15 minutes before slicing thinly.
5 Arrange one slice of beef on each croûte (you may need to cut the slices in half if they are too big), and top with ½ teaspoon of the horseradish

cream and a small sprig of fresh thyme. Serve immediately.

NUTRITION PER PIECE
Protein 3 g; Fat 3 g; Carbohydrate 3 g; Dietary Fibre 0.5 g; Cholesterol 10 mg; 215 kJ (50 Cal)

NOTE: Grated horseradish is readily available in small jars preserved in vinegar. Don't confuse it with horseradish sauce, which already has a cream base.

THINK AHEAD: The beef and croûtes can be prepared the day before serving. Leave the beef whole, covered, in the refrigerator and slice just before assembling. Store the

croûtes in an airtight container lined with paper towels to absorb any excess oil.

VARIATION: For a spicy variation on this classic canapé, marinate the beef fillet in ⅓ cup (80 ml/2¾ fl oz) olive oil, 2 cloves crushed garlic, 1 teaspoon paprika and ½ teaspoon cayenne pepper. Top with a simple garlic cream, made by combining 1 clove crushed garlic with ½ cup (125 ml/4 fl oz) lightly whipped thick cream and some salt and cracked black pepper to taste.

Fold the horseradish and lemon juice into the whisked cream.

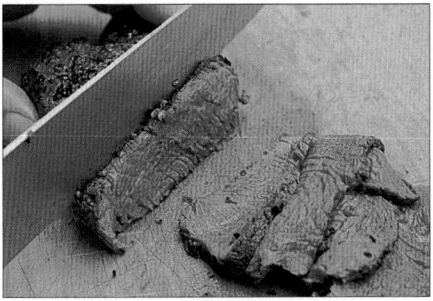

Rest the beef, then thinly slice across the grain with a sharp knife.

WON TON STACKS WITH TUNA AND GINGER

Preparation time: 20 minutes
Total cooking time: 10 minutes
Makes 24

1½ tablespoons sesame seeds
12 fresh won ton wrappers
½ cup (125 ml/4 fl oz) peanut or
    vegetable oil
150 g (5 oz) piece fresh tuna fillet
    (see NOTE)
¼ cup (60 g/2 oz) Japanese
    mayonnaise
50 g (1¾ oz) pickled ginger
50 g (1¾ oz) snow pea sprouts
2 teaspoons mirin
2 teaspoons soy sauce
¼ teaspoon sugar

1 Lightly toast the sesame seeds in a small dry frying pan over low heat for 2–3 minutes, or until golden.
2 Cut the won ton wrappers into quarters to give 48 squares in total. Heat the oil in a small saucepan over medium heat and cook the wrappers in batches for 1–2 minutes, or until they are golden and crisp. Drain on crumpled paper towels.
3 Thinly slice the tuna into 24 slices. Spoon approximately ¼ teaspoon of the mayonnaise onto 24 of the won ton squares. Place a slice of tuna on the mayonnaise and top with a little of the pickled ginger, snow pea sprouts and sesame seeds.
4 Mix the mirin, soy sauce and sugar together in a small bowl and drizzle a little over each stack. Season with pepper. Top with the remaining

24 won ton squares (lids). Serve immediately or the stacks will absorb the dressing and become soggy.

NUTRITION PER STACK
Protein 2.5 g; Fat 6 g; Carbohydrate 4 g;
Dietary Fibre 0.5 g; Cholesterol 3.5 mg;
335 kJ (80 Cal)

NOTE: For this recipe, you need good-quality tuna. Sashimi tuna is the best quality, but if you can't get that, buy only the freshest tuna with as little sinew as possible.

THINK AHEAD: The won ton wrappers can be fried the day before serving. Store them in an airtight container large enough that they are not cramped. Place sheets of paper towels between each layer.

Using a sharp knife, cut the won ton wrappers into four equal squares.

Cook the won ton squares in the hot oil until they are crisp and golden.

Using a sharp knife, cut the tuna into very thin, even slices.

THAI CHICKEN SAUSAGE ROLLS

Preparation time: 20 minutes
Total cooking time: 15 minutes
Makes 24

200 g (6½ oz) chicken breast fillet,
    roughly chopped
150 g (5 oz) mild pancetta, chopped
1 clove garlic, crushed
3 spring onions, chopped
2 tablespoons chopped fresh
    coriander
2 bird's eye chillies, seeded and finely
    chopped
1 teaspoon fish sauce
1 egg
1 teaspoon grated fresh ginger
375 g (12 oz) block frozen puff pastry
1 egg yolk
2 tablespoons sesame seeds
sweet chilli sauce, to serve
fresh coriander, to serve

1 Preheat the oven to moderate 180°C (350°F/Gas 4). Put the chicken, pancetta, garlic, spring onion, coriander, chilli, fish sauce, whole egg and ginger in a food processor and process until just combined.
2 Roll out the pastry to a rectangle 30 cm x 40 cm (12 inches x 16 inches). Halve lengthways. Take half the filling and, with floured hands, roll it into a long sausage and place along the long edge of one piece of pastry. Brush the edges with water and fold the pastry over, pressing down to seal. Place the sealed edge underneath. Repeat with the remaining pastry and filling.
3 Using a sharp knife, cut the sausage rolls into 3 cm (1¼ inch) lengths on the diagonal; discard the end pieces. Brush the tops with egg yolk, then sprinkle with sesame seeds. Bake for 10–15 minutes, or until golden. Serve with sweet chilli sauce and garnished with fresh coriander.

NUTRITION PER SAUSAGE ROLL
Protein 4.5 g; Fat 6 g; Carbohydrate 5.5 g;
Dietary Fibre 0.5 g; Cholesterol 29 mg;
385 kJ (90 Cal)

THINK AHEAD: You can make the sausage rolls a day ahead. Reheat in

a moderate 180°C (350°F/Gas 4) oven for 10–12 minutes, or until they are warmed through.

VARIATION: For spicy lamb sausage rolls, follow the method outlined for the basic sausage roll, but change the filling. Mix 375 g (12 oz) lamb mince, ½ cup (40 g/1¼ oz) fresh breadcrumbs, ½ small grated onion, 2 teaspoons soy sauce, 1 teaspoon grated fresh ginger, 1 teaspoon soft brown sugar, ½ teaspoon ground coriander, ¼ teaspoon each of ground cumin and sambal oelek. Lightly sprinkle the uncooked sausage rolls with poppy seeds after glazing and bake for 10–15 minutes.

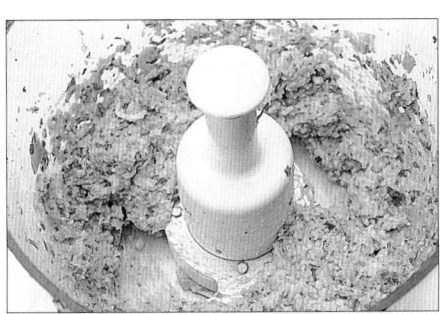

Mix the filling ingredients in the food processor until combined.

Place the sausage filling along one long edge of the pastry.

35

STUFFED CHILLIES

Preparation time: 15 minutes
Total cooking time: 30 minutes
Makes 24

1 teaspoon cumin seeds
12 mild small jalapeño or similar mild
    oblong-shaped fat chillies,
    approximately 4 cm x 3 cm
    (1½ inches x 1¼ inches)
1 tablespoon olive oil
2 cloves garlic, finely chopped
½ small red onion, finely chopped
½ cup (125 g/4 oz) cream cheese,
    softened
¼ cup (30 g/1 oz) coarsely grated
    Cheddar
2 tablespoons finely chopped drained
    sun-dried tomatoes
1 teaspoon finely chopped lime rind
1 tablespoon chopped fresh
    coriander
pinch of smoky paprika
½ cup (50 g/1¾ oz) coarse dry
    breadcrumbs
2 teaspoons lime juice
coriander leaves, to garnish

1 Preheat the oven to moderately hot 200°C (400°F/Gas 6). Line a baking tray with baking paper. Toast the cumin seeds in a small dry frying pan for 1–2 minutes, or until fragrant. Cool slightly, then grind to a powder.
2 Halve the chillies lengthways. Wearing gloves, remove the seeds and membranes. Bring a saucepan of water to the boil, add the chillies and cook for 1 minute, or until the water comes back to the boil. Drain, rinse under cold water, then return to a saucepan of fresh boiling water for another minute before draining, rinsing under cold water, then draining well again.

3 Heat the oil in a non-stick frying pan and cook the garlic and onion over medium–low heat for 5 minutes, or until the onion softens.
4 Mash the cream cheese in a bowl, add the Cheddar, sun-dried tomatoes, lime rind, coriander, paprika, cumin and half the breadcrumbs and mix well. Stir in the cooked onion and season. Fill each chilli with one heaped teaspoon of the mixture, then lay them on the baking tray and scatter with the remaining breadcrumbs.
5 Bake for 20 minutes. Remove; squeeze some lime juice over the top and garnish with coriander leaves.

NUTRITION PER PIECE
Protein 1.5 g; Fat 3 g; Carbohydrate 2 g;
Dietary Fibre 0.5 g; Cholesterol 6.5 mg;
165 kJ (40 Cal)

NOTE: Test the heat of the chillies by placing your tongue on the flesh after blanching twice. If they are still too hot, blanch again.

THINK AHEAD: The chillies can be stuffed the day before serving but they are best crumbed and baked on the day they are to be served.

Wearing gloves to protect your hands, remove the seeds and membrane.

Fill the chillies with a heaped teaspoon of the spicy cream cheese mixture.

Sprinkle the stuffed chillies with breadcrumbs to create a crunchy topping.

LENTIL PATTIES WITH CUMIN SKORDALIA

Preparation time: 40 minutes +
30 minutes refrigeration
Total cooking time: 55 minutes
Makes 32

1 cup (185 g/6 oz) brown lentils
1 teaspoon cumin seeds
½ cup (90 g/3 oz) burghul (bulgur
    wheat)
1 tablespoon olive oil
3 cloves garlic, crushed
4 spring onions, thinly sliced
1 teaspoon ground coriander
3 tablespoons chopped fresh parsley
3 tablespoons chopped fresh mint
2 eggs, lightly beaten
oil, for deep-frying

SKORDALIA
500 g (1 lb) floury potatoes, cut into
    2 cm (¾ inch) cubes (see NOTES)
3 cloves garlic, crushed
½ teaspoon ground cumin
pinch of ground white pepper
¾ cup (185 ml/6 fl oz) olive oil
2 tablespoons white vinegar

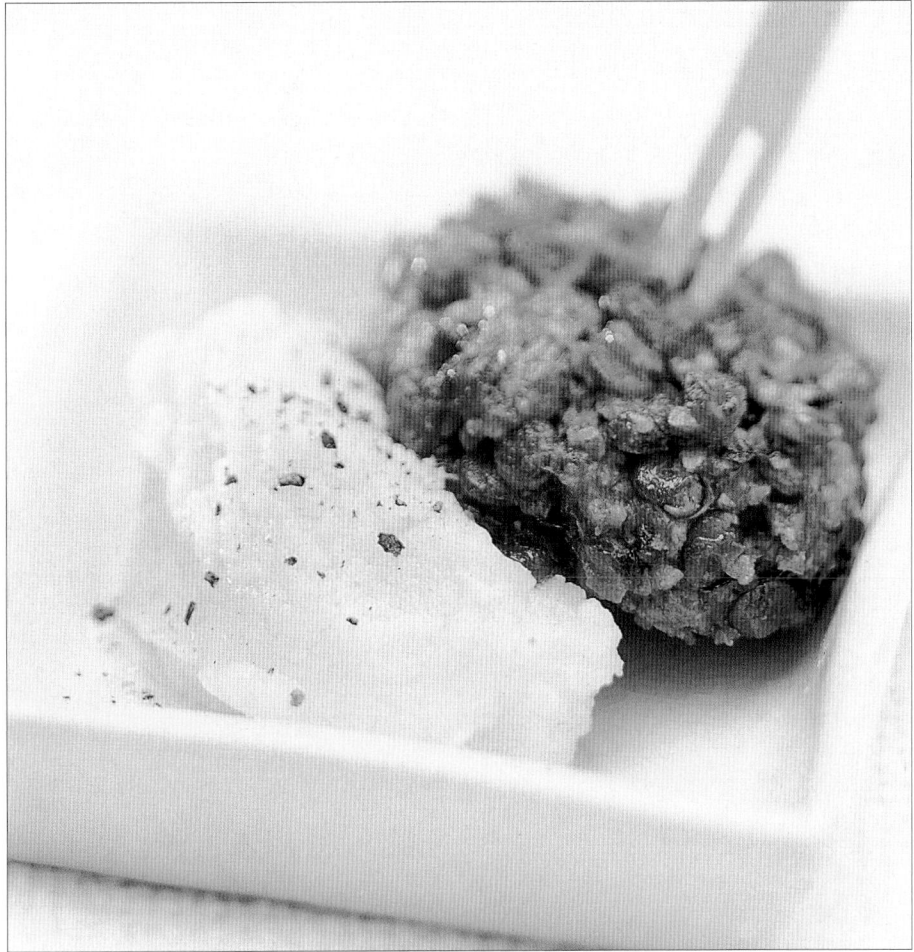

1 To make the patties, place the lentils in a saucepan, add 2½ cups (625 ml/ 20 fl oz) water and bring to the boil. Reduce the heat to low and cook, covered, for 30 minutes, or until soft. Meanwhile, toast the cumin seeds in a dry frying pan over low heat for 1–2 minutes, or until fragrant. Grind.
2 Remove the lentils from the heat and stir in the burghul. Set aside to cool a little.
3 Heat the olive oil in a small frying pan, add the crushed garlic and spring onion and cook for 1 minute, then add the coriander and cumin and cook for a further 30 seconds. Stir into the lentil mixture along with the parsley, mint and egg. Mix until well combined, then chill for 30 minutes.
4 To make the skordalia, cook the potato in a large saucepan of boiling water for 10 minutes, or until very soft. Drain, then mash until quite smooth. Stir in the garlic, cumin, white pepper and 1 teaspoon salt. Gradually pour in the oil, mixing well with a wooden spoon. Stir in the white vinegar.

5 Roll tablespoons of the lentil mixture into balls, then flatten slightly to form small patties. Fill a deep heavy-based saucepan or deep-fryer one-third full of oil and heat to 180°C (350°F), or until a cube of bread browns in 15 seconds. Cook the patties in batches for 1–2 minutes per batch, or until crisp and browned. Drain on crumpled paper towels. Serve the lentil patties warm with the skordalia.

NUTRITION PER PATTY
Protein 2.5 g; Fat 9 g; Carbohydrate 6 g; Dietary Fibre 1.5 g; Cholesterol 13 mg; 465 kJ (110 Cal)

NOTES: Use King Edward, russet or pontiac potatoes for the skordalia. Do not make skordalia with a food processor—the processing will turn the potato into a gluey mess.

THINK AHEAD: Skordalia will keep in an airtight container for up to 2–3 days in the fridge. The lentil patties can be frozen, uncooked, for up to 2 months or will keep in the refrigerator for 2 days.

Gradually pour the olive oil into the mashed potato, mixing at the same time.

Roll the mixture into balls and gently flatten with your hand to form patties.

VEGETABLE DUMPLINGS

Preparation time: 40 minutes +
  15 minutes soaking
Total cooking time: 20 minutes
Makes 24

8 dried Chinese mushrooms
1 tablespoon oil
2 teaspoons finely chopped fresh
  ginger
2 garlic cloves, crushed
100 g (3½ oz) Chinese chives,
  chopped
100 g (3½ oz) water spinach, cut into 1
  cm (½ inch) lengths
¼ cup (60 ml/2 fl oz) chicken stock
2 tablespoons oyster sauce
1 tablespoon cornflour
1 teaspoon soy sauce
1 teaspoon rice wine
¼ cup (45 g/1½ oz) water chestnuts,
  chopped
chilli sauce, to serve

WRAPPERS
200 g (6½ oz) wheat starch (see NOTE)
1 teaspoon cornflour
oil, for kneading

1 Place the mushrooms in a bowl and soak in 2 cups (500 ml/16 fl oz) hot water for 15 minutes. Finely chop the mushroom caps.
2 Heat the oil in a frying pan over high heat, add the ginger, garlic and a pinch of salt and white pepper and cook for 30 seconds. Add the chives and spinach and cook for 1 minute.
3 Combine the stock, oyster sauce, cornflour, soy sauce and rice wine, and add to the spinach mixture along with the water chestnuts and mushrooms. Cook for 1–2 minutes, or until the mixture thickens, them

remove from the heat and cool completely.
4 To make the wrappers, combine the wheat starch and cornflour in a bowl. Make a well in the centre and add ¾ cup (185 ml/6 fl oz) boiling water, a little at a time, while bringing the mixture together with your hands. When it is combined, immediately knead it, using lightly oiled hands until the dough forms a shiny ball.
5 Keeping the dough covered with a cloth while you work, pick walnut-sized pieces from the dough, and using well-oiled hands, squash them between the palms of your hands then roll out as thinly as possible into circles no larger than 10 cm (4 inches)

in diameter. Place 1 tablespoon of the filling in the centre of the circle. Pinch the edges of the wrapper together to enclose the filling and form a tight ball.
6 Fill a wok or saucepan one-third full of water and bring to the boil. Put the dumplings in a bamboo steamer lined with baking paper, leaving a gap between each one. Cover and steam for 7–8 minutes. Serve with chilli sauce.

NUTRITION PER DUMPLING
Protein 0.5 g; Fat 1 g; Carbohydrate 8.5 g;
Dietary Fibre 0.5 g; Cholesterol 0 mg; 185 kJ
(45 Cal)

Use lightly oiled hands to roll the dumpling wrapper dough into a ball.

Roll out the small pieces of dough into flat rounds, taking care not to tear them.

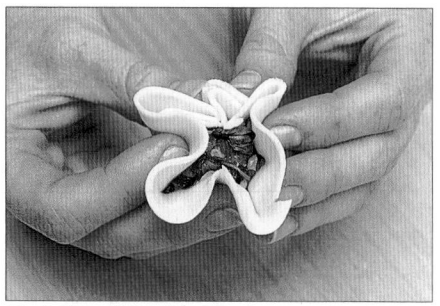

Pinch the edges of the wrapper together so that the filling is enclosed.

MACADAMIA-CRUSTED CHICKEN STRIPS WITH MANGO SALSA

**Preparation time: 25 minutes +
30 minutes refrigeration
Total cooking time: 15 minutes
Makes 24**

12 chicken tenderloins (700 g/
1lb 2½ oz), larger ones cut in half
seasoned plain flour, for dusting
2 eggs, lightly beaten
250 g (8 oz) macadamias, finely
chopped
2 cups (160 g/5½ oz) fresh
breadcrumbs
oil, for deep-frying

MANGO SALSA
1 small mango, very finely diced
2 tablespoons finely diced red onion
2 tablespoons roughly chopped fresh
coriander leaves
1 fresh green chilli, seeded and finely
chopped
1 tablespoon lime juice

1 Cut the chicken into strips. Dust the chicken strips with the flour, then dip them in the egg and, finally, coat them in the combined nuts and breadcrumbs. Chill for at least 30 minutes to firm up.
2 To make the salsa, combine all the ingredients in a small bowl and season to taste with salt and black pepper.
3 Fill a large heavy-based saucepan or deep-fryer one-third full of oil and heat to 180°C (350°F), or until a cube of bread dropped in the oil browns in 15 seconds. Cook the chicken strips in batches for 2–3 minutes, or until golden brown all over, taking

care not to burn the nuts. Drain on crumpled paper towels. Serve the chicken strips warm with the salsa.

NUTRITION PER PIECE
Protein 8 g; Fat 13.5 g; Carbohydrate 6 g; Dietary Fibre 1 g; Cholesterol 43 mg; 740 kJ (175 Cal)

THINK AHEAD: These are best made on the day they are to be served.

VARIATIONS: The chicken strips are also very tasty served with sweet chilli sauce. Try a different coating using almonds or peanuts.

Cut the chicken tenderloins into even bite-size strips before dusting with flour.

Using your hands, coat the chicken strips in the macadamia crumbs.

TURKISH BREAD WITH HERBED ZUCCHINI

Preparation time: 15 minutes
Total cooking time: 35 minutes
Makes 48

½ large loaf Turkish bread
1 tablespoon sesame seeds
½ cup (125 ml/4 fl oz) vegetable oil

HERBED ZUCCHINI
1 tablespoon olive oil
2 cloves garlic, finely chopped
4 x 100 g (3½ oz) small zucchini,
    roughly chopped
1 large carrot, thinly sliced
2 tablespoons chopped fresh flat-leaf
    parsley
2 tablespoons chopped fresh mint
2 teaspoons lemon juice
½ teaspoon ground cumin

1 Split the Turkish bread horizontally through the middle and open it out. Cut the bread into 3 cm (1¼ inch) squares; you should end up with 48 squares.

2 Toast the sesame seeds in a large dry non-stick frying pan over low heat for 2–3 minutes, or until golden. Remove from the pan. Heat the vegetable oil in the same pan and cook the bread in batches for 1–2 minutes each side, or until crisp and golden. Drain on crumpled paper towels.

3 Heat the olive oil in a saucepan over medium heat and cook the garlic for 1 minute. Add the zucchini and carrot and cook over medium heat for 2 minutes. Season with salt and ground black pepper. Add 1 tablespoon water, cover and simmer over low heat for 15 minutes, or until the vegetables are soft. Spoon into a bowl and mash roughly with a potato masher. Add the parsley, mint, lemon juice and cumin. Season to taste.

4 Spoon 2 teaspoons of the zucchini mixture over each square of bread and scatter with sesame seeds. Serve warm or at room temperature.

NUTRITION PER PIECE
Protein 0.5 g; Fat 2.5 g; Carbohydrate 2 g; Dietary Fibre 0.5 g; Cholesterol 0 mg; 140 kJ (35 Cal)

THINK AHEAD: The herbed zucchini can be prepared up to 2 days in advance. Reheat just before serving.

Split the bread in half horizontally, then cut it into 3 cm (1¼ inch) squares.

Use a potato masher to mash the zucchini and carrot mixture.

MEDITERRANEAN TWISTS

Preparation time: 15 minutes
Total cooking time: 30 minutes
Makes 24

2 tablespoons olive oil
2 onions, thinly sliced
⅓ cup (80 ml/2¾ fl oz) dry white wine
3 teaspoons sugar
1 cup (30 g/1 oz) chopped fresh
    flat-leaf parsley
8 anchovies, drained and finely
    chopped
1 cup (130 g/4½ oz) coarsely grated
    Gruyère
6 sheets filo pastry
60 g (2 oz) unsalted butter, melted

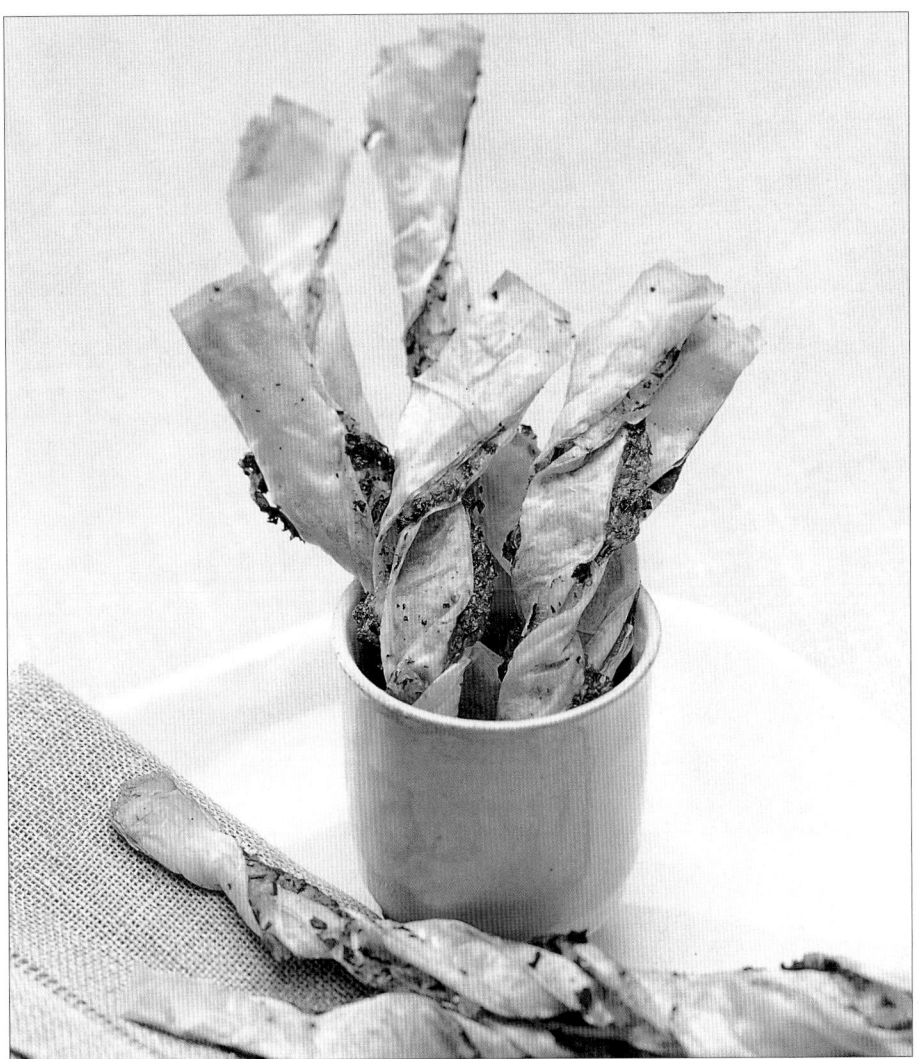

1 Preheat the oven to hot 220°C (425°F/Gas 7) and warm a baking tray. Heat the oil in a medium frying pan and cook the onion over low heat for 5 minutes. Add the white wine and sugar, and cook for 10–15 minutes, or until the onion is soft and golden. Remove from the heat and cool.
2 Combine the parsley, anchovies, grated Gruyère and cooled onion mixture in a bowl.
3 Keeping the filo covered while you work, take one sheet, brush lightly with the butter, cover with another sheet and repeat until you have three buttered sheets. Spread the parsley mixture over the pastry and top with the remaining three sheets, buttering each layer as before. Press down firmly, then cut the pastry in half widthways, then cut each half into strips 1.5–2 cm (⅝–¾ inch) wide. Brush with butter, then gently twist each strip. Season with black pepper, place on a baking tray and bake for 10 minutes, or until crisp and golden.

NUTRITION PER TWIST
Protein 2.5 g; Fat 5 g; Carbohydrate 3 g; Dietary Fibre 0.5 g; Cholesterol 12 mg; 290 kJ (70 Cal)

THINK AHEAD: Make the Mediterranean twists up to 2 days ahead and store them in an airtight container lined with thick paper towels to absorb any excess butter. To refresh them, warm them in a moderate 180°C (350°F/Gas 4) oven for 10 minutes before serving.

VARIATION: There are many variations to these twists, but a great one to try is Parmesan and thyme twists. Simply substitute the Gruyère with ¾ cup (75 g/2½ oz) of coarsely grated Parmesan and replace the parsley with 2 teaspoons of thyme.

Cook the onion with the wine and sugar until it is soft and golden.

Gently spread the parsley mixture over the sheets of filo pastry.

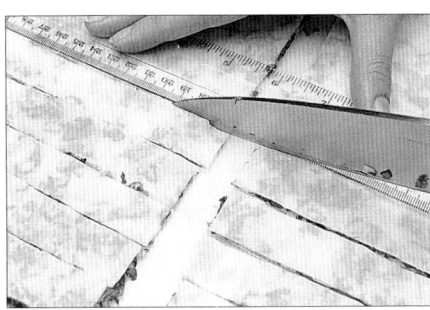

Use a ruler and a very sharp knife to help you cut thin strips from the pastry.

ASPARAGUS AND PROSCIUTTO BUNDLES WITH HOLLANDAISE

Preparation time: 10 minutes
Total cooking time: 15 minutes
Makes 24

24 spears fresh asparagus, trimmed
8 slices prosciutto, cut into thirds lengthways

HOLLANDAISE
175 g (6 oz) butter
4 egg yolks
1 tablespoon lemon juice
ground white pepper

1 Blanch the asparagus in boiling salted water for 2 minutes, then drain and refresh in cold water. Pat dry, then cut the spears in half. Lay the bottom half of each spear next to its tip, then secure by wrapping a piece of prosciutto around the bundle.
2 To make the hollandaise, melt the butter in a small saucepan. Skim any froth off the top. Cool the butter a little. Combine the egg yolks and 2 tablespoons of water in a heatproof bowl placed over a saucepan of simmering water, making sure the base of the bowl does not touch the water. Using a wire whisk, beat for about 3 minutes, or until the mixture is thick and foamy. Make sure the bowl does not get too hot or you will

end up with scrambled eggs. Add the butter slowly, a little at a time at first, whisking well between each addition. Keep adding the butter in a thin stream, whisking continuously, until all the butter has been used. Try to avoid using the milky whey in the bottom of the pan, but don't worry if a little gets in. Stir in the lemon juice and season with salt and white pepper. Place in a bowl and serve warm with the asparagus.

NUTRITION PER BUNDLE
Protein 2 g; Fat 7 g; Carbohydrate 0.5 g;
Dietary Fibre 0.5 g; Cholesterol 51.5 mg;
300 kJ (70 Cal)

Briefly cook the asparagus in boiling water, then drain.

Wrap the tip and bottom end of each spear in a piece of prosciutto.

Gradually whisk the melted butter into the hollandaise mixture.

TAMARI NUT MIX

Preparation time: 15 minutes
Total cooking time: 25 minutes
Serves 10–12

250 g (8 oz) mixed nuts
(almonds, brazil nuts,
peanuts, walnuts)
125 g (4 oz) pepitas (see NOTE)
125 g (4 oz) sunflower seeds
125 g (4 oz) cashew nuts
125 g (4 oz) macadamia nuts
½ cup (125 ml/4 fl oz) tamari

1 Preheat the oven to very slow
140°C (275°F/Gas 1). Lightly grease
two large baking trays.
2 Place the mixed nuts, pepitas,
sunflower seeds, cashew nuts and
macadamia nuts in a large bowl. Pour
the tamari over the nuts and seeds
and toss together well, coating them
evenly in the tamari. Leave for
10 minutes.
3 Spread the nut and seed mixture
evenly over the baking trays and bake
for 20–25 minutes, or until dry roasted.
Cool completely and store in an
airtight container for up to 2 weeks.

NUTRITION PER SERVE (12)
Protein 11.5 g; Fat 36 g; Carbohydrate 4 g;
Dietary Fibre 5 g; Cholesterol 0 mg;
1604 kJ (383 cal)

NOTE: Pepitas are peeled pumpkin
seeds—they are available at most
supermarkets and health-food stores.

STORAGE: Once stored, the nuts may
become soft. If they do, spread them
out flat on a baking tray and bake in
a slow (150°C/300°F/Gas 2) oven for
5–10 minutes.

Stir the tamari through the nuts, pepitas and
sunflower seeds.

Spread the nut mixture evenly over two lightly
greased baking trays.

Dry-roast the tamari-coated nuts in the oven for
20–25 minutes.

OLIVE AND POTATO BALLS WITH PESTO

Preparation time: 20 minutes +
 30 minutes refrigeration
Total cooking time: 30 minutes
Makes 30

650 g (1 lb 5 oz) floury potatoes
    (e.g. russet, King Edward)
1 tablespoon olive oil
1 onion, finely chopped
2 cloves garlic, finely chopped
½ cup (80 g/2¾ oz) pitted Kalamata
    olives, sliced
⅓ cup (40 g/1¼ oz) plain flour
¼ cup (25 g/¾ oz) grated Parmesan
¼ cup (15 g/½ oz) shredded fresh basil
1 egg
¾ cup (45 g/1½ oz) dry Japanese
    breadcrumbs
oil, for deep-frying
¼ cup (60 g/2 oz) pesto
2 slices prosciutto, sliced into thin
    strips

1 Peel the potatoes, then cut into
4 cm (1½ inch) chunks and boil
for 15 minutes, or until tender. Test
with the point of a sharp knife – if the
potato comes away easily, it should
be ready. Drain well, then mash with
a potato masher.
2 Heat the olive oil in a frying pan
and cook the onion over medium
heat for 4–5 minutes, or until soft.
Add the garlic and cook for an extra
minute. Remove from the heat, cool
and add to the potato. Mix in the
olives, flour, Parmesan, basil and egg,
and a little salt and freshly cracked
black pepper. Shape the mixture into
30 small balls, then refrigerate for 30
minutes. Roll the balls in breadcrumbs,
pressing the breadcrumbs on firmly so
that the balls are evenly coated.
3 Fill a deep heavy-based saucepan
or deep-fryer one-third full of oil and
heat to 180°C (350°F), or until a cube
of bread dropped in the oil browns in
15 seconds. Cook the olive and potato
balls in batches for 2–3 minutes, or
until golden. Drain on paper towels.
Top each potato ball with ½ teaspoon
of the pesto and a piece of prosciutto
before serving.

NUTRITION PER BALL
Protein 2 g; Fat 5 g; Carbohydrate 6 g; Dietary
Fibre 0.5 g; Cholesterol 8.5 mg; 290 kJ (70 Cal)

NOTE: Japanese breadcrumbs give
a good crisp coating, but normal
breadcrumbs can also be used.

THINK AHEAD: The balls can be
frozen for up to 2 months before
cooking or refrigerated for 2 days.

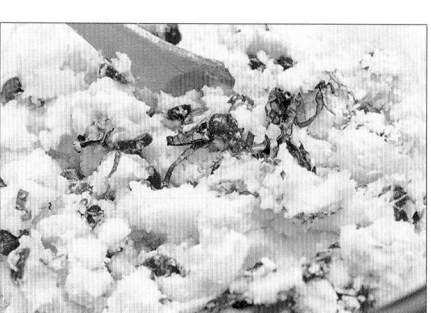

Mix the rest of the ingredients into the mashed
potato until well combined.

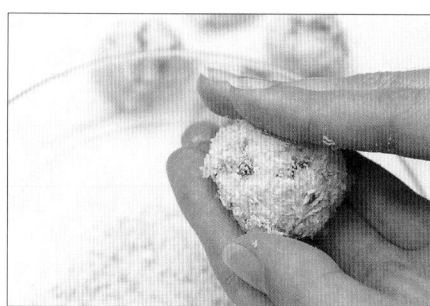

Once the balls have firmed in the refrigerator,
roll them in the breadcrumbs.

ZUCCHINI AND HALOUMI FRITTERS

Preparation time: 15 minutes
Total cooking time: 25 minutes
Makes 45

300 g (10 oz) zucchini
4 spring onions, thinly sliced
200 g (6½ oz) haloumi, coarsely grated
¼ cup (30 g/1 oz) plain flour
2 eggs
1 tablespoon chopped fresh dill,
    plus sprigs, to garnish
¼ cup (60 ml/2 oz) oil
1 lemon, cut into very thin slices,
    seeds removed
⅓ cup (90 g/3 oz) thick Greek-style
    yoghurt

1 Coarsely grate the zucchini and squeeze out as much liquid as possible in your hands or in a clean tea towel. Combine the zucchini with the spring onion, haloumi, flour, eggs and dill. Season well with salt and cracked black pepper.

2 Heat the oil in a large heavy-based frying pan. Form fritters (using heaped teaspoons of the mixture) and cook in batches for 2 minutes each side, or until golden and firm. Drain on crumpled paper towels.

3 Cut each slice of lemon into quarters or eighths, depending on the size, to make small triangles.

4 Top each fritter with ½ teaspoon yoghurt, a piece of lemon and a small sprig of dill.

NUTRITION PER FRITTER
Protein 1.5 g; Fat 4 g; Carbohydrate 1 g; Dietary Fibre 0 g; Cholesterol 12 mg; 170 kJ (40 Cal)

NOTE: The fritters are best prepared and cooked just before serving. If you allow them to sit, the haloumi tends to go a little tough.

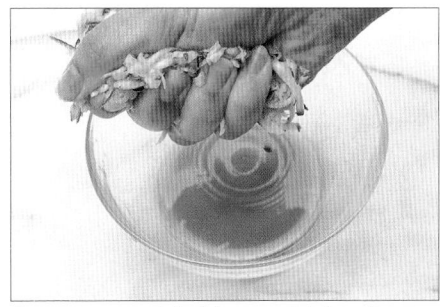

Squeeze as much liquid as possible from the grated zucchini.

Cook the fritters until they are nicely golden on both sides.

DRESSED-UP BABY POTATOES

Preparation time: 25 minutes
Total cooking time: 45 minutes
Makes 24

24 even bite-sized new potatoes,
    washed and dried
⅓ cup (80 ml/2¾ fl oz) olive oil
1 tablespoon drained capers,
    patted dry
1 rasher bacon
1 tablespoon cream
10 g (¼ oz) butter
½ cup (125 g/4 oz) sour cream
1 tablespoon chopped fresh chives
1 tablespoon red or black caviar

1 Preheat the oven to moderate
180°C (350°F/Gas 4). Line a baking
tray with baking paper. Place the
potatoes in a bowl and toss with half
the olive oil. Sprinkle with salt and
black pepper, then put on the baking
tray and bake for 40 minutes, or until
cooked through, rotating them 2–3
times so that they brown evenly.
2 Meanwhile, heat the remaining oil
in a frying pan and cook the capers
over high heat, or until they open into
small flowers. Drain on paper towels.
Cook the bacon under a hot grill until
crispy. Cool, then finely chop.
3 Remove the potatoes from the
oven. When cool enough to handle,
cut a thin lid from each potato.
Discard the lids. Use a melon baller

or small teaspoon to scoop out the
flesh from the middle of the potatoes,
leaving a 1 cm (½ inch) shell. Put the
potato flesh in a bowl and mash
thoroughly with the cream, butter
and salt and black pepper to taste.
Spoon the mash back into the
potatoes.
4 Top each potato with a small
dollop of sour cream. Divide them
into four groups of six and use a
different topping for each group:
capers, bacon, chives and caviar.

NUTRITION PER POTATO
Protein 2.5 g; Fat 4.5 g; Carbohydrate 9.5 g;
Dietary Fibre 1.5 g; Cholesterol 13 mg; 370 kJ
(90 Cal)

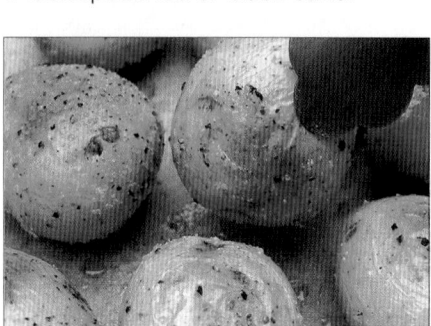

Turn the potatoes once or twice during cooking
so they brown evenly.

Once the capers have opened into small flowers,
drain them on paper towels.

Scoop out a small amount of flesh from the
potatoes, reserving the flesh.

SESAME AND WASABI-CRUSTED TUNA CUBES

Preparation time: 10 minutes
Total cooking time: 5 minutes
Makes about 40

Ginger and soy dipping sauce
2 cm x 2 cm (¾ inch x ¾ inch) piece
    fresh ginger, cut into julienne strips
2 tablespoons Japanese soy sauce
2 tablespoons mirin
1 teaspoon wasabi paste
¼ teaspoon sesame oil

TUNA CUBES
600 g (1¼ lb) fresh tuna steaks
1 teaspoon wasabi powder
⅓ cup (50 g/1¾ oz) black sesame
    seeds
¼ cup (60 ml/2 fl oz) oil

1 To make the dipping sauce, place the ginger, Japanese soy sauce, mirin, wasabi paste and sesame oil in a small bowl and mix together well. Set aside until needed.
2 Cut the tuna into 2 cm (¾ inch) cubes using a very sharp knife. Put the tuna cubes in a large bowl. Add the combined wasabi powder and black sesame seeds to the bowl and toss well until the tuna cubes are evenly coated in powder and seeds.
3 Heat a wok over high heat, add half the oil and swirl to coat. Add half the tuna and cook, tossing gently, for 1–2 minutes, or until lightly golden on the outside but still pink in the middle. Drain on crumpled paper towels and repeat with the remaining oil and tuna. Arrange the tuna cubes on a platter with the dipping sauce in the centre and serve with toothpicks so that your guests can pick up the cubes.

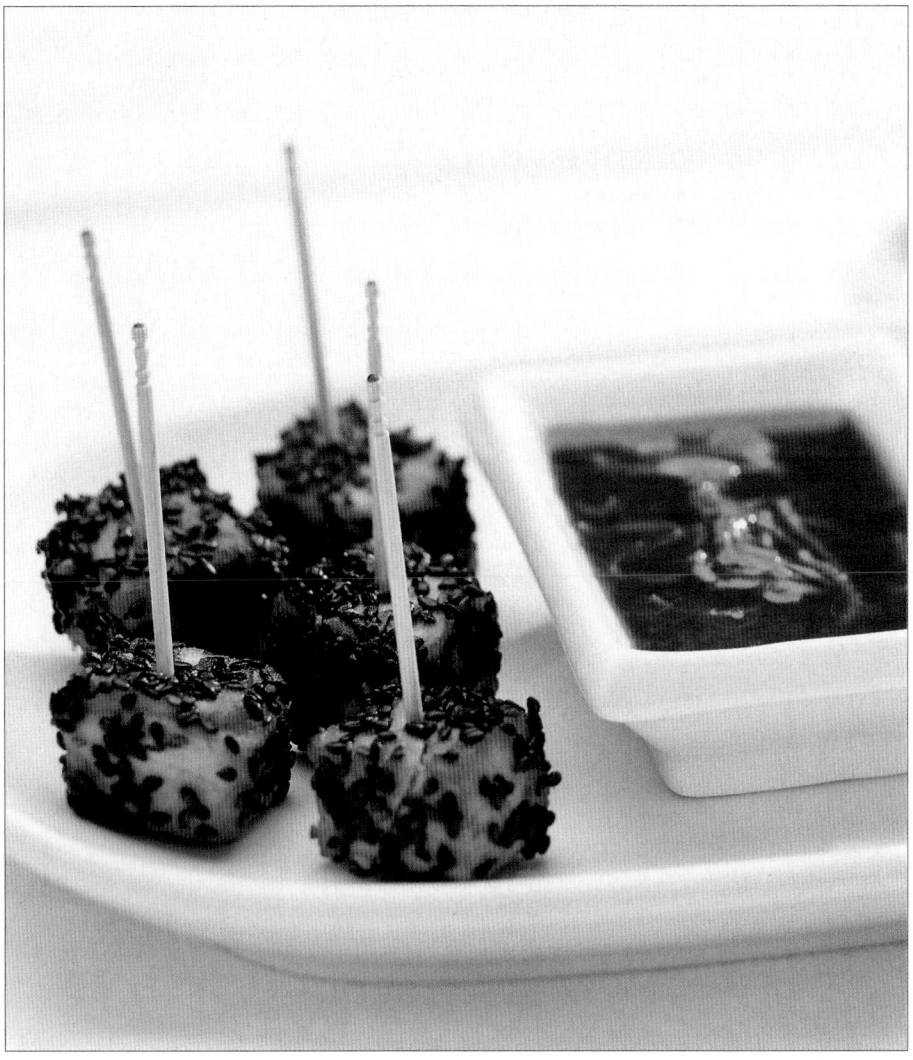

NUTRITION PER PIECE
Protein 4 g; Fat 3 g; Carbohydrate 0 g; Dietary Fibre 0 g; Cholesterol 5.5 mg; 175 kJ (40 Cal)

THINK AHEAD: The dipping sauce will keep in the refrigerator for up to 1 week, but the tuna is best if cooked no more than 3 hours in advance.

VARIATION: The tuna cubes are also very nice served with a chilli and lime dipping sauce instead of the ginger and soy one in the recipe. To make the dipping sauce, dissolve 2 tablespoons grated palm sugar or soft brown sugar in a small bowl with 2 tablespoons lime juice. Add 1 tablespoon fish sauce and 1 seeded and finely chopped fresh red bird's eye chilli. Mix together well. This sauce will keep in the refrigerator for 2–3 days.

Mix all the dipping sauce ingredients together in a small bowl.

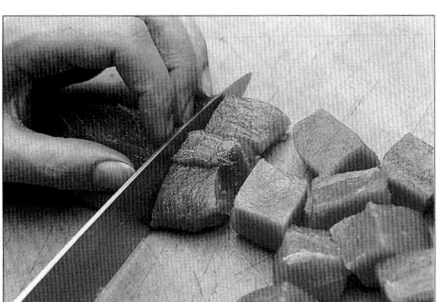

Use a sharp knife to cut the tuna steaks into even 2 cm (¾ inch) cubes.

Coat the tuna cubes in the black sesame seeds and wasabi powder.

GOAT'S CHEESE FRITTERS WITH ROASTED CAPSICUM SAUCE

**Preparation time: 20 minutes +
  30 minutes refrigeration
Total cooking time: 30 minutes
Makes 30**

ROASTED CAPSICUM SAUCE
2 red capsicums
2 tablespoons olive oil
1 small red onion, finely chopped
1 clove garlic
⅓ cup (80 ml/2¾ fl oz) chicken
    or vegetable stock

420 g (14 oz) ricotta, well drained
400 g (13 oz) goat's cheese, crumbled
2 tablespoons chopped fresh chives
¼ cup (30 g/1 oz) flour
2 eggs, lightly beaten
1 cup (100 g/3½ oz) dry breadcrumbs
oil, for deep-frying

1 Cut the capsicums into 2–3 pieces, removing the seeds and membrane. Place, skin-side-up, under a hot grill until the skin blackens and blisters. Cool in a plastic bag, then peel away the skin and roughly chop the flesh.
2 Heat the oil in a frying pan over medium heat and cook the onion and garlic for 4–5 minutes, or until softened. Add the capsicum and stock. Bring to the boil, then remove from the heat, cool slightly and place in a food processor. Pulse until combined, but still a little lumpy. Season with salt and freshly ground black pepper and chill until needed.
3 Combine the ricotta, goat's cheese and chives in a bowl. Add the flour and egg, then season and mix well.
4 Put the breadcrumbs in a bowl. Roll a level tablespoon of the cheese mixture into a ball with damp hands, then flatten slightly and coat in the breadcrumbs. Repeat with the remaining mixture. Refrigerate for 30 minutes.
5 Fill a deep heavy-based saucepan or deep-fryer one-third full of oil and heat to 180°C (350°F), or until a cube of bread browns in 15 seconds. Cook the fritters in batches for 1 minute, or until browned, then remove from the

pan and drain well on crumpled paper towels. Serve warm with the roasted capsicum sauce.

NUTRITION PER FRITTER
Protein 5 g; Fat 8 g; Carbohydrate 4 g; Dietary Fibre 0.5 g; Cholesterol 26 mg; 420 kJ (100 Cal)

THINK AHEAD: The uncooked fritters can be frozen for up to 2 months or refrigerated for 2 days. The roasted capsicum sauce can be made up to 5 days in advance and kept in the refrigerator until needed.

Using a pulse action, process the capsicum mixture until well combined.

Cover all of the fritters with an even coating of breadcrumbs.

MEXICAN BITES

**Preparation time: 40 minutes +
  30 minutes refrigeration**
Total cooking time: 5 minutes
Makes 36

740 g (1½ lb) can kidney beans,
  drained
1 teaspoon ground cumin
2 tablespoons olive oil
¼ teaspoon cayenne pepper
1 avocado
1 small clove garlic, crushed
2 tablespoons sour cream
2 tablespoons lime juice
1 vine-ripened tomato, seeded
  and finely chopped
2 tablespoons finely chopped fresh
  coriander
250 g (8 oz) packet round tortilla chips

1 To make the refried beans, put the
kidney beans in a bowl and mash
with a potato masher, then add the
cumin. Heat 1½ tablespoons of oil
in a large non-stick frying pan and
add the cayenne and mashed kidney
beans. Cook the mixture over
medium–high heat for 2–3 minutes,
stirring constantly. Allow to cool, then
refrigerate for 30 minutes, or until cold.
2 Scoop the avocado flesh into a
food processor and add the garlic,
sour cream and 1 tablespoon of the
lime juice. Process for a few minutes
until it is a thick creamy paste, then
add salt to taste. Refrigerate.
3 To make the salsa, mix together the
tomato, coriander and the remaining
oil and lime juice in a small bowl.
Refrigerate until needed.
4 To assemble, lay out 36 round
tortilla chips. Put a heaped teaspoon

of refried beans in the centre of each
chip, add a teaspoon of the avocado
cream and top each with half a
teaspoon of the tomato salsa.

NUTRITION PER PIECE
Protein 1.5 g; Fat 5 g; Carbohydrate 6.5 g;
Dietary Fibre 1.5 g; Cholesterol 1.4 mg; 315 kJ
(75 Cal)

THINK AHEAD: The bean purée can
be made 3 days in advance. Make
the salsa up to 2 hours beforehand.
Assemble just before serving.

Roughly mash the red kidney beans with a
potato masher.

Blend the avocado mixture until a thick, creamy
paste is formed.

Make the salsa by combining the tomato,
coriander, oil and lemon juice.

PEKING DUCK ROLLS

Preparation time: 35 minutes +
   10 minutes resting
Total cooking time: 5 minutes
Makes 24

1 cup (125 g/4 oz) plain flour
½ teaspoon sesame oil
½ large Chinese roast duck
6 spring onions, cut into 24 pieces
   6 cm (2½ inches) long
1 Lebanese cucumber, seeded and
   cut into 6 cm x 5 mm (2½ inch x
   ¼ inch) batons
2–3 tablespoons hoisin sauce
2 teaspoons toasted sesame seeds
24 chives, blanched

1 Sift the flour into a small bowl, make a well in the centre, and pour in the sesame oil and ½ cup (125 ml/ 4 fl oz) boiling water. Combine well until the mixture becomes a slightly sticky soft dough. If needed, add a few teaspoons more of boiling water at a time if the mixture is still a bit dry. Knead the dough on a floured work surface for about 5 minutes, or until smooth. Cover and rest for about 10 minutes.
2 Shred the duck meat with your fingers and cut the skin into strips.
3 Roll the dough into a sausage shape and divide into 24 pieces, then roll each piece to an 8–9 cm (3–3½ inch) round with a rolling pin on a lightly floured board. Once they are rolled out, lay them out in a single layer and cover with plastic wrap or a tea towel while you are rolling out the others to prevent them from drying out.
4 Heat a non-stick frying pan over medium–high heat, and dry-fry them in batches for about 20 seconds each side. Do not overcook, or they will be too crispy for rolling. The pancakes should have slight brown speckles on them. Stack each pancake on a plate, and keep warm. If they cool down too much, reheat them by placing on a plate, covering with plastic wrap and microwaving for 20–30 seconds on High, or wrapping them in foil and baking in a warm (170°C/325°F/Gas 3) oven until warmed through.

5 Arrange a piece of spring onion, some cucumber strips, duck flesh and skin on each pancake. Drizzle with ½ teaspoon hoisin sauce and sprinkle with toasted sesame seeds. Roll the pancake up firmly and tie with a blanched chive strip to hold it in place. Serve immediately.

NUTRITION PER ROLL
Protein 4 g; Fat 5 g; Carbohydrate 6 g; Dietary Fibre 0.5 g; Cholesterol 20 mg; 330 kJ (80 Cal)

THINK AHEAD: You can make the pancakes 2–3 days ahead and wrap them tightly in plastic wrap until ready to serve. To reheat, put them on a plate, cover with plastic wrap and microwave for 20–30 seconds on high.

Roll each portion of dough into a neat round with a rolling pin.

Tightly roll the pancakes to enclose the filling, then secure with a blanched chive.

VEGETABLE FRITTATA WITH HUMMUS AND BLACK OLIVES

Preparation time: 35 minutes
Total cooking time: 40 minutes
Makes 30 pieces

2 large red capsicums
600 g (1¼ lb) orange sweet potato,
    cut into 1 cm (½ inch) slices
¼ cup (60 ml/2 fl oz) olive oil
2 leeks, finely sliced
2 cloves garlic, crushed
250 g (8 oz) zucchini, thinly sliced
500 g (1 lb) eggplant, cut into 1 cm
    (½ inch) slices
8 eggs, lightly beaten
2 tablespoons finely chopped fresh
    basil
1¼ cups (125 g/4 oz) grated
    Parmesan
200 g (6½ oz) hummus
black olives, pitted and halved, to
    garnish

1 Cut the capsicums into large pieces, removing the seeds and membrane. Place, skin-side-up, under a hot grill until the skin blackens and blisters. Cool in a plastic bag, then peel.
2 Cook the sweet potato in a saucepan of boiling water for 4–5 minutes, or until just tender. Drain.
3 Heat 1 tablespoon of the oil in a deep round 23 cm (9 inch) frying pan and stir the leek and garlic over medium heat for 1 minute, or until soft. Add the zucchini and cook for 2 minutes, then remove from the pan.
4 Heat the remaining oil in the same pan and cook the eggplant in batches for 2 minutes each side, or until golden. Line the base of the pan with half the eggplant and spread with the leek mixture. Cover with the roasted capsicum, then with the remaining eggplant and finally the sweet potato.
5 Put the eggs, basil, Parmesan and pepper in a jug, mix well and pour over the vegetables. Cook over low heat for 15 minutes, or until almost cooked. Place the pan under a hot grill for 2–3 minutes, or until golden and cooked. Cool before inverting onto a board. Trim the edges and cut into 30 squares. Top each square with a dollop of hummus and half an olive.

NUTRITION PER PIECE
Protein 4.5 g; Fat 6 g; Carbohydrate 5 g;
Dietary Fibre 2 g; Cholesterol 52 mg;
387 kJ (92 cal)

Lay the roasted capsicum pieces over the leek and zucchini mixture.

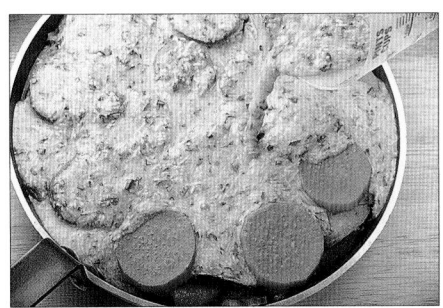
Pour the egg mixture over the vegetables so that they are covered.

Cook the frittata under a hot grill until it is golden brown on top.

POLENTA WEDGES WITH BOCCONCINI AND TOMATO

Preparation time: 30 minutes +
1 hour setting
Total cooking time: 40 minutes
Makes 48

1 tablespoon olive oil
1⅔ cups (250 g/8 oz) polenta
¾ cup (75 g/2½ oz) grated Parmesan
2½ tablespoons pesto
150 g (5 oz) bocconcini, thinly sliced
12 cherry tomatoes, cut into quarters
½ cup (15 g/½ oz) fresh basil, larger
    leaves torn

1 Lightly grease a 20 cm x 30 cm (8 inch x 12 inch) baking tin with the olive oil. Bring 1 litre (4 cups) lightly salted water to the boil in a saucepan. Once water is boiling, add polenta in a steady stream, stirring continuously to prevent lumps forming. Reduce the heat to very low and simmer, stirring regularly, for 20–25 minutes, or until the polenta starts to come away from the side of the pan.
2 Stir the Parmesan into polenta and season with salt and pepper. Spoon polenta into the baking tray, smooth the top with the back of a wet spoon and leave for 1 hour, or until set.
3 Once the polenta has set, carefully tip it out onto a board and cut into 5 cm (2 inch) squares, then cut each square into two triangles. Chargrill the polenta in batches on a preheated chargrill pan for 2–3 minutes on each side, or until warmed through.

4 Spread each triangle with 1 teaspoon of the pesto, then top with a slice of bocconcini and a tomato quarter. Season and grill for 1–2 minutes, or until the cheese is just starting to melt. Garnish with the fresh basil and serve immediately.

NUTRITION PER PIECE
Protein 1.5 g; Fat 1.5 g; Carbohydrate 3.5 g; Dietary Fibre 0.5 g; Cholesterol 3 mg; 155 kJ (35 Cal)

THINK AHEAD: The polenta can be made up to 3 days ahead. Assemble up to 2 hours before serving, then grill at the last moment.

Add the polenta to the boiling water in a fine, steady stream to avoid lumps.

Stir the grated Parmesan through the cooked polenta until well combined and melted.

Chargrill the wedges of polenta until they are warmed through.

DOLMADES

Preparation time: 40 minutes
  + 15 minutes soaking
Total cooking time: 45 minutes
Makes 24

200 g (6½ oz) packet vine leaves
  in brine
1 cup (250 g/8 oz) medium-grain rice
1 small onion, finely chopped
1 tablespoon olive oil
50 g (1¾ oz) pine nuts, toasted
2 tablespoons currants
2 tablespoons chopped fresh dill
1 tablespoon finely chopped fresh
  mint
1 tablespoon finely chopped fresh
  flat-leaf parsley
⅓ cup (80 ml/2¾ fl oz) olive oil, extra
2 tablespoons lemon juice
2 cups (500 ml/16 fl oz) chicken stock
  or vegetable stock

1 Place the vine leaves in a bowl, cover with hot water and soak for 15 minutes. Remove and pat dry. Cut off any stems. Reserve some leaves to line the saucepan and discard any with holes. Meanwhile, soak the rice in boiling water for 10 minutes to soften, then drain.
2 Place the rice, onion, oil, pine nuts, currants, herbs and some salt and pepper in a large bowl, and mix well.
3 Lay a leaf vein-side-down on a flat surface. Place 1 tablespoon of filling in the middle of the leaf, fold the stalk end over the filling, then the left and right sides into the middle, then roll firmly towards the tip. The dolmade should resemble a cigar. Repeat with the remaining filling and leaves.
4 Using the reserved vine leaves, line the bottom of a large heavy-based

saucepan. Drizzle with 1 tablespoon of the extra oil. Place the dolmades in the pan, packing them tightly in one layer. Pour the lemon juice and remaining olive oil over them.
5 Pour the chicken stock over the dolmades and cover with an inverted plate to stop them moving around while cooking. Bring to the boil, then reduce the heat and simmer, covered, for 45 minutes. Remove with a slotted spoon. May be served warm or cold.

NUTRITION PER DOLMADE
Protein 1.5 g; Fat 4 g; Carbohydrate 9.5 g; Dietary Fibre 0.5 g; Cholesterol 0 mg; 335 kJ (80 Cal)

NOTE: Any unused leaves can be stored in brine in an airtight container in the refrigerator for up to 1 week.

Fold the sides of the vine leaf into the middle and roll up towards the tip.

Pack the dolmades tightly into the pan and pour on the oil and lemon juice.

Remove the cooked dolmades from the pan with a slotted spoon.

Dips

Dips are one of the easiest options for feeding the hordes at any gathering. They can be made well in advance and simply need to be placed on a side table for your guests to help themselves.

GUACAMOLE

Ready in under 15 minutes

2 large ripe avocados
2 tablespoons lime juice
1 tomato, seeded and finely diced
1 fresh red chilli, finely chopped
2 tablespoons finely diced red onion
1½ tablespoons chopped fresh
    coriander leaves
1½ tablespoons sour cream
1 tablespoon olive oil
½ teaspoon ground cumin
pinch of cayenne pepper

Mash the avocado and lime juice in a bowl. Stir in the tomato, chilli, onion, coriander, sour cream, olive oil and cumin. Season with cayenne pepper and some salt and pepper. Spoon into a serving bowl and sprinkle with cayenne pepper. Makes 1⅓ cups. Ideal with crudités, tortilla shards, or corn chips.

TARAMASALATA

Ready in under 15 minutes

4 slices white bread, crusts removed
⅓ cup (80 ml/2¾ fl oz) milk
200 g (6½ oz) smoked cod or grey
    mullet roe
1 egg yolk
1 clove garlic, crushed
150–170 ml (5–5½ fl oz) olive oil
2 tablespoons lemon juice
1 tablespoon chopped fresh parsley

Soak the bread in milk for 5 minutes. Squeeze out the excess liquid and transfer to a food processor. Add the roe, egg yolk and garlic and process until smooth. With the motor running, slowly pour in the oil, stopping when the dip is thick and holds its form. Add the juice and parsley. Season and add more juice if necessary. Makes 1⅓ cups. Ideal with crudités

WARM CHEESE DIP

Ready in about 15 minutes

40 g (1¼ oz) butter
3 spring onions, finely chopped
2 jalapeño chillies, finely chopped
½ teaspoon ground cumin
¾ cup (185 g/6 oz) sour cream
2 cups (250 g/8 oz) grated Cheddar
green Tabasco, to drizzle

Melt the butter in a saucepan and add the spring onion, chilli and cumin. Cook, without browning, over low heat, stirring often, for 6–8 minutes. Stir in the sour cream and, when it is warm, add the grated Cheddar. Stir constantly until the cheese melts and the mixture is glossy and smooth. Transfer to a bowl, drizzle with a little Tabasco and serve warm. Makes 2 cups. Ideal with Parmesan puff straws or tortilla shards.

RED CAPSICUM SKORDALIA

Ready in about 30 minutes

1 large floury potato (e.g. russet,
    King Edward), cut into large
    cubes
2 large red capsicums, seeded
    and cut into large flattish pieces
100 g (3½ oz) slivered almonds,
    toasted
4 cloves garlic, crushed
200 ml (6½ fl oz) olive oil
2 tablespoons red wine vinegar

Boil the potato until tender, then drain well and return to the pan. Mash with a potato masher, then cool. Meanwhile, put the capsicum, skin-side-up, under a hot grill and cook until the skin blackens and blisters. Transfer to a plastic bag and leave to cool. Peel the skin and roughly chop the flesh. Finely grind the nuts in a food processor, add the garlic and capsicum and blend until smooth. With the motor running, slowly add the oil, then the vinegar. Transfer to a bowl and fold in the mashed potato. Mix well. Makes 2½ cups. Ideal with crudités, orange sweet potato wedges or deep-fried cheese ravioli.

BABA GANOUJ

Ready in about 1 hour 30 minutes

2 eggplants (1 kg/2 lb)
⅓ cup (80 ml/2¾ fl oz) lemon juice
2 tablespoons tahini
1½ tablespoons olive oil
3 cloves garlic, crushed
½ teaspoon ground cumin
pinch of cayenne pepper
1 tablespoon finely chopped fresh
    flat-leaf parsley
black olives, to garnish

Preheat the oven to moderately hot 200°C (400°F/Gas 6). Pierce each of the eggplants a few times with a fork, then, using tongs to hold the eggplant, cook over an open flame for about 5 minutes, or until the skin is black and blistered all over. Transfer the eggplants to a roasting tin and bake for 35–40 minutes, or until they are soft and wrinkled. Place in a colander over a bowl to drain off any bitter juices and stand for 30 minutes, or until cool. Carefully peel the skin from the eggplant, and place the flesh in a food processor with the lemon juice, tahini, oil, crushed garlic, cumin and cayenne pepper. Process until smooth and creamy. Season with salt and stir in the chopped parsley. Spread the baba ganouj onto a serving plate and garnish with the black olives. Makes 1⅓ cups. Ideal with tortilla shards.

Clockwise, from top left: Red capsicum skordalia, Baba ganouj, Warm cheese dip, Guacamole, Taramasalata.

Clockwise, from top left: Hummus, Green Mexican salsa, White bean dip, Warm crab and lemon dip, Dhal.

HUMMUS

Prepare a day ahead

200 g (6½ oz) dried chickpeas
⅓ cup (80 ml/2¾ fl oz) olive oil
3–4 tablespoons lemon juice
2 cloves garlic, crushed
2 tablespoons tahini
1 tablespoon ground cumin

Soak the chickpeas in cold water for 8 hours or overnight. Drain. Place in a saucepan, cover with cold water, bring to the boil and boil for 50–60 minutes. Drain the chickpeas well, reserving ¾–1 cup (185–250 ml) of the cooking liquid. Place in a food processor with the oil, lemon juice, garlic, tahini, cumin and ½ teaspoon salt. Blend well until the mixture begins to look thick and creamy. With the motor running, gradually add the reserved cooking liquid until the mixture reaches the desired consistency. Makes 2½ cups. Ideal with herbed lavash, herb grissini, crudités, or fresh or toasted pitta bread.

GREEN MEXICAN SALSA

Ready in under 15 minutes

300 g (10 oz) can tomatillos, drained
    (see NOTE)
1 small onion, chopped
1 jalapeño chilli, finely chopped
3 cloves garlic, crushed
2 tablespoons chopped fresh
    coriander leaves
1–2 teaspoons lime juice

Place the tomatillos in a food processor with the onion, chilli, crushed garlic and 1 tablespoon of the coriander. Process until smooth, then blend in the lime juice to taste. Add the rest of the coriander and process just long enough to mix it through the dip. Makes 2 cups. Ideal served with tortilla shards or corn chips.

NOTE: Tomatillos resemble green tomatoes with a papery husk. They are extensively used in Mexican cooking.

WHITE BEAN DIP

Ready in under 15 minutes

2 x 400 g (13 oz) cans lima
    or cannellini beans, drained
    and rinsed
½ cup (125 ml/4 fl oz) olive oil
⅓ cup (80 ml/2¾ fl oz) lemon juice
3 cloves garlic, finely chopped
1 tablespoon finely chopped fresh
    rosemary

Place the beans in a food processor with the olive oil, lemon juice, garlic, rosemary and 1 teaspoon salt. Process until smooth, then season with freshly cracked black pepper. Makes 3 cups. Ideal with herb grissini, orange sweet potato wedges, tortilla shards, or Turkish bread.

THINK AHEAD: This dip improves with age, so you can make it up to 2 days ahead of time.

DHAL

Ready in about 30 minutes

1 cup (250 g/8 oz) red lentils,
    rinsed
¼ teaspoon ground turmeric
1 tablespoon oil
1 tablespoon cumin seeds
½ teaspoon brown mustard seeds
1 onion, finely chopped
1 tablespoon grated fresh ginger
2 long fresh green chillies, seeded
    and finely chopped
⅓ cup (80 ml/2¾ fl oz) lemon juice
2 tablespoons finely chopped fresh
    coriander leaves

Place the lentils in a saucepan with 3 cups (750 ml/24 fl oz) cold water. Bring to the boil, then reduce the heat and stir in the turmeric. Simmer, covered, for 20 minutes, or until they are quite tender. Meanwhile, heat the oil in a saucepan over medium heat, and cook the cumin and mustard seeds for 5–6 minutes, or until the seeds begin to pop. Add the onion, ginger and chilli and cook for 5 minutes, or until the onion is golden. Add the lentils, fresh basil leaves and ½ cup (125 ml/4 fl oz) water. Season

with salt, reduce the heat and simmer for 10 minutes. Spoon into a bowl, stir in the lemon juice and garnish with the coriander. Makes 3 cups. Ideal with herbed lavash or spicy poppadoms.

WARM CRAB AND LEMON DIP

Ready in about 30 minutes

80 g (2¾ oz) butter
2 cloves garlic, crushed
3 French shallots, thinly sliced
1 teaspoon mustard powder
½ teaspoon cayenne pepper
½ cup (125 ml/4 fl oz) cream
150 g (5 oz) cream cheese
½ cup (60 g/2 oz) grated Cheddar
350 g (11 oz) can crab meat, drained
2 tablespoons lemon juice
2 teaspoons Worcestershire sauce
3 teaspoons chopped fresh tarragon
½ cup (40 g/1¼ oz) fresh breadcrumbs
1 tablespoon chopped fresh parsley

Preheat the oven to warm 170°C (325°F/Gas 3). Melt half the butter in a saucepan, then cook the garlic and shallots for 2–3 minutes, or until just softened. Add the mustard powder, cayenne pepper and cream. Bring the mixture to a simmer and slowly whisk in the cream cheese, a little at a time. When the cream cheese is completely incorporated, whisk in the Cheddar and allow to cook, stirring constantly, over very low heat for 1–2 minutes, or until smooth. Remove from the heat and add the crab meat, lemon juice, Worcestershire sauce and 2 teaspoons of the tarragon. Season to taste with salt and cracked black pepper. Mix, then transfer to a small baking dish. Melt the remaining butter in a small saucepan, add the breadcrumbs, parsley and remaining tarragon and stir until just combined. Sprinkle over the crab mixture and bake for 15 minutes, or until golden. Serve warm. Makes 2½ cups. Ideal with Parmesan puff straws or Turkish bread.

Dippers

You can either serve these dippers with one of the home-made dips on the previous pages, or jazz up ready-made dips. Serve in large bowls or on platters.

DEEP-FRIED CHEESE RAVIOLI

Ready in under 15 minutes

oil, for deep-frying
300 g (10 oz) fresh cheese ravioli

Fill a deep heavy-based saucepan or deep-fryer one-third full of oil and heat to 180°C (350°F), or until a cube of bread dropped into the oil browns in 15 seconds. Cook the ravioli in batches until golden brown. Remove from the oil and drain on crumpled paper towels. Sprinkle with salt and cracked black pepper and serve hot. Makes about 30. Ideal with red capsicum skordalia or green Mexican salsa. Also good on their own.

MIXED ASIAN CRISPS

Ready in under 15 minutes

oil, for deep-frying
16 cassava crackers, broken into small pieces (see NOTE)
16 round won ton wrappers
16 small uncooked plain prawn crackers
1 sheet toasted nori, shredded

Fill a deep heavy-based saucepan or deep-fryer one third full of oil and heat to 180°C (350°F), or until a cube of bread dropped into the oil browns in 15 seconds. Deep-fry the cassava pieces until crisp. Remove with a slotted spoon and drain on paper towels. Repeat with the won ton wrappers and prawn chips. When they are all cool, combine and toss with the nori. Makes a big bowl. Best on their own or with a Thai dipping sauce.

NOTE: Cassava crackers are made from the flour of the dried cassava root and are available from most Asian speciality food stores.

HERBED LAVASH

Ready in about 15 minutes

½ cup (125 ml/4 fl oz) olive oil
3 cloves garlic, crushed
6 slices lavash bread
2 teaspoons sea salt flakes
2 teaspoons dried mixed Italian herbs

Preheat the oven to moderate 180°C (350°F/Gas 4). Heat the oil and garlic in a small saucepan over low heat until the oil is warm and the garlic is fragrant but not browned. Lightly brush the lavash bread on both sides with the garlic oil. Cut each piece of bread into eight triangular wedges and position them side-by-side on baking trays. Sprinkle the upper side of the bread with the sea salt and herbs. Bake the lavash for 10 minutes, or until crisp. Makes about 48 pieces. Ideal with hummus or dhal .

CRUDITES

Ready in about 15 minutes

100 g (3½ oz) baby green beans, trimmed
170 g (5½ oz) asparagus, trimmed and halved
100 g (3½ oz) baby corn
24 sugar snap peas
2 heads of endive, trimmed
1 head of radicchio, trimmed
12 baby carrots, trimmed, leaving the leafy tops intact
2 red capsicums, sliced into 1 cm (½ inch) wide slices
fresh herbs (e.g. dill, chervil, coriander), to serve
lime quarters, to serve

Fill a large bowl with plenty of iced water and set it aside. Bring a large saucepan of salted water to the boil and blanch the beans, asparagus,

corn and peas in separate batches until sweet and tender, but still firm to the bite. Remove with a slotted spoon and refresh in the iced water, then pat dry. Separate the endive and radicchio leaves. Arrange all the vegetables, including the carrots and capsicum, on a serving plate with your favourite dip. Garnish with fresh herbs and lime quarters. Makes enough for a platter.

PARMESAN PUFF STRAWS

Ready in under 30 minutes

4 sheets ready-rolled puff pastry
50 g (1¾ oz) butter, melted
1⅔ cups (165 g/5½ oz) finely grated Parmesan
1 egg, lightly beaten

Preheat the oven to moderately hot 200°C (400°F/Gas 6). Lightly brush the puff pastry with the butter, then sprinkle each sheet with ¼ cup (25 g/ ¾ oz) of the cheese and season with salt and pepper. Fold each sheet in half, bringing the top edge down towards you. Brush the tops of each sheet with the egg. Sprinkle each with 2 tablespoons of extra grated Parmesan and season with salt. Using a very sharp knife, cut the dough vertically into 1 cm (½ inch) wide strips. Transfer each of the strips to a baking tray lined with baking paper, spacing them evenly apart. Leave room for them to puff up without touching each other. Grab each end of the pastry and stretch and twist in the opposite direction. Bake for 8–10 minutes or until lightly browned. Makes 80. Ideal with warm cheese dip or warm crab and lemon dip. Also good on their own.

Clockwise, from top left: Deep-fried cheese ravioli, Mixed Asian crisps, Crudités, Parmesan puff straws, Herbed lavash.

Clockwise, from top left: Tortilla shards, Spicy poppadoms, Herb grissini, Spring onion flatbreads, Orange sweet potato wedges.

TORTILLA SHARDS

Ready in under 15 minutes

2 tablespoons sweet paprika
¼ teaspoon cayenne pepper
oil, for deep-frying
8 large flour tortillas, cut into
    long triangles

Combine the paprika and cayenne pepper in a small bowl. Fill a deep heavy-based saucepan one-third full of oil and heat to 180°C (350°F), or until a cube of bread dropped into the oil browns in 15 seconds. Drop the tortilla shards in the oil in batches and deep-fry until crisp. Drain on crumpled paper towels and sprinkle lightly with the paprika mix while still hot. Serves 8–10. Ideal with guacamole, baba ganouj, green Mexican salsa or white bean dip.

SPICY POPPADOMS

Ready in about 15 minutes

3 green cardamom seeds
1½ tablespoons coriander seeds
1 tablespoon cumin seeds
2 cloves
1 teaspoon black peppercorns
1 bay leaf, crushed
1 teaspoon ground mace
¼ teaspoon ground cinnamon
pinch of ground chilli
oil, for deep-frying
24 large poppadoms, broken
    into quarters

Toast the cardamom, coriander and cumin seeds, cloves, peppercorns and bay leaf in a dry frying pan over low heat for 2–3 minutes, or until richly fragrant. Cool for 5 minutes, then grind to a fine powder. Stir in the mace, cinnamon and chilli. Fill a wide, large saucepan one-third full with oil and heat to 180°C (350°F), or until a cube of bread dropped into the oil browns in 15 seconds. Deep-fry the pieces of poppadom, a few at a time, until crisp and golden. Drain on crumpled paper towels and sprinkle with the spice mix while still hot. Makes a large bowl. Ideal with dhal.

ORANGE SWEET POTATO WEDGES

Ready in about 30 minutes

1.3 kg (2 lb 10 oz) orange sweet
    potato, peeled and sliced into
    6 cm x 2 cm (2½ inch x ¾ inch)
    wedges
2 tablespoons olive oil
1 tablespoon fennel seeds
1 tablespoon coriander seeds
½ teaspoon cayenne pepper
1 teaspoon sea salt flakes

Preheat the oven to moderately hot 200°C (400°F/Gas 6). Place the sweet potato in a large baking dish and toss with the oil. In a mortar and pestle, pound together the fennel and coriander seeds until they are roughly crushed. Add to the orange sweet potato along with the cayenne and sea salt flakes. Toss well and bake for about 30 minutes, or until browned and crisp. Serve warm. Serves 6–8. Ideal with red capsicum skordalia or white bean dip. Also great on their own.

SPRING ONION FLATBREADS

Ready in under 1 hour

2 teaspoons oil
185 g (6 oz) spring onions, thinly
    sliced
1 clove garlic, crushed
½ teaspoon grated fresh ginger
1¾ cups (215 g/7 oz) plain flour
1½ tablespoons chopped fresh
    coriander
oil, for shallow-frying

Heat the oil in a frying pan, and cook the spring onion, garlic and ginger for 2–3 minutes, or until soft. Combine the flour and 1 teaspoon salt in a bowl. Stir in the onion mixture and the chopped coriander. Gradually stir in 1 cup (250 ml/8 fl oz) boiling water, stopping when a loose dough forms. Knead the dough with floured hands for 2 minutes, or until smooth. Cover with plastic wrap and rest for 30 minutes. Break off walnut-sized pieces of dough and roll out into thin ovals.

Fill a large frying pan with 2 cm (¾ inch) oil and heat over medium heat. When the oil is shimmering, cook the breads 2–3 at a time for 25–30 seconds each side, or until crisp and golden. Drain on paper towels and serve warm. Makes 40. Ideal with dhal.

HERB GRISSINI

Ready in under 2 hours

7 g (¼ oz) sachet dried yeast
1 teaspoon sugar
4 cups (500 g/1 lb) plain flour
¼ cup (60 ml/2 fl oz) olive oil
½ cup (15 g/½ oz) chopped fresh
    flat-leaf parsley
¼ cup (15 g/½ oz) chopped fresh basil
2 teaspoons sea salt flakes

Combine the yeast, sugar and 1¼ cups (315 ml/10 fl oz) warm water in a small bowl and leave in a warm place for 5–10 minutes, or until it is foamy. If the mixture does not foam, the yeast is dead and you will need to start again with another sachet of yeast. Sift the flour and 1 teaspoon salt into a bowl. Stir in the yeast mixture and oil to form a dough, adding more water if necessary. Gather into a ball and turn out onto a lightly floured surface. Knead for 10 minutes, or until soft and elastic. Add the parsley and basil, and knead for 1–2 minutes to incorporate evenly. Place the dough in a lightly oiled bowl and cover with plastic wrap. Leave in a warm place for 1 hour, or until doubled in volume. Preheat the oven to very hot 230°C (450°F/Gas 8) and lightly grease two large baking trays. Punch down the dough and knead for 1 minute. Divide into 24 portions, and roll each portion into a 30 cm (12 inch) long stick. Place the dough sticks on the trays and lightly brush with water. Sprinkle with the sea salt flakes. Bake for 15 minutes, or until crisp and golden. Makes 24. Ideal with white bean dip or hummus.

Soups & Starters

ROAST PUMPKIN SOUP

Preparation time: 20 minutes
Total cooking time: 55 minutes
Serves 6

1.25 kg (2 lb 8 oz) pumpkin, peeled
    and cut into chunks
2 tablespoons olive oil
1 large onion, chopped
2 teaspoons ground cumin
1 large carrot, chopped
1 celery stick, chopped
1 litre chicken or vegetable stock
sour cream, to serve
finely chopped fresh parsley, to serve
ground nutmeg, to serve

1 Preheat the oven to moderate
180°C (350°F/Gas 4). Place the
pumpkin chunks on a greased baking
tray and lightly brush with half the
olive oil. Bake for 25 minutes, or until
the pumpkin is softened and slightly
browned around the edges.
2 Heat the remaining oil in a large
saucepan. Cook the onion and cumin
for 2 minutes, then add the carrot and
celery and cook for 3 minutes more,
stirring frequently. Add the roasted
pumpkin and stock. Bring to the boil,
then reduce the heat and simmer for
20 minutes.
3 Allow to cool a little then purée
in batches in a blender or food
processor. Return the soup to the pan
and gently reheat without boiling.
Season to taste with salt and cracked
black pepper. Top with sour cream
and sprinkle with chopped parsley
and ground nutmeg before serving.

NUTRITION PER SERVE
Protein 5 g; Fat 8.5 g; Carbohydrate 15 g;
Dietary Fibre 3.5 g; Cholesterol 4.5 mg;
665 kJ (160 Cal)

NOTE: Butternut pumpkin is often
used in soups as it has a sweeter
flavour than other varieties.

HINT: If the soup is too thick, thin
it down with a little stock.

Lightly brush the pumpkin chunks with oil and
bake until softened.

Transfer the cooled mixture to a blender or food
processor and purée in batches.

PORK AND VEAL TERRINE

**Preparation time: 20 minutes + overnight
  refrigeration**
Total cooking time: 1 hour 20 minutes
Serves 6

8–10 thin slices rindless bacon
1 tablespoon olive oil
1 onion, chopped
2 cloves garlic, crushed
1 kg (2 lb) pork and veal mince
1 cup (80 g/2¾ oz) fresh breadcrumbs
1 egg, beaten
¼ cup (60 ml/2 fl oz) brandy
3 teaspoons chopped fresh thyme
¼ cup (15 g/½ oz) chopped fresh
    parsley

1 Preheat the oven to moderate
180°C (350°F/Gas 4). Lightly grease
a 25 cm x 11 cm (10 inch x 4½ inch)
terrine. Line the terrine with the
bacon so that it hangs over the sides.
2 Heat the oil in a frying pan, add
the onion and garlic and cook for
2–3 minutes, or until the onion is
soft. Mix the onion with the mince,
breadcrumbs, egg, brandy, thyme and
parsley in a large bowl. Season with
salt and pepper. Fry a small piece of
the mixture to check the seasoning,
and adjust if necessary.
3 Spoon the mixture into the bacon-
lined terrine, pressing down firmly.
Fold the bacon over the top of the
terrine, cover with foil and place
in a baking dish.
4 Place enough cold water in the
baking dish to come halfway up
the side of the terrine. Bake for
1–1¼ hours, or until the juices run
clear when the terrine is pierced with
a skewer. Remove the terrine from
the water-filled baking dish and pour
off the excess juices. Cover with foil,
then put a piece of heavy cardboard,
cut to fit, on top of the terrine. Put
weights or food cans on top of the
cardboard to compress the terrine.
Refrigerate overnight, then cut into
slices to serve.

NUTRITION PER SERVE
Protein 15 g; Fat 7.5 g; Carbohydrate 10 g;
Dietary Fibre 1 g; Cholesterol 60 mg;
800 kJ (190 Cal)

STORAGE TIME: The terrine can
be made ahead of time and stored,
covered, in the refrigerator for up
to 5 days.

Line the terrine dish with the bacon strips so that
they drape over the sides.

Mix together the onion mixture, mince,
breadcrumbs, egg, brandy and herbs.

Press the mixture firmly into the terrine dish and
fold the bacon over the top.

LEEK AND POTATO SOUP

Preparation time: 20 minutes
Total cooking time: 45 minutes
Serves 4

cooking oil spray
2 leeks, white part only, sliced
3 cloves garlic, crushed
1 teaspoon ground cumin
1 kg (2 lb) potatoes, chopped

5 cups (1.25 litres) vegetable stock
½ cup (125 ml/4 fl oz) skim milk

1 Lightly spray a non-stick frying pan with oil. Add the leek, garlic and 1 tablespoon water to prevent sticking, then cook over low heat, stirring frequently, for 25 minutes, or until the leek turns golden. Add the cumin and cook for 2 minutes.
2 Put the potato in a large pan with the leek mixture and stock, bring to

the boil, reduce the heat and simmer for 10–15 minutes, or until tender. Purée in a processor or blender until smooth. Return to the pan.
3 Stir in the milk, season and heat through before serving.

NUTRITION PER SERVE
Protein 8 g; Fat 1 g; Carbohydrate 35 g;
Dietary Fibre 5.5 g; Cholesterol 1 mg;
795 kJ (190 cal)

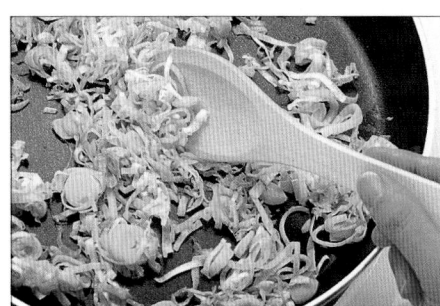
Stir the leek and garlic over low heat for about 25 minutes, until golden.

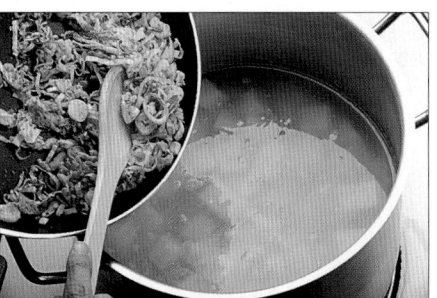
Add the cooked leek mixture to the chopped potato and stock.

Purée the soup in a food processor or blender, in batches if necessary.

CRISP POLENTA WITH MUSHROOMS

**Preparation time: 30 minutes +
   30 minutes refrigeration**
Total cooking time: 40 minutes
Serves 4

1 litre vegetable stock
1 cup (150 g/5 oz) polenta
2 tablespoons low-fat margarine
1 tablespoon grated fresh Parmesan
rocket, to serve
fresh Parmesan, shaved, to serve

MUSHROOM SAUCE
10 g (¼ oz) dried porcini mushrooms
1 tablespoon olive oil
800 g (1 lb 10 oz) mixed mushrooms
   (field, Swiss brown), thickly sliced
4 cloves garlic, finely chopped
2 teaspoons chopped fresh thyme
¾ cup (185 ml/6 fl oz) dry white wine
½ cup (125 ml/4 fl oz) vegetable stock
½ cup (30 g/1 oz) chopped fresh
   parsley

1 Bring the stock to the boil in a large saucepan. Add the polenta in a thin stream, stirring constantly. Simmer for 20 minutes over very low heat, stirring frequently, or until the mixture starts to leave the side of the pan. Add the margarine and Parmesan. Season. Grease a shallow 20 cm (8 inch) square cake tin. Pour in the polenta, smooth the surface and refrigerate for 30 minutes, or until set.
2 To make the mushroom sauce, soak the dried porcini mushrooms in ½ cup (125 ml/4 fl oz) boiling water for 10 minutes, or until softened. Drain, reserving ⅓ cup (80 ml/2¾ fl oz) of the liquid.
3 Heat the oil in a large frying pan. Add the mixed mushrooms and cook over high heat for 4–5 minutes, or until softened. Add the porcini, garlic and thyme, then season and cook for 2–3 minutes. Add the wine and cook until it has evaporated. Add the stock and soaking liquid, then reduce the heat and cook for a 3–4 minutes, or until the stock has reduced and thickened. Stir in the parsley.
4 Cut the polenta into 4 squares and grill until golden on both sides. Place one on each serving plate and top with the mushrooms. Garnish with rocket and Parmesan shavings.

NUTRITION PER SERVE
Protein 15 g; Fat 11 g; Carbohydrate 35 g;
Dietary Fibre 7 g; Cholesterol 1.5 mg;
1390 kJ (330 Cal)

Cook the porcini and mixed mushrooms over high heat until softened.

Grill squares of polenta until golden on both sides.

HOT AND SOUR LIME SOUP WITH BEEF

Preparation time: 20 minutes
Total cooking time: 35 minutes
Serves 4

1 litre beef stock
2 stems lemon grass, white part
    only, halved
3 cloves garlic, halved
2.5 cm x 2.5 cm (1 inch x 1 inch)
    piece fresh ginger, sliced
95 g (3 oz) fresh coriander, leaves
    and stalks separated
2 1.5 cm x 4 cm (⅝ inch x 1½ inch)
    strips lime rind
2 star anise
3 small fresh red chillies, seeded
    and finely chopped
4 spring onions, thinly sliced on
    the diagonal
500 g (1 lb) fillet steak, trimmed
2 tablespoons fish sauce
1 tablespoon grated palm sugar
2 tablespoons lime juice
fresh coriander leaves, extra,
    to garnish

1 Place the stock, lemon grass, garlic, ginger, coriander stalks, rind, star anise, 1 teaspoon chopped chilli, half the spring onion, and 1 litre water in a saucepan. Bring to the boil and simmer, covered, for 25 minutes. Strain and return the liquid to the pan.
2 Heat a chargrill pan until very hot. Brush with olive oil and sear the steak on both sides until browned on the outside, but very rare in the centre.
3 Reheat the soup, adding the fish sauce and palm sugar. Season and add the lime juice to taste (you may want more than 2 tablespoons)—you should achieve a hot and sour flavour.

4 Add the remaining spring onion and the chopped coriander leaves to the soup. Slice the beef across the grain into thin strips. Curl the strips into a decorative pattern, then place in four deep serving bowls. Pour the soup over the beef and garnish with the remaining chilli and coriander leaves.

NUTRITION PER SERVE
Protein 31 g; Fat 7 g; Carbohydrate 7 g; Dietary Fibre 0.5 g; Cholesterol 84 mg; 900 kJ (215 Cal)

Bring the soup to the boil, then reduce the heat and simmer for 25 minutes.

Brown the fillet steak on a hot, lightly oiled chargrill pan.

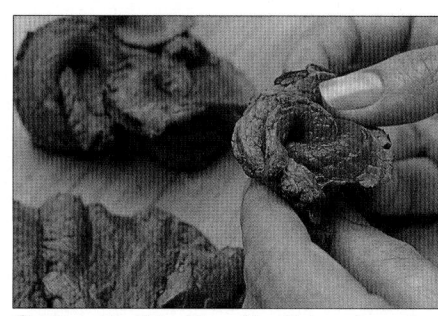

Gently curl the thin strips of beef into a decorative pattern.

CHICKEN CURRY LAKSA

Preparation time: 30 minutes
Total cooking time: 25 minutes
Serves 4

LAKSA PASTE
1 large onion, roughly chopped
5 cm (2 inch) piece fresh ginger, chopped
8 cm (3 inch) piece galangal, peeled and chopped
1 stem lemon grass, white part only, roughly chopped
2 cloves garlic
1 fresh red chilli, seeded and diced
2 teaspoons vegetable oil
2 tablespoons mild curry paste

500 g (1 lb) chicken breast fillets, cut into cubes
2 cups (500 ml/16 fl oz) chicken stock
60 g (2 oz) rice vermicelli
50 g (1¾ oz) dried egg noodles
400 ml (13 fl oz) light coconut milk
10 snow peas, halved
3 spring onions, finely chopped
1 cup (90 g/3 oz) bean sprouts
½ cup (15 g/½ oz) fresh coriander leaves

1 To make the laksa paste, process the onion, ginger, galangal, lemon grass, garlic and chilli in a food processor until finely chopped. Add the oil and process until the mixture has a paste-like consistency. Spoon into a large wok, add the curry paste and stir over low heat for 1–2 minutes, until aromatic. Take care not to burn.
2 Increase the heat to medium, add the chicken and stir for 2 minutes, or until the chicken is well coated. Stir in the chicken stock and mix well. Bring slowly to the boil, then simmer for 10 minutes, or until the chicken is cooked through.
3 Meanwhile, cut the vermicelli into shorter lengths. Cook the vermicelli and egg noodles separately in large pans of boiling water for 5 minutes

each. Drain and rinse in cold water.
4 Just prior to serving, add the light coconut milk and snow peas to the chicken and heat through. To serve, divide the vermicelli and noodles among four warmed serving bowls. Pour the hot laksa over the top and garnish with the spring onion, bean sprouts and coriander leaves.

NUTRITION PER SERVE
Protein 30 g; Fat 8 g; Carbohydrate 4.5 g;
Dietary Fibre 3 g; Cholesterol 65 mg;
945 kJ (225 cal)

HINT: If you prefer a more fiery laksa, use a medium or hot brand of curry paste or increase the amount of chillies in your laksa paste.

Over low heat, stir the curry paste into the onion mixture until aromatic.

Just before serving, stir the light coconut milk into the chicken until heated.

CHARGRILLED VEGETABLE TERRINE

Preparation time: 30 minutes + overnight refrigeration
Total cooking time: Nil
Serves 8

350 g (11 oz) ricotta
2 cloves garlic, crushed
8 large slices chargrilled eggplant, drained (see NOTE)
10 slices chargrilled red capsicum, drained
8 slices chargrilled zucchini, drained
45 g (1½ oz) rocket leaves
3 marinated artichokes, drained and sliced
85 g (3 oz) semi-dried tomatoes, drained and chopped
100 g (3½ oz) marinated mushrooms, drained and halved

1 Line a 24 x 13 x 6 cm (9 x 5 x 2½ inch) loaf tin with plastic wrap, leaving a generous amount hanging over the sides. Place the ricotta and garlic in a bowl and beat until smooth. Season with salt and pepper to taste and set aside.
2 Line the base of the tin with half the eggplant, cutting and fitting to cover the base. Top with a layer of half the capsicum, then all the zucchini slices. Spread evenly with the ricotta mixture and press down firmly. Place the rocket leaves on top of the ricotta. Arrange the artichoke, tomato and mushrooms in three rows lengthways on top of the ricotta.
3 Top with another layer of capsicum and finish with the eggplant. Fold the overhanging plastic wrap over the top of the terrine. Put a piece of cardboard on top and weigh it down with

weights or small food cans. Refrigerate the terrine overnight.
4 To serve, peel back the plastic wrap and turn the terrine out onto a plate. Remove the plastic wrap and cut into thick slices.

NUTRITION PER SERVE
Protein 6 g; Fat 5 g; Carbohydrate 3 g; Dietary Fibre 2 g; Cholesterol 20 mg; 350 kJ (85 cal)

NOTE: You can buy chargrilled eggplant, capsicum and zucchini and marinated mushrooms and artichokes at delicatessens.

STORAGE TIME: Cover any leftovers with plastic wrap and store in the refrigerator for up to 2 days.

Put the ricotta and crushed garlic in a bowl and beat until smooth.

Arrange the mushrooms, tomato and artichoke in three rows over the rocket.

Cover the terrine with cardboard and weigh down with small food cans.

MIXED MUSHROOMS IN BRIOCHE

Preparation time: 15 minutes
Total cooking time: 20 minutes
Serves 6

750 g (1½ lb) mixed mushrooms
    (Swiss brown, shiitake, button,
    field, oyster)
75 g (2½ oz) butter
4 spring onions, chopped
2 cloves garlic, crushed
½ cup (125 ml/4 fl oz) dry white wine
300 ml (10 fl oz) cream
2 tablespoons chopped fresh thyme
6 small brioche (see NOTE)

1 Preheat the oven to moderate 180°C (350°F/Gas 4). Wipe the mushrooms with a clean damp cloth to remove any dirt. Cut the larger mushrooms into thick slices but leave the smaller ones whole.
2 Heat the butter in a large frying pan over medium heat. Add the spring onion and garlic and cook for 2 minutes. Increase the heat, add the mushrooms and cook, stirring frequently, for 5 minutes, or until the mushrooms are soft and all the liquid has evaporated. Pour in the wine and boil for 2 minutes to reduce slightly.
3 Stir in the cream and boil for a further 5 minutes to reduce and slightly thicken the sauce. Season to taste with salt and cracked black pepper. Stir in the thyme and set aside for 5 minutes.
4 Slice the top off the brioche and, using your fingers, pull out a quarter of the bread. Place the brioche and their tops on a baking tray and warm in the oven for 5 minutes.
5 Place each brioche on an individual serving plate. Spoon the mushroom sauce into each brioche, allowing it to spill over one side. Replace the top and serve warm.

NUTRITION PER SERVE
Protein 7.5 g; Fat 33 g; Carbohydrate 15 g;
Dietary Fibre 4 g; Cholesterol 100 mg;
1587 kJ (380 cal)

NOTE: You can use bread rolls, but the flavour won't be as good.

Cut the large mushrooms into thick slices, but leave the smaller ones whole.

Cook the mushrooms, stirring frequently, until they are soft.

Add the cream to the sauce and cook until it has thickened slightly.

Slice off the top of each brioche and pull out a quarter of the bread.

CARROT TIMBALES WITH CREAMY SAFFRON AND LEEK SAUCE

Preparation time: 25 minutes
Total cooking time: 1 hour
Serves 6 as a starter

60 g (2 oz) butter
2 leeks, sliced
2 cloves garlic, crushed
1 kg (2 lb) carrots, sliced
1½ cups (375 ml/12 fl oz) vegetable
   stock
1½ tablespoons finely chopped fresh
   sage
¼ cup (60 ml/2 fl oz) cream
4 eggs, lightly beaten

CREAMY SAFFRON AND
   LEEK SAUCE
40 g (1¼ oz) butter
1 small leek, finely sliced
1 large clove garlic, crushed
¼ cup (60 ml/2 fl oz) white wine
pinch of saffron threads
⅓ cup (90 g/3 oz) crème fraîche

1 Preheat the oven to warm 170°C (325°F/Gas 3). Lightly grease six ¾ cup (185 ml) timbale moulds. Heat the butter in a saucepan and cook the leek for 3–4 minutes, or until soft. Add the garlic and carrot and cook for a further 2–3 minutes. Pour in the stock and 2 cups (500 ml/16 fl oz) water, bring to the boil, then reduce the heat and simmer, covered, for 5 minutes, or until the carrot is tender. Strain, reserving 3/4 cup (185 ml/ 6 fl oz) of the liquid.
2 Blend the carrot mixture, ½ cup (125 ml/4 fl oz) of the reserved liquid and the sage in a food processor or blender until smooth. Cool the mixture slightly and stir in the cream and egg. Season and pour into the prepared moulds. Place the moulds in a roasting tin filled with enough hot water to come halfway up their sides. Bake for 30–40 minutes, or until just set.
3 To make the sauce, melt the butter in a saucepan and cook the leek for 3–4 minutes without browning. Add the garlic and cook for 30 seconds. Add the wine, remaining reserved liquid and saffron and bring to the boil. Reduce the heat and simmer for 5 minutes, or until reduced. Stir in the crème fraîche.
4 Turn out the timbales onto serving plates and serve with the sauce.

NUTRITION PER SERVE
Protein 7 g; Fat 25 g; Carbohydrate 11 g;
Dietary Fibre 6 g; Cholesterol 187 mg;
1258 kJ (300 cal)

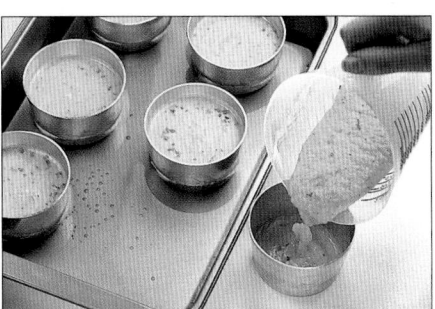

Pour the mixture into the prepared moulds and place in a roasting tin.

Cook the leek, garlic, wine, reserved liquid and saffron on low heat until reduced.

Carefully turn out the carrot timbales onto serving plates.

71

EGGPLANT AND CORIANDER TOSTADAS

Preparation time: 20 minutes
Total cooking time: 30 minutes
Serves 4 as a starter

1 small eggplant, cut into cubes
½ red capsicum, cut into cubes
½ red onion, cut into thin wedges
2 tablespoons olive oil
1 large clove garlic, crushed
1 small loaf wood-fired bread, cut into
    12 slices
1 small ripe tomato, halved
2 tablespoons chopped fresh mint

2 tablespoons chopped fresh
    coriander roots, stems and leaves
60 g (2 oz) slivered almonds, toasted

1 Preheat the oven to very hot 240°C (475°F/Gas 9). Put the eggplant, capsicum, onion and oil in a large bowl and mix to coat with the oil. Spread out in a single layer in a large roasting tin. Bake for 15 minutes, then turn and bake for a further 10 minutes, or until tender. Transfer to a bowl, add the garlic and season to taste with salt and pepper.
2 Place the bread on a baking tray and bake for 4 minutes, or until crisp. Rub the cut side of the tomato onto

one side of each bread slice, squeezing the tomato to get as much liquid as possible, then finely chop the tomato flesh and add to the vegetables with the mint and coriander.
3 Spoon the vegetables onto the tomato side of the bread and sprinkle with the almonds. Serve immediately.

NUTRITION PER SERVE
Protein 10 g; Fat 18 g; Carbohydrate 34 g;
Dietary Fibre 5 g; Cholesterol 0 mg;
1415 kJ (340 cal)

NOTE: You can roast the vegetables and toast the almonds up to a day ahead. Store in an airtight container.

Spread the oil-coated vegetables in a single layer in a large roasting tin.

Tip the roasted vegetables into a bowl and mix with the garlic and seasoning.

Rub the cut side of the tomato onto one side of each slice of bread.

POTATO, BROCCOLI AND CORIANDER SOUP

Preparation time: 15 minutes
Total cooking time: 30 minutes
Serves 6

500 g (1 lb) broccoli
cooking oil spray
2 onions, finely chopped
2 cloves garlic, finely chopped
2 teaspoons ground cumin
1 teaspoon ground coriander
750 g (1½ lb) potatoes, cubed
2 small chicken stock cubes
1½ cups (375 ml/12 fl oz) skim milk

3 tablespoons finely chopped fresh coriander

1 Cut the broccoli into small pieces. Lightly spray the base of a large saucepan with cooking oil, then place over medium heat and add the onion and garlic. Add 1 tablespoon water to prevent sticking. Cover and cook, stirring occasionally, over low heat for 5 minutes, or until the onion has softened and is lightly golden. Add the ground cumin and coriander and cook for 2 minutes.

2 Add the potato and broccoli to the pan, stir well and add the stock cubes and 1 litre of water. Slowly bring to

the boil, reduce the heat, cover and simmer over low heat for 20 minutes, or until the vegetables are tender. Allow to cool slightly.

3 Blend the soup in batches in a food processor or blender until smooth. Return to the pan and stir in the milk. Slowly reheat, without boiling. Stir the chopped coriander through and season well before serving.

NUTRITION PER SERVE
Protein 10 g; Fat 0.5 g; Carbohydrate 20 g; Dietary Fibre 6 g; Cholesterol 2 mg; 580 kJ (140 cal)

Chop all the broccoli into small, even-sized florets for quick cooking.

Stir the ground cumin and coriander into the onion and cook for about 2 minutes.

Purée the mixture in batches, in a food processor or blender, until it is smooth.

SOBA NOODLE SOUP

**Preparation time: 15 minutes +
 5 minutes standing**
Total cooking time: 10 minutes
Serves 4

250 g (8 oz) packet soba noodles
2 dried shiitake mushrooms
2 litres (64 fl oz) vegetable stock
120 g (4 oz) snow peas, cut into thin
  strips
2 small carrots, cut into thin strips
2 cloves garlic, finely chopped
6 spring onions, cut into 5 cm (2 inch)
  lengths and sliced lengthways

3 cm (1 inch) piece ginger, cut into
  julienne strips
⅓ cup (80 ml/2¾ fl oz) soy sauce
¼ cup (60 ml/2 fl oz) mirin or sake
1 cup (90 g/3 oz) bean sprouts
fresh coriander, to garnish

1 Cook the noodles according to the
packet instructions. Drain.
2 Soak the mushrooms in ½ cup
(125 ml/4 fl oz) boiling water until
soft. Drain, reserving the liquid.
Remove the stalks and finely slice
the mushrooms.
3 Combine the vegetable stock,
mushrooms, reserved liquid, snow
peas, carrot, garlic, spring onion and

ginger in a large saucepan. Bring
slowly to the boil, then reduce the
heat to low and simmer for 5 minutes,
or until the vegetables are tender.
Add the soy sauce, mirin and bean
sprouts. Cook for a further 3 minutes.
4 Divide the noodles among four
large serving bowls. Ladle the hot
liquid and vegetables over the top
and garnish with coriander.

NUTRITION PER SERVE
Protein 13 g; Fat 1.5 g; Carbohydrate 30 g;
Dietary Fibre 6 g; Cholesterol 11 mg;
1124 kJ (270 cal)

Cut the ginger into julienne strips (thin strips the
size and shape of matchsticks).

After soaking the mushrooms, drain and finely
slice them.

Simmer the vegetables for 5 minutes, or until
they are tender.

SEAFOOD RAVIOLI IN GINGERY SOUP

Preparation time: 30 minutes
Total cooking time: 20 minutes
Serves 4

8 raw prawns
1 carrot, chopped
1 onion, chopped
1 celery stick, chopped
3 spring onions, thinly sliced
6 cm (2½ inch) piece fresh ginger,
    thinly shredded
1 tablespoon mirin
1 teaspoon kecap manis
1 tablespoon soy sauce
4 large scallops
100 g (3½ oz) boneless white fish fillet
1 egg white
200 g (6½ oz) round gow gee
    wrappers
⅓ cup (10 g/¼ oz) fresh coriander
    leaves

1 To make the soup, peel the prawns, reserve 4 for the ravioli filling and chop the rest into small pieces and reserve. Put the prawn heads and shells in a large pan, cook over high heat until starting to brown, then cover with 1 litre water. Add the carrot, onion and celery, bring to the boil, reduce the heat and simmer for 10 minutes. Strain and discard the prawn heads, shells and vegetables. Return the stock to a clean pan and add the spring onion, ginger, mirin, kecap manis and soy sauce. Set aside.
2 To make the ravioli, chop the whole reserved prawns with the scallops and fish in a food processor until smooth. Add enough egg white to bind. Lay half the gow gee wrappers on a work surface and place a rounded teaspoon of filling in the centre of each. Brush the edges with water. Top each with another wrapper and press the edges to seal, eliminating air bubbles as you go. Trim with a fluted cutter. Cover with plastic wrap.
3 Bring a large pan of water to the boil. Meanwhile, heat the stock and leave simmering. Just prior to serving, drop a few ravioli at a time into the boiling water. Cook for 2 minutes, remove with a slotted spoon and divide among heated bowls. Cook the chopped reserved prawns in the same water for 2 minutes; drain. Pour the hot stock over the ravioli and serve, sprinkled with the chopped cooked prawns and coriander leaves.

NUTRITION PER SERVE
Protein 17 g; Fat 7 g; Carbohydrate 65 g;
Dietary Fibre 4.5 g; Cholesterol 125 mg;
1765 kJ (420 cal)

Stir the prawn heads and shells in a pan over high heat until lightly browned.

Brush the edge of one wrapper with water, then cover with another.

Cook each batch of ravioli for 2 minutes, then remove with a slotted spoon.

CHICKEN AND VEGETABLE SOUP

Preparation time: 1 hour + refrigeration
Total cooking time: 1 hour 25 minutes
Serves 6–8

1.5 kg (3 lb) chicken
2 carrots, roughly chopped
2 celery sticks, roughly chopped
1 onion, quartered
4 fresh parsley sprigs
2 bay leaves
4 black peppercorns
50 g (1¾ oz) butter
2 tablespoons plain flour
2 potatoes, chopped
250 g (8 oz) butternut pumpkin, cut into bite-sized pieces
2 carrots, extra, cut into matchsticks
1 leek, cut into matchsticks
3 celery sticks, extra, cut into matchsticks
100 g (3½ oz) green beans, cut into short lengths, or baby green beans, halved
200 g (6½ oz) broccoli, cut into small florets
100 g (3½ oz) sugar snap peas, trimmed
50 g (1¾ oz) English spinach leaves, shredded
½ cup (125 ml/4 fl oz) cream
¼ cup (15 g/½ oz) chopped fresh parsley

1 Place the chicken in a large pan with the carrot, celery, onion, parsley, bay leaves, 2 teaspoons of salt and the peppercorns. Add 3 litres of water. Bring to the boil, then reduce the heat and simmer for 1 hour, skimming the surface as required. Allow to cool for at least 30 minutes. Strain and reserve the liquid.

2 Remove the chicken and allow to cool until it is cool enough to handle. Discard the skin, then cut or pull the flesh from the bones and shred into small pieces. Set the chicken meat aside.

3 Heat the butter in a large pan over medium heat and, when foaming, add the flour. Cook, stirring, for 1 minute. Remove from the heat and gradually stir in the stock. Return to the heat and bring to the boil, stirring constantly. Add the potato, pumpkin and extra carrot and simmer for 7 minutes. Add the leek, extra celery and beans and simmer for a further 5 minutes. Finally, add the broccoli and sugar snap peas and cook for a further 3 minutes.

4 Just before serving, add the chicken, spinach, cream and chopped parsley. Reheat gently but do not allow the soup to boil. Keep stirring until the spinach has wilted. Season to taste with salt and freshly ground black pepper. Serve the soup immediately.

NUTRITION PER SERVE (8)
Protein 50 g; Fat 15 g; Carbohydrate 15 g;
Dietary Fibre 6 g; Cholesterol 130 mg;
1700 kJ (400 cal)

HINT: Do not overcook the vegetables. They should be tender yet crispy.

NOTE: The chicken stock (up to the end of Step 1) can be made 1 day ahead and kept, covered, in the refrigerator. This can, in fact, be beneficial—before reheating the stock, spoon off the fat which will have formed on the surface.

Cut the extra celery into short lengths, then into matchsticks.

Using a knife, trim the tops from the sugar snap peas, pulling down to remove the string.

Add the parsley sprigs and bay leaves to the chicken and vegetables in the pan.

Remove the skin from the cooled chicken, then shred the meat.

Add the potato, pumpkin and extra carrot to the boiling soup.

Pour in the cream and stir until the spinach has just wilted.

ROASTED ORANGE SWEET POTATO AND DITALINI PATTIES

Preparation time: 15 minutes
Total cooking time: 1 hour 10 minutes
Serves 4

2 orange sweet potatoes
(about 800 g/1 lb 10 oz in total)
½ cup (90 g/3 oz) ditalini
30 g (1 oz) toasted pine nuts
2 cloves garlic, crushed
4 tablespoons finely chopped
fresh basil
½ cup (50 g/1¾ oz) grated Parmesan
⅓ cup (35 g/1¼ oz) dry breadcrumbs
plain flour, for dusting
olive oil, for shallow-frying

1 Preheat the oven to very hot 250°C (500°F/Gas 10). Pierce the sweet potatoes several times with a fork, then place in a roasting tin and roast for about 1 hour, or until soft. Remove from the oven and cool. Meanwhile, cook the pasta in a large saucepan of boiling water until al dente. Drain and rinse under running water.
2 Peel the sweet potato and mash the flesh with a potato masher or fork, then add the pine nuts, garlic, basil, Parmesan, breadcrumbs and the pasta and combine. Season.
3 Shape the mixture into eight even patties (about 1.5 cm/⅝ inch thick) with floured hands, then lightly dust the patties with flour. Heat the oil in a large frying pan and cook the patties in batches over medium heat

for 2 minutes each side, or until golden and heated through. Drain on crumpled paper towels, sprinkle with salt and serve immediately. Great with a fresh green salad.

NUTRITION PER SERVE
Protein 13.5 g; Fat 15 g; Carbohydrate 51 g;
Dietary Fibre 5.5 g; Cholesterol 12 mg;
1650 kJ (395 Cal)

NOTE: To save time, drop spoonfuls of the mixture into the pan and flatten with an oiled spatula.

SERVING SUGGESTION: The patties are great with aïoli—mix 1 clove of crushed garlic into ⅓ cup (90 g/3 oz) whole-egg mayonnaise with a squeeze of lemon juice and season.

Test if the sweet potatoes are cooked with the point of a sharp knife.

When the sweet potatoes are cool enough to handle, peel them with your fingers.

Dusting your hands with flour before handling the mixture will prevent the patties from sticking.

BOUILLABAISSE

Preparation time: 40 minutes
Total cooking time: 30 minutes
Serves 6–8

ROUILLE
1 small red capsicum
1 long red chilli
1 slice white bread, crusts removed
2 cloves garlic
1 egg yolk
⅓ cup (80 ml/2¾ fl oz) olive oil

300 g (10 oz) raw medium prawns
18–24 black mussels
200 g (6½ oz) scallops
1.5 kg (3 lb) assorted white fish fillets
2 tablespoons oil
1 fennel bulb, thinly sliced
1 onion, chopped
5 ripe tomatoes, peeled, chopped
1.25 litres fish stock

pinch of saffron threads
1 bouquet garni
5 cm (2 inch) strip orange rind
chopped fresh parsley, to garnish

1 For the rouille, cut the capsicum and chilli into large pieces and discard the seeds and membrane. Grill skin-side-up until the skins blacken and blister. Cool in a plastic bag, then peel. Soak the bread in ¼ cup (60 ml/2 fl oz) water, then squeeze out excess liquid. Combine the capsicum, chilli, bread, garlic and yolk in a food processor. With the motor running, add the oil in a stream, until the mixture is smooth.
2 Peel the prawns and pull out the dark vein from each back, starting at the head. Scrub the mussels and pull out the beards. Discard any broken mussels, or open ones that don't close when tapped. Slice or pull off any vein, membrane or hard white muscle from each scallop, leaving any roe

attached. Cut the fish into 2 cm (¾ inch) pieces. Cover and refrigerate the seafood.
3 Heat the oil in a large saucepan over medium heat, and cook the fennel and onion for 10 minutes, or until golden. Add the tomato and cook for 3 minutes. Stir in the stock, saffron, bouquet garni and rind. Bring to the boil and cook for 10 minutes. Reduce the heat, add the fish, prawns and mussels and simmer for 4–5 minutes, or until the mussels open (discard any unopened ones). Add the scallops and cook for 1 minute. Remove the bouquet garni and orange rind.
4 Ladle the bouillabaisse into bowls, garnish with the parsley and serve with the rouille.

NUTRITION PER SERVE (8)
Protein 58 g; Fat 23 g; Carbohydrate 7.5 g; Dietary Fibre 2.8 g; Cholesterol 246 mg; 1975 kJ (470 Cal)

CHINESE MUSHROOM AND CHICKEN SOUP

**Preparation time: 20 minutes +
10 minutes soaking
Total cooking time: 10 minutes
Serves 4**

3 dried Chinese mushrooms
185 g (6 oz) thin dried egg noodles
1 tablespoon oil
4 spring onions, julienned
1 tablespoon soy sauce
2 tablespoons rice wine, mirin or
    sherry (see NOTE)
1.25 litres chicken stock
½ small barbecued chicken, shredded
50 g (1¾ oz) sliced ham, cut into strips

1 cup (90 g/3 oz) bean sprouts
fresh coriander leaves, to serve
thinly sliced red chilli, to serve

1 Soak the mushrooms in boiling water for 10 minutes to soften them. Squeeze dry then remove the tough stem from the mushrooms and slice them thinly.
2 Cook the noodles in a large pan of boiling water for 3 minutes, or according to the manufacturer's directions. Drain and cut the noodles into shorter lengths with scissors.
3 Heat the oil in a large heavy-based pan. Add the mushrooms and spring onion. Cook for 1 minute, then add the soy sauce, rice wine and stock. Bring slowly to the boil and cook for

1 minute. Reduce the heat then add the noodles, shredded chicken, ham and bean sprouts. Heat through for 2 minutes without allowing the soup to boil.
4 Use tongs to divide the noodles among four bowls, ladle in the remaining mixture, and garnish with coriander leaves and sliced chilli.

NUTRITION PER SERVE
Protein 25 g; Fat 10 g; Carbohydrate 35 g; Dietary Fibre 3 g; Cholesterol 80 mg; 1426 kJ (340 cal)

NOTE: Rice wine and mirin are available at Asian food stores.

Use a fork to shred the meat from the barbecued chicken.

Put the mushrooms in a bowl, cover with boiling water and leave to soak.

Cut the noodles into shorter lengths to make them easier to eat.

PEA AND HAM SOUP

Preparation time: 15 minutes +
overnight soaking
Total cooking time: 2 hours,
10 minutes
Serves 8

500 g (1 lb) yellow or green split peas
1 leek
1 tablespoon oil
2 carrots, chopped
1 celery stick, chopped
2 cloves garlic, crushed
750 g (1½ lb) meaty ham bone

1 Put the split peas in a large bowl, cover with water and soak overnight.
2 Cut the leek in half lengthways and wash thoroughly in cold water to remove any dirt. Slice thickly. Heat the oil in a large heavy-based pan, and add the leek, carrot, celery and garlic. Cook, stirring, for 2–3 minutes, then add the drained peas, the ham bone and 2.5 litres water. Bring to the boil, then reduce the heat and simmer for 2 hours, stirring occasionally.
3 Remove the ham bone and set it aside to cool. Cool the soup a little then purée in batches in a blender or food processor and return to the

pan. Remove the meat from the bone, chop and return the meat to the soup. Season to taste with salt and black pepper, reheat gently and serve hot.

NUTRITION PER SERVE
Protein 17 g; Fat 8 g; Carbohydrate 8.5 g;
Dietary Fibre 4 g; Cholesterol 30 mg;
725 kJ (175 Cal)

NOTE: If you forget to soak the split peas overnight, rinse them and cook the soup until the peas are tender.

Soak the split peas in water overnight, then drain before adding to the soup.

Add the peas, ham bone and water to the pan and bring to the boil.

Remove the meat from the bone and cut into small chunks.

ASPARAGUS WITH POACHED QUAIL EGGS AND LIME HOLLANDAISE

Preparation time: 15 minutes
Total cooking time: 10 minutes
Serves 4

32 asparagus spears
2 tablespoons virgin olive oil
2 teaspoons cracked black pepper
2 teaspoons white vinegar
12 quail eggs
2 egg yolks
150 g (5 oz) butter, melted
2 tablespoons lime juice
paprika, to serve
shavings of good-quality Parmesan,
    to serve

1 Trim the asparagus, brush with a little of the oil, then roll in the pepper, shaking off any excess.
2 Half fill a deep frying pan with water and bring to a gentle simmer, then add the vinegar—this will stop the egg white separating from the yolk as it cooks. Crack a quail egg into a small bowl before gently sliding it into the pan. Repeat with the other eggs. (You will probably need to cook them in two batches.) Cook for 1–2 minutes, or until the egg white turns opaque, then carefully remove from the pan with an egg slide and keep warm.
3 Heat the remaining oil in a large frying pan and cook the asparagus over high heat for 2–3 minutes, or until tender and bright green.
4 To make the hollandaise, place the egg yolks in a blender or whisk by hand and slowly add the melted butter in a thin, steady stream. Mix until all the butter has been added and the mixture has thickened

slightly. Add the lime juice, season to taste with salt and freshly cracked black pepper, then mix well.
5 Divide the asparagus among four warmed serving plates, top with three quail eggs per person, drizzle with some of the hollandaise and sprinkle with paprika and Parmesan shavings. Best served immediately.

NUTRITION PER SERVE
Protein 30 g; Fat 50 g; Carbohydrate 2 g;
Dietary Fibre 1 g; Cholesterol 425 mg;
2933 kJ (701 Cal)

Trim the asparagus, brush with oil and roll in cracked black pepper.

Gently slide each cracked quail egg into simmering water, one at a time.

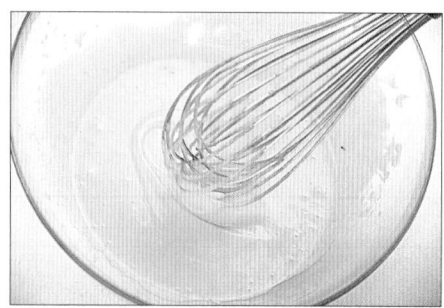

Whisk the egg yolks and butter together until slightly thickened.

CARAMELISED ONION, ROCKET AND BLUE CHEESE TARTS

Preparation time: 30 minutes +
30 minutes refrigeration
Total cooking time: 1 hour 10 minutes
Serves 6

PASTRY
2 cups (250 g/8 oz) plain flour
125 g (4 oz) butter, chilled and cut
    into cubes
¼ cup (25 g/¾ oz) finely grated
    Parmesan
1 egg, lightly beaten
¼ cup (60 ml/2 fl oz) chilled water

FILLING
2 tablespoons olive oil
3 onions, thinly sliced
100 g (3½ oz) baby rocket leaves
100 g (3½ oz) blue cheese, lightly
    crumbled
3 eggs, lightly beaten
¼ cup (60 ml/2 fl oz) cream
½ cup (50 g/1¾ oz) finely grated
    Parmesan
pinch grated fresh nutmeg

1 To make the pastry, sift the flour into a large bowl and add the butter. Rub the butter into the flour with your fingertips until it resembles fine breadcrumbs. Stir in the Parmesan.
2 Make a well in the centre of the dry ingredients, add the egg and water and mix with a flat-bladed knife, using a cutting action, until the mixture comes together in beads.
3 Gently gather the dough together and lift out onto a lightly floured work surface. Press into a ball and flatten it slightly into a disc, wrap in plastic wrap and refrigerate for 30 minutes.
4 Preheat the oven to moderately hot 200°C (400°F/Gas 6). Divide the pastry into six. Roll the dough out between two sheets of baking paper to fit six round 8 cm x 3 cm deep (3 inch x 1¼ inch deep) fluted loose-bottomed tart tins, remove the top sheet of paper and invert the pastry into the tins. Use a small ball of pastry to help press the pastry into the tins, allowing any excess to hang over the sides. Roll the rolling pin over the tins to cut off any excess.

5 Line the pastry shells with a piece of crumpled baking paper and pour in some baking beads or uncooked rice. Bake for 10 minutes, then remove the paper and beads and return the pastry to the oven for 10 minutes, or until the base is dry and golden. Cool slightly. Reduce the oven to moderate 180°C (350°F/Gas 4).
6 Heat the oil in a large frying pan, add the onion and cook over medium heat for 20 minutes, or until the onion is caramelised and golden. (Don't rush this step.)

7 Add the rocket and stir until wilted. Remove from the pan and cool.
8 Divide the onion mixture among the tart bases, then sprinkle with the blue cheese. Whisk together the eggs, cream, Parmesan and nutmeg and pour over each of the tarts. Place on a baking tray and bake for 25 minutes. Serve hot or cold with a green salad.

NUTRITION PER SERVE
Protein 18 g; Fat 40 g; Carbohydrate 33 g; Dietary Fibre 2.5 g; Cholesterol 215 mg; 2388 kJ (570 Cal)

Rub the butter into the flour until it resembles fine breadcrumbs.

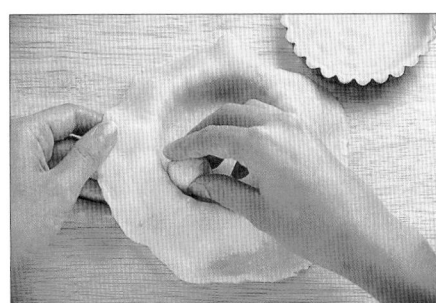

Use a small ball of pastry to press the pastry into the tins.

SMOKED HADDOCK CHOWDER

Preparation time: 20 minutes
Total cooking time: 35 minutes
Serves 4–6

500 g (1 lb) smoked haddock
   or smoked cod
1 potato, diced
1 celery stick, diced
1 onion, finely chopped
50 g (1¾ oz) butter
1 rasher bacon, finely chopped
2 tablespoons plain flour
½ teaspoon mustard powder
½ teaspoon Worcestershire sauce
1 cup (250 ml/8 fl oz) milk

3 tablespoons chopped fresh parsley
cream, for serving, optional

1 Put the fish in a deep frying pan, add 1.25 litres water and bring to the boil. Reduce the heat and simmer for 8 minutes, or until the fish flakes easily. Drain, reserving the liquid. Discard the skin and bones and flake the fish. Set aside.
2 Put the potato, celery and onion in a large saucepan with 3 cups (750 ml/24 fl oz) of the reserved liquid. Bring to the boil, then reduce the heat and simmer for 8 minutes, or until the vegetables are tender. Set aside.
3 Melt the butter in a large saucepan over low heat, add the bacon and cook for 3 minutes. Stir in the flour, mustard powder and Worcestershire sauce and cook for 1 minute, or until pale and foaming. Remove from the heat and gradually stir in the milk. Return to the heat and stir until the mixture boils and thickens. Reduce the heat and simmer for 2 minutes. Stir in the reserved vegetables and liquid, add the parsley and fish and simmer over low heat for 5 minutes, or until heated through. Season, to taste. If you wish, you can serve with a swirl of cream.

NUTRITION PER SERVE (6)
Protein 21.5 g; Fat 14.5 g; Carbohydrate 9 g;
Dietary Fibre 1 g; Cholesterol 93 mg;
1058 kJ (254 Cal)

Simmer the haddock in water until the fish flakes easily when tested with a fork.

Stir with a wooden spoon until the flour mixture is pale and foaming.

When the milk is stirred through, return the pan to the heat and stir until thick.

PRAWN COCKTAILS

Preparation time: 20 minutes
Total cooking time: Nil
Serves 6

COCKTAIL SAUCE
1 cup (250 g/8 oz) whole-egg
    mayonnaise
¼ cup (60 ml/2 fl oz) tomato sauce
2 teaspoons Worcestershire sauce
½ teaspoon lemon juice
1 drop Tabasco sauce

1 kg (2 lb) cooked medium prawns
lettuce, for serving
lemon wedges, for serving
sliced bread, for serving

1 For the cocktail sauce, mix all the
ingredients together in a bowl, then
season with salt and pepper.
2 Peel the prawns, leaving some with
tails intact to use as a garnish.
Remove the tails from the rest. Gently
pull out the dark vein from each
prawn back, starting at the head end.
Add the prawns without tails to the
sauce and mix to coat.
3 Arrange lettuce in serving dishes
or bowls. Spoon some prawns into
each dish. Garnish with the reserved
prawns, drizzling with some dressing.
Serve with lemon wedges and bread.

NUTRITION PER SERVE
Protein 42.5 g; Fat 16 g; Carbohydrate 34 g;
Dietary Fibre 4 g; Cholesterol 311 mg;
1900 kJ (454 Cal)

NOTE: You can make the cocktail
sauce several hours ahead and
refrigerate. Stir in 2 tablespoons
of thick cream for a creamier sauce.

Mix all the cocktail sauce ingredients together
in a bowl.

Carefully pull the shells off the prawns, leaving the
tails intact.

Put the prawns in with the cocktail sauce and mix
gently until well coated.

TWICE-BAKED CHEESE SOUFFLÉS

Preparation time: 30 minutes +
   10 minutes standing + refrigeration
Total cooking time: 45 minutes
Serves 4

1 cup (250 ml/8 fl oz) milk
2 cloves
1 onion, halved
1 bay leaf
3 black peppercorns
60 g (2 oz) butter
¼ cup (30 g/1 oz) self-raising flour
2 eggs, at room temperature,
   separated
125 g (4 oz) Gruyère, grated
1 cup (250 ml/8 fl oz) cream
½ cup (50 g/1¾ oz) grated Parmesan

1 Preheat the oven to moderate 180°C (350°F/Gas 4). Grease four ½ cup (125 ml/4 fl oz) ramekins. Heat the milk, clove-studded onion, bay leaf and peppercorns until about to boil, then remove from the heat and leave for 10 minutes. Strain.
2 Melt the butter, add the flour and cook over medium heat for 1 minute, or until golden. Remove from the heat and gradually stir in the milk, then return to the heat and stir until the mixture boils and thickens. Simmer for 1 minute. Transfer to a bowl, add the egg yolks and Gruyère, and mix.
3 Whisk the egg whites in a clean dry bowl until soft peaks form, then fold into the milk mixture. Divide among the ramekins and run your finger around the rim. Place in a roasting tin with enough boiling water to come halfway up the sides of the dishes. Bake for 15 minutes, or until puffed. Cool, then chill for up to 2 days.
4 To serve, preheat the oven to moderately hot 200°C (400°F/Gas 6), remove the soufflés from the ramekins and place each in an ovenproof dish. Pour the cream over the top, sprinkle with Parmesan and bake for 20 minutes, or until golden.

NUTRITION PER SERVE
Protein 22 g; Fat 55 g; Carbohydrate 12 g;
Dietary Fibre 0 g; Cholesterol 262 mg;
2672 kJ (638 Cal)

Cook the butter and flour mixture until it is golden.

Stir the mixture constantly until it boils and thickens.

Using a balloon whisk, beat the egg whites until soft peaks form.

Place the soufflés in individual dishes and pour on the cream.

OXTAIL SOUP

Preparation time: 20 minutes + chilling
Total cooking time: 3 hours 20 minutes
Serves 4

1 tablespoon plain flour
1 kg (2 lb) oxtail, chopped into 5 cm
    (2 inch) pieces (ask your butcher
    to do this)
1 tablespoon oil
2 litres beef stock
1 onion, chopped
1 celery stick, chopped
2 carrots, chopped
1 swede or turnip, peeled and
    chopped
3 whole cloves
12 peppercorns

2 bay leaves
1 tablespoon plain flour, extra
2 tablespoons port
1 tablespoon tomato paste
⅓ cup (20 g/¾ oz) finely chopped fresh
    parsley

1 Season the flour, put it in a plastic bag with the oxtail and shake to coat. Shake off excess flour. Heat the oil in a large pan, add the oxtail and cook in batches, tossing continually, for 5 minutes, or until evenly browned. Return all the oxtail to the pan.
2 Add the stock, 1½ cups (375 ml/ 12 fl oz) water, vegetables, cloves, peppercorns, bay leaves and ½ teaspoon salt. Bring slowly to the boil then reduce the heat and simmer, covered, for 3 hours.

3 Strain the vegetables and meat, reserving the liquid. Discard the vegetables and leave the meat to cool. Pull the meat from the bone, shred and refrigerate. Meanwhile, refrigerate the stock until the fat has solidified on the surface and can be removed with a spoon. Add the meat.
4 Put the soup in a clean pan. Mix together the extra flour, port and tomato paste, and add to the pan. Bring to the boil, stirring, until the soup thickens slightly. Simmer for 10 minutes, then stir in the parsley.

NUTRITION PER SERVE
Protein 25 g; Fat 7.5 g; Carbohydrate 9.5 g;
Dietary Fibre 2.5 g; Cholesterol 65 mg;
1700 kJ (405 Cal)

Put the seasoned flour and oxtail pieces in a plastic bag and shake to coat.

Heat the oil and cook the oxtail pieces in batches until browned.

Use a spoon to remove the solidified fat from the surface of the stock.

Bruschetta

To make basic bruschetta, cut a crusty Italian loaf into twelve 1.5 cm (⅝ inch) diagonal slices. Toast or grill the slices until golden. Bruise 2 garlic cloves with the flat of a knife, peel and rub the cloves over both sides of the hot bread. Drizzle the tops with a little extra virgin olive oil and finish with one of these delicious toppings.

ANCHOVY, TOMATO AND OREGANO

Seed and roughly chop 3 vine-ripened tomatoes and mix with 1 small chopped red onion, a 90 g (3 oz) jar drained, minced anchovy fillets and 2 tablespoons olive oil. Spoon some of the mixture onto each bruschetta. Drizzle with extra virgin olive oil, and garnish with chopped fresh oregano and freshly ground black pepper.

BLACK OLIVE PATE, ROCKET AND FETA

Place 100 g (3½ oz) trimmed baby rocket leaves, 75 g (2½ oz) crumbled Greek feta and 2 tablespoons olive oil in a bowl, and mix together well. Spread 2 teaspoons of black olive pâté onto each bruschetta slice and top with the feta mixture. Drizzle with extra virgin olive oil and season with sea salt and freshly ground black pepper.

SUN-DRIED TOMATO PESTO, ARTICHOKE AND BOCCONCINI

Spread 1 teaspoon of good-quality sun-dried tomato pesto onto each slice of bruschetta. Slice 12 (360 g/ 12 oz) bocconcini and place on top of the pesto. Chop 55 g (2 oz) drained marinated artichoke hearts in oil and place over the bocconcini slices. Sprinkle with some finely chopped fresh flat-leaf parsley.

PESTO, RED CAPSICUM AND PARMESAN

Cut 3 medium red capsicums into large flattish pieces and remove the seeds and membrane. Cook the capsicum pieces, skin-side-up, under a hot grill until the skin blackens and blisters. Place in a plastic bag and leave to cool. When cool enough to handle, peel away the skin. Discard the skin and cut the flesh into 1 cm (½ inch) strips. Spread 2 teaspoons good-quality basil pesto onto each slice of the bruschetta. Top with the red capsicum strips and 50 g (1¾ oz) fresh Parmesan shards. Drizzle with extra virgin olive oil and season with sea salt and ground black pepper.

MUSHROOM AND GOAT'S CHEESE

Preheat the oven to moderate 180°C (350°F/Gas 4). Mix ½ cup (125 ml/ 4 fl oz) olive oil with 3 chopped garlic cloves, 2 tablespoons chopped fresh flat-leaf parsley and 1 tablespoon dry sherry. Place 6 large field mushrooms on a foil-lined baking tray and spoon on all but 2 tablespoons of the mixture. Bake for 20 minutes, or until soft. Mix 150 g (5 oz) goat's cheese with 1 teaspoon chopped fresh thyme, then spread over the bruschetta. Warm the remaining oil mixture. Cut the mushrooms in half and place one half on each bruschetta. Drizzle with the remaining oil. Season with sea salt and ground black pepper.

TOMATO AND BASIL

Place 4 seeded and roughly chopped large vine-ripened tomatoes, ½ cup (15 g/½ oz) roughly torn fresh basil leaves, 2 tablespoons olive oil and ½ teaspoon caster sugar in a bowl and mix together well. Season with plenty of sea salt and black pepper and set the mixture aside for 10–15 minutes so the flavours have time to infuse and develop. Cut a ripe vine-ripened tomato in half and rub it on the oiled side of the slices of bruschetta, squeezing the tomato to extract as much of the liquid as possible. Carefully spoon 2 tablespoons of the tomato mixture onto each slice of bruschetta and serve immediately.

Left to right: Anchovy, tomato and oregano bruschetta; Black olive pâté, rocket and feta bruschetta; Sun-dried tomato pesto, artichoke and bocconcini bruschetta; Pesto, red capsicum and Parmesan bruschetta; Mushroom and goat's cheese bruschetta; Tomato and basil bruschetta.

LENTIL AND VEGETABLE SOUP WITH SPICED YOGHURT

Preparation time: 30 minutes
Total cooking time: 40 minutes
Serves 6

2 tablespoons olive oil
1 small leek (white part only), chopped
2 cloves garlic, crushed
2 teaspoons curry powder
1 teaspoon ground cumin
1 teaspoon garam masala
1 litre vegetable stock
1 fresh bay leaf
1 cup (185 g/6 oz) brown lentils
450 g (14 oz) butternut pumpkin, peeled and cut into 1 cm (½ inch) cubes
400 g (13 oz) can chopped tomatoes
2 zucchini, cut in half lengthways and sliced
200 g (6½ oz) broccoli, cut into small florets
1 small carrot, diced
½ cup (80 g/2¾ oz) peas
1 tablespoon chopped fresh mint

SPICED YOGHURT
1 cup (250 g/8 oz) thick plain yoghurt
1 tablespoon chopped fresh coriander leaves
1 clove garlic, crushed
3 dashes Tabasco sauce

1 Heat the oil in a saucepan over medium heat. Add the leek and garlic and cook for 4–5 minutes, or until soft and golden. Add the curry powder, cumin and garam masala and cook for 1 minute, or until fragrant.
2 Add the stock, bay leaf, lentils and pumpkin. Bring to the boil, then reduce the heat to low and simmer for 10–15 minutes, or until the lentils are tender. Season well.
3 Add the tomatoes, zucchini, broccoli, carrot and 2 cups (500 ml/16 fl oz) water, and simmer for 10 minutes, or until the vegetables are tender. Add the peas and simmer for 2–3 minutes.
4 Combine the yoghurt, coriander, garlic and Tabasco in a bowl. Add a dollop of the yoghurt to each serving of soup and garnish with the mint.

NUTRITION PER SERVE
Protein 17 g; Fat 10 g; Carbohydrate 26 g; Dietary Fibre 10 g; Cholesterol 6.5 mg; 1100 kJ (260 Cal)

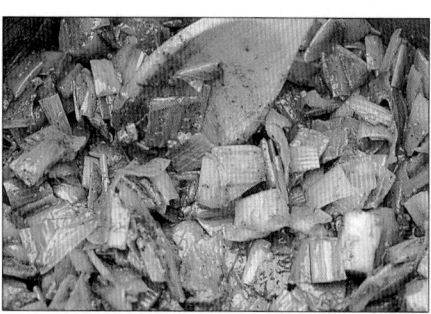

Stir in the curry powder, cumin and garam masala and cook until fragrant.

Simmer the lentils and vegetables over low heat until the lentils are tender.

Combine the yoghurt, coriander, garlic and Tabasco sauce.

SALMON CARPACCIO

**Preparation time: 30 minutes
+ 30 minutes freezing
Total cooking time: Nil
Serves 4**

500 g (1 lb) good-quality salmon
3 vine-ripened tomatoes
1 tablespoon baby capers, well
   rinsed and drained
1 tablespoon chopped fresh dill
1 tablespoon extra virgin olive oil
1 tablespoon lime juice
ciabatta bread, for serving

1 Wrap the salmon piece in foil and freeze for 20–30 minutes, or until partly frozen.
2 Meanwhile, cut a cross in the base of each tomato, place in a bowl and pour in enough boiling water to cover. Stand for 2–3 minutes, until the skin softens, then drain and peel. Cut each tomato in half, scoop out the seeds with a teaspoon and dice the flesh. Place in a bowl and stir in the capers and dill.
3 Remove the salmon from the freezer and unwrap. Using a very sharp knife, carefully cut the salmon into thin slices, cutting across the grain. Divide the salmon equally among four plates, arranging in a single layer, or use a serving platter.
4 Whisk together the olive oil and lime juice in a small bowl and season with a large pinch of salt or sea salt. Drizzle this dressing over the salmon just before serving. Season with ground black pepper and serve immediately with the tomato mixture and slices of ciabatta bread.

NUTRITION PER SERVE
Protein 36.5 g; Fat 12 g; Carbohydrate
32.5 g; Dietary Fibre 3 g; Cholesterol
60 mg; 1635 kJ (390 Cal)

NOTE: For this recipe, you can also use very fresh, good-quality tuna or smoked salmon. If you don't have a lot of time, the salmon can be thinly sliced without partially freezing it—use a very sharp knife.

Cut the peeled tomatoes in half and scoop out the seeds with a teaspoon.

Freezing the salmon makes it easier to cut into very thin slices.

CHARGRILLED BABY OCTOPUS

**Preparation time: 15 minutes
  + overnight marinating
Total cooking time: 10 minutes
Serves 4**

1 kg (2 lb) baby octopus
¾ cup (185 ml/6 fl oz) red wine
2 tablespoons balsamic vinegar
2 tablespoons soy sauce
2 tablespoons hoisin sauce
1 clove garlic, crushed

1 Cut off the octopus heads below the eyes with a sharp knife. Discard heads and guts. Push the beaks out with your index finger, remove and discard. Wash the octopus thoroughly under running water and drain on crumpled paper towels. If the octopus are large, cut tentacles into quarters.
2 Put the octopus in a large bowl. Stir together the wine, vinegar, soy sauce, hoisin sauce and garlic in a jug and pour over the octopus. Toss to coat, then cover and refrigerate for several hours, or overnight.
3 Heat a chargrill pan or barbecue hotplate until very hot and then lightly oil. Drain the octopus, reserving the marinade. Cook in batches for 3–5 minutes, or until the octopus flesh turns white. Brush the marinade over the octopus during cooking. Be careful not to overcook or the octopus will be tough. Serve warm or cold. Delicious with a green salad and lime wedges.

NUTRITION PER SERVE
Protein 42.5 g; Fat 3.5 g; Carbohydrate 4 g; Dietary Fibre 1 g; Cholesterol 497.5 mg; 1060 kJ (255 cal)

Remove and discard the head from each octopus with a sharp knife.

Push the beaks through the centre with your index finger.

Brush the octopus all over with the reserved marinade while cooking.

CHILLI, CORN AND RED CAPSICUM SOUP

Preparation time: 20 minutes
Total cooking time: 45 minutes
Serves 4

1 coriander sprig
4 corn cobs
30 g (1 oz) butter
2 red capsicums, diced
1 small onion, finely chopped
1 small red chilli, finely chopped
1 tablespoon plain flour
2 cups (500 ml/16 fl oz)
   vegetable stock
½ cup (125 ml/4 fl oz) cream

1 Trim the leaves off the coriander and finely chop the root and stems. Cut the kernels off the corn cobs.
2 Heat the butter in a large saucepan over medium heat. Add the corn kernels, capsicum, onion and chilli and stir to coat the vegetables in the butter. Cook, covered, over low heat, stirring occasionally, for 10 minutes, or until the vegetables are soft. Increase the heat to medium and add the coriander root and stem. Cook, stirring, for 30 seconds, or until fragrant. Sprinkle with the flour and stir for a further minute. Remove from the heat and gradually add the vegetable stock, stirring together. Add 2 cups (500 ml/16 fl oz) water and

return to the heat. Bring to the boil, reduce the heat to low and simmer, covered, for 30 minutes, or until the vegetables are tender. Cool slightly.
3 Ladle about 2 cups (500 ml/16 fl oz) of the soup into a blender and purée until smooth. Return the purée to the soup in the saucepan, pour in the cream and gently heat until warmed through. Season to taste with salt. Sprinkle with the coriander leaves to serve. Delicious with grilled cheese on pitta bread.

NUTRITION PER SERVE
Protein 5.5 g; Fat 20 g; Carbohydrate 24 g;
Dietary Fibre 4 g; Cholesterol 62 mg;
1269 kJ (303 cal)

Using a sharp knife, cut all the kernels from the corn cob.

Trim the leaves and finely chop the root and stems of the coriander.

Simmer for 30 minutes, or until the vegetables are tender.

TOMATO DITALINI SOUP

Preparation time: 15 minutes
Total cooking time: 20 minutes
Serves 4

2 tablespoons olive oil
1 large onion, finely chopped
2 celery sticks, finely chopped
3 vine-ripened tomatoes
1.5 litres chicken or vegetable stock
½ cup (90 g/3 oz) ditalini pasta
2 tablespoons chopped fresh
   flat-leaf parsley

1 Heat the oil in a large saucepan over medium heat. Add the onion and celery and cook for 5 minutes, or until they have softened.
2 Score a cross in the base of each tomato, then place them in a bowl of boiling water for 1 minute. Plunge into cold water and peel the skin away from the cross. Halve the tomatoes and scoop out the seeds. Roughly chop the flesh. Add the stock and tomato to the onion mixture and bring to the boil. Add the pasta and cook for 10 minutes, or until al dente. Season and sprinkle with parsley. Serve with crusty bread.

NUTRITION PER SERVE
Protein 8 g; Fat 11 g; Carbohydrate 23 g;
Dietary Fibre 3.5 g; Cholesterol 0 mg;
925 kJ (220 Cal)

Cook the onion and garlic until they are soft and translucent.

Halve the tomatoes horizontally and scoop out the seeds with a teaspoon.

CREAMY PRAWN BISQUE

Preparation time: 25 minutes
Total cooking time: 25 minutes
Serves 4–6

500 g (1 lb) raw medium prawns
60 g (2 oz) butter
2 tablespoons plain flour
2 litres fish stock
½ teaspoon paprika
1 cup (250 ml/8 fl oz) cream
⅓ cup (80 ml/2¾ fl oz) dry sherry
1–2 tablespoons cream, extra,
   for serving
paprika, extra, optional, to garnish

1 Peel the prawns and gently pull out the dark vein from each back, starting at the head end. Reserve the heads and shells. Melt the butter in a saucepan, add the prawn heads and shells and cook, stirring, over medium heat for 5 minutes, lightly crushing the heads with a wooden spoon.
2 Add the flour to the saucepan and stir until combined. Add the fish stock and paprika and stir until the mixture boils. Reduce the heat and simmer, covered, over low heat for 10 minutes. Strain the mixture through a fine sieve set over a bowl, then return the liquid to the saucepan. Discard the shells. Add the prawns to the saucepan and cook over low heat for 2–3 minutes.

Cool slightly, then process in batches in a blender or food processor until smooth. Return to the saucepan.
3 Add the cream and sherry to the pan and stir to heat through. Season, to taste, with salt and freshly ground black pepper. Serve topped with a swirl of cream and sprinkled with paprika, if desired.

NUTRITION PER SERVE (6)
Protein 22.5 g; Fat 32 g; Carbohydrate 4 g; Dietary Fibre 0 g; Cholesterol 249.5 mg; 1679 kJ (400 Cal)

NOTE: A few of the small cooked prawns can be reserved for garnishing.

Gently pull out the dark vein from each prawn back, starting at the head end.

Use a wooden spoon to lightly crush the prawn heads.

After cooking for 10 minutes, strain the mixture through a fine sieve into a bowl.

THAI FISH CAKES

Preparation time: 20 minutes
Total cooking time: 20 minutes
Serves 4–6

500 g (1 lb) redfish fillets, chopped
1 stem lemon grass, white part
   only, chopped
2 tablespoons fish sauce
5 spring onions, chopped
3 tablespoons chopped fresh
   coriander
1 clove garlic, crushed
140 ml (4½ fl oz) can coconut milk
1 tablespoon sweet chilli sauce
1 egg
5 snake beans, finely sliced
oil, for shallow-frying
200 g (6½ oz) mixed lettuce leaves

SAUCE
⅓ cup (90 g/3 oz) sugar
2 tablespoons sweet chilli sauce
½ small Lebanese cucumber, diced

1 Place the fish, lemon grass, fish
sauce, spring onion, coriander, garlic,
coconut milk, sweet chilli sauce and
egg in a food processor or blender
and blend until smooth. Transfer to
a bowl and fold in the snake beans.
With wet hands, shape into twelve
7 cm (2¾ inch) fish cakes, about 1 cm
(½ inch) high. Place on a plate, cover
and refrigerate until ready to use.
2 For the sauce, stir the sugar and
⅓ cup (80 ml/2¾ fl oz) water in
a small saucepan over low heat for
2 minutes, or until all the sugar has
dissolved. Increase the heat and
simmer for 5 minutes, or until slightly
thickened. Remove from the heat and
stir in the sweet chilli sauce. Cool
and stir in the diced cucumber.

3 Heat the oil in a deep, heavy-based
frying pan and cook the fish cakes
over medium heat for 1–2 minutes
on each side, or until cooked through.
4 Divide the lettuce among the plates
and arrange the fish cakes on top.
Serve with the sauce.

NUTRITION PER SERVE (6)
Protein 21 g; Fat 11 g; Carbohydrate 19 g;
Dietary Fibre 1.5 g; Cholesterol 88.5 mg;
1055 kJ (250 Cal)

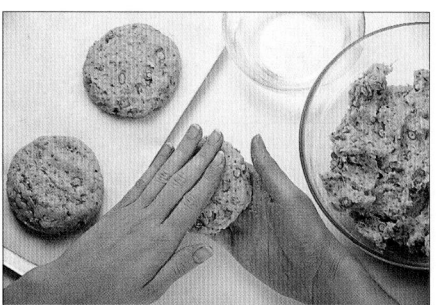

Shape the mixture into 12 patties about 7 cm
(2¾ inch) across and 1 cm (1/2 inch) high.

Remove from the heat and stir the sweet chilli
sauce into the sugar syrup.

Cook the fish cakes on both sides, turning with a
spatula, until cooked through.

MINESTRONE

Preparation time: 30 minutes
Total cooking time: 2 hours 30 minutes
Serves 8

1 tablespoon olive oil
1 onion, finely chopped
2 cloves garlic, crushed
2 carrots, diced
2 potatoes, diced
2 celery sticks, finely chopped
2 zucchini, finely chopped
2 cups (150 g/5 oz) shredded
   cabbage
125 g (4 oz) green beans, chopped

2 litres beef stock
425 g (14 oz) can chopped tomatoes
½ cup (80 g/2¾ oz) macaroni
440 g (14 oz) can borlotti or red
   kidney beans, drained
grated Parmesan, to serve
fresh thyme sprigs, to serve

1 Heat the oil in a large heavy-based pan. Add the onion and garlic and cook over low heat for 5 minutes. Add the carrot, potato and celery and cook, stirring, for a further 5 minutes.
2 Add the zucchini, cabbage and green beans to the pan and cook, stirring, for 5 minutes. Add the stock and chopped tomatoes. Bring slowly

to the boil, then reduce the heat, cover and leave to simmer for 2 hours.
3 Add the macaroni and beans, and cook for 15 minutes, or until the pasta is tender. Serve hot with a sprinkling of Parmesan and garnished with a sprig of fresh thyme.

NUTRITION PER SERVE
Protein 20 g; Fat 4 g; Carbohydrate 55 g;
Dietary Fibre 10.5 g; Cholesterol 0 mg;
1320 kJ (314 Cal)

NOTE: Any type of pasta can be used for minestrone, though smaller shapes are easier to manage on a soup spoon.

Finely shred the cabbage. You'll find this easiest if you use a large sharp knife.

Heat the oil in a pan, add the onion and garlic and cook, stirring, over low heat.

Add the zucchini, shredded cabbage and beans to the pan.

SAN CHOY BAU

**Preparation time: 25 minutes
+ 10 minutes soaking
Total cooking time: 8 minutes
Serves 4**

4 dried Chinese mushrooms
oil, for cooking
¼ cup (30 g/1 oz) slivered almonds,
    chopped
125 g (4 oz) water chestnuts, drained
    and finely chopped
1 carrot, finely chopped
4 spring onions, finely chopped
250 g (8 oz) lean pork mince
4 coriander roots, finely chopped
1 tablespoon grated fresh ginger
12 lettuce leaves
hoisin sauce, to serve

SAUCE
1 tablespoon light soy sauce
1 tablespoon lime juice
1 teaspoon sesame oil
¼ cup (15 g/½ oz) chopped coriander
2 tablespoons chopped mint

1 Soak the mushrooms in a bowl of hot water for 10 minutes, or until softened. Discard the tough stems and chop the mushrooms finely. Set aside.
2 To make the sauce, combine the soy sauce, lime juice, oil, coriander and mint. Set aside.
3 Heat the wok until very hot, add 1 tablespoon of the oil and swirl it around to coat the side. Stir-fry the almonds, water chestnuts, carrot and spring onion for 1 minute, or until lightly cooked but not browned—they should still be crisp. Remove from the wok and set aside.
4 Reheat the wok and add 1 tablespoon of the oil. Stir-fry the pork

mince, coriander root, ginger and mushrooms over medium-high heat for 2–3 minutes, or until the pork changes colour, but do not overcook the pork or it will be tough.
5 Add the sauce and stir to combine. Return the vegetable mixture to the wok and stir-fry for 1–2 minutes, or until heated through and the mixture is well combined. Spoon the pork

mixture into the lettuce leaves and sprinkle with the hoisin sauce, to taste. Serve more hoisin sauce for dipping.

NUTRITION PER SERVE
Protein 3.5 g; Fat 20 g; Carbohydrate 15 g;
Dietary Fibre 5 g; Cholesterol 0 mg;
1525 kJ (365 cal)

Water chestnuts are available canned. Drain them and then chop.

Soak the Chinese mushrooms, then discard the tough stems and finely chop them.

Stir-fry the pork mince with the coriander root, ginger and mushrooms.

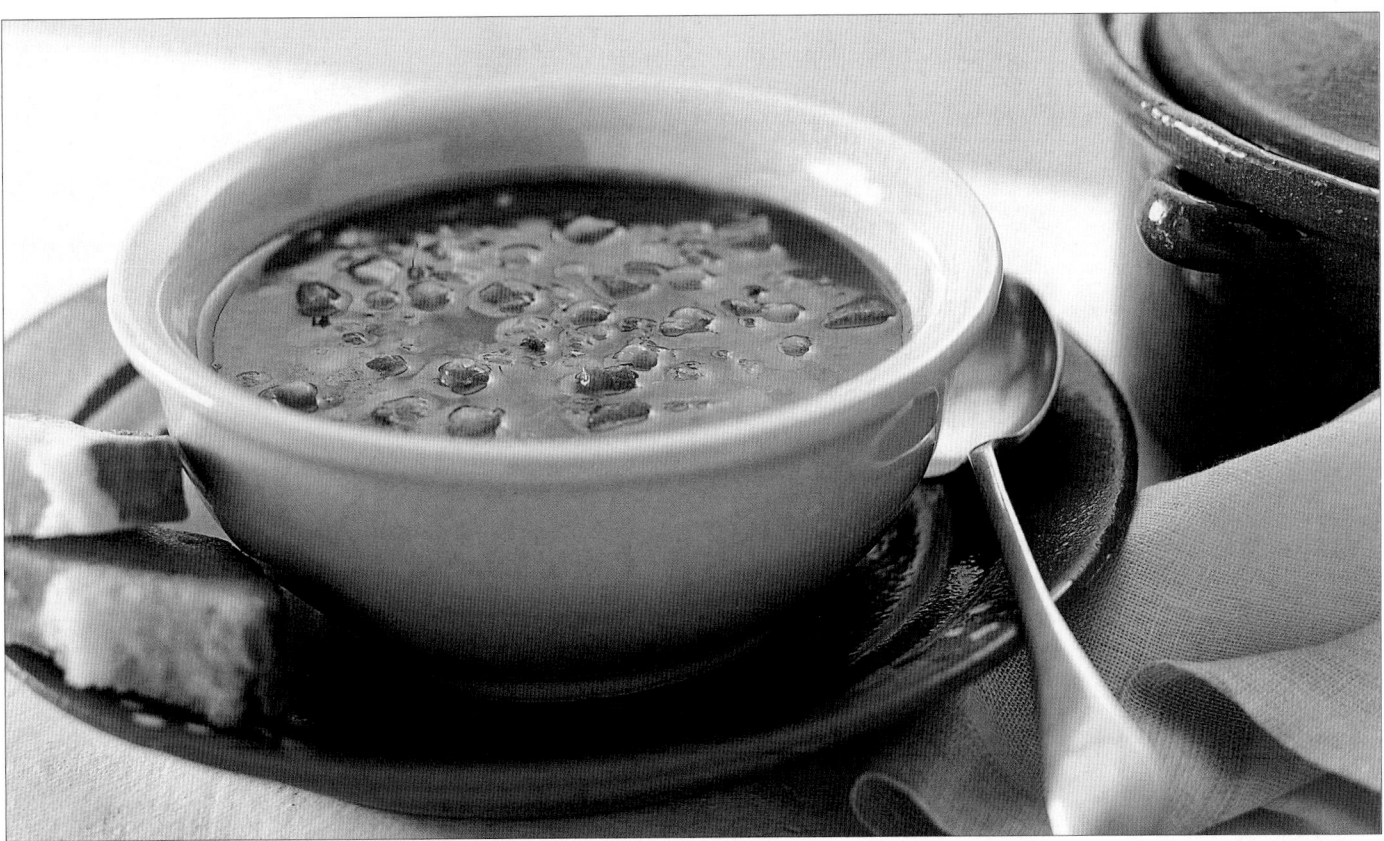

CHICKPEA SOUP

Preparation time: 15 minutes + overnight soaking
Total cooking time: 1 hour 30 minutes
Serves 4

1½ cups (330 g/11 oz) dried
    chickpeas
½ onion
1 bay leaf
½ head garlic, unpeeled (8 cloves)
2 tablespoons olive oil
1 celery stick, chopped
1 large onion, extra, finely chopped
3 cloves garlic, extra, chopped
1 teaspoon ground cumin
1 teaspoon paprika
¼ teaspoon dried chilli powder
3 teaspoons chopped fresh oregano
1 litre vegetable stock
2 tablespoons lemon juice
olive oil, extra to drizzle

1 Place the chickpeas in a bowl and cover with water. Soak overnight, then drain. Transfer the chickpeas to a saucepan and add the onion, bay leaf, garlic and 1.5 litres water. Bring to the boil, then reduce the heat and simmer for 1 hour, or until the chickpeas are tender. Drain, reserving 2 cups (500 ml/16 fl oz) cooking liquid. Discard the onion, bay leaf and garlic.
2 Heat the oil in the same saucepan, add the celery and extra onion, and cook over medium heat for 5 minutes, or until golden. Add the extra garlic and cook for a further 1 minute. Add the cumin, paprika, chilli powder and 2 teaspoons of the oregano, and cook, stirring, for 1 minute. Return the chickpeas to the pan and stir to coat with the spices.
3 Pour in the vegetable stock and reserved cooking liquid, bring to the boil, then reduce the heat and simmer for 20 minutes. Stir in the lemon juice and remaining oregano and serve drizzled with olive oil.

NUTRITION PER SERVE
Protein 16 g; Fat 20 g; Carbohydrate 34 g;
Dietary Fibre 12 g; Cholesterol 0 mg;
1565 kJ (374 Cal)

Cook the chickpeas, onion, bay leaf and garlic until the chickpeas are tender.

Add the cooked chickpeas to the pan and stir to coat in the spices.

Stir in the lemon juice and remaining fresh oregano.

99

SPAGHETTI BOLOGNESE

Preparation time: 30 minutes
Total cooking time: 1 hour 20 minutes
Serves 6

cooking oil spray
2 onions, finely chopped
2 cloves garlic, finely chopped
2 carrots, finely chopped
2 celery sticks, finely chopped
400 g (13 oz) lean beef mince
1 kg (2 1b) tomatoes, chopped
½ cup (125 ml/4 fl oz) red wine

350 g (11 oz) spaghetti
¼ cup (15 g/½ oz) finely chopped fresh
  parsley

1 Lightly spray a large saucepan with oil. Place over medium heat and add the onion, garlic, carrot and celery. Stir for 5 minutes, or until the vegetables have softened. Add 1 tablespoon water, if necessary, to prevent sticking.

2 Increase the heat to high, add the mince and cook for 5 minutes, or until browned. Stir constantly to prevent the meat sticking. Add the tomato,

wine and 1 cup (250 ml/8 fl oz) water. Bring to the boil, reduce the heat and simmer, uncovered, for about 1 hour, until the sauce has thickened.

3 Cook the spaghetti in a large pan of rapidly boiling salted water for 10–12 minutes, or until al dente, then drain. Stir the parsley through the sauce, season with salt and pepper and serve over the pasta.

NUTRITION PER SERVE
Protein 9 g; Fat 8 g; Carbohydrate 50 g;
Dietary Fibre 7 g; Cholesterol 0 mg;
1695 kJ (405 cal)

Finely chop both the onions and then fry with the garlic, carrot and celery.

Stir the meat constantly and break up any lumps with the back of the spoon.

Simmer the bolognese sauce uncovered until the liquid has reduced and the sauce thickened.

ITALIAN SUMMER TART

**Preparation time: 40 minutes +
    50 minutes refrigeration
Total cooking time: 1 hour
Serves 4–6**

1½ cups (185 g/6 oz) plain flour
90 g (3 oz) butter, chilled and cubed
1 egg yolk
2–3 tablespoons iced water

FILLING
1 tablespoon olive oil
2 small red onions, sliced
1 tablespoon balsamic vinegar
1 teaspoon soft brown sugar
1 tablespoon fresh thyme leaves
170 g (51/2 oz) jar marinated
    quartered artichokes, drained
2 slices prosciutto, cut into strips
12 black olives

1 Place the flour and butter in a food processor and process for 15 seconds, or until the mixture resembles fine breadcrumbs. Add the egg yolk and water. Process in short bursts until the mixture just comes together, adding a little extra water if necessary. Turn out onto a floured surface and gather into a ball. Cover with plastic wrap and refrigerate for at least 30 minutes.
2 Roll the pastry between two sheets of baking paper until large enough to fit a 35 x 10 cm (14 x 4 inch) loose-based tart tin.Press it well into the sides and trim off the excess. Cover and refrigerate for 20 minutes.
3 Preheat the oven to 190°C (375°F/Gas 5). Cover the pastry shell with baking paper and fill evenly with baking beads, rice or beans. Bake for 15 minutes. Remove the paper and beads and bake for a further 15 minutes, or until the pastry is golden and dry. Cool on a wire rack.
4 Heat the oil in a pan, add the onion slices and cook, stirring occasionally, for 15 minutes. Add the balsamic vinegar and brown sugar and cook for a further 15 minutes. Remove from the heat, stir through the thyme leaves and set aside to cool.
5 Spread the onion evenly over the pastry shell. Arrange the quartered artichoke pieces on top, then fill the spaces between the artichokes with rolled-up pieces of prosciutto and the black olives. Serve the tart at room temperature.

NUTRITION PER SERVE (6)
Protein 6 g; Fat 15 g; Carbohydrate 25 g;
Dietary Fibre 2 g; Cholesterol 70 mg;
1155 kJ (275 cal)

Once the mixture resembles fine crumbs, add the egg yolk and a little water.

Fill the spaces with rolled-up pieces of prosciutto and black olives.

FRIED WHITEBAIT

Preparation time: 10 minutes
Total cooking time: 5 minutes
Serves 6

750 g whitebait
1½ cups (185 g/6 oz) plain flour
4 tablespoons ready-made
 Moroccan spices
1 teaspoon cayenne pepper
oil, for deep-frying

mixed lettuce leaves, for serving
lemon wedges, for serving

1 Rinse the whitebait under cold water, then drain and pat dry with paper towels.
2 Stir the flour in a bowl with the Moroccan spices, cayenne pepper and 1 teaspoon salt. Add the whitebait and toss to coat. Shake off any excess.
3 Fill a wok or deep heavy-based saucepan one third full of oil and

heat to 190°C (375°F), or until a cube of bread dropped in the oil browns in 10 seconds. Cook the whitebait in batches for 30 seconds, or until golden brown. Drain on crumpled paper towels and season with salt. Serve on a bed of lettuce with lemon wedges.

NUTRITION PER SERVE
Protein 30 g; Fat 10.5 g; Carbohydrate 26 g; Dietary Fibre 3.5 g; Cholesterol 87.5 mg; 1330 kJ (315 Cal)

Rinse all the whitebait under cold running water, then drain and pat dry.

Toss the dried whitebait in the flour and spice mixture and shake off any excess.

Deep-fry the coated whitebait in batches for about 30 seconds, until golden brown.

CORN AND CRAB SOUP

Preparation time: 15 minutes
Total cooking time: 10 minutes
Serves 4

1½ tablespoons oil
6 cloves garlic, chopped
6 red Asian shallots, chopped
2 stems lemon grass, white
   part only, finely chopped
1 tablespoon grated fresh
   ginger
1 litre chicken stock
1 cup (250 ml/8 fl oz) coconut milk

2½ cups (375 g/12 oz) frozen corn
   kernels
2 x 170 g (5 1/2 oz) cans crab meat,
   drained
2 tablespoons fish sauce
2 tablespoons lime juice
1 teaspoon shaved palm sugar
   or soft brown sugar

1 Heat the oil in a large saucepan, then add the chopped garlic, shallots and lemon grass and the grated ginger and cook, stirring, over medium heat for 2 minutes.
2 Pour the chicken stock and coconut milk into the saucepan and bring to the boil, stirring occasionally. Add the corn kernels and continue to cook for 5 minutes.
3 Add the drained crab meat, fish sauce, lime juice and sugar to the saucepan and stir until the crab is heated through. Season with salt and black pepper, to taste. Ladle into bowls and serve immediately.

NUTRITION PER SERVE
Protein 15 g; Fat 11 g; Carbohydrate 21.5 g;
Dietary Fibre 3.5 g; Cholesterol 71.5 mg;
1016 kJ (240 Cal)

Peel off the outer layers of the Asian shallots before chopping.

Shave off thin slices of the palm sugar with a sharp knife.

When the soup comes to the boil, add the corn kernels and cook for 5 minutes.

CHUNKY VEGETABLE SOUP

Preparation time: 25 minutes
Total cooking time: 1 hour 30 minutes
Serves 6

50 g (1¾ oz) butter
1 leek, chopped
1 celery stick, chopped
1 large carrot, chopped
1 large potato, chopped
1 parsnip, peeled and chopped
1 swede or turnip, peeled and
   chopped
225 g (7 oz) sweet potato, chopped

½ cup (115 g/4 oz) soup mix
   (see NOTE)
2 litres vegetable stock or water
1 cup (155 g/5 oz) frozen peas
125 g (4 oz) green beans, chopped
¼ cup (15 g/½ oz) chopped fresh mint
⅓ cup (20 g/¾ oz) chopped fresh
   parsley

1 Heat the butter in a large heavy-based pan, and cook the leek, celery, carrot, potato, parsnip, swede or turnip and sweet potato, stirring, for 5 minutes.
2 Add the soup mix and stock or water. Bring slowly to the boil, then reduce the heat and simmer, covered,

for 1¼ hours, or until the soup mix has softened.
3 Add the peas and beans and cook for a further 10 minutes, or until tender. Stir in the chopped mint and parsley. Season to taste with salt and cracked black pepper. Serve hot. Delicious with crusty bread.

NUTRITION PER SERVE
Protein 3 g; Fat 7 g; Carbohydrate 15 g; Dietary Fibre 4 g; Cholesterol 20 mg; 555 kJ (135 Cal)

NOTE: Soup mix is a combination of dried beans and pulses.

Measure ½ cup (115 g/4 oz) of the soup mix before adding to the vegetables.

Top and tail the beans, then chop them into short lengths.

Add the soup mix and stock or water and slowly bring to the boil.

SCALLOPS ON ASIAN RISOTTO CAKES

Preparation time: 35 minutes +
  3 hours 10 minutes refrigeration
Total cooking time: 40 minutes
Serves 4

2 cups (500 ml/16 fl oz) vegetable
  stock
2 tablespoons mirin
1 stem lemon grass (white part only),
  bruised
2 kaffir lime leaves
3 fresh coriander roots
2 tablespoons fish sauce
1 tablespoon butter
2–3 tablespoons peanut oil
3 red Asian shallots, thinly sliced
4 spring onions, chopped
3 cloves garlic, chopped
2 tablespoons finely chopped fresh
  ginger
1¼ teaspoons white pepper
⅔ cup (140 g/4½ oz) arborio rice
2 tablespoons toasted unsalted
  chopped peanuts
1 cup (50 g/1¾ oz) chopped fresh
  coriander leaves
2 cloves garlic, chopped, extra
1 teaspoon finely chopped fresh
  ginger, extra
¼ cup (60 ml/2 fl oz) lime juice
1–2 teaspoons grated palm sugar
vegetable oil, for shallow-frying
plain flour, to dust
1 tablespoon vegetable oil, extra
16 large white scallops without roe,
  trimmed

1 Heat the stock, mirin, lemon grass, lime leaves, coriander roots, half the fish sauce and 1 cup (250 ml/8 fl oz) water in a saucepan, bring to the boil, then reduce the heat and keep at a low simmer.

2 Heat the butter and 1 tablespoon of the peanut oil in a large saucepan over medium heat until bubbling. Add the shallots, spring onion, garlic, ginger and 1 teaspoon of the white pepper and cook for 2–3 minutes, or until fragrant and the onion is soft. Stir in the rice and toss until well coated.

3 Add ½ cup (125 ml/4 fl oz) of the stock (avoid the lemon grass and coriander roots). Stir constantly over medium heat until nearly all the liquid is absorbed. Continue adding the stock ½ cup (125 ml/4 fl oz) at a time, stirring constantly, for 20–25 minutes, or until all the stock is absorbed and the rice is tender and creamy. Remove from the heat, cool, then cover and refrigerate for 3 hours, or until cold.

4 To make the pesto, combine the peanuts, coriander, extra garlic and ginger and the remaining pepper in a blender or food processor and process until finely chopped. With the motor running, slowly add the lime juice, sugar and remaining fish sauce and peanut oil and process until smooth—you might not need all the oil.

5 Divide the risotto into four balls, then mould into patties. Cover and refrigerate for 10 minutes. Heat the oil in a large frying pan over medium heat. Dust the patties with flour and cook in batches for 2 minutes each side, or until crisp. Drain on paper towels. Cover and keep warm.

6 Heat the extra oil in a clean frying pan over high heat. Cook the scallops in batches for 1 minute each side.

7 Serve each cake with scallops, some pesto and lime wedges, if desired.

NUTRITION PER SERVE
Protein 12 g; Fat 32 g; Carbohydrate 36 g;
Dietary Fibre 2 g; Cholesterol 30 mg;
1987 kJ (475 Cal)

Stir the rice until the stock is absorbed and the
rice is tender and creamy.

Cook the flour-dusted patties until crisp
and golden.

GARLIC PRAWNS

Preparation time: 20 minutes
Total cooking time: 15 minutes
Serves 4

1.25 kg (2½ lb) raw prawns, peeled,
    tails intact, deveined
80 g (2¾ oz) butter, melted
¾ cup (185 ml/6 fl oz) olive oil
8 cloves garlic, crushed
2 spring onions, thinly sliced

1 Preheat the oven to very hot 250°C (500°F/Gas 10). Cut a slit down the back of each prawn.
2 Combine the butter and oil and divide among four 2 cup (500 ml/16 fl oz) cast iron pots. Divide half the crushed garlic among the pots.
3 Place the pots on a baking tray and heat in the oven for 10 minutes, or until the mixture is bubbling. Remove and divide the prawns and remaining garlic among the pots. Return to the oven for 5 minutes, or until the prawns are cooked. Stir in the spring onion. Season, to taste. Serve with crusty bread to mop up the juices.

NUTRITION PER SERVE
Protein 20 g; Fat 61 g; Carbohydrate 1 g;
Dietary Fibre 1 g; Cholesterol 192.5 mg;
2620 kJ (625 Cal)

NOTE: This is the traditional way to make garlic prawns but they can be successfully made in a cast iron frying pan in the oven or on the stovetop.

Carefully cut a slit down the back of each prawn with a sharp knife.

When the mixture in the pots is bubbling, remove from the oven.

Divide the prawns and remaining crushed garlic among the pots.

FRENCH ONION SOUP

Preparation time: 30 minutes
Total cooking time: 1 hour 30 minutes
Serves 4

50 g (1¾ oz) butter
1 tablespoon olive oil
1 kg (2 lb) onions, thinly sliced into
 rings
3 x 420 g (14 oz) cans chicken or beef
 consommé
½ cup (125 ml/4 fl oz) dry sherry
½ French bread stick
⅓ cup (35 g/1¼ oz) grated Parmesan
1 cup (125 g/4 oz) finely grated
 Cheddar or Gruyère
1 tablespoon finely chopped fresh
 parsley, to serve

1 Heat the butter and oil in a large saucepan, then add the onion and cook, stirring frequently, over low heat for 45 minutes, or until softened and translucent. Do not rush this stage—cook the onion thoroughly so that it caramelises and the flavours develop.
2 Add the consommé, sherry and 1 cup (250 ml/8 fl oz) water. Bring to the boil, then reduce the heat and simmer for 30 minutes. Season to taste.
3 Meanwhile, slice the bread into four thick slices and arrange them in a single layer under a hot grill. Toast one side, turn and sprinkle with Parmesan, and toast until crisp and golden and the cheese has melted.
4 Put the bread slices into serving bowls. Ladle in the hot soup, sprinkle with the cheese and parsley and serve.

NUTRITION PER SERVE
Protein 20 g; Fat 30 g; Carbohydrate 30 g;
Dietary Fibre 5 g; Cholesterol 70 mg;
1925 kJ (460 Cal)

Using a large sharp knife, cut the onions into thin rings.

Heat the oil and butter in a large pan and add the onion.

Stir frequently over low heat until the onion is softened and translucent.

TOM YUM GOONG

Preparation time: 25 minutes
Total cooking time: 45 minutes
Serves 4–6

500 g (1 lb) raw medium prawns
1 tablespoon oil
2 tablespoons tom yum paste
2 tablespoons tamarind purée
2 teaspoons ground turmeric
1 teaspoon chopped small red
   chillies
4 kaffir lime leaves, shredded
2 tablespoons fish sauce
2 tablespoons lime juice

2 teaspoons grated palm sugar
   or soft brown sugar
kaffir lime leaves, shredded, extra,
   to garnish

1 Peel the prawns, leaving the tails intact. Remove the vein from each prawn. Reserve the shells and heads. Cover and refrigerate the prawn meat. Heat the oil in a wok and cook the shells and heads over medium heat, stirring frequently, for 10 minutes, or until the shells turn orange.
2 Add 1 cup (250 ml/8 fl oz) water and the tom yum paste to the wok. Bring to the boil and cook for 5 minutes, or until reduced slightly.

Add another 2 litres water, bring to the boil, reduce the heat and simmer for 20 minutes. Strain, discard the shells and heads, and return the stock to the pan.
3 Add the tamarind, turmeric, chilli and lime leaves to the pan, bring to the boil and cook for 2 minutes. Add the prawns and cook for 5 minutes, or until pink. Stir in the fish sauce, lime juice and sugar. Garnish with shredded kaffir lime leaves.

NUTRITION PER SERVE (6)
Protein 15 g; Fat 5 g; Carbohydrate 11 g;
Dietary Fibre 1.3 g; Cholesterol 158 mg;
608 kJ (145 Cal)

Finely shred the kaffir lime leaves with a sharp knife.

Cook the water and tom yum paste until reduced slightly.

Stir in the tamarind, turmeric, chilli and lime leaves and cook for 2 minutes.

CHICKEN AND CORN SOUP

Preparation time: 15 minutes
Total cooking time: 20 minutes
Serves 6

3 corn cobs
1 tablespoon oil
4 spring onions, finely chopped
2 teaspoons grated fresh ginger
1 litre chicken stock
1 tablespoon rice wine, mirin or sherry
1 tablespoon soy sauce
½ small barbecued chicken, shredded
1 tablespoon cornflour
1 teaspoon sesame oil
420 g (13 oz) can creamed corn
fresh thyme sprigs, to garnish

1 Cut the corn kernels from the cobs—you will need about 2 cups (400 g/13 oz). Heat the oil in a large pan, and add the spring onion and ginger. Cook for 1 minute, or until softened, then add the corn, stock, rice wine and soy sauce. Bring slowly to the boil, then reduce the heat and simmer for 10 minutes, or until the corn is cooked through. Add the chicken.
2 In a bowl, blend the cornflour with 3 tablespoons water or stock to make a smooth paste. Add to the soup with the sesame oil and simmer, stirring constantly, until slightly thickened. Stir in the creamed corn and heat for 2–3 minutes without allowing to boil. Season and serve hot, garnished with the thyme sprigs.

NUTRITION PER SERVE
Protein 14 g; Fat 8 g; Carbohydrate 30 g;
Dietary Fibre 5 g; Cholesterol 45 mg;
1077 kJ (255 cal)

NOTE: If fresh corn is unavailable, use a 440 g (14 oz) can of drained corn kernels.

Use a fork to shred the meat from the barbecued chicken.

Remove the husks from the corn cobs and cut off the kernels.

Blend the cornflour and water or stock to make a smooth paste.

SPICED LENTIL SOUP

**Preparation time: 10 minutes +
    20 minutes standing**
Total cooking time: 50 minutes
Serves 4

1 eggplant
¼ cup (60 ml/2 fl oz) olive oil
1 onion, finely chopped
2 teaspoons brown mustard seeds
2 teaspoons ground cumin
1 teaspoon garam masala
¼ teaspoon cayenne pepper (optional)
2 large carrots, cut into cubes
1 celery stick, diced
400 g (13 oz) can crushed tomatoes
1 cup (110 g/3½ oz) puy lentils
1 litre chicken stock
¾ cup (35 g/1¼ oz) roughly chopped
    fresh coriander leaves
½ cup (125 g/4 oz) Greek-style plain
    yoghurt

1 Cut the eggplant into cubes, place
in a colander, sprinkle with salt and
leave for 20 minutes. Rinse well and
pat dry with paper towels.
2 Heat the oil in a large saucepan
over medium heat. Add the onion and
cook for 5 minutes, or until soft. Add
the eggplant, stir to coat in oil and
cook for 3 minutes, or until softened.
3 Add all the spices and cook,
stirring, for 1 minute, or until fragrant
and the mustard seeds begin to pop.
Add the carrot and celery and cook
for 1 minute. Stir in the tomato, lentils
and stock and bring to the boil.
Reduce the heat and simmer for
40 minutes, or until the lentils are
tender and the liquid is reduced to
a thick stew-like soup. Season to taste
with salt and cracked black pepper.
4 Stir the coriander into the soup just
before serving. Ladle the soup into
four warmed bowls and serve with
a dollop of the yoghurt on top.

NUTRITION PER SERVE
Protein 11 g; Fat 16 g; Carbohydrate 20 g;
Dietary Fibre 8.5 g; Cholesterol 5 mg;
1148 kJ (274 Cal)

Cook the chopped onion in a large saucepan
until soft.

Add the spices to the vegetables and stir
until fragrant.

Simmer the mixture until thick and the lentils
are tender.

MEDITERRANEAN RICOTTA TARTS

Preparation time: 20 minutes +
  20 minutes cooling
Total cooking time: 30 minutes
Serves 4

⅓ cup (35 g/1¼ oz) dry breadcrumbs
2 tablespoons virgin olive oil
1 clove garlic, crushed
½ red capsicum, quartered and cut
    into 5 mm (¼ inch) wide strips
1 zucchini, cut into 5 cm x 5 mm
    (2 inch x ¼ inch) strips
2 slices prosciutto, chopped
375 g (12 oz) firm ricotta (see NOTE)
⅓ cup (40 g/1¼ oz) grated Cheddar
⅓ cup (35 g/1¼ oz) grated Parmesan
2 tablespoons shredded fresh basil
4 black olives, pitted and sliced

1 Preheat the oven to moderate 180°C (350°F/Gas 4). Lightly grease four 8 cm x 2.5 cm deep (3 inch x 1 inch deep) fluted tart tins. Lightly sprinkle 1 teaspoon of the breadcrumbs on the base and side of each tin.
2 To make the topping, heat half the oil in a frying pan, add the garlic, capsicum and zucchini and cook, stirring, over medium heat for 5 minutes, or until the vegetables are soft. Remove from the heat and add the prosciutto. Season to taste.
3 Combine the ricotta with the cheeses and remaining breadcrumbs. Season. Press the mixture into the tins and smooth the surface. Sprinkle with basil.
4 Scatter the topping over the ricotta mixture, top with the olives, then drizzle with the remaining oil.
5 Bake for 20 minutes, or until the tarts are slightly puffed and golden around the edges. Cool completely (the tarts will deflate on cooling) and carefully remove from the tins. Do not refrigerate.

NUTRITION PER SERVE
Protein 20 g; Fat 27 g; Carbohydrate 8 g;
Dietary Fibre 1 g; Cholesterol 66 mg;
1457 kJ (348 Cal)

NOTE: Use firm ricotta or very well-drained ricotta, or the tarts will be difficult to remove from the tins.

Sprinkle breadcrumbs over the base and side of each tin.

Cook the vegetables in a frying pan over medium heat until soft.

Press the ricotta mixture into the tins, then smooth the surface.

Bake the tarts until they are puffed and golden around the edges.

THAI BEEF SOUP

Preparation time: 20 minutes
Total cooking time: 30 minutes
Serves 4

3 tablespoons oil
1 onion, finely chopped
1 teaspoon grated fresh ginger
1 teaspoon grated galangal
2 cloves garlic, crushed
2 stalks lemongrass (white part only),
    finely chopped
4 red chillies, seeds removed, finely
    chopped
4 macadamia nuts, crushed
1 tablespoon tom yum paste
2 400 g (13 oz) cans coconut milk
3 cups (750 ml/24 fl oz) beef stock
3 teaspoons sugar
100 g (3½ oz) green beans, halved
1 carrot, julienned
300 g (10 oz) fresh Hokkien noodles
100 g (3½ oz) bean sprouts
55 g (2 oz) thinly sliced cooked beef,
    cut into strips
fresh coriander leaves, to garnish

1 Heat the oil in a heavy-based saucepan, then add the onion, ginger, galangal, garlic, lemongrass, chilli and macadamias. Cook, stirring, over moderate heat for 3–4 minutes, or until the mixture becomes fragrant and changes colour. Add the tom yum paste and stir briefly before gradually adding the coconut milk and stock, stirring constantly to mix the paste into the liquid. Add the sugar and ½ teaspoon salt and bring to the boil. Reduce the heat to low and simmer for 10 minutes. Add the beans and carrot, and cook for 5 minutes more. Skim any fat from the top.
2 Add the noodles, sprouts and beef just before serving, and cook just long enough to heat through. Garnish with coriander leaves. This dish is best eaten from a large, deep bowl with chopsticks and a soup spoon.

NUTRITION PER SERVE
Protein 20 g; Fat 58 g; Carbohydrate 65 g;
Dietary Fibre 8.5 g; Cholesterol 25 mg;
3599 kJ (860 Cal)

Peel the galangal and finely grate with a wooden grater.

Wearing protective gloves, remove the seeds and finely chop the chillies.

Use a sharp knife to cut the carrot into julienne strips.

Stir in the onion, ginger, galangal, garlic, lemongrass, chilli and macadamias.

TUNA PARCELS

**Preparation time: 15 minutes
+ 20 minutes standing
Total cooking time: 50 minutes
Serves 6**

PANCAKES
1¼ cups (155 g/5 oz) plain flour
¼ cup (45 g/1½ oz) rice flour
2 eggs, lightly beaten
melted butter or oil, for greasing

FILLING
1 tablespoon oil
1 onion, finely chopped
2 cloves garlic, crushed
½ cup (80 g/2¾ oz) capers
½ cup (75 g/2½ oz) black olives, pitted,
   chopped
1 tomato, diced
250 g (8 oz) English spinach, roughly
   chopped
3 tablespoons chopped fresh
   flat-leaf parsley
1 tablespoon lemon juice
185 g (6 oz) can tuna in springwater,
   drained and flaked

2 eggs, lightly beaten
2 teaspoons cornflour
⅓ cup (80 ml/2¾ fl oz) olive oil,
   for shallow-frying

1 Sift the flours into a bowl, make a well and gradually whisk in the eggs and 2½ cups (625 ml/20 fl oz) water. Mix to a smooth lump-free batter. Cover and leave for 20 minutes.
2 Heat a frying pan and brush lightly with melted butter or oil. Pour ¼ cup (60 ml/2 fl oz) batter into the pan and swirl to make a 16–20 cm (6½–8 inch) pancake. Cook over low heat for 1 minute, or until bubbles appear on the surface and the underside is golden. Turn and cook for 20 seconds. Repeat to make 12 pancakes.
3 For the filling, heat the oil in a frying pan, add the onion and garlic and cook over medium heat for 2–3 minutes, or until the onion is soft. Add the capers, olives and tomato and cook, stirring occasionally, for 5–8 minutes, or until the liquid has evaporated. Reduce the heat to low, add the spinach, cover and steam for

2 minutes, or until wilted. Remove from the heat and stir in the parsley, lemon juice and tuna. Cool and drain any excess liquid. Season with salt and freshly ground black pepper.
4 For the coating, lightly stir the eggs, cornflour and ¼ cup (60 ml/2 fl oz) water together in a shallow dish.
5 Lay the pancakes on a work surface. Place 1 tablespoon of filling in the centre of each. Fold into a neat parcel and secure with a toothpick.

6 Heat the oil in a frying pan over medium heat. Dip the filled pancakes into the egg coating, allowing any excess to drain off. Fry the pancakes in batches for 3 minutes each side, or until golden and heated through. Serve the parcels hot.

NUTRITION PER SERVE
Protein 17.5 g; Fat 22.5 g; Carbohydrate 28.5 g; Dietary Fibre 4 g; Cholesterol 140.5 mg; 1610 kJ (385 Cal)

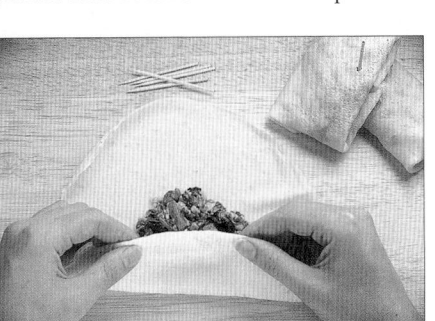
Place a tablespoon of filling in the centre of each pancake, fold over and secure.

Turn the pancakes over and cook until golden and heated through.

CHICKEN TIKKA

Preparation time: 30 minutes
+ overnight marinating
Total cooking time: 15 minutes
Makes 10 skewers

¼ onion, chopped
2 cloves garlic, crushed
1 tablespoon grated fresh ginger
2 tablespoons lemon juice
1 teaspoon grated lemon rind
3 teaspoons ground coriander
3 teaspoons ground cumin
3 teaspoons garam masala
⅓ cup (90 g/3 oz) plain yoghurt
1 teaspoon salt
750 g (1½ lb) chicken thigh fillets, cut
   into cubes

1 Soak 10 wooden skewers in water for 30 minutes to prevent burning.
2 In a food processor, finely chop the onion, garlic, ginger, lemon juice, rind, coriander, cumin and garam masala. Stir in the yoghurt and salt.
3 Thread 4–5 chicken cubes onto each skewer and place in a large shallow dish. Coat the skewers with the spice mixture. Marinate for several hours or overnight, covered, in the refrigerator.

4 Cook the skewers in batches on a barbecue or chargrill pan, or under a hot grill, for 3–4 minutes on each side, or until golden brown and cooked.

NUTRITION PER SKEWER
Protein 15 g; Fat 4 g; Carbohydrate 1 g;
Dietary Fibre 0 g; Cholesterol 55 mg;
420 kJ (100 cal)

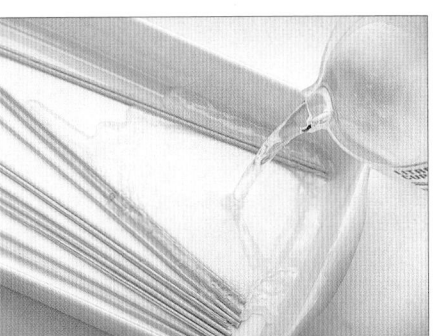

Soak the skewers in water so that they do not burn during cooking.

Finely chop the onion, garlic, ginger, lemon juice, lemon rind and spices in a food processor.

Take the skewers and thread 4–5 pieces of chicken onto each one.

Cook the skewers for 3–4 minutes on each side, or until golden brown.

CHICKPEA AND HERB DUMPLING SOUP

Preparation time: 30 minutes
Total cooking time: 35 minutes
Serves 4

1 tablespoon oil
1 onion, chopped
2 cloves garlic, crushed
2 teaspoons ground cumin
1 teaspoon ground coriander
¼ teaspoon chilli powder
2 x 300 g (10 oz) cans chickpeas, drained
3½ cups (875 ml/28 fl oz) vegetable stock
2 x 425 g (14 oz) cans chopped tomatoes

1 tablespoon chopped fresh coriander leaves
1 cup (125 g/4 oz) self-raising flour
25 g (¾ oz) butter, chopped
2 tablespoons grated fresh Parmesan
2 tablespoons mixed chopped fresh herbs (chives, flat-leaf parsley and coriander leaves)
¼ cup (60 ml/2 fl oz) milk

1 Heat the oil in a large saucepan and cook the onion over medium heat for 2–3 minutes, or until soft. Add the garlic, cumin, ground coriander and chilli, and cook for 1 minute, or until fragrant. Add the chickpeas, stock and tomato. Bring to the boil, then reduce the heat and simmer, covered, for 10 minutes. Stir in the coriander.
2 To make the dumplings, sift the flour into a bowl and add the chopped butter. Rub the butter into the flour with your fingertips until it resembles fine breadcrumbs. Stir in the cheese and mixed fresh herbs. Make a well in the centre, add the milk and mix with a flat-bladed knife until just combined. Bring the dough together into a rough ball, divide into eight portions and roll into small balls.
3 Add the dumplings to the soup, cover and simmer for 20 minutes, or until a skewer comes out clean when inserted into the centre of the dumplings.

NUTRITION PER SERVE
Protein 17 g; Fat 16 g; Carbohydrate 50 g;
Dietary Fibre 12 g; Cholesterol 23 mg;
1767 kJ (422 cal)

Stir the chopped coriander into the simmering chickpea mixture.

Add the milk to the dumpling mixture and mix with a flat-bladed knife.

Pierce the dumplings with a skewer to test if they are cooked.

SMOKED SALMON BREAD BASKETS

Preparation time: 20 minutes + cooling
Total cooking time: 10 minutes
Makes 24

250 g (8 oz) smoked salmon
1 loaf white sliced bread
¼ cup (60 ml/2 fl oz) olive oil
⅓ cup (90 g/3 oz) whole-egg
    mayonnaise
2 teaspoons extra virgin olive oil
1 teaspoon white wine vinegar
1 teaspoon finely chopped fresh dill
3 teaspoons horseradish cream
3 tablespoons salmon roe

1 Preheat the oven to 180°C (350°F/ Gas 4). Cut the salmon into strips. Flatten the bread to 1 mm (¹⁄₁₆ inch) with a rolling pin. Cut out 24 rounds with a 7 cm (2¾ inch) cutter. Brush both sides of the rounds with olive oil and push into the holes of two 12-hole flat-based patty tins. Bake for 10 minutes, or until crisp. Cool.
2 Stir the mayonnaise in a bowl with the extra virgin olive oil, vinegar, dill and horseradish until combined.
3 Arrange folds of salmon in each cooled bread case and top each with 1 teaspoon of mayonnaise mixture. Spoon ½ teaspoon of salmon roe on top of each before serving.

NUTRITION PER TART
Protein 6 g; Fat 6 g; Carbohydrate 14 g;
Dietary Fibre 1 g; Cholesterol 15 mg;
530 kJ (125 cal)

NOTE: The bread cases can be made a day in advance and, when completely cold, stored in an airtight container. If they soften, you can crisp them on a baking tray in a moderate oven for 5 minutes. Cool before filling.

Gently push the oiled circles of bread into the patty tin holes.

Fold the strips of salmon to fit into the cooled bread cases.

117

CHICKEN LIVER PATE WITH PISTACHIO NUTS AND PROSCIUTTO

Preparation time: 20 minutes +
   3 hours refrigeration
Total cooking time: 15 minutes
Serves 10

6 very thin slices prosciutto
2 tablespoons butter
¼ cup (60 ml/2 fl oz) olive oil
80 g (2¾ oz) finely diced bacon
1 onion, finely chopped
2 cloves garlic, crushed
500 g (1 lb) chicken livers
3 bay leaves
⅓ cup (80 ml/2¾ fl oz) sherry or brandy
125 g (4 oz) butter, extra, softened
⅓ cup (50 g/1¾ oz) pistachio nuts,
   toasted

1 Line a 1.5 litre loaf tin with foil. Then line with the prosciutto so that it hangs over the sides, making sure each slice overlaps. Heat the butter and oil and cook the bacon, onion and garlic for 5–6 minutes, or until the onion is softened but not browned.
2 Trim the chicken livers of any fat and veins. Add them to the pan with the bay leaves. Increase the heat to hot and cook for 3–4 minutes, or until the livers are brown on the outside, but still pink on the inside.
3 Add the sherry and simmer, stirring, for 3 minutes, or until the liquid has almost disappeared. Remove the bay leaves. Process the mixture in a food processor until very fine. Gradually add the butter and blend until smooth. Season, then stir in the pistachios.
4 Spoon the pâté mixture into the tin and fold the prosciutto over to enclose it. Refrigerate for at least 3 hours before serving. Cut into slices to serve.

NUTRITION PER SERVE
Protein 4 g; Fat 20 g; Carbohydrate 2 g;
Dietary Fibre 0.5 g; Cholesterol 48 mg;
938 kJ (224 cal)

NOTE: The flavour, colour and texture of the pâté will improve after 2 days, and it will also become easier to slice. Keep refrigerated for 3–4 days.

Line the loaf tin with the prosciutto with each slice overlapping.

Remove the fat and veins from the chicken livers before cooking.

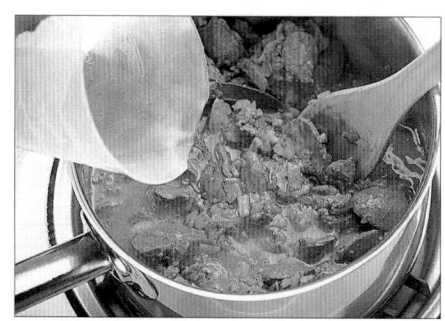

Add the sherry and simmer until most of the liquid has disappeared.

Stir the toasted pistachio nuts through the chicken liver mixture.

BOREKAS

Preparation time: 30 minutes
Total cooking time: 20 minutes
Makes 24

225 g (7 oz) feta cheese,
    crumbled
200 g (6½ oz) cream cheese,
    slightly softened
2 eggs, lightly beaten
¼ teaspoon ground nutmeg
20 sheets filo pastry
60 g (2 oz) butter, melted
3 tablespoons sesame seeds

1 Preheat the oven to moderate 180°C (350°F/Gas 4). Place the feta, cream cheese, egg and nutmeg in a bowl and mix until just combined— the mixture will be lumpy.
2 Work with five sheets of pastry at a time, keeping the rest covered with a damp tea towel. Lay each sheet on a work surface, brush with melted butter and lay them on top of each other. Use a ruler as guidance to cut the filo into six equal strips.
3 Place 1 tablespoon of the filling at one end of a strip, leaving a narrow border. Fold the pastry over to enclose the filling and form a triangle.

Continue folding the triangle over until you reach the end of the pastry, tucking any excess pastry under. Repeat with the remaining ingredients to make 24 triangles, and place on a lined baking tray.
4 Lightly brush with the remaining melted butter and sprinkle with sesame seeds. Bake for 15–20 minutes, or until puffed and golden.

NUTRITION PER BOREKA
Protein 4.5 g; Fat 8.5 g; Carbohydrate 6.5 g; Dietary Fibre 0.5 g; Cholesterol 35 mg; 505 kJ (120 cal)

Mix together the feta, cream cheese, egg and nutmeg until just combined.

Using a straight edge for guidance, cut the filo sheets into six even strips.

Fold the pastry over the filling, then continue folding until the end.

GAZPACHO

**Preparation time: 40 minutes
+ 3 hours refrigeration
Total cooking time: Nil
Serves 4–6**

750 g (1½ lb) ripe tomatoes
1 Lebanese cucumber, chopped
1 green capsicum, chopped
2–3 cloves garlic, crushed
1–2 tablespoons finely chopped
    black olives
⅓ cup (80 ml/2¾ fl oz) red or white
    wine vinegar
¼ cup (60 ml/2 fl oz) olive oil
1 tablespoon tomato paste

ACCOMPANIMENTS
1 onion, finely chopped
1 red capsicum, finely chopped
2 spring onions, finely chopped
1 Lebanese cucumber, finely chopped
2 hard-boiled eggs, chopped
chopped fresh mint or parsley
croutons

1 To peel the tomatoes, score a cross in the base of each tomato. Cover with boiling water for 30 seconds, then plunge into cold water. Drain and peel away the tomato skin from the cross. Chop the flesh so finely that it is almost a purée.
2 Mix together the tomato, cucumber, capsicum, garlic, olives, vinegar, oil, and tomato paste, and season to taste with salt and freshly ground black pepper. Cover and refrigerate for 2–3 hours.
3 Use 2–3 cups (750 ml/24 fl oz) of chilled water to thin the soup to your taste. Serve chilled, with the chopped onion, capsicum, spring onion, cucumber, boiled egg, herbs and croutons served separately for diners to add to their own bowls.

NUTRITION PER SERVE (6)
Protein 5 g; Fat 2 g; Carbohydrate 7 g;
Dietary Fibre 4 g; Cholesterol 70 mg;
310 kJ (75 cal)

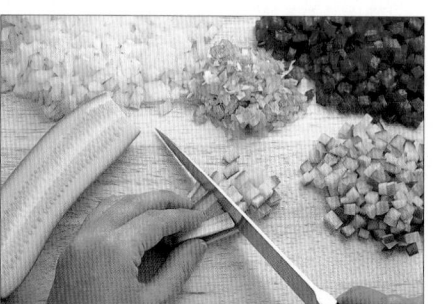

Halve the cucumber lengthways, cut into strips and chop finely.

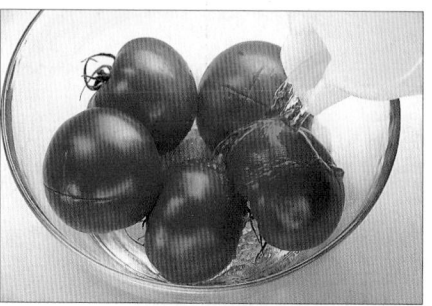

Put the tomatoes in a heatproof bowl and cover with boiling water.

Using a sharp knife, chop the tomato flesh very finely to a purée.

LENTIL AND SPINACH SOUP

**Preparation time: 25 minutes
Total cooking time: 1 hour
Serves 8**

½ cup (95 g/3 oz) brown lentils
2 tablespoons vegetable oil
1 leek, chopped
1 onion, chopped
1 stick celery, chopped
600 g (1¼ lb) potatoes, chopped

4 cups (1 litre/32 fl oz) vegetable stock
250 g (8 oz) English spinach

1 Put the lentils in a pan. Cover with water and bring to the boil, reduce the heat and simmer for 20 minutes, or until tender; drain.
2 Heat the oil in a large pan. Cook the leek, onion and celery for 5 minutes, or until softened. Add the potato and cook, stirring, for 10 minutes. Add the vegetable stock and bring to the boil. Reduce the heat and simmer, covered, for 20 minutes, until potato is tender.

3 Remove the stalks from the spinach, wash the leaves well, add to the soup and cook for 1–2 minutes. Let the soup cool for a couple of minutes, then purée in a food processor or blender. Return to the pan, add the lentils and reheat gently before serving.

NUTRITION PER SERVE
Protein 5 g; Fat 5 g; Carbohydrate 15 g;
Dietary Fibre 4 g; Cholesterol 0 mg;
505 kJ (120 cal)

Place the lentils in a pan and cover with plenty of cold water.

Cook the leek, onion and celery until soft, then add the chopped potato.

Add the cooked and drained lentils to the puréed soup in the pan.

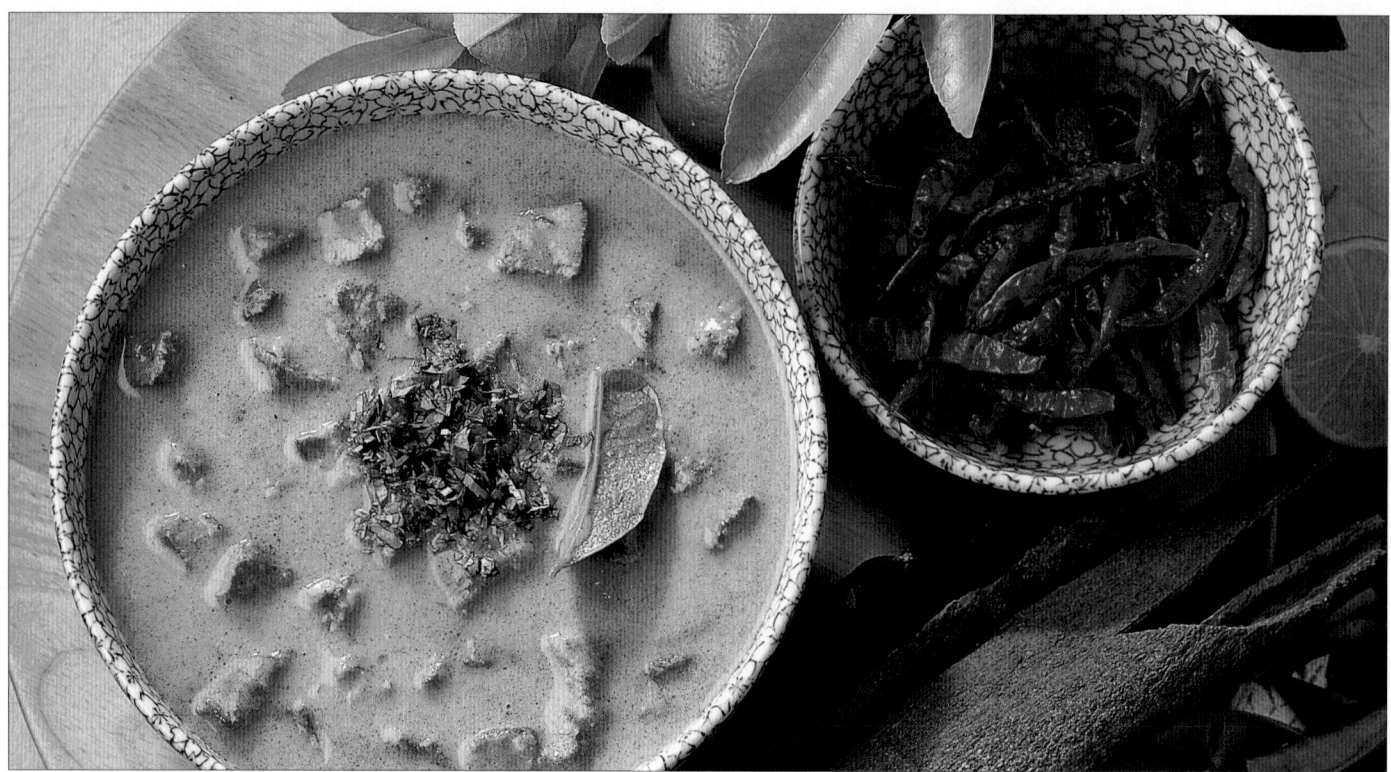

SPICY LAMB SOUP

Preparation time: 40 minutes
Total cooking time: 1 hour 30 minutes
Serves 4–6

2 large onions, roughly chopped
3 red chillies, seeded and chopped (or
    2 teaspoons dried chilli)
3–4 cloves garlic
2.5 cm (1 inch) piece of fresh ginger,
    chopped
1 teaspoon ground black pepper
5 cm (2 inch) lemon grass, white part
    only, finely chopped
½ teaspoon ground cardamom
2 teaspoons ground cumin
½ teaspoon ground cinnamon
1 teaspoon ground turmeric
2 tablespoons peanut oil

1.5 kg (3 lb) lamb neck chops
2–3 tablespoons vindaloo paste
2½ cups (600 ml/20 fl oz) coconut
    cream
3 tablespoons soft brown sugar
2–3 tablespoons lime juice
4 kaffir lime leaves

1 Put the onion, chilli, garlic, ginger, pepper, lemon grass, cardamom, cumin, cinnamon and turmeric in a food processor and process to a paste. Heat half the oil in a large pan and brown the chops in batches. Drain on paper towels.
2 Add the remaining oil to the pan and cook the spice and vindaloo pastes for 2–3 minutes. Add the chops and 1.75 litres water, cover and bring to the boil. Reduce the heat and simmer, covered, for 1 hour. Remove

the chops from the pan and stir in the coconut cream. Remove the meat from the bones, shred and return to the pan.
3 Add the sugar, lime juice and leaves. Simmer, uncovered, over low heat for 20–25 minutes, until slightly thickened.

NUTRITION PER SERVE (6)
Protein 55 g; Fat 38 g; Carbohydrate 17 g;
Dietary Fibre 3 g; Cholesterol 166 mg;
2602 kJ (622 cal)

STORAGE: Can be stored in an airtight container in the fridge for 2 days. Bring to the boil when reheating, simmer for 2–3 minutes, then serve.

HINT: This soup is quite spicy even without the addition of the vindaloo paste. Vary the amount of paste added if you prefer a milder taste.

Wear disposable gloves when working with chillies to avoid smarting.

Process the onion with the chilli, garlic and spices to make a paste.

Trim away any excess fat from the lamb chops before cooking.

DEEP-FRIED SALT-AND-PEPPER SQUID

Preparation time: 30 minutes +
15 minutes marinating
Total cooking time: 10 minutes
Serves 6 as a starter

1 kg (2 lb) squid hoods, halved
lengthways
1 cup (250 ml/8 fl oz) lemon juice
1 cup (125 g/4 oz) cornflour
1½ tablespoons salt
1 tablespoon ground white pepper
2 teaspoons caster sugar

4 egg whites, lightly beaten
oil, for deep-frying
fresh coriander sprigs and lemon
wedges, for serving

1 Open out the squid hoods, wash and pat dry. Score a shallow diamond pattern on the inside, then cut into 5 x 3 cm (2 x 1 inch) pieces. Place in a flat non-metallic dish and pour on the lemon juice. Cover and refrigerate for 15 minutes. Drain well and pat dry.
2 Combine the cornflour, salt, white pepper and sugar in a bowl. Dip the squid into the egg white and lightly coat with the cornflour mixture,

shaking off any excess.
3 Fill a deep heavy-based pan one-third full of oil and heat to 180°C (350°F), or until a cube of bread dropped into the oil turns golden brown in 15 seconds. Deep-fry the squid, in batches, for 1 minute each batch, or until the squid turns white and curls up. Drain on crumpled paper towels. Garnish with coriander sprigs and serve with lemon wedges.

NUTRITION PER SERVE
Protein 31 g; Fat 9 g; Carbohydrate 22 g;
Dietary Fibre 0.5 g; Cholesterol 332 mg;
1225 kJ (290 cal)

Lightly score the squid with a diamond pattern and then cut into small rectangles.

Lightly coat the squid in the cornflour mixture, shaking off any excess.

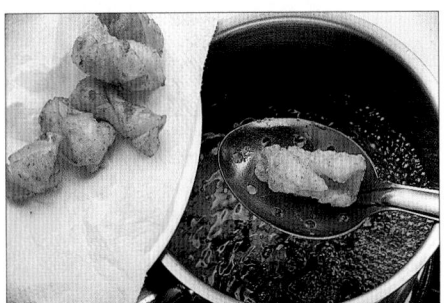

When the squid is golden and curled up, remove from the oil with a slotted spoon.

INDIVIDUAL VEGETABLE TERRINES WITH A SPICY TOMATO SAUCE

Preparation time: 40 minutes
Total cooking time: 50 minutes
Serves 4 as a starter

½ cup (125 ml/4 fl oz) oil
2 zucchini, sliced on the diagonal
500 g (1 lb) eggplant, sliced
1 small fennel bulb, sliced
1 red onion, sliced
300 g (10 oz) ricotta cheese
60 g (2 oz) Parmesan, grated
1 tablespoon chopped fresh
    flat-leaf parsley
1 tablespoon chopped fresh chives
1 red capsicum, grilled, peeled and
    cut into large pieces
1 yellow capsicum, grilled, peeled and
    cut into large pieces

SPICY TOMATO SAUCE
1 tablespoon oil
1 onion, finely chopped
2 cloves garlic, crushed
1 red chilli, seeded and chopped
425 g (14 oz) can chopped tomatoes
2 tablespoons tomato paste

1 Heat 1 tablespoon of the oil in a large frying pan. Cook the vegetables in separate batches over high heat for 5 minutes, or until golden, adding the remaining oil as needed. Drain each vegetable separately on paper towels.
2 Preheat the oven to moderately hot 200°C (400°F/Gas 6). Place the cheeses and herbs in a small bowl and mix together well. Season to taste.
3 Lightly grease four 1¼ cup (315 ml/10 fl oz) ramekins and line with baking paper. Using half the eggplant, put a layer in the base of each dish. Layer the zucchini, capsicum, cheese mixture, fennel and onion over the eggplant. Cover with the remaining eggplant and press down firmly. Bake for 10–15 minutes, or until hot. Leave for 5 minutes before turning out.
4 To make the sauce, heat the oil in a saucepan and cook the onion and garlic for 2–3 minutes, or until soft. Add the chilli, tomato and tomato paste and simmer for 5 minutes, or until thick and pulpy. Purée in a food processor. Return to the saucepan and keep warm. Spoon over the terrines.

NUTRITION PER SERVE
Protein 18 g; Fat 48 g; Carbohydrate 16 g; Dietary Fibre 8.5 g; Cholesterol 48 mg; 2346 kJ (560 cal)

Cook the capsicums under a hot grill until blackened. Cool, peel, then cut into pieces.

Layer the fennel over the cheese mixture, then add a layer of onion.

Simmer the tomato sauce for 5 minutes, or until thick and pulpy.

CLAM CHOWDER

Preparation time: 25 minutes
Total cooking time: 45 minutes
Serves 4

30 g (1 oz) butter
2 rashers bacon, finely chopped
1 large onion, finely chopped
4 potatoes, cut into small cubes
2 cups (500 ml/16 fl oz) fish stock
1 bay leaf
½ cup (125 ml/4 fl oz) milk
4 x 105 g (3½ oz) cans baby clams,
    drained and chopped

¼ cup (15 g/½ oz) finely chopped fresh
    parsley
1 cup (250 ml/8 fl oz) cream

1 Heat the butter in a large saucepan.
Cook the bacon and onion for
2–3 minutes, or until softened. Stir
in the potato. Cook for a further
2–3 minutes, then gradually pour
on the stock. Add the bay leaf.
2 Bring the mixture to the boil, then
reduce the heat and simmer, covered,
for 20 minutes, or until the potato is
cooked. Simmer for 10 minutes, or
until the soup is reduced and slightly
thickened. Discard the bay leaf.

3 Add the milk, chopped clams,
parsley and cream. Stir to reheat,
but do not allow the soup to boil.
Season with salt and freshly ground
black pepper.

NUTRITION PER SERVE
Protein 20 g; Fat 40 g; Carbohydrate 20 g;
Dietary Fibre 3 g; Cholesterol 250 mg;
2090 kJ (500 cal)

Peel and cut the potatoes into strips and then
into small cubes.

Remove the bay leaf from the chowder with a pair
of tongs.

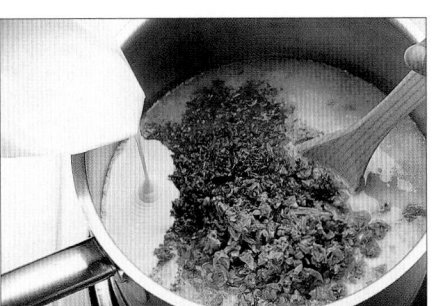

Add the milk, chopped clams and parsley, and
pour in the cream.

BARLEY SOUP WITH GOLDEN PARSNIPS

Preparation time: 30 minutes + overnight soaking
Total cooking time: 2 hours 20 minutes
Serves 6

200 g (6½ oz) pearl barley
1 tablespoon oil
2 onions, chopped
2 cloves garlic, finely chopped
2 carrots, chopped
2 potatoes, chopped
2 celery sticks, chopped
2 bay leaves, torn in half
2 litres chicken stock
½ cup (125 ml/4 fl oz) milk
40 g (1¼ oz) butter

3 parsnips, cubed
1 teaspoon soft brown sugar
chopped fresh parsley, to serve

1 Soak the barley in water overnight. Drain. Place in a saucepan with 2 litres water. Bring to the boil, then reduce the heat and simmer, partially covered, for 1¼ hours, or until tender. Drain the barley.
2 Heat the oil in a large saucepan, add the onion, garlic, carrot, potato and celery, and cook for 3 minutes. Stir well and cook, covered, for 15 minutes over low heat, stirring occasionally.
3 Add the barley, bay leaves, stock, milk, 2 teaspoons of salt and 1 teaspoon of pepper. Bring to the boil, then reduce the heat and simmer the

soup, partially covered, for 35 minutes. If the soup is too thick, add about 1 cup (250 ml/8 fl oz) cold water, a little at a time, until the soup reaches your preferred consistency.
4 While the soup is simmering, melt the butter in a frying pan, add the parsnip and toss in the butter. Sprinkle with the sugar and cook until golden brown and tender. Serve the parsnip on top of the soup and sprinkle with the parsley.

NUTRITION PER SERVE
Protein 7 g; Fat 10 g; Carbohydrate 40 g; Dietary Fibre 8 g; Cholesterol 20 mg; 1190 kJ (285 cal)

Using a sharp knife, chop the carrots, potatoes and celery.

Add the drained barley to the cooked vegetables and stir in.

Sprinkle the soft brown sugar over the parsnip in the frying pan.

SPICY PORK WON TONS

Preparation time: 25 minutes
Total cooking time: 10 minutes
Serves 6 as a starter

1 teaspoon sesame oil
1 teaspoon peanut oil
2 cloves garlic, crushed
2 spring onions, finely chopped
2 small red chillies, finely chopped
2 teaspoons grated fresh ginger
300 g (10 oz) pork mince
1 tablespoon hoisin sauce
2 tablespoons unsalted peanuts,
    chopped
1 tablespoon chopped fresh coriander
250 g (8 oz) won ton wrappers
oil, for deep-frying

DIPPING SAUCE
½ cup (125 ml/4 fl oz) salt-reduced soy
    sauce
1 tablespoon soft brown sugar
1 teaspoon chilli oil

1 Heat both oils in a non-stick frying pan. Add the garlic, spring onion, chilli and ginger and cook over medium heat for 2 minutes. Increase the heat to high, add the pork mince and cook, breaking up any lumps with a fork or wooden spoon, for 5 minutes, or until the mince is brown.
2 Remove the pan from the heat and stir in the hoisin, peanuts and coriander. Place 2 teaspoons of the mixture into the centre of a wrapper. Brush the edge of the won ton lightly with water and place another wrapper on top. Repeat with the remaining wrappers and pork mince.
3 Deep-fry the won tons in batches for 3 minutes, or until crisp and golden. Drain on paper towels.
4 To make the sauce, place the soy sauce, brown sugar and chilli oil in a small pan and simmer over medium heat for 5 minutes, or until the sauce thickens slightly. Pour into a bowl and serve with the won tons.

NUTRITION PER SERVE
Protein 20 g; Fat 12 g; Carbohydrate 30 g;
Dietary Fibre 2 g; Cholesterol 32 mg;
1280 kJ (300 cal)

Take the pan off the heat and stir the hoisin, peanuts and coriander into the mince.

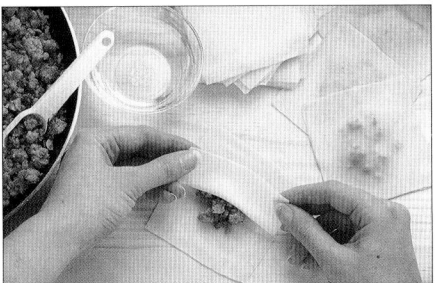
Brush the edge of a won ton with water and place another wrapper on top.

Deep-fry the won tons until crisp. Place on paper towels to drain off the excess oil.

127

SCOTCH BROTH

Preparation time: 20 minutes
Total cooking time: 2½ hours
Serves 10

750 g (1½ lb) neck lamb chops or
 lamb shanks
250 g (8 oz) pearl barley or soup mix
 (see NOTE)
1 carrot, peeled and diced
1 turnip, peeled and diced
1 parsnip, peeled and diced
1 onion, finely chopped
1 small leek, thinly sliced
1 cup (75 g/2½ oz) shredded cabbage
½ cup (15 g/½ oz) chopped parsley

1 Cut away any excess fat from the meat. Put the meat in a large heavy-based pan with 10 cups (2½ litres) water. Bring to the boil, reduce the heat and simmer, covered, for 1 hour. Skim any froth from the surface frequently. Meanwhile, soak the pearl barley or soup mix in a large bowl of water for about 1 hour.
2 Add the carrot, turnip, parsnip, onion and leek to the pan. Drain the barley or soup mix and add to the pan. Stir well to combine, cover and simmer for a further 1½ hours. Stir in the cabbage 10 minutes before the end of cooking time. (Add more water at this stage if you like a thinner soup.)
3 Remove the meat from the pan using tongs. Leave to cool before

removing the meat from the bones. Chop the meat finely and return it to the soup. Add parsley and season with salt and pepper.

NUTRITION PER SERVE
Protein 21 g; Fat 2 g; Carbohydrate 20 g;
Dietary Fibre 4 g; Cholesterol 50 mg;
750 kJ (180 cal)

STORAGE TIME: May be kept covered and refrigerated for up to 3 days. Suitable to freeze up to 1 month.

NOTE: Soup mix is a combination of pearl barley, split peas and lentils. Both pearl barley and soup mix are readily available from supermarkets.

Instead of a spoon, use paper towels to skim any froth from the surface.

Drain the barley or soup mix and add to the pan of simmering meat and vegetables.

Use tongs to lift the bones out of the soup and then cut the meat from the bones.

SPICY POTATO AND CHICKPEA PANCAKES

Preparation time: 30 minutes + resting
Total cooking time: 20 minutes
Serves 4 as a starter

600 g (1¼ lb) waxy potatoes
1 small onion
3 tablespoons chopped fresh
    coriander
2 spring onions, finely sliced
4 tablespoons besan (chickpea flour)
2 teaspoons harissa (see NOTE)
¾ teaspoon salt
¼ teaspoon ground black pepper
pinch of cayenne pepper
1 egg, beaten
vegetable oil, for shallow-frying
1 teaspoon ground coriander
¼ teaspoon ground turmeric
¾ teaspoon cumin seeds

1 Grate the potatoes and onion, place in a bowl and cover with cold water.
2 Put the fresh coriander, spring onion, besan, harissa, salt, pepper and cayenne into another bowl. Mix together and stir in the egg. Heat 2 tablespoons of oil in a large non-stick frying pan and fry the ground coriander, turmeric and cumin seeds over medium-high heat, stirring, for 25–30 seconds. Add to the bowl.
3 Drain the potato and onion and wring out in a tea towel to dry. Add to the other ingredients and mix with your hands. Cover and set aside for 30 minutes. Wipe out the frying pan with paper towel and preheat the oven to very slow 120°C (250°F/Gas ½).
4 Heat 1–2 tablespoons of the oil in the frying pan. Spoon a heaped tablespoon of potato mixture into the pan and flatten to a rough circle. Cook for 2–3 minutes on each side, or until golden. Keep warm while cooking the remainder of the mixture.

NUTRITION PER SERVE
Protein 10 g; Fat 15 g; Carbohydrate 30 g;
Dietary Fibre 6 g; Cholesterol 45 mg;
1315 kJ (315 cal)

NOTE: Harissa should be available from large supermarkets, otherwise try speciality shops.

Grate the potato and onion and soak in cold water to remove the starch.

Use about a heaped tablespoonful of mixture to make each pancake.

PUMPKIN AND PESTO CHICKEN IN FILO PASTRY

Preparation time: 30 minutes
Total cooking time: 50 minutes
Serves 4

4 chicken breast fillets
1 tablespoon oil
250 g (8 oz) pumpkin
1 bunch English spinach
12 sheets filo pastry
100 g (3½ oz) butter, melted
¼ cup (25 g/¾ oz) dry breadcrumbs
100 g (3½ oz) ricotta
⅓ cup (90 g/3 oz) pesto (see NOTE)
1 tablespoon pine nuts, chopped

1 Preheat the oven to moderately hot 200°C (400°F/Gas 6). Season the chicken fillets with salt and pepper. Heat half the oil in a frying pan and fry the chicken until browned on both sides, then remove from the pan.
2 Cut the peeled pumpkin into 5 mm (¼ inch) slices. Heat the remaining oil in the same pan and fry the pumpkin until lightly browned on both sides. Allow to cool.
3 Put the spinach leaves into a bowl of boiling water and stir until just wilted. Drain well and pat dry with paper towels. Layer 3 sheets of filo pastry, brushing each with some of the melted butter, sprinkling between layers with some of the breadcrumbs.
4 Wrap each chicken breast in a quarter of the spinach and place on one short side of the filo, leaving a 2 cm (¾ inch) gap. Top the chicken with a quarter of the pumpkin slices, then spread a quarter of the ricotta down the centre of the pumpkin. Top with a tablespoon of the pesto.

5 Fold the sides of the pastry over the filling, then roll the parcel up until it sits on the unsecured end. Repeat with the remaining ingredients. Place the parcels on a lightly greased baking tray, brush with any remaining butter and sprinkle with the pine nuts. Bake for 15 minutes, then cover loosely with foil and bake for a further 20 minutes, or until the pastry is golden brown.

NUTRITION PER SERVE
Protein 35 g; Fat 40 g; Carbohydrate 30 g; Dietary Fibre 2.5 g; Cholesterol 132 mg; 2635 kJ (630 cal)

NOTE: Bottled pesto is not suitable for this recipe—you can either make your own or use fresh pesto from a delicatessen.

Remove the spinach from the bowl of boiling water and drain well.

Top the chicken breast fillet with a quarter of the pumpkin slices.

Fold the sides of the pastry over the filling, then roll up until it sits on the unsecured end.

OLIVE SPIRALS

Preparation time: 25 minutes +
1 hour 40 minutes rising
Total cooking time: 35 minutes
Makes 12 spirals

7 g (¼ oz) dried yeast
1 teaspoon sugar
4 cups (500 g/1 lb) plain flour
1 teaspoon salt
2 tablespoons olive oil
2 cups (250 g/8 oz) pitted black olives
½ cup (50 g/1¾ oz) finely grated
    Parmesan
3 cloves garlic, chopped
1 tablespoon oil

1 Mix the yeast, sugar and ½ cup (125 ml/4 fl oz) warm water in a bowl. Cover and set aside in a warm place for 10 minutes, or until frothy.
2 Sift the flour and salt into a bowl and make a well in the centre. Add the frothy yeast, oil and 1 cup (250 ml/ 8 fl oz) of warm water. Mix to a soft dough and gather into a ball. Turn out onto a floured surface and knead for 10 minutes, or until smooth. Cover loosely with greased plastic wrap and set aside for 1 hour, or until well risen.
3 Process the olives, Parmesan and garlic in a food processor until chopped. With the motor running, add the tablespoon of oil and process to a paste.

4 Punch down the dough and knead for 1 minute. Roll out to a rectangle 42 x 35 cm (18 x 14 inches). Spread with the olive paste, leaving a border along one long side. Roll up lengthways, ending with the clear long side.
5 Cut into 12 slices and place close together on a greased baking tray. Cover with a damp tea towel and set aside for 30 minutes, or until well risen. Preheat the oven to moderately hot 200°C (400°F/Gas 6). Bake for 35 minutes, or until golden brown.

NUTRITION PER SPIRAL
Protein 8 g; Fat 8 g; Carbohydrate 40 g;
Dietary Fibre 3 g; Cholesterol 4 mg;
1050 kJ (250 cal)

Spread the rectangle of dough with olive paste and roll up lengthways.

Using a serrated knife, cut the rolled log into 12 equal slices.

Place the spirals close together on the baking tray so that they touch while cooking.

CHINESE PORK AND NOODLE SOUP

Preparation time: 25 minutes + overnight refrigeration + 1 hour refrigeration
Total cooking time: 4 hours
Serves 4–6

STOCK
1.5 kg (3 lb) chicken bones (chicken necks, backs, wings), washed
3 cloves garlic, sliced
2 slices fresh ginger, 1 cm (½ inch) thick
4 spring onions, white part only

150 g (5 oz) Chinese cabbage, shredded
1 tablespoon peanut oil
2 teaspoons sesame oil
4 cloves garlic, crushed
1 tablespoon grated fresh ginger
300 g (10 oz) pork mince
1 egg white
¼ teaspoon ground white pepper
2 tablespoons light soy sauce
1 tablespoon Chinese rice wine
1½ tablespoons cornflour
½ cup (15 g/½ oz) fresh coriander leaves, finely chopped
6 spring onions, thinly sliced
200 g (6½ oz) fresh thin egg noodles

1 To make the stock, place the bones and 3.5 litres water in a large saucepan and bring to a simmer—do not boil. Cook for 30 minutes, removing any scum that rises to the surface. Add the garlic, ginger and spring onion, and cook, partially covered, at a low simmer for 3 hours. Strain through a fine sieve, then cool. Cover and refrigerate overnight. Remove the layer of fat from the surface once it has solidified.

2 Bring a large saucepan of water to the boil and cook the cabbage for 2 minutes, or until soft. Drain, cool and squeeze out the excess water.
3 Heat the peanut oil and 1 teaspoon of the sesame oil in a small frying pan, and cook the garlic and ginger for 1 minute, or until the garlic just starts to brown. Allow to cool.
4 Combine the mince, cabbage, garlic mixture, egg white, white pepper, soy sauce, rice wine, cornflour, half the coriander and half the spring onion. Cover and refrigerate for 1 hour. Shape tablespoons of the mixture into balls.
5 Bring 1.5 litres of the stock (freeze the leftover stock) to the boil in a wok over high heat. Reduce the heat

to medium and simmer for 1–2 minutes. Add the pork balls and cook, covered, for 8–10 minutes, or until they rise to the surface and are cooked through.
6 Bring a large saucepan of water to the boil. Cook the noodles for 1 minute, then drain and rinse. Divide among serving bowls and ladle the soup and balls on top. Garnish with the remaining spring onion, coriander and sesame oil.

NUTRITION PER SERVE (6)
Protein 17 g; Fat 9.5 g; Carbohydrate 23 g;
Dietary Fibre 2 g; Cholesterol 35 mg;
1030 kJ (245 cal)

Place all the meatball ingredients in a bowl and combine with your hands.

Once the pork balls have been shaped, add them to the wok one by one.

The pork balls are cooked when they rise to the surface.

HONEY CHICKEN WINGS

**Preparation time: 10 minutes +
  2 hours marinating**
Total cooking time: 15 minutes
Serves 4

12 chicken wings
4 tablespoons soy sauce
1 clove garlic, crushed
3 tablespoons sherry
3 tablespoons vegetable oil
3 tablespoons honey

1 Rinse the chicken wings and pat dry with paper towels. Tuck the wing tips to the underside and put in a shallow, non-metallic dish. Combine the soy sauce, garlic, sherry and oil and pour over the chicken. Cover with plastic wrap and refrigerate for 2 hours, turning occasionally.
2 Cook the chicken on a hot, lightly oiled barbecue grill or flatplate for 5 minutes on each side or until cooked through, turning occasionally. Place the honey in a small heatproof bowl on the edge of the barbecue to warm and thin down a little.
3 Brush the wings with honey and grill for 2 minutes more.

NUTRITION PER SERVE
Protein 46 g; Fat 8 g; Carbohydrate 21 g;
Dietary Fibre 2 g; Cholesterol 100 mg;
1411 kJ (337 cal)

VARIATION: Try apricot jam instead of the honey for basting. If you prefer a slightly hotter flavour, add some bottled crushed chilli pepper.

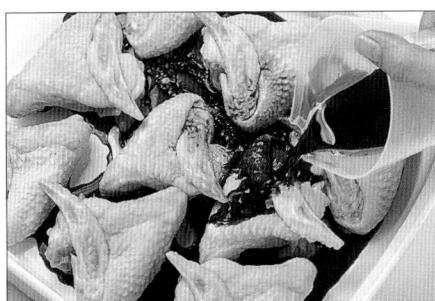

Put the chicken wings in a shallow, non-metallic dish and leave to marinate.

During the 2 hours of marinating, turn the chicken wings occasionally.

Once the wings are cooked through, brush with the honey and cook for a little longer.

133

CREAMY SPINACH AND CHICKEN SOUP

Preparation time: 40 minutes
Total cooking time: 55 minutes
Serves 6

1 tablespoon oil
1 kg (2 lb) chicken pieces
1 carrot, chopped
2 celery sticks, chopped
1 onion, chopped
6 black peppercorns
2 cloves garlic, chopped
1 bouquet garni
800 g (1 lb 10 oz) white sweet potato, chopped

2 bunches (about 500 g/1 lb) English spinach
½ cup (125 ml/4 fl oz) cream

1 Heat the oil in a large pan, add the chicken pieces in batches and brown well. Drain on paper towels. Pour off the excess fat, leaving 1 tablespoon in the pan. Return the chicken to the pan with the carrot, celery, onion, peppercorns, garlic, bouquet garni and 1.5 litres of water.

2 Bring the soup to the boil, reduce the heat and simmer for 40 minutes. Strain, returning the stock to the pan. Pull the chicken meat from the bones, shred and set aside.

3 Add the sweet potato to the stock in the pan. Bring to the boil, then reduce the heat and simmer until tender. Add the spinach leaves and cook until wilted. Process in batches in a food processor until finely chopped.

4 Return the spinach to the pan, add the shredded chicken and stir in the cream. Season to taste. Reheat gently before serving but do not allow the soup to boil.

NUTRITION PER SERVE
Protein 40 g; Fat 15 g; Carbohydrate 25 g;
Dietary Fibre 4 g; Cholesterol 110 mg;
1720 kJ (410 cal)

To make a bouquet garni, tie parsley, thyme and a bay leaf with string.

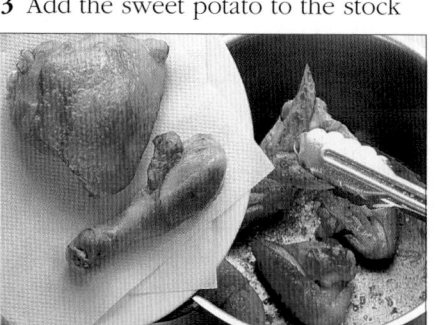

Brown the chicken in batches, then drain on paper towels.

Add the spinach leaves to the soup and cook, stirring, until just wilted.

BEEF KEBABS WITH MINT YOGHURT DRESSING

Preparation time: 30 minutes +
**   2 hours marinating**
Total cooking time: 10 minutes
Makes 8 kebabs

500 g (1 lb) lean beef fillet, cubed
½ cup (125 ml/4 fl oz) olive oil
⅓ cup (80 ml/2¾ fl oz) lemon juice
1 tablespoon chopped fresh rosemary
1 red onion, cut into wedges
200 g (6½ oz) slender eggplants,
   sliced

MINT YOGHURT DRESSING
1 cup (250 g/8 oz) plain yoghurt
1 clove garlic, crushed
1 small Lebanese cucumber, grated
2 tablespoons chopped fresh mint

1 Leave 8 wooden skewers to soak in cold water to prevent scorching. Put the beef in a non-metallic bowl, combine the olive oil, lemon juice and rosemary and pour over the beef. Cover and refrigerate for 2 hours.
2 To make the mint yoghurt dressing, mix together the yoghurt, garlic, cucumber and mint and season with salt and pepper.

3 Drain the beef and thread onto the skewers, alternating pieces of beef with the onion wedges and slices of eggplant.
4 Cook the kebabs on a hot, lightly oiled barbecue grill or flatplate, turning often, for 5–10 minutes, or until the beef is cooked through and tender. Serve with the dressing.

NUTRITION PER KEBAB
Protein 15 g; Fat 15 g; Carbohydrate 3 g;
Dietary Fibre 1 g; Cholesterol 40 mg;
1010 kJ (240 cal)

Marinate the beef in a non-metallic bowl so that the acidic citrus marinade doesn't react.

Cut the slender eggplants (aubergines) into slices before threading onto the skewers.

Alternate cubes of beef with pieces of eggplant and wedges of onion.

CURRIED SWEET POTATO SOUP

Preparation time: 20 minutes
Total cooking time: 40 minutes
Serves 6

1 tablespoon oil
1 large onion, chopped
2 cloves garlic, crushed
3 teaspoons curry powder
1.25 kg (2 lb 8 oz) orange sweet
    potato, peeled and cubed
4 cups (1 litre) chicken stock
1 large apple, peeled, cored and grated

½ cup (125 ml/4 fl oz) light coconut milk

1 Heat the oil in a large pan over medium heat and cook the onion for 10 minutes, stirring occasionally, until very soft. Add the garlic and curry powder and cook for a minute further.
2 Add the sweet potato, stock and apple. Bring to the boil, reduce the heat and simmer, partially covered, for 30 minutes, until very soft.
3 Cool the soup a little before processing in batches until smooth. Return to the pan, stir in the coconut milk and reheat gently without boiling. Serve with warm pitta bread.

NUTRITION PER SERVE
Protein 5 g; Fat 8 g; Carbohydrate 35 g;
Dietary Fibre 5.5 g; Cholesterol 0 mg;
975 kJ (233 cal)

STORAGE TIME: Can be kept in the fridge for 1 day without the coconut milk: add this when you reheat.

HINT: The soup will become quite thick on standing. Thin with stock or water if necessary.

Add the garlic and curry powder to the softened onion and cook for another minute.

Stir in the stock with the cubed sweet potato and grated apple.

Once the soup has been processed stir in the coconut milk.

STEAMED PRAWN NORI ROLLS

**Preparation time: 15 minutes
+ 1 hour refrigeration
Total cooking time: 5 minutes
Makes 25 rolls**

500 g (1 lb) peeled raw prawns,
    deveined
1½ tablespoons fish sauce
1 tablespoon sake
2 tablespoons chopped fresh
    coriander
1 large fresh kaffir lime leaf,
    finely shredded
1 tablespoon lime juice
2 teaspoons sweet chilli sauce

1 egg white, lightly beaten
5 sheets nori

DIPPING SAUCE
¼ cup (60 ml/2 fl oz) sake
¼ cup (60 ml/2 fl oz) soy sauce
1 tablespoon mirin
1 tablespoon lime juice

1 Process the prawns in a food
processor or blender with the fish
sauce, sake, coriander, kaffir lime leaf,
lime juice and sweet chilli sauce, until
smooth. Add the egg white and pulse
for a few seconds to just combine.
2 Lay the nori sheets on a flat surface
and spread some prawn mixture over
each sheet, leaving a 2 cm (1 inch)
border at one end. Roll up tightly,

cover and refrigerate for 1 hour to
firm. Using a sharp knife, trim the
ends and cut into 2 cm (1 inch)
lengths.
3 Place the rolls in a lined bamboo
steamer. Cover the steamer and place
it over a wok of simmering water,
making sure it doesn't touch the
water. Steam the rolls for 5 minutes,
or until heated thoroughly.
4 For the dipping sauce, thoroughly
mix all the ingredients together in a
small bowl. Serve with the nori rolls.

NUTRITION PER ROLL
Protein 4 g; Fat 0.5 g; Carbohydrate 0.5 g;
Dietary Fibre 0.5 g; Cholesterol 39.5 mg;
95 kJ (23 cal)

Spread prawn mixture over each nori sheet,
leaving a 2 cm (1 inch) border at one end.

Roll each sheet up tightly, then cover and
refrigerate to firm.

Cut the nori rolls into short lengths with a very
sharp knife.

CHICKEN QUESADILLAS

Preparation time: 45 minutes
  + 1 hour marinating
Total cooking time: 20–30 minutes
Serves 4

4 large green chillies
3 large red chillies
2 chicken breast fillets
3 tablespoons wholegrain mustard
2 tablespoons honey
4 flour tortillas
3 cups (375 g/12 oz) grated Cheddar
6 spring onions, thinly sliced
1–2 small red chillies, thinly sliced,
    optional
1–2 small green chillies, thinly sliced,
    optional
oilve oil, for cooking

GREEN CHILLI SALSA
3 long green chillies, thinly sliced
2 tomatoes, peeled, seeded and
    chopped
1 onion, finely chopped
⅓ cup (10 g/¼ oz) fresh coriander
    leaves, finely chopped
2 tablespoons lime juice

1 Place the large chillies under a hot grill and cook for 5–8 minutes, turning frequently, until the skins are blackened. Place the chillies in a plastic bag and leave to cool. Remove the skin and seeds. Cut them in half, then slice the flesh into thin strips.
2 Place the chicken in a deep dish. Combine the mustard and honey and add to the chicken. Turn the meat until well coated with the mixture. Cover and refrigerate for 1 hour. Place the chicken under a hot grill and cook for 4 minutes each side, or until

tender. Cool slightly, then cut into thin strips.
3 To make the green chilli salsa, combine the chilli, tomato, onion, coriander and lime juice in a bowl and mix well, adding a little more lime juice if desired. Set aside to allow the flavours to combine.
4 Lightly grease a large, heavy-based frying pan and warm over medium heat. Place one tortilla in the pan and sprinkle with a quarter of the Cheddar and half the spring onion, roasted chilli, chicken and sliced chilli. Sprinkle with a third of the remaining Cheddar and top with another tortilla.
5 Brush lightly with a little oil, invert the quesadilla onto a plate and then slide back into the pan so that the top becomes the bottom. Cook for a few minutes longer, just until the Cheddar has melted and the underside looks golden and crisp. Slide the quesadilla onto a plate and keep warm.
6 Repeat with another tortilla, adding half of the remaining Cheddar, the remaining spring onion, roasted chilli, chicken and sliced chilli. Top with the rest of the Cheddar and the last tortilla. Serve immediately, cut into halves or triangles, with the salsa.

NUTRITION PER SERVE
Protein 45 g; Fat 35 g; Carbohydrate 40 g;
Dietary Fibre 5 g; Cholesterol 125 mg;
2665 kJ (635 cal)

NOTE: Flour tortillas are available from most supermarkets, in the bread section—they may need trimming slightly to fit in the frying pan.

Remove the blackened skins from the grilled, cooled chillies.

Turn the chicken to coat well with the mustard and honey mixture.

Combine all the salsa ingredients in a bowl and mix well.

Sprinkle one of the tortillas with a quarter of the grated Cheddar.

Cover the Cheddar, chicken, chilli and spring onion filling with another tortilla.

Invert the quesadilla onto a plate, then slide it back into the pan.

PRAWN LAKSA

Preparation time: 45 minutes
Total cooking time: 50 minutes
Serves 4

1 kg (2 lb) raw medium prawns
⅓ cup (80 ml/2¾ fl oz) oil
2–6 small fresh red chillies, seeded
1 onion, roughly chopped
3 cloves garlic, halved
2 cm x 2 cm (¾ inch x ¾ inch) piece
    fresh ginger or galangal, chopped
3 stems lemon grass (white part only),
    chopped
1 teaspoon ground turmeric
1 tablespoon ground coriander
2 teaspoons shrimp paste
2½ cups (625 ml/20 fl oz) coconut
    cream
2 teaspoons grated palm sugar or soft
    brown sugar
4 fresh kaffir lime leaves, crushed
1–2 tablespoons fish sauce
200 g (6½ oz) packet fish balls
190 g (6½ oz) packet fried tofu puffs
250 g (8 oz) dried rice vermicelli
125 g (4 oz) bean sprouts
⅓ cup (20 g/¾ oz) chopped fresh mint
2 teaspoons fresh coriander leaves

1 Peel the prawns and gently pull out the dark vein from each prawn back, starting at the head end. Reserve the heads, shells and tails. Cover and refrigerate the prawn meat.
2 Heat 2 tablespoons of the oil in a wok or large saucepan and add the prawn shells and heads. Stir over medium heat for 10 minutes, or until orange, then add 1 litre water. Bring to the boil, then reduce the heat and simmer for 15 minutes. Strain the stock through a fine sieve, discarding the shells. Clean the pan.

3 Finely chop the chillies (use 2 for mild flavour, increase for hot), onion, garlic, ginger and lemon grass with the turmeric, coriander and ¼ cup (60 ml/2 fl oz) of the prawn stock in a food processor.
4 Heat the remaining oil in the pan, add the chilli mixture and shrimp paste, and stir over medium heat for 3 minutes, or until fragrant. Pour in the remaining stock and simmer for 10 minutes. Add the coconut cream, sugar, lime leaves and fish sauce, and simmer for 5 minutes. Add the prawns and simmer for 2 minutes, or until firm and light pink. Add the fish

balls and tofu puffs, and simmer gently until just heated through.
5 Soak the rice vermicelli in a bowl of boiling water for 2 minutes, then drain and divide it among serving bowls. Top with the bean sprouts and ladle the soup over the top. Sprinkle with the mint and coriander.

NUTRITION PER SERVE
Protein 58 g; Fat 58 g; Carbohydrate 71 g;
Dietary Fibre 9 g; Cholesterol 514 mg;
4331 kJ (1031 cal)

Stir and toss the prawn heads, shells and tails until the heads turn bright orange.

Process the chilli, onion, garlic, ginger, lemon grass, spices and stock.

Add the prawns to the pan and simmer until they turn light pink.

LAMB HOTPOT

**Preparation time: 40 minutes +
1 hour refrigeration
Total cooking time: 2 hours
Serves 4**

2 tablespoons olive oil
8 lamb shanks
2 onions, sliced
4 cloves garlic, finely chopped
3 bay leaves, torn in half
1–2 teaspoons hot paprika
2 teaspoons sweet paprika
1 tablespoon plain flour
¼ cup (60 g/2 oz) tomato paste
1.5 litres vegetable stock
4 potatoes, chopped
4 carrots, sliced
3 celery sticks, thickly sliced
3 tomatoes, seeded and chopped

1 To make the lamb stock, heat
1 tablespoon of the oil in a large,
heavy-based saucepan over medium
heat. Brown the shanks well in two
batches, then drain on paper towels.
2 Add the remaining oil to the pan
and cook the onion, garlic and bay
leaves over low heat for 10 minutes,
stirring regularly. Add the paprikas
and flour and cook, stirring, for
2 minutes. Gradually add the combined
tomato paste and vegetable stock.
Bring to the boil, stirring continuously,
and return the shanks to the pan.
Reduce the heat to low and simmer,
covered, for 1½ hours, stirring
occasionally.
3 Remove and discard the bay leaves.
Remove the shanks, allow to cool
slightly and then cut the meat from
the bone. Discard the bone. Cut the
meat into pieces and refrigerate.
Refrigerate the stock for about 1 hour,
or until fat forms on the surface and
can be spooned off.
4 Return the meat to the stock along
with the potato, carrot and celery, and
bring to the boil. Reduce the heat and
simmer for 15 minutes. Season, and
add the chopped tomato to serve.

NUTRITION PER SERVE
Protein 70 g; Fat 15 g; Carbohydrate 30 g;
Dietary Fibre 8 g; Cholesterol 170 mg;
2200 kJ (525 cal)

Halve the tomatoes and scoop out the seeds with
a teaspoon.

Brown the shanks in 2 batches, remove with
tongs and drain on paper towels.

Stir the paprikas and flour into the onion mixture
until it just begins to colour.

Spoon off the fat that forms on the surface of
the soup.

MEXICAN BEAN CHOWDER

Preparation time: 20 minutes + overnight soaking
Total cooking time: 1 hour 15 minutes
Serves 6

¾ cup (155 g/5 oz) dried red kidney beans
¾ cup (165 g/5½ oz) dried Mexican black beans (see NOTE)
1 tablespoon oil
1 onion, chopped
2 cloves garlic, crushed
½–1 teaspoon chilli powder
1 tablespoon ground cumin
2 teaspoons ground coriander
2 x 400 g (13 oz) cans chopped tomatoes
3 cups (750 ml/24 fl oz) vegetable stock
1 red capsicum, chopped
1 green capsicum, chopped
440 g (14 oz) can corn kernels
2 tablespoons tomato paste
grated Cheddar, to serve
sour cream, to serve

1 Soak the kidney beans and black beans in separate bowls in plenty of cold water overnight. Drain. Place in a large saucepan, cover with water and bring to the boil. Reduce the heat and simmer for 45 minutes, or until tender. Drain.
2 Heat the oil in a large saucepan, add the onion and cook over medium heat until soft. Add the garlic, chilli powder, cumin and coriander, and cook for 1 minute. Stir in the tomato, stock, capsicum, corn and tomato paste. Cook, covered, for 25–30 minutes. Add the beans during the last 10 minutes of cooking. Stir occasionally.
3 Serve topped with the grated Cheddar and a spoonful of sour cream.

NUTRITION PER SERVE
Protein 20 g; Fat 7 g; Carbohydrate 40 g; Dietary Fibre 20 g; Cholesterol 3 mg; 1250 kJ (300 cal)

NOTE: Mexican black beans are also known as black turtle beans.

Soak the red kidney beans and black beans in separate bowls overnight.

Add the tomato, stock, capsicum, corn and tomato paste.

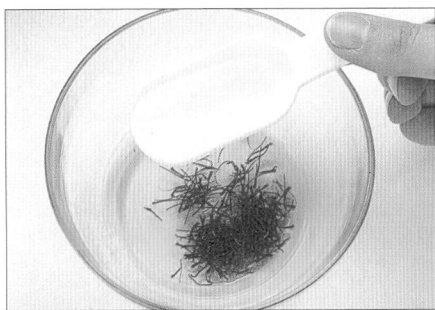

MEDITERRANEAN FISH SOUP

Preparation time: 30 minutes
Total cooking time: 45 minutes
Serves 4

½ teaspoon saffron threads
3 teaspoons oil
2 large onions, thinly sliced
1 leek, white part only, chopped
4 cloves garlic, finely chopped
1 bay leaf, torn
½ teaspoon dried marjoram
1 teaspoon grated orange rind
2 tablespoons dry white wine

1 red capsicum, cut into chunks
500 g (1 lb) tomatoes, chopped
125 ml (4 fl oz) crushed tomatoes
2 cups (500 ml/16 fl oz) fish stock
2 tablespoons tomato paste
2 teaspoons soft brown sugar
500 g (1 lb) firm white fish, cut into
   bite-sized pieces
3 tablespoons chopped fresh parsley

1 Soak the saffron in 2 tablespoons boiling water; set aside. Heat the oil in a large heavy-based pan over low heat. Add the onion, leek, garlic, bay leaf and marjoram. Cover and cook for 10 minutes, shaking the pan occasionally, until the onion is soft.

Add the rind, wine, capsicum and tomato, cover and cook for 10 minutes.
2 Stir in the crushed tomatoes, stock, tomato paste, sugar and saffron (with liquid). Bring to the boil and then simmer, uncovered, for 15 minutes.
3 Add the fish to the soup, cover and cook for 8 minutes, or until tender. Season and add the parsley.

NUTRITION PER SERVE
Protein 30 g; Fat 7.5 g; Carbohydrate 15 g;
Dietary Fibre 5 g; Cholesterol 90 mg;
1020 kJ (245 cal)

Soak the saffron threads in 2 tablespoons boiling water to release the flavour.

Add the orange rind, wine, capsicum and tomato, cover and cook for 10 minutes.

Add the fish pieces to the soup, cover and cook until tender.

POTATO AND CORIANDER SAMOSAS

Preparation time: 1 hour
Total cooking time: 30 minutes
Makes 24

50 g (1¾ oz) butter
2 teaspoons grated fresh ginger
2 teaspoons cumin seeds
1 teaspoon Madras curry powder
½ teaspoon garam masala
500 g (1 lb) waxy potatoes, peeled
    and finely diced
¼ cup (30 g/1 oz) sultanas
½ cup (90 g/3 oz) frozen baby peas
½ cup (15 g/½ oz) fresh coriander
    leaves
3 spring onions, sliced
1 egg, lightly beaten
oil, for deep-frying
thick plain yoghurt, to serve

SAMOSA PASTRY
3¾ cups (465 g/15 oz) plain flour,
    sifted
1 teaspoon baking powder
1½ teaspoons salt
110 g (3½ oz) butter, melted
½ cup (125 g/4 oz) thick plain yoghurt

1 Heat the butter in a large non-stick frying pan, add the ginger, cumin seeds, curry powder and garam masala and fry lightly for 1 minute. Add the potato and 3 tablespoons water and cook over low heat for 15–20 minutes, or until the potato is tender. Toss the sultanas, peas, coriander leaves and spring onion through the potato, remove from the heat and set aside to cool.
2 To make the samosa pastry, combine the flour, baking powder and salt in a large bowl. Make a well in the centre and add the butter, yoghurt and ¾ cup (185 ml/6 fl oz) of water. Using a flat-bladed knife, bring the dough together. Turn out onto a lightly floured surface and bring together to form a smooth ball. Divide the dough into four to make it easier to work with. Roll one piece out until it is very thin. Cover the remaining pastry until you are ready to use it.
3 Using a 12 cm (5 inch) diameter bowl or plate as a guide, cut out six circles. Place a generous tablespoon of potato filling in the centre of each circle, brush the edges of the pastry with egg and fold over to form a semi-circle. Make repeated folds on the rounded edge by folding a little piece of the pastry back as you move around the edge. Continue with the remaining pastry and filling.
4 Heat the oil in a deep heavy-based pan or deep-fryer to 180°C (350°F), or until a cube of bread dropped into the oil browns in 15 seconds. It is important not to have the oil too hot or the samosas will burn before the pastry has cooked. Add the samosas two or three at a time and cook until golden. If they rise to the surface as they puff up, you may need to use a large, long-handled slotted spoon to hold them in the oil to cook the other side. Drain on paper towels. Serve with yoghurt.

NUTRITION PER SAMOSA
Protein 3 g; Fat 6 g; Carbohydrate 20 g;
Dietary Fibre 1 g; Cholesterol 15 mg;
570 kJ (135 cal)

HINT: The samosa pastry becomes very tough if overworked. Use lightly floured hands when working the dough to prevent it sticking and work as quickly as you can.

Toss the sultanas, peas, coriander leaves and spring onion through the potato.

Mix the butter, yoghurt and water into the flour mixture to make a batter.

Cut six circles from each sheet of pastry, using a bowl or plate as a guide.

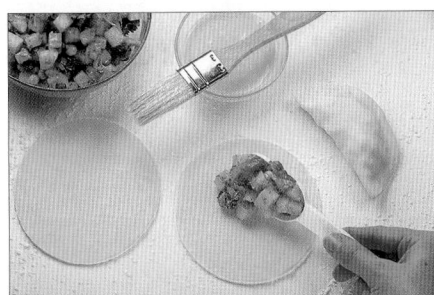

Use a generous tablespoon of filling mixture for each samosa.

Make folds on the edge of the pastry, folding a piece back as you move around.

Remove the cooked samosas from the oil with a slotted spoon.

COCK-A-LEEKIE

**Preparation time: 10 minutes
+ 2 hours refrigeration
Total cooking time: 1 hour 40 minutes
Serves 4–6**

1.5 kg (3 lb) chicken
250 g (8 oz) chicken giblets, optional
(see NOTE)
1 onion, sliced
2 litres chicken stock
4 leeks, thinly sliced
¼ teaspoon ground coriander
pinch nutmeg
1 bouquet garni

12 pitted prunes
pinch cayenne pepper
3 fresh thyme sprigs
fresh thyme sprigs, extra, to serve

1 Put the chicken in a large pan and add the giblets, onion and stock. Bring to the boil, skimming the surface as required. Add the leek, coriander, nutmeg and bouquet garni. Reduce the heat, cover and simmer for 1¼ hours.
2 Remove the chicken and bouquet garni from the pan and lift out the giblets with a slotted spoon. Cool the stock, then refrigerate for 2 hours. Spoon off the fat from the surface and discard. Remove the chicken meat from the bones and shred. Discard the skin and carcass.
3 Return the chicken to the soup with the prunes, cayenne pepper and thyme. Simmer for 20 minutes. Season to taste and garnish with the extra thyme sprigs.

NUTRITION PER SERVE (6)
Protein 60 g; Fat 6 g; Carbohydrate 7 g;
Dietary Fibre 1 g; Cholesterol 125 mg;
1310 kJ (315 cal)

NOTE: The chicken giblets are optional but will give great flavour.

Trim the ends from the leeks and slice thinly, including some green parts.

Add the chicken stock to the pan with the chicken, giblets (if using) and onion.

Add the cayenne pepper, prunes and thyme sprigs to the soup and stir to combine.

PEPPER AND ALMOND BREAD

Preparation time: 10 minutes +
3 hours standing
Total cooking time: 1 hour 10 minutes
Makes about 70 pieces

2 teaspoons black peppercorns
2 egg whites
⅓ cup (90 g/3 oz) caster sugar
¾ cup (90 g/3 oz) plain flour
¼ teaspoon ground ginger
¼ teaspoon ground cinnamon
1 cup (155 g/5 oz) almonds

1 Preheat the oven to moderate 180°C (350°F/Gas 4). Grease an 8 x 26 cm (3 x 10½ inch) bar tin. Line the base and sides with baking paper. Lightly crush the peppercorns with the back of a spoon or in a mortar and pestle.

2 Beat the egg whites and sugar with electric beaters for 4 minutes, or until the mixture turns white and thickens. Sift the flour, ginger and cinnamon and fold in with the almonds and the crushed peppercorns.

3 Spread the mixture into the tin. Bake for 35 minutes, or until lightly browned. Cool in the tin for at least 3 hours, before turning out onto a board. (You can wrap the bread in foil and slice the next day at this stage.) Using a serrated knife, cut the bread into 3 mm (⅛ inch) slices. Place the slices in a single layer on baking trays. Bake in a slow 150°C (300°F/Gas 2) oven for about 25–35 minutes, or until the slices are dry and crisp. Allow to cool completely before serving. Serve with soups as an alternative to plain bread.

NUTRITION PER PIECE
Protein 1 g; Fat 1.5 g; Carbohydrate 2.5 g; Dietary Fibre 0 g; Cholesterol 0 mg; 95 kJ (25 cal)

NOTE: To make a traditional sweet almond bread, simply omit the peppercorns.

Use the back of a large metal spoon to lightly crush the peppercorns.

Beat the egg whites and caster sugar until the mixture turns white and thickens.

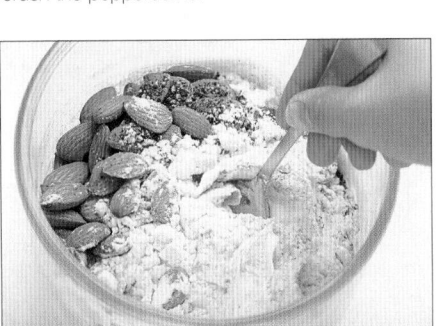

Fold the flour, spices, almonds and peppercorns into the egg white mixture.

Cut the bread into thin slices and arrange them in a single layer on baking trays.

WARM ASPARAGUS AND EGG SALAD WITH HOLLANDAISE

Preparation time: 5 minutes
Total cooking time: 15 minutes
Serves 4

HOLLANDAISE SAUCE
175 g (6 oz) butter
4 egg yolks
1 tablespoon lemon juice

4 eggs, at room temperature
310 g (10 oz) asparagus spears,
    trimmed
Parmesan shavings, to serve

1 To make the hollandaise, melt the butter in a small saucepan and skim off any froth. Remove from the heat and cool. Mix the egg yolks and 2 tablespoons water in another small saucepan for 30 seconds, or until pale and foamy. Place the saucepan over very low heat and whisk for 2–3 minutes, or until thick and foamy—do not overheat or it will scramble. Remove from the heat. Gradually add the butter, whisking well after each addition (avoid using the whey at the bottom). Stir in the lemon juice and season. If the sauce is runny, return to the heat and whisk until thick—do not scramble.
2 Place the eggs in a saucepan half filled with water. Bring to the boil and cook for 6–7 minutes, stirring occasionally to centre the yolks. Drain and cover with cold water until cooled a little, then peel off the shells.
3 Plunge the asparagus into a large saucepan of boiling water and cook for 3 minutes, or until just tender. Drain and pat dry. Divide among four plates. Spoon on the hollandaise. Cut the eggs in half and arrange two halves on each plate. Sprinkle with Parmesan shavings to serve.

NUTRITION PER SERVE
Protein 13 g; Fat 47 g; Carbohydrate 1.5 g;
Dietary Fibre 1 g; Cholesterol 475 mg;
1995 kJ (477 cal)

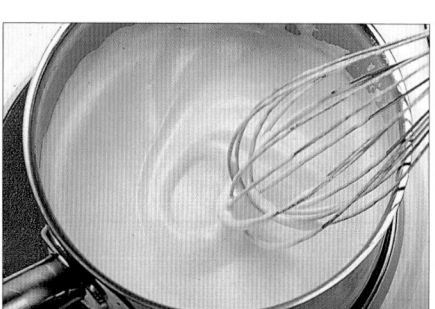

Whisk the yolks over very low heat until they are thick and foamy and the whisk leaves a trail.

Gradually add the cooled butter, whisking well after each addition.

Cook the asparagus in a large saucepan of boiling water until just tender.

HOT BEEF BORSCHT

Preparation time: 30 minutes
Total cooking time: 2 hours 50 minutes
Serves 4–6

500 g (1 lb) gravy beef, cut into large
   pieces
500 g (1 lb) fresh beetroot
1 onion, finely chopped
1 carrot, cut into short strips
1 parsnip, cut into short strips
1 cup (75 g/2½ oz) finely shredded
   cabbage
sour cream and chopped fresh chives,
   to serve

1 Put the beef and 1 litre water in a large, heavy-based saucepan, and bring slowly to the boil. Reduce the heat, cover and simmer for 1 hour. Skim the surface as required.
2 Cut the stems from the beetroot, wash well and place in a large, heavy-based saucepan with 1 litre water. Bring to the boil, then reduce the heat and simmer for 40 minutes, or until tender. Drain, reserving 1 cup (250 ml/ 8 fl oz) of the liquid. Cool, then peel and grate the beetroot.
3 Remove the meat from the stock, cool and dice. Skim any fat from the surface of the stock. Return the meat to the stock and add the onion, carrot, parsnip, beetroot and reserved liquid. Bring to the boil, reduce the heat, cover and simmer for 45 minutes.
4 Stir in the cabbage and simmer for a further 15 minutes. Season to taste. Serve with the sour cream and chives.

NUTRITION PER SERVE (6)
Protein 20 g; Fat 10 g; Carbohydrate 10 g;
Dietary Fibre 5 g; Cholesterol 80 mg;
940 kJ (225 cal)

To avoid stains, wear rubber gloves to grate the cooled beetroot.

Allow the meat to cool, then cut it into dice using a sharp knife.

Pour the reserved beetroot liquid into the soup and bring to the boil.

Pasta & Rice

CHICKEN AND VEGETABLE LASAGNE

Preparation time: 45 minutes
Total cooking time: 1 hour 20 minutes
Serves 8

500 g (1 lb) chicken breast fillets
cooking oil spray
2 cloves garlic, crushed
1 onion, chopped
2 zucchini, chopped
2 celery sticks, chopped
2 carrots, chopped
300 g (10 oz) pumpkin, diced
2 x 400 g (13 oz) cans
    tomatoes, chopped
2 sprigs fresh thyme
2 bay leaves
½ cup (125 ml/4 fl oz) white wine
2 tablespoons tomato paste
2 tablespoons chopped fresh basil
500 g (1 lb) English spinach
500 g (1 lb) reduced-fat cottage
    cheese
450 g (14 oz) ricotta
¼ cup (60 ml/2 fl oz) skim milk
½ teaspoon ground nutmeg
⅓ cup (35 g/1¼ oz) grated Parmesan
300 g (10 oz) instant or fresh lasagne
    sheets

1 Preheat the oven to moderate 180°C (350°F/Gas 4). Trim any fat from the chicken breasts, then finely mince in a food processor. Heat a large, deep, non-stick frying pan, spray lightly with oil and cook the chicken mince in batches until browned. Remove.
2 Add the garlic and onion to the pan and cook until softened. Return the chicken to the pan and add the zucchini, celery, carrot, pumpkin, tomato, thyme, bay leaves, wine and tomato paste. Simmer, covered, for 20 minutes. Remove the bay leaves and thyme and stir in the fresh basil.
3 Shred the spinach and set aside. Mix the cottage cheese, ricotta, skim milk, nutmeg and half the Parmesan.
4 Spoon a little of the tomato mixture over the base of a casserole dish and top with a single layer of pasta. Top with half the remaining tomato mixture, then the spinach and spoon over half the cottage cheese mixture. Continue with another layer of pasta, the remaining tomato and another layer of pasta. Spread the remaining cottage cheese mixture on top and sprinkle with Parmesan. Bake for 40–50 minutes, or until golden. The top may puff up slightly but will settle on standing.

NUTRITION PER SERVE
Protein 40 g; Fat 10 g; Carbohydrate 35 g;
Dietary Fibre 7 g; Cholesterol 70 mg;
1790 kJ (430 cal)

Cut any fat from the chicken fillets and then finely mince in a food processor.

Add the vegetables to the pan with the bay leaves, thyme, wine and tomato paste.

ASIAN MUSHROOM RISOTTO

**Preparation time: 20 minutes +
  20 minutes soaking
Total cooking time: 45 minutes
Serves 4**

10 g (¼ oz) dried Chinese mushrooms
2 cups (500 ml/16 fl oz) vegetable
    stock
2 tablespoons soy sauce
⅓ cup (80 ml/2¾ fl oz) mirin
150 g (5 oz) Swiss brown mushrooms
150 g (5 oz) oyster mushrooms
100 g (3½ oz) fresh shiitake
    mushrooms
150 g (5 oz) shimeji mushrooms
1 tablespoon butter
1 tablespoon olive oil
1 onion, finely chopped
3 cloves garlic, crushed
1 tablespoon finely chopped fresh
    ginger
2 cups (440 g/14 oz) arborio rice
100 g (3½ oz) enoki mushrooms,
    trimmed
2 tablespoons snipped fresh chives
shaved Parmesan, to garnish

1 Put the Chinese mushrooms in a bowl, cover with 2½ cups (625 ml/ 20 fl oz) hot water and soak for 20 minutes, then drain, reserving the liquid. Remove the stems and thinly slice the caps.
2 Heat the vegetable stock, soy sauce, mirin, reserved mushroom liquid and 1 cup (250 ml/8 fl oz) water in a large saucepan. Bring to the boil, then keep at a low simmer, skimming off any scum that forms on the surface.
3 Trim and slice the Swiss brown, oyster and shiitake mushrooms, discarding any woody ends. Trim the shimeji and pull apart into small clumps. Melt the butter in a large saucepan over medium heat, add all the mushrooms except the Chinese and enoki and cook, stirring, for 3 minutes, or until wilted, then remove from the pan.
4 Add the oil to the pan, then add the chopped onion and cook, stirring, for 4–5 minutes, or until soft and just starting to brown. Add the garlic and ginger and stir well until fragrant. Add

the rice and stir for 1 minute, or until it is well coated in the oil mixture.
5 Gradually add ½ cup (125 ml/4 fl oz) of the hot stock to the rice. Stir constantly over medium heat until nearly all the liquid has been absorbed. Continue adding more stock, a little at a time, stirring for 20–25 minutes, until all the stock has been absorbed and the rice is tender.

6 Add all the mushrooms and stir well. Season and garnish with the chives and shaved Parmesan.

NUTRITION PER SERVE
Protein 17 g; Fat 15 g; Carbohydrate 92 g;
Dietary Fibre 8 g; Cholesterol 28 mg;
2397 kJ (573 cal)

Divide the shimeji and slice the Swiss brown,
oyster and shiitake mushrooms.

Stir the rice constantly until nearly all the liquid
has been absorbed.

PENNE WITH PROSCIUTTO

Preparation time: 15 minutes
Total cooking time: 25 minutes
Serves 4

2 teaspoons olive oil
6 thin slices prosciutto, chopped
1 onion, finely chopped
1 tablespoon chopped fresh rosemary
825 g (1 lb 11 oz) can Italian tomatoes
500 g (1 lb) penne or macaroni
grated Parmesan, for serving

1 Heat the oil in a heavy-based frying pan. Add the prosciutto and onion and cook, stirring occasionally, over low heat for 5 minutes, or until golden.
2 Add the rosemary and tomato and season to taste. Simmer for 10 minutes.
3 Meanwhile, cook the pasta in a large pan of rapidly boiling water until al dente. Drain. Divide the pasta among serving bowls and top with the sauce. Sprinkle with a little grated Parmesan to serve.

NUTRITION PER SERVE
Protein 20 g; Fat 9 g; Carbohydrate 65 g;
Dietary Fibre 6 g; Cholesterol 20 mg;
1725 kJ (410 cal)

NOTE: Rosemary is a herb commonly used in Mediterranean cooking and lends a distinctive flavour to the dish. Fresh basil or parsley could be used but dried rosemary is not suitable.

You can cut up the tomato with a pair of kitchen scissors while it is still in the can.

Cook the prosciutto and onion over low heat until they are golden.

Add the rosemary and tomatoes and leave to simmer for 10 minutes.

TURKISH LAMB AND RICE PILAU

Preparation time: 20 minutes
+ 1 hour standing
Total cooking time: 35 minutes
Serves 4–6

1 large eggplant (500 g/1 lb), cut into
    1 cm (½ inch) cubes
½ cup (125 ml/4 fl oz) olive oil
1 large onion, finely chopped
1 teaspoon ground cinnamon
2 teaspoons ground cumin
1 teaspoon ground coriander
300 g (10 oz) long-grain rice
2 cups (500 ml/16 fl oz) chicken stock
500 g (1 lb) lamb mince
½ teaspoon allspice
2 tablespoons olive oil, extra
2 tomatoes, cut into wedges
3 tablespoons toasted pistachios
2 tablespoons currants
2 tablespoons chopped fresh
    coriander leaves

1 Place the eggplant in a colander, sprinkle generously with salt and leave to stand for 1 hour. Rinse well and squeeze dry in a tea towel. Heat 2 tablespoons oil in a large, deep frying pan with a lid, and cook the eggplant over medium heat for 5–8 minutes, or until golden and cooked. Drain on paper towels.
2 Heat the remaining oil in the pan and cook the onion for 2–3 minutes, or until soft but not brown. Stir in ½ teaspoon cinnamon, 1 teaspoon cumin and ½ teaspoon ground coriander. Stir in the rice, then add the stock, season and bring to the boil. Reduce the heat and simmer, covered, for 15 minutes, adding water if the pilau starts to dry out.

3 Meanwhile, place the meat in a bowl with the allspice and remaining cumin, cinnamon and coriander. Season and mix together well. Roll into macadamia nut-size balls. Heat the extra oil in a frying pan, add the meatballs in batches and cook over medium heat for 5 minutes, or until lightly browned and cooked through. Remove and drain on paper towels. Add the tomato to the pan and cook for 3–5 minutes or until

turning lightly golden. Remove.
4 Stir the eggplant, pistachios, currants and meatballs through the rice (this should be quite dry). Spoon onto plates, place the cooked tomato around the edges and garnish with the coriander leaves.

NUTRITION PER SERVE (6)
Protein 25 g; Fat 40 g; Carbohydrate 45 g;
Dietary Fibre 5 g; Cholesterol 55 mg;
2609 kJ (623 Cal)

Add the stock to the pan and bring to the boil.

Roll the lamb mixture into macadamia nut-size balls.

Stir the eggplant, pistachios, currants and meatballs through the rice.

CHICKEN RAVIOLI WITH BUTTERED SAGE SAUCE

Preparation time: 15 minutes
Total cooking time: 10 minutes
Serves 4

500 g (1 lb) fresh or dried chicken-
    filled ravioli or agnolotti
60 g (2 oz) butter
4 spring onions, chopped
2 tablespoons chopped fresh sage
½ cup grated Parmesan, to serve
fresh sage leaves, extra, to serve

1 Add the ravioli to a large pan of rapidly boiling water and cook until just tender. Drain the pasta, then return to the pan.
2 While the ravioli is cooking, melt the butter in a heavy-based pan. Add the spring onion and sage, and stir for 2 minutes. Season with salt and ground black pepper.
3 Add the sauce to the pasta and toss well. Pour onto a warmed serving platter and sprinkle with the Parmesan and sage leaves. Serve immediately.

NUTRITION PER SERVE
Protein 16 g; Fat 24 g; Carbohydrate 18 g;
Dietary Fibre 2 g; Cholesterol 74 mg;
1445 kJ (345 cal)

HINT: Bite through a piece of ravioli to test whether it is done.

Cook the ravioli in a large pan of boiling water until just tender.

Add the spring onion and sage to the melted butter, and stir for 2 minutes.

Add the sage sauce to the ravioli and toss until well combined.

157

PASTA E FAGIOLI (HEARTY PASTA AND BEAN SOUP)

Preparation time: 15 minutes
Total cooking time: 20 minutes
Serves 4

1 tablespoon olive oil
1 onion, finely chopped
3 cloves garlic, crushed
2 x 290 g (10 oz) cans mixed beans, drained
1.75 litres chicken stock (see NOTE)
100 g (3½ oz) conchigliette
1 tablespoon chopped fresh tarragon

1 Heat the oil in a saucepan over low heat. Add the onion and cook for 5 minutes, then add the garlic and cook for a further 1 minute, stirring frequently. Add the beans and chicken stock, cover the pan with a lid, increase the heat and bring to the boil.

2 Add the pasta and cook until al dente. Stir in the tarragon, then season with salt and cracked black pepper. Serve accompanied by crusty bread.

Add the beans and the chicken stock to the pan.

NUTRITION PER SERVE
PROTEIN 12 G; FAT 6.5 G; CARBOHYDRATE 34 G; DIETARY FIBRE 8 G; CHOLESTEROL 0 MG; 1015 KJ (240 CAL)

NOTE: The flavour of this soup is really enhanced by using a good-quality stock. Either make your own or use the tetra packs of liquid stock that are available at the supermarket.

TAGLIATELLE WITH ASPARAGUS, PEAS AND HERB SAUCE

Preparation time: 20 minutes
Total cooking time: 25 minutes
Serves 4

375 g (12 oz) dried or 500 g (1 lb)
   fresh tagliatelle
1 cup (250 ml/8 fl oz) chicken or
   vegetable stock
2 leeks (white part only), thinly sliced
3 cloves garlic, crushed
1½ cups (235 g/7½ oz) fresh peas
1 tablespoon finely chopped fresh
   mint
400 g (13 oz) asparagus spears,
   trimmed and cut into 5 cm (2 inch)
   lengths
¼ cup (15 g/½ oz) finely chopped fresh
   parsley
½ cup (30 g/1 oz) shredded fresh basil
⅓ cup (80 ml/2¾ fl oz) light cream
pinch nutmeg
1 tablespoon grated fresh Parmesan
2 tablespoons extra virgin olive oil,
   to drizzle

1 Bring a saucepan of salted water to the boil and cook the tagliatelle until al dente. Drain well.
2 Place ½ cup (125 ml/4 fl oz) stock and the leek in a large, deep, frying pan. Cook over low heat, stirring often, for 4–5 minutes. Stir in the garlic, peas and mint and cook for 1 minute. Add the remaining stock and ½ cup (125 ml/4 fl oz) water and bring to the boil. Simmer for 5 minutes. Add the asparagus, parsley and basil, and season well. Simmer for a further 3–4 minutes, or until the asparagus is just tender. Gradually increase the heat to reduce the sauce to a light coating consistency. Stir in the cream, nutmeg and Parmesan and adjust the seasoning.
3 Toss the tagliatelle with the sauce to coat. Drizzle each serving with olive oil and garnish with extra grated Parmesan, if desired.

NUTRITION PER SERVE
Protein 21 g; Fat 11 g; Carbohydrate 76 g;
Dietary Fibre 9 g; Cholesterol 32 mg; 2080 kJ
(495 Cal)

Stir the garlic, peas and mint into the stock and leek mixture.

Once the sauce has reduced, stir in the cream, nutmeg and grated Parmesan.

CHICKEN AND PUMPKIN CANNELLONI

Preparation time: 1 hour
Total cooking time: 2 hours
Serves 6

500 g (1 lb) butternut pumpkin, with
  skin and seeds
30 g (1 oz) butter
100 g (3½ oz) pancetta, roughly
  chopped
2 teaspoons olive oil
2 cloves garlic, crushed
500 g (1 lb) chicken thigh fillets, minced
½ teaspoon garam masala
2 tablespoons chopped fresh flat-leaf
  parsley
150 g (5 oz) goats cheese
50 g (1¾ oz) ricotta
375 g (12 oz) fresh lasagne sheets
1 cup (100 g/3½ oz) grated Parmesan

TOMATO SAUCE
30 g (1 oz) butter
1 clove garlic, crushed
2 x 425 g (14 oz) cans chopped
  tomatoes
¼ cup (7 g/¼ oz) chopped fresh flat-
  leaf parsley
¼ cup (60 ml/2 fl oz) white wine

1 Preheat the oven to hot 220°C (425°F/Gas 7). Brush the pumpkin with 10 g (¼ oz) of the butter and bake on a baking tray for 1 hour, or until tender. When the pumpkin has cooked and while it is still hot, remove the seeds. Scrape out the flesh and mash it with a fork. Set aside to cool.
2 Add another 10 g (¼ oz) of the butter to a heavy-based frying pan and cook the pancetta over medium heat for 2–3 minutes. Remove from the pan and drain on paper towels.

3 In the same pan, heat the remaining butter and the olive oil. Add the garlic and stir for 30 seconds. Add the chicken in small batches and brown, making sure the chicken is cooked through. Remove from the pan and set aside to cool on paper towels. Reduce the oven temperature to moderately hot 200°C (400°F/Gas 6).
4 Combine the pumpkin with the pancetta and chicken in a bowl. Mix in the garam marsala, parsley, goats cheese, ricotta and some salt and black pepper. Cut the lasagne sheets into rough 15 cm (6 inch) squares. Place 3 tablespoons of the filling at one end of each square and roll up. Repeat with the rest of the lasagne sheets and filling.
5 To make the tomato sauce, melt the butter in a heavy-based pan and add the garlic. Cook for 1 minute, then add the tomato and simmer over medium heat for 1 minute. Add the parsley and white wine, and simmer gently for another 5 minutes. Season with salt and pepper, to taste.
6 Spread a little of the tomato sauce over the bottom of a 3 litre capacity ovenproof dish and arrange the cannelloni on top in a single layer. Spoon the remaining tomato sauce over the cannelloni and sprinkle with the Parmesan. Bake for 20–25 minutes, or until the cheese is golden.

NUTRITION PER SERVE
Protein 44 g; Fat 26 g; Carbohydrate 55 g; Dietary Fibre 6.5 g; Cholesterol 113 mg; 2670 kJ (638 cal)

NOTE: You can use instant cannelloni tubes instead of the lasagne sheets. Stand the tubes on end on a chopping board and spoon in the filling.

Roughly chop the pancetta slices with a large cook's knife.

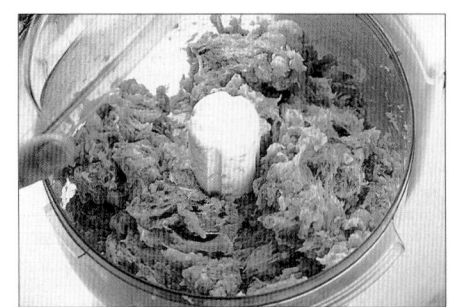

Finely mince the chicken thigh fillets using a food processor.

Scrape out the flesh of the cooked pumpkin and mash with a fork.

Combine the pumpkin, pancetta, chicken and other filling ingredients in a bowl.

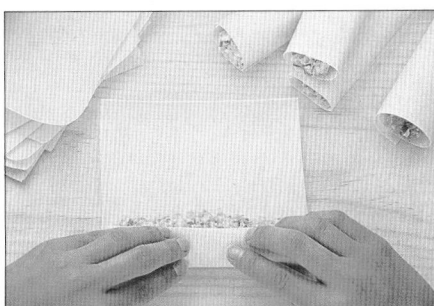

Place 3 tablespoons of the filling onto the end of each lasagne sheet and roll up.

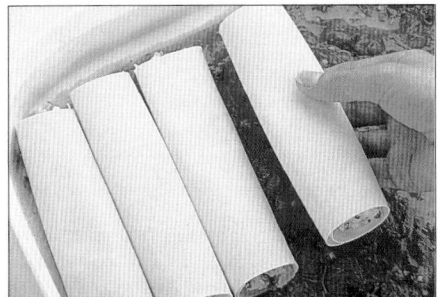

Arrange the cannelloni tubes over a little of the tomato sauce in the dish.

ASIAN BARLEY PILAU

Preparation time: 10 minutes +
   15 minutes standing
Total cooking time: 35 minutes
Serves 4

15 g (½ oz) dried sliced mushrooms
2 cups (500 ml/16 fl oz) vegetable
   stock
½ cup (125 ml/4 fl oz) dry sherry
1 tablespoon oil
3 large French shallots, thinly sliced
2 large cloves garlic, crushed
1 tablespoon grated fresh ginger
1 teaspoon Sichuan peppercorns,
   crushed (see NOTE)
1½ cups (330 g/11 oz) pearl barley
500 g (1 lb) choy sum, cut into short
   lengths
3 teaspoons kecap manis
1 teaspoon sesame oil

1 Place the mushrooms in a bowl and cover with boiling water, then leave for 15 minutes. Strain, reserving ½ cup (125 ml/4 fl oz) of the liquid.
2 Bring the stock and sherry to the boil in a saucepan, then reduce the heat, cover and simmer until needed.
3 Heat the oil in a large saucepan and cook the shallots over medium heat for 2–3 minutes, or until soft. Add the garlic, ginger and pepper-corns and cook for 1 minute. Add the barley and mushrooms and mix well. Stir in the stock and mushroom liquid, then reduce the heat and simmer, covered, for 25 minutes, or until the liquid has evaporated.
4 Meanwhile, steam the choy sum until wilted. Add to the barley mixture. Stir in the kecap manis and sesame oil to serve.

NUTRITION PER SERVE
Protein 13 g; Fat 8.5 g; Carbohydrate 52 g;
Dietary Fibre 13 g; Cholesterol 0 mg;
1552 kJ (370 cal)

NOTE: You can buy Sichuan peppercorns at Asian food stores.

French shallots are like small onions. Peel them and then slice thinly.

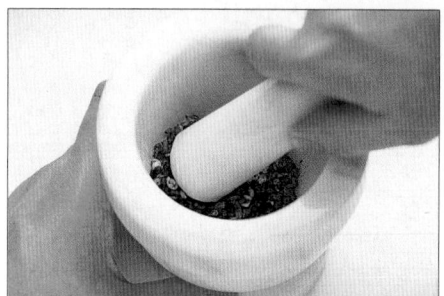

Use a mortar and pestle to crush the Sichuan peppercorns.

Strain the mushrooms, reserving some of the liquid for flavouring the pilau.

Reduce the heat and simmer the pilau until the liquid has evaporated.

RISOTTO WITH SCALLOPS AND MINTED PEAS

Preparation time: 15 minutes
Total cooking time: 35 minutes
Serves 4–6

1 litre chicken, fish or vegetable stock
2¾ cups (360 g/12 oz) fresh or frozen
    baby peas
2 tablespoons light sour cream
2 tablespoons finely shredded mint
1 tablespoon olive oil
1 small onion, finely chopped
2 cloves garlic, finely chopped
150 g (5 oz) arborio rice
16 large scallops (without roe)
1 tablespoon grated fresh Parmesan
4 fresh mint leaves, to garnish
lemon wedges, to serve

1 Bring the stock to the boil and add the peas. Simmer for 1–2 minutes, or until the peas are tender, then remove with a slotted spoon and keep the stock at a low simmer. Blend 1¾ cups (230 g/7½ oz) of the peas with the sour cream in a food processor until smooth. Season, then stir in 1 tablespoon of the mint.
2 Place the oil in a large shallow saucepan and cook the onion over low heat for 4–5 minutes, or until just soft. Add the garlic and cook for 30 seconds. Stir in the rice to coat. Increase the heat to medium.
3 Add 1 cup (250 ml/8 fl oz) stock to the rice mixture and cook, stirring constantly, until all the liquid has evaporated. Add the stock, ½ cup (125 ml/4 fl oz) at a time until the rice is cooked and the mixture is creamy. This will take about 20 minutes.

4 Lightly season the scallops. Heat a chargrill pan or hotplate, add the scallops and sear on both sides until cooked to your liking.
5 Fold the pea purée through the risotto with the whole peas and Parmesan. Divide the risotto among serving bowls and place the scallops on top. Sprinkle with the remaining mint, garnish with a fresh mint leaf and serve with a wedge of lemon.

NUTRITION PER SERVE (6)
Protein 12.5 g; Fat 6 g; Carbohydrate 27.5 g;
Dietary Fibre 4.5 g; Cholesterol 17 mg;
895 kJ (215 Cal)

Process the peas and sour cream in a food processor until smooth.

Fold the pea purée, reserved whole peas and Parmesan through the risotto.

PAELLA

Preparation time: 25 minutes
Total cooking time: 45 minutes
Serves 6

500 g (1 lb) raw prawns
300 g (10 oz) skinless firm white fish
fillets (see NOTE)
250 g (8 oz) black mussels
200 g (6½ oz) calamari rings
2 tablespoons olive oil
1 large onion, diced
3 cloves garlic, finely chopped
1 small red capsicum, thinly sliced
1 small red chilli, seeded and chopped
2 teaspoons paprika
1 teaspoon ground turmeric
2 tomatoes, peeled and diced
1 tablespoon tomato paste
2 cups (400 g/12 oz) long-grain rice
½ cup (125 ml/4 fl oz) white wine
5 cups (1.25 litres) fish stock
3 tablespoons chopped fresh
flat-leaf parsley, for serving
lemon wedges, for serving

1 Peel the prawns, leaving the tails intact. Gently pull out the dark vein from each prawn back, starting at the head end. Cut the fish fillets into cubes. Scrub the mussels and pull out the hairy beards. Discard any broken mussels or any that don't close when tapped. Refrigerate the seafood, covered, until ready to use.
2 Heat the oil in a paella pan or a large deep frying pan with a lid. Add the onion, garlic, capsicum and chilli to the pan and cook over medium heat for 2 minutes, or until the onion and capsicum are soft. Add the paprika, turmeric and 1 teaspoon salt and stir-fry for 1–2 minutes, or until aromatic.

3 Add the tomato and cook for 5 minutes, or until softened. Add the tomato paste. Stir in the rice until it is well coated.
4 Pour in the wine and simmer until almost absorbed. Add all the fish stock and bring to the boil. Reduce the heat and simmer for 20 minutes, or until almost all the liquid is absorbed into the rice. There is no need to stir the rice, but you may occasionally wish to fluff it up with a fork.
5 Add the mussels to the pan, poking the shells into the rice, cover and cook for 2–3 minutes over low heat. Add the prawns and cook for 2–3 minutes. Add the fish, cover and cook for 3 minutes. Finally, add the calamari rings and cook for 1–2 minutes. By this time, the mussels should have opened—discard any unopened ones. The prawns should be pink and the fish should flake easily when tested with a fork. The calamari should be white, moist and tender. Cook for another 2–3 minutes if the seafood is not quite cooked, but avoid overcooking as the seafood will toughen and dry out.
6 Serve with parsley and lemon wedges and a green salad.

NUTRITION PER SERVE
Protein 44.5 g; Fat 14.5 g; Carbohydrate 60 g;
Dietary Fibre 3.5 g; Cholesterol 217 mg;
2360 kJ (560 cal)

NOTE: You can use just fish, or other seafood such as scampi, octopus and crabs. If using just fish, choose one with few bones and chunky flesh, such as ling, blue-eye or warehou.

Protect your hands with rubber gloves when seeding the chilli.

Peel and pull out the dark vein from along the back of each prawn.

Add the paprika and turmeric to the pan and stir until aromatic.

Add the rice to the pan and stir with a wooden spoon until well coated.

Simmer the mixture until almost all the liquid is absorbed into the rice.

Cook the calamari rings for 1–2 minutes. Don't overcook or they will be tough.

BLUE CHEESE GNOCCHI

Preparation time: 20 minutes
Total cooking time: 20 minutes
Serves 8 as a starter

500 g (1 lb) potatoes, quartered
1¼ cups (155 g/5 oz) plain flour

SAUCE
300 ml (10 fl oz) cream
125 g (4 oz) gorgonzola cheese,
    roughly chopped
2 tablespoons chopped fresh chives

1 Cook the potatoes in boiling salted water for 15–20 minutes or in the microwave until tender. Stir through a generous amount of salt. Drain the potatoes, then mash until completely smooth. Transfer to a bowl.

2 Sprinkle the flour into the bowl with one hand while kneading it into the potato mixture with the other hand. Continue kneading until all the flour is worked in and the dough is smooth. This should take a few minutes and will be sticky at first.

3 Divide the dough into three and roll each portion into a sausage that is 2 cm thick. Cut into 2.5 cm lengths and, using floured hands, press each gnocchi against a fork to flatten it and indent one side (the indentation helps the sauce coat the gnocchi).

4 Bring a large pan of water to the boil. Drop in the gnocchi, then reduce the heat and simmer until they rise to the surface. This will take 2–3 minutes. Lift out of the water with a slotted spoon and drain well. Arrange on a warm serving dish and keep warm.

5 Put the cream into a small pan and bring to the boil. Boil rapidly, stirring constantly, for about 5 minutes, or until reduced by one third. Remove from the heat and stir in the cheese. Season with salt and pepper, and pour over the gnocchi. Scatter the chives over the top and serve immediately.

NUTRITION PER SERVE
Protein 10 g; Fat 22 g; Carbohydrate 22 g;
Dietary Fibre 1.5 g; Cholesterol 65 mg;
1370 kJ (325 cal)

Add the flour with one hand while kneading it into the potato with the other.

Gently knead the mixture until all the flour is mixed in and the dough is smooth.

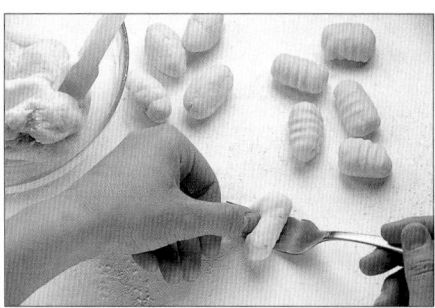

Press the gnocchi against a fork to flatten it and indent one side.

Drop the gnocchi into boiling water and simmer until they rise.

SPAGHETTI WITH MEATBALLS

Preparation time: 40 minutes
Total cooking time: 30 minutes
Serves 4

MEATBALLS
500 g (1 lb) beef mince
½ cup (40 g/1¼ oz) fresh breadcrumbs
1 onion, finely chopped
2 cloves garlic, crushed
2 teaspoons Worcestershire sauce
1 teaspoon dried oregano
¼ cup (30 g/1 oz) plain flour
2 tablespoons olive oil

SAUCE
2 x 400 g (13 oz) cans chopped
   tomatoes
1 tablespoon olive oil
1 onion, finely chopped
2 cloves garlic, crushed
2 tablespoons tomato paste
½ cup (125 ml/4 fl oz) beef stock
2 teaspoons sugar

500 g (1 lb) spaghetti
grated Parmesan, to serve

1 Combine the mince, breadcrumbs, onion, garlic, Worcestershire sauce and oregano and season to taste. Use your hands to mix the ingredients well. Roll level tablespoons of the mixture into balls, dust lightly with the flour and shake off the excess. Heat the oil in a deep frying pan and cook the meatballs in batches, turning often, until browned all over. Drain well.

2 To make the sauce, purée the tomatoes in a food processor or blender. Heat the oil in the cleaned frying pan. Add the onion and cook over medium heat for a few minutes until soft and lightly golden. Add the garlic and cook for 1 minute more. Add the puréed tomatoes, tomato paste, stock and sugar to the pan and stir to combine. Bring the mixture to the boil, and add the meatballs. Reduce the heat and simmer for 15 minutes, turning the meatballs once. Season with salt and pepper.

3 Meanwhile, cook the spaghetti in a large pan of boiling water until just tender. Drain, divide among serving plates and top with the meatballs and sauce. Serve with grated Parmesan.

NUTRITION PER SERVE
Protein 45 g; Fat 30 g; Carbohydrate 112 g;
Dietary Fibre 11 g; Cholesterol 85 mg;
3875 kJ (925 Cal)

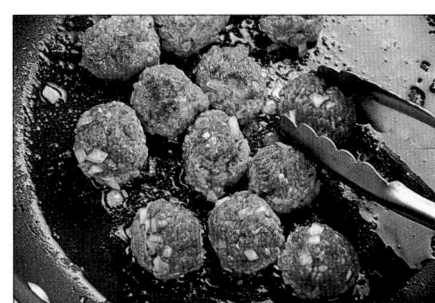

With clean hands, roll the mixture into balls and dust with flour.

Cook the meatballs in batches, turning frequently, until browned all over.

167

RICE WITH CHICKEN AND SEAFOOD

Preparation time: 40 minutes
Total cooking time: 40 minutes
Serves 4–6

500 g (1 lb) raw medium prawns
500 g (1 lb) mussels
200 g (6½ oz) calamari tubes
¼ cup (60 ml/2 fl oz) oil
2 chorizo sausages, thickly sliced
500 g (1 lb) chicken pieces
300 g (10 oz) pork fillet, thickly sliced
4 cloves garlic, crushed
2 red onions, chopped
¼ teaspoon saffron threads, soaked in
    hot water
¼ teaspoon turmeric
4 large tomatoes, peeled, seeded and
    chopped

2 cups (440 g/14 oz) short-grain rice
1.25 litres hot chicken stock
125 g (4 oz) green beans, cut into
    4 cm (1½ inch) lengths
1 red capsicum, cut into thin strips
1 cup (155 g/5 oz) fresh peas

1 Peel the prawns. Devein, leaving the tails intact. Scrub the mussels and remove the beards. Cut the calamari tubes into 5 mm (¼ inch) thin slices. Heat 1 tablespoon of the oil in a large, heavy-based pan and add the chorizo. Cook over medium heat for 5 minutes, or until browned. Drain on paper towels. Add the chicken pieces and cook for 5 minutes, or until golden, turning once. Drain on paper towels.
2 Add the pork to the pan and cook for 3 minutes, or until browned, turning once. Drain on paper towels.

Heat the remaining oil in the pan, add the garlic, onion, drained saffron and turmeric, and cook over medium heat for 3 minutes, or until the onion is soft. Add the tomato and cook for 3 minutes, or until soft.
3 Add the rice and stir for 5 minutes, or until the rice is translucent. Stir in the hot chicken stock, bring to the boil, cover and simmer for 10 minutes. Add the chicken, cover and cook for 20 minutes. Add the pork, prawns, mussels, calamari, chorizo and vegetables. Cover and cook for 10 minutes, or until the liquid has been absorbed.

NUTRITION PER SERVE (6)
Protein 66 g; Fat 12 g; Carbohydrate 66 g;
Dietary Fibre 6 g; Cholesterol 278 mg;
2695 kJ (644 cal)

Drain the cooked chorizo sausage slices on paper towels.

Cook the pork slices until they are browned on both sides.

Add the rice to the pan and stir until the rice is translucent.

KITCHEREE (SEASONED RICE AND LENTILS)

Preparation time: 15 minutes
Total cooking time: 25 minutes
Serves 6

1½ cups (300 g/10 oz) basmati rice
1½ cups (300 g/10 oz) split mung
   beans (mung lentils)
2 tablespoons oil
1 onion, sliced
3 bay leaves
1 teaspoon cumin seeds
2 pieces cassia bark
1 tablespoon cardamom seeds
6 cloves
¼ teaspoon black peppercorns

1 Wash the rice and lentils, then drain and set aside.
2 Heat the oil in a frying pan, add the onion, bay leaves and spices, and cook over low heat for 5 minutes, or until the onion is softened and the spices are fragrant. Add the rice and lentils, and cook, stirring, for 2 minutes. Pour in 1.25 litres water and salt to taste. Bring to the boil, then reduce the heat and cook, covered, over low heat for 15 minutes. Stir gently to avoid breaking the grains and cook, uncovered, over low heat for 3 minutes, or until all the moisture has evaporated. Serve hot with Indian curries.

NUTRITION PER SERVE
Protein 6 g; Fat 10 g; Carbohydrate 44 g; Dietary Fibre 3 g; Cholesterol 0 mg; 1217 kJ (290 Cal)

NOTE: To avoid serving with the whole spices left intact, tie the spices in a piece of muslin and add it to the pan along with the boiling water. Discard when the dish is cooked.

Cook the onion and spices together until the onion is soft and the spices fragrant.

Stir gently until all the excess moisture has evaporated.

169

LASAGNE

Preparation time: 40 minutes
Total cooking time: 1 hour 35 minutes
Serves 8

2 teaspoons olive oil
1 large onion, chopped
2 carrots, finely chopped
2 celery sticks, finely chopped
2 zucchini, finely chopped
2 cloves garlic, crushed
500 g (1 lb) lean beef mince
2 x 400 g (13 oz) cans crushed
   tomatoes
½ cup (125 ml/4 fl oz) beef stock
2 tablespoons tomato paste
2 teaspoons dried oregano
375 g (12 oz) instant or fresh lasagne
   sheets

CHEESE SAUCE
⅓ cup (40 g/1¼ oz) cornflour
3 cups (750 ml/24 fl oz) skim milk
100 g (3½ oz) reduced-fat cheese,
   grated

1 Heat the olive oil in a large non-stick frying pan. Add the onion and cook for 5 minutes, until soft. Add the carrot, celery and zucchini and cook, stirring constantly, for 5 minutes, or until the vegetables are soft. Add the crushed garlic and cook for another minute. Add the beef mince and cook over high heat, stirring, until well browned. Break up any lumps of meat with a wooden spoon.
2 Add the crushed tomato, beef stock, tomato paste and dried oregano to the pan and stir to thoroughly combine. Bring the mixture to the boil, then reduce the heat and simmer gently, partially covered, for 20 minutes, stirring occasionally to prevent the mixture sticking to the pan.
3 Preheat the oven to moderate 180°C (350°F/Gas 4). Spread a little of the meat sauce into the base of a 23 x 30 cm (9 x 12 inch) ovenproof dish. Arrange a layer of lasagne sheets in the dish, breaking some of the sheets, if necessary, to fit in neatly.
4 Spread half the meat sauce over the top to cover evenly. Cover with another layer of lasagne sheets, a layer of meat sauce, then a final layer of lasagne sheets.
5 To make the cheese sauce, blend a little of the milk with the cornflour, to form a smooth paste, in a small pan. Gradually blend in the remaining milk and stir constantly over low heat until the mixture boils and thickens. Remove from the heat and stir in the grated cheese until melted. Spread evenly over the top of the lasagne and bake for 1 hour.
6 Check the lasagne after 25 minutes. If the top is browning too quickly, cover loosely with non-stick baking paper or foil. Take care when removing the baking paper or foil that the topping does not come away with the paper. Leave the lasagne to stand for 15 minutes before cutting into portions for serving.

NUTRITION PER SERVE
Protein 15 g; Fat 12 g; Carbohydrate 50 g;
Dietary Fibre 5 g; Cholesterol 10 mg;
1885 kJ (450 cal)

STORAGE TIME: Can be frozen for up to 2–3 months. When required, thaw overnight in the refrigerator, then reheat, covered with foil, for about 30 minutes in a moderate oven.

Chop the garlic and crush using the flat side of a large knife.

Add the vegetables to the pan and stir constantly until soft.

When you add the meat, break up any lumps with a wooden spoon.

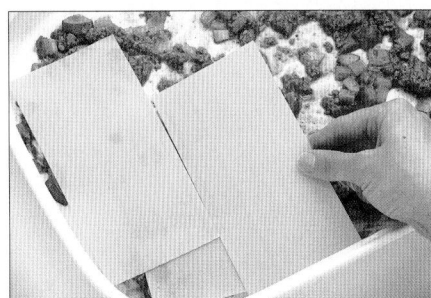
Spread a little of the meat sauce over the base and cover evenly with lasagne sheets.

Remove the pan from the heat and stir in the cheese until melted.

Spread the cheese sauce evenly over the top of the lasagne.

FUSILLI WITH TUNA, CAPERS AND PARSLEY

Preparation time: 15 minutes
Total cooking time: 10 minutes
Serves 4

425 g (14 oz) can tuna in spring water, drained
2 tablespoons olive oil
2 cloves garlic, finely chopped
2 small red chillies, finely chopped
½ cup (30 g/1 oz) finely chopped fresh parsley

3 tablespoons capers (see HINT)
3 tablespoons lemon juice
375 g (12 oz) fusilli

1 Place the tuna in a bowl and flake lightly with a fork. Combine the oil, garlic, chilli, capers, parsley and lemon juice. Pour over the tuna and mix lightly. Season well.
2 Meanwhile, cook the pasta in a large pan of rapidly boiling salted water for 10 minutes, or until al dente. Reserve ½ cup (125 ml/4 fl oz) of the cooking water, then drain the pasta. Toss the tuna mixture through the pasta, adding enough of the reserved water to give a moist consistency. Serve immediately.

NUTRITION PER SERVE
Protein 35 g; Fat 13 g; Carbohydrate 65 g; Dietary Fibre 5 g; Cholesterol 55 mg; 2270 kJ (545 cal)

HINT: Generally, the smaller the caper the tastier, so use baby ones if you can find them.

Finely chop the chillies. Remove the seeds if you prefer a milder taste.

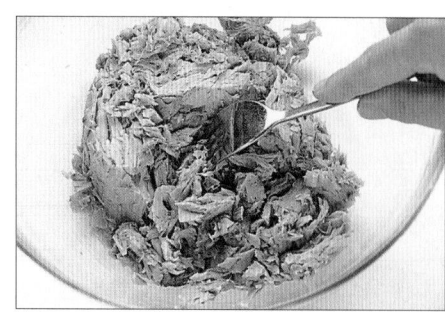
Break the tuna into flakes with a fork and then mix with the dressing.

Cook the pasta in a large pan of rapidly boiling salted water.

PUMPKIN AND BROAD BEAN RISOTTO

Preparation time: 35 minutes
Total cooking time: 50 minutes
Serves 4

350 g (11 oz) pumpkin
cooking oil spray
1 tablespoon olive oil
1 large onion, finely chopped
2 cloves garlic, finely chopped
3 cups (750 ml/24 fl oz) vegetable
    stock
1 cup (220 g/7 oz) arborio rice
200 g (6½ oz) Swiss brown
    mushrooms, halved
4 tablespoons grated Parmesan

2 cups (310 g/10 oz) frozen broad
    beans, defrosted, peeled

1 Preheat the oven to moderately hot 200°C (400°F/Gas 6). Cut the pumpkin into small chunks, place on a baking tray and spray lightly with oil. Bake, turning occasionally, for 20 minutes, or until tender. Set aside, covered.
2 Meanwhile, heat the oil in a large heavy-based pan, add the onion and garlic, cover and cook for 10 minutes over low heat. Put the stock in a different pan and keep at simmering point on the stove top.
3 Add the rice to the onion and stir for 2 minutes. Gradually stir in ½ cup (125 ml/4 fl oz) of the hot stock, until

absorbed. Stir in another ½ cup (125 ml/4 fl oz) of hot stock until absorbed. Add the mushrooms and continue adding the remaining stock, a little at a time, until it is all absorbed and the rice is just tender (this will take about 25 minutes).
4 Stir in the cooked pumpkin and the broad beans. Sprinkle with the grated Parmesan.

NUTRITION PER SERVE
Protein 20 g; Fat 12 g; Carbohydrate 60 g;
Dietary Fibre 10 g; Cholesterol 20 mg;
1775 kJ (425 cal)

Put the chunks of pumpkin on a baking tray and spray with oil.

Add the stock to the rice, a little at a time, and stir until absorbed.

Add the mushrooms, then continue stirring in the stock until absorbed.

173

RED LENTIL PILAU

Preparation time: 15 minutes
Total cooking time: 25 minutes
Serves 4–6

GARAM MASALA
1 tablespoon coriander seeds
1 tablespoon cardamom pods
1 tablespoon cumin seeds
1 teaspoon whole black peppercorns
1 teaspoon whole cloves
1 small cinnamon stick, crushed

3 tablespoons oil
1 onion, chopped

3 cloves garlic, chopped
1 cup (200 g/6½ oz) basmati rice
1 cup (250 g/8 oz) red lentils
3 cups (750 ml/24 fl oz) hot vegetable
   stock
spring onions, thinly sliced

1 To make the garam masala, place all the spices in a dry frying pan and shake over medium heat for 1 minute, or until fragrant. Blend in a spice grinder, blender or mortar and pestle to make a fine powder.
2 Heat the oil in a large saucepan. Add the onion, garlic and 3 teaspoons garam masala. Cook over medium heat for 3 minutes, or until soft.

3 Stir in the rice and lentils and cook for 2 minutes. Add the hot stock and stir well. Slowly bring to the boil, then reduce the heat and simmer, covered, for 15–20 minutes, or until the rice is cooked and all the stock has been absorbed. Gently fluff the rice with a fork. Garnish with spring onion.

NUTRITION PER SERVE (6)
Protein 13 g; Fat 11 g; Carbohydrate 42 g;
Dietary Fibre 7 g; Cholesterol 0 mg;
1333 kJ (318 cal)

NOTE: If time is short you can, of course, use ready-made garam masala instead of making your own.

Finely chop all the spices in a spice grinder until they make a fine powder.

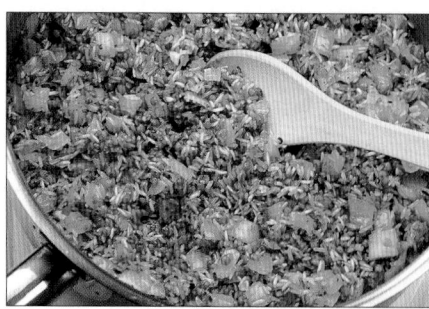

Stir the rice and lentils into the onion and garlic mixture and cook for 2 minutes.

Simmer, covered, until the rice is cooked and all the stock has been absorbed.

FETTUCINE CARBONARA

Preparation time: 10 minutes
Total cooking time: 25 minutes
Serves 4

500 g (1 lb) fettucine
3 eggs, lightly beaten
½ cup (125 ml/4 oz) cream
⅓ cup (35 g/1¼ oz) finely grated
    Parmesan
20 g (¾ oz) butter
250 g (8 oz) bacon, rind removed,
    cut into thin strips
2 cloves garlic, crushed
4 spring onions, finely chopped

1 Bring a large pan of water to the boil, add the fettucine and cook for 10–12 minutes, or until just tender.
2 Whisk together the eggs, cream and Parmesan and season generously.

3 Meanwhile, melt the butter in a frying pan, add the bacon strips and cook for 5–8 minutes, or until lightly golden. Add the garlic and spring onion and cook for 2–3 minutes more. Remove from the heat.
4 Drain the pasta, and transfer to a large serving bowl. While the pasta is still hot pour in the egg mixture and toss well to combine (the heat from the pasta should be sufficient to cook the egg). Add the bacon mixture and toss through the pasta. Season to taste with cracked black pepper and serve immediately.

NUTRITION PER SERVE
Protein 35 g; Fat 30 g; Carbohydrate 90 g;
Dietary Fibre 6.5 g; Cholesterol 235 mg;
3213 kJ (765 Cal)

Whisk together the eggs, cream, cheese, salt and pepper.

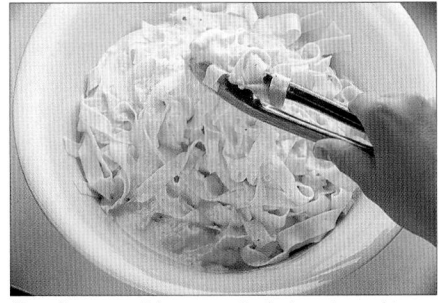

Pour the egg mixture over the hot pasta and toss to combine.

LEEK AND PROSCIUTTO RISOTTO WITH PARSLEY PISTOU

Preparation time: 10 minutes
Total cooking time: 45 minutes
Serves 2

PARSLEY PISTOU
¼ cup (60 ml/2 fl oz) extra virgin olive
    oil
1 clove garlic, crushed
2 tablespoons chopped fresh
    flat-leaf parsley

100 g (3½ oz) prosciutto
3 cups (750 ml/24 fl oz) chicken stock
60 g (2 oz) butter
2 leeks, halved lengthways and sliced
1 celery stick, sliced thinly
2 cups (440 g/14 oz) arborio rice
½ cup (125 ml/4 fl oz) dry white wine
2 teaspoons fresh thyme

1 To make the pistou, combine the oil, garlic, parsley and ½ teaspoon cracked pepper in a blender or mortar and pestle and blend until combined.
2 Place the prosciutto on an oven tray lined with foil and cook under a hot grill for 3 minutes, or until crisp—be careful not to burn it. Cool, then break into small pieces.
3 Put the stock and 3 cups (750 ml/ 24 fl oz) water in a pan, bring to the boil, then reduce to simmering.
4 Heat the butter over medium heat in a large heavy-based pan. When foaming, add the leek and cook, stirring occasionally, for 7 minutes, or until soft. Add the celery and rice and stir for 1 minute, or until the rice is coated in the butter. Add the wine, allow it to boil until almost dry, then add ½ cup (125 ml/4 fl oz) of the hot

stock and stir over low heat with a wooden spoon until all the liquid is absorbed. Continue adding the stock a ladleful at a time, stirring continuously until it is completely absorbed before the next addition. The risotto will be ready after 20–25 minutes when the rice grains are swollen and the mixture appears creamy. You may not need to use all the stock. The rice should be just

tender, when bitten, but not chalky. Stir in the prosciutto and thyme, and season to taste with salt. Spoon into serving bowls and swirl through some of the pistou. Serve immediately.

NUTRITION PER SERVE
Protein 15 g; Fat 55 g; Carbohydrate 175 g;
Dietary Fibre 7 g; Cholesterol 75 mg;
5465 kJ (1305 Cal)

Stir in the celery and rice until the rice is coated in butter.

Add the wine and allow the mixture to boil until almost dry.

Pour in a ladleful of stock and stir until completely absorbed.

PENNE WITH RICOTTA AND BASIL SAUCE

Preparation time: 20 minutes
Total cooking time: 15 minutes
Serves 4

2 bacon rashers
2 teaspoons olive oil
2–3 cloves garlic, crushed
1 onion, finely chopped
2 spring onions, finely chopped
250 g (8 oz) ricotta
325 g (11 oz) penne

½ cup (30 g/1 oz) finely chopped fresh basil
8 cherry tomatoes, halved

1 Remove the fat and rind from the bacon and chop roughly. Heat the oil in a pan, add the bacon, garlic, onion and spring onion and stir over medium heat for 5 minutes, or until cooked. Remove from the heat, stir in the ricotta and chopped basil and beat until smooth.
2 Meanwhile, cook the pasta in a large pan of rapidly boiling salted water for 10 minutes, or until al

dente. Just prior to draining the pasta, add about a cup of the pasta water to the ricotta mixture to thin the sauce. Add more water if you prefer an even thinner sauce. Season well.
3 Drain the pasta and stir the sauce and tomato halves into the pasta.

NUTRITION PER SERVE
Protein 20 g; Fat 10 g; Carbohydrate 65 g;
Dietary Fibre 5 g; Cholesterol 40 mg;
1885 kJ (450 cal)

Remove from the heat and stir in the ricotta and chopped basil.

Bring a large pan of salted water to a rapid boil before adding the pasta.

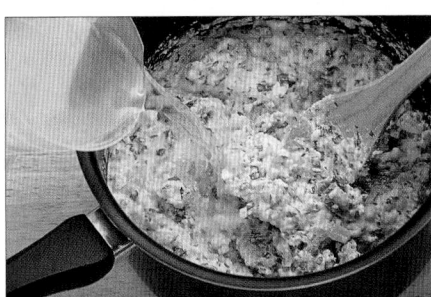

Thin the ricotta mixture with about a cup of the water from the cooked pasta.

PRAWNS WITH JASMINE RICE

Preparation time: 15 minutes
Total cooking time: 30 minutes
Serves 4

1 tablespoon peanut oil
8 spring onions, sliced
1 tablespoon finely chopped fresh
    ginger
1 tablespoon finely sliced lemon grass,
    white part only
2 teaspoons crushed coriander seeds
    (see NOTE)
2 cups (400 g/13 oz) jasmine rice
4 cups (1 litre) vegetable stock
1 tablespoon shredded lime rind
1 kg (2 lb) raw prawns, peeled,
    deveined and chopped
2 tablespoons lime juice
1 cup (30 g/1 oz) fresh coriander
    leaves
fish sauce, for serving

1 Heat the oil in a saucepan, add the spring onion and cook over low heat for 4 minutes, or until soft. Add the ginger, lemon grass, coriander seeds and rice, and stir for 1 minute.
2 Add the stock and lime rind and bring to the boil while stirring. Reduce the heat to very low and cook, covered, for 15–20 minutes, or until the rice is tender.
3 Remove the pan from the heat and stir in the prawns. Cover and leave for 4–5 minutes, or until the prawns are cooked. Add the lime juice and coriander leaves and flake the rice with a fork. Sprinkle with a few drops of fish sauce to serve.

NUTRITION PER SERVE
Protein 59 g; Fat 12 g; Carbohydrate 80 g;
Dietary Fibre 3 g; Cholesterol 373 mg;
2850 kJ (681 cal)

NOTE: To crush coriander seeds, place in a small plastic bag and, using a rolling pin, crush until fine.

Peel and devein the prawns and chop them into small pieces.

Add the ginger, lemon grass, coriander seeds and rice to the saucepan.

Add the lime juice and coriander leaves and flake the rice with a fork.

CREAMY PASTA GNOCCHI WITH PEAS AND PROSCIUTTO

Preparation time: 15 minutes
Total cooking time: 20 minutes
Serves 4

100 g (3½ oz) thinly sliced prosciutto
3 teaspoons oil
2 eggs
1 cup (250 ml/8 fl oz) cream
⅓ cup (35 g/1¼ oz) finely grated
   Parmesan
2 tablespoons chopped fresh
   flat-leaf parsley
1 tablespoon chopped fresh chives
250 g (8 oz) fresh or frozen peas
500 g (1 lb) pasta gnocchi

1 Cut the prosciutto into 5 mm (¼ inch) wide strips. Heat the oil in a frying pan over medium heat, add the prosciutto and cook for 2 minutes, or until crisp. Drain on paper towels. Place the eggs, cream, Parmesan and herbs in a bowl and whisk well.
2 Bring a large saucepan of salted water to the boil. Add the peas and cook for 5 minutes, or until just tender. Leaving the pan on the heat, use a slotted spoon and transfer the peas to the bowl of cream mixture, and then add ¼ cup (60 ml/2 fl oz) of the cooking liquid to the same bowl. Using a potato masher or the back of a fork, roughly mash the peas.
3 Add the gnocchi to the boiling water and cook until al dente. Drain well, then return to the pan. Add the cream mixture, then warm through over low heat, gently stirring for about 30 seconds until the gnocchi is coated in the sauce. Season to taste with salt and cracked black pepper. Divide among warmed plates, top with the prosciutto and serve immediately.

NUTRITION PER SERVE
Fat 32.5 g; Protein 21 g; Carbohydrate 41 g; Dietary Fibre 6 g; Cholesterol 201 mg; 2260 kJ (540 Cal)

NOTE: Be careful not to overheat or cook for too long as the egg will begin to set and the result will look like a scrambled egg sauce.

Cook the prosciutto strips over medium heat until crisp, then drain on paper towels.

Roughly mash the peas using a potato masher or the back of a fork.

Gently stir the mixture until the gnocchi is coated in the sauce.

179

SEAFOOD AND HERB RISOTTO

Preparation time: 40 minutes
Total cooking time: 50 minutes
Serves 4

150 g (5 oz) white boneless fish fillet
    such as sea perch
8 black mussels (200 g/6½ oz)
8 raw prawns (250 g/8 oz)
7 cups (1.75 litres) chicken stock
cooking oil spray
2 onions, finely chopped
2 cloves garlic, finely chopped
1 celery stick, finely chopped
2 cups (440 g/14 oz) arborio rice (see
    NOTE)
2 tablespoons chopped fresh parsley
1 tablespoon chopped fresh oregano
1 tablespoon chopped fresh thyme
    leaves
2 tablespoons grated Parmesan

1 Cut the fish fillet into small cubes. Scrub the mussels well and remove the beards. Discard any musssels that are broken or open and do not close when tapped. Peel and devein the prawns, leaving the tails intact. Put the seafood in a bowl and refrigerate until required.
2 Put the stock in a saucepan and bring to the boil, then reduce the heat until just gently simmering.
3 Lightly spray a large saucepan with cooking oil and heat over medium heat. Add the onion, garlic and celery and cook for 2–3 minutes. Add 2 tablespoons water, cover and cook for 5 minutes, or until the vegetables have begun to soften. Add the arborio rice and 2 tablespoons water and stir over medium heat for 3–4 minutes, or until the rice grains are well coated.

4 Gradually add ½ cup (125 ml/ 4 fl oz) of the hot stock to the rice mixture, stirring constantly over low heat with a wooden spoon, until all the stock has been absorbed. Repeat the process, adding ½ cup of liquid each time until all but a small amount of stock is left and the rice is just tender.
5 Meanwhile, bring a small amount of water to the boil in a saucepan. Add the mussels, cover and cook for about 3 minutes, shaking the pan occasionally, until the mussels have opened. Drain the mussels and discard any that have not opened in the cooking time.
6 Add the fish and prawns and the remaining hot stock to the rice. Stir well and continue to cook for about 5–10 minutes, or until the seafood is just cooked and the rice is tender and creamy. Remove from the heat, add the cooked mussels, cover and set aside for 5 minutes. Stir the herbs and Parmesan through the risotto, then season well. Serve immediately.

NUTRITION PER SERVE
Protein 40 g; Fat 5 g; Carbohydrate 90 g; Dietary Fibre 4 g; Cholesterol 175 mg; 2395 kJ (570 cal)

NOTE: Arborio has a fatter and shorter grain than other short-grain rice. The chief ingredient of risotto, arborio has a high starch content which gives the dish its creamy texture. This is the reason you can't successfully use another type of rice.

Scrub the mussels thoroughly and pull off the beards. Discard any open mussels.

Add the arborio rice to the pan and stir over the heat until the rice is well coated.

Stir in the stock a little at a time, not adding any more until the last portion has been absorbed.

Risotto is ready when the rice has absorbed all the hot stock.

Put the mussels in a pan of boiling water, cover and cook for 3 minutes to open them.

Stir the chopped herbs and grated Parmesan through the risotto.

FRESH VEGETABLE LASAGNE WITH ROCKET

Preparation time: 20 minutes
Total cooking time: 20 minutes
Serves 4

BALSAMIC SYRUP
⅓ cup (80 ml/2¾ fl oz) balsamic vinegar
1½ tablespoons brown sugar

1 cup (150 g/5 oz) fresh or frozen
   peas
16 asparagus spears, trimmed and
   cut into 5 cm (2 inch) lengths
2 large zucchini, cut into thin ribbons
2 fresh lasagne sheets, each sheet
   24 cm x 35 cm (9½ inch x 14 inch)
100 g (3½ oz) rocket leaves
1 cup (30 g/1 oz) fresh basil, torn
2 tablespoons extra virgin olive oil
250 g (8 oz) low-fat ricotta
150 g (5 oz) semi-dried tomatoes
Parmesan shavings, to garnish

1 To make the syrup, place the vinegar and sugar in a saucepan and stir over medium heat until the sugar dissolves. Reduce the heat and simmer for 3 minutes, or until the sauce becomes syrupy. Remove from the heat.
2 Bring a saucepan of salted water to the boil. Blanch the peas, asparagus and zucchini in separate batches until just tender, removing each batch with a slotted spoon and refreshing in cold water. Reserve the cooking liquid and return to the boil.
3 Cook the lasagne sheets in the boiling water for 1–2 minutes, or until al dente. Refresh in cold water and drain. Cut each in half lengthways.
4 Toss the vegetables and the rocket with the basil and olive oil. Season.
5 To assemble, place one strip of

pasta on a serving plate—one-third on the centre of the plate and two-thirds overhanging one side. Place some of the salad on the centre one-third, topped with some ricotta and tomato. Season and fold over one-third of the lasagne sheet. Top with another layer of salad, ricotta and tomato. Fold back the final layer of pasta and garnish with a little salad

and tomato. Repeat with the remaining pasta, salad, ricotta and tomato to make four servings. Just before serving, drizzle with balsamic syrup and garnish with Parmesan.

NUTRITION PER SERVE
Protein 18 g; Fat 16 g; Carbohydrate 36 g;
Dietary Fibre 6 g; Cholesterol 63 mg;
1515 kJ (360 Cal)

Simmer the balsamic vinegar and brown sugar until it becomes syrupy.

Toss the peas, asparagus, zucchini, rocket, basil and olive oil together.

Fold one third of the lasagne sheet over the salad mix, ricotta and tomato.

VEGETARIAN PAELLA

**Preparation time: 20 minutes + overnight
    soaking**
Total cooking time: 40 minutes
Serves 6

1 cup (200 g/6½ oz) dried haricot
    beans
¼ teaspoon saffron threads
2 tablespoons olive oil
1 onion, diced
1 red capsicum, cut into
    1 cm x 4 cm (½ inch x 1½ inch)
    strips
5 cloves garlic, crushed
1¼ cups (275 g/9 oz) paella rice or
    arborio
1 tablespoon sweet paprika
½ teaspoon mixed spice
3 cups (750 ml/24 fl oz) vegetable
    stock
400 g (13 oz) can diced tomatoes
1½ tablespoons tomato paste
1 cup (150 g/5 oz) fresh or frozen soy
    beans
100 g (3½ oz) silverbeet leaves
    (no stems), shredded
400 g (13 oz) can artichoke hearts,
    drained and quartered
4 tablespoons chopped fresh
    coriander leaves

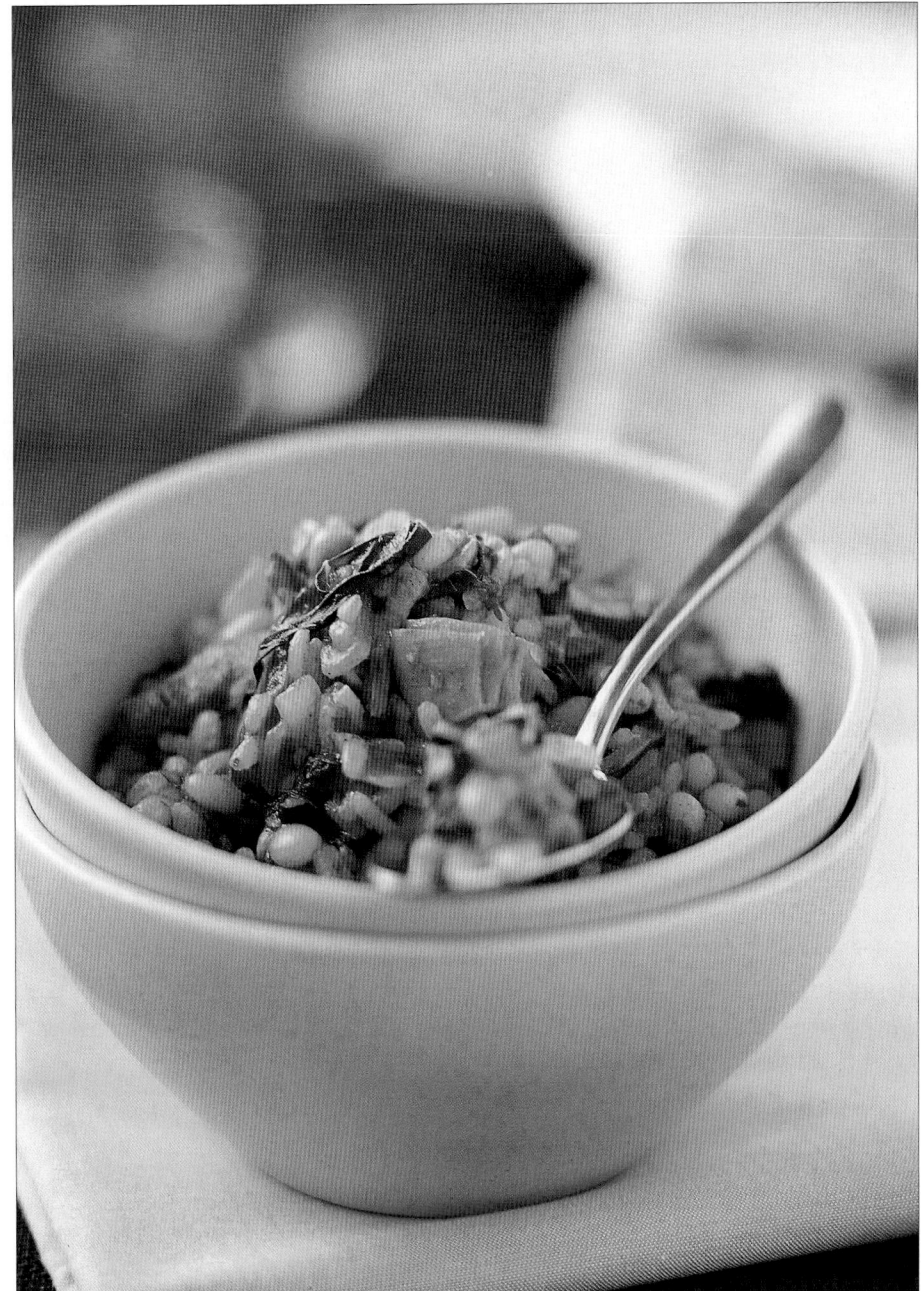

1 Place the haricot beans in a large
bowl, cover with cold water and soak
overnight. Drain and rinse well.
2 Place the saffron threads in a small
frying pan over medium–low heat.
Dry-fry, shaking the pan, for 1 minute,
or until darkened. Remove from the
heat and when cool, crumble into a
small bowl. Pour in ½ cup (125 ml)
warm water and allow to steep.
3 Heat the oil in a paella or frying pan.
Add the onion and capsicum and cook
over medium–high heat for 4 minutes,
or until the onion softens. Stir in the
garlic and cook for 1 minute. Reduce
the heat and add the beans, rice,
paprika, mixed spice and ½ teaspoon
salt. Stir to coat. Add the saffron water,
stock, tomatoes and tomato paste and
bring to the boil. Cover, reduce the
heat and simmer for 20 minutes.
4 Stir in the soy beans, silverbeet and
artichoke hearts and cook, covered,
for 8 minutes, or until all the liquid

is absorbed and the rice and beans
are tender. Turn off the heat and
leave for 5 minutes. Stir in the
coriander just before serving.

NUTRITION PER SERVE
Protein 16 g; Fat 8 g; Carbohydrate 55 g;
Dietary Fibre 12 g; Cholesterol 0 mg;
1510 kJ (360 Cal)

Allow the crumbled saffron threads to steep in
warm water.

Add the haricot beans, rice, paprika, mixed spice
and salt and stir to coat.

MUSHROOM RISOTTO

Preparation time: 15 minutes
Total cooking time: 40 minutes
Serves 4

1.5 litres (48 fl oz) vegetable stock
2 cups (500 ml/16 fl oz) white wine
2 tablespoons olive oil
60 g (2 oz) butter
2 leeks, thinly sliced
1 kg (2 lb) flat mushrooms, sliced
500 g (1 lb) arborio rice
¾ cup (75 g/2½ oz) grated Parmesan,
    plus Parmesan shavings, to serve
3 tablespoons chopped fresh flat-leaf
parsley
balsamic vinegar and fresh flat-leaf
    parsley, to serve

1 Place the stock and wine in a large saucepan and keep at simmering point on the stove top.
2 Heat the oil and butter in a large saucepan. Add the leek and cook over medium heat for 5 minutes, or until soft and golden. Add the mushrooms to the pan and cook for 5 minutes, or until tender. Add the rice and stir for 1 minute, or until translucent.
3 Add ½ cup (125 ml/4 fl oz) hot stock, stirring constantly over medium heat until the liquid is absorbed. Continue adding the stock, a little at a time, stirring constantly for 20–25 minutes, or until all the rice is tender and creamy (you may not need all the stock, or you may need to add a little water if you run out).
4 Stir in the Parmesan and chopped parsley and heat for 1 minute, or until all the cheese has melted. Serve drizzled with balsamic vinegar and topped with Parmesan shavings.

NUTRITION PER SERVE
Protein 26 g; Fat 30 g; Carbohydrate 105 g;
Dietary Fibre 11 g; Cholesterol 56 mg;
3299 kJ (788 cal)

Cook the leek and mushrooms in a large saucepan until tender.

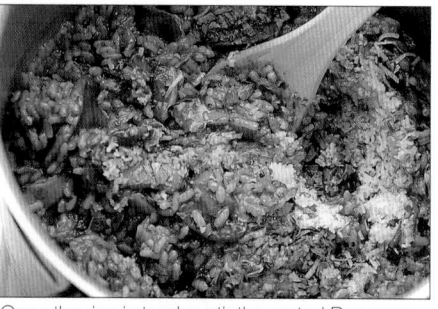

Stir the rice constantly until most of the liquid has been absorbed.

Once the rice is tender, stir the grated Parmesan and parsley into the risotto.

SAVOURY RICE AND EGGS

Preparation time: 20 minutes
Total cooking time: 12 minutes
Serves 4

2 tablespoons ghee (see NOTE) or oil
1 onion, finely chopped
½ red capsicum, finely chopped
10 spring onions, thinly sliced
2–3 small red chillies, seeded and
    finely chopped
2–3 cloves garlic, finely chopped
1 tablespoon grated fresh ginger
125 g (4 oz) Chinese barbecued pork,
    finely chopped
6 eggs, lightly beaten

4 cups (740 g/1½ lb) cold cooked
    jasmine rice
1–2 teaspoons seasoning sauce
⅓ cup (20 g/¾ oz) chopped coriander
onion flakes, to garnish

1 Heat the wok until very hot, add the ghee and swirl it around to coat the side. Stir-fry the onion, capsicum, spring onion, chilli, garlic and ginger over medium-high heat for 2–3 minutes, or until the vegetables are cooked but not brown. Add the barbecued pork and toss to combine.
2 Reduce the heat, then pour in the beaten eggs. Season well with salt and pepper. Gently stir the egg mixture until it is creamy and almost set. Add the rice and gently stir-fry to incorporate all the ingredients and heat the mixture through.
3 Sprinkle with the seasoning sauce and stir in the coriander. Serve the savoury rice immediately, sprinkled with onion flakes.

NUTRITION PER SERVE
Protein 15 g; Fat 20 g; Carbohydrate 60 g;
Dietary Fibre 3.5 g; Cholesterol 295 mg;
2105 kJ (500 cal)

NOTE: Ghee is a form of clarified butter. It is the main type of fat used in Indian cooking and is available in most supermarkets.

Cut the Chinese barbecued pork into slices, then chop it finely.

Add the barbecued pork to the onion mixture and toss to combine.

Add the egg, season well and stir gently until the mixture is creamy.

CHICKEN AGNOLOTTI

Preparation time: 45 minutes +
   30 minutes standing
Total cooking time: 2 hours 45 minutes
Serves 4

PASTA
2 cups (250 g/8 oz) plain flour
3 eggs
1 tablespoon olive oil
1 egg yolk, extra

FILLING
125 g (4 oz) chicken mince
75 g (2½ oz) ricotta or cottage cheese
60 g (2 oz) chicken livers, trimmed and
   chopped
30 g (1 oz) prosciutto, chopped
1 slice salami, chopped
2 tablespoons grated Parmesan
1 egg, beaten
1 tablespoon chopped fresh parsley
1 clove garlic, crushed
¼ teaspoon mixed spice

TOMATO SAUCE
2 tablespoons olive oil
1 onion, finely chopped
2 cloves garlic, crushed
2 x 425 g (14 oz) cans tomatoes
¼ cup (15 g/½ oz) chopped fresh basil
½ teaspoon mixed herbs

1 To make the pasta, sift the flour and a pinch of salt onto a board. Make a well in the centre of the flour. In a bowl, whisk together the eggs, oil and 1 tablespoon water. Add the egg mixture gradually to the flour, working in with your hands until the mixture forms a ball. Knead on a lightly floured surface for 5 minutes, or until smooth and elastic. Place the dough in a lightly oiled bowl and cover with plastic wrap. Allow to stand for 30 minutes.

2 To make the filling, place the chicken, cheese, liver, prosciutto, salami, Parmesan, egg, parsley, garlic, mixed spice and some salt and ground black pepper in a food processor. Process until finely chopped. Set aside.

3 To make the tomato sauce, heat the oil in a medium pan. Add the onion and garlic and stir over low heat until the onion is tender. Increase the heat, add the undrained, crushed tomatoes, basil, herbs, and salt and pepper, to taste. Stir to combine, then bring to the boil. Reduce the heat and simmer for 15 minutes. Remove from the heat.

4 Roll out half the pasta dough until 1 mm (⅟₁₆ inch) thick. Cut with a knife or fluted pastry cutter into 10 cm (4 inch) strips. Place teaspoons of filling at 5 cm (2 inch) intervals down one side of each strip. Whisk together the extra egg yolk and ¼ cup (60 ml/ 2 fl oz) water. Brush along one side of the dough and between the filling. Fold the dough over the filling to meet the other side. Repeat with the remaining filling and dough.

5 Press the edges of the dough together firmly to seal. Cut between the mounds of filling with a knife or a fluted pastry cutter.

6 Cook the ravioli in batches in a large pan of rapidly boiling water for 10 minutes each batch. Reheat the tomato sauce in a large pan. Add the cooked ravioli and toss well until the sauce is evenly distributed. Simmer, stirring, for 5 minutes, then serve.

NUTRITION PER SERVE
Protein 30 g; Fat 25 g; Carbohydrate 60 g; Dietary Fibre 6 g; Cholesterol 223 mg; 2534 kJ (605 cal)

Knead the pasta mixture on a lightly floured surface until smooth and elastic.

Place the filling ingredients in a food processor and process until finely chopped.

Stir the tomatoes, basil, mixed herbs and salt and pepper into the onion mixture.

Place teaspoons of the filling at 5 cm (2 inch) intervals down one side of each strip.

Use a fluted pastry cutter or knife to cut between the mounds of filling.

Add the cooked ravioli to the tomato sauce, and toss until combined.

SPAGHETTI WITH CHILLI CALAMARI

Preparation time: 15 minutes
Total cooking time: 30 minutes
Serves 4

500 g (1 lb) calamari, cleaned
500 g (1 lb) spaghetti
1 tablespoon olive oil
1 leek, chopped
2 cloves garlic, crushed
1–2 teaspoons chopped chilli
½ teaspoon cayenne pepper
425 g (14 oz) can crushed tomatoes
½ cup (125 ml/4 fl oz) fish stock
1 tablespoon chopped fresh basil
2 teaspoons chopped fresh sage
1 teaspoon chopped fresh marjoram

1 Pull the tentacles from the body of the calamari. Using your fingers, pull the quill from the pouch of the calamari. Pull the skin away from the flesh and discard. Use a sharp knife to slit the tubes up one side. Lay out flat and score one side in a diamond pattern. Cut each tube into four.
2 Cook the spaghetti in a large pan of rapidly boiling salted water until al dente. Drain and keep warm.
3 Heat the oil in a large frying pan. Add the leek and cook for 2 minutes. Add the garlic and stir over low heat for 1 minute. Stir in the chilli and cayenne. Add the tomato, stock and herbs and bring to the boil. Reduce the heat and simmer for 5 minutes.
4 Add the calamari to the pan. Simmer for another 5–10 minutes, or until tender. Serve the chilli calamari over the spaghetti.

NUTRITION PER SERVE
Protein 35 g; Fat 15 g; Carbohydrate 90 g;
Dietary Fibre 10 g; Cholesterol 250 mg;
2670 kJ (640 cal)

Pull the clear quill from the pouch of the calamari and then pull the skin away from the flesh.

Add the calamari to the pan and simmer for another few minutes, until tender.

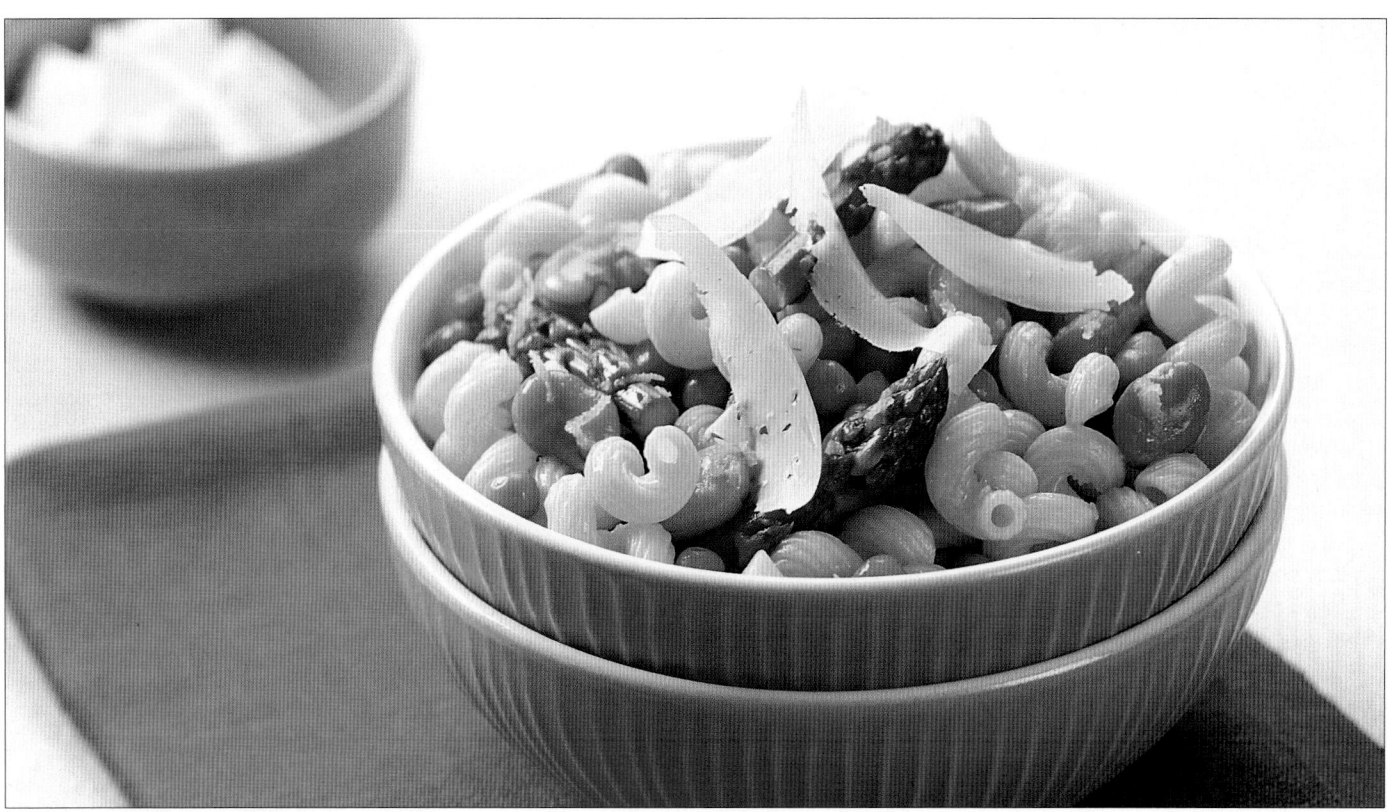

COTELLI WITH SPRING VEGETABLES

Preparation time: 15 minutes
Total cooking time: 20 minutes
Serves 4

500 g (1 lb) cotelli
2 cups (310 g/10 oz) frozen peas
2 cups (310 g/10 oz) frozen broad
  beans, blanched and peeled
⅓ cup (80 ml/2¾ fl oz) olive oil
6 spring onions, cut into 3 cm
  (1¼ inch) pieces
2 cloves garlic, finely chopped
1 cup (250 ml/8 fl oz) chicken stock
12 thin fresh asparagus spears,
  cut into 5 cm (2 inch) lengths
1 lemon

1 Cook the pasta in a large saucepan of boiling water until al dente. Drain, then return to the pan. Meanwhile, place the peas in a saucepan of boiling water and cook them for 1–2 minutes, or until tender. Remove with a slotted spoon and plunge into cold water. Add the broad beans to the same saucepan of boiling water and cook for 1–2 minutes, then drain and plunge into cold water. Remove and slip the skins off.

2 Heat 2 tablespoons of the oil in a frying pan. Add the spring onion and garlic and cook over medium heat for 2 minutes, or until softened. Pour in the stock and cook for 5 minutes, or until slightly reduced. Add the asparagus and cook for 3–4 minutes, or until bright green and just tender.

Stir in the peas and broad beans and cook for 2–3 minutes, or until heated through.

3 Toss the remaining oil through the pasta, then add the vegetable mixture, ½ teaspoon finely grated lemon rind and ¼ cup (60 ml/2 fl oz) lemon juice. Season to taste with salt and cracked black pepper and toss together well. Divide among four bowls and top with shaved Parmesan, if desired.

NUTRITION PER SERVE
Protein 24.5 g; Fat 20.5 g; Carbohydrate 102.5 g; Dietary Fibre 18.5 g; Cholesterol 0 mg; 2935 kJ (700 Cal)

The skins should slip easily off the broad beans after they have been boiled.

Cook the asparagus until the spears are bright green and tender.

Gently toss the pasta with the vegetable mixture until they are well combined.

CHICKEN BIRYANI

**Preparation time: 1 hour 30 minutes
+ 3–4 hours marinating
Total cooking time: about 2 hours
Serves 6**

MARINADE
6 cardamom pods
3 onions, peeled
3 cloves garlic
5 cm (2 inch) piece ginger, sliced
8 cloves or ¼ teaspoon ground cloves
1 teaspoon whole black
    peppercorns
1 teaspoon ground cumin
1 teaspoon ground cinnamon
1½ tablespoons poppy seeds
¼ teaspoon ground nutmeg
1 teaspoon salt
2 tablespoons lemon juice
250 g (8 oz) natural yoghurt

1 kg (2 lb) chicken pieces, cut into
    small pieces
⅓ cup (80 ml/2¾ fl oz) oil
3 bay leaves
2 whole cardamom pods, lightly
    crushed
3 onions, very thinly sliced
2 tablespoons raisins
1½ cups (300 g/10 oz) long-grain
    white rice
¼ cup (60 ml/2 fl oz) milk
1 teaspoon sugar
1 teaspoon saffron threads
plain yoghurt, to serve
¼ cup (40 g/1¼ oz) toasted cashews,
    to serve

1 To make the marinade, crush the cardamom pods with the flat side of a large knife blade to release the seeds; discard the pods. Chop the onions, garlic and ginger in a food processor.

Add the cardamom seeds, cloves, peppercorns, cumin, cinnamon, poppy seeds, nutmeg, salt and lemon juice, and process to a smooth paste. Stir in the yoghurt and set aside.
2 Prick the skin of the chicken with a fork (this helps the flavour infuse into the chicken) and place in a large mixing bowl. Add the marinade and mix well to thoroughly coat the chicken, then refrigerate for 3–4 hours, or overnight.
3 Heat about 3 tablespoons of the oil in a heavy-based frying pan over low heat. Add the bay leaves and whole cardamom pods and toss in the oil. Cook for 2 minutes, being careful not to burn. Remove the bay leaves and set aside; discard the cardamom pods. Add the onion and fry over low heat for 8 minutes, or until a rich golden colour. Remove with a slotted spoon, leaving the oil in the pan. Drain on paper towels. Quickly fry the raisins until plump; set aside with the onions. Reserve the remaining oil.
4 Place the chicken and the marinade in a heavy-based flameproof casserole dish and bring slowly to the boil. Cover and simmer for 15 minutes. Using tongs or a slotted spoon, remove the chicken, leaving as much marinade in the pan as possible. Reduce the marinade down, cooking it over low heat until only about 1 cup (250 ml/8 fl oz) remains. Return the chicken to the pan and toss to coat in the thickened sauce. Cover and set aside while preparing the rice.
5 Add the rice to a large pan of boiling water and cook for 7 minutes. (Do not cook the rice until tender.) Drain the rice into a colander. Meanwhile, heat the milk and sugar, pour into a bowl, add the saffron and soak for 5 minutes.

6 Preheat the oven to slow 150°C (300°F/Gas 2). Spoon the rice over the spice-coated chicken and pour over the saffron mixture. Streak the orange colour gently through the rice with a fork. Pour over the reserved

Crush the cardamom pods to release the seeds with the flat side of a knife.

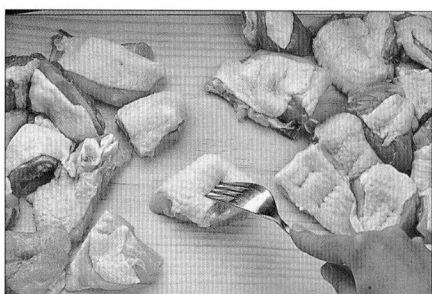

Prick the skin of the chicken with a fork to help the flavour infuse into the meat.

Remove the onion with a slotted spoon, keeping as much oil as possible in the pan.

flavoured oil, and scatter with bay leaves. Cover the dish tightly with foil and bake for 1 hour, or until the rice and chicken are tender. Serve topped with the onion, raisins, yoghurt and cashews.

NUTRITION PER SERVE
Protein 40 g; Fat 45 g; Carbohydrate 60 g; Dietary Fibre 4 g; Cholesterol 140 mg; 3305 kJ (785 cal)

NOTE: Biryani is a very regal and special dish, which is usually served at elaborate weddings. It is definitely worth all the effort to cook, so do not cut corners.

Cook the marinade over low heat until reduced and thickened.

Add the saffron threads to the heated milk and sugar mixture.

Gently streak the saffron mixture through the rice using a fork.

ZUCCHINI PASTA BAKE

Preparation time: 15 minutes
Total cooking time: 40 minutes
Serves 4

200 g (6½ oz) risoni
40 g (1¼ oz) butter
4 spring onions, thinly sliced
400 g (13 oz) zucchini, grated
4 eggs
½ cup (125 ml/4 fl oz) cream
100 g (3½ oz) ricotta (see NOTE)
⅔ cup (100 g/3½ oz) grated mozzarella
¾ cup (75 g/2½ oz) grated Parmesan

1 Preheat the oven to moderate 180°C (350°F/Gas 4). Cook the pasta in a large saucepan of boiling water until al dente. Drain well. Meanwhile, heat the butter in a frying pan, add the spring onion and cook for 1 minute, then add the zucchini and cook for a further 4 minutes, or until soft. Cool slightly.
2 Place the eggs, cream, ricotta, mozzarella, risoni and half of the Parmesan in a bowl and mix together well. Stir in the zucchini mixture, then season with salt and pepper. Spoon the mixture into four 2 cup (500 ml/ 16 fl oz) greased ovenproof dishes, but do not fill to the brim. Sprinkle with the remaining Parmesan and cook for 25–30 minutes, or until firm and golden.

NUTRITION PER SERVE
Protein 28.5 g; Fat 40.5 g; Carbohydrate 39 g; Dietary Fibre 4.5 g; Cholesterol 310.5 mg; 2635 kJ (630 Cal)

NOTE: With such simple flavours, it is important to use good-quality fresh ricotta from the delicatessen or the deli section of your local supermarket.

Cook the grated zucchini until it is soft, taking care not to burn it.

Spoon the mixture into four ovenproof dishes. Take care to not fill them to the top.

FENNEL RISOTTO BALLS WITH CHEESY FILLING

Preparation time: 30 minutes +
1 hour refrigeration
Total cooking time: 50 minutes
Serves 4–6

1.5 litres (48 fl oz) vegetable stock
1 tablespoon oil
30 g (1 oz) butter
2 cloves garlic, crushed
1 onion, finely chopped
2 fennel bulbs, finely sliced
1 tablespoon balsamic vinegar
½ cup (125 ml/4 fl oz) white wine
3 cups (650 g/1 lb 5 oz) arborio rice
½ cup (50 g/1¾ oz) grated Parmesan
½ cup (25 g/¾ oz) snipped chives
1 egg, lightly beaten
150 g (5 oz) sun-dried tomatoes, chopped
100 g (3½ oz) mozzarella, diced
½ cup (90 g/3 oz) frozen peas, thawed
flour, for dusting
3 eggs, lightly beaten, extra
2 cups (200 g/6½ oz) dry breadcrumbs
oil, for deep-frying

1 Heat the stock in a saucepan and keep at simmering point.
2 Heat the oil and butter in a large saucepan and cook the garlic and onion for 3 minutes, or until soft. Add the fennel and cook for 10 minutes, or until it starts to caramelize. Add the vinegar and wine, increase the heat and boil until the liquid evaporates. Add the rice and stir for 1 minute, or until translucent.
3 Add ½ cup (125 ml/4 fl oz) hot stock, stirring constantly over medium heat until the liquid is absorbed. Continue adding the stock, a little at a time, stirring for 20–25 minutes, or until the rice is tender and creamy. Stir in the Parmesan, chives, egg and tomato. Tip into a bowl, cover and leave to cool.
4 Place the mozzarella and peas in a bowl and mash together. Season.
5 With wet hands, shape the risotto into 14 even balls. Flatten each ball out, slightly indenting the centre. Place a heaped teaspoon of the pea mash into the indentation, then reform to make a ball. Roll each ball in seasoned flour, then dip in the extra egg and roll in breadcrumbs. Place on a foil-covered tray and chill for 30 minutes.
6 Fill a deep heavy-based saucepan one third full of oil and heat until a cube of bread dropped into the oil browns in 15 seconds. Cook the risotto balls in batches for 5 minutes, or until golden and crisp and the cheese has melted inside. Drain on crumpled paper towels and season with salt. If the cheese has not melted, cook the balls on a tray in a moderate 180°C (350°F/Gas 4) oven for 5 minutes.

NUTRITION PER SERVE (6)
Protein 11 g; Fat 9.5 g; Carbohydrate 48 g; Dietary Fibre 2.5 g; Cholesterol 65 mg; 1377 kJ (329 cal)

Stir the Parmesan, chives, egg and sun-dried tomato into the risotto.

Place a heaped teaspoon of the cheesy pea mixture into the middle of each ball.

FETTUCINE WITH CHERRY TOMATOES, AVOCADO AND BACON

Preparation time: 15 minutes
Total cooking time: 25 minutes
Serves 4

4 cloves garlic, unpeeled
⅓ cup (80 ml/2¾ fl oz) olive oil
250 g (8 oz) cherry tomatoes
300 g (10 oz) short cut bacon
    (see NOTE)
350 g (11 oz) fresh fettucine
1 tablespoon white wine vinegar
2 tablespoons roughly chopped
    fresh basil
2 ripe avocados, diced
whole fresh basil leaves, to garnish

1 Preheat the oven to moderately hot 200°C (400°F/Gas 6). Place the garlic at one end of a roasting tin and drizzle with 2 tablespoons of the olive oil. Place the tomatoes at the other end and season well. Bake for 10 minutes, then remove the garlic. Return the tomatoes to the oven for a further 5–10 minutes, or until soft.
2 Cook the bacon under a hot grill for 4–5 minutes each side, or until crisp and golden. Roughly chop. Meanwhile, cook the pasta in a large saucepan of boiling water until al dente. Drain well and transfer to a large bowl. Drizzle 1 tablespoon of the olive oil over the pasta and toss well. Season to taste with salt and freshly ground black pepper and keep warm.

3 Slit the skin of each garlic clove and squeeze the garlic out. Place in a screw-top jar with the vinegar, chopped basil and remaining oil and shake well to combine. Add the tomatoes and their juices, bacon and avocado to the fettucine, pour on the dressing and toss well. Garnish with the basil leaves and serve with a green salad and crusty bread.

NUTRITION PER SERVE
Protein 27.5 g; Fat 44 g; Carbohydrate 50.5 g; Dietary Fibre 4 g; Cholesterol 106.5 mg; 2960 kJ (705 Cal)

NOTE: Short cut bacon is the meaty end of the bacon rasher and is also sold as eye bacon.

Bake the tomatoes until they are wrinkled and quite soft.

Grill the bacon until it is crisp and golden, but take care to not burn it.

The roasted garlic should slip out of its skin quite easily.

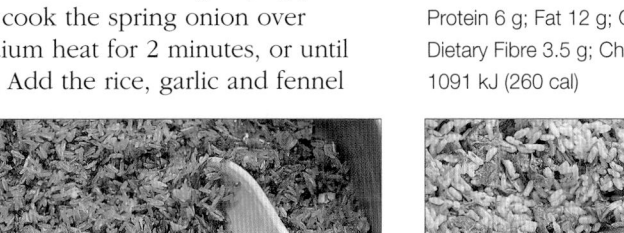

GREEN PILAU WITH CASHEWS

Preparation time: 15 minutes
Total cooking time: 1 hour 10 minutes
Serves 6

200 g (6½ oz) baby English spinach
⅔ cup (100 g/3½ oz) cashew nuts, chopped
2 tablespoons olive oil
6 spring onions, chopped
1½ cups (300 g/10 oz) long-grain brown rice
2 cloves garlic, finely chopped
1 teaspoon fennel seeds

2 tablespoons lemon juice
2½ cups (600 ml/20 fl oz) vegetable stock
3 tablespoons chopped fresh mint
3 tablespoons chopped fresh flat-leaf parsley

1 Preheat the oven to moderate 180°C (350°F/Gas 4). Shred the English spinach leaves.
2 Place the cashew nuts on a baking tray and roast for 5–10 minutes, or until golden brown—watch carefully.
3 Heat the oil in a large frying pan and cook the spring onion over medium heat for 2 minutes, or until soft. Add the rice, garlic and fennel seeds and cook, stirring frequently, for 1–2 minutes, or until the rice is evenly coated. Increase the heat to high, add the lemon juice, stock and 1 teaspoon salt and bring to the boil. Reduce to low, cover and cook for 45 minutes without lifting the lid.
4 Remove from the heat and sprinkle with the spinach and herbs. Leave, covered, for 8 minutes, then fork the spinach and herbs through the rice. Season. Serve sprinkled with cashews.

NUTRITION PER SERVE
Protein 6 g; Fat 12 g; Carbohydrate 32 g;
Dietary Fibre 3.5 g; Cholesterol 0 mg;
1091 kJ (260 cal)

Wash the spinach thoroughly, trim away any stalks and shred the leaves.

Fork the spinach and herbs through the rice and sprinkle with cashews to serve.

Stir the rice until it is evenly coated and starts to stick to the pan.

SEAFOOD LASAGNE

Preparation time: 15 minutes
Total cooking time: 50 minutes
Serves 6

250 g (8 oz) fresh lasagne sheets
1 tablespoon olive oil
30 g (1 oz) butter
1 onion, finely chopped
2 cloves garlic, crushed
400 g (13 oz) raw medium prawns, peeled and deveined
500 g (1 lb) skinless firm white fish fillets, cut into 2 cm (¾ inch) pieces
250 g (8 oz) scallops with roe, membrane removed
750 g (1½ lb) bottled tomato pasta sauce
1 tablespoon tomato paste
1 teaspoon soft brown sugar
½ cup (60 g/2 oz) grated Cheddar
¼ cup (25 g/¾ oz) grated Parmesan

CHEESE SAUCE
120 g (4 oz) butter
⅔ cup (85 g/3 oz) plain flour
1.5 litres milk
2 cups (250 g/8 oz) grated Cheddar
1 cup (100 g/3½ oz) grated Parmesan

1 Preheat the oven to moderate 180°C (350°F/Gas 4). Lightly grease a 27 cm x 21 cm (10¾ inch x 8½ inch), 2.5 litre ovenproof dish and line with the lasagne sheets.
2 Heat the oil and butter in a large saucepan. Add the onion and cook for 2–3 minutes, or until softened. Add the garlic and cook for 30 seconds. Cook the prawns and fish pieces for 2 minutes, then add the scallops and cook for 1 minute. Stir in the pasta sauce, tomato paste and sugar and simmer for 5 minutes.

3 For the cheese sauce, melt the butter over low heat in a saucepan, stir in the flour and cook for 1 minute, or until pale and foaming. Remove from the heat and gradually stir in the milk. Return to the heat and stir until the sauce boils and thickens. Reduce the heat, simmer for 2 minutes, then stir in the cheeses. Season, to taste.
4 Spoon one-third of the seafood sauce over the lasagne sheets. Top

with one-third of the cheese sauce. Arrange lasagne sheets over the top. Repeat to make three layers. Sprinkle with the combined cheeses and bake for 30 minutes or until golden. Leave for 10 minutes before slicing.

NUTRITION PER SERVE
Protein 70.5 g; Fat 63 g; Carbohydrate 50 g; Dietary Fibre 4.6 g; Cholesterol 332 mg; 4321 kJ (1033 Cal)

Cut the fish fillets into even-sized pieces with a sharp knife.

Stir the sauce over low heat until it boils and thickens.

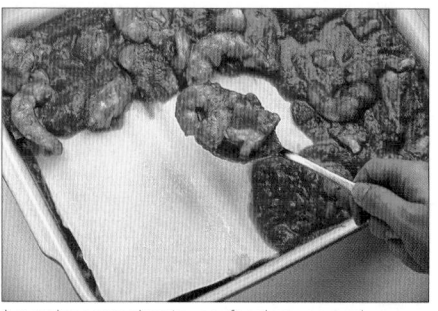

Layer lasagne sheets, seafood sauce and cheese sauce in the dish.

ASPARAGUS AND PISTACHIO RISOTTO

Preparation time: 10 minutes
Total cooking time: 30 minutes
Serves 4–6

1 litre (32 fl oz) vegetable stock
1 cup (250 ml/8 fl oz) white wine
⅓ cup (80 ml/2¾ fl oz) extra virgin olive oil
1 red onion, finely chopped
2 cups (440 g/14 oz) arborio rice
310 g (10 oz) asparagus spears, trimmed and cut into short lengths
½ cup (125 ml/4 fl oz) cream
1 cup (100 g/3½ oz) grated Parmesan
½ cup (40 g/1¼ oz) shelled pistachio nuts, toasted and roughly chopped

1 Heat the stock and wine in a large saucepan and keep at simmering point on the stove top.
2 Heat the oil in another large saucepan. Add the onion and cook over medium heat for 3 minutes, or until soft. Add the rice and stir for 1 minute, or until translucent.
3 Add ½ cup (125 ml/4 fl oz) hot stock, stirring constantly until the liquid is absorbed. Continue adding more stock, a little at a time, stirring constantly for 20–25 minutes, or until the rice is tender and creamy (you may not need to add all the stock, or you may not have quite enough and will need to add a little water as well—every risotto is different). Add the asparagus during the last 5 minutes of cooking.
4 Remove from the heat and leave for 2 minutes, then stir in the cream and Parmesan and season well. Serve sprinkled with pistachios.

NUTRITION PER SERVE (6)
Protein 15 g; Fat 30 g; Carbohydrate 60 g; Dietary Fibre 3.5 g; Cholesterol 45 mg; 2425 kJ (580 cal)

Add the rice to the saucepan and stir until the grains are translucent.

Add the stock a little at a time, stirring until it is completely absorbed.

Leave the risotto to stand for 2 minutes, then stir in the cream and Parmesan.

POTATO GNOCCHI WITH TOMATO SAUCE

Preparation time: 1 hour
Total cooking time: 45 minutes
Serves 4

500 g (1 lb) floury potatoes, unpeeled
1 egg yolk
3 tablespoons grated Parmesan
1 cup (125 g/4 oz) plain flour

TOMATO SAUCE
425 g (14 oz) can tomatoes
1 small onion, chopped
1 celery stick, chopped
1 small carrot, chopped
1 tablespoon shredded fresh basil
1 teaspoon chopped fresh thyme
1 clove garlic, crushed
1 teaspoon caster sugar

1 Steam or boil the potatoes until just tender. Drain thoroughly and allow to cool for 10 minutes before peeling and mashing them.

2 Measure 2 cups of the mashed potato into a large bowl, mix in the egg yolk, Parmesan, ¼ teaspoon of salt and some black pepper. Slowly add flour until you have a slightly sticky dough. Knead for 5 minutes, adding more flour if necessary, until a smooth dough is formed.

3 Divide the dough into four portions and roll each portion on a lightly floured surface to form a sausage shape, about 2 cm (¾ inch) thick.

4 Cut the rolls into 2.5 cm (1 inch) slices and shape each piece into an oval. Press each oval into the palm of your hand against a floured fork, to flatten slightly and indent one side with a pattern. As you make the gnocchi place them in a single layer on a baking tray and cover until ready to use.

5 To make the tomato sauce, mix all the ingredients with salt and pepper in a pan. Bring to the boil, reduce the heat to medium-low and simmer for 30 minutes, stirring occasionally. Allow to cool, then process in a food processor or blender, until smooth. Reheat if necessary before serving.

6 Cook the gnocchi in batches in a large pan of boiling salted water for 2 minutes, or until the gnocchi float to the surface. Drain well. Serve the gnocchi tossed through the sauce.

NUTRITION PER SERVE
Protein 10 g; Fat 4 g; Carbohydrate 45 g;
Dietary Fibre 5 g; Cholesterol 50 mg;
1125 kJ (270 cal)

NOTES: The gnocchi can be prepared several hours in advance and arranged on a tray in a single layer to prevent them sticking together. Cover and keep refrigerated.

Gnocchi was traditionally made using potatoes baked in their skins. This results in a drier dough that is easy to work with, so if you have time you can use this method.

Slowly add flour to the potato mixture, until a slightly sticky dough is formed.

Knead the dough for about 5 minutes or until smooth, adding flour if necessary.

Roll each portion into a sausage shape, on a lightly floured surface.

Press each oval with a floured fork to flatten slightly and make an indentation.

Put all the ingredients for the sauce in a pan and season with salt and pepper.

Cook the gnocchi in a large pan of boiling water until they float to the surface.

SPINACH AND RICOTTA GNOCCHI

**Preparation time: 45 minutes +
  1 hour refrigeration**
Total cooking time: 15 minutes
Serves 6 as a starter

4 slices white bread
½ cup (125 ml/4 fl oz) milk
500 g (1 lb) frozen spinach, thawed
250 g (8 oz) ricotta cheese
2 eggs
60 g (2 oz) Parmesan, grated
¼ cup (30 g/1 oz) plain flour
Parmesan shavings, to serve

GARLIC BUTTER SAUCE
100 g (3½ oz) butter
2 cloves garlic, crushed
3 tablespoons chopped fresh basil
1 ripe tomato, diced

1 Remove the crusts from the bread and soak in milk in a shallow dish for 10 minutes. Squeeze out any excess milk from the bread. Squeeze out any excess liquid from the spinach.
2 Place the bread, spinach, ricotta, eggs and Parmesan in a bowl and mix thoroughly. Refrigerate, covered, for 1 hour. Fold the flour in well.
3 Lightly dust your hands in flour and roll heaped teaspoons of the mixture into dumplings. Lower batches of the gnocchi into a large saucepan of boiling salted water. Cook for about 2 minutes, or until the gnocchi rise to the surface. Transfer to a serving plate and keep warm.
4 To make the sauce, combine all the ingredients in a small saucepan and cook over medium heat for 3 minutes, or until the butter is nutty brown. Drizzle over the gnocchi and sprinkle with the shaved Parmesan.

NUTRITION PER SERVE (6)
Protein 17 g; Fat 26 g; Carbohydrate 16 g;
Dietary Fibre 5 g; Cholesterol 137 mg;
1504 kJ (360 cal)

Gently squeeze out any excess milk from the soaked bread.

With floured hands, roll teaspoons of the mixture into dumplings.

Cook the gnocchi in batches until they rise to the surface of the water.

CHICKEN AND PORK PAELLA

Preparation time: 30 minutes
Total cooking time: 1 hour
Serves 6

¼ cup (60 ml/2 fl oz) olive oil
1 large red capsicum, seeded and cut into 5 mm (¼ inch) strips
600 g (1¼ lb) chicken thigh fillets, cut into 3 cm (1¼ inch) cubes
200 g (6½ oz) chorizo sausage, cut into 2 cm (¾ inch) slices
200 g (6½ oz) mushrooms, thinly sliced
3 cloves garlic, crushed
1 tablespoon lemon zest
700 g (1lb 7 oz) tomatoes, roughly chopped
200 g (6½ oz) green beans, cut into 3 cm lengths
1 tablespoon chopped fresh rosemary
2 tablespoons chopped fresh flat-leaf parsley
¼ teaspoon saffron threads dissolved in ¼ cup (60 ml/2 fl oz) hot water
2 cups (440 g/14 oz) short-grain rice
3 cups (750 ml/24 fl oz) hot chicken stock
6 lemon wedges

1 Heat the olive oil in a large, deep frying pan or paella pan over medium heat. Add the capsicum and cook for 6 minutes, or until softened. Remove from the pan.
2 Add the chicken to the pan and cook for 10 minutes, or until brown on all sides. Remove. Add the sausage to the pan and cook for 5 minutes, or until golden on all sides. Remove.
3 Add the mushrooms, garlic and lemon zest, and cook over medium heat for 5 minutes. Stir in the tomato and capsicum, and cook for a further

5 minutes, or until the tomato is soft.
4 Add the beans, rosemary, parsley, saffron mixture, rice, chicken and sausage. Stir briefly and add the stock. Do not stir at this point. Reduce the heat and simmer for 30 minutes. Remove from the heat, cover and leave to stand for 10 minutes. Serve with lemon wedges.

NUTRITION PER SERVE
Protein 34 g; Fat 20 g; Carbohydrate 63 g; Dietary Fibre 5 g; Cholesterol 72 mg; 2388 kJ (571 Cal)

NOTE: Paellas are not stirred to the bottom of the pan during cooking in the hope that a crust of rice will form. This is considered one of the best parts of the paella. For this reason, it is important to not use a non-stick frying pan. Paellas are traditionally served at the table from the pan.

Cut the chorizo sausage into 2 cm (3/4 inch) thick slices.

Add the tomato and capsicum and cook until the tomato is soft.

Pour the chicken stock into the pan and do not stir.

CHICKEN PILAF WITH SPICES

Preparation time: 25 minutes
Total cooking time: 40 minutes
Serves 4

1.5 kg (3 lb) chicken pieces
⅓ cup (80 ml/2¾ fl oz) oil
¼ cup (40 g/1¼ oz) unblanched whole
   almonds
2 onions, thinly sliced
3 cloves garlic, crushed
1 teaspoon whole black peppercorns
1 teaspoon turmeric
1 teaspoon cumin seeds
2 bay leaves
5 whole cloves
1 cinnamon stick
2 cups (440 g/14 oz) long-grain rice
1 litre chicken stock

½ cup (80 g/2¾ oz) fresh or frozen
   peas
¼ cup (30 g/1 oz) sultanas
3 hard-boiled eggs, peeled and
   quartered
fresh coriander leaves, to serve

1 Trim the chicken of excess fat and sinew. Heat half the oil in a large pan. Add the chicken pieces in batches and cook over medium heat for 5–10 minutes, or until the chicken is brown all over. Drain on paper towels. Heat 1 tablespoon of the oil in a pan. Add the almonds and cook over medium heat for 2 minutes, or until the nuts are brown. Remove from the pan and set aside.
2 Heat the remaining oil in a large pan. Add the onion and garlic and cook gently over low heat for 2 minutes, stirring occasionally. Add

the peppercorns, turmeric, cumin, bay leaves, cloves and cinnamon stick. Fry over high heat for 1 minute, or until fragrant. Stir in the rice, making sure it is well coated with the spices.
3 Add the stock, browned chicken pieces and salt to taste. Bring to the boil, then reduce the heat and simmer, covered, for 20 minutes. Add the peas and sultanas and simmer for a further 5 minutes, or until all the liquid is absorbed and the chicken is tender (you may need to add extra stock or water). Remove the bay leaves and cinnamon stick and discard. Serve the pilaf with quartered eggs, topped with almonds and fresh coriander leaves.

NUTRITION PER SERVE
Protein 67 g; Fat 38 g; Carbohydrate 14 g;
Dietary Fibre 4 g; Cholesterol 280 mg;
2755 kJ (658 cal)

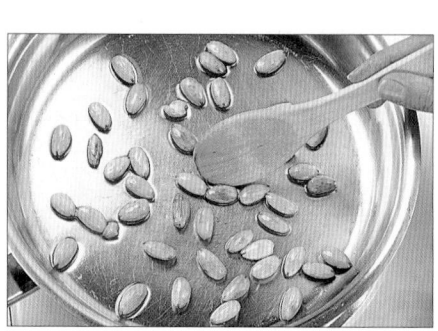

Cook the almonds in 1 tablespoon of the oil until they are brown.

Stir the rice into the onion and spice mixture, making sure it is well coated.

Add the peas and sultanas to the pan and simmer for 5 minutes.

CARROT AND PUMPKIN RISOTTO

Preparation time: 15 minutes
Total cooking time: 35 minutes
Serves 4

90 g (3 oz) butter
1 onion, finely chopped
250 g (8 oz) pumpkin, diced
2 carrots, diced
2 litres (64 fl oz) vegetable stock
2 cups (440 g/14 oz) arborio rice
90 g (3 oz) Romano cheese, grated
    (see NOTE)
¼ teaspoon nutmeg

1 Heat 60 g (2 oz) of the butter in a large, heavy-based pan. Add the onion and fry for 1–2 minutes, or until soft. Add the pumpkin and carrot and cook for 6–8 minutes, or until tender. Mash slightly with a potato masher. In a separate saucepan keep the stock at simmering point.
2 Add the rice to the vegetables and cook for 1 minute, stirring constantly until the grains are translucent. Ladle in ½ cup (125 ml/4 fl oz) hot stock and stir well. Reduce the heat and add the stock little by little, stirring constantly for 20–25 minutes, or until the rice is tender and creamy. (You may not need to add all the stock, or

you may run out and need to use a little water. Every risotto is different.)
3 Remove from the heat, add the remaining butter, cheese, nutmeg and pepper and fork through. Cover and leave for 5 minutes before serving.

NUTRITION PER SERVE
Protein 27 g; Fat 34 g; Carbohydrate 95 g;
Dietary Fibre 5 g; Cholesterol 100 mg;
3318 kJ (793 cal)

NOTE: Romano is a hard, Italian grating cheese similar to Parmesan. Parmesan is a good substitute.

Heat the butter in a large pan and fry the onion until soft.

Cook the pumpkin and carrot until tender, then mash a little.

The secret to good risotto is to add the stock a little at a time and stir constantly.

203

PUMPKIN AND BASIL LASAGNE

Preparation time: 20 minutes
Total cooking time: 1 hour 25 minutes
Serves 4

650 g (1 lb 5 oz) pumpkin
2 tablespoons olive oil
500 g (1 lb) ricotta cheese
⅓ cup (50 g/1¾ oz) pine nuts, toasted
¾ cup (35 g/1 oz) fresh basil
2 cloves garlic, crushed
35 g (1 oz) Parmesan, grated
125 g (4 oz) fresh lasagne sheets
185 g (6 oz) mozzarella, grated

1 Preheat the oven to moderate 180°C (350°F/Gas 4). Lightly grease a baking tray. Cut the pumpkin into thin slices and arrange in a single layer on the tray. Brush with oil and cook for 1 hour, or until softened, turning halfway through cooking.
2 Place the ricotta, pine nuts, basil, garlic and Parmesan in a bowl and mix well with a wooden spoon.
3 Brush a square 20 cm (8 inch) ovenproof dish with oil. Cook the pasta according to the packet instructions. Arrange one third of the pasta sheets over the base of the dish and spread with the ricotta mixture. Top with half of the remaining lasagne sheets.

4 Arrange the pumpkin evenly over the pasta with as few gaps as possible. Season with salt and cracked black pepper and top with the final layer of pasta sheets. Sprinkle with mozzarella. Bake for 20–25 minutes, or until the cheese is golden. Leave for 10 minutes, then cut into squares.

NUTRITION PER SERVE
Protein 24 g; Fat 32 g; Carbohydrate 33 g; Dietary Fibre 4.5 g; Cholesterol 37 mg; 2166 kJ (517 cal)

NOTE: If the pasta has no cooking instructions, blanch them one at a time until softened. Then drain and spread on tea towels to dry.

Mix together the ricotta, pine nuts, basil, garlic and Parmesan.

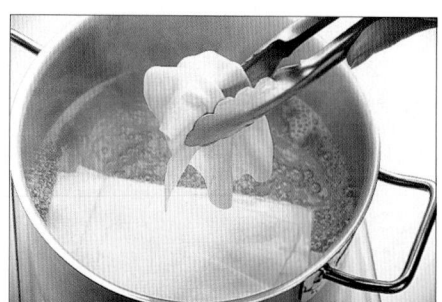

Cook the pasta according to the packet instructions until al dente.

Place the pumpkin on top of the lasagne sheet, leaving as few gaps as possible.

VEAL AGNOLOTTI WITH ALFREDO SAUCE

Preparation time: 10 minutes
Total cooking time: 10 minutes
Serves 4–6

625 g (1¼ lb) veal agnolotti
90 g (3 oz) butter
1½ cups (150 g/5 oz) grated
   Parmesan
300 ml (9½ fl oz) cream
2 tablespoons chopped fresh
   marjoram

1 Cook the pasta in a large saucepan of boiling water until al dente. Drain and return to the pan.
2 Just before the pasta is cooked, melt the butter in a saucepan over low heat. Add the Parmesan and cream and bring to the boil. Reduce the heat and simmer, stirring constantly, for 2 minutes, or until the sauce has thickened slightly. Stir in the marjoram and season with salt and cracked black pepper. Toss the sauce through the pasta until well coated and serve immediately.

NUTRITION PER SERVE (6)
Protein 21.5 g; Fat 48.5 g; Carbohydrate 39.5 g; Dietary Fibre 3.5 g; Cholesterol 156.5 mg; 2835 kJ (680 Cal)

VARIATION: Marjoram can be replaced with any other fresh herb you prefer—for example, try parsley, thyme, chervil or dill.

Test the agnolotti by biting through one. They should be still firm to the tooth, but not chewy.

Simmer, stirring, until the Alfredo sauce has thickened slightly.

SPAGHETTI MARINARA

Preparation time: 40 minutes
Total cooking time: 50 minutes
Serves 6

TOMATO SAUCE
2 tablespoons olive oil
1 onion, finely chopped
1 carrot, sliced
2 cloves garlic, crushed
425 g (14 oz) can crushed tomatoes
½ cup (125 ml/4 fl oz) white wine
1 teaspoon sugar

20 black mussels
¼ cup (60 ml/2 fl oz) white wine
¼ cup (60 ml/2 fl oz) fish stock
1 clove garlic, crushed
375 g (12 oz) spaghetti
30 g (1 oz) butter
125 g (4 oz) calamari rings
125 g (4 oz) skinless firm white
    fish fillets, cubed
200 g (6½ oz) raw medium prawns,
    peeled and deveined
10 g (¼ oz) fresh flat-leaf parsley,
    chopped
200 g (6½ oz) can clams, drained

1 For the sauce, heat the oil in a deep frying pan, add the onion and carrot and stir over medium heat for 10 minutes, or until the vegetables are golden. Add the garlic, tomato, wine and sugar and bring to the boil. Reduce the heat and gently simmer for 30 minutes, stirring occasionally.
2 Scrub the mussels and pull out the hairy beards. Discard any broken ones, or open ones that don't close when tapped. Rinse well. Heat the wine with the stock and garlic in a large frying pan. Add the mussels. Cover and shake the pan over high heat for 4–5 minutes. After 3 minutes, start removing the opened mussels. After 5 minutes, discard any unopened mussels. Reserve the liquid.
3 Cook the spaghetti in a large pan of rapidly boiling salted water for 12 minutes, or until al dente. Drain.
4 Meanwhile, melt the butter in a frying pan, add the calamari, fish and prawns in batches and stir-fry for 2 minutes, or until just cooked through. Add the seafood to the

tomato sauce with the reserved liquid, mussels, parsley and clams. Stir until the seafood is heated through. Add the spaghetti to the pan and toss well.

NUTRITION PER SERVE
Protein 34.5 g; Fat 14 g; Carbohydrate 51.5 g; Dietary Fibre 5 g; Cholesterol 139 mg; 2090 kJ (495 Cal)

SUGGESTED FISH: Blue-eye, groper, striped marlin.

NOTE: Buy the seafood and prepare your own marinara mix, rather than buying prepared marinara mixes.

Stir-fry the calamari rings, fish and prawns until just cooked through.

After adding the seafood and liquid to the sauce, stir until heated through.

MACARONI CHEESE

Preparation time: 15 minutes
Total cooking time: 35 minutes
Serves 4

225 g (7 oz) macaroni
80 g (2¾ oz) butter
1 onion, finely chopped
3 tablespoons plain flour
2 cups (500 ml/16 fl oz) milk
2 teaspoons wholegrain mustard
250 g (8 oz) Cheddar, grated
30 g (1 oz) fresh breadcrumbs

1 Cook the pasta in rapidly boiling salted water until al dente. Drain.

Preheat the oven to moderate 180°C (350°F/Gas 4) and grease a casserole.
2 Melt the butter in a large pan over low heat and cook the onion for 5 minutes, or until softened. Stir in the flour and cook for 1 minute, or until pale and foaming. Remove from the heat and gradually stir in the milk. Return to the heat and stir until the sauce boils and thickens. Reduce the heat and simmer for 2 minutes. Stir in the mustard and about three-quarters of the cheese. Season to taste.
3 Mix the pasta with the cheese sauce. Spoon into the dish and sprinkle the breadcrumbs and remaining cheese over the top. Bake for 15 minutes, or until golden brown and bubbling.

NUTRITION PER SERVE
Protein 30 g; Fat 45 g; Carbohydrate 60 g; Dietary Fibre 4 g; Cholesterol 130 mg; 3087 kJ (737 cal)

Cook the onion in the butter over medium heat until softened.

PROSCIUTTO AND SWEET POTATO PENNE

Preparation time: 10 minutes
Total cooking time: 15 minutes
Serves 4

500 g (1 lb) penne
500 g (1 lb) orange sweet potato, diced
2 tablespoons extra virgin olive oil
5 spring onions, sliced
2 small cloves garlic, crushed
8 thin slices prosciutto, chopped
125 g (4 oz) sun-dried tomatoes in oil, drained and sliced
¼ cup (15 g/½ oz) shredded fresh basil leaves

1 Cook the penne in a large pan of rapidly boiling salted water until al dente. Drain well and return to the pan to keep warm.
2 Meanwhile, steam the sweet potato for 5 minutes, or until tender. Heat the oil in a saucepan, add the spring onion, garlic and sweet potato and stir over medium heat for 2–3 minutes, or until the spring onion is soft. Add the prosciutto and tomato and cook for a further 1 minute.
3 Add the sweet potato mixture to the penne and toss over low heat until heated through. Add the basil and season with black pepper. Serve immediately with crusty bread.

NUTRITION PER SERVE
Protein 20 g; Fat 20 g; Carbohydrate 115 g;
Dietary Fibre 11 g; Cholesterol 5 mg;
3065 kJ (732 cal)

NOTE: Orange sweet potato is also known as kumera.

Cook the spring onion, garlic and sweet potato for 2–3 minutes.

Add the sweet potato mixture to the cooked pasta and heat through.

THAI FRIED RICE WITH DRIED SHRIMP

**Preparation time: 25 minutes +
overnight refrigeration of rice
Total cooking time: 20 minutes
Serves 4**

3 tablespoons oil
1 egg, beaten with 2 teaspoons water
2 cloves garlic, chopped
3 spring onions, chopped
½ cup (45 g/1½ oz) dried shrimp,
    roughly chopped
4 cups (750 g/1½ lb) cold cooked rice
    (see NOTE)

1 tablespoon fish sauce
2 teaspoons light soy sauce
1 cup (30 g/1 oz) fresh coriander
    leaves
¼ pineapple, cut into pieces
1 cucumber, cut into pieces
chilli sauce, for serving

1 Heat 1 tablespoon of oil in a wok
or large frying pan. Pour in the egg
and swirl the wok until set. Cut into
quarters, flip each quarter and cook
the other side. Remove from the wok
and cut into thin strips.
2 Add the remaining oil, reheat the
wok and add the garlic, spring onions
and shrimp. Stir-fry for 2 minutes.

Add the rice to the wok and stir-fry
for 5 minutes over high heat, tossing
constantly until heated through.
3 Add the sauces, coriander and
omelette strips. Toss well. Arrange
the rice on a serving platter. Serve
with the combined pineapple and
cucumber, and chilli sauce on the side.

NUTRITION PER SERVE
Protein 12 g; Fat 15 g; Carbohydrate 60 g;
Dietary Fibre 3 g; Cholesterol 100 mg;
1800 kJ (430 cal)

NOTE: Rice should be refrigerated
overnight before making fried rice to
let the grains dry out and separate.

Cut the omelette into quarters to make it easy to
turn over and cook the other side.

Stir-fry the garlic, spring onions and shrimp for
2 minutes.

Just before serving, add the sauces, coriander
leaves and omelette strips to the wok.

ITALIAN OMELETTE

Preparation time: 20 minutes
Total cooking time: 15 minutes
Serves 4

2 tablespoons olive oil
1 onion, finely chopped
125 g (4 oz) ham, sliced
6 eggs
3 tablespoons milk
2 cups (350 g/11 oz) cooked fusilli or
    spiral pasta (see NOTE)
¼ cup (25 g/¾ oz) grated Parmesan

2 tablespoons chopped fresh parsley
1 tablespoon chopped fresh basil
½ cup (60 g/2 o) grated Cheddar

1 Heat half the oil in pan. Add the onion and stir over low heat until tender. Add the ham and stir for 1 minute. Transfer to a plate.
2 Whisk together the eggs, milk, salt and pepper. Stir in the pasta, Parmesan, herbs and onion mixture.
3 Preheat the grill to hot. Heat the remaining oil in the same pan. Pour the egg mixture into the pan. Sprinkle with Cheddar. Cook over medium heat until the omelette begins to set around the edges then place under the grill until lightly browned on top. Cut into wedges for serving.

NUTRITION PER SERVE
Protein 30 g; Fat 32 g; Carbohydrate 30 g;
Dietary Fibre 2 g; Cholesterol 327 mg;
2206 kJ (530 cal)

NOTE: To get 2 cups of cooked pasta you will need to start with about 150 g (5 oz) of uncooked dried pasta.

Cook the onion until it is tender and then add the ham and cook for 1 minute.

Whisk together the eggs and milk, then stir in the pasta, Parmesan, herbs and onion mixture.

Pour into the pan and then sprinkle with the Cheddar. Flash under the grill to finish cooking.

FARMHOUSE PASTA

Preparation time: 10 minutes
Total cooking time: 15 minutes
Serves 4

375 g (12 oz) pasta
1 large potato, cut into small cubes
400 g (13 oz) broccoli
⅓ cup (80 ml/2¾ fl oz) olive oil
3 cloves garlic, crushed
1 small fresh red chilli, finely chopped
2 x 400 g (13 oz) cans diced tomatoes
¼ cup (30 g/1 oz) grated Pecorino
  cheese

1 Bring a large saucepan of salted water to the boil and cook the pasta and potato together for 8–10 minutes, or until the pasta is al dente. Drain and return to the saucepan. Meanwhile, trim the broccoli into florets and discard the stems. Place in a saucepan of boiling water and cook for 1–2 minutes, then drain and plunge into iced water. Drain and add to the cooked pasta and potato.
2 Heat the oil in a saucepan, add the garlic and chilli and cook for 30 seconds. Add the tomato and simmer for 5 minutes, or until slightly reduced and thickened. Season to taste with salt and cracked black pepper.
3 Pour the tomato mixture over the pasta, potato and broccoli. Toss well and stir over low heat until warmed through. Serve sprinkled with grated Pecorino cheese.

NUTRITION PER SERVE
Protein 20 g; Fat 22 g; Carbohydrate 77 g; Dietary Fibre 11 g; Cholesterol 6 mg; 2445 kJ (585 cal)

Blanch the broccoli in boiling water for a couple of minutes then cool in iced water.

Simmer the tomato sauce for 5 minutes or until it has thickened.

Toss together the tomato sauce, pasta, potato and broccoli.

KEDGEREE

Preparation time: 20 minutes
Total cooking time: 30 minutes
Serves 4

600 g (1¼ lb) smoked haddock
50 g (1½ oz) butter
1 onion, finely chopped
2 teaspoons curry powder
1 teaspoon ground cumin
1 teaspoon ground coriander
2 teaspoons seeded and finely sliced
   green chilli
1 cup (200 g/6½ oz) basmati rice
2¾ cups (660 ml/22 fl oz) chicken or
   fish stock
1 cinnamon stick
⅓ cup (80 ml/2¾ fl oz) cream
2 hard-boiled eggs, finely chopped
2 tablespoons chopped fresh parsley
2 tablespoons chopped fresh
   coriander

1 Poach the haddock in batches in a large shallow pan, skin-side up: cover with boiling water and simmer very gently for about 10 minutes. The fish is cooked when the flesh can be flaked easily with a fork. Drain and pat dry with paper towels. Remove the skin and flake into bite-size chunks.
2 Heat the butter in a large saucepan and add the onion. Cook until golden, then add the curry powder, cumin, coriander and chilli. Cook, stirring, for 1 minute. Add the rice, stir well, then pour in the stock and add the cinnamon. Cover tightly and simmer over gentle heat for about 12 minutes, or until the rice is tender.
3 Remove the cinnamon and gently stir in the haddock. Fold through the cream, chopped egg and the herbs. Season and serve immediately.

NUTRITION PER SERVE
Protein 45 g; Fat 25 g; Carbohydrate 45 g;
Dietary Fibre 2 g; Cholesterol 255 mg;
2355 kJ (560 cal)

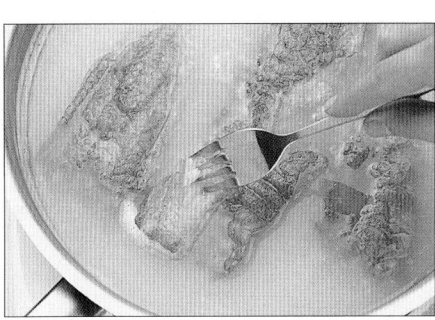

When the fish is cooked, the flesh will flake easily when tested with a fork.

Add the rice to the onion, curry powder, cumin, coriander and chilli and stir well.

Fold through the cream, chopped egg, parsley and coriander.

PENNE WITH SUN-DRIED TOMATOES AND LEMON

Preparation time: 10 minutes
Total cooking time: 15 minutes
Serves 4

250 g (8 oz) penne
3 tablespoons olive oil
3 rashers bacon, chopped
1 onion, chopped
⅓ cup (80 ml/2¾ fl oz) lemon juice
1 tablespoon fresh thyme leaves
⅓ cup (50 g/1½ oz) chopped sun-dried
    tomatoes
½ cup (90 g/3 oz) pine nuts, toasted

1 Cook the pasta in a large pan of rapidly boiling salted water until al dente. Drain well and return to the pan to keep warm.
2 Heat the oil in a large pan. Add the bacon and onion and stir over medium heat for 4 minutes or until the bacon is brown and the onion has softened. Add the pasta, lemon juice, thyme, tomato and pine nuts. Stir over low heat for 2 minutes to heat through.

NUTRITION PER SERVE
Protein 13 g; Fat 25 g; Carbohydrate 47 g;
Dietary Fibre 5 g; Cholesterol 10 mg;
1972 kJ (471 cal)

NOTE: Sun-dried tomatoes will become bitter if heated too much. Variation: Use pancetta instead of bacon, if preferred.

Add the pasta to the pan with the lemon juice, thyme, tomato and pine nuts.

PASTA WITH BRAISED OXTAIL AND CELERY

Preparation time: 20 minutes
Total cooking time: 3 hours 45 minutes
Serves 4

1.5 kg (3 lb) oxtail, jointed
3 tablespoons plain flour, seasoned
3 tablespoons olive oil
1 onion, finely chopped
2 cloves garlic, crushed
2 cups (500 ml/16 fl oz) beef stock
425 g (14 oz) can crushed tomatoes
1 cup (250 ml/8 fl oz) dry white wine
6 whole cloves
2 bay leaves
3 celery stalks, finely chopped

500 g (1 lb) penne
30 g (1 oz) butter or margarine
3 tablespoons grated Parmesan

1 Preheat the oven to warm 160°C (315°F/Gas 2–3). Dust the oxtail in the seasoned flour, shaking off the excess. Heat half the oil in a large pan and brown the oxtail over high heat in batches. Transfer the meat to a large casserole dish.
2 Wipe the pan clean with paper towels, add the remaining oil and the onion and garlic. Cook over low heat until the onion is tender. Stir in the stock, tomatoes, wine, cloves and bay leaves and season with salt and pepper. Bring to the boil and then pour over the oxtail.

3 Bake, covered, for 2½–3 hours. Add the celery and bake, uncovered, for another 30 minutes. Meanwhile, cook the pasta in a large pan of rapidly boiling salted water until al dente. Drain well and return to the pan to keep warm. Toss with butter and Parmesan. Serve the oxtail and sauce with the pasta.

NUTRITION PER SERVE
Protein 82 g; Fat 30 g; Carbohydrate 100 g;
Dietary Fibre 8 g; Cholesterol 700 mg;
4388 kJ (1048 cal)

HINT: Seasoned flour is plain flour to which seasonings of your choice have been added, for example: herbs, salt, pepper or dried mustard.

Heat the oil in a large pan and brown the oxtail in batches.

Stir in the stock, crushed tomatoes, wine, cloves and bay leaves and season to taste.

Bake the oxtail covered, then add the celery and bake uncovered for a further 30 minutes.

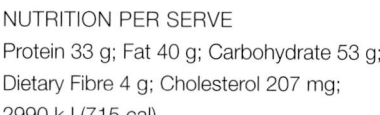

SMOKED CHICKEN LINGUINE

Preparation time: 15 minutes
Total cooking time: 20 minutes
Serves 4

1 tablespoon olive oil
1 leek, thinly sliced
3 large cloves garlic, finely chopped
½ cup (125 ml/4 fl oz) dry white wine
300 g (10 oz) Swiss brown mushrooms, sliced
2 teaspoons chopped fresh thyme
300 ml (10 fl oz) thick cream
2 smoked chicken breast fillets, thinly sliced (see NOTE)
350 g (11 oz) fresh linguine

1 Heat the oil in a saucepan. Add the leek and cook, stirring, over low heat for 3–4 minutes, or until soft. Add the garlic and cook for another minute. Pour in the wine and simmer for 2–3 minutes, or until the liquid has reduced by half.

2 Increase the heat to medium, add the mushrooms and thyme and cook for 5 minutes, or until any excess liquid has been absorbed, then add the cream and sliced chicken. Reduce the heat and simmer for 4–5 minutes, or until the sauce has slightly thickened.

3 Meanwhile, cook the pasta in a large pan of rapidly boiling salted water until al dente. Drain and divide among serving plates. Spoon on the sauce and serve.

NUTRITION PER SERVE
Protein 33 g; Fat 40 g; Carbohydrate 53 g; Dietary Fibre 4 g; Cholesterol 207 mg; 2990 kJ (715 cal)

NOTE: Buy smoked chicken at the deli section of good supermarkets.

Cook the leek in the oil for 3–4 minutes, or until it is soft.

Add the cream and chicken and simmer until the sauce has slightly thickened.

BEEF VERMICELLI CAKE

Preparation time: 10 minutes +
  10 minutes standing
Total cooking time: 50 minutes
Serves 4–6

90 g (3 oz) butter
1 onion, chopped
500 g (1 lb) beef mince
800 g (1 lb 10 oz) bottled tomato
  pasta sauce
2 tablespoons tomato paste
250 g (8 oz) vermicelli
¼ cup (30 g/1 oz) plain flour
1¼ cups (315 ml/10 oz) milk
1¼ cups (150 g/5 oz) grated
  Cheddar

1 Preheat the oven to moderate 180°C (350°F/Gas 4). Lightly grease a 24 cm (10 inch) round deep springform tin. Melt a tablespoon of the butter in a large deep frying pan and cook the onion over medium heat for 2–3 minutes, or until soft. Add the beef mince, breaking up any lumps with the back of a spoon, and cook for 4–5 minutes, or until browned. Stir in the pasta sauce and tomato paste, reduce the heat and simmer for 20–25 minutes. Season well.

2 Cook the pasta in a large pan of rapidly boiling salted water until al dente. Drain well and rinse. Meanwhile, melt the remaining butter in a saucepan over low heat. Stir in the flour and cook for 1 minute, or until pale and foaming. Remove from the heat and gradually stir in the milk. Return to the heat and stir constantly until the sauce boils and thickens. Reduce the heat and simmer for 2 minutes.

3 Spread half the pasta over the base of the tin, then cover with half the meat sauce. Cover with the remaining pasta, pressing down with the palm of your hand. Spoon on the remaining meat sauce and then pour on the white sauce. Sprinkle with cheese and cook for 15 minutes. Leave to stand for 10 minutes before removing from the tin. Cut into wedges to serve.

NUTRITION PER SERVE (6)
Protein 34 g; Fat 32 g; Carbohydrate 47 g;
Dietary Fibre 6 g; Cholesterol 121 mg;
2535 kJ (605 cal)

Cook the mince until browned, breaking up any lumps with a spoon.

Cook the sauce, stirring, until it comes to the boil and thickens.

Spread half the pasta into the tin and then cover with half the meat sauce.

BAKED CHICKEN AND LEEK RISOTTO

Preparation time: 10 minutes
Total cooking time: 40 minutes
Serves 6

1 tablespoon oil
1 leek, thinly sliced
2 chicken breast fillets, cubed
2 cups (440 g/14 oz) arborio rice
¼ cup (60 ml/2 fl oz) white wine
5 cups (1.25) litres chicken stock
⅓ cup (30 g/1 oz) grated Parmesan
2 tablespoons fresh thyme leaves
fresh thyme leaves and Parmesan, for
    serving

1 Preheat the oven to slow 150°C (300°F/Gas 2) and place a 5 litre ovenproof dish with a lid in the oven to warm. Heat the oil in a saucepan over medium heat, add the leek and cook for 2 minutes, or until soft.
2 Add the chicken and cook, stirring, for 2–3 minutes, or until it colours. Add the rice and stir so that it is well coated. Cook for 1 minute.
3 Add the wine and stock and bring to the boil. Pour the mixture into the warm ovenproof dish and cover. Place in the oven and cook for 30 minutes, stirring halfway through. Remove from the oven and stir through the Parmesan and thyme leaves. Season to taste. Sprinkle with extra thyme leaves and a little Parmesan and serve.

NUTRITION PER SERVE
Protein 28 g; Fat 15 g; Carbohydrate 60 g;
Dietary Fibre 3 g; Cholesterol 75 mg;
2014 kJ (480 cal)

Cook the leek for a couple of minutes over medium heat until it is soft.

Add the arborio rice to the pan and stir until it is well coated.

Cook the risotto in the oven for 30 minutes, then remove and stir in the Parmesan and thyme.

BASMATI RICE, CASHEW AND PEA SALAD

Preparation time: 30 minutes +
** 30 minutes standing**
Total cooking time: 20 minutes
Serves 6

40 g (1¼ oz) butter or ghee
½ teaspoon turmeric
300 g (10 oz) basmati rice
½ teaspoon salt
200 g (6½ oz) fresh or frozen peas, thawed
¼ cup (60 ml/2 fl oz) peanut oil
1 teaspoon yellow mustard seeds
1 teaspoon cumin seeds
¼ cup (30 g/1 oz) currants
1 clove garlic, crushed
1–2 small green chillies, finely chopped
1 teaspoon Madras curry powder
100 ml (3½ fl oz) coconut cream
50 g (1¾ oz) glacé ginger, cut into thin strips
¼ small red onion, finely chopped
1 tablespoon chopped fresh mint leaves
1 tablespoon chopped fresh coriander
½ cup (30 g/1 oz) shredded coconut
100 g (3½ oz) roasted cashew nuts, coarsely chopped
2 teaspoons shredded coconut, to garnish

1 Melt the butter or ghee in a heavy-based pan and stir in the turmeric. Add the rice and salt, and stir for 10–15 seconds, then pour in 1½ cups (375 ml/12 fl oz) of water. Stir over high heat until boiling, then reduce the heat until gently simmering. Simmer, tightly covered, and cook for 13 minutes without removing the lid. Remove the pan from the heat and leave for 10 minutes without removing the lid, then fluff gently with a fork. Add the peas, transfer to a large bowl and allow to cool.
2 Heat 2 teaspoons of the oil in a pan and stir in the mustard and cumin seeds. When the mustard seeds start to pop, add the currants, garlic, chilli and curry powder. Stir to combine, but do not brown. Stir in the coconut cream, remove from the heat and transfer to the bowl of rice and peas.
3 Add the ginger, onion, herbs and the remaining oil. Toss well, and set aside for at least 30 minutes. Just before serving, toss through the coconut and cashew nuts. Garnish with the shredded coconut.

NUTRITION PER SERVE
Protein 9 g; Fat 30 g; Carbohydrate 55 g; Dietary Fibre 6 g; Cholesterol 15 mg; 2110 kJ (500 cal)

NOTE: Rice salads often improve if made in advance. This dish may be prepared up to 24 hours in advance, but add the cashew nuts and coconut just before serving to keep them crisp.

Cut the glacé ginger into thin strips and chop the red onion and mint.

Add the rice and salt to the melted butter and turmeric in the pan.

Add the currants, garlic, chilli and curry powder to the mustard and cumin seeds.

VEAL TORTELLINI WITH CREAMY MUSHROOM SAUCE

Preparation time: 15 minutes
Total cooking time: 20 minutes
Serves 4

500 g (1 lb) veal tortellini
¼ cup (60 ml/2 fl oz) olive oil
600 g (1¼ lb) Swiss brown
   mushrooms, thinly sliced
2 cloves garlic, crushed
½ cup (125 ml/4 fl oz) dry white wine
300 ml (10 fl oz) thick cream
pinch of grated nutmeg
3 tablespoons finely chopped fresh
   flat-leaf parsley
30 g (1 oz) Parmesan, grated

1 Cook the pasta in a large pan of rapidly boiling salted water until al dente. Drain and return to the pan to keep warm. Meanwhile, heat the oil in a frying pan over medium heat. Add the mushrooms and cook, stirring occasionally, for 5 minutes, or until softened. Add the garlic and cook for 1 minute, then stir in the wine and cook for 5 minutes, or until the liquid has reduced by half.

2 Add the cream, nutmeg and parsley, stir to combine and cook for 3–5 minutes, or until the sauce thickens slightly. Season with salt and cracked black pepper. Divide the tortellini among four serving plates and spoon on the mushroom sauce. Sprinkle with Parmesan and serve.

NUTRITION PER SERVE
Protein 24 g; Fat 53 g; Carbohydrate 50 g;
Dietary Fibre 8.5 g; Cholesterol 125 mg;
3275 kJ (785 cal)

Heat the oil in a frying pan, add the mushrooms and cook until softened.

Add the cream, nutmeg and parsley and stir until the sauce thickens slightly.

SALMON AND PASTA MORNAY

Preparation time: 10 minutes
Total cooking time: 15 minutes
Serves 4

400 g (13 oz) small shell pasta
30 g (1 oz) butter
6 spring onions, chopped
2 cloves garlic, crushed
1 tablespoon plain flour
1 cup (250 ml/8 fl oz) milk
1 cup (250 g/8 oz) sour cream
1 tablespoon lemon juice
425 g (14 oz) can salmon, drained and
  flaked
½ cup (15 g/½ oz) chopped fresh
  parsley

1 Cook the pasta in a large pan of rapidly boiling salted water until al dente. Drain and return to the pan to keep warm.
2 Meanwhile, melt the butter in a pan and cook the onion and garlic over low heat for 3 minutes or until soft. Add the flour and stir for 1 minute. Mix together the milk, cream and lemon juice and slowly add to the pan, stirring constantly. Stir over medium heat for 3 minutes or until the sauce boils and thickens.
3 Add the salmon and parsley to the sauce and stir for 1 minute to heat through. Toss with the pasta and season before serving.

NUTRITION PER SERVE
Protein 39 g; Fat 42 g; Carbohydrate 78 g;
Dietary Fibre 6 g; Cholesterol 192 mg;
3530 kJ (852 cal)

STORAGE: The sauce can be kept for up to a day, covered in the fridge. Cook the pasta and reheat the sauce just before serving.

VARIATION: Use canned tuna instead of salmon. Add 1 teaspoon of mustard to the sauce.

Combine the milk, cream and lemon juice and stir slowly into the sauce.

Once the sauce is cooked, add the drained pasta to the pan and toss well.

CAJUN SCALLOPS WITH PASTA AND BUTTERY CORN SAUCE

Preparation time: 15 minutes
Total cooking time: 15 minutes
Serves 4

350 g (11 oz) small pasta shells
20 large scallops, without roe
2 tablespoons Cajun spice mix
2 tablespoons corn oil
250 g (8 oz) butter
3 cloves garlic, crushed
400 g (13 oz) can corn kernels, drained
¼ cup (60 ml/2 fl oz) lime juice
4 tablespoons finely chopped fresh coriander leaves

1 Cook the pasta in a large pan of rapidly boiling salted water until al dente. Drain and return to the pan to keep warm. Meanwhile, pat the scallops dry with paper towel and lightly coat in the spice mix. Heat the oil in a large frying pan and cook the scallops for 1 minute each side over high heat (ensuring they are well spaced), then remove from the pan, cover and keep warm.
2 Reduce the heat to medium, add the butter and cook for 4 minutes, or until foaming and golden brown. Remove from the heat, add the garlic, corn and lime juice. Gently toss the corn mixture through the pasta with 2 tablespoons of the coriander and season well. Divide among four serving plates, top with the scallops, drizzle with any juices and sprinkle with the remaining coriander.

NUTRITION PER SERVE
Protein 20 g; Fat 61 g; Carbohydrate 75 g;
Dietary Fibre 7 g; Cholesterol 174.5 mg;
3850 kJ (920 cal)

NOTES: Scallops should not be crowded when they are cooked or they will release all their juices, causing them to stew and toughen.

Cook the scallops over high heat, making sure they are well spaced in the pan.

Cook the butter for 4 minutes, or until it is foaming and golden brown.

INDIVIDUAL CHICKEN AND PASTA CASSEROLES

Preparation time: 15 minutes
Total cooking time: 45 minutes
Serves 4

200 g (6½ oz) spiral pasta
425 g (14 oz) can cream of mushroom
  or broccoli soup
1 cup (250 g/8 oz) sour cream
1 teaspoon curry powder
1 barbecued chicken
250 g (8 oz) broccoli, cut into small
  pieces
1 cup (80 g/2¾ oz) fresh breadcrumbs
1½ cups (185 g/6 oz) grated Cheddar

1 Preheat the oven to moderate 180°C (350°F/Gas 4). Bring a saucepan of salted water to the boil, add the pasta and cook for 10–12 minutes, or until al dente. Drain.

2 Combine the soup, sour cream and curry powder, and season with freshly ground black pepper.

3 Remove the meat from the chicken. Discard the carcass and roughly chop the chicken. Combine the chicken with the cooked pasta, broccoli and soup mixture. Spoon the mixture into four lightly greased 2 cup (500 ml/ 16 fl oz) ovenproof dishes, and sprinkle with the combined breadcrumbs and grated cheese. Bake for 25–30 minutes, or until the cheese melts.

NUTRITION PER SERVE
Protein 67 g; Fat 47 g; Carbohydrate 55 g;
Dietary Fibre 7.5 g; Cholesterol 254 mg;
3812 kJ (911 cal)

Cook the pasta in a saucepan of salted boiling water until al dente.

Combine the cream of mushroom soup, sour cream and curry powder.

Combine the chicken with the pasta, broccoli and soup mixture.

BEEF AND SPINACH CANNELLONI

Preparation time: 35 minutes
Total cooking time: 1 hour 10 minutes
Serves 4–6

FILLING
1 tablespoon olive oil
1 onion, chopped
1 clove garlic, crushed
500 g (1 lb) beef mince
250 g (8 oz) frozen spinach, thawed
3 tablespoons tomato paste
½ cup (125 g/4 oz) ricotta
1 egg
½ teaspoon ground oregano

BECHAMEL SAUCE
1 cup (250 ml/8 fl oz) milk
1 sprig fresh parsley
5 peppercorns
30 g (1 oz) butter
1 tablespoon plain flour
½ cup (125 ml/4 fl oz) cream

TOMATO SAUCE
425 g (14 oz) can tomato purée
2 tablespoons chopped fresh basil
1 clove garlic, crushed
½ teaspoon sugar

12–15 instant cannelloni tubes
1 cup (150 g/5 oz) grated mozzarella
½ cup (60 g/2 oz) grated Parmesan

1 Preheat the oven to moderate 180°C (350°F/Gas 4). Lightly oil a large shallow ovenproof dish. To make the filling, heat the oil in a frying pan. Add the onion and garlic and stir over low heat until the onion is tender. Add the mince and brown well, breaking up any lumps with a fork as it cooks. Add the spinach and tomato paste. Cook, stirring, for 1 minute. Remove from the heat. Mix together the ricotta, egg, oregano and some salt and pepper. Add to the mince mixture and stir well.

2 To make the Béchamel sauce, put the milk, parsley and peppercorns in a small pan. Bring to the boil. Remove from the heat and cool for 10 minutes. Strain, discarding the flavourings. Melt the butter in a small pan and stir in the flour. Cook, stirring, for 1 minute. Remove from the heat. Gradually blend in the strained milk, stirring until smooth. Return to the heat and cook, stirring constantly over medium heat, until the sauce boils and thickens. Reduce the heat and simmer for 3 minutes. Add the cream and season with salt and pepper.

3 To make the tomato sauce, put all the ingredients in a pan and bring to the boil. Reduce the heat and simmer for 5 minutes.

4 Spoon the filling into a piping bag and fill the cannelloni tubes (or fill with a teaspoon).

5 Spoon a little of the tomato sauce in the base of the dish. Arrange the cannelloni on top.

6 Pour Béchamel sauce over the cannelloni, followed by the remaining tomato sauce. Sprinkle the combined cheeses over the top. Bake for 30–35 minutes or until golden.

NUTRITION PER SERVE (6)
Protein 40 g; Fat 30 g; Carbohydrate 68 g; Dietary Fibre 9 g; Cholesterol 120 mg; 3010 kJ (720 Cal)

Brown the mince and add the spinach, then add the ricotta mixture.

Add the milk slowly to the Béchamel sauce, stirring constantly to prevent lumps.

Put all the tomato sauce ingredients in a pan and stir until the sauce comes to the boil.

You can use a piping bag to fill the cannelloni, but if you don't have one a teaspoon will do.

Spoon tomato sauce into the dish and then top with a layer of cannelloni.

Pour Béchamel sauce over the cannelloni and then top with the remaining tomato sauce.

CRAB, CAMEMBERT AND FUSILLI FRITTATA

Preparation time: 15 minutes
Total cooking time: 50 minutes
Serves 4–6

1 cup (90 g/3 oz) fusilli
1 tablespoon olive oil
1 very small red onion, finely chopped
1 large Roma tomato, roughly chopped
⅓ cup (60 g/2 oz) semi-dried tomatoes, roughly chopped
2 tablespoons finely chopped fresh coriander leaves
⅔ cup (150 g/5 oz) cooked fresh or canned crab meat
150 g (5 oz) Camembert, rind removed, cut into small pieces
6 eggs plus 2 egg yolks

1 Cook the pasta in a large pan of rapidly boiling salted water until al dente. Drain and set aside to cool a little.

2 Meanwhile, heat half the oil in a small frying pan over low heat, add the onion and cook for 4–5 minutes, or until softened but not browned. Transfer to a bowl and add the Roma tomato, semi-dried tomatoes and coriander. Squeeze out any excess moisture from the crab meat and add to the bowl. Add half the cheese and the cooled pasta. Mix well. Beat together the six eggs and the two extra yolks, then stir into the frittata mixture. Season with salt and pepper.
3 Heat the remaining oil in the frying pan, pour in the frittata mixture and cook over low heat for 25 minutes. Preheat the grill to low. Scatter the remaining Camembert over the frittata before placing it under the grill for 10–15 minutes, or until cooked and golden brown on top. Remove from the grill and leave for 5 minutes. Cut into slices and serve immediately.

NUTRITION PER SERVE (6)
Protein 19 g; Fat 17 g; Carbohydrate 13 g;
Dietary Fibre 2 g; Cholesterol 293 mg;
1155 kJ (275 cal)

Add the cooked pasta to the mixture and then the eggs.

Cook the frittata over low heat for 25 minutes and then place under the grill to brown.

SPANISH CHICKEN AND RICE STEW

Preparation time: 10 minutes
Total cooking time: 1 hour
Serves 4

¼ cup (60 ml/2 fl oz) olive oil
4 chicken thighs and 6 drumsticks
1 large red onion, finely chopped
1 large green capsicum, two-thirds diced and one-third julienned
3 teaspoons sweet paprika
400 g (13 oz) can diced tomatoes
1¼ cups (275 g/9 oz) paella or arborio rice (see NOTE)
½ teaspoon ground saffron

1 Heat 2 tablespoons of the oil in a large deep frying pan over high heat. Season the chicken pieces well and brown in batches. Remove the chicken from the pan.
2 Reduce the heat to medium and add the remaining oil. Add the onion and the diced capsicum, and cook gently for 5 minutes. Stir in the sweet paprika and cook for 30 seconds. Add the tomato and simmer for 1–3 minutes, or until it thickens.
3 Stir in 3½ cups (875 ml/28 fl oz) boiling water, then add the rice and saffron. Return the chicken to the pan and stir to combine. Season to taste. Bring to the boil, then cover, reduce the heat to medium–low and simmer for 20–30 minutes, or until the liquid has been absorbed and the chicken is tender. Stir in the julienned capsicum, then allow to stand, covered, for 3–4 minutes before serving.

NUTRITION PER SERVE
Protein 92 g; Fat 45 g; Carbohydrate 57 g; Dietary Fibre 2.5 g; Cholesterol 433 mg; 4150 kJ (990 cal)

NOTE: Paella rice is a medium round grain from Spain. Calasparra is the most commonly available variety and can be purchased from fine food stores or Spanish delicatessens.

Add the tomato to the capsicum mixture, and simmer until it thickens.

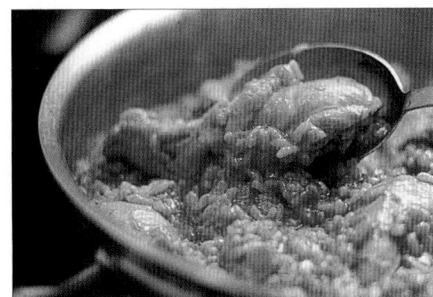
Simmer until the liquid has been absorbed and the chicken is tender.

SPAGHETTI WITH HERBS, BABY SPINACH AND GARLIC CRUMBS

Preparation time: 15 minutes
Total cooking time: 15 minutes
Serves 4

375 g (12 oz) spaghetti
125 g (4 oz) day-old crusty Italian
   bread, crusts removed
100 ml (3½ fl oz) extra virgin olive oil,
   plus extra for serving
4 cloves garlic, finely chopped
400 g (13 oz) baby English spinach
   leaves
4 tablespoons chopped fresh basil

½ cup (30 g/1 oz) chopped fresh flat-
   leaf parsley
1 tablespoon fresh thyme leaves
30 g (1 oz) shaved Parmesan

1 Cook the pasta in a large pan of rapidly boiling salted water until al dente. Drain and return to the pan to keep warm, reserving ½ cup (125 ml/4 fl oz) of the cooking water.
2 To make the garlic breadcrumbs, mix the bread in a food processor or blender until coarse crumbs form. Heat 1 tablespoon oil in a saucepan. Add the breadcrumbs and half the garlic and toss for 2–3 minutes, or until lightly golden. Remove and clean the pan with paper towels.

3 Heat 2 tablespoons of the oil in the same pan. Add the spinach and remaining garlic, toss together for 1 minute, then add the herbs. Cook, tossing frequently, for a further 1 minute to wilt the herbs a little and to heat through. Toss through the pasta with the remaining oil and reserved pasta water. Divide among serving bowls and scatter with the garlic crumbs. Serve hot sprinkled with Parmesan and drizzled with extra virgin olive oil.

NUTRITION PER SERVE
Protein 19 g; Fat 23.5 g; Carbohydrate 82 g;
Dietary Fibre 9 g; Cholesterol 7 mg;
2590 kJ (620 cal)

Cook the spaghetti until al dente, then drain and return to the pan to keep warm.

Cook the breadcrumbs and half the garlic until lightly golden.

Add the spinach and remaining garlic to the oil in the pan and toss together over the heat.

CHICKEN RAVIOLI WITH FRESH TOMATO SAUCE

Preparation time: 40 minutes
Total cooking time: 40 minutes
Serves 4

TOMATO SAUCE
1 large onion, chopped
2 cloves garlic, crushed
⅓ cup (90 g/3 oz) tomato paste
¼ cup (60 ml/2 fl oz) red wine
⅔ cup (170 ml/5½ fl oz) chicken stock
2 tomatoes, chopped
1 tablespoon chopped fresh basil

RAVIOLI
200 g (6½ oz) chicken mince
1 tablespoon chopped fresh basil
¼ cup (25 g/¾ oz) grated Parmesan
3 spring onions, finely chopped
50 g (1¾ oz) ricotta
250 g (8 oz) packet round won ton or gow gee wrappers

1 To make the tomato sauce, heat 1 tablespoon of oil in a pan and cook the onion and garlic for 2–3 minutes, then stir in the tomato paste, wine, stock and tomato and simmer for 20 minutes. Stir in the basil.

2 To make the ravioli, combine the chicken mince, basil, Parmesan, spring onion, ricotta and some salt and black pepper. Lay 24 of the wrappers on a flat surface and brush with a little water. Place slightly heaped teaspoons of the mixture onto the centre of each wrapper. Place another wrapper on top and press the edges together.

3 Bring a large pan of water to the boil. Add the ravioli, a few at a time, and cook for 2–3 minutes, or until just tender. Drain well and serve with the tomato sauce.

NUTRITION PER SERVE
Protein 24 g; Fat 6 g; Carbohydrate 50 g;
Dietary Fibre 6 g; Cholesterol 37 mg;
1517 kJ (363 cal)

For the tomato sauce, add the basil to the tomato mixture.

For the ravioli, combine the Parmesan, chicken, basil, spring onion and ricotta.

Place the mixture between two wrappers and press together to make the ravioli.

NASI GORENG

Preparation time: 25 minutes
Total cooking time: 15 minutes
Serves 4–6

5–8 long red chillies, seeded and
    chopped
2 teaspoons shrimp paste
8 cloves garlic, finely chopped
oil, for cooking
2 eggs, lightly beaten
350 g (12 oz) chicken thigh fillets, cut
    into thin strips
200 g (6½ oz) peeled raw prawns,
    deveined
8 cups (1.5 kg/3 lb) cold cooked rice
    (see NOTE)
⅓ cup (80 ml/2¾ fl oz) kecap manis
⅓ cup (80 ml/2¾ fl oz) soy sauce
2 small Lebanese cucumbers, finely
    chopped
1 large tomato, finely chopped
lime wedges, to serve

1 Mix the chilli, shrimp paste and garlic to a paste in a food processor.
2 Heat the wok until very hot, add 1 tablespoon of the oil and swirl it around to coat the side. Add the beaten eggs and push the egg up the edges of the wok to form a large omelette. Cook for 1 minute over medium heat, or until the egg is set, then flip it over and cook the other side for 1 minute. Remove from the wok and cool before slicing into strips.
3 Reheat the wok, add 1 tablespoon of the oil and stir-fry the chicken and half the chilli paste over high heat until the chicken is just cooked. Remove the chicken from the wok.
4 Reheat the wok, add 1 tablespoon of the oil and stir-fry the prawns and the remaining chilli paste until

cooked. Remove from the wok and set aside.
5 Reheat the wok, add 1 tablespoon of the oil and the rice, and toss over medium heat for 4–5 minutes to heat through. Add the kecap manis and soy sauce and toss constantly until all of the rice is coated in the sauces. Return the chicken and prawns to the wok, and toss to heat through. Season well. Transfer to a serving bowl and top with the omelette strips,

cucumber and tomato. Serve with the lime wedges.

NUTRITION PER SERVE (6)
Protein 30 g; Fat 10 g; Carbohydrate 70 g;
Dietary Fibre 3.5 g; Cholesterol 140 mg;
2105 kJ (505 cal)

NOTE: Rice should be refrigerated overnight before making fried rice to let the grains dry out and separate.

Remove the seeds from the chillies and finely chop the flesh.

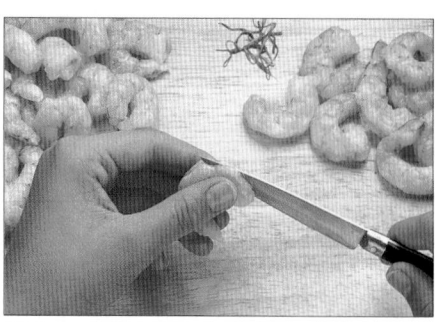
Slit the peeled prawns down the backs to remove the vein.

Process the chilli, shrimp paste and garlic until a paste forms.

BAKED SEAFOOD PASTA

Preparation time: 15 minutes
Total cooking time: 45 minutes
Serves 4–6

250 g (8 oz) lasagne sheets
500 g (1 lb) boneless fish fillets
125 g (4 oz) scallops, cleaned
500 g (1 lb) raw prawns, peeled and
 deveined
125 g (4 oz) butter
1 leek, sliced
⅔ cup (90 g/3 oz) plain flour
2 cups (500 ml/16 fl oz) milk
2 cups (500 ml/16 fl oz) dry white wine
1 cup (125 g/4 oz) grated Cheddar
½ cup (125 ml/4 fl oz) cream
½ cup (60 g/2 oz) grated Parmesan
2 tablespoons chopped fresh parsley

1 Preheat the oven to moderate
180°C (350°F/Gas 4). Line a greased
shallow 24 x 30 cm (10 x 12 inch)
ovenproof dish with lasagne sheets,
breaking them to fill any gaps. Chop
the fish and scallops into even-sized
pieces. Chop the prawns.
2 Melt the butter in a large pan and
cook the leek, stirring, for 1 minute.
Add the flour and cook, stirring, for
1 minute. Remove from the heat and
slowly stir in the milk and wine until
smooth. Return to medium heat and
stir constantly until the sauce boils
and thickens. Reduce the heat and
simmer for 3 minutes. Stir in the
cheese and seafood, season and
simmer for 1 minute.
3 Spoon half the seafood sauce over
the lasagne sheets. Top with another
layer of lasagne sheets. Continue
layering, finishing with lasagne
sheets.
4 Pour the cream over the top.
Sprinkle with the combined Parmesan
and parsley and bake for 30 minutes
or until bubbling and golden.

NUTRITION PER SERVE (6)
Protein 57 g; Fat 28 g; Carbohydrate 45 g;
Dietary Fibre 3 g; Cholesterol 264 mg;
3000 kJ (720 cal)

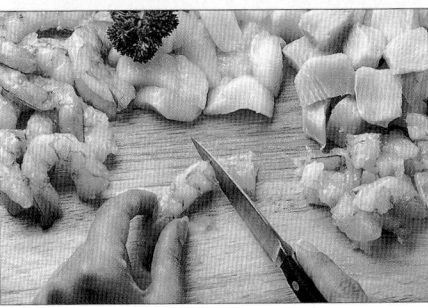

Cut the fish and scallops into bite-sized pieces
and chop the prawns.

Slowly stir in the wine and milk and stir until the
sauce is smooth.

Build up the layers of seafood sauce and lasagne
sheets in the dish.

Mix together the Parmesan and parsley and
sprinkle over the top.

SPINACH RAVIOLI WITH SEMI-DRIED TOMATOES AND PINE NUT SALSA

Preparation time: 15 minutes
Total cooking time: 15 minutes
Serves 4

625 g (1¼ lb) spinach ravioli
3½ tablespoons olive oil
⅓ cup (60 g/2 oz) pine nuts
150 g (5 oz) semi-dried tomatoes,
    thinly sliced
270 g (9 oz) jar roasted capsicums,
    drained and thinly sliced
2 tablespoons finely chopped fresh
    flat-leaf parsley
2 tablespoons finely chopped fresh
    mint
1½ tablespoons balsamic vinegar
30 g (1 oz) shaved Parmesan

1 Cook the pasta in a large pan of rapidly boiling salted water until al dente. Drain and return to the pan to keep warm. Heat ½ teaspoon of the oil in a frying pan and gently cook the pine nuts until golden. Remove from the pan and roughly chop.
2 Add the remaining oil to the pan and add the tomato, capsicum, parsley, mint and vinegar. Stir to warm

through. Remove from the heat and season to taste. Stir in the pine nuts. Divide the pasta among four serving plates, spoon on the sauce and top with the Parmesan. Serve immediately.

NUTRITION PER SERVE
Protein 20 g; Fat 30 g; Carbohydrate 47 g;
Dietary Fibre 9 g; Cholesterol 32 mg;
2225 kJ (530 cal)

Cook the pine nuts in a little oil until they are lightly golden and then chop.

Remove the sauce from the heat and stir in the pine nuts.

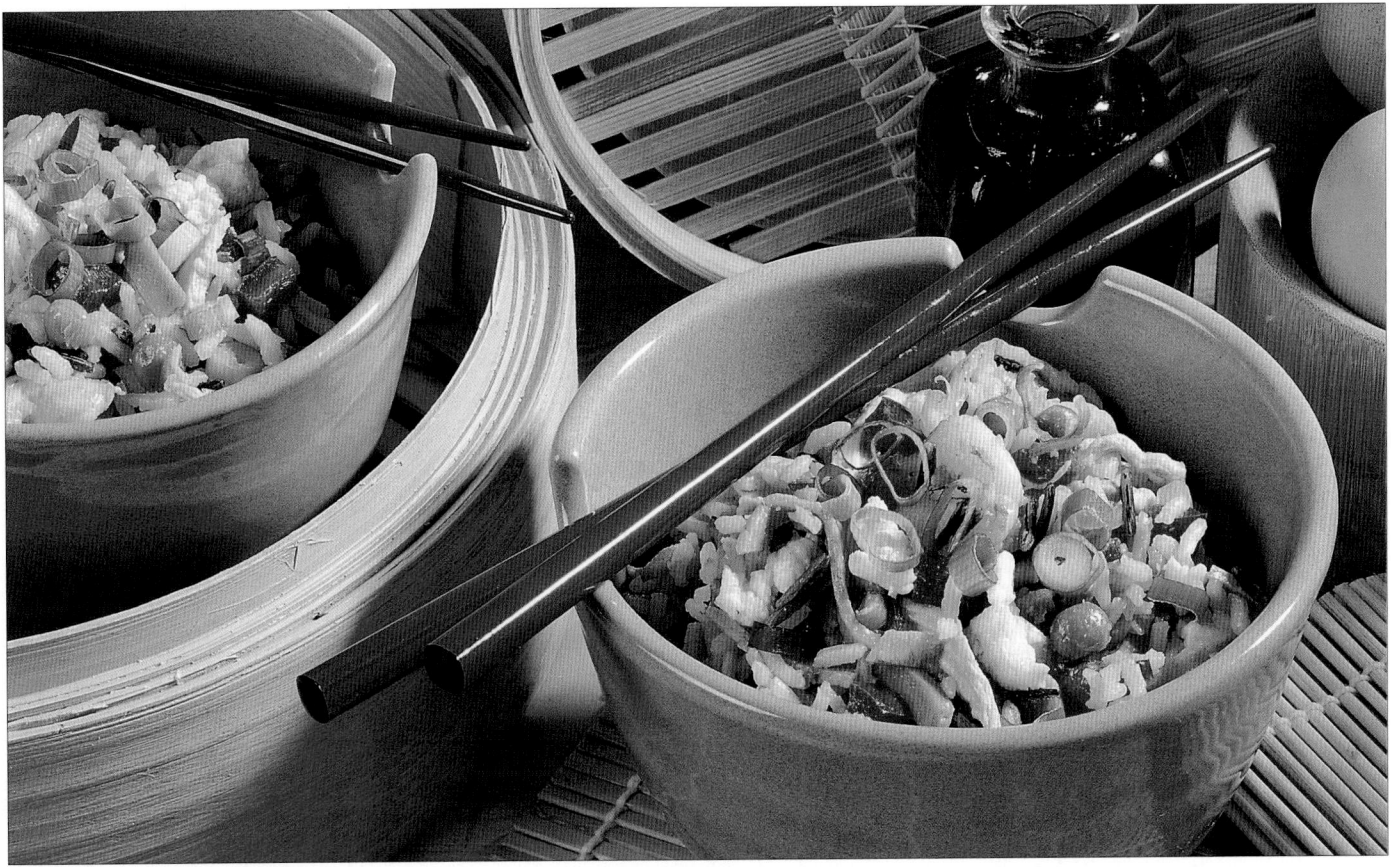

PRAWN FRIED RICE

Preparation time: 20 minutes
Total cooking time: 15 minutes
Serves 6

oil, for cooking
4 egg whites, lightly beaten
2 cloves garlic, crushed
350 g (12 oz) raw prawns, peeled, deveined and halved lengthways
100 g (3½ oz) cooked chicken, shredded
½ cup (80 g/2¾ oz) frozen peas
180 g (6 oz) sliced ham, cut into small strips
1 red capsicum, diced

4 spring onions, sliced
4 cups (750 g/1½ lb) cooked white and wild rice blend (see HINT)
1½ tablespoons soy sauce
3 teaspoons fish sauce
1½ teaspoons soft brown sugar

1 Heat 2 teaspoons of the oil in a wok and pour in the egg white. Cook over low heat, stirring until the egg is just cooked and slightly scrambled, then remove and set aside.
2 Reheat the wok, add a little more oil and stir-fry the garlic, prawns, chicken, peas, ham and capsicum for 3–4 minutes, or until the prawns are cooked through.
3 Add the spring onion, rice, soy and fish sauces and sugar and toss for 30 seconds, or until heated through. Add the egg, toss lightly and serve.

NUTRITION PER SERVE
Protein 35 g; Fat 3 g; Carbohydrate 105 g; Dietary Fibre 4 g; Cholesterol 120 mg; 2500 kJ (600 cal)

HINT: You will need to cook 1⅓ cups (260 g/8 oz) rice to get 4 cupfuls. For fried rice it is best to steam or boil your rice a day in advance and leave it in the fridge overnight. This allows the grains to separate.

Stir the egg white over low heat until just cooked and slightly scrambled.

Stir-fry the garlic, prawns, chicken, peas, ham and capsicum.

When the prawns are cooked through, add the spring onion, rice, sauces and sugar.

VEGETARIAN LASAGNE

Preparation time: 1 hour
Total cooking time: 1 hour 30 minutes
Serves 8

500 g (1 lb) fresh spinach lasagne
　　sheets
½ cup (30 g/1 oz) fresh basil leaves,
　　coarsely chopped
2 tablespoons fresh breadcrumbs
3 tablespoons pine nuts
2 teaspoons paprika
1 tablespoon grated Parmesan

RICOTTA FILLING
750 g (1½ lb) ricotta
½ cup (50 g/1¾ oz) grated Parmesan
pinch of nutmeg

TOMATO SAUCE
1 tablespoon olive oil
2 onions, chopped
2 cloves garlic, crushed
800 g (1 lb 10 oz) can crushed tomatoes
1 tablespoon tomato paste

BECHAMEL SAUCE
60 g (2 oz) butter
½ cup (60 g/2 oz) plain flour
2 cups (500 ml/16 fl oz) milk
2 eggs, lightly beaten
⅓ cup (30 g/1 oz) grated Parmesan

1 Lightly grease a 25 x 32 cm (10 x 13 inch) baking dish. Cut the pasta sheets into large pieces and cook, a couple at a time, in boiling water for 3 minutes. Drain and spread on damp tea towels until needed.
2 To make the ricotta filling, put the ricotta and Parmesan cheeses and nutmeg in a bowl and mix together well. Season with black pepper and set aside.

3 To make the tomato sauce, heat the oil in a frying pan, add the onion and cook for about 10 minutes, stirring occasionally, until very soft. Add the garlic and cook for 1 more minute. Add the tomato and tomato paste and stir until well combined. Stir until the mixture comes to the boil. Reduce the heat and simmer uncovered for 15 minutes, or until thickened, stirring occasionally.
4 To make the Béchamel sauce, heat the butter in a small pan. When starting to foam, add the flour and stir for 3 minutes, or until just coloured. Remove from the heat; add the milk gradually, stirring after each addition, then return to the heat and stir until the sauce boils and thickens. Remove from the heat and stir in the eggs. Return to moderate heat and stir until almost boiling, but do not boil. Add the cheese and season to taste. Put plastic wrap onto the surface to prevent a skin forming. Preheat the oven to 200°C (400°F/Gas 6).
5 Put a layer of lasagne sheets in the dish. Spread with a third of the ricotta filling, sprinkle with basil, then top with a third of the tomato sauce. Repeat the layers, finishing with pasta.
6 Pour over the Béchamel sauce, spread until smooth, then sprinkle with the combined breadcrumbs, pine nuts, paprika and Parmesan. Bake for 45 minutes, or until browned. Leave to stand for 10 minutes before serving.

NUTRITION PER SERVE
Protein 22 g; Fat 30 g; Carbohydrate 16 g;
Dietary Fibre 14 g; Cholesterol 130 mg;
1750 kJ (416 cal)

Cook the lasagne in a large pan of boiling water, a couple of sheets at a time.

Simmer the tomato sauce, uncovered, for 15 minutes until it has thickened.

Stir the Béchamel sauce over the heat until it boils and thickens.

Placing plastic wrap onto the surface of the sauce will stop a skin forming.

Use the back of a spoon to spread a layer of tomato sauce over the ricotta filling.

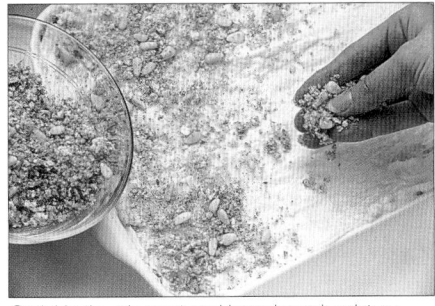

Sprinkle the pine nut and breadcrumb mixture over the Béchamel sauce.

SESAME TOFU RICE

**Preparation time: 20 minutes +
overnight refrigeration of rice +
30 minutes marinating**
Total cooking time: 10 minutes
Serves 4

300 g (10 oz) firm tofu
2 teaspoons sesame oil
2 tablespoons soy sauce
1 tablespoon sesame seeds
2 tablespoons oil
3 zucchini, sliced
150 g (5 oz) button mushrooms,
    halved or quartered
1 large red capsicum, cut into squares
2 cloves garlic, crushed
3 cups (550 g/1 lb 2 oz) cold cooked
    brown rice (see NOTE)
1–2 tablespoons soy sauce, extra

1 Drain the tofu and pat dry with paper towels. Cut into cubes, place in a glass or ceramic bowl and add the sesame oil and soy sauce. Stir well and leave in the fridge to marinate for 30 minutes, stirring occasionally.
2 Heat the wok until very hot, add the sesame seeds and dry-fry until lightly golden. Tip onto a plate to cool.
3 Reheat the wok, add the oil and swirl it around to coat the side. Remove the tofu from the dish with a slotted spoon and reserve the marinade. Stir-fry the tofu over high heat, turning occasionally, for about 3 minutes, or until browned. Remove from the wok and set aside.
4 Add the vegetables and garlic, and cook, stirring often, until they are just tender. Add the rice and tofu, and stir-fry until heated through.
5 Add the toasted sesame seeds, the reserved marinade and extra soy sauce to taste. Toss to coat the tofu and vegetables, then serve immediately.

NUTRITION PER SERVE
Protein 15 g; Fat 20 g; Carbohydrate 50 g;
Dietary Fibre 5.5 g; Cholesterol 0 mg;
1815 kJ (435 cal)

NOTE: Rice should be refrigerated overnight before making fried rice to let the grains dry out and separate.

Dry-fry the sesame seeds until they are lightly golden brown.

AGNOLOTTI WITH CREAMY TOMATO SAUCE AND BACON

Preparation time: 10 minutes
Total cooking time: 20 minutes
Serves 4

4 rashers bacon
625 g (1 lb 5 oz) veal or chicken
    agnolotti
1 tablespoon olive oil
2 cloves garlic, finely chopped
⅔ cup (120 g/4 oz) thinly sliced semi-
    dried tomatoes
1 tablespoon chopped fresh thyme
1½ cups (375 ml/12 fl oz) cream
1 teaspoon finely grated lemon rind
⅓ cup (30 g/1 oz) grated Parmesan

1 Grill the bacon for 5 minutes on each side, or until crisp and golden. Drain on paper towels and then break into pieces.
2 Cook the pasta in a large pan of rapidly boiling salted water until al dente. Drain and return to the pan to keep warm. Heat the oil in a frying pan and cook the garlic over medium heat for 1 minute, or until just golden. Add the semi-dried tomatoes and thyme and cook for 1 minute.
3 Add the cream, bring to the boil, then reduce the heat and simmer for 6–8 minutes, or until thickened and reduced by one-third. Season and add the lemon rind and 2 tablespoons of the Parmesan. Serve over the pasta, topped with the remaining Parmesan and bacon pieces. Serve immediately.

NUTRITION PER SERVE
Protein 32 g; Fat 61 g; Carbohydrate 65 g; Dietary Fibre 7.5 g; Cholesterol 212 mg; 3895 kJ (930 cal)

Grill the bacon until it is crisp, then drain on paper towels and break into pieces.

Add the semi-dried tomatoes and thyme to the garlic and cook for 1 minute more.

Add the cream to the sauce and simmer until it has thickened.

PASTA WITH BABY SPINACH, ROASTED PUMPKIN & TOMATO

Preparation time: 15 minutes
Total cooking time: 1 hour
Serves 4

750 g (1½ lb) pumpkin
2 tablespoons olive oil (see NOTES)
16 unpeeled cloves garlic
250 g (8 oz) cherry tomatoes, halved
500 g (1 lb) pasta
200 g (6½ oz) baby English spinach
    leaves
200 g (6½ oz) marinated Persian feta
    (see NOTES)
¼ cup (60 ml/2 fl oz) sherry vinegar
2 tablespoons walnut oil

1 Preheat the oven to moderately hot 200°C (400°F/Gas 6). Cut the pumpkin into large cubes, place in a roasting tin and drizzle with oil. Roast for 30 minutes, then add the garlic. Arrange the tomatoes on a baking tray. Put all the vegetables in the oven and roast for 10–15 minutes, or until tender. Don't overcook the tomatoes or they will break up.
2 Cook the pasta in a large pan of rapidly boiling salted water until al dente. Drain and return to the pan to keep warm.
3 Toss together the pasta, tomatoes, pumpkin, garlic and spinach.
4 Drain the feta, reserving ¼ cup (60 ml/2 fl oz) marinade. Whisk this with the vinegar and walnut oil. Pour over the pasta and sprinkle with feta.

NUTRITION PER SERVE
Protein 29 g; Fat 34 g; Carbohydrate 105 g; Dietary Fibre 13 g; Cholesterol 34 mg; 3524 kJ (842 cal)

NOTES: If you can find it, use Parmesan-infused olive oil. It is available at gourmet food stores and adds depth of flavour.
Persian feta is softer and creamier than other feta and is marinated in oil, herbs and garlic.

VARIATION: Toss in 200 g marinated Kalamata olives for added flavour.

Drizzle the cubes of pumpkin with olive oil, using Parmesan-infused oil if available.

Roast the pumpkin, garlic and tomatoes until they are tender.

Cook the pasta in a large saucepan of boiling water until al dente.

SPAGHETTI VONGOLE

Preparation time: 25 minutes + soaking
Total cooking time: 35 minutes
Serves 4

1 kg (2 lb) small fresh clams in shells,
  cleaned (see NOTE) or 750 g
  (1½ lb) canned clams in brine
1 tablespoon lemon juice
⅓ cup (80 ml/2¾ fl oz) olive oil
3 cloves garlic, crushed
2 x 425 g (14 oz) cans crushed
  tomatoes
250 g (8 oz) spaghetti
4 tablespoons chopped fresh parsley

1 Place the cleaned clams in a large
pan with the lemon juice. Cover the
pan tightly and shake over medium
heat for 7–8 minutes until the shells
open (discard any clams that do not
open in this time). Remove the clams
from their shells. If using canned
clams, rinse well, drain and set aside.
2 Heat the oil in a large pan. Add the
garlic and cook over low heat for
5 minutes. Add the tomatoes and stir
well. Bring to the boil and simmer,
covered, for 20 minutes. Add the clams
to the sauce and season with black
pepper. Stir until heated through.
3 Meanwhile, cook the pasta in a
large pan of rapidly boiling salted
water until al dente. Drain well and
return to the pan. Add the sauce and
chopped parsley and toss gently.

NUTRITION PER SERVE
Protein 35 g; Fat 25 g; Carbohydrate 55 g;
Dietary Fibre 7 g; Cholesterol 355 mg;
2420 kJ (580 cal)

NOTE: To clean the clams, any sand
and grit needs to be drawn out of the
shells. Combine 2 tablespoons each of
salt and plain flour with enough water
to make a paste. Add to a large
bucket or bowl of cold water and
soak the clams in this mixture
overnight. Drain and scrub the shells
well, then rinse thoroughly and drain
again.

If using canned clams, rinse them thoroughly and
then drain well.

Add the clams to the sauce and season with
ground black pepper.

Cook the spaghetti in a large pan of rapidly boiling
water while the sauce is cooking.

Add the clam sauce and the parsley to the warm
pasta in the pan and toss gently.

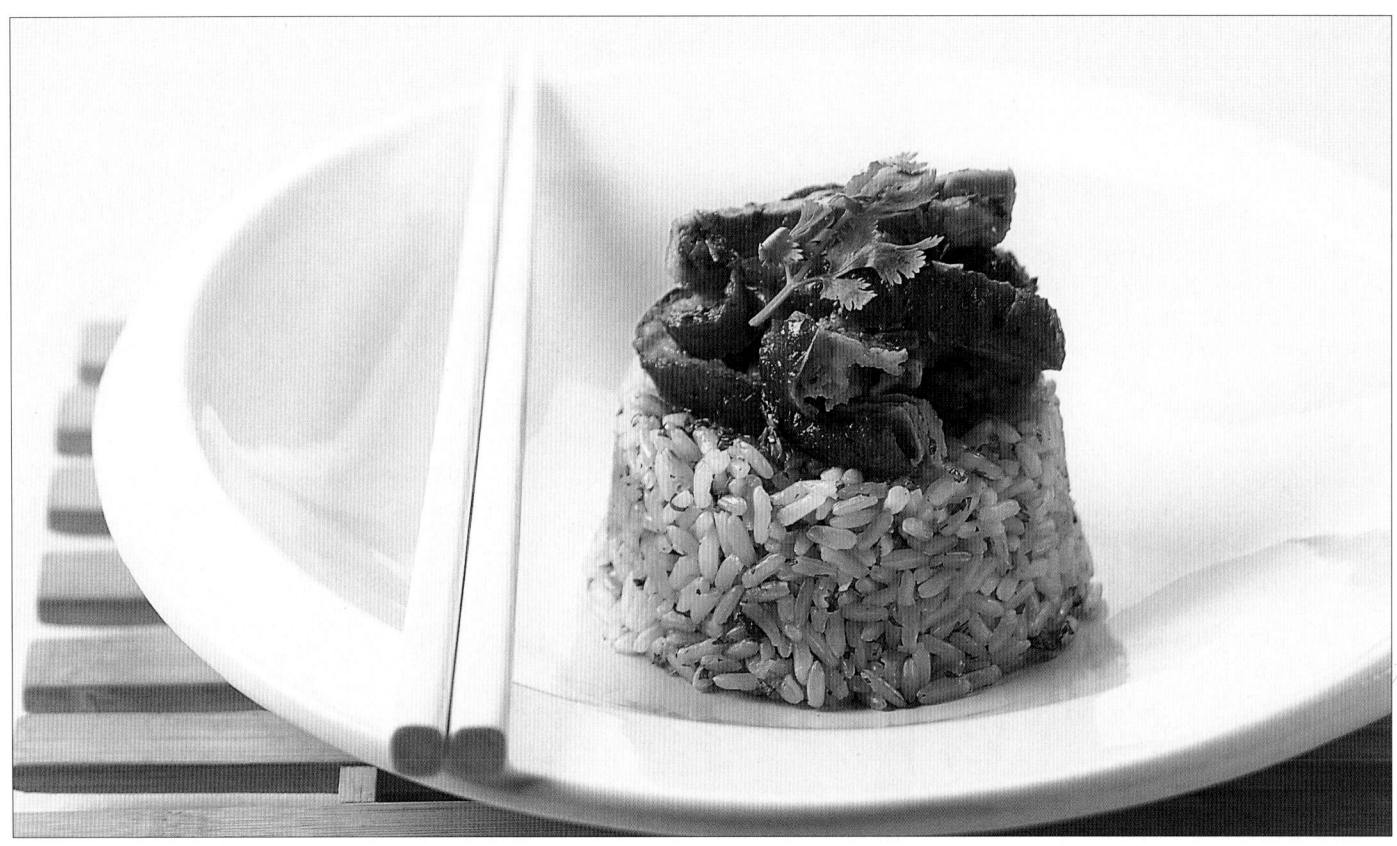

RICE CAKES WITH CHINESE ROAST DUCK

**Preparation time: 15 minutes +
2 hours refrigeration
Total cooking time: 20 minutes
Serves 4**

1 kg (2 lb) Chinese barbecued duck
2 cloves garlic, crushed
200 ml (6½ fl oz) orange juice
2 tablespoons soy sauce
4 tablespoons chopped fresh
   coriander
2 cups (500 ml/16 fl oz) chicken stock
1¼ cups (250 g/8 oz) quick-cooking
   brown rice

1 Remove the meat from the duck, cut into large slices and place in a large non-metallic bowl. Whisk together the garlic, orange juice, soy sauce and 2 tablespoons coriander and pour over the duck. Toss to coat, cover and refrigerate for 2 hours.
2 Place the chicken stock in a saucepan and bring to the boil. Add the rice, then reduce the heat and simmer rapidly until tunnels appear. Reduce the heat to very low, cover and cook for 10–12 minutes, or until tender. Stir in the remaining coriander. Divide the rice among four ½ cup (125 ml/4 fl oz) ramekins. Keep warm.
3 Drain the duck, reserving the marinade. Heat a large frying pan,

add the duck and stir until warmed through. Heat the marinade until boiling in a separate pan. To serve, turn the timbales out onto four serving plates and arrange the duck over the top. Spoon on some reserved marinade and garnish with a few coriander leaves.

NUTRITION PER SERVE
Protein 66 g; Fat 26 g; Carbohydrate 55 g;
Dietary Fibre 3 g; Cholesterol 350 mg;
3007 kJ (718 cal)

NOTE: For something special, try peeling and segmenting 2 oranges and arrange the segments around the bottom of the timbales. Sprinkle with some toasted black sesame seeds.

You can buy barbecued duck in any Chinatown. Cut the meat into large slices.

Cook the rice until it is tender and then stir in the remaining coriander.

Drain the duck, reserving the marinade, and then heat through in a frying pan.

FRIED RICE WITH CORIANDER AND BASIL

Preparation time: 20 minutes + overnight standing
Total cooking time: 20 minutes
Serves 4

2 tablespoons oil
2.5 cm (1 inch) piece of pork fat, chopped
4 cloves garlic, chopped
2 tablespoons grated fresh ginger
2 teaspoons chopped red chillies
2 chicken thigh fillets, diced
100 g (3½ oz) pork loin, diced
2½ cups (470 g/15 oz) cold cooked jasmine rice (see NOTE)
1 tablespoon fish sauce
2 teaspoons light soy sauce
2 spring onions, chopped
1 cup (30 g/1 oz) fresh Thai basil leaves, chopped
½ cup (15 g/½ oz) fresh coriander leaves, chopped

1 Heat the oil to very hot in a wok. Stir-fry the pork fat, garlic, ginger and chillies for 2 minutes.
2 Add the diced chicken and pork to the wok and stir-fry for 3 minutes or until the meat changes colour. Break up any lumps in the rice; add to the wok and toss well to warm through. Add the sauces and toss through with the spring onions and herbs.

NUTRITION PER SERVE
Protein 40 g; Fat 14 g; Carbohydrate 100 g; Dietary Fibre 3 g; Cholesterol 70 mg; 2900 kJ (690 cal)

NOTE: Rice should be refrigerated overnight before making fried rice to let the grains dry out and separate.

Cut the pork loin into small dice with a sharp knife. You can use any lean cut of pork.

Add the pork fat, garlic, ginger and chillies to the wok and stir with a wooden spoon.

Break up any lumps in the cold rice. Add to the wok and toss to heat through.

RICH BEEF AND MUSHROOM LASAGNE

Preparation time: 30 minutes
Total cooking time: 2 hours
Serves 8

1 tablespoon olive oil
2 cloves garlic, crushed
1 onion, chopped
1 carrot, grated
1 celery stalk, diced
125 g (4 oz) mushrooms, chopped
600 g (1¼ lb) minced beef
2½ cups (600 ml/20 fl oz) Italian
    tomato passata
1 teaspoon dried oregano leaves
300 g (10 oz) instant lasagne sheets
1 cup (100 g/3½ oz) grated Parmesan

CHEESE SAUCE
60 g (2 oz) butter
⅓ cup (40 g/1¼ oz) plain flour
1 litre milk
½ teaspoon ground nutmeg
1 cup (125 g/4 oz) grated Cheddar

1 Heat the oil in a large heavy-based pan. Add the garlic, onion, carrot, celery and mushroom. Cook, stirring, over medium heat for 2–3 minutes, or until the onion has softened. Increase the heat, add the mince and stir for a further 3–4 minutes, or until the mince has browned and is well broken up.
2 Add the tomato passata, oregano and 2 cups (500 ml/16 fl oz) water. Bring to the boil, stirring, then lower the heat and simmer for 1 hour, or until the mixture has thickened. Stir occasionally.
3 To make the cheese sauce, melt the butter in a heavy-based pan. Add the flour and cook, stirring, for 1 minute until pale and foaming.

Remove from the heat, gradually add the milk and stir until smooth. Return to the heat and stir continuously for 3–4 minutes, or until the sauce boils and thickens. Cook over low heat for 1 minute. Stir in the nutmeg and Cheddar. Season.
4 To assemble, preheat the oven to moderate 180°C (350°F/Gas 4). Grease a 2.5 litre baking dish. Arrange four lasagne sheets over the base of the baking dish. Spread one-third of the meat mixture over the sheets, then pour over about ¾ cup (185 ml/

6 fl oz) of the cheese sauce. Repeat with two more layers of each. Top with the four remaining lasagne sheets, then with the remaining sauce and finish with the Parmesan. Bake for 45 minutes, or until golden. Leave to stand for 5 minutes before serving.

NUTRITION PER SERVE
Protein 35 g; Fat 30 g; Carbohydrate 45 g; Dietary Fibre 5 g; Cholesterol 110 mg; 2560 kJ (610 cal)

When the mince has browned, add the passata, water and oregano.

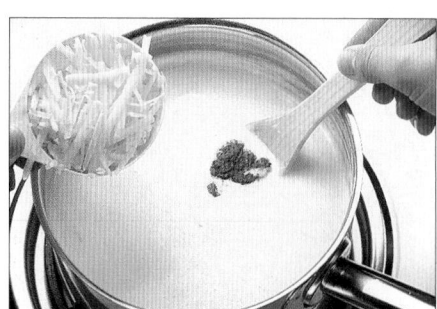

Cook, stirring, until the sauce thickens, then add the nutmeg and Cheddar.

Finish layering with the last four sheets of lasagne, the sauce and the Parmesan.

FISH AND MACARONI CASSEROLE

Preparation time: 20 minutes
Total cooking time: 50 minutes
Serves 4

1 cup (155 g/5 oz) macaroni
30 g (1 oz) butter
1 onion, chopped
500 g (1 lb) white fish fillets, cut into
    2 cm (¾ inch) cubes
1 tablespoon chopped fresh thyme
100 g (3½ oz) butter mushrooms,
    sliced
½ teaspoon hot English mustard
1 tablespoon plain flour
1 cup (250 ml/8 fl oz) chicken stock
½ cup (125 ml/4 fl oz) cream
½ cup (125 g/4 oz) sour cream

1 cup (80 g/2¾ oz) fresh breadcrumbs
1 cup (125 g/4 oz) grated Cheddar
½ cup (50 g/1¾ oz) grated fresh
    Parmesan
2 tablespoons chopped fresh parsley

1 Preheat the oven to moderate 180°C (350°F/Gas 4). Cook the macaroni in a large saucepan of rapidly boiling water until just tender. Drain and set aside.
2 Heat the butter in a heavy-based saucepan over medium heat. Cook the onion for 3 minutes, or until golden. Add the fish, thyme and mushrooms. Cook for 5 minutes, or until the fish is tender. Remove from the pan and keep warm.
3 Stir the mustard and flour into the pan. Add the stock and cream gradually. Stir constantly over medium

heat for 3 minutes, or until the mixture boils and thickens. Boil for 1 minute, then remove from the heat. Stir in the sour cream.
4 Transfer the mixture to a large bowl, and stir in the macaroni, fish and mushrooms. Spoon into a large ovenproof dish. Combine the breadcrumbs, cheese and parsley. Sprinkle over the macaroni mixture. Bake for 30 minutes, or until golden. Serve with a green salad.

NUTRITION PER SERVE
Protein 49 g; Fat 50 g; Carbohydrate 46 g;
Dietary Fibre 3.5 g; Cholesterol 217 mg;
3465 kJ (830 cal)

HINT: If you prefer, you can use a drained can of tuna instead of the fresh fish.

Cook the macaroni in a large saucepan of boiling water until just tender.

Add the fish, thyme and mushrooms to the pan, and cook until the fish is tender.

Gradually add the stock and cream, stirring until the mixture boils and thickens.

Chicken

CHICKEN AND LEEK PIE

Preparation time: 20 minutes
Total cooking time: 40 minutes
Serves 4

50 g (1¾ oz) butter
2 large leeks, washed and thinly sliced
4 spring onions, sliced
1 clove garlic, crushed
¼ cup (30 g/1 oz) plain flour
1½ cups (375 ml/12 fl oz) chicken
  stock
½ cup (125 ml/4 fl oz) cream
1 medium barbecued chicken,
  chopped
2 sheets puff pastry, thawed
¼ cup (60 ml/2 fl oz) milk

1 Preheat the oven to moderately hot 200°C (400°F/Gas 6). In a pan, melt the butter and add the leek, spring onion and garlic. Cook over low heat for 6 minutes, or until the leek is soft but not browned. Sprinkle in the flour and mix well. Pour in the stock gradually and cook, stirring well, until the mixture is thick and smooth.
2 Stir in the cream and the chicken. Put the mixture in a shallow 20 cm (8 inch) pie dish and set aside to cool.

3 Cut a circle out of one of the sheets of pastry to cover the top of the pie. Brush around the rim of the pie dish with a little milk. Put the pastry on top and seal around the edge firmly. Trim off any overhanging pastry and decorate the edge with the back of a fork. Cut the other sheet into 1 cm (½ inch) strips and roll each strip up loosely into a spiral. Arrange the spirals on top of the pie, starting from the middle and leaving a gap between each one. The spirals may not cover the whole surface of the pie. Make a few small holes between the spirals to let out any steam, and brush the top of the pie lightly with milk. Bake for 25–30 minutes, or until the top is brown and crispy. Make sure the spirals look well cooked and are not raw in the middle.

NUTRITION PER SERVE
Protein 25 g; Fat 55 g; Carbohydrate 40 g;
Dietary Fibre 3 g; Cholesterol 185 mg;
3105 kJ (740 cal)

NOTE: Make small pies by placing the mixture into 4 greased 1¼ cup (315 ml/10 fl oz) round ovenproof dishes. Cut the pastry into 4 rounds to fit. Bake for 15 minutes, or until crisp.

Seal the edge firmly and trim off any overhanging pastry with a sharp knife.

Roll up the strips of pastry into spirals and arrange them on top of the pie.

TANDOORI CHICKEN SALAD

Preparation time: 20 minutes
+ overnight marinating
Total cooking time: 15 minutes
Serves 4

4 chicken breast fillets
2–3 tablespoons tandoori paste
200 g (6½ oz) thick plain yoghurt
1 tablespoon lemon juice
½ cup (15 g/½ oz) fresh coriander
    leaves
½ cup (60 g/2 oz) slivered almonds,
    toasted
snow pea sprouts, to serve

CUCUMBER AND YOGHURT
DRESSING
1 Lebanese cucumber, grated
200 g (6½ oz) thick plain yoghurt
1 tablespoon chopped fresh mint
2 teaspoons lemon juice

1 Cut the chicken breast fillets into thick strips. Combine the tandoori paste, yoghurt and lemon juice in a large bowl, add the chicken strips and toss to coat well. Refrigerate and leave to marinate overnight.

2 To make the dressing, put the grated cucumber in a medium bowl. Add the yoghurt, chopped mint and lemon juice, and stir until well combined. Refrigerate until needed.

3 Heat a large non-stick frying pan, add the marinated chicken in batches and cook, turning frequently, until cooked through. Cool and place in a large bowl. Add the coriander leaves and toasted almonds, and toss until well combined. Serve on a bed of snow pea sprouts, with the dressing served separately.

NUTRITION PER SERVE
Protein 35 g; Fat 15 g; Carbohydrate 7 g;
Dietary Fibre 2 g; Cholesterol 70 mg;
1230 kJ (290 cal)

NOTE: The quality of the tandoori paste used will determine the flavour and look of the chicken. There are many home-made varieties available from supermarkets and delicatessens.

Combine the tandoori paste with the yoghurt and lemon juice.

Using a metal grater, coarsely grate the unpeeled Lebanese cucumber.

Cook the marinated chicken strips in batches, turning frequently.

HONEY CHICKEN

Preparation time: 15 minutes
Total cooking time: 25 minutes
Serves 4

oil, for cooking
500 g (1 lb) chicken thigh fillets,
    cut into cubes
1 egg white, lightly beaten
⅓ cup (40 g/1¼ oz) cornflour
2 onions, thinly sliced
1 green capsicum, cubed
2 carrots, cut into batons
100 g (3½ oz) snow peas, sliced
¼ cup (90 g/3 oz) honey

2 tablespoons toasted almonds

1 Heat a wok until very hot, add
1½ tablespoons of the oil and swirl it
around to coat the side. Dip half of
the chicken into the egg white, then
lightly dust with the cornflour. Stir-fry
over high heat for 4–5 minutes, or
until the chicken is golden brown and
just cooked. Remove from the wok
and drain on paper towels. Repeat
with the remaining chicken, then
remove all the chicken from the wok.
2 Reheat the wok, add 1 tablespoon
of the oil and stir-fry the sliced onion
over high heat for 3–4 minutes, or
until slightly softened. Add the

capsicum and carrot, and cook,
tossing, for 3–4 minutes, or until
tender. Stir in the snow peas and
cook for 2 minutes.
3 Increase the heat, add the honey
and toss the vegetables until well
coated. Return the chicken to the wok
and toss until it is heated through and
is well coated in the honey. Remove
from the heat and season well with
salt and pepper. Serve immediately,
sprinkled with the almonds.

NUTRITION PER SERVE
Protein 35 g; Fat 20 g; Carbohydrate 35 g;
Dietary Fibre 4 g; Cholesterol 60 mg;
1815 kJ (435 cal)

Trim the excess fat from the chicken, and cut the chicken into cubes.

Dip the chicken into the egg white, then lightly dust with the cornflour.

Stir-fry the chicken pieces until golden brown and just cooked.

CHICKEN CACCIATORE

Preparation time: 45 minutes
Total cooking time: 1 hour 20 minutes
Serves 4

4 tomatoes
1.5 kg (3 lb) chicken pieces
20 g (¾ oz) butter
1 tablespoon oil
20 g (¾ oz) butter, extra
1 large onion, chopped
2 cloves garlic, chopped
1 small green capsicum, chopped
150 g (5 oz) mushrooms, thickly sliced
1 tablespoon plain flour
1 cup (250 ml/8 fl oz) white wine
1 tablespoon white wine vinegar
2 tablespoons tomato paste
½ cup (90 g/3 oz) small black olives
⅓ cup (20 g/¾ oz) chopped fresh
   parsley

1 Score a cross in the base of each tomato. Put the tomatoes in a bowl of boiling water for 30 seconds, then transfer to a bowl of cold water. Drain and peel the skin away from the cross. Halve the tomatoes and remove the seeds with a teaspoon. Chop the flesh. Preheat the oven to moderate 180°C (350°F/Gas 4).
2 Remove excess fat from the chicken pieces and pat dry with paper towels. Heat half the butter and oil in a large flameproof casserole. Cook half the chicken over high heat until browned all over, then set aside. Heat the remaining butter and oil and cook the remaining chicken. Set aside.
3 Heat the extra butter in the casserole and cook the onion and garlic for 2–3 minutes. Add the capsicum and mushrooms, and cook, stirring, for 3 minutes. Stir in the flour and cook for 1 minute. Add the wine,

vinegar, tomato and tomato paste and cook, stirring, for 2 minutes, or until slightly thickened.
4 Return the chicken to the casserole and make sure it is covered by the tomato and onion mixture. Place in the oven and cook, covered, for 1 hour, or until the chicken is tender. Stir in the olives and parsley. Season with salt and cracked black pepper and serve with pasta.

NUTRITION PER SERVE
Protein 55 g; Fat 15 g; Carbohydrate 9.5 g;
Dietary Fibre 5 g; Cholesterol 125 mg;
1675 kJ (401 cal)

NOTE: If you prefer a thicker sauce, remove the cooked chicken from the casserole and reduce the sauce over high heat until slightly thickened. Return all the chicken to the casserole and add the olives and parsley.

Drain the tomatoes, then peel away the skin from the cross.

Cut the tomatoes in half and remove the seeds with a teaspoon.

Cook the chicken in batches over high heat until browned all over.

APRICOT CHICKEN

Preparation time: 10 minutes
Total cooking time: 1 hour
Serves 6

6 chicken thigh cutlets
425 ml (14 fl oz) can apricot nectar
40 g (1¼ oz) packet French onion
   soup mix
425 g (14 oz) can apricot halves in
   natural juice, drained
¼ cup (60 g/2 oz) sour cream

1 Preheat the oven to moderate 180°C (350°F/Gas 4). Remove the skin from the chicken thigh cutlets. Put the chicken in an ovenproof dish. Mix the apricot nectar with the French onion

soup mix until well combined, and pour over the chicken.
2 Bake, covered, for 50 minutes, then add the apricot halves and bake for a further 5 minutes. Stir in the sour cream just before serving. Delicious served with creamy mashed potato or rice to soak up the juices.

NUTRITION PER SERVE
Protein 23 g; Fat 6 g; Carbohydrate 10 g;
Dietary Fibre 0 g; Cholesterol 63 mg;
780 kJ (187 cal)

NOTE: If you are looking for a healthy alternative, you can use low-fat sour cream in place of the full-fat version.

Pour in the apricot nectar and stir to combine with the soup mix.

Add the apricot halves to the chicken and bake for 5 minutes more.

CHICKEN CHOW MEIN

Preparation time: 25 minutes
+ 1 hour marinating
Total cooking time: 20 minutes
Serves 4–6

500 g (1 lb) chicken thigh fillets,
    cut into small cubes
1 tablespoon cornflour
2 tablespoons soy sauce
1 tablespoon oyster sauce
2 teaspoons sugar
oil, for cooking
2 onions, thinly sliced
2 cloves garlic, finely chopped
1 tablespoon finely chopped fresh
    ginger
1 green capsicum, cubed
2 celery sticks, diagonally sliced
8 spring onions, cut into short pieces
100 g (3½ oz) mushrooms, thinly sliced
½ cup (80 g/2¾ oz) water chestnuts,
    thinly sliced
2 teaspoons cornflour, extra
1 tablespoon sherry
½ cup (125 ml/4 fl oz) chicken stock

1 tablespoon soy sauce, extra
90 g (3 oz) Chinese cabbage, finely
    shredded
200 g (6½ oz) ready-prepared fried
    noodles

1 In a glass or ceramic bowl, combine the chicken with the cornflour, soy sauce, oyster sauce and sugar. Cover and refrigerate for 1 hour.
2 Heat the wok until very hot, add 1 tablespoon of the oil and swirl it around to coat the side. Stir-fry the chicken in two batches over high heat for 4–5 minutes, or until cooked. Add oil between batches. Remove all the chicken from the wok and set it aside.
3 Reheat the wok, add 1 tablespoon of the oil and stir-fry the onion over medium-high heat for 3–4 minutes, or until the onion is slightly softened. Add the garlic, ginger, capsicum, celery, spring onion, mushrooms and water chestnuts to the wok. Stir-fry over high heat for 3–4 minutes.
4 Combine the extra cornflour with the sherry, chicken stock and soy sauce. Add to the wok and bring to

the boil. Simmer for 1–2 minutes, or until the sauce thickens slightly. Stir in the cabbage and cook, covered, for 1–2 minutes, or until the cabbage is just wilted. Return the chicken to the wok and toss until heated through. Season with salt and pepper. Arrange the noodles around the edge of a large platter and spoon the chicken mixture into the centre. Serve immediately.

NUTRITION PER SERVE (6)
Protein 25 g; Fat 8.5 g; Carbohydrate 20 g;
Dietary Fibre 4 g; Cholesterol 55 mg;
1110 kJ (265 cal)

Combine the cornflour, sherry, stock and soy sauce, and pour into the wok.

STUFFED CHICKEN BREASTS

Preparation time: 40 minutes
Total cooking time: 45 minutes
Serves 6

1 tablespoon olive oil
1 onion, finely chopped
2 cloves garlic, crushed
100 g (3½ oz) ham, finely chopped
1 green capsicum, finely chopped
2 tablespoons finely chopped pitted
    black olives
⅓ cup (35 g/1¼ oz) grated Parmesan
6 chicken breast fillets
plain flour, to coat

2 eggs, lightly beaten
1½ cups (150 g/5 oz) dry
    breadcrumbs
¼ cup (60 ml/2 fl oz) olive oil

1 Heat the oil in a pan and add the onion, garlic, ham and capsicum. Cook, stirring, over medium heat for 5 minutes, or until the onion is soft. Remove and place in a heatproof bowl. Add the olives and Parmesan.
2 Cut a deep pocket in the side of each chicken fillet, cutting almost through to the other side.
3 Fill each fillet with the ham mixture and secure with toothpicks along the opening of the pocket. Coat each fillet with the flour, shaking off any

excess. Dip into the beaten egg and then coat with the breadcrumbs. Heat the oil in a large pan and cook the fillets, in batches, over medium-high heat for 15–20 minutes, turning halfway through, until golden and cooked through. To serve, remove the toothpicks, then cut diagonally into thin slices.

NUTRITION PER SERVE
Protein 35 g; Fat 20 g; Carbohydrate 20 g;
Dietary Fibre 2 g; Cholesterol 115 mg;
1660 kJ (395 cal)

Cut a deep pocket in the side of each fillet, cutting almost through to the other side.

Spoon the filling into each fillet, securing the pocket openings with toothpicks.

Coat the chicken breasts in the beaten egg and breadcrumbs before cooking.

NOODLES WITH CHICKEN AND FRESH BLACK BEANS

Preparation time: 15 minutes
Total cooking time: 15 minutes
Serves 2–3

2 teaspoons salted black beans
oil, for cooking
2 teaspoons sesame oil
500 g (1 lb) chicken thigh fillets, cut into thin strips
3 cloves garlic, very thinly sliced
4 spring onions, chopped
1 teaspoon sugar

1 red capsicum, sliced
100 g (3½ oz) green beans, cut into short pieces
300 g (10 oz) Hokkien noodles
2 tablespoons oyster sauce
1 tablespoon soy sauce

1 Rinse the black beans in running water. Drain and roughly chop.
2 Heat a wok until very hot, add 1 tablespoon of oil and the sesame oil and swirl it around to coat the side. Stir-fry the chicken in three batches, until well browned, tossing regularly. Remove from the wok and set aside.
3 Reheat the wok, add 1 tablespoon of the oil and stir-fry the garlic and spring onion for 1 minute. Add the black beans, sugar, capsicum and green beans, and cook for 1 minute. Sprinkle with 2 tablespoons of water, cover and steam for 2 minutes.
4 Gently separate the noodles and add to the wok with the chicken, oyster sauce and soy sauce, and toss well to combine. Cook, covered, for about 2 minutes, or until the noodles are just softened.

NUTRITION PER SERVE (3)
Protein 50 g; Fat 20 g; Carbohydrate 50 g;
Dietary Fibre 2 g; Cholesterol 85 mg;
2490 kJ (595 cal)

Cut the chicken thigh fillets into thin strips, removing any excess fat.

Roughly chop the rinsed and drained black beans with a sharp knife.

Add the black beans, sugar, capsicum and green beans to the garlic and spring onion mixture.

MIDDLE-EASTERN BAKED CHICKEN

Preparation time: 30 minutes
Total cooking time: 1 hour 15 minutes
Serves 6

1.6 kg (3¼ lb) chicken
½ cup (125 ml/4 fl oz) boiling water
½ cup (95 g/3 oz) instant couscous
4 pitted dates, chopped
4 dried apricots, chopped
1 tablespoon lime juice
20 g (¾ oz) butter
2 tablespoons olive oil
1 onion, chopped
1–2 cloves garlic, chopped
1 teaspoon salt
¼ teaspoon cracked black pepper
1 teaspoon ground coriander
2 tablespoons chopped fresh parsley
1 teaspoon ground cumin

1 Prepare a kettle barbecue for indirect cooking at medium heat. Place a drip tray underneath the top grill.
2 Remove the giblets and any fat from the chicken. Wipe the chicken with paper towels. Pour boiling water over the couscous and leave to soak for 15 minutes. Soak the dates and apricots in the lime juice and set aside.
3 Heat the butter and half the oil in a pan and cook the onion and garlic for 3–4 minutes, or until translucent. Remove from the heat and add the couscous, dates, apricots, coriander, parsley and some salt and pepper. Mix well. Spoon into the chicken cavity and close with a skewer. Tie the legs with string.
4 Rub the chicken with the combined salt, cracked black pepper, cumin and remaining oil. Place the chicken in the centre of a large piece of greased foil. Wrap the chicken securely. Place on the barbecue over the drip tray. Cover the barbecue and cook for 50 minutes. Open the foil, crimping the edges to form a tray. Cook for 20 minutes, or until the chicken is tender and golden. Stand for 5–6 minutes before carving.

NUTRITION PER SERVE
Protein 46 g; Fat 14 g; Carbohydrate 5.5 g;
Dietary Fibre 1 g; Cholesterol 110 mg;
1378 kJ (329 cal)

Remove the giblets and any large deposits of fat from the chicken.

Combine the onion, garlic, couscous, dates, apricots, salt, pepper, coriander and parsley.

Rub the chicken skin all over with the combined salt, cracked pepper, cumin and remaining oil.

Open the foil and crimp the edges to form a tray to retain the cooking liquid.

BUTTER CHICKEN

Preparation time: 30 minutes
** + 4 hours marinating**
Total cooking time: 20 minutes
Serves 4

1 kg (2 lb) chicken thigh fillets
1 teaspoon salt
¼ cup (60 ml/2 fl oz) lemon juice
1 cup (250 g/8 oz) yoghurt
1 onion, chopped
2 cloves garlic, crushed
3 cm (1¼ inch) piece ginger, grated
1 green chilli, chopped
3 teaspoons garam masala
2 teaspoons yellow food colouring
1 teaspoon red food colouring
½ cup (125 ml/4 fl oz) tomato purée
2 cm (¾ inch) piece ginger, extra, finely
    grated
1 cup (250 ml/8 fl oz) cream
2 teaspoons sugar
¼ teaspoon chilli powder
1 tablespoon lemon juice, extra
1 teaspoon ground cumin
100 g (3½ oz) butter

1 Cut the chicken into 2 cm (¾ inch) thick strips. Sprinkle with the salt and lemon juice.
2 Place the yoghurt, onion, garlic, ginger, chilli and 2 teaspoons of the garam masala in a food processor and blend until smooth.
3 Combine the food colourings in a small bowl. Brush over the chicken and turn the strips to coat the meat all over. Add the yoghurt mixture and toss to combine. Cover and refrigerate for 4 hours. Remove the chicken from the marinade and allow to drain for 5 minutes.
4 Preheat the oven to hot 220°C (425°F/Gas 7). Place the chicken in a shallow baking dish and bake for 15 minutes, or until it is tender. Drain off any excess juice, cover loosely with foil and keep warm.
5 Mix together the tomato purée and ½ cup (125 ml/4 fl oz) water in a large jug. Add the ginger, cream, remaining garam marsala, sugar, chilli powder, lemon juice and cumin, and stir to thoroughly combine.
6 Melt the butter in a large pan over medium heat. Stir in the tomato mixture and bring to the boil. Cook for 2 minutes, then reduce the heat and add the chicken pieces. Stir to coat the chicken with the sauce and simmer for a further 2 minutes, or until completely heated through. Serve with rice and garnish with some shredded kaffir lime leaves.

NUTRITION PER SERVE
Protein 55 g; Fat 60 g; Carbohydrate 10 g; Dietary Fibre 2 g; Cholesterol 330 mg; 3390 kJ (805 cal)

NOTE: The chicken can also be marinated overnight in the refrigerator. It is important to always use a non-metallic dish when marinating.

HINT: Kaffir lime leaves are available from most supermarkets, Asian food stores and good fruit and vegetable shops.

VARIATION: Chicken pieces can be substituted for the chicken thigh fillets. Score the thickest part of the meat with a knife and then bake for 30–40 minutes, or until tender.

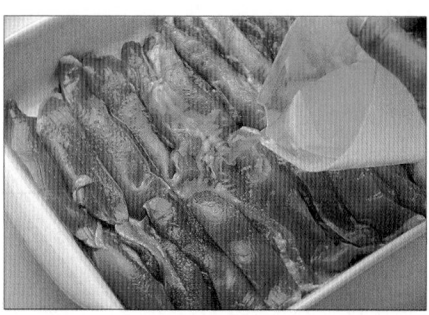

Sprinkle the salt and lemon juice over the strips of chicken.

Process the yoghurt, onion, garlic, ginger, chilli and garam masala.

Brush the food colourings over the chicken, coating the meat thoroughly.

Drain any excess juice from the baked chicken pieces in the baking dish.

Add the ginger, cream, garam masala, sugar, chilli, lemon juice and cumin.

Add the chicken pieces to the pan and stir to coat with the sauce.

TERIYAKI CHICKEN WINGS

Preparation time: 15 minutes
  + 3 hours marinating
Total cooking time: 15 minutes
Serves 4

8 chicken wings
¼ cup (60 ml/2 fl oz) soy sauce
2 tablespoons sherry
2 teaspoons grated fresh ginger
1 clove garlic, crushed
1 tablespoon honey

1 Pat the chicken wings dry with paper towels. Trim any excess fat from the wings, and tuck the tips under to form a triangle.

2 Place the wings in a shallow non-metal dish. Combine the soy sauce, sherry, ginger, garlic and honey in a jug, and mix well. Pour the mixture over the chicken wings. Refrigerate, covered, for several hours or overnight. Lightly brush two sheets of aluminium foil with oil. Place 4 wings in a single layer on each piece of foil and wrap completely.

3 Preheat a barbecue grill or flatplate to high. Cook the parcels on the hot barbecue for 10 minutes. Remove the parcels from the heat and unwrap. Place the wings directly on a lightly greased grill for 3 minutes, or until brown. Turn the wings frequently and brush with any remaining marinade.

NUTRITION PER SERVE
Protein 43 g; Fat 4.5 g; Carbohydrate 6 g;
Dietary Fibre 0 g; Cholesterol 95 mg;
998 kJ (238 cal)

Tuck the tips of the chicken wings under to form a triangle.

Place four chicken wings on each piece of foil and wrap completely.

Place the wings directly on a lightly greased grill and cook until brown.

CHICKEN FAJITAS

**Preparation time: 35 minutes
+ 3 hours marinating
Total cooking time: 10 minutes
Serves 4**

4 chicken breast fillets
2 tablespoons olive oil
¼ cup (60 ml) lime juice
2 cloves garlic, crushed
1 teaspoon ground cumin
¼ cup (15 g/½ oz) chopped fresh
    coriander leaves
8 flour tortillas
1 tablespoon olive oil, extra
2 onions, sliced

2 green capsicums, cut into thin strips
1 cup (125 g/4 oz) grated Cheddar
1 large avocado, sliced
1 cup (250 g/8 oz) bottled tomato
    salsa

1 Trim the chicken of fat and sinew, and cut into thin strips. Place the chicken strips in a shallow non-metal dish. Combine the oil, lime juice, garlic, cumin and coriander in a jug, and mix well. Pour the mixture over the chicken. Refrigerate, covered, for several hours or overnight.
2 Preheat a barbecue grill or flatplate to high. Wrap the tortillas in foil and place on a cool part of the barbecue grill to warm through for 10 minutes.

Heat the oil on a flatplate. Cook the onion and capsicum for 5 minutes, or until soft. Move the vegetables to a cooler part of the plate to keep warm.
3 Place the chicken and marinade on the flatplate and cook for 5 minutes, or until just tender. Transfer the chicken, vegetables and wrapped tortillas to a serving platter. Make up individual fajitas by placing the chicken, onion and capsicum, cheese and avocado over the tortillas. Top with the salsa and roll up to enclose the filling.

NUTRITION PER SERVE
Protein 88 g; Fat 59 g; Carbohydrate 116 g;
Dietary Fibre 9.5 g; Cholesterol 173 mg;
5660 kJ (1352 cal)

Combine the oil, lime juice, garlic, cumin and coriander, and pour over the chicken.

Cook the onion and capsicum on the flatplate until soft.

Cook the chicken and marinade on the flatplate until just tender.

CHARGRILLED CHICKEN

Preparation time: 20 minutes
+ 2 hours marinating
Total cooking time: 1 hour
Serves 4

4 chicken breast fillets
2 tablespoons honey
1 tablespoon wholegrain mustard
1 tablespoon soy sauce
2 red onions, cut into wedges
8 Roma tomatoes, halved lengthways
2 tablespoons soft brown sugar

2 tablespoons balsamic vinegar
cooking oil spray
snow pea sprouts, for serving

1 Preheat the oven to moderate 180°C (350°F/Gas 4). Trim the chicken of any excess fat and place in a shallow dish. Combine the honey, mustard and soy sauce and pour over the chicken, tossing to coat. Cover and refrigerate for 2 hours, turning once.

2 Place the onion wedges and tomato halves on a baking tray covered with baking paper. Sprinkle with the sugar and drizzle with the balsamic vinegar. Bake for 40 minutes.

3 Heat a chargrill pan and lightly spray with oil. Remove the chicken from the marinade and cook for 4–5 minutes on each side, or until cooked through. Slice the chicken and serve with the snow pea sprouts, tomato halves and onion wedges.

NUTRITION PER SERVE
Protein 25 g; Fat 2.5 g; Carbohydrate 30 g; Dietary Fibre 3 g; Cholesterol 50 mg; 990 kJ (235 cal)

Drizzle the balsamic vinegar over the onion wedges and tomato halves.

Cook the marinated chicken in a hot, lightly oiled chargrill pan.

Pour the marinade over the chicken and toss to coat thoroughly.

SWEET CHILLI CHICKEN

Preparation time: 15 minutes +
2 hours marinating
Total cooking time: 20 minutes
Serves 6

1 kg (2 lb) chicken thigh fillets
2 tablespoons lime juice
½ cup (125 ml/4 fl oz) sweet chilli
    sauce
¼ cup (60 ml/2 fl oz) kecap manis
    (see NOTE)

1 Trim any excess fat from the chicken thigh fillets and cut them in half. Transfer to a shallow non-metal dish.

2 Place the lime juice, sweet chilli sauce and kecap manis in a bowl and whisk to combine.

3 Pour the marinade over the chicken, cover and refrigerate for 2 hours.

4 Chargrill for 10–15 minutes, turning once, or until the chicken is tender and cooked through and the marinade has caramelized.

NUTRITION PER SERVE
Protein 35 g; Fat 4.5 g; Carbohydrate 4 g; Dietary Fibre 1 g; Cholesterol 85 mg; 880 kJ (210 cal)

NOTE: Kecap manis (ketjap manis) is a thick Indonesian sauce, similar to—but sweeter than—soy sauce, and is generally flavoured with garlic and star anise. Store in a cool, dry place and refrigerate after opening. If not available, use soy sauce sweetened with a little soft brown sugar.

Trim the excess fat from the thigh fillets, and cut them in half.

To make the marinade, whisk together the lime juice, sweet chilli sauce and kecap manis.

Pour the marinade over the chicken, then cover and refrigerate.

CHICKEN MARYLANDS WITH REDCURRANT SAUCE

Preparation time: 25 minutes
  + 2 hours marinating
Total cooking time: 30 minutes
Serves 4

4 chicken marylands (drumstick and thigh)
½ cup (125 ml/4 fl oz) red wine
1 tablespoon finely chopped fresh thyme
1 tablespoon finely chopped rosemary
1 tablespoon olive oil
½ cup (160 g/5½ oz) redcurrant jelly

1 Trim the chicken of excess fat and sinew. Place the chicken in a shallow non-metal dish. Combine the wine, thyme and rosemary in a small jug and pour over the chicken. Refrigerate, covered, for 2 hours or overnight, turning the chicken occasionally.
2 Preheat the oven to moderately hot 200°C (400°F/Gas 6). Drain the chicken and reserve the marinade. Place the chicken in a baking dish and brush with the oil. Bake for 30 minutes, or until tender, turning occasionally.
3 Combine the reserved marinade and redcurrant jelly in a small pan. Stir over medium heat until smooth, then bring to the boil. Reduce the heat and simmer, uncovered, for 15 minutes. Pour over the chicken and serve with rosemary and some berries.

NUTRITION PER SERVE
Protein 37 g; Fat 8.5 g; Carbohydrate 5 g; Dietary Fibre 0 g; Cholesterol 00 mg; 1112 kJ (266 cal)

Pour the wine, thyme and rosemary mixture over the chicken marylands.

Place the marinated chicken in a baking dish and brush with the oil.

Combine the reserved marinade and redcurrant jelly in a small pan and stir until smooth.

CHICKEN WITH FIGS AND LEMON

Preparation time: 20 minutes
Total cooking time: 35 minutes
Serves 4

4 large chicken thigh cutlets
1 lemon
½ teaspoon ground ginger
½ teaspoon garam masala
1 tablespoon soy sauce
2 tablespoons olive oil
½ cup (125 ml/4 fl oz) sweet white wine
1 tablespoon ginger wine
¼ cup (60 ml/2 fl oz) lemon juice
2 chicken stock cubes, crumbled
6 plump dried figs, halved
2 teaspoons thinly sliced glacé ginger

1 Trim the chicken of fat and sinew. Preheat the oven to moderate 180°C (350°F/Gas 4). Remove the lemon rind with a vegetable peeler and slice the rind into long thin strips. Place the rind in a small pan with a little water. Boil for 2 minutes, then drain and set aside.
2 Combine the ginger, garam masala and soy sauce. Rub the mixture all over the chicken pieces.
3 Heat the oil in a heavy-based pan. Cook the chicken over medium heat for 5 minutes on each side, or until well browned but not cooked through. Drain the chicken on paper towels. Transfer to a shallow ovenproof dish.
4 Add the white wine, ginger wine, juice, stock cubes and any remaining marinade to the same pan. Bring to the boil. Add the figs and glacé ginger. Remove from the heat and spoon over the chicken. Bake for 20 minutes, or until the chicken is tender, turning once. Serve with the lemon rind.

NUTRITION PER SERVE
Protein 20 g; Fat 12 g; Carbohydrate 7 g; Dietary Fibre 2 g; Cholesterol 44 mg; 1018 kJ (245 cal)

Remove the rind from the lemon and cut it into long thin strips.

Place the grilled chicken cutlets in a shallow ovenproof dish.

Add the fig halves and glacé ginger to the boiling wine mixture.

CHICKEN WITH BAKED EGGPLANT AND TOMATO

Preparation time: 30 minutes
Total cooking time: 1 hour 30 minutes
Serves 4

1 red capsicum
1 eggplant
3 tomatoes, cut into quarters
200 g (6½ oz) large button
   mushrooms, halved
1 onion, cut into thin wedges
cooking oil spray
1½ tablespoons tomato paste
½ cup (125 ml/4 fl oz) chicken stock
¼ cup (60 ml/2 fl oz) white wine

2 lean slices bacon
4 chicken breast fillets
4 small fresh rosemary sprigs

1 Preheat the oven to moderately hot 200°C (400°F/Gas 6). Cut the capsicum and eggplant into bite-sized pieces and combine with the tomato, mushrooms and onion in a baking dish. Spray with oil and bake for 1 hour, or until starting to brown and soften, stirring once.
2 Pour the combined tomato paste, stock and wine into the dish and bake for 10 minutes, or until thickened.
3 Meanwhile, discard the fat and rind from the bacon and cut in half. Wrap a strip of bacon around each chicken breast and secure it underneath with a toothpick. Poke a sprig of fresh rosemary underneath the bacon. Pan-fry in a lightly oiled, non-stick frying pan over medium heat until golden on both sides. Cover and cook for 10–15 minutes, or until the chicken is tender and cooked through. Remove the toothpicks. Serve the chicken on the vegetable mixture, surrounded with the sauce.

NUTRITION PER SERVE
Protein 35 g; Fat 4.5 g; Carbohydrate 8 g;
Dietary Fibre 5 g; Cholesterol 70 mg;
965 kJ (230 cal)

Spray the vegetables lightly with the cooking oil before baking.

When the vegetables have softened, add the combined tomato paste, stock and wine.

Wrap a strip of bacon around the chicken and secure underneath with a toothpick.

ORANGE ROASTED CHICKENS

Preparation time: 15 minutes +
  3 hours marinating
Total cooking time: 40 minutes
Serves 8

2 x 800 g (1 lb 10 oz) chickens
100 g (3½ oz) butter, softened
2 cloves garlic, crushed
1 tablespoon finely grated orange
  rind
½ cup (60 ml/2 fl oz) orange
  juice

1 Preheat the oven to hot 220°C (425°F/Gas 7). Using kitchen scissors, cut the chickens in half through the backbone and breastbone. Pat dry with paper towels and wipe the inside.
2 Combine the butter, garlic and orange rind and beat well. Gently loosen the skin of the chickens by sliding your fingers between the flesh and the skin. Push the orange butter under the skin as evenly as possible. Put the chickens onto a ceramic dish and pour on the orange juice. Cover and refrigerate for 3 hours, or preferably overnight.
3 Drain the chicken pieces well and arrange cut-side down on roasting racks inside two baking dishes. Pour 2 tablespoons of water into each baking dish.
4 Roast for 30–40 minutes, or until the chickens are golden brown. Cover with foil and allow to rest for 15 minutes. Cut into quarters to serve.

NUTRITION PER SERVE
Protein 30 g; Fat 15 g; Carbohydrate 1 g; Dietary Fibre 0 g; Cholesterol 95 mg; 990 kJ (235 cal)

NOTE: If you can, use freshly squeezed orange juice.

Cut the chickens in half through the backbone and breastbone.

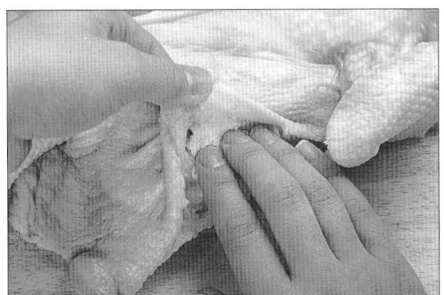

Loosen the skin of the chickens and spread the orange butter underneath.

Put the chicken pieces cut-side down on roasting racks inside the baking dishes.

263

CHICKEN POT PIES WITH HERB SCONES

Preparation time: 25 minutes
Total cooking time: 35 minutes
Serves 6

60 g (2 oz) butter
1 onion, chopped
⅓ cup (40 g/1¼ oz) plain flour
2⅔ cups (670 ml/22 fl oz) milk
1 cup (125 g/4 oz) grated Cheddar
2 teaspoons wholegrain mustard
2½ cups (450 g/14 oz) chopped
    cooked chicken
2 cups (200 g/6½ oz) frozen mixed
    vegetables

TOPPING
2 cups (250 g/8 oz) self-raising flour
15 g (½ oz) butter

1 cup (250 ml/8 fl oz) milk
2 tablespoons chopped fresh parsley
1 tablespoon milk, extra

1 Preheat the oven to hot 210°C (415°F/Gas 6–7). Lightly grease six 1 cup (250 ml/8 fl oz) individual dishes with oil or melted butter. Heat the butter in a large heavy-based pan. Add the onion and cook over medium heat until soft. Add the flour and stir over the heat for 1 minute, or until lightly golden and bubbling. Gradually add the milk, stirring constantly over the heat until the sauce boils and thickens. Remove from the heat. Stir in the Cheddar, mustard, chicken and vegetables. Spoon the mixture evenly into the prepared dishes.
2 To make the topping, place the flour in a bowl. Using your fingertips, rub the butter into the flour for 2 minutes,

or until the mixture is fine and crumbly. Make a well in the centre. Stir in the milk and parsley with a flat-bladed knife. Using a cutting action, stir until the mixture is soft and sticky. Turn onto a floured surface.
3 Gather the dough into a smooth ball and pat out to a 2.5 cm (1 inch) thickness. Cut rounds from the pastry with a 4.5 cm (1¾ inch) cutter. Re-roll the pastry cuttings to cut more rounds. Place three rounds on top of each chicken pot. Brush the tops with the extra milk. Bake for 25 minutes, or until the scones are browned and cooked and the chicken mixture is heated through.

NUTRITION PER SERVE
Protein 17 g; Fat 30 g; Carbohydrate 14 g;
Dietary Fibre 0.5 g; Cholesterol 95 mg;
1656 kJ (396 cal)

Stir the cheese, mustard, chicken and vegetables into the milk mixture.

Stir the milk and parsley into the flour mixture using a flat-bladed knife.

Place three scone rounds on top of each of the chicken pots.

MUSTARD CHICKEN AND ASPARAGUS QUICHE

Preparation time: 25 minutes
  + 40 minutes refrigeration
Total cooking time: 1 hour 20 minutes
Serves 8

2 cups (250 g/8 oz) plain flour
100 g (3½ oz) cold butter, chopped
1 egg yolk

FILLING
150 g (5 oz) asparagus, chopped
25 g (¾ oz) butter
1 onion, chopped
¼ cup (60 g/2 oz) wholegrain mustard
200 g (6½ oz) soft cream cheese
½ cup (125 ml/4 fl oz) cream
3 eggs, lightly beaten
200 g (6½ oz) cooked chicken, chopped
½ teaspoon black pepper

1 Process the flour and butter until crumbly. Add the egg yolk and ¼ cup (60 ml/2 fl oz) of water. Process in short bursts until the mixture comes together. Add a little extra water if needed. Turn onto a floured surface and gather into a ball. Cover with plastic wrap and chill for 30 minutes. Grease a deep loose-based flan tin measuring 19 cm (7½ inches) across the base.
2 Roll out the pastry and line the tin. Trim off any excess with a sharp knife. Place the flan tin on a baking tray and chill for 10 minutes. Preheat the oven to moderately hot 200°C (400°F/Gas 6). Cover the pastry with baking paper and fill evenly with baking beads. Bake for 10 minutes. Remove the paper and beads and bake for about 10 minutes, or until the pastry is lightly browned and dry.

Cool. Reduce the oven to moderate 180°C (350°F/Gas 4).
3 To make the filling, boil or steam the asparagus until tender. Drain and pat dry with paper towels. Heat the butter in a pan and cook the onion until translucent. Remove from the heat and add the mustard and cream cheese, stirring until the cheese has melted. Cool. Add the cream, eggs, chicken and asparagus and mix well.

4 Spoon the filling into the pastry shell and sprinkle with the pepper. Bake for 50 minutes to 1 hour, or until puffed and set. Cool for at least 15 minutes before cutting.

NUTRITION PER SERVE
Protein 15 g; Fat 30 g; Carbohydrate 25 g; Dietary Fibre 2 g; Cholesterol 190 mg; 1860 kJ (440 cal)

When the flour and butter mixture is crumbly, add the egg yolk.

Dry the asparagus well to prevent excess moisture from softening the quiche.

Add the mustard and cream cheese and stir until the cheese has melted.

CHICKEN WITH CORIANDER CHUTNEY AND SPICED EGGPLANT

**Preparation time: 1 hour 10 minutes
+ overnight refrigeration +
30 minutes soaking
Total cooking time: 1 hour 10 minutes
Serves 4**

1 cup (250 g/8 oz) low-fat natural
    yoghurt
1 tablespoon lemon juice
½ onion, roughly chopped
2 cloves garlic, finely chopped
2 teaspoons grated fresh ginger
½ teaspoon ground cumin
750 g (1½ lb) chicken thighs, trimmed
    of fat, cut into large cubes
4 pieces naan bread
low-fat natural yoghurt, to serve

SPICED EGGPLANT
1 large eggplant
1 tablespoon oil
1 onion, finely chopped
3 teaspoons finely chopped fresh
    ginger
2 cloves garlic, crushed
½ teaspoon ground turmeric
1 teaspoon ground cumin
1 tomato, finely diced
2 teaspoons lemon juice

CORIANDER CHUTNEY
¼ cup (60 ml/2 fl oz) lemon juice
2 cups (100 g/3½ oz) roughly chopped
    fresh coriander leaves and stems
½ onion, finely chopped
1 tablespoon finely chopped fresh
    ginger
½ jalapeño pepper, seeded, diced
1 teaspoon sugar

1 Combine the yoghurt, lemon juice, onion, garlic, ginger and cumin in a large non-metallic bowl, add the chicken and toss. Cover and refrigerate overnight.

2 Preheat the oven to very hot 240°C (475°F/Gas 9). Soak eight wooden skewers in water for 30 minutes. To make the spiced eggplant, prick the eggplant a few times, put on a baking tray and bake for 35–40 minutes, or until soft and wrinkled. Cool. Reduce the oven to moderately hot 200°C (400°F/Gas 6).

3 To make the chutney, put the lemon juice, coriander and 3 tablespoons water in a food processor and process until smooth. Add the remaining ingredients and season.

4 Cut the eggplant in half, scoop out the flesh and coarsely chop. Heat the oil in a frying pan over medium heat. Add the onion and cook for 5 minutes, or until soft. Add the ginger and garlic and cook for 2 minutes, or until fragrant. Add the spices and cook for 1 minute, then add the tomato and ¼ cup (60 ml/2 fl oz) water and simmer for 5 minutes, or until the tomato is soft and the mixture thick. Stir in the eggplant and lemon juice and season. Cook for 2 minutes, then remove from the heat and keep warm.

5 Thread the chicken onto skewers and chargrill over medium heat for 4–6 minutes each side, or until tender.

6 Heat the naan in the oven for 5 minutes. Put on a plate and spread some eggplant in the centre. Lay 2 chicken skewers on top and drizzle with chutney and yoghurt.

NUTRITION PER SERVE
Protein 50 g; Fat 15 g; Carbohydrate 26 g;
Dietary Fibre 5.5 g; Cholesterol 105 mg;
1956 kJ (467 cal)

Combine the marinade ingredients in a bowl and add the chicken.

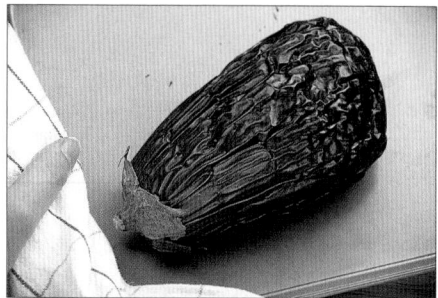
Roast the eggplant on a baking tray until very soft and wrinkled.

Process the coriander, lemon juice and water until you have a smooth paste.

Cut the eggplant in half, scoop out the flesh and coarsely chop.

Simmer until the tomato has softened and the mixture has thickened.

Chargrill the chicken skewers until they are tender and cooked through.

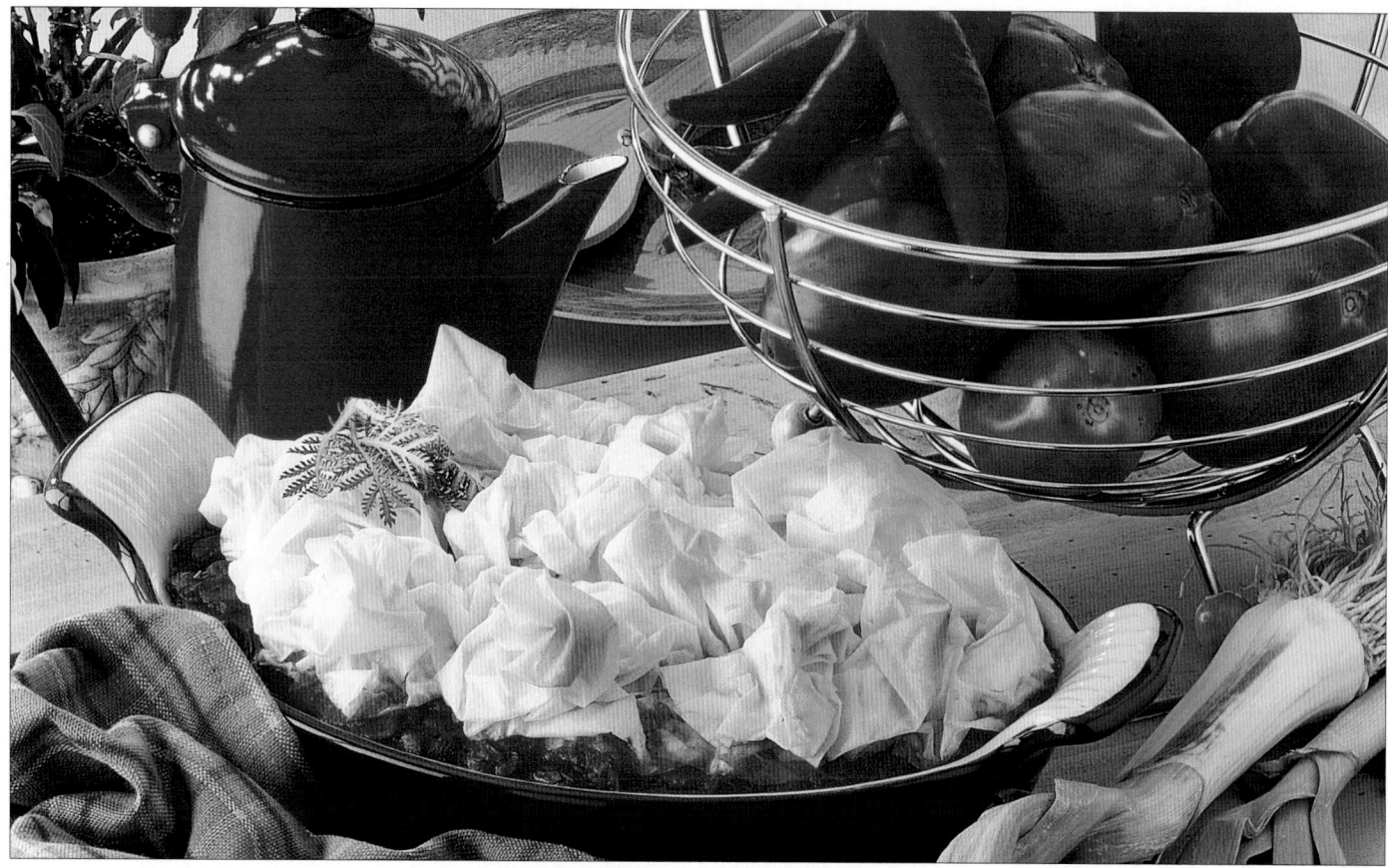

CHILLI CHICKEN PIE

Preparation time: 45 minutes
Total cooking time: 1 hour 20 minutes
Serves 4–6

2 tablespoons olive oil
1 onion, chopped
750 g (1½ lb) chicken breast fillets,
    chopped
3 cloves garlic, crushed
1 teaspoon chilli powder
2 teaspoons cumin seeds
1 tablespoon plain flour
2 x 410 g (13 oz) cans chopped
    tomatoes
1 tablespoon soft brown sugar

1 red capsicum, thinly sliced
375 g (12 oz) can red kidney beans,
    rinsed and drained
15 sheets filo pastry
100 g (3½ oz) butter, melted

1 Heat half the oil in a large frying pan and cook the onion until softened and golden. Remove from the pan, add the remaining oil and brown the chicken over high heat.
2 Stir in the garlic, chilli powder and cumin seeds and cook for 1 minute. Return the onion to the pan, stir in the flour and cook for 30 seconds. Stir in the chopped tomatoes.
3 Add the sugar and capsicum and simmer over low heat for 40 minutes,

or until reduced and thickened. Increase the heat and, stirring constantly to prevent burning, add the kidney beans. Allow to cool, then spoon into a 20 x 28 cm (8 x 11 inch) casserole dish. Preheat the oven to moderate 180°C (350°F/Gas 4).
4 Cut the filo sheets in half, brush with the melted butter and scrunch up. Place on top of the filling, to cover it completely. Brush with the remaining butter and bake for 25–30 minutes, or until golden.

NUTRITION PER SERVE (6)
Protein 40 g; Fat 25 g; Carbohydrate 35 g;
Dietary Fibre 7 g; Cholesterol 105 mg;
2175 kJ (515 cal)

Stir the garlic, chilli powder and cumin seeds into the browned chicken.

Add the kidney beans to the filling mixture, stirring constantly to prevent the mixture from burning.

Scrunch up the sheets of filo pastry and arrange them on top of the filling.

SPICY CHICKEN TARTS

Preparation time: 50 minutes
Total cooking time: 45 minutes
Makes 8

2 large onions, finely chopped
400 g (13 oz) eggplant, cubed
2 cloves garlic, crushed
2 x 410 g (13 oz) cans chopped
    tomatoes
1 tablespoon tomato paste
3 teaspoons soft brown sugar
1 tablespoon red wine vinegar
¼ cup (15 g/½ oz) chopped fresh
    parsley
4 sheets ready-rolled shortcrust pastry

2 teaspoons ground cumin seeds
2 teaspoons ground coriander
1 teaspoon paprika
400 g (13 oz) chicken breast fillets
oil, for cooking
sour cream, to serve
fresh coriander leaves, to serve

1 Fry the onion in a little oil until golden. Add the eggplant and garlic and cook for a few minutes. Stir in the tomato, tomato paste, sugar and vinegar. Bring to the boil, then reduce the heat, cover and simmer for 20 minutes. Uncover and simmer for 10 minutes, or until thick. Add the parsley and season. Preheat the oven to moderately hot 190°C (375°F/Gas 5).

2 Grease 8 small pie tins measuring 7.5 cm (3 inches) across the base, line with the pastry and decorate the edges. Prick the bases using a fork. Bake for 15 minutes, or until golden.
3 Mix the cumin, coriander and paprika together. Coat the chicken pieces in the spices. Heat some oil in a frying pan and cook the chicken until brown and cooked through. Cut diagonally. Fill the pie shells with the eggplant mixture and add the chicken, sour cream and coriander leaves.

NUTRITION PER SERVE
Protein 20 g; Fat 35 g; Carbohydrate 45 g;
Dietary Fibre 5 g; Cholesterol 65 mg;
2315 kJ (550 cal)

Simmer the tomato mixture to reduce the liquid, then add the parsley.

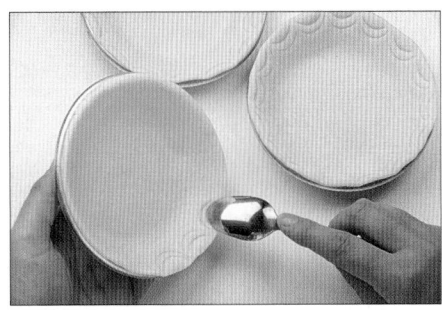
Use a spoon to decorate the edge of the uncooked pastry cases.

Coat the chicken fillets in the combined cumin, coriander and papriika.

CHICKEN BURGER WITH TARRAGON MAYONNAISE

Preparation time: 25 minutes
Total cooking time: 20 minutes
Serves 6

1 kg (2 lb) chicken mince
1 small onion, finely chopped
2 teaspoons lemon rind
2 tablespoons sour cream
1 cup (80 g/2¾ oz) fresh breadcrumbs
6 onion bread rolls

TARRAGON MAYONNAISE
1 egg yolk
1 tablespoon tarragon vinegar
½ teaspoon French mustard

1 cup (250 ml/8 fl oz) olive oil

1 Place the chicken mince in a mixing bowl. Add the onion, lemon rind, sour cream and breadcrumbs. Using your hands, mix until thoroughly combined. Divide the mixture into 6 equal portions and shape into 1.5 cm (⅝ inch) thick patties.
2 Preheat a barbecue grill or flatplate to high. Lightly oil the hot barbecue. Cook the patties for 7 minutes each side, turning once. Serve the patties on the onion rolls with the mayonnaise.
3 To make the tarragon mayonnaise, place the egg yolk, half the vinegar and the mustard in a small mixing bowl. Whisk together for 1 minute, or

until light and creamy. Add the oil about 1 teaspoon at a time, whisking constantly until the mixture thickens. Increase the flow of oil to a thin stream and continue whisking until all of the oil has been incorporated. Stir in the remaining vinegar and season with salt and white pepper.

NUTRITION PER SERVE
Protein 40 g; Fat 47 g; Carbohydrate 11 g;
Dietary Fibre 1 g; Cholesterol 122 mg;
2628 kJ (628 cal)

HINT: The mayonnaise can also be made in a food processor. Add the oil in a thin stream, with the motor constantly running, until the mixture thickens and turns creamy.

Mix the chicken mince, onion, lemon rind, sour cream and breadcrumbs together.

Cook the patties for 7 minutes each side, turning once, or until they are cooked through.

Once the mayonnaise mixture has thickened, add the oil in a steady stream.

SPICY GARLIC CHICKEN

Preparation time: 30 minutes
Total cooking time: 1 hour
Serves 4–6

1.4 kg (2 lb 13 oz) chicken
1 small bunch coriander
2 tablespoons olive oil
4 cloves garlic, crushed
2 red onions, thinly sliced
1 large red capsicum, cut into squares
1 teaspoon ground ginger
1 teaspoon chilli powder
1 teaspoon caraway seeds, crushed
1 teaspoon ground turmeric
2 teaspoons ground coriander
2 teaspoons ground cumin
½ cup (60 g/2 oz) raisins
½ cup (90 g/3 oz) black olives
1 teaspoon finely grated lemon rind

1 Trim the chicken of excess fat and sinew. Cut the chicken into 12 serving pieces. Finely chop the coriander roots, reserving the leaves.
2 Heat the oil in a large heavy-based pan. Add the garlic, onion, capsicum, ginger, chilli powder, caraway seeds, turmeric, coriander, cumin and coriander roots. Cook over medium heat for 10 minutes.
3 Add the chicken pieces and stir until combined. Add 1½ cups (375 ml/12 fl oz) water and bring to the boil. Reduce the heat and simmer for 45 minutes, or until the chicken is tender and cooked through.
4 Add the raisins, black olives and lemon rind and simmer for a further 5 minutes. Serve with pasta or rice. May be served sprinkled with the reserved coriander leaves.

NUTRITION PER SERVE
Protein 33 g; Fat 13 g; Carbohydrate 13 g;
Dietary Fibre 2 g; Cholesterol 105 mg;
1236 kJ (295 cal)

VARIATION: Chicken pieces may be used instead of whole chicken.

Wash the coriander and finely chop the roots, reserving the leaves.

Heat the oil in a large pan and add the garlic, onion, capsicum and spices.

Add the chicken pieces to the mixture and stir until combined.

Add the raisins, olives and lemon rind to the chicken mixture.

SMOKED FIVE-SPICE CHICKEN

**Preparation time: 30 minutes
+ overnight marinating
Total cooking time: 35 minutes
Serves 6**

1 x 1.7 kg (3½ lb) chicken
¼ cup (60 ml/2 fl oz) soy sauce
1 tablespoon finely grated fresh ginger
2 pieces dried mandarin or tangerine
    peel
1 star anise
¼ teaspoon five-spice powder
¼ cup (45 g/1½ oz) soft brown sugar

1 Wash the chicken in cold water. Pat dry with paper towels. Discard any large deposits of fat from inside the chicken. Place the chicken in a large bowl with the soy sauce and grated ginger. Cover and refrigerate for several hours or overnight, turning occasionally.
2 Place a small rack in the base of a pan large enough to hold the chicken. Add water to this level. Place the chicken on the rack and bring the water to the boil. Cover tightly, reduce the heat and steam for 15 minutes. Turn off the heat and allow to stand, covered, for another 15 minutes. Transfer the chicken to a bowl.

3 Wash the pan and line with three or four large pieces of aluminium foil. Pound the dried peel and star anise in a mortar and pestle or crush with a rolling pin until the pieces are the size of coarse breadcrumbs. Add the five-spice powder and sugar, and spread over the foil.
4 Replace the rack in the pan and place the chicken on it. Place the pan over medium heat and, when the spice mixture starts smoking, cover tightly. Reduce the heat to low and smoke the chicken for 20 minutes. Test for doneness by piercing the thigh with a skewer. The juices should run clear. Remove chicken from pan and allow to cool before jointing it or chopping it Chinese-style.

NUTRITION PER SERVE
Protein 46 g; Fat 4.5 g; Carbohydrate 10 g;
Dietary Fibre 0 g; Cholesterol 100 mg;
1126 kJ (270 cal)

VARIATION: If you wish to save on cooking time, try the same method using half chicken-breast fillets. Six fillets will take 7 minutes to steam; smoking will take 8 minutes each side. Overnight marinating is not necessary in this instance.

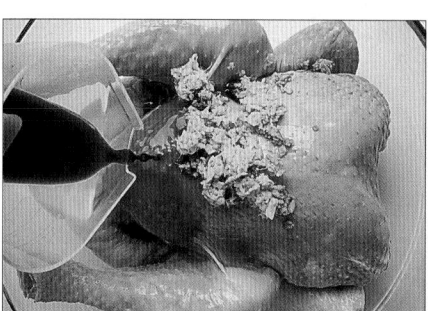

Place the chicken in a large bowl with the soy sauce and grated ginger.

Steam the chicken on a rack in a pan with water in the base.

Pound the dried peel with the star anise in a mortar and pestle.

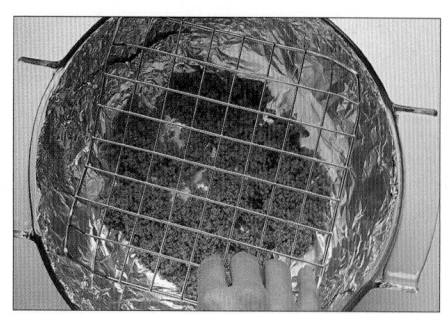

Line the pan with foil and add the combined peel, star anise, five-spice powder and sugar.

Marinades & Glazes

LIME AND GINGER GLAZE

In a small pan combine ½ cup (160 g/5½ oz) lime marmalade, ¼ cup (60 ml/2 fl oz) lime juice, 2 tablespoons sherry, 2 tablespoons soft brown sugar and 2 teaspoons finely grated fresh ginger. Stir over low heat until it reaches a liquid consistency. Pour over 1 kg (2 lb) chicken wings and toss well to combine. Cover and refrigerate for 2 hours or overnight. Cook in a moderately hot 190°C (375°F/Gas 5) oven for 40 minutes, or until cooked through. Makes 1 cup (250 ml/8 fl oz).

HONEY SOY MARINADE

Combine ¼ cup (90 g/3 oz) honey, ¼ cup (60 ml/2 fl oz) soy sauce, 1 crushed garlic clove, 2 tablespoons sake and ½ teaspoon Chinese five-spice powder. Remove excess fat from 500 g (1 lb) chicken thigh fillets. Pour on the marinade and toss well. Cover and refrigerate for 2 hours or overnight. Cook on a hot barbecue for 10 minutes, turning once, or until cooked through. Makes ⅔ cup (170 ml/5½ fl oz).

REDCURRANT GLAZE

In a small saucepan combine a 340 g (11 oz) jar redcurrant jelly, 2 tablespoons lemon juice, 2 tablespoons brandy and 1 teaspoon chopped fresh thyme, and stir over low heat until it reaches a liquid consistency. Pour the marinade over 500 g (1 lb) chicken breast fillets and toss well to combine. Cover and refrigerate for 2 hours or overnight. Cook in a moderately hot 190°C (375°F/Gas 5) oven for 20 minutes, or until cooked through. Makes 1 cup (250 ml/8 fl oz).

TANDOORI MARINADE

Soak 8 bamboo skewers in water for 30 minutes to prevent burning. Combine 2 tablespoons tandoori paste, 1 cup (250 g/8 oz) plain yoghurt and 1 tablespoon lime juice. Cut 500 g (1 lb) tenderloins in half lengthwise and thread onto skewers. Pour over the marinade and toss well to combine. Cover and refrigerate for 1–2 hours. Place under a hot grill and cook, basting with the marinade, until cooked through. Makes 1¼ cups (315 ml/10 fl oz).

MEXICAN MARINADE

Combine 440 g (14 oz) bottled taco sauce, 2 tablespoons lime juice and 2 tablespoons chopped fresh coriander leaves. Pour the marinade over 1 kg (2 lb) scored chicken drumsticks and toss well to combine. Cover and refrigerate for 2 hours or overnight. Cook in a moderately hot 190°C (375°F/Gas 5) oven for 30 minutes, or until cooked through. Makes 1¼ cups (315 ml/10 fl oz).

THAI MARINADE

Combine 2 tablespoons fish sauce, 2 tablespoons lime juice, 1 crushed garlic clove, 1 finely chopped lemon grass stem, 2 teaspoons soft brown sugar, ½ cup (125 g/4 oz) coconut cream and 2 tablespoons chopped fresh coriander leaves. Pour the marinade over 1 kg (2 lb) chicken drumettes and toss well to combine. Cover and refrigerate for 2 hours or overnight. Cook in a moderately hot 190°C (375°F/Gas 5) oven for 30 minutes, or until cooked through. Makes ¾ cup (185 ml/6 fl oz).

Clockwise from top left: Lime and ginger glaze; Tandoori marinade; Mexican marinade; Thai marinade; Redcurrant glaze; Honey soy marinade.

CHICKEN MOLE

Preparation time: 25 minutes
Total cooking time: 1 hour
Serves 4

8 chicken drumsticks
plain flour, for dusting
cooking oil spray
1 large onion, finely chopped
2 cloves garlic, finely chopped
1 teaspoon ground cumin
1 teaspoon chilli powder
2 teaspoons cocoa powder
440 g (14 oz) can tomatoes, roughly
    chopped
440 ml (14 fl oz) tomato purée

1 cup (250 ml/8 fl oz) chicken stock
toasted almonds, to garnish
chopped fresh parsley, to garnish

1 Remove and discard the chicken skin. Wipe the chicken with paper towels and lightly dust with flour. Spray a large, deep, non-stick pan with oil. Cook the chicken for 8 minutes over high heat, turning until golden brown. Remove and set aside.
2 Add the onion, garlic, cumin, chilli powder, cocoa, 1 teaspoon salt, ½ teaspoon black pepper and ¼ cup (60 ml/2 fl oz) water to the pan and cook for 5 minutes, or until softened.
3 Stir in the tomato, tomato purée and chicken stock. Bring to the boil, then add the chicken drumsticks, cover and simmer for 45 minutes, or until tender. Uncover and simmer for 5 minutes, until the mixture is thick. Garnish with the almonds and parsley. Delicious with kidney beans.

NUTRITION PER SERVE
Protein 25 g; Fat 7 g; Carbohydrate 10 g;
Dietary Fibre 4 g; Cholesterol 100 mg;
910 kJ (220 cal)

NOTE: This is a traditional Mexican dish, usually flavoured with a special type of dark chocolate rather than cocoa powder.

Pull the skin off the chicken drumsticks, then wipe the chicken with paper towels.

Turn the chicken until brown on all sides, then remove from the pan.

Stir in the onion, garlic, cumin, chilli powder, cocoa, salt, pepper and water.

MOROCCAN CHICKEN

Preparation time: 20 minutes +
  2 hours marinating
Total cooking time: 1 hour 25 minutes
Serves 4

8 large chicken drumsticks
3 cloves garlic, crushed
1 teaspoon grated fresh ginger
1 teaspoon ground turmeric
2 teaspoons ground cumin
1 teaspoon ground cardamom
1 teaspoon finely grated lemon rind
2 tablespoons oil
1 onion, sliced
2 cups (500 ml/16 fl oz) chicken stock

6 pitted dates, chopped
⅓ cup (20 g/¾ oz) shredded coconut

1 Trim the chicken of excess fat and sinew. Place the chicken in a large bowl. Combine the garlic, ginger, turmeric, cumin, cardamom and rind in a small bowl. Add to the chicken and stir to completely coat. Cover and marinate for 2 hours.
2 Preheat the oven to moderate 180°C (350°F/Gas 4). Heat the oil in a large heavy-based frying pan. Cook the chicken quickly over medium heat until well browned. Drain on paper towels. Place the chicken in an ovenproof casserole dish.
3 Add the onion to the pan and

cook, stirring, for 5 minutes, or until soft. Add the cooked onion, chicken stock, dates and shredded coconut to the casserole dish. Cover and bake for 1 hour 15 minutes, or until the chicken is tender, stirring occasionally.

NUTRITION PER SERVE
Protein 47 g; Fat 18 g; Carbohydrate 9 g;
Dietary Fibre 2.8 g; Cholesterol 100 mg;
1622 kJ (388 cal)

NOTE: The chicken may be left to marinate overnight in the refrigerator.

VARIATION: Dried apricots or prunes are great alteratives to dates.

Add the combined garlic, ginger, turmeric, cumin, cardamom and lemon rind to the chicken.

Drain the chicken on paper towels, then place in an ovenproof casserole dish.

Add the onion, stock, dates and coconut to the casserole dish.

CHICKEN IN RICH MUSHROOM SAUCE

Preparation time: 40 minutes
Total cooking time: 1 hour 10 minutes
Serves 4

1.4 kg (2 lb 13 oz) chicken
1 onion, sliced
2 whole cloves
8–10 peppercorns
1 teaspoon salt
90 g (3 oz) butter
500 g (1 lb) mushrooms, sliced
2 cloves garlic, crushed
2 tablespoons plain flour
½ cup (125 ml/4 fl oz) cream
1 tablespoon French mustard
1 cup (125 g/4 oz) grated Cheddar
½ cup (80 g/2¾ oz) stale breadcrumbs
¼ cup (15 g/½ oz) finely chopped fresh
    parsley

1 Preheat the oven to moderate 180°C (350°F/Gas 4). Trim the chicken of excess fat and sinew. Cut the chicken into 10 portions. Place the chicken, onion, cloves, peppercorns and salt into a 2 litre ovenproof dish with 3 cups (750 ml/24 fl oz) water. Bake for 30 minutes. Remove the chicken from the dish and strain the liquid into a bowl, reserving 2 cups (500 ml/ 16 fl oz). Melt half the butter in a frying pan. Add the mushrooms and cook until soft. Add the garlic and cook for 2 minutes. Transfer the mixture to a bowl.
2 Melt the remaining butter in the pan. Add the flour and cook for 2 minutes. Gradually add the reserved liquid and stir until smooth. Bring to the boil. Remove from the heat and stir in the cream, mustard and mushrooms.

3 Return the chicken and sauce to the dish. Sprinkle with the combined Cheddar, breadcrumbs and parsley. Bake for 30 minutes.

NUTRITION PER SERVE
Protein 75 g; Fat 60 g; Carbohydrate 16 g; Dietary Fibre 4.5 g; Cholesterol 275 mg; 3727 kJ (890 cal)

Place the chicken, onion, cloves, peppercorns and salt into an ovenproof dish.

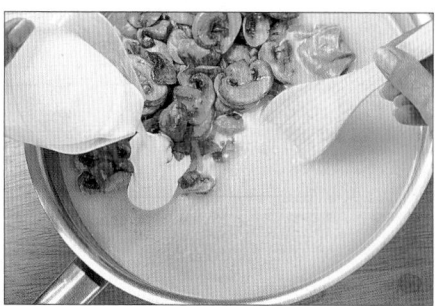

Remove the sauce from the heat and stir in the cream, mustard and mushrooms.

Sprinkle the chicken and sauce with the combined cheese, breadcrumbs and parsley.

CREAMY TOMATO AND CHICKEN STEW

Preparation time: 35 minutes
Total cooking time: 50 minutes
Serves 4–6

4 slices bacon
2 tablespoons oil
50 g (1¾ oz) butter
300 g (10 oz) small button
    mushrooms, halved
1.5 kg (3 lb) chicken pieces
2 onions, chopped
2 cloves garlic, crushed
400 g (13 oz) can tomatoes
1 cup (250 ml/8 fl oz) chicken stock
1 cup (250 ml/8 fl oz) cream
2 tablespoons chopped fresh parsley
2 tablespoons fresh lemon thyme
    leaves

1 Chop the bacon into large pieces. Place a large, heavy-based pan over medium heat. Brown the bacon, then remove and set aside on paper towels.
2 Heat half the oil and a third of the butter in the pan until foaming, then stir in the mushrooms and cook until softened and golden brown. Remove from the pan with a slotted spoon.
3 Add the remaining oil to the pan with a little more butter. When the oil is hot, brown the chicken pieces in batches over high heat until the skin is golden all over and a little crisp. Remove from the pan.
4 Heat the remaining butter in the pan. Add the onion and garlic and cook over medium-high heat for about 3 minutes, or until softened. Pour in the tomatoes, stock and cream. Return the bacon, mushrooms and chicken pieces to the pan and simmer over medium-low heat for 25 minutes. Stir in the herbs, season with salt and freshly ground pepper and simmer for another 5 minutes before serving.

NUTRITION PER SERVE (6)
Protein 70 g; Fat 40 g; Carbohydrate 7 g;
Dietary Fibre 3 g; Cholesterol 215 mg;
2650 kJ (630 cal)

When the oil and butter are foaming, add the mushrooms and cook until soft.

Brown the chicken pieces in batches over high heat until the skin is golden and crisp.

Add the tomatoes, stock and cream to the softened onion and garlic.

CHICKEN IN TANGY LIME MARMALADE SAUCE

Preparation time: 25 minutes
Total cooking time: 20 minutes
Serves 4

500 g (1 lb) chicken thigh fillets, cut into strips
5 cm (2 inch) piece ginger, cut into paper-thin slices
4 spring onions, thinly sliced
oil, for cooking
1 red capsicum, thinly sliced
1 tablespoon mirin
1 tablespoon lime marmalade
2 teaspoons grated lime rind
2 tablespoons lime juice

1 Put the chicken, ginger, spring onion and some ground black pepper in a dish. Toss well to combine.
2 Heat a wok until very hot, add 1 tablespoon of the oil and swirl it around to coat the side. Stir-fry the chicken mixture in three batches over high heat for about 3 minutes, or until it is golden brown and cooked through. Reheat the wok in between each batch, adding more oil when necessary. Remove all the chicken from the wok and set aside.

3 Reheat the wok, add the capsicum and stir-fry for 30 seconds. Add the mirin, marmalade, lime rind and juice, and season with salt and freshly ground black pepper. Cover and steam for 1 minute. Add the chicken and cook, uncovered, for 2 minutes, or until heated through.

NUTRITION PER SERVE
Protein 30 g; Fat 10 g; Carbohydrate 5.5 g;
Dietary Fibre 0 g; Cholesterol 60 mg;
1050 kJ (250 cal)

HINT: Choose young ginger with thin skin as it will be tender and easy to slice.

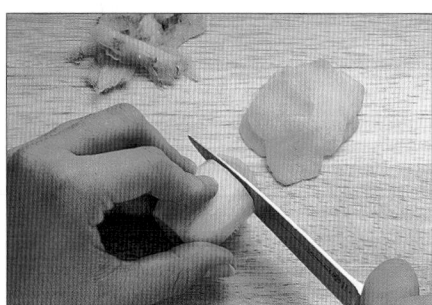

Peel the skin from the ginger, and cut it into paper-thin slices.

Remove the seeds and membrane from the capsicum, and cut it into thin slices.

Combine the chicken, ginger, spring onion and some black pepper.

CHICKEN WITH OLIVES AND SUN-DRIED TOMATOES

Preparation time: 20 minutes
Total cooking time: 15 minutes
Serves 4

olive oil, for cooking
600 g (1¼ lb) chicken breast fillets, cut diagonally into thin slices
1 red onion, thinly sliced
3 cloves garlic, finely chopped
2 tablespoons white wine vinegar
1 teaspoon sambal oelek
1 tablespoon lemon juice

12 Kalamata olives, pitted and quartered lengthways
¼ cup (40 g/1¼ oz) sun-dried tomatoes, cut into thin strips
¼ cup (15 g/½ oz) finely chopped fresh parsley
1 tablespoon shredded fresh basil

1 Heat a wok until very hot, add 2 teaspoons of the oil and swirl it around to coat the side. Stir-fry the chicken slices in two batches until browned and cooked through, adding more oil in between each batch. Remove all the chicken from the wok and keep warm.
2 Reheat the wok, add 1 tablespoon of the oil and stir-fry the onion until it is soft and golden. Add the garlic and cook for 1 minute. Return the warm chicken to the wok. Add the vinegar, sambal oelek and lemon juice, and toss well.
3 Stir in the olive pieces, sun-dried tomato, parsley and basil, and season with salt and ground black pepper. Heat through thoroughly.

NUTRITION PER SERVE
Protein 35 g; Fat 15 g; Carbohydrate 2.5 g; Dietary Fibre 1.5 g; Cholesterol 75 mg; 1420 kJ (335 cal)

Trim the fat from the chicken breast fillets, and cut into thin diagonal slices.

Sambal oelek is a paste made from salt, vinegar and chilli.

Drain the sun-dried tomatoes and cut them into thin strips.

CHICKEN AND HAM PIE

Preparation time: 40 minutes
Total cooking time: 1 hour
Serves 6

PASTRY
3 cups (375 g/12 oz) plain flour
180 g (6 oz) butter, chopped
⅓ cup (80 ml/2¾ fl oz) iced water

FILLING
1 kg (2 lb) chicken mince
½ teaspoon dried thyme
½ teaspoon dried sage
2 eggs, lightly beaten
3 spring onions, finely chopped
2 teaspoons finely grated lemon rind
1 teaspoon French mustard
⅓ cup (80 ml/2¾ fl oz) cream
100 g (3½ oz) sliced leg ham, finely
    chopped
1 egg, lightly beaten, extra

1 Preheat the oven to moderate 180°C (350°F/Gas 4). Process the flour and butter in a food processor for 20 seconds, or until the mixture is fine and crumbly. Add almost all the water and process for 20 seconds, or until mixture comes together. Add more water if needed. Turn onto a lightly floured surface and press together until smooth. Roll out two-thirds of the pastry and line a 20 cm (8 inch) springform tin, bringing the pastry up 2 cm (¾ inch) higher than the sides. Cover with plastic wrap. Set the pastry trimmings aside.

2 To make the filling, place the chicken, thyme, sage, eggs, spring onion, lemon rind, mustard and cream in a large bowl and stir with a wooden spoon until well combined. Place half the chicken mixture into the pastry-lined tin and smooth the surface. Top with the chopped ham, then the remaining chicken mixture.

3 Brush around the inside edge of the pastry with the egg. Roll out the remaining pastry and lay over the top of the mixture. Press the edges of the pastry together. Trim the pastry edges with a sharp knife.

4 Turn the pastry edges down. Use your index finger to make indentations around the inside edge. Decorate the top of the pie with pastry trimmings. Brush the top of the pie with beaten egg and bake for 1 hour, or until golden brown. Serve the pie warm or at room temperature.

NUTRITION PER SERVE
Protein 52 g; Fat 38 g; Carbohydrate 52 g;
Dietary Fibre 3 g; Cholesterol 277 mg;
3180 kJ (759 cal)

Process the flour and butter until the mixture is fine and crumbly.

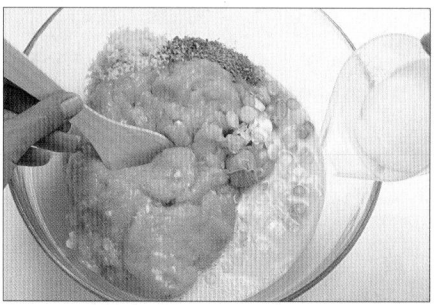
Stir the chicken, thyme, sage, eggs, spring onion, lemon rind, mustard and cream until combined.

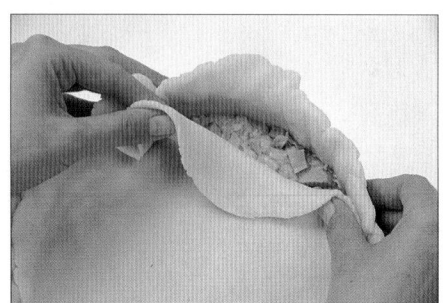
Lay the pastry over the top of the mixture and press the edges together.

Turn the pastry down and make indentations around the inside edge.

COQ AU VIN

Preparation time: 20 minutes
Total cooking time: 1 hour
Serves 6

2 fresh thyme sprigs
4 fresh parsley sprigs
2 bay leaves
2 kg (4 lb) chicken pieces
plain flour, seasoned with salt and
    freshly ground pepper
¼ cup (60 ml/2 fl oz) oil
4 thick bacon rashers, sliced
12 pickling onions
2 cloves garlic, crushed
2 tablespoons brandy
1½ cups (375 ml/12 fl oz) red wine

1½ cups (375 ml/12 fl oz) chicken
    stock
¼ cup (60 g/2 oz) tomato paste
250 g (8 oz) button mushrooms
fresh herbs, for sprinkling

1 To make the bouquet garni, wrap the thyme, parsley and bay leaves in a small square of muslin and tie well with string, or tie them between two 5 cm (2 inch) lengths of celery.

2 Toss the chicken in flour to coat, shaking off any excess. In a heavy-based pan, heat 2 tablespoons of oil and brown the chicken in batches over medium heat. Drain on paper towels.

3 Wipe the pan clean with paper towels and heat the remaining oil.

Add the bacon, onions and garlic and cook, stirring, until the onions are browned. Add the chicken, brandy, wine, stock, bouquet garni and tomato paste. Bring to the boil, reduce the heat and simmer, covered, for 30 minutes.

4 Stir in the mushrooms and simmer, uncovered, for 10 minutes, or until the chicken is tender and the sauce has thickened. Remove the bouquet garni, sprinkle with fresh herbs and serve with crusty French bread.

NUTRITION PER SERVE
Protein 80 g; Fat 20 g; Carbohydrate 7 g;
Dietary Fibre 2 g; Cholesterol 180 mg;
2420 kJ (580 cal)

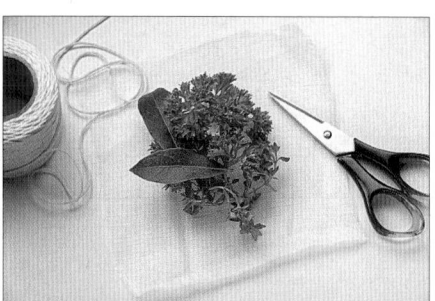

Wrap the thyme, parsley and bay leaves in a small square of muslin.

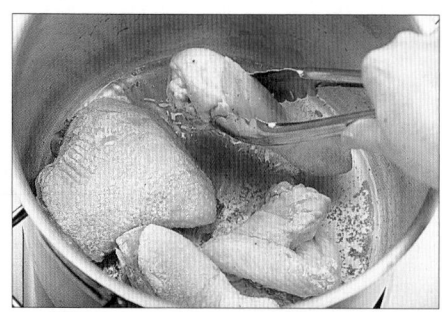

In batches, brown the chicken in the hot oil over medium heat.

Return the chicken to the pan with the liquids, bouquet garni and tomato paste.

CHICKEN DUMPLINGS IN GREEN CURRY

**Preparation time: 25 minutes
+ 2–3 hours refrigeration
Total cooking time: 35 minutes
Serves 3–4**

500 g (1 lb) chicken mince
3 spring onions, finely chopped
2 tablespoons small fresh coriander
leaves
1 stem lemon grass, white part only,
thinly sliced
¼ cup (60 ml/2 fl oz) fish sauce
1 teaspoon chicken stock powder
1½ cups (280 g/9 oz) cooked jasmine
rice

1 egg, plus 1 egg white
2 teaspoons oil
2 tablespoons green curry paste
2 x 400 ml (13 fl oz) cans coconut milk
4 fresh kaffir lime leaves
½ cup (15 g/½ oz) fresh basil leaves
1 tablespoon lemon juice

1 Mix together the chicken mince, spring onion, coriander leaves, lemon grass, 2 tablespoons of the fish sauce, stock powder and some pepper. Add the rice and mix well with your hands.

2 In a separate bowl, beat the egg and egg white with electric beaters until thick and creamy and then fold into the chicken mixture. With lightly floured hands, roll tablespoons of

the mixture into balls. Place on a tray, cover and refrigerate for 2–3 hours, or until firm.

3 Heat the oil in a large frying pan, add the green curry paste and stir over medium heat for 1 minute. Gradually stir in the coconut milk, then reduce the heat to simmer. Add the lime leaves and chicken dumplings to the sauce; cover and simmer for 25–30 minutes, stirring occasionally. Stir in the basil leaves, remaining fish sauce and lemon juice. Serve with steamed rice.

NUTRITION PER SERVE (4)
Protein 37 g; Fat 46 g; Carbohydrate 30 g;
Dietary Fibre 4.5 g; Cholesterol 110 mg;
2815 kJ (672 cal)

Beat the egg and egg white with electric beaters until thick and creamy.

Flour your hands and roll tablespoons of the mixture into balls.

When the sauce is simmering, add the lime leaves and chicken dumplings.

CHICKEN KEBABS WITH CURRY MAYONNAISE

Preparation time: 25 minutes
+ 30 minutes marinating
Total cooking time: 10 minutes
Serves 4

600 g (1¼ lb) chicken breast fillets
4 large spring onions
1 small green capsicum
1 small red capsicum
¼ cup (60 ml/2 fl oz) olive oil
1 teaspoon freshly ground black
    pepper
½ teaspoon ground turmeric
1½ teaspoons ground coriander

CURRY MAYONNAISE
¾ cup (185 g/6 oz) whole-egg
    mayonnaise
1 tablespoon hot curry powder
¼ cup (60 g/2 oz) sour cream
1 tablespoon sweet fruit or mango
    chutney, mashed
¼ cup (45 g/1½ oz) peeled, finely
    chopped cucumber
½ teaspoon toasted cumin seeds
1 tablespoon finely chopped fresh
    mint
1 teaspoon finely chopped fresh mint,
    extra

1 Preheat a barbecue grill or flatplate to high. Trim the chicken of excess fat and sinew. Cut the chicken into 3 cm (1¼ inch) cubes. Cut the spring onions into 3 cm (1¼ inch) lengths. Cut the red and green capsicum into 3 cm (1¼ inch) squares.
2 Thread the chicken, spring onion and capsicum onto skewers. Arrange the kebabs, side by side, in a shallow, non-metal dish. Combine the oil, pepper, turmeric and coriander in a jug. Pour over the kebabs and place in the refrigerator to marinate for 30 minutes.
3 To make the curry mayonnaise, combine the mayonnaise, curry powder, sour cream, chutney, cucumber, cumin seeds and mint in a bowl, and mix well. Spoon the mixture into a dish or jug for serving and sprinkle with the extra chopped mint.
4 Lightly oil the hot barbecue grill or flatplate. Cook the kebabs for 2–3 minutes each side, or until cooked through and tender. Serve with the curry mayonnaise.

NUTRITION PER SERVE
Protein 36 g; Fat 40 g; Carbohydrate 14 g; Dietary Fibre 2 g; Cholesterol 110 mg; 2316 kJ (553 cal)

Cut the chicken, spring onions and capsicums into even-sized pieces.

Pour the oil mixture over the chicken kebabs, and marinate for 30 minutes.

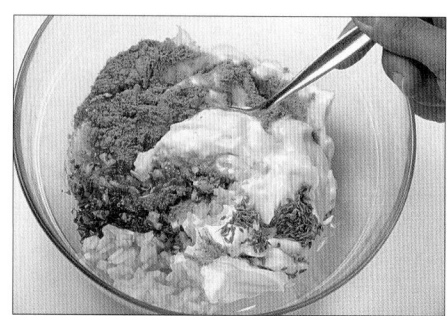
Combine the curry mayonnaise ingredients in a bowl and mix well.

FAMILY CHICKEN PIE

Preparation time: 40 minutes
+ 20 minutes chilling
Total cooking time: 1 hour
Serves 6

PASTRY
2 cups (250 g/8 oz) self-raising flour
125 g (4 oz) butter, chopped
1 egg

FILLING
1 barbecued chicken
30 g (1 oz) butter
1 onion, finely chopped
310 g (10 oz) can creamed corn
1¼ cups (315 ml/10 fl oz) cream

1 To make the pastry, process the
flour and butter in a food processor
for 15 seconds, or until the mixture is
fine and crumbly. Add the egg and
2–3 tablespoons water and process for
30 seconds, or until the mixture just
comes together. Turn onto a lightly
floured surface and gather together
into a smooth ball. Cover with plastic
wrap and refrigerate for 20 minutes.
2 Meanwhile, to make the filling,
remove the meat from the chicken
carcass and shred finely. Heat the
butter in a pan and cook the onion
over medium heat for 3 minutes. Add
the chicken, corn and cream. Bring to
the boil, then reduce the heat and
simmer for 10 minutes. Remove from
the heat and allow to cool slightly.
3 Preheat the oven to moderate 180°C
(350°F/Gas 4). Roll half the pastry
between two sheets of plastic wrap to
cover the base and side of a 23 cm
(9 inch) pie dish. Spoon the chicken
mixture into the pastry-lined dish.
4 Roll the remaining pastry to cover
the top of the pie. Brush with milk.
Press the edges together to seal. Trim
the edges with a sharp knife. Roll the
excess pastry into two long ropes and
twist together. Brush the pie edge with
a little milk and place the pastry rope
around the rim. Bake for 45 minutes.

NUTRITION PER SERVE
Protein 18 g; Fat 48 g; Carbohydrate 44 g;
Dietary Fibre 4 g; Cholesterol 212 mg;
2832 kJ (676 cal)

Add the egg and water to the flour and butter
mixture and process.

Add the chicken, corn and cream to the onion
and bring to the boil.

Roll half the pastry out between two sheets of
plastic wrap.

Brush the pie edge with a little milk, then place
the pastry rope around the rim of the pie.

CHICKEN AND LEEK COBBLER

Preparation time: 1 hour
Total cooking time: 1 hour
Serves 4–6

50 g (1¾ oz) butter
1 kg (2 lb) chicken breast fillets, cut into thick strips
1 large (225 g/7 oz) leek, trimmed and thinly sliced
1 celery stick, thinly sliced
1 tablespoon plain flour
1 cup (250 ml/8 fl oz) chicken stock
1 cup (250 ml/8 fl oz) cream
3 teaspoons Dijon mustard
3 teaspoons drained and rinsed green peppercorns

TOPPING
400 g (13 oz) potatoes, quartered
1⅓ cups (165 g/5½ oz) self-raising flour
½ teaspoon salt
¼ cup (30 g/1 oz) grated mature Cheddar
100 g (3½ oz) cold butter, chopped
1 egg yolk, lightly beaten, to glaze

1 Melt half the butter in a pan. When it begins to foam, add the chicken and cook until golden. Remove from the pan. Add the remaining butter and cook the leek and celery over medium heat until soft. Return the chicken to the pan.
2 Sprinkle the flour over the chicken and stir for about 1 minute. Remove from the heat and stir in the stock and cream. Mix well, making sure that there are no lumps. Return to the heat. Bring to the boil, then reduce the heat and simmer for about 20 minutes. Add the mustard and peppercorns and season to taste with salt and freshly ground black pepper. Transfer the mixture to a 1.25–1.5 litre capacity casserole dish and allow to cool. Preheat the oven to moderately hot 200°C (400°F/Gas 6).
3 To make the topping, cook the potato in a pan of boiling water until tender. Drain and mash until smooth. Place the flour and salt in a food processor and add the cheese and butter. Process in short bursts until the mixture forms crumbs. Add this mixture to the mashed potato and bring together with your hands to form a dough.
4 Roll out the dough on a floured surface, until it is 1 cm (½ inch) thick. Cut into circles with a 6 cm (2½ inch) diameter pastry cutter. Keep re-rolling the pastry scraps until all the dough is used. Carefully lift the circles up with your fingers, and arrange them so that they overlap on top of the cooled chicken and leek filling.
5 Brush the dough circles with the egg yolk and add a little milk if more glaze is needed. Bake for 30 minutes, or until the filling is heated through and the pastry is golden.

NUTRITION PER SERVE (6)
Protein 45 g; Fat 30 g; Carbohydrate 30 g; Dietary Fibre 4 g; Cholesterol 185 mg; 2405 kJ (570 cal)

NOTE: For a lower-fat variation, you can use a non-stick frying pan to cook the chicken in Step 1. You can also replace the mature Cheddar with low-fat Cheddar and reduce the amount of butter used in the filling.

Rinse the leeks thoroughly before cooking, and slice very thinly.

Remove the pan from the heat and stir in the chicken stock and cream.

Add the mustard and peppercorns to the simmering chicken and leek mixture.

Bring together the crumb mixture and mashed potato with your hands.

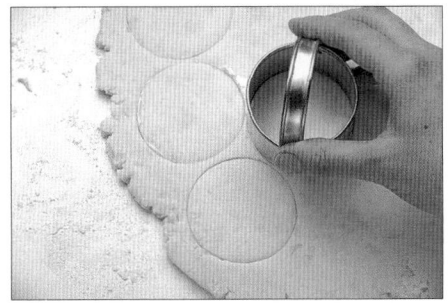
Roll out the dough and cut circles from it with a pastry cutter.

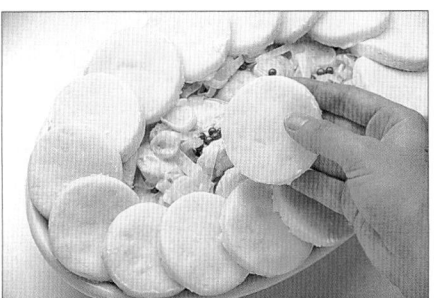
Arrange the circles, overlapping, on top of the cooled filling mixture.

SPICED LIVER CURRY

Preparation time: 25 minutes
** + 2 hours marinating**
Total cooking time: 20 minutes
Serves 4

¼ cup (60 ml/2 fl oz) dark soy sauce
3 cloves garlic, crushed
1 tablespoon sesame seeds, toasted
1 teaspoon sesame oil
500 g (1 lb) chicken livers, trimmed
    and sliced
2 tablespoons olive oil
1 onion, sliced
1 red capsicum, sliced
1 teaspoon ground coriander
1 teaspoon ground cumin
2 tablespoons peanut oil
½ cup (125 ml/4 fl oz) chicken stock
100 g (3½ oz) snow peas, trimmed

1 Combine the soy sauce, garlic, sesame seeds and sesame oil with 2 tablespoons water. Place the liver in a dish and pour over the marinade. Cover and refrigerate for 2 hours.
2 Heat half the olive oil in a large, heavy-based pan and cook the onion and capsicum over medium-low heat for 5–10 minutes, or until softened. Remove from the pan and set aside.
3 Sprinkle the liver with coriander and cumin and season well with freshly ground black pepper. Remove from the dish, reserving the marinade.
4 Heat the remaining olive oil and the peanut oil in a pan and add the liver. Cook over high heat, turning often, for about 3–5 minutes, or until firm but still slightly pink inside. Return the onion, capsicum and reserved marinade to the pan. Add the stock and snow peas, and simmer gently for 2–3 minutes. Serve immediately, with rice if desired. Garnish with toasted sesame seeds.

NUTRITION PER SERVE
Protein 35 g; Fat 35 g; Carbohydrate 5 g;
Dietary Fibre 2 g; Cholesterol 705 mg;
2042 kJ (485 cal)

Trim and slice the chicken livers, making sure to remove any membrane.

Mix together the marinade ingredients and then pour over the liver to coat.

Sprinkle the coriander and cumin over the liver and season well.

Add the chicken stock and snow peas, then simmer gently for 2–3 minutes.

STEAMED LEMON GRASS AND GINGER CHICKEN WITH ASIAN GREENS

Preparation time: 25 minutes
Total cooking time: 40 minutes
Serves 4

200 g (6½ oz) fresh egg noodles
4 chicken breast fillets
2 stems lemon grass
5 cm (2 inch) piece fresh ginger, cut
    into julienne strips
1 lime, thinly sliced
2 cups (500 ml/16 fl oz) chicken stock
1 bunch (350 g/12 oz) choy sum,
    cut into 10 cm (4 inch) lengths
800 g (1 lb 10 oz) Chinese broccoli,
    cut into 10 cm (4 inch) lengths
3 tablespoons kecap manis
3 tablespoons soy sauce
1 teaspoon sesame oil
toasted sesame seeds, to garnish

1 Cook the egg noodles in a sauce-pan of boiling water for 5 minutes, then drain and keep warm.
2 Cut each chicken breast fillet horizontally through the middle so that you are left with eight thin flat chicken fillets.
3 Cut the lemon grass into lengths that are about 5 cm (2 inches) longer than the chicken fillets, then cut in half lengthways. Place one piece of lemon grass onto one half of each chicken breast fillet, top with some ginger and lime slices, then top with the other half of the fillet.
4 Pour the stock into a wok and bring to a simmer. Place two of the chicken fillets in a paper-lined bamboo steamer. Place the steamer over the wok and steam over the simmering stock for 12–15 minutes, or

until the chicken is tender. Remove the chicken from the steamer, cover and keep warm. Repeat with the other fillets.
5 Steam the greens in the same way for 3 minutes, or until tender. Bring the stock in the wok to the boil.
6 Place the kecap manis, soy sauce and sesame oil in a bowl and whisk together well.
7 Divide the noodles among four

serving plates and ladle the boiling stock over them. Top with a pile of Asian greens, then add the chicken and generously drizzle each serve with the sauce. Sprinkle with toasted sesame seeds and serve.

NUTRITION PER SERVE
Protein 65 g; Fat 7.5 g; Carbohydrate 37 g;
Dietary Fibre 9 g; Cholesterol 119 mg;
2045 kJ (488 cal)

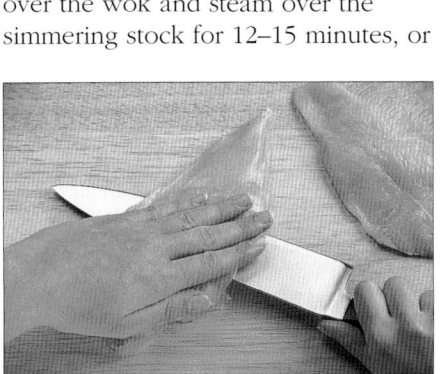
Cut each chicken breast in half horizontally through the middle.

Top the bottom half of each fillet with lemon grass, ginger and lime.

Steam the lemon grass chicken fillets until cooked and tender.

SZECHWAN PEPPER CHICKEN STIR-FRY

Preparation time: 25 minutes
  + 2 hours marinating
Total cooking time: 20 minutes
Serves 4

3 teaspoons Szechwan pepper
500 g (1 lb) chicken thigh fillets, cut
    into strips
2 tablespoons soy sauce
1 clove garlic, crushed
1 teaspoon grated fresh ginger
3 teaspoons cornflour
100 g (3½ oz) dried thin egg noodles
oil, for cooking
1 onion, sliced
1 yellow capsicum, cut into thin strips
1 red capsicum, cut into thin strips
100 g (3½ oz) sugar snap peas
¼ cup (60 ml/2 fl oz) chicken stock

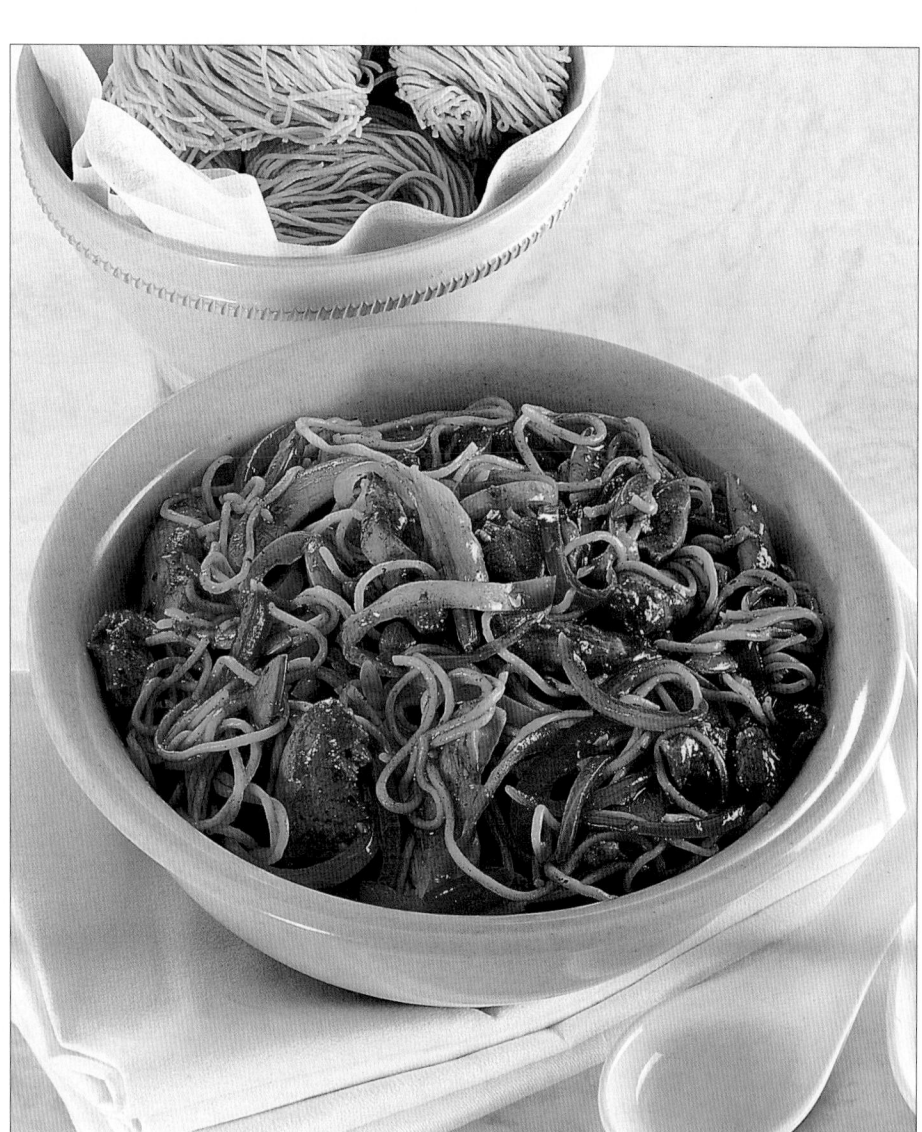

1 Heat a wok until very hot and dry-fry the Szechwan pepper for 30 seconds. Remove from the wok and crush with a mortar and pestle or in a spice mill or small food processor.
2 Combine the chicken pieces with the soy sauce, garlic, ginger, cornflour and Szechwan pepper in a glass or ceramic bowl. Cover and refrigerate for 2 hours.
3 Bring a large pan of water to the boil, add the egg noodles and cook for 5 minutes, or until tender. Drain, then drizzle with a little oil and toss it through the noodles to prevent them from sticking together. Set aside.
4 Heat the wok until very hot, add 1 tablespoon of the oil and swirl it around to coat the side. Stir-fry the chicken in batches over medium-high heat for 5 minutes, or until golden

brown and cooked. Add more oil when necessary. Remove from the wok and set aside.
5 Reheat the wok, add 1 tablespoon of the oil and stir-fry the onion, capsicum and sugar snap peas over high heat for 2–3 minutes, or until the vegetables are tender. Add the chicken stock and bring to the boil.

6 Return the chicken and egg noodles to the wok and toss over high heat until the mixture is well combined. Serve immediately.

NUTRITION PER SERVE
Protein 35 g; Fat 15 g; Carbohydrate 25 g;
Dietary Fibre 3 g; Cholesterol 65 mg;
1515 kJ (360 cal)

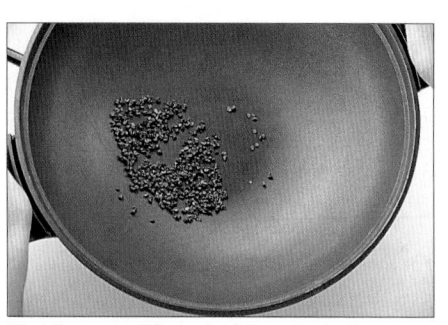

Heat the wok until very hot, then dry-fry the Szechwan pepper.

Crush the Szechwan pepper with a mortar and pestle.

Toss the oil through the noodles to prevent them from sticking.

BAKED CHICKEN AND ARTICHOKE PANCAKES

Preparation time: 30 minutes
Total cooking time: 1 hour
Serves 4

1 teaspoon baking powder
1⅓ cups (165 g/5½ oz) plain flour
¼ teaspoon salt
2 eggs
300 ml (10 fl oz) milk
90 g (3 oz) butter
2½ cups (600 ml/20 fl oz) chicken
    stock
2 egg yolks
1 cup (250 ml/8 fl oz) cream
1 teaspoon lemon juice
300 g (10 oz) cooked chicken,
    chopped roughly
350 g (11 oz) artichoke hearts, drained
    and sliced
2 teaspoons chopped fresh thyme
2 teaspoons chopped fresh parsley
100 g (3½ oz) grated Parmesan

1 Sift the baking powder, 1 cup (125 g/4 oz) flour and salt into a large bowl and make a well in the centre. Whisk the eggs and milk in a jug and pour into the well, whisking until just smooth. Heat a frying pan and brush lightly with melted butter. Add ¼ cup (60 ml/2 fl oz) batter and cook over medium heat until the underside is brown. Turn over and cook the other side. Transfer to a plate and cover with a tea towel while cooking the remaining batter.
2 Melt the butter in a pan and stir in the remaining flour. Cook for 2 minutes, then remove from the heat. Slowly whisk in the chicken stock until smooth. Whisk in the combined egg yolks and cream. Return to the heat and bring slowly to the boil, stirring constantly. Boil for 30 seconds to thicken the sauce, then remove from the heat and stir in the lemon juice. Season with salt and freshly ground black pepper.
3 Preheat the oven to moderately hot 200°C (400°F/Gas 6). Grease a 3 litre ovenproof dish with melted butter. Line the base with 2 pancakes, slightly overlapping. Spoon half of the chicken, artichokes and herbs evenly over the pancakes. Pour a third of the sauce over the top and layer with another two pancakes. Repeat, finishing with a layer of 3 pancakes. Spread the remaining sauce over the top, sprinkle with the Parmesan and bake for 30–35 minutes, or until golden brown.

NUTRITION PER SERVE
Protein 40 g; Fat 60 g; Carbohydrate 37 g;
Dietary Fibre 4 g; Cholesterol 305 mg;
3568 kJ (850 cal)

Heat a frying pan, add the batter and cook until the underside is brown.

Slowly whisk in the combined yolks and cream, away from the heat.

Line the dish with pancakes, then spoon in half the chicken and artichoke filling.

THAI GREEN CURRY CHICKEN PIES

Preparation time: 45 minutes
+ 30 minutes refrigeration
Total cooking time: 45 minutes
Serves 4

1 cup (125 g/4 oz) plain flour
65 g (2¼ oz) cold butter, chopped

FILLING
200 g (6½ oz) green beans
1 tablespoon oil
1 tablespoon Thai green curry paste
½ cup (125 ml/4 fl oz) coconut milk
500 g (1 lb) chicken thigh fillets, cut
  into bite-sized pieces
2 kaffir lime leaves
2 teaspoons fish sauce
1 tablespoon lime juice
2 teaspoons soft brown sugar
1 tablespoon cornflour
1 egg, lightly beaten, to glaze

1 Process the flour and butter in a
food processor until the mixture
resembles fine breadcrumbs. Add
1–2 tablespoons of cold water.
Process in short bursts until the
mixture just comes together, adding a
little extra water if necessary. Turn
out onto a lightly floured surface and
quickly bring together into a ball.
Cover with plastic wrap and
refrigerate for at least 30 minutes.
2 Cut the beans into short lengths.
Heat the oil in a wok or heavy-based
frying pan. Add the curry paste and
cook for 1 minute, stirring constantly.
Add the coconut milk and ¼ cup
(60 ml/2 fl oz) of water and bring to
the boil. Add the chicken, beans and
kaffir lime leaves and stir through.
Simmer gently for 15 minutes, or until

the chicken is cooked. Add the fish
sauce, lime juice and sugar. In a small
bowl, mix together the cornflour and
1 tablespoon of water to a smooth
consistency. Add to the curry and stir
constantly until the sauce thickens
and begins to bubble. Remove the
kaffir lime leaves, and divide the
mixture between four ½ cup (125 ml/4
fl oz) capacity ramekins.
3 Divide the pastry into 4 equal
pieces. Roll each piece between two
sheets of baking paper until it is
slightly larger than the top of the
ramekins. Brush the edges of the
ramekins with the beaten egg and
cover with the pastry. Press the edges
around the rim to seal. Trim off any
excess pastry with a sharp knife.
Decorate the edges of the pastry with
the end of a teaspoon. Cut a small air
hole in the top of each pie to allow
the steam to escape during cooking.
Brush with the beaten egg. Place the
ramekins on a baking tray and bake
for 20–25 minutes, or until the pastry
is golden brown. Serve immediately.

NUTRITION PER SERVE
Protein 35 g; Fat 30 g; Carbohydrate 30 g;
Dietary Fibre 3 g; Cholesterol 175 mg;
2225 kJ (530 cal)

NOTE: Coconut milk varies greatly in
quality. You may get a 'curdled' or
'split' appearance, however this will
not affect the flavour.

HINT: Dried kaffir lime leaves can be
stored for up to 1 year if kept in a
sealed plastic bag.

Cook the curry paste for 1 minute, then add the
coconut milk.

Add the chicken, beans and kaffir lime leaves to
the wok or pan.

Add the cornflour mixture to the curry and stir
until it thickens and bubbles.

Remove the kaffir lime leaves before spooning the mixture into the ramekins.

Roll out each piece of pastry and place over the top of the ramekins.

Glaze the pastry crusts with a little beaten egg to give a golden finish.

CHICKEN WITH ROASTED RED CAPSICUM SAUCE

Preparation time: 30 minutes
Total cooking time: 1 hour 15 minutes
Serves 4

2 red capsicums
1 tablespoon olive oil
1 red onion, roughly chopped
1–2 cloves garlic, crushed
425 g (14 oz) can chopped tomatoes
½ cup (30 g/1 oz) chopped fresh
    parsley
½ cup (30 g/1 oz) chopped fresh basil
    leaves
1 tablespoon tomato paste
1 tablespoon caster sugar
4 chicken breast fillets

1 Cut the capsicums into quarters, remove the membrane and seeds and grill, skin-side-up, until blackened. Cool in a plastic bag for 10 minutes, peel away the skin and chop roughly.
2 Heat the oil in a pan and cook the onion and garlic for 2 minutes, or until soft but not brown. Add the tomatoes, parsley, basil, tomato paste, sugar and 1½ cups (375 ml/12 fl oz) water.
3 Add the chopped capsicum and cook, stirring often, over very low heat for 45 minutes to 1 hour, or until thick. Leave to cool slightly, then purée in batches in a food processor. Season.
4 Grill the chicken under a preheated grill for 5 minutes on each side, or until cooked through and tender. Serve with the sauce.

NUTRITION PER SERVE
Protein 27 g; Fat 7.5 g; Carbohydrate 9 g;
Dietary Fibre 2 g; Cholesterol 55 mg;
886 kJ (210 cal)

Once the capsicum skin has been blackened it should peel away easily.

Cook the onion and garlic until they are softened but not browned.

Add the chopped capsicum to the sauce and cook for up to 1 hour, or until thick.

CHICKEN WITH LEMON AND CAPERS

Preparation time: 15 minutes
Total cooking time: 15 minutes
Serves 4

olive oil, for cooking
1 red onion, cut into thin wedges
25 g (¾ oz) butter
800 g (1 lb 10 oz) chicken breast
    fillets, cut into bite-sized pieces
rind of 1 lemon, cut into thin strips
2 tablespoons baby capers, rinsed
    well and drained
⅓ cup (80 ml/2¾ fl oz) lemon juice
¼ cup (15 g/½ oz) shredded basil

1 Heat the wok until very hot, add 2 teaspoons of the oil and swirl it around to coat the side. Add the red onion wedges and stir-fry until softened and golden. Remove from the wok and set aside.

2 Reheat the wok, add 2 teaspoons of the oil and half the butter, and stir-fry the chicken in two batches until it is browned, adding more oil and butter between batches. Return all the chicken to the wok with the onion.

3 Stir in the lemon rind, capers and lemon juice. Toss well and cook until warmed through. Add the shredded basil and season with salt and black pepper. Delicious served with creamy mashed potato.

NUTRITION PER SERVE
Protein 45 g; Fat 20 g; Carbohydrate 2.5 g;
Dietary Fibre 1 g; Cholesterol 115 mg;
1550 kJ (370 cal)

Peel the red onion, then cut it in half and cut it into thin wedges.

Use a zester to remove thin strips of rind from the lemon, without getting the pith from underneath.

Stir-fry the red onion wedges until they are soft and golden.

ROAST CHICKEN WITH BREADCRUMB STUFFING

Preparation time: 40 minutes
Total cooking time: 1 hour 30 minutes
Serves 6

3 slices bacon, finely chopped
6 slices wholegrain bread, crusts
  removed
3 spring onions, chopped
2 tablespoons chopped pecans
2 teaspoons currants
¼ cup (15 g/½ oz) finely chopped fresh
  parsley
1 egg, lightly beaten
¼ cup (60 ml/2 fl oz) milk
1.4 kg (2 lb 13 oz) chicken
40 g (1¼ oz) butter, melted
1 tablespoon oil
1 tablespoon soy sauce
1 clove garlic, crushed
1½ cups (375 ml/12 fl oz) chicken
  stock
1 tablespoon plain flour

1 Preheat the oven to moderate 180°C (350°F/Gas 4). Cook the bacon in a dry frying pan over high heat for 5 minutes, or until crisp. Cut the bread into 1 cm (½ inch) cubes and place in a bowl. Mix in the bacon, spring onion, pecans, currants, parsley and combined egg and milk. Season.
2 Remove the giblets and any large amounts of fat from the cavity of the chicken. Pat the chicken dry with paper towels. Spoon the bacon mixture into the chicken cavity. Tuck the wings under the chicken and tie the legs securely with string.
3 Place the chicken on a rack in a deep baking dish. Brush with the combined butter, oil and soy sauce. Pour any remaining mixture into the baking dish with the garlic and half the stock. Roast the chicken for 1–1¼ hours, or until brown and tender, basting occasionally with the pan juices. Pierce between the thigh and body to the bone and check that any juices running out are clear. If they are pink, continue cooking. Put the chicken on a serving dish. Cover loosely with foil and leave in a warm place for 5 minutes before carving.
4 Discard all but 1 tablespoon of the pan juices from the baking dish. Transfer the baking dish to the stove. Add the flour to the pan juices and blend to a smooth paste. Stir constantly over low heat for 5 minutes, or until the mixture browns. Gradually add the remaining stock and stir until the mixture boils and thickens. Add a little extra stock or water if the gravy is too thick. Season with salt and cracked black pepper and strain into a jug. Serve the chicken and gravy with snow peas and roast potatoes.

NUTRITION PER SERVE
Protein 33 g; Fat 20 g; Carbohydrate 15 g; Dietary Fibre 3 g; Cholesterol 110 mg; 1530 kJ (365 cal)

Pat the chicken dry and spoon the stuffing into the chicken cavity.

Tuck the wings under the chicken and tie the legs securely with string.

CHICKEN AND BROCCOLI BAKE

Preparation time: 20 minutes
Total cooking time: 1 hour
Serves 6

30 g (1 oz) butter
4 chicken breast fillets, cut into cubes
6 spring onions, sliced
2 cloves garlic, crushed
2 tablespoons plain flour
1½ cups (375 ml/12 fl oz) chicken
    stock
2 teaspoons Dijon mustard
280 g (9 oz) broccoli, cut into florets
1 kg (2 lb) potatoes, cut into quarters
2 tablespoons milk
60 g (2 oz) butter, extra
2 eggs
⅓ cup (30 g/1 oz) flaked toasted
    almonds
snipped fresh chives, to garnish

1 Preheat the oven to moderate 180°C (350°F/Gas 4). Heat half the butter in a large frying pan, and cook the chicken in batches until browned and cooked through. Remove from the pan. In the same pan melt the remaining butter and cook the spring onion and garlic for 2 minutes. Stir in the flour and mix well. Pour in the stock and cook, stirring, until the mixture boils and thickens. Add the mustard and then stir in the chicken. Season well.
2 Meanwhile, steam or microwave the broccoli until just tender, taking care not to overcook it. Refresh the broccoli in iced water and drain well.
3 Boil the potato in plenty of salted water for 15–20 minutes, or until tender. Drain and mash well with the milk, extra butter and eggs. Put the broccoli in a 2.5 litre ovenproof dish and pour in the chicken mixture. Pipe or spoon the mashed potato over the top. Sprinkle with the almonds and bake for 25 minutes, or until the top is browned and cooked through. Scatter the chives over the top before serving.

NUTRITION PER SERVE
Protein 25 g; Fat 20 g; Carbohydrate 25 g; Dietary Fibre 5.5 g; Cholesterol 135 mg; 1610 kJ (385 cal)

Use a large sharp knife to cut the chicken breasts into cubes.

Add the chicken to the pan and cook in batches until browned.

Pour in the stock and stir over heat until the mixture thickens.

CHICKEN, CHILLI JAM AND NOODLE STIR-FRY

**Preparation time: 15 minutes +
    20 minutes soaking**
Total cooking time: 10 minutes
Serves 4

250 g (8 oz) flat rice stick noodles
    (1 cm/½ inch wide)
400 g (13 oz) chicken breast fillet
1 onion
1 red capsicum
1 tablespoon peanut oil
2 tablespoons chilli jam (see NOTE)
2 teaspoons fish sauce
2 tablespoons light soy sauce
90 g (3 oz) bean sprouts
90 g (3 oz) unsalted cashew nuts
1 cup (30 g/1 oz) loosely packed fresh
    basil
2 tablespoons fresh basil, extra,
    to garnish

1 Place the noodles in a large heatproof bowl, cover with warm water and soak for 15–20 minutes. Drain well.
2 Cut the chicken breast fillets into 5 mm (¼ inch) slices against the grain. Halve the onion and cut into thin wedges. Cut the capsicum in half, remove the seeds and membrane, then cut into thin strips with a sharp knife.
3 Heat a wok over high heat, add the peanut oil and swirl to coat the side. Cook the onion for 1–2 minutes, or until lightly golden. Add the chicken slices and cook for a further 3–5 minutes, or until browned and almost cooked through. Stir in the chilli jam, then add the capsicum and cook for another minute.
4 Add the fish sauce, soy sauce, bean sprouts, cashew nuts, basil and the noodles to the wok and toss until warmed through and well combined. Garnish with the extra basil and serve immediately.

NOTE: Chilli jam is made with tomato, onion, chilli, oil, tamarind, garlic, sugar, salt, spices and vinegar. It is available in Asian food stores.

NUTRITION PER SERVE
Fat 23 g; Protein 30.5 g; Carbohydrate
35 g; Dietary Fibre 4 g; Cholesterol 66 mg;
1960 kJ (470 Cal)

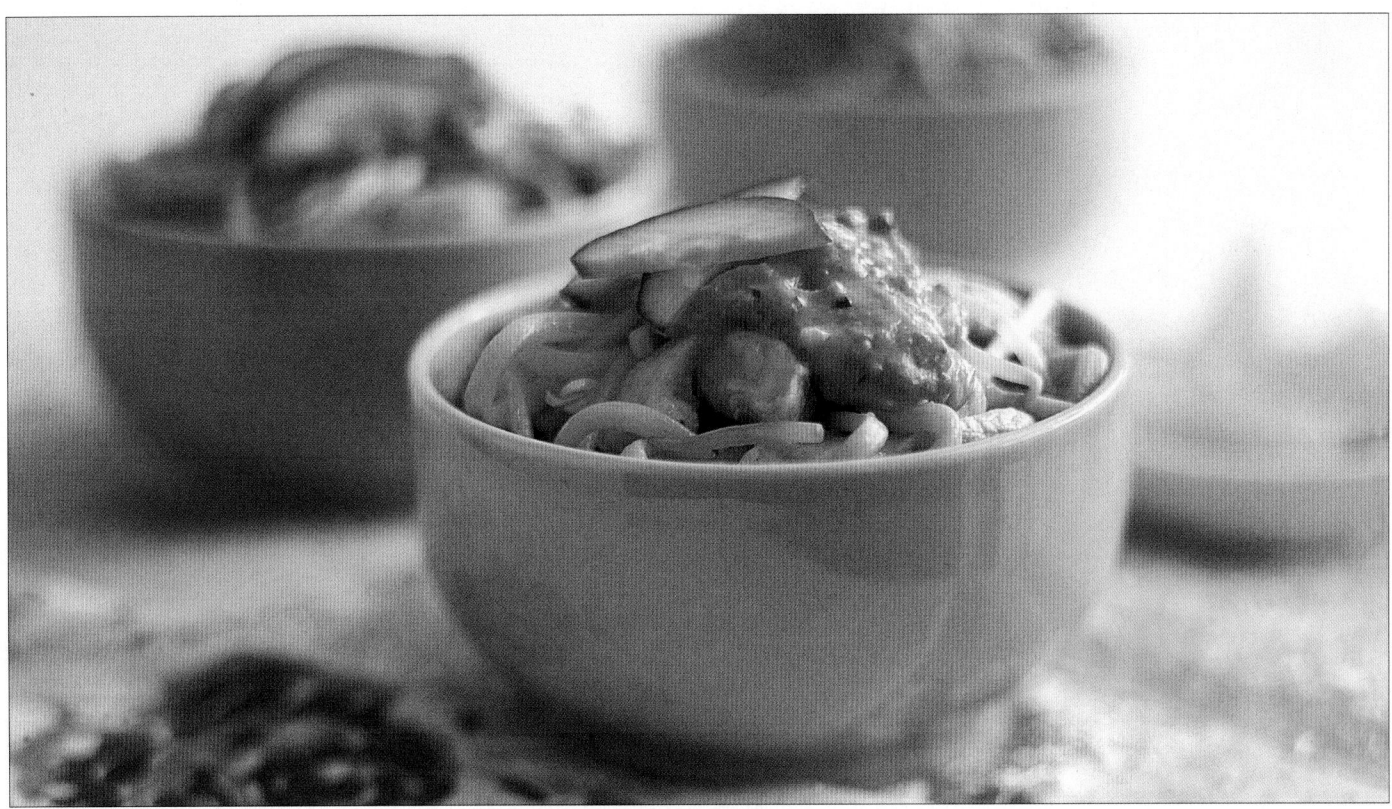

CHICKEN SATAY NOODLES

**Preparation time: 20 minutes +
 5 minutes soaking**
Total cooking time: 25 minutes
Serves 4

PEANUT SAUCE
1 tablespoon peanut oil
8 red Asian shallots, finely chopped
8 cloves garlic, crushed
1 tablespoon finely chopped fresh
   ginger
4 small fresh red chillies, finely chopped
1 cup (250 g/8 oz) crunchy peanut
   butter
1½ tablespoons light soy sauce
¼ cup (60 ml/2 fl oz) fish sauce
400 ml (13 fl oz) coconut milk
4 tablespoons grated palm sugar
2 fresh kaffir lime leaves
⅓ cup (80 ml/2¾ fl oz) lime juice

400 g (13 oz) Hokkien noodles
2 tablespoons peanut oil
1 small white onion, finely chopped
2 cloves garlic, finely chopped
1 small fresh red chilli, finely chopped
400 g (13 oz) chicken tenderloins,
   tendon removed, halved

200 g (6½ oz) bean sprouts
150 g (5 oz) spring onions, chopped
1 Lebanese cucumber, cut in half
   lengthways and sliced
lime wedges, to serve

1 To make the peanut sauce, heat
a wok over medium heat, add the
oil and swirl to coat. Add the shallots,
garlic, ginger and chilli and cook for
5 minutes. Reduce the heat to low,
add the remaining sauce ingredients
and simmer for 10 minutes, or until
thickened. Remove and keep warm.
Discard the kaffir lime leaves before
serving. If the sauce is too thick, stir
in 2 tablespoons water.
2 Place the noodles in a large
heatproof bowl, cover with boiling
water and allow to soak for 1 minute,

or until they are tender and separated.
Drain well.
3 Heat a clean wok over high heat,
add the oil and swirl to coat. Stir-fry
the onion, garlic and chilli for
30 seconds. Add the chicken and
cook for 3–4 minutes, or until brown.
Stir in the bean sprouts and spring
onion and cook for 30 seconds, then
add the noodles and toss together for
1–2 minutes, or until heated through.
4 Divide the noodle mixture among
the serving bowls and top with the
sauce. Garnish with the cucumber
slices and serve with the lime wedges.

NUTRITION PER SERVE
Fat 83 g; Protein 57 g; Carbohydrate 82 g;
Dietary Fibre 17 g; Cholesterol 103 mg;
5415 kJ (1295 Cal)

Cut the tendon from the chicken tenderloins using
a sharp knife.

Remove the kaffir lime leaves from the peanut
sauce before serving.

MEDITERRANEAN CHICKEN

Preparation time: 30 minutes
Total cooking time: 1 hour 10 minutes
Serves 4

8 chicken thigh cutlets
2 tablespoons olive oil
150 g (5 oz) French shallots
4 cloves garlic
½ cup (125 ml/4 fl oz) white wine
425 g (14 oz) can chopped tomatoes
12 Kalamata olives
1 tablespoon red wine vinegar
2 teaspoons tomato paste
1 tablespoon fresh oregano leaves
1 tablespoon chopped fresh basil
1 teaspoon sugar
4 slices prosciutto
1 teaspoon grated lemon rind
½ cup (30 g/1 oz) chopped fresh
   parsley
1 tablespoon capers, rinsed

1 Preheat the oven to moderate 180°C (350°F/Gas 4). Remove the skin and fat from the chicken thighs. Heat half the oil in a large pan and brown the chicken over high heat for 3–4 minutes on each side. Arrange the chicken in a large flameproof casserole dish.

2 Heat the remaining oil in the same pan. Add the shallots and garlic and cook over medium heat for 4 minutes, or until soft but not brown. Add the wine and bring to the boil.

3 Add the tomatoes, olives, vinegar, tomato paste, oregano, basil and sugar. Season with salt and black pepper. Boil, stirring, for 2 minutes, then pour over the chicken and cover with a tight-fitting lid. Bake for

45 minutes, or until the chicken is tender.

4 Meanwhile, place the prosciutto in a single layer in a frying pan. Dry-fry for 3 minutes, or until crisp, turning once. Break into large chunks and set aside.

5 Arrange the chicken on a serving dish, cover and keep warm. Transfer the casserole to the stove top and boil the pan juices for 5 minutes, or until thickened, stirring occasionally. Spoon the juices over the chicken and sprinkle with the lemon rind, parsley and capers. Top with the prosciutto.

NUTRITION PER SERVE
Protein 75 g; Fat 25 g; Carbohydrate 15 g;
Dietary Fibre 8 g; Cholesterol 155 mg;
2390 kJ (570 cal)

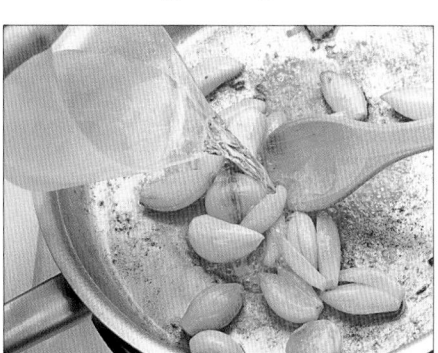

Cook the shallots and garlic until soft, then add the wine.

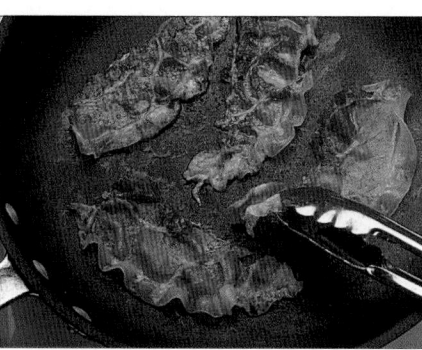

Place the prosciutto slices in a single layer in a dry frying pan and fry until crisp.

CREAMY CHICKEN, SAGE AND TARRAGON PIE

Preparation time: 25 minutes
Total cooking time: 1 hour 10 minutes
Serves 4–6

1.5 kg (3 lb) chicken thigh fillets
2 tablespoons olive oil
2 slices bacon, finely chopped
1 onion, roughly chopped
4 fresh sage leaves, chopped
1 tablespoon chopped fresh tarragon
45 g (1½ oz) butter, melted
2 tablespoons plain flour
½ cup (125 ml/4 fl oz) milk
220 g (7 oz) can creamed corn
2 sheets ready-rolled puff pastry
1 egg, lightly beaten

1 Preheat the oven to hot 210°C (415°F/Gas 6–7). Brush a 23 cm (9 inch) pie dish with butter. Cut the chicken into bite-sized pieces. Heat the oil in a large frying pan. Add the chicken, bacon and onion, and cook over medium heat for 5 minutes, or until browned. Add the sage, tarragon, 1 cup (250 ml/8 fl oz) water, salt and pepper. Bring to the boil, then reduce the heat and simmer, covered, for 25 minutes, or until the chicken is tender. Drain, reserving the juices.
2 Melt the butter in a heavy-based pan. Add the flour and stir over low heat for 1 minute. Remove from heat and gradually add the milk and reserved juice, stirring until smooth. Return to the heat and stir over medium heat until thickenened. Stir in the chicken mixture and corn. Spoon into the dish.
3 Brush a sheet of pastry with egg and top with a second sheet. Brush the rim of the pie dish with egg and place the pastry over the filling. Trim any excess.
4 Decorate the pie with pastry. Brush with egg and make a few slits in the top. Bake for 15 minutes, then reduce the heat to 180°C (350°F/Gas 4) and bake for 10–15 minutes, or until crisp and golden. Leave for 5 minutes.

NUTRITION PER SERVE
Protein 66 g; Fat 40 g; Carbohydrate 34 g;
Dietary Fibre 2.5 g; Cholesterol 217 mg;
3150 kJ (753 cal)

Add the salt, pepper, tarragon, sage and water to the chicken mixture.

Add the chicken mixture and corn to the sauce, and stir to combine.

Place the pastry over the filling, then trim the excess with a sharp knife.

Brush the pie with the beaten egg and make a few slits to allow the steam to escape.

CHICKEN AND RED WINE CASSEROLE

Preparation time: 15 minutes
Total cooking time: 1 hour 50 minutes
Serves 4–6

30 g (1 oz) butter
125 g (4 oz) bacon, roughly chopped
1.5 kg (3 lb) skinless chicken pieces
350 g (11 oz) baby onions
2 tablespoons plain flour
3 cups (750 ml/24 fl oz) red wine
250 g (8 oz) mushrooms, sliced
1 tablespoon fresh thyme leaves, to
   garnish

1 Preheat the oven to moderate 180°C (350°F/Gas 4). Melt the butter in a large flameproof casserole dish over medium heat. Add the bacon and cook until golden, then remove.

Add the chicken pieces and cook, in batches, for 4–5 minutes, or until browned. Remove. Add the onions and cook for 2–3 minutes, or until browned, then remove from the dish.
2 Stir the flour in to the dish, then remove from the heat and slowly pour in the red wine, while stirring. Return to the heat, bring to the boil and return the bacon and chicken to the dish. Cover and bake for 1 hour.

Return the onions to the dish and add the mushrooms. Cook for a further 30 minutes. Season to taste with salt and freshly ground black pepper, and garnish with the thyme. Serve with mashed potato, if desired.

NUTRITION PER SERVE (6)
Protein 65 g; Fat 11 g; Carbohydrate 11 g;
Dietary Fibre 2 g; Cholesterol 150 mg;
2040 kJ (487 cal)

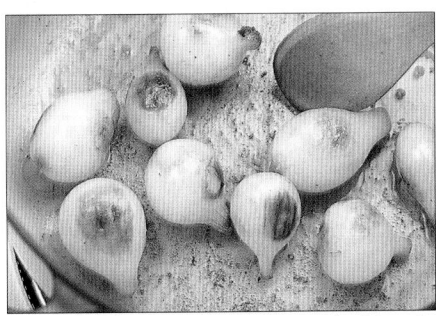
Cook the whole onions in the casserole dish until they are browned.

Return the cooked bacon and chicken pieces to the casserole dish.

MEXICAN CHICKEN CASSEROLE

Preparation time: 15 minutes
Total cooking time: 1 hour
Serves 4

¾ cup (165 g/5½ oz) short-grain rice
300 g (10 oz) can red kidney beans, drained and thoroughly rinsed
3½ tablespoons chopped fresh coriander leaves
1 tablespoon oil
600 g (1¼ lb) chicken thigh fillets
2 x 200 g (6½ oz) jars spicy taco sauce
2 cups (250 g/8 oz) grated Cheddar
½ cup (125 g/4 oz) sour cream

1 Preheat the oven to moderate 180°C (350°F/Gas 4). Lightly grease a 7 cm (2¾ inch) deep, 21 cm (8½ inch) round casserole dish. Bring a large saucepan of water to the boil, add the rice and cook for 10–12 minutes, stirring occasionally. Drain.
2 In the prepared dish, combine the beans and 1½ tablespoons of the coriander, then add the rice and toss together. Lightly press the mixture so the beans are mixed into the rice and the mixture is flat.
3 Heat the oil in a large frying pan over medium–high heat. Sauté the chicken thighs for 3 minutes, then turn over. Add the spicy taco sauce, and cook for a further 3 minutes.
4 To assemble, spread half the cheese over the rice. Arrange the chicken and sauce on top in a star shape, sprinkle with 1½ tablespoons of the coriander, then sprinkle with the remaining cheese. Cover with foil.
5 Bake for 35–40 minutes, or until the mixture is bubbling and the cheese is melted and slightly browned— remove the foil for the last 5 minutes of cooking. Cut into four servings with a knife and scoop out carefully, keeping the layers intact. Serve sprinkled with the remaining coriander and a dollop of sour cream.

NUTRITION PER SERVE
Protein 52 g; Fat 50 g; Carbohydrate 66 g; Dietary Fibre 6 g; Cholesterol 235 mg; 3825 kJ (915 cal)

Arrange the chicken thighs and sauce on top of the cheese in a star shape.

Bake the casserole until it is bubbling and the cheese is melted.

CHICKEN CORDON BLEU

Preparation time: 15 minutes
+ 30 minutes refrigeration
Total cooking time: 20 minutes
Serves 4

4 (460 g/14 oz) chicken
  breast fillets
4 thick slices Swiss cheese
4 slices double-smoked ham or
  pastrami
⅓ cup (40 g/1¼ oz) seasoned plain
  flour
1 egg, lightly beaten
½ cup (50 g/1¾ oz) dry breadcrumbs
½ cup (125 ml/4 fl oz) oil

1 Trim the chicken of excess fat and
sinew. Using a sharp knife, cut into
the thickest section of each fillet
without cutting right through. Open
the fillet out flat and season with salt
and freshly ground black pepper.
2 Place a slice of cheese and ham on
one side of each fillet. Fold the
remaining half of the fillet over to
enclose the filling.
3 Carefully coat each fillet with flour,
then shake off the excess. Dip into
the egg, then coat with the
breadcrumbs. Place on a foil-lined
baking tray. Place, covered, in the
refrigerator for 30 minutes.
4 Heat the oil in a medium heavy-
based pan. Add the chicken and cook
in two batches over medium heat for
4 minutes each side, or until the
chicken is golden and cooked
through. Add more oil between
batches if necessary. Serve the
chicken immediately.

NUTRITION PER SERVE
Protein 40 g; Fat 40 g; Carbohydrate 16 g;
Dietary Fibre 1 g; Cholesterol 130 mg;
2438 kJ (582 cal)

Cut into the thickest section of each chicken fillet
without cutting right through.

Place a slice of cheese and a slice of ham on
one side of each fillet.

Shake the excess flour from the chicken, then dip
into the beaten egg.

Cook the chicken in the oil for 4 minutes each
side, or until golden and cooked through.

LIME STEAMED CHICKEN

Preparation time: 15 minutes
Total cooking time: 15 minutes
Serves 4

2 limes, thinly sliced
4 chicken breast fillets
1 bunch (500 g/1 lb) bok choy
1 bunch (500 g/1 lb) choy sum
1 teaspoon sesame oil
1 tablespoon peanut oil
½ cup (125 ml/4 fl oz) oyster sauce
⅓ cup (80 ml/2¾ fl oz) lime juice

1 Line the base of a bamboo steamer with the lime and place the chicken on top. Season. Place over a wok with a little water in the base, cover and steam for 8–10 minutes, or until the chicken is cooked through. Cover the chicken and keep warm. Remove the water from the wok.
2 Wash and trim the greens. Heat the oils in the wok and cook the greens for 2–3 minutes, or until just wilted.
3 Mix together the oyster sauce and lime juice and pour over the greens. Serve the chicken on top of the greens with some extra lime slices.

NUTRITION PER SERVE
Protein 60 g; Fat 12 g; Carbohydrate 10 g; Dietary Fibre 4.5 g; Cholesterol 120 mg; 1665 kJ (398 cal)

NOTE: The Asian green vegetables used in this recipe, bok choy and choy sum, can be replaced by any green vegetables, such as broccoli, snow peas, or English spinach.

Line the base of the steamer with lime slices and then arrange the chicken on top.

Heat the oils in a wok and stir-fry the Asian greens until they are just wilted.

Mix together the oyster sauce and lime juice and pour over the greens.

CHICKEN PAPRIKA WITH DUMPLINGS

Preparation time: 20 minutes
Total cooking time: 1 hour 10 minutes
Serves 4–6

2 tablespoons oil
1.6 kg (3¼ lb) chicken, cut into
    10 pieces
1 large onion, chopped
1 clove garlic, crushed
1 teaspoon sweet paprika
1 teaspoon dried thyme
2 tablespoons plain flour
½ cup (125 ml/4 fl oz) chicken stock
410 g (13 oz) can peeled tomatoes,
    crushed
2 carrots, sliced

DUMPLINGS
1 cup (125 g/4 oz) self-raising flour
20 g (¾ oz) butter, chopped
2 teaspoons finely chopped parsley
2 teaspoons finely chopped chives
½ teaspoon dried mixed herbs
⅓ cup (80 ml/2¾ fl oz) buttermilk

1 Heat the oil in a frying pan. Brown the chicken in batches over medium–high heat, then place in a deep 3 litre casserole dish.
2 Add the onion and garlic to the pan, stirring until soft. Reduce the heat to low. Add the paprika, thyme and flour, and cook, stirring, for 2 minutes. Gradually stir in the stock. Add the tomato, and season. Pour the mixture over the chicken. Add the carrot. Cover and bake for 30 minutes.
3 To make the dumplings, sift the flour into a bowl. Rub in the butter until fine and crumbly. Stir in the herbs and almost all the buttermilk. Mix to a soft dough, adding more buttermilk if necessary. Turn the dough out onto a floured surface and gather into a ball. Divide into 8 portions and roll each into a ball. Arrange the dumplings on top of the casserole. Bake, uncovered, for 20 minutes. Serve immediately.

NUTRITION PER SERVE (6)
Protein 44 g; Fat 36 g; Carbohydrate 25 g;
Dietary Fibre 3 g; Cholesterol 200 mg;
2480 kJ (595 cal)

Brown the chicken pieces in batches in a frying pan over medium heat.

Rub the butter into the flour until the mixture is fine and crumbly.

Divide the dough into 8 portions and roll each portion into a ball.

Arrange the dumplings on top of the casserole, then bake for 20 minutes.

LITTLE CHICKEN AND VEGETABLE POT PIES

**Preparation time: 45 minutes +
20 minutes chilling
Total cooking time: 1 hour 20 minutes
Makes 6**

1¼ cups (150 g/5 oz) plain flour
90 g (3 oz) butter, chilled and
    cubed
1 tablespoon finely chopped fresh
    thyme
1 tablespoon finely chopped fresh
    flat-leaf parsley
3–4 tablespoons iced water

FILLING
750 g (1½ lb) chicken breast fillets
1 lemon, quartered
5 spring onions
2 bay leaves
1½ cups (375 ml/12 fl oz) chicken
    stock
¼ cup (60 ml/2 fl oz) dry white wine
60 g (2 oz) butter
1 large onion, thinly sliced
1 tablespoon finely chopped fresh
    tarragon
100 g (3½ oz) button mushrooms,
    thinly sliced
¾ cup (90 g/3 oz) plain flour
2 large carrots, cut into small cubes
1 celery stick, cut into small cubes
½ cup (90 g/3 oz) peas
1 egg, lightly beaten, to glaze

1 To make the pastry, sift the flour and ¼ teaspoon salt into a large bowl. Add the butter and rub it into the flour with your fingertips until the mixture resembles fine breadcrumbs. Stir in the chopped herbs. Make a well in the centre of the mixture, add almost all the water and mix with a flat-bladed knife, using a cutting action, until the mixture comes together in beads, adding a little more water if necessary.

2 Gently gather the dough together and lift it out onto a lightly floured work surface. Press together into a ball. Flatten slightly into a disc, wrap in plastic wrap and refrigerate for at least 20 minutes to let the dough relax.

3 Preheat the oven to 180°C (350°F/ Gas 4). Place the chicken, lemon, 4 of the spring onions, the bay leaves, chicken stock, wine, 1½ cups (375 ml/ 12 fl oz) water and ½ teaspoon salt in a large saucepan. Bring to the boil over high heat. Reduce the heat and simmer for 20 minutes, or until the chicken is cooked through. Remove the chicken from the liquid with a slotted spoon and set aside. Return the liquid to the heat and boil for 10 minutes, or until it has reduced to 2 cups (500 ml/16 fl oz), then strain into a bowl and set aside. Roughly cut the chicken into small pieces.

4 Melt the butter in a large saucepan over medium heat. When it is sizzling, add the onion and cook for 2–3 minutes, or until soft. Add the tarragon and mushrooms and cook, stirring occasionally, for 3–4 minutes, or until the mushrooms are soft. Add the flour and cook, stirring constantly, for 3 minutes. Pour in the reserved poaching liquid, bring to the boil and cook, stirring often, for 2 minutes, or until slightly thickened. Remove from the heat, then stir in the carrot, celery, peas and chicken. Divide the filling evenly among six 1½ cup (375 ml/ 12 fl oz) ramekins.

5 Divide the dough into six even portions. Roll out each portion into

a flat disc, 12 cm (4½ inches) in diameter (or use a cutter). Moisten the ramekin rims and cover with pastry rounds, pressing down firmly to seal the edges. Re-roll any pastry trimmings to make decorations. Prick the pie tops with a fork, then brush with the egg. Bake for about 30 minutes, or until the pies are golden.

NUTRITION PER PIE
Protein 28 g; Fat 25 g; Carbohydrate 36 g; Dietary Fibre 4 g; Cholesterol 154 mg; 1990 kJ (475 cal)

Roughly cut the poached chicken breasts into small pieces.

Stir the carrot, celery, peas and chicken into the thickened mixture.

Roll out each portion of dough to a 12 cm circle or use a cutter for neat edges.

Cover the filling with the pastry tops, pressing down firmly to seal the edges.

THAI CHICKEN CUTLETS

Preparation time: 20 minutes
+ 1 hour marinating
Total cooking time: 20 minutes
Serves 4–6

12 chicken thigh fillets (1.25 kg/2½ lb)
6 cloves garlic
1 teaspoon black peppercorns
3 fresh coriander roots and stems,
    roughly chopped
¼ teaspoon salt

CHILLI GARLIC DIP
4–5 dried red chillies
2 large cloves garlic, chopped
¼ cup (60 g/2 oz) sugar
⅓ cup (80 ml/2¾ fl oz) cider or rice
    vinegar
pinch salt
¼ cup (60 ml/2 fl oz) boiling water

1 Trim the chicken thigh fillets of any excess fat and sinew.
2 Place the garlic, peppercorns, coriander and salt in a food processor bowl. Process for 20–30 seconds, or until the mixture forms a smooth paste. (This can also be done using a mortar and pestle.) Place the chicken in a shallow non-metal dish. Spread the garlic mixture over the chicken. Refrigerate the chicken, covered, for 1 hour.
3 To make the chilli garlic dip, soak the chillies in hot water for 20 minutes. Drain the chillies and chop finely. Place in a mortar with the garlic and sugar, and grind to a smooth paste. Place the mixture in a small pan and add the vinegar, salt and boiling water. Bring to the boil, then reduce the heat and simmer for 2–3 minutes. Set aside to cool.
4 Preheat a barbecue grill or flatplate to high. Grease the barbecue and cook the chicken for 5–10 minutes on each side, turning once. Serve with the chilli garlic dip.

NUTRITION PER SERVE (6)
Protein 47 g; Fat 5 g; Carbohydrate 0.5 g;
Dietary Fibre 1 g; Cholesterol 105 mg;
1005 kJ (240 cal)

Using a sharp knife, trim any excess fat and sinew from the chicken.

Place the garlic, peppercorns, coriander and salt in a food processor bowl.

Grind the chilli, garlic and sugar to a smooth paste using a mortar and pestle.

Cook the chicken on a greased barbecue grill or flat plate.

CHINESE BRAISED CHICKEN

Preparation time: 10 minutes
Total cooking time: 1 hour
Serves 4–6

1 cup (250 ml/8 fl oz) soy sauce
1 cinnamon stick
⅓ cup (90 g/3 oz) sugar
⅓ cup (80 ml/2¾ fl oz) balsamic
    vinegar
2.5 cm (1 inch) piece fresh ginger,
    thinly sliced
4 cloves garlic
¼ teaspoon dried chilli flakes
1.5 kg (3 lb) chicken pieces (skin
    removed)
1 tablespoon sesame seeds, toasted

1 Combine 1 litre water with the soy sauce, cinnamon stick, sugar, balsamic vinegar, ginger, garlic and chilli flakes in a saucepan. Bring to the boil, then reduce the heat and simmer for 5 minutes.
2 Add the chicken pieces and simmer, covered, for 50 minutes, or until cooked through. Serve the chicken on a bed of steamed greens, drizzled with the poaching liquid and sprinkled with toasted sesame seeds.

NUTRITION PER SERVE (6)
Protein 45 g; Fat 10 g; Carbohydrate 16 g;
Dietary Fibre 0.5 g; Cholesterol 140 mg;
1420 kJ (339 cal)

Add the chicken to the simmering soy sauce mixture and cook for 50 minutes.

SPICY APRICOT CHICKEN

Preparation time: 10 minutes
Total cooking time: 20 minutes
Serves 4

750 g (1½ lb) chicken thigh fillets,
    cut into 5 cm (2 inch) pieces
plain flour, for coating
2 tablespoons oil
2 teaspoons red curry paste
2 spring onions, sliced
415 g (13 oz) can apricot halves in
    light syrup
½ cup (125 ml/4 fl oz) chicken stock

200 g (6½ oz) plain yoghurt
2 tablespoons chopped fresh
    coriander leaves
fresh coriander leaves, extra, to
    garnish

1 Lightly coat the chicken in the flour. Heat the oil in a saucepan, add the curry paste and stir over low heat for 1 minute. Add the spring onion and chicken, and cook, stirring, over medium heat for 2–3 minutes, or until the chicken is golden.
2 Drain the apricots and reserve ½ cup (125 ml/4 fl oz) apricot juice. Add the reserved juice, apricots and stock to the pan. Bring to the boil, then reduce the heat and simmer for 10 minutes, or until the chicken is tender.
3 Mix together the yoghurt and coriander, and place a spoonful of the mixture over each serving of chicken. Garnish with extra coriander leaves. Serve with couscous or rice.

NUTRITION PER SERVE
Protein 45 g; Fat 15 g; Carbohydrate 15 g;
Dietary Fibre 2 g; Cholesterol 100 mg;
1622 kJ (388 cal)

Cook the chicken and spring onion until the chicken is golden.

Add the apricot juice, apricots and stock to the pan, and bring to the boil.

Mix together the yoghurt and coriander to serve with the chicken.

MADRID CHICKEN

Preparation time: 10 minutes
Total cooking time: 1 hour
Serves 4

1 orange
1 tablespoon olive oil
4 chicken breasts (skin and excess fat
    removed)
2 chorizo sausages (about 200 g/
    6½ oz), cut into 1 cm (½ inch) slices
1 cup (250 ml/8 fl oz) chicken stock
1 cup (250 g/8 oz) bottled tomato
    pasta sauce
12 Kalamata olives
Kalamata olives, extra,
    to garnish
fresh flat-leaf parsley,
    to garnish

1 Using a vegetable peeler, carefully cut 4 thin strips of orange rind (about 1 x 4 cm/½ x 1½ inches). Remove the peel and pith from the orange, and segment the flesh.
2 Heat the oil in a saucepan and brown the chicken and chorizo slices, in batches if necessary. (Leave the meat side of the chicken browning for 5 minutes.) Add the stock, tomato sauce and orange rind. Bring to the boil, then reduce the heat and simmer, covered, for 25 minutes.
3 Remove the lid, turn the chicken over and continue to simmer, uncovered, for about 25 minutes, or until the chicken is tender and the sauce reduced. Season with salt and freshly ground black pepper, and stir through the olives and orange segments. Garnish with extra olives and flat-leaf parsley.

NUTRITION PER SERVE
Protein 75 g; Fat 30 g; Carbohydrate 12 g;
Dietary Fibre 3.5 g; Cholesterol 250 mg;
2553 kJ (610 cal)

NOTE: Chorizo sausages can be replaced with any spicy sausages.

Remove the peel and pith from the orange, and cut the flesh into segments.

Brown the chicken breasts and chorizo slices in the hot oil.

Stir the Kalamata olives and orange segments through the stew.

LEMON AND ROSEMARY CHICKEN STEW

Preparation time: 10 minutes
Total cooking time: 30 minutes
Serves 4

8 large chicken drumsticks
60 g (2 oz) butter
2 cloves garlic, crushed
2 teaspoons finely grated lemon rind
2 tablespoons chopped fresh
    rosemary
1 tablespoon plain flour

1½ cups (375 ml/12 fl oz) chicken
    stock
2 tablespoons lemon juice

1 Using a sharp knife, make two deep cuts in the thickest part of each chicken drumstick.
2 Melt the butter in a large frying pan. Add the drumsticks and cook over medium heat for 2 minutes on each side, or until brown. Add the garlic, lemon rind and rosemary.
3 Blend the flour, stock and lemon juice until smooth. Add to the pan and bring to the boil. Reduce the heat

and simmer, covered, for 25 minutes, or until the drumsticks are tender, stirring occasionally. Season, and serve immediately.

NUTRITION PER SERVE
Protein 68 g; Fat 54 g; Carbohydrate 3.5 g;
Dietary Fibre 0.5 g; Cholesterol 430 mg;
3205 kJ (765 cal)

HINT: To check whether chicken is cooked, insert a skewer into the thickest part. If the juice runs clear, the chicken is cooked.

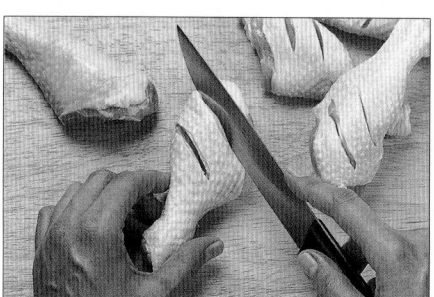

Make two deep cuts in the thickest part of the chicken drumsticks.

Add the crushed garlic, lemon rind and rosemary to the drumsticks.

Pour the stock mixture into the pan, then bring to the boil.

CHICKEN WITH BALSAMIC VINEGAR

Preparation time: 5 minutes
Total cooking time: 50 minutes
Serves 4

2 tablespoons olive oil
8 (1.2 kg/2 lb 6½ oz) chicken pieces
½ cup (125 ml/4 fl oz) chicken stock
½ cup (125 ml/4 fl oz) dry white wine
½ cup (125 ml/4 fl oz) balsamic vinegar
40 g (1¼ oz) chilled butter

1 Heat the oil in a large casserole dish over medium heat and cook the chicken, in batches, for 7–8 minutes, until browned. Pour off any excess fat.
2 Add the stock, bring to the boil, then reduce the heat and simmer, covered, for 30 minutes, or until the chicken is cooked through.
3 Add the white wine and vinegar and increase the heat to high. Boil for 1 minute, or until the liquid has thickened. Remove from the heat, stir in the butter until melted, and season. Spoon the sauce over the chicken to serve, accompanied by roast potatoes and salad.

NUTRITION PER SERVE
Protein 40 g; Fat 25 g; Carbohydrate 0.5 g;
Dietary Fibre 0 g; Cholesterol 165 mg;
1790 kJ (430 cal)

NOTE: Use a good-quality balsamic vinegar, as the cheaper varieties can be too acidic.

Cook the chicken pieces in batches until they are browned all over.

Simmer the chicken and stock, covered, until the chicken is cooked through.

Remove the pan from the heat and stir in the butter until melted.

CHICKEN BALLOTINE

Preparation time: 40 minutes
Total cooking time: 1 hour 45 minutes
Serves 8

1.6 kg (3¼ lb) chicken
2 red capsicums
1 bunch (1 kg /2 lb) silverbeet
30 g (1 oz) butter
1 onion, finely chopped
1 clove garlic, crushed
½ cup (50 g/1¾ oz) grated Parmesan
1 cup (80 g/2¾ oz) fresh breadcrumbs
1 tablespoon chopped fresh oregano
200 g (6½ oz) ricotta

1 To bone the chicken, cut through the skin on the centre back with a sharp knife. Separate the flesh from the bone down one side to the breast, being careful not to pierce the skin. Follow along the bones closely with the knife, gradually easing the meat from the thigh, drumstick and wing. Cut through the thigh bone where it meets the drumstick and cut off the wing tip. Repeat on the other side, then lift the rib cage away, leaving the flesh in one piece and the drumsticks still attached to the flesh. Scrape all the meat from the drumsticks and wings, discarding the bones. Turn the wing and drumstick flesh inside the chicken and lay the chicken out flat, skin-side down. Refrigerate.

2 Preheat the oven to moderate 180°C (350°F/Gas 4). Quarter the capsicums and remove the membranes and seeds. Place skin-side up under a hot grill until the skin blisters and blackens. Place in a plastic bag and allow to cool, then peel off the skin.

3 Remove the stalks from the silverbeet and finely shred the leaves.

Melt the butter in a large frying pan and add the onion and garlic. Cook over medium heat for about 5 minutes, or until soft. Add the silverbeet leaves and stir until wilted and all the moisture has evaporated. In a food processor, process the silverbeet and onion mixture with the Parmesan, breadcrumbs, oregano and half the ricotta. Season to taste with salt and cracked pepper.

4 Spread the silverbeet mixture over the chicken and lay the capsicum over the silverbeet. Form the remaining ricotta into a roll and place across the width of the chicken. Fold the sides of the chicken in over the filling so they overlap slightly, and tuck the ends in neatly. Secure with toothpicks and tie with string at 3 cm (1¼ inch) intervals.

5 Lightly grease a large piece of aluminium foil and place the chicken in the centre. Roll the chicken up securely in the foil, sealing the ends well. Place on a baking tray and bake for 1¼–1½ hours, or until the juices run clear when a skewer is inserted into the centre. Allow to cool, then refrigerate until cold before removing the foil, toothpicks and string. Cut into 1 cm (½ inch) slices to serve.

NUTRITION PER SERVE
Protein 40 g; Fat 12 g; Carbohydrate 9 g; Dietary Fibre 1.5 g; Cholesterol 105 mg; 1290 kJ (310 cal)

NOTE: If you are not confident about boning a chicken, ask your butcher to do it for you. To be on the safe side, it might be worth ordering your boned chicken a day in advance.

Using a sharp knife, cut through the skin on the centre back.

Separate the flesh from the bone down one side to the breast.

With your knife, gradually ease the meat from the thigh, drumstick and wing.

Use a sharp knife to cut off the wing tips through the joint.

Lay the chicken out flat and cover with the silverbeet mixture and capsicum quarters.

Roll the chicken up to enclose the filling and secure with toothpicks.

CHICKEN AND LEMON MEATBALLS

Preparation time: 20 minutes
+ 30 minutes refrigeration
Total cooking time: 10 minutes
Serves 4

500 g (1 lb) chicken mince
2 cloves garlic, crushed
1 cup (80 g/2¾ oz) fresh white
　breadcrumbs
1 teaspoon grated lemon rind
1 teaspoon fresh lemon thyme leaves
1 egg, lightly beaten

1 tablespoon olive oil
2 tablespoons lemon juice

YOGHURT MINT SAUCE
200 g (6½ oz) plain yoghurt
1 tablespoon shredded fresh mint
rinsed, chopped skin from ¼ of a
　preserved lemon

1 Using your hands, mix the chicken mince, garlic, breadcrumbs, lemon rind, thyme, egg and some salt and black pepper together in a large bowl. Wet your hands and form tablespoons of the mixture into balls and place on a lined tray. Refrigerate for 30 minutes.

2 To make the yoghurt mint sauce, mix the yoghurt, mint and preserved lemon rind together.
3 Heat the oil in a non-stick frying pan and cook the chicken meatballs in two batches, until golden on all sides and cooked through. Sprinkle with the lemon juice, transfer to a serving dish and sprinkle with more salt. Serve with the yoghurt mint sauce.

NUTRITION PER SERVE
Protein 35 g; Fat 11 g; Carbohydrate 16 g;
Dietary Fibre 1 g; Cholesterol 116 mg;
1300 kJ (310 cal)

Combine the chicken, garlic, breadcrumbs, lemon rind, thyme, egg, salt and pepper.

Using wet hands, roll tablespoons of the mixture into balls.

Cook the meatballs in batches until golden and cooked through.

BRAISED CHICKEN AND LEEK IN WINE

Preparation time: 15 minutes
Total cooking time: 1 hour
Serves 4

2 tablespoons oil
1.2 kg (2 lb 6½ oz) chicken pieces
1 leek, thinly sliced
5 spring onions, thinly sliced on the
    diagonal
2 tablespoons fresh marjoram
150 ml (5 fl oz) white wine
400 ml (13 fl oz) chicken stock
100 ml (3½ fl oz) cream

1 Score the chicken drumsticks. Heat 1 tablespoon of the oil in a frying pan and cook the chicken pieces in batches for 3–4 minutes, or until browned.

2 Heat the remaining oil in a large casserole dish and cook the leek, spring onion and marjoram for 4 minutes, or until soft. Add the chicken and wine, and cook for 2 minutes. Add the stock, cover and bring to the boil. Reduce the heat and simmer for 30 minutes. Stir in the cream and simmer, uncovered, for 15 minutes, or until the chicken is tender. Season to taste. Serve with steamed rice.

Use a sharp knife to score the thickest part of the chicken drumsticks.

NUTRITION PER SERVE
Protein 48 g; Fat 30 g; Carbohydrate 2.5 g;
Dietary Fibre 1 g; Cholesterol 190 mg;
2065 kJ (493 cal)

Add the stock to the chicken and wine mixture, then cover and bring to the boil.

CHICKEN MARSALA

Preparation time: 20 minutes
Total cooking time: 1 hour 10 minutes
Serves 4

¼ cup (60 ml/2 fl oz) olive oil
3 leeks, thinly sliced
1 teaspoon finely chopped fresh
 rosemary
3 bay leaves, torn
1 kg (2 lb) chicken pieces
seasoned plain flour
1 large eggplant, cut into cubes
2 zucchini, roughly chopped
½ cup (125 ml/4 fl oz) Marsala
300 ml (10 fl oz) chicken stock
2 cups (500 ml/16 fl oz) tomato purée

200 g (6½ oz) button mushrooms,
 halved

1 Heat the oil in a large, heavy-based saucepan. Fry the leek, rosemary and bay leaves over low heat for 5 minutes, or until soft, stirring occasionally. Remove with a slotted spoon, leaving as much oil in the pan as possible.
2 Toss the chicken pieces in the seasoned flour. Add the chicken to the pan and brown well in batches over medium heat. Return all the chicken to the pan with the leek mixture.
3 Add the eggplant and zucchini, and cook, stirring, for 2–3 minutes, or until softened, turning the chicken over. Add the Marsala and stock, and

cook for 15 minutes over medium–high heat.
4 Add the tomato purée and season well with salt and pepper. Bring to the boil, turning the chicken pieces in the sauce. Reduce the heat to a very gentle simmer, then cover and cook for 35 minutes. Add the mushrooms and cook, uncovered, for 5 minutes.

NUTRITION PER SERVE
Protein 63 g; Fat 20 g; Carbohydrate 13 g;
Dietary Fibre 9 g; Cholesterol 125 mg;
2200 kJ (530 cal)

NOTE: Marsala is a famous Italian fortified wine. It has a smoky, rich flavour and ranges from dry to sweet.

Remove the softened leeks and herbs from the pan with a slotted spoon.

Add the chopped eggplant and zucchini to the chicken and leek mixture.

Stir in the tomato purée and season well with salt and pepper.

PAN-FRIED CHICKEN TENDERLOINS WITH VEGETABLES

Preparation time: 25 minutes
Total cooking time: 20 minutes
Serves 4

2 tablespoons oil
6 slices prosciutto, cut crossways into
   1 cm strips
500 g (1 lb) chicken tenderloins
1 red onion, chopped
2 cloves garlic, crushed
1 small red chilli, chopped
1 tablespoon plain flour
1½ cups (375 ml/12 fl oz) chicken
   stock
150 g (5 oz) asparagus, halved
250 g (8 oz) beans, halved
¼ cup (15 g/½ oz) chopped fresh
   chives

1 Heat 1 tablespoon of the oil in a frying pan. Stir-fry the prosciutto over medium-high heat for 2 minutes, or until crisp. Lift out with a slotted spoon and drain on paper towels.
2 Add the chicken to the pan and cook over high heat for 1 minute on each side, or until brown, turning once. Remove from the pan and drain on paper towels.
3 Heat the remaining oil in a pan. Add the onion, garlic and chilli and stir-fry over medium-high heat for 2 minutes, or until softened. Add the flour and stir for 1 minute.
4 Add the stock gradually, stirring over the heat until the mixture boils and thickens. Add the asparagus and beans and reduce the heat to low. Cook, covered, for 3–5 minutes, or until the vegetables are tender. Return the chicken tenderloins to the pan and cook for 1 minute, or until heated through. Stir in the chopped chives and serve hot, sprinkled with the prosciutto strips.

NUTRITION PER SERVE
Protein 4.5 g; Fat 10 g; Carbohydrate 6.5 g;
Dietary Fibre 3 g; Cholesterol 2.5 mg;
263 kJ (135 cal)

HINT: Serve this dish with penne pasta or steamed potatoes.

Trim the asparagus spears and beans, then cut them in half.

Fry the chicken over high heat, then remove and drain on paper towels.

Sprinkle the flour over the onion mixture and stir for 1 minute.

Cook the asparagus and beans in the stock mixture until they are tender.

CHICKEN WITH FETA AND OLIVES

Preparation time: 15 minutes
Total cooking time: 1 hour
Serves 4

2 tablespoons oil
8 (1.2 kg/2 lb 6½ oz) chicken pieces
1 onion, chopped
25 g (¾ oz) fresh oregano, leaves picked
2 tablespoons tomato paste
2 x 425 g (14 oz) cans crushed tomatoes

150 g (5 oz) black olives
150 g (5 oz) feta, crumbled

1 Heat half the oil in a saucepan and cook the chicken pieces, in batches, for 3–4 minutes, or until golden. Remove from the pan and set aside.
2 In the same saucepan, heat the reamining oil and cook the onion and half the oregano leaves for 3 minutes, or until the onion is soft. Add the tomato paste to the onion mixture and stir for 2 minutes, then add the tomato and the chicken pieces.
3 Simmer, covered, for 40–50 minutes, or until the chicken is cooked through.

Add the olives and remaining oregano leaves. To serve, spoon into bowls and top with the crumbled feta.

NUTRITION PER SERVE
Protein 50 g; Fat 28 g; Carbohydrate 11 g;
Dietary Fibre 5 g; Cholesterol 165 mg;
2110 kJ (505 cal)

Cook the chicken pieces in the hot oil until they are golden.

Cook the onion and half the oregano leaves until the onion is soft.

Add the olives and remaining oregano leaves to the chicken.

CRISP-SKINNED CHICKEN

Preparation time: 1 hour + cooling
Total cooking time: 25 minutes
Serves 4

1.3 kg (2 lb 10 oz) chicken
1 tablespoon honey
1 star anise
1 strip dried mandarin peel (see NOTE)
1 teaspoon salt
oil, for deep-frying
2 lemons, cut into wedges

FIVE-SPICE SALT
2 tablespoons sea salt
1 teaspoon white peppercorns
½ teaspoon five-spice powder
½ teaspoon ground white pepper

1 Place the chicken in a pan and cover with cold water. Add the honey, star anise, mandarin peel and salt, and bring to the boil. Reduce the heat and simmer for 15 minutes. Turn off the heat and leave the chicken, covered, for 15 minutes. Transfer the chicken to a plate, and cool. Cut the chicken in half lengthways. Place on paper towels, uncovered, in the refrigerator for 20 minutes.
2 Heat the oil in a wok or deep, heavy- based pan. It is hot enough to use when a piece of bread dropped into the oil turns brown in 30 seconds. Very gently lower in half the chicken, skin-side down. Cook for 6 minutes, then turn and cook for another 6 minutes, making sure all the skin comes in contact with the oil. Drain

on paper towels. Repeat with the remaining chicken.
3 To make the five-spice salt, put the sea salt and peppercorns in a pan and dry-fry until fragrant and the salt is slightly browned. Crush in a mortar and pestle. Mix with the five-spice powder and white pepper. Joint the chicken and serve sprinkled with the five-spice salt and with lemon wedges.

NUTRITION PER SERVE
Protein 45 g; Fat 15 g; Carbohydrate 7 g;
Dietary Fibre 1.5 g; Cholesterol 100 mg;
1482 kJ (355 cal)

NOTE: To make dried mandarin peel, remove all of the pith from strips of peel and bake in a moderate 180°C (350°F/Gas 4) oven for 15 minutes.

Use poultry scissors to cut the cooled chicken in half lengthways.

Gently lower half the chicken, skin-side down, into the oil.

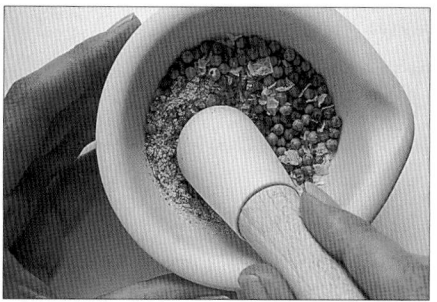

Crush the sea salt and white peppercorns in a mortar and pestle.

BALTI CHICKEN

Preparation time: 25 minutes
Total cooking time: 1 hour
Serves 6

1 kg (2 lb) chicken thigh fillets
⅓ cup (80 ml/2¾ fl oz) oil
1 large red onion, finely chopped
4–5 cloves garlic, finely chopped
1 tablespoon grated fresh ginger
2 teaspoons ground cumin
2 teaspoons ground coriander
1 teaspoon ground turmeric
½ teaspoon chilli powder
425 g (14 oz) can chopped tomatoes
1 green capsicum, seeded and diced
1–2 small green chillies, seeded and
  finely chopped
4 tablespoons chopped fresh
  coriander
2 chopped spring onions, to garnish

1 Remove any excess fat or sinew from the chicken thigh fillets and cut into four or five even-sized pieces.
2 Heat a large wok over high heat, add the oil and swirl to coat the side. Add the onion and stir-fry over medium heat for 5 minutes, or until softened but not browned. Add the garlic and ginger and stir-fry for 3 more minutes.
3 Add the spices, 1 teaspoon salt and ¼ cup (60 ml/2 fl oz) water. Increase the heat to high and stir-fry for 2 minutes, or until the mixture has thickened. Take care not to burn.
4 Add the tomato and 1 cup (250 ml/ 8 fl oz) water and cook, stirring often, for a further 10 minutes, or until the mixture is thick and pulpy and the oil comes to the surface.
5 Add the chicken to the pan, reduce the heat and simmer, stirring often,

for 15 minutes. Add the capsicum and chilli and simmer for 25 minutes, or until the chicken is tender. Add a little water if the mixture is too thick. Stir in the coriander and garnish with the spring onion.

NUTRITION PER SERVE
Protein 40 g; Fat 17 g; Carbohydrate 5 g; Dietary Fibre 2 g; Cholesterol 83 mg; 1370 kJ (327 cal)

NOTE: This curry is traditionally cooked in a Karahi or Balti pan— a wok is a good substitute.

Remove any excess fat or sinew from the chicken, then cut into even-size pieces.

Add the spices, salt and water to the wok and cook until thickened.

Cook, stirring, until the curry thickens and the oil comes to the surface.

CHILLI CON POLLO

Preparation time: 10 minutes
Total cooking time: 45 minutes
Serves 4

1 tablespoon olive oil
1 onion, finely chopped
500 g (1 lb) chicken mince
1–2 teaspoons mild chilli powder
440 g (14 oz) can chopped tomatoes
2 tablespoons tomato paste
1–2 teaspoons soft brown sugar
425 g (13 oz) can red kidney beans,
    rinsed and drained

1 Heat the oil in a large saucepan. Add the onion and cook over medium heat for 3 minutes, or until soft. Increase the heat and add the chicken. Cook until browned, breaking up any lumps with a wooden spoon.
2 Add the chilli powder and cook for 1 minute. Add the tomato, tomato paste and ½ cup (125 ml/4 fl oz) water and stir well.
3 Bring to the boil, then reduce the heat and simmer for 30 minutes. Stir through the sugar to taste and the kidney beans and heat through. Season and serve with baked corn chips and low-fat natural yoghurt.

NUTRITION PER SERVE
Protein 37 g; Fat 8.5 g; Carbohydrate 20 g;
Dietary Fibre 9 g; Cholesterol 60 mg;
1305 kJ (312 cal)

Cook the mince until it has browned, breaking up any lumps with a wooden spoon.

Add the tomato, tomato paste and water and stir well to combine.

Simmer for 30 minutes, then stir in the kidney beans and heat through.

CHICKEN DIANE

Preparation time: 10 minutes
Total cooking time: 15 minutes
Serves 4

8 (880 g/1 lb 13 oz) chicken thigh
    fillets
90 g (3 oz) butter
2 cloves garlic, crushed
1 tablespoon Worcestershire sauce
2 tablespoons finely chopped fresh
    parsley
⅓ cup (80 g/2¾ oz) sour cream
2 tablespoons cream

1 Trim the chicken thigh fillets of any excess fat and sinew. Melt the butter in a heavy-based frying pan over medium heat. Add the garlic and cook for 1 minute.
2 Add the chicken fillets and cook over medium heat for 4 minutes on each side, or until the chicken is cooked through. Remove the chicken fillets from the pan and set aside. Keep warm.
3 Add the Worcestershire sauce, chopped fresh parsley, sour cream and cream to the frying pan and stir over medium heat for 1 minute. Season to taste with salt and freshly ground black pepper. Return the chicken fillets to the pan and spoon the sauce over them. Serve the chicken with the sauce and some steamed green beans.

NUTRITION PER SERVE
Protein 50 g; Fat 18 g; Carbohydrate 2 g;
Dietary Fibre 0.5 g; Cholesterol 150 mg;
1540 kJ (370 cal)

NOTES: This dish is best cooked just before serving.
Do not allow the sauce to boil or the sour cream will separate and the sauce will have an unpleasant, curdled appearance.

VARIATION: Chicken breast fillets may be used in place of the chicken thigh fillets in this recipe.

Using a large sharp knife, finely chop the fresh parsley.

Cook the chicken in the butter and garlic mixture for 4 minutes on each side.

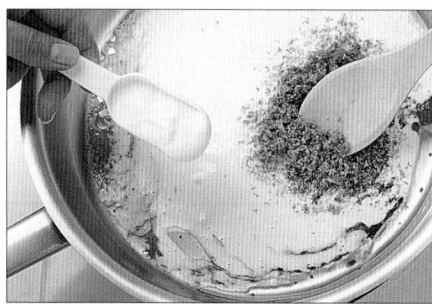

Add the Worcestershire sauce, parsley, sour cream and cream to the frying pan.

CHICKEN AND CHEESE BURGERS

Preparation time: 40 minutes
Total cooking time: 10–15 minutes
Makes 6

oil, for cooking
1 large onion, finely chopped
750 g (1½ lb) chicken mince
1 teaspoon paprika
1–2 teaspoons chopped red chilli
¾ cup (60 g/2 oz) fresh breadcrumbs
⅓ cup (90 g/3 oz) sour cream
2 tablespoons chopped fresh lemon
    thyme or chives
90 g (3 oz) Cheddar
30 g (1 oz) butter
1–2 cloves garlic, crushed

6 crusty bread rolls
lettuce, tomato, extra sour cream,
    pickled cucumbers and sweet chilli
    sauce, to serve

1 Heat a little oil in a frying pan. Add the onion and cook over medium heat until golden. Drain the onion on paper towels and cool slightly.
2 Using your hands, mix together in a large bowl the onion, chicken mince, paprika, chilli, breadcrumbs, sour cream, lemon thyme and some salt and freshly ground black pepper. Divide the mixture into 6 equal portions and shape into round balls. Cut the cheese into 6 pieces. Press a piece of cheese into the centre of each ball and mould the mixture to completely enclose the cheese. Flatten the balls slightly to make patties.
3 Heat the butter and 1 tablespoon of oil in a large frying pan. Add the garlic. When the mixture is foaming, add the patties, pressing with a spatula to flatten slightly. Cook over medium heat for 2–3 minutes each side, or until the patties are browned and the cheese melted.
4 Split the bread rolls in half. Toast and spread with a little butter if you wish. Fill with lettuce and tomato slices, a chicken patty, sour cream, some pickled cucumbers and sweet chilli sauce.

NUTRITION PER BURGER
Protein 40 g; Fat 19 g; Carbohydrate 37 g;
Dietary Fibre 3 g; Cholesterol 107 mg;
2010 kJ (480 cal)

Transfer the cooked onion to a plate covered with paper towels, to drain.

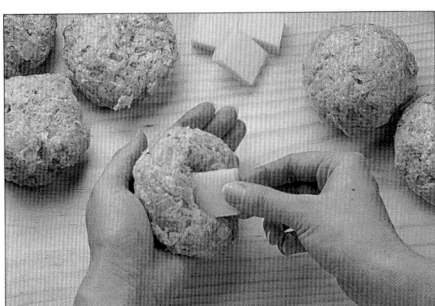

Press a portion of cheese into the centre of each ball and completely enclose.

When the mixture is foaming, add the patties to the pan.

CHICKEN IN MUSHROOM AND PAPRIKA SAUCE

Preparation time: 25 minutes
Total cooking time: 20 minutes
Serves 4

4 chicken breast fillets
¼ cup (30 g/1 oz) plain flour
30 g (1 oz) butter
1 tablespoon oil
1 onion, finely chopped
2 cloves garlic, crushed
250 g (8 oz) button mushrooms, thinly sliced
1 tablespoon sweet paprika
1 tablespoon tomato paste
½ cup (125 ml/4 fl oz) chicken stock

⅓ cup (80 g/2¾ oz) sour cream
2 tablespoons finely chopped fresh parsley

1 Trim the chicken of excess fat and sinew, and cut into bite-sized pieces. Coat the chicken pieces with the flour by shaking together in a plastic bag. Heat half the butter and oil in a large frying pan, add the chicken in small batches and cook over medium heat for 5 minutes, or until browned. Drain on paper towels.
2 Heat the remaining butter and oil in the same pan. Add the onion and garlic and cook over medium heat for 2 minutes, or until the onion has softened. Add the mushrooms and cook for 1–2 minutes, or until tender.

Remove from the heat. Add the paprika and cooked chicken, and stir to combine.
3 Combine the tomato paste with the stock in a small bowl. Add to the pan and stir until well combined with the chicken mixture. Season to taste. Return to the heat and bring to the boil. Reduce the heat and simmer, covered, for 5 minutes, or until the chicken is cooked through. Stir in the sour cream and warm through, but do not boil. Serve sprinkled with the parsley.

NUTRITION PER SERVE
Protein 54 g; Fat 25 g; Carbohydrate 10 g;
Dietary Fibre 3 g; Cholesterol 156 mg;
2007 kJ (480 cal)

Place the chicken pieces and flour into a plastic bag and shake to coat.

Remove from the heat, add the chicken and paprika, and stir to combine.

Stir the sour cream into the chicken mixture and warm through, but do not boil.

SPICY ROAST CHICKEN

Preparation time: 30 minutes
Total cooking time: 1 hour 20 minutes
Serves 6

3 small dried red chillies
1 teaspoon fennel seeds
1 teaspoon cumin seeds
1 teaspoon coriander seeds
⅛ teaspoon salt
1.5 kg (3 lb) chicken
2 cloves garlic, crushed
1 tablespoon peanut oil
2 onions, chopped
250 g (8 oz) pork mince
½ cup (80 g/2¾ oz) peanuts, roasted
    and roughly chopped
¼ cup (60 ml/2 fl oz) lime juice
1 tablespoon chopped fresh mint
2 tablespoons chopped fresh
    coriander leaves
1 teaspoon oil, extra
½ cup (125 ml/4 fl oz) coconut milk

1 Preheat the oven to moderate 180°C (350°F/Gas 4). Place the chillies, fennel, cumin, coriander seeds and salt in a small food processor or mortar and pestle and process or grind until the spices are blended to a powder.
2 Remove any fat from the chicken and rub the skin and cavity with garlic.
3 Heat the oil in a wok and cook the onion over medium heat for 3 minutes, or until golden. Add the pork and cook for 10 minutes, or until brown. Remove from the heat, stir in the peanuts, juice, mint and coriander. Allow the mixture to cool slightly before stuffing the chicken. Tightly secure the opening with a wooden skewer and tie the legs together.
4 Brush the chicken lightly with oil and then rub the skin with the spice mixture. Place the chicken on a rack in a baking dish and bake for 30 minutes. Remove from the oven and baste with the coconut milk and pan juices. Bake for 40 minutes, basting frequently, or until the chicken is tender. Remove the skewer and string before serving.

NUTRITION PER SERVE
Protein 52 g; Fat 20 g; Carbohydrate 5 g;
Dietary Fibre 2 g; Cholesterol 105 mg;
1695 kJ (405 cal)

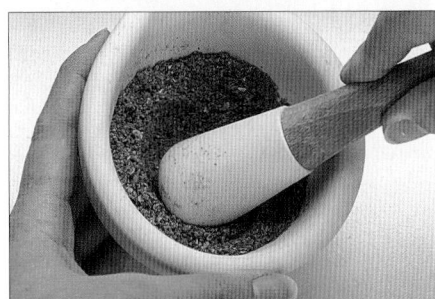

Grind the chillies, fennel, cumin, coriander and salt until they form a powder.

Cook the chopped onion in the wok until soft and golden.

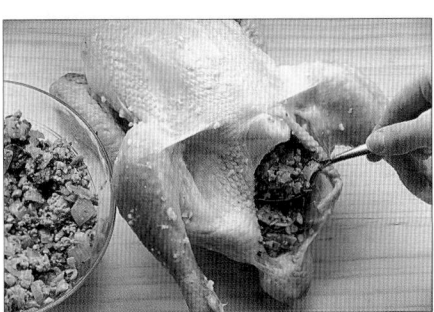

Spoon the prepared cooled filling into the cavity of the chicken.

Rub the spice mixture all over the surface of the chicken, using your fingers.

INDONESIAN CHICKEN IN COCONUT MILK

Preparation time: 15 minutes
  + 1 hour marinating time
Total cooking time: 50 minutes
Serves 4

8 large or 12 small chicken drumsticks
2 teaspoons crushed garlic
1 teaspoon salt
½ teaspoon ground black pepper
2 teaspoons ground cumin
2 teaspoons ground coriander
½ teaspoon ground fennel
½ teaspoon ground cinnamon
¼ cup (60 ml/2 fl oz) oil
2 onions, thinly sliced
¾ cup (185 ml/6 fl oz) coconut milk
1 tablespoon lemon juice or malt
  vinegar

1 Pat the chicken drumsticks dry with paper towels. Place the chicken in a large glass or ceramic bowl. Combine the garlic, salt, pepper, cumin, coriander, fennel, cinnamon and 2 tablespoons of the oil. Rub the mixture thoroughly over the chicken. Cover and marinate for 1 hour in the refrigerator.

2 Heat the remaining oil in a large pan. Add the onion and cook, stirring, until it is soft and golden. Add the chicken drumsticks and cook quickly over medium-high heat until they are well browned.

3 Combine the coconut milk, 1 cup (250 ml/8 fl oz) water and the lemon juice. Pour over the chicken, cover and simmer until the chicken is tender and the sauce is well reduced. (This should take about 40 minutes.) Serve the chicken with rice.

NUTRITION PER SERVE
Protein 44 g; Fat 28 g; Carbohydrate 4.5 g;
Dietary Fibre 2 g; Cholesterol 95 mg;
1870 kJ (445 cal)

Rub the garlic and spice mixture thoroughly over the chicken drumsticks.

Add the marinated chicken to the onion and cook over medium-high heat until well browned.

Combine the coconut milk, water and lemon juice, and pour over the chicken.

CHICKEN WITH SALSA VERDE

Preparation time: 10 minutes
Total cooking time: 10 minutes
Serves 6

SALSA VERDE
1 clove garlic
2 cups (60 g/2 oz) firmly packed fresh flat-leaf parsley
⅓ cup (80 ml/2¾ fl oz) extra virgin olive oil

3 tablespoons chopped fresh dill
1½ tablespoons Dijon mustard
1 tablespoon sherry vinegar
1 tablespoon baby capers, drained

6 large chicken breast fillets

1 Place all the ingredients for the salsa verde in a food processor or blender and process until almost smooth.
2 Cook the chicken fillets on a very hot, lightly oiled barbecue grill or flatplate for 4–5 minutes each side, or until cooked through.

3 Cut each chicken fillet into three on the diagonal and arrange on serving plates. Top with a spoonful of salsa verde and season to taste.

NUTRITION PER SERVE
Protein 50 g; Fat 18 g; Carbohydrate 0 g; Dietary Fibre 0.5 g; Cholesterol 110 mg; 1510 kJ (360 cal)

STORAGE: The salsa verde can be kept for a day in the fridge.

Put all the salsa verde ingredients in the food processor and process until almost smooth.

Cook the chicken on a very hot barbecue until it is cooked through.

To serve, slice each fillet into three on the diagonal and top with salsa verde.

CURRIED CHICKEN PIE

Preparation time: 40 minutes
Total cooking time: 1 hour
Serves 6

PASTRY
2 cups (250 g/8 oz) plain flour
1 teaspoon ground turmeric
1 teaspoon ground cumin
125 g (4 oz) butter, cubed
1 egg, lightly beaten
2–3 tablespoons cold water

1 cooked chicken (barbecued or
    poached)
40 g (1¾ oz) butter, extra
1 onion, chopped
2 tablespoons curry powder
1 teaspoon cumin seeds
1 tablespoon plain flour
1½ cups (375 ml/12 fl oz) chicken
    stock
½ cup (125 ml/4 fl oz) cream
1 tablespoon mango chutney
200 g (6½ oz) sweet potato, cubed
    and cooked
milk, for glazing

1 To make the pastry, place the flour, turmeric, cumin and butter in a food processor. Process the mixture for about 15 seconds, or until fine and crumbly. Add the egg and 2–3 tablespoons cold water to bring the mixture together. Turn out onto a lightly floured surface and press together until smooth. Cover with plastic wrap and refrigerate for 20 minutes while making the filling.
2 Remove the skin and bones from the chicken and chop the meat into bite-sized pieces. Heat the butter in a large pan or deep frying pan and cook the onion until soft and transparent. Add the curry powder and cumin seeds and cook for 1 minute longer.

3 Add the flour and cook for another 30 seconds. Remove from the heat and stir in the stock gradually, making sure the mixture is smooth between each addition. Return to the heat and cook, stirring, until the sauce bubbles and thickens. Add the cream, mango chutney, sweet potato and chicken meat. Simmer for 5 minutes, then season to taste with salt and black pepper. Remove from the heat and cool completely. Preheat the oven to moderately hot 190°C (375°F/Gas 5).
4 Divide the pastry into two portions. Roll out one half on a lightly floured surface until it is large enough to cover the base and side of a 23 cm (9 inch) pie dish. Line the dish with the pastry and spoon the chicken mixture into the base.
5 Roll out the remaining pastry to cover the top of the pie. Brush the adjoining edges with water and press together. Trim the edges with a sharp knife. Roll out the trimmings and cut into decorative shapes. Brush the underneath of the shapes with milk and press gently on to the pie.
6 Brush the top of the pie with milk and bake for 40 minutes, or until the top is golden brown. Serve hot or at room temperature.

NUTRITION PER SERVE
Protein 30 g; Fat 50 g; Carbohydrate 40 g;
Dietary Fibre 5 g; Cholesterol 240 mg;
2795 kJ (710 cal)

NOTE: It is very important that the filling is cold when added to the pastry, otherwise it will cause the pastry to become soggy.

Add the egg and enough water to bring the mixture together.

After removing the skin and bones, chop the chicken meat into bite-sized pieces.

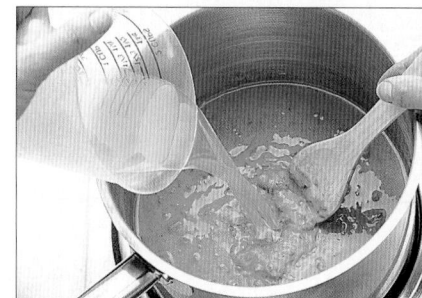
Stir in the stock, making sure the mixture is smooth after each addition.

Spoon the chicken mixture into the pastry in the pie dish.

Seal the adjoining edges of the pie and trim with a sharp knife.

Brush the top of the pie with milk before placing in the oven.

BLACKENED CAJUN SPICED CHICKEN

**Preparation time: 15 minutes +
30 minutes standing**
Total cooking time: 1 hour
Serves 4

1½ tablespoons onion powder
1½ tablespoons garlic powder
2 teaspoons paprika
1 teaspoon white pepper
2 teaspoons dried thyme
½–1 teaspoon chilli powder (see
    NOTE)
8 chicken drumsticks, scored

1 Combine the herbs, spices and
1 teaspoon salt in a plastic bag. Place
the drumsticks in the bag and shake
until all the pieces are coated. Leave
the chicken in the fridge for at least
30 minutes to allow the flavours to
develop, or overnight if time permits.
2 Cook the chicken on a lightly oiled
barbecue grill for 55–60 minutes, or
until slightly blackened and cooked
through. Brush lightly with some oil
to prevent drying out during cooking.

NUTRITION PER SERVE
Protein 25 g; Fat 7 g; Carbohydrate 0 g;
Dietary Fibre 0 g; Cholesterol 103 mg;
660 kJ (160 cal)

NOTE: Chilli powder is very hot, so
only use ½ teaspoon if you prefer a
milder flavour.

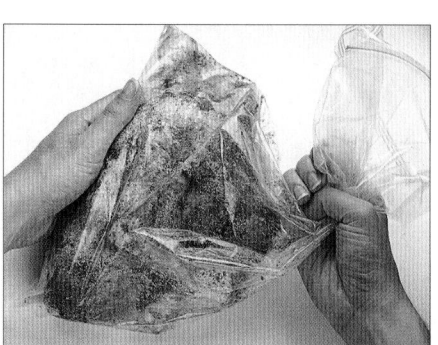

Put the herbs, spices and salt in a freezer bag,
add the chicken and shake to coat.

Cook the chicken for 55–60 minutes, or until
slightly blackened.

CITRUS CHICKEN DRUMSTICKS

**Preparation time: 20 minutes +
  3 hours marinating**
Total cooking time: 20 minutes
Serves 4

8 chicken drumsticks
4 tablespoons orange juice
4 tablespoons lemon juice
1 teaspoon grated orange rind
1 teaspoon grated lemon rind
1 teaspoon sesame oil
1 tablespoon olive oil
1 spring onion, finely chopped

1 Score the thickest part of the chicken so that it cooks evenly. Place in a shallow non-metallic dish.
2 Combine the juices, rinds, oils and spring onion and pour over chicken. Cover and leave in the fridge for at least 3 hours, turning occasionally. Drain the chicken, reserving marinade.

3 Cook the drumsticks on a hot, lightly oiled barbecue grill or flatplate for 15–20 minutes, or until tender. Brush occasionally with the reserved marinade. Serve immediately.

NUTRITION PER SERVE
Protein 24 g; Fat 13 g; Carbohydrate 3 g;
Dietary Fibre 0 g; Cholesterol 103 mg;
949 kJ (227 cal)

Score the thickest part of the chicken with a knife so that it cooks evenly.

Put the chicken in a non-metallic dish so that the citrus in the marinade doesn't react.

While the chicken is cooking, brush it occasionally with the marinade.

CHICKEN PROVENCALE

Preparation time: 15 minutes
Total cooking time: 1 hour 20 minutes
Serves 6

1 tablespoon olive oil
1.5 kg (3 lb) chicken pieces
1 onion, chopped
1 red capsicum, chopped
⅓ cup (80 ml/2¾ fl oz) white wine
⅓ cup (80 ml/2¾ fl oz) chicken stock
425 g (14 oz) can chopped tomatoes
2 tablespoons tomato paste
½ cup (90 g/3 oz) black olives
4 tablespoons shredded fresh basil

1 Heat the oil in a saucepan over high heat, add the chicken, in batches, and cook for 3–4 minutes, or until browned. Return all the chicken to the pan and add the onion and capsicum. Cook for 2–3 minutes, or until the onion is soft.

2 Add the wine, stock, tomatoes, tomato paste and olives and bring to the boil. Reduce the heat, cover and simmer for 30 minutes. Remove the lid, turn the chicken pieces over and cook for another 30 minutes, or until the chicken is tender and the sauce thickened. Season to taste, sprinkle with the basil and serve with rice.

NUTRITION PER SERVE
Protein 35 g; Fat 10 g; Carbohydrate 5 g;
Dietary Fibre 2 g; Cholesterol 115 mg;
1133 kJ (270 cal)

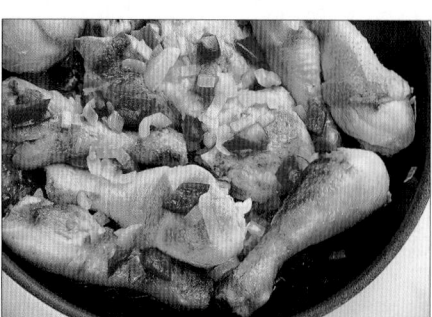

Once the chicken is browned, return it all to the pan with the onion and capsicum.

Just before serving, season and sprinkle with the shredded basil.

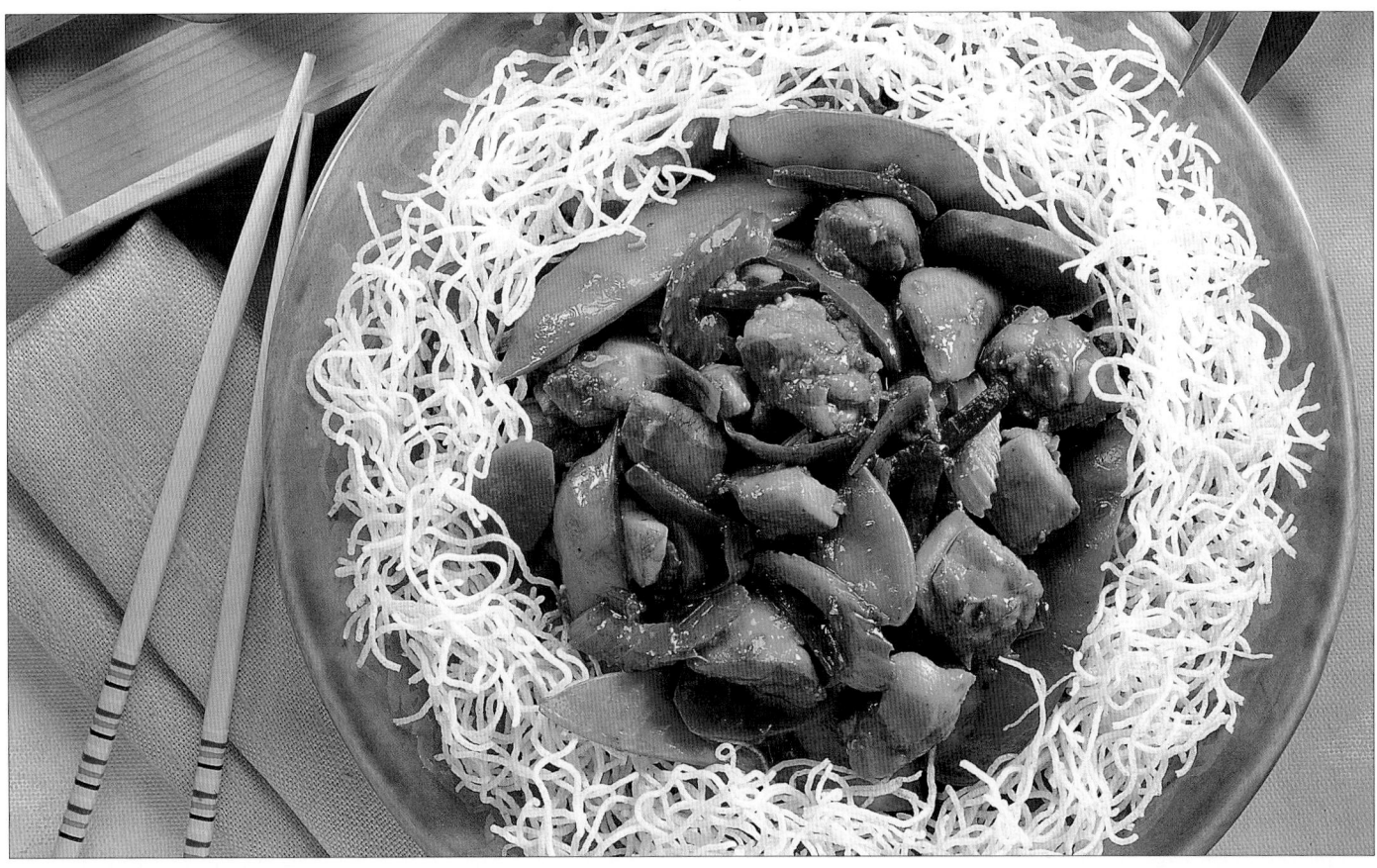

SOY CHICKEN AND CRISPY NOODLES

Preparation time: 30 minutes
Total cooking time: 35 minutes
Serves 4–6

750 g (1½ lb) chicken thigh fillets
3 teaspoons cornflour
⅓ cup (80 ml/2¾ fl oz) soy sauce
oil, for deep-frying
100 g (3½ oz) dried rice vermicelli
1 clove garlic, crushed
2 teaspoons grated fresh ginger
1 carrot, sliced
2 sticks celery, sliced
1 red capsicum, sliced

1 green capsicum, sliced
100 g (3½ oz) snow peas, trimmed
6 spring onions, sliced
¼ cup (60 ml/2 fl oz) chicken stock

1 Cut the chicken into 2 cm (¾ inch) cubes. Mix the cornflour with half the soy sauce; add the chicken, then cover and refrigerate until ready to use.
2 Heat the oil in a large pan. Break the vermicelli into small pieces. Drop a noodle into the oil: if it fizzes and puffs, the oil is hot enough. Add the noodles in small amounts and cook until puffed and white. Drain on paper towels and set aside.
3 Heat 1 tablespoon of oil in a wok,

add the chicken and stir-fry in batches over high heat for about 4 minutes, or until cooked. Remove the chicken from the wok and set aside.
4 Heat 1 tablespoon of oil in the wok and cook the garlic and ginger for 30 seconds. Add the vegetables and cook, tossing well, for 2–3 minutes.
5 Add the chicken, stock and remaining soy sauce and stir until boiled and thickened. Transfer to serving plates and arrange the noodles around the outside of the plates.

NUTRITION PER SERVE (6)
Protein 30 g; Fat 9 g; Carbohydrate 20 g;
Dietary Fibre 2 g; Cholesterol 85 mg;
1150 kJ (275 cal)

Mix the cornflour with half the soy sauce and then add the chicken and leave to marinate.

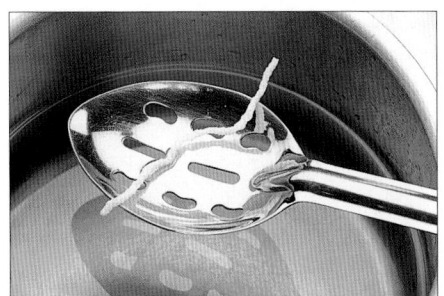

To test if the oil is hot, add one noodle. If the noodle fizzes and puffs, the oil is hot enough.

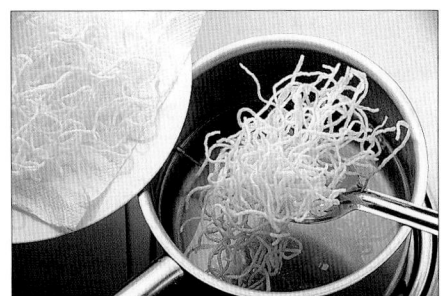

Cook the noodles in the hot oil until they are puffed and white.

GRILLED CHICKEN SKEWERS

**Preparation time: 20 minutes +
   2 hours marinating**
Total cooking time: 10 minutes
Serves 4

32 chicken tenderloins
24 (180 g/6 oz) cherry tomatoes
6 cap mushrooms, cut into quarters
2 cloves garlic, crushed
rind of 1 lemon, grated
2 tablespoons lemon juice
1 tablespoon olive oil
1 tablespoon fresh oregano leaves,
   chopped

1 Soak 8 wooden skewers for at least
30 minutes to prevent burning.
Thread a piece of chicken onto each
skewer, followed by a tomato, then a
piece of mushroom. Repeat three
times for each skewer.
2 Combine the garlic, lemon rind,
lemon juice, olive oil and chopped
oregano, pour over the skewers and
toss well. Marinate for at least 2
hours.

3 Place the skewers on a grill plate
and cook under high heat for
5 minutes each side, basting while
cooking, or until the chicken is cooked
and the tomatoes have shrivelled
slightly. Serve hot with a green salad.

NUTRITION PER SERVE
Protein 34 g; Fat 8 g; Carbohydrate 1 g;
Dietary Fibre 1 g; Cholesterol 75 mg;
909 kJ (217 cal)

NOTE: The skewers can be made in
advance and marinated for up to a
day before cooking.

Thread the chicken, tomato and mushrooms onto the skewers.

Leave the skewers in the marinade for at least 2 hours and overnight if possible.

Grill the skewers, basting with the marinade as they cook.

CURRIED CHICKEN NOODLES

Preparation time: 20 minutes
Total cooking time: 10 minutes
Serves 4

100 g (3½ oz) dried rice vermicelli
oil, for cooking
500 g (1 lb) chicken breast fillets, cut
   into thin strips
2 cloves garlic, crushed
1 teaspoon grated fresh ginger
2 teaspoons Asian-style curry powder
1 red onion, sliced

1 red capsicum, cut into thin strips
2 carrots, cut into matchsticks
2 zucchini, cut into matchsticks
1 tablespoon soy sauce

1 Place the vermicelli in a large bowl, cover with boiling water and soak for 5 minutes. Drain well and place on a tea towel to dry.
2 Heat the wok until very hot, add 1 tablespoon of the oil and swirl it around to coat the side. Stir-fry the chicken in batches over high heat until browned and tender. Remove all the chicken and drain on paper towels.
3 Reheat the wok, add 1 tablespoon of the oil and stir-fry the garlic, ginger, curry powder and onion for 1–2 minutes, or until fragrant. Add the capsicum, carrot and zucchini to the wok, and stir-fry until well coated in the spices. Add 1 tablespoon water and stir-fry for 1 minute.
4 Add the drained noodles and chicken to the wok. Add the soy sauce and toss well. Season with salt before serving.

NUTRITION PER SERVE
Protein 30 g; Fat 15 g; Carbohydrate 25 g;
Dietary Fibre 4 g; Cholesterol 60 mg;
1495 kJ (355 cal)

Trim any excess fat from the chicken and cut the chicken into thin strips.

Cut the carrot into strips, the size and shape of matchsticks.

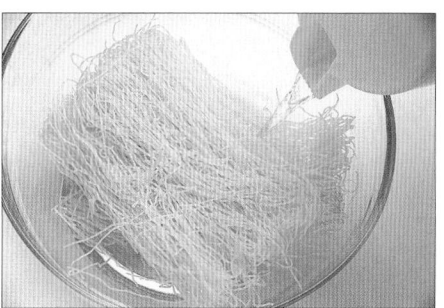

Soak the dried rice vermicelli in boiling water for 5 minutes.

SESAME CHICKEN AND SHANGHAI NOODLES

Preparation time: 20 minutes
Total cooking time: 15 minutes
Serves 4

600 g (1¼ lb) Shanghai noodles
1 tablespoon olive oil
1 tablespoon fresh ginger, cut into
  matchsticks
1 long red chilli, seeded and finely
  chopped
500 g (1 lb) chicken breast fillets, thinly
  sliced
2 cloves garlic, crushed
¼ cup (60 ml/2 fl oz) salt-reduced soy
  sauce
3 teaspoons sesame oil
700 g (1 lb 7 oz) baby bok choy, sliced
  lengthways into eighths
2 tablespoons sesame seeds, toasted

1 Cook the noodles in a saucepan of boiling water for 4–5 minutes, or until tender. Drain and rinse under cold water. Drain again.
2 Heat the oil in a wok and swirl to coat. Add the ginger and chilli and stir-fry for 1 minute. Add the chicken and stir-fry for a further 3–5 minutes, or until browned and almost cooked.
3 Add the garlic and cook for a further 1 minute. Pour in the soy sauce and sesame oil and toss to coat. Add the bok choy and noodles and stir-fry until the bok choy is tender and the noodles are warmed through. Place in individual serving bowls, sprinkle with sesame seeds and serve.

NUTRITION PER SERVE
Protein 45 g; Fat 19 g; Carbohydrate 80 g;
Dietary Fibre 6 g; Cholesterol 102 mg;
2850 kJ (680 cal)

Cut each baby bok choy into eighths with a sharp knife.

Cook the noodles until tender, drain and rinse, then drain again.

Stir-fry the chicken in the ginger and chilli mixture until browned and almost cooked.

CHICKEN, LEEK AND SWEET POTATO ONE-POT

Preparation time: 15 minutes
Total cooking time: 1 hour 40 minutes
Serves 4

600 g (1¼ lb) orange sweet potato
2 tablespoons olive oil
1.5 kg (3 lb) chicken pieces
1 leek, cut into 2 cm (¾ inch) slices
2 cloves garlic, crushed
2 tablespoons plain flour
2 cups (500 ml/16 fl oz) chicken stock
2 tablespoons fresh thyme

1 Preheat the oven to hot 220°C (425°F/Gas 7). Peel the sweet potato and cut it into chunks. Heat 1 tablespoon of the oil in a large flameproof casserole dish. Cook the chicken in batches for 3–4 minutes, or until browned. Set aside. Add the remaining oil and cook the leek and garlic for 2 minutes, or until soft.
2 Add the flour to the dish and cook, stirring, for about 1 minute to brown the flour. Gradually add the stock, stirring until the sauce boils and thickens. Remove from the heat. Return the chicken to the pan.
3 Add the sweet potato and half the thyme. Bake, covered, for 1½ hours, or until the chicken is cooked through and the sweet potato is tender. Season, and scatter with the remaining thyme. Serve with steamed rice.

NUTRITION PER SERVE
Protein 80 g; Fat 25 g; Carbohydrate 25 g; Dietary Fibre 4 g; Cholesterol 260 mg; 2778 kJ (665 cal)

Brown the chicken pieces, in batches, until they are browned all over.

Gradually add the stock to the flour mixture, then stir until the sauce boils and thickens.

Add the sweet potato pieces to the casserole dish, along with half the thyme.

Beef

OSSO BUCO AND GREMOLATA PIE

Preparation time: 40 minutes
Total cooking time: 2 hours 50 minutes
Serves 4–6

1 kg veal shanks, each 3.5 cm
   (1¼ inch) thick (6 pieces)
plain flour, to coat
2 tablespoons olive oil
1 onion, finely chopped
1 carrot, finely chopped
1 celery stick, finely diced
2 cloves garlic, finely chopped
⅔ cup (170 ml/5½ oz) beef stock
400 g (13 oz) can chopped tomatoes
⅔ cup (170 ml/5½ fl oz) dry white wine
1 teaspoon dried oregano

GREMOLATA
4 tablespoons finely chopped
   fresh flat-leaf parsley
1–2 cloves garlic, finely chopped
1 tablespoon grated lemon rind

PARMESAN POLENTA
1 cup (150 g/5 oz) instant polenta
½ cup (125 ml/4 fl oz) cream
½ cup (50 g/1¾ oz) grated Parmesan

1 Coat the veal with flour. Heat
1 tablespoon of the oil in a large
frying pan over high heat. Cook and
turn the veal until brown, then set
aside. Preheat the oven to moderate
180°C (350°F/Gas 4).

2 Heat the remaining oil in a 2 litre
flameproof casserole dish. Cook the
onion, carrot, celery and garlic over
low heat for 8 minutes, or until soft
but not brown.

3 Place the meat in a single layer on
top of the vegetables. Add the stock,
tomato, wine and oregano, and season
with salt and black pepper. Cover and
bake for 1½–2 hours, or until the meat
is tender and falling off the bones and
the liquid reduced and thickened.

4 Using tongs, remove the bones and
any fatty sinew from the veal. If you
like the marrow, spoon it out and
return it to the pan. Spoon the hot
mixture evenly into an oval 1.25 litre
ovenproof dish. Combine the
gremolata ingredients and sprinkle
half over the filling.

5 Cook the polenta according to the
manufacturer's instructions, then stir
in the cream and Parmesan. Season
with black pepper. Spread evenly
over the osso buco and rough up
with a fork. Bake for 25–30 minutes,
until bubbling. Leave for 5 minutes.
Sprinkle with the remaining
gremolata.

NUTRITION PER SERVE (6)
Protein 42.5 g; Fat 17.5 g; Carbohydrate
23.5 g; Dietary Fibre 3.0 g; Cholesterol
171.5 mg; 1835 kJ (440 Cal)

When the meat is tender and falling off the
bones, remove the bones and fatty sinew.

Spread the polenta topping evenly over the
osso buco.

PESTO BEEF SALAD

Preparation time: 30 minutes
Total cooking time: 25 minutes
Serves 8 as a starter

100 g (3½ oz) button mushrooms
1 large yellow capsicum
1 large red capsicum
cooking oil spray
100 g (3½ oz) lean fillet steak
1½ cups (135 g/4½ oz) penne

PESTO
1 cup (50 g/1¾ oz) tightly packed basil
    leaves
2 cloves garlic, chopped
2 tablespoons pepitas (pumpkin seeds)

1 tablespoon olive oil
2 tablespoons orange juice
1 tablespoon lemon juice

1 Cut the mushrooms into quarters. Cut the capsicums into large flat pieces, removing the seeds and membrane. Place skin-side-up under a hot grill until blackened. Leave covered with a tea towel until cool, then peel away the skin and chop the flesh.
2 Spray a non-stick frying pan with oil and cook the steak over high heat for 3–4 minutes each side until it is medium-rare. Remove and leave for 5 minutes before cutting into thin slices. Season with a little salt.
3 To make the pesto, finely chop the basil leaves, garlic and pepitas in a

food processor. With the motor running, add the oil, orange and lemon juice. Season well.
4 Meanwhile, cook the penne in a large pan of rapidly boiling salted water until al dente. Drain, then toss with the pesto in a large bowl.
5 Add the capsicum pieces, steak slices and mushroom quarters to the penne and toss to distribute evenly. Serve immediately.

NUTRITION PER SERVE
Protein 8 g; Fat 5 g; Carbohydrate 15 g;
Dietary Fibre 2 g; Cholesterol 7 mg;
660 kJ (135 cal)

When the capsicum has cooled, peel away the skin and dice the flesh.

Cook the steak in a non-stick frying pan until it is medium-rare.

Add the oil with the orange and lemon juice, in a thin stream.

VEAL CUTLETS IN CHILLI TOMATO SAUCE

Preparation time: 35 minutes
Total cooking time: 35 minutes
Serves 4

5 slices wholemeal bread
3 tablespoons fresh parsley
3 cloves garlic
4 thick veal cutlets, trimmed
3 tablespoons skim milk
2 teaspoons olive oil
1 onion, finely chopped
1 tablespoon capers, drained
1 teaspoon canned green
 peppercorns, chopped
1 teaspoon chopped red chilli
2 tablespoons balsamic vinegar
1 teaspoon soft brown sugar
2 tablespoons tomato paste
440 g (14 oz) can chopped tomatoes

1 Preheat the oven to moderate 180°C (350°F/Gas 4). Place a rack in a small baking dish. Chop the bread, parsley and garlic in a food processor to make fine breadcrumbs.
2 Season the cutlets on both sides with salt and black pepper. Pour the milk into a bowl and put the breadcrumbs on a plate. Dip the veal in the milk, then coat in the crumbs, pressing the crumbs on. Transfer to the rack and bake for 20 minutes.
3 Heat the oil in a small pan over medium heat. Add the onion, capers, peppercorns and chilli, cover and cook for 8 minutes. Stir in the vinegar, sugar and tomato paste and stir until boiling. Stir in the tomato, reduce the heat and simmer for 15 minutes.
4 Remove the cutlets from the rack and wipe the dish. Place about three-quarters of the tomato sauce in the base and put the cutlets on top. Spoon the remaining sauce over the cutlets and return to the oven. Reduce the oven to slow 150°C (300°F/Gas 2) and bake for 10 minutes to heat through.

NUTRITION PER SERVE
Protein 15 g; Fat 6 g; Carbohydrate 20 g; Dietary Fibre 5 g; Cholesterol 25 mg; 845 kJ (200 cal)

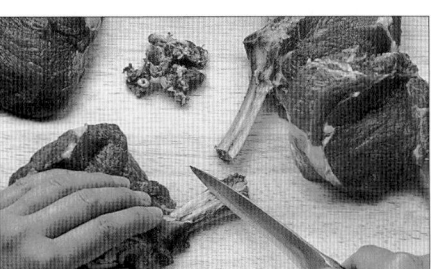
Trim the veal cutlets of any excess fat and gristle and then season with salt and pepper.

Dip the seasoned cutlets in the milk, then press into the breadcrumb mixture.

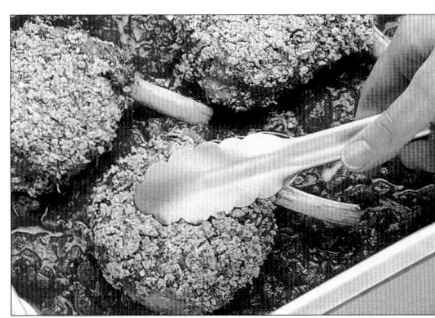
Put the cutlets on top of the tomato sauce, then top with the remaining sauce.

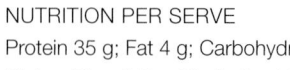

BEEF STROGANOFF

Preparation time: 20 minutes
Total cooking time: 25 minutes
Serves 4

500 g (1 lb) rump steak
cooking oil spray
1 onion, sliced
¼ teaspoon paprika
250 g (8 oz) button mushrooms,
    halved
2 tablespoons tomato paste

½ cup (125 ml/4 fl oz) beef stock
½ cup (125 ml/4 fl oz) low-fat
    evaporated milk
3 teaspoons cornflour
3 tablespoons chopped fresh parsley

1 Remove any excess fat from the steak and slice into thin strips. Cook in batches in a large, lightly greased non-stick frying pan over high heat, until just cooked. Remove from the pan.
2 Lightly spray the pan and cook the onion, paprika and mushrooms over medium heat until the onion has softened. Add the meat, tomato paste, stock and ½ cup (125 ml/4 fl oz) water. Bring to the boil, then reduce the heat and simmer for 10 minutes.
3 In a small bowl, mix the evaporated milk with the cornflour. Add to the pan and stir until the sauce boils and thickens. Sprinkle with parsley.

NUTRITION PER SERVE
Protein 35 g; Fat 4 g; Carbohydrate 8 g;
Dietary Fibre 2.5 g; Cholesterol 85 mg;
900 kJ (215 cal)

Slice the rump steak into thin strips after removing any excess fat.

Stir the onion, paprika and mushrooms until the onion has softened.

Stir the evaporated milk into the cornflour until the mixture is smooth.

THAI BEEF SALAD

Preparation time: 20 minutes + cooling
Total cooking time: 5 minutes
Serves 6

oil, for cooking
500 g (1 lb) beef fillet or lean rump,
    thinly sliced
2 cloves garlic, crushed
¼ cup (15 g/½ oz) finely chopped
    coriander roots and stems
1 tablespoon grated palm sugar
⅓ cup (80 ml/2¾ fl oz) lime juice
2 tablespoons fish sauce
2 small red chillies, seeded,
    finely sliced

2 red Asian shallots, finely sliced
2 telegraph cucumbers, sliced into
    thin ribbons
1 cup (30 g/1 oz) mint leaves
1 cup (90 g/3 oz) bean sprouts
¼ cup (30 g/1 oz) chopped roasted
    peanuts

1 Heat the wok until very hot, add
1 tablespoon of the oil and swirl it
around to coat the side. Add half the
beef and cook for 1–2 minutes, or
until medium rare. Remove from the
wok and set aside. Repeat with the
rest of the beef.
2 Place the garlic, coriander, palm
sugar, lime juice, fish sauce,
¼ teaspoon ground white pepper and

¼ teaspoon salt in a bowl, and stir
until all the sugar has dissolved. Add
the chilli and shallots and mix well.
3 Pour the sauce over the beef while
still hot, mix well, then cool to room
temperature.
4 In a separate bowl, toss together
the cucumber and mint leaves, and
refrigerate until required.
5 Place the cucumber and mint on a
serving platter, and top with the beef,
bean sprouts and roasted peanuts.
Serve immediately.

NUTRITION PER SERVE
Protein 22 g; Fat 13 g; Carbohydrate 7.5 g;
Dietary Fibre 2 g; Cholesterol 50 mg;
1041 kJ (248 cal)

Small red chillies are the hottest type. Remove
the seeds and white membrane, and finely slice.

Pour the sauce over the hot stir-fried beef and
leave to cool.

Toss together the cucumber and mint leaves and
leave in the fridge.

MADRAS BEEF CURRY

Preparation time: 20 minutes
Total cooking time: 1 hour 40 minutes
Serves 4

1 kg (2 lb) skirt or chuck steak
1 tablespoon oil
1 onion, chopped
3–4 tablespoons Madras
    curry paste

¼ cup (60 g/2 oz) tomato paste
1 cup (250 ml/8 fl oz) beef stock

1 Trim the meat of any fat or sinew and cut it into bite-sized cubes. Heat the oil in a large frying pan, add the onion and cook over medium heat for 10 minutes, or until browned.
2 Add the curry paste and stir for 1 minute, or until fragrant. Then add the meat and cook, stirring, until coated with the curry paste. Stir in the tomato paste and stock. Reduce the heat and simmer, covered, for 1 hour 15 minutes. Uncover and simmer for 15 minutes, or until the meat is tender.

NUTRITION PER SERVE
Protein 53 g; Fat 15 g; Carbohydrate 4.5 g;
Dietary Fibre 1.5 g; Cholesterol 170 mg;
1514 kJ (362 cal)

STORAGE TIME: This dish can be refrigerated for 2–3 days.

Trim the meat of any excess fat or sinew and cut into cubes.

Cook the chopped onion in a large frying pan until it is browned.

Add the meat to the pan and stir to coat in the curry paste.

VEAL, LEMON AND CAPER STEW

Preparation time: 30 minutes
Total cooking time: 2 hours
Serves 6

1 tablespoon olive oil
50 g (1¾ oz) butter
1 kg (2 lb) stewing veal,
   cut into 4 cm (1½ inch) chunks
300 g (10 oz) French shallots
3 leeks, cut into large chunks
2 cloves garlic, crushed
1 tablespoon plain flour
2 cups (500 ml/16 fl oz)
   chicken stock
1 teaspoon grated lemon rind
⅓ cup (80 ml/2¾ fl oz) lemon juice
2 bay leaves
2 tablespoons capers, drained and
   well rinsed

1 Preheat the oven to moderate 180°C (350°F/Gas 4). Heat the oil and half the butter in a large, heavy-based pan. Brown the veal in batches over medium-high heat and transfer to a large casserole dish.
2 Blanch the shallots in boiling water for 30 seconds, then peel and add to the pan with the leeks. Gently cook for 5 minutes, or until soft and golden. Add the garlic, cook for 1 minute, then transfer to the casserole dish.
3 Melt the remaining butter in the pan, add the flour and cook for 30 seconds. Remove from the heat, add the stock and stir until well combined. Return to the heat and cook, stirring, until the sauce begins to bubble.
4 Pour the sauce into the casserole dish and stir in the lemon rind, lemon juice and bay leaves. Cover and bake for 1–1½ hours, or until the veal is tender. During the last 20 minutes of cooking, remove the lid to allow the sauces to reduce a little. Stir in the capers and season with salt and pepper before serving.

NUTRITION PER SERVE
Protein 40 g; Fat 13 g; Carbohydrate 5 g;
Dietary Fibre 2 g; Cholesterol 160 mg;
1300 kJ (300 cal)

Add the leeks and peeled shallots to the pan and gently fry until soft and golden.

Remove the pan from the heat and stir in the stock, scraping up the brown bits.

KEEMA CURRY (MINCED BEEF AND PEA CURRY)

Preparation time: 15 minutes
Total cooking time: 40 minutes
Serves 6

2 tablespoons oil
2 onions, chopped
1 clove garlic, finely chopped
1 tablespoon finely chopped fresh
   ginger
3 large green chillies, seeded and
   finely chopped
1½ tablespoons ground coriander
1 tablespoon ground cumin
2 teaspoons ground turmeric

750 g (1½ lb) potatoes, cut into
   1.5 cm (⅝ inch) cubes
1.5 kg (3 lb) minced beef
225 g (7 oz) frozen peas
⅔ cup (170 ml/5½ fl oz) coconut
   cream
1 tablespoon fresh coriander leaves,
   chopped

1 Heat the oil in a large saucepan, add the onion and cook, stirring frequently, for 5 minutes, or until lightly golden. Add the garlic, ginger and chilli, and cook for 1 minute, then add the coriander, cumin and turmeric and cook for a further 1 minute.

2 Add the potato and ½ cup (125 ml/ 4 fl oz) water to the pan, and combine well. Cook, covered, over medium

heat for 15 minutes. Add the beef and cook, uncovered, stirring frequently, over high heat, for 4–5 minutes, or until the mince is lightly browned. Break up any lumps with the back of a spoon. Stir in the peas and coconut cream.

3 Bring to the boil and cook, stirring occasionally, for 10 minutes, or until the curry is almost dry and the peas are cooked through. Season with salt and garnish with the coriander leaves. Serve with naan or pitta bread.

NUTRITION PER SERVE
Protein 56 g; Fat 34 g; Carbohydrate 20 g;
Dietary Fibre 5 g; Cholesterol 158 mg;
2548 kJ (609 Cal)

Cook the onion in a large saucepan for 5 minutes, or until lightly golden.

Break up any lumps in the mince with the back of a spoon.

Bring to the boil and cook, stirring, until the curry is almost dry.

BEEF POT ROAST

Preparation time: 15 minutes
Total cooking time: 3 hours 15 minutes
Serves 6

300 g (10 oz) small pickling onions
2 carrots
3 parsnips, peeled
30 g (1 oz) butter
1–1.5 kg (2–3 lb) piece of silverside,
    trimmed of fat (see NOTE)
¼ cup (60 ml/2 fl oz) dry red wine
1 large tomato, finely chopped
1 cup (250 ml/8 fl oz) beef stock

1 Put the onions in a heatproof bowl and cover with boiling water. Leave for 1 minute, then drain well. Allow to cool and then peel off the skins.

2 Cut the carrots and parsnips in half lengthways then into even-sized pieces. Heat half the butter in a large heavy-based pan that will tightly fit the meat (it will shrink during cooking), add the onions, carrot and parsnip and cook, stirring, over medium-high heat until browned. Remove from the pan.

3 Add the remaining butter to the pan and add the meat, browning well all over. Increase the heat to high and pour in the wine. Bring to the boil, then add the tomato and stock. Return to the boil, then reduce the heat to low, cover and simmer for 2 hours, turning once. Add the vegetables and simmer, covered, for 1 hour.

4 Remove the meat from the pan and put it on a board ready for carving.

Cover with foil and leave it to stand while you finish the sauce.

5 Increase the heat to high and boil the pan juices with the vegetables for 10 minutes to reduce and thicken slightly. Skim off any fat and taste before seasoning. Serve the meat and vegetables with the pan juices. Serve with mustard.

NUTRITION PER SERVE
Protein 60 g; Fat 10 g; Carbohydrate 95 g;
Dietary Fibre 3.5 g; Cholesterol 185 mg;
1690 kJ (405 cal)

NOTE: Eye of silverside is a tender, long shaped cut of silverside which carves easily into serving-sized pieces. A regular piece of silverside or topside may be substituted.

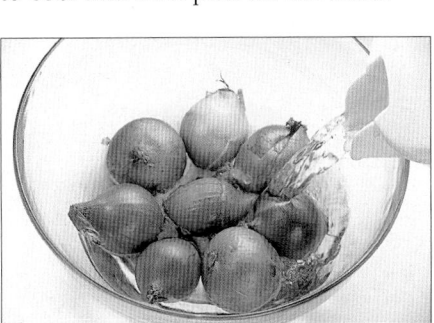

Put the pickling onions in a bowl and cover with boiling water.

Add the piece of meat to the pan and brown well on all sides.

Put the vegetables in with the meat, then cover and simmer for 1 hour.

CHILLI CON CARNE

Preparation time: 25 minutes + overnight soaking
Total cooking time: 2 hours 15 minutes
Serves 6

185 g (6 oz) dried black eye beans
650 g (1 lb 5 oz) tomatoes
1½ tablespoons oil
900 g (1 lb 13 oz) trimmed chuck
    steak, cut into chunks
3 onions, thinly sliced
2 cloves garlic, chopped
2 teaspoons ground cumin
1 tablespoon paprika
½ teaspoon ground allspice
1–2 teaspoons chilli powder
1 tablespoon soft brown sugar
1 tablespoon red wine vinegar

1 Put the beans in a bowl, cover with plenty of water and leave overnight to soak. Drain well. Score a cross in the base of each tomato. Put the tomatoes in a bowl of boiling water for 30 seconds, then transfer to a bowl of cold water. Drain and peel the skin away from the cross. Halve the tomatoes and remove the seeds with a teaspoon. Chop the flesh finely.
2 Heat 1 tablespoon of the oil in a large heavy-based pan and add half the meat. Cook over medium-high heat for 2 minutes, or until well browned. Remove from the pan and repeat with the remaining meat, then remove from the pan.
3 Add the rest of the oil to the pan and add the onion. Cook over medium heat for 5 minutes, or until softened. Add the garlic and spices and cook, stirring, for 1 minute, or until aromatic. Add 2 cups (500 ml/16 fl oz) water and stir. Return the meat

to the pan with the beans and tomatoes. Bring to the boil, then reduce the heat to low and simmer, partially covered, for 2 hours, or until the meat is tender and the chilli con carne is thick and dryish, stirring occasionally. Towards the end of the cooking time the mixture may start to catch, so add a little water if

necessary. Stir through the sugar and vinegar, and season with salt to taste. Serve with flour tortillas, grated low-fat cheese and lime wedges.

NUTRITION PER SERVE
Protein 43 g; Fat 10 g; Carbohydrate 54 g; Dietary Fibre 10 g; Cholesterol 100 mg; 2040 kJ (486 cal)

Soak the black eye beans in a bowl of water overnight before cooking them.

Drain the tomatoes then carefully peel the skin away from the cross.

Remove the tomato seeds with a teaspoon and then finely chop the flesh.

SILVERSIDE AND PARSLEY SAUCE

Preparation time: 20 minutes + soaking
Total cooking time: 2 hours
Serves 6

1.5 kg (3 lb) corned silverside
1 teaspoon black peppercorns
5 whole cloves
2 bay leaves, torn
2 tablespoons soft brown sugar

PARSLEY SAUCE
30 g (1 oz) butter
1½ tablespoons plain flour
400 ml (13 fl oz) skim milk
½ cup (125 ml/4 fl oz) beef stock

2 tablespoons chopped fresh
  parsley

1 Soak the corned beef in cold water for 45 minutes, changing the water 3–4 times to reduce the saltiness.
2 Put the beef in a large heavy-based pan with the peppercorns, cloves, bay leaves, brown sugar and enough cold water to just cover. Bring to the boil, then reduce the heat to very low and simmer for 1½–1¾ hours. Turn the meat every 30 minutes and add more water when needed. Do not let the water boil or the beef will be tough. Remove from the pan, wrap in foil and leave to stand for at least 15 minutes before carving. (Save the liquid and use for cooking vegetables.)

3 To make the parsley sauce, melt the butter in a pan over medium heat, and stir in the flour. Cook, stirring with a wooden spoon, for 1 minute. Remove the pan from the heat and pour in the milk and stock, whisking until smooth. Return the pan to the heat and cook, whisking constantly, until the sauce boils and thickens. Reduce the heat and simmer for 2 minutes more. Stir in the parsley and season to taste.
4 Slice the meat across the grain and serve with the sauce.

NUTRITION PER SERVE
Protein 50 g; Fat 15 g; Carbohydrate 10 g;
Dietary Fibre 0 g; Cholesterol 100 mg;
1625 kJ (390 cal)

Soak the corned beef in cold water to help eliminate some of the saltiness.

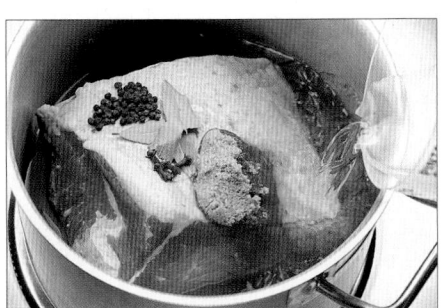

Put the beef, peppercorns, cloves, bay leaves and sugar in a pan and cover with water.

Make sure you turn the meat every half hour or so and don't boil the water or the meat will toughen.

NOODLES WITH BEEF

Preparation time: 20 minutes
Total cooking time: 20 minutes
Serves 4–6

500 g (1 lb) fresh rice noodle sheets
2 tablespoons peanut oil
2 eggs, lightly beaten
500 g (1 lb) rump steak, thinly sliced
   across the grain
¼ cup (60 ml/2 fl oz) kecap manis
1½ tablespoons soy sauce
1½ tablespoons fish sauce
300 g (10 oz) Chinese broccoli (gai
   larn), cut into 5 cm (2 inch) lengths
¼ teaspoon ground white pepper
lemon wedges, to serve

1 Cut the noodle sheets lengthways into 2 cm strips. Cover with boiling water, then gently separate the strips.

2 Heat a wok over medium heat, add 1 tablespoon of the oil and swirl to coat the side. Add the egg, swirl to coat and cook for 1–2 minutes, or until set. Remove, roll up and cut into shreds.

3 Reheat the wok over high heat, add the remaining oil and swirl to coat. Stir-fry the beef in batches for 3 minutes, or until brown. Remove the beef to a side plate.

4 Reduce the heat to medium, add the noodles and stir-fry for 2 minutes. Combine the kecap manis, soy sauce and fish sauce in a bowl. Add to the wok with the broccoli and white pepper, then stir-fry for a further 2 minutes. Return the egg and beef to the wok and stir-fry for another 3 minutes, or until the broccoli has wilted and the noodles are soft but not falling apart. Serve with the lemon wedges on the side.

NUTRITION PER SERVE (6)
Protein 24 g; Fat 12 g; Carbohydrate 19 g;
Dietary Fibre 1.5 g; Cholesterol 121 mg;
1175 kJ (280 Cal)

NOTE: Rice noodles should not be refrigerated as they are very difficult to separate when cold.

Cut the noodle sheets lengthways into even strips.

BEEF WITH OYSTER SAUCE

Preparation time: 15 minutes
Total cooking time: 5 minutes
Serves 4

1½ teaspoons cornflour
½ cup (125 ml/4 fl oz) beef stock
2 tablespoons oyster sauce
1 teaspoon finely crushed garlic
1 teaspoon caster sugar
1 tablespoon oil
350 g (11 oz) rump steak, finely sliced

250 g (8 oz) beans, topped and tailed, cut into 5 cm (2 inch) lengths
1 small red capsicum, sliced
½ cup (60 g/2 oz) bean sprouts

1 Dissolve the cornflour in a little of the stock. Mix with the remaining stock, oyster sauce, garlic and sugar and set aside.
2 Heat the wok until very hot, add the oil and swirl it around to coat the side. Add the beef in batches and stir-fry over high heat for 2 minutes, or until it browns.

3 Add the beans and capsicum and stir-fry another minute.
4 Add the cornflour mixture to the wok and cook until the sauce boils and thickens. Stir in the bean sprouts and serve immediately.

NUTRITION PER SERVE
Protein 23 g; Fat 12 g; Carbohydrate 10 g;
Dietary Fibre 2.5 g; Cholesterol 60 mg;
1016 kJ (243 cal)

Brown the steak in batches so the wok doesn't overcrowd and reduce the temperature.

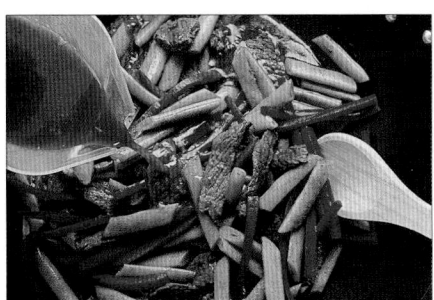

Add the beans and capsicum to the browned meat and stir-fry for 1 minute.

Add the mixture of stock and cornflour and stir until the sauce boils and thickens.

CORIANDER BEEF

Preparation time: 15 minutes
+ 1–2 hours marinating
Total cooking time: 15 minutes
Serves 4

500 g (1 lb) rump steak, cut into thin
   strips
4 cloves garlic, finely chopped
1 tablespoon finely chopped fresh
   ginger
½ cup (25 g/¾ oz) chopped coriander
   roots, stems and leaves
¼ cup (60 ml/2 fl oz) oil
oil, extra, for cooking

2 red onions, thinly sliced
½ red capsicum, thinly sliced
½ green capsicum, thinly sliced
1 tablespoon lime juice
½ cup (25 g/¾ oz) chopped coriander
   leaves, extra

1 Place the beef strips in a glass or
ceramic bowl. Add the garlic, ginger,
coriander and oil. Mix together well,
then cover and refrigerate for
1–2 hours.
2 Heat the wok until very hot and
stir-fry the meat in three batches over
high heat for 2–3 minutes, or until the
meat is just cooked. Remove all the
meat from the wok and keep it warm.

3 Heat 1 tablespoon oil, add the
onion and cook over medium-high
heat for 3–4 minutes, or until the
onion is slightly softened. Add the
capsicum, and cook, tossing
constantly, for 3–4 minutes, or until
the capsicum is slightly softened.
4 Return all the meat to the wok with
the lime juice and extra coriander.
Toss well, then remove from the heat
and season well with salt and cracked
black pepper. Serve immediately.

NUTRITION PER SERVE
Protein 30 g; Fat 25 g; Carbohydrate 5 g;
Dietary Fibre 2 g; Cholesterol 85 mg;
1620 kJ (385 cal)

Finely chop the roots, stems and leaves of the
coriander.

Stir-fry the marinated meat in batches until it is
just cooked.

Add the capsicum and toss constantly until it is
slightly softened.

STEAK AND KIDNEY PUDDING

Preparation time: 25 minutes
Total cooking time: 5 hours
Serves 4

2¾ cups (340 g/11 oz) self-raising flour
150 g (5 oz) butter, frozen and grated
700 g (1 lb 7 oz) chuck steak, cut into
    2 cm (¾ inch) pieces
200 g (6½ oz) ox kidney, cleaned and
    cut into 2 cm (¾ inch) pieces
1 small onion, finely chopped
2 teaspoons finely chopped fresh
    parsley
1 tablespoon plain flour
1 teaspoon Worcestershire sauce
¾ cup (185 ml/6 fl oz) beef stock

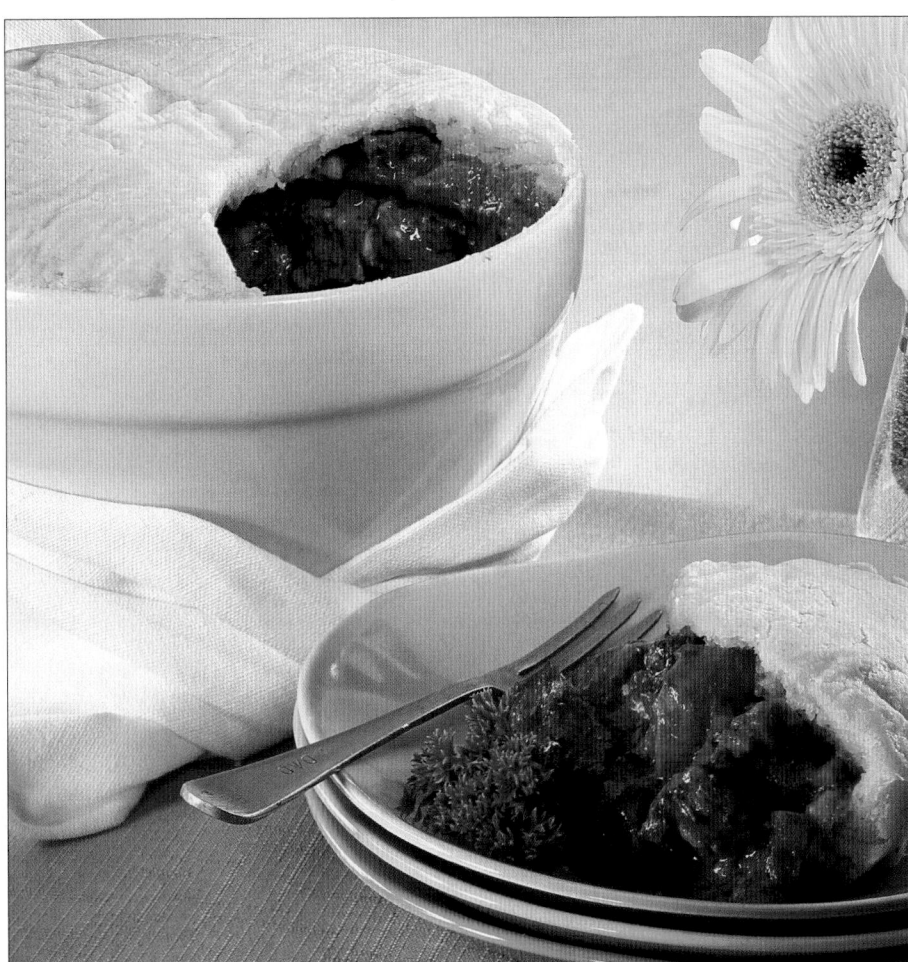

1 Grease a 1.5 litre pudding basin with melted butter, and put a round of baking paper in the bottom. Place the empty basin in a large pan on a trivet or upturned saucer and pour in enough cold water to come halfway up the side of the basin. Remove the basin and put the water on to boil.
2 Sift the flour into a bowl and add the butter and a large pinch of salt. Mix together with a flat-bladed knife and add enough water to form a soft dough. Reserve one-third of the dough and roll the rest out to a circle about 1 cm (¾ inch) thick. Sprinkle with flour and fold it in half. Using a rolling pin, roll the straight edge away from you, making sure the two halves don't stick together—this helps form a bag shape. Fit the bag into the pudding basin and stretch it to fit, leaving a little hanging over the edge, and brush out any excess flour.
3 Mix the steak, kidney, onion, parsley and flour together in a bowl.

Season and add the Worcestershire sauce. Put the mixture into the pastry case and add enough stock or water to come three-quarters of the way up the meat. Roll out the remaining pastry to form a lid the same size as the top of the bowl. Fold overhanging pastry into the bowl and dampen the edge with water. Put the lid on and press the edges together securely.
4 Lay a sheet of foil then a sheet of baking paper on the work surface, and make a large pleat in the middle. Grease with melted butter. Place paper-side-down across the top of the

basin and tie string securely around the rim and over the top of the basin to make a handle. This is used to lift the pudding in and out of the pan.
5 Lower the basin into the simmering water and cover with a tight-fitting lid. Cook for 5 hours, checking every hour and topping up with boiling water as needed. Serve from the basin.

NUTRITION PER SERVE
Protein 55 g; Fat 40 g; Carbohydrate 63 g;
Dietary Fibre 3.7 g; Cholesterol 370 mg;
3402 kJ (813 Cal)

Roll the straight edge away from you to form a bag shape.

Fit the bag into the basin, leaving a little pastry hanging over the edge.

Pour in enough stock or water to come three-quarters of the way up the meat.

COTTAGE PIE

Preparation time: 30 minutes
Total cooking time: 1 hour 30 minutes
Serves 6–8

2 tablespoons olive oil
2 onions, chopped
2 carrots, diced
1 celery stick, diced
1 kg (2 lb) beef mince
2 tablespoons plain flour
1½ cups (375 ml/12 fl oz) beef stock
1 tablespoon soy sauce
1 tablespoon Worcestershire sauce
2 tablespoons tomato sauce
1 tablespoon tomato paste
2 bay leaves
2 teaspoons chopped fresh flat-leaf
   parsley

TOPPING
800 g (1 lb 10 oz) potatoes, diced
400 g (13 oz) parsnips, diced
30 g (1 oz) butter
½ cup (125 ml/4 fl oz) milk

1 Heat the oil in a large frying pan over medium heat and cook the onion, carrot and celery, stirring occasionally, for 5 minutes, or until softened and lightly coloured. Add the mince and cook for 7 minutes, then stir in the flour and cook for 2 minutes. Add the stock, soy sauce, Worcestershire sauce, tomato sauce, tomato paste and bay leaves and simmer over low heat for 30 minutes, stirring occasionally. Leave to cool. Remove the bay leaves and stir in the parsley.
2 To make the topping, boil the potato and parsnip in salted water for

15–20 minutes, or until cooked through. Drain, return to the pan and mash with the butter and enough of the milk to make a firm mash.
3 Preheat the oven to 180°C (350°F/ Gas 4) and lightly grease a 2.5 litre ovenproof dish. Spoon the filling into the dish and spread the topping over it. Fluff with a fork. Bake for 25 minutes, or until golden.

NUTRITION PER SERVE (8)
Protein 31 g; Fat 18 g; Carbohydrate 27 g; Dietary Fibre 4 g; Cholesterol 78 mg; 1640 kJ (390 cal)

Mash the potato and parsnip together with a potato masher.

Spoon the cooled meat filling into the a lightly greased dish.

OSSO BUCO WITH GREMOLATA

Preparation time: 30 minutes
Total cooking time: 2 hours 40 minutes
Serves 4

2 tablespoons olive oil
1 onion, finely chopped
1 clove garlic, crushed
1 kg (2 lb) veal shin slices (osso buco)
2 tablespoons plain flour
410 g (13 oz) can tomatoes, roughly chopped
1 cup (250 ml/8 fl oz) white wine
1 cup (250 ml/8 fl oz) chicken stock

GREMOLATA
2 tablespoons finely choppped fresh parsley
2 teaspoons grated lemon rind
1 teaspoon finely chopped garlic

1 Heat 1 tablespoon oil in a large shallow casserole. Add the onion and cook over low heat until soft and golden. Add the garlic. Cook for 1 minute, then remove from the dish.
2 Heat the remaining oil and brown the veal in batches, then remove. Return the onion to the casserole and stir in the flour. Cook for 30 seconds and remove from the heat. Slowly stir in the tomatoes, wine and stock, combining well with the flour. Return the veal to the casserole.

3 Return to the heat and bring to the boil, stirring. Cover and reduce the heat to low so that the casserole is just simmering. Cook for 2½ hours, or until the meat is very tender and almost falling off the bones.
4 To make the gremolata, combine the parsley, lemon rind and garlic in a bowl. Sprinkle over the osso buco and serve with risotto or plain rice.

NUTRITION PER SERVE
Protein 50 g; Fat 15 g; Carbohydrate 9.5 g; Dietary Fibre 2.5 g; Cholesterol 165 mg; 1700 kJ (405 cal)

HINT: Try to make this a day in advance to give the flavours time to develop and blend.

Heat the oil in the casserole and cook the veal pieces in batches until browned.

Add the tomatoes, white wine and stock and mix until well combined.

Make the traditional gremolata topping by mixing together the parsley, lemon rind and garlic.

CALVES' LIVER WITH WINE AND PARSLEY

Preparation time: 15 minutes
Total cooking time: 20 minutes
Serves 4

600 g (1¼ lb) calves' liver, thinly sliced
   (ask your butcher to do this)
oil, for cooking
50 g (1¾ oz) butter
2 onions, thinly sliced
2 tablespoons plain flour
½ cup (125 ml/4 fl oz) Riesling
1 cup (30 g/1 oz) chopped parsley

1 Cut the liver into thin strips. Heat the wok until very hot, add 2 teaspoons of the oil with 10 g (¼ oz) butter and swirl it around to coat the side. Stir-fry the onion for 3–4 minutes, or until softened. Remove from the wok.
2 Season the flour with salt and pepper and use to coat the liver. Reheat the wok, add a little more of the oil and butter, and stir-fry the floured liver in four batches until browned. Add more oil and butter to the wok if necessary. Remove all the liver from the wok.
3 Reheat the wok, then add the wine and boil until it has reduced by two-thirds. Return the onion and liver to the wok, add the parsley and toss well. Season and serve immediately.

NUTRITION PER SERVE
Protein 30 g; Fat 35 g; Carbohydrate 10 g; Dietary Fibre 1.5 g; Cholesterol 440 mg; 2025 kJ (485 cal)

Ask your butcher to thinly slice the calves' liver, then you can cut it into thin strips.

Toss the liver in the flour that has been seasoned with salt and black pepper.

Stir-fry the liver in small batches so that it fries rather than stews.

MEATBALLS IN TOMATO SAUCE

Preparation time: 40 minutes
Total cooking time: 1 hour 40 minutes
Serves 6

500 g (1 lb) lean veal mince
1 onion, very finely chopped
4 cloves garlic, finely chopped
1 egg white, lightly beaten
1 cup (80 g/2¾ oz) fresh white
    breadcrumbs
½ cup (30 g/1 oz) finely chopped fresh
    parsley
3 tablespoons finely chopped fresh
    oregano
cooking oil spray
1.5 kg (3 lb) ripe tomatoes
2 onions, finely sliced
½ cup (125 g/4 oz) tomato paste
½ teaspoon sugar
350 g (11 oz) penne

1 Combine the veal mince, onion, half the garlic, the egg white, breadcrumbs, two-thirds of the parsley and 1 tablespoon of the oregano in a large bowl. Season and mix well with your hands. Shape into 36 small balls. Spray a large non-stick frying pan with oil. Cook a third of the meatballs over high heat for 4–5 minutes, or until browned, turning constantly to prevent the meatballs sticking. Remove from the pan and repeat with the remaining meatballs.
2 Score a cross in the base of each tomato, place in a heatproof bowl and cover with boiling water. Leave for 1 minute, or until the skins start to come away. Drain, plunge into a bowl of iced water, then peel away the skin and roughly chop the flesh.
3 Lightly spray the base of a large,

deep non-stick saucepan. Add the sliced onion and remaining garlic and cook over low heat for 2–3 minutes, stirring constantly. Add 2 tablespoons water, cover and cook gently for 5 minutes to soften the onion. Stir in the tomato and tomato paste. Cover and simmer for 10 minutes, uncover and simmer gently for 40 minutes. Add the meatballs, cover and simmer for another 15–20 minutes, or until the meatballs are just cooked. Add the

sugar, remaining parsley and oregano and season well.
4 Cook the penne in a large pan of boiling salted water until al dente, then drain. Serve with the meatballs.

NUTRITION PER SERVE
Protein 15 g; Fat 8 g; Carbohydrate 60 g;
Dietary Fibre 9 g; Cholesterol 60 mg;
1321 kJ (316 cal)

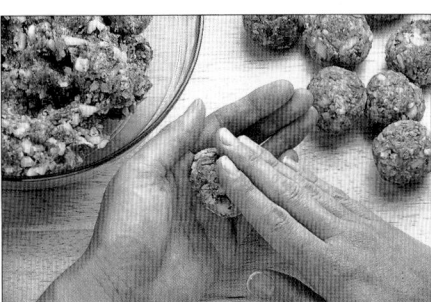
When the veal mixture is thoroughly combined, shape into balls.

Score a cross in the base of each tomato so that you can peel off the skin.

Remove the tomatoes from the hot water, plunge into iced water, then peel.

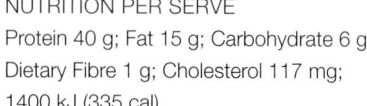

ASIAN PEPPERED BEEF

**Preparation time: 10 minutes
+ 2 hours marinating
Total cooking time: 12 minutes
Serves 4**

600 g (1¼ lb) skirt steak, thinly sliced
2 cloves garlic, finely chopped
2 teaspoons finely chopped fresh
    ginger
2 onions, thinly sliced
2 tablespoons Chinese rice wine
1 teaspoon sesame oil
1 tablespoon soy sauce
1 tablespoon oyster sauce

2 teaspoons sugar
1 teaspoon Sichuan peppercorns,
    crushed
1 tablespoon black peppercorns,
    crushed
2 spring onions, chopped into
    2.5 cm (1 inch) lengths
oil, for cooking

1 Place the beef strips in a large bowl. Add the garlic, ginger, onion, rice wine, sesame oil, soy sauce, oyster sauce, sugar and peppercorns, and mix together well. Cover and marinate in the refrigerator for at least 2 hours.
2 Drain, discarding any excess liquid, and stir in the spring onion.

3 Heat the wok until very hot, add 1 tablespoon of the oil and swirl it around to coat the side. Add half the beef and stir-fry for 6 minutes, or until seared and cooked to your liking. Repeat with the rest of the beef. Serve immediately.

NUTRITION PER SERVE
Protein 40 g; Fat 15 g; Carbohydrate 6 g;
Dietary Fibre 1 g; Cholesterol 117 mg;
1400 kJ (335 cal)

NOTE: The wok needs to be searing hot for this recipe. The beef is easier to thinly slice if you put it in the freezer for half an hour beforehand.

Crush the Sichuan peppercorns in a mortar and pestle to release their flavour.

Chop the spring onions into short lengths for quick and even stir-frying.

Place the beef strips in a large bowl with all the marinade ingredients.

VEAL PIE WITH JERUSALEM ARTICHOKE AND POTATO TOPPING

Preparation time: 40 minutes
Total cooking time: 1 hour 15 minutes
Serves 4–6

1 tablespoon olive oil
500 g (1 lb) lean veal mince
2 onions, finely chopped
3 cloves garlic, crushed
150 g (5 oz) bacon, diced
½ teaspoon dried rosemary
2 tablespoons plain flour
pinch of cayenne pepper
½ cup (125 ml/4 fl oz) dry white wine
150 ml (5 fl oz) cream
1 egg, lightly beaten
2 hard-boiled eggs, roughly chopped

TOPPING
500 g (1 lb) Jerusalem artichokes
400 g (13 oz) potatoes
100 g (3½ oz) butter

1 To make the filling, heat the oil in a large frying pan and cook the mince, onion, garlic, bacon and rosemary, stirring often, for 10 minutes, or until the veal changes colour. Stir in the flour and cayenne pepper and cook for 1 minute. Pour in the wine and ½ cup (125 ml/4 fl oz) water. Season well. Simmer for 5 minutes, or until the sauce is very thick, then stir in the cream, beaten egg and chopped egg.
2 Preheat the oven to 210°C (415°F/Gas 6–7). Lightly grease a 21 cm (8 inch) springform tin. Peel and chop

the artichokes and potatoes and boil together for 12–15 minutes until tender. Drain, add the butter, then mash until smooth.
3 Spoon the filling into the tin then spread with the topping. Bake for 15 minutes, then reduce the heat to 180°C (350°F/Gas 4) and bake for 30 minutes, or until golden on top.

NUTRITION PER SERVE (6)
Protein 31 g; Fat 38 g; Carbohydrate 17 g; Dietary Fibre 4 g; Cholesterol 258 mg; 2265 kJ (540 cal)

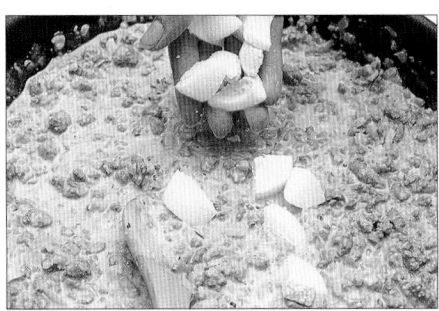

When the sauce has thickened, stir in the cream, beaten egg and chopped egg.

Mash the cooked potato and artichoke with butter until smooth.

MUSAMAN (THAI BEEF CURRY WITH POTATO AND PEANUTS)

Preparation time: 30 minutes
Total cooking time: 1 hour 45 minutes
Serves 4

1 tablespoon tamarind pulp
2 tablespoons oil
750 g (1½ lb) lean stewing beef, cubed
2 cups (500 ml/16 fl oz) coconut milk
4 cardamom pods, bruised
2 cups (500 ml/16 fl oz) coconut cream
2–3 tablespoons Musaman curry
  paste
8 pickling onions, peeled (see NOTE)
8 baby potatoes, peeled (see NOTE)
2 tablespoons fish sauce
2 tablespoons palm sugar
½ cup (70 g/2¼ oz) unsalted peanuts,
  roasted and ground
fresh coriander leaves, to garnish

1 Combine the tamarind pulp and ½ cup (125 ml/4 fl oz) boiling water and leave to cool. Mash the pulp until dissolved, then strain and reserve the liquid. Discard the pulp.
2 Heat the oil in a wok or a large saucepan and cook the beef in batches over high heat for 5 minutes, or until browned. Reduce the heat and add the coconut milk and cardamom to the pan, and simmer for 1 hour, or until the beef is tender. Remove the beef, strain and reserve the beef and cooking liquid.
3 Heat the coconut cream in the wok and stir in the curry paste. Cook for 5 minutes, or until the oil starts to separate from the cream.
4 Add the onions, potatoes, fish sauce, palm sugar, peanuts, beef mixture, reserved liquid and tamarind

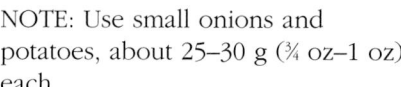

water, and simmer for 25–30 minutes. Garnish with fresh coriander leaves. Serve with rice.

NUTRITION PER SERVE
Protein 52 g; Fat 77 g; Carbohydrate 35 g; Dietary Fibre 7.5 g; Cholesterol 115 mg; 4324 kJ (1033 Cal)

NOTE: Use small onions and potatoes, about 25–30 g (¾ oz–1 oz) each.

Mash the tamarind pulp with a fork, then strain and reserve the liquid.

Cook the beef in batches over high heat until browned.

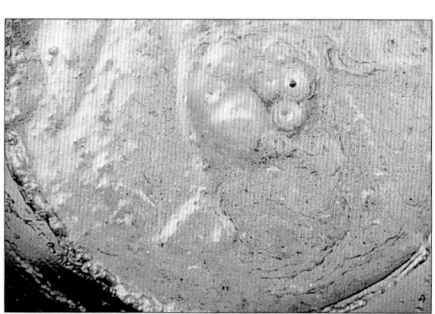

Cook until the oil starts to separate from the cream.

RENDANG (INDONESIAN DRY BEEF CURRY)

Preparation time: 20 minutes
Total cooking time: 2 hours 30 minutes
Serves 6

1.5 kg (3 lb) chuck steak
2 onions, roughly chopped
2 cloves garlic, crushed
400 ml (13 oz) coconut milk
2 teaspoons ground coriander seeds
½ teaspoon ground fennel seeds
2 teaspoons ground cumin seeds
¼ teaspoon ground cloves
4–6 small red chillies, chopped
1 stem lemon grass, white part only,
   bruised, cut lengthways

1 tablespoon lemon juice
2 teaspoons grated palm sugar or soft
   brown sugar

1 Trim the meat of excess fat or sinew and cut into 3 cm (1¼ inch) cubes.
2 Place the onion and garlic in a food processor, and process until smooth, adding water, if necessary.
3 Place the coconut milk in a large saucepan and bring to the boil, then reduce the heat to medium and cook, stirring occasionally, for 15 minutes, or until the milk has reduced by half and the oil has separated. Do not allow the milk to brown.
4 Add the coriander, fennel, cumin and cloves to the pan, and stir for 1 minute. Add the meat and cook for

2 minutes, or until it changes colour. Add the onion mixture, chilli, lemon grass, lemon juice and sugar. Cook, covered, over medium heat for 2 hours, or until the liquid has reduced and the mixture has thickened. Stir frequently to prevent it sticking to the bottom of the pan.
5 Uncover and continue cooking until the oil from the coconut milk begins to emerge again, letting the curry develop colour and flavour. Be careful that it does not burn. The curry is cooked when it is brown and dry.

NUTRITION PER SERVE
Protein 53 g; Fat 20 g; Carbohydrate 5.5 g;
Dietary Fibre 1.5 g; Cholesterol 168 mg;
1775 kJ (424 Cal)

Process the onion and garlic in a food processor until smooth.

Cook the coconut milk over medium heat until reduced and the oil has separated.

Continue to cook until the oil from the coconut milk begins to emerge again.

CURRIED BEEF SAUSAGES

Preparation time: 20 minutes
Total cooking time: 45 minutes
Serves 6–8

1 onion, chopped
2 cloves garlic
1 teaspoon chopped fresh ginger
2 teaspoons curry powder
1 teaspoon chilli powder
1½ teaspoons paprika
3 teaspoons poppy seeds
2 tablespoons oil

1.25 kg (2 lb 8 oz) medium-size good-
    quality beef sausages
6 tomatoes, skinned, quartered and
    seeded
2 tablespoons mango chutney
1⅔ cups (420 ml/13 fl oz) coconut
    milk

1 Place the onion, garlic, ginger, curry powder, chilli powder, paprika and poppy seeds in a food processor, and process until smooth.
2 Heat 1 tablespoon of the oil in a saucepan and cook for 6–8 minutes, or until browned. Remove and wipe

out the pan with paper towels. Leave the sausages to cool and slice into 1 cm (½ inch) thick pieces.
3 Heat the remaining oil in the pan, add the spice paste and cook, stirring, for 2 minutes, or until fragrant. Mix in the tomato, mango chutney, coconut milk and sausages, and simmer, covered, for 20 minutes, stirring occasionally.

NUTRITION PER SERVE (8)
Protein 22 g; Fat 50 g; Carbohydrate 10 g;
Dietary Fibre 6 g; Cholesterol 90 mg;
2407 kJ (575 Cal)

Place the paste ingredients in a food processor and process until smooth.

Cook the sausages in batches in a large frying pan until browned on all sides.

Wipe out the pan with paper towels to remove any excess oil.

FRESH RICE NOODLES WITH BEEF

**Preparation time: 10 minutes
+ 30 minutes marinating
Total cooking time: 15 minutes
Serves 4–6**

2 cloves garlic, crushed
2 teaspoons chopped fresh ginger
1 tablespoon oyster sauce
2 teaspoons soy sauce
500 g (1 lb) beef, thinly sliced
oil, for cooking

1 kg (2 lb) fresh rice noodles, sliced
    into 2 cm (1 inch) strips
100 g (3½ oz) garlic chives, chopped
2½ tablespoons oyster sauce, extra
3 teaspoons soy sauce, extra
1 teaspoon sugar

1 Combine the garlic, ginger, oyster and soy sauces, add the beef and toss to coat. Cover and refrigerate for 30 minutes.

2 Heat the wok until very hot, add 1 tablespoon of the oil and swirl it around to coat the side. Add half the beef and stir-fry for 5 minutes, or until cooked. Remove and repeat with the remaining beef. Add another tablespoon of oil, then add the noodles and stir-fry for 3–5 minutes, or until softened.

3 Add the garlic chives and stir-fry until just wilted. Stir in the extra oyster and soy sauces and sugar, return the beef to the wok and toss to heat through. Serve immediately.

NUTRITION PER SERVE (6)
Protein 33 g; Fat 13 g; Carbohydrate 40 g;
Dietary Fibre 1.5 g; Cholesterol 50 mg;
1295 kJ (310 cal)

Buy the fresh rice noodle as a block and cut it into thin strips.

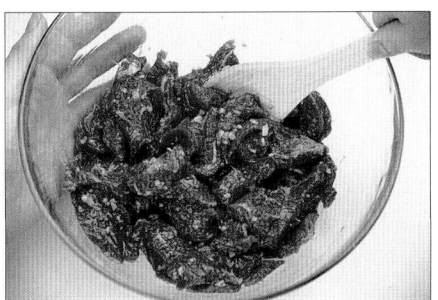

Mix together the garlic, ginger, oyster and soy sauces to marinate the beef.

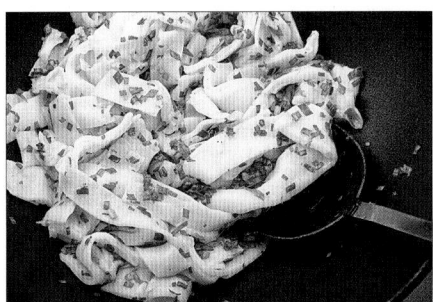

Stir-fry the noodles until they are softened, then add the garlic chives.

BEEF IN RED WINE

Preparation time: 20 minutes
Total cooking time: 2 hours 15 minutes
Serves 4

2 tablespoons olive oil
1 kg (2 lb) trimmed chuck steak, cubed
12 baby onions, halved, with root base left intact
4 rashers bacon, rind removed, chopped
2 cloves garlic, finely chopped
3 tablespoons plain flour
1½ cups (375 ml/12 fl oz) red wine
2 tablespoons port
2 bay leaves
5 sprigs fresh parsley
3 sprigs fresh thyme
1 thin slice lemon rind
1½ cups (375 ml/12 fl oz) beef or chicken stock
500 g (1 lb) flat mushrooms, halved

1 Heat 1 tablespoon of oil in a large heavy-based pan, and cook the steak in small batches over high heat for 2 minutes, or until well browned. Remove from the pan.
2 Heat the remaining oil in the same pan, and add the onion, bacon and garlic. Stir over medium–high heat for 5 minutes, or until the onion is browned. Return the beef to the pan, add the flour, and stir for 1 minute. Remove the pan from the heat, and gradually stir in the wine and port, mixing the flour in well. Return the pan to the heat and bring to the boil, stirring, then reduce the heat and simmer for 3 minutes, or until the sauce boils and thickens slightly.
3 Make a bouquet garni by wrapping the bay leaves, parsley, thyme and lemon rind in a piece of muslin and tying with string. Add the bouquet garni, stock and mushrooms to the pan, bring to the boil, then reduce the heat to low and simmer, covered, for 2 hours, or until the beef is tender, stirring occasionally. Remove the bouquet garni, and season. Serve with mashed potato and baby carrots.

NUTRITION PER SERVE
Protein 65 g; Fat 20 g; Carbohydrate 12 g; Dietary Fibre 4.5 g; Cholesterol 185 mg; 2332 kJ (557 Cal)

Chop the baby onions in half, leaving the root base intact.

Cook the steak in batches until well browned all over.

Gradually add the wine and port, and stir to mix in the flour.

MEATLOAF

Preparation time: 25 minutes
Total cooking time: 1 hour 15 minutes
Serves 6

125 g (4 oz) bacon, trimmed and
    chopped
500 g (1 lb) beef mince
500 g (1 lb) pork mince
1 onion, coarsely grated
2 cloves garlic, crushed
2 cups (160 g/5½ oz) fresh
    breadcrumbs
2 teaspoons fresh thyme leaves
1 egg, lightly beaten
1 tablespoon red wine vinegar
2 teaspoons soft brown sugar

1 Preheat the oven to moderate 180°C (350°F/Gas 4). Lightly grease a loaf tin then line with a single sheet of baking paper, leaving the paper to overhang on the long sides of the tin.
2 Heat a non-stick frying pan, add the chopped bacon, and cook, stirring, until crispy. Drain on paper towels.
3 Place the mince, onion, garlic, breadcrumbs, thyme, egg, vinegar, sugar and bacon in a bowl. Season and combine, using your hands. Don't overmix or the meatloaf will become too dense when cooked.
4 Spoon the mixture into the loaf tin and press down gently. Smooth the top and cook in the oven for 1 hour 10 minutes, or until browned and cooked through. Test if it is cooked by pushing a metal skewer or sharp knife into the centre, leaving it for 3 seconds, and then pulling it out and holding it against your wrist. If it is really hot, it is cooked through; if not, cook a little longer. Leave for 5 minutes and pour the cooking juices into a jug. Lift out the meatloaf using the overhanging baking paper. Cut into slices with a serrated knife and drizzle with the cooking juices. Serve with tomato sauce, peas, corn and potatoes.

NUTRITION PER SERVE
Protein 45 g; Fat 13 g; Carbohydrate 20 g;
Dietary Fibre 1.5 g; Cholesterol 135 mg;
1588 kJ (380 Cal)

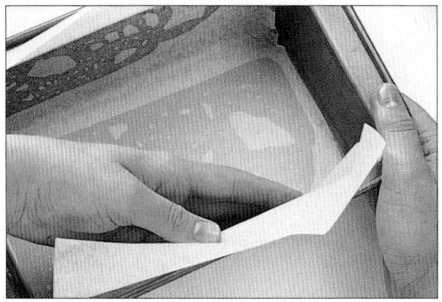

Line the tin with baking paper, allowing it to overhang the long sides of the tin.

Spoon the mixture into the tin and gently press down with the back of a spoon.

BURGUNDY BEEF PIE

Preparation time: 30 minutes + cooling
Total cooking time: 3 hours 10 minutes
Serves 6

2 tablespoons olive oil
40 g (1¼ oz) butter
185 g (6 oz) bacon, diced
1.25 kg (2 lb 8 oz) chuck steak,
    trimmed and cut into 2.5 cm
    (1 inch) cubes
2 onions, diced
3 cloves garlic, crushed
2 carrots, cut into 1.5 cm (⅝ inch)
    cubes
¼ cup (30 g/1 oz) plain flour
1¼ cups (315 ml/10 fl oz) Burgundy
1½ cups (375 ml/10 fl oz) beef stock
2 tablespoons tomato paste
1 teaspoon chopped fresh thyme
1 bay leaf
275 g (9 oz) small Swiss brown
    mushrooms, halved
pinch of ground nutmeg
3 tablespoons chopped fresh flat-leaf
    parsley
375 g (12 oz) puff pastry
1 egg, lightly beaten

1 Heat 1 tablespoon of oil and 20 g (¾ oz) of butter in a large, heavy-based, flameproof casserole dish or saucepan over medium heat. Add the bacon and cook for 2–3 minutes. Transfer to a plate. Increase the heat to high, add the beef to the pan in batches and cook, turning, for 7–8 minutes, or until browned. Add to the bacon.
2 Heat the remaining oil in the pan over medium heat, add the onion and garlic and cook for 4–5 minutes. Add the carrot and cook, stirring once or twice, for 5 minutes. Stir in the flour, add the beef, bacon, wine, stock and tomato paste and stir for 5 minutes, or until the sauce has thickened slightly and is smooth. Add the thyme and bay leaf and season. Reduce the heat, cover and cook for 1¼ hours, or until the meat is tender, adding ¼ cup (60 ml/2 fl oz) hot water, if necessary, to make a thick gravy.
3 Meanwhile, melt the remaining butter in a frying pan over low heat. Add the mushrooms and fry until

golden. Stir in the nutmeg and parsley.
4 Preheat the oven to moderately hot 200°C (400°F/Gas 6) and grease a 2 litre oval ovenproof dish that has 5–6 cm (2–2½ inch) sides. Roll out the pastry between two sheets of baking paper until about 5 mm (¼ inch) thick and slightly larger than the dish. Roll out the scraps to a 35 cm x 10 cm (14 inch x 4 inch) strap, 5 mm (¼ inch) thick. Cut into 1.5 cm (⅝ inch) strips.
5 Remove the bay leaf from the meat, then stir in the mushrooms. Spoon into the dish. Cover with the pastry

lid, press the edges firmly down onto the lip of the dish, then trim any excess. Brush the edges with egg. Make three 2.5 cm (1 inch) slits in the centre. Take a strip of pastry and twist a tight scroll. Repeat with the other strips. Run them around the rim, pressing joins together. Brush with egg and bake for 1 hour, or until golden.

NUTRITION PER SERVE
Protein 58 g; Fat 34.5 g; Carbohydrate
31 g; Dietary Fibre 4 g; Cholesterol
220 mg; 2930 kJ (700 Cal)

Cook the beef mixture until the sauce has thickened slightly and is smooth.

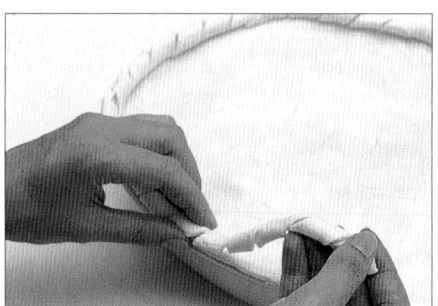

Twist the strips of pastry to form long, tight scrolls and place them around the pie rim.

THAI BEEF AND PUMPKIN CURRY

Preparation time: 20 minutes
Total cooking time: 1 hour 30 minutes
Serves 6

2 tablespoons oil
750 g (1½ lb) blade steak,
   thinly sliced
4 tablespoons Musaman curry paste
2 cloves garlic, finely chopped
1 onion, sliced lengthways
6 curry leaves, torn
3 cups (750 ml/24 fl oz) coconut milk
3 cups (450 g/14 oz) butternut
   pumpkin, roughly diced

2 tablespoons chopped unsalted
   peanuts
1 tablespoon palm sugar
2 tablespoons tamarind purée
2 tablespoons fish sauce
curry leaves, to garnish

1 Heat a large wok or frying pan over high heat. Add the oil and swirl to coat the side. Add the meat in batches and cook for 5 minutes, or until browned. Remove the meat from the wok.
2 Add the Musaman curry paste, chopped garlic, onion and torn curry leaves to the wok, and stir to coat. Return the meat to the wok and cook, stirring, over medium heat for 2 minutes.

3 Add the coconut milk to the wok, then reduce the heat and simmer for 45 minutes. Add the diced pumpkin and simmer for 25–30 minutes, or until the meat and the vegetables are tender and the sauce has thickened.
4 Stir in the peanuts, palm sugar, tamarind purée and fish sauce, and simmer for 1 minute. Garnish with curry leaves. Serve with pickled vegetables and rice.

NUTRITION PER SERVE
Protein 33 g; Fat 43 g; Carbohydrate 16 g;
Dietary Fibre 4.5 g; Cholesterol 66 mg;
2403 kJ (574 Cal)

Cut the meat across the grain and at an angle into thin slices.

Add the meat to the wok and cook in batches until browned.

Simmer until the meat and vegetables are tender and the sauce has thickened.

BEEF TERIYAKI WITH CUCUMBER SALAD

Preparation time: 20 minutes +
  30 minutes refrigeration +
  10 minutes resting
Total cooking time: 20 minutes
Serves 4

4 scotch fillet steaks
⅓ cup (80 ml/2¾ fl oz) soy sauce
2 tablespoons mirin
1 tablespoon sake (optional)
1 clove garlic, crushed
1 teaspoon grated fresh ginger
1 teaspoon sugar
1 teaspoon toasted sesame seeds

CUCUMBER SALAD
1 large Lebanese cucumber, peeled,
    seeded and diced
½ red capsicum, diced
2 spring onions, sliced thinly on
    the diagonal
2 teaspoons sugar
1 tablespoon rice wine vinegar

1 Place the steaks in a non-metallic dish. Combine the soy, mirin, sake, garlic and ginger and pour over the steaks. Cover with plastic wrap and refrigerate for at least 30 minutes.
2 To make the cucumber salad, place the cucumber, capsicum and spring onion in a small bowl. Place the sugar, rice wine vinegar and ¼ cup (60 ml/ 2 fl oz) water in a small saucepan and stir over medium heat until the sugar dissolves. Increase the heat and simmer rapidly for 3–4 minutes, or until slightly thickened. Pour over the cucumber salad, stir to combine and leave to cool completely.
3 Spray a chargrill or hot plate with oil spray and heat until very hot. Drain the steaks and reserve the marinade. Cook for 3–4 minutes on each side, or until cooked to your liking. Remove and rest the meat for 5–10 minutes before slicing.
4 Meanwhile, place the sugar and the reserved marinade in a small saucepan and heat, stirring, until the sugar has dissolved. Bring to the boil, then simmer for 2–3 minutes, remove from the heat and keep warm.
5 Slice each steak into 1 cm strips, being careful to keep the steak in its shape. Arrange the steak on each plate. Spoon on some of the marinade, a spoonful of cucumber salad and garnish with sesame seeds. Serve with steamed rice and the remaining cucumber salad.

NUTRITION PER SERVE
Protein 23 g; Fat 5 g; Carbohydrate 6 g; Dietary Fibre 1 g; Cholesterol 67 mg; 720 kJ (170 Cal)

Combine the cucumber, capsicum and spring onion with the dressing.

Cook the steaks for 3–4 minutes on each side, or until cooked to your liking.

SAUSAGES AND MASH WITH ONION GRAVY

Preparation time: 10 minutes
Total cooking time: 50 minutes
Serves 4

1½ cups (375 ml/12 fl oz) beef stock
2 teaspoons cornflour
2 teaspoons balsamic vinegar
1 tablespoon oil
6 onions, sliced
1.5 kg (3 lb) potatoes, chopped
60 g (2 oz) butter
½ cup (125 ml/4 fl oz) cream
8 beef sausages

1 Mix together 1 tablespoon stock with the cornflour, and stir to dissolve, ensuring there are no lumps. Add to the remaining stock with the vinegar.
2 To make the onion gravy, heat the oil in a large frying pan, add the onion and cook over low heat for 35–40 minutes, or until the onion is soft and beginning to caramelise.

Increase the heat and slowly add the stock mixture, stirring constantly until the mixture thickens. Remove from the heat and set aside.
3 Meanwhile, put the potatoes in a large pan of boiling water and cook for 15–20 minutes, or until tender. Drain the potatoes and return them to the pan with the butter and cream. With a potato masher, mash until smooth and creamy. Season to taste with salt and cracked black pepper.
4 Prick the sausages and cook under a hot grill, turning once, for 10 minutes, or until cooked through.

5 Gently warm the gravy and serve with sausages and mashed potato. Delicious with baked zucchini.

NUTRITION PER SERVE
Protein 30 g; Fat 70 g; Carbohydrate 63 g; Dietary Fibre 13 g; Cholesterol 160 mg; 4280 kJ (1025 Cal)

NOTE: The gravy can be warmed in the microwave just before serving.

Cook the onion in the oil until soft and beginning to caramelise.

Slowly pour in the stock mixture and stir constantly until the gravy thickens.

BEEF PIE

Preparation time: 35 minutes + chilling
Total cooking time: 2 hours 30 minutes
Serves 6

FILLING
2 tablespoons oil
1 kg (2 lb) trimmed chuck steak, cubed
1 large onion, chopped
1 large carrot, finely chopped
2 cloves garlic, crushed
2 tablespoons plain flour
1 cup (250 ml/8 fl oz) beef stock
2 teaspoons fresh thyme leaves
1 tablespoon Worcestershire sauce

PASTRY
2 cups (250 g/8 oz) plain flour
150 g (5 oz) cold butter, chopped
1 egg yolk
3–4 tablespoons iced water
1 egg yolk and 1 tablespoon milk, to glaze

1 Heat 1 tablespoon of the oil in a large pan and cook the meat in batches until browned all over. Remove from the pan and set aside. Heat the remaining oil, then add the onion, carrot and garlic and cook over medium heat until browned.
2 Return the meat to the pan and stir through the flour. Cook for 1 minute, then remove from the heat and slowly stir in the beef stock, mixing the flour in well. Add the thyme leaves and Worcestershire sauce, and bring to the boil. Season to taste with salt and cracked black pepper.
3 Reduce the heat to very low, cover and simmer for 1½–2 hours, or until the meat is tender. During the last 15 minutes of cooking, remove the lid

and allow the liquid to reduce so that the sauce is very thick and suitable for filling a pie. Allow to cool completely.
4 To make the pastry, sift the flour into a large bowl and add the butter. Using your fingertips, rub the butter into the flour until it resembles fine breadcrumbs. Add the egg yolk and 2 tablespoons of iced water, and mix with a knife using a cutting action until the mixture comes together in beads, adding a little more water if necessary. Turn out onto a lightly floured surface and gather together to form a smooth dough. Wrap in plastic wrap and refrigerate for 30 minutes.
5 Preheat the oven to moderately hot 200°C (400°F/Gas 6). Divide the pastry into two pieces and roll out one of the pieces on a sheet of baking paper until large enough to line a 23 cm (9 inch) pie dish. Line the pie dish with the pastry. Fill with the cold filling and roll out the remaining piece of pastry until large enough to fully cover the dish. Dampen the edges of the pastry with your fingers dipped in water. Lay the top piece of pastry over the pie and gently press the bottom and top pieces of pastry together. Trim the overhanging edges with a sharp knife, reroll the scrap pieces to make decorative shapes and press on the pie.
6 Cut a few slits in the top of the pastry to allow the steam to escape. Beat together the egg yolk and milk, and brush it over the top of the pie. Cook in the oven for 20–30 minutes, or until the pastry is golden and the filling is hot.

NUTRITION PER SERVE
Protein 40 g; Fat 35 g; Carbohydrate 35 g;
Dietary Fibre 3 g; Cholesterol 235 mg;
2580 kJ (615 Cal)

Add the butter and rub it into the flour with your fingertips.

Mix the egg yolk and water into the flour mixture with a flat-bladed knife.

Gather the mixture together to form a smooth dough.

The baking paper will help you lift the pastry into the pie dish.

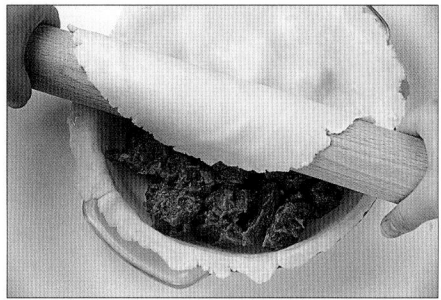

Spoon in the filling then top with the second piece of pastry.

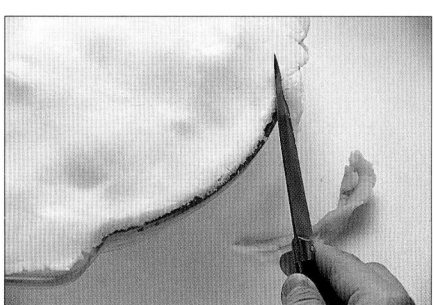

Press the pieces of pastry together and trim off the excess with a sharp knife.

VEAL GOULASH

Preparation time: 25 minutes
Total cooking time: 2 hours
Serves 4

500 g (1 lb) veal, cut into 2.5 cm
   (1 inch) pieces
2 tablespoons plain flour
2 tablespoons olive oil
2 onions, thinly sliced
2 cloves garlic, finely chopped
1 tablespoon sweet Hungarian paprika
1 teaspoon ground cumin
440 g (14 oz) can diced tomatoes
2 carrots, sliced
½ red capsicum, chopped
½ green capsicum, chopped

1 cup (250 ml/8 fl oz) beef stock
½ cup (125 ml/4 fl oz) red wine
½ cup (125 g/4 fl oz) sour cream
chopped fresh parsley, to garnish

1 Put the veal and flour in a plastic bag and shake to coat the veal with flour. Shake off any excess. Heat 1 tablespoon oil in a large deep heavy-based pan over medium heat. Brown the meat well in batches, then remove the meat and set aside.
2 Add the remaining oil to the pan. Cook the onion, garlic, paprika and cumin for 5 minutes, stirring frequently. Return the meat and any juices to the pan with the tomato, carrot and capsicum. Cover and cook for 10 minutes.

3 Add the stock and wine and season with salt and pepper. Stir well, then cover and simmer over very low heat for 1½ hours. Stir in half the sour cream, season with more salt and pepper if needed and serve garnished with parsley and the remaining sour cream. Delicious served with buttered boiled small potatoes or noodles.

NUTRITION PER SERVE
Protein 30 g; Fat 25 g; Carbohydrate 15 g;
Dietary Fibre 4.5 g; Cholesterol 144 mg;
1790 kJ (430 Cal)

NOTE: If you prefer your sauce to be a little thicker, cook, uncovered, for 5 minutes over high heat before adding the sour cream.

Remove any excess fat then cut the veal into 2.5 cm (1 inch) pieces.

Put the veal and flour in a plastic bag and shake to coat.

Heat the oil in a pan, add the veal and brown well in batches.

MARINATED LEMON GRASS BEEF

**Preparation time: 15 minutes
+ 3–4 hours marinating
Total cooking time: 15 minutes
Serves 4**

500 g (1 lb) rump steak, cut into thin
   strips
3 stems lemon grass, white part only,
   finely chopped
1 onion, finely chopped
3 cloves garlic, finely chopped
2 tablespoons fish sauce
2 teaspoons sugar
1 tablespoon oil
¼ cup (40 g/1¼ oz) chopped roasted
   peanuts

1 Put the steak in a large glass or
ceramic bowl. Mix the lemon grass,
onion, garlic, fish sauce, sugar and oil
to make a marinade. Pour over the
meat and toss well. Cover and
refrigerate for 3–4 hours.
2 Heat the wok until very hot and
stir-fry the beef in two batches over
high heat until it is just browned. Toss
constantly to make sure the small
pieces of onion and lemon grass don't
catch on the wok and burn.
3 Return all the meat to the wok. Add
the roasted peanuts and toss quickly
until combined. Serve immediately.

NUTRITION PER SERVE
Protein 35 g; Fat 8.5 g; Carbohydrate 6 g;
Dietary Fibre 2 g; Cholesterol 85 mg;
980 kJ (235 cal)

Using a large sharp knife, cut the rump steak into
thin strips.

Finely chop the lemon grass, using only the white
part of the stems.

Pour the lemon grass, onion, garlic, fish sauce,
sugar and oil over the meat.

TRADITIONAL ROAST BEEF WITH YORKSHIRE PUDDINGS

Preparation time: 15 minutes
Total cooking time: 1 hour 45 minutes
Serves 6

2.5 kg (5 lb) piece roasting beef
2 cloves garlic, crushed
1 tablepoon plain flour
2 tablespoons red wine
1¼ cups (315 ml/10 fl oz) beef stock

YORKSHIRE PUDDINGS
2 cups (250 g/8 oz) plain flour
4 eggs
400 ml (13 fl oz) milk

1 Preheat the oven to very hot 240°C (475°F/Gas 9). Rub the outside of the beef with garlic and cracked black pepper. Place on a rack in a baking dish, and roast for 15 minutes.
2 To make the Yorkshire puddings, sift the flour and a pinch of salt into a bowl, and make a well in the centre. Add the eggs and whisk. Gradually pour in the milk and whisk to a smooth batter. Pour into a jug, cover and leave for about 30 minutes.
3 Reduce the heat to moderate 180°C (350°F/Gas 4), and roast the meat for 50–60 minutes for a rare result, or a little longer for well done. Cover the meat loosely with foil and leave in a warm place for 10–15 minutes. Increase the oven temperature to hot 220°C (425°F/Gas 7).
4 Pour the pan juices into a jug, then separate the oil from the meat juices, reserving both. Put 1 teaspoon of the oil in each hole of a 12-hole, deep patty pan (if there is not enough of the oil, use vegetable oil). Heat in the oven for 2–3 minutes, or until just smoking. Pour in the pudding batter to three-quarters full, return to the oven and bake for 5 minutes. Reduce the oven to moderately hot 200°C (400°F/Gas 6) and bake for 10 minutes, or until risen, crisp and golden.
5 Meanwhile, put the baking dish with the reserved meat juices on the stove over low heat. Add the flour and stir, scraping the bottom of the pan to release any sediment. Cook over medium heat, stirring constantly, until the flour is browned. Combine the wine and stock, and gradually stir into the flour mixture. Cook, stirring constantly, until the gravy boils and thickens. Simmer for 3 minutes.
6 Serve the sliced roast beef on a warm plate with the gravy, hot Yorkshire puddings, Brussels sprouts and roast potatoes.

NUTRITION PER SERVE
Protein 100 g; Fat 20 g; Carbohydrate 35 g; Dietary Fibre 2 g; Cholesterol 335 mg; 3085 kJ (740 Cal)

NOTE: Cuts of beef suitable for this recipe include rib eye roast, rump or Scotch fillet.

Rub garlic over the outside of the meat and season with cracked pepper.

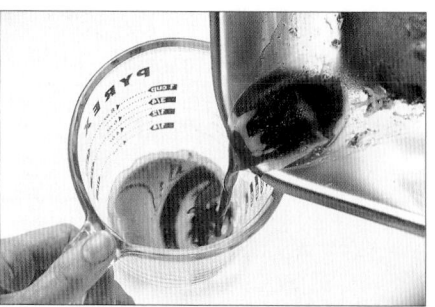
Pour the pan juices into a jug and allow the oil to separate from the meat juices.

Pour the pudding batter into the holes until three-quarters full.

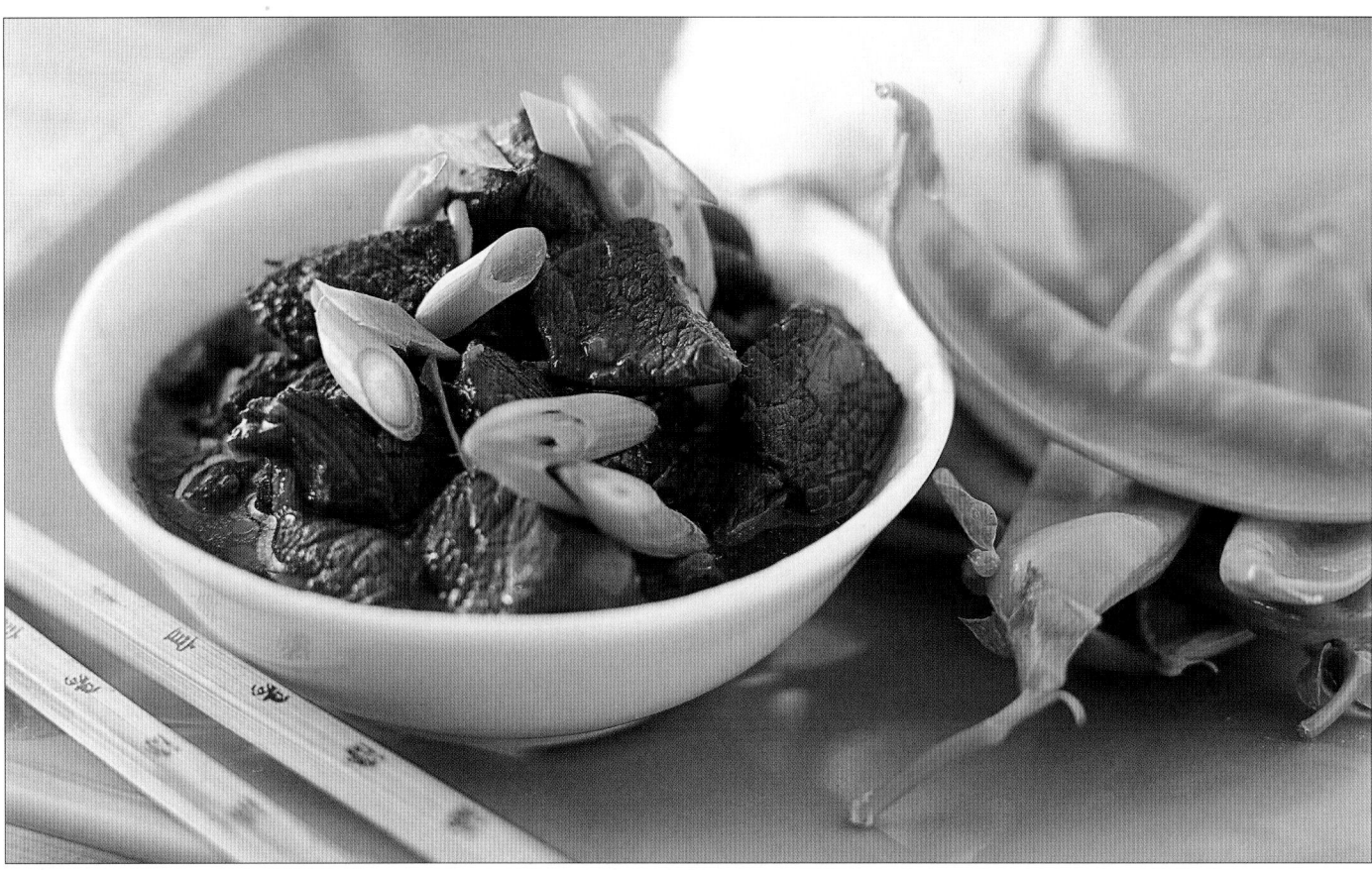

CHINESE BEEF IN SOY

**Preparation time: 20 minutes +
    overnight marinating**
Total cooking time: 1 hour 45 minutes
Serves 4

700 g (1 lb 7 oz) chuck steak, trimmed
    and cut into 2 cm cubes
⅓ cup (80 ml/2¾ fl oz) dark soy sauce
2 tablespoons honey
1 tablespoon wine vinegar
3 tablespoons soy bean oil
4 cloves garlic, chopped
8 spring onions, finely sliced
1 tablespoon finely grated fresh ginger
2 star anise

½ teaspoon ground cloves
1½ cups (375 ml/12 fl oz) beef stock
½ cup (125 ml/4 fl oz) red wine
spring onions, extra, sliced, to garnish

1 Place the meat in a non-metallic
dish. Combine the soy sauce, honey
and vinegar in a small bowl, then
pour over the meat. Cover with
plastic wrap and marinate for at least
2 hours, or preferably overnight.
Drain, reserving the marinade, and
pat the cubes dry.
2 Place 1 tablespoon of the oil in
a saucepan and brown the meat in
3 batches, for 3–4 minutes per batch—
add another tablespoon of oil, if
necessary. Remove the meat. Add the

remaining oil and fry the garlic, spring
onion, ginger, star anise and cloves
for 1–2 minutes, or until fragrant.
3 Return all the meat to the pan, add
the reserved marinade, stock and
wine. Bring to the boil and simmer,
covered, for 1 hour 15 minutes. Cook,
uncovered, for a further 15 minutes,
or until the sauce is syrupy and the
meat is tender.
4 Garnish with the extra sliced spring
onion and serve immediately with
rice.

NUTRITION PER SERVE
Protein 37 g; Fat 20 g; Carbohydrate 12 g;
Dietary Fibre 0.5 g; Cholesterol 117 mg;
1657 kJ (395 Cal)

Finely grate a piece of fresh ginger on a wooden
ginger grater.

Cook the cubes of beef, in batches, until brown
all over.

Simmer the beef, marinade, stock and wine until
the sauce is thick and syrupy.

381

BEEF FILLET WITH ROASTED TOMATO BEARNAISE

**Preparation time: 35 minutes +
  30 minutes standing
Total cooking time: 2 hours 15 minutes
Serves 4**

6 Roma tomatoes
½ teaspoon sugar
⅓ cup (80 ml/2¾ fl oz) olive oil
1½ teaspoons sea salt flakes
¼ cup (60 ml/2 fl oz) tarragon vinegar
4 black peppercorns
½ cup (125 ml/4 fl oz) dry white wine
3 French shallots, chopped
1 large Pontiac potato
1 large orange sweet potato
1 large parsnip
1 celeriac
4 fillet steaks (200 g/6½ oz each)
2 egg yolks
175 g (6 oz) butter, chilled and cut into
    cubes
2 teaspoons finely chopped tarragon
sprigs fresh tarragon, to garnish

1 Preheat the oven to moderate 180°C (350°F/Gas 4). Cut the tomatoes into quarters and toss with the sugar, 1 tablespoon of the oil and ½ teaspoon of the salt. Spread in a single layer in a roasting tin, then roast for 1½ hours, or until they are slightly shrivelled and darkened. Remove from the oven and cover with foil for 15 minutes, or until cool enough to handle. Increase the oven to moderately hot 200°C (400°F/Gas 6). Peel the tomatoes, purée, and push through a sieve—you will have about ⅓ cup (80 ml/2¾ fl oz) liquid.
2 Place the vinegar, peppercorns, wine and shallots in a small saucepan over medium heat and cook for

5 minutes, or until reduced to 1 tablespoon. Strain into a small heatproof bowl.
3 Peel the vegetables and cut into neat 2 cm (¾ inch) cubes. Toss the cubes with the remaining sea salt flakes and half the remaining olive oil, then spread out in a single layer in a roasting tin. Roast for 25–30 minutes, or until crisp. Reduce the heat to very low to keep warm until ready to serve.
4 Meanwhile, tie the steaks into neat rounds, then lightly season on both sides. Heat the remaining oil in a large heavy-based frying pan over high heat, then add the steaks, making sure they are well spaced. Cook for about 4 minutes each side, or until done to your liking. Remove the string. Transfer to a warm plate, cover with foil and rest for 10–15 minutes.
5 To make the Béarnaise, whisk the egg yolks into the vinegar mixture. Sit the bowl on top of a small saucepan of barely simmering water, making sure the bowl does not touch the water, and whisk for about 1 minute, or until the mixture starts to thicken, then gradually whisk in a couple of cubes of butter at a time until you have used up the butter or you have achieved a thick, glossy sauce—this should take about 6–7 minutes. Remove from the heat and stir in the tomato purée and chopped tarragon. Season to taste.
6 To serve, place one quarter of the root vegetables onto each plate and top with a steak. Stir the Béarnaise, then spoon over the top, garnish with fresh tarragon and serve immediately.

NUTRITION PER SERVE
Protein 54 g; Fat 66 g; Carbohydrate 37 g;
Dietary Fibre 11 g; Cholesterol 335 mg;
4105 kJ (980 Cal)

Roast the tomato quarters until slightly shrivelled and darkened.

Push the cooled tomato purée through a sieve to remove any remaining solids.

Cook the vinegar mixture until it has reduced to 1 tablespoon liquid.

Roast the vegetable cubes until they are crisp and golden.

Cook the steaks in a large frying pan until cooked to your liking.

Add the butter a few cubes at a time, and whisk until thick and glossy.

VEAL CUTLETS WITH CELERIAC PURÉE AND CAPERBERRIES

Preparation time: 30 minutes +
  2 hours refrigeration +
  10 minutes resting
Total cooking time: 25 minutes
Serves 4

8 veal cutlets, trimmed
4 long sprigs rosemary
2 teaspoons lemon zest
½ cup (125 ml/4 fl oz) white wine
  vinegar
1 clove garlic, crushed
½ cup (125 ml/4 fl oz) lemon juice
¼ cup (60 ml/2 fl oz) oil
1 celeriac, peeled and chopped
750 g (1½ lb) Pontiac potatoes,
  chopped
24 caperberries
lemon zest, to garnish

1 Trim the cutlets so that only the eye remains. Wrap the rosemary around four of the veal cutlets and secure with kitchen string. Place all the cutlets in a large non-metallic dish.

2 Combine the zest, vinegar, garlic, lemon juice and 2 tablespoons of the oil. Pour over the cutlets, season with pepper, cover and chill for 2 hours.
3 Preheat the oven to moderately hot 200°C (400°F/Gas 6). Drain the cutlets, reserving the marinade. Heat the remaining oil in a frying pan and cook the cutlets in batches over high heat for 2 minutes, or until brown on both sides. Transfer to a roasting tin and roast for 10 minutes, or until cooked to your liking. Rest for 10 minutes.
4 Meanwhile, cook the celeriac and potato in a large saucepan of boiling water for 15 minutes, or until very soft. Drain, then mash well and push through a sieve until smooth. You

may need to add a little milk if it is too thick. Season with salt and pepper. Keep warm.
5 Pour the reserved marinade and caperberries into a small saucepan and bring to the boil for 2 minutes, or until slightly reduced.
6 To serve, spoon a large mound of the purée on each plate and top with a plain cutlet, then a rosemary-covered cutlet. Pour the sauce over the cutlets and add the caperberries. Garnish with lemon zest.

NUTRITION PER SERVE
Protein 88 g; Fat 22 g; Carbohydrate 32 g;
Dietary Fibre 8.5 g; Cholesterol 300 mg;
2904 kJ (694 Cal)

Wrap the rosemary around half of the cutlets and secure with string.

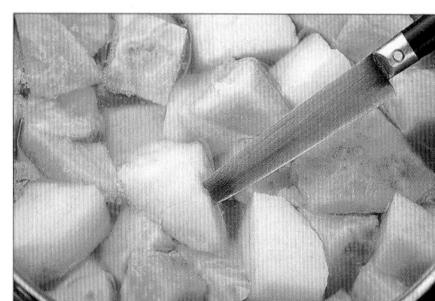

Cook the potato and celeriac until they are very soft.

MOROCCAN BEEF PIES

**Preparation time: 45 minutes +
  30 minutes refrigeration**
Total cooking time: 1 hour 20 minutes
Serves 4

1 tablespoon oil
2 cloves garlic, crushed
1 onion, cut into thin wedges
2 teaspoons ground cumin
2 teaspoons ground ginger
2 teaspoons paprika
pinch saffron threads
500 g (2 lb) round steak, cut into
    2 cm (¾ inch) cubes
1½ cups (375 ml/12 fl oz) beef stock
1 small cinnamon stick
100 g (3½ oz) pitted prunes, halved
2 carrots, sliced
1 teaspoon grated orange rind
2 cups (250 g/8 oz) plain flour
125 g (4 oz) butter, chilled and cut
    into cubes
1 egg, lightly beaten
¼ preserved lemon, rinsed, pith and
    flesh removed, finely chopped
    (optional)
200 g (6½ oz) thick plain yoghurt

1 Heat the oil in a large saucepan, add the garlic and onion and cook for 3 minutes, or until softened. Add the cumin, ginger, paprika and saffron and stir for 1 minute, or until fragrant. Add the meat and toss until coated in the spices. Add the stock, cinnamon stick, prunes and carrot. Bring to the boil, reduce the heat and simmer, covered, for 30 minutes. Increase the heat to medium, add the orange rind and cook, uncovered, for 20 minutes, or until the liquid has reduced and thickened slightly. Remove the cinnamon stick and cool completely.

2 To make the pastry, sift the flour into a large bowl. Rub the butter into the flour with your fingertips until it resembles fine breadcrumbs. Make a well in the centre and add the egg and 1–2 tablespoons water and mix with a flat-bladed knife, using a cutting action, until the mixture comes together in beads.
3 Gently gather the dough together and lift out onto a lightly floured work surface. Press together into a ball, wrap in plastic wrap and refrigerate for 30 minutes.
4 Preheat the oven to moderately hot 200°C (400°F/Gas 6). Grease four 9 cm (3½ inch) pie tins. Divide the dough

into four pieces. Roll each piece of dough out between two sheets of baking paper to a 20 cm (8 inch) circle. Press the pastry into the tins, leaving the excess overhanging.
5 Divide the filling among the tins. Fold over the excess pastry, pleating as you go. Place on a baking tray and bake for 20–25 minutes, or until the pastry is golden. Combine the preserved lemon and yoghurt and serve with the pies.

NUTRITION PER SERVE
Protein 40 g; Fat 40 g; Carbohydrate 64 g;
Dietary Fibre 6.5 g; Cholesterol 205 mg;
3183 kJ (760 Cal)

Cook the beef mixture until the liquid has reduced and thickened slightly.

Gently gather the dough together and press into a ball.

Fold the excess pastry in neat pleats over the beef filling.

FIVE-SPICE BEEF WITH ASIAN MUSHROOMS

Preparation time: 20 minutes +
10 minutes resting
Total cooking time: 30 minutes
Serves 4

¼ cup (60 ml/2 fl oz) soy sauce
¼ cup (60 ml/2 fl oz) mirin
¼ cup (60 ml/2 fl oz) sake
2 tablespoons soft brown sugar
3 teaspoons five-spice powder
1 teaspoon sea salt flakes
4 fillet steaks (200 g/6½ oz each)
600 g (1¼ lb) orange sweet potato,
    chopped
20 g (¾ oz) butter
⅓ cup (90 g/3 oz) sour cream
2 cloves garlic, crushed
1 teaspoon ground ginger
1 tablespoon peanut oil
10 g (½ oz) butter, for frying, extra
1 teaspoon chopped fresh ginger
1 clove garlic, crushed, extra
100 g (3½ oz) shiitake mushrooms,
    sliced
100 g (3½ oz) shimeji mushrooms,
    pulled apart
100 g (3½ oz) enoki mushrooms
toasted sesame seeds, to serve

1 Place the soy sauce, mirin, sake and sugar in a small saucepan and boil over high heat for 5 minutes, or until reduced and thickened slightly. Remove from the heat and cover.
2 Rub the combined five-spice powder and sea salt flakes into the steaks.
3 Boil the orange sweet potato for 12 minutes, or until soft. Drain well, then add the butter, sour cream, garlic and ground ginger and mash together until smooth and creamy. Season, cover and keep warm.
4 Heat the oil in a large frying pan over high heat. When very hot, cook the steaks for 4–5 minutes each side for a medium–rare result, or until done to your liking. Remove from the pan, cover with foil and rest for 10 minutes.

5 Melt the extra butter in a frying pan over medium heat until just sizzling, then stir in the fresh ginger and extra garlic. Add the shiitake and shimeji mushrooms and stir for 3 minutes, or until wilted. Add the trimmed enoki, remove from the heat, cover and keep warm. Gently reheat the sauce and mashed sweet potato.
6 To serve, dollop mash on four plates, sit a steak on top, then spoon on the sauce. Top with mushrooms, sprinkle with sesame seeds and serve.

NUTRITION PER SERVE
Protein 47 g; Fat 28 g; Carbohydrate 13 g;
Dietary Fibre 2.5 g; Cholesterol 180 mg;
2105 kJ (505 Cal)

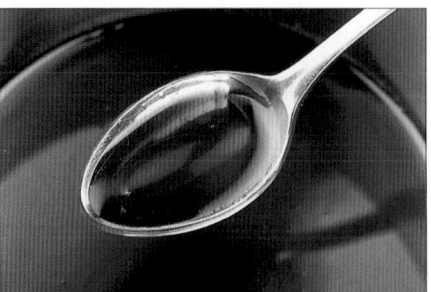
Boil until the sauce has reduced and thickened slightly.

Cook the mushrooms, stirring, until they are wilted.

BEEF FILLET WITH ONION MARMALADE AND CREAMY POTATO GRATIN

**Preparation time: 30 minutes +
  2 hours refrigeration
Total cooking time: 1 hour 10 minutes
Serves 4**

1 cup (250 ml/8 fl oz) port
¼ cup (60 ml/2 fl oz) balsamic vinegar
2 cloves garlic, crushed
4 beef eye fillet steaks
1 tablespoon olive oil

ONION MARMALADE
¼ cup (60 ml/2 fl oz) olive oil
500 g (1 lb) onions, thinly sliced
¼ cup (45 g/1½ oz) soft brown sugar
75 ml (2½ fl oz) red wine vinegar

POTATO GRATIN
4 large potatoes, thinly sliced
1 onion, thinly sliced
1 cup (250 ml/8 fl oz) cream
50 g (1¾ oz) Gruyère cheese, grated

1 Put the port, vinegar and garlic in a non-metallic dish and mix together well. Add the beef and stir to coat. Cover and refrigerate for 2 hours.

Drain, reserving the marinade.
2 To make the marmalade, heat the oil in a large non-stick frying pan, add the onion and sugar and cook over medium heat for 30–40 minutes, or until caramelised. Stir in the red wine vinegar, bring to the boil and cook for 10 minutes, or until thick and sticky. Remove from the heat and keep warm.
3 Meanwhile, preheat the oven to moderate 180°C (350°F/Gas 4). Lightly grease four ½ cup (125 ml/4 fl oz) soufflé dishes, then fill with alternating layers of potato and onion. Combine the cream and cheese, and season, then pour into the dishes. Place on a baking tray and bake for 45 minutes, or until the potato is cooked. Remove from the heat and keep warm.

4 Heat the oil in a large frying pan, add the steaks and cook over high heat for 3–5 minutes each side, or until cooked to your liking. Remove from the pan and keep warm, then add the reserved marinade to the pan and boil for 5–6 minutes, or until reduced by about half.
5 Spoon some of the sauce onto four serving plates, place a steak on the sauce, top with a generous mound of onion marmalade and a gratin. Serve with steamed greens.

NUTRITION PER SERVE
Protein 53 g; Fat 59 g; Carbohydrate 43 g;
Dietary Fibre 4.5 g; Cholesterol 232 mg;
4048 kJ (967 Cal)

Cook the onion marmalade until it is very thick and sticky.

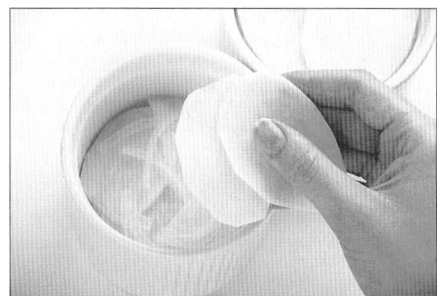

Lay alternate layers of potato and onion in the soufflé dishes.

CORNISH PASTIES

Preparation time: 35 minutes +
30 minutes refrigeration
Total cooking time: 45 minutes
Makes 6 pasties

2½ cups (310 g/10 oz) plain flour
125 g (4 oz) butter, chilled and
    chopped
160 g (5½ oz) round steak, finely
    chopped
1 small potato, finely chopped
1 small onion, finely chopped
1 small carrot, finely chopped
1–2 teaspoons Worcestershire sauce
2 tablespoons beef stock
1 egg, lightly beaten

1 Grease a baking tray. Place the flour, butter and a pinch of salt in a food processor and process for 15 seconds, or until crumbly. Add 4–5 tablespoons of water and process in short bursts until the mixture comes together (add more water if needed). Turn out onto a floured surface and gather together into a ball. Cover with plastic wrap and refrigerate for 30 minutes. Preheat the oven to hot 210°C (415°F/Gas 6–7).
2 Place the steak, potato, onion, carrot, Worcestershire sauce and stock in a large bowl and combine well. Season with salt and pepper.
3 Divide the dough into six portions. Roll out each portion to 3 mm (⅛ inch) thick and use a 16 cm (6½ inch) diameter plate as a guide to cut out 6 circles. Divide the filling evenly and put in the centre of each pastry circle.
4 Brush the edges of the pastry with beaten egg and form into a semicircle. Pinch the edges to form a frill and arrange on the tray. Brush with the remaining beaten egg and bake for 15 minutes. Lower the heat to moderate 180°C (350°F/Gas 4). Cook for 25–30 minutes, or until golden.

NUTRITION PER PASTY
Protein 15 g; Fat 20 g; Carbohydrate 40 g;
Dietary Fibre 3 g; Cholesterol 100 mg;
1665 kJ (395 Cal)

Process the flour, butter and salt until the mixture resembles fine breadcrumbs.

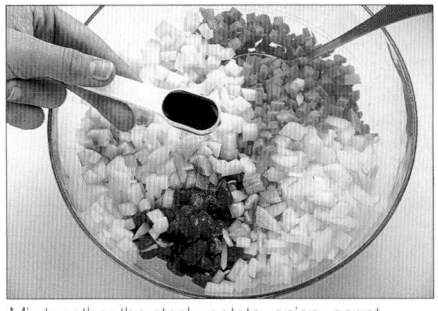

Mix together the steak, potato, onion, carrot, Worcestershire sauce and stock.

Fold the pastry over the filling to form a semi-circle and pinch to close.

BEEF, STOUT AND POTATO PIE

Preparation time: 30 minutes
Total cooking time: 3 hours 10 minutes
Serves 6

2 tablespoons olive oil
1.25 kg (2½ lb) chuck steak, cut into
    3 cm (1¼ inch) cubes, excess fat
    trimmed
2 onions, sliced
2 rashers bacon, roughly chopped
4 cloves garlic, crushed
2 tablespoons plain flour
440 ml (14 fl oz) can stout
1½ cups (375 ml/12 fl oz) beef stock
1½ tablespoons chopped fresh thyme
2 large potatoes, thinly sliced
olive oil, for brushing

1 Heat 1 tablespoon of the oil over high heat in a large, heavy-based flameproof casserole dish, add the beef in batches and cook, turning occasionally, for 5 minutes, or until the meat is nicely coloured. Remove from the dish. Reduce the heat to low, add the remaining oil to the dish, then cook the onion and bacon for 10 minutes, stirring occasionally. Add the garlic and cook for another minute. Return the beef to the pan.
2 Sprinkle the flour over the beef, cook for a minute, stirring, and then gradually add the stout, stirring constantly. Add the stock, increase the heat to medium–high and bring to the boil. Stir in the thyme, season well, then reduce the heat and simmer for 2 hours, or until the beef is tender and the mixture has thickened.
3 Preheat the oven to moderately hot 200°C (400°F/Gas 6). Lightly grease a 1.25 litre ovenproof dish and pour in the beef mixture. Arrange potato slices in a single overlapping layer over the top to cover the meat. Brush with olive oil and sprinkle with salt. Bake for 30–40 minutes, or until the potato is golden.

NUTRITION PER SERVE
Protein 48.5 g; Fat 13 g; Carbohydrate 14 g;
Dietary Fibre 2 g; Cholesterol 146 mg;
1665 kJ (400 Cal)

Gradually add the stout to the beef mixture, stirring constantly.

Arrange the potato slices in a single overlapping layer to cover the meat.

BEEF CARBONNADE

Preparation time: 15 minutes
Total cooking time: 3 hours 25 minutes
Serves 4

1 leek, green part only
1 bay leaf
1 sprig fresh thyme
1 sprig celery leaves
4 sprigs fresh parsley
2 tablespoons butter
1 tablespoon oil
1 kg (2 lb) chuck or stewing steak, cubed
2 onions, sliced
2 cloves garlic, crushed
2 tablespoons plain flour
1½ cups (375 ml/12 fl oz) brown ale or stout
1 long bread stick
2 teaspoons French mustard
2 teaspoons butter, softened

1 To make a bouquet garni, wrap the green part of the leek around the bay leaf, thyme sprig, celery leaves and parsley, then tie with string. Leave a long tail to the string for easy removal.

2 Preheat the oven to moderate 180°C (350°F/Gas 4). Heat the butter and oil in a large pan and cook the beef in batches for 3–4 minutes, or until well browned. Remove from the pan. Lower the heat and cook the onion and garlic for 4 minutes, or until translucent. Sprinkle in the flour, stir well, then cook for 1 minute. Combine the beer with 1½ cups (375 ml/12 fl oz) water and add the pan. Stir well, scraping the pan to incorporate ingredients that are stuck to the base. Bring to the boil and return the meat to the pan. Add the bouquet garni and return to the boil. Transfer to a 2.5 litre casserole dish, cover well with foil and cook gently in the oven for 2½ hours.

3 Cut the bread into 2 cm (¾ inch) slices and spread with the combined mustard and butter. Remove the casserole from the oven, take out the bouquet garni and skim off any fat. Put the bread slices on the surface of the casserole, mustard-side-up, and press down gently to cover with juice. Return to the oven and cook, uncovered, for another 30–40 minutes, or until the bread becomes crusty. Serve with steamed green vegetables.

NUTRITION PER SERVE
Protein 60 g; Fat 25 g; Carbohydrate 30 g; Dietary Fibre 3.5 g; Cholesterol 195 mg; 2455 kJ (585 Cal)

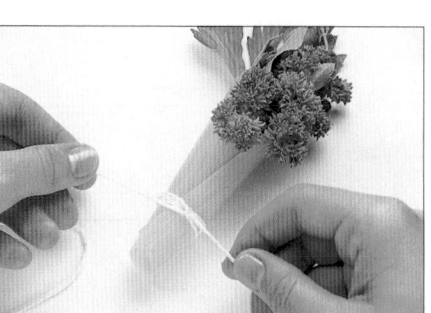

Leave a long tail of string on the bouquet garni for easy removal.

Cook the beef in batches until well browned all over.

CHILLI CON CARNE PIE

**Preparation time: 25 minutes +
  20 minutes chilling**
Total cooking time: 2 hours 15 minutes
Serves 6–8

1½ cups (185 g/6 oz) plain flour
100 g (3½ oz) butter, chilled and cubed
¾ cup (90 g/3 oz) grated Cheddar
1–2 tablespoons iced water

FILLING
2 tablespoons olive oil
1 onion, chopped
2 cloves garlic, chopped
¼ teaspoon chilli powder
2 teaspoons ground cumin
1 teaspoon ground coriander
¼ teaspoon cayenne pepper
1 teaspoon paprika
1 teaspoon dried oregano
750 g (1½ lb) beef mince
2 tablespoons tomato paste
½ cup (125 ml/4 fl oz) dry red wine
425 g (14 oz) can crushed tomatoes
1 tablespoon wholegrain mustard
300 g (10 oz) can red kidney beans,
  drained and rinsed
2 tablespoons chopped fresh
  flat-leaf parsley
1 tablespoon chopped fresh oregano
⅔ cup (170 g/5½ oz) sour cream

1 Sift the flour into a bowl and rub in the butter with your fingertips until the mixture resembles fine breadcrumbs. Stir in the cheese. Make a well and add almost all the water. Mix with a flat-bladed knife, using a cutting action, until the dough comes together, adding more water if necessary.
2 Gather the dough together and lift out onto a lightly floured surface. Press it into a ball and flatten slightly into a disc. Cover in plastic wrap and refrigerate for at least 20 minutes.
3 Heat the oil in a large saucepan over medium heat and cook the onion for 5 minutes, or until softened. Add the garlic, spices and dried oregano and cook for 2 minutes. Add the mince and cook over high heat for 5 minutes, or until brown. Stir in the tomato paste and cook for 1 minute. Pour in the wine and simmer for 3 minutes. Add the tomato and

mustard, bring to the boil, then reduce the heat and simmer for 30 minutes.
4 Add the kidney beans to the beef and cook for 30 minutes, or until any excess moisture has evaporated. Stir in the fresh herbs. Season well.
5 Preheat the oven to 200°C (400°F/Gas 6). Lightly grease a 23 cm (9 inch) pie dish and spoon in the beef filling. Roll out the pastry to fit the top of the dish, then trim away the excess pastry and crimp the edges. Make two or

three cuts in the top to let the steam escape. Bake for 10 minutes, then reduce the oven to 180°C (350°F/Gas 4) and cook for 40–45 minutes, or until the top is golden. Cover the top with foil if it is browning too much. Serve with sour cream.

NUTRITION PER SERVE (8)
Protein 27 g; Fat 32 g; Carbohydrate 24 g;
Dietary Fibre 4 g; Cholesterol 111 mg;
2085 kJ (500 cal)

Simmer the chilli con carne filling until the excess liquid has evaporated.

Use a rolling pin to help you lift the pastry top over the filling.

QUICK BEEF AND NOODLE SALAD

Preparation time: 15 minutes
Total cooking time: 10 minutes
Serves 4

500 g (1 lb) rump steak
1 tablespoon peanut oil
2 tablespoons oyster sauce
2 teaspoons mild curry powder
1 tablespoon soft brown sugar
1 small Lebanese cucumber, thinly
    sliced
1 red onion, sliced
1 red capsicum, cut into thin strips
1 small red chilli, seeded and chopped
¼ cup (15 g/½ oz) chopped mint
⅓ cup (60 g/2 oz) chopped unsalted
    peanuts or cashews
500 g (1 lb) Hokkien noodles

DRESSING
½ cup (125 ml/4 fl oz) rice vinegar
    (see NOTE)
2 tablespoons fish sauce
¼ cup (60 g/2 oz) caster sugar
2 teaspoons finely chopped fresh
    ginger
1 small red chilli, seeded and chopped
1 tablespoon chopped coriander
    leaves

1 Remove all visible fat from the meat. Combine the peanut oil, oyster sauce, curry powder and brown sugar in a small bowl.
2 Heat a wok over medium heat. Add the steak and cook for 6–8 minutes, turning and basting with half the sauce during cooking. Remove the steak from the wok.
3 To make the dressing, whisk together all the ingredients.

4 Place the cucumber, onion, capsicum and chilli in a large bowl. Add the mint and nuts. Thinly slice the meat, add to the bowl with the dressing and lightly toss to combine. If you have time, leave for a few minutes to marinate.
5 Place the noodles in the same wok and stir-fry over medium heat for 1–2 minutes. Stir in the remaining basting sauce and toss until heated through. Divide the noodles among serving bowls and top with the salad. Serve immediately.

NUTRITION PER SERVE
Protein 50 g; Fat 17 g; Carbohydrate 115 g;
Dietary Fibre 5.5 g; Cholesterol 105 mg;
3405 kJ (815 cal)

NOTE: Rice vinegar is available in Asian grocery stores.

While you cook the steak, turn it and baste often with the sauce.

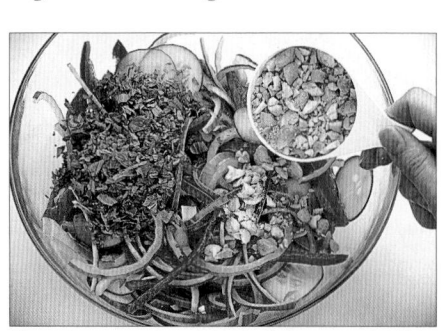
Place the cucumber, onion, capsicum and chilli in a large bowl and add the mint and nuts.

Stir the remaining basting sauce into the noodles in the wok.

FAMILY-STYLE MEAT PIE

**Preparation time: 30 minutes + cooling +
20 minutes refrigeration**
Total cooking time: 1 hour 45 minutes
Serves 6

1 tablespoon oil
1 onion, chopped
1 clove garlic, crushed
750 g (1 lb 8 oz) beef mince
1 cup (250 ml/8 fl oz) beef stock
1 cup (250 ml/8 fl oz) beer
1 tablespoon tomato paste
1 tablespoon vegetable yeast extract
1 tablespoon Worcestershire sauce
2 teaspoons cornflour
375 g (12 oz) shortcrust pastry
375 g (12 oz) puff pastry
1 egg, lightly beaten

1 Heat the oil in a large saucepan over medium heat, add the onion and cook for 5 minutes, or until golden. Increase the heat to high, add the garlic and mince and cook, breaking up any lumps, for about 5 minutes, or until the mince changes colour.
2 Add the stock, beer, tomato paste, yeast extract, Worcestershire sauce and ½ cup (125 ml/4 fl oz) water. Reduce the heat to medium and cook for 1 hour, or until there is little liquid left. Combine the cornflour with 1 tablespoon water, then stir into the mince and cook for 5 minutes, or until the mixture is thick and glossy. Remove from the heat and leave to cool completely.
3 Lightly grease a 23 cm (9 inch) top, 18 cm (7 inch) base, 3 cm (1¼ inch) deep pie tin. Roll the shortcrust pastry out between two sheets of baking paper until it is large enough to line the base and side of the tin. Remove the top sheet of paper and invert the pastry into the tin, then remove the remaining sheet of paper. Use a ball of pastry to help press the pastry into the tin, allowing any excess to hang over.
4 Roll out the puff pastry between two sheets of baking paper to a 24 cm (9½ inch) circle. Spoon the cooled filling into the pastry shell and smooth it down. Brush the pastry edges with beaten egg, then place the puff pastry over the top. Cut off any overhang with a sharp knife. Press the top and bottom pastries together, then scallop the edges with a fork or your fingers, and refrigerate for 20 minutes. Preheat the oven to moderately hot 200°C (400°F/Gas 6) and heat a baking tray.
5 Brush the remaining egg over the top of the pie, place on the hot tray on the bottom shelf of the oven (this helps make a crisp crust for this pie) and bake for 25–30 minutes, or until the pastry is golden and well puffed.

NUTRITION PER SERVE
Protein 38 g; Fat 43.5 g; Carbohydrate 52 g; Dietary Fibre 2.5 g; Cholesterol 129.5 mg; 3120 kJ (745 Cal)

Spoon the cooled meat filling evenly into the pastry shell.

Trim the edges of the puff pastry with a very sharp knife.

PASTICCIO (MEAT AND PASTA BAKE)

Preparation time: 25 minutes
  + 15 minutes resting
Total cooking time: 2 hours
Serves 4–6

¼ cup (60 ml/2 fl oz) olive oil
1 onion, finely chopped
2 cloves garlic, crushed
80 g (2¾ oz) pancetta, finely chopped
500 g (1 lb) beef mince
1 teaspoon chopped fresh oregano
60 g (2 oz) small button mushrooms, sliced
115 g (4 oz) chicken livers, trimmed and finely chopped
¼ teaspoon ground nutmeg
pinch cayenne pepper
¼ cup (60 ml/2 fl oz) dry white wine
2 tablespoons tomato paste
1½ cups (375 ml/12 fl oz) beef stock
2 tablespoons grated Parmesan
1 egg, beaten
150 g (5 oz) macaroni
100 g (3½ oz) ricotta cheese
2 tablespoons milk
pinch cayenne pepper, extra
pinch ground nutmeg, extra
1 egg, beaten, extra
1 cup (100 g/3½ oz) grated Parmesan, extra

BECHAMEL SAUCE
40 g (1¼ oz) butter
1½ tablespoons plain flour
pinch ground nutmeg
300 ml (10 fl oz) milk
1 small bay leaf

1 Preheat the oven to moderate 180°C (350°F/Gas 4). Lightly grease a 1.5 litre ovenproof dish. Heat the oil in a large frying pan over medium heat and cook the onion, garlic and pancetta, stirring, for 5 minutes, or until the onion is golden. Add the beef, increase the heat and stir for 5 minutes, or until browned.

2 Add the oregano, mushrooms, chicken livers, nutmeg and cayenne, season and cook for 2 minutes, or until the livers change colour. Add the wine and cook over high heat for 1 minute, or until evaporated. Stir in tomato paste and stock. Reduce heat and simmer for 45 minutes, or until thickened. Beat the Parmesan and egg together, and quickly stir into sauce.

3 Cook the macaroni in lightly salted boiling water until al dente. Blend the ricotta, milk, extra cayenne, extra nutmeg, extra egg and ¼ cup (25 g/ ¾ oz) extra Parmesan. Season. Drain the macaroni, add to the ricotta mixture and mix well.

4 To make the Béchamel sauce, melt the butter in a small saucepan. Stir in the flour and cook over low heat until beginning to turn golden, then stir in the nutmeg. Remove from the heat and gradually stir in the milk. Add the bay leaf and season. Return to low heat and simmer, stirring, until thickened. Discard the bay leaf.

5 Spread half the meat sauce in the dish, layer half the pasta over the top and sprinkle with half the remaining Parmesan. Layer with remaining meat sauce and pasta. Press down firmly with the back of a spoon. Spread the Béchamel sauce over the top and sprinkle with remaining Parmesan. Bake for 45–50 minutes, or until golden. Rest for 15 minutes before serving.

NUTRITION PER SERVE (6)
Protein 43 g; Fat 40 g; Carbohydrate 27 g; Dietary Fibre 2.5 g; Cholesterol 192 mg; 2670 kJ (638 Cal)

Cook the mixture for 2 minutes, or until the chicken livers change colour.

Add the tomato paste and stock, then simmer until thickened.

Stir the cooked, drained macaroni through the ricotta mixture.

Gradually add the milk to the butter and flour to make the Béchamel sauce.

Spoon half the pasta and ricotta mixture over the meat sauce.

Pour the Béchamel sauce evenly over the top pasta layer.

MANDARIN BEEF

**Preparation time: 25 minutes
+ 15 minutes marinating
Total cooking time: 5 minutes
Serves 4**

350 g (11 oz) boned rib eye steak,
    finely sliced
2 teaspoons soy sauce
2 teaspoons dry sherry
1 teaspoon chopped fresh ginger
1 teaspoon sesame oil
oil, for cooking
¼ teaspoon ground white pepper
2 teaspoons finely chopped dried
    mandarin or tangerine rind
2 teaspoons soy sauce, extra
1½ teaspoons caster sugar
1½ teaspoons cornflour
4 tablespoons beef stock

1 Place the meat in a bowl. Mix the soy, sherry, ginger and sesame oil together, add to the meat and toss well. Leave to marinate for 15 minutes.
2 Heat the wok until very hot, add 1 tablespoon of the oil and swirl it around to coat the side. Add the beef and stir-fry over high heat for 2 minutes, or until the meat is browned on all sides.
3 Add the pepper, dried mandarin or tangerine rind, extra soy sauce and sugar. Stir-fry briefly.
4 Dissolve the cornflour in a little of the stock and then add the remaining stock. Pour the whole lot into the wok. Stir until the sauce boils and thickens. Serve immediately.

NUTRITION PER SERVE
Protein 20 g; Fat 8 g; Carbohydrate 9 g;
Dietary Fibre 0 g; Cholesterol 60 mg;
785 kJ (188 cal)

VARIATION: For a hotter dish, fry a whole dried chilli in the hot oil and then discard the chilli before adding the beef to the wok.

The thickened sauce is optional. You can dry-fry the marinated beef and serve with fine noodles instead of the more traditional rice.

Make a marinade from the soy sauce, sherry, ginger and sesame oil and toss over the meat.

Add the pepper, mandarin or tangerine rind, soy sauce and sugar to the meat.

Dissolve the cornflour in the stock and then add to the wok to make a sauce.

BEEF AND CARAMELISED ONION PIE

**Preparation time: 40 minutes +
20 minutes cooling**
Total cooking time: 2 hours 20 minutes
Serves 6–8

⅓ cup (80 ml/2¾ fl oz) oil
2 large red onions, thinly sliced
1 teaspoon dark brown sugar
1 kg (2 lb) lean rump steak, diced
¼ cup (30 g/1 oz) plain flour, seasoned
2 cloves garlic, crushed
225 g (7 oz) button mushrooms, sliced
1 cup (250 ml/8 fl oz) beef stock
150 ml (5 fl oz) stout
1 tablespoon tomato paste
1 tablespoon Worcestershire sauce
1 tablespoon chopped fresh thyme
350 g (11 oz) potatoes, diced
2 carrots, diced
600 g (1¼ lb) quick flaky pastry
1 egg, lightly beaten

1 Heat 2 tablespoons of the oil in a frying pan over medium heat and cook the onion for 5 minutes, or until light brown, then add the sugar and cook for 7–8 minutes, or until the onion caramelises. Remove from the pan. Wipe the pan clean.
2 Toss the beef in flour and shake off the excess. Heat the remaining oil in the same pan and cook the meat in batches over high heat until browned. Return all the meat to the pan, add the garlic and mushrooms and cook for 2 minutes. Add the stock, stout, tomato paste, Worcestershire sauce and thyme. Bring to the boil, then reduce the heat and simmer, covered, for 1 hour. Add the potato and carrot and simmer for 30 minutes. Remove from the heat and allow to cool.
3 Preheat the oven to 190°C (375°F/ Gas 5). Grease a 1.25 litre pie dish. Pour in the filling, then top with the onion. Roll the pastry out between two sheets of baking paper until it is 2.5 cm (1 inch) wider than the pie dish. Cut a 2 cm (¾ inch) strip around the edge of the pastry circle, brush with water and place damp-side-down on the rim of the dish.
4 Cover with the remaining pastry, pressing the edges together. Knock up the rim by making small slashes in the edges of the pastry with the back of a knife. Re-roll the trimmings and use them to decorate the pie. Brush with egg and bake for 25 minutes, or until golden.

NUTRITION PER SERVE (8)
Protein 36 g; Fat 32 g; Carbohydrate 47 g; Dietary Fibre 4 g; Cholesterol 113 mg; 2615 kJ (625 cal)

Spoon the caramelised onion over the filling in the pie dish.

Place the strip of pastry damp-side-down on the rim of the dish.

397

BEEF BOURGUIGNON

Preparation time: 10 minutes
Total cooking time: 2 hours
Serves 6

1 kg (2 lb) topside or round steak
plain flour, seasoned with salt and
    pepper
3 rashers bacon, rind removed
1 tablespoon oil
12 pickling onions
1 cup (250 ml/ 8 fl oz) red wine
2 cups (500 ml/16 fl oz) beef stock
1 teaspoon dried thyme
200 g (6½ oz) button mushrooms
2 bay leaves

1 Trim the steak of fat and sinew and cut into 2 cm (¾ inch) cubes. Lightly toss in the seasoned flour to coat, shaking off the excess.
2 Cut the bacon into 2 cm (¾ inch) squares. Heat the oil in a large pan and quickly cook the bacon over medium heat. Remove the bacon from the pan, then add the meat and brown well in batches. Remove and set aside. Add the onions to the pan and cook until golden.
3 Return bacon and meat to pan with the remaining ingredients. Bring to the boil, reduce the heat and simmer, covered, for 1½ hours, or until the meat is very tender, stirring now and then. Remove the bay leaves to serve.

NUTRITION PER SERVE
Protein 40 g; Fat 7 g; Carbohydrate 5 g;
Dietary Fibre 1 g; Cholesterol 90 mg;
1150 kJ (275 cal)

STORAGE TIME: Refrigerate in an airtight container for up to 3 days.

Trim the meat of any fat and sinew and cut it into cubes.

Return the bacon and meat to the pan and add the remaining ingredients.

BEEF AND VEGETABLE CASEROLE

Preparation time: 40 minutes
Total cooking time: 1 hour 40 minutes
Serves 6

500 g (1 lb) lean round steak
cooking oil spray
1 onion, sliced
3 cloves garlic, crushed
2 teaspoons ground cumin
1 teaspoon dried thyme leaves
2 bay leaves
400 g (13 oz) can chopped tomatoes
500 g (1 lb) potatoes, chopped
2 large carrots, thickly sliced
4 zucchini, thickly sliced
250 g (8 oz) mushrooms, halved
250 g (8 oz) yellow squash, halved
2 tablespoons tomato paste
½ cup (125 ml/4 fl oz) red wine
⅓ cup (20 g/¾ oz) chopped fresh
    parsley

1 Preheat the oven to moderate 180°C (350°F/Gas 4). Remove any excess fat and sinew from the meat and cut into 2 cm (¾ inch) cubes. Spray a deep, non-stick frying pan with oil and fry the meat in batches until brown. Remove from the pan. Spray the pan again, add the onion and cook until lightly golden. Add the garlic, cumin, thyme and bay leaves and stir for 1 minute.

2 Return the meat and any juices to the pan, tossing to coat with spices. Add 1½ cups (375 ml/12 fl oz) water and the tomato, scraping the pan. Simmer for 10 minutes, or until thickened. Mix in a large casserole dish with the vegetables, tomato paste and wine.

3 Bake, covered, for 1 hour. Stir well, then uncover and bake for 20 minutes. Season, remove the bay leaves and stir in the parsley.

NUTRITION PER SERVE
Protein 25 g; Fat 4 g; Carbohydrate 20 g; Dietary Fibre 6.5 g; Cholesterol 50 mg; 930 kJ (220 cal)

Discard any excess fat and sinew from the steak and cut the steak into cubes.

When the onion is golden, add the garlic, cumin, thyme and bay leaves.

Pour the wine into the casserole dish and stir through the vegetables.

CHINESE BEEF AND SNOW PEAS

Preparation time: 10 minutes
Total cooking time: 5 minutes
Serves 4

400 g (13 oz) rump steak, finely sliced (see HINT)
2 tablespoons soy sauce
½ teaspoon grated fresh ginger
oil, for cooking
200 g (6½ oz) snow peas, trimmed

1½ teaspoons cornflour
½ cup (125 ml/4 fl oz) beef stock
1 teaspoon soy sauce, extra
¼ teaspoon sesame oil

1 Put the meat in a glass or ceramic bowl. Mix the soy and ginger and add to the meat. Stir well. Heat the wok until very hot, add 2 tablespoons of the oil and swirl it around to coat the side. Add the beef and snow peas and stir-fry over high heat for 2 minutes, or until the meat changes colour.

2 Dissolve the cornflour in a little of the stock. Add to the wok with the remaining stock, extra soy and oil.
3 Stir until the sauce boils and thickens. Serve immediately.

NUTRITION PER SERVE
Protein 27 g; Fat 13 g; Carbohydrate 9 g;
Dietary Fibre 3 g; Cholesterol 67 mg;
1088 kJ (260 cal)

HINT: To make the beef easier to slice, freeze it until it is just firm and thinly slice while it is still frozen.

Stir-fry the beef and snow peas over high heat until the meat browns.

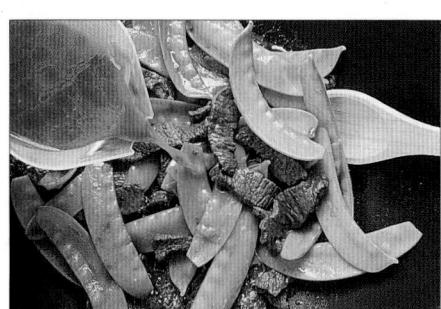

Dissolve the cornflour in a little of the stock and add to the wok with the rest of the stock.

Stir the beef and snow peas until the sauce comes to the boil and thickens.

BEEF AND LENTIL CURRY

Preparation time: 45 minutes +
  10 minutes soaking
Total cooking time: 1 hour 50 minutes
Serves 6

3–4 small dried red chillies
1 tablespoon oil
2 red onions, cut into thin wedges
4 cloves garlic, finely chopped
1 tablespoon grated fresh ginger
1 tablespoon garam masala
3 cardamom pods, lightly crushed
1 cinnamon stick
2 teaspoons ground turmeric
750 g (1½ lb) chuck or gravy beef,
  diced
400 g (13 oz) can chopped tomatoes
½ cup (90 g/3 oz) brown or green
  lentils
½ cup (125 g/4 oz) red lentils
200 g (6½ oz) pumpkin, diced
150 g (5 oz) baby eggplant, quartered
  lengthways, diced
125 g (4 oz) baby English spinach
  leaves
1 tablespoon tamarind purée
2 tablespoons grated palm sugar

1 Soak the chillies in boiling water for 10 minutes, drain and finely chop.
2 Heat the oil in a large saucepan. Add the onion and cook, stirring, over medium heat for 5 minutes, or until soft. Add the garlic and ginger, and cook for a further 2 minutes.
3 Add the chilli, garam masala, cardamom pods, cinnamon stick, turmeric and ½ teaspoon coarsely ground black pepper. Cook, stirring, for 2 minutes, or until fragrant. Add the beef and stir constantly for 3–4 minutes, or until the meat changes colour and is well coated in the spices.

4 Add the tomato, lentils, 1 teaspoon salt and 3 cups (750 ml) water. Simmer, covered, for 1 hour, or until the lentils are tender. Stir frequently to prevent any of the mixture sticking to the base of the pan. Add a little extra water, if necessary.
5 Add the pumpkin and eggplant to the pan, and cook, covered, for 20 minutes, or until the beef and vegetables are tender and the sauce thickens. Stir in the spinach, tamarind purée and palm sugar, and cook,

covered, for a further 10 minutes. Remove the cinnamon stick and serve.

NUTRITION PER SERVE
Protein 34 g; Fat 14 g; Carbohydrate 22 g; Dietary Fibre 6.5 g; Cholesterol 84 mg; 1452 kJ (347 cal)

NOTE: This dish is traditionally served with rice which is cooked pilaf-style with well-browned, slow-cooked onion slices.

Lightly crush the cardamom pods with the back of a heavy knife.

Add the beef to the pan and stir to coat with the fragrant spices.

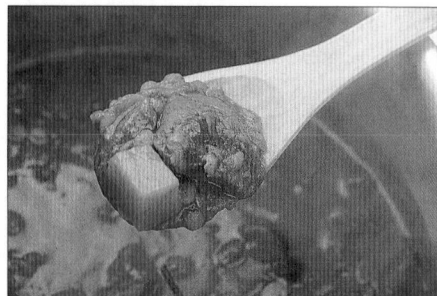

Cook until the beef and vegetables are tender and the sauce thickens.

STEAK WITH ROASTED RED ONION SAUCE

Preparation time: 20 minutes
Total cooking time: 1 hour 20 minutes
Serves 4

250 g (8 oz) red onions, thinly sliced
500 g (1 lb) pickling onions
2 cloves garlic
1 tablespoon olive oil
750 g (1½ lb) Roma tomatoes
½ teaspoon salt
2 tablespoons chopped fresh oregano
220g (7 oz) can Italian peeled
    tomatoes
2 teaspoons muscatel liqueur or
    brandy
2 teaspoons soft brown sugar
4 scotch or rump fillet steaks, trimmed

1 Preheat the oven to moderately hot 200°C (400°F/Gas 6). Place the red onion, pickling onions and garlic cloves in a large roasting tin with half the olive oil. Roll the onions in the oil so that they are lightly coated.
2 Halve the tomatoes lengthways and add to the tin. Drizzle with the remaining olive oil, salt and oregano and roast for 1 hour.
3 Use a pair of kitchen scissors to roughly cut up the canned tomatoes, while they are still in the tin. Spoon the chopped tomatoes and their juice into the roasting tin, taking care not to break up the roasted tomatoes. Drizzle the muscatel or brandy over the top and sprinkle with the brown sugar. Return to the oven and roast for a further 20 minutes.
4 Chargrill the steaks on a lightly oiled chargrill pan until cooked to your liking. Serve with the hot sauce.

NUTRITION PER SERVE
Protein 60 g; Fat 15 g; Carbohydrate 13 g;
Dietary Fibre 5 g; Cholesterol 143 mg;
1900 kJ (450 cal)

SERVING SUGGESTION: This sauce is a great low-fat condiment for serving with grilled meats at barbecues.

Red onions will give a lovely colour to the sauce. Peel them and slice thinly.

Add the tomatoes to the roasting tin and sprinkle with oil, salt and oregano.

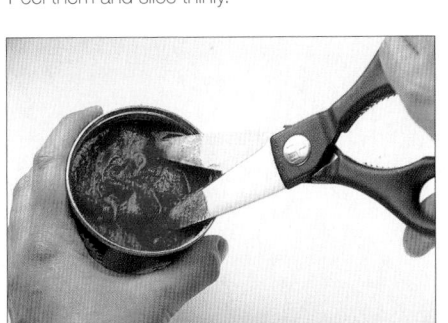

Use scissors to chop up tinned tomatoes without losing the juice.

Drizzle the muscatel or brandy over the pan and sprinkle with soft brown sugar.

HONEY AND BLACK PEPPER BEEF

Preparation time: 15 minutes
Total cooking time: 10 minutes
Serves 4

oil, for cooking
500 g (1 lb) round steak, cut into thin
    strips
2 cloves garlic, crushed
1 onion, sliced
300 g (10 oz) sugar snap peas

2 tablespoons honey
2 teaspoons soy sauce
2 tablespoons oyster sauce
3 teaspoons cracked black pepper

1 Heat the wok until very hot, add
1 tablespoon of the oil and swirl it
around to coat the side. Stir-fry the
beef in batches over high heat.
Remove and drain on paper towels.
2 Reheat the wok, add 1 tablespoon
of the oil and stir-fry the garlic, onion
and sugar snap peas until softened.
Remove from the wok and set aside.

3 Add the honey, soy sauce, oyster
sauce and cracked pepper to the
wok. Bring to the boil, then reduce
the heat and simmer for 3–4 minutes,
or until the sauce thickens slightly.
4 Increase the heat, return the meat
and vegetables to the wok, and toss
for 2–3 minutes, or until well
combined and heated through.

NUTRITION PER SERVE
Protein 30 g; Fat 15 g; Carbohydrate 20 g;
Dietary Fibre 4.5 g; Cholesterol 70 mg;
1400 kJ (335 cal)

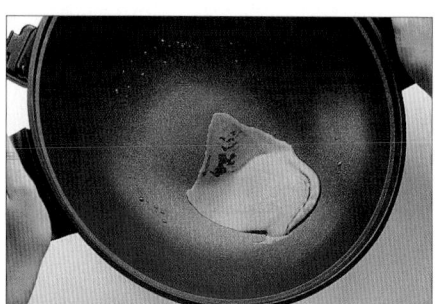

Heat the wok before adding the oil, then add the
oil and swirl to coat the side.

Once the beef is cooked, remove it from the wok
and drain on paper towels.

Add the honey, soy sauce, oyster sauce and
cracked pepper and bring to the boil.

CHUNKY VEAL AND CAPSICUM PIE

**Preparation time: 40 minutes +
10 minutes resting + cooling**
Total cooking time: 2 hours
Serves 6

⅓ cup (80 ml/2¾ fl oz) olive oil
3 capsicums, seeded and cut into
   2.5 cm (1 inch) pieces
2 cloves garlic, crushed
1 kg (2 lb) neck, shoulder or breast of
   veal, cut into small pieces
¼ cup (30 g/1 oz) plain flour, seasoned
40 g (1½ oz) butter
2 onions, finely chopped
8 French shallots, peeled
¼ teaspoon cayenne pepper
2 teaspoons red wine vinegar
¾ cup (185 ml/6 fl oz) chicken stock
2 tablespoons chopped fresh flat-leaf
   parsley
375 g (12 oz) shortcrust pastry
1 egg, lightly beaten, to glaze

1 Heat half the oil in a large
saucepan and cook the capsicum over
medium heat for 2–3 minutes. Add
the garlic, cover the pan and reduce
the heat to low. Cook gently for
5 minutes, then remove from the pan.
2 Put the veal and flour in a plastic
bag and shake until the veal is evenly
coated, shaking off any excess. Heat
the butter and the remaining oil over
high heat in the same saucepan and
cook the veal in batches until evenly
browned. Return all the veal to the
pan, add the onion, shallots and
cayenne and reduce the heat to low.
Cook, covered, for 10 minutes. Stir
in the vinegar, cover and turn off the
heat. Leave for 10 minutes.
3 Add the capsicum, stock and
parsley to the meat, bring to the boil,
then reduce the heat to low. Cover
and simmer for 20 minutes, or until
the meat is tender.
4 Uncover and cook for another
30–40 minutes to reduce the liquid
until it thickens and darkens. Season
to taste and cool slightly. Preheat the
oven to 200°C (400°F/Gas 6) and
preheat a baking tray. Lightly grease
an 18 cm (7 inch) pie dish.
5 Spoon the filling into the pie dish,
levelling the surface. Roll the dough
out between two sheets of baking
paper to a size slightly larger than the
top of the pie dish. Carefully cover
the filling and press the pastry over
the edge to seal. Trim the edges.
Decorate with pastry trimmings and
brush the top with egg. Place on the
hot tray and bake for 30 minutes, or
until golden.

NUTRITION PER SERVE
Protein 44 g; Fat 37 g; Carbohydrate 33 g;
Dietary Fibre 2.5 g; Cholesterol 201 mg;
2660 kJ (635 cal)

Spoon the filling into the lightly greased pie dish,
then level the surface.

BEEF POT ROAST WITH EGGPLANT

Preparation time: 20 minutes
Total cooking time: 1 hour 25 minutes
Serves 4

2 tablespoons oil
1 kg (2 lb) piece lean topside beef
1 cup (250 ml/8 fl oz) beef stock
1 onion, sliced
1 clove garlic, crushed
4 large tomatoes, peeled, seeded and chopped
1 teaspoon ground cumin
1 teaspoon ground turmeric
1 teaspoon finely grated lemon rind

2 tablespoons lemon juice
1 medium eggplant, cut into 3 cm (1¼ inch) cubes
1 sweet potato, halved and cut into 1 cm (½ inch slices)
2 tablespoons plain flour
1 tablespoon chopped fresh coriander

1 Heat the oil in a deep heavy-based saucepan. Add the meat and cook over medium–high heat until well browned on all sides.
2 Remove the pan from the heat and add the stock, onion, garlic, tomato, cumin, turmeric, lemon rind and lemon juice. Cover, bring slowly to simmering point over low heat and simmer for 45 minutes.

3 Add the eggplant and sweet potato, and cook, uncovered, for 30 minutes, or until the meat and vegetables are tender. Remove the meat and leave it in a warm place, covered with foil, for 10 minutes before slicing.
4 Combine the flour and ¼ cup (60 ml/2 fl oz) water to make a smooth paste. Add to the sauce with the coriander, stir over medium heat until the sauce boils and thickens, and cook for 3 minutes. Pour over the sliced meat to serve.

NUTRITION PER SERVE
Protein 60 g; Fat 18 g; Carbohydrate 18 g;
Dietary Fibre 4.5 g; Cholesterol 123 mg;
1985 kJ (475 cal)

Cook the beef in the hot oil until it is well browned all over.

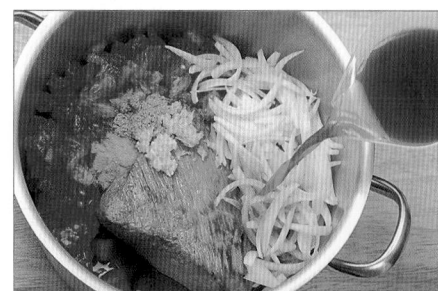
Add the stock, onion, garlic, tomato, cumin, turmeric, lemon rind and juice to the beef.

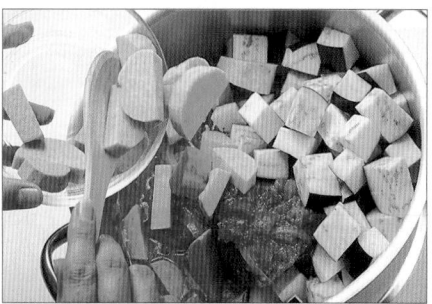
Add the eggplant and sweet potato, and cook until the meat and vegetables are tender.

SPICY BURGERS WITH AVOCADO SALSA

Preparation time: 25 minutes
Total cooking time: 10 minutes
Serves 6

1 kg (2 lb) beef mince
1 small onion, finely chopped
3 teaspoons chopped chilli
1 teaspoon ground cumin
2 tablespoons tomato paste

2 tablespoons chopped fresh coriander
6 bread rolls

AVOCADO SALSA
1 avocado
2 tablespoons lime juice
1 small tomato, chopped
125 g (4 oz) can corn kernels, drained

1 With your hands, mix together the mince, onion, chilli, cumin, tomato paste and coriander. Divide into six portions and shape into burgers.

2 Cook on a hot, lightly oiled grill or flatplate for 4–5 minutes each side.
3 To make the salsa, dice the avocado and toss with lime juice. Add the tomato and corn and toss lightly. Sandwich the burgers in the bread rolls and serve with the salsa.

NUTRITION PER SERVE
Protein 44 g; Fat 29 g; Carbohydrate 49 g;
Dietary Fibre 5 g; Cholesterol 105 mg;
2649 kJ (633 cal)

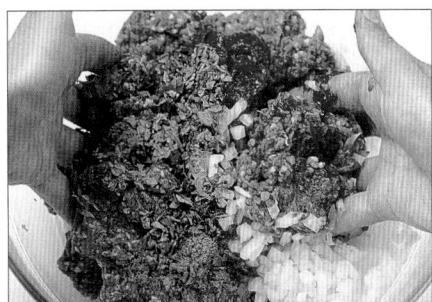

The most thorough way to mix the ingredients together is to use your hands.

Cook the burgers on a lightly oiled barbecue grill or flatplate, turning once.

Mix together the salsa ingredients: the lime juice will prevent the avocado browning.

COUNTRY BEEF STEW

Preparation time: 40 minutes
Total cooking time: 2 hours 10 minutes
Serves 8

1 small eggplant, cubed
2–3 tablespoons olive oil
2 red onions, sliced
2 cloves garlic, crushed
1 kg (2 lb) chuck steak, cubed
1 teaspoon ground coriander
½ teaspoon allspice
¾ teaspoon sweet paprika
6 ripe tomatoes, chopped
1 cup (250 ml/8 fl oz) red wine
3 cups (750 ml/24 fl oz) beef stock

2 tablespoons tomato paste
250 g (8 oz) baby new potatoes,
    halved
2 celery sticks, sliced
3 carrots, chopped
2 bay leaves
3 tablespoons chopped fresh parsley

1 Put the eggplant in a colander, sprinkle generously with salt and leave for 20 minutes. Rinse, pat dry with paper towels and set aside.
2 Heat the oil in a large heavy-based pan and cook the onion for 5 minutes until soft; add the garlic and cook for 1 minute. Remove and set aside. Add the eggplant and brown for 5 minutes. Remove and set aside. Brown the

meat in batches over medium heat, sprinkle with the spices, season and cook for 1–2 minutes. Add the tomato, onion, wine, stock and tomato paste and bring to the boil. Reduce the heat and simmer, covered, for 25 minutes.
3 Add the potato, celery, carrot and bay leaves, bring to the boil, reduce the heat, cover and simmer for 1 hour. Add the eggplant and simmer for 30 minutes, uncovered. Lift out the bay leaves and stir in the parsley.

NUTRITION PER SERVE
Protein 30 g; Fat 10 g; Carbohydrate 10 g;
Dietary Fibre 4 g; Cholesterol 85 mg;
1160 kJ (280 cal)

Put the eggplant in a colander and sprinkle with salt to draw out any bitterness.

Add the tomato, onion, wine, stock and tomato paste to the pan.

Add the potato, celery, carrot and bay leaves to the pan.

BEEF AND RED WINE PIES

Preparation time: 50 minutes
Total cooking time: 2 hours 40 minutes
Makes 6

¼ cup (60 ml/2 fl oz) oil
1.5 kg (3 lb) chuck steak, cubed
2 onions, chopped
1 clove garlic, crushed
¼ cup (30 g/1 oz) plain flour
1¼ cups (315 ml/10 fl oz) dry red wine
2 cups (500 ml/16 fl oz) beef stock
2 bay leaves
2 sprigs fresh thyme
2 carrots, chopped
4 sheets ready-rolled shortcrust pastry
1 egg, lightly beaten
4 sheets ready-rolled puff pastry

1 Heat 2 tablespoons of the oil in a large pan, add the meat and fry in batches until browned all over. Remove all the meat from the pan. Heat the remaining oil in the same pan, add the onion and garlic and cook, stirring, until golden brown. Add the flour and stir over medium heat for 2 minutes, or until well browned.
2 Remove from the heat and gradually stir in the combined wine and stock. Return to the heat and stir until the mixture boils and thickens. Return the meat to the pan with the bay leaves and thyme, and simmer for 1 hour. Add the carrot and simmer for 45 minutes, or until the meat and carrot are tender and the sauce has thickened. Season to taste, and remove the bay leaves and thyme sprigs. Cool.
3 Preheat the oven to 200°C (400°F/Gas 6). Lightly grease six 9 cm (3½ inch) metal pie tins. Cut the shortcrust pastry sheets in half

diagonally. Line the base and side of each pie tin with the pastry and trim the edges. Line each pie with baking paper and fill with baking beads. Place on a baking tray and bake for 8 minutes. Remove the paper and beads and bake for a further 8 minutes, or until the pastry is lightly browned. Cool.
4 Spoon the filling into the pastry cases and brush the edge with some of the beaten egg. Cut the puff pastry

sheets in half diagonally and cover the tops of the pies. Trim the excess, pressing the edges with a fork to seal. Cut a slit in the top of each pie. Brush the tops with the remaining egg, and bake for 20–25 minutes, or until the pastry is golden brown.

NUTRITION PER PIE
Protein 60 g; Fat 47 g; Carbohydrate 51 g; Dietary Fibre 3 g; Cholesterol 200 mg; 3648 kJ (873 cal)

Fry the steak in batches in a large pan until browned all over.

Line the base and side of each pie tin with the shortcrust pastry.

Cover the filling with puff pastry and trim off the excess with a sharp knife.

BEEF CASSEROLE WITH CARAWAY DUMPLINGS

Preparation time: 1 hour
Total cooking time: 1 hour 15 minutes
Serves 6

1.5 kg (3 lb) round or topside steak, trimmed and cut into 3 cm (1¼ inch) cubes
½ cup (60 g/2 oz) plain flour
¼ teaspoon ground black pepper
⅓ cup (80 ml/2¾ fl oz) olive oil
1 clove garlic, crushed
2 onions, sliced
1 teaspoon ground sweet paprika
½ teaspoon ground cinnamon
⅓ cup (80 ml/ 2¾ fl oz) red wine
½ cup (125 ml/4 fl oz) beef stock
½ teaspoon dried mixed herbs
⅔ cup (160 g/5½ oz) tomato pasta sauce
3 large red capsicums

DUMPLINGS
1½ cups (185 g/6 oz) self-raising flour
65 g (2¼ oz) butter
½ cup (125 ml/4 fl oz) milk
1 teaspoon caraway seeds
1 tablespoon milk, extra

1 Preheat the oven to moderate 180°C (350°F/Gas 4). Toss the meat lightly in the combined flour and pepper, and shake off any excess.
2 Heat 2 tablespoons of the oil in a heavy-based saucepan. Cook the meat quickly in small batches over medium–high heat until well browned. Drain on paper towels.
3 Heat the remaining oil in the pan. Cook the garlic and onion over medium heat, stirring, for 2 minutes, or until soft.

4 Return the meat to the pan with the spices, wine, stock, mixed herbs and tomato pasta sauce. Bring to the boil, then remove from the heat and transfer to a deep casserole dish. Bake, covered, for 45 minutes. Remove from the oven and remove the lid. Increase the oven to very hot 240°C (475°F/Gas 9).
5 Halve the capsicums lengthways and remove the seeds. Grill, skin-side up, under a hot grill for 10 minutes, or until the skin blackens and blisters. Remove from the grill and allow to cool. Carefully peel off the skins. Cut the capsicum into 2 cm (¾ inch) wide strips. Arrange the roasted capsicum over the meat.
6 To make the dumplings, process the flour and butter in a food processor for 10 seconds, or until fine and crumbly. Add the milk all at once and process for 10 seconds, or until a soft dough is formed. Turn the dough onto a lightly floured surface. Add the caraway seeds and knead for 1 minute, or until smooth. Press the dough out to a 1 cm (½ inch) round. Cut 4 cm (1½ inch) rounds using a fluted cutter. Top the casserole with the dumplings and brush with the extra milk. Return the casserole to the oven, uncovered, for 15 minutes, or until the dumplings are puffed and golden.

NUTRITION PER SERVE
Protein 61 g; Fat 31 g; Carbohydrate 40 g; Dietary Fibre 2.5 g; Cholesterol 176 mg; 2880 kJ (685 cal)

Use a large, sharp knife to trim the steak and cut it into cubes.

Cook the meat quickly in small batches in the hot oil until browned.

Cook the garlic and onion over medium heat, stirring, until soft.

Return the meat to the pan with the spices, wine, stock, mixed herbs and tomato pasta sauce.

Carefully peel the blackened skin from the grilled capsicum pieces.

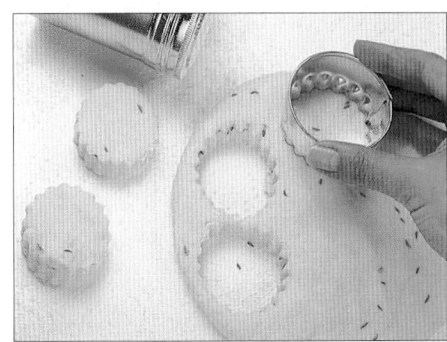

Use a fluted cutter to cut rounds from the dough to make dumplings.

SPICED BEEF

Preparation time: 20 minutes
Total cooking time: 1 hour 40 minutes
Serves 4–6

⅓ cup (60 g/2 oz) soft brown sugar
1 teaspoon ground cinnamon
1 teaspoon ground nutmeg
1 teaspoon ground cardamom
1 teaspoon ground black pepper
1.5 kg (3 lb) piece fresh silverside, trimmed
1 orange, quartered
1 large onion, quartered
¼ cup (60 ml/2 fl oz) red wine vinegar

1 Preheat the oven to warm 160°C (315°F/Gas 2–3). Combine the sugar, cinnamon, nutmeg, cardamom and pepper in a small bowl. Rub the mixture all over the meat, pressing it on firmly with your fingers. Place the meat in a deep casserole dish.
2 Place the orange and onion around the meat, and pour in the vinegar combined with 1 cup (250 ml/8 fl oz) water. Bake, covered, for 1–1½ hours, or until the meat is tender.
3 Remove the meat from the dish, cover and set aside. Remove the orange pieces from the cooking liquid. Strain the remaining cooking liquid into a shallow saucepan and cook, uncovered, for 10 minutes, or until reduced by half. Serve the meat warm or cold, accompanied by the sauce.

NUTRITION PER SERVE (6)
Protein 56 g; Fat 5.5 g; Carbohydrate 10 g; Dietary Fibre 0.5 g; Cholesterol 168 mg; 1325 kJ (315 cal)

NOTES: To serve the silverside cold, refrigerate it overnight in the cooking liquid before draining.
A whole piece of rump or topside steak may be used in place of the fresh silverside.

Use your fingers to press the spice mixture over the silverside.

Pour the combined vinegar and water over the beef, orange and onion.

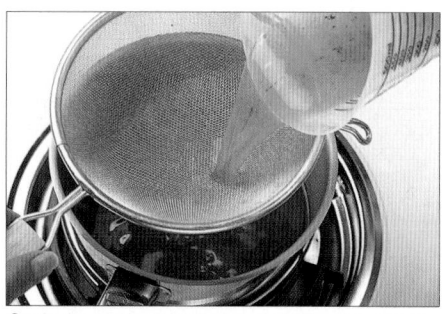

Strain the cooking liquid into a shallow saucepan and cook until it is reduced by half.

BEEF AND HOKKIEN NOODLE STIR-FRY

Preparation time: 15 minutes +
   10 minutes soaking
Total cooking time: 15 minutes
Serves 4

350 g (11 oz) beef fillet, partially frozen
   (see HINT)
100 g (3½ oz) snow peas
600 g (1¼ lb) fresh Hokkien noodles
2 tablespoons peanut oil
1 large onion, cut into thin wedges
1 large carrot, sliced thinly on the
   diagonal
1 red capsicum, cut into thin strips
2 cloves garlic, crushed
1 teaspoon grated fresh ginger
200 g (6½ oz) fresh shiitake
   mushrooms, sliced
¼ cup (60 ml/2 fl oz) oyster sauce
2 tablespoons light soy sauce
1 tablespoon soft brown sugar
½ teaspoon five-spice powder

1 Cut the steak into thin slices. Top and tail the snow peas and slice in half diagonally. Soak the noodles in a large bowl of boiling water for 10 minutes.

2 Heat a wok to very hot, add half the peanut oil and stir-fry the steak in batches until brown. Remove.

3 Heat the remaining peanut oil in the wok until very hot and stir-fry the onion, carrot and capsicum for 2–3 minutes, or until tender. Add the garlic, ginger, snow peas and shiitake mushrooms and cook for another minute. Return the steak to the wok.

4 Separate the noodles with a fork, then drain. Add to the wok, tossing well. Combine the oyster sauce with the soy sauce, brown sugar, five-spice powder and 1 tablespoon water and pour over the noodles. Toss until warmed through.

NUTRITION PER SERVE
Protein 38 g; Fat 10 g; Carbohydrate 92 g;
Dietary Fibre 7 g; Cholesterol 78 mg;
2555 kJ (610 cal)

HINT: Partially freezing the meat will firm it up and make it easier to slice thinly.

Cut the partially frozen beef fillet into thin slices with a sharp knife.

Add the garlic, ginger, snow peas and shiitake mushrooms and cook for another minute.

BEEF, POTATO AND CAPSICUM CASSEROLE

Preparation time: 35 minutes
Total cooking time: 2 hours 20 minutes
Serves 4–6

300 g (10 oz) French shallots
2 tablespoons olive oil
1 kg (2 lb) gravy beef, cut into 4 cm
    (1½ inch) cubes
4 cloves garlic, crushed
3 teaspoons paprika
1 teaspoon fennel seeds
½ teaspoon ground cumin
1 tablespoon plain flour
½ cup (125 ml/4 fl oz) red wine
2 tablespoons brandy
½ teaspoon dried thyme

½ teaspoon dried oregano
1 bay leaf
1½ cups (375 ml/12 fl oz) beef stock
1 tablespoon honey
400 g (13 oz) potatoes, cut into large
    chunks
2 red capsicums, chopped
½ cup (125 g/4 oz) sour cream
chopped fresh chives, to serve

1 Preheat the oven to moderate 180°C (350°F/Gas 4). Place the shallots in a bowl, cover with boiling water and leave for 30 seconds. Drain and peel.
2 Heat the oil in a large, heavy-based saucepan, then brown the meat in batches over medium–high heat, and transfer to a large casserole dish.
3 Add the shallots to the pan and cook over medium heat until soft and

golden. Add the garlic, paprika, fennel seeds and cumin; cook until fragrant.
4 Add the flour, cook for 30 seconds, then remove from the heat. Stir in the red wine and brandy. Return to the heat and add the thyme, oregano, bay leaf and stock. Stir until the mixture bubbles, then add to the meat.
5 Cover and bake for 1½ hours, then add the honey, potato and capsicum. Cook, uncovered, for 30 minutes, or until the potato is tender. Season to taste. Serve with a dollop of sour cream and a sprinkling of chives.

NUTRITION PER SERVE (6)
Protein 40 g; Fat 20 g; Carbohydrate 30 g;
Dietary Fibre 3 g; Cholesterol 140 mg;
1790 kJ (430 cal)

Drain the blanched shallots, then carefully peel off the skin.

Brown the meat in batches in the hot oil over medium–high heat.

Add the red wine and brandy to the spice mixture, and stir well.

VEAL AND FENNEL CASEROLE

Preparation time: 20 minutes
Total cooking time: 2 hours 15 minutes
Serves 4–6

1 tablespoon oil
30 g (1 oz) butter
4 veal shanks, cut into 4 cm (1½ inch) pieces (see NOTE)
1 large onion, sliced
1 clove garlic, crushed
2 celery sticks, thickly sliced
3 carrots, thickly sliced
2 small fennel bulbs, quartered
¼ cup (30 g/1 oz) plain flour

425 g (14 oz) can crushed tomatoes
⅓ cup (80 ml/2¾ fl oz) white wine
1 cup (250 ml/8 fl oz) chicken stock
1 tablespoon chopped fresh thyme
12 black olives

1 Preheat the oven to moderate 180°C (350°F/Gas 4). Heat the oil and butter in a large, heavy-based saucepan and brown the meat quickly in batches on both sides over high heat. Transfer to a large, shallow casserole dish.
2 Add the onion and garlic to the pan, and cook over medium heat until soft. Add the celery, carrot and fennel, and cook for 2 minutes. Add the flour, stir until golden, then add

the tomato, wine, stock and thyme. Bring to the boil, reduce the heat and simmer for 5 minutes, or until thickened. Season with salt and freshly ground pepper.
3 Add the sauce to the veal; cover and bake for 1½–2 hours, or until tender. Scatter with olives to serve.

NUTRITION PER SERVE (6)
Protein 20 g; Fat 8 g; Carbohydrate 10 g;
Dietary Fibre 3 g; Cholesterol 80 mg;
840 kJ (200 cal)

NOTE: Many butchers sell veal shanks already cut into pieces. You will need 12 medium pieces for this recipe.

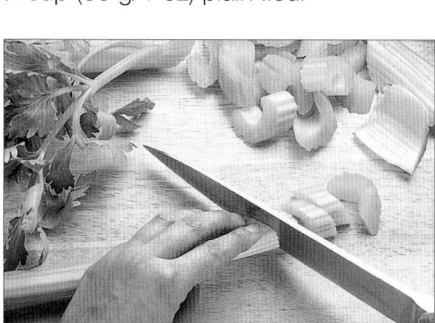
Trim the leaves and base from the celery sticks, then cut into thick slices.

Heat the oil and butter, then brown the meat in batches over high heat.

Add the celery, carrot and fennel to the onion and garlic, and cook for 2 minutes.

PANANG BEEF (THAI BEEF AND PEANUT CURRY)

Preparation time: 30 minutes +
**   5 minutes soaking**
Total cooking time: 1 hour 30 minutes
Serves 4–6

CURRY PASTE
8–10 large dried red chillies
6 red Asian shallots, chopped
6 cloves garlic, chopped
1 teaspoon ground coriander
1 tablespoon ground cumin
1 teaspoon white pepper
2 stems lemon grass (white part only), bruised and sliced
1 tablespoon chopped fresh galangal
6 coriander roots
2 teaspoons shrimp paste
2 tablespoons roasted peanuts
peanut oil, if needed

1 tablespoon peanut oil
400 ml (13 fl oz) can coconut cream (do not shake the can)
1 kg (2 lb) round or blade steak, thinly sliced
400 ml (13 fl oz) can coconut milk
4 kaffir lime leaves, whole
⅓ cup (90 g/3 oz) crunchy peanut butter
¼ cup (60 ml/2 fl oz) lime juice
2½ tablespoons fish sauce
3–4 tablespoons palm sugar or soft brown sugar
fresh Thai basil leaves, to garnish
1 tablespoon chopped peanuts, extra, to garnish (optional)

1 To make the curry paste, soak the chillies in boiling water for 5 minutes, or until soft. Remove the stem and seeds, then chop. Place all the curry paste ingredients in a food processor and process to a smooth paste. Add a little peanut oil if it is too thick.
2 Place the oil and the thick cream from the top of the coconut cream (reserving the rest) in a large saucepan over high heat. Add 6–8 tablespoons of the curry paste and cook, stirring, for 5 minutes, or until fragrant. Cook for 5–10 minutes, or until the coconut cream splits and becomes oily.

3 Add the beef, the reserved coconut cream, coconut milk, lime leaves and peanut butter, and cook for 8 minutes, or until the beef just starts to change colour. Reduce the heat and simmer for 1 hour, or until the beef is tender.
4 Stir in the lime juice, fish sauce and palm sugar, and transfer to a serving dish. Garnish with the Thai basil leaves, and extra peanuts, if desired, and serve immediately.

NUTRITION PER SERVE (6)
Protein 8 g; Fat 30 g; Carbohydrate 5.5 g;
Dietary Fibre 4 g; Cholesterol 0 mg;
1293 kJ (310 cal)

Place all the curry paste ingredients in a food processor and process until smooth.

Cook the coconut cream and curry paste until it splits and becomes oily.

PAPRIKA VEAL WITH CARAWAY NOODLES

Preparation time: 10 minutes
Total cooking time: 1 hour 35 minutes
Serves 4

¼ cup (60 ml/2 fl oz) oil
1 kg (2 lb) veal shoulder, diced
1 large onion, thinly sliced
3 cloves garlic, finely chopped
¼ cup (60 g/2 oz) Hungarian paprika
½ teaspoon caraway seeds
2 x 400 g (13 oz) cans chopped tomatoes, one drained
350 g (11 oz) fresh fettuccine
40 g (1¼ oz) butter, softened

1 Heat half the oil in a large saucepan over medium–high heat, then brown the veal in batches for 3 minutes per batch. Remove the veal from the pan and set aside with any pan juices.
2 Add the remaining oil to the pan and sauté the onion and garlic over medium heat for 5 minutes, or until softened. Add the paprika and ¼ teaspoon of the caraway seeds, and stir for 30 seconds.
3 Add the chopped tomatoes and their liquid plus ½ cup (125 ml/4 fl oz) water. Return the veal to the pan with any juices, increase the heat to high and bring to the boil. Reduce the heat to low, then cover and simmer for 1¼ hours, or until the meat is tender and the sauce has thickened.
4 About 15 minutes before the veal is ready, cook the pasta in a large saucepan of rapidly boiling salted water according to the packet instructions until al dente. Drain, then return to the pan. Stir in the butter and the remaining caraway seeds. Serve immediately with the paprika veal.

NUTRITION PER SERVE
Protein 68 g; Fat 25 g; Carbohydrate 73 g; Dietary Fibre 10 g; Cholesterol 231 mg; 3340 kJ (800 cal)

Brown the veal in batches over medium–high heat for 3 minutes.

Cover and simmer until the meat is tender and the sauce has thickened.

417

WARM CITRUS BEEF SALAD

Preparation time: 25 minutes
Total cooking time: 15 minutes
Serves 4

oil, for cooking
500 g (1 lb) rump or sirloin steak, cut into thin strips
1 onion, sliced
2 cloves garlic, crushed
1 teaspoon grated fresh ginger
1 teaspoon grated lemon rind (see HINT)
1 teaspoon grated orange rind
1 tablespoon lemon juice
1 tablespoon orange juice
100 g (3½ oz) rocket leaves
40 g (1¼ oz) snow pea sprouts
1 lemon, segmented
1 orange, segmented

1 Heat the wok until very hot, add 1 tablespoon of the oil and swirl it around to coat the side. Stir-fry the beef in batches until well browned, adding more oil when necessary. Remove all the beef from the wok and set aside.
2 Reheat the wok, add 1 tablespoon of the oil and stir-fry the onion, garlic and ginger for 3–4 minutes, or until tender. Return the meat to the wok along with the combined lemon and orange rind and juice.
3 Bring to the boil, then toss the rocket through the beef mixture and cook until the rocket is just wilted. Serve immediately on a bed of snow pea sprouts, surrounded by the lemon and orange segments.

NUTRITION PER SERVE
Protein 30 g; Fat 15 g; Carbohydrate 7 g; Dietary Fibre 3 g; Cholesterol 85 mg; 1145 kJ (275 cal)

HINT: Grate the rind you need from the lemon and orange, before peeling and segmenting them to add to the stir-fry. Collect the juice in a bowl as you segment them.

To segment the orange, cut a slice off the top and bottom to stabilize the orange.

Remove the rind and pith, following the curve of the orange.

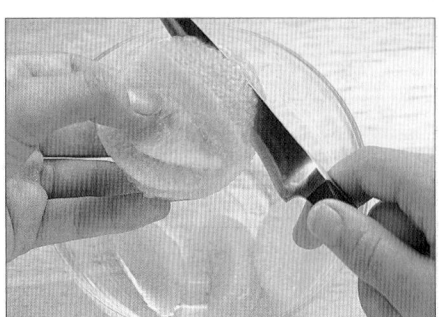

Cut out the segments by slicing between the membrane and flesh on each side.

Return the meat to the wok with the citrus rind and juice.

MEXICAN BEEF STEW

Preparation time: 30 minutes
Total cooking time: 1 hour 30 minutes
Serves 6

500 g (1 lb) Roma tomatoes, halved
6 flour tortillas
1–2 fresh red chillies, finely chopped
1 tablespoon olive oil
1 kg (2 lb) stewing beef, cubed
½ teaspoon black pepper
2 onions, thinly sliced
1½ cups (375 ml/12 fl oz) beef stock
¼ cup (60 g/2 oz) tomato paste
375 g (12 oz) can kidney beans, drained
1 teaspoon chilli powder
½ cup (125 g/4 oz) sour cream

1 Preheat the oven to moderate 180°C (350°F/Gas 4). Grill the tomatoes, skin-side up, under a hot grill for 6–8 minutes, or until the skin is black and blistered. Cool, remove the skin and roughly chop the flesh.
2 Bake 2 of the tortillas for 4 minutes, or until crisp. Break into pieces and put in a food processor with the tomato and chilli. Process for 30 seconds, or until almost smooth.
3 Heat the oil in a large heavy-based saucepan. Brown the beef in batches, season with pepper, then remove. Add the onion to the pan and cook for 5 minutes. Return the meat to the pan. Stir in the processed mixture, stock and tomato paste, and bring to the boil. Reduce the heat, cover and simmer for 1¼ hours. Add the beans

and chilli powder, and heat through.
4 Grill the remaining tortillas for 2–3 minutes on each side, then cool and cut into wedges. Serve the stew with the sour cream, and toasted tortilla wedges on the side.

NUTRITION PER SERVE
Protein 50 g; Fat 20 g; Carbohydrate 40 g;
Dietary Fibre 8 g; Cholesterol 125 mg;
2235 kJ (535 cal)

HINT: If this stew becomes thick during cooking, thin it with a little extra stock.

Grill the tomatoes until the skin is black and blistered and it will peel away easily.

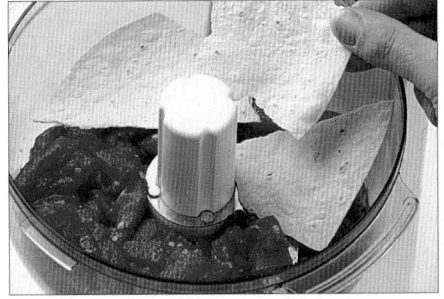

Once the tortillas are crisp, break into pieces and put in the food processor.

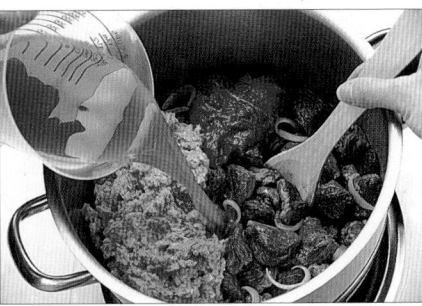

Stir the processed mixture, stock and tomato paste into the beef mixture.

THAI BRAISED BEEF WITH SPINACH AND LEEKS

Preparation time: 10 minutes
  + 2 hours marinating
Total cooking time: 25 minutes
Serves 4

400 g (13 oz) beef fillet
2 tablespoons light soy sauce
2 tablespoons fish sauce
oil, for cooking
4 coriander roots, finely chopped
¼ cup (15 g/½ oz) chopped coriander
    leaves and stems
2 teaspoons cracked black
    peppercorns
2 cloves garlic, crushed

1 tablespoon soft brown sugar
1 leek, sliced
20 English spinach leaves, stalks
    removed
3 tablespoons lime juice

1 Cut the beef into 2.5 cm (1 inch) thick pieces and place in a bowl. Place the sauces, 1 tablespoon oil, coriander, peppercorns, garlic and brown sugar in a blender and mix until smooth. Pour the marinade over the beef, cover and refrigerate for 2 hours.
2 Drain the beef, reserving the marinade. Heat the wok until very hot, add 1 tablespoon of the oil and swirl it around to coat the side. Stir-fry the beef in batches, browning well.
3 Return all the meat to the wok and add the reserved marinade and ½ cup (125 ml/4 fl oz) water. Reduce the heat and simmer for 8 minutes. Remove the meat and keep warm. Simmer the sauce for 10 minutes, then remove from the wok and set aside. Slice the beef into large bite-sized pieces.
4 Wipe out the wok and heat 1 tablespoon oil. Add the leek and stir-fry for 2 minutes. Add the spinach and cook for 30 seconds or until softened. Serve with the meat with the sauce poured over the top. Drizzle with lime juice and serve immediately.

NUTRITION PER SERVE
Protein 24 g; Fat 20 g; Carbohydrate 7 g;
Dietary Fibre 1.5 g; Cholesterol 67 mg;
1220 kJ (290 cal)

Place the pieces of beef in a bowl and pour the marinade over the top.

Brown the beef in batches if necessary so that you don't overcrowd the wok.

Add the spinach to the leek and toss it for about 30 seconds, or until softened.

COCINO MADRILENO

Preparation time: 25 minutes + overnight soaking
Total cooking time: 2 hours 45 minutes
Serves 6–8

1 cup (220 g/7 oz) dried chickpeas
1 kg (2 lb) chicken, trussed
500 g (1 lb) piece lean beef brisket
250 g (8 oz) piece smoke-cured bacon
125 g (4 oz) tocino, streaky bacon or speck
1 pig's trotter
200 g (6½ oz) chorizo
1 onion, studded with 2 cloves
1 bay leaf
1 morcilla blood sausage (optional)
250 g (8 oz) green beans, sliced lengthways
250 g (8 oz) green cabbage, cut into sections through the heart
300 g (10 oz) silverbeet leaves, stalks removed
4 small potatoes
2 leeks, cut into 10 cm (4 inch) lengths
pinch saffron threads
75 g (2½ oz) dried rice vermicelli

1 Soak the chickpeas in cold water overnight. Drain and rinse. Tie loosely in a muslin bag.

2 Put 3 litres cold water in a very large, deep saucepan. Add the chicken, beef, bacon and tocino, and bring to the boil. Add the chickpeas, pig's trotter and chorizo, return to the boil, then add the onion, bay leaf and ½ teaspoon salt. Simmer, partially covered, for 2½ hours.

3 After 2 hours, bring a saucepan of water to the boil, add the morcilla and gently boil for 5 minutes. Drain and set aside. Tie the green beans loosely in a muslin bag. Pour 1 litre water into a large saucepan and bring to the boil. Add the beans, cabbage, silverbeet, potatoes, leek and saffron with 1 teaspoon of salt. Return to the boil and simmer for 30 minutes.

4 Strain the stock from both the meat and vegetable pans, and combine in a large saucepan. Bring to the boil, adjust the seasoning and add the vermicelli. Simmer for 6–7 minutes. Release the chickpeas and pile them in the centre of a large warm platter. Discard the tocino, then slice the meats and sausages. Arrange the meats and sausages in groups around the chickpeas at one end of the platter. Release the beans. Arrange the vegetables in groups around the other end. Spoon a little of the simmering broth (minus the vermicelli) over the meat, then pour the rest (with the vermicelli) into a soup tureen. Serve at once. It is traditional to serve the two dishes together, although the broth is eaten first.

NUTRITION PER SERVE (8)
Protein 51 g; Fat 27 g; Carbohydrate 26 g;
Dietary Fibre 8 g; Cholesterol 158 mg;
2290 kJ (545 cal)

Using a sharp knife, cut the green beans into long slices.

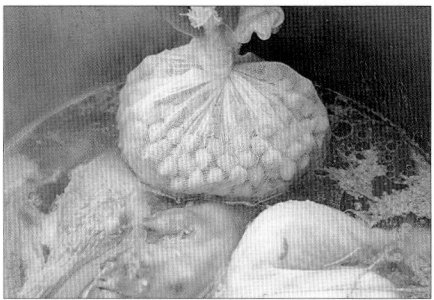

Add the chickpeas, pig's trotter and chorizo to the saucepan.

VEAL STEAKS WITH CAPER BUTTER

Preparation time: 10 minutes
Total cooking time: 6 minutes
Serves 4

50 g (1¾ oz) butter, softened
2 tablespoons dry white wine
2 tablespoons capers, finely chopped
2 teaspoons finely grated lemon rind
8 small veal steaks, about 500 g (1 lb)

1 Mix together the butter, white wine, capers, lemon rind and some salt and black pepper with a wooden spoon. Cover and refrigerate until required.
2 Cook the veal steaks on a hot, lightly oiled barbecue flatplate or grill for 2–3 minutes on each side. Remove, place on warm plates and top with the caper butter. Serve immediately.

NUTRITION PER SERVE
Protein 30 g; Fat 15 g; Carbohydrate 0 g;
Dietary Fibre 0 g; Cholesterol 135 mg;
990 kJ (235 cal)

Use a sharp knife to finely chop the capers so that they mix smoothly with the butter.

Mix the butter, white wine, capers, lemon rind and salt and pepper.

Cook the veal for 2–3 minutes on each side on a hot barbecue flatplate.

BEEF SATAY STICKS WITH PEANUT SAUCE

**Preparation time: 30 minutes +
  at least 3 hours marinating
Total cooking time: 15 minutes
Serves 4**

800 g (1 lb 10 oz) rump steak
⅓ cup (80 ml/2¾ fl oz) soy sauce
2 tablespoons oil
2 cloves garlic, crushed
1 teaspoon grated fresh ginger

PEANUT SAUCE
1 cup (250 ml/8 fl oz) pineapple juice
1 cup (250 g/8 oz) peanut butter
½ teaspoon garlic powder

½ teaspoon onion powder
2 tablespoons sweet chilli sauce
3 tablespoons soy sauce

1 Trim the steak of excess fat and sinew. Slice across the grain evenly into long, thin strips. Thread onto skewers, bunching them thickly along three-quarters of the skewer. Place in a shallow non-metal dish.
2 Mix the soy sauce, oil, garlic and ginger together and pour over the satays. Cover with plastic wrap and refrigerate for several hours or overnight, turning occasionally.
3 Cook on a hot, lightly oiled barbecue grill or flatplate for 8–10 minutes or until tender, turning the skewers occasionally.

4 To make the peanut sauce, combine the juice, peanut butter, garlic and onion powders and sauces in a small pan and stir over medium heat for 5 minutes or until smooth. Serve warm with the satay sticks.

NUTRITION PER SERVE
Protein 70 g; Fat 55 g; Carbohydrate 17 g; Dietary Fibre 9 g; Cholesterol 134 mg; 3500 kJ (838 cal)

STORAGE: The sauce can be made a day in advance and stored in the fridge. If it thickens too much on standing, add a little warm water when reheating.

Trim the meat and then slice across the grain into long, thin strips.

Thread the meat onto skewers and then leave to marinate in a non-metallic dish.

To make the peanut sauce, stir all the ingredients over medium heat until smooth.

BRAISED OXTAIL CASSEROLE

Preparation time: 15 minutes
Total cooking time: 2 hours
Serves 6

¼ cup (60 ml/2 fl oz) oil
16 small pieces oxtail, about 1.5 kg
　　(3 lb)
4 baby potatoes, halved
1 large onion, chopped
2 carrots, chopped
250 g (8 oz) button mushrooms
2 tablespoons plain flour
3 cups (750 ml/24 fl oz) beef stock

1 teaspoon dried marjoram leaves
2 tablespoons Worcestershire
　　sauce

1 Preheat the oven to moderate 180°C (350°F/Gas 4). Heat 2 table-spoons of the oil in a saucepan over medium-high heat. Cook the oxtail quickly in small batches until well browned. Place in a deep casserole dish and add the potato.
2 Heat the remaining oil in the pan. Cook the onion and carrot, stirring, over medium heat for 5 minutes. Transfer to the casserole dish. Add the mushrooms to the pan, and cook, stirring, for 5 minutes. Stir in the flour.

Reduce the heat to low, and stir for 2 minutes.
3 Add the stock gradually, stirring until the liquid boils and thickens. Add the marjoram and Worcestershire sauce. Pour into the casserole dish. Bake, covered, for 1½ hours. Stir, then bake, uncovered, for a further 30 minutes.

NUTRITION PER SERVE
Protein 35 g; Fat 53 g; Carbohydrate 16 g;
Dietary Fibre 3.5 g; Cholesterol 102 mg;
2825 kJ (675 cal)

Cook the oxtail pieces in small batches in the hot oil.

Cook the onion and carrot, stirring, for 5 minutes over medium heat.

Pour the sauce over the oxtail and vegetables in the casserole dish.

BEEF AND SPINACH

Preparation time: 20 minutes
  + 2 hours marinating
Total cooking time: 15 minutes
Serves 4

500 g (1 lb) rump or sirloin steak, cut
    into thin strips
¼ cup (60 ml/2 fl oz) sweet chilli sauce
2 tablespoons soy sauce
1 clove garlic, crushed
2 teaspoons grated fresh ginger
1 tablespoon sherry
oil, for cooking

2 onions, cut into wedges
500 g (1 lb) English spinach leaves,
    shredded

1 Combine the steak with the sweet
chilli sauce, soy sauce, garlic, ginger
and sherry. Cover and refrigerate for
at least 2 hours, or overnight.
2 Drain the meat. Heat the wok until
very hot, add 1 tablespoon of the oil
and swirl it around to coat the side.
Stir-fry the meat in batches over high
heat until it is well browned, adding
more oil when necessary. Remove
from the wok and set aside.
3 Reheat the wok, add 1 tablespoon

of the oil and stir-fry the onion
wedges for 3–4 minutes, or until
tender. Return the meat to the wok.
4 Just before serving, toss the English
spinach through the beef mixture
until the spinach is just wilted. Serve
immediately.

NUTRITION PER SERVE
Protein 35 g; Fat 15 g; Carbohydrate 6.5 g;
Dietary Fibre 5 g; Cholesterol 85 mg;
1200 kJ (285 cal)

Carefully slice the rump or sirloin steak into thin
strips across the grain.

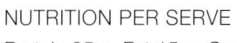

Drain all the liquid from the marinated meat, using
a sieve.

Toss the English spinach through the stir-fry until
the spinach is just wilted.

BEEF AND PEPPERCORN STEW

Preparation time: 15 minutes
Total cooking time: 2 hours
Serves 4

1 kg (2 lb) chuck steak, cut into 3 cm (1¼ inch) cubes
2 teaspoons cracked black peppercorns
40 g (1¼ oz) butter
2 tablespoons oil
1 large onion, thinly sliced
2 cloves garlic, sliced
1½ tablespoons plain flour
2 tablespoons brandy
3 cups (750 ml/24 fl oz) beef stock

1 tablespoon Worcestershire sauce
2 teaspoons Dijon mustard
500 g (1 lb) baby new potatoes
¼ cup (60 ml/2 fl oz) cream
2 tablespoons chopped fresh parsley

1 Toss the steak in the peppercorns. Heat half the butter and half the oil in a large heavy-based saucepan. Brown half the steak over high heat, then remove and set aside. Heat the remaining butter and oil, and brown the remaining steak. Remove from the pan and set aside.
2 Add the onion and garlic to the pan and cook, stirring, until the onion is golden. Add the flour and stir until browned. Remove from the heat.

3 Combine the brandy, beef stock, Worcestershire sauce and mustard, and gradually stir into the onion mixture. Return to the heat, add the steak and any juices, then simmer, covered, for 1¼ hours.
4 Add the potatoes and simmer, uncovered, for a further 30 minutes, or until the meat and potatoes are tender. Stir in the cream and parsley, and season to taste with salt and freshly ground pepper.

NUTRITION PER SERVE
Protein 60 g; Fat 30 g; Carbohydrate 20 g; Dietary Fibre 3 g; Cholesterol 215 mg; 2580 kJ (615 cal)

Cut the steak into 3 cm (11/4 inch) cubes, using a sharp knife.

Add the brandy, stock, Worcestershire sauce and mustard to the onion mixture.

Add the potatoes and simmer, uncovered, for a further 30 minutes, or until tender.

VEAL WITH SKORDALIA AND TOMATO BEANS

Preparation time: 45 minutes
Total cooking time: 40 minutes
Serves 4

SKORDALIA
350 g (11 oz) potatoes
3 tablespoons toasted blanched
   almonds
2 cloves garlic
1 tablespoon white wine vinegar
⅓ cup (80 ml/2¾ fl oz) olive oil

TOMATO BEANS
6 tomatoes, peeled, seeded and
   chopped
3 cloves garlic, chopped
1 teaspoon caster sugar
300 g (10 oz) can cannellini beans
⅓ cup (20 g/¾ oz) chopped fresh
   parsley

8 veal cutlets
lemon pepper seasoning
Parmesan shavings, to garnish

1 To make the skordalia, cut the potatoes into large pieces and boil for 15–20 minutes, or until tender. Drain and cool. Finely chop the toasted almonds in a food processor. Mash the potato and stir in the almonds, garlic and vinegar. Gradually pour in the olive oil, stirring constantly, until all the oil is incorporated. Season well.
2 To make the beans, heat a little olive oil in a heavy-based pan and add the tomato, garlic and sugar. Bring to the boil, reduce the heat and simmer, stirring frequently, for 15 minutes, or until thickened. Stir in the rinsed and drained beans and parsley. Season.

3 Trim the veal of fat and sinew and coat liberally with the lemon pepper. Cook on a hot, lightly oiled barbecue grill or flatplate for 3 minutes each side, depending on the thickness of the cutlets. Serve with the beans and skordalia, topped with Parmesan.

NUTRITION PER SERVE
Protein 35 g; Fat 25 g; Carbohydrate 35 g;
Dietary Fibre 5 g; Cholesterol 85 mg;
2200 kJ (525 cal)

Peel the cooked potatoes, then mash with a potato masher.

Mix the beans, parsley and salt and pepper into the tomatoes.

Trim the veal cutlets of any excess fat and sinew before they are barbecued.

KOREAN BEEF

Preparation time: 20 minutes
+ 30 minutes freezing
+ 2 hours marinating
Total cooking time: 15 minutes
Serves 4–6

500 g (1 lb) scotch fillet or sirloin steak
¼ cup (40 g/1¼ oz) sesame seeds
½ cup (125 ml/4 fl oz) shoyu
    (Japanese soy sauce)
2 cloves garlic, finely chopped
3 spring onions, finely chopped
1 tablespoon sesame oil
1 tablespoon oil

1 Freeze the steak for 30 minutes for ease of slicing. Dry-fry the sesame seeds over low heat for 3–4 minutes, shaking the pan until golden. Cool and then grind in a food processor or with a mortar and pestle.
2 Slice the steak into thin strips, cutting across the grain. Combine the meat, shoyu, garlic, spring onion and half the crushed seeds in a non-metallic bowl and toss until the meat is well coated. Cover and marinate in the fridge for 2 hours.
3 Combine the oils and use to brush a very hot barbecue flatplate. Cook the meat in batches, searing each side for about 1 minute (don't overcook or the steak will be chewy). Oil and reheat the grill between batches. Sprinkle the steak with the remaining crushed seeds to serve.

NUTRITION PER SERVE (6)
Protein 19 g; Fat 15 g; Carbohydrate 0.5 g;
Dietary Fibre 1 g; Cholesterol 42 mg;
893 kJ (213 cal)

Freeze the meat for 30 minutes and then thinly slice across the grain.

Combine the meat with shoyu, garlic, spring onion and half the sesame seeds.

Take care not to overcook the meat when searing it on both sides.

STEAK AND KIDNEY STEW

Preparation time: 35 minutes
Total cooking time: 2 hours 30 minutes
Serves 4–6

1 kg (2 lb) chuck steak, trimmed
8 lamb's kidneys
¼ cup (60 ml/2 fl oz) oil
1 rasher bacon, rind removed, cut
    into long, thin strips
40 g (1¼ oz) butter
1 large onion, chopped
300 g (10 oz) button mushrooms,
    halved
1 cup (250 ml/8 fl oz) Muscat
2–3 cloves garlic, crushed
¼ teaspoon ground allspice
½ teaspoon paprika
2 teaspoons coriander seeds, lightly
    crushed
1 tablespoon wholegrain mustard
1 cup (250 ml/8 fl oz) beef stock
2–3 tablespoons soft brown sugar
1–2 teaspoons fresh thyme
1–2 teaspoons fresh rosemary

1 Cut the steak into 2–3 cm (1 inch) cubes. Cut the kidneys in half, remove the core and any fat, then slice them in half again.
2 Heat 1 teaspoon of the oil in a large, heavy-based saucepan. Add the bacon and cook over medium heat until just crisp. Remove and set aside.
3 Heat 2 tablespoons of the oil and 30 g (1 oz) of the butter in the pan. Brown the steak cubes in batches, then set aside.
4 Add the onion to the pan and cook for 3 minutes, or until soft and golden. Add the mushrooms and cook, stirring, for 3 minutes, until starting to brown. Stir in half the Muscat and simmer for 3–4 minutes. Remove and set aside.

5 Add the remaining oil and butter to the pan. Stir in the garlic, allspice, paprika and coriander, and cook for 1 minute. Add the kidney and cook until just starting to brown. Stir in the mustard and remaining Muscat, and simmer for 2 minutes.
6 Stir in the bacon, steak, onion and mushrooms. Stir in the stock, bring to the boil, then reduce the heat, cover and simmer for 1 hour. Add the sugar.

Simmer, covered, for 40 minutes, then uncovered for 20 minutes, stirring in the herbs during the last 10 minutes.

NUTRITION PER SERVE (6)
Protein 40 g; Fat 20 g; Carbohydrate 15 g; Dietary Fibre 2 g; Cholesterol 155 mg; 1830 kJ (440 cal)

Halve the kidneys and remove the cores and fat. Slice in half again.

Add half the Muscat to the onion and mushrooms, and simmer for 3–4 minutes.

Add the kidney to the pan-fried spices and cook until just starting to brown.

PEPPERED STEAKS WITH MANGO SALSA

**Preparation time: 10 minutes
  + 30 minutes chilling
Total cooking time: 15 minutes
Serves 6**

6 fillet steaks
2 tablespoons black peppercorns
1 tablespoon white mustard seeds
2 tablespoons oil

MANGO AND AVOCADO SALSA
1 large ripe mango
1 large ripe avocado
1 spring onion, finely sliced
1 tablespoon lime juice
dash of Tabasco sauce

1 Trim the meat of excess fat and flatten with a meat mallet to even thickness. Nick the edges to prevent curling. Crush the peppercorns and mustard seeds briefly in a blender until coarsely cracked.

2 Rub oil over the steaks, then press on the peppercorn mixture to coat both sides. Store in the fridge, covered in plastic, for 30 minutes.

3 To make the salsa, peel the mango and dice the flesh. Peel the avocado and dice the flesh. Mix together the mango, avocado and remaining ingredients and toss well. Refrigerate, covered, until needed.

4 Cook the steaks on a hot, lightly oiled barbecue flatplate or grill for 2 minutes on each side to sear, turning only once. For rare steaks, cook for a further minute each side. For medium and well done, move the steaks to a cooler part of the barbecue and cook for a further 3–6 minutes each side. Serve with the salsa.

NUTRITION PER SERVE
Protein 28 g; Fat 20 g; Carbohydrate 3.5 g;
Dietary Fibre 1 g; Cholesterol 84 mg;
1302 kJ (311 cal)

Place the steaks between two sheets of plastic and flatten with a meat mallet.

Mix together the black pepper and white mustard seeds and press onto the steaks.

Cook the steaks on a hot barbecue flatplate for 3–6 minutes each side, depending on taste.

CREAMY VEAL AND MUSHROOM STEW

Preparation time: 20 minutes
Total cooking time: 2 hours
Serves 4

750 g (1½ lb) veal steaks, cut into
   1 cm (½ inch) strips
¼ cup (30 g/1 oz) plain flour
30 g (1 oz) butter
1 clove garlic, crushed
1 tablespoon Dijon mustard
1 cup (250 ml/8 fl oz) cream

½ cup (125 ml/4 fl oz) white wine
1 tablespoon chopped fresh thyme
1 cup (250 ml/8 fl oz) chicken stock
375 g (12 oz) button mushrooms,
   halved

1 Toss the meat in the flour, shaking off the excess. Heat the butter and garlic in a heavy-based saucepan. Add the meat and cook quickly in small batches over medium heat until well browned. Drain on paper towels.
2 Return the meat to the pan and add the mustard, cream, wine, thyme and stock. Bring to the boil, then reduce

the heat and simmer, covered, for 1½ hours, stirring occasionally.
3 Add the mushrooms and cook for a further 15 minutes, or until the meat is tender. Delicious served with pasta and steamed vegetables.

NUTRITION PER SERVE
Protein 47 g; Fat 38 g; Carbohydrate 8.5 g;
Dietary Fibre 3 g; Cholesterol 258 mg;
2425 kJ (580 cal)

Toss the veal strips in the flour, shaking off any excess flour.

Return the meat to the pan with the mustard, cream, wine, thyme and stock.

Add the mushrooms and cook for a further 15 minutes, or until the meat is tender.

431

MUSTARD BURGERS WITH TOMATO AND ONION SALSA

Preparation time: 20 minutes
Total cooking time: 10 minutes
Makes 8 burgers

1 kg (2 lb) beef mince
3 tablespoons wholegrain mustard
2 teaspoons Dijon mustard
1 teaspoon beef stock powder
1 cup (90 g/3 oz) fresh breadcrumbs
 (see NOTE)
1 egg
1 teaspoon black pepper
¼ red capsicum, chopped

TOMATO AND ONION SALSA
1 small red onion, diced
4 tomatoes, diced
2 tablespoons red wine vinegar
1½ teaspoons caster sugar
2 teaspoons lemon juice

1 Mix together the beef mince, mustards, stock powder, breadcrumbs, egg, pepper and capsicum with your hands. Divide into eight portions and shape into burgers.
2 Cook the burgers on a hot, lightly oiled barbecue grill or flatplate for 2–3 minutes each side.
3 To make the tomato and onion salsa, put all the ingredients in a bowl and mix together well.

NUTRITION PER BURGER
Protein 27 g; Fat 14 g; Carbohydrate 13 g;
Dietary Fibre 1.5 g; Cholesterol 80 mg;
1210 kJ (290 cal)

NOTE: The breadcrumbs are best if made from slightly stale bread.

STORAGE: The burgers can be made a day in advance and kept, covered, in the fridge. The salsa will also keep, covered, in the fridge for a day.

VARIATION: Instead of Dijon, use German or American mustard for a mild-tasting burger. English mustard will make a strong-tasting, hot burger.

Put all the burger ingredients in a bowl and mix together thoroughly with your hands.

Divide the mixture into eight portions and shape each one into a burger.

To make the tomato and onion salsa, simply mix together all the ingredients.

BEEF IN BEER WITH CAPERS

Preparation time: 25 minutes
Total cooking time: 3 hours 20 minutes
Serves 4–6

1 kg (2 lb) gravy beef
seasoned plain flour
olive oil, for cooking
4 cloves garlic, finely chopped
2 cups (500 ml/16 fl oz) beef stock
1½ cups (375 ml/12 fl oz) beer
2 onions, chopped
3 bay leaves
⅓ cup (55 g/2 oz) stuffed or pitted
    green olives, sliced

6 anchovies
2 tablespoons capers, drained

1 Cut the beef into 4 cm (1½ inch) chunks. Lightly coat in the flour. Heat ¼ cup (60 ml/2 fl oz) of oil in a deep heavy-based pan, add the garlic, then brown the beef over high heat.
2 Add the stock, beer, onion and bay leaves, season well and bring to the boil. Reduce the heat and gently simmer, covered, for 2½ hours, stirring about three times during cooking. Remove the lid and simmer for 30 minutes more. Stir, then mix in the olives.
3 Heat 2 teaspoons of oil in a small pan. Add the anchovies and capers,

gently breaking up the anchovies. Cook over medium heat for 4 minutes, or until brown and crisp. To serve, place the meat on serving plates, drizzle with the sauce, sprinkle with anchovies and capers, and season with salt and freshly cracked pepper.

NUTRITION PER SERVE (6)
Protein 40 g; Fat 6 g; Carbohydrate 4 g;
Dietary Fibre 1 g; Cholesterol 115 mg;
965 kJ (230 cal)

NOTE: The capers should be squeezed very dry before being added to the pan, or they will spit in the hot oil.

Using a sharp knife, cut the gravy beef into large chunks.

Add the stock, beer, onion and bay leaves to the browned beef.

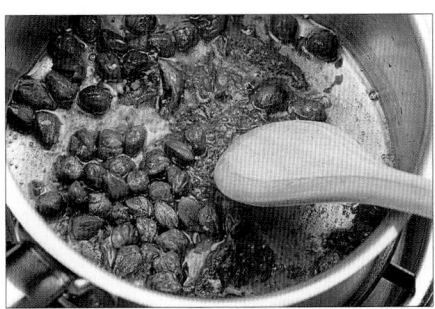

Fry the anchovies and capers in a little hot oil until brown and crisp.

BEEF POT ROAST PROVENCALE

Preparation time: 15 minutes
Total cooking time: 2 hours 15 minutes
Serves 6

2 tablespoons oil
2 kg (4 lb) rolled beef brisket, trimmed
3 cups (750 ml/24 fl oz) beef stock
1 cup (250 ml/8 fl oz) red wine
¼ cup (60 ml/2 fl oz) brandy
2 onions, quartered
3 cloves garlic, crushed
3 tomatoes, peeled, seeded and chopped
2 bay leaves
¼ cup (15 g/½ oz) chopped fresh parsley
2 tablespoons fresh thyme leaves
12 pitted black olives
6 small carrots, thickly sliced
2 tablespoons plain flour

1 Heat the oil in a deep heavy-based saucepan. Cook the meat over medium–high heat until browned all over, then remove from the heat.
2 Add the stock to the pan with the wine, brandy, onion, garlic, tomato, bay leaves, parsley and thyme. Cover and bring to simmering point over low heat. Simmer for 1½ hours.

3 Add the olives and carrot, and cook for 30 minutes. Remove the meat and leave it in a warm place, covered with foil, for 10 minutes before slicing.
4 Combine the flour and ¼ cup (60 ml/2 fl oz) water to make a smooth paste. Add to the sauce, stir over medium heat until the sauce thickens, and cook for 3 minutes. Pour over the sliced meat to serve.

NUTRITION PER SERVE
Protein 70 g; Fat 11 g; Carbohydrate 11.5 g; Dietary Fibre 2.5 g; Cholesterol 150 mg; 2005 kJ (480 cal)

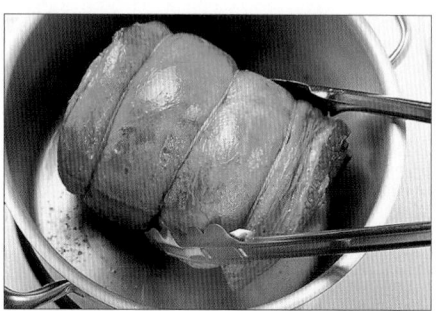
Cook the meat in the oil over medium–high heat until it is browned all over.

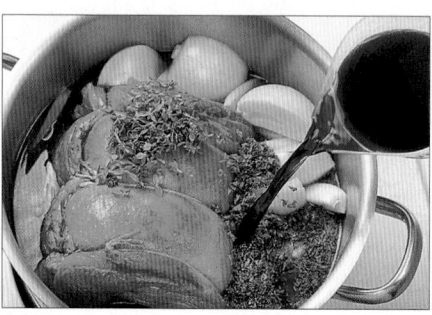
Add the stock to the pan with the wine, brandy, onion, garlic, tomato and herbs.

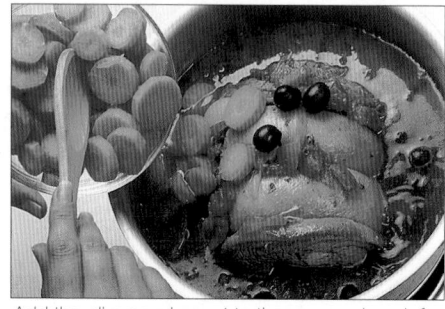
Add the olives and carrot to the pan, and cook for 30 minutes.

BRAISED BEEF IN RED WINE

Preparation time: 10 minutes
Total cooking time: 2 hours
Serves 6

¼ cup (30 g/1 oz) plain flour
¼ teaspoon ground black pepper
1 kg (2 lb) lean round or chuck steak, cut into 3 cm (1¼ inch) cubes
1 tablespoon oil
15 g (½ oz) butter
12 baby onions
1 cup (250 ml/8 fl oz) beef stock
1 cup (250 ml/8 fl oz) red wine
2 tablespoons tomato paste
1 tablespoon French mustard
1 bay leaf
¼ teaspoon mixed dried herbs

1 Combine the flour and pepper. Toss the meat in the seasoned flour, shaking off the excess.
2 Heat the oil and butter in a heavy-based saucepan. Cook the meat quickly in batches over medium–high heat until well browned. Drain on paper towels.

3 Add the onions to the pan and cook over medium heat until golden brown. Return the meat to the pan and stir in the stock, wine, tomato paste, mustard and herbs. Bring to the boil, then reduce the heat and simmer, covered, for 1½ hours, or until the meat is tender, stirring occasionally.

NUTRITION PER SERVE
Protein 37 g; Fat 10 g; Carbohydrate 7.5 g; Dietary Fibre 1.5 g; Cholesterol 110 mg; 1235 kJ (295 cal)

Toss the meat in the seasoned flour, shaking off the excess.

Cook the meat in batches until well browned, then drain on paper towels.

Stir in the stock, wine, tomato paste, mustard and herbs, then simmer until the meat is tender.

Lamb

LAMB KORMA

Preparation time: 30 minutes +
1 hour marinating
Total cooking time: 1 hour 10 minutes
Serves 4–6

2 kg (4 lb) leg of lamb, boned
1 onion, chopped
2 teaspoons grated fresh ginger
3 cloves garlic
2 teaspoons ground coriander
2 teaspoons ground cumin
1 teaspoon cardamom seeds
large pinch cayenne pepper
2 tablespoons ghee or oil
1 onion, extra, sliced
2½ tablespoons tomato paste
½ cup (125 g/4 oz) plain yoghurt
½ cup (125 ml/4 fl oz) coconut cream
½ cup (95 g/3 oz) ground almonds
toasted slivered almonds, to serve

1 Trim any excess fat or sinew from the leg of lamb, then cut the meat into 3 cm (1¼ inch) cubes and place in a large bowl.
2 Place the onion, ginger, garlic, coriander, cumin, cardamom seeds, cayenne pepper and ½ teaspoon salt in a food processor, and process to a smooth paste. Add the spice mixture to the lamb and mix well to coat. Leave to marinate for 1 hour.
3 Heat the ghee in a large saucepan, add the extra sliced onion and cook, stirring, over low heat for 7 minutes, or until the onion is soft. Add the lamb mixture and cook, stirring constantly, for 8–10 minutes, or until the lamb changes colour. Stir in the tomato paste, yoghurt, coconut cream and ground almonds.
4 Reduce the heat and simmer, covered, stirring occasionally, for 50 minutes, or until the meat is tender. Add a little water if the mixture becomes too dry. Season with salt and pepper, and garnish with the slivered almonds. Serve with rice.

NUTRITION PER SERVE (6)
Protein 80 g; Fat 23 g; Carbohydrate 5 g;
Dietary Fibre 2 g; Cholesterol 240 mg;
2280 kJ (545 Cal)

NOTE: Korma curries can also be made using beef or chicken. Korma refers to the style of curry—rich and smooth, and including almonds.

Trim any excess fat or sinew from the lamb and cut into cubes.

Process the spice mixture until it forms a smooth paste.

LAMB CUTLETS WITH CANNELLINI BEAN PUREE

**Preparation time: 30 minutes +
   1 hour refrigeration**
Total cooking time: 20 minutes
Serves 4

8 lamb cutlets
4 cloves garlic
1 tablespoon chopped fresh rosemary
2 teaspoons olive oil
2 x 400 g (13 oz) cans cannellini
   beans, drained
1 teaspoon ground cumin
½ cup (125 ml/4 fl oz) lemon juice
cooking oil spray
2 tablespoons balsamic vinegar

1 Trim the cutlets of excess fat from the outside edge and scrape the fat away from the bones. Place in a single layer in a shallow dish. Thinly slice 2 garlic cloves and mix with the rosemary, oil and ½ teaspoon salt and cracked black pepper. Pour over the meat, cover and refrigerate for 1 hour.
2 Rinse the beans and purée with the remaining garlic, the cumin and half the lemon juice in a food processor. Transfer to a pan, then set aside.
3 Lightly spray a non-stick frying pan with oil and cook the cutlets over medium heat for 1–2 minutes on each side. Add the vinegar and cook for 1 minute, turning to coat. Remove the cutlets and cover to keep warm. Add the remaining lemon juice to the pan and simmer for 2–3 minutes, or until the sauce thickens slightly. Warm the purée over medium heat and serve with the cutlets.

NUTRITION PER SERVE
Protein 30 g; Fat 8 g; Carbohydrate 45 g;
Dietary Fibre 3.5 g; Cholesterol 50 mg;
1560 kJ (375 cal)

Peel 2 of the garlic cloves and thinly slice with a sharp knife.

Trim all the excess fat from the cutlets, scraping any away from the bones.

After cooking the cutlets lightly on each side, add the vinegar to the pan.

MUNG BEAN VERMICELLI WITH LAMB AND PEANUTS

**Preparation time: 35 minutes +
    25 minutes soaking +
    1 hour marinating
Total cooking time: 15 minutes
Serves 4**

6 dried Chinese mushrooms
100 g (3½ oz) mung bean vermicelli
300 g (10 oz) lamb fillet, thinly sliced
    across the grain
¼ cup (60 ml/2 fl oz) soy sauce
2 teaspoons sugar
1½ tablespoons sesame oil
5 cloves garlic, finely chopped
¼ cup (60 ml/2 fl oz) peanut oil
2 small fresh red chillies, finely
    chopped
1 large carrot, julienned
2 small zucchini, julienned
175 g (6 oz) baby English spinach
    leaves, trimmed
5 spring onions, thinly sliced on the
    diagonal
⅓ cup (60 g/2 oz) unsalted peanuts,
    crushed
¼ cup (7 g/¼ oz) fresh coriander
    leaves, chopped
white pepper, to taste

1 Place the Chinese mushrooms in a heatproof bowl, cover with boiling water and soak for 20 minutes, or until softened. Drain and squeeze out the excess water. Discard the woody stems, then thinly slice the caps. Place the noodles in a heatproof bowl, cover with boiling water and soak for 3–4 minutes, or until softened. Drain and cut into 8 cm (3 inch) lengths with scissors.
2 Place the lamb in a non-metallic bowl. Combine the soy sauce, sugar, 1 tablespoon of sesame oil and half the garlic, pour over the lamb and turn until well coated. Cover with plastic wrap and marinate for 1 hour.
3 Heat a large wok over high heat, add 1 tablespoon of the peanut oil and 1 teaspoon of the sesame oil and swirl to coat. Stir-fry the lamb in two batches (adding another 1 tablespoon of the peanut oil and 1 teaspoon of the sesame oil with each batch), for

2 minutes, or until brown. Remove and keep warm.
4 Wipe the wok clean with paper towels, then return to high heat. Add the remaining peanut oil and swirl to coat. Stir-fry the chilli and remaining garlic for 30 seconds. Add the carrot and zucchini and cook for 2 minutes. Add the spinach, spring onion and mushrooms and cook for 1 minute. Return the lamb and any juices to the wok and stir-fry for 1–2 minutes to heat through. Add the noodles with half the crushed peanuts and coriander, season to taste with white pepper and toss together until well combined. Garnish with the remaining peanuts and coriander.

NUTRITION PER SERVE
Protein 21.5 g; Fat 27.5 g; Carbohydrate 20 g; Dietary Fibre 5 g; Cholesterol 48.5 mg; 1715 kJ (410 Cal)

Return the lamb to the wok with any of the pan juices.

TAGINE OF LAMB WITH QUINCE AND LEMON

Preparation time: 25 minutes
Total cooking time: 2 hours 10 minutes
Serves 4

1.5 kg (3 lb) boned shoulder of lamb, cut into 12 even pieces
1 onion, finely chopped
2 cloves garlic, crushed
1 cinnamon stick
1 teaspoon ground ginger
½ teaspoon saffron threads
1 large quince, peeled, seeded and cut into 12 pieces
¼ cup (90 ml/3 fl oz) honey
1 teaspoon ground cinnamon
½ preserved lemon

1 Trim the lamb of excess fat and place in a large pan. Add the onion, garlic, cinnamon stick, ginger and saffron and enough cold water to cover. Slowly bring to the boil, stirring occasionally. Reduce the heat, cover and simmer for 45 minutes. Transfer the meat to a casserole dish.

2 Add the quince, honey and ground cinnamon to the cooking liquid and simmer for 15 minutes, or until the quince is tender. Discard the cinnamon, remove the quince and add to the meat, reserving the liquid.

3 Preheat the oven to moderate 180°C (350°F/Gas 4). Boil the cooking liquid for 30 minutes, or until reduced by half, then pour over the meat and quince. Remove and discard the flesh from the lemon. Slice the rind thinly, then add to the meat. Cover and bake for 40 minutes, or until the meat is tender.

NUTRITION PER SERVE
Protein 80 g; Fat 15 g; Carbohydrate 20 g; Dietary Fibre 3 g; Cholesterol 250 mg; 2160 kJ (515 cal)

HINT: As you work, place the peeled quince in water with a little lemon juice to prevent discolouring.

Add the onion, garlic, cinnamon stick, ginger, saffron and cold water to the lamb.

Add the quince, honey and ground cinnamon to the cooking liquid.

Remove and discard the flesh from the preserved lemon and slice the rind thinly.

WARM LAMB SALAD

**Preparation time: 15 minutes
+ 3 hours refrigeration
Total cooking time: 15 minutes
Serves 4–6**

2 tablespoons red curry paste
(use the recipe on page 246 or
ready-made paste)
¼ cup (15 g/½ oz) chopped coriander
leaves
1 tablespoon finely grated fresh ginger
3–4 tablespoons peanut oil
750 g (1½ lb) lamb fillets, thinly sliced
200 g (6½ oz) snow peas
600 g (1¼ lb) packet thick fresh rice
noodles
1 red capsicum, thinly sliced

1 Lebanese cucumber, thinly sliced
6 spring onions, thinly sliced

MINT DRESSING
1½ tablespoons peanut oil
¼ cup (60 ml/2 fl oz) lime juice
2 tablespoons soft brown sugar
3 teaspoons fish sauce
3 teaspoons soy sauce
⅓ cup (20 g/¾ oz) chopped mint
leaves
1 clove garlic, crushed

1 Combine the curry paste, coriander, ginger and 2 tablespoons oil in a bowl. Add the lamb and coat well. Cover and refrigerate for 2–3 hours.
2 Steam or boil the snow peas until just tender, refresh under cold water and drain.

3 Cover the noodles with boiling water. Leave for 5 minutes, or until tender, and drain.
4 To make the dressing, put all the ingredients in a jar and shake well.
5 Heat a wok until very hot, add 1 tablespoon oil and swirl to coat. Add half the lamb and stir-fry for 5 minutes, or until tender. Repeat with the remaining lamb, using more oil if needed.
6 Place the lamb, snow peas, noodles, capsicum, cucumber and spring onion in a large bowl, drizzle with the dressing and toss before serving.

NUTRITION PER SERVE (6)
Protein 32 g; Fat 20 g; Carbohydrate 33 g;
Dietary Fibre 3 g; Cholesterol 83 mg;
1850 kJ (442 cal)

Mix together the curry paste, coriander, ginger and 2 tablespoons oil.

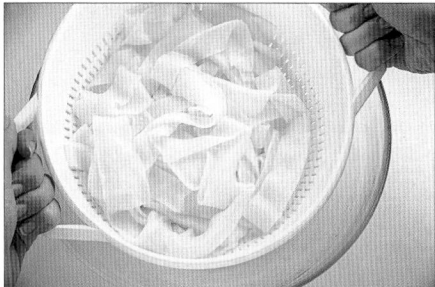

Leave the thick fresh rice noodles in boiling water until they are tender, then drain.

Put all the dressing ingredients in a screw-top jar and shake well to mix them.

NAVARIN OF LAMB

Preparation time: 20 minutes
Total cooking time: 1 hour 45 minutes
Serves 4

1.25 kg (2 lb 8 oz) boned shoulder or
    leg of lamb (ask your butcher to
    bone the meat)
1 tablespoon oil
1 small onion, quartered
1 clove garlic, crushed
2 rashers bacon, rind removed, finely
    chopped
12 large bulb spring onions, stems
    removed
1 tablespoon plain flour
1 cup (250 ml/8 fl oz) chicken stock
1 tablespoon tomato paste

1 turnip, swede or parsnip, peeled
    and cubed
1 large carrot, thickly sliced
4–6 new potatoes, halved
½ cup (60 g/2 oz) frozen peas

1 Remove any excess fat from the lamb and cut the meat into bite-sized cubes. Preheat the oven to slow 150°C. (300°F/Gas 2). Heat the oil in a heavy-based non-stick frying pan. Cook the onion, garlic, bacon and spring onions over medium heat for 5 minutes, or until the onion is soft. Remove with a slotted spoon to a large heatproof casserole dish.
2 Add the lamb to the frying pan and brown quickly in batches. When all the meat is browned return it to the pan and sprinkle with the flour. Stir

for 1 minute to combine, then pour on the stock and tomato paste. Stir until thickened and smooth and pour into the casserole.
3 Stir in the turnip, swede or parsnip, carrot and potato. Cover with a tight-fitting lid and bake for 1¼ hours, stirring a couple of times. Add the peas and cook for another 15 minutes, or until the lamb is tender. Season to taste before serving.

NUTRITION PER SERVE
Protein 9 g; Fat 12 g; Carbohydrate 22 g;
Dietary Fibre 7 g; Cholesterol 30 mg;
970 kJ (235 cal)

STORAGE TIME: Keep covered and refrigerated for up to 3 days.

Remove the onion, spring onion, garlic and bacon to a casserole dish.

Return all the browned meat to the pan and sprinkle with flour.

Add the turnip, carrot and potato to the meat in the casserole dish.

LAMB WITH ROAST PUMPKIN AND CAPSICUM SAUCE

Preparation time: 30 minutes
Total cooking time: 1 hour 20 minutes
Serves 4

500 g (1 lb) pumpkin (jap, butternut or
  golden nugget)
2 cloves garlic, crushed
1 tablespoon olive oil
1 red capsicum
2 teaspoons cumin seeds
2 teaspoons coriander seeds
1 cup (250 ml/8 fl oz) vegetable stock
750 g (1 lb 8 oz) lamb backstrap

1 Preheat the oven to 200°C.
(400°F/Gas 6). Cut the pumpkin into
wedges and put in a baking dish.
Combine the garlic and oil and
drizzle over the pumpkin. Season
well with salt and pepper. Cook for
1 hour or until tender. Cool slightly.
2 Cut the capsicum into large flat
pieces, removing the membranes and
seeds. Place, skin-side-up, under a
hot grill for 10 minutes, or until the
skin blackens and blisters. Cool
under a tea towel or in a plastic bag,
peel away the skin and cut the flesh
into strips.
3 Put the cumin and coriander seeds
in a small frying pan and dry-fry for
5 minutes. Grind in a small food
processor or mortar and pestle.
Remove the skin from the pumpkin
and put the flesh, ground spices and
stock in a food processor. Purée the
mixture until smooth, then transfer to
a pan and heat through gently. Add
the capsicum strips and stir through.
4 Lightly spray a chargrill pan with
oil. Cook the lamb for 3–4 minutes
on each side. Leave to rest for
5 minutes before slicing. Serve with
the sauce.

NUTRITION PER SERVE
Protein 60 g; Fat 15 g; Carbohydrate 22 g;
Dietary Fibre 7 g; Cholesterol 210 mg;
2330 kJ (550 cal)

Drizzle the combined garlic and oil over the
pumpkin and season well.

Peel the blackened skin away from the capsicum
and cut the flesh into strips.

Put the cumin and coriander seeds in a dry frying
pan and toast for 5 minutes.

Purée the roast pumpkin, dry-fried spices and
stock until smooth.

LAMB BACKSTRAPS WITH SPICY LENTILS AND RAITA

Preparation time: 30 minutes +
   30 minutes standing
Total cooking time: 1 hour
Serves 4

SPICY LENTILS
2 tablespoons olive oil
1 onion, chopped
1 carrot, diced
3 cloves garlic, finely chopped
2 teaspoons ground coriander
½ teaspoon ground cinnamon
½ teaspoon ground cloves
1 teaspoon ground turmeric
2 teaspoons ground cumin
½ teaspoon cayenne pepper
1 large tomato, diced
1 cup (185 g/6 oz) brown lentils
chopped fresh coriander, to garnish

RAITA
1 Lebanese cucumber, seeded and
   grated
1 cup (250 g/8 oz) plain yoghurt
½ small red onion, finely chopped
1 clove garlic, crushed
3 tablespoons fresh coriander leaves,
   chopped
1 tablespoon lemon juice
½ teaspoon ground cumin
pinch cayenne pepper

LAMB
2.5 cm (1 inch) cinnamon stick
2 teaspoons cardamom seeds
2 cloves
2 teaspoons cumin seeds
½ teaspoon chilli flakes
1 tablespoon coriander seeds
2 x 25 cm (10 inch) lamb backstraps
   or loin fillets (250 g/8 oz each)
1 tablespoon olive oil

1 To make the spicy lentils, heat the oil in a large saucepan, add the onion and carrot and cook, stirring, for 7 minutes, or until the onion is soft. Stir in the garlic and cook for 2–3 minutes, then add the spices and stir for 1 minute, or until fragrant. Add the tomato, washed lentils, 1 teaspoon salt and 1 litre water. Bring to the boil, then reduce the heat and simmer for 30–40 minutes, or until the lentils are soft and most of the liquid is absorbed. Add more water if it is too dry. Season.
2 Meanwhile, to prepare the raita, toss the cucumber with 1 teaspoon salt and drain for 30 minutes. Rinse. Squeeze the cucumber to remove excess liquid and combine with remaining ingredients.
3 Preheat the oven to very hot 240°C (475°F/Gas 9). Preheat a baking tray. Combine the spices for the lamb in a dry frying pan and toast, shaking the pan frequently, over medium heat for 2 minutes, or until smoking and fragrant. Grind the spices together coarsely. Season the lamb, then rub on the spice blend.
4 Heat a large frying pan over medium heat. Add the oil, then the lamb and brown each side for 2 minutes. Transfer to the hot baking tray and roast for 3–5 minutes, or until cooked to your liking. Remove from the oven, cover with foil and rest for 8 minutes. Cut the meat across the grain into 1 cm (½ inch) slices.
5 Place a mound of lentils in the centre of each plate. Arrange 6–8 lamb pieces around the lentils, then add a dollop of raita. Garnish with coriander.

NUTRITION PER SERVE
Protein 43 g; Fat 22 g; Carbohydrate 24 g; Dietary Fibre 9 g; Cholesterol 92 mg; 1975 kJ (472 Cal)

Cook the onion and carrot until the onion has softened.

Simmer the lentils until soft and most of the liquid has been absorbed.

Squeeze the cucumber to remove any excess liquid.

Toast the spices in a dry frying pan until fragrant. Take care to not burn them.

Rub the spice blend on the seasoned lamb backstraps.

Cook the lamb backstraps until browned on both sides.

LANCASHIRE HOTPOT

Preparation time: 20 minutes
Total cooking time: 2 hours
Serves 8

8 forequarter chops, cut 2.5 cm
    (1 inch) thick
4 lamb kidneys, cut into quarters,
    cores removed
3 tablespoons plain flour
30 g (1 oz) butter
4 potatoes, thinly sliced
2 large onions, sliced
2 celery sticks, chopped
1 large carrot, peeled and chopped
1¾ cups (440 ml/14 fl oz) chicken or
    beef stock
200 g (6½ oz) button mushrooms,
    sliced
2 teaspoons chopped fresh thyme
1 tablespoon Worcestershire sauce

1 Preheat the oven to warm 160°C (315°F/Gas 2–3). Lightly brush a large casserole dish with oil. Trim the meat of fat and sinew and toss the chops and kidneys in flour, shaking off the excess. Heat the butter in a large frying pan and brown the chops quickly on both sides. Remove chops from pan and brown the kidneys. Layer half the potato slices in the base of the dish and place chops and kidneys on top.
2 Add the onion, celery and carrot to the pan and cook until the carrot begins to brown. Layer on top of the chops and kidneys. Sprinkle the remaining flour over the base of the pan and cook, stirring, until dark brown. Gradually pour in the stock and bring to the boil, stirring. Add the mushrooms, salt, pepper, thyme and Worcestershire sauce, reduce the heat and leave to simmer for 10 minutes.

Pour into the casserole dish.
3 Layer the remaining potato over the top of the casserole, to cover the meat and vegetables. Cover and cook in the oven for 1¼ hours. Remove the lid and cook for a further 30 minutes, or until the potatoes are brown.

NUTRITION PER SERVE
Protein 40 g; Fat 10 g; Carbohydrate 11 g;
Dietary Fibre 3 g; Cholesterol 170 mg;
1227 kJ (295 cal)

Toss the kidneys in flour and then brown in the pan you used for browning the chops.

Stir in the mushrooms, seasoning, thyme and Worcestershire sauce.

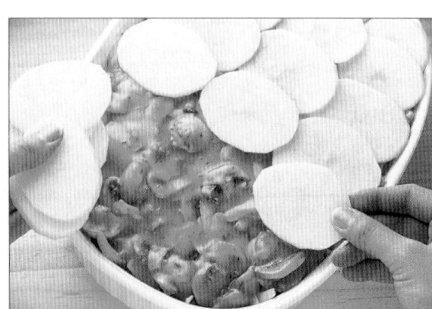

Layer the remaining potato over the top of the casserole, covering the meat and vegetables.

MINTED PESTO LAMB

Preparation time: 20 minutes
Total cooking time: 15 minutes
Serves 4

2 cups (40 g/1¼ oz) mint leaves
2 cloves garlic
¼ cup (40 g/1¼ oz) toasted pine nuts
½ cup (50 g/1¾ oz) grated Parmesan
¼ cup (60 ml/2 fl oz) olive oil
oil, for cooking
500 g (1 lb) lamb fillet, thinly sliced
1 onion, sliced
300 g (10 oz) mixed mushrooms, such as enoki, oyster, button, shimeji or Swiss brown

1 Place the mint, garlic, pine nuts and Parmesan in a food processor, and process for 10 seconds, or until finely chopped. With the motor running, gradually add the olive oil to form a paste. Season well.
2 Heat the wok until very hot, add 1 tablespoon of the oil and stir-fry the lamb in batches over medium-high heat until well browned. Remove all the lamb from the wok.
3 Reheat the wok, add 1 tablespoon of the oil and stir-fry the onion for 3–4 minutes, or until tender. Add the mushrooms and cook for 2 minutes.
4 Stir in the mint pesto. Return the lamb to the wok and toss over high heat for 5 minutes, or until the

mushrooms are soft and the lamb is heated through. Season well.

NUTRITION PER SERVE
Protein 35 g; Fat 40 g; Carbohydrate 3 g; Dietary Fibre 3 g; Cholesterol 95 mg; 2145 kJ (510 cal)

Prepare the mushrooms, cutting any particularly large mushrooms in half.

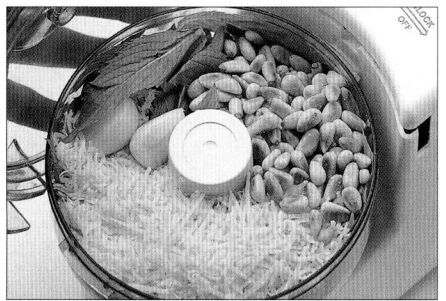

Mix the mint, garlic, pine nuts and Parmesan in a food processor to make mint pesto.

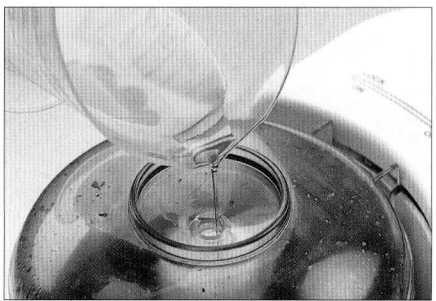

Gradually pour the olive oil into the food processor while the motor is running.

SLOW-COOKED SHANKS

Preparation time: 20 minutes
Total cooking time: 3 hours
Serves 4

1 tablespoon oil
4 lamb shanks
2 red onions, sliced
10 cloves garlic, peeled
400 g (13 oz) can chopped tomatoes
½ cup (125 ml/4 fl oz) dry white wine
1 bay leaf

1 teaspoon grated lemon rind
1 large red capsicum, chopped
3 tablespoons chopped fresh parsley

1 Preheat the oven to warm 170°C (325°F/Gas 3). Heat the oil in a large flameproof casserole dish, add the shanks in batches and cook over high heat until browned on all sides. Return all the lamb to the casserole.
2 Add the onion and garlic to the casserole and cook until softened. Add the tomato, wine, bay leaf, lemon rind, capsicum and ½ cup (125 ml/4 fl oz) water and bring to the boil.
3 Cover the casserole and cook in the oven for 2–2½ hours, or until the meat is tender and falling off the bone and the sauce has thickened. Season to taste. Sprinkle the parsley over the top before serving. Serve with couscous or soft polenta.

NUTRITION PER SERVE
Protein 35 g; Fat 10 g; Carbohydrate 9 g;
Dietary Fibre 4.5 g; Cholesterol 85 mg;
1275 kJ (305 cal)

Add the onion and garlic to the casserole and cook until softened.

Add the tomato, wine, bay leaf, lemon rind, capsicum and water.

Heat the oil in a pan and brown the lamb shanks in batches.

ROGAN JOSH

Preparation time: 25 minutes
Total cooking time: 1 hour 40 minutes
Serves 6

1 kg (2 lb) boned leg of lamb
1 tablespoon oil
2 onions, chopped
½ cup (125 g/4 oz) low-fat natural
   yoghurt
1 teaspoon chilli powder
1 tablespoon ground coriander
2 teaspoons ground cumin
1 teaspoon ground cardamom
½ teaspoon ground cloves
1 teaspoon ground turmeric
3 cloves garlic, crushed

1 tablespoon grated fresh ginger
400 g (13 oz) can chopped tomatoes
¼ cup (30 g/1 oz) slivered almonds
1 teaspoon garam masala
chopped fresh coriander leaves, for
   serving

1 Trim the lamb of any fat or sinew
and cut into small cubes.
2 Heat the oil in a large saucepan,
add the onion and cook, stirring, for
5 minutes, or until soft. Stir in the
yoghurt, chilli powder, coriander,
cumin, cardamom, cloves, turmeric,
garlic and ginger. Add the tomato and
1 teaspoon salt and simmer for
5 minutes.
3 Add the lamb and stir until coated.
Cover and cook over low heat,

stirring occasionally, for 1–1½ hours,
or until the lamb is tender. Uncover
and simmer until the liquid thickens.
4 Meanwhile, toast the almonds in a
dry frying pan over medium heat for
3–4 minutes, shaking the pan gently,
until the nuts are golden brown.
Remove from the pan at once to
prevent them burning.
5 Add the garam masala to the curry
and mix through well. Sprinkle the
slivered almonds and coriander leaves
over the top and serve.

NUTRITION PER SERVE
Protein 40 g; Fat 13 g; Carbohydrate 5.5 g;
Dietary Fibre 2 g; Cholesterol 122 mg;
1236 kJ (295 cal)

Cook the onion in the oil for 5 minutes, or until it
is soft.

Remove the lid from the pan and simmer until the
liquid thickens.

Toast the almonds in a dry frying pan until they
are golden brown.

SATAY LAMB

Preparation time: 20 minutes
Total cooking time: 15 minutes
Serves 4–6

oil, for cooking
500 g (1 lb) lamb fillet, thinly sliced
1 onion, chopped
2 cloves garlic, crushed
2 teaspoons grated fresh ginger
1–2 red chillies, seeded and finely
    chopped
1 teaspoon ground cumin
1 teaspoon ground coriander
½ cup (125 g/4 oz) crunchy peanut
    butter
1 tablespoon soy sauce
2 tablespoons lemon juice
½ cup (125 ml/4 fl oz) coconut cream

1 Heat the wok until very hot, add 1 tablespoon oil and swirl it around to coat the side. Stir-fry the lamb in batches over high heat until it is well browned and cooked, adding more oil when necessary. Remove the lamb from the wok and set aside.
2 Reheat the wok, add 1 tablespoon of the oil and stir-fry the onion over medium heat for 2–3 minutes, or until soft and transparent. Stir in the garlic, ginger, chilli, cumin and coriander, and cook for 1 minute.
3 Stir in the peanut butter, soy sauce, lemon juice, coconut cream and ½ cup (125 ml/4 fl oz) water. Slowly bring to the boil. Return the lamb to the wok and stir until heated through.

NUTRITION PER SERVE (6)
Protein 25 g; Fat 25 g; Carbohydrate 5 g;
Dietary Fibre 3 g; Cholesterol 55 mg;
1390 kJ (330 cal)

Stir-fry the onion over medium heat until it is soft and transparent.

Add the garlic, ginger, chilli, cumin and coriander to the onion.

Add the peanut butter, soy sauce, lemon juice, coconut cream and water to the wok.

MEDITERRANEAN LAMB CASSEROLE

Preparation time: 15 minutes
Total cooking time: 1 hour
Serves 4

1 tablespoon olive oil
750 g (1½ lb) lamb from the bone, diced
1 large onion, sliced
2 cloves garlic, crushed
2 carrots, chopped
2 parsnips, chopped
400 g (13 oz) can chopped tomatoes
2 tablespoons tomato paste
2 teaspoons chopped fresh rosemary
½ cup (125 ml/4 fl oz) red wine
1 cup (250 ml/8 fl oz) chicken stock

1 Heat the oil in large saucepan and cook the lamb, in batches, for 3–4 minutes, or until browned. Remove from the pan and keep warm. Add the onion and garlic to the pan and cook for 2–3 minutes, or until the onion is soft.
2 Return the lamb and juices to the pan. Add the carrots, parsnips, tomatoes, tomato paste, rosemary, wine and stock and bring to the boil. Reduce the heat and cover the pan. Simmer the casserole for 50 minutes, or until the lamb is tender and the sauce has thickened. Serve with soft polenta or couscous.

NUTRITION PER SERVE
Protein 45 g; Fat 12 g; Carbohydrate 12 g;
Dietary Fibre 4.5 g; Cholesterol 125 mg;
1517 kJ (362 cal)

Add the onion and garlic to the pan and cook until the onion is soft.

Simmer until the lamb is tender and the sauce has thickened.

MONGOLIAN LAMB

Preparation time: 15 minutes
Total cooking time: 12 minutes
Serves 4

oil, for cooking
500 g (1 lb) lamb backstrap
    (tender eye of the lamb loin),
    cut into thin strips
2 cloves garlic, crushed
4 spring onions, thickly sliced
2 tablespoons soy sauce
⅓ cup (80 ml/2¾ fl oz) dry sherry
2 tablespoons sweet chilli sauce
2 teaspoons sesame seeds, toasted

1 Heat the wok until very hot, add 1 tablespoon of the oil and swirl it around to coat the side of the wok. Stir-fry the lamb strips in batches over high heat, adding more oil whenever necessary. Remove all the lamb from the wok.
2 Reheat the wok, add 1 tablespoon of oil and stir-fry the garlic and spring onion for 2 minutes. Remove from the wok and set aside. Add the soy sauce, sherry and sweet chilli sauce to the wok. Bring to the boil, reduce the heat and simmer for 3–4 minutes, or until the sauce thickens slightly.
3 Return the meat, with any juices, and the spring onion to the wok, and toss to coat with the sauce. Serve sprinkled with the toasted sesame seeds.

NUTRITION PER SERVE
Protein 30 g; Fat 20 g; Carbohydrate 7 g;
Dietary Fibre 1.5 g; Cholesterol 80 mg;
1445 kJ (345 cal)

Slice the lamb backstrap into thin strips with a sharp knife.

Stir-fry the lamb strips in batches over high heat so that they fry rather than stew.

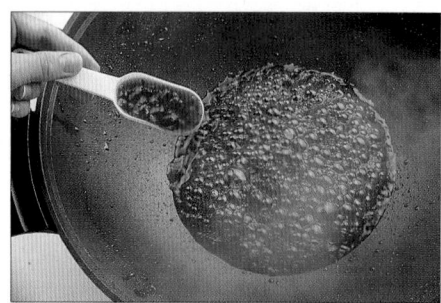

Add the soy sauce, sherry and sweet chilli sauce to the wok and bring to the boil.

LAMB WITH CANNELLINI BEANS AND ROSEMARY

Preparation time: 20 minutes
Total cooking time: 10 minutes
Serves 4

2 tomatoes
oil, for cooking
600 g (1¼ lb) lamb fillet,
    diagonally sliced
3 cloves garlic, finely chopped
1 teaspoon cumin seeds
2 teaspoons finely chopped
    rosemary
2 tablespoons red wine vinegar
1 tablespoon lemon juice
300 g (10 oz) can cannellini beans,
    rinsed
1 tablespoon flat-leaf parsley leaves

1 Score a cross in the base of each tomato with a sharp knife. Put the tomatoes in a heatproof bowl and cover with boiling water for 30 seconds. Transfer to iced water and then peel the skin away from the cross and remove the stalks. Scoop out the seeds with a teaspoon and finely chop the flesh into cubes.
2 Heat the wok until very hot, add 2 teaspoons of the oil and swirl it around to coat the side. Stir-fry the lamb in two batches over very high heat until it is browned.
3 Return all the lamb to the wok and add the garlic, cumin seeds and rosemary. Cook for 1 minute. Reduce the heat and add the vinegar and lemon juice. Stir to combine, scraping any bits from the bottom of the wok.
4 Add the tomato and cannellini beans and stir-fry until warmed through. Season with salt and black pepper, then scatter with the parsley.

NUTRITION PER SERVE
Protein 35 g; Fat 6 g; Carbohydrate 3 g;
Dietary Fibre 3 g; Cholesterol 100 mg;
890 kJ (210 cal)

Peel the skin in a downwards motion, away from the cross. Remove the stalk.

Cut the tomatoes in half and scoop out the seeds with a teaspoon.

Using a sharp knife, chop the tomatoes into very fine cubes.

SWEET MUSTARD LAMB STIR-FRY

Preparation time: 15 minutes
Total cooking time: 15 minutes
Serves 4

oil, for cooking
500 g (1 lb) lamb fillet, cut into thin
    strips
2 cloves garlic, crushed
250 g (8 oz) snow peas
1 onion, cut into large wedges
20 g (¾ oz) butter
¼ cup (60 g/2 oz) wholegrain mustard
1 tablespoon honey
½ cup (125 ml/4 fl oz) cream
2 tablespoons brandy, optional

1 Heat the wok until very hot, add
1 tablespoon of the oil and swirl it
around to coat the side. Stir-fry the
lamb strips in batches over high heat.
Remove from the wok and set aside.
2 Heat 1 tablespoon of the oil in the
wok and add the crushed garlic, snow
peas and onion wedges. Stir-fry over
medium heat for 3–4 minutes, or until
the onion softens slightly. Remove
from the wok and keep warm.
3 Reduce the heat and add the butter,
wholegrain mustard, honey, cream
and brandy to the wok. Simmer the
sauce gently for 3–4 minutes. Return
the meat and the snow pea mixture to
the wok and stir until the meat and
vegetables are heated through and
combined with the sauce.

NUTRITION PER SERVE
Protein 30 g; Fat 30 g; Carbohydrate 15 g;
Dietary Fibre 4 g; Cholesterol 140 mg;
2030 kJ (485 cal)

Remove any fat or sinew from the lamb fillet and
cut the lamb into thin strips.

Stir-fry the lamb slices in batches over high heat
so that the meat browns.

Heat the oil and add the garlic, snow peas and
onion wedges.

PEPPERED LAMB AND ASPARAGUS

**Preparation time: 35 minutes
+ 20 minutes marinating
Total cooking time: 20 minutes
Serves 4**

400 g (13 oz) lamb fillets
2 teaspoons green peppercorns,
    finely chopped
3 cloves garlic, finely chopped
1 tablespoon vegetable oil
1 onion, cut into small wedges
⅓ cup (80 ml/2¾ fl oz) dry sherry
1 green capsicum, cut into strips

½ teaspoon sugar
16 small asparagus spears, chopped,
    tough ends discarded
200 g (6½ oz) broccoli florets
2 tablespoons oyster sauce
garlic chives, snipped, to garnish

1 Trim away any sinew from the lamb and cut the lamb into bite-sized pieces. Combine in a bowl with the green peppercorns, garlic and oil, then toss well and set aside for 20 minutes.

2 Heat a wok over high heat until slightly smoking. Add the lamb and stir-fry in batches until browned. Remove, cover and keep warm.

3 Reheat the wok and stir-fry the onion and 2 teaspoons of the sherry for 1 minute. Add the capsicum, sugar and a large pinch of salt. Cover and steam for 2 minutes. Add the asparagus, broccoli and the remaining sherry and stir-fry for 1 minute. Cover and steam for 3 minutes, or until the vegetables are just tender. Return the lamb to the wok, add the oyster sauce and stir well. Top with the chives.

NUTRITION PER SERVE
Protein 25 g; Fat 12 g; Carbohydrate 8 g;
Dietary Fibre 4 g; Cholesterol 65 mg;
1100 kJ (265 cal)

Trim the lamb of any excess fat or sinew, then cut into bite-sized pieces.

Stir-fry the lamb over high heat until brown and just cooked.

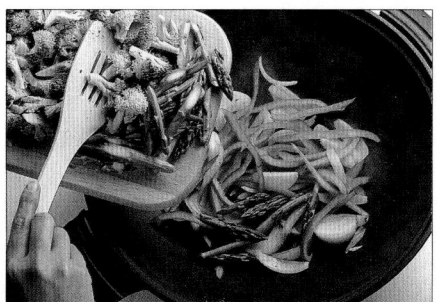

Add the asparagus and broccoli to the capsicum and onion.

ROSEMARY-INFUSED LAMB AND LENTIL CASSEROLE

Preparation time: 20 minutes
Total cooking time: 2 hours 30 minutes
Serves 6

1 tablespoon olive oil
1 onion, finely sliced
2 cloves garlic, crushed
1 small carrot, finely chopped
2 teaspoons cumin seeds
¼ teaspoon chilli flakes
2 teaspoons finely chopped fresh
    ginger
1 kg (2 lb) boned leg of lamb, cut into
    4 cm (1½ inch) cubes
2 teaspoons fresh rosemary leaves,
    chopped
3 cups (750 ml/24 fl oz) chicken stock
1 cup (185 g/6 oz) green or brown
    lentils
3 teaspoons soft brown sugar
2 teaspoons balsamic vinegar

1 Preheat the oven to moderate 180°C (350°F/Gas 4). Heat half the oil in a large, heavy-based pan. Add the onion, garlic and carrot and cook over medium heat for about 5 minutes, or until soft and golden. Add the cumin seeds, chilli flakes and ginger, cook for 1 minute, then transfer to a large casserole dish.
2 Heat the remaining oil in the pan and brown the lamb in batches over high heat. Transfer to the casserole.
3 Add the rosemary to the pan and stir in 2½ cups (625 ml/20 fl oz) of the stock. Heat until the stock is bubbling, then pour into the casserole dish. Cover the dish and bake in the oven for 1 hour.
4 Add the lentils, sugar and vinegar and cook for 1 hour more, or until the lentils are cooked. If the mixture is too thick, stir in the remaining stock. Season with salt and pepper to taste and serve.

NUTRITION PER SERVE
Protein 45 g; Fat 15 g; Carbohydrate 15 g;
Dietary Fibre 5 g; Cholesterol 120 mg;
1618 kJ (385 cal)

When the oil is hot, add the onion, garlic and carrot and cook until soft and golden.

After browning the lamb, add the rosemary and stock to the pan.

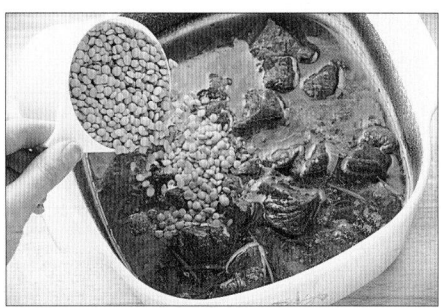

Bake the casserole for 1 hour, then add the lentils, sugar and vinegar.

BASIC LAMB CURRY

Preparation time: 40 minutes
Total cooking time: 2 hours 10 minutes
Serves 6

⅓ cup (80 ml/2¾ fl oz) oil
1.5 kg (3 lb) lamb, cut into 3 cm
    (1¼ inch) cubes
2 large onions, finely chopped
4–6 cloves garlic, chopped
1 tablespoon grated fresh ginger
2 small red chillies, seeded and
    chopped
1 tablespoon ground cumin
1 tablespoon ground coriander
2 teaspoons ground turmeric
½ teaspoon chilli powder
2 x 400 g (13 oz) cans crushed
    tomatoes
1 tablespoon tomato paste
4 tablespoons chopped fresh
    coriander

1 Heat 1 tablespoon of the oil in a large saucepan, add a third of the lamb and cook over high heat for 4 minutes, or until browned. Remove. Repeat twice more with the remaining lamb and 2 more tablespoons oil. Remove all the lamb from the pan.
2 Heat the remaining oil in the saucepan. Add the onion and cook over medium heat, stirring frequently, for 10 minutes, or until golden. Add the garlic, ginger and chilli, and cook for 2 minutes, then add the ground spices and cook, stirring, for a further 3 minutes, or until fragrant.
3 Add the tomato, tomato paste, the lamb and 1 teaspoon salt. Mix well, then reduce the heat and simmer, covered, for 1½ hours, or until the meat is tender. Stir occasionally.
4 Uncover, increase the heat and cook for 10 minutes to allow the sauce to reduce and thicken. Garnish with the coriander and serve with rice or boiled potatoes.

NUTRITION PER SERVE
Protein 57 g; Fat 25 g; Carbohydrate 7 g;
Dietary Fibre 3 g; Cholesterol 165 mg;
2030 kJ (485 Cal)

Brown the lamb in a large saucepan in three batches.

Cook the onion, stirring frequently, until softened and golden.

SAAG GOSHT (LAMB AND SPINACH CURRY)

Preparation time: 30 minutes
Total cooking time: 2 hours 20 minutes
Serves 6

1 kg (2 lb) English spinach
½ cup (125 ml/4 fl oz) oil
1.5 kg (3 lb) lamb, cut into
   3 cm (1¼ inch) cubes (see NOTE)
2 red onions, finely chopped
6 cloves garlic, crushed
1½ tablespoons grated fresh ginger
2 bay leaves
2 tablespoons ground coriander
1 tablespoon ground cumin
1 teaspoon ground turmeric
2 large vine-ripened tomatoes, peeled,
   seeded and chopped
2–3 small green chillies, seeded and
   finely chopped
100 g (3½ oz) plain thick yoghurt
1 cinnamon stick
2 teaspoons garam masala

1 Preheat the oven to warm 170°C (325°F/Gas 3). Trim the spinach and quickly blanch in simmering water. Drain, cool slightly and squeeze to remove any excess moisture, then place in a food processor and process until smooth.
2 Heat half the oil in a large saucepan. Add the lamb pieces in batches and cook over high heat for 4–5 minutes, or until browned. Remove the lamb from the pan.
3 Heat the remaining oil in the saucepan. Add the onion and cook, stirring frequently, for 10 minutes, or until golden brown but not burnt. Add the garlic, ginger and bay leaves, and cook, stirring, for 3 more minutes.

4 Add the spices and cook, stirring, for 2 minutes, or until fragrant. Add the tomato and chilli, and stir over low heat for 5 minutes, or until the tomato is thick and pulpy. Remove from the heat and cool for 5 minutes. Transfer to a 4 litre ovenproof casserole dish and stir in the yoghurt.
5 Add the meat to the dish and add the cinnamon stick and 1 teaspoon salt. Bake, covered, for 1 hour and then uncovered for a further 15 minutes. Stir in the spinach and garam masala, and cook, stirring

occasionally, for 15 minutes, or until the meat is tender. Remove the bay leaves and cinnamon stick, and serve with rice or pilaf.

NUTRITION PER SERVE
Protein 60 g; Fat 30 g; Carbohydrate 5 g;
Dietary Fibre 6.5 g; Cholesterol 170 mg;
2240 kJ (533 Cal)

NOTE: Ask your butcher to bone and cut a leg of lamb into 3 cm (1¼ inch) cubes. A 2.2 kg (4 lb 7 oz) leg will yield about 1.5 kg (3 lb) meat.

Squeeze the blanched spinach to remove any excess moisture.

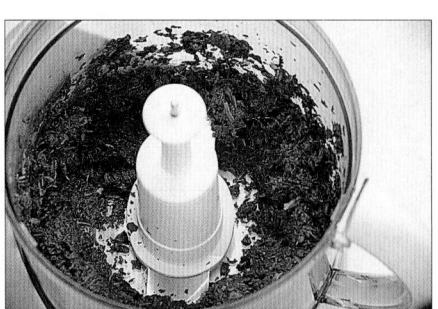

Process the spinach in a food processor until smooth.

Stir over low heat until the tomato is thick and pulpy.

LAMB AND EGGPLANT PIE

Preparation time: 20 minutes
+ 30 minutes cooling
Total cooking time: 1 hour 45 minutes
Serves 8–10

2 eggplants, cut into 2.5 cm
   (1 inch) cubes
¼ cup (60 ml/2 fl oz) olive oil
3 onions, finely chopped
3 cloves garlic, chopped
1 teaspoon paprika
½ teaspoon ground cinnamon
¼ teaspoon ground nutmeg
650 g (1 lb 5 oz) lamb mince
¼ cup (60 g/2 oz) tomato paste
1 cup (250 ml/8 fl oz) dry red wine
425 g (14 oz) can crushed tomatoes
1 cup (250 ml/8 fl oz) beef stock
200 g (6½ oz) Greek-style natural
   yoghurt
2 eggs, lightly beaten
200 g (6½ oz) feta, crumbled
11 sheets filo pastry
olive oil spray

1 Preheat the oven to moderately hot 200°C (400°F/Gas 6) and grease a baking tray. Toss the eggplant with 2 tablespoons olive oil and place on the tray. Bake for 30 minutes, or until tender and brown. Remove, drain off any excess oil and set aside.
2 Meanwhile, heat the remaining oil in a large, deep frying pan over medium heat and cook the onion for 5 minutes, or until soft. Add the garlic and spices and cook for another minute.
3 Increase the heat to high, add the mince and cook for 5 minutes, or until brown. Add the tomato paste and cook for 2 minutes. Pour in the wine and cook for 3 minutes, stirring occasionally. Add the tomato and stock, bring to the boil, then reduce the heat and simmer for 30 minutes, or until the liquid has evaporated. Stir in the eggplant, then set aside for 30 minutes to cool completely.
4 Increase the oven to hot 220°C (425°F/Gas 7). Lightly grease a 2 litre pie dish. Combine the yoghurt, eggs and feta in a bowl.
5 Layer 6 sheets of filo in the base

and sides of the pie dish, spraying the top of each sheet with olive oil. Top with all the lamb mixture, then pour in the yoghurt and feta mixture. Fold the overhanging pastry over the top of the filling, then top with another 5 filo sheets, spraying each sheet, to cover completely.
6 Bake on the lowest shelf for

30 minutes, then cook on the middle shelf for another 20–30 minutes, or until the pastry is crisp and golden.

NUTRITION PER SERVE (10)
Protein 22.5 g; Fat 17.5 g; Carbohydrate 14.5 g; Dietary Fibre 2.5 g; Cholesterol 98 mg; 1340 kJ (320 Cal)

Spoon the lamb and eggplant mixture into the pie dish.

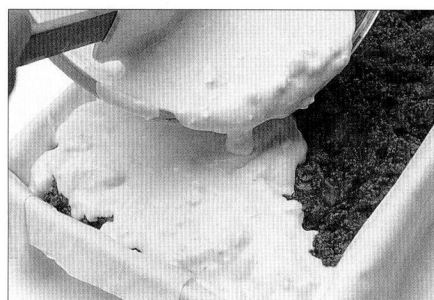

Pour the yoghurt and feta mixture over the lamb and eggplant mixture.

LAMB MEATBALLS

Preparation time: 25 minutes
Total cooking time: 1 hour 10 minutes
Serves 4–6

1 kg (2 lb) lamb mince
1 onion, finely chopped
2 small green chillies, finely chopped
3 teaspoons grated fresh ginger
3 cloves garlic, crushed
1 teaspoon ground cardamom
⅓ cup (25 g/¾ oz) fresh breadcrumbs
1 egg, lightly beaten
2 tablespoons ghee or oil

SAUCE
1 tablespoon ghee or oil
1 onion, sliced
1 green chilli, finely chopped
3 teaspoons grated fresh ginger
2 cloves garlic, crushed
1 teaspoon ground turmeric
3 teaspoons ground coriander
2 teaspoons ground cumin
1 teaspoon chilli powder
2 tablespoons white vinegar
¾ cup (185 g/3 oz) plain yoghurt
1¼ cups (315 ml/10 fl oz) coconut milk

1 Line a baking tray. Combine the mince with the onion, chilli, ginger, garlic, cardamom, breadcrumbs, egg, salt and pepper. Roll tablespoons into balls, and place on the tray.
2 Heat the ghee in a large frying pan, add the meatballs in batches and cook over medium heat for 10 minutes, or until browned all over.
3 To make the sauce, heat the ghee in the pan, add the onion, chilli, ginger, garlic and turmeric, and cook, stirring, over low heat for 8 minutes, or until the onion is soft. Add the coriander, cumin, chilli powder, vinegar, meatballs and 1⅓ cups (350 ml/11 fl oz) water, and stir gently. Simmer, covered, for 30 minutes. Stir in the combined yoghurt and coconut milk, and simmer, partially covered, for another 10 minutes. Serve with rice.

NUTRITION PER SERVE (6)
Protein 38 g; Fat 40 g; Carbohydrate 8.5 g;
Dietary Fibre 2.5 g; Cholesterol 165 mg;
2253 kJ (538 Cal)

Roll tablespoons of the mince mixture into bite-sized balls.

Cook the meatballs in batches until golden brown.

Cook the onion, chilli, ginger, garlic and turmeric until the onion is soft.

Stir the combined yoghurt and coconut milk into the curry.

SHEPHERD'S PIE

Preparation time: 30 minutes
Total cooking time: 1 hour 20 minutes
Serves 6

1 kg (2 lb) potatoes
30 g (1 oz) butter
2 tablespoons milk
1 tablespoon oil
1 large onion, finely chopped
1 kg (2 lb) lamb mince
1 carrot, finely chopped
2 tablespoons plain flour
1 cup (250 ml/8 fl oz) vegetable stock
2 tablespoons Worcestershire sauce
1 cup (155 g/5 oz) frozen peas

1 Peel the potatoes and cut into chunks. Cook in a large pan of boiling water for 15–20 minutes, or until tender. Drain the potato well and return to the pan over low heat, and stir to evaporate any excess water. Remove from the heat, add the butter and milk, and mash with a potato masher until smooth. Season with salt and cracked pepper. Preheat the oven to moderate 180°C (350°F/Gas 4).

2 Meanwhile, heat the oil in a large frying pan and add the onion. Cook, stirring occasionally, until soft and just beginning to colour. Add the mince, increase the heat and cook until browned, breaking up any lumps with a wooden spoon as the meat cooks.

3 Add the carrot to the pan and cook for a few minutes until just tender. Sprinkle on the flour and cook, stirring, for 1 minute. Slowly add the stock, stirring constantly. Add the Worcestershire sauce. Bring to the boil and cook for 2–3 minutes, or until the gravy thickens. Season to taste with salt and pepper. Stir in the peas and transfer the mixture to a 2 litre ovenproof dish.

4 Spoon the mashed potato onto the meat mixture and spread out evenly. Use a fork to swirl the surface. Bake for 40–50 minutes, or until the potato is golden.

NUTRITION PER SERVE
Protein 40 g; Fat 20 g; Carbohydrate 30 g; Dietary Fibre 5 g; Cholesterol 105 mg; 1995 kJ (475 Cal)

Cook the mince until browned, breaking up any lumps as you go.

Sprinkle the flour over the mince mixture and stir to blend it in.

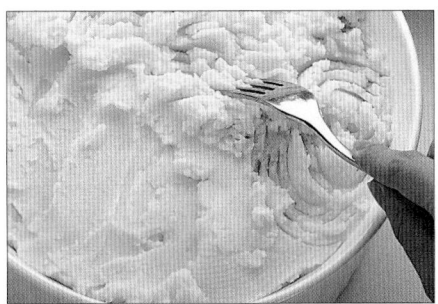

Use a fork to swirl the surface of the mashed potato.

LAMB CASSEROLE WITH BEANS

Preparation time: 25 minutes + overnight soaking
Total cooking time: 2 hours 15 minutes
Serves 6

1½ cups (300 g/10 oz) borlotti beans or red kidney beans
1 kg (2 lb) boned leg lamb
1½ tablespoons olive oil
2 rashers bacon, rind removed, chopped
1 large onion, chopped
2 cloves garlic, crushed
1 large carrot, chopped
2 cups (500 ml/16 oz) dry red wine
1 tablespoon tomato paste
1½ cups (375 ml/12 fl oz) beef stock
2 large sprigs fresh rosemary
2 sprigs fresh thyme

1 Put the beans in a bowl and cover with plenty of water. Leave to soak overnight, then drain well.
2 Preheat the oven to warm 160°C (315°F/Gas 2–3). Trim any excess fat from the lamb and cut into 3 cm (1¼ inch) pieces.
3 Heat 1 tablespoon oil in a large flameproof casserole. Add half the meat and toss over medium–high heat for 2 minutes, or until browned. Remove from the pan and repeat with the remaining lamb.
4 Heat the remaining olive oil in the casserole and add the bacon and onion. Cook over medium heat for 3 minutes, or until the onion is translucent. Add the garlic and carrot, and cook for 1 minute, or until aromatic.
5 Return the meat and any juices to the pan, increase the heat to high and add the wine. Bring to the boil and cook for 2 minutes. Add the beans, tomato paste, stock, rosemary and thyme, bring to the boil, then cover and cook in the oven for 2 hours, or until the meat is tender. Stir occasionally during cooking. Skim off any excess fat, remove the sprigs of herbs and season. Serve with bread.

NUTRITION PER SERVE
Protein 50 g; Fat 10 g; Carbohydrate 48 g; Dietary Fibre 9 g; Cholesterol 117 mg; 2367 kJ (565 Cal)

Remove any excess fat from the lamb then cut it into 3 cm (11/4 inch) pieces.

Heat the oil then add the lamb and toss until browned all over.

Return the meat and juices to the pan, add the wine, and bring to the boil.

MEDITERRANEAN BURGERS

Preparation time: 15 minutes
Total cooking time: 20 minutes
Serves 4

1 large red capsicum
500 g (1 lb) lamb mince
1 egg, lightly beaten
1 small onion, grated
3 cloves garlic, crushed
2 tablespoons pine nuts, chopped
1 tablespoon finely chopped fresh
mint
1 tablespoon finely chopped fresh
parsley
1 teaspoon ground cumin
2 teaspoons chilli sauce
1 tablespoon olive oil
4 Turkish or pide bread rolls
1 cup (220 g/7 oz) ready-made
hummus
100 g (3½ oz) baby rocket
1 small Lebanese cucumber,
cut into ribbons
chilli sauce, to serve (optional)

1 Cut the capsicum into large pieces, removing the seeds and membrane. Place, skin-side-up, under a hot grill until the skin blackens and blisters. Cool in a plastic bag, then peel and cut into thick strips.
2 Combine the mince, egg, onion, garlic, pine nuts, fresh herbs, cumin and chilli sauce in a large bowl. Mix with your hands and roll into four even-sized balls. Press the balls into large patties about 9 cm (3½ inches) in diameter.
3 Heat the oil in a large frying pan and cook the patties over medium heat for 6 minutes each side, or until

well browned and cooked through, then drain on paper towels.
4 Halve the rolls and toast both sides.
5 Spread the cut sides of the rolls with hummus, then lay rocket leaves, roasted capsicum and cucumber ribbons over the base. Place a patty on the salad and top with the other half of the roll. Serve with chilli sauce.

NUTRITION PER SERVE
Protein 40 g; Fat 30 g; Carbohydrate 54 g; Dietary Fibre 7 g; Cholesterol 124 mg; 2758 kJ (660 Cal)

Cook the capsicum under a hot grill until the skin blackens and blisters.

Roll the mince mixture into even-sized balls and then flatten into patties.

LAMB HOTPOT WITH RICE NOODLES

Preparation time: 20 minutes
  + 2 hours marinating
Total cooking time: 2 hours
Serves 4

2 cloves garlic, crushed
2 teaspoons grated fresh ginger
1 teaspoon five-spice powder
¼ teaspoon ground white pepper
2 tablespoons Chinese rice wine
1 teaspoon sugar
1 kg (2 lb) boneless lamb shoulder, trimmed and cut into 3 cm pieces
30 g (1 oz) whole dried Chinese mushrooms
1 tablespoon peanut oil
1 large onion, cut into wedges
2.5 cm (1 inch) piece fresh ginger, julienned
1 teaspoon Sichuan peppercorns, crushed or ground
2 tablespoons sweet bean paste
1 teaspoon black peppercorns, ground and toasted
2 cups (500 ml/16 fl oz) chicken stock
¼ cup (60 ml/2 fl oz) oyster sauce
2 star anise
¼ cup (60 ml/2 fl oz) Chinese rice wine, extra
80 g (3 oz) can sliced bamboo shoots
100 g (3½ oz) can water chestnuts, drained and sliced
400 g (13 oz) fresh rice noodles, cut into 2 cm (¾ inch) wide strips
1 spring onion, sliced on the diagonal

1 Combine the garlic, grated ginger, five-spice powder, white pepper, rice wine, sugar and 1 teaspoon salt in a large bowl. Add the lamb and toss to coat. Cover and marinate for 2 hours.
2 Meanwhile, soak the mushrooms in boiling water for 20 minutes. Drain. Discard the stems and slice the caps.
3 Heat a wok over high heat, add the oil and swirl to coat. Stir-fry the onion, julienned ginger and Sichuan pepper for 2 minutes. Cook the lamb in three batches, stir-frying for 2–3 minutes each batch, or until starting to brown. Stir in the bean paste and ground peppercorns and cook for 3 minutes, or until the lamb is brown. Add the stock and transfer to a 2 litre

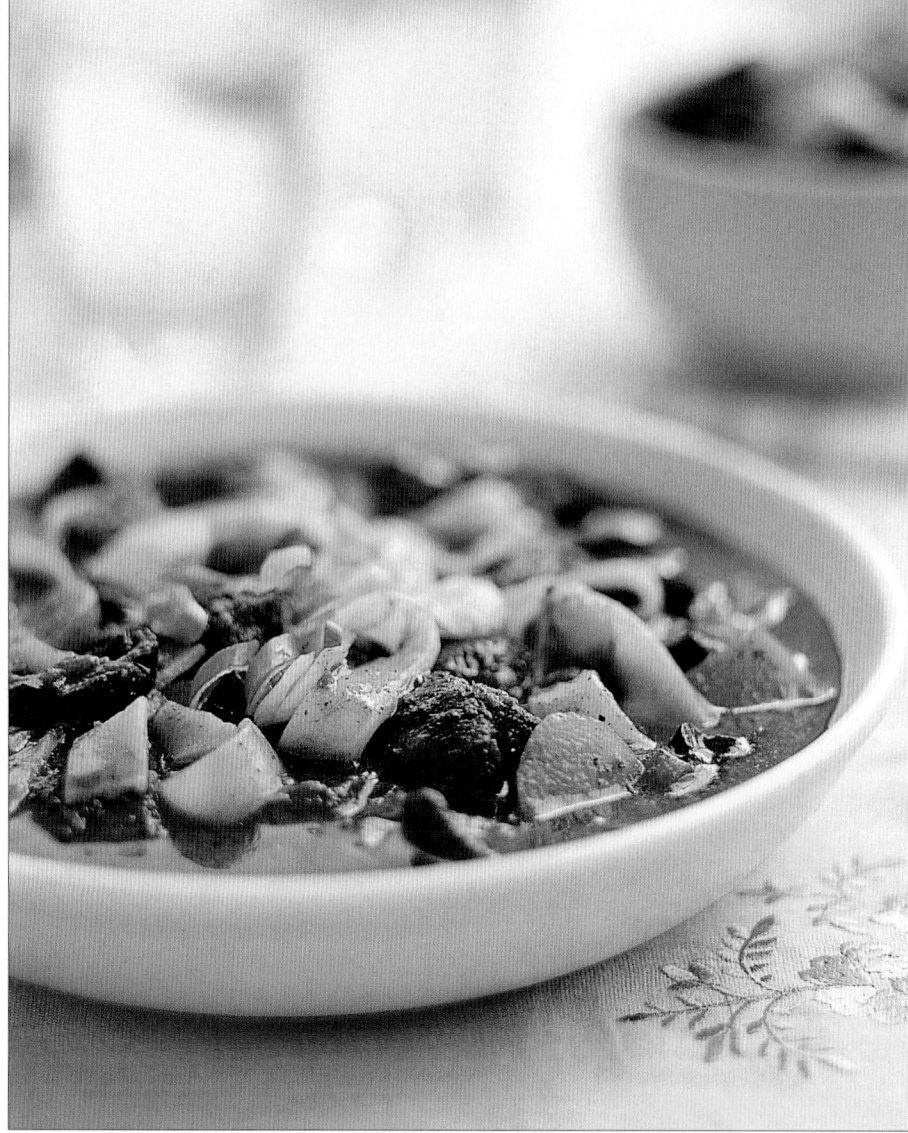

flameproof clay pot or casserole dish. Stir in the oyster sauce, star anise and extra rice wine and simmer, covered, over low heat for 1 hour 30 minutes, or until the lamb is tender. Stir in the drained bamboo shoots and water chestnuts and cook for 20 minutes. Add the mushrooms.
4 Cover the noodles with boiling water and gently separate. Drain and rinse, then add to the hotpot, stirring for 1–2 minutes, or until heated through. Sprinkle with spring onion.

NUTRITION PER SERVE
Protein 58 g; Fat 20.5 g; Carbohydrate 56.5 g; Dietary Fibre 4 g; Cholesterol 167.5 mg; 2805 kJ (670 Cal)

Stir the bean paste into the lamb and onion mixture.

Stir the bamboo shoots and water chestnuts into the hotpot.

LAMB KOFTA CURRY

Preparation time: 25 minutes
Total cooking time: 35 minutes
Serves 4

500 g (1 lb) minced lean lamb
1 onion, finely chopped
1 clove garlic, finely chopped
1 teaspoon grated fresh ginger
1 small fresh chilli, finely chopped
1 teaspoon garam masala
1 teaspoon ground coriander
¼ cup (45 g/1½ oz) ground almonds
2 tablespoons chopped fresh
    coriander leaves

SAUCE
2 teaspoons oil
1 onion, finely chopped
3 tablespoons Korma curry paste
400 g (13 oz) can chopped tomatoes
½ cup (125 g/4 oz) low-fat plain
    yoghurt
1 teaspoon lemon juice

1 Combine the lamb, onion, garlic, ginger, chilli, garam masala, ground coriander, ground almonds and 1 teaspoon salt in a large bowl. Shape the mixture into walnut-sized balls with your hands.
2 Heat a large non-stick frying pan and cook the koftas in batches until brown on both sides—they don't have to be cooked all the way through.
3 Meanwhile, to make the sauce, heat the oil in a large saucepan over low heat. Add the onion and cook for 6–8 minutes, or until soft and golden. Add the curry paste and cook until fragrant. Add the chopped tomatoes and simmer for 5 minutes. Stir in the yoghurt (1 tablespoon at a time) and the lemon juice until combined.

4 Place the koftas in the tomato sauce. Cook, covered, over low heat for 20 minutes. Serve over steamed rice and garnish with the chopped coriander.

NUTRITION PER SERVE
Protein 32 g; Fat 23 g; Carbohydrate 10 g;
Dietary Fibre 5 g; Cholesterol 88 mg;
1575 kJ (375 Cal)

Roll the lamb mixture into walnut-sized balls with your hands.

Add the chopped tomatoes and simmer for 5 minutes.

Add the koftas to the tomato sauce and cook over low heat for 20 minutes.

TAPENADE-COATED LAMB RACKS WITH FETA AND COUSCOUS

**Preparation time: 30 minutes +
  15 minutes standing
Total cooking time: 1 hour 10 minutes
Serves 4**

2 teaspoons capers
15 g drained anchovy fillets
1 clove garlic
¾ cup (90 g/3 oz) sliced pitted black
  olives
1½ tablespoons lemon juice
1½ tablespoons extra virgin olive oil
1 tablespoon cognac
8 small ripe Roma tomatoes, halved
150 g (5 oz) Bulgarian feta (see NOTE)
4 lamb racks with 3 cutlets each
1½ cups (375 ml/12 fl oz) chicken stock
1 tablespoon olive oil
1 red onion, thinly sliced
1 tablespoon baby capers
1 cup (185 g/6 oz) couscous
1 teaspoon orange zest
25 g (¾ oz) butter
1½ tablespoons chopped fresh mint

1 Preheat the oven to moderate 180°C (350°F/Gas 4). To make the tapenade, put the capers, anchovy fillets, garlic, olives and lemon juice in a food processor and process until finely chopped. While the motor is running, slowly pour in the extra virgin olive oil and cognac. Season with pepper.
2 Place the tomatoes on a wire rack in a roasting tin, sprinkle with salt and pepper and roast for 40 minutes, or until slightly dried. Sprinkle with the crumbled feta. Increase the oven to hot 220°C (425°F/Gas 7).
3 Trim and clean the lamb racks, then coat them in the tapenade and place in a roasting tin. Cook for 20–25 minutes, or until cooked to your liking. Rest for 10 minutes before carving into cutlets.
4 Bring the stock to the boil in a saucepan. Meanwhile, heat the olive oil in a frying pan, add the onion and baby capers and cook over medium heat for 5 minutes, or until the onion is tender. Transfer to a bowl, add the couscous, zest and butter, and cover with the stock. Leave for 5 minutes,

or until all the liquid has been absorbed. Fluff with a fork to separate the grains, adding half the mint.
5 To serve, place a mound of couscous in the centre of each of four serving plates. Top with a cutlet, then a piece of tomato, another cutlet, another tomato half and finish with a cutlet. Lean two pieces of tomato up against the side of each stack, sprinkle with the remaining mint and serve.

NUTRITION PER SERVE
Protein 38 g; Fat 30 g; Carbohydrate 36 g;
Dietary Fibre 3.5 g; Cholesterol 124 mg;
2394 kJ (572 Cal)

NOTE: Bulgarian feta has a distinctive flavour, but you can use normal feta. Hint: To save time, use ½ cup (155 g/ 5 oz) good-quality bought tapenade.

Bake the tomatoes on a wire rack until they are slightly dried.

Trim the fat from the lamb racks and clean the bones.

WELSH LAMB PIE

Preparation time: 20 minutes + cooling
Total cooking time: 2 hours 35 minutes
Serves 6

750 g (1½ lb) boned lamb shoulder, cubed
¾ cup (90 g/3 oz) plain flour, seasoned
2 tablespoons olive oil
200 g (6½ oz) bacon, finely chopped
2 cloves garlic, chopped
4 large leeks, sliced
1 large carrot, chopped
2 large potatoes, diced
1¼ cups (315 ml/10 fl oz) beef stock
1 bay leaf
2 teaspoons chopped fresh parsley
375 g (12 oz) quick flaky pastry
1 egg, lightly beaten, to glaze

1 Toss the meat in the flour. Heat the oil in a large frying pan over medium heat and brown the meat in batches for 4–5 minutes, then remove from the pan. Cook the bacon in the pan for 3 minutes. Add the garlic and leek and cook for 5 minutes, or until soft.
2 Put the meat in a large saucepan, add the leek and bacon, carrot, potato, stock and bay leaf and bring to the boil, then reduce the heat, cover and simmer for 30 minutes. Uncover and simmer for 1 hour, or until the meat is cooked and the liquid has thickened. Season to taste. Remove the bay leaf, stir in the parsley and set aside to cool.
3 Preheat the oven to 200°C (400°F/ Gas 6). Place the filling in an 18 cm (7 inch) pie dish. Roll out the pastry between two sheets of baking paper until large enough to cover the pie. Trim the edges and pinch to seal.
4 Decorate the pie with pastry trimmings. Cut two slits in the top for steam to escape. Brush with egg and bake for 45 minutes, or until the pastry is crisp and golden.

NUTRITION PER SERVE
Protein 42 g; Fat 28 g; Carbohydrate 43 g; Dietary Fibre 5 g; Cholesterol 147 mg; 2465 kJ (590 cal)

Cook the filling until the liquid has thickened and then remove the bay leaf.

Cut out shapes from the pastry trimmings to decorate the pie.

CABBAGE ROLLS

Preparation time: 30 minutes
Total cooking time: 1 hour 35 minutes
Makes 12 large rolls

1 tablespoon olive oil
1 onion, finely chopped
large pinch allspice
1 teaspoon ground cumin
large pinch ground nutmeg
2 bay leaves
1 large head of cabbage
500 g (1 lb) lamb mince
1 cup (220 g/7 oz) short-grain
    white rice
4 cloves garlic, crushed
⅓ cup (50 g/1¾ oz) toasted pine nuts
2 tablespoons finely chopped fresh
    mint
2 tablespoons finely chopped fresh
    flat-leaf parsley
1 tablespoon finely chopped raisins
1 cup (250 ml/8 fl oz) olive oil, extra
⅓ cup (80 ml/2¾ fl oz) lemon juice
extra virgin olive oil, to drizzle
lemon wedges, to serve

1 Heat the oil in a saucepan, add the onion and cook over medium heat for 10 minutes, or until golden. Add the allspice, cumin and nutmeg, and cook for 2 minutes, or until fragrant. Remove from the pan.
2 Bring a very large saucepan of water to the boil and add the bay leaves. Remove the tough outer leaves and about 5 cm (2 inch) of the core from the cabbage with a sharp knife, then place the cabbage into the boiling water. Cook for 5 minutes, then carefully loosen a whole leaf with tongs and remove. Continue to cook and remove the leaves until you reach the core. Drain, reserving the cooking liquid, and set aside to cool.
3 Take 12 equal-size leaves and cut a small 'v' from the core end of each leaf to remove the thickest part, then trim the firm central veins so that the leaf is as flat as possible. Place three-quarters of the remaining leaves into a very large saucepan to prevent the rolls catching on the base.
4 Combine the mince, onion mixture, rice, garlic, pine nuts, mint, parsley and raisins in a bowl, and season

well. With the core end of the leaf closest to you, shape 2 tablespoons of the mince mixture into an oval and place in the centre of the leaf. Roll up, tucking in the sides to enclose the filling. Repeat with the other 11 leaves and filling. Place the rolls tightly in a single layer in the saucepan, seam-side-down.
5 Combine 2½ cups (625 ml/20 fl oz) of the cooking liquid with the extra olive oil, lemon juice and 1 teaspoon salt, and pour over the rolls (the

liquid should just cover the rolls). Top with the remaining leaves. Cover and bring to the boil, then reduce the heat and simmer for 1 hour 15 minutes, or until the filling is cooked. Remove from the pan and drizzle with extra virgin olive oil. Serve with lemon wedges.

NUTRITION PER ROLL
Protein 13 g; Fat 26 g; Carbohydrate 20 g;
Dietary Fibre 4 g; Cholesterol 28 mg;
1510 kJ (360 Cal)

Cook the cabbage in boiling water and remove the outer leaves as they cook.

Roll up the cabbage leaf, tucking in the sides, to enclose the filling.

LAMB SHANK PIE

Preparation time: 30 minutes + 2 hours chilling
Total cooking time: 3 hours 10 minutes
Serves 6

8 lamb shanks
½ cup (60 g/2 oz) plain flour
2 tablespoons olive oil
4 red onions, quartered
8 cloves garlic, peeled
1 cup (250 ml/8 fl oz) red wine
1 litre beef stock
2 tablespoons finely chopped fresh rosemary
6 whole black peppercorns
¼ cup (30 g/1 oz) cornflour
375 g (12 oz) puff pastry
1 egg, lightly beaten

1 Preheat the oven to 220°C (425°F/ Gas 7). Lightly dust the shanks with flour, shaking off the excess. Heat the oil in a large frying pan and cook the shanks for 2 minutes each side, or until well browned. Transfer to a deep roasting tin and add the onion, garlic, wine, stock, rosemary and pepper-corns. Cover and bake for 1 hour.

2 Stir the mixture, uncover and return to the oven for 1 hour 10 minutes, stirring occasionally, until the meat falls off the bones.

3 Remove the lamb bones with tongs. Mix the cornflour with 2 tablespoons water, then stir into the tin. Return to the oven for 10 minutes, or until thickened. Transfer to a large bowl, cool, then refrigerate for at least 2 hours, or overnight.

4 Preheat the oven to moderate 180°C (350°F/Gas 4). Grease a 23 cm (9 inch) pie plate with a rim. Spoon in the filling. Roll the pastry out between two sheets of baking paper until a little wider than the plate. Cut a 2 cm (¾ inch) strip around the edge of the pastry, brush with water and place damp-side-down on the rim. Cover with the pastry circle, pressing down on the edges. Use the back of a knife to make small slashes around the edge. Trim, then re-roll the scraps to decorate. Brush with egg and bake for 45 minutes, or until the pastry is golden and has risen.

NUTRITION PER SERVE
Protein 50 g; Fat 24 g; Carbohydrate 47 g; Dietary Fibre 3 g; Cholesterol 157 mg; 2625 kJ (630 cal)

Cook the lamb shanks until the meat is so tender it is falling off the bones.

Stir the cornflour mixture into the tin and continue cooking until the sauce thickens.

MOUSSAKA (LAMB AND EGGPLANT BAKE)

Preparation time: 20 minutes
+ 40 minutes standing
Total cooking time: 1 hour 50 minutes
Serves 6

2 large ripe tomatoes
1.5 kg (3 lb) eggplant, cut into 5 mm
    (¼ inch) slices
½ cup (125 ml/4 fl oz) light olive oil
1 tablespoon olive oil
2 onions, finely chopped
2 large cloves garlic, crushed
½ teaspoon ground allspice
1¼ teaspoons ground cinnamon
750 g (1½ lb) lamb mince
2 tablespoons tomato paste
½ cup (125 ml/4 fl oz) white wine
3 tablespoons chopped fresh
    flat-leaf parsley

WHITE SAUCE
50 g (1¾ oz) butter
½ cup (60 g/2 oz) plain flour
600 ml (20 fl oz) milk
pinch ground nutmeg
⅓ cup (35 g/1¼ oz) finely grated
    kefalotyri or Parmesan
2 eggs, lightly beaten

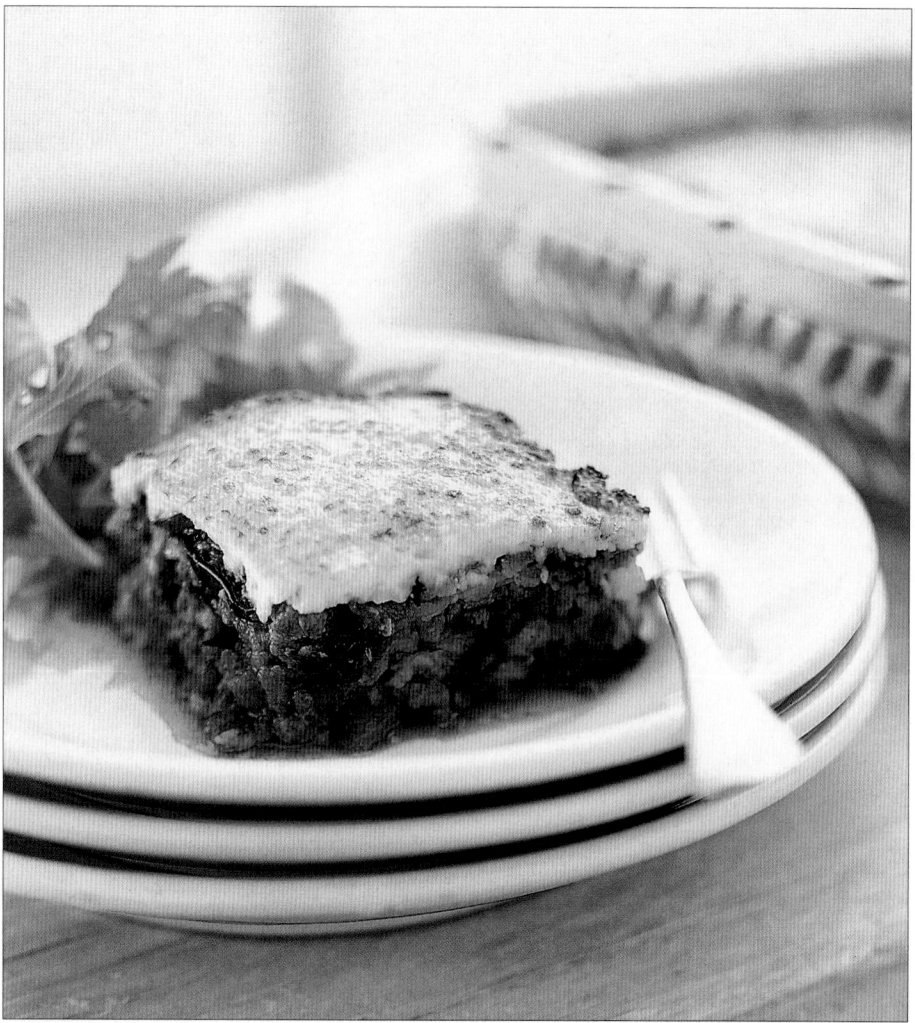

1 Preheat the oven to moderate 180°C (350°F/Gas 4). Cut a cross in the base of each tomato. Place in boiling water for 1 minute, then plunge into cold water and peel away from the cross. Roughly chop. Lay the eggplant on a tray, sprinkle with salt and leave for 30 minutes. Rinse and pat dry.
2 Heat 2 tablespoons olive oil in a frying pan, and cook the eggplant in 4–5 batches for 1–2 minutes each side, or until golden and soft. Add more oil as needed.
3 Heat the olive oil in a saucepan, add the onion and cook over medium heat for 5 minutes. Add the garlic, allspice and cinnamon, and cook for 30 seconds. Add the mince and cook for 5 minutes, or until browned, breaking up any lumps. Add the tomato, tomato paste and wine, and simmer over low heat for 30 minutes, or until the liquid has evaporated. Stir in the parsley and season to taste.

4 Meanwhile, to make the white sauce, melt the butter in a saucepan over medium heat. Add the flour and cook for 1 minute. Remove from the heat and gradually stir in the milk and nutmeg. Return to the heat and simmer for 2 minutes. Add 1 tablespoon of the cheese and stir well. Stir in the egg just before using.
5 Line the base of a 3 litre 25 cm x 30 cm (10 inch x 12 inch) ovenproof dish with a third of the eggplant. Spoon on half the meat and cover

with a second layer of eggplant. Spoon on the remaining meat and cover with the remaining eggplant. Spread the white sauce over the top and sprinkle with the remaining cheese. Bake for 1 hour, then leave for 10 minutes before slicing.

NUTRITION PER SERVE
Protein 34 g; Fat 47 g; Carbohydrate 15 g;
Dietary Fibre 7 g; Cholesterol 173 mg;
2609 kJ (623 Cal)

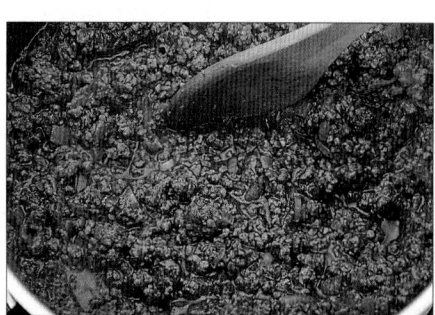

Cook the tomato and mince mixture until the liquid has evaporated.

Pour the white sauce over the final layer of eggplant.

GRILLED LAMB PITTAS WITH FRESH MINT SALAD

**Preparation time: 20 minutes +
  30 minutes refrigeration
Total cooking time: 15 minutes
Serves 4**

1 kg (2 lb) lean minced lamb
1 cup (60 g/2 oz) finely chopped fresh
  flat-leaf parsley
½ cup (25 g/¾ oz) finely chopped fresh
  mint
1 onion, finely chopped
1 clove garlic, crushed
1 egg
1 teaspoon chilli sauce
4 small wholemeal pitta pockets

MINT SALAD
3 small vine-ripened tomatoes
1 small red onion, finely sliced
1 cup (20 g/¾ oz) fresh mint
1 tablespoon olive oil
2 tablespoons lemon juice

1 Place the lamb, parsley, mint,
onion, garlic, egg and chilli sauce in a
large bowl and mix together well.
Shape into eight small patties. Chill
for 30 minutes. Preheat the oven to
warm 160°C (315°F/Gas 2–3).
2 To make the mint salad, slice the
tomatoes into thin rings and place
in a bowl with the onion, mint, olive
oil and lemon juice. Season well with
salt and freshly ground black pepper.
Gently toss to coat.

3 Wrap the pitta breads in foil and
warm in the oven for 5–10 minutes.
4 Heat a chargrill or hot plate and
brush with a little oil. When very hot,
cook the patties for 3 minutes on
each side. Do not turn until a nice
crust has formed on the base or they
will fall apart when you move them.
5 Remove the pitta breads from the
oven. Cut the pockets in half, fill each
half with some mint salad and a lamb
patty. Serve with some low-fat
yoghurt, if desired.

NUTRITION PER SERVE
PROTEIN 59 G; FAT 24 G; CARBOHYDRATE
29 G; DIETARY FIBRE 8 G; CHOLESTEROL
211 MG; 2390 KJ (570 CAL)

Mix the lamb, herbs, onion, garlic, egg and chilli
sauce together with your hands.

Toss together the tomato and onion slices, mint,
oil and lemon juice.

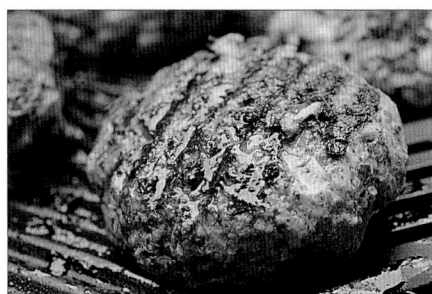

Chargrill the patties on a lightly oiled surface until
a crust has formed.

LAMB BACKSTRAPS ON EGGPLANT MASH AND OLIVE SALSA

Preparation time: 45 minutes +
overnight refrigeration +
10 minutes resting
Total cooking time: 3 hours
Serves 4

2 tablespoons lemon juice
2 teaspoons ground cumin
½ cup (125 ml/4 fl oz) olive oil
4 lamb backstraps or loin fillets
    (200 g/6½ oz each), trimmed
1 kg lamb bones
1 onion, chopped
3 cloves garlic, peeled and bruised
1 carrot, chopped
1 celery stick, chopped
1 bay leaf
1 cup (250 ml/8 oz) white wine
2½ tablespoons ground cumin, extra
2 large eggplants
500 g (1 lb) desiree potatoes
2 teaspoons tahini
¼ teaspoon sesame oil
3 cloves garlic, crushed, extra

OLIVE SALSA
⅔ cup (12 g/¼ oz) fresh mint, finely
    chopped
2 tablespoons finely chopped pitted
    black olives
2 tablespoons finely diced red
    capsicum
1 tablespoon sesame seeds, toasted
1 tablespoon finely chopped red onion

1 To make the marinade, put the lemon juice, cumin and 2 tablespoons of the olive oil in a flat non-metallic, shallow dish and mix together. Add the lamb backstraps and stir to coat them well. Cover and refrigerate overnight.
2 Preheat the oven to hot 220°C (425°F/Gas 7). Pour 1 tablespoon of the remaining oil into a very large saucepan over medium heat, add the lamb bones and cook for a few minutes, or until well browned. Add the onion, garlic, carrot, celery, bay leaf, wine and extra cumin to the pan and stir well. Cover with cold water and bring to the boil, then reduce the heat and simmer for 2 hours,

skimming off any scum that forms on the surface. Remove the bones, then strain the stock through a fine sieve into a smaller saucepan and leave off the heat for 10 minutes, then remove any fat that has settled on top. Simmer for an hour, or until the sauce thickens slightly—you should have about ⅓ cup (80 ml/2¾ fl oz) sauce. Remove from the heat, season to taste, cover and keep warm.
3 Meanwhile, prick the eggplants all over with a fork, then place in a roasting tin and bake for 45 minutes, or until they are quite wrinkled. Remove from the oven and place in a colander over a bowl to catch any bitter juices. Reduce the oven temperature to moderately hot 190°C (375°F/Gas 5). When the eggplants are cool enough to handle comfortably, cut them in half and carefully scoop out the flesh. Process the flesh in a food processor until smooth.
4 Roughly chop the potatoes, then place them in a saucepan. Cover the potato with cold water, then bring to the boil and cook for 12 minutes, or until soft. Drain well, then add the tahini, sesame oil, extra garlic and 2 tablespoons of the remaining olive oil. Mash well, then season to taste with salt and cracked black pepper. Stir in the eggplant purée.

5 To make the olive salsa, combine all the ingredients in a bowl and season to taste.
6 Heat the remaining oil in a large heavy-based frying pan over high heat, then add the lamb backstraps in batches, spacing them well apart. Cook each side for 2 minutes. Remove from the pan and place in a roasting tin in the oven for 5 minutes for a medium-rare result, or until cooked to your liking. Remove from the oven, cover with foil and rest for 10 minutes. Reheat the mash if needed.
7 To serve, place a large spoonful of the eggplant mash on each plate. Drain any juices from the rested lamb into the sauce and bring to a simmer. Slice the very ends off each backstrap, then cut on a slight angle into thin slices. Overlap the slices on the mash and top with one quarter of the olive salsa. Drizzle the sauce around the edge of the plate.

NUTRITION PER SERVE
Protein 50 g; Fat 40 g; Carbohydrate 25 g;
Dietary Fibre 9 g; Cholesterol 132 mg;
2927 kJ (699 Cal)

Cook the lamb bones until they are well browned all over.

Simmer the sauce until it has reduced and thickened slightly.

Cut the cooled eggplant in half and scoop out the flesh.

Stir the eggplant purée through the potato mash until they are evenly combined.

LAMB BURGER WITH WEDGES

Preparation time: 30 minutes
Total cooking time: 1 hour
Serves 4

1 red capsicum
1 yellow capsicum
1 green capsicum
400 g (13 oz) baking potatoes
  (pontiac or desiree)
garlic oil spray
300 g (10 oz) lean lamb mince
2 teaspoons chopped fresh thyme
2 tablespoons chopped fresh parsley
2 tomatoes (140 g/4½ oz), seeded and
  finely chopped
1 large onion, finely chopped
⅓ cup (25 g/¾ oz) fresh breadcrumbs
1 egg white, lightly beaten
4 slices low-fat cheese
1 large red onion, thinly sliced
2 teaspoons olive oil
4 hamburger buns
40 g (1¼ oz) rocket

1 Cut the capsicums into quarters and remove the membranes and seeds. Grill, skin-side up, until the skin blackens and blisters. Place in a bowl and cover with plastic wrap. When cool enough to handle, peel off the skin and cut the capsicums into strips.

2 Preheat the oven to moderately hot 200°C (400°F/Gas 6). Line a baking tray with foil. Cut the potatoes into medium wedges. Spray well with the oil spray, then season and toss. Lay out evenly on the baking tray. Bake for 40 minutes, or until crisp and golden, turning once.

3 Meanwhile, combine the mince, thyme, parsley, tomato, onion, breadcrumbs, egg white and 1 teaspoon ground black pepper. Form into four even-sized patties. Heat a non-stick frying pan over medium heat and cook the patties on each side for 5 minutes, or until cooked. Put a slice of cheese on top to melt slightly. Remove from the pan. Cook the onion in the olive oil for 4–5 minutes over medium heat until softened a little. Cut the buns in half and toast each side until crisp.

4 To assemble, layer the bun with a little rocket, the patty with cheese, onion, one strip each of red, yellow and green capsicum, and top with more rocket and the top of the bun. Cut in half and serve with wedges.

NUTRITION PER SERVE
Protein 34.5 g; Fat 14 g; Carbohydrate 52 g; Dietary Fibre 5.5 g; Cholesterol 65.5 mg; 1995 kJ (475 Cal)

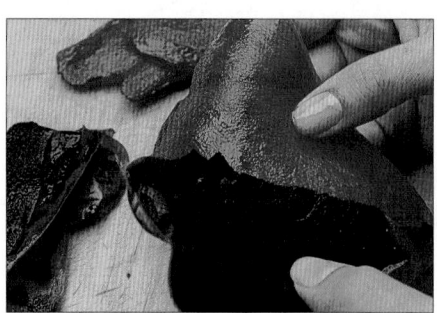

Peel the blackened and blistered skin from the capsicum.

Using your hands, form the mince mixture into even-sized patties.

SOUVLAKE (SKEWERED LAMB)

Preparation time: 20 minutes
  + overnight marinating
  + 30 minutes standing
Total cooking time: 10 minutes
Serves 4

1 kg (2 lb) boned leg lamb, trimmed,
    cut into 2 cm (¾ inch) cubes
¼ cup (60 ml/2 fl oz) olive oil
2 teaspoons finely grated lemon rind
⅓ cup (80 ml/2¾ fl oz) lemon juice
2 teaspoons dried oregano
½ cup (125 ml/4 fl oz) dry white wine

2 large cloves garlic, finely chopped
2 fresh bay leaves
1 cup (250 g/8 oz) Greek-style plain
    yoghurt
2 cloves garlic, crushed, extra

1 Place the lamb in a non-metallic bowl with 2 tablespoons of the olive oil, the lemon rind and juice, oregano, wine, garlic and bay leaves. Season with black pepper and toss to coat. Cover and refrigerate overnight.
2 Place the yoghurt and extra garlic in a bowl, mix together well and leave for 30 minutes.
3 Drain the lamb and pat dry. Thread onto 8 skewers and cook on a

barbecue or chargrill plate, brushing with the remaining oil, for 8 minutes, or until brown on the outside and still a little rare in the middle. Drizzle with the garlic yoghurt and serve with warm pitta bread and a salad.

NUTRITION PER SERVE
Protein 43 g; Fat 20 g; Carbohydrate 4 g;
Dietary Fibre 0 g; Cholesterol 126 mg;
1660 kJ (397 Cal)

NOTE: If using wooden skewers, soak them in water for 30 minutes to prevent burning during cooking.

Toss the lamb to coat well with the spicy marinade.

Pat the drained lamb dry and thread onto eight skewers.

Brush the remaining oil over the lamb skewers during cooking.

MOROCCAN LAMB PIE

Preparation time: 30 minutes + cooling
Total cooking time: 2 hours 40 minutes
Serves 6–8

3 tablespoons olive oil
2 onions, finely chopped
4 cloves garlic, crushed
1¼ teaspoons ground cinnamon
1¼ teaspoons ground cumin
1¼ teaspoons ground coriander
½ teaspoon ground ginger
large pinch of cayenne pepper
1.2 kg (2 lb 7 oz) boned lamb leg, cut
    into small cubes
1½ cups (375 ml/12 fl oz) chicken stock
2 teaspoons grated lemon rind
1 tablespoon lemon juice
2 carrots, cut into small cubes
⅓ cup (60 g/2 oz) ground almonds
½ cup (30 g/1 oz) chopped fresh
    coriander
500 g (1 lb) puff pastry
1 egg, lightly beaten

1 Heat the oil in a large saucepan.
Add the onion, garlic, cinnamon,
cumin, ground coriander, ginger and
cayenne pepper and cook, stirring,
over medium heat for 30–40 seconds.
Add the lamb and stir until coated in
the spices. Add the stock, lemon rind
and lemon juice and cook, covered,
over low heat for 45 minutes.
2 Add the carrot, cover and simmer
for another 45 minutes, or until the
lamb is tender. Stir in the almonds,
increase the heat and boil for
30 minutes, or until the sauce
becomes very thick. Stir in the fresh
coriander, season and leave to cool.
3 Preheat the oven to 200°C (400°F/
Gas 6) and heat a baking tray. Grease
a 20 cm (8 inch) pie dish. Roll out the
pastry to a 40 cm (16 inch) round and
neaten the edge with a sharp knife.
Line the dish with the pastry, leaving
the rest overhanging the edge.
4 Spoon the filling into the dish,
levelling the surface. Fold the
overhanging pastry over the filling,
forming loose pleats. Using kitchen
scissors, cut out Vs of pastry where it
falls into deep folds towards the
middle. This reduces the thickness so
that the pastry can bake evenly.

5 Brush with egg and bake on the
hot tray in the centre of the oven for
20 minutes. Reduce the oven to
moderate 180°C (350°F/Gas 4), cover
the pie with foil and bake for another
20 minutes.

NUTRITION PER SERVE (8)
Protein 39 g; Fat 31 g; Carbohydrate 26 g;
Dietary Fibre 3 g; Cholesterol 115 mg;
2230 kJ (535 cal)

Boil the lamb mixture for 30 minutes, or until the
sauce becomes very thick.

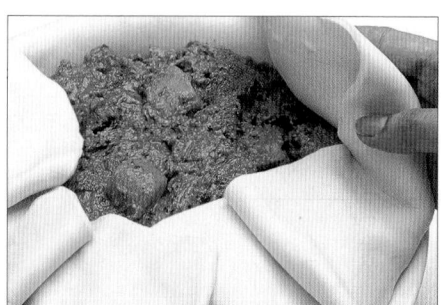
Fold the overhanging pastry up and over the
filling, in loose pleats.

BALTI-STYLE LAMB

Preparation time: 15 minutes
Total cooking time: 1 hour 25 minutes
Serves 4

1 kg (2 lb) lamb leg steaks, cut into
    3 cm (1¼ inch) cubes
1 tablespoon Balti masala paste
2 tablespoons ghee or oil
3 cloves garlic, crushed
1 tablespoon garam masala
1 large onion, finely chopped
4 tablespoons Balti masala paste,
    extra
2 tablespoons chopped fresh
    coriander leaves
fresh coriander leaves, extra,
    to garnish

1 Preheat the oven to moderately hot 190°C (375°F/Gas 5). Place the meat, masala paste and 1½ cups (375 ml/12 fl oz) boiling water in a 4 litre ovenproof casserole dish, and combine. Cook, covered, in the oven for 30–40 minutes, or until almost cooked through. Drain, reserving the stock.

2 Heat the ghee in a wok, add the garlic and garam masala, and stir-fry over medium heat for 1 minute. Add the onion and cook for 5–7 minutes, or until the onion is soft and golden brown. Increase the heat, add the extra masala paste and the lamb. Cook for 5 minutes to brown the meat. Slowly add the reserved stock and simmer over low heat, stirring occasionally, for 15 minutes.

3 Add the chopped coriander leaves and 1 cup (250 ml/8 fl oz) water and simmer for 15 minutes, or until the meat is tender and the sauce has thickened slightly. Season with salt and ground black pepper. Garnish with the extra coriander leaves and serve with roti or naan bread.

NUTRITION PER SERVE
Protein 58 g; Fat 8.5 g; Carbohydrate 3.5 g;
Dietary Fibre 1 g; Cholesterol 167 mg;
1368 kJ (327 Cal)

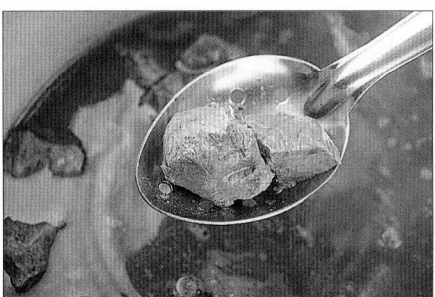

Cook the meat until almost cooked through, then drain, reserving the liquid.

Cook the onion over medium heat until soft and golden brown.

Simmer until the meat is tender and the sauce has thickened slightly.

LAMB CUTLETS WITH PARMESAN POLENTA AND RATATOUILLE

**Preparation time: 25 minutes +
  10 minutes cooling
Total cooking time: 2 hours 35 minutes
Serves 4**

1 kg (2 lb) lamb bones
1 onion, chopped
1 large carrot, chopped
1 celery stick, chopped
1 bay leaf
1 teaspoon black peppercorns
4 cloves garlic, peeled and bruised
6 Roma tomatoes, chopped
1 cup (250 ml/8 fl oz) red wine
2 cups (500 ml/16 fl oz) sherry
4 sprigs fresh thyme
1 red onion
1 eggplant
1 small red capsicum
1 small green capsicum
1 small yellow capsicum
1 zucchini
1 tablespoon finely chopped fresh
  thyme
2 tablespoons olive oil
1 litre chicken stock
1 cup (170 g/5½ oz) instant polenta
40 g (1¼ oz) butter
½ cup (50 g/1¾ oz) finely grated
  Parmesan
2 tablespoons olive oil, for pan-frying,
  extra
12 lamb cutlets
2 tablespoons finely chopped parsley

1 Cook the lamb bones in a saucepan over medium heat, stirring occasionally, for 5 minutes, or until browned. Add the onion, carrot, celery, bay leaf, peppercorns, garlic, tomato, wine, sherry, thyme and 1 litre cold water. Bring to the boil, then reduce the heat and simmer for 2 hours, skimming off any scum. Remove the bones, then strain into a saucepan and simmer for 30 minutes, or until thickened—you should have about ¾ cup (185 ml/6 fl oz) sauce. Cover and keep warm.

2 Meanwhile, preheat the oven to moderately hot 200°C (400°F/Gas 6). To make the ratatouille, cut the onion, eggplant, capsicums and zucchini into 1.5 cm (⅝ inch) cubes and combine in a large roasting tin. Add the thyme and drizzle with the oil. Season, then spread in a single layer. Roast, stirring occasionally, for 30–35 minutes, or until just cooked and starting to brown. Remove from the oven and cover with foil. Reduce the heat to moderate 180°C (350°F/Gas 4).

3 While the ratatouille is cooking, bring the chicken stock to the boil, then slowly pour in the polenta, stirring constantly. Cook, stirring, for 8–10 minutes, or until the polenta is smooth and thick. Stir in the butter and Parmesan. Season and keep warm.

4 Heat 1 tablespoon of the extra olive oil in a frying pan over high heat and sear the cutlets in batches for 1 minute each side, then place in a single layer in a roasting tin. Bake for 4–5 minutes for a medium-rare result. Remove from the oven, cover and rest for 10 minutes. If necessary, reheat the ratatouille in the oven for 5 minutes. Stir in the parsley just before serving.

5 To serve, dollop polenta onto each plate, top with three cutlets and some ratatouille. Drizzle with the sauce.

NUTRITION PER SERVE
Protein 35 g; Fat 39 g; Carbohydrate 42 g;
Dietary Fibre 8 g; Cholesterol 105 mg;
3466 kJ (828 Cal)

Cook the lamb bones until they are well browned all over.

Simmer the liquid, skimming off any scum that forms on top.

Simmer the strained liquid in a clean saucepan until just thickened.

Toss the vegetables, thyme and oil together, then cook until just browned.

Cook the polenta, stirring constantly, until it is smooth and thick.

Sear the lamb cutlets in batches for 1 minute each side.

ROSEMARY LAMB COBBLER

Preparation time: 30 minutes
Total cooking time: 2 hours
Serves 4–6

600 g (1¼ lb) boned lamb leg, cut into
    small chunks
¼ cup (30 g/1 oz) plain flour, seasoned
30 g (1 oz) butter
2 tablespoons olive oil
8 spring onions, chopped
3 cloves garlic, crushed
2 cups (500 ml/16 fl oz) beef stock
1 cup (250 ml/8 fl oz) dry white wine
2 teaspoons wholegrain mustard
2 teaspoons finely chopped
    fresh rosemary
2 celery sticks, sliced
1 teaspoon grated lemon rind
1 teaspoon lemon juice
½ cup (125 g/4 oz) sour cream

COBBLER TOPPING
¾ cup (185 ml/6 fl oz) milk
1 egg
2 tablespoons melted butter
1½ cups (185 g/6 oz) plain flour
2 teaspoons baking powder
1 teaspoon finely chopped
    fresh rosemary
2 tablespoons finely chopped
    fresh flat-leaf parsley

1 Put the lamb pieces and flour in a plastic bag and shake well to evenly coat the lamb. Shake off any excess.
2 Heat the butter and 1 tablespoon of the olive oil in a large saucepan over high heat, then cook half the lamb for 5 minutes, or until well browned. Add the remaining oil if needed and cook the remaining lamb.
3 Add half the spring onion to the pan with the garlic and cook for 30 seconds, or until the spring onion is softened. Return all the lamb to the pan with the stock, wine, mustard, rosemary, celery, lemon rind and juice and bring to the boil. Reduce the heat and simmer, stirring occasionally, for 1¼ hours, or until the lamb is tender and the sauce has thickened.
4 Remove from the heat and stir a little of the sauce into the sour cream, then stir it all back into the lamb mixture with the remaining spring onion. Leave to cool while you make the topping.
5 Preheat the oven to 190°C (375°F/ Gas 5). To make the topping, combine the milk, egg and melted butter in a large bowl. Add the combined sifted flour and baking powder with the herbs, 1 teaspoon salt and some cracked black pepper and stir until you have a thick, sticky batter—you may need to add a little more flour if it is too wet, or milk if it is too dry.
6 Spoon the lamb into a deep 18 cm (7 inch) pie dish and, using two spoons, cover the top with small dollops of the batter, leaving a little space for spreading. Cook for 30 minutes, or until the topping is risen and golden.

NUTRITION PER SERVE (6)
Protein 31 g; Fat 28 g; Carbohydrate 31 g;
Dietary Fibre 2.5 g; Cholesterol 153 mg;
2180 kJ (520 cal)

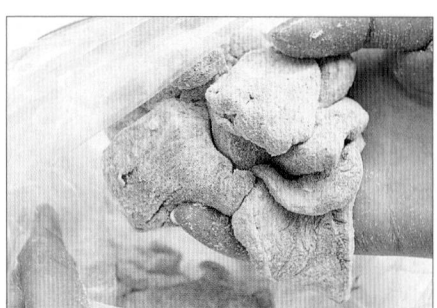
Put the lamb and flour in a plastic bag and shake until the meat is lightly covered.

Cook the lamb in two batches in a large saucepan until it is nicely browned.

Simmer the mixture until the meat is tender and the sauce has thickened.

Stir a little of the meaty sauce into the sour cream.

Stir the batter for the cobbler topping until it is thick and sticky.

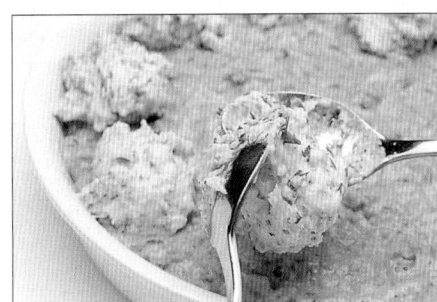

Add spoonfuls of the batter to the top of the pie, leaving a little room for spreading.

LAMB CUTLETS WITH BEETROOT, BEAN AND POTATO SALAD

Preparation time: 15 minutes + overnight refrigeration
Total cooking time: 45 minutes
Serves 4

2 cloves garlic, crushed
2 tablespoons finely chopped fresh thyme
1½ tablespoons lemon juice
1 tablespoon walnut oil
2 tablespoons extra virgin olive oil
12 lamb cutlets, trimmed
6 baby beetroots, trimmed
500 g (1 lb) kipfler potatoes, unpeeled
250 g (8 oz) baby green beans
2 tablespoons olive oil

DRESSING
1 clove garlic, crushed
3½ tablespoons lemon juice
⅓ cup (80 ml/2¾ fl oz) extra virgin olive oil
1 tablespoon walnut oil
¼ cup (30 g/1 oz) chopped walnuts

1 Combine the garlic, thyme, lemon juice, walnut oil and extra virgin olive oil in a shallow, non-metallic dish, add the cutlets and toss well. Cover with plastic wrap and refrigerate overnight.
2 Cook the beetroots in boiling water for 20 minutes, or until tender. Drain. Meanwhile, cook the potatoes in lightly salted boiling water for 12 minutes, or until tender. Drain.
3 When cool enough to handle, peel the beetroots and potatoes. Cut each beetroot into six wedges and thickly slice the potatoes.
4 Cook the beans in lightly salted boiling water for 4 minutes. Drain, refresh under cold water, then drain

again. Pat dry with paper towels.
5 Heat the olive oil in a large frying pan over high heat and cook the cutlets in batches for 4–5 minutes, or until cooked to your liking, turning once.
6 Whisk the garlic, lemon juice, extra virgin olive oil and walnut oil in a large bowl. Add the potatoes, beans and walnuts and toss gently. Season and arrange over the beetroot. Top with the cutlets and serve.

NUTRITION PER SERVE
Protein 30 g; Fat 55 g; Carbohydrate 25 g; Dietary Fibre 6.5 g; Cholesterol 70 mg; 2990 kJ (714 Cal)

Peel the beetroots and cut each one into six wedges.

Cook the cutlets in batches until done to your liking.

LAMB NECK CURRY

Preparation time: 30 minutes
Total cooking time: 1 hour 35 minutes
Serves 4–6

1 tablespoon oil
8 best lamb neck chops (see NOTE)
2 onions, sliced
3 cloves garlic, finely chopped
2 teaspoons finely chopped fresh
  ginger
1 small green chilli, seeded and finely
  chopped
½ teaspoon ground cumin
1 teaspoon ground fennel
1½ teaspoons ground turmeric
1½ teaspoons chilli powder
2 teaspoons garam masala
1 star anise
1 cinnamon stick
5 curry leaves
2 bay leaves
2 cups (500 ml/16 fl oz) beef stock
8 tomatoes, peeled and quartered

1 Heat the oil in a large frying pan, add the lamb and cook in batches for 5–8 minutes, or until browned. Place in a large saucepan.

2 Add the onion to the frying pan and cook, stirring frequently, for 5 minutes, or until soft and browned. Stir in the garlic, ginger and green chilli and cook for 1 minute. Then stir in the cumin, fennel, turmeric, chilli powder, garam masala, star anise, cinnamon stick, curry leaves and bay leaves, and cook, stirring to prevent sticking, for a further 1 minute.

3 Add 2 tablespoons cold water to the frying pan, mix well, and then add the beef stock. Bring to the boil, then pour over the lamb. Stir in the tomato, reduce the heat and simmer, covered, for 1 hour 15 minutes. Serve with jasmine rice tossed with coriander.

NUTRITION PER SERVE (6)
Protein 17 g; Fat 7 g; Carbohydrate 5 g; Dietary Fibre 5 g; Cholesterol 48 mg; 658 kJ (157 Cal)

NOTE: Best lamb neck chops come from the meat just under the shoulder and are sweeter, leaner and meatier than lamb neck.

Cook the lamb neck chops in batches until browned.

Stir the spices to prevent them sticking to the base of the pan.

INDIAN-STYLE SPICY LAMB AND APRICOT PIE

**Preparation time: 40 minutes +
20 minutes refrigeration + cooling
Total cooking time: 2 hours 45 minutes
Serves 8–10**

2½ cups (310 g/10 oz) plain flour
160 g (5½ oz) ghee, chilled and cut
    into small pieces
1 teaspoon cumin seeds
1 teaspoon sugar
3–6 tablespoons iced water

FILLING
1.4 kg (2 lb 13 oz) boned lamb
    shoulder, cubed (see NOTES)
1 cup (250 g/8 oz) natural yoghurt
2 teaspoons garam masala
1½ tablespoons grated fresh ginger
1 teaspoon chilli powder
2 teaspoons ghee
2 onions, sliced
3 cloves garlic, crushed
1 long fresh green chilli, finely
    chopped
6 cardamom pods, crushed
1 teaspoon ground coriander
2 teaspoons ground cumin
2 x 425 g (14 oz) cans crushed
    tomatoes
100 g (3½ oz) dried apricots, halved,
    soaked in 1 cup (250 ml/8 fl oz)
    warm water
½ cup (125 g/4 oz) thick natural
    yoghurt, to serve

1 To make the pastry, sift the flour into a food processor and add the ghee, cumin seeds, sugar and 1 teaspoon salt. Process until mixture resembles fine breadcrumbs, then gradually add the water until the pastry comes together in beads. Do not over-process. Gently gather dough together into a ball, place on a lightly floured surface and press into a disc. Refrigerate for 20 minutes.

2 Combine the lamb, yoghurt, garam masala, ginger, chilli powder and ½ teaspoon salt in a large bowl.

3 Heat the ghee in a large saucepan, add the onion and cook over medium heat for 10 minutes, or until soft and golden. Add the garlic and fresh chilli and cook for 1 minute, then add the remaining spices and cook for another minute.

4 Add the lamb and yoghurt mixture to the pan and cook, stirring often, until combined. Add the tomato, bring to the boil, reduce the heat and simmer for 1¼ hours, then add the apricots and simmer for another 15 minutes, or until the lamb is tender. Set aside to cool.

5 Preheat the oven to 220°C (425°F/ Gas 7). Preheat a baking tray. Grease a deep 23 cm (9 inch) fluted tart tin or pie dish. Roll out two-thirds of the pastry between two sheets of baking paper until large enough to fit the tin. Remove the top sheet of paper and invert the pastry into the tin. Fill the pastry shell with the lamb curry. Brush the edges with a little water. Roll out the remaining pastry between the sheets of baking paper until large enough to cover the top of the pie dish. Position the lid on top of the filling. Make two or three slits for the steam to escape, then trim the pastry edges with a sharp knife.

6 Place the pie on the heated baking tray and bake on the lowest shelf for 30 minutes. Move to the centre shelf and bake for another 30 minutes, or until brown. Leave for 10 minutes before slicing. Serve with a dollop of thick yoghurt.

NUTRITION PER SERVE (10)
Protein 19 g; Fat 21 g; Carbohydrate 34 g;
Dietary Fibre 4 g; Cholesterol 94 mg;
1660 kJ (395 cal)

NOTES: Ask your butcher to bone the lamb shoulder for you.
Because of the ghee content in the pastry for this pie, it is very difficult to make successfully by hand. It is better to use a food processor as described in the recipe. The filling mixture may seem a little runny when ready to go in the pie, but once it is cooked the sauce thickens.

Gently gather the dough together into a ball and place on a lightly floured surface.

Add the spices to the onion mixture and cook for another minute.

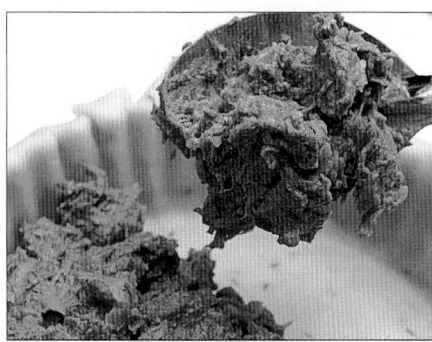

Spoon the lamb curry mixture into the pastry shell. The filling will thicken when baked.

Make steam holes on top of the pie and trim the pastry edges with a sharp knife.

LAMB WITH MIXED GREENS

Preparation time: 10 minutes
Total cooking time: 15 minutes
Serves 4

500 g (1 lb) lamb fillets, cut into strips
    about 2.5 cm (1 inch) wide
1 egg white, lightly beaten
1 tablespoon cornflour
2–3 tablespoons oil
2.5 cm (1 inch) piece fresh ginger,
    thinly sliced
2 cloves garlic, crushed
2 tablespoons soy sauce
2 leeks, finely sliced
250 g (8 oz) baby English spinach
    leaves, torn
1 small bunch bok choy, cut into short
    lengths
¾ cup (115 g/4 oz) frozen peas
1 teaspoon sugar
3 tablespoons chicken stock
dash of chilli sauce

1 Season the strips of lamb with salt and pepper, dip in the egg white and dust with cornflour.
2 Heat half the oil in a wok and add the ginger, garlic and soy sauce. Stir-fry over high heat for 30 seconds. Add the lamb and stir-fry for 1 minute or until browned. Reduce the heat, cover and cook for 3 minutes. Remove the lamb from the wok.
3 Heat the remaining oil in the wok and add the leek. Stir-fry over high heat for 3 minutes, or until the leek has softened.
4 Add the spinach, bok choy and frozen peas to the wok and stir-fry for 1 minute. Reduce the heat and cover the wok to steam the vegetables for 2 minutes. Combine the sugar, stock and chilli sauce and add to the wok. Add the lamb and stir well. Stir-fry for 2 minutes or until the lamb and vegetables are just tender.

NUTRITION PER SERVE
Protein 35 g; Fat 30 g; Carbohydrate 7 g; Dietary Fibre 5 g; Cholesterol 100 mg; 1775 kJ (425 cal)

Season the meat with salt and pepper, then dip in the egg white and cornflour.

Add the spinach, bok choy and frozen peas to the wok and stir-fry for 1 minute.

LAMB WITH BORLOTTI BEANS

Preparation time: 20 minutes + overnight soaking
Total cooking time: 2 hours
Serves 6

1 cup (200 g/6½ oz) dried borlotti beans
1 tablespoon olive oil
12 lamb loin chops
1 onion, finely chopped
1 celery stick, chopped
1 carrot, chopped
3 cloves garlic, finely chopped
½ teaspoon dried chilli flakes
1 teaspoon cumin seeds
2 cups (500 ml/16 fl oz) lamb or chicken stock
2 bay leaves
¼ cup (60 ml/2 fl oz) lemon juice
⅓ cup (20 g/¾ oz) chopped fresh parsley
1 tablespoon shredded fresh mint

1 Soak the beans overnight in cold water. Drain, rinse well and set aside.
2 Preheat the oven to moderate 180°C (350°F/Gas 4). Heat the oil in a large heavy-based saucepan. Brown the lamb over high heat in batches, then transfer to a casserole dish.
3 Add the onion, celery and carrot to the pan, and cook over low heat for 10 minutes, or until soft and golden. Add the garlic, chilli and cumin seeds, and cook for 1 minute, then transfer to the casserole dish.
4 Add the stock, beans and bay leaves. Cover tightly and bake for 1½–1¾ hours, or until the lamb is very tender and the beans are cooked. Season with salt and freshly cracked black pepper. Stir in the lemon juice, parsley and mint just before serving.

NUTRITION PER SERVE
Protein 30 g; Fat 8 g; Carbohydrate 20 g; Dietary Fibre 5 g; Cholesterol 65 mg; 1185 kJ (280 cal)

When the oil is hot, brown the lamb over high heat in batches.

Add the onion, celery and carrot to the pan, and cook until soft and golden.

Add the stock, drained borlotti beans and bay leaves to the casserole.

MOROCCAN LAMB WITH PISTACHIO COUSCOUS

**Preparation time: 40 minutes +
 2 hours marinating**
Total cooking time: 20 minutes
Serves 4

MOROCCAN MARINADE
3 tablespoons olive oil
1 tablespoon lemon juice
2 teaspoons honey
1–2 cloves garlic, crushed
1 teaspoon ground cumin
½ teaspoon ground turmeric
½ teaspoon ground
    cinnamon
¼ teaspoon cayenne pepper

8–10 small lamb fillets
pinch of saffron
1½ cups (375 ml/12 fl oz) hot chicken
    stock
250 g (8 oz) couscous
1 tablespoon olive oil
1 red onion, chopped
1 red chilli, seeded and chopped
2 cloves garlic, crushed
½ cup (75 g/2½ oz) currants
100 g (3½ oz) shelled pistachio nuts
grated rind of 1 lemon
grated rind of 1 orange
3 tablespoons chopped fresh mint

1 Mix together all the marinade ingredients. Put the lamb in a shallow, non-metallic dish, add the marinade, cover and refrigerate for 2 hours.

2 Add the saffron to the hot stock and pour over the couscous. Set aside for 10 minutes, then stir to remove lumps.
3 Heat the oil in a frying pan, add the onion, chilli and garlic and cook for 3 minutes. Add the currants and nuts and cook for 5 minutes. Stir in the lemon and orange rind and the mint. Stir through the couscous.
4 Cook the lamb on a hot, lightly oiled barbecue grill or flatplate, turning once, until browned all over. Cook for 2–3 minutes more, turning frequently. Serve with the couscous.

NUTRITION PER SERVE
Protein 45 g; Fat 40 g; Carbohydrate 50 g;
Dietary Fibre 5 g; Cholesterol 110 mg;
3030 kJ (720 cal)

Mix together all the ingredients for the Moroccan marinade and pour over the lamb.

Stir the onion, chilli, garlic, currants, nuts, rind and mint through the couscous.

Cook the lamb on a hot barbecue until browned all over and then cook for a little longer.

LAMB SHANKS WITH GARLIC

Preparation time: 20 minutes
Total cooking time: 1 hour 25 minutes
Serves 6

6 large lamb shanks
1 tablespoon oil
2 leeks, sliced
1 sprig fresh rosemary
1 cup (250 ml/8 fl oz) dry white wine
1 bulb garlic
oil, for brushing

1 Preheat the oven to moderate 180°C (350°F/Gas 4). Season the lamb shanks. Heat the oil in a frying pan over medium–high heat. Cook the lamb shanks quickly in batches until well browned. Drain on paper towels, then place in a casserole dish.
2 Cook the leek in the frying pan until tender. Add to the lamb shanks with the rosemary and wine.
3 Cut the garlic horizontally through the centre. Brush the cut surfaces with a little oil. Place cut-side up in the casserole, but not covered by liquid. Bake, covered, for 1 hour. Remove the lid and bake for a further 15 minutes. Discard the rosemary. Serve with steamed vegetables and crusty bread on which to spread the roasted garlic.

NUTRITION PER SERVE
Protein 33 g; Fat 18 g; Carbohydrate 2 g;
Dietary Fibre 2 g; Cholesterol 101 mg;
1350 kJ (320 cal)

Cook the shanks quickly in batches in the oil in a frying pan.

Cook the leek in the frying pan, stirring, until the leek is tender.

Place the cut garlic bulb on top of the lamb shanks and leek.

LAMB AND MUSTARD STEW

Preparation time: 15 minutes
Total cooking time: 1 hour 40 minutes
Serves 4

750 g (1½ lb) lean lamb fillets, cut into
   2.5 cm (1 inch) cubes
½ cup (60 g/2 oz) plain flour
1 tablespoon oil
16 baby onions
1 cup (250 ml/8 fl oz) white wine

1 cup (250 ml/8 fl oz) chicken stock
½ cup (125 g/4 oz) Dijon mustard
2 tablespoons chopped fresh thyme

1 Toss the lamb cubes in the flour, shaking off any excess. Heat the oil in a heavy-based saucepan over high heat. Add the lamb in small batches and cook for 3 minutes, or until well browned, turning occasionally. Drain on paper towels.
2 Return the lamb to the pan. Add the onions, wine, stock, mustard and thyme. Bring to the boil, then reduce

the heat to low and simmer, covered, for 1 hour, stirring occasionally. Remove the lid and simmer for another 30 minutes, or until the lamb is tender. Serve with pasta.

NUTRITION PER SERVE
Protein 46 g; Fat 11 g; Carbohydrate 18 g;
Dietary Fibre 2.5 g; Cholesterol 124 mg;
1655 kJ (395 cal)

NOTE: A small, boned leg of lamb is ideal for this dish.

Toss the lamb cubes in the flour, shaking off any excess flour.

Brown the lamb in small batches, turning occasionally, then drain on paper towels.

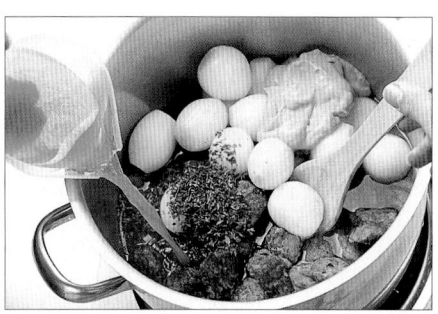

Add the onions, wine, stock, mustard and thyme to the pan.

LAMB SATAYS WITH CHILLI PEANUT SAUCE

Preparation time: 25 minutes +
  1 hour marinating
Total cooking time: 15 minutes
Serves 4

600 g (1¼ lb) lamb fillet
2 cloves garlic, crushed
½ teaspoon ground black pepper
6 teaspoons finely chopped lemon
  grass
2 tablespoons soy sauce
2 teaspoons sugar
¼ teaspoon ground turmeric

CHILLI PEANUT SAUCE
1½ cups (250 g/8 oz) unsalted roasted
  peanuts
2 tablespoons vegetable oil
1 onion, roughly chopped
1 clove garlic, roughly chopped
1 tablespoon sambal oelek
1 tablespoon soft brown sugar
1 tablespoon kecap manis
  or soy sauce
1 teaspoon grated fresh ginger
1½ teaspoons ground coriander
1 cup (250 ml/8 fl oz) coconut cream
¼ teaspoon ground turmeric

1 Trim the lamb, cut into thin strips and thread onto skewers, bunching along three-quarters of the length. Place in a shallow non-metallic dish. Mix together the garlic, pepper, lemon grass, soy sauce, sugar and turmeric and brush over the meat. Leave to marinate for 1 hour.
2 To make the chilli peanut sauce, roughly grind the peanuts in a food processor for 10 seconds. Heat the oil in a small pan. Add the onion and garlic and cook over medium heat for

3–4 minutes or until translucent. Add the sambal oelek, sugar, kecap manis, ginger and coriander. Cook, stirring, for 2 minutes. Add the coconut cream, turmeric and ground peanuts. Reduce the heat and cook for 3 minutes, or until thickened. Season well and then process for 20 seconds, or until the sauce is almost smooth.
3 Cook the skewers on a hot, lightly oiled barbecue grill or flatplate for 2–3 minutes on each side.

NUTRITION PER SERVE
Protein 51 g; Fat 57 g; Carbohydrate 16 g;
Dietary Fibre 7 g; Cholesterol 99 mg;
3241 kJ (774 cal)

STORAGE: Satays can be marinated for up to 2 days, covered in the fridge. The sauce will keep for 3–4 days in a screw-top jar in the fridge.

Thread the strips of lamb onto the skewers and then marinate for 1 hour.

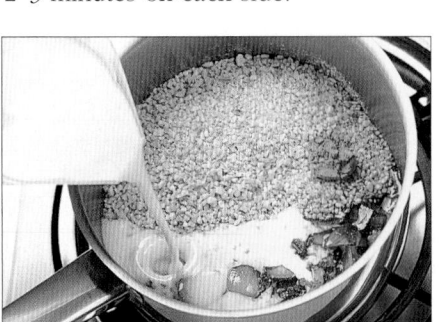

Coarsely grind the peanuts in a processor and then heat with the other sauce ingredients.

Process the sauce until it is almost smooth and then serve with the skewers.

LAMB AND FILO PIE

Preparation time: 20 minutes
Total cooking time: 50 minutes
Serves 6

2 tablespoons oil
2 onions, chopped
1 clove garlic, chopped
1 teaspoon ground cumin
1 teaspoon ground coriander
½ teaspoon ground cinnamon
1 kg (2 lb) lamb mince
3 tablespoons chopped fresh parsley
2 tablespoons chopped fresh mint
1 tablespoon tomato paste
10 sheets filo pastry
250 g (8 oz) unsalted butter, melted

1 Heat the oil in a large frying pan. Add onion and garlic and cook for 3 minutes or until just soft. Add ground cumin, coriander and cinnamon, and cook, stirring, for another minute.
2 Add the mince to the pan and cook over medium–high heat for 10 minutes or until the meat is brown and all the liquid has evaporated. Use a fork to break up any lumps. Add the herbs, tomato paste and a little salt and mix well. Set aside to cool.
3 Preheat the oven to 180°C (350°F/Gas 4). Lightly grease a 33 x 23 cm (13 x 9 inch) ovenproof dish with butter or oil. Remove 3 sheets of filo and cover the rest with a damp tea towel to prevent them drying out. Brush one sheet of pastry with melted butter. Place another 2 sheets of filo on top and brush the top one with butter. Line the dish with these sheets, letting the excess overhang.
4 Spread the lamb filling over the pastry and then fold the overhanging pastry back over the filling. Butter 2 sheets of filo, place one on top of the other and fold in half. Place over the top of the filling and tuck in the edges. Butter the remaining 4 sheets and cut roughly into squares. Scrunch these over the top of the pie. Bake for 40 minutes or until crisp and golden.

NUTRITION PER SERVE
Protein 47 g; Fat 46 g; Carbohydrate 17 g; Dietary Fibre 5 g; Cholesterol 105 mg; 2784 kJ (665 cal)

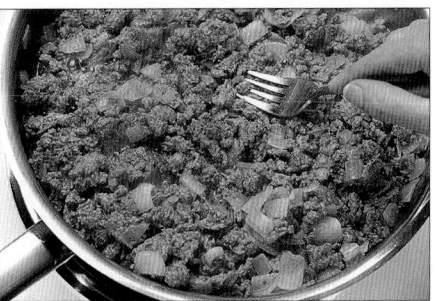
As the mince cooks, press down on any lumps, using a fork to break them up.

Gently brush each top sheet of filo pastry with melted butter.

Spread the lamb over the pastry and then fold the overhanging pastry over the filling.

Scrunch the squares of pastry roughly and arrange them over the top of the pie.

LAMB SHANKS WITH PUY LENTILS

Preparation time: 25 minutes
Total cooking time: 1 hour 45 minutes
Serves 4

⅓ cup (80 ml/2¾ fl oz) olive oil
4 French-trimmed lamb shanks
    (280 g/9 oz each) (see NOTE)
6 cloves garlic, unpeeled
1 onion, thinly sliced
1 red capsicum, sliced
2 cloves garlic, crushed
400 g (13 oz) can peeled tomatoes,
    chopped
1 cup (250 ml/8 fl oz) white wine
1 bay leaf
1 cinnamon stick
2 strips orange rind
1½ cups (320 g/11 oz) Puy lentils
400 g (13 oz) can cannellini beans,
    rinsed and drained
2 spring onions, sliced
pinch saffron threads
1 teaspoon ground coriander
1 teaspoon ground cumin
¼ cup (7 g/¼ oz) chopped fresh
    flat-leaf parsley

1 Preheat the oven to moderately hot 200°C (400°F/Gas 6). Heat half the oil in a large, deep flameproof casserole dish, add the shanks in batches and cook over medium heat for 4 minutes, or until the shanks are brown on all sides. Remove from the dish.
2 Place the unpeeled garlic cloves on a baking tray and drizzle with half the remaining oil.
3 Add the onion, capsicum and crushed garlic to the casserole dish and cook until golden. Stir in the tomato, wine, bay leaf, cinnamon stick

and orange rind, return all the shanks, then cover and transfer to the oven. Cook for 1 hour, then uncover and cook for a further 30 minutes, or until the shanks are tender and the meat is just falling off the bone. Keep warm. Add the tray with the garlic cloves to the oven 15 minutes before the shanks will be ready, and cook until they are soft. Cool slightly, then peel.
4 Meanwhile, place the lentils in a saucepan, cover with 1.5 litres water and bring to the boil. Cook over high heat for 20 minutes, or until tender. Drain, reserving the cooking liquid.
5 Place the garlic in a food processor with the cannellini beans and a little of the reserved lentil cooking liquid, and process until smooth and creamy, then season to taste with salt and cracked black pepper. Cover and keep warm. Add more of the cooking liquid if it starts to thicken and dry out.
6 Heat the remaining oil in a large frying pan, add the spring onion and spices, and cook over medium heat for 3 minutes, or until fragrant. Stir in the lentils and parsley, and cook until warmed through.
7 Place a mound of lentils on each plate, stand the shanks in the lentils and drizzle with some of the cooking liquid. Serve a spoonful of the bean purée on the side.

NUTRITION PER SERVE
Protein 70 g; Fat 35 g; Carbohydrate 45 g;
Dietary Fibre 2 g; Cholesterol 130 mg;
3437 kJ (820 cal)

NOTE: French-trimmed lamb shanks are lamb shanks that have the meat scraped back to make a neat lamb 'drumstick'. You can use regular lamb shanks instead.

Cook the lamb shanks in batches until brown all over.

Add the onion, capsicum and garlic to the dish, and cook until golden.

Cook the lamb shanks until the meat is just falling off the bone.

When the garlic is cool enough to handle, peel off the skin.

Cover the Puy lentils with water and cook until they are tender.

Process the cannellini bean mixture until smooth and creamy.

SKEWERED LAMB WITH CHILLI AIOLI

Preparation time: 25 minutes + 3 hours marinating
Total cooking time: 15 minutes
Makes 12 skewers

1.5 kg (3 lb) leg of lamb, boned and cubed
½ cup (125 ml/4 fl oz) olive oil
½ cup (125 ml/4 fl oz) lemon juice
2 cloves garlic, crushed
1 teaspoon cracked black pepper
1 tablespoon Dijon mustard
1 tablespoon chopped fresh oregano

CHILLI AIOLI
2–3 small red chillies, seeds and stems removed
3 cloves garlic
½ teaspoon ground black pepper
3 egg yolks
2 tablespoons lemon juice
200 ml (6½ fl oz) olive oil

1 Put the lamb in a large, non-metallic bowl. Add the combined olive oil, lemon juice, garlic, pepper, mustard and oregano. Toss well, cover and refrigerate for at least 3 hours.
2 Soak 12 wooden skewers in water to prevent scorching. Drain the lamb, reserving the marinade. Thread the lamb onto the skewers and cook on a hot, lightly oiled barbecue grill or flatplate until well browned, brushing with the marinade occasionally.
3 To make the chilli aioli, chop the chillies and garlic for 30 seconds in a food processor. Add the black pepper, egg yolks and 2 teaspoons of lemon juice. With the motor running, slowly pour in the oil in a fine stream. Increase the flow as the aioli thickens. Add the remaining lemon juice and season to taste. Serve with the skewered lamb.

NUTRITION PER SKEWER
Protein 20 g; Fat 15 g; Carbohydrate 0 g; Dietary Fibre 0 g; Cholesterol 55 mg; 810 kJ (190 cal)

Mix the lamb pieces with the marinade to thoroughly coat the meat.

Thread four pieces of marinated lamb onto each soaked skewer.

Pour the oil in a fine stream into the food processor with the motor running.

KASHMIR LAMB WITH SPINACH

Preparation time: 20 minutes
Total cooking time: 1 hour 30 minutes
Serves 4

2 tablespoons oil
750 g (1½ lb) diced leg of lamb
2 large onions, chopped
3 cloves garlic, crushed
5 cm (2 inch) piece of fresh ginger, grated
2 teaspoons ground cumin
2 teaspoons ground coriander
2 teaspoons turmeric
¼ teaspoon ground cardamom
¼ teaspoon ground cloves
3 bay leaves
1½ cups (375 ml/12 fl oz) chicken stock
½ cup (125 ml/4 fl oz) cream
2 bunches English spinach leaves, washed and chopped

1 Heat the oil in a heavy-based pan and brown the lamb in batches. Remove from the pan. Add the onions, garlic and ginger and cook for 3 minutes, stirring regularly. Add the cumin, coriander, turmeric, cardamom and cloves and cook, stirring, for 1–2 minutes or until fragrant. Return the lamb to the pan with any juices. Add the bay leaves and stock.

2 Bring to the boil and then reduce the heat, stir well, cover and simmer for 35 minutes. Add the cream and cook, covered, for a further 20 minutes or until the lamb is very tender.
3 Add the spinach and cook until the spinach has softened. Season to taste before serving.

NUTRITION PER SERVE
Protein 45 g; Fat 25 g; Carbohydrate 3 g; Dietary Fibre 2 g; Cholesterol 165 mg; 1820 kJ (435 cal)

STORAGE: Curry is best cooked a day in advance and refrigerated. Do not add the spinach until reheating.

Return the browned lamb to the pan and add the bay leaves.

Stir in the cream and simmer, covered, until the lamb is very tender.

It will only take a few minutes for the spinach to soften and reduce.

LAMB WITH EGGPLANT, TOMATO AND PESTO

Preparation time: 30 minutes
Total cooking time: 25 minutes
Serves 4

PESTO
2 cups (100 g/3½ oz) fresh basil leaves
2 cloves garlic, crushed
⅓ cup (50 g/1¾ oz) pine nuts
¾ cup (185 ml/6 fl oz) olive oil
¾ cup (75 g/2½ oz) grated Parmesan
1 eggplant
4 Roma tomatoes, halved

6 lamb fillets
60 g (2 oz) goats cheese

1 To make the pesto, finely chop the basil, garlic and pine nuts in a food processor. With the motor running slowly, gradually pour in the olive oil. Add the Parmesan and process briefly.
2 Cut the eggplant into thick slices and brush with some olive oil. Cook the eggplant on a hot barbecue grill or flatplate, brushing with a little more oil, for 3–4 minutes each side, or until golden brown and softened. Remove and keep warm. Add the tomatoes and cook, brushing with olive oil, until soft. Remove and keep warm.
3 Sprinkle each lamb fillet liberally with black pepper. Wipe the barbecue clean and lightly oil. Cook the lamb for 3–4 minutes, until cooked through but still pink inside. Slice diagonally and serve with the eggplant, tomato and a little pesto. Crumble the goats cheese over the top.

NUTRITION PER SERVE
Protein 35 g; Fat 75 g; Carbohydrate 5 g;
Dietary Fibre 5 g; Cholesterol 95 mg;
3490 kJ (830 cal)

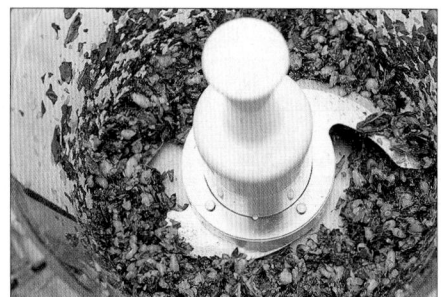

Make the pesto in a food processor, finely chopping the basil, garlic and pine nuts first.

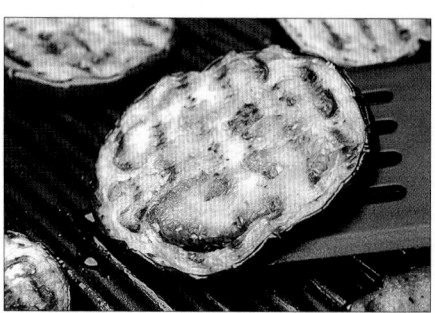

Brush the slices of eggplant with olive oil and then grill until golden brown and softened.

The lamb should be cooked through but still pink inside. Slice diagonally to serve.

LAMB CHOPS WITH CITRUS POCKETS

Preparation time: 25 minutes
Total cooking time: 15 minutes
Serves 4

4 lamb chump chops, about 250 g
    (8 oz) each
2 tablespoons lemon juice

CITRUS FILLING
3 spring onions, finely chopped
1 celery stick, finely chopped
2 teaspoons grated fresh ginger
¾ cup (60 g/2 oz) fresh breadcrumbs
2 tablespoons orange juice
2 teaspoons finely grated orange rind
1 teaspoon chopped fresh rosemary

1 Cut a deep, long pocket in the side of each lamb chop.
2 Mix together all the filling ingredients and spoon into the pockets in the lamb.
3 Cook on a hot, lightly oiled barbecue flatplate or grill, turning once, for 15 minutes, or until the lamb is cooked through but still pink in the centre. Drizzle with the lemon juice.

NUTRITION PER SERVE
Protein 35 g; Fat 5 g; Carbohydrate 15 g;
Dietary Fibre 1 g; Cholesterol 105 mg;
1080 kJ (335 cal)

Cut a deep, long pocket in the side of each lamb chop, right through the skin and fat.

Mix together all the filling ingredients and then spoon into the lamb pockets.

Cook the lamb chops on a hot barbecue flatplate, turning once.

499

LAMB SHANKS IN TOMATO SAUCE ON POLENTA

Preparation time: 10 minutes
Total cooking time: 2 hours 30 minutes
Serves 4

2 tablespoons olive oil
1 large red onion, sliced
4 French-trimmed lamb shanks
   (about 250 g/8 oz each)
2 cloves garlic, crushed
400 g (13 oz) can peeled, chopped
   tomatoes
½ cup (125 ml/4 fl oz) red wine
2 teaspoons chopped fresh rosemary
1 cup (150 g/5 oz) instant polenta
50 g (1¾ oz) butter
½ cup (50 g/1¾ oz) grated fresh
   Parmesan

1 Preheat the oven to warm 160°C (315°F/Gas 2–3). Heat the oil in a 4 litre flameproof casserole dish over medium heat and sauté the onion for 3–4 minutes, or until softening and becoming transparent. Add the lamb shanks and cook for 2–3 minutes, or until lightly browned. Add the garlic, tomato and wine, then bring to the boil and cook for 3–4 minutes. Stir in the rosemary. Season with ¼ teaspoon each of salt and pepper.
2 Cover and bake for 2 hours. Remove the lid, return to the oven and simmer for a further 15 minutes, or until the lamb just starts to fall off the bone. Check periodically that the sauce is not too dry, adding water if needed.
3 About 20 minutes before serving, bring 1 litre water to the boil in a saucepan. Add the polenta in a thin stream, whisking continuously, then reduce the heat to very low. Simmer for 8–10 minutes, or until thick and coming away from the side of the pan. Stir in the butter and Parmesan. To serve, spoon the polenta onto serving plates, top with the shanks and tomato sauce.

NUTRITION PER SERVE
Protein 39 g; Fat 36.5 g; Carbohydrate 31 g;
Dietary Fibre 3 g; Cholesterol 137 mg;
2615 kJ (625 cal)

LAMB CUTLETS WITH ROSEMARY MARINADE

Preparation time: 15 minutes +
20 minutes marinating
Total cooking time: 10 minutes
Serves 4

12 lamb cutlets
3 tablespoons olive oil
2 tablespoons chopped fresh
   rosemary
1½ teaspoons cracked black pepper
1 bunch fresh rosemary, extra

1 Trim the cutlets of excess fat and sinew. Place in a shallow, non-metallic dish and brush with oil.
2 Scatter half the chopped rosemary and pepper on the meat and set aside for 20 minutes. Turn the meat over and brush with the remaining oil. Scatter with the remaining rosemary and pepper. Tie the extra bunch of rosemary to the handle of a wooden spoon.
3 Cook the cutlets on a hot, lightly oiled barbecue grill or flatplate for 2–3 minutes on each side. As the cutlets cook, bat frequently with the rosemary spoon. This will release flavoursome oils into the cutlets. When the cutlets are almost done, remove the rosemary from the spoon and drop it on the fire, where it will flare up briefly and infuse rosemary smoke into the cutlets. Serve with barbecued lemon slices.

NUTRITION PER SERVE
Protein 23 g; Fat 22 g; Carbohydrate 0 g;
Dietary Fibre 0 g; Cholesterol 71 mg;
1195 kJ (285 cal)

Trim the lamb cutlets of excess fat and sinew and then place in a shallow dish.

Scatter half the chopped rosemary and pepper over the meat.

As the lamb is cooking, bat it frequently with the rosemary spoon to add flavour.

LAMB WITH SALSA VERDE AND POLENTA WEDGES

**Preparation time: 40 minutes +
   20 minutes**
Total cooking time: 35 minutes
Serves 4

SALSA VERDE
1 cup (20 g/¾ oz) fresh parsley leaves
1 cup (50 g/1¾ oz) fresh basil leaves
1 cup (20 g/¾ oz) fresh mint leaves
½ cup (30 g/1 oz) fresh dill
2 tablespoons capers
1–2 cloves garlic
1 tablespoon caster sugar
1 teaspoon grated lemon rind
1 tablespoon lemon juice
1 slice white bread
2–3 anchovy fillets
⅓ cup (80 ml/2¾ fl oz) olive oil

POLENTA WEDGES
2 cups (500 ml/16 fl oz) chicken stock
1 cup (150 g/5 oz) polenta (cornmeal)
50 g (1¾ oz) butter
½ cup (125 ml/4 fl oz) cream

12 lamb cutlets, trimmed

1 To make the salsa verde, chop the herbs, capers, garlic, sugar, lemon rind, juice, bread and anchovies in a food processor. With the motor running, add the oil in a thin stream and blend until smooth.
2 To make the polenta, heat the stock until boiling. Add the polenta, stirring over low heat for 20 minutes until it leaves the side of the pan. Stir in the butter and cream and season. Grease a deep 23 cm (9 inch) round cake tin, spoon in the polenta and smooth the top. Set in the fridge for 20 minutes.
3 Turn out the polenta, cut into wedges and brush with melted butter. Cook on a hot, lightly oiled barbecue grill or flatplate for 2–3 minutes each side, or until brown.
4 Cook the lamb for 2 minutes on each side, or until cooked through but still just pink inside.

NUTRITION PER SERVE
Protein 30 g; Fat 50 g; Carbohydrate 35 g;
Dietary Fibre 3 g; Cholesterol 150 mg;
2985 kJ (710 cal)

Trimming the lamb bones of any excess fat or sinew makes them easier to hold.

Finely chop the ingredients for the salsa verde in a food processor.

When the polenta leaves the side of the pan, stir in the butter and cream.

Cut the polenta into wedges and brush with melted butter.

INDIAN-STYLE LAMB COUSCOUS SALAD

Preparation time: 25 minutes
Total cooking time: 35 minutes
Serves 6

250 g (8 oz) lamb backstrap
    (tender eye of the lamb loin)
1 tablespoon mild curry powder
2 tablespoons pepitas
    (pumpkin seeds)
2 tablespoons sesame seeds
2 teaspoons cumin seeds
2 teaspoons coriander seeds
1 tablespoon oil
2 tablespoons lemon juice
1 onion, chopped
1 carrot, chopped
125 g (4 oz) orange sweet potato,
    cubed
1 clove garlic, finely chopped
1 cup (185 g/6 oz) couscous
¼ cup (50 g/1¾ oz) raisins

1 Sprinkle the lamb with the combined curry powder and a pinch of salt, then turn to coat well. Cover with plastic wrap and refrigerate while preparing the salad.
2 Place the pepitas and sesame seeds in a dry frying pan and cook, stirring, over medium-high heat until the seeds begin to brown. Add the cumin and coriander seeds and continue stirring until the pepitas are puffed and begin to pop. Remove from the heat and allow to cool.
3 Heat the oil in a pan, add the lamb and cook over medium-high heat for 5–8 minutes, or until browned and tender. Remove from the pan, drizzle with half the lemon juice and leave to cool to room temperature. Turn the meat occasionally to coat in the

lemon juice while cooling.
4 Using the same pan, stir the onion, carrot and sweet potato over high heat until the onion is translucent. Reduce the heat to medium, add 3 tablespoons water, cover and cook for about 3 minutes, or until the vegetables are tender. Stir in the chopped garlic and remaining lemon juice.
5 Pour 1 cup (250 ml/8 fl oz) boiling water into a heatproof bowl and add the couscous. Stir until combined. Leave for about 2 minutes, or until the water has been absorbed. Fluff gently with a fork to separate the grains. Add the vegetable mixture,

raisins and most of the toasted nuts and seeds, reserving some to sprinkle over the top, and toss until just combined. Spoon the mixture onto a serving plate. Slice the lamb thinly and arrange over the salad. Drizzle with any leftover lemon juice and sprinkle with the nuts and seeds.

NUTRITION PER SERVE
Protein 15 g; Fat 10 g; Carbohydrate 30 g;
Dietary Fibre 3 g; Cholesterol 30 mg;
1135 kJ (270 cal)

Sprinkle the lamb backstrap with the combined curry powder and salt.

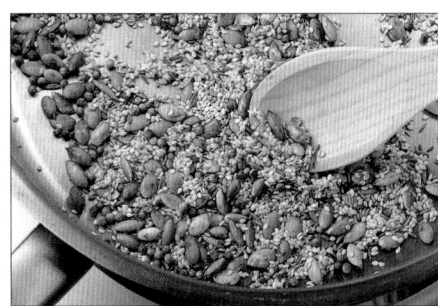

Fry the seeds in a dry frying pan until the pepitas puff up.

When the water has been absorbed, fluff the couscous gently with a fork.

GARLIC LAMB WITH WILTED MUSHROOMS AND NOODLES

Preparation time: 30 minutes
Total cooking time: 20 minutes
Serves 4

350 g (12 oz) lamb fillet,
    cut into diagonal strips
8 Asian shallots, very thinly sliced
4 cloves garlic, finely chopped
1½ tablespoons oil
1 teaspoon soft brown sugar
1 teaspoon salt
1 teaspoon freshly ground black
    pepper

300 g (10 oz) fresh egg noodles
oil, extra, for cooking
200 g (6½ oz) button mushrooms,
    sliced
150 g (5 oz) small oyster mushrooms
2 tablespoons teriyaki sauce
75 g (2½ oz) fresh garlic chives,
    cut into short pieces

1 Combine the lamb, shallots, garlic, oil, brown sugar, salt and pepper in a bowl. Mix well.
2 Cook the noodles in boiling salted water for 3 minutes, or until just tender. Rinse with cold water.
3 Heat the wok until very hot, add 1 tablespoon of oil and swirl it around to coat the side. Stir-fry the lamb in three batches until browned, adding a little more oil when needed. Remove all the meat from the wok.
4 Add the button mushrooms to the wok with 2 teaspoons of water and stir-fry for 1 minute. Add the oyster mushrooms and teriyaki sauce and toss well. Cover and steam for about 10 seconds.
5 Return all the lamb and any juices to the wok with the noodles and chives. Toss well to heat through. Serve immediately.

NUTRITION PER SERVE
Protein 30 g; Fat 20 g; Carbohydrate 40 g;
Dietary Fibre 3 g; Cholesterol 60 mg;
1920 kJ (460 cal)

Trim any fat from the lamb fillet and cut the fillet into diagonal strips.

Asian shallots look rather like large cloves of garlic with a pink papery skin.

Stir-fry the marinated lamb in batches, tossing constantly until it is well browned.

SPICY LAMB AND EGGPLANT

Preparation time: 15 minutes
Total cooking time: 20 minutes
Serves 4

oil, for cooking
1 onion, finely chopped
500 g (1 lb) eggplant,
    peeled and cut into batons
600 g (1¼ lb) lamb fillet, cut diagonally
    into thin slices
2 cloves garlic, finely chopped
1 small red chilli, seeded and finely
    chopped
1 tablespoon ground cumin

1 tablespoon ground coriander
2 teaspoons ground turmeric
1 teaspoon ground cinnamon
1 cup (250 ml/8 fl oz) thick coconut
    cream
1 tablespoon chopped mint
2 tablespoons chopped parsley
lemon wedges, to serve

1 Heat the wok until very hot, add 2 teaspoons of the oil and swirl it around to coat the side. Stir-fry the onion until soft and golden. Remove from the wok and set aside.
2 Add 1 tablespoon of the oil to the wok and cook the eggplant in two batches over high heat until golden brown and cooked through. Remove

and drain on paper towels.
3 Reheat the wok and add 2 teaspoons of the oil. Stir-fry the lamb in two batches over high heat until browned and just cooked.
4 Return all the lamb to the wok with the onion and eggplant. Add the garlic, chilli and spices, and cook for 1 minute. Pour in the coconut cream and bring to the boil.
5 Stir in the fresh herbs and season with salt and pepper. Serve with the lemon wedges.

NUTRITION PER SERVE
Protein 35 g; Fat 30 g; Carbohydrate 7 g;
Dietary Fibre 5 g; Cholesterol 100 mg;
1775 kJ (425 cal)

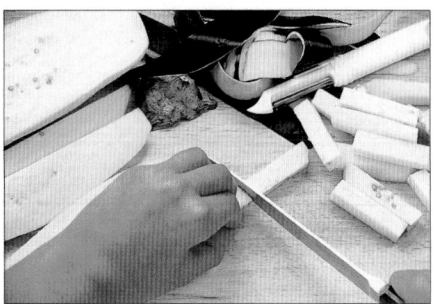

Peel the eggplant, remove the ends and cut the eggplant into batons.

Cook the eggplant in the oil until it has turned golden brown.

Return the lamb, onion and eggplant to the wok and add the garlic, chilli and spices.

LAMB CHOP CASSEROLE

Preparation time: 15 minutes
Total cooking time: 1 hour 15 minutes
Serves 4

6–8 lamb chump chops (see NOTE)
1 tablespoon oil
1 large onion, finely chopped
⅓ cup (90 g/3 oz) redcurrant jelly
1 teaspoon grated lemon rind
1 tablespoon lemon juice
1 tablespoon barbecue sauce
1 tablespoon tomato sauce
½ cup (125 ml/4 fl oz) chicken stock

1 Trim any fat from the lamb. Preheat the oven to moderate180°C (350°F/ Gas 4). Heat the oil in a large heavy-based frying pan; add the chops and cook over medium-high heat for 2–3 minutes, turning once, until well browned. Remove from the pan and put in a casserole dish.
2 Add the onion to the frying pan and cook over medium heat, stirring frequently, for 5 minutes or until the onion is softened. Add the jelly, lemon rind and juice, barbecue and tomato sauces and stock. Stir for 2–3 minutes until heated through. Pour over the chops and stir well, cover and place in the oven. Cook for 1 hour, or until the meat is tender, turning 2–3 times. Lift out the chops onto a side plate and leave them to keep warm.
3 Pour the sauce into a pan and boil rapidly for 5 minutes until the sauce has thickened and reduced. Return the chops to the sauce before serving.

NUTRITION PER SERVE
Protein 30 g; Fat 11 g; Carbohydrate 13 g;
Dietary Fibre 1 g; Cholesterol 95 mg;
1150 kJ (275 cal)

STORAGE TIME: Keep covered and refrigerated for up to 2 days. Suitable to freeze for up to 1 month.

NOTE: Other lamb chop cuts can be used instead of chump.

Once the chops have been well browned, put them in a casserole dish.

Pour the sauce over the chops in the dish and stir to combine.

Use a pair of tongs to turn the chops a couple of times during cooking.

LAMB PITTA

**Preparation time: 20 minutes +
15 minutes marinating
Total cooking time: 5 minutes
Serves 4**

400 g (13 oz) lamb leg steaks
2 teaspoons finely grated lemon rind
3 teaspoons finely chopped fresh
   oregano
2 cloves garlic, finely chopped
2 tablespoons olive oil
1 red onion, thinly sliced
4 small pitta breads

½ cup (125 g/4 oz) hummus
½ cup (125 g /4 oz) plain yoghurt
1 small Lebanese cucumber, thinly
   sliced
1 small red chilli, seeds removed,
   finely chopped
snow pea sprouts

1 Trim the lamb of excess fat and cut into thin strips. Mix together the lemon rind, oregano, garlic, olive oil and some cracked black pepper in a non-metallic bowl. Add the lamb and refrigerate for 15 minutes.
2 Cook the lamb and onion on a very hot, lightly oiled barbecue flatplate for

2–3 minutes, turning to brown the meat quickly and soften the onion. Remove from the plate and keep warm. Place the pitta breads on the flatplate and warm both sides.
3 Spread each round of bread with a little of the hummus and yoghurt. Add the barbecued lamb and onion and scatter with the cucumber, chilli and a few snow pea sprouts.

NUTRITION PER SERVE
Protein 40 g; Fat 20 g; Carbohydrate 65 g;
Dietary Fibre 5 g; Cholesterol 70 mg;
2550 kJ (605 cal)

The seeds contain the heat of the chilli. Scrape them out with a knife.

Mix together the lemon rind, oregano, garlic, olive oil and some ground pepper.

Cook the lamb and onion for 2–3 minutes, turning to brown the meat quickly.

KIDNEY KEBABS

**Preparation time: 15 minutes
 + 20 minutes marinating
Total cooking time: 5–10 minutes
Serves 4**

200 g (6½ oz) lamb kidneys
3 cloves garlic, finely chopped
2 bay leaves, torn into small pieces
3 tablespoons olive oil
300 g (10 oz) chicken breast fillets
150 g (5 oz) double-smoked ham
2 small onions
2 tablespoons dry sherry

1 Soak 8 bamboo skewers in water to prevent scorching. Trim the kidneys of any sinew or fat and cut into bite-sized pieces. Combine the garlic, bay leaves and olive oil. Add the kidneys, cover and marinate in the refrigerator for about 20 minutes.
2 Cut the chicken and ham into bite-sized pieces and cut the onions into small wedges.
3 Drain the kidneys, keeping the marinade. Thread the pieces of onion, kidney, chicken and ham alternately onto the skewers.
4 Cook the kebabs on a hot, lightly oiled barbecue grill or flatplate for

about 5–10 minutes, brushing lightly with the marinade and sherry as they cook and turning them regularly. Cook until golden brown.

NUTRITION PER SERVE
Protein 35 g; Fat 20 g; Carbohydrate 2 g;
Dietary Fibre 1 g; Cholesterol 225 mg;
1335 kJ (315 cal)

VARIATION: Chicken livers can be used instead of the lamb kidneys.

Trim the kidneys of any sinew or fat and cut into bite-sized pieces.

Thread the pieces of onion, kidney, chicken and ham alternately onto the skewers.

While the skewers are cooking, brush them lightly with the marinade and sherry.

LAMB'S LIVER AND BACON STEW

Preparation time: 10 minutes
Total cooking time: 30 minutes
Serves 6

1 lamb's liver, about 750 g (1½ lb) (see NOTE)
¼ cup (30 g/1 oz) cornflour
¼ teaspoon ground black pepper
6 rashers bacon, cut into large pieces
2 tablespoons oil
2 onions, thinly sliced
1 beef stock cube, crumbled

1 Wash the liver and cut it into thin slices, discarding any veins or discoloured spots. Pat the liver dry with paper towels. Combine the cornflour and pepper. Toss the liver slices in the seasoned cornflour, shaking off the excess.
2 Cook the bacon in a heavy-based saucepan until crisp, then drain on paper towels. Heat the oil in the pan and cook the onion gently until golden, then remove from the pan.
3 Cook the liver quickly in small batches over medium heat until well browned, then drain on paper towels. Return the liver, bacon and onion to the pan. Dissolve the stock cube in 1 cup (250 ml/8 fl oz) boiling water, then gradually add to the pan. Stir over medium heat for 10 minutes, or until the liquid boils and thickens. Serve the stew immediately.

NUTRITION PER SERVE
Protein 36 g; Fat 30 g; Carbohydrate 9 g;
Dietary Fibre 0.5 g; Cholesterol 573 mg;
1850 kJ (440 cal)

NOTE: Soaking the liver in milk for 30 minutes before cooking will result in a milder taste.

Toss the liver slices in the seasoned cornflour, shaking off the excess.

Cook the bacon in a heavy-based saucepan until crisp, then drain on paper towels.

Return the cooked bacon, liver slices and onion to the pan.

BOMBAY LAMB CURRY

Preparation time: 25 minutes
Total cooking time: 1 hour 25 minutes
Serves 4–6

1.5 kg (3 lb) leg lamb, boned (ask your
    butcher to do this)
2 tablespoons ghee or oil
2 onions, finely chopped
2 cloves garlic, crushed
2 small green chillies, finely chopped
5 cm (2 inch) piece of fresh ginger,
    grated
1½ teaspoons turmeric
2 teaspoons ground cumin
3 teaspoons ground coriander
½–1 teaspoon chilli powder
1–1½ teaspoons salt
425 g (14 oz) can crushed tomatoes
2 tablespoons coconut cream

1 Cut the meat into cubes, removing
any skin and fat. You will have about
1 kg (2 lb) meat remaining. Heat the
ghee or oil in a large heavy-based
frying pan. Add the onion and cook,
stirring frequently, over medium-high
heat for 10 minutes until golden
brown. Add the garlic, chillies and
ginger and stir for a further 2 minutes,
taking care not to burn them.
2 Mix together the turmeric, cumin,
coriander and chilli powder. Stir to a
smooth paste with 2 tablespoons
water and add to the frying pan. Stir
for 2 minutes, taking care not to burn.
3 Add the meat a handful at a time,
stirring well to coat with spices. It is
important to make sure all the meat is
well-coated and browned.
4 Add the salt to taste and stir in the
tomatoes. Bring to the boil, cover and
reduce the heat to low. Simmer for
30 minutes and then stir in the
coconut cream. Simmer for another 30
minutes, or until the lamb is tender.

NUTRITION PER SERVE (6)
Protein 58 g; Fat 13 g; Carbohydrate 5 g;
Dietary Fibre 1.5 g; Cholesterol 165 mg;
1565 kJ (375 cal)

STORAGE: Keep covered and
refrigerated for up to 3 days. The
flavour of curry improves if kept for
at least a day.

Cut the meat into bite-sized chunks, removing
any fat as you cut.

Once the onion is golden brown, stir in the garlic,
chilli and ginger.

Blend the ground spices to a smooth paste with
a little water.

Add the meat a handful at a time to make sure it
is thoroughly coated with the spices.

TANDOORI LAMB PIE

Preparation time: 45 minutes +
** 20 minutes chilling**
Total cooking time: 1 hour 30 minutes
Serves 4–6

1 cup (125 g/4 oz) plain flour
60 g (2 oz) butter, chilled and cubed
2 teaspoons coriander seeds
2 teaspoons cumin seeds
2 teaspoons poppy seeds
1 egg yolk
2 tablespoons iced water

FILLING
850 g (1 lb 11 oz) boned lamb
    shoulder
2 tablespoons oil
2 onions, chopped
1 clove garlic, crushed
2 teaspoons grated fresh ginger
1 teaspoon chilli powder
2 teaspoons garam masala
1 teaspoon ground cumin
½ teaspoon ground turmeric
2 carrots, chopped
1¼ cups (315 ml/10 fl oz) beef stock
1 tablespoon plain flour
1 teaspoon sugar
2 tablespoons lemon juice
200 g (6½ oz) yoghurt
1 egg yolk, lightly beaten, to glaze

1 To make the pastry, mix the flour and butter in a food processor until the mixture is crumbly. Season with a pinch of salt. Add the coriander, cumin and poppy seeds and process until combined. Then add the egg yolk and water. Process in short bursts until the mixture just comes together, adding a little extra water if necessary. Turn out onto a floured surface and quickly bring together into a ball. Cover with plastic wrap and refrigerate for at least 20 minutes.
2 To make the filling, trim any excess fat from the lamb and cut into large cubes. Heat the oil in a pan and brown the lamb in batches. Return all the lamb to the pan. Add the onion and cook until translucent. Add the garlic, ginger and spices and stir over the heat for about 1 minute, or until aromatic. Stir in the carrot and stock. Bring to the boil, reduce the heat and simmer, covered, for 50 minutes, or until the lamb is tender. Remove from the heat. Mix together the flour and 2 tablespoons of water, until smooth. Stir into the meat, return to the heat and then stir until the mixture boils and thickens. Add the sugar, lemon juice and yoghurt and stir well. Season with a good pinch of salt.
3 Spoon the mixture into a deep 20 cm (8 inch) square or round pie dish and allow to cool. Preheat the oven to 200°C (400°F/Gas 6).
4 Roll out the pastry on a sheet of baking paper until it is large enough to cover the pie dish. Place the pastry over the filling and pinch the edges decoratively with your fingers. Then brush with the lightly beaten egg yolk and bake for 25–30 minutes, or until the pastry is browned and crisp.

NUTRITION PER SERVE (6)
Protein 40 g; Fat 25 g; Carbohydrate 25 g; Dietary Fibre 3 g; Cholesterol 185 mg; 1920 kJ (455 cal)

STORAGE: The pie can be stored, covered, in the fridge for up to a day before baking.

Add the coriander, cumin and poppy seeds to the food processor.

Brown the lamb in batches, returning all the meat to the pan.

Stir the chopped carrot and beef stock into the lamb mixture.

Add the sugar, lemon juice and yoghurt to the pan and stir well.

Roll out the pastry until it is large enough to cover the pie dish.

Cover the filling with the pastry and pinch the edges for a decorative finish.

GREEK-STYLE LAMB

Preparation time: 20 minutes
Total cooking time: 8 minutes
Serves 4

400 g (13 oz) lamb fillets
2 tablespoons olive oil
1 large red onion, sliced
3 zucchini, thinly sliced
200 g (6½ oz) cherry tomatoes, halved
3 cloves garlic, crushed
⅓ cup (60 g/2 oz) pitted black olives, halved
2 tablespoons lemon juice

2 tablespoons oregano, finely chopped
100 g (3½ oz) feta cheese, crumbled
⅓ cup (60 g/2 oz) pine nuts, toasted

1 Cut the lamb fillets across the grain into thin strips. Heat a wok, then add the olive oil and heat for 30 seconds, swirling the wok to coat the base and side. Add the lamb in small batches and stir-fry each batch over high heat for 1–2 minutes or until browned. Remove all the lamb from the wok.
2 Add the onion and zucchini to the wok. Stir-fry over high heat for 2 minutes or until just tender. Add the cherry tomatoes and crushed garlic. Stir-fry for 1–2 minutes until the tomatoes have just softened. Return the meat to the wok and stir over high heat until heated through.
3 Remove the wok from the heat. Add the olives, lemon juice and oregano and toss until well combined. Sprinkle with crumbled feta cheese and pine nuts before serving.

NUTRITION PER SERVE
Protein 28 g; Fat 20 g; Carbohydrate 4 g;
Dietary Fibre 3 g; Cholesterol 83 mg;
1273 kJ (300 cal)

Before you start, toast the pine nuts for a couple of minutes under a hot grill or in the oven.

Cut the lamb fillets across the grain so that the strips hold together.

Stir-fry the lamb strips in small batches so they brown rather than stew.

LAMB TAGINE

Preparation time: 15 minutes +
   1 hour marinating
Total cooking time: 1 hour 45 minutes
Serves 6–8

1.5 kg (3 lb) leg or shoulder of lamb,
   cut into 2.5 cm (1 inch) pieces
3 cloves garlic, chopped
⅓ cup (80 ml/2¾ fl oz) olive oil
2 teaspoons ground cumin
1 teaspoon ground ginger
1 teaspoon ground turmeric
1 teaspoon paprika
½ teaspoon ground cinnamon
2 onions, thinly sliced
600 ml (20 fl oz) beef stock
¼ preserved lemon, pulp discarded,
   rind rinsed and cut into thin strips
425 g (14 oz) can chickpeas,
   drained
35 g (1¼ oz) cracked green olives
¼ cup (15 g/½ oz) chopped fresh
   coriander leaves

1 Place the lamb pieces in a non-metallic bowl, add the chopped garlic, 2 tablespoons of the olive oil and the ground cumin, ginger, turmeric, paprika, cinnamon, and ½ teaspoon ground black pepper and 1 teaspoon salt. Mix well to coat, then leave to marinate for 1 hour.
2 Heat the remaining olive oil in a large saucepan, add the lamb in batches and cook over high heat for 2–3 minutes, or until browned. Remove from the pan. Add the onion and cook for 2 minutes, then return the meat to the pan and add the beef stock. Reduce the heat and simmer, covered, for 1 hour.
3 Add the preserved lemon strips, drained chickpeas and olives, and cook, uncovered, for a further 30 minutes, or until the lamb is tender and the sauce has reduced and thickened. Stir in the coriander. Serve in bowls with couscous.

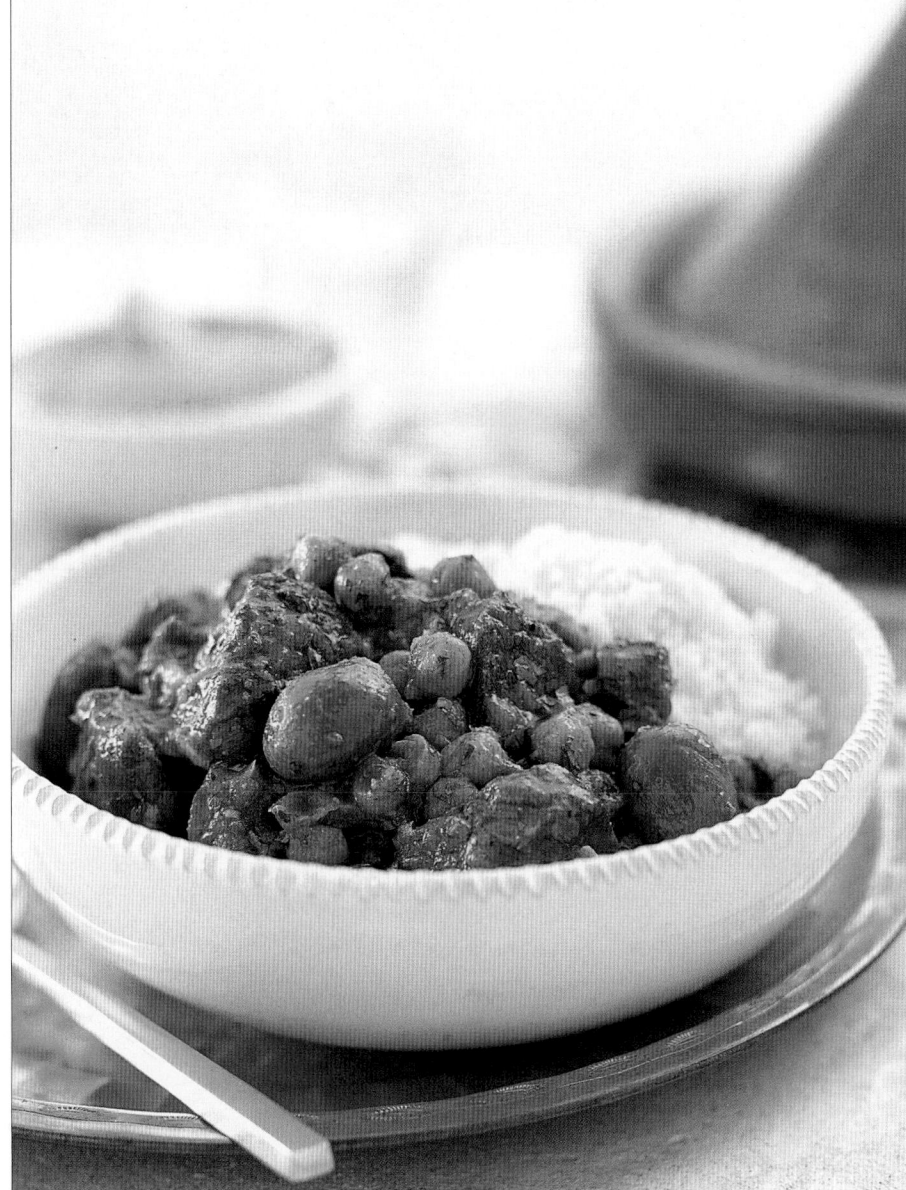

NUTRITION PER SERVE (8)
Protein 50 g; Fat 20 g; Carbohydrate 11 g;
Dietary Fibre 5.5 g; Cholesterol 124 mg;
1765 kJ (422 cal)

Coat the lamb in the spice marinade, then leave for 1 hour.

Cook the lamb in batches over high heat for 2–3 minutes, or until browned.

Add the preserved lemon strips, chickpeas and cracked green olives to the pan.

Pork

PHAD THAI

Preparation time: 25 minutes
Total cooking time: 10–15 minutes
Serves 4

250 g (8 oz) thick rice stick noodles
2 tablespoons oil
3 cloves garlic, chopped
2 teaspoons chopped red chillies
150 g (5 oz) pork, thinly sliced
100 g (3½ oz) peeled raw prawns, chopped
½ bunch garlic chives, chopped
2 tablespoons fish sauce
2 tablespoons lime juice
2 teaspoons soft brown sugar
2 eggs, beaten
1 cup (90 g/3 oz) bean sprouts
sprigs of coriander
3 tablespoons chopped roasted peanuts
crisp-fried onion, soft brown sugar and chopped peanuts, to serve

1 Soak the rice stick noodles in warm water for 10 minutes or until they are soft. Drain and set aside. Heat the wok until very hot, then add the oil and swirl to coat the side. When the oil is very hot, add the garlic, chilli and pork and stir-fry for 2 minutes.
2 Add the prawns and stir-fry for 3 minutes. Add the garlic chives and drained noodles to the wok; cover and cook for another minute.
3 Add the fish sauce, lime juice, sugar and eggs to the wok. Toss well until heated through.
4 Serve immediately, sprinkled with the bean sprouts, sprigs of fresh coriander and chopped peanuts. Traditionally served with crisp-fried onion, soft brown sugar and more chopped peanuts on the side.

NUTRITION PER SERVE
Protein 20 g; Fat 17 g; Carbohydrate 20 g; Dietary Fibre 2 g; Cholesterol 145 mg; 1334 kJ (320 cal)

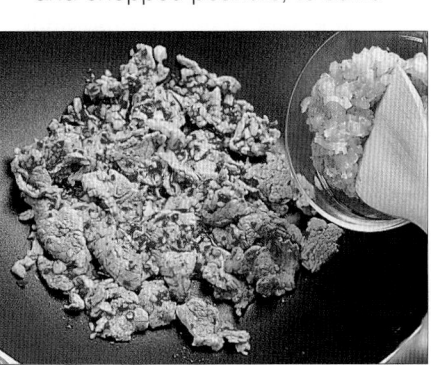

After stir-frying the pork for 2 minutes, stir in the chopped prawns.

Use two wooden spoons or a pair of tongs to toss the stir-fry.

ITALIAN PORK WITH FENNEL

Preparation time: 15 minutes
Total cooking time: 15 minutes
Serves 4

140 g (4½ oz) fennel bulb, thinly sliced
oil, for cooking
30 g (1 oz) butter
600 g (1¼ lb) pork fillet, cut into thin
    strips
1 tablespoon lemon juice
¼ cup (60 ml/2 fl oz) chicken stock
2 tablespoons baby capers, rinsed

Parmesan shavings, to serve
1 tablespoon chopped fennel, to serve

1 Blanch the fennel in boiling water
for 1 minute. Drain and cool under
cold running water, then drain again.
2 Heat the wok until very hot, add
1 tablespoon of the oil and half the
butter and swirl it around to coat the
side. When the butter begins to sizzle,
add the sliced fennel. Stir-fry until
golden and tender. Remove from the
wok and keep warm.
3 Reheat the wok, add 2 teaspoons of
the oil and half the remaining butter.
Stir-fry the pork in two batches until

browned, adding more oil and butter
between batches. Return the pork and
fennel to the wok and add the lemon
juice and stock.
4 Add the capers and stir them
through the pork mixture, scraping
any bits from the bottom of the wok.
Season with salt and pepper, then
scatter with the Parmesan and extra
fennel. Serve immediately.

NUTRITION PER SERVE
Protein 40 g; Fat 20 g; Carbohydrate 2 g;
Dietary Fibre 1 g; Cholesterol 105 mg;
1525 kJ (365 cal)

Remove the top from the fennel and thinly slice
the bulb.

To make Parmesan shavings, draw a vegetable
peeler along the block.

Stir-fry the fennel in the oil and butter until it is
golden and tender.

HUNGARIAN-STYLE PORK AND LENTIL STEW

Preparation time: 20 minutes
Total cooking time: 1 hour
Serves 4

1 tablespoon olive oil
2 onions, chopped
500 g (1 lb) lean diced pork
2 teaspoons sweet Hungarian paprika
1 teaspoon hot paprika
½ teaspoon dried thyme
2 tablespoons tomato paste

2 teaspoons soft brown sugar
¼ cup (60 g/2 oz) red lentils
1½ cups (375 ml/12 fl oz) beef stock
1 tomato, to garnish
2 tablespoons low-fat natural yoghurt

1 Heat the olive oil in a large, deep saucepan over high heat. Add the onion, pork and paprika and stir for 3–4 minutes, until browned.
2 Add the thyme, tomato paste, sugar, lentils, stock and salt and pepper. Bring to the boil, reduce the heat to very low and cook, covered, for 20 minutes, stirring occasionally to

prevent sticking. Uncover and cook for 15–20 minutes, or until thickened.
3 Remove from the heat and set aside for 10 minutes. To prepare the tomato, cut in half and scoop out the seeds. Slice the flesh into thin strips.
4 Just before serving, stir the yoghurt into the stew. Scatter with tomato. Serve with plain boiled rice.

NUTRITION PER SERVE
Protein 35 g; Fat 8 g; Carbohydrate 13 g;
Dietary Fibre 4 g; Cholesterol 70 mg;
1110 kJ (265 cal)

Stir the onion, pork and paprika until the pork is browned on all sides.

Add the thyme, tomato paste, sugar, lentils and beef stock to the pan and bring to the boil.

To make the tomato garnish, remove the seeds and slice the flesh into thin strips.

PORK WITH SNAKE BEANS

Preparation time: 15 minutes
Total cooking time: 20 minutes
Serves 4

1 tablespoon oil
400 g (13 oz) pork fillet, cut into
    thick slices
2 onions, thinly sliced
150 g (5 oz) snake beans, diagonally
    sliced (see NOTE)
3 cloves garlic, finely chopped
1 tablespoon finely chopped
    fresh ginger
1 red capsicum, thinly sliced
6 spring onions, diagonally sliced
2 tablespoons sweet chilli sauce

1 Heat the wok until very hot, add half the oil and swirl it around to coat the side of the wok. Stir-fry the pork in two batches over high heat for 3–4 minutes, or until it is just cooked, adding a little more oil if necessary for the second batch. Remove all the pork from the wok.
2 Heat the remaining oil in the wok over medium heat and add the sliced onion. Cook for 3–4 minutes, or until the onion has softened slightly. Add the sliced snake beans and cook for 2–3 minutes. Add the garlic, ginger, capsicum and spring onion, and toss well. Increase the heat and cook for 3–4 minutes.
3 Return the pork to the wok, add the sweet chilli sauce and toss well. Remove from the heat and season with salt and pepper. Serve immediately.

NUTRITION PER SERVE
Protein 25 g; Fat 12 g; Carbohydrate 8 g;
Dietary Fibre 4 g; Cholesterol 50 mg;
1005 kJ (240 cal)

NOTE: If you can't find snake beans you can use ordinary green beans in this recipe.

Top and tail the snake beans, then cut them into diagonal pieces.

BOSTON BAKED BEANS

Preparation time: 25 minutes +
  6 hours soaking
Total cooking time: 1 hour 35 minutes
Serves 6

1¾ cups (350 g/11 oz) dried cannellini
    beans (see NOTE)
1 whole ham hock
2 onions, chopped
2 tablespoons tomato paste
1 tablespoon Worcestershire sauce
1 tablespoon molasses
1 teaspoon French mustard
¼ cup (45 g/1½ oz) brown sugar
½ cup (125 ml/4 fl oz) tomato juice

1 Cover the beans with cold water and soak for at least 6 hours or overnight (see NOTE).
2 Drain the beans, rinse them well and place in a large pan. Add the ham hock and cover with cold water. Bring to the boil, then reduce the heat and simmer, covered, for 25 minutes, or until the beans are tender. Preheat the oven to warm 160°C (315°F/Gas 2–3).
3 Remove the ham hock from the pan and set aside to cool. Drain the beans, reserving 1 cup (250 ml/8 fl oz) of the cooking liquid. Trim the ham of all skin, fat and sinew, then roughly chop the meat and discard the bone.
4 Transfer the meat and beans to a 2 litre casserole dish. Add the reserved liquid and all remaining ingredients. Mix gently, then cover and bake for 1 hour. Serve with toast.

NUTRITION PER SERVE
Protein 28 g; Fat 5 g; Carbohydrate 30 g;
Dietary Fibre 2 g; Cholesterol 60 mg;
1090 kJ (260 cal)

NOTE: Any type of dried bean can be used in this recipe.
If you don't have 6 hours to soak the beans, to quick-soak beans, place them in a pan, add hot water to cover, bring slowly to the boil, then remove from the heat. Leave to soak for 1 hour before draining and using. Cooked beans can be frozen in small quantities.

Place the drained beans in a large pan. Add the ham hock and cover with cold water.

Trim the ham of all fat, skin and sinew, then roughly chop the meat.

Add the reserved liquid and remaining ingredients to the meat and beans.

PORK AND CORIANDER STEW

Preparation time: 15 minutes
 + overnight marinating
Total cooking time: 1 hour 20 minutes
Serves 6

1½ tablespoons coriander seeds
800 g (1 lb 10 oz) pork fillet, cubed
1 tablespoon plain flour
2 tablespoons olive oil
1 large onion, thinly sliced
1½ cups (375 ml/12 fl oz) red wine
1 cup (250 ml/8 fl oz) chicken stock
1 teaspoon sugar
fresh coriander sprigs, to garnish

1 Crush the coriander seeds in a mortar and pestle. Combine the pork, crushed seeds and ½ teaspoon cracked pepper in a bowl. Cover and marinate overnight in the fridge.
2 Toss the flour and pork. Heat the oil in a large frying pan and cook the pork in batches over high heat for 1–2 minutes, or until brown. Remove.
3 Add the onion to the frying pan and cook over medium heat for 2–3 minutes, or until just golden. Return the meat to the pan, add the red wine, stock and sugar, and season. Bring to the boil, then reduce the heat and simmer, covered, for 1 hour.
4 Remove the meat. Return the pan to the heat and boil over high heat for 3–5 minutes, or until reduced and slightly thickened. Pour over the meat and top with the coriander.

NUTRITION PER SERVE
Protein 30 g; Fat 12 g; Carbohydrate 2.5 g;
Dietary Fibre 0 g; Cholesterol 65 mg;
1180 kJ (282 cal)

Coat the pork fillet pieces in the ground coriander and pepper.

Remove the meat from the pan and set aside to keep warm.

Boil the liquid until it has reduced and is slightly thickened.

PORK WITH PEAR AND CORIANDER SALSA

Preparation time: 35 minutes
Total cooking time: 10 minutes
Serves 4

3 beurre bosc pears
3–4 tablespoons lime juice
¾ cup (25 g/¾ oz) coriander leaves,
   finely chopped

1 red onion, finely diced
½ teaspoon chilli flakes
1 teaspoon finely grated lime rind
cooking oil spray
4 pork steaks, butterflied

1 Cut the pears into quarters, remove the cores and chop into small dice. Sprinkle with the lime juice.
2 Combine the pear, onion, coriander, chilli flakes and lime rind and season.

3 Lightly spray a frying pan with oil and cook the pork steaks for 5 minutes on each side, or until cooked through. Serve with the salsa.

NUTRITION PER SERVE
Protein 24 g; Fat 7 g; Carbohydrate 17 g;
Dietary Fibre 3 g; Cholesterol 53 mg;
930 kJ (234 cal)

NOTE: Use pears that are just ready to eat, not overripe and floury fruit.

To dice an onion, slice it almost to the root, two or three times.

Then slice through vertically, leaving the root to hold it together. Then chop finely.

Cut the pears into quarters, then remove the cores and chop into dice.

GOAN PORK CURRY

Preparation time: 50 minutes
Total cooking time: 1 hour 50 minutes
Serves 6

2 teaspoons cumin seeds
2 teaspoons black mustard seeds
1 teaspoon cardamom seeds
    (see NOTE)
1 teaspoon ground turmeric
1 teaspoon ground cinnamon
½ teaspoon black peppercorns
6 whole cloves
5 small dried red chillies
⅓ cup (80 ml/2¾ fl oz) white vinegar
1 tablespoon soft brown sugar
1 tablespoon oil
1 large onion, chopped
6–8 cloves garlic, crushed
1 tablespoon finely grated fresh ginger
1.5 kg (3 lb) pork leg, cut into cubes

1 Dry-fry the spices and chillies in a large frying pan for 2 minutes, or until fragrant. Place in a spice grinder or food processor and grind until finely ground. Transfer to a bowl and stir in the vinegar, sugar and 1 teaspoon salt to form a paste.
2 Heat half the oil in a large saucepan. Add the onion and cook for 5 minutes, or until lightly golden. Place the onion in a food processor with 2 tablespoons water and process until smooth. Stir into the spice paste.
3 Place the garlic and ginger in a small bowl, mix together well and stir in 2 tablespoons water.
4 Heat the remaining oil in the pan over high heat. Add the meat and cook in 3–4 batches for 8 minutes, or until well browned. Return all the meat to the pan and stir in the garlic and ginger mixture. Add the spice and onion mix and 1 cup (250 ml/ 8 fl oz) hot water. Simmer the curry, covered, for 1 hour, or until the pork is tender. Uncover, bring to the boil and cook, stirring frequently, for 10 minutes, or until the sauce has reduced and thickened slightly. Serve with rice.

NUTRITION PER SERVE
Protein 59 g; Fat 12 g; Carbohydrate 5 g; Dietary Fibre 1 g; Cholesterol 115 mg; 1643 kJ (392 cal)

NOTE: Crush cardamom pods with the blade of a heavy knife and open with your fingers to remove the seeds.

Place the dry-fried spices in a spice grinder and finely grind.

Process the fried onion with 2 tablespoons water and then stir into the spice paste.

Bring the curry to the boil and cook until the sauce reduces and thickens slightly.

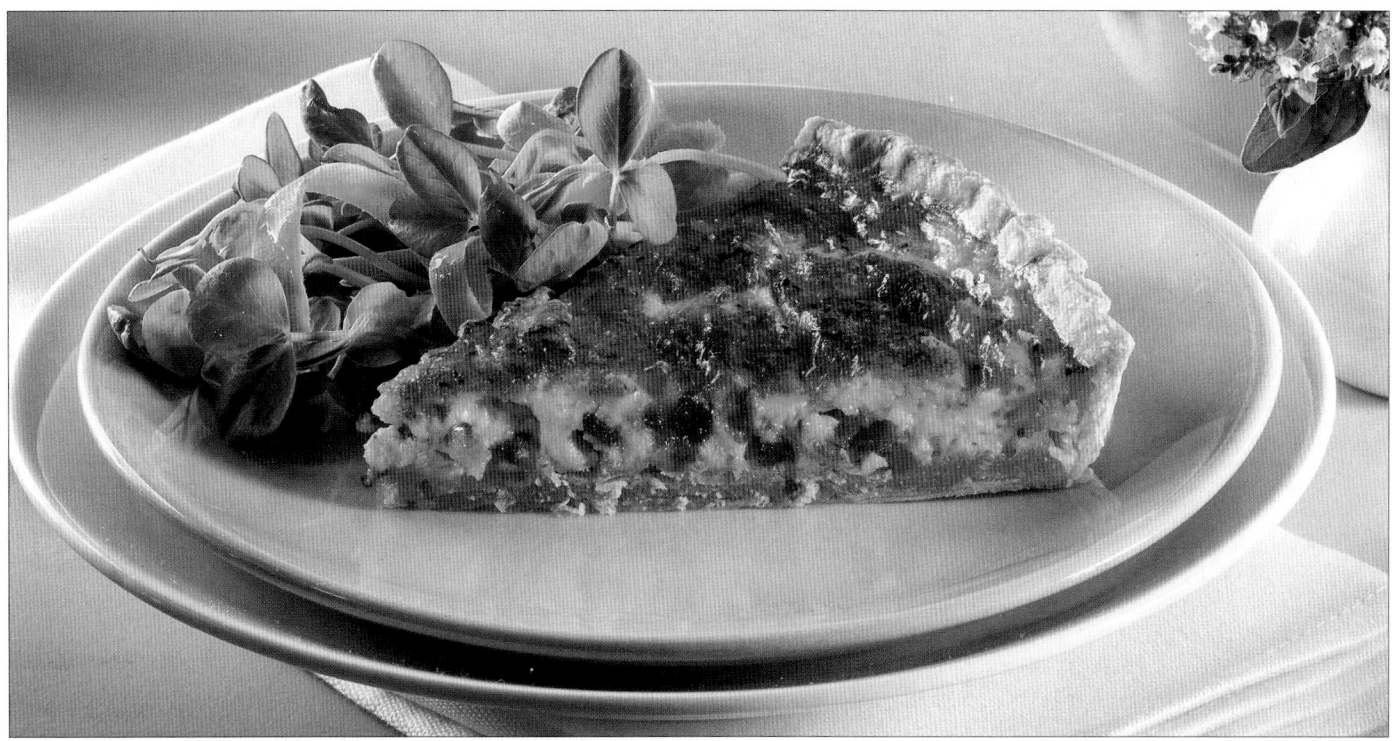

QUICHE LORRAINE

Preparation time: 35 minutes + chilling
Total cooking time: 1 hour 5 minutes
Serves 6

1¼ cups (155 g/5 oz) plain flour
90 g (3 oz) cold butter, chopped
2–3 tablespoons iced water
4 rashers bacon, rind removed
75 g (2½ oz) Gruyère, finely grated
3 eggs
½ cup (125 ml/4 fl oz) cream
½ cup (125 ml/4 fl oz) milk

1 Sift the flour into a bowl and rub in the butter with your fingertips until the mixture resembles fine breadcrumbs. Make a well in the centre and add the water. Using a cutting action, mix with a flat-bladed knife until the mixture comes together in beads. Gently gather the dough together and lift onto a floured surface. Press into a ball and flatten it slightly. Wrap in plastic wrap and refrigerate for 15 minutes. Preheat the oven to moderately hot 200°C (400°F/Gas 6).

2 Roll the dough out between two sheets of baking paper until large enough to line a 23 cm (9 inch) fluted flan tin. Remove the top sheet of paper and invert the pastry into the tin (draping it over the rolling pin may help). Use a small ball of pastry to help press the pastry into the tin, leaving any excess to hang over the side. Roll the rolling pin over the tin to cut off any excess, and then refrigerate for 15 minutes.

3 Line the pastry shell with enough crumpled greaseproof paper to cover the base and side of the tin. Pour in some baking beads and bake for 15 minutes. Remove the paper and beads and return the pastry to the oven for 10 minutes, or until the base is dry. Cool completely before filling. Reduce the oven to moderate 180°C (350°F/Gas 4).

4 Cut the bacon into short, thin strips and cook in a frying pan until brown and crisp. Drain, then spread evenly over the pastry base. Sprinkle the cheese over the bacon. In a jug, whisk together the eggs, cream and milk. Stand the tin on a baking tray, and pour the egg mixture into the pastry shell. Bake for 35–40 minutes, or until set and lightly golden.

NUTRITION PER SERVE
Protein 15 g; Fat 28 g; Carbohydrate 20 g;
Dietary Fibre 1 g; Cholesterol 180 mg;
1640 kJ (390 Cal)

Add the water and mix together with a flat-bladed knife.

Roll out the dough until it is large enough to line the tin.

Remove any excess pastry by rolling a rolling pin over the top of the tin.

CARAMEL PORK WITH SHANGHAI NOODLES

Preparation time: 15 minutes
Total cooking time: 2 hours 30 minutes
Serves 4

500 g (1 lb) Shanghai noodles
700 g (1 lb 5 oz) boneless pork belly
2 teaspoons peanut oil
150 g (5 oz) caster sugar
5 cloves garlic, crushed
5 slices fresh ginger, 5 mm (¼ inch)
    thick
2 stems lemon grass (white part only),
    bruised
1 teaspoon ground white pepper
2 cups (500 ml/16 fl oz) chicken stock
3½ tablespoons fish sauce
100 g (3½ oz) canned bamboo shoots,
    well drained
4 spring onions, cut into
    3 cm (1¼ inch) pieces
1 tablespoon lime juice
1 tablespoon chopped fresh coriander
    leaves (optional)

1 Cook the Shanghai noodles in a large saucepan of boiling water for 4–5 minutes, or until tender. Rinse, drain and cut into 10 cm lengths.
2 Preheat the oven to moderate 180°C (350°F/Gas 4). Cut the pork belly across the grain into 1 cm thick slices then cut each slice into 2 cm (¾ inch) pieces. Heat the oil in a 4 litre clay pot or flameproof casserole dish over medium–high heat. Cook the pork in two batches for about 5 minutes, or until it starts to brown all over. Remove the pork and drain the fat.
3 Add the sugar and 2 tablespoons water to the casserole dish, stirring until the sugar has dissolved and scraping up any sediment that may

have stuck to the bottom. Increase the heat to high and cook for 2–3 minutes without stirring until dark golden, being careful not to burn—you should just be able to smell the caramel.
4 Return the pork to the casserole dish, then add the garlic, ginger, lemon grass, white pepper, stock, 2 tablespoons of the fish sauce and 1½ cups (375 ml/12 fl oz) water and stir to combine. Bake, covered, for 1 hour then remove the lid and cook for another hour, or until the pork is very tender. Carefully remove the ginger slices and the lemon grass.

5 Add the noodles to the casserole dish with the bamboo shoots, spring onion, lime juice and remaining fish sauce and stir to combine. Return the dish to the oven for 10 minutes to heat through. Stir in the chopped coriander, if desired, and serve immediately with steamed Asian greens.

NUTRITION PER SERVE
Protein 48.5 g; Fat 7.5 g; Carbohydrate 73 g; Dietary Fibre 4 g; Cholesterol 166 mg; 2305 kJ (550 Cal)

Cut the pork belly across the grain into 1 cm thick slices.

Return the browned pork pieces to the caremel in the hotpot.

Remove the ginger slices and lemon grass from the hotpot.

SWEET AND SOUR PORK

Preparation time: 25 minutes
+ 30 minutes marinating
Total cooking time: 20 minutes
Serves 4

500 g (1 lb) pork fillet, thickly sliced
2 tablespoons cornflour
1 tablespoon sherry
1 tablespoon soy sauce
1 tablespoon sugar
oil, for cooking
1 large onion, thinly sliced
1 green capsicum, cut into cubes
2 small carrots, thinly sliced
1 small Lebanese cucumber, seeded
    and chopped
5 spring onions, cut into short lengths
440 g (14 oz) can pineapple pieces in
    juice, drained, juice reserved
¼ cup (60 ml/2 fl oz) white vinegar
½ teaspoon salt

1 Place the pork in a shallow glass or ceramic bowl. Combine the cornflour with the sherry, soy sauce and half the sugar and add to the pork. Cover and refrigerate for 30 minutes.

2 Drain the pork, reserving the marinade. Heat the wok until very hot, add 1 tablespoon of oil and swirl to coat the side. Stir-fry half the pork over high heat for 4–5 minutes, or until the pork is golden brown and just cooked. Remove from the wok and cook the remaining pork, adding a little more oil if necessary. Remove all the pork from the wok.

3 Reheat the wok, add 1 tablespoon of oil and stir-fry the onion over high heat for 3–4 minutes, or until slightly softened. Add the capsicum and carrot, and cook for 3–4 minutes, or until tender. Stir in the marinade, cucumber, spring onion, pineapple, vinegar, salt, remaining sugar and 4 tablespoons of the reserved pineapple juice.

4 Bring to the boil and simmer for 2–3 minutes, or until the sauce has thickened slightly. Return the pork to the wok and toss until the pork is heated through. Serve immediately with steamed rice.

NUTRITION PER SERVE
Protein 25 g; Fat 12 g; Carbohydrate 25 g;
Dietary Fibre 4 g; Cholesterol 50 mg;
1325 kJ (315 cal)

Peel the carrots, if necessary, and cut them into thin diagonal slices.

Halve the cucumber lengthways and scoop out the seeds with a teaspoon.

Stir-fry the pork until it is golden brown and just cooked through.

TOURTIERE

Preparation time: 40 minutes +
20 minutes chilling + cooling
Total cooking time: 1 hour
Serves 6

2¼ cups (280 g/9 oz) plain flour
½ teaspoon baking powder
120 g (4 oz) butter, chilled and cubed
½ teaspoon finely chopped fresh
    thyme
1 teaspoon lemon juice
1 egg, lightly beaten
1–2 tablespoons iced water

FILLING
1 small carrot
1 baby fennel bulb, thick outer
    leaves removed
4 French shallots
30 g (1 oz) butter
200 g (6½ oz) bacon, chopped
3 cloves garlic, crushed
500 g (1 lb) pork mince
1 teaspoon finely chopped fresh
    thyme
1 teaspoon finely chopped fresh sage
¼ teaspoon ground nutmeg
¾ cup (185 ml/6 fl oz) chicken stock
250 g (8 oz) potatoes, cut into small
    cubes
1 egg, lightly beaten

1 To make the pastry, sift the flour, baking powder and ¼ teaspoon salt into a large bowl and rub in the chilled butter with your fingertips until the mixture resembles fine breadcrumbs. Stir in the thyme, then make a well in the centre and add the lemon juice, egg and a little of the water. Mix with a flat-bladed knife, using a cutting action, until the mixture comes together in beads, adding more water if necessary.
2 Gently gather the dough together and lift out onto a lightly floured work surface. Press into a ball and flatten slightly into a disc, wrap in plastic wrap and chill for at least 20 minutes.
3 Finely chop the carrot, fennel and shallots in a food processor. Heat the butter in a large frying pan over medium heat and add the chopped vegetables, bacon, garlic and mince.

Cook, stirring often, for 10 minutes, or until the pork changes colour, then stir in the thyme, sage and nutmeg. Season well with salt and cracked black pepper. Add ¼ cup (60 ml/ 2 fl oz) of stock and simmer for 10 minutes, or until it is absorbed. Set aside to cool.
4 Preheat the oven to 200°C (400°F/ Gas 6) and heat a baking tray. Grease an 18 cm (7 inch) pie dish. Place the remaining stock in a small saucepan with the potato and simmer for about 10 minutes, or until tender. Do not drain. Mash coarsely, then stir into the pork mixture.
5 Divide the dough into two portions, one slightly larger than the other. Roll out the larger portion between two sheets of baking paper until large enough to line the base and side of the dish. Spoon in the filling, levelling the surface. Brush the exposed pastry with beaten egg.
6 Roll out the remaining dough between the sheets of baking paper until large enough to cover the pie. Trim the edges and crimp to seal. Brush the surface with egg and make 6–8 small slits over the surface. Bake on the hot baking tray in the centre of the oven for 30 minutes until golden.

NUTRITION PER SERVE
Protein 33 g; Fat 30 g; Carbohydrate 42 g; Dietary Fibre 3.5 g; Cholesterol 189 mg; 2350 kJ (560 cal)

NOTE: The flavour of a tourtière improves over 24 hours and it is excellent served cold.

Remove the thick outer leaves from the baby fennel before chopping.

Cook the pork mixture, stirring often, until the meat changes colour.

Mash the potato and stock together, then stir into the pork mixture.

Trim the edges of the pastry to fit and then crimp them to seal.

BARBECUED PORK AND BROCCOLI

Preparation time: 25 minutes
Total cooking time: 10 minutes
Serves 4–6

1 tablespoon oil
1 large onion, thinly sliced
2 carrots, cut into matchsticks
200 g (6½ oz) broccoli, chopped
6 spring onions, diagonally sliced
1 tablespoon finely chopped fresh
    ginger

3 cloves garlic, finely chopped
400 g (13 oz) Chinese barbecued
    pork, thinly sliced
2 tablespoons soy sauce
2 tablespoons mirin
2 cups (180 g/6 oz) bean sprouts

1 Heat the wok until very hot, add the oil and swirl it around to coat the side. Stir-fry the onion over medium heat for 3–4 minutes, or until slightly softened. Add the carrot, broccoli, spring onion, ginger and garlic and cook for 4–5 minutes, tossing the mixture constantly.

2 Increase the heat to high and add the barbecued pork. Toss constantly until the pork is well mixed with the vegetables and is heated through. Add the soy sauce and mirin, and toss until the ingredients are well coated. (The wok should be hot enough for the sauce to reduce into a glaze.) Add the bean sprouts and season well with salt and pepper. Serve immediately.

NUTRITION PER SERVE (6)
Protein 20 g; Fat 15 g; Carbohydrate 6.5 g;
Dietary Fibre 6 g; Cholesterol 40 mg;
920 kJ (220 cal)

Peel the carrots, if necessary, and cut them into even-sized matchsticks.

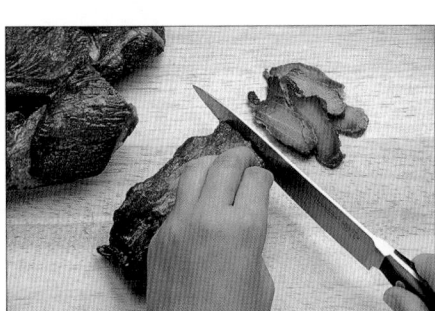

Cut the pieces of Chinese barbecued pork into thin slices.

Add the pork to the wok and toss until it is well mixed with the vegetables.

PORK WITH SAGE AND APPLES

Preparation time: 25 minutes
Total cooking time: 20 minutes
Serves 4

500 g (1 lb) pork fillet, cut into strips
2 tablespoons oil
2 cloves garlic, finely chopped
40 g (1¼ oz) butter
1 large onion, thinly sliced
2 Granny Smith apples, cut into thin
   wedges

1 tablespoon soft brown sugar
2 tablespoons brandy
1 tablespoon chopped fresh sage
150 ml (5 fl oz) cream

1 Combine the pork, oil and garlic in a glass or ceramic bowl, and season well with salt and pepper.
2 Heat the wok and melt the butter over medium heat until foaming. Add the onion and apple and toss well. Sprinkle with the brown sugar and cook, stirring regularly, for 4 minutes, or until the apple is golden and softened. Remove from the wok.

3 Reheat the wok until very hot. Stir-fry the pork in batches over high heat for 2 minutes, tossing regularly until it turns white. Return all the pork to the wok with the apple. Add the brandy, sage and cream, and season well. Stir to combine. Serve immediately.

NUTRITION PER SERVE
Protein 30 g; Fat 35 g; Carbohydrate 15 g;
Dietary Fibre 2.5 g; Cholesterol 140 mg;
2190 kJ (525 cal)

HINT: Never overcook the pork or it will be dry and tough.

Cut the Granny Smith apples into thin wedges, leaving the skin on.

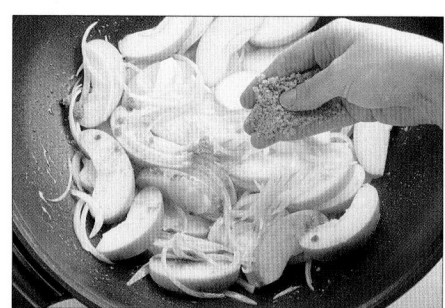
Sprinkle the brown sugar over the apple and onion in the wok.

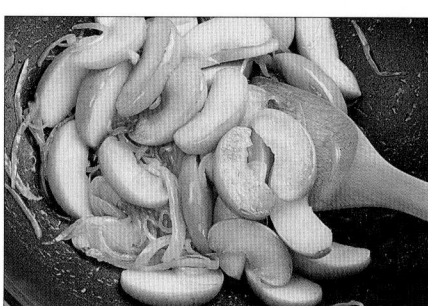
Cook the apple and onion, stirring regularly, until the apple is golden.

PORK, BEER AND CHICKPEA STEW

Preparation time: 35 minutes
Total cooking time: 1 hour 30 minutes
Serves 4

2 teaspoons ground cumin
1 teaspoon ground coriander
½ teaspoon chilli powder
¼ teaspoon ground cinnamon
400 g (13 oz) lean diced pork,
    trimmed
1 tablespoon plain flour
1 tablespoon olive oil
1 large onion, finely chopped
3 cloves garlic, finely chopped
2 large carrots, chopped
2 celery sticks, sliced
½ cup (125 ml/4 fl oz) chicken stock
½ cup (125 ml/4 fl oz) beer
2 ripe tomatoes, chopped
310 g (10 oz) can chickpeas, rinsed
2 tablespoons chopped fresh parsley

1 Cook the spices in a dry frying pan over low heat, shaking the pan, for 1 minute, or until aromatic.

2 Combine the pork, trimmed of all fat, with the spices and flour in a plastic bag and toss well. Remove the pork and shake off the excess flour. Heat the oil in a large heavy-based pan over high heat and cook the pork, tossing regularly, for 8 minutes, or until lightly browned.

3 Add the onion, garlic, carrot, celery and half the stock to the pan and toss well. Cover and cook for 10 minutes. Add the remaining stock, beer and tomato and season to taste. Bring to the boil, reduce the heat, cover with a tight-fitting lid, then simmer over low heat for 1 hour. Gently shake the pan occasionally, but do not remove the lid during cooking. Stir in the chickpeas and fresh parsley. Simmer, uncovered, for 5 minutes and serve.

NUTRITION PER SERVE
Protein 40 g; Fat 10 g; Carbohydrate 35 g; Dietary Fibre 15 g; Cholesterol 50 mg; 1720 kJ (410 cal)

Chop the carrots into quite small pieces and thinly slice the celery sticks.

Dry-fry the spices over low heat, stirring the spices and shaking the pan.

Cook the flour-coated pork, tossing regularly, until lightly browned.

CITRUS CHILLI PORK WITH CASHEW NUTS

Preparation time: 20 minutes
Total cooking time: 12 minutes
Serves 4

2 tablespoons oil
375 g (12 oz) pork fillet, thinly sliced
2 small red chillies, seeded and finely
    chopped
6 spring onions, chopped
1 tablespoon mild curry paste
2 tablespoons fish sauce
1–2 tablespoons lime juice
2 teaspoons crushed palm sugar
2 teaspoons cornflour
½–1 teaspoon seasoning sauce

⅓ cup (50 g/1¾ oz) roasted unsalted
    cashews
shredded lime rind, to garnish

1 Heat the wok until very hot, add the oil and swirl it around to coat the side. Stir-fry the pork slices, chilli and spring onion in batches over high heat for 2 minutes, or until the pork just changes colour. Stir in the curry paste and stir-fry for 1 minute. Remove from the wok and set aside.
2 Combine the fish sauce, lime juice, sugar and cornflour with ½ cup (125 ml/4 fl oz) water. Pour into the wok and stir for 1 minute, or until heated through and slightly thickened. Return the meat to the wok and toss until heated through.

3 Stir in the seasoning sauce, to taste, and cashews. Top with the lime rind.

NUTRITION PER SERVE
Protein 25 g; Fat 20 g; Carbohydrate 9 g;
Dietary Fibre 1 g; Cholesterol 45 mg;
1215 kJ (290 cal)

Crush the palm sugar, using the flat blade of a large knife.

THAI RED PORK AND PUMPKIN CURRY

Preparation time: 20 minutes
Total cooking time: 25 minutes
Serves 4

1 tablespoon oil
1–2 tablespoons red curry paste (use the recipe on page 246 or ready-made paste)
500 g (1 lb) lean pork, cubed
1 cup (250 ml/8 fl oz) coconut milk

350 g (11 oz) butternut or Japanese pumpkin, peeled and cubed
6 kaffir lime leaves
¼ cup (60 ml/2 fl oz) coconut cream
1 tablespoon fish sauce
1 teaspoon soft brown sugar
2 red chillies, thinly sliced

1 Heat the oil in a wok, add the curry paste and stir for 1 minute.
2 Add the pork to the wok and stir-fry over medium-high heat until golden brown. Add the coconut milk, pumpkin, kaffir lime leaves and 125

ml (4 fl oz) water, reduce the heat and simmer for 15 minutes, or until the pork is tender.
3 Add the coconut cream, fish sauce and brown sugar and stir to combine. Scatter chilli over the top to serve.

NUTRITION PER SERVE
Protein 30 g; Fat 11 g; Carbohydrate 9 g; Dietary Fibre 1.5 g; Cholesterol 62 mg; 1085 kJ (260 cal)

NOTE: Butternut and Japanese pumpkins are tender, sweet varieties.

Add the curry paste to the hot oil and stir with a wooden spoon for 1 minute.

Add the pork pieces to the wok and stir-fry over medium-high heat until golden brown.

Add the coconut cream, fish sauce and brown sugar to the wok and stir well.

PORK BALL CURRY WITH EGG NOODLES

Preparation time: 15 minutes
Total cooking time: 20 minutes
Serves 4

200 g (6½ oz) pork mince
3 cloves garlic, chopped
2 stems lemon grass (white part only),
    finely chopped
2.5 cm (1 inch) piece ginger, grated
1 tablespoon oil
1–2 tablespoons green curry paste
    (use the recipe on page 246 or
    ready-made paste)
1½ cups (375 ml/12 fl oz) coconut milk
2 tablespoons fish sauce

2 teaspoons soft brown sugar
½ cup (15 g/½ oz) chopped Thai basil
    leaves
200 g (6½ oz) fresh egg noodles
sliced spring onions, coriander leaves
    and sliced chillies, to serve

1 Finely chop the pork mince with a cleaver or large knife. Combine the mince, garlic, lemon grass and ginger in a bowl and mix thoroughly. Form teaspoonfuls into small balls.

2 Heat the oil in a wok, add the curry paste and cook over low heat, stirring constantly, for 1 minute or until fragrant. Add the coconut milk and 1 cup (250 ml/8 fl oz) water to the wok. Stir until boiling, then reduce the heat and simmer for 5 minutes.

Add the pork balls and simmer for 5 minutes or until cooked. Add the fish sauce, brown sugar and Thai basil.

3 Cook the noodles in boiling water for 4 minutes or until tender, then drain. Toss with the pork balls and curry sauce and then serve immediately, as the noodles will soak up the sauce. Scatter spring onions, coriander and chillies over the top.

NUTRITION PER SERVE
Protein 20 g; Fat 25 g; Carbohydrate 42 g;
Dietary Fibre 3.5 g; Cholesterol 34 mg;
1980 kJ (475 cal)

Mix together the mince, garlic, lemon grass and ginger and form into meatballs.

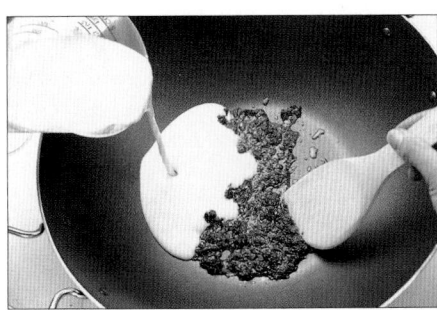

Add the coconut milk and water to the wok and stir until boiling.

Add the noodles to rapidly boiling water and cook for 4 minutes.

HAM, CHEESE AND POTATO PIE

Preparation time: 25 minutes +
** cooling + 10 minutes standing**
Total cooking time: 1 hour 45 minutes
Serves 6–8

¼ cup (60 ml/2 fl oz) olive oil
3 onions, finely chopped
1 clove garlic, finely chopped
300 g (10 oz) ham, chopped
430 g (14 oz) desiree potatoes, diced
2 cups (250 g/8 oz) grated Cheddar
2 eggs
⅓ cup (80 ml/2¾ fl oz) cream
2 teaspoons chopped chives
4 sheets puff pastry
1 egg, lightly beaten, to glaze

1 Heat the oil in a large frying pan over medium heat. Add the onion and garlic and cook, stirring occasionally, for 5 minutes, or until the onion softens. Add the ham and potato and cook, stirring occasionally, for 5–7 minutes, or until the potato softens slightly. Transfer to a large

bowl and stir in the Cheddar.
2 Mix together the eggs and cream and pour into the bowl. Add the chives and mix thoroughly. Season and leave to cool.
3 Preheat the oven to 200°C (400°F/ Gas 6). Grease an 18 cm (7 inch) pie dish. Line the pie dish with two sheets of puff pastry, and brush the edge with beaten egg. Spoon the filling into the pie dish.
4 Cut the remaining sheets of pastry into quarters, and each quarter into three equal lengths. Place the strips, overlapping, around the top of the pie, leaving the centre open. Press down the edges so that the top and

bottom layers stick together, then trim the edges with a sharp knife.
5 Brush the top of the pie with the beaten egg, and bake in the oven for 30 minutes. Reduce the temperature to 180°C (350°F/Gas 4) and cook the pie for another hour, covering the top with foil if it is browning too much. Leave for 10 minutes before serving.

NUTRITION PER SERVE (8)
Protein 24 g; Fat 44 g; Carbohydrate 39 g;
Dietary Fibre 3 g; Cholesterol 153 mg;
2700 kJ (645 cal)

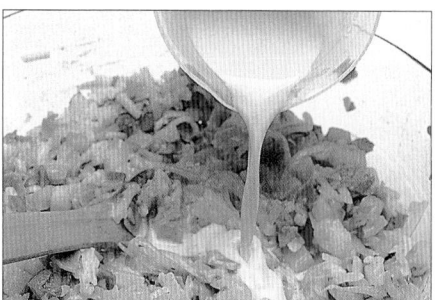

Pour the creamy egg mixture into the bowl with the ham and cheese.

Overlap the pastry strips around the pie, leaving a gap in the middle.

SRI LANKAN FRIED PORK CURRY

Preparation time: 45 minutes
Total cooking time: 1 hour 40 minutes
Serves 6

⅓ cup (80 ml/2¾ fl oz) oil
1.25 kg (2½ lb) boned pork shoulder, cut into 3 cm (1¼ inch) cubes
1 large red onion, finely chopped
3–4 cloves garlic, crushed
1 tablespoon grated fresh ginger
10 curry leaves
½ teaspoon fenugreek seeds
½ teaspoon chilli powder
6 cardamom pods, bruised
2 tablespoons Sri Lankan curry powder
1 tablespoon white vinegar
⅓ cup (105 g/3½ oz) tamarind concentrate
270 ml (9 fl oz) coconut cream

1 Heat half the oil in a large saucepan over high heat, add the meat and cook in batches for 6 minutes, or until well browned. Remove from the saucepan.
2 Heat the remaining oil in the saucepan, add the onion and cook over medium heat for 5 minutes, or until lightly browned. Add the garlic and ginger, and cook for 2 minutes.

Stir in the curry leaves, spices and curry powder, and cook for 2 minutes, or until fragrant. Stir in the vinegar and 1 teaspoon salt.
3 Return the meat to the pan, add the tamarind and 1¼ cups (315 ml/10 fl oz) water and simmer, covered, for 50 minutes, or until the meat is tender. Stir occasionally. Stir in the coconut cream and simmer, uncovered, for 15 minutes, or until the sauce reduces and thickens. Serve with rice.

NUTRITION PER SERVE
Protein 48 g; Fat 25 g; Carbohydrate 3 g;
Dietary Fibre 1 g; Cholesterol 100 mg;
1800 kJ (430 Cal)

Cook the meat in batches for 6 minutes, or until well browned.

Cook the onion over medium heat until lightly browned.

Simmer, uncovered, until the sauce has reduced and thickened.

MA POR TOFU

Preparation time: 15 minutes
+ 10 minutes marinating
Total cooking time: 15 minutes
Serves 4

3 teaspoons cornflour
2 teaspoons soy sauce
1 teaspoon oyster sauce
1 clove garlic, finely chopped
250 g (8 oz) pork mince
1 tablespoon oil

3 teaspoons red bean chilli paste
3 teaspoons preserved bean curd
750 g (1½ lb) firm tofu, drained, cubed
2 spring onions, sliced
3 teaspoons oyster sauce, extra
2 teaspoons soy sauce, extra
1½ teaspoons sugar

1 Put the cornflour, soy and oyster sauces and the garlic in a bowl and mix well. Add the mince, toss to coat and leave for 10 minutes.
2 Heat a wok until very hot, add the oil and swirl to coat the base and side of the wok with oil. Add the mince and stir-fry for 5 minutes, or until browned. Add the chilli paste and bean curd, and cook for 2 minutes, or until fragrant.
3 Add the remaining ingredients and stir for 3–5 minutes, or until the tofu is heated through.

NUTRITION PER SERVE
Protein 26 g; Fat 12 g; Carbohydrate 5 g;
Dietary Fibre 0 g; Cholesterol 30 mg;
1092 kJ (260 cal)

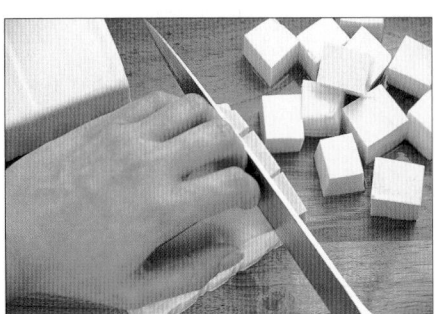

Drain the firm tofu from the liquid you buy it in, and cut it into cubes.

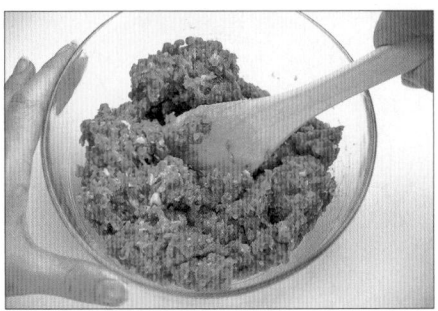

Add the minced pork to the cornflour, soy sauce, oyster sauce and garlic.

Stir-fry the pork mince until it is browned, then add the chilli paste and bean curd.

SESAME PORK

Preparation time: 10 minutes
Total cooking time: 20 minutes
Serves 4

2 tablespoons sesame seeds
3 tablespoons peanut oil
600 g (1¼ lb) pork fillets, thinly
    sliced
2 tablespoons hoisin sauce
2 tablespoons teriyaki sauce
2 teaspoons cornflour
2 teaspoons sesame oil
8 spring onions, sliced on the
    diagonal
2 cloves garlic, crushed

2 teaspoons finely grated fresh ginger
2 carrots, julienned
200 g (6½ oz) snake beans, cut into
    short lengths

1 Preheat the oven to moderate 180°C (350°F/Gas 4). Place the sesame seeds on an oven tray and bake for 5 minutes, or until browned.
2 Heat a wok until very hot, add 1 tablespoon oil and swirl to coat. Add half the pork and stir-fry for 3 minutes, or until browned. Remove. Repeat with the remaining pork. Remove.
3 Combine the hoisin and teriyaki sauces, cornflour and 1 tablespoon water and mix until smooth.
4 Reheat the wok until very hot, add the remaining peanut oil and the sesame oil and swirl to coat. Add the spring onion, garlic and ginger, and stir-fry for 1 minute, or until fragrant.
5 Add the carrot and beans, and stir-fry for 3 minutes, or until almost cooked but still crunchy. Return the pork to the wok, add the cornflour mixture and stir until the sauce boils and thickens. Simmer until the meat is tender and the vegetables are just cooked. Toss through the sesame seeds and serve immediately.

NUTRITION PER SERVE
Protein 38 g; Fat 27 g; Carbohydrate 7.5 g;
Dietary Fibre 4.5 g; Cholesterol 75 mg;
1766 kJ (420 cal)

Cut the snake beans into shorter lengths for easy stir-frying.

Cook the pork in two batches, so that it fries rather than stews.

Mix together the hoisin and teriyaki sauces, cornflour and 1 tablespoon of water.

PORK SCHNITZEL WITH CURRY SAUCE

Preparation time: 25 minutes
Total cooking time: 30 minutes
Serves 4

1 tablespoon oil
1 onion, cut into thin wedges
2 large carrots, cut into 2 cm (¾ inch) cubes
1 large potato, cut into 2 cm (¾ inch) cubes
60 g (2 oz) Japanese curry paste block, broken into small pieces (see NOTE)
flour, for coating
4 x 120 g (4 oz) pork schnitzels, pounded to 4 mm (¼ inch) thickness
2 eggs, lightly beaten
150 g (5 oz) Japanese breadcrumbs (panko)
oil, for deep-frying
pickled ginger, pickled daikon, umeboshi (baby pickled plums), crisp fried onions, to garnish

1 Heat the oil in a saucepan, add the onion, carrot and potato, and cook over medium heat for 10 minutes, or until starting to brown. Add 2 cups (500 ml/16 fl oz) water and the curry paste, and stir until the curry paste dissolves and the sauce becomes a smooth consistency. Reduce the heat and simmer for 10 minutes, or until the vegetables are cooked through. Season to taste with salt and freshly ground black pepper.

2 Season the flour well with salt and pepper. Dip each schnitzel into the flour, shake off any excess and dip into the beaten egg, allowing any excess to drip off. Coat with the Japanese breadcrumbs by pressing each side of the schnitzel firmly into the crumbs on a plate.

3 Fill a deep heavy-based saucepan one-third full of oil and heat to 180°C (350°F), or until a cube of bread dropped into the oil browns in 15 seconds. Cook the schnitzels, one at a time, turning once or twice, for 5 minutes, or until golden brown all over and cooked through. Drain on crumpled paper towels.

4 Slice each schnitzel into 5–6 pieces and arrange, keeping the original shape, over cooked rice. Ladle some of the curry sauce over the schnitzels. Garnish with fried onions and serve with the pickles on the side.

NUTRITION PER SERVE
Protein 38 g; Fat 22 g; Carbohydrate 40 g; Dietary Fibre 5 g; Cholesterol 150 mg; 2145 kJ (513 Cal)

NOTE: Japanese curry is available from Asian grocers as a block or powder.

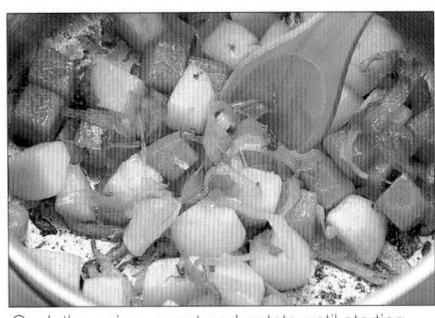

Cook the onion, carrot and potato until starting to brown.

Coat the schnitzels in flour, egg and then Japanese breadcrumbs.

CHINESE BARBECUED PORK PIES

Preparation time: 35 minutes
+ 1 hour refrigeration
Total cooking time: 45 minutes
Makes 4

2 tablespoons cornflour
¼ cup (60 ml/ 2 fl oz) oyster sauce
¼ cup (60 ml/2 fl oz) rice wine
2 tablespoons kecap manis
2 tablespoons lime juice
1 tablespoon grated fresh ginger
½ teaspoon ground white pepper
400 g (13 oz) Chinese barbecued
    pork, cut into 1 cm (½ inch) dice
150 g (5 oz) snow peas, sliced
2 cups (100 g/3½ oz) thinly sliced
    Chinese cabbage
375 g (12 oz) shortcrust pastry
375 g (12 oz) puff pastry
milk, for brushing
1 teaspoon sesame seeds

1 Preheat the oven to moderate 180°C (350°F/Gas 4). Grease four 11 cm (4½ inch) top, 9 cm (3½ inch) base and 3 cm (1¼ inch) deep metal pie dishes. Mix the cornflour with 2 tablespoons water. Heat a large frying pan over low heat and add the oyster sauce, rice wine, kecap manis, lime juice, ginger, white pepper and the cornflour mixture. Simmer for 2 minutes, or until very thick. Add the pork, snow peas and cabbage. Cook, stirring, for 5 minutes. Cool, then refrigerate for 1 hour, or until cold.
2 Meanwhile, roll out the shortcrust pastry between two sheets of baking paper until it is 3 mm (⅛ inch) thick. Cut out four 16 cm (6½ inch) rounds. Line the pie dishes with the pastry, then refrigerate.

3 When the filling is cold, fill the pastry shells. Roll out the puff pastry between the baking paper to 3 mm (⅛ inch) thick and cut out four rounds large enough to cover the tops of the pie dishes. Cover the pies with the puff pastry rounds and trim any excess. Use a fork to seal the edges and prick a few holes in the top. Brush the lids with milk, sprinkle with sesame seeds, and bake for 35 minutes, or until golden.

NUTRITION PER PIE
Protein 35 g; Fat 60.5 g; Carbohydrate 86 g; Dietary Fibre 7 g; Cholesterol 112.5 mg; 4360 kJ (1040 Cal)

Add the pork, snow peas and cabbage and cook, stirring, for 5 minutes.

Cut four 16 cm (61/2 inch) rounds of shortcrust pastry and use them to line the pie dishes.

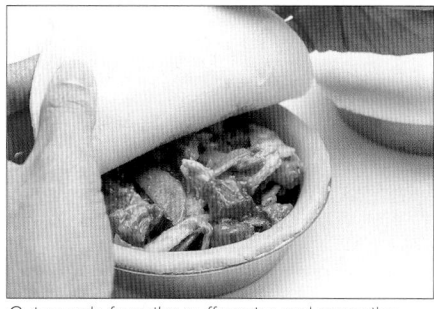

Cut rounds from the puff pastry and cover the tops of the pies.

ROAST LEG OF PORK

Preparation time: 30 minutes
Total cooking time: 3 hours 45 minutes
Serves 8

4 kg (8 lb) leg of pork
oil and salt, to rub on pork

GRAVY
1 tablespoon brandy or Calvados
2 tablespoons plain flour
1½ cups (375 ml/12 fl oz) chicken
    stock
½ cup (125 ml/4 fl oz) unsweetened
    apple juice

1 Preheat the oven to very hot 250°C (500°F/Gas 10). Score the rind of the pork with a sharp knife at 2 cm (¾ inch) intervals. Rub in some oil and salt to ensure crisp crackling. Place the pork, rind-side-up, on a rack in a large baking dish.
2 Add a little water to the dish. Roast for 30 minutes, or until the rind begins to crackle and bubble. Reduce the heat to moderate 180°C (350°F/Gas 4). Roast for 2 hours 40 minutes (20 minutes per 500 g/1 lb) then roast for a further 30 minutes. The pork is cooked if the juices run clear when the flesh is pierced with a skewer. Do not cover the pork or the crackling will soften. Leave in a warm place for 10 minutes.
3 To make the gravy, drain off all except 2 tablespoons of the pan juices from the baking dish. Place on top of the stove over moderate heat, add the brandy and stir quickly to lift the sediment from the bottom of the pan. Cook for 1 minute. Remove from the heat, stir in the flour and mix well. Return the pan to the heat and cook for 2 minutes, stirring constantly. Gradually add the stock and apple juice, and cook, stirring constantly, until the gravy boils and thickens. Season to taste with salt and cracked pepper. Slice the pork and serve with the crackling, gravy, apple sauce and baked apple wedges and vegetables.

NUTRITION PER SERVE
Protein 157 g; Fat 8.5 g; Carbohydrate
2.4 g; Dietary Fibre 0 g; Cholesterol
305 mg; 3050 kJ (730 Cal)

NOTE: Cook the pork just before serving. Any leftover pork can be refrigerated, covered, for up to 3 days.

Use a sharp knife to score the pork rind at regular intervals.

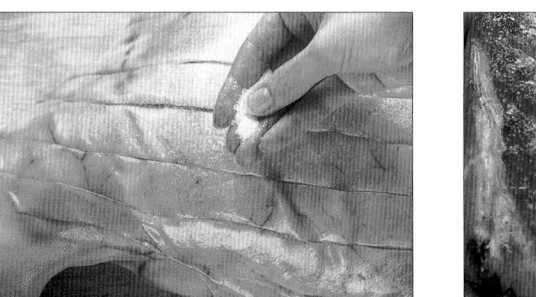

Rub oil and salt into the rind to make sure the crackling will be crisp.

Test the pork by piercing with a skewer—if the juices run clear, the flesh is cooked.

BURMESE PORK CURRY

Preparation time: 30 minutes
Total cooking time: 1 hour
Serves 6

2 stems lemon grass, white part only, sliced
1 red onion, chopped
1 clove garlic
1 teaspoon grated fresh ginger
2 large red dried chillies
1 teaspoon fenugreek seeds, roasted and ground
1 teaspoon yellow mustard seeds, roasted and ground
2 teaspoons paprika
750 g (1½ lb) lean boneless shoulder pork, cut into cubes
2 tablespoons Worcestershire sauce
2 tablespoons fish sauce
6 chat potatoes, peeled and sliced
2 small red onions, diced
1 tablespoon oil
2 tablespoons mango chutney

1 Put the lemon grass, onion, garlic, ginger, chillies, fenugreek seeds, yellow mustard seeds, paprika and Worcestershire sauce in a processor or blender and mix to a thick paste.
2 Place the pork in a bowl, sprinkle with the fish sauce and ¼ teaspoon ground black pepper and toss to coat.
3 Place the potato and onion in another bowl, add 3 tablespoons of the paste and toss to coat. Add the remaining paste to the pork. Mix well.
4 Heat the oil in a saucepan or wok over medium heat. Add the pork and cook in batches, stirring, for 8 minutes, or until the meat begins to brown. Remove from the pan. Add the potato and onion and cook, stirring, for 5 minutes, or until soft and starting to brown.
5 Return the meat to the pan and stir in 3 cups (750 ml/24 fl oz) water, adding 1 cup (250 ml/8 fl oz) at a time. Stir in the mango chutney, then reduce the heat and simmer for 30 minutes, or until the meat and potatoes are tender.

NUTRITION PER SERVE
Protein 30 g; Fat 8.5 g; Carbohydrate 16 g; Dietary Fibre 2.5 g; Cholesterol 60 mg; 1126 kJ (270 cal)

Process all the spice paste ingredients to make a thick paste.

Heat the oil in a saucepan or wok and brown the pork in batches.

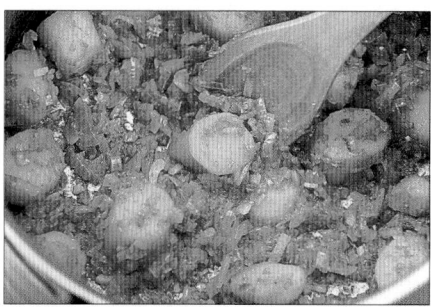

Add the potato and onion and cook until they are starting to brown.

GAME PIE

**Preparation time: 50 minutes
  + overnight setting
Total cooking time: 5 hours
Serves 4–6**

JELLY
any bones reserved from the game
    meat
2 pig's trotters
1 onion, quartered
1 carrot, roughly chopped
1 celery stick, chopped
2 bay leaves
6 black peppercorns

FILLING
250 g (8 oz) pork belly, finely diced
4 rashers streaky bacon, chopped
400 g (13 oz) game meat (e.g. rabbit,
    pheasant), removed from carcass
    and finely diced (bones reserved)
½ small onion, finely chopped
½ teaspoon ground nutmeg
½ teaspoon ground cinnamon
2 dried juniper berries, crushed
1 teaspoon chopped fresh thyme

PASTRY
4 cups (500 g/1 lb) plain flour
90 g (3 oz) lard
1 egg, lightly beaten, to glaze

1 To make the stock for the jelly, place all the ingredients and 1.75 litres water in a large saucepan and bring to the boil over high heat. Remove any froth that forms on the surface. Reduce the heat and simmer for 3 hours, skimming off any froth occasionally. Strain, return to the pan and cook uncovered until the liquid has reduced to about 2 cups (500 ml/ 16 fl oz). Cool, then refrigerate.

2 To make the filling, combine all the ingredients in a bowl. Season well.

3 To make the pastry, sift the flour and ½ teaspoon salt into a large bowl and make a well in the centre. Bring 200 ml (6½ fl oz) water and the lard to the boil in a saucepan. Pour the boiling liquid into the flour and mix with a wooden spoon to form a dough. Gather together and lift onto a lightly floured work surface. Press together until smooth. Keep the dough warm by covering with foil and putting it in a warm place.

4 Preheat the oven to 190°C (375°F/ Gas 5). Grease an 18 cm (7 inch) springform tin. While the pastry is still warm, roll out two-thirds of the dough between two sheets of baking paper and line the base and side of the tin, leaving some overhanging. Spoon the filling into the tin, pressing down well. Roll out the remaining dough to about 4 mm (¼ inch) thick and 20 cm (8 inches) across. Place on top of the tin and pinch the edges together to seal. Trim the edges and cut a small hole in the top of the pie.

5 Roll out the pastry trimmings to make decorations, securing to the pie top with a little beaten egg. Glaze the top of the pie with egg and bake for 1 hour 20 minutes. Cover the top with foil after about 45 minutes to prevent it colouring too much.

6 Remove the pie from the oven and allow to cool for about 25 minutes. Gently remove from the tin, brush the top and sides with beaten egg and place on a baking tray. Return to the oven and cook for another 20 minutes until golden brown and firm to touch. Remove from the oven and cool.

7 Warm the jelly to a pouring consistency. Place a small piping nozzle into the hole in the pie and pour in a little of the jelly. Leave to settle, then pour in more jelly until the pie is full (see HINT). Fill the pie completely so there are no gaps when the jelly sets. Refrigerate overnight but serve at room temperature.

NUTRITION PER SERVE (6)
Protein 40 g; Fat 20 g; Carbohydrate 63 g;
Dietary Fibre 3.5 g; Cholesterol 113 mg;
2455 kJ (585 cal)

HINT: If there is some jelly left, you can freeze it and use it to add flavour to soups, casseroles or sauces.

Line the tin with the warm pastry, leaving some overhanging the edge.

Place the dough on top of the filling and pinch the edges together to seal.

Use a small, sharp knife to cut a hole in the top of the pie.

Insert a nozzle into the hole and pour in a little of the liquid jelly.

MEDITERRANEAN PIE

**Preparation time: 25 minutes +
  20 minutes refrigeration**
Total cooking time: 35 minutes
Serves 4

3 cups (375 g/12 oz) plain flour
1 egg, lightly beaten
½ cup (125 ml/4 fl oz) buttermilk
100 ml (3½ fl oz) olive oil

FILLING
2 tablespoons olive oil
100 g (3½ oz) button mushrooms,
    sliced
400 g (13 oz) can tomatoes, drained
    and roughly chopped
100 g (3½ oz) sliced salami
180 g (6 oz) jar artichokes, drained
4 tablespoons fresh basil leaves, torn
100 g (3½ oz) mozzarella, grated
¼ cup (30 g/1 oz) grated Parmesan
milk, to brush

1 Preheat the oven to 210°C (415°F/
Gas 6–7). Grease a large baking tray
and place in the oven to heat up. Sift
the flour into a large bowl and add
the egg and buttermilk. Add the oil
and mix with a large metal spoon
until the mixture comes together and
forms a soft dough (add a little water
if the mixture is too dry). Turn onto a
lightly floured surface and gather
together into a smooth ball. Cover
with plastic wrap and refrigerate for
20 minutes.
2 Heat the oil in a large frying pan,
add the button mushrooms and cook
over medium heat for 5 minutes,
or until they have softened and
browned a little.
3 Divide the pastry in half and roll
each portion, between two sheets of
baking paper, into a 30 cm (12 inch)
round. Layer the chopped tomato,

salami, mushrooms, artichokes, basil
leaves, mozzarella and Parmesan on
one of the pastry rounds, leaving a
narrow border. Season well.
4 Brush the border with milk. Top
with the remaining pastry circle to
enclose the filling, then pinch and
seal the edges together. Make three
slits in the top. Brush the top with
milk. Place on the preheated tray and
bake for 30 minutes, or until golden.

NUTRITION PER SERVE
Protein 30 g; Fat 52 g; Carbohydrate 75 g;
Dietary Fibre 7 g; Cholesterol 95 mg;
3675 kJ (880 cal)

Gently gather the dough together to form a
smooth ball.

Brush the pastry border with milk to help the top
layer of pastry stick.

TERIYAKI PORK WITH SOYA BEANS

Preparation time: 20 minutes +
2 hours refrigeration + 10 minutes
resting
Total cooking time: 30 minutes
Serves 4

1½ tablespoons soy sauce
3 teaspoons grated fresh ginger
1 clove garlic, crushed
¼ cup (60 ml/2 fl oz) peanut oil
¼ cup (60 ml/2 fl oz) dry sherry
700 g (1 lb 6½ oz) pork fillet
2 tablespoons honey
300 g (10 oz) frozen soya beans
4 baby bok choy, sliced in half
    lengthways
3 teaspoons sesame oil
2 teaspoons finely chopped fresh
    ginger, extra
1 clove garlic, crushed, extra
sesame seeds, toasted, to garnish
    (optional)

1 Combine the soy sauce, ginger, garlic and 2 tablespoons each of the peanut oil and sherry in a large shallow non-metallic dish. Add the pork and toss gently to coat. Cover and refrigerate for 2 hours, turning the meat occasionally. Preheat the oven to moderate 180°C (350°F/Gas 4).
2 Remove the pork and drain well, reserving the marinade. Pat the pork dry with paper towels. Heat the remaining peanut oil in a large frying pan and cook the pork over medium heat for 5–6 minutes, or until browned all over. Transfer to a baking tray and roast for 10–15 minutes. Cover with foil and rest for 10 minutes.
3 Put the reserved marinade, honey, the remaining sherry and ⅓ cup

(80 ml/2¾ oz) water in a small saucepan and bring to the boil. Reduce the heat and simmer for 3–4 minutes, or until reduced to a glaze. Keep the glaze hot.
4 Cook the soya beans in a large covered saucepan of lightly salted boiling water for 1 minute, then add the bok choy and cook for a further 2 minutes. Drain. Heat the sesame oil in the same pan, add the extra ginger and garlic and heat for 30 seconds.

Return the soya beans and bok choy to the pan and toss gently.
5 Slice the pork. Put the vegetables on a large serving dish and top with the pork slices. Spoon the glaze over the pork, sprinkle with sesame seeds and serve immediately.

NUTRITION PER SERVE
Protein 48 g; Fat 25 g; Carbohydrate 6.5 g;
Dietary Fibre 5 g; Cholesterol 86 mg;
1899 kJ (455 Cal)

Cook the pork fillets until browned
all over.

Simmer the marinade, honey and sherry mixture
until reduced to a glaze.

Toss together the soya beans, bok choy, ginger
and garlic.

CYPRIOT PORK AND CORIANDER STEW

Preparation time: 15 minutes
+ overnight marinating
Total cooking time:
1 hour 20 minutes
Serves 4–6

1½ tablespoons coriander seeds
800 g (1 lb 10 oz) pork fillet, cut into
    2 cm (¾ inch) dice
1 tablespoon plain flour
¼ cup (60 ml/2 fl oz) olive oil
1 large onion, thinly sliced
1½ cups (375 ml/12 fl oz) red wine
1 cup (250 ml/8 fl oz) chicken stock
1 teaspoon sugar
fresh coriander sprigs, to garnish

1 Crush the coriander seeds in a mortar and pestle. Combine the pork, crushed seeds and ½ teaspoon cracked pepper in a bowl. Cover and marinate overnight in the fridge.
2 Combine the flour and pork and toss. Heat 2 tablespoons oil in a frying pan and cook the pork in batches over high heat for 1–2 minutes, or until brown. Remove.
3 Heat the remaining oil, add the onion and cook over medium heat for 2–3 minutes, or until just golden. Return the meat to the pan, add the red wine, stock and sugar, and season. Bring to the boil, then reduce the heat and simmer, covered, for 1 hour.
4 Remove the meat. Return the pan to the heat and boil over high heat for 3–5 minutes, or until reduced and slightly thickened. Pour over the meat and top with the coriander.

NUTRITION PER SERVE (6)
Protein 30 g; Fat 12 g; Carbohydrate 2.5 g;
Dietary Fibre 0 g; Cholesterol 65 mg;
1180 kJ (282 Cal)

Coat the pork fillet pieces in the ground coriander and pepper.

Heat some oil in a frying pan and cook the pork in batches until brown.

Remove the meat from the pan and keep warm while making the sauce.

Boil the liquid until reduced and slightly thickened.

SPICY NOODLES WITH PORK AND TOFU

Preparation time: 20 minutes
Total cooking time: 15 minutes
Serves 4

250 g (8 oz) Hokkien noodles
1 tablespoon oil
500 g (1 lb) pork fillet, thinly sliced
2 cloves garlic, crushed
2 cm x 2 cm (¾ inch x ¾ inch) piece fresh ginger, julienned
100 g (3½ oz) snow peas, sliced
100 g (3½ oz) fresh shiitake mushrooms, sliced
½ teaspoon five-spice powder
2 tablespoons hoisin sauce
2 tablespoons soy sauce
¼ cup (60 ml/2 fl oz) vegetable stock
200 g (6½ oz) fried tofu, sliced
100 g (3½ oz) soy bean sprouts
fried red Asian shallot flakes, to garnish

1 Cook the noodles in a large saucepan of boiling water for 2–3 minutes, or until tender. Drain.
2 Heat a wok over high heat, add half the oil and swirl to coat. Add the pork in two batches and stir-fry for 2 minutes each batch, or until browned. Remove from the wok.
3 Add a little more oil if necessary, then add the garlic and ginger and stir-fry for 30 seconds, or until fragrant. Add the snow peas, mushrooms and five-spice powder and cook for a further 1 minute. Pour in the hoisin sauce, soy sauce and stock and cook, stirring constantly, for 1–2 minutes. Add the tofu, soy bean sprouts, noodles and pork and toss to warm through.
4 Serve immediately, garnished with the fried shallot flakes.

NUTRITION PER SERVE
Protein 45 g; Fat 16 g; Carbohydrate 55 g; Dietary Fibre 9.5 g; Cholesterol 75 mg; 2293 kJ (548 Cal)

Use a sharp knife to slice the pork fillets into thin slices.

Stir-fry the pork slices in batches until browned all over.

Add the hoisin and soy sauces and stock and cook for a further 1–2 minutes.

PORK AND VEAL PIE

Preparation time: 40 minutes +
30 minutes refrigeration
Total cooking time: 1 hour 40 minutes
Serves 8

2 sheets ready-rolled shortcrust pastry
2 tablespoons oil
1 onion, finely chopped
1 clove garlic, crushed
1 kg (2 lb) lean pork and veal mince
2 tablespoons chopped fresh parsley
   leaves
2 tablespoons chopped fresh thyme
   leaves
2 eggs
4 cups (320 g/11 oz) fresh white
   breadcrumbs
4 gherkins, roughly chopped
125 g (4 oz) ham steak, diced
1 sheet ready-rolled puff pastry

1 Grease a shallow 22.5.cm (9 inch) flan tin. Cut one sheet of pastry in half and join to the other pastry sheet, pressing the join together. Line the base and side of the tin and trim the edge. Refrigerate for 30 minutes. Preheat the oven to moderately hot 200°C (400°F/Gas 6).
2 Put the flan tin on a baking tray. Cover the base of the pastry with baking paper and baking beads or rice. Bake blind for 10 minutes, then remove the paper and beads and bake for a further 10–15 minutes, or until lightly browned. Allow to cool.
3 Heat the oil in a frying pan and fry the onion and garlic over medium heat for 5 minutes, or until soft. Remove from the heat. Combine the mince, herbs, ¼ cup (60 ml/2 fl oz) water, 1 egg and the breadcrumbs in a food processor until fine but not

smooth. Place in a bowl and add the onion mixture, gherkins and ham. Season well. Mix well and fry a small amount of mixture to taste for seasoning.
4 Press the mixture firmly into the cold pastry base, forming a dome shape. Lightly beat the remaining egg and brush the edges of the pastry. Place the puff pastry over the mince to make a lid, and press the edges firmly to seal. Trim any excess pastry.
5 Brush the pastry all over with the rest of the egg and make two small

slashes in the top of the pie. Using the back of a knife, decorate the top of the pie with a lattice pattern.
6 Bake for 20 minutes, then reduce the oven to moderate 180°C (350°F/Gas 4) and bake for 50 minutes, or until the pastry is golden brown. Serve cold with salad and pickles.

NUTRITION PER SERVE
Protein 40 g; Fat 25 g; Carbohydrate 55 g; Dietary Fibre 3.5 g; Cholesterol 170 mg; 2625 kJ (625 Cal)

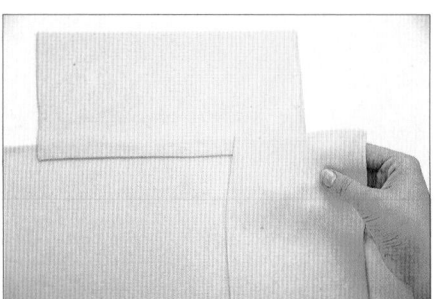

Cut one piece of shortcrust pastry in half and join to the other sheet of pastry.

Press the meat mixture into the pastry base, forming a dome shape.

Cover with the puff pastry and press the edges of the two pastries firmly together.

LEAN PORK STEW WITH ASIAN FLAVOURS

Preparation time: 20 minutes
Total cooking time: 50 minutes
Serves 4

2 teaspoons olive oil
2 cloves garlic, crushed
1 tablespoon julienned fresh ginger
1 teaspoon Sichuan pepper, crushed
1 star anise
800 g (1 lb 10 oz) pork fillet, cut into
   3 cm (1¼ inch) cubes
1 cup (250 ml/8 fl oz) chicken stock
1 tablespoon light soy sauce
1 tablespoon cornflour
2 teaspoons chilli bean paste
250 g (8 oz) Chinese broccoli, cut into
   4 cm (1½ inch) lengths

1 Heat the olive oil in a heavy-based saucepan over high heat. Add the garlic, ginger, Sichuan pepper and star anise and cook for 30 seconds, or until fragrant. Stir in the pork to coat.
2 Add the stock, soy sauce and 1 cup (250 ml/8 fl oz) water to the pan and bring to the boil. Reduce the heat and simmer for 40 minutes, or until the pork is tender. Combine the cornflour with 2 tablespoons of the cooking liquid, stirring until smooth. Add to the pan and stir over medium heat for 3–4 minutes, or until the mixture thickens slightly.
3 Stir in the bean paste and Chinese broccoli and cook for a further 2 minutes, or until the broccoli is just tender. Serve with steamed rice.

NUTRITION PER SERVE
Protein 47 g; Fat 7 g; Carbohydrate 4 g;
Dietary Fibre 3 g; Cholesterol 190 mg;
1135 kJ (270 Cal)

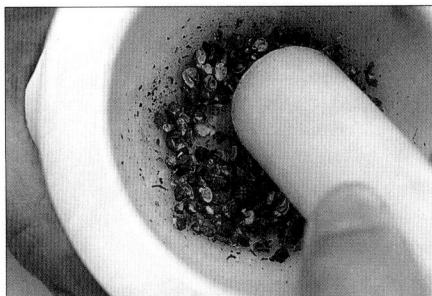
Crush the Sichuan pepper in a mortar and pestle before heating it with the other spices.

Cut the Chinese broccoli into 4 cm (1½ inch) lengths, using a sharp knife.

Stir the cornflour mixture into the stew until the mixture thickens slightly.

PORK PIES

Preparation time: 20 minutes
Total cooking time: 1 hour 15 minutes
Makes 6

400 g (13 oz) pork mince
¼ cup (35 g/1¼ oz) shelled pistachios,
    chopped
½ apple, finely chopped
1 teaspoon finely chopped
    sage leaves
2¼ cups (280 g/9 oz) plain flour
80 g (2¾ oz) butter
1 egg, lightly beaten
1 egg yolk
½ cup (125 ml/4 fl oz) vegetable stock
½ cup (125 ml/4 fl oz) unsweetened
    apple juice
1½ teaspoons gelatine

1 Preheat the oven to moderately
hot 200°C (400°F/Gas 6). Combine
the mince, pistachios, apple and sage
in a large bowl and season very well
with salt and cracked black pepper.
Fry a teaspoon of the filling and
adjust the seasoning if necessary.
Cover and refrigerate until needed.
2 Put the flour and ½ teaspoon of salt
in a large bowl and make a well in
the centre. Put the butter in a small
pan with ⅓ cup (100 ml/3½ fl oz) of
water and bring to the boil. Pour into
the centre of the well, add the beaten
egg and mix to form a smooth dough.
3 Grease six ⅓ cup (80 ml/2¾ fl oz)
capacity muffin holes. Set aside one
third of the dough and divide the rest
into six portions. Roll each portion
into a small circle and line the muffin
cups with the dough, leaving a little
dough hanging over the side of each
cup. Divide the filling among the
pastry-filled cups, packing the filling

down and making a small dome
shape in the centre—the filling will
shrink as it cooks. Divide the remaining dough into six portions and roll
each into a small circle to make the
lids. Brush the edges with water and
lay one on top of each pie. Fold up
the pastry hanging over the edge and
roll or crimp it. Cut a small hole in
the top of each pie. Brush with the
egg yolk mixed with a tablespoon of
water.
4 Put the muffin tin on a baking tray
and bake for 30 minutes; then check
the pastry tops. If they are still pale,
bake for another 5–10 minutes. Leave
to rest for 5 minutes, then lift the pies
out of the muffin tray, put them on
the baking tray and bake for 15
minutes, or until the sides of the pies
are golden brown (be careful not to
break the pies when you move them).
5 Bring the stock and half the apple
juice to the boil in a small saucepan.
Sprinkle the gelatine over the surface
of the remaining apple juice and
leave to go spongy, then pour on the
boiling stock and mix until the
gelatine dissolves. Place a small
funnel (a piping nozzle works well)
in the hole of each pie and pour in a
little of the gelatine mixture. Leave to
settle, then pour in a little more until
the pies are full. It is important to fill
the pies completely to make sure
there are no gaps when the gelatine
mixture sets. You may need more or
less liquid, depending on how much
the meat shrinks. Allow to cool
completely before serving.

NUTRITION PER PIE
Protein 25 g; Fat 17 g; Carbohydrate 32 g;
Dietary Fibre 2.5 g; Cholesterol 25 mg;
1565 kJ (375 Cal)

Mix together the mince, pistachios, apple and
sage and season with salt and pepper.

Bring the melted butter and water to the boil and
pour into the centre of the well.

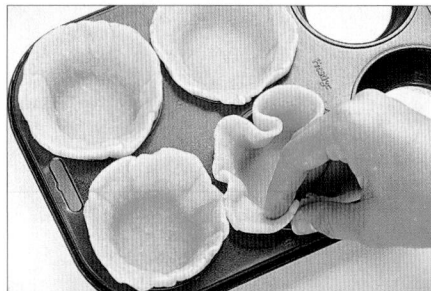

Line the muffin holes, leaving a little dough
hanging over the sides.

Spoon the filling into the pastry shells and pack firmly into a dome shape.

Put the dough lids on top, then fold up the pastry hanging over the side and roll it.

Put a funnel in the hole of the pie and pour in some of the gelatine mixture.

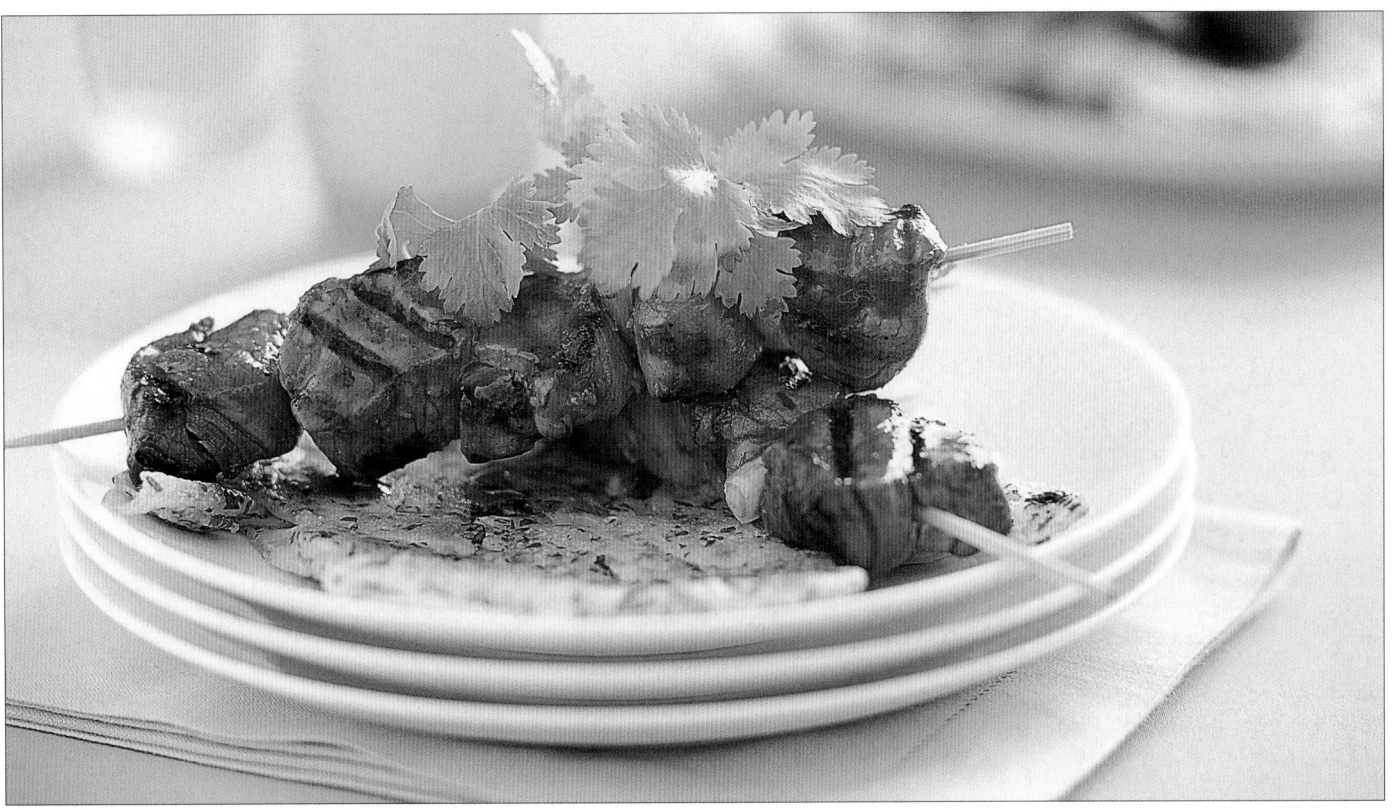

PORK SKEWERS ON RICE NOODLE CAKES

**Preparation time: 20 minutes +
30 minutes soaking +
overnight marinating
Total cooking time: 30 minutes
Serves 4**

1 kg (2 lb) pork fillet, cut into 2 cm
(¾ inch) cubes
8 spring onions, cut into 3 cm
(1¼ inch) lengths
2 tablespoons rice wine vinegar
2 teaspoons chilli bean paste
3 tablespoons char sui sauce
400 g (13 oz) fresh flat rice noodles
1 cup (30 g/1 oz) fresh coriander
leaves, chopped

3 spring onions, extra, sliced
1 tablespoon vegetable oil
fresh coriander sprigs, to garnish

1 Soak eight bamboo skewers in
water for 30 minutes. Thread the pork
and spring onion alternately on the
skewers. Combine the vinegar, bean
paste and char sui sauce in a shallow
non-metallic dish. Add the skewers
and turn to coat. Cover with plastic
wrap and refrigerate overnight.
2 Drain the skewers, reserving the
marinade. Heat a grill plate until
very hot and cook the skewers for
1–2 minutes on each side, or until
brown and cooked through. Remove
and keep warm. Place the reserved
marinade in a small saucepan and
bring to the boil.

3 Separate the noodles with your
hands, add the coriander and extra
spring onion and toss together. Divide
into four portions. Heat the oil in
a non-stick frying pan over medium
heat. Place one portion in the pan,
pressing down very firmly with a
spatula to form a pancake. Cook
on each side for 3–4 minutes, or
until golden. Remove and keep warm.
Repeat with the remaining noodles.
4 To serve, place each noodle cake
on a serving plate and top with two
skewers. Drizzle with the marinade
and garnish with the coriander sprigs.

NUTRITION PER SERVE
Protein 59.5 g; Fat 11.5 g; Carbohydrate
46.5 g; Dietary Fibre 3 g; Cholesterol 237.5 mg;
2240 kJ (535 Cal)

Thread the pork cubes and pieces of spring
onion alternately onto each skewer.

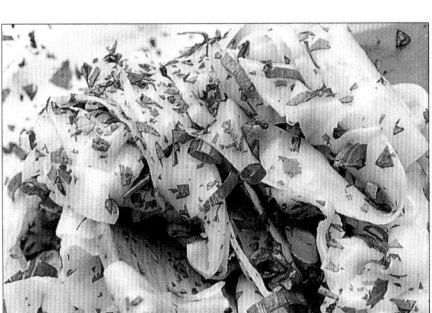

Toss the coriander and spring onion through the
flat rice noodles.

Press the noodles firmly with a spatula to form a
pancake, then cook until golden.

EGG AND BACON PIE

Preparation time: 20 minutes
+ 30 minutes refrigeration + cooling
Total cooking time: 50 minutes
Serves 4–6

PASTRY
450 g (14 oz) plain flour
125 g (4 oz) butter, chilled and cubed
250 g (8 oz) mascarpone

1 tablespoon olive oil
300 g (10 oz) bacon, diced
2 onions, halved and thinly sliced
1 tablespoon chopped fresh
    flat-leaf parsley
6 eggs
1 egg yolk

1 Sift the flour into a large bowl and rub in the butter with your fingertips until the mixture resembles fine breadcrumbs. Add the mascarpone and mix with a flat-bladed knife, using a cutting action, until the mixture begins to form lumps which leave the side of the bowl.
2 Turn the dough out onto a lightly floured surface and gently gather into a smooth ball. Flatten slightly into a disc, then cover in plastic wrap and refrigerate for 30 minutes.
3 Preheat the oven to warm 170°C (325°F/Gas 3). Lightly grease a 23 cm (9 inch) top, 18 cm (7 inch) base and 3 cm (1¼ inch) deep metal pie dish. Place a baking tray in the oven to preheat. Heat the oil in a frying pan and cook the bacon and onion over medium heat, stirring occasionally, for 5–7 minutes, or until just browning. Stir in the parsley. Set aside to cool.
4 Divide the pastry into two portions, one slightly larger than the other. Roll out the larger portion between two sheets of baking paper until large enough to line the base and side of the pie dish. Line the pie dish. Place the onion and bacon in the pastry shell and make six well-spaced holes in the mixture with the back of a spoon. Crack an egg into each of the holes. Brush the rim of the pastry with water. Roll out the remaining pastry between the baking paper until large enough to cover the top of the pie. Lift

it onto the pie. Trim the excess pastry and seal the edges well. Re-roll the trimmings and make leaves to decorate the pie. Brush with egg yolk and bake on the hot tray for 40 minutes. Cover if it browns too quickly. Leave for 10 minutes before serving.

NUTRITION PER SERVE (6)
Protein 29.5 g; Fat 43.5 g; Carbohydrate 58.5 g; Dietary Fibre 3.5 g; Cholesterol 332 mg; 3085 kJ (735 Cal)

Add the mascarpone and mix with a flat-bladed knife until lumps start to form.

Crack an egg into each hole in the onion and bacon filling mixture.

THAI-SPICED GRILLED PORK TENDERLOIN AND GREEN MANGO SALAD

Preparation time: 45 minutes +
 2 hours refrigeration
Total cooking time: 10 minutes
Serves 4 as a main (6 as an entrée)

2 stems lemon grass (white part only),
 thinly sliced
1 clove garlic
2 red Asian shallots
1 tablespoon coarsely chopped fresh
 ginger
1 red bird's-eye chilli, seeded
1 tablespoon fish sauce
½ cup (15 g/½ oz) fresh coriander
1 teaspoon grated lime rind
1 tablespoon lime juice
2 tablespoons oil
2 pork tenderloins, trimmed
steamed jasmine rice (optional)

DRESSING
1 large red chilli, seeded and finely
 chopped
2 cloves garlic, finely chopped
3 fresh coriander roots, finely chopped
1¼ tablespoons grated palm sugar
2 tablespoons fish sauce
¼ cup (60 ml/2 fl oz) lime juice

SALAD
2 green mangoes or 1 small green
 papaya, peeled, pitted and cut into
 julienne strips
1 carrot, grated
½ cup (45 g/1½ oz) bean sprouts
½ red onion, thinly sliced
3 tablespoons roughly chopped fresh
 mint
3 tablespoons roughly chopped fresh
 coriander leaves
3 tablespoons roughly chopped fresh
 Vietnamese mint

1 Place the lemon grass, garlic, shallots, ginger, chilli, fish sauce, coriander, lime rind, lime juice and oil in a blender or food processor and process until a coarse paste forms. Transfer the mixture to a non-metallic dish and coat the pork in the marinade. Cover with plastic wrap and refrigerate for at least 2 hours, but no longer than 4 hours.

2 To make the salad dressing, mix all the ingredients together in a bowl.
3 Combine all the salad ingredients in a large bowl.
4 Preheat a grill or chargrill pan and cook the pork over medium heat for 4–5 minutes each side, or until cooked through. Remove from the heat, rest for 5 minutes, then slice.
5 Toss the dressing and salad together. Season to taste with salt and cracked black pepper. Arrange the sliced pork in a circle in the centre of each plate and top with salad. To make this a main course, serve with steamed jasmine rice, if desired.

NUTRITION PER SERVE (4)
Protein 60 g; Fat 14 g; Carbohydrate 20 g;
Dietary Fibre 3 g; Cholesterol 122 mg;
1860 kJ (444 Cal)

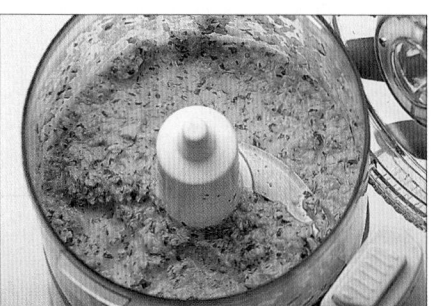

Process the marinade ingredients to a coarse paste.

Cook the pork on a chargrill pan until cooked through.

SPICY SAUSAGE STIR-FRY

Preparation time: 40 minutes
Total cooking time: 15 minutes
Serves 4

2 tablespoons oil
500 g (1 lb) potato, cubed
500 g (1 lb) orange sweet potato, cubed
6 chorizo sausages, diagonally sliced
2 cloves garlic, thinly sliced
1 red onion, cut into wedges
200 g (6½ oz) broccoli, chopped
1 red capsicum, cut into short thick strips
½ cup (125 ml/4 fl oz) tomato purée
2 tablespoons chopped fresh parsley

1 Heat the wok until very hot, add the oil and swirl it around to coat the side. Stir-fry the potato and sweet potato over medium heat until tender and golden. Remove and drain on paper towels, then place on a serving plate and cover to keep warm.
2 Add the sausage to the wok and stir-fry in batches over high heat for 3–4 minutes, or until crisp. Remove and drain on paper towels.
3 Add the garlic and onion to the wok and stir-fry for 2 minutes, or until the onion softens. Add the broccoli and capsicum, and stir-fry for 1 minute. Return the sausage to the wok, add the tomato purée and toss to combine. Add the parsley and season with salt and black pepper. Toss well and serve on top of the stir-fried potato.

NUTRITION PER SERVE
Protein 20 g; Fat 30 g; Carbohydrate 40 g;
Dietary Fibre 8 g; Cholesterol 55 mg;
2390 kJ (570 cal)

Peel the skin from the sweet potato and cut the flesh into cubes.

Chorizo is a spicy Spanish sausage. Cut the chorizo into thick diagonal slices.

Stir-fry the potato and sweet potato in the hot oil until tender and golden.

BACON, TURKEY AND CIDER PIE

Preparation time: 45 minutes
+ 20 minutes refrigeration
Total cooking time: 4 hours
Serves 6

PASTRY
3¼ cups (405 g/13 oz) plain flour
1 teaspoon baking powder
200 g (6½ oz) lard, chilled and roughly
    chopped
3–4 tablespoons iced water

4 carrots
4 celery sticks (including leafy tops)
9 spring onions
3 onions
1.5 kg (3 lb) smoked bacon bones
2 teaspoons whole black peppercorns
1.5 litres apple cider
60 g (2 oz) butter
500 g (1 lb) turkey breast fillet, cut into
    2 cm (¾ inch) cubes
½ cup (60 g/2 oz) seasoned plain flour
1 egg, lightly beaten

1 Sift the flour and baking powder into a large bowl and add the lard and ½ teaspoon salt. Rub the lard into the flour with your fingertips until the mixture resembles fine breadcrumbs. Make a well in the centre, add almost all the water and mix with a flat-bladed knife, using a cutting action, until the mixture comes together in beads, adding more water, a teaspoon at a time, if necessary. Turn out onto a lightly floured surface and gather together into a smooth ball. Flatten slightly into a disc, wrap in plastic wrap and refrigerate for at least 20 minutes.
2 Roughly chop two of the carrots, three of the celery sticks (including the leafy tops), six of the spring onions and cut two of the onions into quarters and place them in a large saucepan with the bacon bones, peppercorns, cider and 2 litres cold water. Bring to the boil over high heat, then reduce the heat and simmer for 2 hours. Remove the bones with tongs, then strain the liquid into a bowl. Return the liquid to the saucepan and simmer for

another hour, or until reduced (you will need 2 cups/500 ml/16 fl oz). Meanwhile, pick the meat from the bacon bones, avoiding any gristle and small bones. You should have 200–250 g (6½ oz–8 oz) meat.
3 Cut the remaining carrots and celery sticks into 1 cm (½ inch) cubes, roughly chop the onion and cut the remaining spring onions into 3 cm (1¼ inch) lengths. Melt half the butter in a large frying pan over medium heat. Add the carrot and onion and cook for 5 minutes, or until the onion is soft and golden. Stir in the celery and spring onion and cook for another 3 minutes, or until all the vegetables have softened. Transfer to a plate.
4 Toss the turkey cubes in seasoned flour. Melt the remaining butter in the large frying pan over medium heat. Add the turkey and cook, turning constantly, for 8 minutes, or until browned all over. Return the vegetables and bacon meat to the pan and stir well, scraping the bottom of the pan to remove any flour. Slowly pour in the reserved stock. Stir for several minutes until the mixture has thickened, then remove from the heat and allow to cool.
5 Preheat the oven to moderate 180°C (350°F/Gas 4) and lightly grease a 25 cm (10 inch) ceramic pie dish. Divide the dough into two portions, one slightly larger than the other. Roll out the larger portion between two sheets of baking paper into a 35 cm (14 inch) circle, not too thin. Line the pie dish with the pastry. Spoon the filling into the shell. Roll out the remaining pastry between the baking paper to a 30 cm (12 inch) circle. Brush around the rim of the pastry base with egg, then place the top on. Trim off any excess pastry and pinch the edges together. If you wish, decorate the edges with pastry leaves. Brush the pie with egg, prick with a fork and bake for 45 minutes, or until golden brown.

NUTRITION PER SERVE
Protein 29 g; Fat 46 g; Carbohydrate 89.5 g; Dietary Fibre 6 g; Cholesterol 124 mg; 3715 kJ (885 Cal)

Gently gather the dough together into a smooth ball.

Using your fingers, remove the meat from the bacon bones.

Pour the reserved stock over the bacon and turkey mixture.

Brush the beaten egg over the rim of the filled pastry.

ITALIAN SAUSAGE CASEROLE

Preparation time: 15 minutes
Total cooking time: 45 minutes
Serves 4

2 large red capsicums
1 tablespoon olive oil
2 large red onions, sliced into thick
    wedges
2 cloves garlic, finely chopped
600 g (1¼ lb) Italian-style thin pork
    sausages
300 g (10 oz) can chickpeas, drained
150 g (5 oz) flat mushrooms, thickly
    sliced
½ cup (125 ml/4 fl oz) dry white wine
2 bay leaves
2 teaspoons chopped fresh rosemary
400 g (13 oz) can diced tomatoes

1 Cut the capsicums into large pieces, removing the seeds and membrane. Place skin-side-up, under a hot grill until the skin blackens and blisters. Allow to cool in a plastic bag. Peel away the skin, and slice diagonally into thick strips.
2 Meanwhile, heat the oil in a non-stick frying pan. Add the onion and garlic, and stir over medium heat for 6 minutes, or until the onion is soft and browned. Remove the onion from the pan. Add the sausages to the same pan. Cook over medium heat, turning occasionally, for 8 minutes, or until the sausages are browned. Remove the sausages and slice diagonally into 3 cm (1¼ inch) pieces.
3 Combine the capsicum, onion, sausage, chickpeas and mushrooms in the pan and cook over medium–high heat for 5 minutes.

4 Add the wine, bay leaves and rosemary. Bring to the boil, then reduce the heat to low and simmer for 3 minutes. Stir in the tomatoes and simmer for 20 minutes, or until the sauce has thickened slightly. Remove the bay leaves and season to taste with sugar, salt and cracked black pepper. Delicious served with fettucine, noodles, grilled ciabatta bread, mashed potato, soft polenta, or Parmesan shavings.

NUTRITION PER SERVE
Protein 20 g; Fat 25 g; Carbohydrate 25 g; Dietary Fibre 9.5 g; Cholesterol 50 mg; 1695 kJ (405 Cal)

STORAGE TIME: This casserole can be stored in the refrigerator for up to 2 days.

Grill the capsicums under a hot grill until the skin blackens and blisters.

Remove the skin from the cooled capsicums and slice them into thin strips.

Use a pair of tongs to hold the sausages as you slice them into 3 cm (¼ inch) pieces.

SAUSAGE AND ONION PIE

Preparation time: 30 minutes
Total cooking time: 55 minutes
Serves 6–8

1 tablespoon olive oil
2 onions, chopped
1 clove garlic, chopped
1 kg (2 lb) pork sausages (see NOTE)
1 tablespoon chopped chives
1 teaspoon chopped fresh
   flat-leaf parsley
1½ teaspoons English mustard
1 egg, lightly beaten
600 g (1¼ lb) shortcrust pastry
1 egg, lightly beaten, to glaze

1 Preheat the oven to 200°C (400°F/ Gas 6) and grease an 18 cm (7 inch) metal pie dish. Heat the oil in a frying pan and cook the onion and garlic for 5 minutes, or until soft and lightly golden. Transfer to a large bowl.
2 Remove the sausage meat from the casings, crumble slightly and add to the onion. Add the chives, parsley and mustard. Season well. Mix well, then stir in the beaten egg.
3 Roll out two-thirds of the pastry between two sheets of baking paper to make a round large enough to fit the base and side of the pie tin. Line the tin with the pastry and trim the edges. Fill with the sausage mixture.
4 Roll out the remaining dough between two pieces of baking paper to a round large enough to cover the pie. Brush the rim of the first piece of pastry with the egg glaze, then cover the top with the pastry and press the edges to seal. Make a small hole in the centre. Use the trimmings to decorate. Brush the pie with beaten egg and bake for 10 minutes. Reduce the oven to 180°C (350°F/Gas 4) and bake for 40 minutes. Serve hot.

NUTRITION PER SERVE (8)
Protein 22 g; Fat 51 g; Carbohydrate 37 g; Dietary Fibre 3.5 g; Cholesterol 148 mg; 2835 kJ (680 cal)

NOTE: It's important to use lean, English-style pork sausages as they contain grains which soak up any excess liquid. Other sausages will make the pie too wet.

Using your fingers, remove the sausage meat from the casings.

Fill the pastry-lined pie dish with the sausage meat filling.

BARBECUED PORK WITH RICE NOODLE CAKE AND CUCUMBER SALAD

Preparation time: 40 minutes +
  5 minutes soaking
Total cooking time: 25 minutes
Serves 4

500 g (1 lb) thin fresh rice noodles,
    at room temperature
2 Lebanese cucumbers, halved
    lengthways and thinly sliced
2 tablespoons chopped fresh
    coriander leaves
1 tablespoon lime juice
1 tablespoon fish sauce
2 teaspoons caster sugar
¼ cup (60 ml/2 fl oz) oil
1 red capsicum, thinly sliced
3 cloves garlic, finely chopped
1 tablespoon white vinegar
¼ cup (60 ml/2 fl oz) black bean sauce
⅓ cup (80 ml/2¾ fl oz) chicken stock
1 tablespoon soft brown sugar
300 g (10 oz) Chinese barbecued
    pork, sliced

1 Pour boiling water over the noodles and leave for 5 minutes, or until softened. Drain, then separate by pulling apart slightly.
2 To make the cucumber salad, toss the cucumber, coriander, lime juice, fish sauce and caster sugar together in a large bowl and leave until needed.
3 Heat 1 tablespoon of the oil in a large non-stick frying pan. Place four 9.5 cm x 2.5 cm deep (3½ inch x 1 inch deep) rings in the frying pan. Fill as firmly as possible with the noodles and press down with the back of a spoon. Cook over medium heat for 10 minutes, or until crisp, pressing the noodles down occasionally. Turn over and repeat on the other side, adding another tablespoon of the oil if necessary. Cover and keep warm.
4 Meanwhile, heat 1 tablespoon of the remaining oil in a wok, add the capsicum and stir-fry over high heat for 2 minutes, or until the capsicum has softened slightly. Add the garlic to the wok and toss for 1 minute, or until softened, then add the vinegar, black bean sauce, stock and sugar. Stir until the sugar has dissolved, then simmer for 2 minutes, or until the sauce thickens slightly. Add the Chinese barbecued pork and stir to coat.
5 To serve, place a noodle cake on each plate and top with some of the barbecued pork mixture. Arrange the salad around the noodle cake and serve.

NUTRITION PER SERVE
Protein 34 g; Fat 28 g; Carbohydrate 100 g; Dietary Fibre 7 g; Cholesterol 70 mg; 3360 kJ (805 Cal)

Soak the noodles in boiling water until they are soft.

Press the noodles down into the rings with the back of a spoon.

Simmer until the sugar dissolves and the sauce slightly thickens.

ROAST PORK, CHINESE CABBAGE AND NOODLE HOTPOT

Preparation time: 15 minutes
Total cooking time: 20 minutes
Serves 4

60 g (2 oz) mung bean vermicelli
250 g (8 oz) Chinese cabbage
1 litre chicken stock
2.5 cm x 2.5 cm (1 inch x 1 inch) piece fresh ginger, thinly sliced
350 g (11 oz) Chinese roast pork, skin removed and reserved (see NOTE)
2 spring onions, thinly sliced on the diagonal
2 tablespoons light soy sauce
1 tablespoon Chinese rice wine
½ teaspoon sesame oil
100 g (3½ oz) Sichuan pickles, roughly chopped (optional)

1 Soak the vermicelli in a large bowl of boiling water for 3–4 minutes, or until soft. Drain and rinse, then drain again thoroughly.
2 Separate the cabbage leaves and remove the leafy ends from the stems. Cut both the cabbage stems and leaves into 2.5 cm (1 inch) squares.
3 Place the chicken stock and ginger slices in a 2 litre flameproof casserole dish and bring to the boil over high heat. Add the cabbage stems and cook for 2 minutes, then add the cabbage leaves and cook for 1 minute. Reduce the heat to medium, add the noodles and cook, covered, for 4–5 minutes, stirring occasionally.
4 Meanwhile, cut the pork into 2.5 cm (1 inch) cubes and add to the casserole dish with the spring onion, soy sauce, rice wine and sesame oil. Stir to combine, then cook, covered, for another 3–4 minutes. Serve with the pickles on the side.

NUTRITION PER SERVE
Protein 31.5 g;Fat 4.5 g; Carbohydrate 13 g; Dietary Fibre 2.5 g; Cholesterol 112 mg; 950 kJ (225 Cal)

NOTE: If desired, grill the reserved pork skin for 1 minute, or until crispy and arrange on top of each serving.

Cut the Chinese cabbage leaves and stems into squares.

CHIANG MAI NOODLES

Preparation time: 20 minutes
Total cooking time: 15 minutes
Serves 4

500 g (1 lb) fresh egg noodles
1 tablespoon oil
3 Asian or French shallots, chopped
6 cloves garlic, chopped
2 teaspoons finely chopped red
    chillies
1–2 tablespoons red curry paste
    (use the recipe on page 246 or
    ready-made paste)

350 g (12 oz) lean pork, finely sliced
1 carrot, cut into thin strips
2 tablespoons fish sauce
2 teaspoons soft brown sugar
3 spring onions, finely sliced
¼ cup (7 g/¼ oz) coriander leaves
nam prik dipping sauce (page 249), for
    serving

1 Cook the noodles in a wok or large pan of rapidly boiling water for 2–3 minutes, or until they are just tender. Drain and keep warm. Heat the oil in a wok until it is very hot. Add the shallots, garlic, chilli and curry paste and stir-fry for 2 minutes or until fragrant. Add the pork in two batches and cook for 3 minutes or until the meat changes colour.

2 Return all the meat to the wok. Add the carrot, fish sauce and brown sugar and bring to the boil. Add the noodles and spring onion and toss well. Top with coriander leaves and serve immediately with nam prik.

NUTRITION PER SERVE
Protein 17 g; Fat 7.5 g; Carbohydrate 92 g;
Dietary Fibre 5 g; Cholesterol 23 mg;
2122 kJ (501 cal)

Use Asian shallots if you can find them. Otherwise French shallots will do.

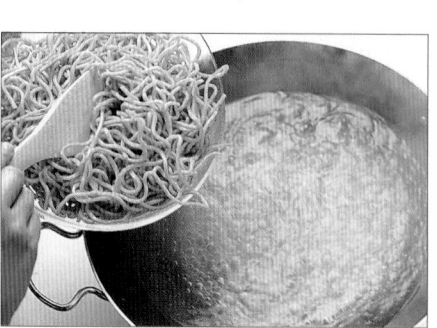
Cook the noodles in a wok or pan of rapidly boiling water until just tender.

Return all the meat to the wok. Add the carrot, fish sauce and brown sugar.

SINGAPORE NOODLES

Preparation time: 20 minutes
Total cooking time: 10 minutes
Serves 4–6

150 g (5 oz) dried rice vermicelli
oil, for cooking
250 g (8 oz) Chinese barbecued pork,
    cut into small pieces
250 g (8 oz) peeled raw prawns, cut
    into small pieces
2 tablespoons Madras curry powder
2 cloves garlic, crushed
100 g (3½ oz) shiitake mushrooms,
    thinly sliced

1 onion, thinly sliced
100 g (3½ oz) green beans, thinly
    sliced on the diagonal
1 tablespoon soy sauce
4 spring onions, thinly sliced on the
    diagonal

1 Place the vermicelli in a large bowl, cover with boiling water and soak for 5 minutes. Drain well and spread out on a clean tea towel to dry.
2 Heat the wok until very hot, add 1 tablespoon of the oil and swirl it around to coat the side. Stir-fry the barbecued pork and the prawn pieces in batches over high heat. Remove from the wok and set aside.

3 Reheat the wok, add 2 tablespoons of the oil and stir-fry the curry powder and garlic for 1–2 minutes, or until fragrant. Add the mushrooms and onion and stir-fry over medium heat for 2–3 minutes, or until the onion and mushrooms are soft.
4 Return the pork and prawns to the wok, add the beans and 2 teaspoons water, and toss to combine. Add the drained noodles, soy sauce and spring onion. Toss well and serve.

NUTRITION PER SERVE (6)
Protein 10 g; Fat 7.5 g; Carbohydrate 25 g;
Dietary Fibre 3 g; Cholesterol 60 mg;
905 kJ (215 cal)

Cut the barbecued pork into slices, then into small pieces.

Put the vermicelli in a heatproof bowl, cover with boiling water and leave to soak.

Stir-fry the curry powder and garlic in the oil until the mixture is fragrant.

CASSOULET

Preparation time: 20 minutes + overnight soaking
Total cooking time: 4 hours
Serves 6

500 g (1 lb) dried haricot beans
1.5 litres beef stock
2 tablespoons oil
500 g (1 lb) pork spareribs, trimmed
250 g (8 oz) diced lamb
250 g (8 oz) garlic or spiced sausage
125 g (4 oz) piece bacon, cut into cubes
2 onions, chopped
2 carrots, chopped
2 cloves garlic, crushed
1 bay leaf
1 sprig fresh parsley
1 sprig fresh thyme
6 black peppercorns
2 cups (160 g/5½ oz) fresh breadcrumbs
60 g (2 oz) butter, chilled and grated

1 Soak the beans overnight in water.
2 Drain the beans and place in a large saucepan with the stock. Bring slowly to the boil, then reduce the heat and simmer for 1 hour, or until tender. Drain the beans, reserving the liquid.
3 Heat the oil in a frying pan. Brown the pork, lamb, sausage and bacon in several batches. Remove and drain on paper towels. Add the onion, carrot and garlic to the pan, and brown well.
4 Preheat the oven to warm 160°C (315°F/Gas 2–3). Layer the meats, beans and vegetables in a large casserole dish. Tie the herbs and peppercorns together in a small piece of muslin, and add to the dish. Pour over the liquid from the beans, cover and bake for 2 hours.
5 Remove and discard the herb bag. Combine the breadcrumbs and butter, and sprinkle over the top of the casserole. Return to the oven for 30 minutes, or until the crust is golden and crisp.

NUTRITION PER SERVE
Protein 55 g; Fat 36 g; Carbohydrate 56 g; Dietary Fibre 19 g; Cholesterol 123 mg; 3140 kJ (750 cal)

Place the soaked haricot beans in a large saucepan with the beef stock.

Add the onion, carrot and garlic to the frying pan, and brown well.

Layer the meats, beans and vegetables in a large casserole dish.

Sprinkle the combined breadcrumbs and butter over the top of the casserole.

PORK AND LENTIL STEW

Preparation time: 20 minutes
Total cooking time: 1 hour
Serves 4

1 tablespoon olive oil
2 onions, chopped
500 g (1 lb) lean diced pork
2 teaspoons sweet Hungarian paprika
1 teaspoon hot paprika
½ teaspoon dried thyme
2 tablespoons tomato paste
2 teaspoons soft brown sugar

¼ cup (60 g/2 oz) red lentils
1½ cups (375 ml/12 fl oz) beef stock
1 tomato
2 tablespoons low-fat plain yoghurt

1 Heat the olive oil in a large, deep saucepan over high heat. Add the onion, pork and paprikas, and stir for 3–4 minutes, or until browned.
2 Add the thyme, tomato paste, sugar, lentils, stock, and salt and freshly ground black pepper. Bring to the boil, then reduce the heat to very low and cook, covered, for 20 minutes, stirring occasionally to prevent sticking. Uncover and cook for another 15–20 minutes, or until thickened.
3 Remove from the heat and set aside for 10 minutes. Cut the tomato in half and scoop out the seeds. Slice the flesh into thin strips.
4 Just before serving, stir the yoghurt into the stew. Scatter with the tomato strips and serve with rice, if desired.

NUTRITION PER SERVE
Protein 35 g; Fat 8 g; Carbohydrate 13 g;
Dietary Fibre 4 g; Cholesterol 70 mg;
1110 kJ (265 cal)

Stir the onion, pork and paprika until the pork is browned on all sides.

Add the beef stock to the saucepan and bring to the boil.

To make the tomato garnish, remove the seeds and slice the flesh into thin strips.

PORK AND TOMATO BURGERS

**Preparation time: 20 minutes +
   15 minutes refrigeration**
Total cooking time: 15 minutes
Serves 4

350 g (11 oz) pork and veal mince
100 g (3½ oz) sun-dried tomatoes,
   chopped
3 spring onions, finely chopped
2 tablespoons chopped fresh basil
1 red capsicum, seeded and sliced
1 tablespoon balsamic vinegar

1 Mix together the mince, sun-dried tomato, spring onion and basil. Season well and knead for 2 minutes, or until a little sticky. Form into four burgers and refrigerate for 15 minutes.
2 Mix the capsicum with a little olive oil. Cook on a hot, lightly oiled barbecue grill or flatplate, tossing well and drizzling with the balsamic vinegar, until just softened. Set aside.
3 Wipe the barbecue clean and reheat. Brush the burgers with a little olive oil and cook for 4–5 minutes each side, or until browned and cooked through. Serve with the chargrilled capsicum.

NUTRITION PER SERVE
Protein 20 g; Fat 10 g; Carbohydrate 5 g;
Dietary Fibre 2 g; Cholesterol 45 mg;
840 kJ (200 cal)

Cook the capsicum, tossing well and drizzling with balsamic vinegar, until softened.

Clean the barbecue plate before you reheat it to cook the burgers.

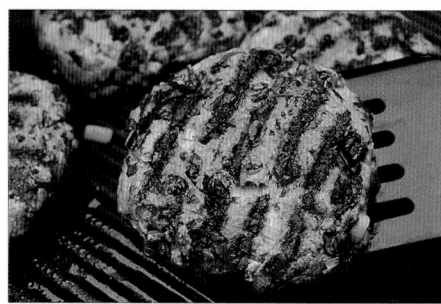

Brush the burgers with a little oil and cook until they are browned.

PORK, PAPRIKA AND POTATO STEW

Preparation time: 15 minutes
Total cooking time: 45 minutes
Serves 4

1 tablespoon paprika
4 thick pork loin cutlets
2 tablespoons olive oil
¼ cup (60 ml/2 fl oz) sherry
   vinegar
¼ teaspoon cayenne pepper
½ cup (125 ml/4 fl oz) tomato
   purée
400 g (13 oz) potatoes, cut into 2 cm
   (¾ inch) cubes
8 French shallots, peeled
200 g (6½ oz) rocket leaves

1 Combine the paprika with ¼ teaspoon each of salt and freshly ground black pepper. Sprinkle over both sides of the pork. Heat the oil over medium heat in a deep frying pan large enough to fit the cutlets in a single layer, and cook the cutlets until brown on both sides.
2 Pour the sherry vinegar into the pan and stir well to scrape up any sediment stuck to the base. Stir in the cayenne pepper, tomato purée and 1 cup (250 ml/8 fl oz) hot water. Bring to the boil, then add the potato and shallots. Reduce the heat and simmer, covered, for 30 minutes, or until the sauce has thickened and reduced by half—check the liquid level once or twice, and add a little more water if necessary. Season.

3 To serve, divide the rocket leaves among four serving plates and place a cutlet on top. Spoon the sauce and potato over the top.

NUTRITION PER SERVE
Protein 41 g; Fat 17 g; Carbohydrate 17 g; Dietary Fibre 3.5 g; Cholesterol 103 mg; 1615 kJ (385 cal)

CHILLI PORK RIBS

Preparation time: 15 minutes + overnight marinating
Total cooking time: 20 minutes
Serves 4–6

1 kg (2 lb) pork spareribs
125 g (4 oz) can puréed tomatoes
2 tablespoons honey
2 tablespoons chilli sauce
2 tablespoons hoisin sauce
2 tablespoons lime juice
2 cloves garlic, crushed
1 tablespoon oil

1 Cut each rib into thirds, then lay them in a single layer in a shallow non-metallic dish.
2 Mix together all the other ingredients except the oil and pour over the meat, turning to coat well. Cover with plastic wrap and refrigerate overnight, turning occasionally.
3 Drain the ribs, reserving the marinade, and cook them over medium heat on a lightly oiled barbecue grill or flatplate. Baste often with the marinade and cook for 15–20 minutes, or until the ribs are tender and well browned, turning occasionally. Season to taste before serving immediately.

NUTRITION PER SERVE (6)
Protein 15 g; Fat 26 g; Carbohydrate 9 g;
Dietary Fibre 0 g; Cholesterol 90 mg;
1399 kJ (333 cal)

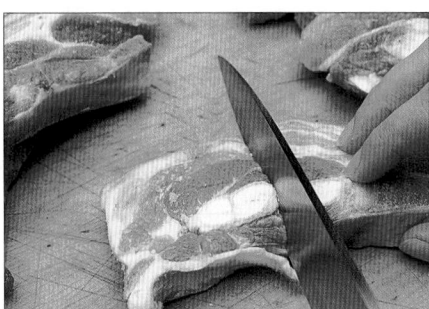
Use a sharp knife to cut each of the pork ribs into thirds, then place in a shallow dish.

Mix together all the ingredients for the marinade and then pour over the ribs.

Turn the ribs and baste often with the marinade while they are cooking.

570

HASH HAM CAKE

Preparation time: 30 minutes +
1 hour refrigeration
Total cooking time: 50 minutes
Serves 6

500 g (1 lb) floury potatoes, quartered
200 g (6½ oz) ham, finely chopped
4 spring onions, finely chopped
1 small gherkin, finely chopped
2 tablespoons chopped fresh parsley
1 egg, lightly beaten
cooking oil spray

1 Cook the potato until tender. Drain and mash in a large bowl.
2 Mix in the ham, spring onion, gherkin, parsley, beaten egg and lots of black pepper. Spread on a plate, cover and refrigerate for at least 1 hour, or overnight, to firm.
3 Spray a heavy-based non-stick frying pan lightly with oil. Add the potato mixture, spread evenly into the pan and smooth the surface with the back of a spoon. Cook over moderate heat for 15 minutes, then slide out onto a plate. Spray the pan with oil again, carefully flip the cake back into the pan and cook for another 15–20 minutes, or until the outside forms a brown crust. Serve hot, cut into wedges.

NUTRITION PER SERVE
Protein 9 g; Fat 10 g; Carbohydrate 10 g;
Dietary Fibre 2 g; Cholesterol 70 mg;
730 kJ (175 cal)

Spread the mixture in a heavy-based frying pan and smooth the surface.

Slide the hash cake onto a plate, then flip back into the pan to cook the other side.

PORK LOIN CHOPS WITH APPLE CHUTNEY

Preparation time: 20 minutes
+ 3 hours marinating
Total cooking time: 25 minutes
Serves 6

6 pork loin chops
⅓ cup (80 ml/2¾ fl oz) white wine
2 tablespoons oil
2 tablespoons honey
1½ teaspoons ground cumin
2 cloves garlic, crushed

APPLE CHUTNEY
3 green apples

½ cup (125 ml/4 fl oz) apple juice
½ cup (125 g/4 oz) fruit chutney
15 g (½ oz) butter

1 Trim the chops of excess fat and sinew. Combine the wine, oil, honey, cumin and garlic. Put the chops in a shallow non-metallic dish and then pour in the marinade and toss well to cover. Store, covered with plastic wrap, in the fridge for at least 3 hours, turning occasionally.
2 To make the chutney, peel and dice the apples. Place in a small pan with the apple juice. Bring to the boil, reduce the heat and simmer, covered, for 7 minutes or until completely soft. Stir in the chutney and butter and

serve warm.
3 Cook the chops on a hot, lightly oiled barbecue grill or flatplate for 8 minutes on each side or until tender, turning once. Serve immediately with the chutney.

NUTRITION PER SERVE
Protein 25 g; Fat 10 g; Carbohydrate 29 g; Dietary Fibre 2 g; Cholesterol 55 mg; 1304 kJ (311 cal)

STORAGE: The chutney can be kept in the fridge for 1 day before use. It is also delicious with roast pork, lamb chops, chicken cutlets or as a relish with a cheese plate. It can be served warm or cold.

Mix together the white wine, oil, honey, cumin and garlic to make a marinade.

Simmer until the apple is soft and then stir in the chutney and butter.

Cook the chops on a hot barbecue for 8 minutes on each side.

GINGER-ORANGE PORK

Preparation time: 15 minutes + 3 hours
marinating
Total cooking time: 20 minutes
Serves 6

6 pork butterfly steaks
1 cup (250 ml/8 fl oz) ginger wine
½ cup (150 g/5 oz) orange marmalade
2 tablespoons oil
1 tablespoon grated fresh ginger

1 Trim the pork steak of excess fat and sinew. Mix together the wine, marmalade, oil and ginger. Place the steaks in a shallow non-metallic dish and add the marinade. Store, covered with plastic wrap, in the fridge for at least 3 hours, turning occasionally. Drain, reserving the marinade.
2 Cook the pork on a hot, lightly oiled barbecue flatplate or grill for 5 minutes each side or until tender, turning once.
3 While the meat is cooking, place the reserved marinade in a small pan. Bring to the boil, reduce the heat and

simmer for 5 minutes, or until the marinade has reduced and thickened slightly. Pour over the pork.

NUTRITION PER SERVE
Protein 45 g; Fat 10 g; Carbohydrate 14 g; Dietary Fibre 0 g; Cholesterol 98 mg; 1461 kJ (349 cal)

HINT: Steaks of uneven thickness may curl when cooked. Prevent this by leaving a layer of fat on the outside and making a few deep cuts in it prior to cooking. Remove before serving.

Put the pork in a shallow non-metallic dish so that the marinade doesn't react.

Cook the pork on a hot barbecue for 5 minutes on each side, or until tender.

Place the leftover marinade in a small pan and boil until reduced and thickened to a sauce.

LION'S HEAD MEATBALLS

**Preparation time: 20 minutes + overnight
  refrigeration +
  20 minutes soaking
Total cooking time: 4 hours 45 minutes
Serves 4**

CHICKEN STOCK
1.5 kg (3 lb) chicken bones (chicken
  necks, backs, wings), washed
2 slices fresh ginger, cut into 1 cm
  (½ inch) thick slices
4 spring onions

6 dried Chinese mushrooms
100 g (3½ oz) mung bean vermicelli
600 g (1¼ lb) pork mince
1 egg white
4 cloves garlic, finely chopped
1 tablespoon finely grated fresh ginger
1 tablespoon cornflour
1½ tablespoons Chinese rice wine
6 spring onions, thinly sliced
2 tablespoons peanut oil
¼ cup (60 ml/2 fl oz) light soy sauce
1 teaspoon sugar
400 g (13 oz) bok choy, halved
  lengthways, leaves separated

1 To make the stock, place the bones and 3.5 litres water in a large saucepan and bring to a simmer—do not let it boil. Remove the scum from the surface and continue doing so over the next 30 minutes. Add the ginger and spring onions, and cook, partially covered, keeping at a low simmer for 3 hours. Strain through a fine sieve. Cool. Cover and refrigerate overnight. Remove the layer of fat from the surface once it has solidified.
2 Soak the Chinese mushrooms in 1 cup (250 ml/8 fl oz) boiling water for 20 minutes. Drain. Discard the stems and thinly slice the caps. Meanwhile, place the vermicelli in a heatproof bowl, cover with boiling water and soak for 3–4 minutes, or until soft. Drain and rinse. Preheat the oven to hot 220°C (425°F/Gas 7).
3 Place the mince, egg white, garlic, ginger, cornflour, rice wine, two-thirds of the spring onion and salt, to taste, in a food processor. Using the pulse button, process until smooth and well combined. Divide the mixture into

eight portions and shape into large balls with wet hands.
4 Place 2 cups (500 ml/16 fl oz) of the stock (freeze any remaining stock) in a large saucepan and bring to the boil over high heat, then remove from the heat and keep warm.
5 Heat the oil in a wok over high heat. Fry the meatballs in batches for 2 minutes each side, or until golden, but not cooked through. Drain.
6 Place the meatballs, mushrooms, soy sauce and sugar in a 2.5 litre ovenproof clay pot or casserole dish, and cover with the hot stock. Bake,

covered, for 45 minutes. Add the bok choy and noodles and bake, covered, for another 10 minutes. Sprinkle with the remaining spring onion, and serve.

NUTRITION PER SERVE
Protein 35 g; Fat 20 g; Carbohydrate 22 g;
Dietary Fibre 4 g; Cholesterol 97 mg;
1720 kJ (410 cal)

HINT: To save time, use 2 cups (500 ml/16 fl oz) purchased stock instead of making your own.

Form the mince mixture into eight large balls using wet hands.

Add the bok choy and noodles to the clay pot containing the meatballs.

PORK SAUSAGE AND SOY BEAN CASSEROLE

Preparation time: 25 minutes + soaking
Total cooking time: 4 hours
Serves 4

1½ cups (325 g/11 oz) dried soy beans
8 thin pork sausages
2 tablespoons soy bean oil, or oil
1 red onion, chopped
4 cloves garlic, chopped
1 large carrot, diced
1 celery stick, diced
2 x 415 g (13 oz) cans chopped
   tomatoes
1 tablespoon tomato paste
1 cup (250 ml/8 fl oz) white wine
2 sprigs fresh thyme
1 teaspoon dried oregano
1 tablespoon fresh oregano, chopped

1 Soak the soy beans in cold water for at least 8 hours. Drain well. Place in a large saucepan with enough fresh water to cover. Bring to the boil, then reduce the heat and slowly simmer for 1¼–2 hours—keep the beans covered with water during cooking; drain.
2 Prick the sausages all over. Cook in a frying pan, turning, for 10 minutes, or until browned. Drain on paper towels.
3 Heat the oil in a 3.5 litre flameproof casserole dish over medium heat. Cook the onion and garlic for 3–5 minutes, or until softened. Add the carrot and celery. Cook, stirring, for 5 minutes. Stir in the tomato, tomato paste, wine, thyme and dried oregano, and bring to the boil. Reduce the heat and simmer, stirring often, for 10 minutes, or until reduced and thickened slightly.
4 Preheat the oven to warm 160°C (315°F/Gas 2–3). Add the sausages, beans and 1 cup (250 ml/8 fl oz) water to the casserole dish. Bake, covered, for 2 hours. Stir occasionally, adding more water to keep the beans covered.
5 Return the casserole dish to the stove, skim off any fat, then reduce the liquid until thickened slightly. Remove the thyme and stir in the oregano.

NUTRITION PER SERVE
Protein 46 g; Fat 58 g; Carbohydrate 20 g;
Dietary Fibre 23 g; Cholesterol 93 mg;
3479 kJ (830 cal)

Drain the soaked and cooked soy beans well in a colander.

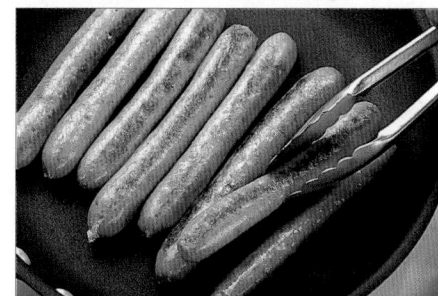

Cook the sausages in a frying pan, turning frequently, until brown all over.

Simmer the tomato mixture until reduced and thickened slightly.

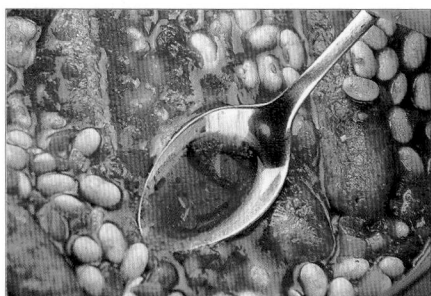

Return the casserole dish to the stove and skim off any fat.

CORN AND BACON CRUSTLESS QUICHES

Preparation time: 30 minutes
Total cooking time: 40 minutes
Makes 4

4 corn cobs
2 teaspoons olive oil
2 rashers bacon, cut into thin strips
1 small onion, finely chopped
3 eggs, lightly beaten
2 tablespoons chopped chives

2 tablespoons chopped fresh parsley
¾ cup (60 g/2 oz) fresh white
    breadcrumbs
⅓ cup (80 ml/2¾ fl oz) cream

1 Preheat the oven to 180°C (350°F/ Gas 4). Lightly grease four ¾ cup (185 ml/6 fl oz) ramekins. Remove the husks from the corn and, using a coarse grater, grate the corn kernels into a deep bowl—there should be about 1½ cups corn flesh and juice.
2 Heat the oil in a pan and cook the bacon and onion for 3–4 minutes, or

until the onion softens. Transfer to a bowl. Stir in the corn, eggs, chives, parsley, breadcrumbs and cream and season well. Spoon into the ramekins.
3 Put the ramekins in a large baking dish. Add enough hot water to come halfway up the sides of the ramekins. Lay foil loosely over the top. Bake for 25–30 minutes or until just set.

NUTRITION PER QUICHE
Protein 13 g; Fat 17 g; Carbohydrate 23 g;
Dietary Fibre 3 g; Cholesterol 175 mg;
1230 kJ (295 cal)

Using the coarse side of the grater, grate the corn kernels into a bowl.

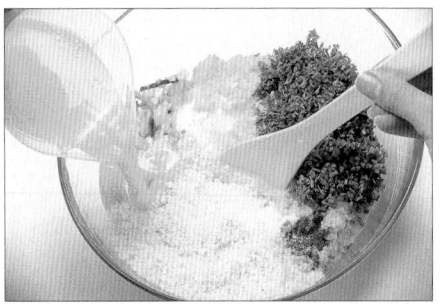

Mix together the cooked onion, bacon, corn, eggs, chives, parsley, breadcrumbs and cream.

Cook the quiches in a bain-marie, made by pouring water into a large baking dish.

PORK, BOK CHOY AND BLACK BEAN STIR-FRY

Preparation time: 20 minutes
Total cooking time: 20 minutes
Serves 4

400 g (13 oz) lean pork leg steaks
2 teaspoons sesame oil
2 onions, finely sliced
2 cloves garlic, finely chopped
2–3 teaspoons chopped fresh ginger
1 red capsicum, cut into strips
500 g (1 lb) baby bok choy, shredded

1 tablespoon canned salted black
    beans, rinsed, roughly chopped
½ cup (90 g/3 oz) water chestnuts,
    finely sliced
2 tablespoons oyster sauce
1 tablespoon soy sauce
2 teaspoons fish sauce

1 Slice the pork steaks into strips across the grain.
2 Heat half the sesame oil in a large non-stick frying pan or wok. Cook the onion, garlic and ginger over high heat for 3–4 minutes, add the capsicum and cook for 2–3 minutes.

Remove from the pan. Heat the remaining sesame oil and stir-fry the pork in batches over high heat.
3 Return the pork to the pan with the onion mixture, black beans, bok choy, water chestnuts and oyster, soy and fish sauces. Toss quickly, lower the heat, cover and steam for 3–4 minutes, or until the bok choy has just wilted.

NUTRITION PER SERVE
Protein 30 g; Fat 3 g; Carbohydrate 20 g;
Dietary Fibre 3.5 g; Cholesterol 55 mg;
910 kJ (215 cal)

Trim the ends from the bok choy, then separate the leaves and shred them with a knife.

Stir-fry the pork strips in batches over high heat until brown.

Toss all the ingredients quickly until combined, then lower the heat.

PORK AND EGGPLANT HOTPOT

Preparation time: 20 minutes
Total cooking time: 1 hour 40 minutes
Serves 4

olive oil, for cooking
375 g (12 oz) slender eggplant, cut
    into 3 cm (1¼ inch) slices
8 bulb spring onions
400 g (13 oz) can chopped tomatoes
2 cloves garlic, crushed
2 teaspoons ground cumin
500 g (1 lb) pork fillet, cut into 3 cm
    (1¼ inch) thick slices
seasoned plain flour
⅔ cup (170 ml/5½ fl oz) cider
1 sprig fresh rosemary

2 tablespoons finely chopped toasted
    almonds

1 Heat ¼ cup (60 ml/2 fl oz) of oil in
a large, heavy-based frying pan.
Brown the eggplant in batches over
high heat, adding oil as needed.
Remove and set aside.
2 Quarter the spring onions along
their length. Add some oil to the pan
and fry the spring onion over medium
heat for 5 minutes. Add the tomato,
garlic and cumin, and cook for
2 minutes. Remove and set aside.
3 Coat the pork in the seasoned flour,
shaking off any excess. Brown in
batches over medium–high heat until
golden, adding oil as needed. Remove
and set aside.
4 Add the cider to the pan and stir

well, scraping down the side and
base. Allow to boil for 1–2 minutes,
then add ½ cup (125 ml/4 fl oz) water.
Reduce the heat and stir in the spring
onion and tomato. Add the pork,
season, and poke the rosemary sprig
into the stew. Partially cover and
simmer gently for 20 minutes.
5 Layer the eggplant on top, partially
cover and cook for 25 minutes, or
until the pork is tender. Just before
serving, gently toss the almonds
through.

NUTRITION PER SERVE
Protein 30 g; Fat 7 g; Carbohydrate 10 g;
Dietary Fibre 5 g; Cholesterol 60 mg;
980 kJ (235 cal)

Fry the eggplant in batches over high heat until
browned on both sides.

Add the cider to the frying pan, scraping the
brown bits from the side and base.

Layer the eggplant over the top of the pork and
tomato mixture.

SPICY PORK SALAD

**Preparation time: 20 minutes
+ 3 hours marinating
Total cooking time: 15 minutes
Serves 6**

1 tablespoon oil
500 g (1 lb) pork mince
2 tablespoons fish sauce
1 tablespoon soy sauce
50 ml (1¾ fl oz) lime juice
1 tablespoon soft brown sugar
10 spring onions, finely chopped

3 stems lemon grass, white part only,
  finely chopped
2 red chillies, seeded and sliced
2 tablespoons each of chopped fresh
  coriander, mint and parsley
lettuce leaves, for serving

1 Heat the oil in a frying pan. Add the mince and cook over medium heat until well browned, breaking up any lumps with a fork as it cooks. Remove from the pan and leave to cool.
2 Combine the fish sauce, soy sauce, lime juice and brown sugar in a bowl. Add the pork mince. Mix in the spring onion, lemon grass, chilli and herbs.
3 Cover and refrigerate for at least 3 hours, stirring occasionally, or overnight. To serve, lay a lettuce leaf on each plate and spoon in some of the pork mixture.

NUTRITION PER SERVE
Protein 20 g; Fat 10 g; Carbohydrate 5 g;
Dietary Fibre 0 g; Cholesterol 50 mg;
875 kJ (210 cal)

Chop the spring onions, lemon grass, chillies, coriander, mint and parsley.

Break up any lumps of the pork mince with a fork as you brown it.

Mix in the spring onion, lemon grass, chilli and herbs and leave to marinate.

BRAISED PORK WITH PRUNES

Preparation time: 15 minutes
Total cooking time: 30 minutes
Serves 4

4 lean pork loin medallions, about
   175 g (6 oz) each
2 cups (500 ml/16 fl oz) chicken
   stock
2 tablespoons oil
1 large onion, cut into wedges
2 cloves garlic, crushed
1 tablespoon fresh thyme leaves

1 large tomato, peeled, seeded and
   finely chopped
½ cup (125 ml/4 fl oz) cream
16 pitted prunes

1 Shape the meat into rounds by securing a length of string around the medallions. Tie with a bow for easy removal. Bring the stock to the boil in a medium saucepan. Reduce the heat to a simmer and cook for 5 minutes, or until reduced to ¾ cup (185 ml/6 fl oz).
2 Heat the oil over high heat in a heavy-based frying pan. Cook the meat for 2 minutes each side to seal, turning once. Drain on paper towels.

3 Add the onion and garlic to the saucepan, and stir for 2 minutes. Return the meat to the pan with the thyme, tomato and stock, then reduce the heat to low. Cover the pan and bring slowly to simmering point. Simmer for 10 minutes, or until the meat is tender, turning once. Add the cream and prunes, and simmer for a further 5 minutes.

NUTRITION PER SERVE
Protein 45 g; Fat 25 g; Carbohydrate 20 g;
Dietary Fibre 4 g; Cholesterol 138 mg;
2015 kJ (480 cal)

Shape the pork medallions into rounds by securing a length of string around each one.

Cook the medallions in the oil for 2 minutes on each side, turning once.

Return the meat to the pan with the thyme, tomato and stock.

HOISIN PORK WITH STIR-FRIED GREENS AND GINGERED RICE

Preparation time: 15 minutes +
10 minutes standing
Total cooking time: 35 minutes
Serves 4

1¼ cups (250 g/8 oz) jasmine rice
500 g (1 lb) pork fillets, thinly sliced
1 tablespoon caster sugar
2 tablespoons oil
½ cup (125 ml/4 fl oz) white wine
    vinegar
1 cup (250 ml/8 fl oz) hoisin sauce
2 tablespoons stem ginger in syrup,
    chopped (see NOTE)
1.25 kg (2½ lb) mixed Asian greens
    (bok choy, choy sum or spinach)

1 Rinse the rice and place in a large saucepan. Add 1¾ cups (435 ml/ 14 fl oz) water and bring to the boil. Cover, reduce the heat to very low and cook for 10 minutes. Remove from the heat and leave to stand, covered, for 10 minutes. Meanwhile, place the pork in a bowl and sprinkle with the sugar. Toss to coat. Heat a wok over high heat, add 1 tablespoon oil and swirl to coat. Add the pork in batches and stir-fry for 3 minutes, or until brown. Remove all the pork from the wok. Add the vinegar to the wok and boil for 3–5 minutes, or until reduced by two-thirds. Reduce the heat, add the hoisin sauce and 1 tablespoon ginger, and simmer for 5 minutes.
2 Reheat the wok over high heat, add the remaining oil and swirl to coat. Add the greens and stir-fry for 3 minutes, or until crisp and cooked. Stir the remaining ginger through the rice, then press into four round teacups or small Asian bowls, smoothing the surface. Unmould the rice onto four serving plates, arrange the pork and greens on the side and drizzle the sauce over the top.

NUTRITION PER SERVE
Protein 50 g; Fat 17 g; Carbohydrate 177 g; Dietary Fibre 20 g; Cholesterol 60 mg; 4523 kJ (1080 cal)

NOTE: Stem ginger is available from Asian food stores. Substitute glacé ginger if it is unavailable.

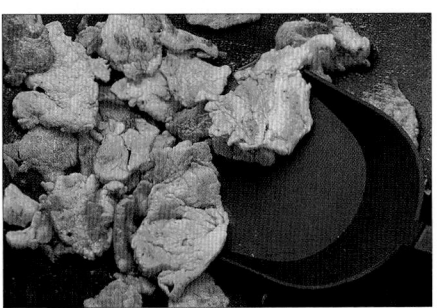
Sprinkle the pork with sugar and then stir-fry until it is brown.

Press the gingered rice into teacups or small Asian bowls to give it a neat shape.

TOMATO AND BACON QUICHE

Preparation time: 45 minutes + 1 hour refrigeration
Total cooking time: 1 hour 10 minutes
Serves 6

1½ cups (185 g/6 oz) plain flour
pinch of cayenne pepper
pinch of mustard powder
125 g (4 oz) butter, chilled and cubed
⅓ cup (40 g/1¼ oz) grated Cheddar
1 egg yolk

FILLING
25 g (¾ oz) butter
100 g (3½ oz) lean bacon, chopped
1 small onion, finely sliced
3 eggs
¾ cup (185 ml/6 fl oz) cream
½ teaspoon salt
2 tomatoes, peeled, seeded and
    chopped into chunks
¾ cup (90 g/3 oz) grated Cheddar

1 Mix the flour, pepper, mustard and butter in a food processor until crumbly. Add the cheese and egg yolk and process in short bursts until the mixture comes together. Add 1–2 tablespoons of cold water if needed. Turn out onto a floured surface and gather into a ball. Wrap in plastic and refrigerate for 30 minutes. Grease a 23 cm (9 inch) loose-based deep tart tin.
2 To make the filling, melt the butter in a frying pan and cook the bacon for a few minutes until golden. Add the onion and cook until soft. Remove from the heat. Lightly beat the eggs, cream and salt together. Add the bacon and onion, then fold in the tomato and Cheddar.

3 Roll out the pastry on a floured surface until large enough to fit the tin. Trim the excess pastry and refrigerate for 30 minutes. Preheat the oven to 180°C (350°F/Gas 4). Cover the pastry with baking paper and spread with a layer of baking beads or rice. Bake for 10 minutes. Remove the paper and beads and bake for 10 minutes.
4 Pour the filling into the pastry shell and bake for 35 minutes until golden.

NUTRITION PER SERVE
Protein 15 g; Fat 45 g; Carbohydrate 25 g;
Dietary Fibre 2 g; Cholesterol 255 mg;
2405 kJ (570 cal)

Remove the rind and excess fat from the bacon and chop the meat.

Cook the bacon in a little butter until golden and then add the onion.

Fold the tomato chunks and Cheddar into the egg and cream mixture.

NOODLES WITH MUSHROOMS AND BARBECUED PORK

Preparation time: 30 minutes
Total cooking time: 6 minutes
Serves 4

8 dried Chinese mushrooms
1 tablespoon oil
4 cloves garlic, chopped
5 cm (2 inch) piece fresh ginger, grated
1–2 teaspoons chopped red chillies
100 g (3½ oz) barbecued pork, cut into small pieces
200 g (6½ oz) fresh egg noodles
2 teaspoons fish sauce
2 tablespoons lime juice
2 teaspoons soft brown sugar
2 tablespoons crisp-fried garlic
2 tablespoons crisp-fried onion
chilli flakes

1 Soak the mushrooms in hot water for 20 minutes. Drain and cut them into quarters.
2 Heat the oil in a large wok. Add the garlic, ginger and chilli and stir-fry for 1 minute over high heat. Add the pork to the wok and stir for 1 minute.
3 Add the egg noodles and mushrooms and toss well. Sprinkle the fish sauce, lime juice and soft brown sugar over the pork and then toss quickly, cover and steam for 30 seconds. Sprinkle the crisp garlic and onion and chilli flakes over the top before serving.

NUTRITION PER SERVE
Protein 16 g; Fat 12 g; Carbohydrate 40 g; Dietary Fibre 3 g; Cholesterol 32 mg; 1375 kJ (328 cal)

Drain the Chinese mushrooms and use a sharp knife to cut them into quarters.

Add the pork pieces to the wok and stir with a wooden spoon for a minute.

Cover the wok and allow the noodles to steam for 30 seconds.

RAISED PORK PIE

Preparation time: 20 minutes + chilling + overnight setting
Total cooking time: 1 hour
Serves 6

1.2 kg (2 lb 7 oz) minced pork
⅔ cup (90 g/3 oz) pistachio nuts, shelled and chopped
2 green apples, peeled and finely chopped
6 fresh sage leaves, finely chopped
4 cups (500 g/1 lb) plain flour
150 g (5 oz) butter
2 eggs, lightly beaten
1 egg yolk, to glaze
200 ml (6½ fl oz) vegetable stock
200 ml (6½ fl oz) unsweetened apple juice
2 teaspoons gelatine

1 Preheat the oven to 200°C (400°F/Gas 6). Mix together the pork, pistachio nuts, apple and sage leaves and season. Fry a piece of the mixture to taste and adjust the seasoning. Cover and refrigerate. Wrap a piece of plastic wrap around a 6 cm (2½ inch) high, 20 cm (8 inch) straight-sided tin, then turn the tin over and grease the outside base and side.
2 Put the flour and 1 teaspoon salt in a bowl and make a well in the centre. Put the butter in a pan with 210 ml (7 fl oz) water, bring to the boil and add to the flour with the eggs. Mix with a wooden spoon until combined, then turn out onto a work surface and bring together to form a smooth dough. Wrap in plastic and refrigerate for 10 minutes.
3 Cut off a third of the pastry and wrap in plastic wrap—do not refrigerate. Roll the remainder into a circle large enough to just cover the outside of the tin. Lift onto a rolling pin and place over the tin, working fast before the pastry sets. Refrigerate until the pastry hardens. Carefully pull out the tin and remove the plastic wrap. Attach a paper collar made of two layers of greased baking paper around the outside of the pastry so it fits snugly and secure with a paper clip at the top and bottom. Fill the pie, then roll out the remaining pastry to form a lid. Attach it to the base with some water, pressing or crimping it to make it look neat. Cut a small hole in the top of the pie.
4 Put the pie on a baking tray, bake for 40 minutes and check the pastry top. If it is still pale, bake for another 10 minutes, then remove the paper. Brush with egg yolk mixed with 1 tablespoon water and bake for another 15 minutes, or until the sides are brown. Cool completely.
5 Bring the stock and half the apple juice to the boil. Sprinkle the gelatine over the surface of the remaining apple juice in a jug and leave to go spongy, then pour into the stock and mix until the gelatine dissolves. Place a small funnel (a piping nozzle works well) in the hole of the pie and pour in a little of the gelatine, leave to settle and then pour in some more until the pie is full. Fill the pie completely so there are no gaps when the gelatine sets. Leave in the fridge overnight.

NUTRITION PER SERVE
Protein 60 g; Fat 35 g; Carbohydrate 72 g; Dietary Fibre 5.5 g; Cholesterol 257 mg; 3545 kJ (845 cal)

STORAGE: If wrapped tightly with plastic wrap, pork pies will last in the fridge for 4–5 days.

Mix together the ingredients for the filling and then fry a little to test the seasoning.

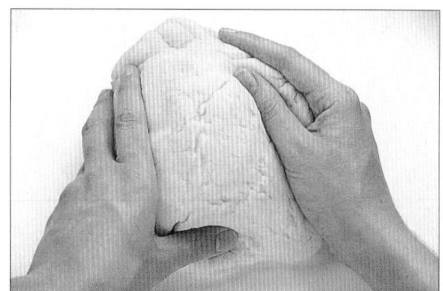

Turn out the dough onto a work surface and then bring together with your hands.

Cover the outside of the tin with the pastry, working fast so that it does not set.

The greased paper collar should fit snugly around the outside of the pastry.

Cut a small hole in the top of the pie to allow the gelatine to be poured in.

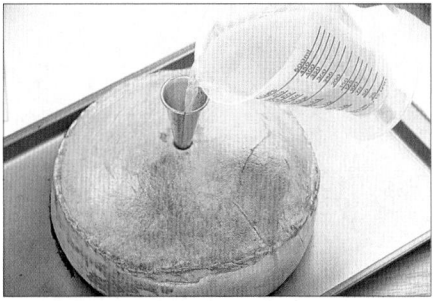
Gradually pour the gelatine into the cooked and cooled pie until it is full.

HAM, LEEK AND POTATO RAGU

Preparation time: 25 minutes
Total cooking time: 45 minutes
Serves 4–6

50 g (1¾ oz) butter
2 tablespoons olive oil
250 g (8 oz) piece double-smoked
    ham, cut into cubes (see NOTE)
3 cloves garlic, finely chopped
3 leeks, sliced
1.5 kg (3 lb) potatoes, peeled and cut
    into large chunks

2 cups (500 ml/16 fl oz) chicken stock
2 tablespoons brandy
½ cup (125 ml/4 fl oz) cream
1 tablespoon each of chopped fresh
    oregano and parsley

1 Heat the butter and oil in a large heavy-based saucepan. Cook the ham, garlic and leek over low heat for 10 minutes, stirring regularly.
2 Add the potato and cook for 10 minutes, stirring regularly.
3 Slowly stir in the combined stock and brandy. Cover and bring to a gentle simmer. Cook for another 15–20 minutes, or until the potato is very tender but still chunky, and the sauce has thickened. Add the cream and herbs, and season with salt and pepper. Simmer for another 5 minutes. Serve with toast.

NUTRITION PER SERVE (6)
Protein 15 g; Fat 25 g; Carbohydrate 40 g;
Dietary Fibre 9 g; Cholesterol 70 mg;
1990 kJ (475 cal)

NOTE: You can use any type of ham for this recipe. A double-smoked ham will give a good flavour.

Heat the butter and oil in a pan, then cook the ham, garlic and leek.

Stir in the stock and brandy, then cover and leave to simmer.

Once the sauce has thickened, add the cream and chopped herbs.

HOT ITALIAN SALAD

Preparation time: 15 minutes
Total cooking time: 15 minutes
Serves 4

olive oil, for cooking
4 slices prosciutto
2 onions, cut into wedges
1 clove garlic, crushed
250 g (8 oz) cherry tomatoes
1 yellow capsicum, cut into squares
1 green capsicum, cut into squares
180 g (6 oz) marinated artichoke
    hearts, halved

100 g (3½ oz) black olives
150 g (5 oz) rocket leaves
1 tablespoon balsamic vinegar
1 tablespoon extra virgin olive oil
Parmesan shavings, to serve

1 Heat the wok until very hot, add 2 teaspoons of the oil and swirl it around to coat the side. Stir-fry the prosciutto until crisp and golden. Drain on paper towels and crumble.
2 Reheat the wok, add 2 teaspoons of the oil and stir-fry the onion and garlic over high heat for 3–4 minutes, or until tender.
3 Stir in the tomatoes, capsicum and

artichokes, and cook for 4–5 minutes, or until tender. Add the olives and rocket and stir-fry until the rocket has just wilted.
4 Combine the vinegar and olive oil, and season. Pour into the wok and toss thoroughly. Serve immediately, sprinkled with the prosciutto and Parmesan shavings.

NUTRITION PER SERVE
Protein 7.5 g; Fat 20 g; Carbohydrate 5 g;
Dietary Fibre 3.5 g; Cholesterol 10 mg;
870 kJ (210 cal)

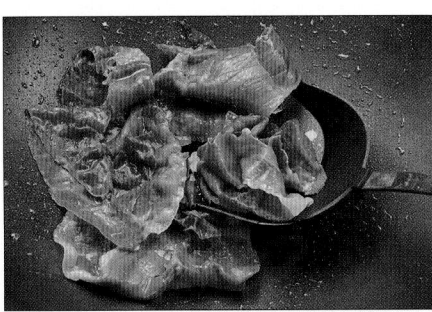

Stir-fry the prosciutto slices until they are crisp and golden.

Drain the prosciutto on paper towels, then crumble into pieces with your fingers.

Stir the tomatoes, capsicum and artichokes into the onion and garlic.

NOODLES WITH BARBECUED PORK AND GREENS

Preparation time: 20 minutes
Total cooking time: 25 minutes
Serves 4

250 g (8 oz) fresh thick egg noodles
1 tablespoon oil
1 tablespoon sesame oil
250 g (8 oz) Chinese barbecued pork, cut into small cubes (see NOTE)
1 large onion, very thinly sliced
2 cloves garlic, finely chopped
400 g (13 oz) green vegetables (beans, broccoli, celery), cut into bite-sized pieces
2 tablespoons hoisin sauce

1 tablespoon kecap manis
100 g (3½ oz) snow peas
3 baby bok choy, leaves separated
230 g (7½ oz) can water chestnuts, sliced

1 Two-thirds fill a pan with water and bring to the boil. Add the noodles and cook for about 3 minutes, or until just tender. Drain well.
2 Heat the wok until very hot, add the oils and swirl them around to coat the side. Stir-fry the pork over medium heat for 2 minutes, or until crisp. Drain on paper towels.
3 Reheat the wok, add the onion and garlic and stir-fry over very high heat for about 1 minute, or until just softened. Add the vegetables and cook, tossing regularly, for 2 minutes,

or until just softened. Stir in the hoisin sauce, kecap manis, snow peas, bok choy, water chestnuts and 1 tablespoon of water. Cook for 2 minutes, covered. Add the noodles and stir-fried pork, and toss gently to combine. Serve immediately.

NUTRITION PER SERVE
Protein 10 g; Fat 20 g; Carbohydrate 60 g;
Dietary Fibre 10 g; Cholesterol 0 mg;
3910 kJ (930 cal)

NOTES: Chinese barbecued pork is also known as char siu. You can buy it at Chinese barbecue shops.
You can use Asian greens instead of beans, broccoli and celery.

Cut the barbecued pork into strips, then into small cubes.

Trim the base of the baby bok choy, then cut them into quarters lengthways.

Drain the can of water chestnuts and then slice them.

PORK AND APPLE BRAISE

Preparation time: 20 minutes
Total cooking time: 40 minutes
Serves 4

1 tablespoon oil
1 large onion, thinly sliced
1 clove garlic, chopped
2 teaspoons soft brown sugar
2 green apples, cut into wedges
4 pork loin steaks or medallions
2 tablespoons brandy
2 tablespoons seeded mustard

1 cup (250 ml/8 fl oz) chicken stock
½ cup (140 g/5 oz) pitted prunes
½ cup (125 ml/4 fl oz) light cream

1 Heat the oil in a large heavy-based pan. Cook the onion and garlic for 10 minutes over low heat, stirring often, until softened and golden brown. Add the sugar and apple and cook, stirring regularly, until the apple begins to brown. Remove the apple and onion from the pan.

2 Reheat the pan and lightly brown the pork steaks, two at a time, then return them all to the pan. Add the brandy and stir until it has nearly all evaporated. Add the mustard and stock. Simmer over low heat, covered, for 15 minutes.

3 Return the apple to the pan with the prunes and cream and simmer for 10 minutes, or until the pork is tender. Season to taste before serving.

NUTRITION PER SERVE
Protein 25 g; Fat 12 g; Carbohydrate 22 g;
Dietary Fibre 4 g; Cholesterol 55 mg;
1250 kJ (298 cal)

HINT: Take care not to overcook pork or it can become tough and dry.

Stir the apple regularly over the heat until it begins to brown.

Brown the pork steaks two at a time and then return them all to the pan.

Put the browned apple back in the pan with the prunes and cream.

LEEK AND HAM QUICHE WITH POLENTA PASTRY

Preparation time: 45 minutes +
   50 minutes refrigeration
Total cooking time: 1 hour 15 minutes
Serves 6

1 cup (125 g/4 oz) plain flour
½ cup (75 g/2½ oz) polenta
90 g (3 oz) butter, chilled and cubed
90 g (3 oz) cream cheese, chilled and
   cubed

LEEK AND HAM FILLING
50 g (1¾ oz) butter
2 leeks, thinly sliced
2 eggs, lightly beaten
1 cup (250 ml/8 fl oz) cream
½ teaspoon ground nutmeg
100 g (3½ oz) ham, chopped
75 g (2½ oz) Swiss cheese, grated

1 Process the flour and polenta briefly to mix together. Add the butter and cream cheese and process for about 15 seconds until the mixture comes together. Add 1–2 tablespoons of water if needed. Turn out onto a floured surface and gather into a ball. Wrap in plastic wrap and refrigerate for 30 minutes.

2 To make the filling, heat the butter in a pan and cook the leeks, covered, stirring often, for 10–15 minutes, or until soft but not brown. Cool. Mix together the beaten eggs, cream and nutmeg and season with pepper.

3 Grease a shallow 21 x 28 cm (8½ x 11 inch) loose-based tart tin with melted butter. Roll the pastry between two sheets of baking paper until large enough to fit the tin. Trim off any excess pastry and refrigerate for 20 minutes. Preheat the oven to 190°C (375°F/Gas 5). Cover the pastry shell with baking paper and spread with a layer of baking beads or rice. Bake for 15 minutes. Remove the paper and beads and bake for a further 15 minutes, or until the pastry is golden and dry. Reduce the oven to 180°C (350°F/Gas 4).

4 Spread the leek over the pastry shell and sprinkle with the ham and cheese. Pour in the cream mixture. Bake for 30 minutes, or until golden and set.

NUTRITION PER SERVE
Protein 15 g; Fat 50 g; Carbohydrate 25 g;
Dietary Fibre 2 g; Cholesterol 210 mg;
2495 kJ (595 cal)

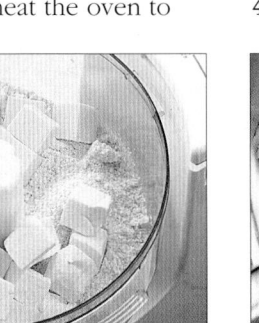
Add the chopped butter and cream cheese to the flour and polenta in the processor.

Cook the leek, stirring frequently, until it is soft but not brown.

Spread the leek over the pastry shell and sprinkle with ham and Swiss cheese.

PORK ROLLS WITH ROASTED CAPSICUM

Preparation time: 40 minutes
Total cooking time: 30 minutes
Serves 4

SAUCE
¾ cup (185 ml/6 fl oz) beef stock
2 teaspoons soy sauce
2 tablespoons red wine
2 teaspoons wholegrain mustard
2 teaspoons cornflour

1 red capsicum
4 x 150 g (5 oz) lean pork leg steaks
⅓ cup (90 g/3 oz) ricotta
2 spring onions, finely chopped
1 clove garlic, crushed
75 g (2½ oz) rocket
4 small lean slices prosciutto (about 35 g/1¼ oz)
cooking oil spray

1 To make the sauce, put the beef stock, soy sauce, red wine and mustard in a pan. Blend the cornflour with 1 tablespoon water and add to the pan. Stir until the mixture boils.
2 Cut the capsicum into quarters and remove the seeds and membrane. Grill until the skin blisters and blackens. Cool under a damp tea towel, peel and cut the flesh into thin strips.
3 Flatten each steak into a thin square between 2 sheets of plastic, using a rolling pin or mallet. Combine the ricotta, onion and garlic in a bowl, then spread evenly over the pork. Top with a layer of rocket and prosciutto. Place a quarter of the capsicum at one end and roll up to enclose the capsicum. Tie with string or secure with toothpicks at even intervals.

4 Spray a non-stick pan with oil and fry the pork rolls over medium heat for 5 minutes, or until well browned. Add the sauce to the pan and simmer over low heat for 10–15 minutes, or until the rolls are cooked. Remove the string or toothpicks. Slice and serve with the sauce.

NUTRITION PER SERVE
Protein 40 g; Fat 5 g; Carbohydrate 3.5 g; Dietary Fibre 1 g; Cholesterol 95 mg; 925 kJ (220 cal)

Flatten the pork between two pieces of plastic wrap, using a rolling pin or mallet.

Secure the pork rolls with string or toothpicks at even intervals.

Add the sauce to the pan and simmer over low heat until cooked through.

PORK SAUSAGE BURGERS WITH MUSTARD CREAM

Preparation time: 20 minutes
Total cooking time: 10 minutes
Serves 6

1 kg (2 lb) pork mince
1 small onion, finely chopped
1 cup (90 g/3 oz) fresh breadcrumbs
2 cloves garlic, crushed
1 egg, lightly beaten

1 teaspoon dried sage
6 bread sticks

MUSTARD CREAM
½ cup (125 g/4 oz) sour cream
1 tablespoon wholegrain mustard
2 teaspoons lemon juice

1 Mix together the mince, onion, breadcrumbs, garlic, egg and sage with your hands. Divide into six portions and shape into sausages.
2 Cook the sausages on a hot, lightly oiled barbecue flatplate or grill for 5–10 minutes, turning occasionally.
3 To make the mustard cream, put the sour cream, mustard and juice in a small bowl and stir together. Sandwich the sausage burgers in the bread sticks and serve with the mustard cream.

NUTRITION PER SERVE
Protein 51 g; Fat 15 g; Carbohydrate 55 g; Dietary Fibre 4 g; Cholesterol 140 mg; 2342 kJ (559 cal)

Divide the mixture into six portions and shape each one into a sausage.

Cook the burgers on a hot, lightly oiled barbecue flatplate or grill.

Stir together the sour cream, mustard and lemon juice and serve with the burgers.

BACON AND WHOLE EGG FILO PIES

Preparation time: 30 minutes
Total cooking time: 30 minutes
Makes 6

1 teaspoon oil
4 spring onions, chopped
6 lean bacon rashers, chopped
½ cup (125 ml/4 fl oz) milk
¼ cup (60 ml/2 fl oz) cream
2 tablespoons chopped fresh parsley
pinch of ground nutmeg
7 eggs
10 sheets filo pastry
melted butter, for brushing

1 Heat the oil in a pan and cook the spring onion and bacon for 2–3 minutes, then set aside to cool. Mix together the milk, cream, parsley, ground nutmeg and 1 egg and season with salt and pepper.

2 Brush 1 sheet of filo pastry with the melted butter, then brush another sheet and lay it on top. Repeat until you have a stack of 5 sheets. Cut into 6 squares. Repeat with the remaining 5 sheets of pastry. Place 2 squares together at an angle to form a rough 8-pointed star and fit into a 1 cup (250 ml/8 fl oz) muffin tin. Repeat with the remaining squares.

3 Preheat the oven to 200°C (400°F/ Gas 6). Divide the spring onion and bacon mixture evenly between the filo pastry cups. Then pour over the egg and cream mixture and carefully break an egg on the top of the pie. Bake for 10 minutes, then reduce the oven to moderate 180°C (350°F/Gas 4) and bake for a further 10–15 minutes, or until the pastry is lightly crisp and golden and the egg is just set. Serve the pies immediately.

NUTRITION PER PIE
Protein 15 g; Fat 15 g; Carbohydrate 10 g; Dietary Fibre 1 g; Cholesterol 245 mg; 1130 kJ (270 cal)

Season the egg, milk, cream, parsley and nutmeg mixture.

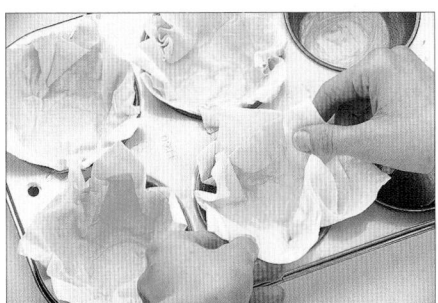

Make an 8-pointed star from two pastry squares and place in the muffin tin.

Carefully break an egg over the filling inside the pastry shell.

Seafood

BARBECUED TUNA AND MEDITERRANEAN VEGETABLES

**Preparation time: 15 minutes
+ 30 minutes marinating
Total cooking time: 20 minutes
Serves 4**

¾ cup (185 ml/6 fl oz) olive oil
3 cloves garlic, crushed
2 tablespoons sweet chilli sauce
1 red capsicum, cut into 3 cm
    (1¼ inch) pieces
1 yellow capsicum, cut into
    3 cm (1¼ inch) pieces
2 large zucchini, cut into 1.5 cm
    (⅝ inch) slices
2 slender eggplant, cut into
    1.5 cm (⅝ inch) slices
olive oil, extra, for brushing
4 tuna steaks

LEMON AND CAPER MAYONNAISE
1 egg yolk
1 teaspoon grated lemon rind
2 tablespoons lemon juice
1 small clove garlic, chopped
¾ cup (185 ml/6 fl oz) olive oil
1 tablespoon baby capers

1 Combine the olive oil, garlic and sweet chilli sauce in a large bowl. Add the capsicum, zucchini and eggplant, toss well, then marinate for 30 minutes.
2 For the mayonnaise, process the egg yolk, rind, lemon juice and garlic together in a food processor or blender until smooth. With the motor running, gradually add the oil in a thin steady stream until the mixture thickens and is a creamy consistency. Stir in the capers and ½ teaspoon salt. Set aside.
3 Heat the barbecue or a chargrill plate, brush with oil and cook the drained vegetables for 4–5 minutes each side, or until cooked through. Set aside and keep warm.
4 Brush the tuna steaks with extra oil and barbecue for 2–3 minutes each side, or until just cooked (tuna should be rare in the centre). Arrange the vegetables and tuna on individual serving plates and serve with the lemon and caper mayonnaise.

NUTRITION PER SERVE
Protein 68 g; Fat 69 g; Carbohydrate 6 g;
Dietary Fibre 3 g; Cholesterol 151 mg;
3885 kJ (925 Cal)

Process the mayonnaise mixture until smooth and creamy.

Turn the vegetables over when browned on one side, then cook through.

THAI-STYLE WHOLE SNAPPER

Preparation time: 10 minutes
Total cooking time: 30 minutes
Serves 6

2 garlic cloves, crushed
1 tablespoon fish sauce
2 tablespoons lemon juice
1 tablespoon grated fresh ginger
2 tablespoons sweet chilli sauce
2 tablespoons chopped fresh coriander

1 tablespoon rice wine vinegar
2 tablespoons white wine
600 g (1¼ lb) whole snapper, cleaned and scaled (ask your fishmonger to do this)
2 spring onions, cut into thin strips

1 Preheat the oven to 190°C (375°F/Gas 5). Place the garlic, fish sauce, lemon juice, ginger, chilli sauce, coriander, rice wine vinegar and wine in a jug and mix together well.
2 Place the snapper on a large piece of foil on a baking tray. Pour the marinade over the fish and sprinkle with the spring onion.
3 Wrap some foil around the fish like a parcel and place in the oven. Bake for 20–30 minutes or until the flesh flakes easily when tested with a fork. Serve immediately with steamed rice.

NUTRITION PER SERVE
Protein 20 g; Fat 2 g; Carbohydrate 5 g;
Dietary Fibre 0 g; Cholesterol 60 mg;
495 kJ (120 cal)

Put the ingredients for the marinade in a jug and mix together well.

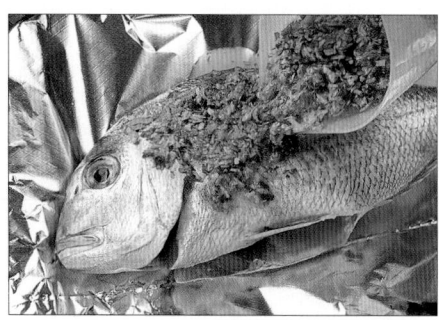
Pour the marinade over the snapper after you have placed it on the aluminium foil.

Cook the fish until the flesh flakes easily when tested with a fork.

SARDINES WITH CHARGRILLED CAPSICUM AND EGGPLANT

Preparation time: 25 minutes
Total cooking time: 35 minutes
Serves 4

2 large red capsicums, quartered and
    seeded
4 finger eggplants, cut into quarters
    lengthways
cooking oil spray

DRESSING
1 tablespoon olive oil
1 tablespoon balsamic vinegar
½ teaspoon soft brown sugar
1 clove garlic, crushed
1 tablespoon chopped fresh chives

16 fresh sardines, butterflied
    (about 300 g/10 oz)
1 slice white bread, crusts removed
⅓ cup (7 g/¼ oz) fresh parsley
1 clove garlic, crushed
1 teaspoon grated lemon rind

1 Preheat the oven to moderate 180°C (350°F/Gas 4). Lightly grease a large baking dish with oil. Preheat the grill and line with foil.
2 Grill the capsicum until the skin is blistered and blackened. Cool under a damp tea towel, peel and slice thickly lengthways. Lightly spray the eggplant with oil and grill each side for 3–5 minutes, until softened.
3 Combine the dressing ingredients in a jar and shake well. Put the capsicum and eggplant in a bowl, pour the dressing over, toss well and set aside.
4 Place the sardines on a baking tray in a single layer, well spaced. Finely

chop the bread, parsley, garlic and lemon rind together in a food processor. Sprinkle over each sardine. Bake for 10–15 minutes, until cooked through. Serve the capsicum and eggplant topped with sardines.

NUTRITION PER SERVE
Protein 20 g; Fat 15 g; Carbohydrate 15 g;
Dietary Fibre 3 g; Cholesterol 85 mg;
1185 kJ (285 cal)

When the capsicum has cooled enough to handle, peel away the skin.

Pour the dressing over the capsicum and eggplant, then toss.

Sprinkle the chopped bread, parsley, garlic and lemon rind over the sardines.

CRUMBED FISH WITH WASABI CREAM

Preparation time: 25 minutes +
**   15 minutes refrigeration**
Total cooking time: 20 minutes
Serves 4

¾ cup (60 g/2 oz) fresh breadcrumbs
¾ cup (25 g/¾ oz) cornflakes
1 sheet nori, torn roughly
¼ teaspoon paprika
4 x 150 g (5 oz) pieces firm white fish
    fillets
plain flour, for dusting
1 egg white
1 tablespoon skim milk
1 spring onion, thinly sliced

WASABI CREAM
½ cup (125 g/4 oz) low-fat natural
    yoghurt
1 teaspoon wasabi (see NOTE)
1 tablespoon low-fat mayonnaise
1 teaspoon lime juice

1 Preheat the oven to moderate 180°C (350°F/Gas 4). Combine the crumbs, cornflakes, nori and paprika in a food processor and process until the nori is finely chopped.
2 Dust the fish lightly with plain flour, dip into the combined egg white and milk, then into the breadcrumb mixture. Press the crumb mixture on firmly, then refrigerate for 15 minutes.
3 Line a baking tray with non-stick baking paper and put the fish on the paper. Bake for 15–20 minutes, or until the fish flakes easily with a fork.
4 To make the wasabi cream, mix the ingredients thoroughly in a bowl. Serve with the fish and sprinkle with a little spring onion.

NUTRITION PER SERVE
Protein 35 g; Fat 6 g; Carbohydrate 25 g;
Dietary Fibre 1 g; Cholesterol 105 mg;
1270 kJ (305 cal)

NOTE: Wasabi paste (a pungent paste, also known as Japanese horseradish) and nori (sheets of paper-thin dried seaweed) are both available from Japanese food stores.

Process the breadcrumbs, cornflakes, nori and paprika together.

Dust the fish with flour, dip in the egg and milk, then press in the breadcrumbs.

Thoroughly mix the wasabi cream ingredients in a bowl and then serve with the fish.

BLACK BEAN AND CHILLI MUSSELS

Preparation time: 10 minutes
Total cooking time: 8 minutes
Serves 4

3 teaspoons salted black beans, rinsed
1 tablespoon shredded fresh ginger
2 cloves garlic, chopped
1 tablespoon sugar
2 tablespoons oyster sauce
1 teaspoon soy sauce
2 teaspoons oil
1 small red chilli, seeded and thinly sliced
1.2 kg (2 lb 6 oz) black mussels, scrubbed, debearded (see NOTE)
2 teaspoons cornflour
4 spring onions, sliced on the diagonal
coriander leaves, to serve

1 Place the black beans, ginger, garlic, sugar, oyster sauce and soy sauce in a small bowl and mash with a fork.
2 Heat a wok over high heat, add the oil and swirl to coat the side. Add the chilli and stir-fry for 30 seconds, then add the black bean mixture and stir-fry for 1 minute, or until fragrant. Add the mussels and stir-fry for 3–5 minutes, or until they open. Discard any that do not open. Reduce the heat to low.
3 Place the cornflour and ½ cup (125 ml/4 fl oz) water in a bowl and stir until smooth. Add to the wok and bring to the boil, stirring until the sauce boils and thickens. Stir through the spring onion and coriander leaves.

NUTRITION PER SERVE
Protein 38 g; Fat 7.5 g; Carbohydrate 19 g; Dietary Fibre 1.5 g; Cholesterol 243 mg; 1240 kJ (295 cal)

NOTE: When buying live mussels make sure they are fresh. Live mussels will have tightly closed shells—some may be slightly opened. Give the shells a tap and if they close this will indicate that they are still alive. Discard any with broken or cracked shells. Always buy extra to allow for the ones that are cracked or do not open during cooking.

Mash together the black beans, ginger, garlic, sugar, oyster and soy sauce.

Stir-fry the mussels for 3–5 minutes, or until they open. Discard any that don't open.

Add the cornflour mixture to the wok and bring to the boil until the sauce thickens.

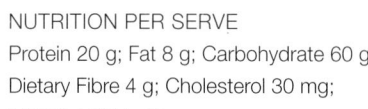

SMOKED SALMON PIZZAS

Preparation time: 20 minutes
Total cooking time: 15 minutes
Serves 6

250 g (8 oz) low-fat ricotta
6 small oval pitta breads
125 g (4 oz) sliced smoked salmon
1 small red onion, sliced
1 tablespoon baby capers

small dill sprigs, to garnish
1 lemon, cut into thin wedges,
   for serving

1 Preheat the oven to moderate 180°C (350°F/Gas 4). Put the ricotta in a bowl, season well with salt and pepper and stir until smooth. Spread the ricotta over the breads, leaving a clear border around the edge.
2 Top each pizza with some smoked salmon slices, then some onion

pieces. Scatter baby capers over the top and bake on a baking tray for 15 minutes, or until the bases are slightly crispy around the edges. Garnish with a few dill sprigs and serve with lemon wedges.

NUTRITION PER SERVE
Protein 20 g; Fat 8 g; Carbohydrate 60 g;
Dietary Fibre 4 g; Cholesterol 30 mg;
1650 kJ (395 cal)

Peel the small red onion and then cut it into thin slices.

Spread the seasoned ricotta over the pitta breads, leaving a border around the edge.

Put some smoked salmon slices over the ricotta, followed by onion and capers.

TUNA WITH CORIANDER NOODLES

Preparation time: 15 minutes
Total cooking time: 10 minutes
Serves 4

¼ cup (60 ml/2 fl oz) lime juice
2 tablespoons fish sauce
2 tablespoons sweet chilli sauce
2 teaspoons grated palm sugar
1 teaspoon sesame oil
1 clove garlic, finely chopped
1 tablespoon virgin olive oil
4 tuna steaks
200 g (6½ oz) dried thin wheat noodles
6 spring onions, thinly sliced

¾ cup (25 g/¾ oz) chopped fresh
   coriander leaves
lime wedges, to garnish

1 To make the dressing, place the lime juice, fish sauce, chilli sauce, sugar, sesame oil and garlic in a small bowl and mix together.
2 Heat the olive oil in a chargrill pan. Add the tuna steaks and cook over high heat for 2 minutes each side, or until cooked to your liking. Transfer the steaks to a warm plate, cover and keep warm.
3 Place the noodles in a large saucepan of lightly salted, rapidly boiling water and return to the boil. Cook for 4 minutes, or until the

noodles are tender. Drain well. Add half the dressing and half the spring onion and coriander to the noodles and gently toss together.
4 Either cut the tuna into even cubes or slice it.
5 Place the noodles on serving plates and top with the tuna. Mix the remaining dressing with the spring onion and coriander and drizzle over the tuna. Garnish with lime wedges.

NUTRITION PER SERVE
Protein 32 g; Fat 10 g; Carbohydrate 5 g;
Dietary Fibre 1 g; Cholesterol 105 mg;
1030 kJ (245 cal)

Cook the tuna steaks in a chargrill pan until cooked to your liking.

Cook the noodles in lightly salted water until they are tender.

Combine the remaining dressing with the spring onion and coriander.

COD WITH PAPAYA AND BLACK BEAN SALSA

Preparation time: 25 minutes
Total cooking time: 5 minutes
Serves 4

1 small red onion, finely chopped
1 papaya (about 500 g/1 lb), peeled, seeded and cubed
1 bird's-eye chilli, seeded and finely chopped
1 tablespoon salted black beans, rinsed and drained
4 blue-eyed cod cutlets
2 teaspoons peanut oil
1 teaspoon sesame oil
2 teaspoons fish sauce
1 tablespoon lime juice
1 tablespoon chopped fresh coriander leaves
2 teaspoons shredded fresh mint

1 Toss together the onion, papaya, chilli and black beans.
2 Cook the cod cutlets in a lightly oiled chargrill pan for 2 minutes each side, or until cooked to your liking.
3 Whisk together the peanut oil, sesame oil, fish sauce and lime juice. Pour over the papaya and black bean salsa and toss. Add the coriander and mint and serve immediately, at room temperature, with the fish.

NUTRITION PER SERVE
Protein 18 g; Fat 6 g; Carbohydrate 5 g; Dietary Fibre 1 g; Cholesterol 40 mg; 540 kJ (130 cal)

NOTE: Black beans have a distinctive taste, so if you are not familiar with them, taste them before adding to the salsa. If you prefer not to add them, the salsa is equally delicious without.

VARIATION: Pawpaw can be used instead of papaya. It is a larger fruit from the same family, with yellower flesh and a less sweet flavour.

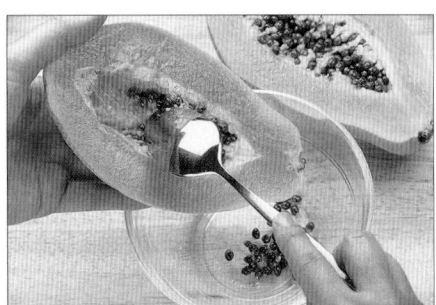
Cut the papaya in half and scoop out the seeds with a spoon.

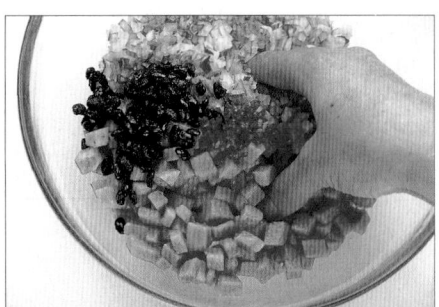
The best way to toss the salsa, without breaking up the fruit, is with your hands.

Whisk together the oil dressing and add to the salsa just before serving.

TUNA WITH LIME AND CHILLI SAUCE

Preparation time: 15 minutes
Total cooking time: 5 minutes
Serves 4

½ cup (25 g/¾ oz) chopped and firmly
    packed fresh mint leaves
½ cup (25 g/¾ oz) chopped fresh
    coriander leaves
1 teaspoon grated lime rind
1 tablespoon lime juice
1 teaspoon grated fresh ginger
1 jalapeno chilli, seeded and finely
    chopped
1 cup (250 g/8 oz) low-fat natural
    yoghurt
4 tuna steaks

1 Mix together the mint, coriander,
lime rind, lime juice, ginger and chilli.
Fold in the yoghurt and season.
2 Cook the tuna in a lightly oiled
chargrill pan for 2 minutes each side.
Serve with the sauce.

NUTRITION PER SERVE
Protein 28 g; Fat 5 g; Carbohydrate 4 g;
Dietary Fibre 1 g; Cholesterol 55 mg;
800 kJ (200 cal)

NOTE: Jalapeno chillies are smooth
and thick-fleshed and are available
both red and green. They are quite
fiery and you can use a less powerful
variety of chilli if you prefer.

It's a good idea to wear gloves to remove the
seeds from chillies, to prevent skin irritation.

Mix together the mint, coriander, lime rind, juice,
ginger and chilli.

Check the taste of the sauce before seasoning
with salt and black pepper.

PRAWN CURRY

Preparation time: 25 minutes
Total cooking time: 15 minutes
Serves 6

1 tablespoon butter
1 onion, finely chopped
1 clove garlic, crushed
1½ tablespoons curry powder
2 tablespoons plain flour
2 cups (500 ml/16 fl oz) skim milk
1½ tablespoons lemon juice

1 kg (2 lb) raw prawns, peeled and
   deveined
2 teaspoons sherry
1 tablespoon finely chopped fresh
   parsley

1 Heat the butter in a large saucepan.
Add the onion and garlic, and cook
for 5 minutes, or until softened. Add
the curry powder and cook for 1
minute, then stir in the flour and cook
for a further 1 minute.
2 Remove from the heat and stir in
the milk until smooth. Return to the
heat and stir constantly until the sauce
has thickened. Simmer for 2 minutes
and then stir in the prawns. Continue
to simmer for 5 minutes, or until the
prawns are just cooked.
3 Stir in the lemon juice, sherry
and parsley and serve immediately
with rice.

NUTRITION PER SERVE
Protein 38 g; Fat 12 g; Carbohydrate 9 g;
Dietary Fibre 1.5 g; Cholesterol 280 mg;
1247 kJ (298 cal)

Add the garlic and onion to the butter and cook until softened.

Return the saucepan to the heat and stir the curry constantly until thickened.

Add the prawns and continue to simmer until they are just cooked.

THAI PRAWN AND NOODLE SALAD

Preparation time: 25 minutes
Total cooking time: 5 minutes
Serves 4

DRESSING
2 tablespoons grated fresh ginger
2 tablespoons soy sauce
2 tablespoons sesame oil
⅓ cup (80 ml/2¾ fl oz) red wine vinegar
3–4 teaspoons sweet chilli sauce
2 cloves garlic, crushed
⅓ cup (80 ml/2¾ fl oz) kecap manis
    (see NOTE)

250 g (8 oz) fine instant noodles
5 spring onions, sliced
2 tablespoons chopped fresh
    coriander
1 red capsicum, chopped
100 g (3½ oz) snow peas, sliced
500 g (1 lb) cooked king prawns,
    peeled, halved and deveined

1 To make the dressing, whisk together the ingredients with a fork.
2 Cook the noodles in a large pan of boiling water for 2 minutes and drain well. Add to the dressing and toss to combine. Leave to cool.
3 Add the remaining ingredients to the noodles and toss gently. Serve at room temperature.

NUTRITION PER SERVE
Protein 35 g; Fat 15 g; Carbohydrate 60 g;
Dietary Fibre 3 g; Cholesterol 235 mg;
2275 kJ (540 cal)

NOTE: Kecap manis (sweet soy sauce) is available from Asian food stores.

Peel and finely grate the fresh ginger on the fine side of the grater.

Add the kecap manis to the other ingredients and mix to combine.

Add the noodles to a large pan of boiling water and cook until tender.

Batters & coatings

When delicious seafood is dipped in flavourful batters or coatings before being cooked, it not only has an extra dimension but retains its moisture and is therefore wonderfully succulent. All these recipes serve four.

SPICY BATTER

Sift 1 cup (125 g/4 fl oz) plain flour into a bowl with 2 teaspoons ground cumin, 2 teaspoons ground coriander, 1 teaspoon chilli powder and ¼ teaspoon ground turmeric. Make a well in the centre and slowly mix in ¾ cup (185 ml/6 fl oz) water and 1 beaten egg. Mix well and set aside for 10 minutes. Fill a deep-fryer or deep, heavy-based saucepan one-third full of oil and heat to 180°C (350°F), or until a cube of bread dropped into the oil browns in 15 seconds. Dip 500 g (1 lb) John dory or flounder fillets in the batter and deep-fry for 2–3 minutes, or until golden and cooked through (the fish will flake easily—test a small piece with a fork). Drain on crumpled paper towels and serve immediately.

SEAWEED BATTER

Shred 1 sheet nori (dried seaweed) into fine strips with scissors. Place in a bowl and mix with 1 cup (125 g/4 fl oz) tempura flour and 1 tablespoon sesame seeds. Make a well in the centre and gradually pour in 1 cup (250 ml/8 fl oz) iced water. Mix gently until just combined (the batter will be lumpy). Fill a deep-fryer or deep, heavy-based saucepan one-third full of oil and heat to 180°C (350°F), or until a cube of bread dropped into the oil browns in 15 seconds. Dip 500 g (1 lb) small, firm, boneless white fish fillets (e.g. ling, perch), or raw medium, peeled prawns with tails intact, or calamari rings, in the batter, shaking off any excess. Deep-fry for 1–2 minutes, or until cooked through (the fish will flake easily—test a small piece with a fork). Drain on crumpled paper towels and serve with a bowl of shoyu (Japanese soy) mixed with a little wasabi paste.

SODA WATER BATTER

Sift 1 cup (125 g/4 oz) plain flour into a large bowl with ¼ teaspoon salt and finely ground black pepper. Make a well in the centre, pour in 1 cup (250 ml/8 fl oz) chilled soda water and mix until just combined (the batter will be lumpy). Beat 1 egg white in a bowl to soft peaks and fold through the batter. Fill a deep-fryer or deep, heavy-based saucepan one-third full of oil and heat to 180°C (350°F), or until a cube of bread dropped into the oil browns in 15 seconds. Dip 500 g (1 lb) firm white fish fillets (e.g. ocean perch or whiting) in the batter, then deep-fry for 3–4 minutes, until crisp and lightly golden and cooked through (the fish will flake easily—test a small piece with a fork). Drain on crumpled paper towels, season with salt and serve immediately. This batter can also be used with prawns and vegetables.

BLACK SESAME CRUST

Mix 2 tablespoons black sesame seeds with 1½ cups (90 g/3 oz) Japanese breadcrumbs in a bowl. Lightly beat an egg in a shallow bowl. Dust 500 g (1 lb) firm white boneless fish fillets (e.g. ling, bream, ocean perch) in seasoned flour, dip lightly in the egg, then press in the bread-crumbs to coat well. Refrigerate on a plate for 30 minutes. Heat enough oil in a large deep frying pan to coat the base. Cook the fish for 2–3 minutes, or until golden brown and cooked through (the fish will flake easily when tested with a fork). Drain on crumpled paper towels and serve immediately. A dipping sauce can be made by mixing ½ cup (125 g/4 oz) Japanese or whole-egg mayonnaise with 2 teaspoons wasabi paste and 3 teaspoons soy sauce in a bowl.

PARMESAN CRUST

Process 4 slices of fresh white bread, crusts removed, in a food processor for 30 seconds to make breadcrumbs. Combine in a large bowl with 1 cup (140 g/4½ oz) roughly chopped, roasted macadamias and ½ cup (50 g/1¾ oz) grated Parmesan. Season with plenty of salt and pepper. Lightly beat an egg in a shallow bowl. Dust 500 g (1 lb) salmon fillets or ocean perch with seasoned flour, dip into the egg, then press in the breadcrumb mixture to coat well. Refrigerate for 30 minutes. Heat enough oil in a large deep frying pan to coat the base. Cook the salmon, over medium heat, for 3–4 minutes on each side, until cooked through (the fish will flake easily—test a small piece with a fork). The coating should be crunchy and golden. Serve immediately.

CHILLI CRUST

Process 6 slices of fresh white bread, crusts removed, in a food processor for 30 seconds to make breadcrumbs. Combine in a large bowl with 3 teaspoons each of chilli flakes and ground cumin and a pinch of chilli powder. Season with salt and pepper. Lightly beat an egg in a shallow bowl. Pat dry 500 g (1 lb) calamari rings, or 750 g (1½ lb) raw medium prawns, peeled and deveined, with paper towels. Dust with flour, then dip in the egg and roll in the breadcrumbs, pressing to coat. Refrigerate for 30 minutes. Fill a deep-fryer or deep, heavy-based saucepan one-third full of oil and heat to 180°C (350°F), or until a cube of bread dropped into the oil browns in 15 seconds. Deep-fry the calamari or prawns for 1 minute, or until golden and cooked. Drain on crumpled paper towels and serve.

Opposite page, from left: Spicy batter (with fish); Seaweed batter (with fish); Soda water batter (with prawns and vegetables).
This page, from left: Black sesame crust (with fish); Parmesan crust (with fish); Chilli crust (with calamari).

CRAB CURRY

Preparation time: 25 minutes
Total cooking time: 20 minutes
Serves 6

4 raw large blue swimmer or mud
   crabs
1 tablespoon oil
1 large onion, finely chopped
2 cloves garlic, crushed
1 stem lemon grass, white part only,
   finely chopped
1 teaspoon sambal oelek
1 teaspoon ground cumin
1 teaspoon ground turmeric
1 teaspoon ground coriander

270 ml (9 fl oz) light coconut cream
2 cups (500 ml/16 fl oz) chicken stock
⅓ cup (20 g/¾ oz) firmly packed fresh
   basil leaves

1 Pull back the apron and remove
the top shell from the crabs. Remove
the intestines and grey feathery gills.
Cut each crab into four pieces. Use a
cracker to crack the claws open; this
will make it easier to eat later and will
also allow the flavours to get into the
crab meat.
2 Heat the oil in a large saucepan or
wok. Add the onion, garlic, lemon
grass and sambal oelek and cook for
2–3 minutes, or until softened.
3 Add the cumin, turmeric, coriander

and ½ teaspoon salt, and cook for a
further 2 minutes, or until fragrant.
4 Stir in the coconut cream and stock.
Bring to the boil, then reduce the
heat, add the crab pieces and cook,
stirring occasionally, for 10 minutes,
or until the liquid has reduced and
thickened slightly and the crabs are
cooked through. Stir in the basil and
serve with steamed rice.

NUTRITION PER SERVE
Protein 0.5 g; Fat 7 g; Carbohydrate 1.5 g;
Dietary Fibre 0.5 g; Cholesterol 20 mg;
290 kJ (70 cal)

Pull back the apron and remove the top shell
from the crab.

Remove the intestines and grey feathery gills from
the crab.

Crack the claws open to allow the flavours to get
into the crab meat while it is cooking.

MUSSELS IN CHUNKY TOMATO SAUCE

Preparation time: 15 minutes
Total cooking time: 30 minutes
Serves 6

1.5 kg (3 lb) black mussels
1 tablespoon olive oil
1 large onion, diced
4 cloves garlic, finely chopped
2 x 400 g (13 oz) cans diced tomatoes
¼ cup (60 g/2 oz) tomato paste
¼ cup (30 g/1 oz) pitted black olives
1 tablespoon capers
½ cup (125 ml/4 fl oz) fish stock
3 tablespoons chopped fresh
    flat-leaf parsley

1 Scrub the mussels with a stiff brush and pull out the hairy beards. Discard any damaged mussels, or any that don't close when tapped.

2 In a large saucepan, heat the olive oil and cook the onion and garlic over medium heat for 1–2 minutes, until softened. Add the tomato, tomato paste, olives, capers and fish stock. Bring to the boil, then reduce the heat and simmer, stirring occasionally, for 20 minutes, or until the sauce is thick.
3 Stir in the mussels and cover the saucepan. Shake or toss the mussels occasionally and cook for

4–5 minutes, or until the mussels begin to open. Remove the pan from the heat and discard any mussels that haven't opened in the cooking time.
4 Just before serving, toss the chopped parsley through.

NUTRITION PER SERVE
Protein 17 g; Fat 12 g; Carbohydrate 11 g;
Dietary Fibre 3 g; Cholesterol 35 mg;
973 kJ (233 cal)

Simmer the chunky tomato sauce, stirring occasionally, until thick.

Cook the mussels until they open. Discard any that don't open in the time.

MARINATED CHILLI SQUID

**Preparation time: 10 minutes
  + 2–3 hours marinating
Total cooking time: 15 minutes
Serves 4**

500 g (1 lb) squid tubes
1 tablespoon finely chopped
    fresh ginger
2–3 teaspoons finely chopped
    red chilli
3 cloves garlic, finely chopped
¼ cup (60 ml/2 fl oz) oil
2 onions, thinly sliced
500 g (1 lb) baby bok choy,
    roughly chopped

1 Wash the squid well and dry with
paper towels. Cut into 1 cm (½ inch)
rings and place in a bowl with the
ginger, chilli, garlic and oil. Toss well.
Cover and refrigerate for 2–3 hours.
2 Heat the wok until very hot and
stir-fry the squid rings over high heat
in three batches for 1–2 minutes,
reserving the marinade. Remove from
the wok as soon as the squid turns
white. Keep the wok very hot and
don't cook the squid for too long or it
will toughen. Remove all the squid
from the wok.
3 Pour the reserved marinade into the
wok and bring to the boil. Add the
onion and cook over medium heat for
3–4 minutes, or until slightly softened.
Add the bok choy, cover and steam
for 2 minutes, or until wilted. Add the
squid and toss. Serve immediately.

NUTRITION PER SERVE
Protein 25 g; Fat 15 g; Carbohydrate 7 g;
Dietary Fibre 2 g; Cholesterol 250 mg;
1105 kJ (265 cal)

Wash the squid tubes well and pat them dry with
paper towels.

Using a sharp knife, slice the washed squid
tubes into rings.

Remove the squid from the wok as soon as it
turns white, or it will be rubbery.

SMOKED SALMON WITH CANNELLINI BEANS

Preparation time: 20 minutes
Total cooking time: 15 minutes
Serves 4

olive oil, for cooking
6 slices white bread, cubed
3 cloves garlic, crushed
6 spring onions, sliced
300 g (10 oz) smoked salmon, cut into thin strips
300 g (10 oz) can cannellini beans, rinsed
4 Roma tomatoes, chopped
175 g (6 oz) iceberg lettuce, shredded
2 tablespoons chopped fresh dill
2 tablespoons lemon juice

1 Heat the wok until very hot, add ⅓ cup (80 ml/2¾ fl oz) oil and swirl it around to coat the side. Stir-fry the bread over high heat until crisp and golden. Remove from the wok and drain the croutons on paper towels.
2 Reheat the wok, add 1 tablespoon of the oil and stir-fry the garlic and half the spring onion for 2 minutes. Remove from the wok.
3 Reheat the wok and stir-fry the salmon until it is slightly crisp. Add the cannellini beans and tomato and cook for 2–3 minutes, or until heated through. Remove the wok from the heat and quickly stir in the lettuce, dill, and the spring onion and garlic mixture.
4 Whisk the lemon juice with 2 tablespoons olive oil to make a dressing and pour over the salad. Add the croutons and toss. Garnish with the remaining spring onion.

NUTRITION PER SERVE
Protein 25 g; Fat 25 g; Carbohydrate 25 g; Dietary Fibre 5 g; Cholesterol 35 mg; 1700 kJ (405 cal)

Make the croutons by stir-frying the bread cubes until crisp and golden.

SALMON WITH LEEK AND CAMEMBERT IN HONEY MUSTARD SAUCE

Preparation time: 10 minutes
Total cooking time: 15 minutes
Serves 4

500 g (1 lb) salmon fillet, cut into thick
    strips
¼ cup (60 g/2 oz) wholegrain mustard
1 tablespoon lime juice
2 tablespoons oil
1 leek, white part only, julienned
2 tablespoons tamari
2 teaspoons fish sauce

1 tablespoon honey
75 g (2½ oz) snow pea sprouts
½ cup (15 g/½ oz) coriander leaves,
    plus extra to garnish
100 g (3½ oz) Camembert, sliced
lime wedges, to serve

1 Place the salmon strips in a glass or ceramic bowl. Add the mustard and lime juice and toss to coat the salmon.
2 Heat the wok until very hot, add the oil and swirl it around to coat the side. Stir-fry the salmon in batches over high heat until it is slightly browned. Remove from the wok.
3 Add 1 tablespoon water to the wok, then add the leek and stir-fry

until it is golden brown. Return the salmon to the wok, with the tamari, fish sauce and honey. Cook until the salmon is heated through.
4 Remove the wok from the heat and toss the snow pea sprouts and coriander leaves through the salmon. Serve topped with the Camembert and extra coriander, and the lime wedges on the side.

NUTRITION PER SERVE
Protein 30 g; Fat 30 g; Carbohydrate 7 g;
Dietary Fibre 2 g; Cholesterol 110 mg;
1770 kJ (420 cal)

Remove the skin from the salmon, pull out any bones, then cut into thick strips.

Cut the leek into julienne strips, using only the white part.

Stir-fry the salmon until it turns a soft pink colour and is slightly browned.

SICHUAN PRAWNS WITH SNOW PEAS

Preparation time: 30 minutes
+ 20 minutes marinating
Total cooking time: 20 minutes
Serves 4

2 teaspoons Sichuan pepper
750 g (1½ lb) raw prawns, peeled and
    deveined, tails intact
2 tablespoons grated fresh ginger
3 cloves garlic, finely chopped
2 tablespoons Chinese rice wine or
    dry sherry
oil, for cooking
2 eggs, lightly beaten
½ red capsicum, cut into strips
½ green capsicum, cut into strips
4 spring onions, cut into pieces
100 g (3½ oz) snow peas
½ teaspoon salt
75 g (2½ oz) roasted unsalted peanuts,
    roughly chopped
50 g (1¾ oz) snow pea sprouts

1 Heat the wok until very hot and dry-fry the Sichuan pepper until it is fragrant. Remove from the wok and crush with a mortar and pestle or in a spice grinder.
2 Combine the prawns with the Sichuan pepper, ginger, garlic and wine in a glass or ceramic dish. Cover and refrigerate for 20 minutes.
3 Heat the wok until very hot, add 1½ tablespoons of the oil and swirl it around to coat the side. Dip three or four prawns in the beaten eggs, then stir-fry for about 1 minute, or until the prawns just change colour and are cooked. Remove from the wok. Repeat with the remaining prawns, reheating the wok to very hot for each batch and adding a little oil when needed.

Remove the prawns from the wok.
4 Add the capsicum, spring onion, snow peas and salt to the wok. Stir-fry for 2 minutes, or until the vegetables are just crisp and tender.
5 Return the prawns to the wok with the peanuts and toss gently to

combine. Serve immediately on a bed of snow pea sprouts.

NUTRITION PER SERVE
Protein 50 g; Fat 20 g; Carbohydrate 8 g;
Dietary Fibre 4.5 g; Cholesterol 370 mg;
1710 kJ (410 cal)

Peel the prawns, leaving the tails intact, and pull out the dark veins from their backs.

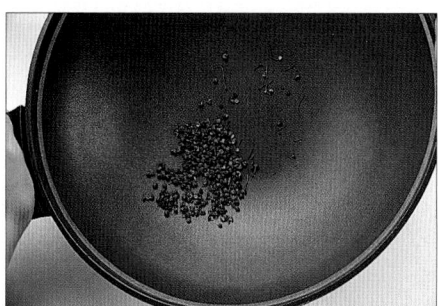

Dry-fry the Sichuan pepper in a hot wok until it becomes fragrant.

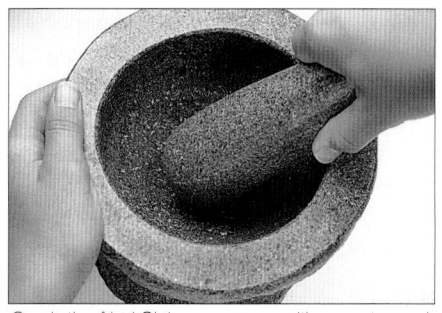

Crush the fried Sichuan pepper with a mortar and pestle or in a spice grinder.

Flavoured butters

These butters melt into the hot seafood and are good to have on hand for adding zing to simply cooked fish or other seafood. All the butters can be stored, wrapped tightly, in the refrigerator for up to 1 week, or frozen for 2–3 months. The amounts are enough for 6 serves.

OLIVE, ANCHOVY AND CAPER

Beat 125 g (4 oz) chopped, slightly softened unsalted butter until smooth. Beat in 2 teaspoons chopped capers, 3 chopped anchovy fillets and 1 tablespoon finely chopped green olives. Spoon the butter onto a piece of greaseproof paper, shape into a 4–5 cm (1¾–2 inch) wide log, roll up and twist the ends to seal. Refrigerate until firm, then cut into 5 mm (¼ inch) slices. Serve on fish such as poached salmon fillets.

SEMI-DRIED TOMATO AND WHITE CASTELLO

Beat 90 g (3 oz) chopped, slightly softened butter until smooth. Fold in 50 g (1¾ oz) finely chopped semi-dried tomatoes, and 50 g (1¾ oz) chopped White Castello cheese. Place on a piece of greaseproof paper, shape into a 4–5 cm (1¾–2 inch) wide log, roll up and twist the ends to seal. Refrigerate until firm, cut into 5 mm (¼ inch) slices and serve on seafood such as seared scallops or prawns.

LEMON AND DILL

Beat 100 g (3½ oz) unsalted chopped, slightly softened butter until smooth. Beat in 2 teaspoons finely chopped fresh dill, ½ teaspoon finely grated lemon rind and 2 tablespoons lemon juice until well combined. Spoon onto a piece of greaseproof paper, shape into a 4–5 cm (1¾–2 inch) wide log, roll up and twist the ends to seal. Refrigerate until firm, then cut into 5 mm (¼ inch) thick slices. Serve on pan-fried fish such as bream.

ROASTED CAPSICUM AND ROCKET

Beat 125 g (4 oz) chopped, slightly softened butter until smooth. Fold in 1 crushed garlic clove, 2 tablespoons finely chopped rocket leaves, 1½ tablespoons finely chopped basil and 60 g (2 oz) roasted red capsicum, finely chopped. Spoon onto greaseproof paper, shape into a 4–5 cm (1¾–2 inch) wide log, roll up and twist the ends. Refrigerate until firm, then cut into 5 mm (¼ inch) thick slices. Serve on chargrilled fish.

PESTO

Process 4 tablespoons fresh basil leaves, 1 tablespoon each of pine nuts and grated Parmesan and 1 crushed garlic clove in a food processor until smooth. Put in a bowl with 125 g (4 oz) chopped, slightly softened butter and beat to combine. Spoon onto greaseproof paper, shape into a wide log, 4–5 cm (1¾–2 inch), roll up and twist the ends. Refrigerate until firm. Cut into 5 mm (¼ inch) slices. Serve on chargrilled tuna or swordfish steaks.

WASABI AND SEAWEED

Beat 125 g (4 oz) chopped, slightly softened butter with electric beaters until smooth. Fold through 2 teaspoons wasabi paste, 1 teaspoon rice vinegar and 1 sheet nori (dried seaweed), finely cut into small pieces with scissors. Spoon onto greaseproof paper, shape into a 4–5 cm (1¾–2 inch) wide log. Roll up and twist the ends to seal. Refrigerate until firm, then cut into 5 mm (¼ inch) thick slices. Serve on chargrilled shellfish such as large prawns or scampi.

SAFFRON AND PARSLEY

Grind ¼ teaspoon saffron threads in a mortar and pestle or spice grinder until powdery. Transfer to a small bowl, add 1 tablespoon hot water and soak for 2 minutes. Beat 125 g (4 oz) chopped, slightly softened butter with electric beaters until smooth. Beat in 2 teaspoons finely chopped parsley and the saffron and water. Spoon onto greaseproof paper, shape into a 4–5 cm (1¾–2 inch) wide log, roll up and twist the ends. Refrigerate until required, then cut into 5 mm (¼ inch) slices. Serve on fish such as pan-fried whiting or ocean perch fillets.

SWEET CHILLI AND CORIANDER

Beat 125 g (4 oz) chopped, slightly softened butter with electric beaters until smooth. Beat in 2 tablespoons sweet chilli sauce, 1 tablespoon chopped coriander, ½ teaspoon grated ginger and 1–2 teaspoons fish sauce. Spoon onto greaseproof paper, shape into a 4–5 cm (1¾–2 inch) wide log and roll up, twisting the ends to seal. Refrigerate until firm, then cut into 5 mm (¼ inch) thick slices. Serve on shellfish such as chargrilled prawns.

Opposite page, clockwise from top left: Olive, anchovy and caper; Semi-dried tomato and white castello; Lemon and dill; Roasted capsicum and rocket; Sweet chilli and coriander; Saffron and parsley; Wasabi and seaweed; Pesto.

SALT-AND-PEPPER SQUID

Preparation time: 40 minutes
  + 20 minutes marinating
Total cooking time: 10 minutes
Serves 4

500 g (1 lb) squid tubes
⅓ cup (80 ml/2¾ fl oz) oil
4 cloves garlic, finely chopped
½ teaspoon sugar
2 teaspoons sea salt
1 teaspoon ground black pepper
150 g (5 oz) baby English spinach
  leaves
100 g (3½ oz) cherry tomatoes,
  quartered
2 tablespoons lime juice
lime quarters, to garnish

1 Cut the squid tubes in half length-ways and open them out. Rinse and pat dry with paper towels. Lay on a chopping board with the inside facing upwards. Honeycomb the squid by scoring along the length of each piece very finely, then diagonally across the width to create a fine diamond pattern. Cut the squid into pieces 5 x 3 cm (2 x 1¼ inches). Combine the squid, oil, garlic, sugar and half the salt and pepper, cover and refrigerate for 20 minutes.
2 Arrange the spinach leaves and tomatoes on a large serving platter.
3 Heat the wok until it is very hot and stir-fry the squid over high heat in several batches, tossing constantly, for 1–2 minutes, or until the squid just turns white and curls. Keep the wok very hot and don't cook the squid for too long or it will toughen.
4 Return all the squid pieces to the wok with the lime juice and the remaining salt and pepper. Stir briefly until heated through. Arrange on top of the spinach and garnish with the lime wedges. Serve immediately.

NUTRITION PER SERVE
Protein 20 g; Fat 15 g; Carbohydrate 3 g;
Dietary Fibre 2 g; Cholesterol 250 mg;
1020 kJ (250 cal)

HINT: Tenderize squid by marinating in puréed papaya or pawpaw mixed with a little milk. Rinse and drain.

Cut the squid tubes in half lengthways, and open them out.

Score very finely along the length, then diagonally to create a diamond pattern.

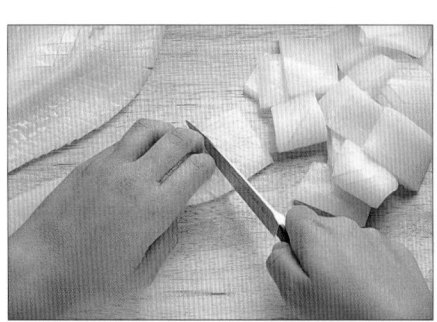

Fold the honeycombed squid tubes over and cut them into pieces.

Stir-fry the squid in batches until it turns white and curls up. Take care not to overcook.

GARLIC AND GINGER PRAWNS

Preparation time: 25 minutes
Total cooking time: 10 minutes
Serves 4

2 tablespoons oil
1 kg (2 lb) raw king prawns,
    peeled, deveined and butterflied,
    tails left intact
3–4 cloves garlic, finely chopped
5 cm (2 inch) piece fresh ginger,
    cut into matchsticks
2–3 small red chillies, seeded and
    finely chopped
6 coriander roots, finely chopped, plus
    a few leaves to garnish
8 spring onions, cut into short lengths
½ red capsicum, thinly sliced
2 tablespoons lemon juice
½ cup (125 ml/4 fl oz) white wine
2 teaspoons crushed palm sugar
2 teaspoons fish sauce

1 Heat the wok until very hot, add
the oil and swirl to coat. Stir-fry the
prawns, garlic, ginger, chilli and
coriander root in two batches for
1–2 minutes over high heat, or until
the prawns turn pink. Remove all the
prawns from the wok and set aside.
2 Add the spring onion and capsicum
to the wok. Cook over high heat for
2–3 minutes. Add the lemon juice,
wine and palm sugar. Cook until the
liquid has reduced by two thirds.
3 Add the prawns and sprinkle with
fish sauce. Toss to heat through.
Garnish with coriander to serve.

NUTRITION PER SERVE
Protein 1 g; Fat 10 g; Carbohydrate 4.5 g;
Dietary Fibre 1.5 g; Cholesterol 0 mg;
550 kJ (130 cal)

Butterfly the peeled prawns by cutting a slit down
the backs and opening them out.

Using a large, sharp knife, finely chop the
coriander roots.

Stir-fry the prawns in two batches with the garlic,
ginger, chilli and coriander root.

CHILLI CRAB

Preparation time: 25 minutes
Total cooking time: 25 minutes
Serves 4

2 x 1 kg (2 lb) mud crabs
2 tablespoons oil
1 onion, chopped
4 cloves garlic, crushed
3 teaspoons grated fresh ginger
2–3 red chillies, finely chopped
440 ml (14 fl oz) tomato purée
1 tablespoon soy sauce
1 tablespoon soft brown sugar
2 teaspoons rice vinegar

1 Wash the crabs well with a scourer. Pull the apron back from underneath the crab and snap it off. Remove the feathery gills and internal organs. Twist off the legs and claws and pull the body apart. Using a cleaver or a heavy-bladed knife, cut the body in half or quarters. Crack the claws by giving them a good hit with the back of a cleaver.
2 Heat the wok until very hot, add the oil and swirl it around to coat the side of the wok. Stir-fry the crab in batches for 2–3 minutes, or until it turns bright red. Remove all the crab from the wok and set aside.
3 Add the onion to the wok and cook for 3 minutes. Add the garlic, ginger and chilli, and cook for 1–2 minutes. Stir in the tomato purée, soy sauce, sugar, vinegar and ½ cup (125 ml/ 4 fl oz) water. Bring to the boil, then reduce the heat and simmer for 5 minutes.
4 Return the crab to the wok and toss to coat with the tomato sauce mixture. Simmer for 8 minutes, turning the crab pieces frequently.

NUTRITION PER SERVE
Protein 65 g; Fat 15 g; Carbohydrate 20 g; Dietary Fibre 3 g; Cholesterol 420 mg; 1185 kJ (450 cal)

Snap the apron off the crab by pulling it back from underneath the crab.

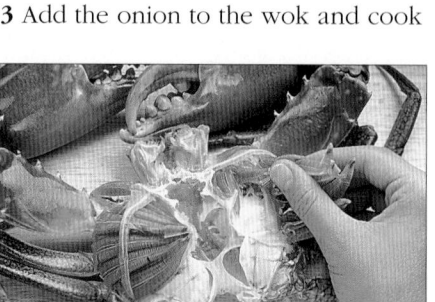
Pull the feathery gills and the internal organs out of the crab.

Using a cleaver, cut the body of the crab in half or into quarters.

FRESH TUNA AND GREEN BEANS

Preparation time: 25 minutes
Total cooking time: 10 minutes
Serves 4

300 g (10 oz) small green beans, topped and tailed
2 tablespoons oil
600 g (1¼ lb) fresh tuna, cut into small cubes
250 g (8 oz) small cherry tomatoes
16 small black olives
2–3 tablespoons lemon juice
2 cloves garlic, finely chopped
8 anchovy fillets, rinsed, dried and finely chopped
¼ cup (15 g/½ oz) small basil leaves (or larger leaves, torn)

1 Bring a small pan of water to the boil. Add the beans and cook for 2 minutes. Drain and refresh under very cold water so they keep their colour. Set aside.
2 Heat the wok until very hot, add the oil and swirl it around to coat the side. Stir-fry the tuna for about 5 minutes, or until it is cooked on the outside, but still pink on the inside.
3 Add the cherry tomatoes, olives and beans and gently toss until heated through. Stir in the lemon juice, garlic and anchovies. Season with salt and black pepper and serve scattered with the basil leaves.

NUTRITION PER SERVE
Protein 40 g; Fat 15 g; Carbohydrate 4 g; Dietary Fibre 4 g; Cholesterol 75 mg; 1390 kJ (330 cal)

Cut the tuna into long strips and then into small cubes.

Rinse and dry the anchovy fillets to reduce their saltiness, then chop them finely.

Tuna is best cooked until it is browned on the outside, but still pink inside.

JAPANESE-STYLE SALMON PARCELS

Preparation time: 40 minutes
Total cooking time: 15 minutes
Serves 4

2 teaspoons sesame seeds
4 x 150 g (5 oz) salmon cutlets or
    steaks
2.5 cm (1 inch) piece fresh ginger
2 celery sticks
4 spring onions
¼ teaspoon dashi granules
3 tablespoons mirin
2 tablespoons tamari

1 Cut 4 squares of baking paper large enough to enclose the salmon steaks. Preheat the oven to very hot 230°C (450°F/Gas 8). Lightly toast the sesame seeds under a hot grill for 1 minute.
2 Wash the salmon and dry with paper towels. Place a salmon cutlet in the centre of each paper square.
3 Cut the ginger into paper-thin slices. Slice the celery and spring onions into short lengths, then lengthways into fine strips. Arrange a bundle of celery and spring onion and several slices of ginger on each salmon steak.
4 Combine the dashi granules, mirin and tamari in a small saucepan. Heat gently until the granules dissolve.

Drizzle over each parcel, sprinkle with sesame seeds and carefully wrap the salmon, folding in the sides to seal in all the juices. Arrange the parcels on a baking tray and cook for about 12 minutes, or until tender. (The paper will puff up when the fish is cooked.) Do not overcook or the salmon will dry out. Serve immediately, as standing time can spoil the fish.

NUTRITION PER SERVE
Protein 20 g; Fat 14 g; Carbohydrate 0 g;
Dietary Fibre 0.5 g; Cholesterol 85 mg;
935 kJ (225 cal)

NOTE: Dashi, mirin and tamari are all available from Japanese food stores.

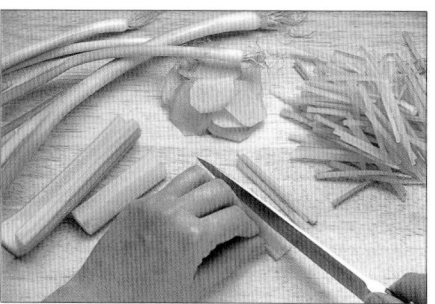

Cut the celery sticks into short lengths, then lengthways into thin julienne strips.

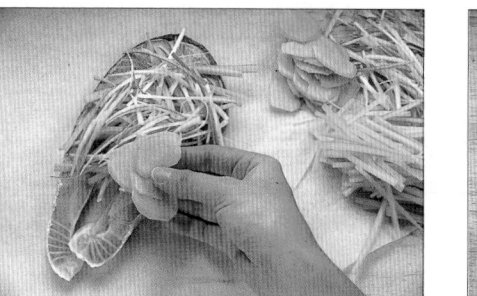

Arrange celery and spring onion strips on the fish and top with ginger slices.

Wrap the salmon in baking paper, folding the sides to seal in the juices.

MALAY FISH CURRY

Preparation time: 25 minutes
Total cooking time: 25 minutes
Serves 4

3–6 red chillies, to taste
1 onion, chopped
4 cloves garlic
3 stems lemon grass, white part only, sliced
5 cm (2 inch) piece fresh ginger, sliced
2 teaspoons shrimp paste
¼ cup (60 ml/2 fl oz) oil
1 tablespoon fish curry powder (see NOTE)
1 cup (250 ml/8 fl oz) coconut milk
1 tablespoon tamarind concentrate
1 tablespoon kecap manis
350 g (11 oz) firm white fish fillets, cut into bite-sized pieces
2 ripe tomatoes, chopped
1 tablespoon lemon juice

1 Combine the chillies, onion, garlic, lemon grass, ginger and shrimp paste in a small food processor and process until roughly chopped. Add 2 tablespoons of oil and process to a smooth paste.
2 Heat the remaining oil in a wok and add the paste. Cook for 3–4 minutes over low heat, stirring constantly until very fragrant. Add the curry powder and stir for another 2 minutes. Add the coconut milk, tamarind, kecap manis and 1 cup (250 ml/8 fl oz) water to the wok. Bring to the boil, stirring occasionally, then reduce the heat and simmer for 10 minutes.
3 Add the fish, tomato and lemon juice and season well. Simmer for 5 minutes or until the fish is just cooked. Serve immediately.

NUTRITION PER SERVE
Protein 22 g; Fat 30 g; Carbohydrate 6.5 g; Dietary Fibre 4 g; Cholesterol 65 mg; 1600 kJ (382 cal)

NOTE: Fish curry powder is a blend of spices suited to seafood flavours. It is available from Asian food stores.

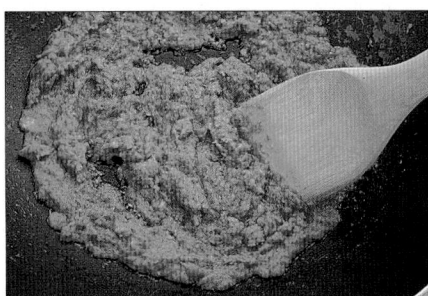
Process the ingredients to make a smooth paste, then stir-fry over low heat for 3–4 minutes.

Add the coconut milk to the paste and simmer the sauce for 10 minutes, stirring occasionally.

Add the fish, tomato and lemon juice and season with salt and pepper.

621

PRAWN OMELETTE

Preparation time: 15 minutes
Total cooking time: 15 minutes
Serves 2–4

2 tablespoons oil
3 cloves garlic, chopped
2 stems lemon grass, white part only, finely chopped
2 coriander roots, finely chopped
1–2 teaspoons chopped red chillies
500 g (1 lb) small raw prawns, peeled
3 spring onions, chopped
½ teaspoon black pepper
1½ tablespoons fish sauce

2 teaspoons soft brown sugar
4 eggs
chilli sauce, for serving

1 Heat half the oil in a wok. Add the garlic, lemon grass, coriander root and chilli and stir-fry for 20 seconds. Add the prawns and stir-fry until they change colour. Add the spring onions, pepper, 1 tablespoon fish sauce and brown sugar; toss well and remove.
2 Beat the eggs, remaining fish sauce and 2 tablespoons water until foamy. Add the remaining oil to the wok and swirl around to coat the side. Heat the wok and, when it is very hot, pour in the egg mixture and swirl around the

wok. Allow the mixture to set underneath, frequently lifting the edge once set, and tilting the wok a little to let the unset mixture run underneath. Repeat until the omelette is nearly set.
3 Place three-quarters of the prawn mixture in the centre of the omelette and fold in the sides to make a square (or simply fold the omelette in half). Slide onto a serving plate and place the remaining prawn mixture on top. Serve with chilli sauce.

NUTRITION PER SERVE (4)
Protein 30 g; Fat 10 g; Carbohydrate 3 g;
Dietary Fibre 1 g; Cholesterol 320 mg;
925 kJ (220 cal)

Add the chopped spring onions, pepper, fish sauce and brown sugar to the prawns.

Tilt the wok and lift the edge of the omelette to let the unset mixture run underneath.

Fold the sides of the omelette over the filling to form a square.

SCALLOPS AND FISH IN GINGER AND LIME

Preparation time: 15 minutes
Total cooking time: 15 minutes
Serves 4

500 g (1 lb) firm white fish fillets
350 g (12 oz) scallops
2 tablespoons oil
5 cm (2 inch) piece fresh ginger, grated
3 spring onions, chopped
1 tablespoon lime juice
2 tablespoons chilli jam

2 teaspoons finely grated lime rind
3 tablespoons coriander leaves

1 Cut the fish into bite-sized pieces and remove any black veins from the scallops. Heat half the oil in a wok and stir-fry the ginger and spring onions for 30 seconds. Remove from the wok.
2 Reheat the wok and, when it is very hot, add the remaining oil. Add the fish and scallops in three batches and stir-fry for 2–3 minutes. Remove from the wok and set aside.
3 Add the lime juice, chilli jam, lime rind and 2 tablespoons water to the

wok and bring to the boil, stirring. Return the fish, scallops, and onion mixture to the wok, tossing gently with the sauce. Serve immediately sprinkled with coriander leaves.

NUTRITION PER SERVE
Protein 37 g; Fat 14 g; Carbohydrate 3 g; Dietary Fibre 0 g; Cholesterol 116 mg; 1185 kJ (283 cal)

NOTE: Seafood should be stir-fried in a very hot wok, but don't cook it for too long or it will become tough.

Pull away any of the large black veins from the scallops.

Stir-fry the fish and scallops in three batches, then remove from the wok.

Return the seafood to the wok and toss gently through the sauce.

SWEET CHILLI SQUID

Preparation time: 20 minutes
Total cooking time: 10 minutes
Serves 4

750 g (1½ lb) squid tubes
1 tablespoon peanut oil
1 tablespoon finely grated fresh ginger
2 cloves garlic, crushed
8 spring onions, chopped
2 tablespoons sweet chilli sauce
2 tablespoons Chinese barbecue
    sauce

1 tablespoon soy sauce
550 g (1 lb 2 oz) bok choy, cut into
    short pieces
1 tablespoon chopped coriander
    leaves

1 Cut the squid tubes open, score diagonal slashes across the inside surface and cut into strips.
2 Heat a wok until very hot, add the oil and swirl to coat. Add the ginger, garlic, spring onion and squid and stir-fry for 3 minutes, or until browned.
3 Add the sauces and 2 tablespoons water to the wok and stir-fry for

2 minutes, or until the squid is just tender. Add the bok choy and coriander, and stir-fry for 1 minute, or until the bok choy is tender.

NUTRITION PER SERVE
Protein 40 g; Fat 8 g; Carbohydrate 4 g;
Dietary Fibre 7.5 g; Cholesterol 375 mg;
1030 kJ (245 cal)

NOTE: Squid should be cooked at a very high temperature but quite quickly. If you cook it for too long it will toughen.

Rinse the bok choy thoroughly, then cut it into short pieces.

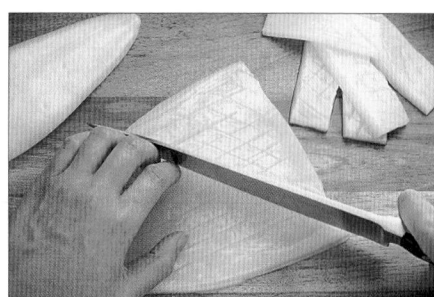
Score diagonal slashes across the inside surface of the squid tubes, then cut into strips.

Stir-fry the squid for 3 minutes. The score marks in the flesh will make it curl nicely.

SMOKED TROUT CAESAR SALAD

Preparation time: 15 minutes
Total cooking time: 20 minutes
Serves 4

⅓ cup (80 ml/2¾ fl oz) extra virgin olive oil
2 cloves garlic, crushed
½ bread stick, thinly sliced
12 quail eggs
2 x 400 g (13 oz) whole smoked trout
2 cos lettuces, torn into pieces
125 g (4 oz) Parmesan, shaved

DRESSING
1 cup (250 g/8 oz) whole-egg mayonnaise
4 anchovy fillets, chopped, reserving 1 teaspoon oil
2 tablespoons lemon juice
2 cloves garlic, crushed, extra
2 tablespoons grated Parmesan

1 Preheat the oven to moderate 180°C (350°F/Gas 4). Stir the oil and garlic together in a bowl. Brush over both sides of the bread slices and bake on a baking tray for 15 minutes, turning once, or until crisp and golden. Cool.
2 Cover the eggs with cold water in a saucepan. Bring to the boil and cook for 5 minutes. Put in cold water to cool. Peel and cut each in half.
3 Place all the dressing ingredients in a food processor or blender and blend until smooth.
4 Remove the skin from the trout, pull the flesh from the bones and flake into pieces. Arrange the lettuce on plates and top with the trout. Spoon the dressing over, then top with the egg, shaved Parmesan and toast. Season with salt and black pepper, to taste.

NUTRITION PER SERVE
Protein 67 g; Fat 66 g; Carbohydrate 27 g; Dietary Fibre 2 g; Cholesterol 425.5 mg; 4065 kJ (970 Cal)

Cut the bread into thin slices and bake on a baking tray until crisp and golden.

Process the dressing ingredients together until smooth.

Use a fork to flake the peeled trout flesh into pieces.

FISH KOFTAS IN TOMATO CURRY SAUCE

Preparation time: 40 minutes
Total cooking time: 30 minutes
Serves 6

750 g (1½ lb) firm fish fillets, such as snapper or ling, roughly chopped
1 onion, chopped
2–3 cloves garlic, chopped
1 tablespoon grated fresh ginger
4 tablespoons chopped fresh coriander leaves
1 teaspoon garam masala
¼ teaspoon chilli powder
1 egg, lightly beaten
oil, for shallow-frying

TOMATO CURRY SAUCE
2 tablespoons oil
1 large onion, finely chopped
3–4 cloves garlic, finely chopped
1 tablespoon grated fresh ginger
1 teaspoon ground turmeric
1 teaspoon ground cumin
1 teaspoon ground coriander
½ teaspoon garam masala
¼ teaspoon chilli powder
2 x 400 g (13 oz) cans crushed tomatoes
3 tablespoons chopped fresh coriander

1 Place the fish in a food processor and process until smooth. Add the onion, garlic, ginger, coriander leaves, garam masala, chilli powder and egg, and process using the pulse button, until well combined. Using wetted hands, form 1 tablespoon of the mixture into a ball. Repeat with the remaining mixture.

2 To make the tomato curry sauce, heat the oil in a large saucepan, add the onion, garlic and ginger, and cook, stirring frequently, over medium heat for 8 minutes, or until lightly golden.

3 Add the spices and cook, stirring, for 2 minutes, or until aromatic. Add the tomato and 1 cup (250 ml/8 fl oz) water, then reduce the heat and simmer, stirring frequently, for 15 minutes, or until reduced and thickened.

4 Meanwhile, heat the oil in a large frying pan to the depth of 2 cm (¾ inch). Add the fish koftas in 3–4 batches and cook for 3 minutes, or until browned all over. Drain on paper towels.

5 Add the koftas to the sauce and simmer over low heat for 5 minutes, or until heated through. Gently fold in the coriander, season with salt to taste and serve with steamed rice and freshly made chapatis.

NUTRITION PER SERVE
Protein 30 g; Fat 15 g; Carbohydrate 7 g; Dietary Fibre 3 g; Cholesterol 118 mg; 1145 kJ (273 Cal)

NOTE: The fish mixture is quite moist. Wetting your hands will stop the mixture from sticking to them.

Using wetted hands, form tablespoons of the mixture into balls.

Cook the onion, garlic and ginger until lightly golden.

CUCUMBER AND WHITE FISH STIR-FRY

Preparation time: 20 minutes
Total cooking time: 20 minutes
Serves 4

½ cup (60 g/2 oz) plain flour
½ cup (60 g/2 oz) cornflour
½ teaspoon Chinese five-spice
750 g (1½ lb) firm white boneless fish
    fillets, such as ling, cut into cubes
2 egg whites, lightly beaten
oil, for deep-frying
1 tablespoon oil
1 onion, cut into wedges
1 telegraph cucumber, seeded, sliced

1 teaspoon cornflour, extra
¾ teaspoon sesame oil
1 tablespoon soy sauce
⅓ cup (80 ml/2¾ fl oz) rice wine vinegar
1½ tablespoons soft brown sugar
3 teaspoons fish sauce

1 Combine the flours and five-spice, and season. Dip the fish in the egg white, drain off any excess, then toss in the flour. Shake off any excess.
2 Fill a large saucepan one third full of oil and heat until a bread cube browns in 15 seconds. Cook the fish in batches for 6 minutes, or until golden brown. Drain and keep warm.
3 Heat a wok until very hot, add 1 tablespoon oil and swirl to coat.

Add the onion and stir-fry for 1 minute. Add the cucumber and stir-fry for 30 seconds.
4 Blend the cornflour with 2 tablespoons water and add to the wok with the sesame oil, soy, vinegar, sugar and fish sauce. Stir-fry for 3 minutes, or until the mixture boils and thickens. Add the fish and toss to coat. Serve immediately.

NUTRITION PER SERVE
Protein 43 g; Fat 16 g; Carbohydrate 35 g;
Dietary Fibre 1 g; Cholesterol 130 mg;
1990 kJ (475 cal)

Use boneless white fish fillets and cut them into bite-sized pieces.

Deep-fry the pieces of fish in oil, cooking in batches so the temperature stays high.

Stir-fry the mixture for 3 minutes, or until it boils and thickens, before adding the fish.

FISH PIE

Preparation time: 10 minutes
Total cooking time: 45 minutes
Serves 4

2 large potatoes (500 g/1 lb), chopped
¼ cup (60 ml/2 fl oz) milk or cream
1 egg
60 g (2 oz) butter
½ cup (60 g/2 oz) grated Cheddar
800 g (1 lb 10 oz) white fish fillets,
    cut into large chunks
1½ cups (375 ml/12 fl oz) milk
1 onion, finely chopped
1 clove garlic, crushed
2 tablespoons plain flour
2 tablespoons lemon juice
2 teaspoons lemon rind
1 tablespoon chopped fresh dill

1 Preheat the oven to moderate 180°C (350°F/Gas 4). Boil or steam the potatoes until tender. Drain and mash well with the milk or cream, egg and half the butter. Mix in half the cheese, then set aside and keep warm.
2 Put the fish in a shallow frying pan and cover with the milk. Bring to the boil, then reduce the heat and simmer for 2–3 minutes, or until the fish flakes when tested with a knife. Drain the fish well, reserving the milk, and set aside.
3 Melt the remaining butter over medium heat in a pan and cook the onion and garlic for 2 minutes. Stir in the flour and cook for 1 minute, or until pale and foaming. Remove from the heat and gradually stir in the reserved milk. Return to the heat and stir constantly until the sauce boils and thickens. Reduce the heat and simmer for 2 minutes. Add the lemon juice, lemon rind and dill, and season.
4 Put the fish into a 1.5 litre ovenproof dish and gently mix in the sauce. Spoon the potato over the fish and top with the remaining cheese. Bake in the oven for 35 minutes, or until the top is browned.

NUTRITION PER SERVE
Protein 55 g; Fat 30 g; Carbohydrate 25 g;
Dietary Fibre 3 g; Cholesterol 255 mg;
2460 kJ (585 Cal)

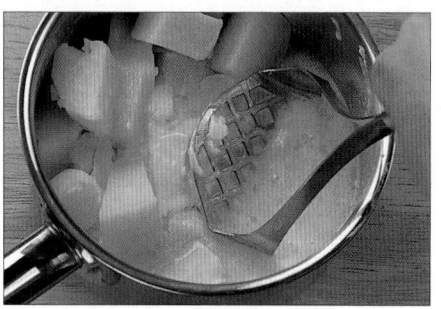

Use a potato masher to mash the potatoes with the milk or cream, egg and butter.

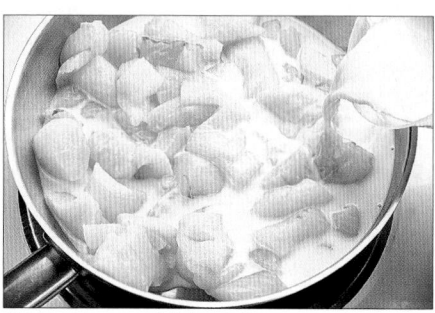

Put the pieces of fish in a frying pan and cover with the milk.

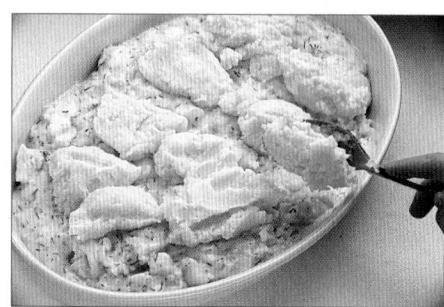

Put spoonfuls of the potato mixture on top of the fish.

TUNA MORNAY

Preparation time: 20 minutes
Total cooking time: 25 minutes
Serves 4

60 g (2 oz) butter
2 tablespoons plain flour
2 cups (500 ml/16 fl oz) milk
½ teaspoon dry mustard
¾ cup (90 g/3 oz) grated Cheddar
425 g (14 oz) can tuna in brine,
    drained
180 g (6 oz) can tuna in brine, drained
2 tablespoons finely chopped fresh
    parsley
2 eggs, hard boiled and chopped
⅓ cup (25 g/¾ oz) fresh breadcrumbs
paprika, to season

1 Preheat the oven to moderate 180°C (350°F/Gas 4). Melt the butter in a small pan, then add the flour and stir over low heat for 1 minute. Remove the pan from the heat and add the milk gradually, stirring until smooth between each addition.
2 Return the pan to the heat and stir constantly until the sauce boils and thickens. Reduce the heat and simmer for 2 minutes. Remove from the heat, whisk in the mustard and ½ cup (60 g/ 2 oz) cheese until melted and smooth.
3 Flake the tuna with a fork, and mix into the sauce, along with the parsley and egg. Season with salt and pepper. Spoon the mixture into four 1-cup (250 ml/8 fl oz) ovenproof ramekins. Mix together the breadcrumbs and remaining cheese and sprinkle over the mornay. Dust very lightly with paprika. Bake for 15–20 minutes, or until the topping is golden brown.

NUTRITION PER SERVE
Protein 55 g; Fat 30 g; Carbohydrate 15 g;
Dietary Fibre 0.5 g; Cholesterol 260 mg;
2320 kJ (555 Cal)

Gradually add the milk, stirring until smooth between each addition.

Use a fork to flake the tuna, then stir it into the sauce.

Sauces & salsas

These sauces and salsas are a perfect accompaniment for a piece of cooked fish or other seafood. Leftovers can be refrigerated in an airtight container for up to three days.

CREAMY TARRAGON SAUCE

Combine ½ cup (125 ml/4 fl oz) fish stock in a small saucepan with 1 crushed clove garlic, 1 teaspoon dried tarragon leaves and 1 thinly sliced spring onion. Bring to the boil, then reduce the heat and simmer for 3 minutes, or until reduced by half. Add 1 cup (250 ml/8 fl oz) thick cream or mascarpone. Reduce the heat to very low and stir until the cream has fully melted. Add ½ teaspoon lemon juice, 2 tablespoons grated Parmesan and salt and ground black pepper, to taste. Simmer for 1 minute, then serve with grilled fish cutlets such as blue-eye. Serves 4–6.

CANNELLINI BEAN AND SEMI-DRIED TOMATO SALSA

Drain a 400 g (13 oz) can cannellini beans and rinse the beans. Put in a bowl and stir with ½ cup (75 g/2½ oz) chopped semi-dried tomatoes, ¼ cup (30 g/1 oz) sliced pitted black olives and ¼ red onion, chopped. Stir in 1 tablespoon olive oil, 3 teaspoons white wine vinegar and 1 tablespoon finely chopped fresh flat-leaf parsley. Cover and refrigerate for 30 minutes, or until required. Serve with fish such as red mullet or snapper. Serves 6.

BUTTER SAUCE

Finely chop two French shallots and place in a small saucepan with ¼ cup (60 ml/2 fl oz) each of white wine vinegar and water. Bring to the boil, then reduce the heat and simmer until reduced to 2 tablespoons. Remove from the heat and strain into a clean saucepan. Return to the heat and whisk in 220 g (7 oz) cubed unsalted butter, a few pieces at a time. The sauce will thicken as the butter is added. Season, to taste, with salt, pepper and lemon juice. Serve with poached fish fillets such as salmon or barramundi, or chargrilled lobster tail. Serves 4–6.

SALSA VERDE

Place 1 cup (20 g/¾ oz) tightly packed fresh flat-leaf parsley, 1 clove crushed garlic, 3 tablespoons fresh dill, 2 tablespoons chopped fresh chives and 4 tablespoons fresh mint in a food processor and process for 30 seconds, or until combined. Add 1 tablespoon lemon juice, 5 anchovy fillets and 3 tablespoons drained, bottled capers and process until mixed. With the motor running, slowly add ½ cup (125 ml/4 fl oz) olive oil in a thin stream and process until all the oil is added and the mixture is smooth. Serve with grilled prawns or fish kebabs (e.g. swordfish or salmon). Serves 4.

ROASTED CAPSICUM AND BASIL SAUCE

Preheat the oven to hot 210°C (415°F/Gas 6–7). Halve two red capsicums and place skin-side-up on a greased baking tray with two cloves unpeeled garlic. Brush with olive oil and bake for 20 minutes, or until the capsicum is soft and the skin is blackened and blistered. Remove and cool the capsicums in a plastic bag. Peel the capsicums and garlic and mix in a food processor or blender for 30 seconds, or until combined. With the motor running, slowly add 100 ml (3½ fl oz) olive oil in a thin stream and blend until all the oil is added and the mixture is smooth. Add 1 tablespoon finely chopped fresh basil, ¼ teaspoon salt and freshly ground black pepper. Serve warm or cold with chargrilled fish such as sardines, swordfish or tuna. Serves 4.

MANGO AVOCADO SALSA

Cut 1 mango and 1 avocado into 1 cm (½ inch) cubes and place in a small bowl with 1 diced small red capsicum. Mix 2 tablespoons lime juice with 1 teaspoon caster sugar in a jug and pour over the mango. Stir in 3 tablespoons chopped fresh coriander leaves. Serve with chilled cooked seafood such as prawns or smoked salmon. Serves 6.

Opposite page, clockwise from top left: Creamy tarragon sauce; Salsa verde; Roasted capsicum and basil sauce; Mango avocado salsa; Butter sauce; Cannellini bean and semi-dried tomato salsa

CAJUN BLACKENED FISH

Preparation time: 10 minutes
Total cooking time: 5 minutes
Serves 4

3 teaspoons paprika
½ teaspoon cayenne pepper
3 teaspoons black pepper
1 teaspoon white pepper
1 teaspoon dried thyme
50 g (1¾ oz) butter
4 x 200 g (6½ oz) firm white fish fillets
2 cloves garlic, crushed
1 lemon, cut into wedges

1 Place the paprika, cayenne pepper, black pepper, white pepper and dried thyme in a bowl and mix well.
2 Melt the butter in a large frying pan over medium heat, then remove the pan from the heat. Brush both sides of the fillets with some of the melted butter, then spread the crushed garlic over the fish. Sprinkle each side of the fillets with the spice mixture.
3 Return the pan to medium heat and cook the fish for 1–2 minutes each side, or until cooked through (the fish will flake easily when tested with a fork). Spoon the pan juices over the fish and serve immediately with the lemon wedges on the side.

NUTRITION PER SERVE
Protein 38 g; Fat 15.5 g; Carbohydrate 3 g; Dietary Fibre 1.5 g; Cholesterol 158 mg; 1265 kJ (300 Cal)

SUGGESTED FISH: Deep-sea perch, ling, ocean perch.

NOTE: For less heat, you can omit the cayenne and white peppers.

Brush the fish with butter, spread with garlic, then sprinkle the spices all over.

Test the fish with a fork. When it is cooked, it will flake apart easily.

HERBED WHOLE SALMON

Preparation time: 15 minutes
Total cooking time: 35 minutes
Serves 6–8

1 teaspoon fennel seeds
2 tablespoons extra virgin olive oil
2 cloves garlic, finely chopped
¼ cup (60 ml/2 fl oz) white wine
¼ teaspoon sugar
1 teaspoon chopped fresh dill
2 kg whole salmon, scaled and
    cleaned
1 lemon, sliced
¾ cup (10 g/¼ oz) fresh dill sprigs

1 Preheat the oven to moderately hot 190°C (375°F/Gas 5). Place the fennel seeds in a dry frying pan and roast over high heat for 30–60 seconds or until fragrant; do not burn. Grind in a spice grinder to form a fine powder. Whisk in a bowl with the olive oil, garlic, wine, sugar and chopped dill.
2 Pat the fish dry with paper towels and make 2 diagonal cuts in the thickest part of the fish on each side. Season, then stuff lemon slices and dill sprigs into the cavity. Place enough foil to cover the fish on a lined baking tray. Place the fish on top and pour on the wine mixture. Wrap loosely and bake for 30–35 minutes, or until the dorsel fin pulls away easily or the

fish flakes easily when tested with a fork (salmon should be rare in the centre so it is moist).
3 Cut with a spoon on the natural marking along the fish, then across in sections and pull away from the bone (remove the skin if you like). Serve with lemon and dill butter, or melted butter mixed with lemon juice.

NUTRITION PER SERVE (8)
Protein 43 g; Fat 28.5 g; Carbohydrate 0.5 g; Dietary Fibre 0.5 g; Cholesterol 1210 mg; 1873 kJ (446 Cal)

SUGGESTED FISH: Ocean trout, snapper, bream.

Push the lemon slices and dill sprigs into the salmon cavity.

Put the fish on a serving plate and cut along the natural line with a spoon.

Cut sections across the fish with the spoon and pull away from the bone.

SALMON FILLETS WITH LEMON HOLLANDAISE SAUCE

Preparation time: 5 minutes
Total cooking time: 10 minutes
Serves 4

LEMON HOLLANDAISE SAUCE
175 g (6 oz) butter
4 egg yolks
2 tablespoons lemon juice

2 tablespoons olive oil
4 salmon fillets with skin on

1 Melt the butter in a small saucepan over low heat. Skim any froth from the surface and discard. Leave to cool. Whisk the yolks and 2 tablespoons water in a separate small saucepan for 30 seconds, or until pale and foamy. Place the saucepan over very low heat and whisk the egg mixture for 2–3 minutes, or until frothy and the whisk leaves a trail behind it as you whisk. Don't let the saucepan get too hot or you will scramble the eggs. Remove from the heat.
2 Whisk the cooled butter into the eggs, a little at a time, whisking well after each addition. Avoid using the milky butter whey from the base of the saucepan. Stir in the lemon juice and season with salt and cracked black pepper. Set aside.
3 Heat the oil in a large non-stick frying pan over high heat and cook the salmon fillets skin-side-down for 2 minutes. Turn over and cook for another 2 minutes, or until cooked to your liking. Serve with the sauce and vegetables of your choice.

NUTRITION PER SERVE
Protein 52.5 g; Fat 78 g; Carbohydrate 0.5 g; Dietary Fibre 0 g; Cholesterol 432 mg; 3860 kJ (920 Cal)

ALTERNATIVE FISH: Tuna, blue-eye.

NOTE: Hollandaise sauce should be made in a heavy-based saucepan. If the sauce separates or curdles, remove from the heat and whisk in an ice cube.

Use a spoon to carefully skim off any froth that forms on top of the butter.

Whisk the egg yolks over very low heat until the whisk leaves a trail behind.

Add a little cooled butter at a time to the eggs, whisking well after each addition.

Use a spatula to turn the fillets over, then cook until done to your liking.

STEAMED FISH WITH GINGER

Preparation time: 10 minutes
Total cooking time: 15 minutes
Serves 4

4 whole bream, each about
    350 g (11 oz), scaled and cleaned
2 tablespoons julienned ginger
¼ cup (60 ml/2 fl oz) peanut oil
2–3 tablespoons soy sauce
6 spring onions, sliced diagonally
45 g (1½ oz) fresh coriander sprigs

1 Make 2 diagonal cuts in the thickest part of each fish on both sides, then put in a lined bamboo or other large steamer. Cover and steam for 10 minutes, or until cooked (the fish will flake easily with a fork).
2 Place each whole fish on a serving plate and scatter some of the fresh julienned ginger over the fish. Heat the oil in a small saucepan over medium heat until the oil begins to smoke. Pour some hot oil over each fish. The oil will sizzle and splatter, so stand back a little (the oil must be very hot or the fish won't go crisp and may seem oily). Drizzle the soy sauce over the fish and garnish with spring onion and coriander sprigs.
3 Serve with steamed rice and steamed or stir-fried Asian vegetables.

NUTRITION PER SERVE
Protein 52.5 g; Fat 27.5 g; Carbohydrate 2 g; Dietary Fibre 1 g; Cholesterol 193 mg; 1950 kJ (465 Cal)

ALTERNATIVE FISH: Whole snapper, flounder.

Cut the spring onions on the diagonal into short pieces.

When the fish is cooked it will flake apart easily when tested with a fork.

Put the cooked fish on serving plates and drizzle some hot oil over each.

FISH FILLETS IN CRISPY BATTER WITH SHIITAKE MUSHROOM SAUCE

Preparation time: 15 minutes
+ 15 minutes soaking
Total cooking time: 15 minutes
Serves 4

SHIITAKE MUSHROOM SAUCE
50 g (1¾ oz) dried shiitake mushrooms
2 tablespoons peanut oil
2 cloves garlic, chopped
2 teaspoons chopped fresh ginger
1 small red chilli, seeded
    and sliced
3 spring onions, sliced diagonally
2 tablespoons oyster sauce
2 tablespoons soy sauce
2 tablespoons Chinese wine
2 teaspoons sugar

BATTER
½ cup (60 g/2 oz) plain flour
½ cup (60 g/2 oz) cornflour
1 teaspoon baking powder
1½ teaspoons salt

4 x 200 g (6½ oz) flounder or
    sole fillets
plain flour, for dusting
oil, for deep-frying
fresh coriander, to garnish

1 Soak the mushrooms in boiling water for 10 minutes, or until soft. Drain, cut off the stalks and thinly slice the mushrooms. Heat the oil in a frying pan or wok and cook the garlic, ginger and chilli over low heat for 1 minute, or until aromatic. Add the mushrooms and spring onion, and cook for 1 minute over medium heat. Combine the oyster and soy sauces, Chinese wine, sugar and ¼ cup (60 ml/ 2 fl oz) water. Add to the pan and cook, stirring for 1–2 minutes, or until combined.
2 Sift all the dry ingredients for the batter and make a well. Add ¾ cup (185 ml/6 oz) chilled water and whisk until combined. Dry the fish with paper towels and dust with flour.
3 Fill a wok one-third full of oil and heat to 180°C (350°F), or until a cube of bread browns in 15 seconds. Dip the fish in batter, drain off any excess

and cook in batches for 5–6 minutes, or until the fish is golden and flakes when tested with a fork. Drain on paper towels, top with the sauce and garnish. Serve with greens and rice.

NUTRITION PER SERVE
Protein 43.5 g; Fat 20 g; Carbohydrate 41.5 g; Dietary Fibre 2.5 g; Cholesterol 131 mg; 2185 kJ (520 Cal)

SUGGESTED FISH: Fillets of ling, flathead, sole.

NOTE: If the sauce is left to stand for too long, the mushrooms will soak up the liquid. If this happens, just add a little more water and reheat. If you prefer fresh shiitake mushrooms, slice 100 g (3½ oz) of them and add to the pan.

Cook the sauce until the ingredients are well combined.

Remove the cooked fish from the oil with a slotted spoon.

CREAMY GARLIC SEAFOOD

Preparation time: 20 minutes
Total cooking time: 20 minutes
Serves 6

12 scallops, with roe
500 g (1 lb) skinless firm white fish fillets
6 raw slipper lobsters or crabs
500 g (1 lb) raw medium prawns, peeled and deveined
50 g (1¾ oz) butter
1 onion, finely chopped
5–6 large cloves garlic, finely chopped
½ cup (125 ml/4 fl oz) white wine
2 cups (500 ml/16 fl oz) cream
1½ tablespoons Dijon mustard
2 teaspoons lemon juice
2 tablespoons chopped fresh flat-leaf parsley

1 Slice or pull off any membrane or hard muscle from the scallops. Cut the fish into 2 cm (¾ inch) cubes. Cut the heads off the slipper lobsters, then use scissors to cut down around the sides of the tail so you can flap open the shell. Remove the flesh in one piece, then slice each piece in half. Refrigerate all the seafood, covered, until ready to use.
2 Melt the butter in a frying pan and cook the onion and garlic over medium heat for 2 minutes, or until the onion is softened (be careful not to burn the garlic—it may turn bitter).
3 Add the wine to the pan and cook for 4 minutes, or until reduced by half. Stir in the cream, mustard and lemon juice and simmer for 5–6 minutes, or until reduced to almost half.
4 Add the prawns to the pan and cook for 1 minute, then add the

slipper lobster meat and cook for another minute, or until white. Add the fish and cook for 2 minutes, or until cooked through (the flesh will flake easily when tested with a fork). Finally, add the scallops and cook for 1 minute. If any of the seafood is still not cooked, cook for another minute or so, but be careful not to overcook as this will result in tough flesh. Remove the frying pan from the heat and toss the parsley through. Season, to taste. Serve with salad and bread.

NUTRITION PER SERVE
Protein 38.5 g; Fat 45.5 g; Carbohydrate 4 g; Dietary Fibre 1 g; Cholesterol 316 mg; 2460 kJ (585 Cal)

SUGGESTED FISH: Perch, ling, bream, tuna, blue-eye.

Use strong kitchen scissors to cut through the sides of each slipper lobster tail.

Pull back the shell and pull out the flesh in one piece.

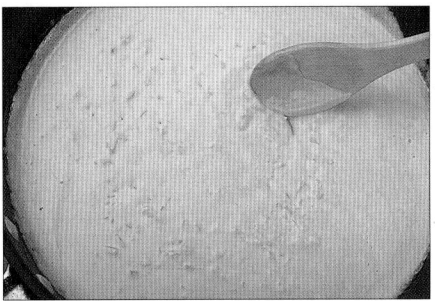

Simmer the sauce for about 5 minutes, or until reduced by almost half.

CALAMARI IN BLACK BEAN AND CHILLI SAUCE

Preparation time: 20 minutes
Total cooking time: 10 minutes
Serves 4

4 squid hoods
2 tablespoons oil
1 onion, cut into 8 wedges
1 red capsicum, sliced
115 g (4 oz) baby corn, cut in halves
3 spring onions, optional, cut
    into 3 cm (1¼ inch) lengths

BLACK BEAN SAUCE
3 teaspoons cornflour
2 tablespoons canned salted black
    beans, washed, drained
2 small red chillies, seeded
    and chopped
2 cloves garlic, finely chopped
2 teaspoons grated fresh ginger
2 tablespoons oyster sauce
2 teaspoons soy sauce
1 teaspoon sugar

1 Open out each squid hood. Score a shallow diamond pattern over the inside surface, without cutting through, then cut into 5 cm (2 inch) squares.
2 For the sauce, mix the cornflour with 1½ cups (125 ml/4 fl oz) water in a small bowl. Place the black beans in a bowl and mash with a fork. Add the chilli, garlic, ginger, oyster and soy sauces, sugar and the cornflour mix and stir.
3 Heat the oil in a wok or frying pan and stir the onion for 1 minute over high heat. Add the capsicum and corn and stir for another 2 minutes.
4 Add the squid to the wok and stir for 1–2 minutes, until the flesh curls up. Add the sauce and bring

to the boil, stirring constantly until the sauce thickens. Stir in the spring onion. Serve with steamed rice noodles.

NUTRITION PER SERVE
Protein 11.5 g; Fat 10.5 g; Carbohydrate 12.5 g; Dietary Fibre 3.5 g; Cholesterol 99.5 mg; 800 kJ (190 Cal)

VARIATION: Instead of squid, you can use fish, cuttlefish, prawns, octopus, or a combination.

NOTE: Black beans are available in cans in Asian food stores.

Score a shallow diamond pattern over the inside surface of each hood.

Toss the prepared squid in the wok until the flesh curls up.

Add the sauce, bring to the boil and stir constantly until the sauce thickens.

FISH HOTPOT WITH GINGER AND TOMATOES

**Preparation time: 20 minutes +
    20 minutes soaking**
Total cooking time: 1 hour
Serves 4

1 tablespoon peanut oil
1 onion, cut into thin wedges
1 small fresh red chilli, sliced
3 cloves garlic, finely chopped
2 cm x 2 cm (¾ x ¾ inch) piece
    fresh ginger, julienned
½ teaspoon ground turmeric
425 g (14 oz) can diced tomatoes
1 litre chicken stock
1 tablespoon tamarind purée
80 g (3 oz) dried flat rice stick
    noodles
600 g (1¼ lb) snapper fillets,
    skin removed, cut into 3 cm
    (1¼ inch) cubes
fresh coriander leaves, to garnish

1 Preheat the oven to hot 220°C (425°F/Gas 7). Heat the oil in a large frying pan over medium–high heat and cook the onion wedges for 1–2 minutes, or until softened. Add the chilli, chopped garlic and ginger and cook for 30 seconds. Add the ground turmeric, tomato, chicken stock and tamarind purée and bring to the boil over high heat. Transfer to a 2.5 litre heatproof hotpot or flameproof casserole dish and cook, covered, in the oven for 40 minutes.
2 Place the noodles in a large heatproof bowl, cover with warm water and soak for 15–20 minutes, or until al dente. Drain, rinse and drain again.
3 Remove the hotpot from the oven and stir in the noodles. Add the fish cubes, then cover and return to the oven for a further 10 minutes, or until the fish is cooked through. Serve sprinkled with some fresh coriander leaves.

NUTRITION PER SERVE
Fat 8 g; Protein 36 g; Carbohydrate 23.5 g;
Dietary Fibre 3 g; Cholesterol 91.5 mg;
1310 kJ (315 Cal)

Gently add all the fish cubes to the hotpot mixture.

FISH AND CHIPS

Preparation time: 25 minutes + soaking
Total cooking time: 30 minutes
Serves 4

1¼ cups (155 g/5 oz) plain flour
1½ cups (375 ml/12 fl oz) beer
4 floury potatoes (e.g. spunta, russet
    or King Edward)
oil, for deep-frying
4 firm white fish fillets
cornflour, for coating
lemon wedges, for serving

1 Sift the flour into a large bowl, make a well and gradually add the beer, whisking to make a smooth lump-free batter. Cover and set aside. Preheat the oven to moderate 180°C (350°F/Gas 4).

2 Cut the potatoes into 1 cm (¾ inch) thick chips. Soak in cold water for 10 minutes, drain and pat dry. Fill a deep heavy-based saucepan one-third full of oil and heat to 160°C (315°F), or until a cube of bread browns in 30 seconds. Cook batches of chips for 4–5 minutes, or until pale golden. Remove with a slotted spoon. Drain on crumpled paper towels.

3 Just before serving, reheat the oil to moderate 180°C (350°F), or until a cube of bread browns in 15 seconds. Cook the chips again, in batches, until crisp and golden. Drain. Keep hot on a baking tray in the oven.

4 Pat the fish dry with paper towels. Dust with cornflour, dip into the batter and drain off any excess. Deep-fry in batches for 5–7 minutes, or until cooked through. Turn with tongs if necessary. Remove with a slotted spoon and drain on crumpled paper towels. Serve with chips and lemon.

NUTRITION PER SERVE
Protein 22.5 g; Fat 18 g; Carbohydrate
51.5 g; Dietary Fibre 4 g; Cholesterol
49 mg; 2035 kJ (485 Cal)

SUGGESTED FISH: Fillets of bream, cod, coley, flake, flathead, pollack or snapper.

Whisk the flour and beer together until you have a smooth lump-free batter.

Cut the peeled potatoes into thick even-sized chips.

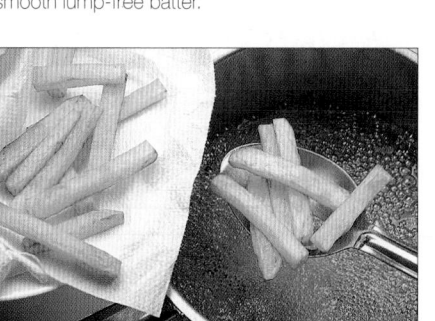

Cook the chips in batches a second time until crisp and golden.

If you need to turn the fish over during cooking, use tongs to handle.

SWORDFISH SKEWERS WITH WHITE BEAN PUREE

Preparation time: 25 minutes +
  30 minutes soaking +
  30 minutes marinating
Total cooking time: 20 minutes
Serves 4

1 kg (2 lb) swordfish steaks, cut into
   3 cm (1¼ inch) cubes
1 tablespoon olive oil
2 tablespoons lemon juice
1 clove garlic, crushed
1 tablespoon chopped fresh rosemary
1 tablespoon chopped fresh thyme
2 tablespoons chopped fresh
   flat-leaf parsley

WHITE BEAN PURÉE
2 x 400 g (13 oz) cans cannellini
   beans
1½ cups (375 ml/12 fl oz) chicken stock
2 fresh bay leaves
2 cloves garlic, crushed
1 teaspoon chopped fresh thyme
½ teaspoon finely grated lemon rind
¼ cup (60 ml/2 fl oz) extra virgin
   olive oil

1 Soak eight wooden skewers in water for at least 30 minutes to prevent them from burning during cooking. Thread the swordfish cubes onto the skewers. Place in a large non-metallic dish and pour on the combined olive oil, lemon juice, garlic, rosemary and thyme. Season well. Cover with plastic wrap and refrigerate for at least 30 minutes.
2 Meanwhile, to make the white bean purée, wash the beans in a colander and place in a large saucepan. Add the chicken stock, bay leaves and ½ cup (125 ml/4 fl oz) water. Bring to

the boil, then reduce the heat and simmer for 10 minutes. Remove from the heat and drain well, reserving 2 tablespoons of the liquid.
3 Place the beans and the reserved liquid in a food processor or blender with the garlic, thyme and lemon rind. Season with salt and freshly ground black pepper and process until smooth. With the motor running, gradually pour in the olive oil in a thin stream. Continue processing until well combined, then keep warm.

4 Heat a chargrill or hot plate until very hot. Cook the skewers, turning regularly and basting with any leftover marinade, for 3–4 minutes, or until cooked through and golden.
5 Serve the skewers warm, sprinkled with parsley and a spoonful of white bean purée on the side.

NUTRITION PER SERVE
Protein 62 g; Fat 21 g; Carbohydrate 18 g;
Dietary Fibre 9 g; Cholesterol 147 mg;
2115 kJ (505 Cal)

Drain the beans over a heatproof bowl and reserve some of the liquid.

Process the beans, garlic, thyme and lemon rind, then the oil, in a food processor.

Chargrill the swordfish skewers until cooked through and golden.

THAI PRAWN CURRY

Preparation time: 30 minutes
Total cooking time: 10 minutes
Serves 4

2 cm x 2 cm (¾ inch x ¾ inch) piece fresh galangal
1 small onion, roughly chopped
3 cloves garlic
4 dried long red chillies
4 whole black peppercorns
2 tablespoons chopped lemon grass, white part only
1 tablespoon chopped fresh coriander root
2 teaspoons grated lime rind

2 teaspoons cumin seeds
1 teaspoon sweet paprika
1 teaspoon ground coriander
3 tablespoons oil
1–2 tablespoons fish sauce
2 kaffir lime leaves
2 cups (500 ml/16 fl oz) coconut cream
1 kg (2 lb) raw medium prawns, peeled and deveined

1 Peel the galangal and thinly slice. Process the onion, garlic, chillies, peppercorns, lemon grass, coriander root, lime rind, cumin seeds, paprika, coriander, 2 tablespoons oil and ½ teaspoon salt in a small food processor until a smooth paste forms.

2 Heat the remaining oil in a frying pan. Add half the curry paste and stir over medium heat for 2 minutes. (Leftover curry paste can be kept in the refrigerator for up to 2 weeks.) Stir in the fish sauce, galangal, kaffir lime leaves and coconut cream.
3 Add the prawns to the pan and simmer for 5 minutes, or until the prawns are cooked and the sauce has thickened slightly. Serve with steamed rice. Can be garnished with shredded kaffir lime leaves and strips of chilli.

NUTRITION PER SERVE
Protein 42 g; Fat 39.5 g; Carbohydrate 9 g; Dietary Fibre 4 g; Cholesterol 279.5 mg; 2310 kJ (550 Cal)

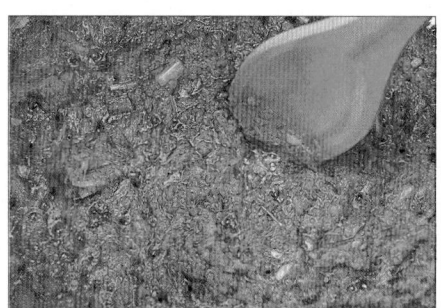

Peel the galangal and use a sharp knife to cut into very thin slices.

Add half the curry paste to the pan and stir over medium heat for 2 minutes.

Add the prawns to the pan and simmer until cooked.

CREAMY SNAPPER PIES

Preparation time: 25 minutes
Total cooking time: 1 hour 20 minutes
Serves 6

2 tablespoons olive oil
4 onions, thinly sliced
1½ cups (375 ml/12 fl oz) fish stock
3½ cups (875 ml/28 fl oz) cream
1 kg (2 lb) skinless snapper fillets, cut
    into large bite-sized pieces
2 sheets ready-rolled puff pastry,
    thawed
1 egg, lightly beaten

1 Preheat the oven to hot 220°C (425°F/Gas 7). Heat the oil in a large deep-sided frying pan, add the onion and stir over medium heat for 20 minutes, or until golden brown and slightly caramelised.
2 Add the stock to the pan, bring to the boil and cook for 10 minutes, or until the liquid has nearly evaporated. Stir in the cream, bring to the boil, then reduce the heat and simmer for 20 minutes, or until the liquid reduces by half or coats the back of a spoon.
3 Divide half the sauce among six 1¼ cup (315 ml/10 fl oz) deep ovenproof dishes. Put some fish in each dish, then top with the sauce.
4 Cut the pastry sheets into rounds slightly larger than the tops of the dishes. Brush the edges of the pastry with a little of the egg. Press onto the dishes. Brush lightly with the remaining beaten egg. Bake for 30 minutes, or until the pastry is crisp, golden and puffed.

NUTRITION PER SERVE
Protein 43 g; Fat 85 g; Carbohydrate 27 g; Dietary Fibre 1.6 g; Cholesterol 345 mg; 4347 kJ (1033 Cal)

ALTERNATIVE FISH: Fillets of bream, sea perch, ling or jewfish. Make sure you remove any bones before cooking.

Stir the sliced onion with a wooden spoon until slightly caramelised.

Reduce the heat and simmer until the liquid coats the back of a spoon.

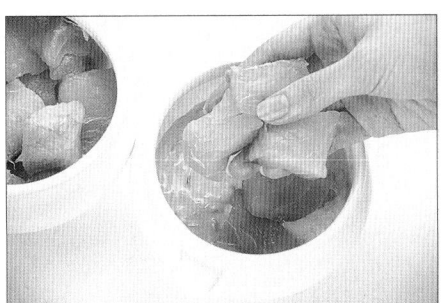

Put some fish in each dish, dividing the pieces equally among the four dishes.

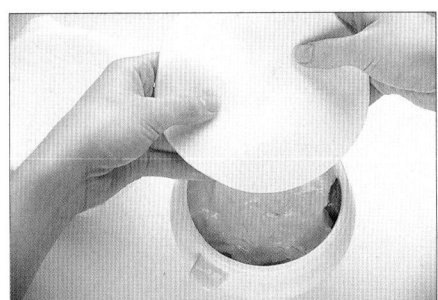

Put a round of pastry on top of each dish and gently press the edges.

LOBSTER MORNAY

Preparation time: 25 minutes
+ 15 minutes standing
Total cooking time: 10 minutes
Serves 2

1 cooked medium lobster
1¼ cups (315 ml/10 fl oz) milk
1 slice onion
1 bay leaf
6 black peppercorns
30 g (1 oz) butter
2 tablespoons plain flour
2 tablespoons cream
60 g (2 oz) Cheddar, grated

1 Using a large sharp knife, cut the lobster in half lengthways through the tail. Lift the lobster meat from the tail and body, reserving both pieces of shell. Crack the legs and prise the meat out. Discard the cream vein and soft body matter. Cut the meat into 2 cm (¾ inch) pieces, cover and refrigerate. Wash and dry the shells.
2 Put the milk, onion, bay leaf and peppercorns in a saucepan. Bring to the boil, then remove from the heat, cover and leave for 15 minutes. Strain.
3 Melt the butter in a saucepan over low heat, stir in the flour and cook for 1 minute, or until pale and foaming. Remove from the heat and gradually stir in the strained milk. Return to the heat and stir until the mixture thickens. Reduce the heat to very low and simmer for 1 minute. Stir in the cream. Season to taste then fold in the lobster meat and stir over low heat for 1 minute, or until warmed through.
4 Spoon half the mixture into each shell and sprinkle with cheese. Cook the lobster under a hot grill for 2 minutes, or until the cheese is golden. Can be served with asparagus.

NUTRITION PER SERVE
Protein 33.5 g; Fat 38 g; Carbohydrate 17.5 g; Dietary Fibre 1 g; Cholesterol 215.5 mg; 2270 kJ (540 Cal)

Use a strong knife to cut the lobster in half lengthways through the tail.

Crack the lobster legs and prise the meat out with a knife.

Add the lobster meat to the sauce and stir over low heat until heated through.

SWEET AND SOUR FISH WITH HOKKIEN NOODLES

Preparation time: 20 minutes
Total cooking time: 20 minutes
Serves 4

425 g (14 oz) Hokkien noodles
1 tablespoon peanut oil
1 clove garlic, crushed
2 teaspoons grated fresh ginger
1 onion, cut into thin wedges
1 carrot, halved lengthways and
    thinly sliced
½ red capsicum, cut into thin strips
½ green capsicum, cut into thin strips
1 celery stick, thinly sliced
½ cup (60 g/2 oz) plain flour
¼ cup (45 g/1½ oz) rice flour
1 teaspoon caster sugar
½ teaspoon ground white pepper
500 g (1 lb) firm white fish fillets (ling,
    flake, snapper), cut into 3–4 cm
    (1¼–1½ inch) cubes
1 egg, beaten with 1 tablespoon water
oil, to deep-fry
2 spring onions, sliced diagonally

SAUCE
¼ cup (60 ml/2 fl oz) rice vinegar
1 tablespoon cornflour
3 tablespoons tomato sauce
2 tablespoons sugar
2 teaspoons light soy sauce
¼ cup (60 ml/2 fl oz) pineapple juice
1 tablespoon dry sherry
2 tablespoons vegetable stock

1 Place the noodles in a heatproof bowl, cover with boiling water and soak for 1 minute. Drain.
2 To make the sauce, combine the vinegar and cornflour, then stir in the tomato sauce, sugar, soy sauce, pineapple juice, sherry, stock and ¾ cup (185 ml/6 fl oz) water.
3 Heat a wok over medium heat, add the oil and swirl to coat the side. Cook the garlic and ginger for 30 seconds. Add the onion, carrot, red and green capsicum and celery and stir-fry for 3–4 minutes. Add the sauce to the wok, increase the heat to high and stir-fry for 1–2 minutes, or until thickened. Remove from the heat and keep warm.
4 Combine the flours, sugar and white pepper in a medium bowl. Dip each piece of fish in the egg, then coat in the flour mix, shaking off any excess. Fill a deep heavy-based saucepan one-third full of oil and heat to 180°C (350°F), or until a cube of bread browns in 15 seconds. Deep-fry the fish in batches for 3 minutes, or until cooked and golden. Drain on paper towels and keep warm.
5 Return the wok with the sauce to medium heat, add the noodles and toss together for 3–4 minutes, or until heated through. Gently toss the fish through, top with the spring onion and serve immediately.

NUTRITION PER SERVE
Protein 41.5 g; Fat 10 g; Carbohydrate 98.5 g; Dietary Fibre 4.5 g; Cholesterol 138 mg; 2760 kJ (660 Cal)

Add the sauce to the wok and stir-fry until the sauce thickens.

GREEK OCTOPUS IN RED WINE STEW

Preparation time: 25 minutes
Total cooking time:
  1 hour 10 minutes
Serves 4–6

1 kg (2 lb) baby octopus
2 tablespoons olive oil
1 large onion, chopped
3 cloves garlic, crushed
1 bay leaf
3 cups (750 ml/24 fl oz) red wine
¼ cup (60 ml/2 fl oz) red wine vinegar
400 g (13 oz) can crushed tomatoes
1 tablespoon tomato paste
1 tablespoon chopped fresh oregano
¼ teaspoon ground cinnamon
small pinch ground cloves
1 teaspoon sugar
2 tablespoons finely chopped fresh
    flat-leaf parsley

1 Cut between the head and tentacles of the octopus, just below the eyes. Grasp the body and push the beak out and up through the centre of the tentacles with your fingers. Cut the eyes from the head by slicing a small round off. Discard the eye section. Carefully slit through one side, avoiding the ink sac, and remove any gut from inside. Rinse the octopus well under running water.
2 Heat the oil in a large saucepan, add the onion and cook over medium heat for 5 minutes, or until starting to brown. Add the garlic and bay leaf, and cook for 1 minute further. Add the octopus and stir to coat in the onion mixture.
3 Stir in the wine, vinegar, tomato, tomato paste, oregano, cinnamon, cloves and sugar. Bring to the boil, then reduce the heat and simmer for 1 hour, or until the octopus is tender and the sauce has thickened slightly. Stir in the parsley and season to taste with salt and pepper. Serve with a Greek salad and crusty bread.

NUTRITION PER SERVE (6)
Protein 29 g; Fat 8.5 g; Carbohydrate 3.5 g;
Dietary Fibre 1.5 g; Cholesterol 332 mg;
1234 kJ (295 Cal)

Cut between the head and the tentacles of the octopus.

Slit the head section and remove any gut from the inside.

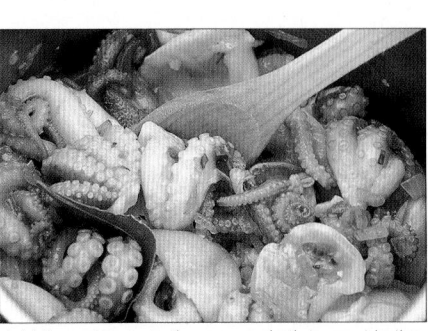
Add the octopus to the pan and stir to coat in the onion mixture.

Simmer until the octopus is tender and the sauce has thickened slightly.

GREEN FISH CURRY

Preparation time: 15 minutes
Total cooking time: 15 minutes
Serves 4

1 tablespoon peanut oil
1 brown onion, chopped
1½ tablespoons green curry paste
1½ cups (375 ml/12 fl oz) coconut milk
700 g (1 lb 6½ oz) boneless firm white
　 fish fillets, cut in bite-sized pieces
3 kaffir lime leaves

1 tablespoon fish sauce
2 teaspoons grated palm sugar
2 tablespoons lime juice
1 long green chilli, finely sliced

1 Heat a wok until very hot, add the oil and swirl to coat. Add the onion and stir-fry for 2 minutes, or until soft. Add the curry paste and stir-fry for 1–2 minutes, or until fragrant. Stir in the coconut milk and bring to the boil.

2 Add the fish and lime leaves to the wok, reduce the heat and simmer, stirring occasionally, for 8–10 minutes, or until the fish is cooked through.

3 Stir in the fish sauce, palm sugar and lime juice. Scatter the chilli slices over the curry before serving with steamed rice.

NUTRITION PER SERVE
Protein 39 g; Fat 29 g; Carbohydrate 4.5 g;
Dietary Fibre 1 g; Cholesterol 123.5 mg;
1820 kJ (435 Cal)

SUGGESTED FISH: Ling, ocean perch, bream, warehou.

To prevent skin irritation, wear rubber gloves when slicing the chilli.

Heat the coconut milk to boiling point before adding the fish.

Gently simmer the fish pieces, stirring occasionally, until cooked through.

SPICY PRAWNS

**Preparation time: 30 minutes +
15 minutes standing
Total cooking time: 1 hour
Serves 4–6**

1 kg (2 lb) raw medium prawns,
   peeled and deveined, tails intact
   (reserve shells and heads)
1 teaspoon ground turmeric
¼ cup (60 ml/2 fl oz) oil
2 onions, finely chopped
4–6 cloves garlic, finely chopped
1–2 small fresh green chillies, seeded
   and chopped
2 teaspoons ground cumin
2 teaspoons ground coriander
1 teaspoon paprika
⅓ cup (90 g/3 oz) plain yoghurt
⅓ cup (80 ml/2¾ fl oz) thick cream
⅓ cup (20 g/¾ oz) chopped fresh
   coriander leaves

1 Bring 1 litre water to the boil in a
large saucepan. Add the reserved
prawn shells and heads, reduce the
heat and simmer for 2 minutes. Skim
any scum that forms on the surface
during cooking with a skimmer or
slotted spoon. Drain, discard the
shells and heads, and return the
liquid to the pan. You will need
3 cups (750 ml/24 fl oz) liquid. Make
up with water, if necessary. Add the
turmeric and peeled prawns, and
cook for 1 minute, or until the prawns
just turn pink. Remove the prawns
and set the stock aside.
2 Heat the oil in a large saucepan.
Cook the onion, stirring, for 8
minutes, or until light golden brown.
Take care not to burn the onion.
Add the garlic and chilli, cook for
2 minutes, then add the cumin,
coriander and paprika, and cook,
stirring, for 2–3 minutes, or until
fragrant.
3 Gradually add the reserved prawn
stock, bring to the boil and cook,
stirring occasionally, for 35 minutes,
or until the mixture has reduced by
half and thickened.
4 Remove from the heat and stir in
the yoghurt. Add the prawns and stir
over low heat for 2–3 minutes, or
until the prawns are warmed through,
but do now allow the mixture to
boil. Stir in the cream and coriander
leaves. Cover and leave to stand for
15 minutes to allow the flavours to
infuse. Reheat gently and serve with
rice.

NUTRITION PER SERVE (6)
Protein 35 g; Fat 17 g; Carbohydrate 3 g;
Dietary Fibre 1 g; Cholesterol 270 mg;
1293 kJ (310 cal)

NOTE: You can remove the prawn
tails, if you prefer.

Skim any scum on the surface with a skimmer or
a slotted spoon.

Boil the mixture, stirring occasionally, until it has
reduced by half and thickened.

CATALAN FISH STEW

Preparation time: 30 minutes
Total cooking time: 40 minutes
Serves 6–8

300 g (10 oz) red mullet fillets
400 g (13 oz) firm white fish fillets
300 g (10 oz) cleaned calamari
1.5 litres fish stock
⅓ cup (80 ml/2¾ fl oz) olive oil
1 onion, chopped
6 cloves garlic, chopped
1 small fresh red chilli, chopped
1 teaspoon paprika
pinch saffron threads
150 ml (5 fl oz) white wine
425 g (14 oz) can crushed tomatoes
16 raw medium prawns, peeled and
    deveined, tails intact
2 tablespoons brandy
24 black mussels, cleaned
1 tablespoon chopped fresh parsley

PICADA
2 tablespoons olive oil
2 slices day-old bread, cubed
2 cloves garlic
5 blanched almonds, toasted
2 tablespoons fresh flat-leaf
    parsley

1 Cut the fish and calamari into 4 cm (1½ inch) pieces. Place the stock in a large saucepan, bring to the boil and boil for 15 minutes, or until reduced by half.
2 To make the picada, heat the oil in a frying pan, add the bread and cook, stirring, for 2–3 minutes, or until golden, adding the garlic for the last minute. Place the almonds, bread, garlic and parsley in a food processor and process, adding enough of the stock to make a smooth paste.

3 Heat 2 tablespoons of the oil in a large saucepan, add the onion, garlic, chilli and paprika, and cook, stirring, for 1 minute. Add the saffron, wine, tomato and stock. Bring to the boil, then reduce the heat and simmer.
4 Heat the remaining oil in a frying pan and quickly fry the fish and calamari for 3–5 minutes. Remove from the pan. Add the prawns, cook for 1 minute and then pour in the brandy. Carefully ignite the brandy with a match and let the flames burn down. Remove from the pan.

5 Add the mussels to the stock and simmer, covered, for 2–3 minutes, or until opened. Discard any that do not open. Add all the seafood and the picada to the pan, stirring until the sauce has thickened and the seafood has cooked through. Season to taste, sprinkle with the parsley, and serve.

NUTRITION PER SERVE (8)
Protein 26 g; Fat 18 g; Carbohydrate 5 g;
Dietary Fibre 1.5 g; Cholesterol 136 mg;
1275 kJ (305 cal)

Process the almonds, bread, garlic, parsley and some of the stock to a smooth paste.

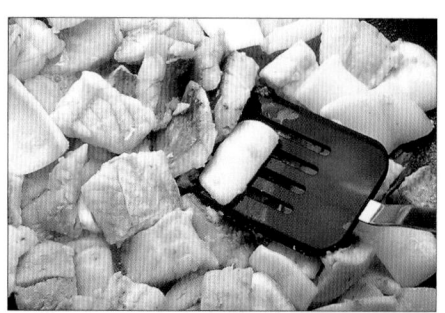

Quickly cook the fish and calamari in the oil in a frying pan.

Add the mussels to the stock and simmer until they open.

FISHERMAN'S PIE

Preparation time: 40 minutes
Total cooking time: 1 hour
Serves 4

800 g (1 lb 10 oz) white fish fillets
1½ cups (375 ml/12 fl oz) milk
1 onion, roughly chopped
2 cloves
50 g (1¾ oz) butter
2 tablespoons plain flour
pinch of ground nutmeg
2 tablespoons chopped fresh parsley
1 cup (150 g/5 oz) peas
750 g (1½ lb) potatoes, quartered
2 tablespoons hot milk
3 tablespoons grated Cheddar

1 Place the fish in a pan and cover with the milk. Add the onion and cloves and bring to the boil. Reduce the heat and simmer for 5 minutes, or until the fish is cooked and flakes easily with a fork.

2 Preheat the oven to 180°C (350°F/ Gas 4). Remove the fish from the pan, reserving the milk and onion. Discard the cloves. Allow the fish to cool then remove any bones and flake into bite-sized pieces with a fork.

3 Heat half of the butter in a pan, stir in the flour and cook, stirring, for 1 minute. Slowly add the reserved milk, stirring constantly until smooth. Cook, stirring, until the sauce begins to bubble, then cook for another minute. Remove from the heat, cool slightly, then add the nutmeg, parsley and peas. Season and gently fold in the fish. Spoon into a 1.25 litre casserole.

4 Cook the potatoes in boiling water until tender. Drain and add the hot milk and remaining butter. Mash until very smooth. Add the cheese. If the mash is very stiff you can add a little more milk, but it should be fairly firm.

5 Spoon the potato over the filling and rough up with a fork. For a neater topping, spoon the potato into a piping bag and pipe over the filling. Bake for 30 minutes to heat through.

NUTRITION PER SERVE
Protein 55 g; Fat 25 g; Carbohydrate 40 g; Dietary Fibre 6 g; Cholesterol 200 mg; 2565 kJ (610 cal)

Cover the fish fillets with the milk and add the onion and cloves.

Heat half the butter in a pan and stir in the flour to make a roux.

For a neat topping to the pie, put the mash in a piping bag and pipe over the filling.

FISH AND LEMON GRASS CASSEROLE

Preparation time: 15 minutes
Total cooking time: 40 minutes
Serves 4

4 fish cutlets (200 g/6½ oz each)
seasoned plain flour
2–3 tablespoons peanut oil
2 onions, sliced
2 stems lemon grass (white part only),
    finely chopped
4 kaffir lime leaves, shredded
1 teaspoon ground cumin
1 teaspoon ground coriander
1 teaspoon finely chopped fresh
    red chilli
¾ cup (185 ml/6 fl oz) chicken stock
1½ cups (375 ml/12 fl oz) coconut milk
¼ cup (15 g/½ oz) chopped fresh
    coriander
2 teaspoons fish sauce

1 Preheat the oven to moderate 180°C (350°F/Gas 4). Toss the fish lightly in the flour. Heat half the oil in a large heavy-based frying pan and cook the fish over medium heat until lightly browned on both sides. Transfer to a shallow ovenproof dish.
2 Heat the remaining oil in the pan. Cook the onion and lemon grass, stirring, for 5 minutes, or until the onion softens. Add the lime leaves, ground spices and chilli, and stir for 2 minutes, or until fragrant.
3 Add the stock and coconut milk to the onion mixture, and bring to the boil. Pour over the fish, then cover and bake for 30 minutes, or until the fish is tender.
4 Transfer the fish to a serving plate. Stir the chopped coriander and the fish sauce into the remaining sauce,

and season to taste with salt and freshly ground pepper. Pour the sauce over the fish to serve.

NUTRITION PER SERVE
Protein 35 g; Fat 40 g; Carbohydrate 6 g;
Dietary Fibre 1 g; Cholesterol 105 mg;
2040 kJ (490 cal)

NOTE: Kaffir lime leaves are glossy and dark green, with double leaves and a floral citrus smell. They can be frozen.

Finely chop the white part of the lemon grass stems, and shred the lime leaves.

Heat half the peanut oil and brown the lightly floured fish over medium heat.

Add the lime leaves, ground spices and chilli to the fried onion and lemon grass.

LOBSTER TAILS WITH AVOCADO SAUCE

Preparation time: 15 minutes + 3 hours marinating
Total cooking time: 10 minutes
Serves 4

3 tablespoons dry white wine
1 tablespoon honey
1 teaspoon sambal oelek
1 clove garlic, crushed
1 tablespoon olive oil
4 raw lobster tails

AVOCADO SAUCE
1 ripe avocado, mashed
3 teaspoons lemon juice
2 tablespoons sour cream
1 small tomato, chopped finely

1 Mix together the wine, honey, sambal oelek, garlic and oil. Cut along the soft shell on the underside of the lobster. Gently pull the shell apart and ease out the flesh.
2 Put the lobster in a shallow, non-metallic dish. Add the marinade and toss to coat. Cover and refrigerate for at least 3 hours.
3 Cook the lobster on a hot, lightly oiled barbecue grill or flatplate for 5–10 minutes, turning frequently. Brush with the marinade until cooked through. Slice into medallions.
4 To make the sauce, mix together the avocado, juice and sour cream. Add the tomato and season well.

NUTRITION PER SERVE
Protein 24 g; Fat 23 g; Carbohydrate 7 g; Dietary Fibre 1 g; Cholesterol 1 mg; 1421 kJ (339 cal)

STORAGE: The sauce will keep for 2–3 hours in the fridge with plastic wrap pressed over its surface.

Use a sharp knife or kitchen scissors to cut the soft shell on the underside of the lobster.

Put the lobster in a shallow, non-metallic dish and leave to marinate.

Mix together the avocado, juice and sour cream before combining with the tomato.

BARBECUED SARDINES

Preparation time: 25 minutes + 2 hours marinating
Total cooking time: 10 minutes
Serves 4

8 large fresh sardines
8 sprigs fresh lemon thyme
3 tablespoons extra virgin olive oil
2 cloves garlic, crushed
1 teaspoon finely grated lemon rind
2 tablespoons lemon juice

1 teaspoon ground cumin
lemon wedges, for serving

1 Carefully slit the sardines from head to tail and remove the gut. Rinse, then pat dry inside and out with paper towels. Place a sprig of fresh lemon thyme in each fish cavity and arrange the fish in a shallow non-metallic dish.
2 Combine the olive oil, garlic, lemon rind, lemon juice and cumin and pour over the fish. Cover and refrigerate for 2 hours.
3 Cook on a hot, lightly oiled

barbecue flatplate for 2–3 minutes each side, basting frequently with the marinade, or until the flesh flakes easily when tested with a fork. Alternatively, barbecue in a sardine cooking rack until tender. Serve with lemon wedges.

NUTRITION PER SERVE
Protein 46 g; Fat 12 g; Carbohydrate 0 g;
Dietary Fibre 1 g; Cholesterol 180 mg;
1200 kJ (245 cal)

Slit the sardine from head to tail with a sharp knife and then remove the gut.

Place a sprig of lemon thyme in the cavity of each fish and put in a shallow dish to marinate.

Cook the sardines until the flesh flakes easily when tested with a fork.

HERB-STUFFED TROUT

Preparation time: 15 minutes
Total cooking time: 10 minutes
Serves 4

4 rainbow trout, about 200 g
    (6½ oz) each
4 sprigs fresh dill
4 sprigs fresh lemon thyme
2 limes, thinly sliced
2 cloves garlic, thinly sliced

2 tablespoons olive oil
100 g (3½ oz) butter, softened
1 teaspoon grated lime rind
1 tablespoon lime juice
1 tablespoon chopped fresh dill

1 Wash the trout under cold water and pat dry with paper towels.
2 Place a sprig of each herb into the cavity of each fish along with the lime slices and garlic.
3 Lightly brush the outside of each fish with the olive oil. Cook on a hot, lightly oiled barbecue grill or flatplate for 5 minutes each side, or until the fish flakes when tested.
4 Place the butter, lime rind and juice and chopped dill into a bowl and mix together. Top each fish with a spoonful of the butter before serving.

NUTRITION PER SERVE
Protein 50 g; Fat 40 g; Carbohydrate 1 g;
Dietary Fibre 1 g; Cholesterol 185 mg;
2290 kJ (545 cal)

Place a sprig of each herb into the cavity of each fish, with the lime and garlic.

Lightly brush the skin of the fish with olive oil so that it becomes crisp.

Cook the fish until the flesh flakes when tested with a fork.

SEAFOOD QUICHE

**Preparation time: 20 minutes +
20 minutes refrigeration
Total cooking time: 1 hour
Serves 4–6**

2 sheets shortcrust pastry

FILLING
30 g (1 oz) butter
300 g (10 oz) mixed raw seafood
    (prawns, scallops, crab meat)
¾ cup (90 g/3 oz) grated Cheddar
3 eggs
1 tablespoon plain flour
¼ teaspoon salt
½ teaspoon black pepper
½ cup (125 ml/4 fl oz) cream
½ cup (125 ml/4 fl oz) milk
1 small fennel, finely sliced
1 tablespoon grated Parmesan

1 Place the sheets of pastry slightly
overlapping and roll out until large
enough to fit a 23 cm (9 inch) loose-
based tart tin. Trim away the excess
pastry. Refrigerate for 20 minutes.
Preheat the oven to 190°C (375°F/
Gas 5). Cover the pastry shell with
baking paper and spread with a layer
of baking beads or rice. Bake for
15 minutes. Remove the paper and
beads and bake for 10 minutes, or
until golden. Cool on a wire rack.
2 Heat the butter in a pan and cook
the seafood for 2–3 minutes. Cool,
then arrange in the pastry shell.
Sprinkle with Cheddar.
3 Beat the eggs together and whisk
in the flour, salt, pepper, cream and
milk. Pour over the seafood filling.
Sprinkle the fennel and Parmesan
over the top.
4 Bake for 30–35 minutes. Leave to
cool slightly before serving.

NUTRITION PER SERVE (6)
Protein 20 g; Fat 35 g; Carbohydrate 30 g;
Dietary Fibre 1 g; Cholesterol 220 mg;
2190 kJ (520 cal)

Fit the pastry into the flan tin, pressing it well into
the sides.

Remove the baking paper and rice from the
pastry shell.

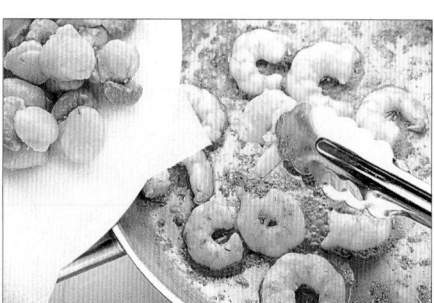

Cook the seafood in the melted butter before
putting into the pastry shell.

Sprinkle the Cheddar over the top of the seafood
in the pastry shell.

FISH FILLETS IN COCONUT MILK

Preparation time: 10 minutes
Total cooking time: 15 minutes
Serves 4

2 long green chillies
2 small red chillies
2 stems lemon grass, white part
    only
2 coriander roots
4 kaffir lime leaves
2.5 cm (1 inch) piece fresh ginger,
    thinly sliced
2 cloves garlic, crushed
3 spring onions, finely sliced
1 teaspoon soft brown sugar
1 cup (250 ml/8 fl oz) coconut milk
400 g (13 oz) firm white fish fillets, cut
    into bite-sized pieces
½ cup (125 ml/4 fl oz) coconut
    cream
1 tablespoon fish sauce
2–3 tablespoons lime juice

1 Heat a wok until hot, then add the whole chillies and roast until just beginning to brown. Remove from the wok, cool and slice.
2 Bruise the lemon grass and coriander roots by crushing them with the flat side of a knife.
3 Add the lemon grass, coriander roots, kaffir lime leaves, ginger, garlic, spring onion, sugar and coconut milk to the wok. Stir and bring to the boil. Reduce the heat and simmer for 2 minutes. Add the fish pieces and simmer gently for 2–3 minutes or until the fish is tender. Stir in the coconut cream.
4 Stir through the chopped green and red chillies, fish sauce, salt and lime juice, to taste and serve immediately.

NUTRITION PER SERVE
Protein 23 g; Fat 22 g; Carbohydrate 6.5 g;
Dietary Fibre 2.5 g; Cholesterol 70 mg;
1323 kJ (316 cal)

Roast the whole chillies in a hot wok until they begin to brown.

Bruise the lemon grass and coriander roots by crushing them with the flat side of a knife.

Add the fish pieces to the wok and simmer gently for 2–3 minutes.

Just before serving, stir in the chillies, fish sauce, salt and lime juice.

PRAWNS WITH MANGO SALSA

**Preparation time: 25 minutes +
  1 hour marinating**
Total cooking time: 5 minutes
Serves 4–6

1 kg (2 lb) raw prawns
⅓ cup (80 ml/2¾ fl oz) lemon juice
⅓ cup (80 ml/2¾ fl oz) olive oil
¼ cup (15 g/½ oz) chopped fresh dill
450 g (14 oz) mango, cubed

1 onion, finely diced
1 red chilli, seeded and finely chopped
1 tablespoon grated lemon rind

1 Peel and devein the raw prawns, keeping the tails intact.
2 Combine the lemon juice, olive oil, dill and a teaspoon of salt in a shallow, non-metallic dish, add the prawns and toss. Cover and refrigerate for 1 hour.
3 Drain the prawns, reserving the marinade, and cook on a very hot, lightly oiled barbecue flatplate for 3 minutes, or until they change colour.
4 Put the reserved marinade in a pan on the stovetop or barbecue and boil for 5 minutes. Mix with the prawns.
5 Mix together the mango, onion, chilli, lemon rind and some salt and pepper. Add the prawns and toss together gently.

NUTRITION PER SERVE (6)
Protein 35 g; Fat 15 g; Carbohydrate 10 g; Dietary Fibre 2 g; Cholesterol 250 mg; 1320 kJ (315 cal)

Peel the prawns and remove the veins from the prawn backs, leaving the tails intact.

Cook the prawns on the very hot barbecue until they change colour.

Mix together the mango, onion, chilli, lemon rind and salt and pepper.

SALMON WITH GREMOLATA AND POTATO GRIDDLE CAKES

Preparation time: 25 minutes
Total cooking time: 15 minutes
Serves 4

GREMOLATA
30 g (1 oz) fresh parsley, finely
   chopped
grated rind of 1 lemon
grated rind of 1 orange
2 cloves garlic, crushed

POTATO GRIDDLE CAKES
250 g (8 oz) potatoes
250 g (8 oz) sweet potatoes, peeled
⅓ cup (20 g/¾ oz) chopped fresh chives
2 tablespoons plain flour
1 egg, lightly beaten
4 salmon fillets, about 200 g (6½ oz)
   each
2–3 teaspoons baby capers, drained

1 For the gremolata, mix the parsley, lemon and orange rind and garlic.
2 To make the potato griddle cake, coarsely grate the peeled potatoes and sweet potatoes and squeeze to remove any excess moisture. Mix with the chives, flour, egg and salt and pepper. Preheat a barbecue flatplate and drizzle with olive oil. Use a heaped tablespoon of mixture to make each patty, flattening slightly. Cook, turning once, for 5 minutes, or until golden.
3 Cook the salmon on the lightly oiled hot plate for 2–3 minutes each side, or until just tender. Serve with the gremolata, griddle cakes and capers.

NUTRITION PER SERVE
Protein 40 g; Fat 30 g; Carbohydrate 20 g; Dietary Fibre 3 g; Cholesterol 185 mg; 2215 kJ (525 cal)

To make the gremolata, mix together the parsley, lemon and orange rind and garlic.

Coarsely grate the potato and sweet potato and then squeeze out any excess moisture.

As you cook the griddle cakes, flatten them slightly with the spatula.

MINI OYSTER PIES

**Preparation time: 30 minutes +
  20 minutes cooling**
Total cooking time: 45 minutes
Makes 30

2 cups (500 ml/16 fl oz) fish stock
1 tablespoon olive oil
2 leeks, chopped
30 g (1 oz) butter
1 tablespoon plain flour
1 teaspoon lemon juice
1 teaspoon chopped fresh chives
8 sheets puff pastry
30 fresh oysters
1 egg, lightly beaten, to glaze

1 Pour the stock into a saucepan and simmer over medium heat for 15 minutes, or until reduced by half—you will need 1 cup (250 ml/8 fl oz).
2 Heat the oil in a saucepan over medium heat. Add the leek and cook, stirring well, for 5 minutes, or until soft and lightly coloured. Transfer to a small bowl to cool slightly.

3 Melt the butter in a small saucepan over low heat. Add the flour and cook, stirring well, for 2 minutes, or until the flour is golden. Remove from the heat and gradually add the fish stock, stirring well. Return to the heat and bring to the boil, stirring constantly for 2 minutes, or until thickened. Add the lemon juice, chives and leek and season well. Set aside to cool for 20 minutes. Preheat the oven to 200°C (400°F/Gas 6) and grease two baking trays.
4 Using a 6 cm (2½ inch) round cutter, cut out 30 circles of pastry and put one oyster and a heaped

teaspoon of the filling on top of each, leaving a narrow border. Lightly brush the edges with beaten egg.
5 Cut thirty 8 cm (3 inch) circles from the remaining pastry. Cover the filling with these rounds and press the edges with a fork to seal. Brush the tops with the remaining beaten egg, put on the trays and bake for 15–20 minutes, or until golden and well puffed.

NUTRITION PER PIE
Protein 3.5 g; Fat 12 g; Carbohydrate 17 g;
Dietary Fibre 1 g; Cholesterol 24 mg;
785 kJ (190 cal)

Gradually add the fish stock and boil, stirring constantly, until thickened.

Place an oyster and a heaped teaspoon of filling on each pastry round.

SQUID WITH PICADA DRESSING

**Preparation time: 40 minutes +
  30 minutes chilling**
Total cooking time: 10 minutes
Serves 6

500 g (1 lb) small squid (see NOTE)
¼ teaspoon salt

PICADA DRESSING
2 tablespoons extra virgin olive oil
2 tablespoons finely chopped fresh
  flat-leaf parsley
1 clove garlic, crushed
¼ teaspoon cracked black pepper

1 To clean the squid, gently pull the tentacles away from the hood (the intestines should come away at the same time). Remove the intestines from the tentacles by cutting under the eyes, then remove the beak, if it remains in the centre of the tentacles, by pushing up with your index finger. Pull away the soft bone.
2 Rub the hoods under cold running water and the skin should come away easily. Wash the hoods and tentacles and drain well. Place in a bowl, add the salt and mix well. Cover and refrigerate for about 30 minutes.
3 For the picada dressing, whisk together the olive oil, parsley, garlic, pepper and some salt.
4 Cook the squid hoods in small

batches on a very hot, lightly oiled barbecue flatplate for 2–3 minutes, or until white and tender. Barbecue or grill the squid tentacles, turning to brown them all over, for 1 minute, or until they curl up. Serve hot, drizzled with the picada dressing.

NUTRITION PER SERVE
Protein 20 g; Fat 10 g; Carbohydrate 1 g;
Dietary Fibre 1 g; Cholesterol 180 mg;
800 kJ (190 cal)

NOTE: A suitably small variety of squid is the bottleneck squid.

STORAGE: Make the picada dressing as close to serving time as possible so the parsley doesn't discolour.

Gently pull the tentacles away from the squid hoods and the intestines should follow.

Cut under the eyes to remove the intestines and then remove the beak.

Rub the hoods under cold running water and remove the skin.

BALSAMIC BABY OCTOPUS

Preparation time: 15 minutes + 3 hours marinating
Total cooking time: 10 minutes
Serves 4

1 kg (2 lb) baby octopus
¾ cup (185 ml/6 fl oz) red wine
2 tablespoons balsamic vinegar
2 tablespoons soy sauce
2 tablespoons hoisin sauce
1 clove garlic, crushed

1 Cut off the octopus heads, below the eyes, with a sharp knife. Discard the heads and guts. Push the beaks out with your index finger, remove and discard. Wash the octopus thoroughly under running water and drain on crumpled paper towels. If the octopus tentacles are large, cut into quarters.
2 Put the octopus in a large bowl. Stir together the wine, vinegar, soy sauce, hoisin sauce and garlic and pour over the octopus. Toss to coat, then cover and refrigerate for at least 3 hours. Drain the octopus, reserving the leftover marinade.

3 Cook on a very hot, lightly oiled barbecue grill or flatplate, in batches, for 3–5 minutes, or until the octopus flesh turns white. Brush the marinade over the octopus during cooking. Be careful not to overcook or the octopus will be tough. Serve warm or cold.

NUTRITION PER SERVE
Protein 42.5 g; Fat 3.5 g; Carbohydrate 4 g;
Dietary Fibre 1 g; Cholesterol 497.5 mg;
1060 kJ (255 cal)

Remove and discard the head from each octopus using a sharp knife.

Push the beaks through the centre with your index finger.

Brush the octopus all over with the reserved marinade while cooking.

SEAFOOD MORNAY CASSEROLE

Preparation time: 25 minutes
Total cooking time: 40 minutes
Serves 4–6

400 g (13 oz) mussels
3 medium white fish fillets, cut into
    3 cm (1¼ inch) cubes
250 g (8 oz) raw medium prawns,
    peeled and deveined
200 g (6½ oz) scallops, trimmed
1 small onion, halved
2 bay leaves
½ lemon, sliced
½ cup (125 ml/4 fl oz) white wine

SAUCE
45 g (1½ oz) butter
1 celery stick, chopped
1 large carrot, finely chopped
1½ tablespoons plain flour
1½ cups (375 ml/12 fl oz) milk
125 g (4 oz) Gruyère cheese, grated
1 cup (130 g/4½ oz) frozen peas

TOPPING
1 cup (80 g/2¾ oz) fresh breadcrumbs
½ cup (45 g/1½ oz) flaked almonds
2 teaspoons finely grated lemon rind
½ teaspoon freshly ground black
    pepper
60 g (2 oz) butter, chopped

1 Preheat the oven to moderate 180°C (350°F/Gas 4). Discard any open mussels, then remove the beards from the rest of the mussels and wash away any grit. Prise open the shells and remove the mussels. Place the fish, prawns, scallops and mussels in a saucepan. Cover with cold water and add the onion, bay leaves, lemon and wine. Bring slowly to the boil. Cover, then reduce the heat to low and simmer for 3–4 minutes. Remove the seafood from the cooking liquid and place it in a lightly greased casserole dish.
2 To make the sauce, heat the butter in a saucepan. Cook the celery and carrot for 1 minute, then add the flour. Stir over low heat for 2 minutes, or until the mixture is lightly golden. Add the milk gradually, stirring until smooth. Stir constantly over medium heat for 3 minutes, or until the mixture boils and thickens. Boil for 1 minute, then remove from the heat and cool the sauce to room temperature.
3 Stir the cheese and peas into the sauce, then pour it over the seafood. Mix gently to combine.

4 To make the topping, combine the breadcrumbs, almonds, rind and pepper in a bowl. Spread evenly over the top of the seafood mixture. Dot with the butter. Bake for 20 minutes, or until the seafood is heated through and the top is golden brown.

NUTRITION PER SERVE (6)
Protein 42 g; Fat 31 g; Carbohydrate 18 g;
Dietary Fibre 3 g; Cholesterol 177 mg;
2165 kJ (515 cal)

NOTE: Any combination of cooked seafood can be used in this recipe. The cooking liquid can replace half the milk, if desired.

Once the shells have been cleaned, prise them open and remove the mussels.

Heat the butter in a medium saucepan and cook the celery and carrot for 1 minute.

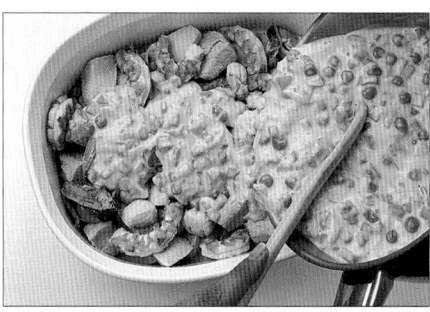

Pour the sauce over the seafood in the casserole dish, and mix gently to combine.

SCALLOPS WITH GREEN PEPPERCORNS

**Preparation time: 20 minutes +
   20 minutes marinating**
Total cooking time: 5 minutes
Serves 4

¼ cup (60 ml/2 fl oz) olive oil
2 teaspoons green peppercorns,
   chopped
2 teaspoons finely grated lime rind
1 teaspoon finely grated fresh ginger
500 g (1 lb) scallops with corals,
   deveined
salad leaves and pickled ginger, to
   serve

1 Combine the oil, peppercorns, rind and fresh ginger. Add the scallops and refrigerate for 20 minutes.
2 Cook the scallops on a very hot, lightly oiled barbecue flatplate, in batches, stirring gently, for about 2 minutes, or until they become lightly golden brown.
3 Serve the scallops on salad leaves and topped with ginger strips.

NUTRITION PER SERVE
Protein 15 g; Fat 15 g; Carbohydrate 1 g;
Dietary Fibre 0 g; Cholesterol 40 mg;
820 kJ (195 cal)

Peel the skin from the fresh ginger and finely grate the flesh.

Mix together the oil, peppercorns, lime rind and ginger to make a marinade.

Cook the scallops on a very hot barbecue flatplate until they are lightly golden brown.

PRAWN AND PEA NOODLE BASKETS

Preparation time: 40 minutes
Total cooking time: 25 minutes
Serves 4

oil, for deep-frying
200 g (6½ oz) fresh egg noodles
700 g (1 lb 7 oz) raw prawns, peeled
    and deveined
2 spring onions, chopped
1 clove garlic, crushed
½ teaspoon finely grated fresh ginger
½ teaspoon sesame oil
½ teaspoon fish sauce
100 g (3½ oz) peas, cooked
3 tablespoons sliced water chestnuts
1 tablespoon fresh mint
2 teaspoons chopped fresh chives
80 g (2¾ oz) snow pea sprouts

1 Half-fill a deep-fryer or large pan with oil and heat to 180°C (350°F). Before the oil is too hot, dip in 2 wire baskets, one slightly smaller than the other, then shake dry. Drop a noodle into the oil: if the oil bubbles and the noodle turns golden in 8–10 seconds, the oil is hot enough.

2 Separate the noodles and divide into four bundles. Arrange the first batch inside the large basket and press the smaller basket inside to mould the noodles. Holding the handles firmly, ease the baskets into the oil, keeping the noodles under. Gently twist the top basket to help stop sticking, tipping from side to side, and cook the noodles to an even golden brown. Drain on paper towels. Repeat with the other noodles.

3 Heat 2 tablespoons of oil in a wok. Stir-fry the prawns, spring onion, garlic and ginger over high heat for 2 minutes, or until the prawns turn pink. Stir in the sesame oil, fish sauce, peas and water chestnuts. Remove from the heat, season and mix in the mint, chives and snow pea sprouts.

4 Pile the prawn and pea mixture into the noodle baskets and serve at once.

NUTRITION PER SERVE:
Protein 40 g; Fat 15 g; Carbohydrate 15 g;
Dietary Fibre 3 g; Cholesterol 260 mg;
1575 kJ (375 cal)

Loosely separate the noodles and divide them into bundles.

Arrange the first bundle of noodles inside the larger basket.

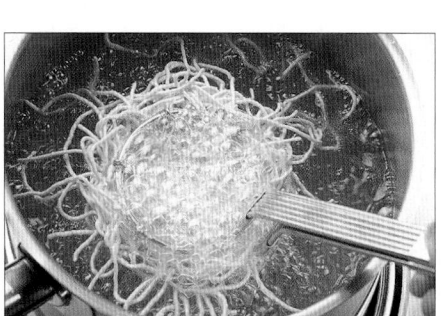

Fit the baskets together, hold firmly, then gently lower them into the oil.

Stir-fry the prawns over high heat until they just turn pink.

SEAFOOD WITH CHILLI PLUM SAUCE

Preparation time: 30 minutes
Total cooking time: 15 minutes
Serves 4

150 g (5 oz) squid tubes
1 kg (2 lb) English spinach
oil, for cooking
500 g (1 lb) raw prawns, peeled and
    deveined
400 g (13 oz) scallops, cleaned
2 cloves garlic, crushed
1–2 red chillies, seeded and finely
    chopped
½ cup (125 ml/4 fl oz) plum sauce

1 teaspoon soft brown sugar
2 tablespoons lime juice
3 spring onions, sliced

1 Rinse the squid tubes, pat dry with paper towels and slice into rings.
2 Rinse the spinach and leave wet (so it won't stick to the wok). Heat the wok until very hot, add the spinach and toss over high heat until wilted. Transfer to a serving plate.
3 Heat the wok until very hot, add 1 tablespoon of the oil and swirl it around to coat the side. Stir-fry the squid rings, prawns and scallops in batches over high heat until they turn opaque and are cooked through. Remove all of the seafood from the

wok and set aside. Heat 1 tablespoon of the oil and cook the garlic and chilli for 1–2 minutes, or until softened.
4 Add the plum sauce, brown sugar and lime juice to the wok. Bring to the boil, then reduce the heat and simmer for 4–5 minutes, or until the sauce thickens. Return the squid rings, prawns and scallops to the wok, add the sliced spring onion and toss to coat in the sauce. Serve the seafood on top of the stir-fried spinach.

NUTRITION PER SERVE
Protein 65 g; Fat 4 g; Carbohydrate 20 g;
Dietary Fibre 7.5 g; Cholesterol 470 mg;
1605 kJ (385 cal)

Peel the prawns and remove the dark veins from their backs.

Cut the hard white muscle and any dark veins from the scallops.

Wash and dry the squid tubes, then cut them into thin rings.

SALMON WITH DILL CREAM

Preparation time: 25 minutes
Total cooking time: 25 minutes
Serves 4

4 small salmon
4 cloves garlic, peeled
2 lemons, sliced
8 fresh bay leaves
8 sprigs fresh flat-leaf parsley
8 sprigs fresh thyme
olive oil, for brushing

DILL CREAM
90 g (3 oz) butter
1 cup (250 ml/8 fl oz) fish stock
1½ teaspoons wholegrain mustard
1 cup (250 ml/8 fl oz) cream
2 tablespoons lemon juice
3 tablespoons chopped fresh dill

1 Wash the fish and pat dry inside and out with paper towels. Place a clove of garlic, a few slices of lemon and a bay leaf in the cavity of each fish. Bundle together a sprig of parsley and thyme and tie a bundle with string onto each fish, near the tail. Reserve the other sprigs. Brush both sides of the fish with a little of the olive oil.

2 For the dill cream, melt the butter in a pan and add the fish stock, mustard and cream. Bring to the boil, then reduce the heat and simmer for 15 minutes, or until the sauce is slightly thickened. Stir in the lemon juice and dill. Season and keep warm.

3 While the dill cream is cooking, cook the fish on a hot, lightly oiled barbecue grill or flatplate for 3–6 minutes on each side, turning carefully, or until cooked through. Discard the herbs. For serving, bundle together a fresh parsley sprig, a thyme sprig and a bay leaf, and tie a bundle near each fish tail. Serve warm with the dill cream.

NUTRITION PER SERVE
Protein 52 g; Fat 78 g; Carbohydrate 1 g;
Dietary Fibre 0 g; Cholesterol 350 mg;
3860 kJ (920 cal)

NOTE: Rainbow trout is also a suitable fish for this recipe.

Wash the fish and pat dry inside and out with paper towels.

Tie together a sprig of parsley and a sprig of thyme and tie to the tail of the fish.

PRAWN, CRAB AND CHEESE QUICHES

Preparation time: 45 minutes +
30 minutes refrigeration
Total cooking time: 40 minutes
Serves 4

2 cups (250 g/8 oz) plain flour
125 g (4 oz) butter, chilled and cubed
2 egg yolks
3–4 tablespoons iced water

FILLING
170 g (5½ oz) can crab meat,
    drained and squeezed dry
4 spring onions, chopped
2 eggs, lightly beaten
1 cup (250 ml/8 fl oz) cream
1 cup (125 g/4 oz) finely grated
    Cheddar
2 tablespoons chopped fresh dill
1 teaspoon grated lemon rind
200 g (6½ oz) small prawns,
    cooked and peeled

1 Process the flour and butter for 15 seconds, or until the mixture resembles fine breadcrumbs. Add the egg yolks and water. Process in short bursts until the mixture comes together. Add a little more water if needed. Turn out onto a floured surface and gather into a ball. Cover with plastic wrap and refrigerate for at least 15 minutes.
2 Grease eight 8 cm (3 inch) loose-based tart tins. Divide the pastry into eight equal pieces and roll out until large enough to fit the tins. Trim off any excess pastry. Cover and refrigerate for 15 minutes. Preheat the oven to 190°C (375°F/Gas 5). Cover the pastry shells with baking paper and spread with a layer of baking beads or rice. Bake for 10 minutes.

Remove the paper and beads and bake for a further 10 minutes.
3 To make the filling, mix together the crab meat, spring onions, beaten eggs, cream, cheese, dill and lemon rind. Divide the prawns among the pastry shells. The crab filling will be quite thick, so use a fork to spread it over the prawns. Bake for 15–20 minutes, or until the filling is golden brown.

NUTRITION PER SERVE
Protein 15 g; Fat 35 g; Carbohydrate 25 g;
Dietary Fibre 1 g; Cholesterol 255 mg;
1990 kJ (475 cal)

Squeeze small amounts of crab meat with your hands to get out a lot of the moisture.

Roll out the pastry until it is large enough to fit the tins, then trim away the excess.

Use a fork to help you spread the crab mixture into the pastry shells.

SEAFOOD CASSEROLE WITH FETA AND OLIVES

Preparation time: 20 minutes
Total cooking time: 35 minutes
Serves 4

500 g (1 lb) fresh mussels
2 tablespoons olive oil
1 large onion, sliced
2 x 400 g (13 oz) cans tomatoes, chopped
2 strips lemon rind
1 tablespoon chopped fresh lemon thyme
⅓ cup (80 ml/2¾ fl oz) dry vermouth or white wine
1 teaspoon sugar

12 raw king prawns, peeled and deveined, tails intact
750 g (1½ lb) firm white fish fillets, cut into bite-size pieces
12 black olives
125 g (4 oz) feta cheese, cubed

1 Discard any open mussels. Scrub the rest of the mussels and remove the beards. Place the mussels in a saucepan of simmering water. As soon as the shells open, place the mussels in a bowl of cold water, discarding any unopened ones. Open them up and leave on their half shells, discarding the other half.
2 Preheat the oven to moderate 180°C (350°F/Gas 4). Heat the oil in a large, heavy-based saucepan and cook the onion over low heat for 5 minutes, or until soft but not brown. Add the tomato, lemon rind, lemon thyme, vermouth and sugar. Bring to the boil, and season to taste. Reduce the heat, cover and simmer for 10 minutes.
3 Place the seafood in a shallow ovenproof dish and cover with the hot sauce. Bake, covered, for 10 minutes. Add the olives and feta, covering the seafood with the sauce. Bake for 10 minutes, or until heated through. Serve immediately.

NUTRITION PER SERVE
Protein 70 g; Fat 25 g; Carbohydrate 10 g;
Dietary Fibre 4 g; Cholesterol 313 mg;
2430 kJ (580 cal)

Peel and devein the prawns, and cut the fish into bite-size pieces.

Scrub the mussels, remove the beards, then place in a saucepan of simmering water.

Add the tomato, lemon rind, lemon thyme, vermouth and sugar to the softened onion.

COCONUT SEAFOOD AND TOFU CURRY

Preparation time: 30 minutes
Total cooking time: 30 minutes
Serves 4

2 tablespoons soy bean oil, or oil
500 g (1 lb) firm white fish (ling, perch), cut into 2 cm (¾ inch) cubes
250 g (8 oz) raw prawns, peeled and deveined, tails intact
2 x 400 ml (13 fl oz) cans coconut milk
1 tablespoon red curry paste
4 fresh or 8 dried kaffir lime leaves
2 tablespoons fish sauce
2 tablespoons finely chopped fresh lemon grass (white part only)
2 cloves garlic, crushed
1 tablespoon finely chopped fresh galangal
1 tablespoon shaved palm sugar or soft brown sugar
300 g (10 oz) silken firm tofu, cut into 1.5 cm (⅝ inch) cubes
½ cup (125 g/4 oz) bamboo shoots, julienned
1 large fresh red chilli, thinly sliced
2 teaspoons lime juice
spring onions, chopped, to garnish
fresh coriander leaves, chopped, to garnish

1 Heat the oil in a large frying pan or wok over medium heat. Sear the fish and prawns for 1 minute on each side. Remove the fish and prawns from the pan.
2 Place ¼ cup (60 ml/2 fl oz) of the coconut milk and the curry paste in the pan, and cook over medium heat for 2 minutes, or until fragrant and the oil separates. Add the remaining coconut milk, kaffir lime leaves, fish sauce, lemon grass, garlic, galangal, palm sugar and 1 teaspoon salt. Cook over low heat for 15 minutes.
3 Add the tofu cubes, bamboo shoots and sliced chilli. Simmer for a further 3–5 minutes. Return to medium heat, add the seafood and lime juice, and cook for a further 3 minutes, or until the seafood is just cooked. Remove from the heat.
4 Serve the curry with steamed rice and garnish with the spring onion and coriander leaves.

NUTRITION PER SERVE
Protein 50 g; Fat 58 g; Carbohydrate 15 g; Dietary Fibre 4 g; Cholesterol 180 mg; 3201 kJ (765 cal)

Peel the prawns, remove the veins and keep the tails intact.

Cook the coconut milk and the curry paste until the oil separates.

Add the tofu, bamboo shoots and chilli, then simmer for 5 minutes.

THAI BABY OCTOPUS

Preparation time: 1 hour
Total cooking time: 15–25 minutes
Serves 6

500 g (1 lb) baby octopus
2 tablespoons oil
3 cloves garlic, chopped
1 tablespoon green or pink
    peppercorns
2–4 small red chillies, finely chopped
1 tablespoon fish sauce

1 Cut off the octopus heads, below the eyes, with a sharp knife. Discard the heads and guts. Push the beaks out with your index finger, remove and discard. Wash the octopus thoroughly under running water and drain on crumpled paper towels. If the octopus tentacles are large, cut into quarters. Put in a shallow dish.
2 Mix together the oil, garlic, peppercorns and chilli, add to the octopus and marinate for 30 minutes. Cook 3 octopus at a time, turning frequently, on a very hot, lightly oiled barbecue flatplate for 3 minutes or until they turn white. Do not overcook. Sprinkle the fish sauce over the top and serve immediately.

NUTRITION PER SERVE
Protein 14 g; Fat 7 g; Carbohydrate 0 g;
Dietary Fibre 0 g; Cholesterol 166 mg;
522 kJ (125 cal)

HINT: This recipe is also suitable for calamari. Wash the tubes, pat dry and cut into strips before marinating and cooking in the same way.

Use a sharp knife to slice off the head of the octopus so you can remove the gut.

Use your index finger to push the beak up so you can remove and discard it.

Cook the octopus, turning frequently, until they turn white.

671

THAI-STYLE STEAMED FISH WITH SPICY TOMATO SAUCE

Preparation time: 25 minutes +
30 minutes standing
Total cooking time: 40 minutes
Serves 4

6 cloves garlic
3 red Asian shallots
3 tomatoes
2 fresh long red chillies
1½ tablespoons lime juice
3½ tablespoons fish sauce
2 cloves garlic, extra
4 coriander roots
6 whole black peppercorns
4 snapper, fins trimmed, cleaned and
    gutted
1 cup (30 g/1 oz) fresh coriander
    leaves

1 Chargrill the skins of the garlic, shallots, tomatoes and chillies over an open gas flame, using a pair of metal tongs, or roast in a preheated very hot (230°C/450°F/Gas 8) oven for 15–20 minutes. When cool enough to handle, peel and discard the skins of all the vegetables. Roughly chop the vegetables and combine with the lime juice and 2 tablespoons of the fish sauce. Leave for 30 minutes.

2 Place the extra garlic, coriander roots and peppercorns in a mortar and pestle and grind to a smooth paste. Add the remaining fish sauce and stir to combine. Score each fish on both sides in a crisscross pattern. Rub the paste on both sides.

3 Line the bottom of a large bamboo steamer with baking paper. Place the fish on the paper and place the steamer over a wok of boiling water. Cover and steam for 15–20 minutes, or until the flesh flakes easily when tested with a fork. Remove the steamer from the wok and slide the fish onto a serving plate. Spoon the tomato sauce over the fish and sprinkle with fresh coriander leaves.

NUTRITION PER SERVE
Protein 34 g; Fat 3 g; Carbohydrate 4 g;
Dietary Fibre 3 g; Cholesterol 92 mg;
750 kJ (180 cal)

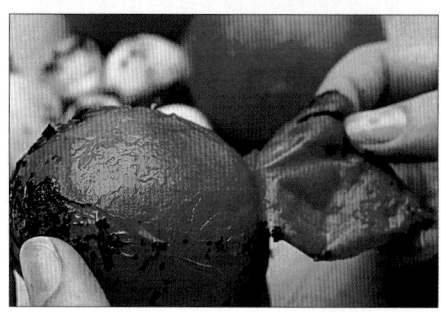
Once the vegetables have been chargrilled, peel off and discard the skins.

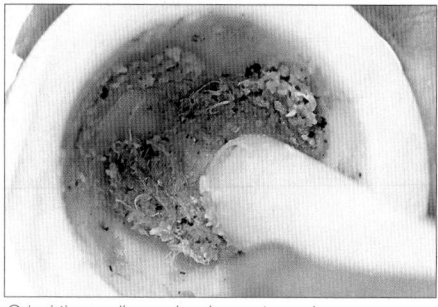
Grind the garlic, coriander roots and peppercorns until smooth.

GARLIC SCALLOPS WITH ANGEL HAIR PASTA

Preparation time: 10 minutes
Total cooking time: 15 minutes
Serves 4

20 large scallops with corals
250 g (8 oz) angel hair pasta
150 ml (5 fl oz) extra virgin olive oil
2 cloves garlic, finely chopped
¼ cup (60 ml/2 fl oz) white wine
1 tablespoon lemon juice
100 g (3½ oz) baby rocket leaves
30 g (1 oz) chopped fresh coriander

1 Pull or trim any veins, membrane or hard white muscle from the scallops. Pat dry with paper towels. Cook the pasta in boiling water until al dente. Drain and toss with 1 tablespoon oil to keep it from sticking.
2 Meanwhile, heat 1 tablespoon oil in a frying pan, add the garlic and cook for a few seconds. Add the combined wine and lemon juice and remove from the heat.
3 Season the scallops with salt and pepper and cook on a hot, lightly oiled barbecue grill or flatplate for 1 minute each side, or until just cooked. Gently reheat the garlic mixture, add the rocket and stir over medium heat for 1–2 minutes, or until wilted. Toss through the pasta with the remaining oil, coriander and scallops.

NUTRITION PER SERVE
Protein 15 g; Fat 37 g; Carbohydrate 45 g;
Dietary Fibre 4 g; Cholesterol 20 mg;
2425 kJ (580 cal)

VARIATION: Add ½ teaspoon dried chilli flakes just before the wine and lemon juice for an added kick.

Drain the pasta and toss with a tablespoon of oil to prevent it sticking.

Cook the garlic for a few seconds and then add the wine and lemon juice.

Cook the scallops for just 1 minute on each side until they are cooked through.

BALINESE SEAFOOD CURRY

Preparation time: 20 minutes +
** 20 minutes marinating**
Total cooking time: 20 minutes
Serves 6

CURRY PASTE
2 tomatoes, peeled, seeded and
  roughly chopped
5 small fresh red chillies, seeded and
  chopped
5 cloves garlic, chopped
2 stems lemon grass (white part only),
  sliced
1 tablespoon coriander seeds,
  dry-roasted and ground
1 teaspoon shrimp powder,
  dry-roasted (see NOTE)
1 tablespoon ground almonds
¼ teaspoon ground nutmeg
1 teaspoon ground turmeric
3 tablespoons tamarind purée

1 tablespoon lime juice
250 g (8 oz) swordfish, cut into 3 cm
  (1¼ inch) cubes
¼ cup (60 ml/2 fl oz) oil
2 red onions, chopped
2 small fresh red chillies, seeded and
  sliced
400 g (13 oz) raw medium prawns,
  peeled and deveined, tails intact
250 g (8 oz) calamari tubes, cut into
  1 cm (½ inch) rings
½ cup (125 ml/4 fl oz) fish stock
fresh Thai basil leaves, shredded, to
  garnish

1 To make the curry paste, place all
the ingredients in a blender or food
processor, and blend to a thick paste.
2 Place the lime juice in a bowl and
season with salt and freshly ground
black pepper. Add the swordfish, toss
to coat well and leave to marinate for
20 minutes.
3 Heat the oil in a saucepan or wok,
add the onion, sliced red chilli and
curry paste, and cook, stirring
occasionally, over low heat for
10 minutes, or until fragrant.
4 Add the swordfish and prawns, and
stir to coat in the curry paste mixture.
Cook for 3 minutes, or until the
prawns just turn pink, then add the
calamari and cook for 1 minute.
5 Add the stock and bring to the boil,
then reduce the heat and simmer for
2 minutes, or until the seafood is
cooked and tender. Season to taste
with salt and freshly ground black
pepper. Garnish with the shredded
fresh basil leaves.

NUTRITION PER SERVE
Protein 30 g; Fat 14 g; Carbohydrate 3.5 g;
Dietary Fibre 2 g; Cholesterol 210 mg;
1100 kJ (263 cal)

NOTE: If you cannot purchase shrimp
powder, place some dried baby
shrimp in a mortar and pestle and
grind to a fine powder. Alternatively,
you can place them in the small bowl
of a food processor and process to a
fine powder.

Remove the seeds from the chillies, and roughly
chop the flesh.

Peel and devein the raw prawns, leaving the
tails intact.

Using a sharp knife, cut the cleaned calamari
tubes into rings.

Place all the curry paste ingredients in a food processor, and blend to a thick paste.

Cook the onion, sliced chilli and curry paste until the mixture is fragrant.

Add the stock and simmer until the seafood is cooked and tender.

CLAMS IN ROASTED CHILLI PASTE

Preparation time: 15 minutes
Total cooking time: 15 minutes
Serves 4

ROASTED CHILLI PASTE
2 tablespoons oil
2 spring onions, sliced
2 cloves garlic, sliced
¼ cup (90 g/3 oz) small dried shrimps
6 small red chillies, seeded
2 teaspoons palm sugar
2 teaspoons fish sauce
2 teaspoons tamarind concentrate
pinch of salt
3 cloves garlic, finely sliced

3 small red chillies, seeded and sliced
    lengthways
1 tablespoon light soy sauce
1 cup (250 ml/8 fl oz) chicken stock
1 kg (2 lb) clams, scrubbed
½ cup (25 g/¾ oz) Thai basil leaves

1 To make the roasted chilli paste, heat the oil in a wok and fry the spring onion, garlic, dried shrimps and chillies until golden brown. Remove with a slotted spoon and keep the oil.
2 Place the onion, garlic, shrimps, chillies and sugar in a mortar and pestle or small food processor and grind until the mixture is well blended. Add the fish sauce, tamarind concentrate and salt. Blend or grind to a fine paste. Transfer to a bowl.

3 Heat the reserved oil in the wok. Add the garlic, chilli, roasted chilli paste and soy sauce. Mix well, then add the chicken stock and bring just to the boil. Add the clams and cook over medium-high heat for 2–3 minutes. Discard any unopened clams. Stir in the basil and serve immediately with steamed jasmine rice.

NUTRITION PER SERVE
Protein 30 g; Fat 15 g; Carbohydrate 90 g;
Dietary Fibre 5 g; Cholesterol 280 mg;
2490 kJ (700 cal)

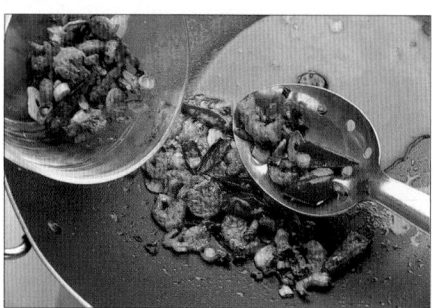

Use a slotted spoon to remove the onion, garlic, shrimps and chillies from the wok.

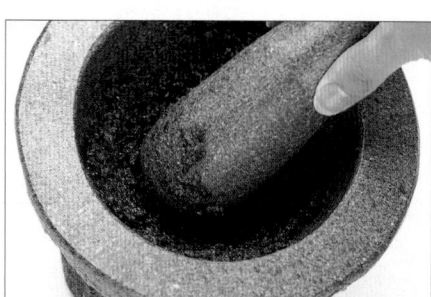

Blend or grind the mixture to obtain a finely textured paste.

Remove any clams that have not opened during the cooking time.

POTATO AND SALMON PARCELS

Preparation time: 30 minutes
Total cooking time: 40 minutes
Makes 12

750 g (1½ lb) floury potatoes, peeled
40 g (1¼ oz) butter
¼ cup (60 ml/2 fl oz) cream
1 cup (125 g/4 oz) grated Cheddar
210 g (7 oz) can red salmon, skin and
　　bones removed, flaked
1 tablespoon chopped fresh dill
4 spring onions, finely chopped
3 sheets puff pastry
1 egg, lightly beaten, to glaze

1 Cut the potatoes into small pieces and cook in a pan of boiling water until tender. Mash with the butter and the cream until there are no lumps. Lightly grease two oven trays.
2 Add the cheese, salmon, dill and spring onion to the potato and mix well. Preheat the oven to 200°C (400°F/Gas 6). Cut each pastry sheet into four squares. Divide the mixture among the squares (approximately ¼ cup in each). Lightly brush the edges with beaten egg. Bring all four corners to the centre to form a point and press together to make a parcel.
3 Put the parcels on the greased trays and glaze with egg. Bake for 15–20 minutes, or until the pastry is golden brown.

NUTRITION PER PARCEL
Protein 30 g; Fat 55 g; Carbohydrate 70 g;
Dietary Fibre 5 g; Cholesterol 180 mg;
3700 kJ (885 cal)

NOTE: Before removing the pastries from the oven, lift them gently off the tray and check that the bottom of the parcels are cooked through. Take care not to overcook the parcels or they may burst open.

HINT: If you like your puff pastry to taste extra buttery, brush it with melted butter before baking.

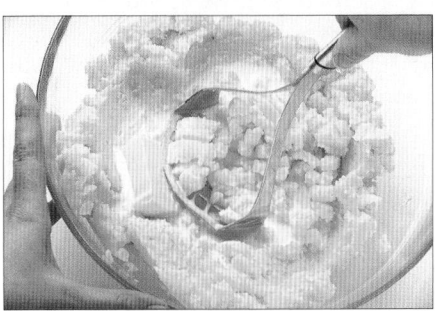

Cook and drain the potato, then mash well with the butter and cream.

Mix the cheese, salmon, dill and spring onion into the mashed potato.

Cut each pastry sheet into four squares and then divide the filling among them.

Bring up the corners to the centre and press together to make a parcel.

SPICY SEAFOOD SKEWERS

Preparation time: 40 minutes
Total cooking time: 15 minutes
Serves 4

SPICE PASTE
2 large red chillies, seeded and
    chopped
1 clove garlic, chopped
2 spring onions, finely chopped
1 teaspoon grated fresh ginger
1 tablespoon grated fresh turmeric
1 small tomato, peeled and seeded
½ teaspoon coriander seeds
2 tablespoons chopped roasted
    peanuts
½ teaspoon dried shrimp paste
2 teaspoons vegetable oil
1 tablespoon tamarind concentrate
1 tablespoon finely chopped lemon
    grass

350 g (11 oz) skinned boneless
    snapper fillet
350 g (11 oz) raw prawns, peeled and
    deveined
1 egg, lightly beaten
2 cups (120 g/4 oz) flaked coconut
4 kaffir lime leaves, shredded
2 tablespoons brown sugar
¾ cup (185 g/6 oz) whole egg
    mayonnaise
3 teaspoons grated lime rind
1 tablespoon chopped fresh coriander

1 Soak 6 thick wooden skewers in
water for 30 minutes.
2 To make the paste, coarsely grind
the chilli, garlic, spring onion, ginger,
turmeric, tomato, coriander, peanuts
and shrimp paste in a food processor.
Heat the oil in a frying pan and cook
the chilli mixture, tamarind and lemon
grass for 5 minutes over medium

heat, stirring frequently, until golden.
Put aside to cool before using.
3 Finely mince the fish and prawns in
a food processor. Add the egg,
coconut, kaffir lime leaves, sugar and
spice paste. Season well with salt and
pepper. Process until well combined.
4 Using wet hands, shape ¼ cup of
mixture around each skewer, then
cook on a hot, lightly oiled barbecue
flatplate or grill for 8–10 minutes,
turning often, until golden. Mix the

mayonnaise, lime rind and coriander
in a bowl and serve with the skewers.

NUTRITION PER SERVE
Protein 45 g; Fat 50 g; Carbohydrate 25 g;
Dietary Fibre 5 g; Cholesterol 245 mg;
2965 kJ (710 cal)

HINT: For extra flavour, try using
trimmed stalks of lemon grass instead
of wooden skewers.

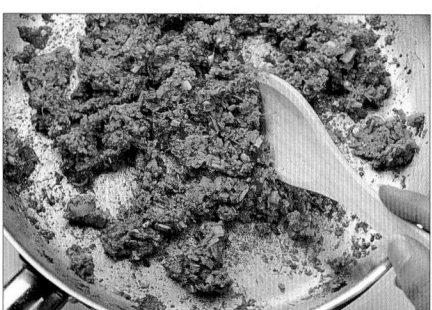

Cook the spice paste in a frying pan until it
becomes golden.

Add the egg, coconut, lime leaves, sugar and
spice paste to the food processor.

Shape the skewers with wet hands so that the
mixture doesn't stick.

SQUID WITH OLIVE OIL AND OREGANO DRESSING

Preparation time: 10 minutes
Total cooking time: 5 minutes
Serves 4

olive oil, for cooking
500 g (1 lb) squid tubes
2 teaspoons sea salt
2 teaspoons ground black pepper
mixed salad leaves, to serve

DRESSING
1 teaspoon grated lemon rind (see HINT)
2 tablespoons lemon juice
4 spring onions, finely sliced
2 teaspoons chopped oregano

1 To make the dressing, mix together 3 tablespoons olive oil with the lemon rind, lemon juice, spring onion and oregano.

2 Rinse the squid tubes in cold water and then pat dry with paper towels. Cut them in half and then into thin strips lengthways.

3 Place the salt and pepper in a bowl, mix well and add the squid strips. Toss to evenly coat.

4 Heat a wok over high heat, add 1 tablespoon of the oil and swirl to coat the side of the wok with oil. Cook the squid strips, in two batches, stir-frying for 1–2 minutes, or until they just change colour. Keep the wok hot and don't cook the squid for too long or it will toughen. Arrange the salad leaves on a serving platter, top with the stir-fried squid and drizzle with the dressing.

NUTRITION PER SERVE
Protein 40 g; Fat 45 g; Carbohydrate 1 g;
Dietary Fibre 1 g; Cholesterol 498 mg;
2449 kJ (585 cal)

HINT: When grating citrus rind, place a piece of baking paper over the grater. It will allow you to grate while making it easier to remove the rind from the grater.

Mix together the olive oil, lemon rind, lemon juice, spring onion and oregano.

Cut the squid hoods in half and then slice into thin strips lengthways.

Add the squid strips to the salt and pepper mixture and toss to coat.

Cook the squid strips in two batches over high heat, taking care not to overcook.

WARM PRAWN AND SCALLOP SALAD

Preparation time: 30 minutes
Total cooking time: 15 minutes
Serves 4

2 teaspoons five-spice powder
1–2 small red chillies, chopped
2–3 cloves garlic, crushed
2 teaspoons sesame oil
oil, for cooking
24 raw prawns, peeled and deveined, tails intact
20 scallops, cleaned
200 g (6½ oz) asparagus, cut into short lengths
150 g (5 oz) snow peas
125 g (4 oz) rocket leaves
2 tablespoons light soy sauce
2 tablespoons lemon juice
1 tablespoon mirin
1 tablespoon honey
6 spring onions, chopped
⅓ cup (20 g/¾ oz) chopped coriander leaves
1 tablespoon sesame seeds, toasted

1 Mix the five-spice powder, chilli, garlic, sesame oil and 2 tablespoons cooking oil in a large glass bowl. Add the prawns and scallops and toss to coat. Cover and refrigerate for at least 10 minutes.
2 Blanch the asparagus and snow peas briefly in a pan of boiling water. Drain and plunge into a bowl of iced water, then drain again. Tear the rocket leaves if they are too big. Arrange the asparagus, snow peas and rocket on four serving plates.
3 Put the soy sauce, lemon juice, mirin, honey and 1 tablespoon oil in a small bowl. Stir to combine.

4 Heat the wok until very hot and stir-fry the prawns, scallops and spring onion over high heat in three or four batches for 3–4 minutes, or until cooked through. Remove from the wok and set aside.
5 Add the sauce and coriander to the wok and bring to the boil. Cook over high heat for 1–2 minutes. Return the seafood to the wok and toss well. Sprinkle with sesame seeds to serve.

NUTRITION PER SERVE
Protein 35 g; Fat 20 g; Carbohydrate 10 g;
Dietary Fibre 5 g; Cholesterol 170 mg;
1515 kJ (360 cal)

Peel the prawns, leaving the tails intact, and pull out the dark veins.

Slice or pull off any vein, membrane or hard white muscle from the scallops.

FISH WITH GINGER

Preparation time: 20 minutes
Total cooking time: 15 minutes
Serves 4

1 tablespoon peanut oil
1 small onion, finely sliced
3 teaspoons ground coriander
600 g (1¼ lb) boneless white fish fillets,
    such as perch, sliced

1 tablespoon julienned fresh ginger
1 teaspoon finely chopped and
    seeded green chilli
2 tablespoons lime juice
2 tablespoons coriander leaves

1 Heat a wok until very hot, add the oil and swirl to coat. Add the onion and stir-fry for 4 minutes, or until soft and golden. Add the ground coriander and cook for 1–2 minutes, or until the mixture is fragrant.

2 Add the fish, ginger and chilli, and stir-fry for 5–7 minutes, or until the fish is cooked through. Stir in the lime juice and season. Garnish with the coriander leaves and serve.

NUTRITION PER SERVE
Protein 30 g; Fat 9 g; Carbohydrate 1 g;
Dietary Fibre 0.4 g; Cholesterol 105 mg;
895 kJ (214 cal)

Peel the fresh ginger and then cut the flesh into julienne strips.

Stir-fry the onion for 4 minutes, or until it is soft and golden.

Add the fish, ginger and chilli to the wok and stir-fry until the fish is cooked through.

INVOLTINI OF SWORDFISH

Preparation time: 30 minutes
Total cooking time: 10 minutes
Serves 4

1 kg (2 lb) swordfish, skin removed,
    cut into four 5 cm (2 inch) pieces
3 lemons
4 tablespoons olive oil
1 small onion, chopped
3 cloves garlic, chopped
2 tablespoons chopped capers
2 tablespoons chopped pitted
    Kalamata olives
⅓ cup (35 g/1 oz) finely grated
    Parmesan
1½ cups (120 g/4 oz) fresh
    breadcrumbs
2 tablespoons chopped fresh parsley
1 egg, lightly beaten
24 fresh bay leaves
2 small white onions, quartered and
    separated into pieces
2 tablespoons lemon juice, extra

1 Cut each swordfish piece horizontally into four slices to give you 16 slices. Place each piece between two pieces of plastic wrap and roll gently with a rolling pin to flatten without tearing. Cut each piece in half to give 32 pieces.
2 Peel the lemons with a vegetable peeler. Cut the peel into 24 even pieces. Squeeze the lemons to give 3 tablespoons of juice.
3 Heat 2 tablespoons olive oil in a pan, add the onion and garlic, and cook over medium heat for 2 minutes. Place in a bowl with the capers, olives, Parmesan, breadcrumbs and parsley. Season, add the egg and mix to bind.
4 Divide the stuffing among the fish pieces and, with oiled hands, roll up to form parcels. Thread four rolls onto each of eight skewers alternating with the bay leaves, lemon peel and onion.
5 Mix the remaining oil with the lemon juice in a small bowl. Cook the skewers on a hot barbecue flatplate for 3–4 minutes each side, basting with the oil and lemon mixture. Serve with a little extra lemon juice drizzled over the top.

NUTRITION PER SERVE
Protein 34 g; Fat 38 g; Carbohydrate 5.5 g;
Dietary Fibre 5 g; Cholesterol 193 mg;
2065 kJ (493 cal)

Roll the swordfish out between two pieces of plastic wrap.

Roll up the fish pieces and filling with oiled hands to form neat parcels.

Thread the rolls, bay leaves, lemon peel and onion onto skewers.

SALMON FILO PIE WITH DILL BUTTER

Preparation time: 25 minutes + cooling
Total cooking time: 50 minutes
Serves 6

¾ cup (150 g/5 oz) medium-grain white rice
90 g (3 oz) butter, melted
8 sheets filo pastry
500 g (1 lb) fresh salmon fillet, cut into small cubes
2 French shallots, finely chopped
1½ tablespoons baby capers
150 g (5 oz) Greek-style yoghurt
1 egg
1 tablespoon grated lemon rind
3 tablespoons chopped fresh dill
¼ cup (30 g/1 oz) dry breadcrumbs
1 tablespoon sesame seeds
2 teaspoons lemon juice

1 Put the rice in a large saucepan and add enough water to cover it by 2 cm (1 inch). Bring to the boil over medium heat, then reduce the heat to low, cover and cook for 20 minutes, or until all the water has been absorbed and tunnels appear on the surface of the rice. Set aside to cool.

2 Preheat the oven to 180°C (350°F/ Gas 4). Grease a 20 x 30 cm (8 x 12 inch) baking tin with melted butter. Cover the filo pastry with a damp tea towel. Mix the salmon with the shallots, capers, rice, yoghurt and egg. Add the lemon rind, 1 tablespoon of the dill and season well.

3 Layer four sheets of pastry in the base of the tin, brushing each one with melted butter and leaving the sides of the pastry overhanging the edge of the tin. Spoon in the salmon filling and pat down well. Fold the overhanging pastry over the filling.

4 Top with four more sheets of filo, brushing each one with melted butter and sprinkling all but the top layer with a tablespoon of breadcrumbs. Sprinkle the top with sesame seeds.

5 Score the top of the pie into diamonds without cutting right through the pastry. Bake for 25–30 minutes on the lowest shelf until golden brown. Reheat the remaining butter, add the lemon juice and remaining dill and pour some over each portion of pie.

NUTRITION PER SERVE
Protein 23 g; Fat 20 g; Carbohydrate 35 g; Dietary Fibre 1 g; Cholesterol 110 mg; 1705 kJ (410 cal)

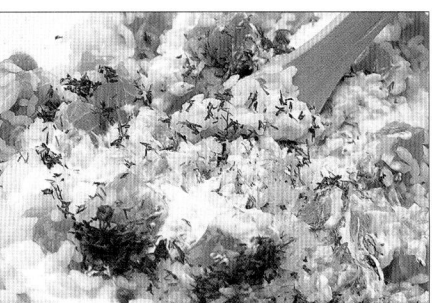

Combine the salmon, shallots, capers, rice, yoghurt, egg, lemon rind and dill.

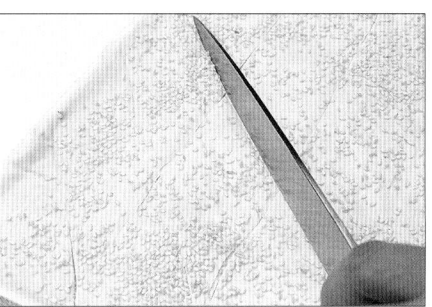

Sprinkle the pie with sesame seeds, then score the top into diamonds.

CORIANDER PRAWNS

Preparation time: 15 minutes +
**   30 minutes marinating**
Total cooking time: 5 minutes
Serves 4

8 very large raw prawns
1 tablespoon sweet chilli sauce
1 teaspoon ground coriander
½ cup (125 ml/4 fl oz) olive oil
⅓ cup (80 ml/2¾ fl oz) lime juice
3 cloves garlic, crushed
1 tomato, peeled, seeded and
    chopped
2 tablespoons roughly chopped
    fresh coriander

1 Remove the heads from the prawns and, with a sharp knife, cut the prawns in half lengthways, leaving the tails attached. Pull out each dark vein.
2 Mix together the sweet chilli sauce and ground coriander with half the olive oil, half the lime juice and half the garlic. Add the prawns, toss to coat, then cover and marinate in the fridge for 30 minutes.
3 Meanwhile, to make the dressing, mix the remaining olive oil, lime juice and garlic in a bowl with the chopped tomato and fresh coriander.
4 Drain the prawns, reserving the marinade and cook, cut-side-down, on a hot, lightly oiled barbecue grill

or flatplate for 1–2 minutes each side, or until cooked through, brushing occasionally with the marinade.
5 Spoon a little of the dressing over the prawns and season well before serving.

NUTRITION PER SERVE
Protein 42 g; Fat 31 g; Carbohydrate 2.5 g;
Dietary Fibre 2 g; Cholesterol 298 mg;
1930 kJ (460 cal)

Cut each prawn through the centre lengthways, leaving the tail attached.

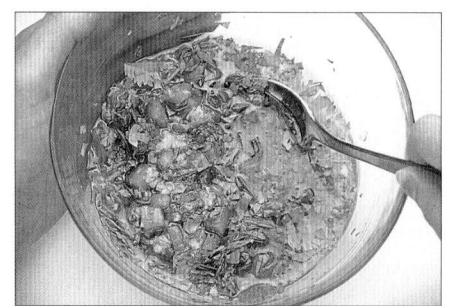

Stir the dressing ingredients together in a bowl until well combined.

Cook both sides of the drained prawns on a hot barbecue grill.

VIETNAMESE FISH

Preparation time: 25 minutes +
20 minutes marinating
Total cooking time: 15 minutes
Serves 6

750 g (1½ lb) small, firm, white fish
2 teaspoons green peppercorns, finely crushed
2 teaspoons chopped red chilli
3 teaspoons fish sauce
2 teaspoons oil
1 tablespoon oil, extra
2 onions, finely sliced
4 cm (1½ inch) piece of fresh ginger, peeled and thinly sliced
3 cloves garlic, finely sliced

2 teaspoons sugar
4 spring onions, cut into short lengths, then finely shredded

LEMON AND GARLIC DIPPING SAUCE
3 tablespoons lemon juice
2 tablespoons fish sauce
1 tablespoon sugar
2 small red chillies, chopped
3 cloves garlic, crushed

1 Cut 2 diagonal slashes in the thickest part of the fish on both sides. In a food processor or mortar and pestle, grind the peppercorns, chilli and fish sauce to a paste and brush over the fish. Leave for 20 minutes.
2 Cook on a hot, lightly oiled barbecue grill or flatplate for 8 minutes on each side, or until the flesh flakes easily when tested.
3 While the fish is cooking, heat the extra oil in a pan and stir the onion over medium heat, until golden. Add the ginger, garlic and sugar and cook for 3 minutes. Place the fish on a serving plate, top with the onion mixture and sprinkle with spring onion.
4 To make the dipping sauce, mix together all the ingredients. Serve with the barbecued fish.

NUTRITION PER SERVE
Protein 27 g; Fat 5 g; Carbohydrate 3 g;
Dietary Fibre 1 g; Cholesterol 88 mg;
705 kJ (168 cal)

Cut diagonal slashes into the thickest part of the fish so that it cooks through evenly.

Lightly brush the chilli mixture over the surface of the fish.

Cook the finely sliced onion over medium heat, stirring until golden.

Vegetarian

MUSHROOM, RICOTTA AND OLIVE PIZZA

Preparation time: 30 minutes + proving
Total cooking time: 1 hour
Serves 6

4 Roma (egg) tomatoes, quartered
¾ teaspoon caster sugar
7 g (¼ oz) dry yeast or
    15 g (½ oz) fresh yeast
½ cup (125 ml/4 fl oz) skim milk
1¾ cups (220 g/7 oz) plain flour
2 teaspoons olive oil
2 cloves garlic, crushed
1 onion, thinly sliced
750 g (1½ lb) cap mushrooms, sliced
1 cup (250 g/8 oz) ricotta cheese
2 tablespoons sliced black olives
small fresh basil leaves

1 Preheat the oven to hot 210°C (415°F/Gas 6–7). Put the tomatoes on a baking tray covered with baking paper, sprinkle with salt, cracked black pepper and ½ teaspoon sugar and bake for 20 minutes, or until the edges are starting to darken.
2 Stir the yeast and remaining sugar with 3 tablespoons warm water until the yeast dissolves. Cover and leave in a warm place until foamy (if the yeast doesn't foam you will have to throw it away and start again). Warm the milk. Sift the flour into a large bowl and stir in the yeast and milk. Mix to a soft dough, then turn onto a lightly floured surface and knead for 5 minutes. Leave, covered, in a lightly oiled bowl in a warm place for 40 minutes, or until doubled in size.
3 Heat the oil in a pan and fry the garlic and onion until soft. Add the mushrooms and stir until they are soft and the liquid has evaporated. Cool.
4 Turn the dough out onto a lightly floured surface and knead lightly. Roll out to a 36 cm (15 inch) circle and transfer to a lightly greased oven or pizza tray. Spread with the ricotta, leaving a border to turn over the filling. Top with the mushrooms, leaving a circle in the centre and arrange the tomato and olives in the circle. Fold the dough edge over onto the mushroom and dust the edge with flour. Bake for 25 minutes, or until the crust is golden. Garnish with basil.

NUTRITION PER SERVE
Protein 15 g; Fat 7.5 g; Carbohydrate 30g;
Dietary Fibre 6 g; Cholesterol 20 mg;
1100 kJ (265 cal)

Leave the yeast in a warm place until it begins to foam and become active.

Spread the ricotta over the pastry, leaving a border to turn over the filling.

BLUE CHEESE AND ONION FLAN

Preparation time: 40 minutes +
  20 minutes refrigeration
Total cooking time: 1 hour 40 minutes
Serves 8

2 tablespoons olive oil
1 kg (2 lb) red onions, very thinly sliced
1 teaspoon soft brown sugar
2 cups (250 g/8 oz) plain flour
100 g (3½ oz) cold butter, cubed
¾ cup (180 ml/6 fl oz) cream
3 eggs
100 g (3½ oz) blue cheese, crumbled
1 teaspoon freshly chopped lemon
   thyme or thyme leaves

1 Heat the oil in a heavy-based pan over low heat. Add the onion and sugar and cook, stirring regularly, for 45 minutes, or until the onion is soft and lightly golden.
2 Process the flour and butter in a food processor for 15 seconds. Add 1–2 tablespoons of iced water and process in short bursts until the mixture just comes together. Turn out onto a floured surface and gather into a ball. Cover with plastic wrap and refrigerate for 10 minutes.
3 Preheat the oven to moderate 180°C (350°F/Gas 4). Roll out the pastry thinly on a lightly floured surface to fit a greased 22 cm (9 inch) round loose-based flan tin. Trim any excess pastry. Chill for 10 minutes. Line with crumpled baking paper and fill with baking beads or rice. Put on a baking tray and bake for 10 minutes. Remove the paper and beads, then bake for 10 minutes, or until lightly golden and dry to the touch.
4 Cool, then gently spread the onion over the base of the pastry shell. Whisk together the cream, eggs, blue cheese, thyme and pepper to taste. Pour into the pastry shell and bake for 35 minutes, or until firm.

NUTRITION PER SERVE
Protein 9 g; Fat 30 g; Carbohydrate 25 g;
Dietary Fibre 1.5 g; Cholesterol 145 mg;
1718 kJ (410 cal)

Turn the dough out onto a lightly floured surface and gather into a ball.

Roll the pastry out thinly and line the greased flan tin, trimming away any excess.

Spread the onion over the cooled pastry base, then pour in the cream mixture.

CHICKPEA CURRY

Preparation time: 10 minutes +
   overnight soaking
Total cooking time: 1 hour 15 minutes
Serves 6

1 cup (220 g/7 oz) dried chickpeas
1 tablespoon oil
2 onions, finely chopped
2 large ripe tomatoes, chopped
½ teaspoon ground coriander
1 teaspoon ground cumin
1 teaspoon chilli powder
¼ teaspoon ground turmeric
1 tablespoon channa masala (see
   NOTE)
1 small white onion, sliced
mint and coriander leaves, to garnish

1 Place the chickpeas in a bowl, cover with water and leave to soak overnight. Drain, rinse and place in a large saucepan. Cover with plenty of water and bring to the boil, then reduce the heat and simmer for 40 minutes, or until soft. Drain.
2 Heat the oil in a large saucepan, add the onion and cook over medium heat for 15 minutes, or until golden brown. Add the tomato, ground coriander and cumin, chilli powder, turmeric and channa masala, and 2 cups (500 ml/16 fl oz) water and cook for 10 minutes, or until the tomato is soft. Add the chickpeas, season and cook for 7–10 minutes, or until the sauce thickens. Garnish with sliced onion and fresh mint and coriander leaves.

NUTRITION PER SERVE
Protein 8 g; Fat 9 g; Carbohydrate 17 g;
Dietary Fibre 6 g; Cholesterol 8.5 mg;
835 kJ (200 cal)

NOTE: Channa (chole) masala is a spice blend available at Indian grocery stores. Garam masala can be used as a substitute but the flavour will be a little different.

Cook the onion over medium heat for 15 minutes, or until golden brown.

Add the soaked chickpeas and cook until the sauce thickens.

TAMARI ROASTED ALMONDS WITH SPICY GREEN BEANS

Preparation time: 10 minutes
Total cooking time: 25 minutes
Serves 4–6

1 tablespoon sesame oil
2½ cups (500 g/1 lb) jasmine rice
2 tablespoons sesame oil, extra
1 long red chilli, seeded and finely
    chopped
2 cm (¾ inch) piece of fresh ginger,
    peeled and grated
2 cloves garlic, crushed

375 g (12 oz) green beans, cut into
    short lengths
½ cup (125 ml/4 fl oz) hoisin sauce
1 tablespoon soft brown sugar
2 tablespoons mirin
250 g (8 oz) tamari roasted almonds,
    roughly chopped (see NOTE)

1 Preheat the oven to moderately hot 200°C (400°F/Gas 6). Heat the oil in a 1.5 litre (48 fl oz) ovenproof dish. Add the rice and stir to coat with oil. Stir in 1 litre (32 fl oz) boiling water. Cover and bake for 20 minutes, or until all the water is absorbed. Keep warm.
2 Meanwhile, heat the extra oil in a wok or large frying pan and cook the

chilli, ginger and garlic for 1 minute, or until lightly browned. Add the beans, hoisin sauce and sugar and stir-fry for 2 minutes. Stir in the mirin and cook for 1 minute, or until the beans are tender but still crunchy.
3 Remove from the heat and stir in the almonds. Serve on a bed of the rice.

NUTRITION PER SERVE (6)
Protein 15 g; Fat 34 g; Carbohydrate 80 g;
Dietary Fibre 9.5 g; Cholesterol 0 mg;
2874 kJ (687 cal)

NOTE: Tamari roasted almonds are available from health-food stores.

When chopping chillies, it's a good idea to wear rubber gloves to prevent chilli burns.

Cook the rice in the oven until all the water has been absorbed.

Stir-fry the beans for 2 minutes, tossing to coat them in the sauce.

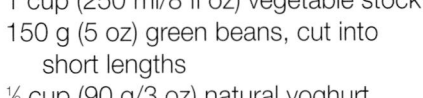

VEGETABLE CURRY

Preparation time: 20 minutes
Total cooking time: 30 minutes
Serves 6

250 g (8 oz) potatoes, diced
250 g (8 oz) pumpkin, diced
200 g (6½ oz) cauliflower, broken into
  florets
150 g (5 oz) yellow squash, cut into
  quarters
1 tablespoon oil
2 onions, chopped
3 tablespoons curry powder
400 g (13 oz) can crushed tomatoes

1 cup (250 ml/8 fl oz) vegetable stock
150 g (5 oz) green beans, cut into
  short lengths
⅓ cup (90 g/3 oz) natural yoghurt
¼ cup (30 g/1 oz) sultanas

1 Bring a saucepan of water to the boil, add the potato and pumpkin, and cook for 6 minutes, then remove. Add the cauliflower and squash, cook for 4 minutes, then remove.
2 Heat the oil in a large saucepan, add the onion and cook, stirring, over medium heat for 8 minutes, or until starting to brown.
3 Add the curry powder and stir for 1 minute, or until fragrant. Stir in the crushed tomato and vegetable stock.
4 Add the parboiled potato, pumpkin, cauliflower and squash and cook for 5 minutes, then add the green beans and cook for a further 2–3 minutes, or until the vegetables are just tender.
5 Add the yoghurt and sultanas, and stir to combine. Simmer for 3 minutes, or until thickened slightly. Season to taste and serve with lemon wedges.

NUTRITION PER SERVE
Protein 7 g; Fat 8.5 g; Carbohydrate 20 g;
Dietary Fibre 7 g; Cholesterol 2.5 mg;
805 kJ (192 cal)

Cook the onion over medium heat until it is starting to brown.

Add the beans and cook until the vegetables are just tender.

Add the yoghurt and sultanas and simmer until thickened slightly.

SOMEN NOODLE SALAD WITH SESAME DRESSING

Preparation time: 25 minutes + cooling
Total cooking time: 5 minutes
Serves 4

SESAME DRESSING
⅓ cup (40 g/1 oz) sesame seeds, toasted
2½ tablespoons Japanese or light soy sauce
2 tablespoons rice vinegar
2 teaspoons sugar
½ teaspoon grated fresh ginger
½ teaspoon dashi granules

125 g (4 oz) dried somen noodles
100 g (3½ oz) snow peas, finely sliced on the diagonal
100 g daikon radish, julienned
1 small (100 g/3½ oz) carrot, julienned
1 spring onion, sliced on the diagonal
60 g (2 oz) baby English spinach leaves, trimmed

2 teaspoons toasted sesame seeds

1 To make the dressing, place the sesame seeds in a mortar and pestle and grind until fine and moist. Combine the soy sauce, rice vinegar, sugar, ginger, dashi granules and ½ cup (125 ml) water in a small saucepan and bring to the boil over high heat. Reduce the heat to medium and simmer, stirring, for 2 minutes, or until the dashi granules have dissolved. Remove from the heat. Cool. Gradually combine with the ground sesame seeds, stirring to form a thick dressing.
2 Cook the noodles in a large saucepan of boiling water for 2 minutes, or until tender. Drain, rinse under cold water and cool completely. Cut into 10 cm lengths using scissors.
3 Place the snow peas in a large shallow bowl with the daikon, carrot, spring onion, English spinach leaves and the noodles. Add the dressing

and toss well to combine. Place in the refrigerator until ready to serve. Just before serving, sprinkle the top with the toasted sesame seeds.

NUTRITION PER SERVE
Fat 7.5 g; Protein 8 g; Carbohydrate 27 g; Dietary Fibre 4 g; Cholesterol 0.5 mg; 885 kJ (210 Cal)

Pour the soy sauce mixture into the sesame seeds, stirring to form a thick dressing.

POLENTA PIE

Preparation time: 20 minutes +
    15 minutes standing + refrigeration
Total cooking time: 50 minutes
Serves 6

2 eggplants, thickly sliced
1⅓ cups (350 ml/11 fl oz) vegetable
    stock
1 cup (150 g/5 oz) fine polenta
½ cup (60 g/2 oz) finely grated
    Parmesan
1 tablespoon olive oil
1 large onion, chopped
2 cloves garlic, crushed
1 large red capsicum, diced
2 zucchini, thickly sliced
150 g (5 oz) button mushrooms, cut
    into quarters
400 g (13 oz) can chopped tomatoes
3 teaspoons balsamic vinegar
olive oil, for brushing

1 Spread the eggplant in a single layer on a board and sprinkle with salt. Leave for 15 minutes, then rinse, pat dry and cut into cubes.
2 Line a 22 cm (9 inch) round cake tin with foil. Pour the stock and 1⅓ cups (350 ml/11 fl oz) water into a saucepan and bring to the boil. Add the polenta in a thin stream and stir over low heat for 5 minutes, or until the liquid is absorbed and the mixture comes away from the side of the pan.
3 Remove from the heat and stir in the cheese until it melts through the polenta. Spread into the prepared tin, smoothing the surface as much as possible. Refrigerate until set.
4 Preheat the oven to moderately hot 200°C (400°F/Gas 6). Heat the oil in a large saucepan with a lid and add the onion. Cook over medium heat,

stirring occasionally, for 3 minutes, or until soft. Add the garlic and cook for a further 1 minute. Add the eggplant, capsicum, zucchini, mushrooms and tomato. Bring to the boil, then reduce the heat and simmer, covered, for 20 minutes, or until the vegetables are tender. Stir occasionally to prevent catching on the bottom of the pan. Stir in the vinegar and season.
5 Transfer the vegetable mixture to a 22 cm (9 inch) ovenproof pie dish, piling it up slightly in the centre.

6 Turn out the polenta, peel off the foil and cut into 12 wedges. Arrange smooth-side-down in a single layer, over the vegetables—don't worry about any gaps. Brush lightly with a little olive oil and bake for 20 minutes, or until lightly brown and crisp.

NUTRITION PER SERVE
Protein 8 g; Fat 8.5 g; Carbohydrate 23 g;
Dietary Fibre 4.5 g; Cholesterol 8 mg;
855 kJ (205 cal)

Cook the polenta, stirring, until all the liquid is absorbed and it is very thick.

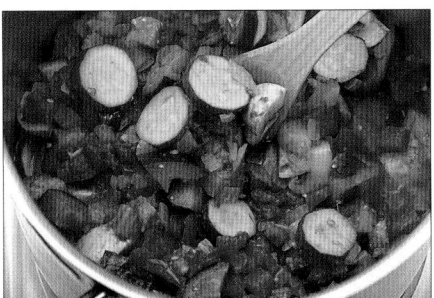

Reduce the heat and simmer until the vegetables are tender.

Arrange the polenta wedges, smooth-side-down, over the vegetable mixture.

CHEESE AND SPINACH PANCAKES

Preparation time: 40 minutes
Total cooking time: 50 minutes
Serves 4

250 g (8 oz) cooked, drained
 English spinach, chopped
½ cup (125 g/4 oz) ricotta cheese
¼ cup (30 g/1 oz) grated Cheddar
freshly grated nutmeg
¼ cup (25 g/¾ oz) grated Parmesan
½ teaspoon paprika
½ cup (40 g/1¼ oz) fresh breadcrumbs

BATTER
1 cup (125 g/4 oz) plain flour
1¼ cups (315 ml/10 fl oz) milk
1 egg
butter, for cooking

CHEESE SAUCE
2 tablespoons butter
¼ cup (30 g/1 oz) plain flour
1¾ cups (440 ml/14 fl oz) milk
1 cup (125 g/4 oz) grated Cheddar

1 Put the spinach, cheeses and nutmeg in a bowl and mix well.
2 To make batter, sift the flour and a pinch of salt into a bowl. Add half the milk and the egg. Whisk until smooth; add remaining milk. Heat a teaspoon of butter in a frying pan and pour in a thin layer of batter. Cook the base until golden, then flip.
3 To make the cheese sauce, melt the butter over low heat, stir in the flour until smooth and cook for 1 minute. Remove from heat and slowly stir in the milk. Bring to the boil, stirring. Remove from the heat and add salt and pepper and the grated cheese.
4 Preheat oven to 180°C (350°F/Gas 4). Divide the filling among the pancakes, roll up and put in a greased ovenproof dish. Pour cheese sauce over pancakes. Mix the Parmesan, paprika and breadcrumbs together and sprinkle over the sauce. Bake for 30 minutes, or until golden brown.

NUTRITION PER SERVE
Protein 18 g; Fat 17 g; Carbohydrate 34 g;
Dietary Fibre 3 g; Cholesterol 96 mg;
1511 kJ (360 cal)

Put the spinach, cheese, pepper and nutmeg in a bowl and mix well.

Cook until both sides of the pancake are golden, then remove with a spatula.

Remove the sauce from the heat and add salt and pepper, to taste, and grated cheese.

Divide the filling among the pancakes, roll up and put in the greased dish.

SPICY BEANS ON BAKED SWEET POTATO

Preparation time: 20 minutes
Total cooking time: 1 hour 30 minutes
Serves 6

3 orange sweet potatoes
  (500 g/1 lb each)
1 tablespoon olive oil
1 large onion, chopped
3 cloves garlic, crushed
2 teaspoons ground cumin
1 teaspoon ground coriander
½ teaspoon chilli powder
400 g (13 oz) can chopped tomatoes
1 cup (250 ml/8 fl oz) vegetable stock
1 large zucchini, cubed
1 green capsicum, cubed
310 g (10 oz) can corn kernels,
  drained
2 x 400 g (13 oz) cans red kidney
  beans, rinsed and drained
3 tablespoons chopped fresh
  coriander leaves
light sour cream and grated reduced-
  fat Cheddar, to serve

1 Preheat the oven to hot 210°C (415°F/Gas 6–7). Rinse the sweet potatoes, then pierce with a small sharp knife. Place them on a baking tray and bake for 1–1½ hours, or until soft when tested with a skewer or sharp knife.
2 Meanwhile, heat the oil in a large saucepan and cook the onion over medium heat for about 5 minutes, stirring occasionally, until very soft and golden. Add the garlic and spices, and cook, stirring, for 1 minute.
3 Add the tomato and stock, stir well, then add the vegetables and beans. Bring to the boil, then reduce the heat and simmer, partially covered, for

20 minutes. Uncover, increase the heat slightly, and cook for a further 10–15 minutes, or until the liquid has reduced and thickened. Stir in the coriander leaves just before serving.
4 To serve, cut the sweet potatoes in half lengthways. Spoon the vegetable mixture over the top. Add a dollop of light sour cream and sprinkle with grated Cheddar cheese.

NUTRITION PER SERVE
Protein 15 g; Fat 5 g; Carbohydrate 72 g;
Dietary Fibre 17 g; Cholesterol 0 mg;
1665 kJ (397 cal)

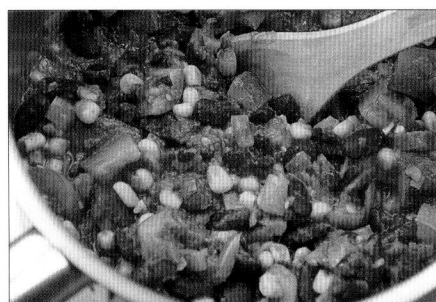
Cook the spicy vegetable mixture until the liquid has reduced.

Cut the baked sweet potatoes in half lengthways and top with the spicy beans.

VEGETABLE STRUDEL PARCELS

Preparation time: 1 hour
Total cooking time: 30 minutes
Serves 4

300 g (10 oz) pumpkin
2 carrots
1 parsnip
2 celery sticks
2 teaspoons sesame oil
1 onion, finely sliced
3 teaspoons finely chopped or
    grated fresh ginger
1 tablespoon dry sherry
1 teaspoon finely grated lemon rind
1 cup (185 g/6 oz) cooked long-grain
    rice
2 tablespoons plum sauce
1 tablespoon sweet chilli sauce
2 teaspoons soy sauce
16 sheets filo pastry
⅓ cup (35 g/1¼ oz) dry breadcrumbs
1 teaspoon butter, melted
1 tablespoon sesame seeds
sweet chilli sauce, for serving

1 Cut the pumpkin, carrots, parsnip and celery into thick matchsticks about 2.5 mm (⅛ inch) wide and 5 cm (2 inches) long.
2 Heat the sesame oil in a heavy-based pan or wok, add the onion and ginger and stir-fry, tossing well until brown, over medium heat. Add the pumpkin, carrot and parsnip, toss well and cook for 1 minute. Sprinkle 2 teaspoons of water all over the vegetables, cover and steam for another minute. Add the celery, sherry and lemon rind, toss and cook for 1 minute. Cover again and let steam for about 1 minute, or until the vegetables are just tender. Stir in the cooked rice and the plum, chilli and soy sauces. Set aside for about 20 minutes to cool.

3 Preheat the oven to moderately hot 190°C (375°F/Gas 5). Remove two sheets of filo pastry, keeping the remaining pastry covered with a damp tea towel. Place one sheet on top of the other, carefully brush the edges lightly with a little water, then scatter some breadcrumbs over the pastry. Top with another 2 sheets of pastry, fold over the edges to make a 2 cm (¾ inch) border and brush lightly with a little water. Press the edges down gently with your finger-tips to make the parcel easier to fold.
4 Place one-quarter of the filling about 5 cm (2 inches) from the short end, then firmly roll into a parcel to encase the filling, ensuring that the seam is underneath. Repeat with the remaining ingredients.
5 Brush the tops very lightly with butter, cut 3 slashes across the top of each and scatter any remaining breadcrumbs and the sesame seeds over the top. Arrange on a lightly greased baking tray and bake for 20–25 minutes, or until crisp and golden. Serve immediately, drizzled with sweet chilli sauce.

NUTRITION PER SERVE
Protein 15 g; Fat 8 g; Carbohydrate 95 g; Dietary Fibre 7 g; Cholesterol 3 mg; 2210 kJ (530 cal)

HINT: Cover the filo pastry that is waiting to be used with a damp tea towel to prevent it drying out.

Cut the pumpkin, carrot, parsnip and celery into similar-sized short matchsticks.

Stir the rice and plum, chilli and soy sauces into the vegetables.

Moisten the pastry before scattering the breadcrumbs over it.

Fold the pastry edges over, brush with water, then press down lightly.

Put the filling on the pastry, then firmly roll it up into a parcel.

Cut 3 slashes on the top of each parcel to allow steam to escape.

ITALIAN ZUCCHINI PIE

Preparation time: 30 minutes +
  30 minutes refrigeration +
  30 minutes draining
Total cooking time: 1 hour
Serves 6

2½ cups (310 g/10 oz) plain flour
⅓ cup (80 ml/2¾ fl oz) olive oil
1 egg, beaten
3–4 tablespoons iced water

FILLING
600 g (1¼ lb) zucchini
150 g (5 oz) provolone cheese, grated
120 g (4 oz) ricotta
3 eggs
2 cloves garlic, crushed
2 teaspoons finely chopped fresh basil
pinch of ground nutmeg
1 egg, lightly beaten, to glaze

1 To make the pastry, sift the flour and ½ teaspoon salt into a large bowl and make a well. Combine the oil, egg and almost all the water and add to the flour. Mix with a flat-bladed knife, using a cutting action, until the mixture comes together in beads, adding a little more water if necessary. Gather into a ball, wrap in plastic wrap and refrigerate for 30 minutes.

2 Preheat the oven to moderately hot 200°C (400°F/Gas 6) and heat a baking tray. Grease an 18 cm (7 inch) pie dish. To make the filling, grate the zucchini and toss with ¼ teaspoon salt. Place in a colander for 30 minutes to drain. Squeeze out any excess liquid with your hands. Place in a large bowl and add the provolone, ricotta, eggs, garlic, basil and nutmeg. Season well and mix thoroughly.

3 Roll out two-thirds of the pastry between two sheets of baking paper until large enough to line the base and side of the dish. Remove the top sheet and invert into the dish.

4 Spoon the filling into the pastry shell and level the surface. Brush the exposed rim of the dough with egg. Roll out two-thirds of the remaining dough between the baking paper to make a lid. Cover the filling with it, pressing the edges together firmly. Trim the edges. Crimp the rim. Prick the top all over with a skewer and brush with egg.

5 Roll the remaining dough into a strip about 30 x 10 cm (12 x 4 inches). Using a long sharp knife, cut this into nine lengths 1 cm (½ inch) wide. Press three ropes together at one end and press these onto the workbench to secure them. Plait the ropes. Make two more plaits with the remaining lengths. Trim the ends and space the plaits parallel across the centre of the pie. Brush with egg. Bake on the hot tray for 50 minutes, or until golden.

NUTRITION PER SERVE
Protein 21 g; Fat 27 g; Carbohydrate 40 g; Dietary Fibre 4 g; Cholesterol 184.5 mg; 2010 kJ (480 cal)

Spoon the zucchini filling into the pastry shell and level the surface.

RED LENTIL AND RICOTTA LASAGNE

Preparation time: 30 minutes + soaking
Total cooking time: 2 hours 10 minutes
Serves 6

½ cup (125 g/4 oz) red lentils
2 teaspoons olive oil
2–3 cloves garlic, crushed
1 large onion, chopped
1 small red capsicum, chopped
2 zucchini, sliced
1 celery stick, sliced
2 x 425 g (14 oz) cans chopped
    tomatoes
2 tablespoons tomato paste
1 teaspoon dried oregano
350 g (12 oz) ricotta
12 dried or fresh lasagne sheets
60 g (2 oz) reduced-fat Cheddar,
    grated

WHITE SAUCE
⅓ cup (40 g/1¼ oz) cornflour
3 cups (750 ml/24 fl oz) skim milk
¼ onion
½ teaspoon ground nutmeg

1 Soak the lentils in boiling water to cover for at least 30 minutes, then drain. Meanwhile, heat the oil in a large pan, add the garlic and onion and cook for 2 minutes. Add the capsicum, zucchini and celery and cook for 2–3 minutes.
2 Add the lentils, tomato, tomato paste, oregano and 1½ cups (375 ml/ 12 fl oz) water. Bring slowly to the boil, reduce the heat and simmer for 30 minutes, or until the lentils are tender. Stir occasionally.
3 To make the white sauce, blend the cornflour with 2 tablespoons of the milk in a pan until smooth. Pour the

remaining milk into the pan, add the onion and stir over low heat until the mixture boils and thickens. Add the nutmeg and season with pepper, then cook over low heat for 5 minutes. Remove the onion.
4 Beat the ricotta with about ½ cup (125 ml/4 fl oz) of the white sauce. Preheat the oven to moderate 180°C (350°F/Gas 4). Spread one-third of the lentil mixture over the base of a 3-litre capacity ovenproof dish. Cover with a layer of lasagne sheets. Spread another third of the lentil mixture over the pasta, then spread the ricotta

evenly over the top. Follow with another layer of lasagne, then the remaining lentils. Pour the white sauce evenly over the top and sprinkle with the grated cheese. Bake for 1 hour, covering loosely with foil if the top starts to brown too much. Leave to stand for 5 minutes before cutting.

NUTRITION PER SERVE
Protein 25 g; Fat 10 g; Carbohydrate 65 g; Dietary Fibre 9 g; Cholesterol 40 mg; 1995 kJ (475 cal)

Chop the onion and capsicum into quite small pieces and slice the zucchini.

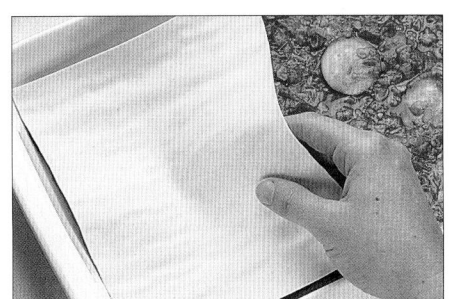

Build up layers of the lentil mixture, lasagne sheets and ricotta.

Pour the white sauce evenly over the top of the lasagne, then sprinkle with cheese.

RATATOUILLE TARTE TATIN

**Preparation time: 45 minutes +
20 minutes refrigeration
Total cooking time: 50 minutes
Serves 6**

1½ cups (185 g/6 oz) plain flour
90 g (3 oz) butter, chopped
1 egg
1 tablespoon oil
30 g (1 oz) butter, extra
2 zucchini, halved lengthways and
  sliced
250 g (8 oz) eggplant, diced
1 red capsicum, diced
1 green capsicum, diced
1 large red onion, diced
250 g (8 oz) cherry tomatoes, halved
2 tablespoons balsamic vinegar
½ cup (60 g/2 oz) grated Cheddar
300 g (10 oz) sour cream
3 tablespoons good-quality pesto

1 Sift the flour into a bowl and add the butter. Rub the butter into the flour with your fingertips until it resembles fine breadcrumbs. Make a well in the centre and add the egg (and 2 tablespoons water if the mixture is too dry). Mix with a flat-bladed knife, using a cutting action, until the mixture comes together in beads. Gather the dough together and lift onto a floured work surface. Press into a ball, flatten slightly into a disc, then wrap in plastic wrap and refrigerate for 20 minutes.
2 Preheat the oven to moderately hot 200°C (400°F/Gas 6). Grease a 25 cm (12 inch) springform tin and line with baking paper. Heat the oil and extra butter in a large frying pan and cook the zucchini, eggplant, capsicums and

onion over high heat for 8 minutes, or until just soft. Add the tomatoes and vinegar and cook for 3–4 minutes.
3 Place the tin on a baking tray and neatly lay the vegetables in the tin, then sprinkle with cheese. Roll the dough out between two sheets of baking paper to a 28 cm (11 inch) circle. Remove the paper and invert the pastry into the tin over the filling. Use a spoon handle to tuck the edge of the pastry down the side of the tin. Bake for 30–35 minutes (some liquid

will leak out), then leave to stand for 1–2 minutes. Remove from the tin and place on a serving plate, pastry-side-down. Mix the sour cream and pesto together in a small bowl. Serve with the tarte tatin.

NUTRITION PER SERVE
Protein 10 g; Fat 40 g; Carbohydrate 29 g;
Dietary Fibre 4.5 g; Cholesterol 144 mg;
2277 kJ (544 cal)

Mix with a flat-bladed knife until the mixture comes together in beads.

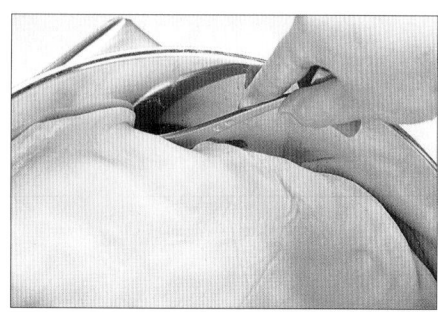

Add the cherry tomatoes and balsamic vinegar and cook for 3–4 minutes.

Use a spoon handle to tuck the edge of the pastry down the side of the tin.

HOKKIEN NOODLE SALAD

Preparation time: 20 minutes
Total cooking time: Nil
Serves 8

900 g (1¾ lb) Hokkien noodles
6 spring onions, sliced diagonally
1 large red capsicum, thinly sliced
200 g (6½ oz) snow peas, sliced
1 carrot, sliced diagonally
60 g (2 oz) fresh mint, chopped
60 g (2 oz) fresh coriander, chopped
100 g (3½ oz) roasted cashew nuts

SESAME DRESSING
2 teaspoons sesame oil
1 tablespoon peanut oil
2 tablespoons lime juice
2 tablespoons kecap manis (see NOTE)
3 tablespoons sweet chilli sauce

1 Gently separate the noodles and place in a large bowl, cover with boiling water and leave for 2 minutes. Rinse and drain.
2 Put the noodles in a large bowl, and add spring onions, capsicum, snow peas, carrot, mint and coriander. Toss together well.

3 To make the dressing, whisk together the oils, lime juice, kecap manis and sweet chilli sauce. Pour the dressing over the salad and toss again. Sprinkle the cashew nuts over the top and serve immediately.

NUTRITION PER SERVE
Protein 10 g; Fat 9 g; Carbohydrate 35 g;
Dietary Fibre 4.5 g; Cholesterol 0 mg;
1115 kJ (265 cal)

NOTE: If you can't find kecap manis, you can use soy sauce sweetened with a little soft brown sugar.

Top and tail the snow peas, then finely slice lengthways with a sharp knife.

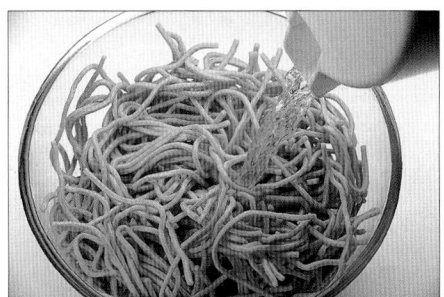

Separate the noodles, then put them in a large bowl and cover with boiling water.

Whisk together the oils, lime juice, kecap manis and sweet chilli sauce.

SPINACH PIE

Preparation time: 45 minutes +
1 hour refrigeration
Total cooking time: 55 minutes
Serves 6

PASTRY
2 cups (250 g/8 oz) plain flour
30 g (1 oz) chilled butter, chopped
¼ cup (60 ml) olive oil

FILLING
500 g (1 lb) English spinach leaves
2 teaspoons olive oil
1 onion, finely chopped
3 spring onions, finely chopped
200 g (6½ oz) feta, crumbled
2 tablespoons chopped fresh flat-leaf
  parsley
1 tablespoon chopped fresh dill
2 tablespoons grated kefalotyri cheese
¼ cup (45 g/1½ oz) cooked white rice
¼ cup (40 g/1½ oz) pine nuts, toasted
  and roughly chopped
¼ teaspoon ground nutmeg
½ teaspoon ground cumin
3 eggs, lightly beaten

1 Lightly grease a shallow 17 x 26 cm (7 x 10 inch) tin. To make the pastry, sift the flour and ½ teaspoon salt into a large bowl. Rub in the butter until it resembles fine breadcrumbs. Make a well in the centre and add the oil. Using your hands, mix together. Add ½ cup (125 ml/4 fl oz) warm water and mix with a flat-bladed knife, in a cutting action, until the mixture comes together in beads. Gently gather the dough together and lift out onto a lightly floured surface. Press into a ball and flatten into a disc. Wrap in plastic wrap and refrigerate for 1 hour.
2 Trim and wash the spinach, then coarsely chop the leaves and stems. Wrap in a tea towel and squeeze out as much moisture as possible. Heat the oil in a frying pan, add the onion and spring onion and cook over low heat, without browning, for 5 minutes, or until softened. Place in a bowl with the spinach and the remaining filling ingredients and mix well. Season.
3 Preheat the oven to moderately hot 200°C (400°F/Gas 6). Roll out just over half the pastry between two

sheets of baking paper, remove the top sheet and invert the pastry into the tin. Use a small ball of pastry to help press the pastry into the tin, allowing any excess to hang over the sides. Spoon the filling into the tin. Roll out the remaining pastry until large enough to cover the top. Place over the filling and press the two pastry edges firmly together to seal. Use a small sharp knife to trim away any extra pastry. Brush the top with a little oil, then score three strips lengthways, then on the diagonal to make a diamond pattern on the surface. Make two slits in the top to allow steam to escape.
4 Bake for 45–50 minutes, covering with foil if the surface becomes too brown. The pie is cooked when it slides when the tin is gently shaken. Turn out onto a rack for 10 minutes, then cut into pieces and serve.

NUTRITION PER SERVE
Protein 19 g; Fat 33 g; Carbohydrate 39 g; Dietary Fibre 5 g; Cholesterol 133 mg; 2207 kJ (527 cal)

Line the tin with the pastry, then spoon the spinach filling into the tin.

Score a diamond pattern in the pastry, then make two slits so steam can escape.

ROAST VEGETABLE TART

Preparation time: 30 minutes
Total cooking time: 1 hour 45 minutes
Serves 4–6

2 slender eggplants, halved and cut
    into thick slices
350 g (11 oz) pumpkin, chopped
2 zucchini, halved and cut into thick
    slices
1–2 tablespoons olive oil
1 large red capsicum, chopped
1 teaspoon olive oil, extra
1 red onion, cut into thin wedges
1 tablespoon Korma curry paste
plain yoghurt, to serve

PASTRY
1½ cups (185 g/6 oz) plain flour
125 g (4 oz) butter, chopped
⅔ cup (100 g/3½ oz) roasted cashews,
    finely chopped
1 teaspoon cumin seeds
2–3 tablespoons chilled water

1 Preheat the oven to moderately hot 200°C (400°F/Gas 6). Put the eggplant, pumpkin and zucchini on a lined oven tray, then brush with oil and bake for 30 minutes. Turn, add the capsicum and bake for 30 minutes. Cool.
2 Meanwhile, heat the extra oil in a frying pan and cook the onion for 2–3 minutes, or until soft. Add the curry paste and cook, stirring, for 1 minute, or until fragrant and well mixed. Cool. Reduce the oven to moderate 180°C (350°F/Gas 4).
3 To make the pastry, sift the flour into a large bowl and add the butter. Rub the butter into the flour with your fingertips until it resembles fine breadcrumbs. Stir in the cashews and cumin seeds. Make a well in the centre and add the water. Mix with a flat-bladed knife, using a cutting action, until the mixture comes together in beads. Gather the dough together and lift out onto a sheet of baking paper. Flatten to a disc, then roll out to a 35 cm (14 inch) circle.
4 Lift onto an oven tray and spread the onion mixture over the pastry, leaving a wide border. Arrange the other vegetables over the onion, piling them slightly higher in the centre. Working your way around, fold the edge of the pastry in pleats over the vegetables. Bake for 45 minutes, or until the pastry is golden. Serve immediately with plain yoghurt.

NUTRITION PER SERVE (6)
Protein 9 g; Fat 34 g; Carbohydrate 33 g;
Dietary Fibre 5 g; Cholesterol 54 mg;
1959 kJ (470 cal)

Spread the onion mixture over the pastry, leaving a good wide border for turning over.

Fold the edge of the pastry over the vegetables in rough pleats.

VEGETABLE TART WITH SALSA VERDE

**Preparation time: 30 minutes +
30 minutes refrigeration**
Total cooking time: 50 minutes
Serves 6

1¾ cups (215 g/7 oz) plain flour
120 g (4 oz) chilled butter, cubed
¼ cup (60 ml/2 fl oz) cream
1–2 tablespoons chilled water
1 large (250 g/8 oz) Desiree potato,
    cut into 2 cm (1 inch) cubes
1 tablespoon olive oil
2 cloves garlic, crushed
1 red capsicum, cut into cubes
1 red onion, sliced into rings
2 zucchini, sliced
2 tablespoons chopped fresh dill
1 tablespoon chopped fresh thyme
1 tablespoon drained baby capers
150 g (5 oz) marinated quartered
    artichoke hearts, drained
⅔ cup (30 g/1 oz) baby English
    spinach leaves

SALSA VERDE
1 clove garlic
2 cups (40 g/1¼ oz) fresh flat-leaf
    parsley
⅓ cup (80 ml/2¾ fl oz) extra virgin olive
    oil
3 tablespoons chopped fresh dill
1½ tablespoons Dijon mustard
1 tablespoon red wine vinegar
1 tablespoon drained baby capers

1 Sift the flour and ½ teaspoon salt into a large bowl. Add the butter and rub it into the flour with your fingertips until it resembles fine breadcrumbs. Add the cream and water and mix with a flat-bladed knife until the mixture comes together in beads. Gather together and lift onto a lightly floured work surface. Press into a ball, then flatten into a disc, wrap in plastic wrap and refrigerate for 30 minutes.

2 Preheat the oven to moderately hot 200°C (400°F/Gas 6). Grease a 27 cm (11 inch) loose-bottomed flan tin. Roll the dough out between two sheets of baking paper large enough to line the tin. Remove the paper and invert the pastry into the tin. Use a small pastry ball to press the pastry into the tin, allowing any excess to hang over the side. Roll a rolling pin over the tin, cutting off any excess. Cover the pastry with a piece of crumpled baking paper, then add baking beads. Place the tin on a baking tray and bake for 15–20 minutes. Remove the paper and beads, reduce the heat to moderate 180°C (350°F/Gas 4) and bake for 20 minutes, or until golden.

3 To make the salsa verde, combine all the ingredients in a food processor and process until almost smooth.

4 Boil the potato until just tender. Drain. Heat the oil in a large frying pan and cook the garlic, capsicum and onion over medium heat for 3 minutes, stirring frequently. Add the zucchini, dill, thyme and capers and cook for 3 minutes. Reduce the heat to low, add the potato and artichokes, and heat through. Season to taste.

5 To assemble, spread 3 tablespoons of the salsa over the pastry. Spoon the vegetable mixture into the case and drizzle with half the remaining salsa. Pile the spinach in the centre and drizzle with the remaining salsa.

NUTRITION PER SERVE
Protein 7 g; Fat 37 g; Carbohydrate 36 g;
Dietary Fibre 4.5 g; Cholesterol 65 mg;
2110 kJ (505 cal)

Rub the butter into the flour and salt with your fingertips until it resembles fine breadcrumbs.

Mix with a flat-bladed knife until the dough comes together in beads.

Press the pastry gently into the side of the greased flan tin.

Bake the pastry case until it is dry to the touch and golden brown.

Mix together the salsa verde ingredients in a food processor until almost smooth.

Spread salsa verde over the pastry base, then fill with the hot vegetables.

MIDDLE EASTERN POTATO CASEROLE

Preparation time: 10 minutes
Total cooking time: 30 minutes
Serves 4

¼ teaspoon saffron threads
1 kg (2 lb) potatoes, cut into large cubes
1 teaspoon olive oil
1 small onion, sliced
½ teaspoon ground turmeric
½ teaspoon ground coriander
1 cup (250 ml/8 fl oz) vegetable stock
1 clove garlic, crushed
¼ cup (30 g/1 oz) raisins
1 teaspoon chopped fresh flat-leaf parsley
1 teaspoon chopped fresh coriander leaves

1 Put the saffron to soak in 1 tablespoon of hot water. Place the potato in a saucepan of cold, salted water. Bring to the boil and cook until tender but still firm. Drain and set aside.
2 Heat the oil in a separate saucepan, add the onion, turmeric and ground coriander and cook over low heat for 5 minutes, or until the onion is soft.

3 Add the potato, vegetable stock and garlic. Bring to the boil, then reduce the heat and simmer for 10 minutes.
4 Add the saffron with its soaking water and the raisins, and cook for 10 minutes, or until the potato is soft and the sauce has reduced and thickened. Stir in the parsley and coriander. Delicious with couscous.

NUTRITION PER SERVE
Protein 10 g; Fat 6 g; Carbohydrate 65 g; Dietary Fibre 8 g; Cholesterol 0.5 mg; 1500 kJ (358 cal)

Soak the saffron threads in 1 tablespoon hot water while you cook the potatoes.

Cook the onion, turmeric and ground coriander until the onion is soft.

Add the potato, stock and garlic to the saucepan and bring to the boil.

PIZZA-TOPPED FOCACCIA

Preparation time: 30 minutes +
1 hour 30 minutes standing
Total cooking time: 40 minutes
Serves 4

7 g (¼ oz) sachet dry yeast
1 teaspoon sugar
2 tablespoons olive oil
2½ cups (310 g/10 oz) plain flour, sifted

PIZZA TOPPING
1 tablespoon tomato paste
1 large red capsicum, thinly sliced
125 g (4 oz) marinated artichoke hearts, quartered
¼ cup (30 g/1 oz) black olives, pitted
200 g (6½ oz) bocconcini, thickly sliced

1 Combine the yeast, ¾ cup (185 ml/ 6 fl oz) of warm water and the sugar in a bowl and set aside in a warm place for 5–10 minutes, or until frothy. Put the oil, flour and 1 teaspoon salt in a large bowl, add the frothy yeast and mix to a soft dough.
2 Turn the dough out onto a lightly floured surface and knead for 10 minutes, or until smooth and elastic. Roll into a ball and place in a large oiled bowl. Cover with oiled plastic wrap and set aside in a warm place for 1 hour, or until the dough has doubled in size.
3 Preheat the oven to moderate 180°C (350°F/Gas 4). Punch down the dough with your fist to expel any air, and knead for 1 minute. Roll into a flat disc large enough to fit into a greased 23 cm (9 inch) springform tin. Press into the tin, cover with a tea towel and leave to rise for about 20 minutes.

4 Spread the tomato paste over the dough and arrange the other topping ingredients, except for the bocconcini, on top. Bake for 20 minutes, remove from the oven and spread the slices of bocconcini over the top, then bake for a further 20 minutes, or until the dough is well risen and firm to the touch in the centre. Cool on a wire rack before cutting and serving.

NUTRITION PER SERVE
Protein 25 g; Fat 20 g; Carbohydrate 60 g; Dietary Fibre 5 g; Cholesterol 30 mg; 2235 kJ (535 cal)

Bocconcini are small balls of mozzarella. Cut them into thick slices with a sharp knife.

On a lightly floured surface, knead the dough until smooth and elastic.

Arrange the capsicum, artichokes and olives over the tomato paste.

VEGETABLE CASSEROLE WITH HERB DUMPLINGS

Preparation time: 30 minutes
Total cooking time: 50 minutes
Serves 4

1 tablespoon olive oil
1 large onion, chopped
2 cloves garlic, crushed
2 teaspoons sweet paprika
1 large potato, chopped
1 large carrot, sliced
400 g (13 oz) can chopped tomatoes
1½ cups (375 ml/12 fl oz) vegetable
    stock
400 g (13 oz) orange sweet potato,
    cubed
150 g (5 oz) broccoli, cut into florets
2 zucchini, thickly sliced
1 cup (125 g/4 oz) self-raising flour
20 g (¾ oz) cold butter, cut into small
    cubes
2 teaspoons chopped fresh flat-leaf
    parsley
1 teaspoon fresh thyme
1 teaspoon chopped fresh rosemary
⅓ cup (80 ml/2¾ fl oz) milk
2 tablespoons light sour cream

1 Heat the oil in a large saucepan and add the onion. Cook over low heat, stirring occasionally, for 5 minutes, or until soft. Add the garlic and paprika and cook, stirring, for 1 minute.
2 Add the potato, carrot, tomato and stock to the pan. Bring to the boil, then reduce the heat and simmer, covered, for 10 minutes. Add the sweet potato, broccoli and zucchini and simmer for 10 minutes, or until tender. Preheat the oven to moderately hot 200°C (400°F/Gas 6).
3 To make the dumplings, sift the flour and a pinch of salt into a bowl

and add the butter. Rub the butter into the flour with your fingertips until it resembles fine breadcrumbs. Stir in the herbs and make a well in the centre. Add the milk, and mix with a flat-bladed knife, using a cutting action, until the mixture comes together in beads. Gather up the dough and lift onto a lightly floured surface, then divide into eight portions. Shape each portion into a ball.

4 Add the sour cream to the casserole. Pour into a 2 litre ovenproof dish and top with the dumplings. Bake for 20 minutes, or until the dumplings are golden and a skewer comes out clean when inserted in the centre.

NUTRITION PER SERVE
Protein 8 g; Fat 10 g; Carbohydrate 27 g;
Dietary Fibre 7.5 g; Cholesterol 16 mg;
967 kJ (230 cal)

Add the remaining vegetables and simmer for 10 minutes, or until they are tender.

Rub the butter into the flour until the mixture resembles fine breadcrumbs.

Divide the dough into eight equal portions and shape each portion into a dumpling.

TEMPEH STIR-FRY

Preparation time: 15 minutes
Total cooking time: 15 minutes
Serves 4

1 teaspoon sesame oil
1 tablespoon peanut oil
2 cloves garlic, crushed
1 tablespoon grated fresh ginger
1 red chilli, finely sliced
4 spring onions, sliced on the diagonal
300 g (10 oz) tempeh, diced
500 g (1 lb) baby bok choy leaves

800 g (1 lb 10 oz) Chinese broccoli, chopped
½ cup (125 ml/4 fl oz) mushroom oyster sauce
2 tablespoons rice vinegar
2 tablespoons fresh coriander leaves
3 tablespoons toasted cashew nuts

1 Heat the oils in a wok over high heat, add the garlic, ginger, chilli and spring onion and cook for 1–2 minutes, or until the onion is soft. Add the tempeh and cook for 5 minutes, or until golden. Remove and keep warm.

2 Add half the greens and 1 tablespoon water to the wok and cook, covered, for 3–4 minutes, or until wilted. Remove and repeat with the remaining greens and more water.
3 Return the greens and tempeh to the wok, add the sauce and vinegar and warm through. Top with the coriander and nuts. Serve with rice.

NUTRITION PER SERVE
Protein 23 g; Fat 15 g; Carbohydrate 12 g; Dietary Fibre 15 g; Cholesterol 0 mg; 2220 kJ (529 cal)

Stir-fry the garlic, ginger, chilli and spring onion for 1–2 minutes.

Add the tempeh to the wok and stir-fry for 5 minutes, or until golden.

Add the greens to the wok in two batches and cook until wilted.

VEGETARIAN PHAD THAI

Preparation time: 20 minutes
Total cooking time: 15 minutes
Serves 4

400 g (13 oz) flat rice-stick noodles
2 tablespoons peanut oil
2 eggs, lightly beaten
1 onion, cut into thin wedges
2 cloves garlic, crushed
1 small red capsicum, thinly sliced
100 g (3½ oz) deep-fried tofu puffs, cut into thin strips
6 spring onions, thinly sliced
½ cup (30 g/1 oz) chopped fresh coriander leaves

¼ cup (60 ml/2 fl oz) soy sauce
2 tablespoons lime juice
1 tablespoon soft brown sugar
2 teaspoons sambal oelek
1 cup (90 g/3 oz) bean shoots
3 tablespoons chopped roasted unsalted peanuts

1 Cook the noodles in a saucepan of boiling water for 5–10 minutes, or until tender. Drain and set aside.
2 Heat a wok over high heat and add enough peanut oil to coat the bottom and side. When smoking, add the egg and swirl to form a thin omelette. Cook for 30 seconds, or until just set. Roll up, remove and thinly slice.
3 Heat the remaining oil in the wok.

Add the onion, garlic and capsicum and cook over high heat for 2–3 minutes, or until the onion softens. Add the noodles, tossing well. Stir in the omelette, tofu, spring onion and half the coriander.
4 Pour in the combined soy sauce, lime juice, sugar and sambal oelek, then toss to coat the noodles. Sprinkle with the bean shoots and top with roasted peanuts and the remaining coriander. Serve immediately.

NUTRITION PER SERVE
Protein 13 g; Fat 21 g; Carbohydrate 34 g;
Dietary Fibre 5 g; Cholesterol 90 mg;
1565 kJ (375 cal)

Buy deep-fried tofu puffs (rather than silken or firm tofu) and cut into thin strips.

Cook the egg, swirling the wok, to make a thin omelette, then roll up and thinly slice.

Stir in the omelette, tofu, spring onion and fresh coriander.

VEGETARIAN CHILLI

Preparation time: 15 minutes
Total cooking time: 40 minutes
Serves 8

¾ cup (150 g/5 oz) burghul (cracked
    wheat)
1 tablespoon olive oil
1 large onion, finely chopped
2 cloves garlic, crushed
1 teaspoon chilli powder
2 teaspoons ground cumin
1 teaspoon cayenne pepper
½ teaspoon ground cinnamon
2 x 400 g (13 oz) cans crushed
    tomatoes
3 cups (750 ml/24 fl oz) vegetable stock

440 g (14 oz) can red kidney beans,
    rinsed and drained
2 x 300 g (10 oz) cans chickpeas,
    rinsed and drained
310 g (10 oz) can corn kernels,
    drained
2 tablespoons tomato paste
corn chips and light sour cream, for
    serving

1 Soak the burghul in 1 cup (250 ml/
8 fl oz) of hot water for 10 minutes.
Heat the oil in a large heavy-based
pan and cook the onion for 10
minutes, stirring often, until soft and
golden.
2 Add the garlic, chilli powder,
cumin, cayenne and cinnamon and
cook, stirring, for a further minute.

3 Add the tomatoes, stock and
burghul. Bring to the boil and simmer
for 10 minutes. Stir in the beans,
chickpeas, corn and tomato paste and
simmer for 20 minutes, stirring often.
Serve with corn chips and sour
cream.

NUTRITION PER SERVE
Protein 7 g; Fat 10 g; Carbohydrate 18 g;
Dietary Fibre 7 g; Cholesterol 8 mg;
780 kJ (185 cal)

STORAGE TIME: Chilli will keep for
up to 3 days in the refrigerator (and
can be frozen for up to 1 month).

Stir the garlic and spices into the pan with the
onion and cook for a minute.

Add the crushed tomatoes, stock and burghul to
the pan.

Stir in the beans, chickpeas, corn kernels and
tomato paste.

POTATO, LEEK AND SPINACH QUICHE

Preparation time: 1 hour +
50 minutes refrigeration
Total cooking time: 2 hours
Serves 6–8

2 cups (250 g/8 oz) plain flour
125 g (4 oz) cold butter, chopped

FILLING
3 potatoes
30 g (1 oz) butter
2 tablespoons oil
2 cloves garlic, crushed
2 leeks, sliced
500 g (1 lb) English spinach, trimmed
1 cup (125 g/4 oz) grated Cheddar
4 eggs
½ cup (125 ml/4 fl oz) cream
½ cup (125 ml/4 fl oz) milk

1 Place the flour in a food processor, add the butter and process for about 15 seconds until the mixture is crumbly. Add 2–3 tablespoons of water and process in short bursts until the mixture just comes together when you squeeze a little between your fingers. Add a little extra water if you think the dough is too dry. Turn out onto a floured surface and quickly bring the mixture together into a ball. Cover the pastry with plastic wrap and refrigerate for at least 30 minutes. Roll the pastry out between two sheets of baking paper until it is large enough to line a deep loose-based fluted flan tin measuring 21 cm (8½ inches) across the base. Place on a baking tray and refrigerate for 20 minutes.
2 Peel and thinly slice the potatoes. Melt the butter and oil together in a frying pan and add the garlic and sliced potatoes. Gently turn the potatoes until they are coated, then cover and cook for 5 minutes over low heat. Remove the potatoes with a slotted spoon, drain on paper towels and set aside. Add the leeks to the pan and cook until they are softened, then remove from the heat.
3 Wash the spinach and put in a large saucepan with just the water clinging to the leaves. Cover the pan and cook for 2 minutes, or until it has just wilted. Cool the spinach and squeeze out any excess water, then spread the leaves out on a paper towel or a tea towel to allow to dry.
4 Preheat the oven to moderate 180°C (350°F/Gas 4). Cover the pastry shell with baking paper and fill evenly with baking beads. Bake for 15 minutes. Remove the paper and beads and bake for a further 15 minutes.
5 Spread half the cheese over the bottom of the pastry base and top with half the potatoes, half the spinach and half the leeks. Repeat these layers again. In a large jug, mix together the eggs, cream and milk and pour over the layered mixture. Bake for 1 hour 20 minutes, or until the filling is firm. Serve warm or cold.

NUTRITION PER SERVE (8)
Protein 15 g; Fat 35 g; Carbohydrate 35 g;
Dietary Fibre 5 g; Cholesterol 180 mg;
2150 kJ (510 cal)

NOTE: Spinach can be kept in a plastic bag and stored for up to 3 days in the refrigerator. It can often be very gritty, so wash thoroughly in a few changes of water. When cooking the spinach, you don't need to add any extra water, just heat it with the water still clinging to the leaves.

Squeeze a little of the pastry with your fingers: it should stick together.

Roll the pastry out between two sheets of baking paper.

Lift out the potatoes with a slotted spoon and drain on paper towels.

Cover the pan and cook the spinach for 2 minutes, or until it has just wilted.

Use your hands to squeeze out the excess water from the cooled spinach.

Build up layers of cheese, potato, spinach and leek in the pastry case.

STIR-FRIED CRISP TOFU IN A HOT BEAN SAUCE

Preparation time: 35 minutes +
  30 minutes marinating
Total cooking time: 15 minutes
Serves 4

500 g (1 lb) firm tofu, cut into
    small cubes
2 tablespoons peanut oil
¼ cup (60 ml/2 fl oz) soy sauce
2 teaspoons finely grated fresh ginger
oil, for cooking
¾ cup (125 g/4 oz) rice flour
2 onions, cut into thin wedges
2 cloves garlic, finely chopped
2 teaspoons soft brown sugar
½ red capsicum, cut into short,
    thin strips
5 spring onions, cut into short pieces
2 tablespoons dry sherry
2 teaspoons finely grated orange rind
2 tablespoons hot bean paste

1 Place the tofu in a glass or ceramic bowl with the peanut oil. Add the soy sauce and ginger, cover and refrigerate for 30 minutes.
2 Drain the tofu, reserving the marinade, and toss several pieces at a time in the rice flour to coat heavily. Heat the wok until very hot, add about ¼ cup (60 ml/2 fl oz) of the oil and swirl it around to coat the side. Add the tofu to the hot oil and stir-fry over medium heat for 1½ minutes, or until golden all over. Remove from the wok and drain on paper towels. Repeat with the remaining tofu. Keep warm. Drain any oil from the wok.
3 Reheat the wok and stir-fry the onion, garlic and sugar for 3 minutes, or until golden. Add the capsicum,

spring onion, sherry, orange rind, bean paste and the reserved tofu marinade. Stir and bring to the boil. Return the tofu to the wok, toss to heat through, and serve.

NUTRITION PER SERVE
Protein 15 g; Fat 8 g; Carbohydrate 40 g;
Dietary Fibre 3 g; Cholesterol 0 mg;
1215 kJ (290 cal)

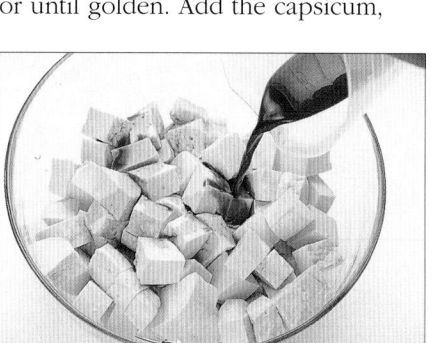

Marinate the tofu in the peanut oil and soy sauce for 30 minutes before cooking.

Drain the tofu in a sieve, then toss it in the rice flour to coat heavily.

Stir-fry the tofu until it is golden on all sides, then drain on paper towels.

PUMPKIN, LEEK AND CORN PIE

Preparation time: 30 minutes
+ cooling
Total cooking time: 1 hour 15 minutes
Serves 6

⅓ cup (80 ml/2¾ oz) olive oil
2 leeks, thinly sliced
2 large cloves garlic, chopped
1 butternut pumpkin (1.7 kg/3 lb 7 oz),
   peeled, seeded and cut into 1 cm
   (½ inch) cubes
3 corn cobs
1½ cups (185 g/6 oz) grated Cheddar
1 teaspoon chopped fresh rosemary
½ cup (15 g/½ oz) chopped fresh
   flat-leaf parsley
12 sheets filo pastry
5 eggs, lightly beaten

1 Preheat the oven to moderate 180°C (350°F/Gas 4). Grease a 32 x 24 cm (13 x 9 inch), 6 cm (2½ inch) deep, ovenproof dish.
2 Heat 1 tablespoon of the oil in a small saucepan and cook the leek and garlic over medium heat for 10 minutes, stirring occasionally, until soft and lightly golden. Transfer to a large bowl and allow to cool.
3 Meanwhile, cook the pumpkin in boiling water for 5 minutes, or until just tender. Drain well and cool. Cook the corn in a large saucepan of boiling water for 7–8 minutes, or until tender. Drain, leave until cool enough to handle, then cut away the kernels. Add these to the bowl with the pumpkin, Cheddar, rosemary and chopped parsley, season generously and mix gently but thoroughly.
4 Place the filo pastry on a clean workbench and cover with a damp tea towel to prevent the pastry drying out. Lightly brush one sheet of filo with oil and place in the dish. Layer five more sheets in the dish, brushing all but the last sheet with oil.
5 Gently stir the eggs into the pumpkin mixture, then spoon into the dish. Cover with the remaining filo pastry, again brushing each layer with oil, and tuck in the edges. Bake for 1 hour, or until the pastry is golden brown and the filling has set.

NUTRITION PER SERVE
Protein 22 g; Fat 29 g; Carbohydrate 37.5 g;
Dietary Fibre 6 g; Cholesterol 180.5 mg;
2080 kJ (495 Cal)

Spoon the pumpkin and corn mixture into the ovenproof dish.

Tuck the edges of the filo pastry into the side of the dish.

LENTIL RISSOLES

Preparation time: 20 minutes +
40 minutes cooling
Total cooking time: 45 minutes
Serves 4

1 tablespoon oil
1 onion, finely chopped
2 large cloves garlic, crushed
2 teaspoons ground cumin
1 teaspoon ground coriander
1 small carrot, finely diced
1 cup (250 g/8 oz) red lentils
1½ cups (120 g/4 oz) fresh wholemeal
   breadcrumbs
⅔ cup (60 g/2 oz) walnuts, finely
   chopped
½ cup (90 g/3 oz) frozen peas
3 tablespoons chopped fresh flat-leaf
   parsley
dry breadcrumbs, for coating
oil, for shallow-frying

1 Heat the oil in a large saucepan. Cook the onion, garlic, cumin and ground coriander over medium heat for 2 minutes, or until the onion has softened. Stir in the carrot, lentils and 2 cups (500 ml/16 fl oz) water. Slowly bring to the boil, then reduce the heat to low and simmer, covered, for 25–30 minutes, or until the lentils are cooked and pulpy, stirring frequently to stop them sticking and burning. Remove the lid during the last 10 minutes to evaporate any remaining liquid.
2 Transfer the mixture to a large bowl, cover with plastic wrap and cool for 10 minutes. Stir in the fresh breadcrumbs, walnuts, peas and parsley. Form into eight 8 cm (3 inch) round rissoles. Cover and refrigerate for 30 minutes, or until they are firm.
3 Evenly coat the rissoles in dry breadcrumbs, shaking off any excess. Heat 1 cm (½ inch) oil in a deep frying pan, add the rissoles and cook in two batches for 3 minutes each side, or until golden brown. Drain on crumpled paper towels, season with salt and serve with a salad.

NUTRITION PER SERVE
Protein 24 g; Fat 20 g; Carbohydrate 50 g; Dietary Fibre 14 g; Cholesterol 0 mg; 2014 kJ (480 cal)

Cover the pan and simmer the lentils until they are cooked and pulpy.

With clean hands, form the mixture into eight round rissoles.

BARBECUE VEGETABLE AND TOFU KEBABS

Preparation time: 40 minutes +
30 minutes marinating
Total cooking time: 30 minutes
Serves 4

500 g (1 lb) firm tofu, cubed
1 red capsicum, cubed
3 zucchini, thickly sliced
4 small onions, cut into quarters
300 g (10 oz) button mushrooms, cut
    into quarters
½ cup (125 ml/4 fl oz) tamari
½ cup (125 ml/4 fl oz) sesame oil
2.5 cm (1 inch) piece ginger, peeled
    and grated
½ cup (175 g/6 oz) honey

PEANUT SAUCE
1 tablespoon sesame oil
1 small onion, finely chopped
1 clove garlic, crushed
2 teaspoons chilli paste
1 cup (250 g/8 oz) smooth peanut
    butter
1 cup (250 ml/8 fl oz) coconut milk
1 tablespoon soft brown sugar
1 tablespoon tamari
1 tablespoon lemon juice
¼ cup (40 g/1¼ oz) peanuts, roasted
    and chopped
¼ cup (40 g/1¼ oz) sesame seeds,
    toasted

1 Soak 12 bamboo skewers in water for 2 hours. Thread the tofu, capsicum, zucchini, onions and mushrooms alternately onto the skewers. Lay out in a large flat dish.
2 Combine the tamari, oil, ginger and honey in a non-metallic bowl. Pour over the kebabs. Leave for 30 minutes. Cook on a hot barbecue or in a chargrill pan, basting and turning, for 10–15 minutes, or until tender. Remove and keep warm.
3 To make the peanut sauce, heat the oil in a large frying pan over medium heat and cook the onion, garlic and chilli paste for 1–2 minutes, or until the onion is soft. Reduce the heat, add the peanut butter, coconut milk, sugar, tamari and lemon juice and stir. Bring to the boil, then reduce the heat and simmer for 10 minutes, or until just thick. Stir in the peanuts. If the sauce is too thick, add water. Serve with the kebabs, sprinkled with sesame seeds.

NUTRITION PER SERVE
Protein 31.5 g; Fat 65 g; Carbohydrate 25.5 g; Dietary Fibre 15 g; Cholesterol 0 mg; 3334 kJ (795 cal)

Thread alternating pieces of tofu and vegetables onto the skewers.

Cook the skewers on a barbecue, occasionally turning and basting them.

Simmer the peanut sauce for 10 minutes, or until just thickened.

THAI TEMPEH

Preparation time: 15 minutes + overnight marinating
Total cooking time: 20 minutes
Serves 4

THAI MARINADE
2 stems lemon grass,
    finely chopped
2 kaffir lime leaves, shredded
2 small red chillies, seeded and finely
    chopped
3 cloves garlic, crushed
2 teaspoons sesame oil
½ cup (125 ml/4 fl oz) lime juice
2 teaspoons shaved palm sugar
½ cup (125 ml/4 fl oz) soy sauce

600 g (1¼ lb) tofu tempeh, cut into
    twelve 5 mm (¼ inch) slices
3 tablespoons peanut oil
1 tablespoon shaved palm sugar
100 g (3½ oz) snow pea sprouts or
    watercress
kaffir lime leaves, finely shredded

1 To make the Thai marinade, mix the lemon grass, lime leaves, chilli, garlic, sesame oil, lime juice, sugar and soy sauce in a non-metallic bowl. Add the tempeh. Cover and marinate overnight in the fridge, turning occasionally.
2 Drain the tempeh, reserving the marinade. Heat half the peanut oil in a frying pan over high heat. Cook the tempeh in batches, turning once, for 5 minutes, or until crispy, adding more oil when needed. Drain on paper towels. Heat the reserved marinade with the palm sugar in a saucepan until syrupy.

3 Put a slice of tempeh on each serving plate and top with some snow pea sprouts. Continue the layers, finishing with the tempeh on top. Drizzle with the reserved marinade and sprinkle with lime leaves.

NUTRITION PER SERVE
Protein 9.5 g; Fat 20 g; Carbohydrate 7 g;
Dietary Fibre 1.5 g; Cholesterol 0 mg;
1102 kJ (262 cal)

Cook the slices of tempeh in batches, turning once, until they are crispy.

Heat the reserved marinade and palm sugar in a saucepan until the mixture is syrupy.

GRILLED POLENTA WITH WILD MUSHROOMS

Preparation time: 30 minutes + chilling
Total cooking time: 1 hour 20 minutes
Serves 6–8

2½ cups (600 ml/20 fl oz) vegetable
    stock
2 cups (300 g/10 oz) polenta
100 g (3½ oz) Parmesan, grated

MUSHROOM SAUCE
1 kg (2 lb) mixed mushrooms (roman,
    oyster and flat)
½ cup (125 ml/4 fl oz) olive oil
½ cup (15 g/½ oz) chopped parsley
4 cloves garlic, finely chopped
1 onion, chopped

1 Put the stock and 2 cups (500 ml/ 16 fl oz) water in a large pan and bring to the boil. Add the polenta and stir constantly for 10 minutes until very thick. Remove from the heat and stir in the Parmesan. Brush a 20 cm (8 inch) round springform tin with oil. Spread the polenta into the tin and smooth the surface. Refrigerate for 2 hours, turn out and cut into 6–8 wedges.

2 To make the sauce, wipe the mushrooms with a damp cloth and roughly chop the larger ones. Put the mushrooms, oil, parsley, garlic and onion in a pan. Stir, cover and leave to simmer for 50 minutes, or until cooked through. Uncover and cook for 10 minutes, or until there is very little liquid left. Set aside.

3 Brush one side of the polenta with olive oil and cook under a preheated grill for 5 minutes, or until the edges are browned. Turn over and brown. Reheat the mushroom sauce and serve spooned over slices of polenta.

NUTRITION PER SERVE (6)
Protein 11 g; Fat 20 g; Carbohydrate 11 g;
Dietary Fibre 4 g; Cholesterol 12 mg;
1103 kJ (214 cal)

Stir the polenta until very thick, remove from the heat and add the Parmesan.

Refrigerate the tin of polenta for 2 hours, then turn out and cut into wedges.

Uncover the mushrooms and let them simmer for 10 minutes, until little liquid is left.

SUMMER BREAD SALAD

Preparation time: 20 minutes
Total cooking time: 15 minutes
Serves 6–8

2 red capsicums
2 yellow capsicums
6 Roma (egg or plum) tomatoes, cut into large chunks
100 g (3½ oz) capers, drained
100 g (3½ oz) black olives
150 g (5 oz) bocconcini, halved
1 Italian wood-fired loaf
2 cups (60 g/2 oz) basil leaves

DRESSING
4 cloves garlic, finely chopped
¼ cup (60 ml/2 fl oz) red wine vinegar
½ cup (125 ml/4 fl oz) extra virgin olive oil

1 Cut the capsicums into large pieces, removing the seeds and white membrane. Place, skin-side-up, under a hot grill, until the skin blackens and blisters. Cool in a plastic bag or under a tea towel, then peel away the skin and cut into thick strips.
2 Put the capsicum, tomato, capers, olives and bocconcini in a bowl and toss to combine.

3 Put the dressing ingredients in a screw-top jar and shake well.
4 Cut the bread into large pieces and put in a bowl. Drizzle with the dressing and mix until well coated. Toss gently with the capsicum mixture and basil leaves.

NUTRITION PER SERVE (8)
Protein 15 g; Fat 25 g; Carbohydrate 35 g; Dietary Fibre 4 g; Cholesterol 25 mg; 1870 kJ (445 cal)

NOTE: This dish is based on the Tuscan favourite that uses leftover crusty bread to make a salad.

Put the grilled capsicum pieces in a plastic bag until cool enough to handle.

Put the grilled capsicum, tomato, capers, olives and bocconcini in a bowl and toss together.

Using a bread knife, cut the wood-fired loaf into large pieces.

GREEN CURRY WITH SWEET POTATO AND EGGPLANT

Preparation time: 15 minutes
Total cooking time: 25 minutes
Serves 4–6

1 tablespoon oil
1 onion, chopped
1–2 tablespoons green curry paste
   (see NOTE)
1 eggplant, quartered and sliced
1½ cups (375 ml/12 fl oz) coconut milk
1 cup (250 ml/8 fl oz) vegetable stock
6 kaffir lime leaves
1 orange sweet potato, cubed

2 teaspoons soft brown sugar
2 tablespoons lime juice
2 teaspoons lime rind

1 Heat the oil in a large wok or frying pan. Add the onion and green curry paste and cook, stirring, over medium heat for 3 minutes. Add the eggplant and cook for a further 4–5 minutes, or until softened.
2 Pour in the coconut milk and vegetable stock, bring to the boil, then reduce the heat and simmer for 5 minutes. Add the kaffir lime leaves and sweet potato and cook for 10 minutes, or until the eggplant and sweet potato are very tender.
3 Mix in the sugar, lime juice and

lime rind until well combined with the vegetables. Season to taste with salt and serve with steamed rice.

NUTRITION PER SERVE (6)
Protein 2.5 g; Fat 17 g; Carbohydrate 10 g; Dietary Fibre 3 g; Cholesterol 0.5 mg; 835 kJ (200 cal)

NOTE: Strict vegetarians should be sure to read the label and choose a green curry paste that doesn't contain shrimp paste. Alternatively, make your own curry pastes.

Eggplants are also known as aubergines. Use a sharp knife to quarter and slice the eggplant.

Stir-fry the onion and curry paste over medium heat for 3 minutes.

Cook, stirring occasionally, until the vegetables are tender.

SPICY VEGETABLE STEW WITH DHAL

**Preparation time: 25 minutes +
2 hours soaking
Total cooking time: 1 hour 35 minutes
Serves 4–6**

DHAL
¾ cup (165 g/5½ oz) yellow split peas
5 cm (2 inch) piece of ginger, grated
2–3 cloves garlic, crushed
1 red chilli, seeded and chopped

3 tomatoes
2 tablespoons oil
1 teaspoon yellow mustard seeds
1 teaspoon cumin seeds
1 teaspoon ground cumin
½ teaspoon garam masala
1 red onion, cut into thin wedges
3 slender eggplants, thickly sliced
2 carrots, thickly sliced
¼ cauliflower, cut into florets
1½ cups (375 ml/12 fl oz) vegetable
    stock
2 small zucchini, thickly sliced
½ cup (90 g/3 oz) frozen peas
½ cup (15 g/½ oz) fresh coriander
    leaves

1 To make the dhal, put the split peas in a bowl, cover with water and soak for 2 hours. Drain. Place in a large saucepan with the ginger, garlic, chilli and 3 cups (750 ml/24 fl oz) water. Bring to the boil, reduce the heat and simmer for 45 minutes, or until soft.
2 Score a cross in the base of each tomato, soak in boiling water for 30 seconds, then plunge into cold water and peel the skin away from the cross. Deseed and roughly chop.
3 Heat the oil in a large saucepan.

Cook the spices over medium heat for 30 seconds, or until fragrant. Add the onion and cook for 2 minutes, or until the onion is soft. Stir in the tomato, eggplant, carrot and cauliflower.
4 Add the dhal and stock, mix together well and simmer, covered, for 45 minutes, or until the vegetables are tender. Stir occasionally. Add the

zucchini and peas during the last 10 minutes of cooking. Stir in the coriander leaves and serve hot.

NUTRITION PER SERVE (6)
Protein 11 g; Fat 7 g; Carbohydrate 20 g;
Dietary Fibre 8.5 g; Cholesterol 17 mg;
780 kJ (186 cal)

Simmer the dhal for 45 minutes, or until the split peas are soft.

Score a cross in the top of each tomato, then soak in hot water to make the skin come away.

Add the dhal and stock to the stew and simmer for 45 minutes, or until the vegetables are tender.

MUSHROOM NUT ROAST WITH TOMATO SAUCE

Preparation time: 25 minutes
Total cooking time: 50 minutes
Serves 6

2 tablespoons olive oil
1 large onion, diced
2 cloves garlic, crushed
300 g (10 oz) cap mushrooms, finely
    chopped
200 g (6½ oz) cashew nuts
200 g (6½ oz) brazil nuts
1 cup (125 g/4 oz) grated Cheddar
30 g (1 oz) Parmesan, grated
1 egg, lightly beaten
2 tablespoons chopped fresh chives

1 cup (80 g/2¾ oz) fresh wholemeal
    breadcrumbs

TOMATO SAUCE
1½ tablespoons olive oil
1 onion, finely chopped
1 clove garlic, crushed
400 g (13 oz) can chopped tomatoes
1 tablespoon tomato paste
1 teaspoon caster sugar

1 Preheat the oven to moderate
180°C (350°F/Gas 4). Grease a 15 x
20 cm (6 x 8 inch) tin and line with
baking paper. Heat the oil in a frying
pan and fry the onion, garlic and
mushrooms over medium heat for
2–3 minutes, or until soft. Cool.
2 Finely chop the nuts in a food

processor, but do not overprocess.
3 Combine the nuts, mushroom
mixture, cheeses, egg, chives and
breadcrumbs in a bowl. Press into the
tin and bake for 45 minutes until firm.
Leave for 5 minutes, then turn out.
4 Meanwhile, to make the sauce, heat
the oil in a frying pan and add the
onion and garlic. Cook over low heat
for 5 minutes, or until soft. Add the
tomato, tomato paste, sugar and
⅓ cup (80 ml) water. Simmer for
3–5 minutes, or until thick. Season.
Serve with the sliced roast.

NUTRITION PER SERVE
Protein 18 g; Fat 44 g; Carbohydrate 16 g;
Dietary Fibre 6.5 g; Cholesterol 55 mg;
2195 kJ (525 cal)

Finely chop the cashews and brazil nuts in a food
processor but don't overprocess.

Press the nutty mushroom mixture into the
prepared tin.

Simmer the tomato sauce for 3–5 minutes, or
until thickened.

MOROCCAN TAGINE WITH COUSCOUS

Preparation time: 20 minutes
Total cooking time: 1 hour
Serves 4–6

2 tablespoons oil
2 onions, chopped
1 teaspoon ground ginger
2 teaspoons ground paprika
2 teaspoons ground cumin
1 cinnamon stick
pinch of saffron threads
1.5 kg (3 lb) vegetables, peeled
   and cut into large chunks (carrot,
   eggplant, orange sweet potato,
   parsnip, potato, pumpkin)
½ preserved lemon, rinsed, pith and
   flesh removed, thinly sliced
400 g (13 oz) can peeled tomatoes
1 cup (250 ml/8 fl oz) vegetable stock
100 g (3½ oz) dried pears, halved
60 g (2 oz) pitted prunes
2 zucchini, cut into large chunks
300 g (10 oz) instant couscous
1 tablespoon olive oil
3 tablespoons chopped fresh flat-leaf
   parsley
⅓ cup (50 g/1¾ oz) almonds

1 Preheat the oven to moderate 180°C (350°F/Gas 4). Heat the oil in a large saucepan or ovenproof dish, add the onion and cook over medium heat for 5 minutes, or until soft. Add the spices and cook for 3 minutes.
2 Add the vegetables and cook, stirring, until coated with the spices and the outside begins to soften. Add the lemon, tomatoes, stock, pears and prunes. Cover, transfer to the oven and cook for 30 minutes. Add the zucchini and cook for 15–20 minutes, or until the vegetables are tender.

3 Cover the couscous with the olive oil and 2 cups (500 ml/16 fl oz) boiling water and leave until all the water has been absorbed. Flake with a fork.
4 Remove the cinnamon stick from the vegetables, then stir in the parsley. Serve on a large platter with

the couscous formed into a ring and the vegetable tagine in the centre, sprinkled with the almonds.

NUTRITION PER SERVE (6)
Protein 8 g; Fat 15 g; Carbohydrate 33 g;
Dietary Fibre 9 g; Cholesterol 0 mg;
1240 kJ (296 cal)

Cook the vegetables until they are coated in spices and the outside starts to soften.

Once all the water has been absorbed, flake the couscous with a fork.

Before serving, remove the cinnamon stick with a pair of tongs.

LENTIL AND CAULIFLOWER CURRY STACKS

Preparation time: 15 minutes
Total cooking time: 50 minutes
Serves 6

60 g (2 oz) ghee or butter
2 onions, thinly sliced
2 tablespoons Madras curry paste
2 cloves garlic, crushed
180 g (6 oz) button mushrooms, sliced
1 litre (32 fl oz) vegetable stock
300 g (10 oz) brown or green lentils
400 g (13 oz) can chopped tomatoes
2 cinnamon sticks
300 g (10 oz) cauliflower, cut into small
    florets
oil, for deep-frying
18 small (8 cm/3 inch) pappadums
plain yoghurt and coriander, to serve

1 Heat the ghee in a large pan over medium heat and cook the onion for 2–3 minutes, or until soft. Add the curry paste, garlic and mushrooms and cook for 2 minutes, or until soft.

2 Add the stock, lentils, tomato and cinnamon and mix well. Bring to the boil and cook for 40 minutes, or until the lentils are tender. Add the cauliflower in the last 10 minutes and cover. If the curry is too wet, continue to cook, uncovered, until the excess liquid has evaporated. Season to taste with salt and cracked black pepper. Remove the cinnamon.

3 Meanwhile, fill a deep heavy-based saucepan one third full of oil and heat until a cube of bread dropped into the oil browns in 15 seconds. Cook the pappadums in batches for 10 seconds, or until golden brown and puffed all over. Drain on crumpled paper towels and season with salt.

4 To assemble, place a pappadum on each serving plate and spoon on a little of the curry. Place a second pappadum on top and spoon on some more curry. Cover with the remaining pappadum and top with a spoonful of yoghurt. Garnish with coriander sprigs and serve immediately (the pappadums will become soggy if left to stand for too long.)

NUTRITION PER SERVE
Protein 16 g; Fat 13 g; Carbohydrate 23 g;
Dietary Fibre 10 g; Cholesterol 24 mg;
1144 kJ (273 cal)

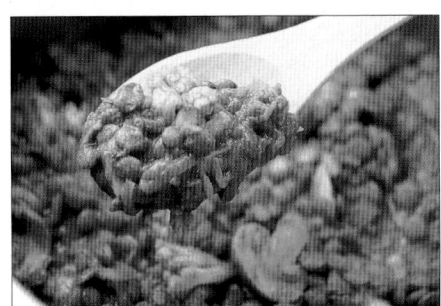
If the curry is too wet, continue cooking to evaporate the excess liquid.

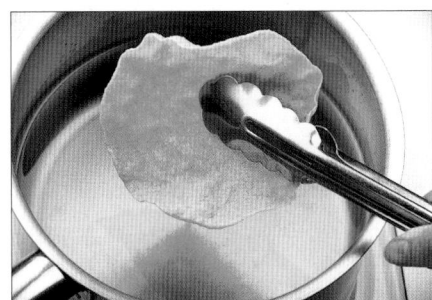
Drop the pappadums into the oil and cook until puffed and golden.

Pestos & tapenades

They are best known as pasta sauces, but pestos and tapenades are also great for spicing up vegetables and soups or serving as dips. Sterilise your jars first with boiling water, then dry in a warm oven.

TRADITIONAL PESTO

Whiz 2 cups (60 g/2 oz) basil leaves, ¼ cup (40 g/1¼ oz) lightly toasted pine nuts, 2 coarsely chopped large cloves of garlic and a pinch of salt in a food processor or blender. With the motor running, slowly pour in ⅓ cup (80 ml/2¾ fl oz) extra virgin olive oil. Add ½ cup (50 g/1¾ oz) freshly grated Parmesan and some black pepper and process until just combined. Transfer to a sterilised jar and cover the surface with a thin layer of extra virgin olive oil. Seal and refrigerate for up to a week. Serve as a pasta sauce, a dip, or a dressing for vegetables. Makes about 1 cup (250 g/ 8 oz).

RED PESTO

Put a 200 g (6½ oz) jar sun-dried tomatoes in oil, ⅓ cup (10 g/¼ oz) fresh basil leaves, ⅓ cup (7 g/¼ oz) fresh flat-leaf parsley leaves, 2 chopped cloves garlic, 2 teaspoons rinsed and drained capers and 4 tablespoons lightly toasted pine nuts in a food processor or blender. Process until finely minced. Keep the motor running while you pour in 2 tablespoons red wine vinegar and ½ cup (125 ml/4 fl oz) extra virgin olive oil. When these are thoroughly blended, add 2 tablespoons freshly grated Parmesan and some pepper. Transfer to a sterilised jar and cover the surface with a thin coating of extra virgin olive oil. Seal and refrigerate for up to 2 weeks. Serve as a pasta sauce if thinned with a little more olive oil, or a dip for crudités. Makes about 1¼ cups (310 g/10 oz).

ROCKET AND PECAN PESTO

Whiz 60 g (2 oz) young rocket leaves, ⅓ cup (7 g/¼ oz) flat-leaf parsley, 12 large pecan halves and 2 coarsely chopped large cloves garlic in a food processor or blender. With the motor running, slowly pour in ½ cup (125 ml/4 fl oz) extra virgin olive oil. Add ⅓ cup (35 g/1¼ oz) grated Parmesan and mix well. Lightly season with salt. Put the pesto in a sterilised jar and cover the surface with a thin coating of extra virgin olive oil. Seal and refrigerate for up to a week. Serve as a dip with crudités and crusty bread or as a pasta sauce. Makes about ¾ cup (185 g/6 oz).

From left to right: Traditional pesto; Red pesto; Rocket and pecan pesto; Olive tapenade; North African tapenade.

OLIVE TAPENADE

Place 1 tablespoon rinsed and drained capers, 1 small clove garlic, 1 cup (125 g/4 oz) sliced pitted black or green olives and 2 tablespoons lemon juice in a food processor or blender. Process until finely chopped. While the motor is still running, pour in 2 tablespoons extra virgin olive oil and 1½ tablespoons Cognac. Season to taste with black pepper. Transfer to a sterilised jar. Seal and refrigerate for up to 2 weeks. Serve as a spread for bread or with crudités.
Makes about 1¼ cups (310 g/10 oz).

NORTH AFRICAN TAPENADE

Put a pinch of saffron in a small bowl with 1 teaspoon hot water and set aside. Whiz ⅔ cup (140 g/4½ oz) pitted green olives, ¼ teaspoon dried oregano, 2 tablespoons toasted pine nuts, 1 chopped clove garlic and ⅛ teaspoon ground cumin in a food processor or blender. With the motor running, add 3 teaspoons lime juice, 3 tablespoons extra virgin olive oil and the saffron and water mixture. Stop processing as soon as the ingredients are blended and transfer to a sterilised jar. Seal and store in the refrigerator for up to 2 weeks. Delicious as a pasta sauce when thinned with a little more olive oil, or on bruschetta.
Makes about 1 cup (250 g/8 oz).

TOFU BURGERS

Preparation time: 25 minutes +
   30 minutes refrigeration
Total cooking time: 30 minutes
Serves 6

1 tablespoon olive oil
1 red onion, finely chopped
200 g (6½ oz) Swiss brown
   mushrooms, finely chopped
350 g (11 oz) hard tofu (see NOTE)
2 large cloves garlic
3 tablespoons chopped fresh basil
2 cups (200 g/6½ oz) dry wholemeal
   breadcrumbs
1 egg, lightly beaten
2 tablespoons balsamic vinegar
2 tablespoons sweet chilli sauce
1½ cups (150 g/5 oz) dry wholemeal
   breadcrumbs, extra
olive oil, for shallow-frying
6 wholemeal or wholegrain bread rolls
½ cup (125 g/4 oz) mayonnaise
100 g (3½ oz) semi-dried tomatoes
60 g (2 oz) rocket leaves
sweet chilli sauce, to serve

1 Heat the oil in a frying pan and cook the onion over medium heat for 2–3 minutes, or until soft. Add the mushrooms and cook for a further 2 minutes. Cool slightly.
2 Blend 250 g (8 oz) of the tofu with the garlic and basil in a food processor until smooth. Transfer to a large bowl and stir in the onion mixture, bread-crumbs, egg, vinegar and sweet chilli sauce. Grate the remaining tofu and fold through the mixture, then refrigerate for 30 minutes. Divide the mixture into six and form into patties, pressing together well. Coat them in the extra breadcrumbs.
3 Heat 1 cm (½ inch) oil in a deep frying pan and cook the patties in two batches for 4–5 minutes each side, or until golden. Turn carefully to prevent them breaking up. Drain on crumpled paper towels and season with salt.
4 Halve the bread rolls and toast under a hot grill. Spread mayonnaise over both sides of each roll. Layer semi-dried tomatoes, a tofu patty and rocket leaves in each roll and drizzle with sweet chilli sauce.

NUTRITION PER SERVE
Protein 23 g; Fat 24 g; Carbohydrate 86 g;
Dietary Fibre 10 g; Cholesterol 37 mg;
2740 kJ (653 cal)

NOTE: Hard tofu (not to be confused with 'firm' tofu) is quite rubbery and firm and won't break up during cooking. It's perfect for patties, stir-frying and pan-frying.

Mix the tofu, garlic and basil in a food processor until smooth.

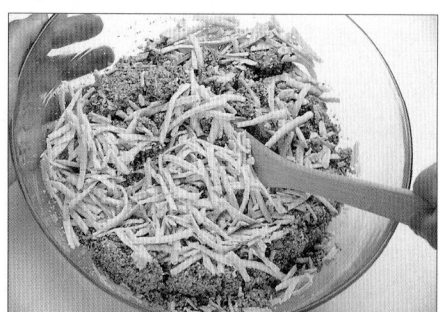

Grate the remaining hard tofu and fold it into the mixture. Refrigerate for 30 minutes.

Be careful when you turn the patties during frying. You don't want them to break up.

BEAN AND CAPSICUM STEW

Preparation time: 20 minutes + overnight
   soaking
Total cooking time: 1 hour 35 minutes
Serves 4–6

1 cup (200 g/6½ oz) dried haricot
   beans (see NOTE)
2 tablespoons olive oil
2 large cloves garlic, crushed
1 red onion, halved and cut into thin
   wedges
1 red capsicum, cubed
1 green capsicum, cubed
2 x 400 g (13 oz) cans chopped
   tomatoes
2 tablespoons tomato paste
2 cups (500 ml/16 fl oz) vegetable
   stock
2 tablespoons chopped fresh basil
⅔ cup (125 g/4 oz) Kalamata olives,
   pitted
1–2 teaspoons soft brown sugar

1 Put the beans in a large bowl,
cover with cold water and soak
overnight. Rinse well, then transfer to
a saucepan, cover with cold water
and cook for 45 minutes, or until just
tender. Drain.
2 Heat the oil in a large saucepan.
Cook the garlic and onion over
medium heat for 2–3 minutes, or until
the onion is soft. Add the red and
green capsicums and cook for a
further 5 minutes.
3 Stir in the tomato, tomato paste,
stock and beans. Simmer, covered, for

40 minutes, or until the beans are
cooked through. Stir in the basil,
olives and sugar. Season with salt and
pepper. Serve hot with crusty bread.

NUTRITION PER SERVE (6)
Protein 10 g; Fat 8 g; Carbohydrate 20 g;
Dietary Fibre 9.5 g; Cholesterol 0 mg;
825 kJ (197 cal)

NOTE: 1 cup of dried haricot beans
yields about 2½ cups cooked beans.
So use 2½ cups tinned haricot or
borlotti beans instead if you prefer.

Cook the garlic and onion until the garlic is soft,
then add the capsicum.

Simmer the stew for 40 minutes, or until the
beans are cooked through.

ROAST VEGETABLE QUICHE

**Preparation time: 45 minutes
+ 25 minutes refrigeration
Total cooking time: 2 hours
30 minutes
Serves 6**

cooking oil spray
1 large potato
400 g (13 oz) pumpkin
200 g (6½ oz) orange sweet potato
2 large parsnips
1 red capsicum
2 onions, cut into wedges
6 cloves garlic, halved
2 teaspoons olive oil
1¼ cups (150 g/5 oz) plain flour
40 g (1¼ oz) butter
45 g (1½ oz) ricotta
1 cup (250 ml/8 fl oz) skim milk
3 eggs, lightly beaten
¼ cup (30 g/1 oz) grated reduced-fat
   Cheddar
2 tablespoons chopped fresh basil

1 Preheat the oven to moderate 180°C (350°F/Gas 4). Lightly spray a 3.5 cm (1¼ inch) deep, 23 cm (9 inch) diameter loose-based flan tin with oil. Cut the potato, pumpkin, sweet potato, parsnips and capsicum into bite-sized chunks, place in a baking dish with the onion and garlic and drizzle with the oil. Season and bake for 1 hour, or until the vegetables are tender. Leave to cool.

2 Mix the flour, butter and ricotta in a food processor, then gradually add up to 3 tablespoons of the milk, enough to form a soft dough. Turn out onto a lightly floured surface and gather together into a smooth ball. Cover and refrigerate for 15 minutes.

3 Roll the pastry out on a lightly floured surface, then ease into the tin, bringing it gently up the side. Trim the edge and refrigerate for another 10 minutes. Increase the oven to moderately hot 200°C (400°F/Gas 6). Cover the pastry with crumpled baking paper and fill with baking beads or uncooked rice. Bake for 10 minutes, remove the beads or rice and paper, then bake for another 10 minutes, or until golden brown.

4 Place the vegetables in the pastry base and pour in the combined remaining milk, eggs, cheese and basil. Reduce the oven temperature to moderate 180°C (350°F/Gas 4) and bake for 1 hour 10 minutes, or until set in the centre. Leave for 5 minutes before removing from the tin to serve.

NUTRITION PER SERVE
Protein 15 g; Fat 10 g; Carbohydrate 45 g;
Dietary Fibre 5.5 g; Cholesterol 115 mg;
1440 kJ (345 cal)

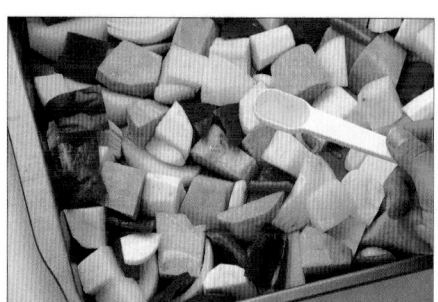

Put the vegetables in a baking dish and drizzle with the olive oil.

Ease the pastry into the flan tin, bring it up the side, then trim the edge.

Mix the milk, eggs, cheese and basil and pour over the vegetables.

![Curried lentils in a bowl garnished with bay leaves]

CURRIED LENTILS

Preparation time: 15 minutes
Total cooking time: 30 minutes
Serves 4

1 cup (250 g/8 oz) red lentils
2 cups (500 ml/16 fl oz) vegetable
  stock
½ teaspoon ground turmeric
50 g (1¾ oz) ghee
1 onion, chopped
2 cloves garlic, finely chopped
1 large green chilli, seeded and finely
  chopped

2 teaspoons ground cumin
2 teaspoons ground coriander
2 tomatoes, chopped
½ cup (125 ml/4 fl oz) coconut milk

1 Rinse the lentils and drain well. Place the lentils, stock and turmeric in a large heavy-based pan. Bring to the boil, reduce the heat and simmer, covered, for 10 minutes, or until just tender. Stir occasionally and check the mixture is not catching on the bottom of the pan.
2 Meanwhile, heat the ghee in a small frying pan and add the onion. Cook until soft and golden and add the garlic, chilli, cumin and coriander. Cook, stirring, for 2–3 minutes until fragrant. Stir the onions and spices into the lentil mixture and then add the tomato. Simmer over very low heat for 5 minutes, stirring frequently.
3 Season to taste and add the coconut milk. Stir until heated through. Serve with naan bread or rice.

NUTRITION PER SERVE
Protein 15 g; Fat 20 g; Carbohydrate 25 g; Dietary Fibre 10 g; Cholesterol 35 mg; 1500 kJ (355 cal)

Stir the lentil mixture occasionally so that it does not stick to the bottom of the pan.

Add the chopped tomato and simmer over very low heat for 5 minutes.

Season the lentils and add the coconut milk. Stir until heated through.

DRY POTATO AND PEA CURRY

Preparation time: 15 minutes
Total cooking time: 20–25 minutes
Serves 4

2 teaspoons brown mustard seeds
2 tablespoons ghee or oil
2 onions, sliced
2 cloves garlic, crushed
2 teaspoons grated fresh ginger
1 teaspoon ground turmeric
½ teaspoon chilli powder

1 teaspoon ground cumin
1 teaspoon garam masala
750 g (1½ lb) potatoes, cubed
⅔ cup (100 g/3½ oz) peas
2 tablespoons chopped mint

1 Heat the mustard seeds in a dry pan until they start to pop. Add the ghee or oil, onion, garlic and ginger and cook, stirring, until the onion is soft.
2 Add the turmeric, chilli powder, cumin, garam marsala and potato, and season with salt and pepper. Stir until the potato is coated with the spice mixture. Add 125 ml (4 fl oz) water and simmer, covered, for about 15–20 minutes, or until the potato is just tender. Stir occasionally to stop the curry sticking to the bottom of the pan.
3 Add the peas and stir until well combined. Simmer, covered, for 3–5 minutes, or until the potato is cooked and all the liquid is absorbed. Stir in the mint and season well.

NUTRITION PER SERVE
Protein 5 g; Fat 10 g; Carbohydrate 30 g;
Dietary Fibre 5 g; Cholesterol 25 mg;
985 kJ (235 cal)

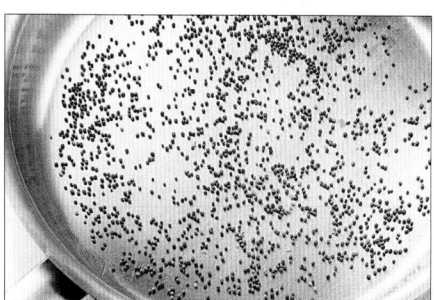

Fry the mustard seeds in a dry pan until they begin to pop.

Add the potato cubes and stir until they are well coated in the spice mixture.

Stir in the chopped mint before seasoning with salt and pepper, to taste.

BEAN NACHOS

Preparation time: 20 minutes
Total cooking time: 10 minutes
Serves 4

4 large ripe tomatoes
2 ripe avocados, mashed
1 tablespoon lime juice
1 tablespoon sweet chilli sauce
1 tablespoon oil
2 small red onions, diced
1 small red chilli, chopped
2 teaspoons ground oregano
2 teaspoons ground cumin
¼ teaspoon chilli powder
1 tablespoon tomato paste

1 cup (250 ml/8 fl oz) white wine
2 x 440 g (14 oz) cans red kidney
  beans, rinsed and drained
3 tablespoons chopped fresh
  coriander leaves
200 g (6½ oz) packet corn chips
⅔ cup (90 g/3 oz) grated Cheddar
sour cream, to serve

1 Score a cross in the base of each tomato. Put them in a bowl of boiling water for 30 seconds, then plunge into cold water and peel the skin away from the cross. Cut in half and scoop out the seeds with a teaspoon. Chop the tomato flesh.

2 Mix together the avocado, lime juice and sweet chilli sauce.

3 Heat the oil in a large frying pan. Cook the onion, chilli, oregano, cumin and chilli powder over medium heat for 2 minutes. Add the tomato, tomato paste and wine and cook for 5 minutes, or until the liquid reduces. Add the beans and coriander.

4 Divide the corn chips into four portions on heatproof plates. Top with the bean mixture and sprinkle with cheese. Flash under a hot grill until the cheese melts. Serve with the avocado mixture and sour cream.

NUTRITION PER SERVE
Protein 26 g; Fat 35 g; Carbohydrate 53 g;
Dietary Fibre 20 g; Cholesterol 20 mg;
2845 kJ (680 cal)

Scoop out the seeds of the tomatoes and roughly chop the flesh.

Cook the onion, chilli, oregano and spices in a large frying pan.

Cook the mixture until the liquid is reduced and the tomato is soft.

SUMMER POTATO PIZZA

Preparation time: 30 minutes
Total cooking time: 40 minutes
Serves 6

7 g (¼ oz) sachet dry yeast
2½ cups (310 g/10 oz) plain flour
2 teaspoons polenta or semolina
2 tablespoons olive oil
2 cloves garlic, crushed
4–5 potatoes, unpeeled, thinly sliced
1 tablespoon fresh rosemary leaves

1 Preheat the oven to hot 210°C (415°F/Gas 6–7). Combine the yeast, ½ teaspoon of salt and sugar and 1 cup (250 ml/8 fl oz) of warm water in a bowl. Cover and leave in a warm place for 10 minutes, or until foamy. Sift the flour into a bowl, make a well in the centre, add the yeast mixture and mix to a dough.
2 Turn the dough out onto a lightly floured surface and knead for 5 minutes, or until smooth and elastic. Roll out to a 30 cm (12 inch) circle. Lightly spray a pizza tray with oil and sprinkle with polenta or semolina.

3 Place the pizza base on the tray. Mix 2 teaspoons of the oil with the garlic and brush over the pizza base. Gently toss the remaining olive oil, potato slices, rosemary leaves, 1 teaspoon of salt and some pepper in a bowl.
4 Arrange the potato slices in overlapping circles over the pizza base and bake for 40 minutes, or until the base is crisp and golden.

NUTRITION PER SERVE
Protein 9 g; Fat 10 g; Carbohydrate 50 g;
Dietary Fibre 4 g; Cholesterol 0 mg;
1415 kJ (340 cal)

Leave the yeast mixture in a warm place until it becomes foamy—this shows it is active.

Knead the dough until firm and elastic, then roll out to fit a pizza tray.

Brush the dough base with garlic oil, then top with a layer of potato slices.

BEAN ENCHILADAS

Preparation time: 20 minutes
Total cooking time: 25 minutes
Serves 4

1 tablespoon light olive oil
1 onion, finely sliced
3 cloves garlic, crushed
1 fresh bird's-eye chilli, finely chopped
2 teaspoons ground cumin
½ cup (125 ml/4 fl oz) vegetable stock
3 tomatoes, peeled, seeded and chopped
1 tablespoon tomato paste
2 x 430 g (14 oz) cans three-bean mix
2 tablespoons chopped fresh coriander leaves
8 flour tortillas
1 small avocado, peeled and chopped
½ cup (125 g/4 oz) light sour cream
½ cup (10 g/¼ oz) fresh coriander sprigs
2 cups (115 g/4 oz) shredded lettuce

1 Heat the oil in a deep frying pan over medium heat. Add the onion and cook for 3–4 minutes, or until just soft. Add the garlic and chilli and cook for a further 30 seconds. Add the cumin, vegetable stock, tomato and tomato paste and cook for 6–8 minutes, or until the mixture is quite thick and pulpy. Season with salt and freshly ground black pepper.
2 Preheat the oven to warm 170°C (325°F/Gas 3). Drain and rinse the beans. Add the beans to the sauce and cook for 5 minutes to heat through, then add the chopped coriander.
3 Meanwhile, wrap the tortillas in foil and warm in the oven for 3–4 minutes.
4 Place a tortilla on a plate and spread with ¼ cup of the bean mixture. Top with some avocado, sour cream, coriander sprigs and lettuce. Roll the enchiladas up, tucking in the ends. Cut each one in half to serve.

NUTRITION PER SERVE
Protein 17 g; Fat 23 g; Carbohydrate 47 g;
Dietary Fibre 13.5 g; Cholesterol 20 mg;
1910 kJ (455 Cal)

Cook the tomato sauce until the mixture is thick and pulpy.

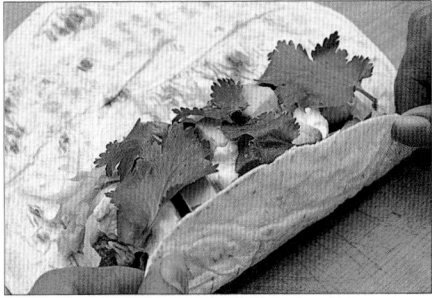

Place the filling in the centre of the tortilla and roll up, tucking in the ends.

MUSHROOM MOUSSAKA

Preparation time: 20 minutes
Total cooking time: 1 hour
Serves 4–6

1 eggplant (250 g/8 oz), cut into
    1 cm (½ inch) slices
1 large potato, cut into 1 cm (½ inch)
    slices
30 g (1 oz) butter
1 onion, finely chopped
2 cloves garlic, finely chopped
500 g (1 lb) flat mushrooms, sliced
400 g (13 oz) can chopped tomatoes
½ teaspoon sugar
40 g (1¼ oz) butter, extra
⅓ cup (40 g/1¼ oz) plain flour
2 cups (500 ml/16 fl oz) milk
1 egg, lightly beaten
40 g (1¼ oz) grated Parmesan

1 Preheat the oven to hot 220°C
(425°F/Gas 7). Line a large baking
tray with foil and brush with oil. Put
the eggplant and potato in a single
layer on the tray and sprinkle with
salt and pepper. Bake for 20 minutes.
2 Melt the butter in a large frying pan
over medium heat. Add the onion and
cook, stirring, for 3–4 minutes, or until
soft. Add the garlic and cook for
1 minute, or until fragrant. Increase the
heat to high, add the mushrooms and
stir continuously for 2–3 minutes, or
until soft. Add the tomato, reduce the
heat and simmer rapidly for 8 minutes,
or until reduced. Stir in the sugar.
3 Melt the extra butter in a large
saucepan over low heat. Add the flour
and cook for 1 minute, or until pale
and foaming. Remove from the heat
and gradually stir in the milk. Return
to the heat and stir constantly until it
boils and thickens. Reduce the heat

and simmer for 2 minutes. Remove
from the heat and, when the bubbles
subside, stir in the egg and Parmesan.
4 Reduce the oven to moderate 180°C
(350°F/Gas 4). Grease a shallow 1.5
litre (48 fl oz) ovenproof dish. Spoon
one third of the mushroom mixture
into the dish. Cover with potato and
top with half the remaining
mushrooms, then the eggplant. Finish

with the remaining mushrooms, pour
on the sauce and smooth the top.
Bake for 30–35 minutes, or until the
edges bubble. Leave for 10 minutes
before serving.

NUTRITION PER SERVE (6)
Protein 12 g; Fat 16 g; Carbohydrate 18 g;
Dietary Fibre 5 g; Cholesterol 77 mg;
1125 kJ (268 cal)

A small amount of sugar added to the tomato
mixture will bring out the flavours.

Remove the saucepan from the heat and stir in
the egg and Parmesan.

Cover the tomato and mushroom mixture with the
potato slices.

CHARGRILLED VEGETABLE AND PARMESAN PIE

Preparation time: 45 minutes +
  1 hour standing
Total cooking time: 1 hour 30 minutes
Serves 6

1 clove garlic, crushed
300 ml (10 fl oz) olive oil
2 large eggplants
1 large orange sweet potato
3 large zucchini
3 red capsicums
3 yellow capsicums
2 tablespoons polenta
90 g (3 oz) Parmesan, grated
1 egg, lightly beaten

PASTRY
450 g (14 oz) plain flour
2 teaspoons cumin seeds
2 teaspoons paprika
100 g (3½ oz) butter, chopped

1 Mix the garlic and oil together. Cut the eggplants and sweet potato into 5 mm (¼ inch) slices and the zucchini into 5 mm (¼ inch) lengths, then brush with the garlic oil. Quarter the capsicums and place, skin-side-up, under a hot grill for 10 minutes, or until the skins blacken and blister. Cool in a plastic bag, then peel.

2 Cook the eggplant, sweet potato and zucchini in batches in a chargrill pan over high heat, turning often, for 5–6 minutes, or until brown and tender. Set aside to cool.

3 Preheat the oven to 180°C (350°F/ Gas 4). Grease a deep 20 cm (8 inch) springform tin. Sift the flour into a bowl and add the cumin, paprika and ½ teaspoon salt. Gently heat the butter in a saucepan with 225 ml (7 fl oz) water. Bring to the boil, pour into the flour and mix with a wooden spoon. When cool enough to handle, tip onto a floured surface and press gently together. Rest for 5 minutes.

4 Set aside one quarter of the dough and roll out the rest between two sheets of baking paper until large enough to line the base and side of the tin, leaving some pastry overhanging. Sprinkle polenta over the base, then layer the red capsicum, zucchini, eggplant, sweet potato and yellow capsicum in the pie, brushing each layer with a little garlic oil, sprinkling with Parmesan and seasoning with salt and pepper as you go.

5 Roll out the remaining pastry between the baking paper to fit the top of the tin. Brush the edges of the bottom layer of pastry with egg. Cover with the pastry lid. Brush the edges with egg and trim with a sharp knife, crimping the edges to seal. Cut a small steam hole in the centre of the pie. Roll out the trimmings and use to decorate. Cook for 1 hour, or until crisp and golden (cover with foil if it browns too quickly). Cool for 1 hour before serving at room temperature.

NUTRITION PER SERVE
Protein 18 g; Fat 54 g; Carbohydrate 68 g; Dietary Fibre 7 g; Cholesterol 86 mg; 3445 kJ (820 cal)

Layer the chargrilled vegetables and grated Parmesan in the pastry case.

CREAMY MUSHROOM PIE

Preparation time: 45 minutes +
35 minutes soaking and chilling
Total cooking time: 1 hour
Serves 4–6

2 cups (250 g/8 oz) plain flour
½ cup (75 g/2½ oz) fine polenta
125 g (4 oz) butter, chilled and cubed
¼ cup (60 ml/2 fl oz) cream
2–3 tablespoons iced water

FILLING
10 g (¼ oz) dried porcini mushrooms
150 g (5 oz) oyster mushrooms
1 large leek
150 g (5 oz) butter
2 large cloves garlic, crushed
200 g (6½ oz) shiitake mushrooms,
    thickly sliced
200 g (6½ oz) Swiss brown
    mushrooms, thickly sliced
350 g (11 oz) field mushrooms, sliced
100 g (3½ oz) enoki mushrooms
2 tablespoons plain flour
½ cup (125 ml/4 fl oz) dry white wine
½ cup (125 ml/4 fl oz) vegetable or
    chicken stock
¼ cup (60 ml/2 fl oz) thick cream
2 tablespoons chopped fresh thyme
1 egg, lightly beaten, to glaze

1 To make the pastry, sift the flour into a large bowl, then stir in the polenta and ½ teaspoon of salt. Add the butter and rub into the dry ingredients with your fingertips until the mixture resembles fine breadcrumbs. Make a well in the centre, pour in the cream and mix with a flat-bladed knife, using a cutting action, until the mixture comes together in beads. Add a little water if the mixture is too dry.
2 Gently gather the dough together and lift out onto a lightly floured work surface. Press together into a ball and then flatten slightly into a disc. Wrap in plastic wrap and refrigerate for 20 minutes.
3 Soak the porcini mushrooms in 3 tablespoons boiling water for about 15 minutes. Cut any large oyster mushrooms into halves. Thoroughly wash the leek and thinly slice it.
4 Preheat the oven to hot 210°C

(415°F/Gas 6–7). Heat a baking tray in the oven. Lightly grease an 18 cm (7 inch) pie dish.
5 Drain the porcini mushrooms, reserving the soaking liquid, then coarsely chop them. Heat the butter in a large, deep frying pan over medium heat and cook the leek and garlic for 7–8 minutes, or until the leek is soft and golden. Add all the mushrooms to the pan and cook, stirring, for 5–6 minutes, or until soft.
6 Add the flour to the pan and stir for 1 minute. Pour in the wine and reserved mushroom soaking liquid and bring to the boil for 1 minute, then pour in the stock and cook for 4–5 minutes, or until the liquid has reduced. Stir in the cream and cook for 1–2 minutes, or until thickened. Stir in the thyme and season. Cool.
7 Divide the pastry into two portions. Roll out one portion between two sheets of baking paper to 2 mm (⅛ inch) thick to line the base and side of the pie dish. Line the pie dish, then spoon in the cooled mushroom filling. Lightly brush the edge of the pastry with egg.
8 Roll out the remaining pastry between the baking paper until about 2 mm (⅛ inch) thick and cover the pie. Pinch the edges together and pierce the top three times with a fork. Trim the edges. Roll the trimmings and cut into mushroom shapes. Arrange over the pie and lightly brush the top with more egg. Place on the hot tray and bake for 35–40 minutes, or until the pastry is golden brown. Set aside for 5 minutes before slicing.

NUTRITION PER SERVE (6)
Protein 14 g; Fat 48 g; Carbohydrate 51 g;
Dietary Fibre 8 g; Cholesterol 173 mg;
2900 kJ (695 cal)

Mix in the cream, using a cutting action, until the mixture comes together in beads.

Add all of the mushrooms to the pan and cook them until they are soft.

Spoon the cooled mushroom filling into the pastry-lined dish.

Cut the pastry trimmings into mushroom shapes to decorate the pie.

STIR-FRIED ASIAN GREENS AND MUSHROOMS

Preparation time: 20 minutes
Total cooking time: 5 minutes
Serves 4

20 stems Chinese broccoli
4 baby bok choy
100 g (3½ oz) shimeji or enoki
    mushrooms
100 g (3½ oz) shiitake mushrooms
1 tablespoon soy sauce
2 teaspoons crushed palm sugar
1 tablespoon oil
4 spring onions, cut into short pieces
5 cm (2 inch) fresh ginger, cut into thin
    strips
1–2 small red chillies, seeded and
    finely chopped
2–3 cloves garlic, crushed
125 g (4 oz) snow peas, halved
1–2 teaspoons seasoning sauce

1 Remove any tough outer leaves from the Chinese broccoli and bok choy. Cut into 4 cm (1½ inch) pieces across the leaves, including the stems. Wash thoroughly, then drain and dry thoroughly. Wipe the mushrooms with a paper towel and trim the ends. Slice the shiitake mushrooms thickly.
2 Combine the soy sauce and palm sugar with ¼ cup (60 ml/2 fl oz) water. Set aside.
3 Heat the wok until very hot, add the oil and swirl it around to coat the side. Stir-fry the spring onion, ginger, chilli and garlic over low heat for 30 seconds, without browning. Increase the heat to high and add the Chinese broccoli, bok choy and snow peas. Stir-fry for 1–2 minutes, or until the vegetables are wilted.
4 Add the prepared mushrooms and

soy sauce mixture. Stir-fry over high heat for 1–2 minutes, or until the mushrooms and sauce are heated through. Sprinkle with the seasoning sauce, to taste, and serve immediately.

NUTRITION PER SERVE
Protein 6.5 g; Fat 10 g; Carbohydrate 15 g;
Dietary Fibre 3 g; Cholesterol 0 mg;
780 kJ (185 cal)

You will need to gently separate the shimeji mushrooms from each other.

Trim the shiitake mushrooms and cut them into thick slices.

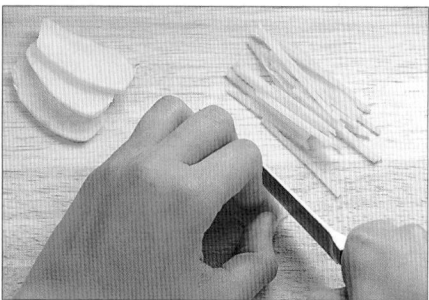

Peel the piece of ginger with a vegetable peeler or sharp knife and cut it into thin strips.

SWEET POTATO AND FENNEL PIE

Preparation time: 20 minutes
  + 30 minutes refrigeration
  + 10 minutes draining
Total cooking time: 1 hour 10 minutes
Serves 6

2 fennel bulbs (500 g/1 lb), thick outer
  leaves removed, sliced
300 g (10 oz) sweet potato, cut into
  1 cm (½ inch) cubes
1 tablespoon dried juniper berries,
  ground
¼ cup (60 ml/2 fl oz) olive oil
300 g (10 oz) ricotta
1 cup (100 g/3½ oz) grated Parmesan
100 g (3½ oz) ground almonds

6 sheets ready-rolled shortcrust pastry
milk, to glaze
3 sheets ready-rolled puff pastry

1 Preheat the oven to moderate 180°C
(350°F/Gas 4). Grease six 11 cm
(4½ inch) (top) 9.5 cm (4 inch (base)
and 2.5 cm (1 inch) (deep) pie tins.
Place the fennel, sweet potato and
juniper berries in a deep roasting tin
and toss with the oil. Season, cover
with foil and cook for 35 minutes, or
until the vegetables have softened.
Drain any oil away, transfer to a bowl
and chill for 30 minutes, or until cold.
2 Combine the ricotta, Parmesan
and ground almonds in a large bowl.
Transfer to a sieve and sit over a bowl
for 10 minutes to drain away any
liquid from the ricotta.

3 Cut a 15 cm (6 inch) round from
each sheet of shortcrust pastry and
line the pie tins, leaving the excess
overhanging. Brush the rims with
milk.
4 Divide the vegetables among the
pastry shells, then top with ricotta
mixture. Cut six 12 cm (4¾ inch)
rounds from the puff pastry, place
over the filled shells and trim. Seal
the edges with a fork and prick a
few holes in the tops. Brush with
milk, then bake for 35 minutes, or
until golden.

NUTRITION PER SERVE
Protein 29.5 g; Fat 86.5 g; Carbohydrate
104.5 g; Dietary Fibre 8.5 g; Cholesterol
102 mg; 5474 kJ (1310 Cal)

Roast the fennel and sweet potato until they
have softened.

Cut a 15 cm (6 inch) round from each sheet of
shortcrust, using a saucer to help you.

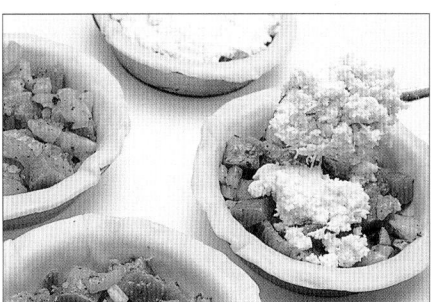

Spoon the ricotta and Parmesan mixture into the
vegetable-filled pie tins.

EGGPLANT PARMIGIANA

Preparation time: 30 minutes
Total cooking time: 1 hour 15 minutes
Serves 6–8

3 tablespoons olive oil
1 onion, diced
2 cloves garlic, crushed
1.25 kg (2½ lb) tomatoes, peeled and
  chopped
1 kg (2 lb) eggplants
250 g (8 oz) bocconcini, sliced
185 g (6 oz) Cheddar cheese, finely
  grated
1 cup (50 g/1¾ oz) basil leaves
½ cup (50 g/1¾ oz) grated Parmesan

1 Heat the oil in a large frying pan;
add the onion and cook over
moderate heat until soft. Add the
garlic and cook for 1 minute. Add the
tomato and simmer for 15 minutes.
Season with salt to taste. Preheat the
oven to moderately hot 200°C
(400°F/Gas 6).
2 Slice the eggplants very thinly and
shallow-fry in oil in batches for
3–4 minutes, or until golden brown.
Drain on paper towels.
3 Place one third of the eggplant in a
7-cup (1.75 litre) ovenproof dish. Top
with half the bocconcini and Cheddar.
Repeat the layers, finishing with a
layer of eggplant.
4 Pour the tomato mixture over the
eggplant. Scatter with torn basil
leaves, then Parmesan. Bake for 40
minutes.

NUTRITION PER SERVE (6)
Protein 19 g; Fat 28 g; Carbohydrate 7 g;
Dietary Fibre 5 g; Cholesterol 60 mg;
1495 kJ (357 cal)

VARIATION: If you prefer not to fry
the eggplant, brush it lightly with oil
and brown lightly under a hot grill.

Shallow-fry the eggplant in batches, then drain on
paper towels.

Arrange layers of eggplant, bocconcini and
Cheddar in the dish.

MUSHROOM QUICHE WITH PARSLEY PASTRY

Preparation time: 30 minutes +
  50 minutes refrigeration
Total cooking time: 1 hour
Serves 4–6

1¼ cups (155 g/5 oz) plain flour
¼ cup (15 g/½ oz) chopped fresh
   parsley
90 g (3 oz) butter, chilled and cubed
1 egg yolk
2 tablespoons iced water

FILLING
30 g (1 oz) butter
1 red onion, chopped
175 g (6 oz) button mushrooms, sliced
1 teaspoon lemon juice
⅓ cup (20 g/¾ oz) chopped fresh
   parsley
⅓ cup (20 g/¾ oz) chopped chives
1 egg, lightly beaten
⅓ cup (80 ml/2¾ oz) cream

1 Process the flour, parsley and butter for 15 seconds, or until crumbly. Add the egg yolk and water. Process in short bursts until the mixture comes together. Add a little more water if needed. Turn out onto a floured surface and gather into a ball. Cover with plastic wrap and refrigerate for at least 30 minutes.

2 Roll out the pastry between two sheets of baking paper until large enough to fit a 35 x 10 cm (14 x 4 inch) loose-based tart tin. Trim away the excess pastry. Refrigerate for 20 minutes. Preheat the oven to 190°C (375°F/Gas 5). Cover the pastry with baking paper and spread with a layer of baking beads or rice. Bake for 15 minutes. Remove the paper and

beads and bake for 10 minutes, or until the pastry is dry. Reduce the oven to 180°C (350°F/Gas 4).

3 To make the mushroom filling, melt the butter in a pan and cook the onion for 2–3 minutes until soft. Add the mushrooms and cook, stirring, for 2–3 minutes until soft. Stir in the lemon juice and herbs. Mix the egg and cream together and season.

4 Spread the mushroom filling into the pastry shell and pour over the egg and cream. Bake for 25–30 minutes, or until the filling has set.

NUTRITION PER SERVE (6)
Protein 6 g; Fat 25 g; Carbohydrate 20 g;
Dietary Fibre 2 g; Cholesterol 130 mg;
1350 kJ (320 cal)

Place the flour and parsley in a food processor and add the butter.

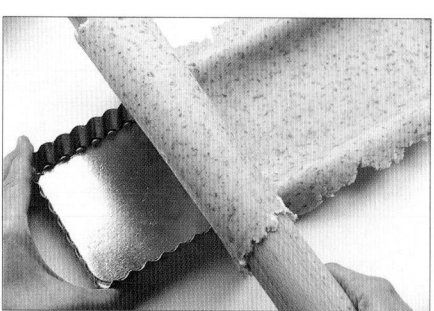

The easiest way to line the tin with pastry is to roll the pastry over the rolling pin to lift it.

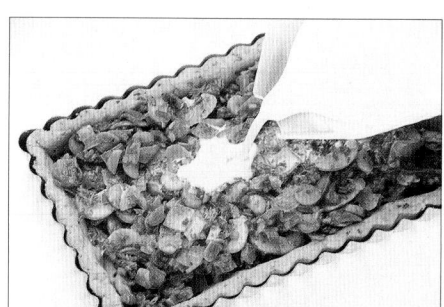

Pour the combined egg and cream over the mushroom filling.

SWEET AND SOUR TOFU WITH NOODLES

Preparation time: 10 minutes
Total cooking time: 5 minutes
Serves 4

100 g (3½ oz) deep-fried tofu puffs
(see NOTE)
2 tablespoons oil
1 onion, sliced
1 red capsicum, cut into squares
3 cloves garlic, crushed
2 teaspoons grated fresh ginger
500 g (1 lb) thin Hokkien noodles

¾ cup (120 g/4 oz) small chunks fresh
pineapple
¼ cup (60 ml/2 fl oz) pineapple juice
¼ cup (60 ml/2 fl oz) hoisin sauce
¼ cup (15 g/½ oz) roughly chopped
fresh coriander

1 Slice the tofu puffs into three, then cut each slice into two or three pieces.
2 Heat the wok until very hot, add the oil and stir-fry the onion and capsicum for 1–2 minutes, or until beginning to soften. Add the garlic and ginger, stir-fry for 1 minute, then add the tofu and stir-fry for 2 minutes.
3 Add the noodles and pineapple chunks and toss until the mixture is combined and heated through. Add the pineapple juice, hoisin sauce and chopped coriander, and toss well. Serve immediately.

NUTRITION PER SERVE
Protein 10 g; Fat 15 g; Carbohydrate 65 g;
Dietary Fibre 3.5 g; Cholesterol 0 mg;
1830 kJ (435 cal)

NOTE: Deep-fried tofu puffs are available from the refrigerated section in Asian grocery stores and some supermarkets. They have a very different texture to ordinary tofu.

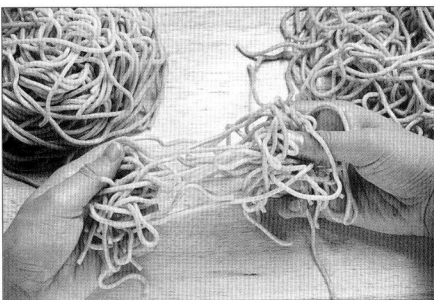

Use your fingers to gently pull apart the strands of Hokkien noodles before use.

Buy deep-fried tofu puffs, not silken tofu. Slice each tofu puff into three, then cut into pieces.

Stir-fry the onion and capsicum until they are beginning to soften.

HOT VEGETABLE CURRY WITH SPICED NOODLES

Preparation time: 40 minutes
Total cooking time: 35 minutes
Serves 4–6

CURRY PASTE
5 red chillies, seeded and chopped
1 stem lemon grass, sliced
1 tablespoon chopped galangal
2 garlic cloves, crushed
1 small onion, chopped
1 tablespoon chopped fresh coriander
10 black peppercorns
2 tablespoons lime juice
2 teaspoons oil

2 tablespoons oil
1½ cups (375 ml/12 fl oz) coconut milk
200 g (6½ oz) green beans, cut into
   short lengths
2 small zucchini, thickly sliced
1 eggplant, cubed
200 g (6½ oz) pumpkin, cubed
5 kaffir lime leaves
2 tablespoons lime juice
¼ cup (15 g/½ oz) chopped fresh
   coriander
½ cup (30 g/1 oz) chopped fresh basil

SPICED NOODLES
2 tablespoons oil
1 small onion, chopped
1 clove garlic, crushed
½–1 teaspoon dried chilli flakes
½ teaspoon garam masala
200 g (6½ oz) thin egg noodles

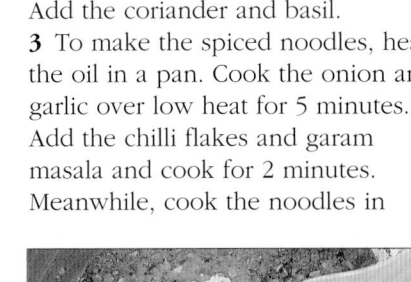

1 To make the curry paste, blend all the ingredients in a food processor or blender to make a smooth paste.
2 Heat the oil in a pan and stir-fry the curry paste for 2 minutes. Add the coconut milk and ½ cup (125 ml/ 4 fl oz) water and bring to the boil. Reduce the heat and add the vegetables, kaffir lime leaves and lime juice. Cook, covered, until tender. Add the coriander and basil.
3 To make the spiced noodles, heat the oil in a pan. Cook the onion and garlic over low heat for 5 minutes. Add the chilli flakes and garam masala and cook for 2 minutes. Meanwhile, cook the noodles in boiling water until tender and drain. Add to the onion mixture and toss well. Serve with the vegetable curry.

NUTRITION PER SERVE (6)
Protein 5 g; Fat 25 g; Carbohydrate 15 g;
Dietary Fibre 5 g; Cholesterol 0 mg;
1415 kJ (335 cal)

Lemon grass and galangal are both available from Asian food stores.

Heat the oil in a pan and stir-fry the curry paste for 2 minutes.

Add the noodles to a large pan of boiling water and cook until tender.

VEGETABLE LATTICE PIE

Preparation time: 40 minutes + chilling
Total cooking time: 1 hour
Serves 6

185 g (6 oz) butter
2 cups (250 g/8 oz) plain flour
3 tablespoons iced water

FILLING
1 tablespoon oil
1 onion, finely chopped
1 small red capsicum, chopped
1 small green capsicum, chopped
150 g (5 oz) pumpkin, chopped
1 small potato, chopped
100 g (3½ oz) broccoli, cut into small
    florets
1 carrot, chopped
3 tablespoons plain flour
1 cup (250 ml/8 fl oz) milk
2 egg yolks
½ cup (60 g/2 oz) grated Cheddar
1 egg, lightly beaten, to glaze

1 Chop 125 g (4 oz) of the butter. Sift the flour into a large bowl and add the chopped butter. Using your fingertips, rub the butter into the flour until the mixture is fine and crumbly. Add almost all the water and use a knife to mix to a firm dough, adding more water if necessary. Turn onto a lightly floured surface and press together until smooth. Divide the dough in half, roll out one portion and line a deep 20 cm (8 inch) fluted flan tin. Refrigerate for 20 minutes. Roll the remaining pastry out to a 25 cm (10 inch) diameter circle. Cut into strips and lay half of them on a sheet of baking paper, leaving a 2 cm (¾ inch) gap between each strip. Interweave the remaining strips to form a lattice pattern. Cover with plastic wrap and refrigerate, keeping flat, until firm.
2 Preheat the oven to 180°C (350°F/ Gas 4). Cut a sheet of greaseproof paper to cover the pastry-lined tin. Spread a layer of baking beads or dried beans or rice over the paper. Bake for 10 minutes, remove from the oven and discard the paper and beans. Bake for another 10 minutes or until golden. Remove and allow to cool.

3 Heat the oil in a frying pan. Add the onion and cook for 2 minutes or until soft. Add the caspicum and cook, stirring, for another 3 minutes. Steam or boil the remaining vegetables until just tender; drain and cool. Combine the onion, capsicum and the other vegetables in a large bowl.
4 Heat the remaining butter in a small pan. Add the flour and cook, stirring, for 2 minutes. Add the milk gradually, stirring until smooth after each addition. Stir until the sauce boils and thickens. Boil for 1 minute and then remove from the heat. Add the egg yolks and cheese and stir until

smooth. Pour over the vegetables and stir together. Pour into the pastry case and brush the edges with egg. Using the baking paper to help, invert the lattice over the vegetables, trim the edges and brush with a little egg. Press the edges lightly to seal to the cooked pastry. Brush the top with egg and bake for 30 minutes or until the pastry is golden.

NUTRITION PER SERVE
Protein 17 g; Fat 39 g; Carbohydrate 48 g;
Dietary Fibre 4 g; Cholesterol 190 mg;
2535 kJ (605 cal)

Add almost all the water to the bowl, mixing with a knife until a firm dough is formed.

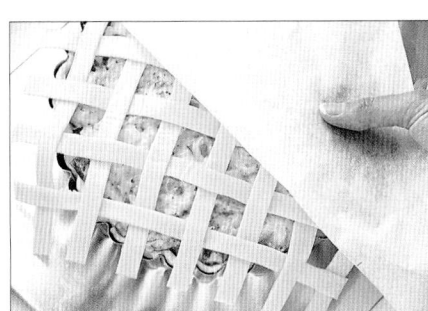

Invert the lattice over the pie and slowly pull away the baking paper.

SPRING VEGETABLES WITH HERBED BUTTER

Preparation time: 20 minutes
Total cooking time: 10 minutes
Serves 6 as an accompaniment

2 tablespoons light olive oil
200 g (6½ oz) asparagus, cut into
    short lengths
115 g (4 oz) baby corn, halved
    lengthways
250 g (8 oz) snow peas
250 g (8 oz) green beans, halved

300 g (10 oz) baby carrots, halved
    lengthways
2 cloves garlic, crushed
50 g (1¾ oz) butter
¼ cup (15 g/½ oz) finely chopped fresh
    parsley
¼ cup (15 g/½ oz) finely chopped chives
¼ cup (15 g/½ oz) shredded fresh basil

1 Heat the wok until very hot, add the oil and swirl it around to coat the side. Stir-fry all the vegetables over high heat for 5 minutes. Cover and cook over low heat for 2 minutes, or until tender.

2 Add the crushed garlic, butter and all the fresh herbs, and toss until the butter has melted and the herbs have wilted slightly. Season well with salt and pepper and serve immediately as an accompaniment.

NUTRITION PER SERVE
Protein 3 g; Fat 12 g; Carbohydrate 8 g;
Dietary Fibre 4 g; Cholesterol 20 mg;
695 kJ (165 cal)

Use a large sharp knife to finely chop the fresh parsley, chives and basil.

Stir-fry the asparagus, snow peas, beans, corn and carrot over high heat.

Add the garlic, butter and herbs to the tender vegetables and toss until the butter melts.

WILD MUSHROOMS WITH SPICES

Preparation time: 30 minutes
Total cooking time: 5 minutes
Serve 4

20 g (¾ oz) butter
1 tablespoon oil
2 cloves garlic, crushed
1 teaspoon ground cumin
1 teaspoon ground coriander
¼ teaspoon sweet paprika
750 g (1½ lb) mixed mushrooms
    (see NOTE), cleaned and
    trimmed

2 tablespoons dry sherry
4 spring onions, sliced
¼ cup (15 g/½ oz) shredded
    fresh basil
2 tablespoons chopped fresh
    flat-leaf parsley

1 Heat the wok until very hot, add the butter and oil and swirl it around the wok. Stir-fry the garlic, cumin, coriander and paprika for 1–2 minutes, or until fragrant. Add the mushrooms and stir-fry for 2 minutes, tossing well.
2 Add the sherry and bring to the boil. Cover and cook for 30 seconds. Toss the spring onion and herbs through the mushroom mixture.

NUTRITION PER SERVE
Protein 7 g; Fat 9.5 g; Carbohydrate 4 g;
Dietary Fibre 5.5 g; Cholesterol 15 mg;
580 kJ (140 cal)

NOTE: Mushrooms such as shimeji, oyster, swiss brown, enoki and button can be used in this recipe. If using enoki mushrooms, add them when the sherry is added as they cook faster than the other mushrooms.

Clean and trim the mushrooms, cutting any larger ones in half.

Stir-fry the garlic, cumin, coriander and paprika until fragrant.

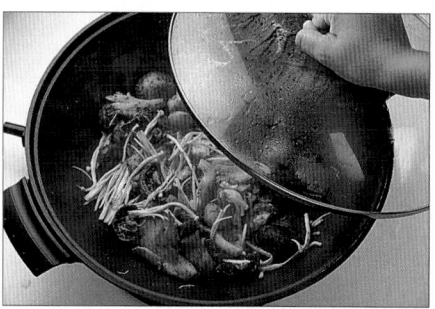

Add the sherry and enoki mushrooms, and cover and cook for 2 minutes.

CHICKPEA PATTIES WITH CARAMELIZED ONION

Preparation time: 20 minutes
Total cooking time: 30 minutes
Serves 4

1 tablespoon olive oil
1 red onion, finely chopped
2 cloves garlic, crushed
1 tablespoon ground cumin
2 x 310 g (10 oz) cans chickpeas
¼ cup (30 g/1 oz) sunflower seeds
½ cup (30 g/1 oz) finely chopped fresh
    coriander leaves
2 eggs, lightly beaten
⅔ cup (75 g/2½ oz) besan flour
oil, for shallow-frying

CARAMELIZED ONION
40 g (1¼ oz) butter
2 red onions, thinly sliced
3 teaspoons soft brown sugar
plain yoghurt, to serve

1 Heat the oil in a frying pan, add the onion and cook over medium heat for 3 minutes, or until soft. Add the garlic and cumin and cook for 1 minute. Allow to cool slightly.
2 Blend the drained chickpeas, sunflower seeds, coriander, egg and onion mixture in a food processor until smooth. Fold in the besan flour and season. Divide the mixture into eight portions and, using floured hands, form into patties. Heat 1 cm (½ inch) oil in a frying pan and cook the patties in two batches over medium heat for 2–3 minutes each side, or until firm. Drain on paper towels. Keep warm.
3 To make the caramelized onion, melt the butter in a small frying pan and cook the onion over medium heat for 10 minutes, stirring occasionally. Add the sugar and cook for 1 minute, or until caramelized. Spoon over the patties with a dollop of yoghurt.

NUTRITION PER SERVE
Protein 35 g; Fat 38 g; Carbohydrate 70 g;
Dietary Fibre 23 g; Cholesterol 116 mg;
3170 kJ (757 cal)

NOTE: Besan flour is also known as chickpea flour.

Fold the besan flour (also known as chickpea flour) into the chickpea purée.

Shallow-fry the chickpea patties in batches, until firm and golden on both sides.

Cook the onion for 10 minutes, then stir in the sugar and cook until caramelized.

SOYA BEAN MOUSSAKA

Preparation time: 25 minutes
Total cooking time: 1 hour
Serves 4

2 eggplants
1 tablespoon oil
1 onion, finely chopped
2 cloves garlic, crushed
2 ripe tomatoes, peeled, seeded and
    chopped
2 teaspoons tomato paste
½ teaspoon dried oregano
½ cup (125 ml/4 fl oz) dry white wine
300 g (10 oz) can soya beans, rinsed
    and drained
3 tablespoons chopped fresh flat-leaf
    parsley
30 g (1 oz) butter
2 tablespoons plain flour
pinch of ground nutmeg
1¼ cups (315 ml/10 fl oz) milk
⅓ cup (40 g/1¼ oz) grated Cheddar

1 Preheat the oven to moderate 180°C
(350°F/Gas 4). Cut the eggplants in
half lengthways. Spoon out the flesh,
leaving a narrow border and place on
a large baking tray, cut-side-up. Use
crumpled foil around the sides of the
eggplant to help support it.
2 Heat the oil in a large frying pan.
Cook the onion and garlic over
medium heat for 3 minutes, or until
soft. Add the tomato, tomato paste,
oregano and wine. Boil for 3 minutes,
or until the liquid is reduced and the
tomato is soft. Stir in the soya beans
and parsley.
3 To make the sauce, melt the butter
in a saucepan. Stir in the flour and
cook over medium heat for 1 minute,
or until pale and foamy. Remove from
the heat and gradually stir in the
nutmeg and milk. Return to the heat
and stir constantly until the sauce
boils and thickens. Pour one third of
the white sauce into the tomato
mixture and stir well.
4 Spoon the mixture into the
eggplant shells. Smooth the surface
before spreading the remaining sauce
evenly over the top and sprinkling
with cheese. Bake for 50 minutes, or
until cooked through. Serve hot.

NUTRITION PER SERVE
Protein 35 g; Fat 33 g; Carbohydrate 20 g;
Dietary Fibre 20 g; Cholesterol 40 mg;
2192 kJ (524 cal)

Scoop out the eggplant flesh, leaving a narrow
border all the way around.

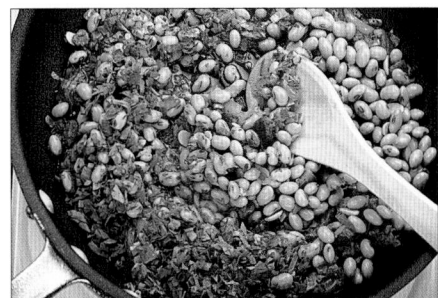
Add the soya beans and parsley to the tomato
mixture and stir well.

POTATO FILO PIES

Preparation time: 1 hour
Total cooking time: 1 hour 20 minutes
Makes 6

6 Roma tomatoes, halved
   lengthways
3 tablespoons olive oil
50 g (1¾ oz) butter
3 cloves garlic, crushed
800 g (1 lb 10 oz) potatoes, unpeeled
   and sliced
500 g (1 lb) English spinach, trimmed
12 sheets filo pastry
100 g (3½ oz) butter, melted
2 tablespoons sesame seeds

1 Preheat the oven to 200°C (400°F/ Gas 6). Place the tomato halves, cut-side-up, on a baking tray, drizzle with 1 tablespoon of the oil and sprinkle with a little salt. Bake for 40 minutes.
2 Heat the butter and remaining oil in a large non-stick pan and cook the garlic and potato, tossing occasionally, for 10 minutes, or until the potato is tender. Set aside on paper towels. Cook the spinach in the pan for 1–2 minutes, or until wilted. Cool and then squeeze out any excess moisture.
3 Reduce the oven to 180°C (350°F/ Gas 4). Work with one sheet of pastry at a time and cover the rest with a damp tea towel. Brush the pastry with melted butter and place another sheet

on top. Brush with butter and repeat with another two layers. Cut in half widthways. Place a few potato slices at one end of each half, leaving a wide border on each side. Top with two tomato pieces and some spinach.
4 Fold in the sides of the pastry and roll up. Place on a lightly greased baking tray, brush with melted butter and sprinkle with sesame seeds. Use the remaining filo and filling to make another five parcels. Bake for 25–30 minutes, or until lightly golden.

NUTRITION PER PIE
Protein 9 g; Fat 30 g; Carbohydrate 35 g;
Dietary Fibre 6 g; Cholesterol 60 mg;
1940 kJ (465 cal)

Build up the layers of filo pastry, brushing each with melted butter.

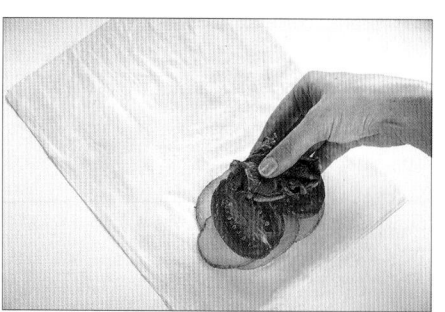

Place a few slices of potato at one end and top with tomato and spinach.

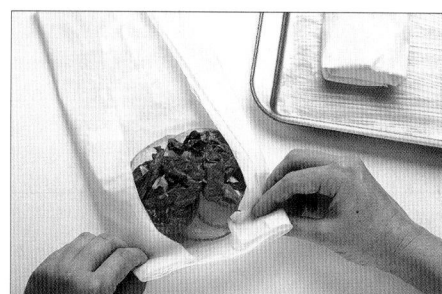

Fold in the sides of the pastry and then roll up around the filling, into a parcel.

COUSCOUS VEGETABLE LOAF

Preparation time: 20 minutes
  + cooling + overnight refrigeration
Total cooking time: 10 minutes
Serves 6

1 litre (32 fl oz) vegetable stock
500 g (1 lb) instant couscous
30 g (1 oz) butter
3 tablespoons olive oil
2 cloves garlic, crushed
1 onion, finely chopped
1 tablespoon ground coriander
1 teaspoon ground cinnamon
1 teaspoon garam masala
250 g (8 oz) cherry tomatoes,
    quartered
1 zucchini, diced
130 g (4½ oz) can corn kernels,
    drained
8 large fresh basil leaves
150 g (5 oz) sun-dried capsicums in oil
1 cup (60 g/2 oz) chopped fresh basil
⅓ cup (80 ml/2¾ fl oz) orange juice
1 tablespoon lemon juice
3 tablespoons chopped fresh flat-leaf
    parsley
1 teaspoon honey
1 teaspoon ground cumin

1 Bring the stock to the boil. Put the couscous and butter in a bowl, cover with the stock; leave for 10 minutes.
2 Heat 1 tablespoon of the oil in a large frying pan and cook the garlic and onion over low heat for 5 minutes, or until the onion is soft. Add the spices and cook for 1 minute, or until fragrant. Remove from the pan.
3 Add the remaining oil to the pan and cook the tomatoes, zucchini and corn over high heat until soft.
4 Line a 3 litre (96 fl oz) loaf tin with plastic wrap, letting it overhang the sides. Arrange the basil leaves in the shape of two flowers in the base of the tin. Drain the capsicums, reserving 2 tablespoons of the oil, then roughly chop. Add the onion mixture, tomato mixture, capsicum and chopped basil to the couscous and mix. Cool.
5 Press into the tin and fold the plastic wrap over to cover. Weigh down with cans of food to compress the loaf and refrigerate overnight.
6 To make the dressing, put the remaining ingredients and reserved capsicum oil in a screw-top jar and shake. Turn out the loaf, cut into slices and serve with the dressing.

NUTRITION PER SERVE
Protein 8.5 g; Fat 19 g; Carbohydrate 67 g;
Dietary Fibre 5 g; Cholesterol 13 mg;
1985 kJ (474 cal)

Cook the tomatoes, zucchini and corn over high heat until soft.

Arrange the basil leaves in the shape of two flowers in the base of the loaf tin.

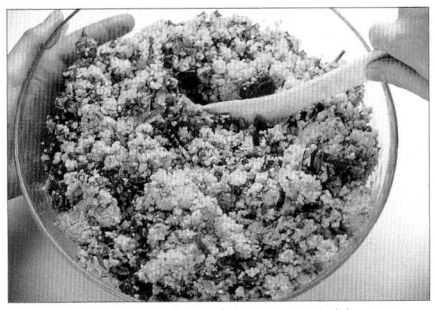

Mix together the onion mixture, vegetables, capsicum, basil and couscous.

BAKED POLENTA WITH THREE CHEESES

Preparation time: 20 minutes
+ 2 hours chilling
Total cooking time: 45 minutes
Serves 4

POLENTA
2½ cups (600 ml/20 fl oz) vegetable
   stock
2 cups (300 g/10 oz) polenta (see
   NOTE)
½ cup (60 g/2 oz) grated Parmesan

CHEESE FILLING
100 g (3½ oz) havarti cheese, sliced
100 g (3½ oz) mascarpone cheese
100 g (3½ oz) blue cheese, crumbled
100 g (3½ oz) butter, sliced thinly
½ cup (60 g/2 oz) grated Parmesan

1 To make the polenta, brush a 7-cup
(1.75 litre/56 fl oz) loaf tin with oil.
Put the stock and 2 cups (500 ml/16 fl
oz) water in a large pan and bring to
the boil. Add the polenta and stir for
10 minutes until very thick.

2 Remove from the heat and stir in
the Parmesan. Spread into the tin and
smooth the surface. Refrigerate for
2 hours, then cut into about 30 thin
slices. Preheat the oven to moderate
180°C (350°F/Gas 4).

3 Brush a large ovenproof dish with
oil. Place a layer of polenta slices on
the base. Top with a layer of half the
combined havarti, mascarpone and
blue cheeses and half the butter. Add
another layer of polenta and top with
the remainder of the three cheeses
and butter. Add a final layer of
polenta and sprinkle the Parmesan on
top. Bake for 30 minutes, or until a
golden crust forms. Serve immediately.

NUTRITION PER SERVE
Protein 20 g; Fat 38 g; Carbohydrate 35 g;
Dietary Fibre 1.5 g; Cholesterol 113 mg;
2351 kJ (560 cal)

NOTE: Polenta is also known as
cornmeal and is available from most
supermarkets and delicatessens.
Havarti is a Danish cheese with a
full flavour.

Add the polenta to the stock and water and stir
constantly until very thick.

Use the back of a spoon to spread the polenta in
the tin.

Build up the layers of sliced polenta, butter and
different cheeses.

Add the final layer of sliced polenta and then
sprinkle with Parmesan cheese.

ROMAN GNOCCHI

**Preparation time: 15 minutes +
1 hour refrigeration**
Total cooking time: 40 minutes
Serves 4

3 cups (750 ml/24 fl oz) milk
½ teaspoon ground nutmeg
¾ cup (90 g/3 oz) semolina
1 egg, beaten
1½ cups (150 g/5 oz) grated
    Parmesan
60 g (2 oz) butter, melted
½ cup (125 ml/4 fl oz) cream
½ cup (60 g/2 oz) grated mozzarella

1 Line a deep 30 x 20 cm (12 x 8 inch) swiss roll tin with baking paper. Put the milk, half the nutmeg and some salt and pepper in a pan and bring to the boil. Reduce the heat and gradually stir in the semolina. Cook, stirring occasionally, for 5–10 minutes or until the semolina is very stiff.
2 Remove from the heat. Add the egg and 1 cup (100 g/3½ oz) Parmesan and stir well. Spread into the tin and refrigerate for 1 hour or until firm.
3 Preheat the oven to moderate 180°C (350°F/Gas 4). Cut the semolina into rounds with a floured 4 cm (1½ inch) cutter. Arrange in a greased shallow casserole dish.

4 Pour the butter over the top and then the cream. Sprinkle with the combined remaining Parmesan and mozzarella cheeses. Sprinkle with the remaining nutmeg. Bake for 20–25 minutes or until golden.

NUTRITION PER SERVE
Protein 33 g; Fat 53 g; Carbohydrate 24 g; Dietary Fibre 0.5 g; Cholesterol 205 mg; 2918 kJ (697 cal)

NOTE: Roman gnocchi is also known as gnocchi alla semolina, to differentiate it from the small potato gnocchi that are boiled and served with pasta sauce.

Cook the semolina for 5–10 minutes, or until it is very stiff.

Use a floured biscuit cutter to cut the gnocchi into circles.

Mix together the grated Parmesan and mozzarella and sprinkle over the gnocchi.

SPICY SWEET POTATO QUICHE

Preparation time: 30 minutes +
  20 minutes refrigeration
Total cooking time: 1 hour 35 minutes
Serves 6

2 cups (250 g/8 oz) plain flour
125 g (4 oz) butter, chilled and cubed
1 egg yolk
2–3 tablespoons iced water

FILLING
30 g (1 oz) butter
1 onion, sliced
1 clove garlic, crushed
2 teaspoons black mustard seeds
2 teaspoons ground cumin
1 teaspoon soft brown sugar
450 g (14 oz) orange sweet potato,
  chopped
2 eggs, lightly beaten
¼ cup (60 ml/2 fl oz) milk
¼ cup (60 ml/2 fl oz) cream
2 tablespoons chopped fresh parsley
2 tablespoons chopped chives

1 Process the flour and butter for about 15 seconds until crumbly. Add the egg yolk and water. Process in short bursts until the mixture comes together. Add a little more water if needed. Turn out onto a floured surface and gather into a ball. Roll the pastry between two sheets of baking paper until large enough to line a shallow 23 cm (9 inch) loose-based fluted tart tin. Trim away the excess pastry. Refrigerate for 20 minutes.
2 Heat the butter in a large pan and cook the onion and garlic for 5 minutes, or until golden. Add the mustard seeds, cumin and brown sugar and stir for 1 minute. Add the sweet potato and cook for 10 minutes over low heat until it has softened slightly. Stir gently, or the sweet potato will break up.
3 Preheat the oven to 180°C (350°F/Gas 4). Cover the pastry shell with baking paper and spread with a layer of baking beads or rice. Bake for 15 minutes, then remove the paper and beads and bake for a further 15 minutes.

4 Put the sweet potato mixture into the pastry shell. Mix together the eggs, milk, cream and herbs and pour over the sweet potato. Bake for 50 minutes, or until set.

NUTRITION PER SERVE
Protein 10 g; Fat 30 g; Carbohydrate 45 g;
Dietary Fibre 4 g; Cholesterol 140 mg;
2015 kJ (480 cal)

Peel the sweet potato and cut into bite-size chunks for the filling.

Add the mustard seeds, cumin and brown sugar to the onion and garlic.

Pour the combined eggs, milk, cream and herbs over the sweet potato mixture.

GADO GADO

Preparation time: 30 minutes
Total cooking time: 35 minutes
Serves 4

6 new potatoes
2 carrots, cut into thick strips
250 g (8 oz) snake beans, cut into
    long lengths
2 tablespoons peanut oil
250 g (8 oz) firm tofu, cubed
100 g (3½ oz) baby English spinach
    leaves
2 Lebanese cucumbers, cut into
    batons
1 large red capsicum, cut into batons
100 g (3½ oz) bean sprouts
5 hard-boiled eggs

PEANUT SAUCE
1 tablespoon peanut oil
1 onion, finely chopped
⅔ cup (150 g/5 oz) peanut butter
¼ cup (60 ml/2 fl oz) kecap manis
2 tablespoons ground coriander
2 teaspoons chilli sauce
¾ cup (185 ml/6 fl oz) coconut cream
1 teaspoon grated palm sugar
1 tablespoon lemon juice

1 Cook the potatoes in boiling water
until tender. Drain and cool slightly.
Cut into quarters. Cook the carrots
and beans separately in boiling water
until just tender. Plunge into iced
water, then drain.
2 Heat the oil in a non-stick frying
pan and cook the tofu in batches until
crisp. Drain on paper towels.
3 To make the peanut sauce, heat the
oil in a pan over low heat and cook
the onion for 5 minutes, or until
golden. Add the peanut butter, kecap
manis, coriander, chilli sauce and
coconut cream. Bring to the boil,
reduce the heat and simmer for
5 minutes. Stir in the sugar and juice
until dissolved.
4 Arrange the vegetables and tofu on
a plate. Halve the eggs and place in
the centre. Serve with the sauce.

NUTRITION PER SERVE
Protein 35 g; Fat 55 g; Carbohydrate 35 g;
Dietary Fibre 15 g; Cholesterol 265 mg;
3175 kJ (755 cal)

Cut the cucumbers and capsicum into even-sized batons.

Cook the snake beans quickly in a pan of boiling water then plunge into iced water.

Heat the oil and cook the tofu in batches until crisp and golden brown.

Add the peanut butter, kecap manis, coriander, chilli sauce and coconut cream to the pan.

PUY LENTILS AND BEAN PUREE ON MUSHROOMS WITH RED WINE SAUCE

Preparation time: 30 minutes
Total cooking time: 35 minutes
Serves 4

4 large (10 cm/4 inch) field
   mushrooms
1 tablespoon olive oil
1 red onion, cut into thin wedges
1 clove garlic, crushed
1 cup (200 g/6½ oz) puy lentils
¾ cup (185 ml/6 fl oz) red wine
1¾ cups (440 ml/14 fl oz) vegetable
   stock
1 tablespoon finely chopped fresh flat-
   leaf parsley
30 g (1 oz) butter
2 cloves garlic, crushed, extra

BEAN PUREE
1 large potato, cut into chunks
2 tablespoons extra virgin olive oil
400 g (13 oz) can cannellini beans,
   drained and rinsed
2 large cloves garlic, crushed
1 tablespoon vegetable stock

RED WINE SAUCE
⅔ cup (170 ml/5½ fl oz) red wine
2 tablespoons tomato paste
1½ cups (375 ml/12 fl oz) vegetable
   stock
1 tablespoon soft brown sugar

1 Remove the stalks from the mushrooms and chop them. Heat the oil in a large saucepan and cook the onion over medium heat for 2–3 minutes, or until soft. Add the garlic and mushroom stalks and cook for a further 1 minute. Stir in the lentils, wine and stock and bring to the boil. Reduce the heat and simmer, covered, for 20–25 minutes, stirring occasionally, or until reduced and the lentils are cooked through. If the mixture is too wet, remove the lid and boil until slightly thick. Stir in the parsley and keep warm.

2 Meanwhile, to make the bean purée, bring a small saucepan of water to the boil over high heat and cook the potato for 10 minutes, or until tender. Drain and mash with a potato masher or fork until smooth. Stir in half the extra virgin olive oil. Combine the cannellini beans and garlic in a food processor bowl. Add the stock and the remaining oil and process until smooth. Transfer to a bowl and fold in the mashed potato. Keep warm.

3 Melt the butter in a deep frying pan. Add the mushrooms and extra garlic and cook in batches over medium heat for 4 minutes each side, or until tender. Remove and keep warm.

4 To make the red wine sauce, add the red wine to the same frying pan, then scrape the bottom to remove any sediment. Add the combined tomato paste, stock and sugar and bring to the boil. Cook for about 10 minutes, or until reduced and thickened.

5 To assemble, place the mushrooms onto serving plates and top with the bean purée. Spoon on the lentil mixture and drizzle with the red wine sauce. Season and serve immediately.

NUTRITION PER SERVE
Protein 23 g; Fat 23 g; Carbohydrate 42 g;
Dietary Fibre 17 g; Cholesterol 20 mg;
2198 kJ (525 cal)

NOTE: The mushrooms tend to shrivel if you keep them warm in the oven—either turn the oven off or find another warm place.

Remove the stalks from the field mushrooms and finely chop them.

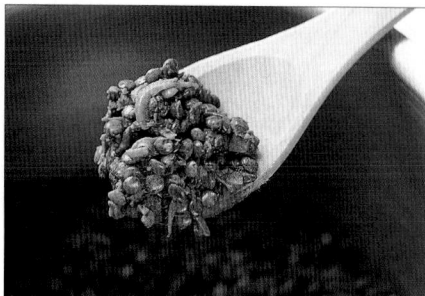
Simmer the lentils until they are cooked through and the liquid is reduced.

Fold the mashed potato into the purée of cannellini beans and garlic.

Fry the mushrooms over medium heat until they are tender, turning once.

Scrape the bottom of the frying pan to stir in any sediment stuck to the pan.

Cook the red wine sauce for 10 minutes, until it is reduced and thickened.

LOW-FAT SPINACH PIE

Preparation time: 25 minutes
Total cooking time: 45 minutes
Serves 6

1.5 kg (3 lb) English spinach
2 teaspoons olive oil
1 onion, chopped
4 spring onions, chopped
750 g (1½ lb) reduced-fat cottage
    cheese
2 eggs, lightly beaten
2 cloves garlic, crushed
pinch of ground nutmeg
¼ cup (15 g/½ oz) chopped fresh mint
8 sheets filo pastry
30 g (1 oz) butter, melted
½ cup (40 g/1¼ oz) fresh breadcrumbs

1 Preheat the oven to 180°C (350°F/ Gas 4). Lightly spray a square 1.5 litre capacity ovenproof dish with oil. Trim and wash the spinach, then place in a large pan with the water clinging to the leaves. Cover and cook for 2–3 minutes, until just wilted. Drain, cool then squeeze dry and chop.

2 Heat the oil in a small pan. Add the onion and spring onion and cook for 2–3 minutes, until softened. Combine in a bowl with the chopped spinach. Stir in the cottage cheese, egg, garlic, nutmeg and mint. Season and mix thoroughly.

3 Brush a sheet of filo pastry with a little butter. Fold in half widthways and line the base and sides of the dish. Repeat with 3 more sheets. Keep the unused sheets moist by covering with a damp tea towel.

4 Sprinkle the breadcrumbs over the pastry. Spread the filling into the dish. Fold over any overlapping pastry. Brush and fold another sheet and

place on top. Repeat with 3 more sheets. Tuck the pastry in at the sides. Brush the top with any remaining butter. Score squares or diamonds on top using a sharp knife. Bake for 40 minutes, or until golden. Cut into squares to serve.

NUTRITION PER SERVE
Protein 35 g; Fat 10 g; Carbohydrate 30 g;
Dietary Fibre 8 g; Cholesterol 75 mg;
1500 kJ (360 cal)

Squeeze any excess moisture out of the cooled spinach with your hands.

Line the base and sides of the dish with the greased and folded filo.

When you have lined the top with pastry, tuck it in at the sides.

COUSCOUS PATTIES

Preparation time: 35 minutes +
   15 minutes refrigeration +
   10 minutes standing
Total cooking time: 30 minutes
Makes 4

1 cup (185 g/6 oz) couscous
4 tablespoons oil
1 eggplant, finely diced
1 onion, finely chopped
1 clove garlic, crushed
2 teaspoons ground cumin
2 teaspoons ground coriander
1 red capsicum, finely diced
2 tablespoons chopped fresh
   coriander
2 teaspoons grated lemon rind

2 teaspoons lemon juice
5 tablespoons natural yoghurt
1 egg, lightly beaten
oil, for shallow-frying

1 Place the couscous in a bowl. Add
1 cup (250 ml/8 fl oz) of boiling
water and leave for 10 minutes, or
until all the water has been absorbed.
Fluff up the grains with a fork.
2 Heat 2 tablespoons of the oil in a
large frying pan and fry the eggplant
until soft and golden, then place in
a bowl. Heat 1 tablespoon of the oil
in the pan. Add the onion, garlic,
cumin and ground coriander. Cook
over medium heat for 3–4 minutes,
or until soft, then add to the bowl.
Heat the remaining oil and cook the
capsicum for 5 minutes, or until soft.

Place in the bowl and stir well.
3 Add the vegetable mixture to the
couscous with the fresh coriander,
lemon rind, lemon juice, yoghurt and
egg. Season to taste and mix well.
4 Using damp hands, divide the
mixture into four portions and form
into large patties—they should be
about 2 cm (¾ inch) thick. Cover and
refrigerate for 15 minutes. Shallow-fry
the patties over medium heat for
5 minutes on each side, or until
golden. Drain the patties well and
serve with yoghurt.

NUTRITION PER PATTY
Protein 9 g; Fat 25 g; Carbohydrate 35 g;
Dietary Fibre 4 g; Cholesterol 5 mg;
1760 kJ (420 cal)

When the couscous has absorbed the water, fluff
up the grains with a fork.

Season the patty mixture with salt and cracked
pepper and mix well.

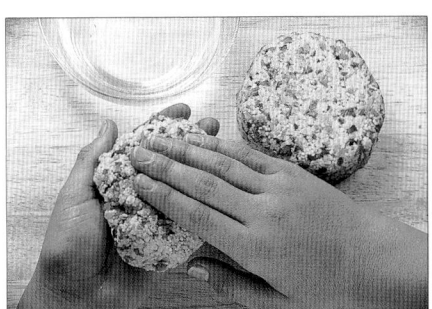

With damp hands, form the mixture into four
large patties.

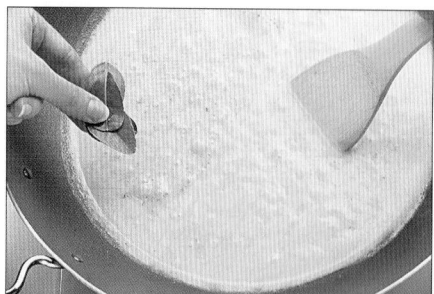

RED VEGETABLE CURRY

Preparation time: 25 minutes
Total cooking time: 20 minutes
Serves 4

225 g (7 oz) bamboo shoots or tips, drained
2 cups (500 ml/16 fl oz) coconut milk
2 tablespoons Thai red curry paste
1 onion, finely chopped
4 kaffir lime leaves
2 potatoes, roughly chopped
200 g (6½ oz) pumpkin, chopped
150 g (5 oz) green beans, chopped

1 red capsicum, chopped
3 small zucchini, chopped
2 tablespoons chopped fresh basil leaves
2 tablespoons lime juice
3 teaspoons soft brown sugar

1 Cut the bamboo shoots in half, discard the tough ends and set the shoots aside. Combine the coconut milk and curry paste in a large wok or pan with ½ cup (125 ml/4 fl oz) water. Bring to the boil, stirring occasionally.
2 Add the onion and kaffir lime leaves and allow to boil for 3 minutes.

3 Add the potato and pumpkin to the wok and cook over medium heat for 8 minutes, or until the pumpkin is nearly cooked. Add the beans, capsicum and zucchini and simmer for another 5 minutes. Add ½ cup (125 ml/4 fl oz) of water if the curry is too thick. Add the bamboo shoots and basil. Add the lime juice and sugar and taste for seasoning. Serve with steamed rice.

NUTRITION PER SERVE
Protein 7 g; Fat 26 g; Carbohydrate 22 g; Dietary Fibre 6.5 g; Cholesterol 0 mg; 1443 kJ (345 cal)

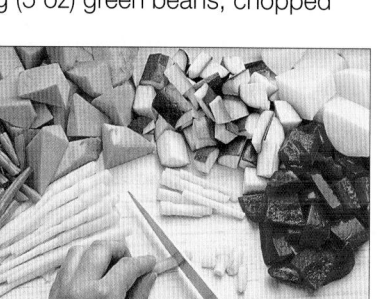

Cut the bamboo shoots in half and discard the tough ends.

Stir in the onion and kaffir lime leaves and boil for 3 minutes.

Add the potato and pumpkin to the curry and simmer until the pumpkin is almost cooked.

TOFU KEBABS WITH MISO PESTO

**Preparation time: 30 minutes +
  1 hour marinating**
Total cooking time: 10 minutes
Serves 4

1 large red capsicum, cubed
12 button mushrooms, halved
6 pickling onions, quartered
3 zucchini, cut into chunks
450 g (14 oz) firm tofu, cubed
½ cup (125 ml/4 fl oz) light olive oil
3 tablespoons light soy sauce
2 cloves garlic, crushed
2 teaspoons grated fresh ginger

MISO PESTO
½ cup (90 g/3 oz) unsalted roasted
  peanuts
2 cups (60 g/2 oz) firmly packed fresh
  coriander leaves
2 tablespoons white miso paste
2 cloves garlic
100 ml (3½ oz) olive oil

1 If using wooden skewers, soak them in water for 30 minutes to prevent scorching. Thread the vegetables and tofu alternately onto 12 skewers, then place in a large non-metallic dish.
2 Mix together the olive oil, soy sauce, garlic and ginger, then pour half over the kebabs. Cover and leave to marinate for 1 hour.

3 To make the miso pesto, finely chop the peanuts, coriander leaves, miso paste and garlic in a food processor. Slowly add the olive oil while the machine is still running and blend to a smooth paste.
4 Cook the kebabs on a hot, lightly oiled barbecue flatplate or grill, turning and brushing with the remaining marinade, for 4–6 minutes, or until the edges are slightly brown. Serve with the miso pesto.

NUTRITION PER SERVE
Protein 8 g; Fat 64 g; Carbohydrate 10 g;
Dietary Fibre 4 g; Cholesterol 0 mg;
2698 kJ (645 cal)

Thread the vegetable pieces and tofu cubes alternately onto the skewers.

Mix the nuts, coriander leaves, miso and garlic in a food processor until finely chopped.

Brush the kebabs with the remaining marinade during cooking.

SILVERBEET PARCELS

Preparation time: 40 minutes
Total cooking time: 1 hour
Serves 6

2 cups (500 ml/16 fl oz) vegetable
    stock
1 tablespoon olive oil
1 onion, chopped
2 cloves garlic, crushed
1 red capsicum, chopped
250 g (8 oz) mushrooms, chopped
½ cup (110 g/3½ oz) arborio rice
60 g (2 oz) Cheddar, grated
¼ cup (15 g/½ oz) shredded fresh basil
6 large silverbeet leaves
2 x 400 g (13 oz) cans chopped
    tomatoes
1 tablespoon balsamic vinegar
1 teaspoon soft brown sugar

1 Heat the vegetable stock in a pan and maintain at simmering point. Heat the oil in a large pan, add the onion and garlic and cook until the onion has softened. Add the capsicum, mushrooms and rice and stir until well combined. Gradually add ½ cup (125 ml/4 fl oz) hot stock, stirring until the liquid has been absorbed. Continue to add the stock, a little at a time, stirring constantly for 20–25 minutes, or until the rice is creamy and tender (you may not need all the stock, or you may need to add a little water if you run out). Remove from the heat, add the cheese and basil and season well.
2 Trim the stalks from the silverbeet and cook the leaves, a few at a time, in a large pan of boiling water for 30 seconds, or until wilted. Drain on a tea towel. Using a sharp knife, cut away any tough white veins from the centre of the leaves without cutting them in half. If necessary, overlap the two sides to make a flat surface. Place a portion of mushroom filling in the centre of each leaf, fold in the sides and roll up carefully. Tie with string.
3 Put the tomato, balsamic vinegar and sugar in a large, deep non-stick frying pan and stir to combine. Add the silverbeet parcels, cover and simmer for 10 minutes. Remove the string and serve with tomato sauce.

NUTRITION PER SERVE
Protein 7.5 g; Fat 6 g; Carbohydrate 20 g;
Dietary Fibre 4 g; Cholesterol 7 mg;
725 kJ (175 cal)

Add the stock, a little at a time, until the rice is tender and has absorbed the stock.

Using a sharp knife, cut away the white veins from the centre of the leaves.

Place the filling in the centre of each leaf, fold in the sides and roll up into parcels.

MEDITERRANEAN VEGETABLE HOTPOT

Preparation time: 20 minutes
Total cooking time: 40 minutes
Serves 4

3 tablespoons olive oil
1 onion, chopped
2 cloves garlic, crushed
1 green capsicum, chopped
1 red capsicum, chopped
3 zucchini, sliced
3 slender eggplant, sliced
2 cups (440 g/14 oz) long-grain rice
1 cup (250 ml/8 fl oz) white wine

100 g (3½ oz) button mushrooms, sliced
3 cups (750 ml/24 fl oz) vegetable stock
400 g (13 oz) can crushed tomatoes
2 tablespoons tomato paste
150 g (5 oz) feta cheese

1 Heat the oil in a large heavy-based pan and cook the onion over medium heat for about 10 minutes, or until very soft but not browned. Add the garlic and cook for a further minute.
2 Add the green and red capsicums and cook, stirring, for 3 minutes, Add the zucchini and eggplant and sitr-fry for a further 5 minutes. Add the rice

and stir-fry for 2 minutes.
3 Add the wine, mushrooms, stock, crushed tomatoes and tomato paste. Stir to combine. Bring to the boil, reduce the heat, cover and simmer for 20 minutes. The rice should be tender. Serve immediately, topped with the crumbled feta cheese.

NUTRITION PER SERVE
Protein 20 g; Fat 25 g; Carbohydrate 92 g; Dietary Fibre 9 g; Cholesterol 25 mg; 2980 kJ (710 cal)

NOTE: Like most hotpots and casseroles, this is best made a day in advance to let the flavours develop.

Cook the onion for 10 minutes, until it is very soft but not browned.

Add the zucchini and eggplant to the pan and stir-fry for a little longer.

Add the wine, mushrooms, stock, crushed tomatoes and tomato paste.

AUTUMN VEGETABLE STEW

Preparation time: 25 minutes
Total cooking time: 30 minutes
Serves 4–6

185 g (6 oz) frozen broad beans, thawed
150 g (5 oz) baby onions
50 g (1¾ oz) butter
2 teaspoons olive oil
400 g (13 oz) small parsnips
150 g (5 oz) Jerusalem artichokes
2 tablespoons plain flour
2⅓ cups (580 ml/19 fl oz) chicken stock
300 ml (10 fl oz) cream
2 teaspoons grated lemon rind
1 teaspoon grated orange rind
400 g (13 oz) baby carrots, trimmed
500 g (1 lb) baby turnips, trimmed

1 Peel and discard the tough outer skin of the broad beans. Carefully peel the onions, leaving the flat root end attached, then cut a cross through the root end of each onion.
2 Heat the butter and oil in a large, heavy-based saucepan until foamy. Add the onions and cook for 7 minutes over low–medium heat, turning often to colour evenly.
3 While the onions are browning, peel the parsnips and artichokes, and cut them into bite-size pieces. Add to the saucepan and toss well. Scatter the flour over the onion, parsnip and artichokes, toss to coat and cook for 2 minutes.
4 Stir in the chicken stock, cream, lemon rind and orange rind. Bring to the boil, stirring, then reduce the heat and simmer for 7 minutes, or until the vegetables are half-cooked.
5 Add the carrots and turnips, and toss well. Cover the pan and cook for 4–5 minutes, or until the vegetables are just tender. Season well with salt and freshly ground pepper, stir in the peeled broad beans to heat through, and serve.

NUTRITION PER SERVE (6)
Protein 7 g; Fat 30 g; Carbohydrate 25 g; Dietary Fibre 10 g; Cholesterol 90 mg; 1665 kJ (400 cal)

NOTES: Baby vegetables have a sweet, delicate flavour. If unavailable, choose the smallest vegetables and cook them for a few minutes longer. Fresh broad beans can be used. Add them with the carrots and turnips.

Skin the broad beans and cut a cross through the root end of the peeled onions.

Peel the small parsnips and Jerusalem artichokes, and cut into bite-sized pieces.

STUFFED EGGPLANTS

Preparation time: 20 minutes
Total cooking time: 1 hour
Serves 4

⅓ cup (60 g/2 oz) brown lentils
2 large eggplants
cooking oil spray
1 red onion, chopped
2 cloves garlic, crushed
1 red capsicum, finely chopped
¼ cup (40 g/1¼ oz) pine nuts, toasted
¾ cup (140 g/4½ oz) cooked
    short-grain rice
440 g (14 oz) can chopped tomatoes
2 tablespoons chopped coriander

1 tablespoon chopped fresh parsley
2 tablespoons grated Parmesan

1 Simmer the brown lentils in a pan of water for 25 minutes, or until soft; drain. Slice the eggplants in half lengthways and scoop out the flesh, leaving a 1 cm (½ inch) shell. Chop the flesh finely.
2 Spray a deep, large non-stick frying pan with oil, add 1 tablespoon water to the pan, then add the onion and garlic and stir until softened. Add the cooked lentils to the pan with the capsicum, pine nuts, rice, tomato and eggplant flesh. Stir over medium heat for 10 minutes, or until the eggplant has softened. Add the fresh coriander

and parsley. Season, then toss until well mixed.
3 Cook the eggplant shells in boiling water for 4–5 minutes, or until tender, or microwave on High (100%) for 8 minutes. Spoon the filling into the eggplant shells and sprinkle with the Parmesan. Grill for 5–10 minutes, or until golden. Serve immediately.

NUTRITION PER SERVE
Protein 15 g; Fat 10 g; Carbohydrate 50 g;
Dietary Fibre 8.5 g; Cholesterol 9.5 mg;
1490 kJ (355 cal)

Scoop out the flesh, leaving a shell on the inside of the eggplant halves.

Stir in the chopped fresh coriander and parsley and season.

Cook the eggplant halves in boiling water for about 5 minutes, or until tender.

FRITTATA

Preparation time: 25 minutes
Total cooking time: 25 minutes
Serves 6

200 g (6½ oz) zucchini, cubed
250 g (8 oz) pumpkin, cubed
300 g (10 oz) potato, cubed
100 g (3½ oz) broccoli florets
3 teaspoons oil
1 small onion, chopped
1 small red capsicum, chopped
2 tablespoons chopped fresh parsley
3 eggs
2 egg whites

1 Steam the zucchini, pumpkin, potato and broccoli until tender.
2 Heat 2 teaspoons of the oil in a non-stick frying pan, about 22 cm (9 inch) diameter. Add the onion and capsicum and cook for 3 minutes, or until tender. Mix with the steamed vegetables, along with the parsley.
3 Brush the pan with the remaining oil. Return all the vegetables to the pan and spread out with a spatula to an even thickness. Beat the eggs and whites together and pour into the pan.
4 Cook over medium heat until the eggs are almost set, but still runny on top. Wrap the handle of the pan in foil to protect it and place under a hot grill to brown the frittata top (pierce gently with a fork to make sure it is cooked through). Cut into wedges to serve.

NUTRITION PER SERVE
Protein 8 g; Fat 5 g; Carbohydrate 10 g;
Dietary Fibre 3 g; Cholesterol 90 mg;
515 kJ (125 cal)

Cook the finely chopped onion and capsicum until tender.

Beat the combined eggs and whites and pour into the pan over the vegetables.

The eggs should be almost set, but still runny on top, before you put them under the grill.

CHILLI NOODLES WITH NUTS

Preparation time: 20 minutes
Total cooking time: 12 minutes
Serves 4

1½ tablespoons oil
1 tablespoon sesame oil
2–3 small red chillies, finely chopped
1 large onion, cut into thin wedges
4 cloves garlic, cut into paper-thin slices
1 red capsicum, cut into strips
1 green capsicum, cut into strips
2 large carrots, cut into thick matchsticks
100 g (3½ oz) green beans

2 celery sticks, cut into matchsticks
2 teaspoons honey
500 g (1 lb) Hokkien noodles, gently separated
100 g (3½ oz) dry-roasted peanuts
100 g (3½ oz) honey-roasted cashews
¼ cup (30 g/1 oz) chopped fresh garlic chives, or 4 spring onions, chopped
sweet chilli sauce and sesame oil, to serve

1 Heat the wok over low heat, add the oils and swirl them around to coat the side. When the oil is warm, add the chilli and heat until very hot.
2 Add the onion and garlic and stir-fry for 1 minute, or until the onion just softens. Add the capsicum, carrot and beans and stir-fry for 1 minute. Add the celery, honey and 1 table-spoon water and season with salt and pepper. Toss well, then cover and cook for 1–2 minutes, or until the vegetables are brightly coloured and just tender.
3 Add the noodles and nuts and toss well. Cook, covered, for 1–2 minutes, or until the noodles are heated through. Stir in the garlic chives and serve, drizzled with the sweet chilli sauce and sesame oil.

NUTRITION PER SERVE
Protein 20 g; Fat 45 g; Carbohydrate 75 g; Dietary Fibre 7 g; Cholesterol 0 mg; 3330 kJ (795 cal)

Peel the cloves of garlic, then cut them into paper-thin slices.

Remove the seeds from the capsicum and cut the flesh into strips.

Heat the chopped chilli in the oil until the oil is very hot.

ASIAN GREENS WITH TERIYAKI TOFU DRESSING

Preparation time: 15 minutes
Total cooking time: 20 minutes
Serves 6

650 g (1 lb 5 oz) baby bok choy
500 g (1 lb) choy sum
440 g (14 oz) snake beans, topped
 and tailed
¼ cup (60 ml/2 fl oz) oil
1 onion, thinly sliced
⅓ cup (60 g/2 oz) soft brown sugar
½ teaspoon ground chilli

2 tablespoons grated fresh ginger
1 cup (250 ml/8 fl oz) teriyaki sauce
1 tablespoon sesame oil
600 g (1¼ lb) silken firm tofu, drained

1 Cut the the baby bok choy and choy sum widthways into thirds. Cut the beans into 10 cm (4 inch) lengths.
2 Heat a wok over high heat, add 1 tablespoon of the oil and swirl to coat the side. Cook the onion in batches for 3–5 minutes, or until crisp. Remove with a slotted spoon and drain on paper towels.
3 Heat 1 tablespoon of the oil in the wok, add half the greens and stir-fry for 2–3 minutes, or until wilted.

Remove and keep warm. Repeat with the remaining oil and greens. Remove. Drain any liquid from the wok.
4 Add the combined sugar, chilli, ginger and teriyaki sauce to the wok and bring to the boil. Simmer for 1 minute. Add the sesame oil and tofu and simmer for 2 minutes, turning once—the tofu will break up. Divide the greens among serving plates, then top with the dressing. Sprinkle with the fried onion.

NUTRITION PER SERVE
Protein 19 g; Fat 11 g; Carbohydrate 20 g;
Dietary Fibre 11 g; Cholesterol 1 mg;
1093 kJ (260 cal)

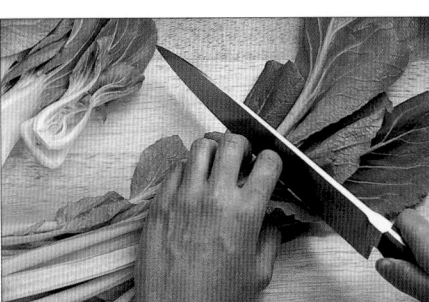

Cut the baby bok choy and choy sum widthways into thirds.

Cook the combined greens in two batches until the leaves are wilted.

Turn the tofu with an egg-flip halfway through cooking—it will break up.

RED CAPSICUM, TOMATO AND ONION TART

Preparation time: 35 minutes +
20 minutes refrigeration
Total cooking time: 1 hour 10 minutes
Serves 6

1 cup (125 g/4 oz) plain flour
½ cup (75 g/2½ oz) wholemeal plain
    flour
100 g (3½ oz) butter, chilled and cubed
1 tablespoon sesame seeds
1 egg, lightly beaten

FILLING
500 g (1 lb) tomatoes, finely chopped
2 tablespoons tomato paste
1 teaspoon dried oregano
½ teaspoon sugar
1 tablespoon olive oil
3 red onions, sliced
1 teaspoon chopped fresh thyme
3 red capsicums
⅓ cup (35 g/1¼ oz) grated Parmesan

1 Process the flours, butter and sesame seeds for about 15 seconds, or until the mixture resembles fine breadcrumbs. Add the egg and process in short bursts until the mixture just comes together. Add a little cold water if necessary. Turn out onto a lightly floured surface and gather into a ball. Wrap in plastic and refrigerate for at least 20 minutes. Preheat the oven to 200°C (400°F/Gas 6) and grease a shallow 19 x 28 cm (7½ x 11 inch) loose-based fluted tart tin.

2 Roll out the pastry on a sheet of baking paper until large enough to line the tin. Press well into the sides and trim away the excess. Prick the pastry all over with a fork and bake for 12 minutes, or until just brown and dry. Allow to cool.

3 Heat the tomatoes, tomato paste, oregano and sugar in a pan. Bring to the boil, then reduce the heat and simmer for 15–20 minutes, or until thick. Allow to cool. Season well.

4 Heat the oil in a pan and add the onion and thyme. Cook until the onion is soft and transparent.

5 Quarter the capsicums and remove the seeds and membrane. Grill, skin-side-up, until the skins have blistered. Cool in a plastic bag. Remove the skins and cut into quarters.

6 Spread the onion evenly over the base of the pastry shell and top with the tomato sauce. Sprinkle with cheese then top with the capsicum. Bake for 30 minutes, or until heated through and the pastry is crisp. Serve hot.

NUTRITION PER SERVE
Protein 10 g; Fat 20 g; Carbohydrate 30 g;
Dietary Fibre 5 g; Cholesterol 80 mg;
1485 kJ (355 cal)

STORAGE: The pastry can be made in advance and kept in the freezer for up to 3 months; or in the fridge for a day. Make sure it is well covered. Allow enough time to bring the pastry to room temperature before rolling it out.

Slice the red onions into large pieces to add texture to the tart filling.

Place the flours, butter and sesame seeds in a food processor.

Lift the pastry into the prepared tin and press it well into the sides.

Heat the tomatoes, tomato paste, oregano and sugar in a pan.

Remove the blistered skin from the capsicums and cut them into pieces.

Spread the onions over the pastry shell and top with the tomato sauce.

LENTIL BHUJIA STEW

**Preparation time: 30 minutes + overnight
soaking + 30 minutes refrigeration
Total cooking time: 1 hour 10 minutes
Serves 4–6**

2 cups (370 g/12 oz) green or brown
    lentils
1 large onion, grated
1 large potato, grated
1 teaspoon ground cumin
1 teaspoon ground coriander
1 teaspoon ground turmeric
¾ cup (90 g/3 oz) plain flour
oil, for shallow-frying
2 cloves garlic, crushed
1 tablespoon grated fresh ginger
1 cup (250 ml/8 fl oz) tomato
    purée
2 cups (500 ml/16 fl oz) vegetable
    stock
1 cup (250 ml/8 fl oz) cream
200 g (6½ oz) green beans, topped,
    tailed and cut in half
2 carrots, sliced
2 hard-boiled eggs, chopped
sprigs fresh rosemary, to garnish

1 Soak the lentils overnight in cold
water. Drain well. Squeeze the excess
moisture from the lentils, onion and
potato using a tea towel. Place them
in a bowl with the ground spices
and flour; mix well and leave for
10 minutes. With floured hands,
shape the mixture into walnut-sized
balls and place on a foil-lined tray.
Cover and refrigerate for 30 minutes.
2 Heat 2 cm (¾ inch) of oil in a
heavy-based frying pan. Cook the
balls in batches over high heat until
golden brown. Drain on paper towels.
3 Heat 2 tablespoons of oil in a
saucepan and gently fry the garlic and

ginger for 2 minutes. Stir in the purée,
stock and cream. Bring to the boil,
then reduce the heat and simmer for
10 minutes. Add the beans, lentil
balls and carrot. Cook, covered, for
30 minutes, stirring twice. Add the
egg and cook for 10 minutes. Garnish
with rosemary to serve.

NUTRITION PER SERVE (6)
Protein 23 g; Fat 30 g; Carbohydrate 45 g;
Dietary Fibre 13 g; Cholesterol 125 mg;
2290 kJ (550 cal)

VARIATION: Split peas can be used in
this recipe in place of the lentils. Soak
them in cold water overnight, then
drain well before using.

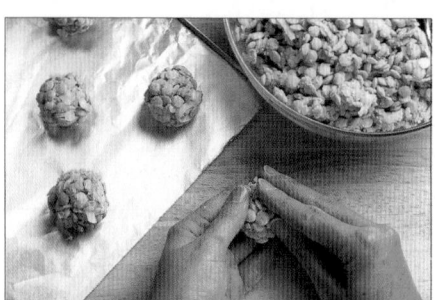

Shape the lentil mixture into walnut-sized balls,
and place on a foil-lined tray.

Fry the lentil balls in oil in batches over high heat,
until golden brown.

Add the beans, lentil balls and carrot to the
simmering sauce.

FRENCH SHALLOT TATIN

**Preparation time: 45 minutes +
  20 minutes refrigeration
Total cooking time: 1 hour
Serves 4–6**

750 g (1½ lb) French shallots
50 g (1¾ oz) butter
2 tablespoons olive oil
⅓ cup (60 g/2 oz) soft brown sugar
3 tablespoons balsamic vinegar

PASTRY
1 cup (125 g/4 oz) plain flour
60g (2 oz) butter, chilled and cubed
2 teaspoons wholegrain mustard
1 egg yolk
1–2 tablespoons iced water

1 Peel the shallots, leaving the bases intact and tips exposed (see Hint).
2 Heat the butter and olive oil in a large pan. Cook the shallots for 15 minutes over low heat, then remove. Add the sugar, vinegar and 3 tablespoons of water to the pan and stir to dissolve the sugar. Add the shallots and simmer over low heat for 15–20 minutes, turning occasionally.
3 Preheat the oven to 200°C (400°F/ Gas 6). To make the pastry, process the flour and butter until crumbly. Add the mustard, egg yolk and water. Process in short bursts until the mixture comes together. Turn out onto a floured surface and gather into a ball. Wrap in plastic wrap and refrigerate for 20 minutes.
4 Grease a shallow 20 cm (8 inch) round sandwich tin. Pack the shallots tightly into the tin and pour over any syrup from the pan. Roll out the pastry on a sheet of baking paper to a circle, 1 cm (½ inch) larger than the

tin. Lift the pastry into the tin and lightly push it down so it is slightly moulded over the shallots. Bake for 20–25 minutes, or until golden brown. Cool for 5 minutes on a wire rack. Place a plate over the tin and turn the tart out.

NUTRITION PER SERVE (6)
Protein 5 g; Fat 25 g; Carbohydrate 25 g;
Dietary Fibre 2 g; Cholesterol 75 mg;
1360 kJ (325 cal)

HINT: Put the unpeeled shallots in boiling water for 30 seconds to make them easier to peel.

Return the shallots to the brown sugar and balsamic vinegar mixture in the pan.

Arrange the shallots over the base of the tin so that they are tightly packed.

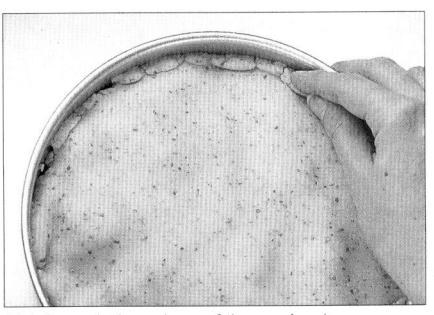

Lightly push the edges of the pastry down so that it moulds over the shallots.

MUSHROOM AND EGGPLANT SKEWERS WITH TOMATO SAUCE

Preparation time: 20 minutes +
15 minutes marinating
Total cooking time: 30 minutes
Serves 4

12 long fresh rosemary sprigs
18 Swiss brown mushrooms,
    halved
1 small eggplant, cubed
3 tablespoons olive oil
2 tablespoons balsamic vinegar
2 cloves garlic, crushed
1 teaspoon sugar

TOMATO SAUCE
5 tomatoes
1 tablespoon olive oil
1 small onion, finely chopped
1 clove garlic, crushed
1 tablespoon tomato paste
2 teaspoons sugar
2 teaspoons balsamic vinegar
1 tablespoon chopped fresh
    flat-leaf parsley

1 Remove the leaves from the lower part of the rosemary sprigs. Reserve a tablespoon of the leaves. Put the mushrooms and eggplant in a large non-metallic bowl. Pour on the combined oil, vinegar, garlic and sugar and toss. Marinate for 15 minutes.
2 To make the tomato sauce, score a cross in the base of each tomato. Put in a bowl of boiling water for 30 seconds, then plunge into cold water. Peel the skin away from the cross. Cut in half and scoop out the seeds with a teaspoon. Dice the flesh.
3 Heat the oil in a saucepan. Cook the onion and garlic over medium heat for 2–3 minutes, or until soft.

Reduce the heat, add the tomato, tomato paste, sugar, vinegar and parsley and simmer for 10 minutes, or until thick.
4 Thread alternating mushroom halves and eggplant cubes onto the rosemary sprigs. Cook on a hot, lightly oiled barbecue grill or flatplate for 7–8 minutes, or until the eggplant is tender, turning occasionally. Serve with the sauce.

NUTRITION PER SERVE
Protein 3 g; Fat 24 g; Carbohydrate 8.5 g;
Dietary Fibre 4 g; Cholesterol 0 mg;
1100 kJ (263 cal)

Simmer the tomato sauce until the liquid has evaporated and the sauce is thick.

Thread alternating mushrooms and eggplant cubes onto the skewers.

VEGETARIAN BURGERS WITH CORIANDER GARLIC CREAM

Preparation time: 30 minutes
Total cooking time: 20 minutes
Makes 10 burgers

1 cup (250 g/8 oz) red lentils
1 tablespoon oil
2 onions, sliced
1 tablespoon tandoori mix powder
425 g (14 oz) can chickpeas, drained
1 tablespoon grated fresh ginger
1 egg
3 tablespoons chopped fresh parsley
2 tablespoons chopped fresh
    coriander
2¼ cups (180 g/6 oz) fresh
    breadcrumbs
plain flour, for dusting

CORIANDER GARLIC CREAM
½ cup (125 g/4 oz) sour cream
½ cup (125 ml/4 fl oz) cream
1 clove garlic, crushed
2 tablespoons chopped fresh
    coriander
2 tablespoons chopped fresh parsley

1 Simmer the lentils in a large pan of water for 8 minutes or until tender. Drain well. Heat the oil in a pan and cook the onion until tender. Add the tandoori mix and stir until fragrant.
2 Put the chickpeas, half the lentils, the ginger, egg and onion mixture in a food processor. Process for 20 seconds or until smooth. Transfer to a bowl. Stir in the remaining lentils, parsley, coriander and breadcrumbs.
3 Divide into 10 portions and shape into burgers. (If the mixture is too soft, refrigerate for 15 minutes to firm.) Toss the burgers in flour and

place on a hot, lightly oiled barbecue grill or flatplate. Cook for 3–4 minutes each side or until browned.
4 For the coriander garlic cream, mix together the sour cream, cream, garlic and herbs. Serve with the burgers.

NUTRITION PER BURGER
Protein 11 g; Fat 14 g; Carbohydrate 26 g;
Dietary Fibre 5 g; Cholesterol 50 mg;
1155 kJ (276 cal)

STORAGE: The burgers can be prepared up to 2 days in advance and stored, covered, in the fridge. The cream can be stored, covered, in the fridge for up to 3 days.

NOTE: The coriander garlic cream is also delicious with chicken or fish burgers.

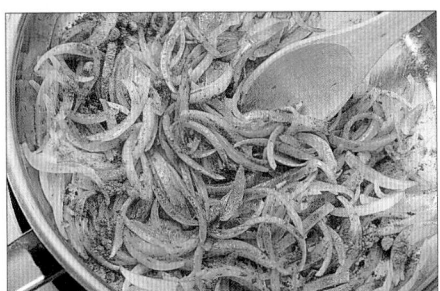

Heat the oil in a pan and cook the onion until tender, then add the tandoori mix.

Process the chickpea mixture, then transfer to a bowl and mix with the other ingredients.

Shape the portions into burgers and then toss in flour, shaking off the excess, before cooking.

TOFU TRIANGLES

**Preparation time: 30 minutes +
   4 hours refrigeration**
Total cooking time: 20 minutes
Serves 4

150 g (5 oz) firm tofu
2 spring onions, chopped
3 teaspoons chopped fresh coriander
   leaves
½ teaspoon grated orange rind
2 teaspoons soy sauce
1 tablespoon sweet chilli sauce
2 teaspoons grated fresh ginger
1 teaspoon cornflour
½ cup (125 ml/4 fl oz) seasoned rice
   vinegar

¼ cup (60 g/2 oz) sugar
1 small Lebanese cucumber, finely
   diced
1 small red chilli, thinly sliced
1 spring onion, extra, thinly sliced on
   the diagonal
2 sheets puff pastry
1 egg, lightly beaten

1 Drain the tofu, then pat dry and cut into small cubes.
2 Put the spring onion, coriander, rind, soy and chilli sauces, ginger, cornflour and tofu in a bowl and gently mix. Cover, then refrigerate for 3–4 hours.
3 To make a dipping sauce, put the vinegar and sugar in a small saucepan and stir over low heat until the sugar dissolves. Remove from the heat and add the cucumber, chilli and extra spring onion. Cool completely.
4 Preheat the oven to 220°C (425°F/ Gas 7). Cut each pastry sheet into four squares. Drain the filling and divide into eight. Place one portion in the centre of each square and brush the edges with egg. Fold into a triangle and seal the edges with a fork.
5 Put the triangles on two lined baking trays, brush with egg and bake for 15 minutes. Serve with the dippping sauce.

NUTRITION PER SERVE
Protein 9 g; Fat 24 g; Carbohydrate 48 g;
Dietary Fibre 2 g; Cholesterol 66 mg;
1946 kJ (464 cal)

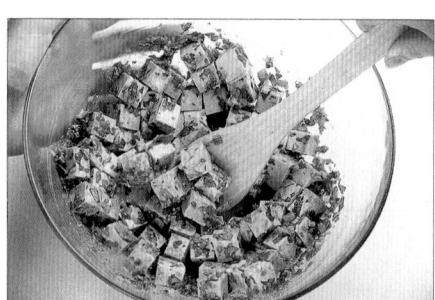
Gently mix the tofu and other ingredients together in a bowl.

Remove the saucepan from the heat and add the spring onion, cucumber and chilli.

Fold the pastry to enclose the filling, then seal the edges with a fork.

GREEN TOFU CURRY

Preparation time: 20 minutes
Total cooking time: 20 minutes
Serves 6

CURRY PASTE
10 small fresh green chillies
50 g (1¾ oz) red Asian shallots, peeled
2 cloves garlic
1 cup (50 g/1¾ oz) finely chopped
    coriander stems and roots
1 stem lemon grass (white part only),
    chopped
2 tablespoons grated fresh galangal
1 tablespoon ground coriander
1 teaspoon ground cumin
1 teaspoon black peppercorns
½ teaspoon ground turmeric
1 tablespoon lime juice

2 tablespoons oil
1 onion, sliced
400 ml (13 fl oz) can coconut cream
4–5 kaffir lime leaves, torn
500 g (1 lb) firm tofu, cut into 2 cm
    (¾ inch) cubes
1 tablespoon lime juice

1 tablespoon shredded fresh Thai basil

1 To make the curry paste, place all the ingredients in a food processor and process until smooth.

2 Heat the oil in a frying pan, add the onion and cook for 5 minutes, or until soft. Add 4 tablespoons curry paste (or more for a stronger flavour) and cook, stirring, for 2 minutes. Stir in the coconut cream and 1 cup (250 ml/8 fl oz) water, and season with salt. Bring to the boil and add the lime leaves and tofu. Reduce the heat and simmer for 8 minutes, stirring often. Stir in the lime juice and Thai basil, and serve.

Place the curry paste ingredients in a food processor and process until smooth.

NUTRITION PER SERVE
Protein 3.5 g; Fat 25 g; Carbohydrate 3 g;
Dietary Fibre 1.5 g; Cholesterol 0 mg;
1020 kJ (242 cal)

NOTE: The recipe for the curry paste makes 1 cup, but you will only need ⅓ cup. Freeze the remaining paste in two portions to use at a later date.

Cook the onion slices for 5 minutes, or until the onion is soft.

Sides & Salads

FRESH BEETROOT AND GOAT'S CHEESE SALAD

Preparation time: 20 minutes
Total cooking time: 30 minutes
Serves 4

1 kg (2 lb) (4 bulbs with leaves) fresh
   beetroot
200 g (6½ oz) green beans
1 tablespoon red wine vinegar
2 tablespoons extra virgin olive oil
1 clove garlic, crushed
1 tablespoon drained capers,
   coarsely chopped
100 g (3½ oz) goat's cheese

1 Trim the leaves from the beetroot. Scrub the bulbs and wash the leaves well. Add the whole bulbs to a large saucepan of boiling water, reduce the heat and simmer, covered, for 30 minutes, or until tender when pierced with the point of a knife. (The cooking time may vary depending on the size of the bulbs.)

2 Meanwhile, bring a saucepan of water to the boil, add the beans and cook for 3 minutes, or until just tender. Remove with a slotted spoon and plunge into a bowl of cold water. Drain well. Add the beetroot leaves to the same saucepan of boiling water and cook for 3–5 minutes, or until the leaves and stems are tender. Drain, plunge into a bowl of cold water, then drain again well.

3 Drain and cool the beetroots, then peel the skins off and cut the bulbs into thin wedges.

4 To make the dressing, put the red wine vinegar, oil, garlic, capers, ½ teaspoon salt and ½ teaspoon pepper in a screw-top jar and shake.

5 To serve, divide the beans, beetroot leaves and bulbs among four serving plates. Crumble goat's cheese over the top and drizzle with the dressing.

NUTRITION PER SERVE
Protein 12 g; Fat 18 g; Carbohydrate 22 g;
Dietary Fibre 9 g; Cholesterol 25 mg;
1256 kJ (300 Cal)

Remove the skin from the beetroot, then cut into thin wedges.

Cook the beetroot leaves until the leaves and stems are tender.

INDIVIDUAL OVEN-BAKED ROSTI

Preparation time: 20–25 minutes
Total cooking time: 55 minutes
Makes 12

500 g (1 lb) waxy potatoes (Desiree, Pontiac), peeled
1 onion
30 g (1 oz) butter, melted

1 Preheat the oven to hot 220°C (425°F/Gas 7). Cook the potatoes in a pan of boiling salted water for 7 minutes, or until just tender. Drain.
2 Prepare a 12-hole muffin tin, with holes measuring 6 cm (2½ inches) at the top and 4.5 cm (1¾ inches) at the base, by brushing with a little of the butter. Grate the potatoes and onion, mix together in a bowl and pour the melted butter over the mixture. Season with salt and mix together well. Using two forks, divide the mixture among the muffin holes, gently pressing it in. Cook the rosti in the oven for 45 minutes, or until golden.
3 Using a small palette knife, loosen each rosti around the edge and lift out. Serve on a warm serving dish.

NUTRITION PER ROSTI
Protein 1 g; Fat 2 g; Carbohydrate 6 g; Dietary Fibre 1 g; Cholesterol 6 mg; 200 kJ (50 cal)

Lightly brush the muffin tin with some of the melted butter.

Use two forks to put some mixture into each hole of the muffin tin.

Before lifting the rosti out, loosen around the edge with a small palette knife.

VIETNAMESE SALAD

**Preparation time: 30 minutes +
10 minutes standing + 30 minutes
refrigeration**
Total cooking time: Nil
Serves 4–6

200 g (6½ oz) dried rice vermicelli
1 cup (140 g/4½ oz) crushed peanuts
½ cup (10 g/¼ oz) fresh Vietnamese
    mint leaves, torn
½ cup (15 g/½ oz) firmly packed fresh
    coriander leaves
½ red onion, cut into thin wedges
1 green mango, cut into julienne strips
1 Lebanese cucumber, halved
    lengthways and thinly sliced on the
    diagonal

LEMON GRASS DRESSING
½ cup (125 ml/4 fl oz) lime juice
1 tablespoon shaved palm sugar
¼ cup (60 ml/2 fl oz) seasoned rice
    vinegar
2 stems lemon grass, finely chopped
2 red chillies, seeded and finely
    chopped
3 kaffir lime leaves, shredded

1 Place the rice vermicelli in a bowl
and cover with boiling water. Leave
for 10 minutes, or until soft, then
drain, rinse under cold water and cut
into short lengths.
2 Place the vermicelli, three-quarters
of the peanuts, the mint, coriander,
onion, mango and cucumber in a
large bowl and toss together.
3 To make the dressing, place all the
ingredients in a jar with a lid and
shake together.
4 Toss the salad and dressing and
refrigerate for 30 minutes. Sprinkle
with the remaining nuts to serve.

NUTRITION PER SERVE (6)
Protein 6.5 g; Fat 13 g; Carbohydrate 19 g;
Dietary Fibre 3 g; Cholesterol 0 mg;
926 kJ (221 cal)

Cut the green mango into julienne strips (the size
and shape of matchsticks).

Using scissors, cut the rice vermicelli into shorter,
more manageable lengths.

Put the salad ingredients in a bowl and toss well,
reserving some of the peanuts to garnish.

ASPARAGUS STIR-FRIED WITH MUSTARD

Preparation time: 10 minutes
Total cooking time: 10 minutes
Serves 2

480 g (15 oz) asparagus
1 tablespoon oil
1 red onion, sliced
1 clove garlic, crushed
1 tablespoon wholegrain mustard
1 teaspoon honey
½ cup (125 ml/4 fl oz) cream

1 Break the woody ends off the asparagus by holding both ends of the spear and bending gently until it snaps at its natural breaking point. Cut the asparagus into 5 cm (2 inch) lengths.

2 Heat the wok until very hot, add the oil and swirl to coat the side. Stir-fry the onion for 2–3 minutes, or until tender. Stir in the crushed garlic and cook for 1 minute. Add the asparagus to the wok and stir-fry for 3–4 minutes, or until tender, being careful not to overcook the asparagus.

3 Remove the asparagus from the wok, set it aside and keep it warm. Combine the wholegrain mustard, honey and cream. Add to the wok and bring to the boil, then reduce the heat and simmer for 2–3 minutes, or until the mixture reduces and thickens slightly. Return the asparagus to the wok and toss it through the cream mixture. Serve immediately.

NUTRITION PER SERVE
Protein 8.5 g; Fat 35 g; Carbohydrate 10 g;
Dietary Fibre 5 g; Cholesterol 85 mg;
1685 kJ (405 cal)

VARIATION: When asparagus is in season, white and purple asparagus are also available. Vary the recipe by using a mixture of the three colours. Do not overcook the purple asparagus or it will turn green as it cooks.

HINT: This dish can also be served on croutons, toasted ciabatta or toasted wholegrain bread as a smart starter or first course.

Gently bend the asparagus spear and the tough woody end will naturally snap off.

Stir-fry the sliced red onion over moderate heat for 2–3 minutes, or until tender.

FENNEL WITH PECORINO CHEESE

Preparation time: 15 minutes
Total cooking time: 25 minutes
Serves 4

4 fennel bulbs
1 clove garlic, crushed
½ lemon, sliced
2 tablespoons olive oil
1 teaspoon salt

3 tablespoons butter, melted
2 tablespoons grated Pecorino cheese

1 Cut the top shoots and base off the fennel and remove the tough outer layers. Cut into segments and place in a pan with the garlic, lemon, oil and salt. Cover with water and bring to the boil. Reduce the heat and simmer for 20 minutes, or until just tender.
2 Drain well and place in a heatproof dish. Drizzle with the butter. Sprinkle with the cheese and season to taste.

3 Place under a preheated grill until the cheese has browned. Best served piping hot.

NUTRITION PER SERVE
Protein 4 g; Fat 23 g; Carbohydrate 3 g;
Dietary Fibre 2.5 g; Cholesterol 43 mg;
990 kJ (235 cal)

NOTE: If Pecorino (a hard sheep's milk cheese) is not available, then use Parmesan instead.

Trim the tops and bases from the fennel and remove the tough outer layers.

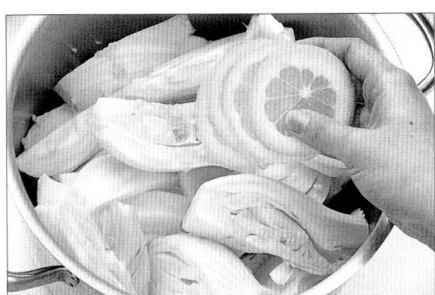

Cut the fennel into segments and put in a pan with the garlic, lemon, oil and salt.

Sprinkle grated Pecorino cheese over the fennel and brown under a grill.

ASPARAGUS AND MUSHROOM SALAD

Preparation time: 20 minutes
Total cooking time: 10 minutes
Serves 4

155 g (5 oz) asparagus spears
1 tablespoon wholegrain mustard
¼ cup (60 ml/2 fl oz) orange juice
2 tablespoons lemon juice
1 tablespoon lime juice
1 tablespoon orange zest
2 teaspoons lemon zest
2 teaspoons lime zest

2 cloves garlic, crushed
¼ cup (90 g/3 oz) honey
400 g (13 oz) button mushrooms,
    halved
150 g (5 oz) rocket
1 red capsicum, cut into strips

1 Snap the woody ends from the asparagus spears and cut in half on the diagonal. Cook in boiling water for 1 minute, or until just tender. Drain, plunge into cold water and set aside.
2 Place the mustard, citrus juice and zest, garlic and honey in a large saucepan and season with pepper. Bring to the boil, then reduce the heat and add the mushrooms, tossing for 2 minutes. Cool.
3 Remove the mushrooms from the sauce with a slotted spoon. Return the sauce to the heat, bring to the boil, then reduce the heat and simmer for 3–5 minutes, or until reduced and syrupy. Cool slightly.
4 Toss the mushrooms, rocket leaves, capsicum and asparagus. Put on a plate and drizzle with the sauce.

NUTRITION PER SERVE
Protein 6 g; Fat 0 g; Carbohydrate 25 g;
Dietary Fibre 5 g; Cholesterol 0 mg;
550 kJ (132 cal)

Use a zester to remove the zest of the orange, lemon and lime.

Toss the mushrooms in the mustard, juices, zest, garlic and honey.

Remove the mushrooms and simmer the sauce until it is reduced and syrupy.

WALDORF SALAD

Preparation time: 20 minutes
Total cooking time: Nil
Serves 4–6

2 red and 2 green apples
2 tablespoons lemon juice
¼ cup (30 g/1 oz) walnut pieces
4 celery sticks, sliced
1 cup (250 g/8 oz) mayonnaise

1 Quarter the apples, remove and discard the seeds and cores, and cut the apples into small pieces.
2 Place the diced apple in a large bowl, drizzle with the lemon juice and toss to coat (this will prevent the apple discolouring). Add the walnut pieces and celery and mix well.
3 Add the mayonnaise to the apple mixture and toss until well coated. Spoon the salad into a lettuce-lined bowl and serve immediately.

NUTRITION PER SERVE (6)
Protein 2 g; Fat 15 g; Carbohydrate 20 g;
Dietary Fibre 3 g; Cholesterol 15 mg;
1020 kJ (240 cal)

NOTE: Waldorf salad can be made up to 2 hours in advance and stored, covered, in the refrigerator. It is named after the Waldorf-Astoria hotel in New York where it was first served.

Using both red and green apples gives the finished salad a colourful appearance.

Pour the lemon juice over the apples and toss to coat—this will prevent them browning.

Add the mayonnaise to the apple mixture and toss until well coated.

Purées & mashes

The success story of the humble mashed potato takes on a new twist with these delicious purées and mashes. These are simple to make and are perfect for soaking up the juices of home-made casseroles or as an accompaniment to lamb chops or juicy steaks.

CREAMED SPINACH PUREE

Wash and roughly chop 1 kg/2 lb) English spinach. Heat 60 g (2 oz) butter in a heavy-based pan and cook the spinach over high heat until it is wilted and the liquid has evaporated. Place in a food processor or blender with ½ cup (125 ml/4 fl oz) cream and purée until smooth. Season to taste with salt, pepper and nutmeg. Combine well and serve. Makes about 2 cups (500 g/1 lb). Serves 4.

NUTRITION PER SERVE
Protein 6 g; Fat 26 g; Carbohydrate 2 g; Dietary Fibre 8 g; Cholesterol 80 mg; 1114 kJ (266 Cal)

ROAST PUMPKIN PUREE

Preheat the oven to moderately hot 200°C (400°F/Gas 6). Seed 750 g (1½ lb) pumpkin and cut into pieces. Place on an oven tray, brush with olive oil and roast for 35 minutes, or until the pumpkin is tender. Remove from the tray, cool slightly, then peel off the skin. Place in a food processor or mash with a masher until you have a purée, then add ¼ cup (60 g/2 oz) sour cream. Season well. Makes about 2 cups (500 g/1 lb). Serves 4.

NUTRITION PER SERVE
Protein 4 g; Fat 9 g; Carbohydrate 13 g; Dietary Fibre 2 g; Cholesterol 20 mg; 623 kJ (149 Cal)

VERY COMFORTING CHEESY MASH

Cut 900 g (1 lb 13 oz) floury potatoes into chunks. Boil for 20 minutes, or until tender. Drain and transfer to a bowl. Add 2 crushed garlic cloves and ⅓ cup (80 ml/2¾ fl oz) cream, and mash, then beat until fluffy. Season. Stir in 300 g (10 oz) grated Gruyère or Cheddar and beat again until the cheese is melted. Makes 1½ cups (500 g/1 lb). Serves 4.

NUTRITION PER SERVE
Protein 25 g; Fat 34 g; Carbohydrate 30 g; Dietary Fibre 4 g; Cholesterol 102 mg; 2220 kJ (530 Cal)

PEA PUREE

Melt 50 g (1¾ oz) butter in a pan over low heat and add 2 crushed garlic cloves. Stir briefly and then add 500 g (1 lb) frozen peas and cover. Increase the heat to moderate and, shaking the pan occasionally, cook the peas for 5 minutes, or until they are tender. Mash roughly with a masher or process in a food processor until you have a coarse purée. Season well. Makes about 2 cups (500 g/1 lb). Serves 4.

NUTRITION PER SERVE
Protein 7.5 g; Fat 11 g; Carbohydrate 8 g; Dietary Fibre 8 g; Cholesterol 32 mg; 650 kJ (155 Cal)

BEETROOT PUREE

Preheat the oven to moderate 180°C (350°F/Gas 4). Wrap 500 g (1 lb) unpeeled beetroot in foil and bake for 50 minutes, or until they feel soft to the touch. Cool, then peel off the skin and cut into pieces. Fry 1 chopped onion in 1 tablespoon olive oil until soft but not browned. Add the beetroot and 1 tablespoon balsamic vinegar and stir until heated through. Mash with a masher or in a food processor, then stir in 2 tablespoons cream. Makes 2 cups (500 g/1 lb). Serves 4.

NUTRITION PER SERVE
Protein 3 g; Fat 9 g; Carbohydrate 12 g; Dietary Fibre 4 g; Cholesterol 14 mg; 592 kJ (142 Cal)

BUTTERBEAN AND ROSEMARY PUREE

Heat 2 tablespoons olive oil in a frying pan over low heat and add 2 crushed garlic cloves. Stir briefly until softened, then add 4 x 300 g (10 oz) cans drained butter beans and 2 table-spoons chopped fresh rosemary and cook until heated through. Season well, then mash roughly with 2 table-spoons olive oil, until smooth. Drizzle with a little extra olive oil if desired. Makes about 1½ cups (375 g/12 oz). Serves 4.

NUTRITION PER SERVE
Protein 4 g; Fat 10 g; Carbohydrate 4 g; Dietary Fibre 6 g; Cholesterol 0 mg; 501 kJ (120 Cal)

LEEK AND CAPER SALAD

Preparation time: 20 minutes
Total cooking time: 20 minutes
Serves 6

5 leeks, white part only
⅓ cup (80 ml/2¾ fl oz) olive oil
2 tablespoons sherry vinegar
2 tablespoons baby capers, rinsed

1 Cut the leeks in half lengthways and wash under cold running water. Cut them into 5 cm (2 inch) lengths, then cut in half again lengthways. Heat the oil in a large heavy-based pan, add the leeks and stir until coated with the oil. Cover and cook over low heat for 15–20 minutes, or until the leeks are soft and tender (but don't let them brown or burn). Cool for 10 minutes.
2 Stir through the vinegar and season to taste with salt and pepper. Transfer to a serving dish and scatter with the baby capers (if baby capers are unavailable, use chopped ordinary-sized capers).

NUTRITION PER SERVE
Protein 1.5 g; Fat 13 g; Carbohydrate 2.5 g;
Dietary Fibre 2 g; Cholesterol 0 mg;
550 kJ (130 cal)

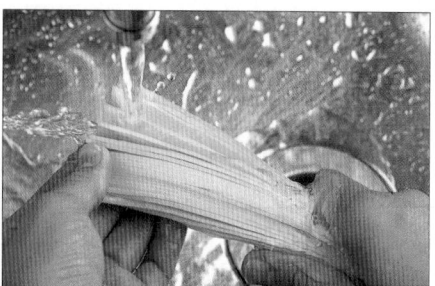

Trim the leeks and wash them thoroughly under cold running water.

Add the leeks to the pan and stir until they are covered with the oil.

Add the vinegar to the cooled leeks and stir until they are well coated.

SEMI-DRIED TOMATOES

**Preparation time: 10 minutes +
 24 hours refrigeration**
Total cooking time: 2 hours 30 minutes
Fills a 500 ml (16 fl oz) jar

16 Roma tomatoes
3 tablespoons fresh thyme, chopped
2 tablespoons olive oil

1 Preheat the oven to warm 160°C (315°F/Gas 2–3). Cut the tomatoes into quarters lengthways and lay them skin-side-down on a wire rack in a baking tray.
2 Sprinkle with 1 teaspoon of salt, 1 teaspoon of cracked black pepper and the thyme and cook in the oven for 2½ hours. Check occasionally to make sure the tomatoes don't burn.
3 Toss the tomatoes in the olive oil and leave to cool before packing into sterilised jars and sealing. Store in the refrigerator for 24 hours before using. Semi-dried tomatoes should be eaten within 3–4 days.

NUTRITION
Analysis is not appropriate for this recipe.

NOTE: To sterilise a storage jar, rinse with boiling water, then place in a warm oven until completely dry. Do not dry with a tea towel.

Cut the tomatoes into quarters and lay them skin-side-down on a wire rack.

Season the tomatoes with salt, cracked pepper and fresh thyme.

Cover the tomatoes with olive oil and toss until well coated.

WILD MUSHROOM SALAD

Preparation time: 15 minutes
Total cooking time: 15 minutes
Serves 4

100 g (3½ oz) hazelnuts
1 mizuna lettuce
90 g (3 oz) baby curly endive
60 g (2 oz) baby English spinach
2 tablespoons hazelnut oil
2 tablespoons light olive oil
500 g (1 lb) wild mushrooms
    (enoki, shimeji, Shiitake, oyster)
150 g (5 oz) strong blue cheese,
    crumbled

TOMATO MUSTARD VINAIGRETTE
½ cup (125 ml/4 fl oz) light olive oil
2 tablespoons tarragon vinegar
1 teaspoon tomato mustard

1 Preheat the oven to moderate 180°C (350°F/Gas 4). Put the hazelnuts on a baking tray and cook for 10 minutes, shaking the tray occasionally. Remove from the oven, cool, and remove the skins by rubbing the nuts together in a tea towel. Coarsely chop the nuts.
2 Remove the tough lower stems from the mizuna and endive, and tear the larger leaves into bite-sized pieces. Wash the mizuna, endive and spinach under cold water, dry completely and refrigerate until well chilled.
3 To make the vinaigrette, whisk the ingredients together and season well.
4 Heat the oils in a frying pan and sauté the mushrooms for 3–4 minutes, or until beginning to soften. Remove from the heat and cool slightly, then stir in the vinaigrette. Arrange the salad greens on serving plates. Spoon the mushrooms over the top and sprinkle with cheese and hazelnuts.

NUTRITION PER SERVE
Protein 10 g; Fat 75 g; Carbohydrate 20 g;
Dietary Fibre 4 g; Cholesterol 40 mg;
3375 kJ (805 cal)

NOTE: Chestnut mushrooms or chanterelles can also be used. Pink oyster mushrooms, if available, make this salad look particularly attractive.

Rub the hazelnuts together in a tea towel to remove the skins.

Remove the tough lower stems from the baby curly endive.

Sauté the mushrooms until they are just beginning to soften.

GREEK SALAD

Preparation time: 20 minutes
Total cooking time: Nil
Serves 6–8

6 tomatoes, cut into thin wedges
1 red onion, cut into thin rings
2 Lebanese cucumbers, sliced

1 cup (185 g/6 oz) Kalamata olives
200 g (6½ oz) feta cheese
½ cup (125 ml/4 fl oz) extra virgin olive
   oil
dried oregano, to sprinkle

1 Combine the tomato wedges with the onion rings, sliced cucumber and Kalamata olives in a large bowl. Season to taste with salt and freshly ground black pepper.

2 Break up the feta into large pieces with your fingers and scatter over the top of the salad. Drizzle with the olive oil and sprinkle with some oregano.

NUTRITION PER SERVE (8)
Protein 6 g; Fat 25 g; Carbohydrate 3 g;
Dietary Fibre 2 g; Cholesterol 15 mg;
1060 kJ (250 cal)

Cut the tomatoes into thin wedges, and cut the red onion into thin rings.

Combine the tomato, onion, cucumber and olives in a large bowl.

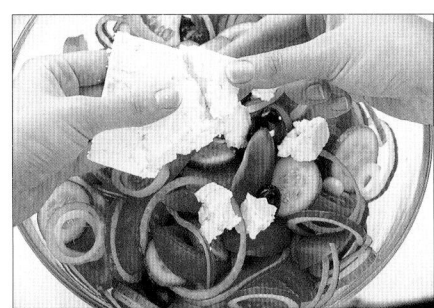

Good feta should break up and crumble nicely. Just use your fingers.

TOMATO, HALOUMI AND SPINACH SALAD

**Preparation time: 15 minutes +
2 hours marinating
Total cooking time: 1 hour
Serves 4**

200 g (6½ oz) haloumi cheese
¼ cup (60 ml/2 fl oz) olive oil
2 cloves garlic, crushed
1 tablespoon chopped fresh oregano
1 tablespoon chopped fresh marjoram
8 egg (Roma) tomatoes, halved
1 small red onion, cut into 8 wedges
   with base intact

¼ cup (60 ml/2 fl oz) olive oil, extra
2 tablespoons balsamic vinegar
150 g (5 oz) baby English spinach
   leaves

1 Cut the haloumi into 1 cm (½ inch) slices lengthways and put in a shallow dish. Mix together the oil, garlic and herbs and pour over the haloumi. Marinate, covered, for 1–2 hours.
2 Preheat the oven to moderately hot 200°C (400°F/Gas 6). Place the tomato and onion in a single layer in a roasting tin, drizzle with 2 tablespoons of the extra olive oil and 1 tablespoon of the vinegar and sprinkle with salt and cracked black pepper. Bake for 50–60 minutes, or until golden.
3 Meanwhile, heat a non-stick frying pan over medium heat. Drain the haloumi and cook for 1 minute each side, or until golden brown.
4 Divide the spinach leaves among four serving plates and top with the tomato and onion. Whisk together the remaining olive oil and balsamic vinegar in a small bowl and drizzle over the salad. Top with the haloumi.

NUTRITION PER SERVE
Protein 14 g; Fat 27 g; Carbohydrate 6.5 g;
Dietary Fibre 4 g; Cholesterol 26 mg;
1333 kJ (320 cal)

Cut the onion into eight wedges, keeping the base intact.

Arrange the tomatoes and onion in a single layer in a roasting tin and bake until golden.

Drain the marinated haloumi and cook for a minute on each side, until golden brown.

SALAD NICOISE

Preparation time: 30 minutes
Total cooking time: 15 minutes
Serves 4

3 eggs
2 vine-ripened tomatoes
175 g (6 oz) baby green beans
½ cup (125 ml/4 fl oz) olive oil
2 tablespoons white wine vinegar
1 large clove garlic, halved
325 g (11 oz) iceberg lettuce heart,
    cut into 8 wedges
1 small red capsicum, seeded and
    thinly sliced
1 celery stick, cut into 5 cm (2 inch)
    thin strips
1 Lebanese cucumber, cut into thin
    5 cm (2 inch) lengths
¼ large red onion, thinly sliced

2 x 185 g (6 oz) cans tuna, drained,
    broken into chunks
12 Kalamata olives
45 g (1½ oz) can anchovy fillets,
    drained
2 teaspoons baby capers
12 small fresh basil leaves

1 Place the eggs in a saucepan of cold water. Bring slowly to the boil, then reduce the heat and simmer for 10 minutes. Stir during the first few minutes to centre the yolks. Cool, then peel and cut into quarters. Meanwhile, score a cross in the base of each tomato. Place in a bowl of boiling water for 1 minute, then plunge into cold water and peel the skin away from the cross. Cut into eighths.
2 Trim the beans and cook them in a saucepan of boiling water for 2 minutes, then refresh quickly under

cold water and drain. Place the oil and vinegar in a jar and shake to combine.
3 Rub the garlic halves over the base and sides of a large salad serving platter. Arrange the lettuce wedges evenly over the base. Layer the tomato, capsicum, celery, cucumber, beans and egg quarters over the lettuce. Scatter with the onion and tuna. Arrange the olives, anchovies, capers and basil leaves over the top, pour the dressing over the salad and serve immediately.

NUTRITION PER SERVE
Protein 63 g; Fat 32 g; Carbohydrate 25 g;
Dietary Fibre 5 g; Cholesterol 228 mg;
2697 kJ (644 Cal)

Using a sharp knife, cut the celery stick into long, thin strips.

Cut the peeled tomatoes into quarters, and again into eighths.

Layer the tomato, capsicum, celery, cucumber, beans and egg over the lettuce.

ORANGE POPPY SEED ROASTED VEGETABLES

Preparation time: 20 minutes
Total cooking time: 50 minutes
Serves 6–8

500 g (1 lb) new potatoes, unpeeled, halved
6 parsnips, peeled and quartered lengthways
500 g (1 lb) orange sweet potato, cut into large pieces
335 g (11 oz) baby carrots, with stalks
6 pickling onions, halved

⅓ cup (80 ml/2¾ fl oz) oil
2 tablespoons poppy seeds
200 g (6½ oz) Brie cheese, thinly sliced

ORANGE DRESSING
½ cup (125 ml/4 fl oz) orange juice
2 cloves garlic, crushed
1 tablespoon Dijon mustard
1 teaspoon white wine vinegar
1 teaspoon sesame oil

1 Preheat the oven to moderately hot 200°C (400°F/Gas 6). Place all the vegetables and the oil in a large deep baking dish. Toss the vegetables to coat with the oil. Bake for 50 minutes, or until the vegetables are crisp and tender, tossing every 15 minutes. Sprinkle with the poppy seeds.
2 Whisk together all the dressing ingredients.
3 Pour the dressing over the warm vegetables and toss to coat. Transfer to a large bowl, top with the Brie and serve immediately, while still warm.

NUTRITION PER SERVE (8)
Protein 10 g; Fat 20 g; Carbohydrate 35 g;
Dietary Fibre 6 g; Cholesterol 25 mg;
1510 kJ (360 cal)

Quarter the parsnips lengthways and cut the sweet potato into large pieces.

Roast the vegetables until they are tender, then sprinkle with the poppy seeds.

Pour the dressing over the warm vegetables and toss to coat.

CAPONATA

Preparation time: 20 minutes +
24 hours refrigeration
Total cooking time: 40 minutes
Serves 8

1 kg (2 lb) eggplant, cubed
¾ cup (185 ml/6 fl oz) olive oil
200 g (6½ oz) zucchini, cubed
1 red capsicum, thinly sliced
2 onions, finely sliced
4 celery sticks, sliced
400 g (13 oz) can crushed tomatoes
3 tablespoons red wine vinegar
2 tablespoons sugar
2 tablespoons drained capers
24 green olives, pitted (see NOTE)
2 tablespoons pine nuts, toasted

1 Put the eggplant in a colander, sprinkle with salt and leave to drain.
2 Heat 3 tablespoons of the oil in a large frying pan and fry the zucchini and capsicum for 5–6 minutes, or until the zucchini is lightly browned. Transfer to a bowl. Add a little more oil to the pan and gently fry the onion and celery for 6–8 minutes, or until softened but not brown. Transfer to the bowl.
3 Rinse the eggplant and pat dry. Add ¼ cup (60 ml/2 fl oz) of the oil to the pan, increase the heat and brown the eggplant in batches. Keep adding more oil to each batch. Drain on paper towels and set aside.
4 Remove any excess oil from the pan and return the vegetables to the pan, except the eggplant.
5 Add ¼ cup (60 ml/2 fl oz) water and the tomatoes. Reduce the heat and simmer for 10 minutes. Add the remaining ingredients and eggplant and mix well. Remove from the

heat and cool. Cover and leave for 24 hours in the refrigerator. Add some pepper, and more vinegar if needed.

NUTRITION PER SERVE
Protein 3.5 g; Fat 25 g; Carbohydrate 8.5 g;
Dietary Fibre 5.5 g; Cholesterol 0 mg;
1160 kJ (280 cal)

NOTE: Green olives stuffed with red pimentos can be used instead of pitted green olives.

STORAGE TIME: Caponata will keep, covered, in the refrigerator for up to 5 days.

You can remove the stones from the olives with an olive pitter.

Increase the heat under the oil and brown the eggplant in batches.

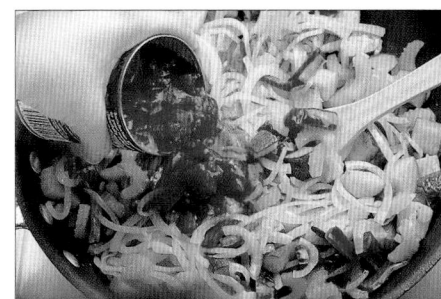

Add the water and crushed tomatoes to the pan and allow to simmer.

POTATO SALAD

Preparation time: 30 minutes
Total cooking time: 5 minutes
Serves 4

600 g (1¼ lb) potatoes, unpeeled, cut
    into bite-sized pieces
1 small onion, finely chopped
1 small green capsicum, chopped
2–3 celery sticks, finely chopped
¼ cup (15 g/½ oz) finely chopped
    parsley

DRESSING
¾ cup (185 g/6 oz) mayonnaise
1–2 tablespoons vinegar or lemon
    juice
2 tablespoons sour cream

1 Cook the potato in a large pan of boiling water for 5 minutes, or until just tender (pierce with a small sharp knife—if the potato comes away easily it is ready). Drain and cool completely.
2 Combine the onion, capsicum, celery and parsley (reserving a little for garnishing) with the cooled potato in a large salad bowl.

3 To make the dressing, mix together the mayonnaise, vinegar and sour cream. Season with salt and pepper. Pour over the salad and toss gently to combine, without breaking the potato. Garnish with the remaining parsley.

NUTRITION PER SERVE
Protein 6 g; Fat 20 g; Carbohydrate 30 g;
Dietary Fibre 4 g; Cholesterol 30 mg;
1355 kJ (320 cal)

NOTE: Any potato is suitable for this recipe. Most potatoes are delicious with their skins left on.

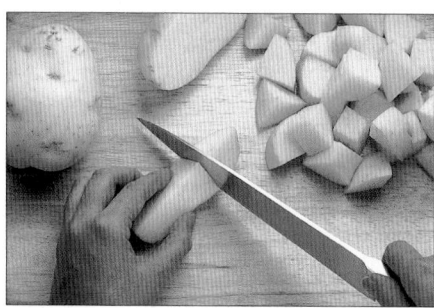

Cut the potatoes into bite-sized pieces, leaving the skins on.

Combine the onion, capsicum, celery and parsley with the cooled potato.

Mix together the mayonnaise, vinegar and sour cream and season, to taste.

STUFFED MUSHROOM SALAD

Preparation time: 25 minutes
Total cooking time: Nil
Serves 4

20 button mushrooms
¼ cup (60 g/2 oz) pesto, chilled
100 g (3½ oz) rocket leaves
1 green oakleaf lettuce
12 small black olives
⅓ cup (50 g/1¾ oz) sliced semi-dried
    or sun-dried tomatoes
1 tablespoon roughly chopped
    basil
Parmesan shavings, to serve

DRESSING
⅓ cup (80 ml/2¾ fl oz) olive oil
1 tablespoon white wine vinegar
1 teaspoon Dijon mustard

1 Trim the mushroom stalks level with the caps and scoop out the remaining stalk with a melon baller. Spoon the pesto into the mushrooms.
2 To make the dressing, whisk together all the ingredients. Season with salt and pepper, to taste.
3 Arrange the rocket and lettuce leaves on a serving plate and top with the mushrooms, olives, tomato and basil. Drizzle the dressing over the salad and top with the Parmesan shavings. Serve immediately.

NUTRITION PER SERVE
Protein 9 g; Fat 35 g; Carbohydrate 2 g;
Dietary Fibre 3 g; Cholesterol 15 mg;
1525 kJ (365 cal)

HINT: Home-made pesto is preferable for this recipe. To make your own, process 1 cup (30 g/1 oz) loosely packed basil leaves, 2 tablespoons pine nuts and ¼ cup (25 g/¾ oz) grated Parmesan in a food processor to form a smooth paste. Gradually pour in ¼ cup (60 ml/2 fl oz) olive oil in a steady stream with the motor running. Process until combined.

Draw a vegetable peeler across a block of Parmesan to make the shavings.

Trim the mushroom stalks so they are level with the caps.

Spoon the chilled pesto into the mushroom caps. Home-made pesto will give the best flavour.

Dressings

Most people think that low-fat eating means no more tangy dressings and creamy sauces. Not so. These dressings will give a lift to salads, meat, fish and even desserts and won't break the fat bank.

HERB, GARLIC AND YOGHURT

Whisk together 200 g (6½ oz) low-fat natural yoghurt, 4 tablespoons skim milk, 1 teaspoon Dijon mustard, 1 tablespoon finely chopped chives, 2 teaspoons finely chopped fresh parsley, 2 teaspoons chopped fresh oregano and 1 crushed clove garlic. Season with salt and pepper. Makes 1 cup (250 ml/8 fl oz).

NUTRITION PER TABLESPOON
Protein 1 g; Fat 0 g; Carbohydrate 1 g; Dietary Fibre 0 g; Cholesterol 0 mg; 50 kJ (10 cal)

BERRY DRESSING

Blend 100 g (3½ oz) fresh or thawed frozen strawberries, 1½ tablespoons oil, 3 tablespoons apple juice, 1 teaspoon lemon juice, 1 tablespoon cider vinegar and some cracked black pepper in a blender until smooth. Season with salt. Makes ¾ cup (185 ml/6 fl oz).

NUTRITION PER TABLESPOON
Protein 0 g; Fat 3 g; Carbohydrate 1 g; Dietary Fibre 0 g; Cholesterol 0 mg; 145 kJ (35 cal)

WALNUT VINAIGRETTE

Combine 2 tablespoons cider vinegar, 1 tablespoon balsamic vinegar, 1½ tablespoons walnut oil, 1 teaspoon Dijon mustard, 2 tablespoons water, ½ teaspoon caster sugar and 2 teaspoons finely chopped fresh parsley in a screw-top jar. Shake the jar, then season. Makes ½ cup (125 ml/4 fl oz).

NUTRITION PER TABLESPOON
Protein 0 g; Fat 5 g; Carbohydrate 1 g; Dietary Fibre 0 g; Cholesterol 0 mg; 210 kJ (50 cal)

ROASTED CAPSICUM SAUCE

Quarter 2 red capsicums, remove the seeds and membrane and grill until the skins blister and blacken. Cool under a damp tea towel before peeling. Cut one quarter into thin strips then set aside. Heat 1 teaspoon oil in a small pan, add 2 finely chopped spring onions and 1 table-psoon water, then stir over heat until the spring onion is soft. Add the remaining capsicum, 3 tablespoons beef stock, 2 table-spoons white wine, 2 tablespoons tomato paste and ¼ teaspoon sugar. Simmer for 2 minutes, then blend until smooth. Season and stir in 1 table-spoon chopped chives. Garnish with red capsicum strips. Makes 1 cup (250 ml/8 fl oz).

NUTRITION PER TABLESPOON
Protein 0.5 g; Fat 0.5 g; Carbohydrate 1.5 g;
Dietary Fibre 0.5 g; Cholesterol 0 mg;
55 kJ (15 cal)

TOMATO SAUCE

Heat 1 teaspoon oil in a pan, add a sliced small leek, 2 tablespoons water and 1 crushed clove garlic. Cover and stir until the leek is soft. Add a 440 g (14 oz) can chopped tomato, 1 table-spoon tomato paste,¼ teaspoon sugar and 2 tablespoons red wine. Stir, then simmer for 5 minutes. Season. Makes 2 cups (500 ml/16 fl oz).

NUTRITION PER TABLESPOON
Protein 0.5 g; Fat 0.5 g; Carbohydrate 1.5 g;
Dietary Fibre 0.5 g; Cholesterol 0 mg;
55 kJ (15 cal)

HUMMUS DRESSING

Drain a 425 g (14 oz) can chickpeas and put in a food processor with ¾ cup (185 ml/6 fl oz) vegetable stock, 1 tablespoon tahini paste and 2 chopped cloves garlic. Stir 1 teaspoon each of ground coriander and cumin in a dry frying pan over medium heat for 3 minutes, or until aromatic. Cool slightly, add to the processor and mix until nearly smooth. Mix in 2 tablespoons lemon juice. Season with cracked pepper and salt. If too thick, add a little water. Makes 1 cup (250 ml/8 fl oz).

NUTRITION PER TABLESPOON
Protein 2 g; Fat 1.5 g; Carbohydrate 4 g;
Dietary Fibre 1.5 g; Cholesterol 0 mg;
160 kJ (40 cal)

SWEET RICOTTA CREAM

Beat together 200 g (6½ oz) ricotta, 100 g (3½ oz) low-fat natural yoghurt, ½ teaspoon finely grated orange rind, 3 tablespoons orange juice and 1 tablepoon caster sugar until smooth. Makes 1 cup (250 ml/8 fl oz).

NUTRITION PER TABLESPOON
Protein 2 g; Fat 1.5 g; Carbohydrate 2.5 g;
Dietary Fibre 0 g; Cholesterol 6.5 mg;
130 kJ (30 cal)

Clockwise, from top left: Berry dressing; Walnut vinaigrette; Hummus dressing; Tomato sauce; Sweet ricotta cream; Roasted capsicum sauce; Herb, garlic and yoghurt.

CAULIFLOWER CHEESE

Preparation time: 15 minutes
Total cooking time: 20 minutes
Serves 4

500 g (1 lb) cauliflower, cut into pieces
30 g (1 oz) butter
30 g (1 oz) plain flour
1¼ cups (315 ml/10 fl oz) warm milk
1 teaspoon Dijon mustard
½ cup (60 g/2 oz) grated Cheddar
½ cup (60 g/2 oz) grated Parmesan
2 tablespoons fresh breadcrumbs
3 tablespoons grated Cheddar, extra

1 Brush a 1.5 litre (48 fl oz) heatproof dish with melted butter or oil. Cook the cauliflower in lightly salted boiling water until just tender. Drain. Place in the dish and keep warm.

2 Melt the butter in a pan. Stir in the flour and cook for 1 minute, or until golden and bubbling. Remove from the heat and whisk in the milk and mustard. Return to the heat and bring to the boil, stirring constantly. Cook, stirring, over low heat for 2 minutes, then remove from the heat. Add the cheeses and stir until melted. Season with salt and white pepper and pour over the cauliflower.

3 Mix together the breadcrumbs and extra Cheddar cheese and sprinkle over the sauce. Grill until the top is browned and bubbling and then serve immediately.

NUTRITION PER SERVE
Protein 22 g; Fat 33 g; Carbohydrate 15 g;
Dietary Fibre 2 g; Cholesterol 88 mg;
1840 kJ (440 cal)

Add the Cheddar and Parmesan and stir until the cheeses have melted.

ASPARAGUS AND RED CAPSICUM SALAD

Preparation time: 20 minutes
Total cooking time: 15 minutes
Serves 4

2 red capsicums
⅓ cup (80 ml/2¾ fl oz) virgin olive oil
1 clove garlic, crushed
2 tablespoons lemon juice
2 tablespoons chopped basil
2 tablespoons pine nuts
310 g (10 oz) fresh asparagus
small black olives

1 Cut the capsicums into large pieces, removing the seeds and white membrane. Place, skin-side-up, under a hot grill until the skin blackens and blisters. Cool under a tea towel or in a plastic bag, then carefully peel away and discard the skin. Finely dice the capsicum flesh.
2 Put the olive oil, garlic, lemon juice and basil in a small bowl and whisk to combine. Add the capsicum and pine nuts, and season with salt and pepper.
3 Remove the woody ends from the asparagus (hold each spear at both ends and bend gently—the woody end will snap off at its natural breaking point). Plunge the asparagus into a large frying pan of boiling water and cook for 3 minutes, or until just tender. Drain and plunge into a bowl of iced water, then drain again and gently pat dry with paper towels.
4 Arrange the asparagus on a large serving platter and spoon the dressing over the top. Garnish with the black olives and perhaps a few lemon wedges to squeeze over the top.

NUTRITION PER SERVE
Protein 4 g; Fat 25 g; Carbohydrate 5 g;
Dietary Fibre 3 g; Cholesterol 0 mg;
1100 kJ (260 cal)

Grill the capsicum pieces until the skin blackens and blisters.

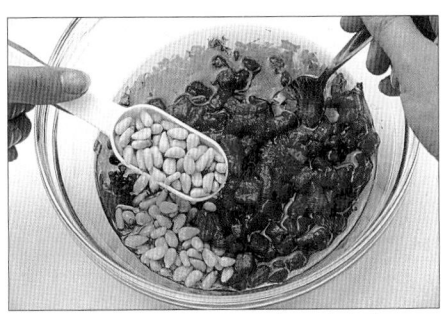
Add the diced capsicum and pine nuts to the other dressing ingredients.

Cook the asparagus in boiling water, then plunge into cold water and pat dry with paper towels.

CARAWAY POLENTA WITH BRAISED LEEKS

Preparation time: 10 minutes
Total cooking time: 30 minutes
Serves 4

6 cups (1.5 litres/48 fl oz) vegetable
   stock
1½ cups (225 g/7½ oz) polenta
2 teaspoons caraway seeds
45 g (1½ oz) butter
2 large leeks, cut into thin strips
250 g (8 oz) Fontina cheese, cubed

1 Place the stock in a large heavy-based pan and bring to the boil. Pour in the polenta in a fine stream, stirring continuously. Add the caraway seeds and then reduce the heat and simmer for about 20–25 minutes, or until the polenta is very soft.
2 Melt the butter in a frying pan over medium heat and add the leeks. Cover and cook gently, stirring often, until wilted. Add the Fontina, stir a couple of times and remove from the heat.
3 Pour the polenta onto plates in nest shapes and spoon the leeks and cheese into the centre.

NUTRITION PER SERVE
Protein 17 g; Fat 25 g; Carbohydrate 40 g;
Dietary Fibre 3 g; Cholesterol 72 mg;
1908 kJ (456 cal)

HINT: Ready-made stock can be quite salty, so use half stock, half water.

NOTE: Polenta is also known as cornmeal and is available from most supermarkets and delicatessens.

Use a sharp knife to cut the leeks into very thin, long strips.

Bring the stock to the boil, then pour in the polenta, stirring continuously.

Cook the leeks in the butter until wilted, then stir in the cheese.

TABBOULEH

**Preparation time: 25 minutes +
    30 minutes refrigeration**
Total cooking time: Nil
Serves 8

1 cup (175 g/6 oz) burghul
2 teaspoons olive oil
1 cup (30 g/1 oz) chopped fresh flat-
    leaf parsley
1 cup (50 g/1¾ oz) chopped fresh mint
¾ cup (90 g/3 oz) finely chopped
spring onions
4 Roma (egg) tomatoes, chopped
½ cup (125 ml/4 fl oz) olive oil
½ cup (125 ml/4 fl oz) lemon juice
2 cloves garlic, crushed

1 Put the burghul in a bowl and pour in 1 cup (250 ml/8 fl oz) boiling water. Mix in the olive oil, then set aside for 10 minutes. Stir again and cool.
2 Add the herbs, spring onion and tomato to the burghul and mix well. Whisk the oil, lemon juice and garlic together and add to the burghul. Mix gently and season well. Cover and chill for 30 minutes before serving.

NUTRITION PER SERVE
Protein 6 g; Fat 20 g; Carbohydrate 7.5 g;
Dietary Fibre 5 g; Cholesterol 0 mg;
1028 kJ (245 cal)

VARIATION: Burghul is also sold as bulgur or cracked wheat. If you prefer, use couscous instead of the burghul in this recipe.

Roma tomatoes are also known as 'egg' or 'plum' tomatoes because of their shape.

Soak the burghul in boiling water and then mix with the olive oil.

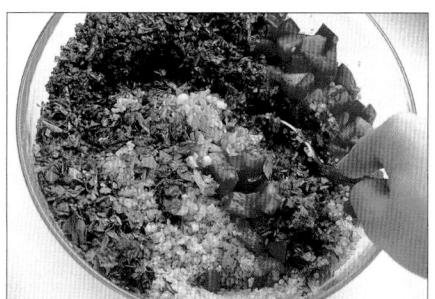

Add the herbs, spring onion and tomato to the burghul and mix well.

SPICY LENTIL SALAD

Preparation time: 30 minutes
Total cooking time: 1 hour 10 minutes
Serves 6

1 cup (220 g/7 oz) brown rice
1 cup (185 g/6 oz) brown lentils
1 teaspoon turmeric
1 teaspoon ground cinnamon
6 cardamom pods
3 star anise
2 bay leaves
¼ cup (60 ml/2 fl oz) sunflower oil
1 tablespoon lemon juice
250 g (8 oz) broccoli florets
2 carrots, cut into julienne strips
1 onion, finely chopped
2 cloves garlic, crushed
1 red capsicum, finely chopped
1 teaspoon garam masala
1 teaspoon ground coriander
1½ cups (250 g/8 oz) fresh or frozen
    peas, thawed

MINT AND YOGHURT DRESSING
1 cup (250 g/8 oz) plain yoghurt
1 tablespoon lemon juice
1 tablespoon chopped fresh mint
1 teaspoon cumin seeds

1 Put 3 cups (750 ml/24 fl oz) water with the rice, lentils, turmeric, cinnamon, cardamom, star anise and bay leaves in a pan. Stir well and bring to the boil. Reduce the heat, cover and simmer gently for 50–60 minutes, or until the liquid is absorbed. Remove the whole spices. Transfer the mixture to a large bowl. Whisk 2 tablespoons of the oil with the lemon juice and fork through the rice mixture.
2 Boil, steam or microwave the broccoli and carrots until tender. Drain and refresh in cold water.

3 Heat the remaining oil in a large pan and add the onion, garlic and capsicum. Stir-fry for 2–3 minutes, then add the garam masala and coriander, and stir-fry for a further 1–2 minutes. Add the vegetables and toss to coat in the spice mixture. Add to the rice and fork through to combine. Cover and refrigerate until cold.
4 To make the dressing, mix the

yoghurt, lemon juice, mint and cumin seeds together, and season with salt and pepper. Spoon the salad into individual serving bowls or onto a platter and serve with the dressing.

NUTRITION PER SERVE
Protein 20 g; Fat 15 g; Carbohydrate 50 g;
Dietary Fibre 10 g; Cholesterol 7 mg;
1605 kJ (380 cal)

Add the cardamom pods, star anise and bay leaves to the pan.

Add the vegetables and toss to coat with the spice mixture.

Mix the yoghurt, lemon juice, mint and cumin seeds together to make a dressing.

PUMPKIN AND CASHEW STIR-FRY

Preparation time: 20 minutes
Total cooking time: 15 minutes
Serves 4–6

oil, for cooking
1 cup (155 g/5 oz) raw cashew nuts
1 leek, white part only, sliced
2 teaspoons ground coriander
2 teaspoons ground cumin
2 teaspoons brown mustard seeds
2 cloves garlic, crushed

1 kg (2 lb) butternut pumpkin, cubed
¾ cup (185 ml/6 fl oz) orange juice
1 teaspoon soft brown sugar

1 Heat the wok until very hot, add 1 tablespoon of the oil and swirl to coat. Stir-fry the cashews until golden, then drain on paper towels. Stir-fry the leek for 2–3 minutes, or until softened. Remove from the wok.
2 Reheat the wok, add 1 tablespoon of the oil and stir-fry the coriander, cumin, mustard seeds and garlic for 2 minutes, or until the spices are fragrant and the mustard seeds begin to pop. Add the pumpkin and stir to coat well. Stir-fry for 5 minutes, or until the pumpkin is brown and tender.
3 Add the orange juice and sugar. Bring to the boil and cook for 5 minutes. Add the leek and three-quarters of the cashews and toss well. Top with the remaining cashews to serve.

NUTRITION PER SERVE (6)
Protein 8 g; Fat 20 g; Carbohydrate 20 g;
Dietary Fibre 4 g; Cholesterol 0 mg;
1240 kJ (295 cal)

Stir-fry the cashews in 1 tablespoon of the oil until they are golden.

Reheat the wok and stir-fry the coriander, cumin, mustard seeds and garlic.

Add the pumpkin and stir to coat well in the spices. Stir-fry until brown and tender.

CHARGRILLED VEGETABLES

**Preparation time: 15 minutes +
40 minutes standing**
Total cooking time: 1 hour
Serves 6

2 eggplants
900 g (1¾ lb) orange sweet potato
4 zucchini
2 red capsicums
600 g (1¼ lb) button mushrooms
⅓ cup (80 ml/2¾ fl oz) olive oil

BASIL DRESSING
½ cup (125 ml/4 fl oz) olive oil
2 cloves garlic, crushed
2 tablespoons balsamic vinegar
½ teaspoon sugar
⅓ cup (20 g/¾ oz) fresh basil leaves

1 Cut the eggplant into 1 cm (½ inch) thick slices. Place on a wire rack and sprinkle liberally with salt. Leave for 30 minutes, then rinse under cold water and pat dry with paper towels.
2 Cut the sweet potato into 5 mm (¼ inch) slices and the zucchini into 1 cm (½ inch) slices lengthways. Quarter the capsicums, remove the seeds and membranes and chargrill, skin-side-down, until the skin blackens and blisters. (Alternatively, cook the capsicums, skin-side-up, under a preheated grill to blister the skins.) Place in a plastic bag and leave to cool. Peel away the skin.
3 Brush the eggplant, sweet potato, zucchini and mushrooms with oil. Chargrill or barbecue in batches until lightly browned and cooked through.
4 To make the basil dressing, put the oil, garlic, vinegar, sugar and basil in a food processor or blender and process until smooth.
5 Combine the chargrilled vegetables with the basil dressing and mix well. Allow to cool, then cover and refrigerate until ready to use. Return to room temperature before serving.

NUTRITION PER SERVE
Protein 9 g; Fat 20 g; Carbohydrate 28 g;
Dietary Fibre 9 g; Cholesterol 0 mg; 1495 kJ
(355 Cal)

Put the slices of eggplant on a wire rack and sprinkle with salt.

Use a sharp knife to cut the sweet potato into slices.

Once cooled, gently peel the blackened skin off the capsicums.

Brush the vegetables with oil and chargrill or barbecue until lightly browned.

CAESAR SALAD

Preparation time: 25 minutes
Total cooking time: 20 minutes
Serves 6

1 small French stick (baguette)
2 tablespoons olive oil
2 cloves garlic, halved
4 rashers bacon
2 cos lettuces
10 anchovy fillets, halved lengthways
1 cup (100 g/3½ oz) freshly shaved
    Parmesan
Parmesan shavings, to serve

DRESSING
2 egg yolks
4 cloves garlic, crushed
1 tablespoon Dijon mustard
4 anchovy fillets
⅓ cup (80 ml/2¾ fl oz) white wine
    vinegar
2 tablespoons Worcestershire sauce
1¾ cups (440 ml/14 fl oz) olive oil

1 Preheat the oven to moderate 180°C (350°F/Gas 4). Cut the bread into 15 thin slices and brush both sides with oil. Bake on a baking tray for 10–15 minutes, or until golden. Cool slightly and rub each side with the cut edge of a garlic clove. Break the bread into pieces to make croûtons.
2 Trim the bacon. Cook under a hot grill until crisp. Drain on paper towels until cool, then break into large pieces.
3 Tear the lettuce into pieces and put in a large serving bowl with the bacon, anchovies, croûtons and Parmesan.
4 Place the egg yolks, garlic, mustard, anchovies, vinegar and Worcestershire sauce in a food processor or blender. Season and process for 20 seconds, or until smooth. With the motor running, add the oil in a thin stream until the dressing is thick and creamy. This makes enough dressing for two salads. Refrigerate the rest for up to 5 days.
5 Drizzle half the dressing over the salad and toss to combine. Sprinkle on the Parmesan shavings.

NUTRITION PER SERVE
Protein 18 g; Fat 50 g; Carbohydrate 20 g;
Dietary Fibre 2 g; Cholesterol 55 mg; 2437 kJ
(582 Cal)

With a sharp knife, cut the anchovy fillets in half lengthways.

Rub both sides of the bread with the cut edge of the garlic clove.

Process the egg, garlic, mustard, anchovies, vinegar and Worcestershire sauce.

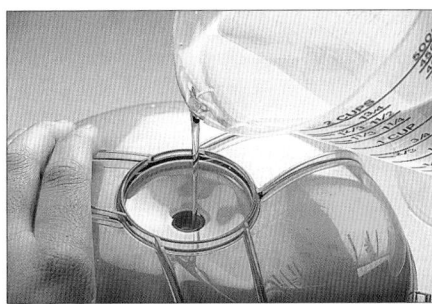
Add the olive oil in a thin stream until the dressing is thick and creamy.

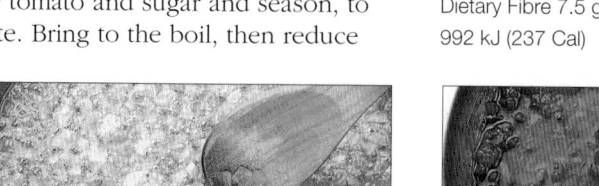

GREEN BEANS WITH TOMATO AND OLIVE OIL

Preparation time: 10 minutes
Total cooking time: 25 minutes
Serves 4

⅓ cup (80 ml/2¾ oz) olive oil
1 large onion, chopped
3 cloves garlic, finely chopped
400 g (13 oz) can diced tomatoes
½ teaspoon sugar

750 g (1½ lb) green beans, trimmed
3 tablespoons chopped fresh flat-leaf parsley

1 Heat the olive oil in a large frying pan, add the onion and cook over medium heat for 4–5 minutes, or until softened. Add the garlic and cook for a further 30 seconds.
2 Add ½ cup (125 ml/4 fl oz) water, the tomato and sugar and season, to taste. Bring to the boil, then reduce the heat and simmer for 10 minutes, or until reduced slightly.
3 Add the beans and parsley and simmer for a further 10 minutes, or until the beans are tender and the tomato mixture is pulpy. Season with salt and black pepper, and serve immediately as a side dish.

NUTRITION PER SERVE
Protein 5.5 g; Fat 20 g; Carbohydrate 9.5 g;
Dietary Fibre 7.5 g; Cholesterol 0 mg;
992 kJ (237 Cal)

The garlic will be easier to chop if you smash it with the back of a knife first.

Cook the chopped onion in the olive oil until softened, but not brown.

Simmer the tomato mixture until reduced and slightly thickened.

LEBANESE TOASTED BREAD SALAD (FATTOUSH)

Preparation time: 15 minutes
Total cooking time: 10 minutes
Serves 6

2 pitta bread rounds (17 cm/7 inches diameter)
6 cos lettuce leaves, shredded
1 large Lebanese cucumber, cubed
4 tomatoes, cut into 1 cm (½ inch) cubes
8 spring onions, chopped
4 tablespoons finely chopped fresh flat-leaf parsley

1 tablespoon finely chopped fresh mint
2 tablespoons finely chopped fresh coriander

DRESSING
2 cloves garlic, crushed
100 ml (3½ fl oz) extra virgin olive oil
100 ml (3½ fl oz) lemon juice

1 Preheat the oven to moderate 180°C (350°F/Gas 4). Split the bread in half through the centre and bake on a baking tray for 8–10 minutes, or until golden and crisp, turning halfway through. Break into pieces.
2 To make the dressing, whisk all the ingredients together in a bowl.
3 Place the bread and remaining salad ingredients in a serving bowl and toss to combine. Pour on the dressing and toss well. Season to taste with salt and freshly ground black pepper. Serve immediately.

NUTRITION PER SERVE
Protein 5.5 g; Fat 17 g; Carbohydrate 24 g; Dietary Fibre 4 g; Cholesterol 0 mg; 1133 kJ (270 Cal)

NOTE: This is a popular Middle Eastern peasant salad which is served as an appetiser or to accompany a light meal.

Split the pitta bread rounds in two through the centre.

Once the bread is golden and crisp, break it into small pieces with your fingers.

Place the bread pieces and salad ingredients in a bowl and toss well.

Oils & Vinegars

Spice up your marinades, vinaigrettes and dressings with these delicious recipes, or simply enjoy the oil with fresh crusty bread. If you sterilise the storage jar first by rinsing it with boiling water and placing it in a warm oven until it is completely dry, most oils and vinegars will keep for up to 6 months.

TARRAGON VINEGAR

Warm 2 cups (500 ml/16 fl oz) white wine vinegar over low heat. Gently bruise 25 g (¾ oz) fresh tarragon leaves in your hands and put in a 2-cup (500 ml/16 fl oz) sterilised wide-necked jar. Pour in the vinegar, seal with a non-metallic lid and shake well. Allow to stand in a warm place for 2 weeks to infuse. Strain and return to the clean sterilised bottle. Add a fresh sprig of tarragon, seal and label. Store in a cool, dark place for up to 6 months. Makes 2 cups (500 ml/16 fl oz).

CHILLI OIL

Place 6 dried chillies and 1 teaspoon chilli powder in a heavy-based pan. Add 3 cups (750 ml/24 fl oz) olive oil, bring to the boil, then lower the heat and simmer for 5 minutes (if it gets too hot the oil will change flavour). Cover with plastic wrap and leave in a cool, dark place for 3 days. Strain the oil into a 3-cup (750 ml/24 fl oz) sterilised bottle. Discard the chillies and add new chillies for decoration. Makes 3 cups (750 ml/24 fl oz). Store in a cool, dark place for up to 6 months.

PARMESAN OIL

Combine 2 cups (500 ml/16 fl oz) olive oil and 100 g (3½ oz) finely grated Reggiano Parmesan in a small pan. Stir over low heat for 10–15 minutes, or until the Parmesan starts to melt and clump together. Remove from the heat and allow to cool. Strain into a 2-cup (500 ml/16 fl oz) sterilised bottle and add 20 g (¾ oz) shaved Parmesan. Seal and label. Store in a cool, dark place for up to 6 months. Makes 2 cups (500 ml/16 fl oz).

INDIAN OIL

Place 1 teaspoon each of garam masala, coriander seeds, cardamom pods and fennel seeds, 3 allspice berries, 3 curry leaves and 1 small dried chilli in a bowl and lightly crush with the back of a spoon. Place in a sterilised bottle with 3 cups (750 ml/ 24 fl oz) peanut or canola oil. Seal and leave for 3 days in a cool, dark place. Strain into a 3-cup (750 ml/24 fl oz) sterilised bottle. Store in a cool, dark place for up to 3 months. Makes about 3 cups (750 ml/24 fl oz).

SPICY APPLE AND CINNAMON VINEGAR

Combine 2 cups (500 ml/16 fl oz) white wine vinegar, ⅓ cup (30 g/1 oz) finely chopped dried apple slices, ¼ teaspoon black peppercorns, 2 bay leaves, ¼ teaspoon yellow mustard seeds, 2 cinnamon sticks, 2 sprigs fresh thyme and 1 garlic clove in a 2-cup (500 ml/16 fl oz) sterilised jar or bottle. Seal and leave in a cool, dark place for 2 weeks. Strain the vinegar and pour into warm sterilised jars. Store in a cool, dark place for up to 6 months. Makes about 2 cups (500 ml/16 fl oz).

RASPBERRY VINEGAR

Place 2⅓ cups (290 g/10 oz) fresh or thawed frozen raspberries in a non-metallic bowl and crush gently with the back of a spoon. Over low heat, warm 2 cups (500 ml/16 fl oz) white wine vinegar. Add the vinegar to the raspberries and mix well. Pour into a 2-cup (500 ml/16 fl oz) sterilised jar and keep in a warm place for 2 weeks, shaking regularly. Strain through a muslin-lined sieve into a small pan. Add 2 teapoons caster sugar and stir over medium heat until the sugar has dissolved. Pour into a warm sterilised jar or bottle. Add 2–3 raspberries, if desired, seal and label. Store in a cool, dark place for up to 6 months. Makes about 2 cups (500 ml/16 fl oz).

SPICED MALT VINEGAR

Place 2 cups (500 ml/16 fl oz) malt vinegar in a pan. Add a 1 cm piece (10 g) fresh ginger cut into four pieces. Add 1 cinnamon stick, 2 teaspoons allspice berries, ½ teaspoon black peppercorns, 1 teaspoon brown mustard seeds, 10 cloves and warm over low heat. Pour into a warm, sterilised, 2-cup (500 ml/16 fl oz) wide-necked jar and seal with a non-metallic lid. Stand in a warm place for 2 weeks. Put some peppercorns into a sterilised 2-cup (500 ml/16 fl oz) bottle. Strain and pour the vinegar into the bottle. Seal and store in a cool, dark place for up to 6 months. Makes 2 cups (500 ml/16 fl oz).

From left to right: Tarragon vinegar; Chilli oil; Parmesan oil; Raspberry vinegar; Spicy apple and cinnamon vinegar; Spiced malt vinegar; Indian oil.

ROASTED FENNEL AND ORANGE SALAD

Preparation time: 30 minutes
Total cooking time: 1 hour
Serves 4

8 baby fennel bulbs
100 ml (3½ fl oz) olive oil
1 teaspoon sea salt
2 oranges
1 tablespoon lemon juice
1 red onion, halved and thinly sliced
100 g (3½ oz) Kalamata olives
2 tablespoons chopped fresh mint
1 tablespoon roughly chopped fresh
   flat-leaf parsley

1 Preheat the oven to moderately hot 200°C (400°F/Gas 6). Trim and reserve the fennel fronds. Remove the stalks and cut a slice off the base of each fennel about 5 mm (¼ inch) thick. Slice each fennel into 6 wedges. Place in a baking dish and drizzle with ¼ cup (60 ml/2 fl oz) of the oil. Add the salt and plenty of pepper to taste. Bake for 40–60 minutes, or until the fennel is tender and slightly caramelised. Cool.
2 Cut a slice off the top and bottom of each orange. Using a small sharp knife, slice off the skin and pith, following the curves of the orange. Remove as much pith as possible. Slice down the side of a segment between the flesh and the membrane. Repeat with the other side and lift the segment out. Do this over a bowl to catch the segments and juices. Repeat with each segment. Squeeze any juice from the membrane. Drain and reserve the juice.
3 Whisk the remaining olive oil into the orange juice and the lemon juice until emulsified. Season well. Combine the orange segments, onion and olives in a serving dish, pour on half the dressing and add half the mint. Mix well. Top with the fennel, drizzle with the remaining dressing, and scatter with the parsley and the remaining mint. Roughly chop the reserved fronds and scatter over the salad.

NUTRITION PER SERVE
Protein 5 g; Fat 25 g; Carbohydrate 19 g;
Dietary Fibre 15 g; Cholesterol 0 mg;
1339 kJ (320 Cal)

Use a sharp knife to slice each of the baby fennels into wedges.

Bake the fennel until tender and slightly caramelised.

Remove the orange skin and pith with a small sharp knife.

Cut the orange between the flesh and the membrane to remove the segments.

WARM CHICKPEA AND SILVERBEET SALAD WITH SUMAC

**Preparation time: 30 minutes
  + overnight soaking
Total cooking time: 2 hours
Serves 4**

250 g (8 oz) dried chickpeas
½ cup (125 ml/4 fl oz) olive oil
1 onion, cut into thin wedges
2 tomatoes
1 teaspoon sugar
¼ teaspoon ground cinnamon
2 cloves garlic, chopped
1.5 kg (3 lb) silverbeet

3 tablespoons chopped fresh mint
2–3 tablespoons lemon juice
1½ tablespoons ground sumac
  (see NOTE)

1 Place the chickpeas in a large bowl, cover with water and leave to soak overnight. Drain and place in a large saucepan. Cover with water and bring to the boil, then simmer for 1¾ hours, or until tender. Drain.
2 Heat the oil in a frying pan, add the onion and cook over low heat for 3–4 minutes, or until soft and just starting to brown. Cut the tomatoes in half, remove the seeds and dice the flesh. Add to the pan with the sugar, cinnamon and garlic, and cook

for 2–3 minutes, or until softened.
3 Wash the silverbeet and dry with paper towel. Trim the stems and finely shred the leaves. Add to the tomato mixture with the chickpeas and cook for 3–4 minutes, or until the silverbeet wilts. Add the mint, lemon juice and sumac, season, and cook for 1 minute. Serve immediately.

NUTRITION PER SERVE
Protein 18 g; Fat 34 g; Carbohydrate 30 g;
Dietary Fibre 20 g; Cholesterol 0 mg;
2080 kJ (497 Cal)

NOTE: Sumac is available from Middle Eastern speciality shops.

Scoop the seeds out of the halved tomatoes with a teaspoon.

Add the tomato, sugar, cinnamon and garlic to the pan and cook until soft.

Add the silverbeet and chickpeas and cook until the spinach is wilted.

OKRA IN TOMATO SAUCE AND CORIANDER

Preparation time: 5 minutes
Total cooking time: 15 minutes
Serves 4–6

¼ cup (60 ml/2 fl oz) olive oil
1 onion, chopped
2 cloves garlic, crushed
500 g (1 lb) fresh okra (see NOTE)
425 g (14 oz) can chopped tomatoes
2 teaspoons sugar
¼ cup (60 ml/2 fl oz) lemon juice
55 g (2 oz) fresh coriander, finely chopped

1 Heat the oil in a large frying pan, add the onion and cook over medium heat for 4 minutes, or until transparent and golden. Add the garlic and cook for a further minute.
2 Add the okra and cook, stirring, for 4–5 minutes, then add the tomato, sugar and juice, and simmer, stirring occasionally, for 3–4 minutes, or until softened. Stir in the coriander, remove from the heat and serve.

NUTRITION PER SERVE (6)
Protein 3.5 g; Fat 10 g; Carbohydrate 5.5 g; Dietary Fibre 4 g; Cholesterol 0 mg; 522 kJ (125 Cal)

NOTE: If fresh okra is not available, you can use an 800 g (1 lb 10 oz) can of okra. Rinse and drain well before adding it to the pan with the

Add the garlic to the onion in the pan and cook for a further minute.

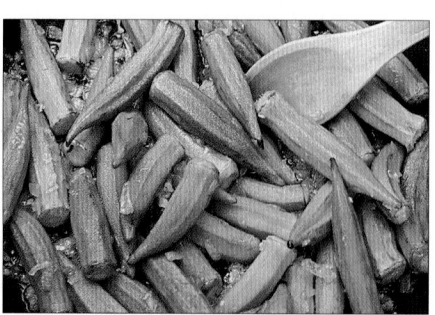

Stir the okra into the onion mixture and simmer for a few minutes.

Stir in the tomato, sugar and lemon juice and simmer until softened.

THREE-BEAN STIR-FRY

Preparation time: 10 minutes
Total cooking time: 5 minutes
Serves 4

1 tablespoon oil
1 red onion, chopped
2 cloves garlic, crushed
1 tablespoon finely chopped thyme
200 g (6½ oz) green beans, cut into
    short lengths
300 g (10 oz) can cannellini beans,
    rinsed
1 cup (170 g/5½ oz) chickpeas, rinsed
    and drained

150 g (5 oz) rocket
2 tablespoons finely chopped parsley
3 tablespoons lemon juice

1 Heat the wok until very hot, add
the oil and swirl it around to coat the
side. Stir-fry the onion for 2 minutes.
Add the garlic and stir-fry until soft.
Stir in the thyme.
2 Add the green beans and stir-fry for
2–3 minutes, or until tender. Add the
cannellini beans and chickpeas, and
stir-fry until heated through. Season,
and spoon the mixture onto the
rocket on a platter. Sprinkle the
parsley on top and drizzle with the
lemon juice to serve.

NUTRITION PER SERVE
Protein 7 g; Fat 6 g; Carbohydrate 10 g;
Dietary Fibre 6.5 g; Cholesterol 0 mg;
530 kJ (125 cal)

Add the green beans to the onion, garlic and
thyme and stir-fry until tender.

817

CHICKPEA AND ROAST VEGETABLE SALAD

**Preparation time: 25 minutes +
30 minutes standing**
Total cooking time: 40 minutes
Serves 8

500 g (1 lb) butternut pumpkin, cubed
2 red capsicums, halved
4 slender eggplants, cut in half
   lengthways
4 zucchini, cut in half lengthways
4 onions, quartered
olive oil, for brushing

2 x 300 g (10 oz) cans chickpeas,
   rinsed and drained
2 tablespoons chopped fresh flat-leaf
   parsley

DRESSING
⅓ cup (80 ml/2¾ fl oz) olive oil
2 tablespoons lemon juice
1 clove garlic, crushed
1 tablespoon chopped fresh thyme

1 Preheat the oven to hot 220°C
(425°F/Gas 7). Brush two baking trays
with oil and lay out the vegetables in
a single layer. Brush lightly with oil.
2 Bake for 40 minutes, or until the
vegetables are tender and begin to
brown slightly on the edges. Cool.
Remove the skins from the capsicum
if you want. Chop the capsicum,
eggplant and zucchini into pieces,
then put the vegetables in a bowl with
the chickpeas and half the parsley.
3 Whisk together all the dressing
ingredients. Season, then toss with the
vegetables. Leave for 30 minutes, then
sprinkle with the rest of the parsley.

NUTRITION PER SERVE
Protein 8.5 g; Fat 12 g; Carbohydrate 20 g;
Dietary Fibre 7.5 g; Cholesterol 0 mg;
935 kJ (225 cal)

Rinse the chickpeas under cold running water
then drain thoroughly.

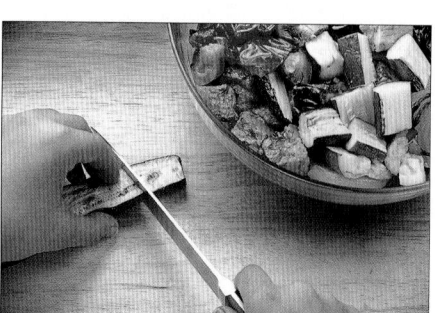

Chop the roasted capsicum, eggplant and
zucchini into small pieces.

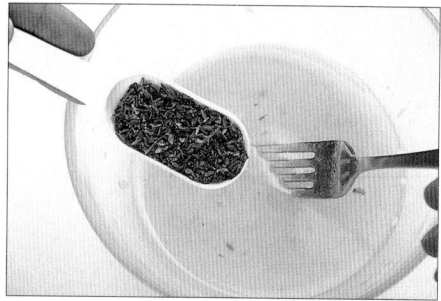

Put the olive oil, lemon juice, garlic and thyme in a
bowl and whisk together.

POTATO GRATIN

Preparation time: 25 minutes
Total cooking time: 1 hour
Serves 4

30 g (1 oz) butter
1 onion, halved and thinly sliced
650 g (1 lb 5 oz) floury potatoes, thinly
    sliced
⅔ cup (90 g/3 oz) grated Cheddar
300 ml (10 fl oz) cream
100 ml (10 fl oz) milk

1 Heat the butter in a frying pan and cook the onion over low heat for 5 minutes, or until it is soft and translucent.
2 Preheat the oven to warm 160°C (315°F/Gas 3). Grease the base and sides of a deep 1 litre (32 fl oz) ovenproof dish. Layer the potato slices with the onion and cheese (reserving 2 tablespoons of cheese for the top). Whisk together the cream and milk, and season with salt and cracked black pepper. Slowly pour over the potato, then sprinkle with the remaining cheese.
3 Bake for 50–60 minutes, or until golden brown and the potato is very soft. Leave to rest for 10 minutes before serving.

NUTRITION PER SERVE
Protein 12 g; Fat 50 g; Carbohydrate 25 g;
Dietary Fibre 3 g; Cholesterol 155 mg;
2465 kJ (590 cal)

VARIATION: For something different, try combining potato and orange sweet potato, layering alternately. For extra flavour, add chopped fresh herbs to the cream and milk mixture.

Peel the onion and slice it in half before cutting into thin slices.

Use a large sharp knife to cut the potatoes into thin slices.

Add the onion to the butter and cook until soft and translucent.

MANY MUSHROOM NOODLES

**Preparation time: 30 minutes
+ 20 minutes soaking
Total cooking time: 15 minutes
Serves 4–6**

30 g (1 oz) dried Chinese mushrooms
1 tablespoon oil
½ teaspoon sesame oil
1 tablespoon grated fresh ginger
4 cloves garlic, crushed
100 g (3½ oz) shiitake mushrooms,
   trimmed, sliced
150 g (5 oz) oyster mushrooms, sliced
150 g (5 oz) shimeji mushrooms,
   trimmed, pulled apart
¾ cup (185 ml/6 fl oz) dashi (see
   NOTE)

¼ cup (60 ml/2 fl oz) soy sauce
¼ cup (60 ml/2 fl oz) mirin
30 g (1 oz) butter
2 tablespoons lemon juice
100 g (3½ oz) enoki mushrooms,
   trimmed, pulled apart
500 g (1 lb) thin Hokkien noodles,
   separated
1 tablespoon chopped chives

1 Soak the Chinese mushrooms in 1½ cups (375 ml/12 fl oz) boiling water for 20 minutes, or until soft. Drain, reserving the liquid. Discard the stems and slice the caps.
2 Heat a wok until very hot, add the oils and swirl to coat. Add the ginger, garlic, shiitake, oyster and shimeji mushrooms and stir-fry for 2 minutes, or until the mushrooms have wilted. Remove from the wok.

3 Combine the dashi, soy, mirin, ¼ teaspoon white pepper and ¾ cup (185 ml) reserved liquid, add to the wok and cook for 3 minutes. Add the butter, lemon juice and 1 teaspoon salt and cook for 1 minute, or until the sauce thickens. Return the mushrooms to the wok, cook for 2 minutes, then stir in the enoki and Chinese mushrooms.
4 Add the noodles and stir for 3 minutes, or until heated through. Sprinkle with chives to serve.

NUTRITION PER SERVE (6)
Protein 15 g; Fat 8.5 g; Carbohydrate 60 g;
Dietary Fibre 5 g; Cholesterol 25 mg;
1610 kJ (385 cal)

NOTE: Dissolve 1½ teaspoons dashi powder in 185 ml (6 fl oz) water.

Soak the Chinese mushrooms in boiling water, then drain, reserving the liquid.

Stir-fry the mushrooms for 1–2 minutes, or until they have wilted.

Add the butter, lemon juice and 1 teaspoon salt to the wok and cook until thickened.

BRAISED BOK CHOY

**Preparation time: 10 minutes
Total cooking time: 5 minutes
Serves 4 (as a side dish)**

2 tablespoons peanut oil
1 clove garlic, crushed
1 tablespoon shredded fresh
   ginger

550 g (1 lb 2 oz) bok choy, separated,
   cut into 8 cm (3 inch) lengths
1 teaspoon sugar
1 teaspoon sesame oil
1 tablespoon oyster sauce

1 Heat a wok until very hot, add the oil, garlic and ginger and stir-fry for 1–2 minutes. Add the bok choy and stir-fry for 1 minute. Add the sugar, a pinch of salt, cracked black pepper

and 3 tablespoons water. Bring to the boil, then reduce the heat and simmer, covered, for 3 minutes, or until the stems are tender but crisp.
2 Stir in the sesame oil and oyster sauce and serve immediately.

NUTRITION PER SERVE
Protein 7 g; Fat 11 g; Carbohydrate 3 g;
Dietary Fibre 6 g; Cholesterol 0 mg;
582 kJ (139 cal)

Separate the leaves of the bok choy and then cut them into shorter lengths.

Heat the wok until very hot, then stir-fry the garlic and ginger in the oil.

Stir-fry the bok choy for 3 minutes, or until the stems are tender but still crisp.

TOMATO AND BOCCONCINI SALAD

Preparation time: 10 minutes
Total cooking time: Nil
Serves 4

3 large vine-ripened tomatoes
250 g (8 oz) bocconcini
    (see NOTE)
12 fresh basil leaves
¼ cup (60 ml/2 fl oz) extra virgin
    olive oil
4 basil leaves, roughly torn, extra,

1 Slice the tomatoes into 1 cm (½ inch) slices, making twelve slices altogether. Slice the bocconcini into twenty-four 1 cm (½ inch) slices.
2 Arrange the tomato slices on a serving plate, alternating them with 2 slices of bocconcini. Place the basil leaves between the bocconcini slices.
3 Drizzle with the oil, sprinkle with the basil and season well with salt and freshly ground black pepper.

NUTRITION PER SERVE
Protein 14 g; Fat 25 g; Carbohydrate 3 g;
Dietary Fibre 1 g; Cholesterol 33 mg;
1221 kJ (292 Cal)

NOTE: This popular summer salad is most successful with very fresh buffalo mozzarella if you can find it. We've used bocconcini in this recipe as it can be difficult to find very fresh mozzarella.

Slice the bocconcini into twenty-four 1 cm (½ inch) thick slices.

Arrange the tomato slices on a serving plate, alternating with the bocconcini.

SPICY FUN SEE NOODLE SALAD

Preparation time: 20 minutes + 5 minutes soaking + 2 hours refrigeration
Total cooking time: 5 minutes
Serves 4

125 g (4 oz) mung bean vermicelli (fun see)
1 teaspoon sesame oil
1 large carrot, julienned
2 sticks celery, julienned
100 g (3½ oz) snow peas, julienned
2 small Lebanese cucumbers
3 spring onions, thinly sliced into long diagonal strips
½ cup (15 g/½ oz) fresh coriander leaves
½ cup (10 g/¼ oz) fresh mint

DRESSING
⅓ cup (70 g/2 oz) Chinese sesame paste

2 teaspoons chilli oil
¼ cup (60 ml/2 fl oz) light soy sauce
1 tablespoon white vinegar
1 tablespoon sugar
¼ teaspoon cayenne pepper
2½ tablespoons chicken stock

1 Place the noodles in a large heatproof bowl, cover with boiling water and soak for 3–4 minutes, or until softened. Drain. Cut in half with scissors, place in a large bowl, add the sesame oil and mix well. Cover and refrigerate for 1 hour, or until needed.
2 Bring a large saucepan of water to the boil, add the carrot, celery, snow peas and 2 teaspoons salt and cook for 30 seconds. Drain and refresh in icy cold water. Drain again and pat dry, making sure that as little moisture as possible remains. Seed and julienne the cucumber, and combine with the vegetables and spring onion. Refrigerate for 1 hour.
3 To make the dressing, place the sesame paste in a bowl and stir well.

Slowly mix in the chilli oil, soy sauce, vinegar, sugar, cayenne pepper and chicken stock.
4 Just before serving, add three quarters of the blanched vegetables and three quarters of the herbs to the chilled noodles. Pour the dressing on top, then toss well. Season to taste with salt and pepper. Transfer to a serving platter and top with the remaining vegetables and herbs.

NUTRITION PER SERVE
Fat 13 g; Protein 6 g; Carbohydrate 25.5 g;
Dietary Fibre 6.5 g; Cholesterol 0 mg;
1020 kJ (245 Cal)

OVEN-BAKED POTATO, LEEK AND OLIVES

Preparation time: 20 minutes
Total cooking time: 1 hour
Serves 4–6

2 tablespoons extra virgin olive oil
1 leek, finely sliced
1½ cups (375 ml/12 fl oz) vegetable stock
2 teaspoons chopped fresh thyme
1 kg (2 lb) potatoes, unpeeled, cut into thin slices
6–8 pitted black olives, sliced
½ cup (60 g/2 oz) grated Parmesan
30 g (1 oz) butter, chopped

1 Preheat the oven to moderate 180°C (350°F/Gas 4). Brush a shallow 1.25 litre (40 fl oz) ovenproof dish with a little olive oil. Heat the remaining oil in a large pan and cook the leek over moderate heat until soft. Add the stock, thyme and potato. Cover and leave to simmer for 5 minutes.
2 Using tongs, lift out half the potato and put in the ovenproof dish. Sprinkle with olives and Parmesan and season with salt and pepper.
3 Layer with the remaining potato, then spoon the leek and stock mixture in at the side of the dish, keeping the top dry.
4 Scatter chopped butter over the potato and then bake, uncovered, for 50 minutes, or until cooked and golden brown. Leave in a warm place for about 10 minutes before serving.

NUTRITION PER SERVE (6)
Protein 7.5 g; Fat 13 g; Carbohydrate 23 g; Dietary Fibre 3 g; Cholesterol 20 mg; 1019 kJ (243 cal)

NOTE: Keeping the top layer of potato dry as you pour in the stock mixture will give the dish a crisp finish.

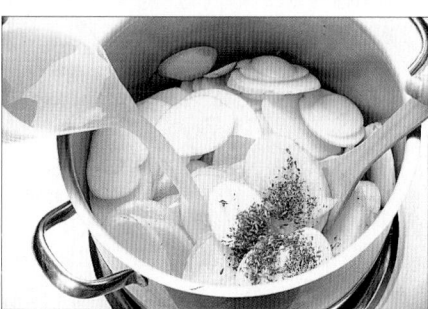

Cook the leek until soft, then add the stock, thyme and potato.

Lift out half the potato with tongs and put into an ovenproof dish.

Spoon the leek and stock mixture around the side, trying to keep the top dry.

Bake, uncovered, until the potatoes on top are golden brown.

LEMON, FENNEL AND ROCKET SALAD

Preparation time: 25 minutes
Total cooking time: 5 minutes
Serves 4

2 lemons
2 oranges
1 large fennel bulb or 2 baby fennel
200 g (6½ oz) rocket
100 g (3½ oz) pecans, chopped
½ cup (90 g/3 oz) stuffed green olives,
    halved lengthways

TOASTED SESAME DRESSING
1 tablespoon sesame oil
1 tablespoon sesame seeds
¼ cup (60 ml/2 fl oz) olive oil
2 tablespoons white wine vinegar
1 teaspoon French mustard

1 Peel the lemons and oranges, removing all the white pith. Cut the fruit into thin slices and remove any seeds. Thinly slice the fennel. Wash and dry the rocket leaves and tear into pieces. Chill the salad while making the dressing.
2 To make the dressing, heat the oil in a small pan over moderate heat. Add the sesame seeds and fry, stirring constantly, until lightly golden. Remove from the heat and cool. Pour the mixture into a small jug, whisk in the remaining ingredients and season with salt and ground black pepper.
3 Combine the fruit, fennel, rocket, pecans and olives in a shallow serving bowl. Drizzle with the dressing.

NUTRITION PER SERVE
Protein 6 g; Fat 40 g; Carbohydrate 10 g;
Dietary Fibre 9 g; Cholesterol 0 mg;
1820 kJ (435 cal)

Cut the peeled lemons and oranges into thin slices and remove any seeds.

Using a large, sharp knife, thinly slice the fennel bulb crossways.

Stir the sesame seeds in the sesame oil until they are lightly golden.

SMOKED CHICKEN CAESAR SALAD

Preparation time: 25 minutes
Total cooking time: 15 minutes
Serves 4

GARLIC CROUTONS
1 thin baguette
45 g (1½ oz) unsalted butter
½ cup (125 ml/4 fl oz) olive oil
4 cloves garlic, crushed

1 cos lettuce, tough outer leaves
    discarded
1 large smoked chicken (about
    950 g/1 lb 14 oz)
1½ cups (150 g/5 oz) Parmesan
    shavings

DRESSING
2 eggs
2 cloves garlic, crushed
2 tablespoons lemon juice
2 teaspoons Dijon mustard
45 g (1½ oz) can anchovy fillets,
    drained
1 cup (250 ml/8 fl oz) olive oil
¼ teaspoon salt
1 teaspoon freshly ground black
    pepper

1 To make the garlic croutons, slice
the baguette diagonally into 1 cm
(½ inch) thick slices. Melt the butter
and olive oil in a large frying pan over
moderate heat. Stir in the crushed
garlic. Fry the bread slices, a few at a
time, until golden. Remove from the
pan and drain on paper towels.
2 Separate the lettuce leaves, wash
and dry thoroughly. Tear the larger
leaves into pieces and refrigerate until
well chilled. Cut the chicken into bite-
sized chunks. Refrigerate while
preparing the dressing.
3 To make the dressing, blend or
process the eggs, garlic, lemon juice,
mustard and anchovies. With the
motor running, gradually pour in the
oil in a thin stream and process until
thick. Season with the salt and pepper.
4 In a large bowl, combine the torn
lettuce leaves, chicken, about half of
the croutons and half the Parmesan.
Add the dressing and toss well.
Arrange 2–3 whole lettuce leaves in
each individual serving bowl, spoon
in the salad and sprinkle with the
remaining croutons and Parmesan.
Season liberally with freshly ground
black pepper and serve immediately.

NUTRITION PER SERVE
Protein 45 g; Fat 120 g; Carbohydrate 10 g;
Dietary Fibre 2 g; Cholesterol 235 mg;
5350 kJ (1275 cal)

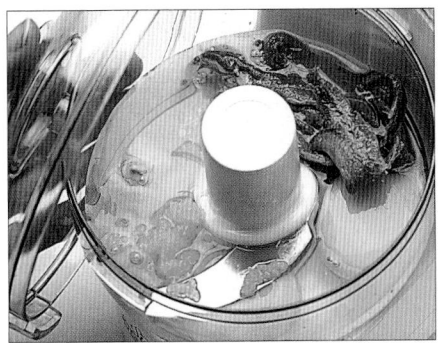

Roughly chop the smoked chicken meat into
bite-sized chunks.

Process the eggs, garlic, lemon juice, mustard
and anchovies.

JAPANESE SPINACH SALAD

Preparation time: 25 minutes
Total cooking time: 5 minutes
Serves 4

2 eggs
1 sheet nori, cut into matchsticks
100 g (3½ oz) baby English spinach
   leaves
1 small red onion, finely sliced
½ small daikon radish, finely sliced
2 Lebanese cucumbers, sliced
30 g (1 oz) pickled ginger, sliced
1 tablespoon toasted sesame seeds

DRESSING
⅓ cup (80 ml/2¾ fl oz) light olive oil
1 tablespoon rice vinegar
1 tablespoon light soy sauce

1 Preheat the grill to hot. Beat the
eggs lightly in a small bowl, add
1 tablespoon water and the nori.
Season well. Heat and grease a 20 cm
(8 inch) omelette pan. Pour in the
mixture to make a thin omelette.
When lightly browned underneath,
place under the grill to set the top,
without colouring. Turn out onto a
board and leave to cool. Cut the
omelette into thin strips.
2 To make the dressing, whisk
together the olive oil, vinegar and soy
sauce until combined.
3 Toss together the spinach leaves,
onion, daikon, cucumber, ginger,
toasted sesame seeds, omelette strips
and dressing in a large bowl.

NUTRITION PER SERVE
Protein 5 g; Fat 25 g; Carbohydrate 15 g;
Dietary Fibre 2 g; Cholesterol 90 mg;
1235 kJ (295 cal)

Peel the daikon radish and cut it into fine slices
with a sharp knife.

Add 1 tablespoon water and the nori to the lightly
beaten eggs.

Once the omelette has cooled, slice it into thin
strips for adding to the salad.

WARM STIR-FRIED SALAD

Preparation time: 15 minutes
Total cooking time: 5 minutes
Serves 2

2 tablespoons olive oil
1 red onion, sliced
1 red capsicum, cut into small
    squares
2 cloves garlic, thinly sliced
250 g (8 oz) cherry tomatoes,
    halved

150 g (5 oz) baby English spinach
    leaves
½ cup (15 g/½ oz) basil leaves
125 g (4 oz) feta cheese,
    crumbled

1 Heat the wok until very hot, add the oil and swirl it around to coat the base and side of the wok. Add the onion, capsicum and garlic to the wok and stir-fry for 2 minutes, or until just beginning to soften. Add the tomatoes, spinach and basil and stir-fry until the leaves have just wilted.

2 Transfer the salad to a serving plate and top with the crumbled feta cheese. Serve immediately.

NUTRITION PER SERVE
Protein 15 g; Fat 35 g; Carbohydrate 7 g;
Dietary Fibre 6 g; Cholesterol 45 mg;
1635 kJ (390 cal)

NOTE: Serve as a main course with crusty bread or pasta or heap onto crostini as a starter.

Remove the seeds from the capsicum and cut the flesh into squares.

Peel the cloves of garlic, then cut each clove into thin slices.

Good-quality feta cheese should crumble easily between your fingers.

ITALIAN-STYLE PRAWN AND PASTA SALAD

Preparation time: 15 minutes
Total cooking time: 15 minutes
Serves 4

DRESSING
⅓ cup (80 ml/2¾ fl oz) olive oil
1½ tablespoons white wine vinegar
1½ tablespoons pine nuts, toasted
1 tablespoon roughly chopped fresh basil
1 tablespoon roughly chopped fresh flat-leaf parsley
1 clove garlic
1 tablespoon grated Parmesan
pinch of sugar

400 g (13 oz) large pasta shells
1 tablespoon olive oil, extra
500 g (1 lb) small cooked prawns
100 g (3½ oz) bocconcini, thinly sliced
125 g (4 oz) chargrilled red capsicum, cut into thin strips
125 g (4 oz) cherry tomatoes, halved
fresh basil leaves, to garnish

1 For the dressing, process all the ingredients together in a blender or food processor until smooth.
2 Cook the pasta in a large pan of rapidly boiling salted water until al dente. Drain well, return to the pan and toss with the extra olive oil. Allow to cool.
3 Peel the prawns and gently pull out the dark vein from each prawn back, starting at the head end.
4 Put the pasta, prawns, bocconcini, capsicum and tomatoes in a serving bowl and pour on the dressing. Toss together well and garnish with basil leaves to serve.

NUTRITION PER SERVE
Protein 51 g; Fat 35 g; Carbohydrate 73 g;
Dietary Fibre 7 g; Cholesterol 257 mg;
3420 kJ (815 cal)

Slice the chargrilled red capsicum into very thin strips.

Process all the dressing ingredients together until well blended and smooth.

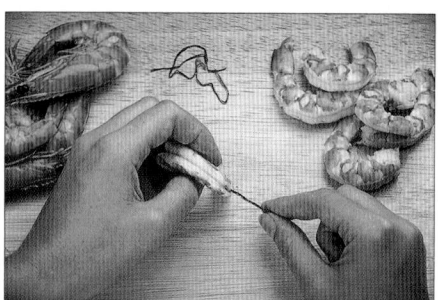

Gently pull out the dark vein from the back of each peeled prawn.

CHILLI LAMB AND CASHEWS

Preparation time: 10 minutes
Total cooking time: 10 minutes
Serves 4

750 g (1½ lb) lamb fillets
4 tablespoons peanut oil
1 cup (150 g/5 oz) cashew nuts
1 large onion, cut into wedges
200 g (6½ oz) snow peas
230 g (7½ oz) sliced bamboo shoots

2 tablespoons chilli sauce
1 tablespoon soy sauce

1 Trim the meat of any fat and sinew and then cut across the grain evenly into thin slices. Heat 2 tablespoons of the oil in a wok, swirling gently to coat the side. Stir-fry the lamb in small batches over high heat until browned but not cooked through. Remove from the wok and drain on paper towels.
2 Heat 1 tablespoon oil in the wok and fry the cashews until golden brown. Remove with a slotted spoon

and drain on paper towels.
3 Heat the remaining oil in the wok and stir-fry the onion and snow peas for 2 minutes. Add the bamboo shoots and stir-fry for 1 minute. Return the meat to the wok with the cashews, chilli and soy sauces. Stir-fry over high heat until the meat is cooked and the sauce is hot. Serve immediately.

NUTRITION PER SERVE
Protein 52 g; Fat 45 g; Carbohydrate 15 g;
Dietary Fibre 7 g; Cholesterol 124 mg;
2784 kJ (665 cal)

Heat the wok, then add 1 tablespoon of oil and heat it up, swirling to coat the side of the wok.

Stir-fry the cashews until they are golden brown, then remove with a slotted spoon.

Return the browned meat to the wok with the fried cashew nuts.

CHICKEN AND WATERCRESS SALAD

Preparation time: 40 minutes
Total cooking time: 10–15 minutes
Serves 4

3 small chicken breast fillets
    (350 g/11 oz)
1 Lebanese cucumber
½ red capsicum
150 g (5 oz) watercress
½ cup (10 g/¼ oz) fresh mint leaves
2 tablespoons finely shredded fresh
    mint
2 chillies, thinly sliced
2 tablespoons crisp-fried onion

DRESSING
¼ cup (60 ml/2 fl oz) lime juice
2 tablespoons coconut milk
1 tablespoon fish sauce
1 tablespoon sweet chilli sauce

1 Line a bamboo steamer with baking paper and steam the chicken, covered, over a wok or pan of simmering water, for 10 minutes or until the chicken is cooked through. Remove from the heat and set aside to cool. Thinly slice the cucumber and cut the slices in half. Slice the capsicum into thin strips.
2 While the chicken is cooling, pick over the watercress and separate the sprigs from the tough stems. Arrange the watercress and whole mint leaves on a serving plate. Using your fingers, tear the chicken into long, thin shreds. Gently toss the shredded chicken, cucumber and capsicum in a bowl. Arrange over the watercress bed.
3 To make the dressing, whisk the lime juice, coconut milk, fish sauce and sweet chilli sauce until combined.

4 Drizzle the dressing over the salad and sprinkle with the shredded mint, sliced chillies and crisp-fried onion.

NUTRITION PER SERVE
Protein 40 g; Fat 6 g; Carbohydrate 3 g;
Dietary Fibre 2.5 g; Cholesterol 82 mg;
966 kJ (230 cal)

NOTE: Crisp-fried, or sometimes deep-fried, onions are available in packets or small jars from Asian supermarkets.

Line a bamboo steamer with baking paper and cook the chicken.

Pick over the watercress to separate the sprigs from the tough stems.

When the chicken is cooked, tear it into shreds, using your fingers.

WARM MARINATED MUSHROOM SALAD

**Preparation time: 25 minutes +
20 minutes marinating
Total cooking time: 5 minutes
Serves 4**

750 g (1½ lb) mixed mushrooms (such as baby button, oyster, Swiss brown, shiitake and enoki)
2 cloves garlic, finely chopped
½ teaspoon green peppercorns, crushed
⅓ cup (80 ml/2¾ fl oz) olive oil

⅓ cup (80 ml/2¾ fl oz) orange juice
250 g (8 oz) salad leaves, watercress or baby spinach leaves
1 teaspoon finely grated orange rind

1 Trim the mushroom stems and wipe the mushrooms with a damp paper towel. Cut any large mushrooms in half. Mix together the garlic, peppercorns, olive oil and orange juice. Pour over the mushrooms and marinate for about 20 minutes.
2 Arrange the salad leaves in a serving dish.
3 Drain the mushrooms, reserving the marinade. Cook the flat and button

mushrooms on a hot, lightly oiled barbecue grill or flatplate for about 2 minutes. Add the softer mushrooms and cook for 1 minute, or until they just soften.
4 Scatter the mushrooms over the salad leaves and drizzle with the marinade. Sprinkle with orange rind and season well.

NUTRITION PER SERVE
Protein 10 g; Fat 15 g; Carbohydrate 5 g;
Dietary Fibre 5 g; Cholesterol 0 mg;
790 kJ (190 cal)

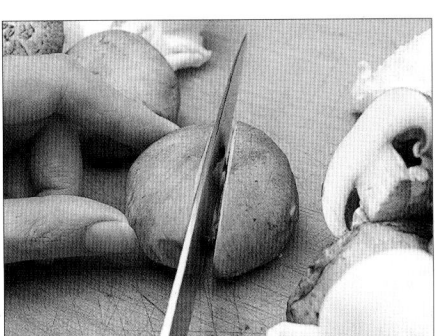

Trim the mushroom stems and wipe clean with paper towel. Cut any large mushrooms in half.

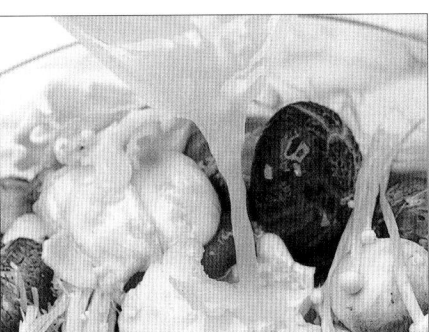

Mix together the garlic, peppercorns, olive oil and orange juice and pour over the mushrooms.

Add the softer mushrooms to the barbecue and just cook for 1 minute.

CARAMELISED ONION AND POTATO SALAD

Preparation time: 20 minutes
Total cooking time: 1 hour
Serves 10

oil, for cooking
6 red onions, thinly sliced
1 kg (2 lb) small waxy potatoes,
    unpeeled
4 rashers bacon, rind removed
⅔ cup (30 g/1 oz) fresh chives,
    snipped
1 cup (250 g/8 oz) mayonnaise

1 tablespoon Dijon mustard
juice of 1 lemon
2 tablespoons sour cream

1 Heat 2 tablespoons of oil in a large heavy-based frying pan, add the onion and cook over medium-low heat for 40 minutes, or until very soft.
2 Cut the potatoes into large chunks (if they are small enough, leave them whole). Cook in boiling water for 10 minutes, or until just tender, then drain and cool slightly. (Do not overcook the potatoes or they will fall apart.)
3 Grill the bacon until crisp, drain on paper towels and cool slightly before coarsely chopping.
4 Put the potato, onion and chives in a large bowl, reserving a few chives for a garnish, and mix well.
5 Put the mayonnaise, mustard, lemon juice and sour cream in a bowl and whisk together. Pour over the salad and toss to coat. Sprinkle with the bacon and garnish with the reserved chives.

NUTRITION PER SERVE
Protein 9 g; Fat 13 g; Carbohydrate 35 g;
Dietary Fibre 4.5 g; Cholesterol 20 mg;
1221 kJ (292 cal)

Cook the sliced onion over medium-low heat until soft and caramelised.

Wash the potatoes and cut them into large chunks or leave whole if they are small enough.

Whisk together the mayonnaise, mustard, lemon juice and sour cream.

EGGPLANT, CAPSICUM, PESTO AND GOAT'S MILK CHEESE STACK

Preparation time: 20 minutes +
30 minutes standing
Total cooking time: 15 minutes
Serves 4 as an entrée

1 kg eggplant, cut into twelve
    1.5 cm slices (ends discarded)
1 large red capsicum
olive oil, for pan-frying
1 cup (45 g) rocket leaves
100 g goat's milk cheese
shredded rocket or basil, to garnish
balsamic vinegar, to serve (optional)
olive oil, to serve (optional)

PESTO
1½ cups (75 g) firmly packed fresh basil
2 cloves garlic
2 tablespoons pine nuts, toasted
1 tablespoon lemon juice
1½ tablespoons grated Parmesan
½ cup (125 ml) olive oil

1 Rub salt generously into the eggplant slices, then sit in a colander for 30 minutes. Rinse under cold water and pat the eggplant dry.

2 Cut the capsicum into large pieces, removing the seeds and membrane. Place, skin-side-up, under a hot grill until the skin blackens and blisters. Cool in a plastic bag, then peel away the skin. Slice thinly.

3 To make the pesto, combine the basil, garlic, pine nuts, lemon juice and Parmesan in a food processor or blender and process until finely minced. With the motor running, slowly pour in the oil and blend until smooth.

4 Lightly cover the base of a frying pan with oil and heat over medium heat. Add the eggplant in batches and cook both sides until golden, adding more oil as needed. Drain on crumpled paper towels and keep warm.

5 To assemble, lay a few rocket leaves on a plate. Place one slice of eggplant on the rocket, then top with some more rocket leaves, a heaped teaspoon of pesto, one eighth of the capsicum and one eighth of the goat's milk cheese. Repeat, making two layers and finish with a final slice of eggplant. Dollop some pesto on the top of the stack, sprinkle with shredded rocket or basil and season with pepper. Repeat, making three more stacks. Drizzle balsamic vinegar and olive oil around the plate, if desired. Serve immediately.

NUTRITION PER SERVE
Protein 12 g; Fat 55 g; Carbohydrate 8.5 g;
Dietary Fibre 7 g; Cholesterol 24 mg;
2397 kJ (573 cal)

Cook the capsicum under a hot grill until the skin blackens and blisters.

Cook both sides of the eggplant until golden, then drain on paper towels.

Add the olive oil and blend until the pesto is smooth.

MEXICANA SALAD

Preparation time: 40 minutes + overnight standing
Total cooking time: 1 hour
Serves 10–12

250 g (8 oz) black-eyed beans
250 g (8 oz) red kidney beans
500 g (1 lb) sweet potato
1 large red onion, chopped
1 large green capsicum, chopped
3 ripe tomatoes, chopped
¼ cup (15 g/½ oz) chopped basil
3 flour tortillas
1 tablespoon oil
2 tablespoons grated Parmesan
¼ cup (60 g/2 oz) sour cream

DRESSING
1 clove garlic, crushed
1 tablespoon lime juice
2 tablespoons olive oil

GUACAMOLE
3 avocados
2 tablespoons lemon juice
1 clove garlic, crushed
1 small red onion, chopped
1 small red chilli, chopped
¼ cup (60 g/2 oz) sour cream
2 tablespoons hot ready-made taco sauce

1 Soak the beans in a large bowl of cold water overnight. Drain and cook in a large pan of rapidly boiling water for 30 minutes, or until just tender. Skim off any scum that appears on the surface during cooking. Do not overcook or they will become mushy. Drain and set aside to cool.
2 Chop the sweet potato into large pieces and cook in boiling water until tender. Drain and combine with the onion, capsicum, tomato and beans. Stir in the basil.
3 To make the dressing, shake the ingredients in a jar until combined. Pour over the salad and toss to coat.
4 Preheat the oven to moderate 180°C (350°F/Gas 4). Using a small knife, cut cactus shapes or large triangles out of the tortillas, brush lightly with the oil and sprinkle with Parmesan. Bake for 5–10 minutes, or until they are crisp and golden.
5 To make the guacamole, mash the avocados with the lemon juice. Add the garlic, onion, chilli, sour cream and taco sauce and mix well.
6 Pile the guacamole in the centre of the salad, top with the sour cream and arrange the cactus shapes on top.

NUTRITION PER SERVE (12)
Protein 15 g; Fat 25 g; Carbohydrate 40 g;
Dietary Fibre 10 g; Cholesterol 15 mg;
1735 kJ (415 cal)

Combine the sweet potato with the onion, capsicum, tomato and beans.

Using a small sharp knife, cut cactus shapes out of the tortillas.

HERBED FETA SALAD

**Preparation time: 20 minutes +
  30 minutes marinating**
Total cooking time: 10 minutes
Serves 8

2 slices thick white bread
200 g (6½ oz) feta cheese
1 clove garlic, crushed
1 tablespoon chopped fresh marjoram
1 tablespoon snipped chives
1 tablespoon chopped fresh basil

2 tablespoons white wine vinegar
⅓ cup (80 ml/2¾ fl oz) olive oil
1 red coral lettuce
1 green mignonette or oak leaf lettuce

1 Preheat the oven to 180°C (350°F/
Gas 4). Remove the crusts from the
bread and cut the bread into small
cubes. Place on an oven tray in a
single layer and bake for 10 minutes,
until crisp and lightly golden. Transfer
to a bowl and cool completely.
2 Cut the feta into small cubes and
put in a bowl. Put the garlic,

marjoram, chives, basil, vinegar and
oil in a screw-top jar and shake well.
Pour over the feta and cover with
plastic wrap. Leave for at least
30 minutes, stirring occasionally.
3 Tear the lettuce into large pieces
and put in a serving bowl. Add the
feta with the dressing and bread
cubes and toss the salad well.

NUTRITION PER SERVE
Protein 6 g; Fat 16 g; Carbohydrate 4 g;
Dietary Fibre 1 g; Cholesterol 17 mg;
750 kJ (180 cal)

Remove the crusts from the bread and then cut it
into small cubes.

Cut the feta into cubes and then pour the
dressing over and leave to marinate.

Add the bread cubes to the salad leaves and
marinated feta.

DEEP-FRIED CALAMARI IN CHICKPEA BATTER WITH PARSLEY SALAD

**Preparation time: 15 minutes +
30 minutes standing**
Total cooking time: 10 minutes
Serves 4 as an entrée

DEEP-FRIED CALAMARI
150 g besan (chickpea flour)
1½ teaspoons bittersweet smoked
    paprika or normal paprika
1½ teaspoons ground cumin
½ teaspoon baking powder
1 cup (250 ml) soda water
oil, for deep-frying
6 calamari, cleaned and sliced
    into rings about 8 mm wide

PARSLEY SALAD
¼ preserved lemon, rinsed, pith
    and flesh removed
¼ cup (60 ml) lemon juice
¼ cup (60 ml) extra virgin olive oil
1 clove garlic, finely chopped
1 cup (20 g) fresh flat-leaf parsley
harissa, to serve (optional)

1 To make the batter, sift the besan, paprika, cumin and baking powder into a bowl, add ¼ teaspoon pepper, mix together and make a well in the centre. Gradually add the soda water, whisking until smooth. Season with salt. Cover, then leave for 30 minutes.
2 Cut the lemon rind into very thin slivers. To make the dressing, whisk the lemon juice, extra virgin olive oil and garlic together in a bowl.
3 Fill a large heavy-based saucepan or wok one third full of oil and heat until a cube of bread dropped into the oil browns in 15 seconds.
4 Dip the calamari into the batter, allowing any excess to drip away.

Cook in batches for 30–60 seconds, or until pale gold and crisp all over. Drain well on crumpled paper towels and keep warm.
5 Add the parsley and lemon slivers to the dressing, tossing to coat the leaves. Divide the leaves among four bowls or plates. Top with the calamari rings and serve with harissa.

NUTRITION PER SERVE
Protein 14 g; Fat 27 g; Carbohydrate 14 g;
Dietary Fibre 5 g; Cholesterol 90 mg;
1470 kJ (350 cal)

Whisk the batter ingredients together until smooth.

Using a sharp knife, cut the lemon rind into very thin slivers.

SUMMER SALAD WITH BASIL DRESSING

Preparation time: 15 minutes
Total cooking time: 5 minutes
Serves 8

2 carrots
6 radishes
150 g (5 oz) snow peas
250 g (8 oz) asparagus
1 cup (30 g/1 oz) fresh basil leaves
½ cup (125 ml/4 fl oz) olive oil
1 tablespoon white wine vinegar
½ teaspoon French mustard
¼ teaspoon sugar

1 Thinly slice the carrots and radishes. Trim the ends from the snow peas and cut into short lengths. Snap the woody ends from the asparagus and put in a pan with a small amount of water.
2 Cook the asparagus over low heat until just tender. Plunge into cold water and then drain and pat dry with paper towels.
3 Put the basil in a food processor and blend until finely chopped. Add the oil, vinegar, mustard and sugar and process until smooth. Store in a screw-top jar until required. Put the vegetables in a large serving bowl and toss together. Add the dressing and toss well.

NUTRITION PER SERVE
Protein 2 g; Fat 15 g; Carbohydrate 4 g;
Dietary Fibre 2 g; Cholesterol 0 mg;
650 kJ (156 cal)

STORAGE: The dressing can be kept in the fridge for up to 2 days.

VARIATION: Make the dressing with fresh coriander instead of basil.

Cut the radishes and carrots into thin slices and cut the snow peas into short lengths.

Plunge the asparagus into cold water to stop the cooking and dry with paper towels.

Blend the basil leaves until finely chopped, then add the other dressing ingredients.

RED CURRY CHICKEN SALAD

**Preparation time: 30 minutes
+ overnight marinating
Total cooking time: 20 minutes
Serves 4**

500 g (1 lb) chicken thigh fillets,
    cut into thin strips
2 teaspoons Thai red curry paste
1 teaspoon chopped red chilli
1 clove garlic, crushed
1 stem lemon grass, white part only,
    finely chopped
cooking oil spray
1 red onion, thinly sliced
2 tomatoes, cut into wedges
½ cup (25 g/¾ oz) chopped fresh mint
¼ cup (15 g/½ oz) chopped coriander
400 g (13 oz) mixed salad leaves
2 tablespoons roasted peanuts

DRESSING
1½ tablespoons soft brown sugar
2 tablespoons fish sauce
2 tablespoons lime juice
2 kaffir lime leaves, shredded
2 teaspoons oil

1 Combine the chicken, curry paste, chilli, garlic and lemon grass. Cover and refrigerate overnight.
2 Lightly spray a non-stick frying pan with oil and cook the chicken in batches until tender and lightly browned; set aside. Add the onion to the pan and cook for 1 minute, or until just soft. Return the chicken and any juices to the pan and add the tomato, mint and coriander, stirring until heated. Set aside until just warm.
3 To make the dressing, put the sugar, fish sauce, lime juice, lime leaves and oil in a jug. Mix until combined. In a large bowl, toss the chicken mixture with the salad leaves and dressing. Sprinkle with the peanuts to serve.

NUTRITION PER SERVE
Protein 25 g; Fat 10 g; Carbohydrate 15 g; Dietary Fibre 2.5 g; Cholesterol 50 mg; 1050 kJ (250 cal)

Remove the fat from the chicken fillets and cut the meat into strips.

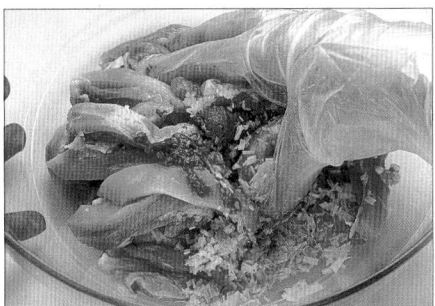

If you find it easier, you can use your hands to mix the chicken and marinade.

Stir the tomatoes and herbs with the chicken, until heated through.

SNOW PEA SALAD

Preparation time: 10 minutes
Total cooking time: Nil
Serves 8

150 g (5 oz) snow peas
250 g (8 oz) fresh asparagus
2 carrots, peeled
425 g (14 oz) can baby corn, drained
230 g (7½ oz) can bamboo shoots,
    drained

DRESSING
3 tablespoons vegetable oil
3 teaspoons sesame oil
1 tablespoon soy sauce

1 Trim the snow peas and cut in half. Snap the woody ends from the asparagus and cut into short lengths. Cut the carrots into matchsticks.
2 Put the snow peas and asparagus in a heatproof bowl and cover with boiling water. Leave for 1 minute, then drain and plunge into iced water. Drain and dry on paper towels.
3 Combine the snow peas, asparagus, carrots, corn and bamboo shoots in a serving bowl. To make the dressing, put the oils and sauce in a small screw-top jar and shake well to combine. Pour over the salad and toss well.

NUTRITION PER SERVE
Protein 3 g; Fat 10 g; Carbohydrate 12 g;
Dietary Fibre 4 g; Cholesterol 0 mg;
603 kJ (144 cal)

NOTE: Sesame oil is a very strongly flavoured oil and should be used sparingly as its flavour tends to dominate. The darker the oil, the stronger the flavour.

Cut all the vegetables into similar-sized strips and pieces so the salad is balanced.

Drain the snow peas and asparagus and then pat dry on paper towels.

Combine all the dressing ingredients in a screw-top jar, then pour over the salad.

WARM PESTO AND PRAWN SALAD

Preparation time: 15 minutes
Total cooking time: 20 minutes
Serves 4

PESTO
2 cloves garlic, crushed
1 teaspoon salt
¼ cup (40 g/1¼ oz) pine nuts, toasted
2 cups (60 g/2 oz) fresh basil
½ cup (60 g/2 oz) grated Parmesan
¼ cup (60 ml/2 fl oz) extra virgin olive oil

500 g (1 lb) pasta
150 g (5 oz) jar capers in brine
3 tablespoons olive oil
2 tablespoons extra virgin olive oil
2 cloves garlic, chopped
2 tomatoes, seeded and diced
150 g (5 oz) thin asparagus, trimmed, halved and blanched
2 tablespoons balsamic vinegar
150 g (5 oz) rocket
20 cooked prawns, peeled, tails intact
shaved Parmesan, to garnish

1 For the pesto, blend the garlic, salt, pine nuts, fresh basil leaves and grated Parmesan in a food processor or blender until thoroughly combined. With the motor running, add the oil in a thin steady stream and process until the pesto is smooth.
2 Cook the pasta in a large pan of rapidly boiling salted water until al dente. Drain well, transfer to a large bowl and toss the pesto through.
3 Pat the drained capers dry with paper towels, then heat the olive oil in a frying pan and fry the capers for 4–5 minutes, stirring occasionally, until crisp. Drain on paper towels.
4 Heat the extra virgin olive oil in a deep frying pan over medium heat

and add the garlic, tomatoes and asparagus. Toss continuously for 1–2 minutes, or until warmed through. Stir in the balsamic vinegar.
5 When the pasta is just warm, not hot (or it will wilt the rocket), toss the tomato mixture, rocket and prawns with the pasta and season with salt and pepper, to taste. Serve sprinkled with capers and shaved Parmesan.

NUTRITION PER SERVE
Protein 42 g; Fat 52 g; Carbohydrate 92 g; Dietary Fibre 10 g; Cholesterol 163 mg; 4195 kJ (1000 cal)

Use two wooden spoons to toss the pesto through the drained pasta.

Fry the drained capers in the hot oil, stirring occasionally, until crisp.

PASTA AND BEAN SALAD WITH CUMIN AND CORIANDER DRESSING

Preparation time: 25 minutes
Total cooking time: 15 minutes
Serves 6

300 g (10 oz) spiral pasta
2 tablespoons sunflower oil
1 leek, sliced
1 red capsicum, seeded and diced
2 cups (125 g/4 oz) finely shredded
    English spinach
150 g (5 oz) button mushrooms,
    halved
300 g (10 oz) can red kidney beans,
    rinsed and drained
300 g (10 oz) can butter beans, rinsed
    and drained
2 tablespoons snipped chives
½ teaspoon coarsely ground black
    pepper
60 g (2 oz) sunflower seeds, toasted

CUMIN AND CORIANDER DRESSING
2 cloves garlic, crushed
½ teaspoon ground cumin
½ teaspoon ground coriander
2 tablespoons cider vinegar
½ cup (125 ml/4 fl oz) olive oil

1 Cook the pasta in a large pan of rapidly boiling salted water until al dente. Drain well.

2 Heat the oil in a large pan, add the leek and capsicum and stir-fry over medium heat for 2–3 minutes. Add the spinach and mushrooms and toss together for about 1 minute, or until the spinach just wilts.

3 To make the dressing, mix the garlic, cumin, coriander and vinegar together. Gradually add the olive oil and whisk to combine.

4 Toss together the pasta, vegetables, beans, chives and black pepper. Toss with the dressing and sprinkle with the sunflower seeds to serve.

NUTRITION PER SERVE
Protein 15 g; Fat 30 g; Carbohydrate 45 g;
Dietary Fibre 10 g; Cholesterol 0 mg;
2215 kJ (525 cal)

Add the spinach and mushrooms to the leek and capsicum and cook until the spinach wilts.

Gradually whisk the oil into the combined garlic, cumin, coriander and vinegar.

Pour the dressing into the salad and toss gently to mix through.

THAI NOODLE SALAD

Preparation time: 25 minutes
Total cooking time: 5 minutes
Serves 4

DRESSING
2 tablespoons grated fresh ginger
2 tablespoons soy sauce
2 tablespoons sesame oil
⅓ cup (80 ml/2¾ fl oz) red wine vinegar
3–4 teaspoons sweet chilli sauce
2 cloves garlic, crushed
⅓ cup (80 ml/2¾ fl oz) kecap manis
    (see NOTE)

250 g (8 oz) fine instant noodles
5 spring onions, sliced
2 tablespoons chopped fresh
    coriander
1 red capsicum, chopped
100 g (3½ oz) snow peas, sliced
500 g (1 lb) cooked king prawns,
    peeled, halved and deveined

1 To make the dressing, put the ingredients in a large bowl and whisk with a fork to combine.
2 Cook the noodles in a large pan of boiling water for 2 minutes and drain well. Add to the dressing and toss to combine. Leave to cool.
3 Add the remaining ingredients to the noodles and toss gently. Serve at room temperature.

NUTRITION PER SERVE
Protein 35 g; Fat 15 g; Carbohydrate 60 g;
Dietary Fibre 3 g; Cholesterol 235 mg;
2275 kJ (540 cal)

NOTE: Kecap manis (sweet soy sauce) is available from Asian food stores.

Peel and finely grate the fresh ginger on the fine side of the grater.

Add the kecap manis to the other ingredients and mix to combine.

Add the noodles to a large pan of boiling water and cook until tender.

Dressings

Mayonnaise is something that most of us expect to buy in a jar in the supermarket and take a chance as to whether it's rich and creamy or, as if often the case, rather gluey and oversweet. Try making your own—it's actually very easy and you'll get a good-quality result every time.

MAYONNAISE

Whisk together 2 egg yolks, 1 teaspoon Dijon mustard and 1 tablespoon lemon juice for 30 seconds, or until light and creamy. Add ¾ cup (185 ml/6 fl oz) olive oil, about a teaspoon at a time, whisking continuously. You can add the oil more quickly as the mayonnaise thickens. Season, to taste, with salt and white pepper.
Alternatively, place the egg yolks, mustard and lemon juice in a food processor and mix for 10 seconds. With the motor running, add the oil in a thin stream. Season, to taste. Makes about 1 cup (250 ml/8 fl oz)

THOUSAND ISLAND DRESSING

Mix together 1½ cups (375 ml/12 fl oz) mayonnaise, 1 tablespoon sweet chilli sauce, 1–2 tablespoons tomato sauce, ¼ red capsicum and ¼ green capsicum, finely chopped, 1 tablespoon chopped chives and ½ teaspoon sweet paprika. Stir well and season. Cover and refrigerate for up to 3 days. Thousand Island dressing is traditionally served on lettuce leaves.
Makes 1⅔ cups (410 ml/13 fl oz)

GREEN GODDESS DRESSING

Mix together 1½ cups (375 ml/12 fl oz) mayonnaise, 4 mashed anchovy fillets, 4 finely chopped spring onions, 1 crushed clove garlic, ¼ cup (7 g/¼ oz) chopped fresh flat-leaf parsley, ¼ cup (15 g/½ oz) finely chopped chives and 1 teaspoon tarragon vinegar. Serve on salad or with barbecued seafood.
Makes about 1⅔ cups (410 ml/13 fl oz)

AIOLI (GARLIC MAYONNAISE)

Mix together 1 cup (250 ml/8 fl oz) mayonnaise with
3 crushed cloves of garlic. Season, to taste, with salt and
pepper. Serve with barbecued seafood, such as prawns.
Makes about 1 cup (250 ml/8 fl oz)

TARTARE SAUCE

Mix together 1½ cups (375 ml/12 fl oz) mayonnaise,
1 tablespoon finely chopped onion, 1 teaspoon lemon
juice, 1 tablespoon chopped gherkins, 1 teaspoon chopped
capers, ¼ teaspoon Dijon mustard and 1 tablespoon finely
chopped fresh parsley. Mix and season with salt and
pepper. Top with a few capers and serve with barbecued
seafood. Makes about 1⅔ cups (410 ml/13 fl oz)

COCKTAIL SAUCE

Mix together 1 cup (250 ml/8 fl oz) mayonnaise,
3 tablespoons tomato sauce, 2 teaspoons Worcestershire
sauce, ½ teaspoon lemon juice and 1 drop of Tabasco
sauce. Season with salt and pepper. Keep, covered, in the
fridge for up to 2 days.
Makes about 1¼ cups (315 ml/10 fl oz)

BLUE CHEESE DRESSING

Mix together ½ cup (125 ml/4 fl oz) mayonnaise, ¼ cup
(60 ml/2 fl oz) thick cream, 1 teaspoon white wine vinegar
and 1 tablespoon finely chopped chives. Crumble 50 g
(1¾ oz) blue cheese into the mixture and gently stir
through. Season with salt and white pepper. Can be kept
refrigerated, covered, for up to 2 days. Serve as a salad
dressing or with barbecued asparagus.
Makes about 1 cup (250 ml/8 fl oz)

CAESAR DRESSING

Cook an egg in boiling water for 1 minute. Break the egg
into a small bowl and add 2 tablespoons white wine or
tarragon vinegar, 2 teaspoons Dijon mustard, 2 chopped
anchovy fillets and 1 crushed clove garlic. Mix together
with a small wire whisk. Add ½ cup (125 ml/4 fl oz) oil in a
thin stream, whisking continuously until the mixture is
smooth and creamy. Keep, covered, in the fridge for up to
2 days. Serve over crisp salad.
Makes about ¾ cup (185 ml/6 fl oz)

Top, from left: Tartare Sauce; Blue Cheese; Thousand Island; Mayonnaise
Bottom, from left: Aioli; Green Goddess; Caesar Dressing; Cocktail Sauce

MEDITERRANEAN PASTA SALAD WITH BLACK OLIVE DRESSING

Preparation time: 30 minutes
Total cooking time: 25 minutes
Serves 4

250 g (8 oz) spiral pasta
1 red capsicum
1 yellow or green capsicum
1 tablespoon sunflower oil
2 tablespoons olive oil
2 cloves garlic, crushed
1 eggplant, cubed
2 zucchini, thickly sliced
2 large ripe tomatoes, peeled, seeded and chopped (see NOTE)
¼ cup (7 g/¼ oz) chopped fresh flat-leaf parsley
1 teaspoon seasoned pepper
150 g (5 oz) feta cheese, crumbled

BLACK OLIVE DRESSING
6 large marinated black olives, pitted
½ cup (125 ml/4 fl oz) olive oil
2 tablespoons balsamic vinegar

1 Cook the pasta in a large pan of rapidly boiling salted water until al dente. Drain well, spread in a single layer on a baking tray to dry, then refrigerate, uncovered, until chilled.
2 Cut the red and yellow capsicum into large pieces, removing the seeds and membrane. Place, skin-side-up, under a hot grill until the skin blackens and blisters. Leave under a tea towel to cool, then peel away the skin. Slice the flesh into thick strips.
3 Heat the sunflower and olive oil in a frying pan. Add the garlic and eggplant and fry quickly, tossing, until lightly browned. Remove from the heat and place in a large bowl. Steam the zucchini for 1–2 minutes, or until just tender. Rinse under cold water, drain and add to the eggplant.
4 To make the dressing, process the olives in a food processor until finely chopped. Gradually add the olive oil, processing until thoroughly combined after each addition. Add the vinegar, season and process to combine.
5 Combine the pasta, capsicum, eggplant, zucchini, tomato, parsley and pepper in a large bowl. Top with the feta and drizzle with the dressing.

NUTRITION PER SERVE
Protein 15 g; Fat 55 g; Carbohydrate 50 g; Dietary Fibre 8 g; Cholesterol 25 mg; 3220 kJ (765 cal)

NOTE: To peel tomatoes, score a cross in the base of each tomato. Leave in a pan of boiling water for 1 minute, then plunge into cold water. Peel the skin away from the cross. To remove the seeds, cut the tomato in half and scoop out the seeds with a teaspoon.

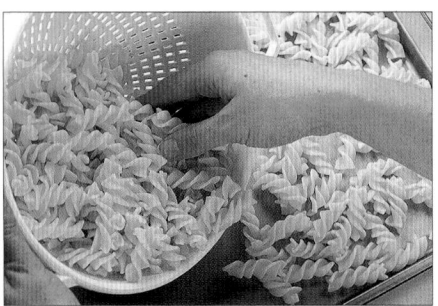
Drain the cooked pasta and spread on a tray to dry and cool.

Remove the seeds and white membrane from the capsicums and cut into large pieces.

Fry the garlic and cubed eggplant quickly until it is lightly browned.

CHICKPEA SALAD

Preparation time: 20 minutes
Total cooking time: Nil
Serves 8

2 large cans chickpeas
    (see NOTE)
3 tomatoes
1 red onion, thinly sliced
1 small red capsicum, cut into thin
    strips
4 spring onions, cut into thin strips
1 cup (60 g/2 oz) chopped fresh
    parsley
2–3 tablespoons chopped fresh mint
    leaves

DRESSING
2 tablespoons tahini (sesame paste)
2 tablespoons fresh lemon juice
3 tablespoons olive oil
2 cloves garlic, crushed
½ teaspoon ground cumin

1 Drain the chickpeas and rinse well. Cut the tomatoes in half and remove the seeds with a spoon. Dice the flesh. Mix the onion, tomato, capsicum and spring onion in a bowl. Add the chickpeas, parsley and mint.
2 To make the dressing, put all the ingredients in a screw-top jar with 2 tablespoons water, season well and shake vigorously to make a creamy liquid. Pour over the salad and toss.

NUTRITION PER SERVE
Protein 4 g; Fat 2 g; Carbohydrate 8 g; Dietary Fibre 3 g; Cholesterol 0 mg; 877 kJ (210 cal)

STORAGE: Can be kept, covered, in the fridge for up to 3 hours.

NOTE: You can also use dried chickpeas, but they will need to be soaked and cooked first. Use 1¾ cups (380 g/12 oz) dried chickpeas and put in a pan with 3.5 litres water and 3 tablespoons olive oil. Partially cover and boil for 2½ hours, or until tender. Rinse, drain well and allow to cool a little before making the salad.

Both canned and dried chickpeas should be rinsed and drained well.

Cut the tomatoes in half and scoop out the seeds with a teaspoon.

The easiest way to make a salad dressing is by shaking the ingredients in a screw-top jar.

FARFALLE SALAD WITH SUN-DRIED TOMATOES AND SPINACH

Preparation time: 20 minutes
Total cooking time: 15 minutes
Serves 4–6

500 g (1 lb) farfalle or spiral pasta
3 spring onions
60 g (2 oz) sun-dried tomatoes, cut into strips
500 g (1 lb) English spinach, trimmed and shredded
⅓ cup (50 g/1¾ oz) pine nuts, toasted
1 tablespoon chopped fresh oregano

DRESSING
3 tablespoons olive oil
1 teaspoon fresh chopped chilli
1 clove garlic, crushed

1 Cook the pasta in a large pan of rapidly boiling salted water until al dente. Drain well and rinse under cold water. Transfer to a large salad bowl. Trim the spring onions and chop finely. Add to the pasta with the tomato, spinach, pine nuts and fresh oregano.
2 To make the dressing, put the oil, chilli and garlic in a small screw-top jar and add salt and pepper to taste. Shake well.
3 Pour the dressing over the salad, toss well and serve immediately.

NUTRITION PER SERVE (6)
Protein 12 g; Fat 8 g; Carbohydrate 60 g;
Dietary Fibre 6 g; Cholesterol 0 mg;
1490 kJ (357 cal)

Put the dressing ingredients in a screw-top jar so you can mix them together by shaking.

Pour the dressing over the salad and then toss together before serving.

TABBOULEH WITH SOY GRITS

Preparation time: 20 minutes +
** soaking**
Total cooking time: Nil
Serves 6–8

150 g fresh flat-leaf parsley
1 cup (180 g) soy grits
2 tablespoons chopped fresh mint
1 small red onion, cut into thin wedges
3 ripe tomatoes, chopped
400 g can chickpeas, rinsed and
    drained

3 tablespoons lemon juice
2 tablespoons extra virgin olive oil
Lebanese or pitta bread, to serve

1 Remove all the parsley leaves from the stalks, roughly chop and place in a large serving bowl.
2 Place the soy grits in a heatproof bowl and pour in ⅔ cup (170 ml) boiling water. Leave to soak for 3 minutes, or until all the water has been absorbed.
3 Add the soy grits to the parsley, along with the mint, onion, tomato and chickpeas. Drizzle with the lemon juice and olive oil. Season well with salt and freshly ground black

pepper and toss together.
4 Serve with Lebanese or pitta bread and Soy bean hummus as a vegetarian meal, or as an accompaniment to barbecued meat, chicken or fish.

NUTRITION PER SERVE (8)
Protein 12 g; Fat 11 g; Carbohydrate 13 g;
Dietary Fibre 6.5 g; Cholesterol 0 mg;
820 kJ (196 cal)

Cut the red onion into thin wedges with a sharp knife.

Allow the grits and water to soak until the liquid has been absorbed.

Toss together the grits, parsley, mint, onion, tomato, chickpeas and dressing.

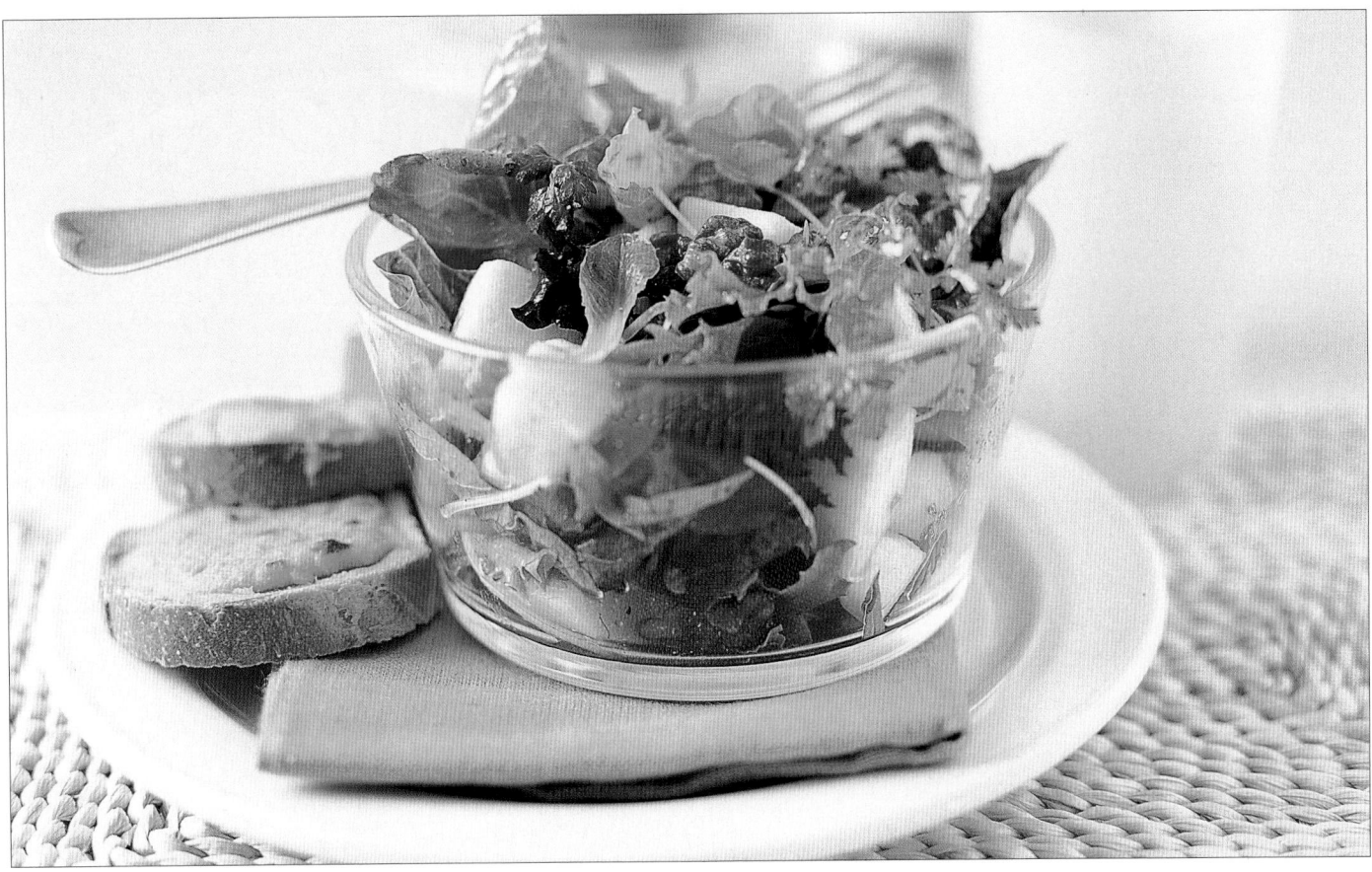

PEAR AND WALNUT SALAD WITH LIME VINAIGRETTE

Preparation time: 25 minutes
Total cooking time: 20 minutes
Serves 4

1 small baguette, cut into 16 thin
    slices
soy bean oil, for brushing
1 clove garlic, cut in half
1 cup (100 g) walnuts
200 g soy cheese
400 g mesclun leaves
2 pears, cut into 2 cm cubes, mixed
    with 2 tablespoons lime juice

LIME VINAIGRETTE
3 tablespoons soy bean oil
¼ cup (60 ml) lime juice
2 tablespoons raspberry vinegar

1 Preheat the oven to moderate 180°C (350°F/Gas 4). Brush the baguette slices with a little oil, rub with the cut side of the garlic, then place on a baking tray. Bake for 10 minutes, or until crisp and golden. Place the walnuts on a baking tray and roast for 5–8 minutes, or until slightly browned—shake the tray to ensure even colouring. Allow to cool for 5 minutes.

2 To make the lime vinaigrette, whisk together the oil, lime juice, raspberry vinegar, 1 teaspoon salt and ½ teaspoon freshly ground black pepper in a small bowl. Set aside until ready to use.

3 Spread some of the soy cheese on each crouton, then cook under a hot grill for 2–3 minutes, or until hot.

4 Place the mesclun, pears and walnuts in a bowl, add the vinaigrette and toss through. Divide the salad among four serving bowls and serve with the soy cheese croutons.

NUTRITION PER SERVE
Protein 24 g; Fat 60 g; Carbohydrate 40 g; Dietary Fibre 7 g; Cholesterol 0 mg; 3310 kJ (790 cal)

Rub each slice of baguette with a cut piece of garlic.

Whisk together the soy bean oil, lime juice, raspberry vinegar, salt and pepper.

Place the soy cheese-topped croutons on a baking tray and grill until hot.

VIETNAMESE CHICKEN AND CABBAGE SALAD

Preparation time: 40 minutes
Total cooking time: 5 minutes
Serves 4

4 cooked chicken thigh fillets
1 cup (125 g/4 oz) thinly sliced
    celery
2 carrots, cut into thin strips
1 cup (75 g/2½ oz) finely shredded
    cabbage
1 small onion, sliced
¼ cup (7 g/¼ oz) fresh coriander leaves
¼ cup (15 g/½ oz) finely shredded fresh
    mint

DRESSING
¼ cup (60 g/2 oz) caster sugar
1 tablespoon fish sauce
1 teaspoon crushed garlic
2 tablespoons white vinegar
1 red chilli, seeded and finely chopped

TOPPING
2 tablespoons peanut oil
1½ teaspoons chopped garlic
⅓ cup (50 g/1¾ oz) roasted peanuts,
    finely chopped
1 tablespoon caster sugar

1 Cut the chicken fillets into long, thin strips. Combine the chicken, celery, carrot, cabbage, onion, coriander and mint in a large bowl.

2 To make the dressing, put the sugar, fish sauce, garlic, vinegar, chilli and 2 tablespoons water in a small bowl. Whisk until sugar has dissolved and the ingredients are combined. Pour dressing over the chicken mixture and toss . Arrange on a serving plate.
3 To make the topping, heat the oil in a wok over moderate heat. Add the garlic and cook, stirring, until pale golden. Stir in the peanuts and sugar. Cool slightly. Sprinkle the topping over the salad just before serving.

NUTRITION PER SERVE
Protein 50 g; Fat 15 g; Carbohydrate 25 g;
Dietary Fibre 3 g; Cholesterol 110 mg;
1820 kJ (435 cal)

Combine the chicken, celery, carrot, cabbage, onion, coriander and mint.

Pour the dressing over the salad and gently toss to combine.

Gently stir the peanuts and sugar into the cooked garlic.

CHICKEN, PRAWN AND GRAPEFRUIT SALAD

Preparation time: 20 minutes
Total cooking time: Nil
Serves 4–6

1 small pink or yellow grapefruit
½ small green pawpaw or green
    mango (about 100 g/3½ oz)
6 cooked prawns, peeled and
    deveined
2 Roma tomatoes, chopped
1 orange, peeled and segmented
125 g (4 oz) cooked chicken,
    shredded or cut into bite-sized
    pieces (see NOTE)
4 spring onions, sliced
2 cloves garlic, sliced
2 tablespoons coarsely chopped fresh
    coriander
1 tablespoon shredded coconut
lettuce leaves, to serve
1 tablespoon roasted, unsalted
    peanuts, finely chopped
2 teaspoons dried shrimp, finely
    chopped

DRESSING
2 teaspoons soft brown sugar
1½ tablespoons fish sauce
¼ cup (60 ml/2 fl oz) lime juice
2 teaspoons chilli sauce

1 Peel the grapefruit, discarding the pith, then cut it into thin segments. Peel the pawpaw and cut it into long, thin strips.
2 Combine the pawpaw, grapefruit, prawns, tomato, orange segments, chicken, spring onion, garlic, coriander and coconut in a bowl.
3 To make the dressing, combine the sugar, fish sauce, lime juice and chilli sauce in a jug and whisk until the sugar has dissolved. Pour the dressing over the salad and toss gently. Serve on a bed of lettuce leaves and sprinkle with the peanuts and dried shrimp.

NUTRITION PER SERVE (6)
Protein 9.5 g; Fat 1.5 g; Carbohydrate 8.5 g;
Dietary Fibre 2.5 g; Cholesterol 34 mg;
376 kJ (98 cal)

NOTE: Use leftover chicken, or pan-fry a chicken breast until tender.

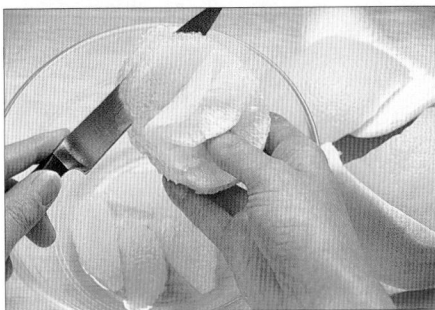

Peel the grapefruit, removing all the white pith. Cut into thin segments.

Cut the peeled pawpaw into long, thin strips, using a sharp knife.

Combine the fruit, chicken, tomato, spring onion, garlic, coriander, coconut and prawns in a bowl.

Whisk the dressing ingredients in a small jug until the sugar has dissolved.

CURLY ENDIVE SALAD WITH CRISP PROSCIUTTO AND GARLIC CROUTONS

Preparation time: 20 minutes
Total cooking time: 5 minutes
Serves 6

1 large bunch curly endive
½ red oak leaf lettuce
2 red onions
4 slices white or brown bread
2 large cloves garlic, crushed
60 g (2 oz) butter, softened
30 g (1 oz) feta cheese, mashed
4–6 thin slices prosciutto
1 large avocado

DRESSING
2 tablespoons olive oil
3 tablespoons sugar
3 tablespoons spicy tomato sauce
1 tablespoon soy sauce
⅓ cup (80 ml/2¾ fl oz) red wine vinegar

1 Tear the endive and lettuce into pieces. Peel and slice the onions and separate into rings. Toss the endive, lettuce and onion in a salad bowl.
2 Toast the bread on one side only. Mash the garlic, butter and feta cheese into a paste and spread over the untoasted side of the bread. Remove the crusts and toast the buttered side of the bread until crisp and golden. Cut into small cubes.
3 Crisp the prosciutto under a very hot grill for a few seconds. Remove and cut into pieces. Cut the avocado into thin wedges.
4 To make the dressing, whisk the oil, sugar, tomato sauce, soy sauce and vinegar together. Add the prosciutto and avocado to the salad and pour over half the dressing. Arrange the croutons on top and serve the remaining dressing in a jug.

NUTRITION PER SERVE
Protein 5 g; Fat 24 g; Carbohydrate 22 g;
Dietary Fibre 2 g; Cholesterol 27 mg;
1356 kJ (324 cal)

STORAGE: The dressing will keep for a day in a screw-top jar.

Peel the red onion, slice it thinly and then separate into rings.

Spread the feta, butter and garlic paste over the untoasted side of the bread.

Crisp the prosciutto under a hot grill and then cut it into pieces.

Whisk together the oil, sugar, tomato sauce, soy sauce and vinegar.

LIME AND PRAWN SALAD

Preparation time: 35 minutes
Total cooking time: 2 minutes
Serves 4

200 g (6½ oz) baby green beans
2 Lebanese cucumbers, sliced
4 spring onions, finely chopped
1 tablespoon finely shredded kaffir
   lime leaves
¼ cup (15 g/½ oz) flaked coconut
750 g (1½ lb) cooked prawns, peeled,
   tails intact
2 teaspoons shredded lime rind

DRESSING
1 tablespoon peanut oil
1 tablespoon nam pla (Thai fish sauce)
1 tablespoon grated palm sugar
1 tablespoon chopped fresh coriander
2 teaspoons soy sauce
1–2 teaspoons sweet chilli sauce
¼ cup (60 ml/2 fl oz) lime juice

1 Cook the beans in a small pan of boiling water for 2 minutes. Drain and cover with cold water, then drain again and pat dry with paper towels.
2 To make the dressing, whisk the ingredients in a bowl.
3 Combine the beans, cucumber, spring onion, lime leaves, flaked coconut and prawns in a large bowl. Add the dressing and toss gently to combine. Place the salad in a large serving bowl and garnish with the shredded lime rind.

NUTRITION PER SERVE
Protein 45 g; Fat 8 g; Carbohydrate 7 g; Dietary Fibre 3 g; Cholesterol 350 mg; 1200 kJ (285 cal)

NOTE: Young lemon leaves can be used in place of the kaffir lime leaves if they are not available.
Soft brown or dark brown sugar may be substituted for the palm sugar.

Cut the cucumbers in half lengthways, then cut into slices.

Lower the beans into a small pan of boiling water and cook for 2 minutes.

Whisk the dressing ingredients in a small bowl until combined.

Desserts

JAM ROLY POLY

Preparation time: 20 minutes
Total cooking time: 35 minutes
Serves 4

2 cups (250 g/8 oz) self-raising flour
125 g (4 oz) butter, roughly chopped
2 tablespoons caster sugar
50 ml (1¾ fl oz) milk
⅔ cup (210 g/7 oz) raspberry jam
1 tablespoon milk, extra

1 Preheat the oven to moderate 180°C (350°F/Gas 4) and line a baking tray with baking paper. Sift the flour into a mixing bowl and, using your fingertips, rub the butter into the flour until the mixture resembles fine breadcrumbs. Stir through the sugar.

2 Add the milk and 50 ml (1¾ fl oz) water, and stir with a flat-bladed knife to form a dough. Turn out onto a lightly floured surface and gather together to form a smooth dough.
3 On a sheet of baking paper, roll out into a rectangle 33 x 23 cm (13 x 9 inches) and 5 mm (¼ inch) thick. Spread with the raspberry jam, leaving a 5 mm (¼ inch) border.
4 Roll up lengthways and place on the tray seam-side down. Brush with the extra milk and bake for 35 minutes, or until golden and cooked. Leave for a few minutes, then slice thickly. Serve warm with custard.

NUTRITION PER SERVE
Protein 7 g; Fat 25 g; Carbohydrate 73 g; Dietary Fibre 3 g; Cholesterol 80 mg; 2330 kJ (555 Cal)

Rub the butter into the flour with your fingertips until it resembles fine breadcrumbs.

Add the milk and water and mix with a flat-bladed knife to form a dough.

Roll out the dough into a rectangle on a sheet of non-stick baking paper.

Spread the jam over the dough, leaving a border around the edge.

LEMON MERINGUE PIE

Preparation time: 1 hour + chilling
Total cooking time: 45 minutes
Serves 6

1½ cups (185 g/6 oz) plain flour
2 tablespoons icing sugar
125 g (4 oz) cold butter, chopped
2–3 tablespoons iced water

FILLING
¼ cup (30 g/1 oz) cornflour
¼ cup (30 g/1 oz) plain flour
1 cup (250 g/8 oz) caster sugar
¾ cup (185 ml/6 fl oz) lemon juice
3 teaspoons grated lemon rind
40 g (1¼ oz) butter
6 eggs, separated
1½ cups (375 g/12 oz) caster sugar, extra
½ teaspoon cornflour, extra

1 Sift the flour into a bowl and add the icing sugar and butter. Using your fingertips, rub in the butter until the mixture resembles breadcrumbs. Add 2 tablespoons water and mix into the flour with a flat-bladed knife using a cutting action until the mixture comes together in small beads, then gather the dough together. Add the remaining water if the dough is too dry.
2 Transfer dough to a sheet of baking paper and roll out until large enough to line a greased 23 cm (9 inch) round pie plate. Ease the pastry into the prepared dish. Trim off any excess pastry and pinch or fork the edge to decorate. Refrigerate for 15 minutes.
3 Preheat the oven to moderate 180°C (350°F/Gas 4). Place a sheet of baking paper in the pie shell and spread a layer of baking beads or rice over the top. Bake for 10–15 minutes, then remove the paper and beads, and bake for a further 10 minutes, or until the pastry is cooked through. Remove from the oven and cool completely.
4 To make the filling, place the flours and sugar in a pan. Whisk in the lemon juice, rind and 1½ cups (375 ml/ 12 fl oz) water. Whisk constantly over medium heat until the mixture boils and thickens, then reduce the heat and cook for 1 minute. Remove from the heat then whisk in the butter and egg yolks, one at a time. Cover the surface with plastic wrap and cool.
5 Preheat the oven to hot 220°C (425°F/Gas 7). Spread the filling into the pastry shell. Place the egg whites and extra sugar in a mixing bowl. Beat with electric beaters on high for 10 minutes, or until the sugar is almost completely dissolved and the meringue is thick and glossy. Beat in the extra cornflour. Spread the meringue over the top of the pie, piling it high towards the centre. Bake for 5–10 minutes, or until lightly browned. Cool before serving.

NUTRITION PER SERVE
Protein 4 g; Fat 18 g; Carbohydrate 80 g;
Dietary Fibre 1.5 g; Cholesterol 53 mg;
2020 kJ (483 Cal)

Remove the paper, beans or rice and bake until the pastry is cooked through.

Whisk the lemon mixture over medium heat until it boils and thickens.

Beat the egg whites and sugar until the meringue is thick and glossy.

MANGO AND PASSIONFRUIT SORBET

Preparation time: 20 minutes + 8 hours freezing
Total cooking time: 5 minutes
Serves 6

1 cup (250 g/8 oz) caster sugar
⅓ cup (90 g/3 oz) passionfruit pulp
½ large mango (200 g/6½ oz), chopped
1 large (250 g/8 oz) peach, chopped
2 tablespoons lemon juice
1 egg white

1 Stir the sugar in a pan with 1 cup (250 ml/8 fl oz) water over low heat until dissolved. Increase the heat, bring to the boil and boil for 1 minute. Transfer to a glass bowl, cool, then refrigerate. Strain the passionfruit pulp, reserving 1 tablespoon of the seeds.
2 Blend the fruit, passionfruit juice and lemon juice in a blender until smooth. With the motor running, add the cold sugar syrup and 150 ml (5 fl oz) water. Stir in the passionfruit seeds. Freeze in a shallow container, stirring occasionally, for about 5 hours, or until almost set.
3 Break up the icy mixture roughly with a fork or spoon, transfer to a bowl and beat with electric beaters until smooth and fluffy. Beat the egg white in a small bowl until firm peaks form, then fold into the mixture until just combined. Spread into a loaf tin and return to the freezer until firm. Transfer to the refrigerator, to soften, 15 minutes before serving.

NUTRITION PER SERVE
Protein 2 g; Fat 0 g; Carbohydrate 50 g;
Dietary Fibre 3 g; Cholesterol 0 mg;
850 kJ (200 cal)

VARIATION: To make a berry sorbet, use 200 g (6½ oz) blackberries or blueberries, 200 g (6½ oz) hulled strawberries and 50 g (1¾ oz) peach flesh. Prepare as above.

Leave the motor running and pour in the cold sugar syrup and water.

Gently fold the egg white into the smooth fruit purée with a metal spoon.

FLOURLESS CHOCOLATE CAKE

Preparation time: 1 hour + overnight refrigeration
Total cooking time: 1 hour 15 minutes
Serves 10

500 g (1 lb) good-quality dark
   chocolate, chopped
6 eggs
2 tablespoons Frangelico or brandy
1½ cups (165 g/5½ oz) ground
   hazelnuts
1 cup (250 ml/8 fl oz) cream, whipped
icing sugar, to dust
thick cream, to serve (optional)

1 Preheat the oven to slow 150°C (300°F/Gas 2). Grease a deep 20 cm (8 inch) round cake tin and line the base with baking paper.
2 Half-fill a saucepan with water and bring to the boil. Remove from the heat and sit the chocolate in a heatproof bowl over the pan, making sure it is not touching the water. Stir occasionally until melted.
3 Put the eggs in a large heatproof bowl and add the Frangelico. Place the bowl over a pan of just simmering water on low heat, making sure the bowl does not touch the water. Beat the mixture with electric beaters on high speed for 7 minutes, or until light and foamy. Remove from the heat.
4 Using a metal spoon, quickly and lightly fold the chocolate and nuts into the egg mixture until just combined. Fold in the cream and pour into the cake tin. Place the tin in a shallow roasting tin. Pour enough hot water into the roasting tin to come halfway up the side of the cake tin. Bake for 1 hour, or until just set. Remove from the roasting tin and cool to room temperature. Cover with plastic wrap and refrigerate overnight.
5 Invert the cake onto a plate and remove the baking paper. Cut into slices, dust lightly with icing sugar and serve with thick cream.

NUTRITION PER SERVE
Protein 9 g; Fat 38 g; Carbohydrate 34 g;
Dietary Fibre 2.5 g; Cholesterol 142 mg;
2135 kJ (510 Cal)

Grease the cake tin with butter or brush with oil, and line the base with baking paper.

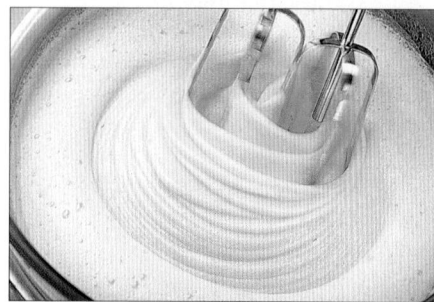

Beat the mixture over simmering water until light and foamy.

Gently fold the whipped cream into the chocolate nut mixture.

Place the cake tin in the roasting tin and bake until just set.

PECAN PIE

Preparation time: 30 minutes + chilling
Total cooking time: 1 hour 15 minutes
Serves 6

1½ cups (185 g/6 oz) plain flour
100 g (3½ oz) cold butter, chopped
2 tablespoons iced water

FILLING
2 cups (200 g/6½ oz) whole pecans
3 eggs
60 g (2 oz) butter, melted
⅔ cup (155 g/5 oz) soft brown sugar
⅔ cup (170 ml/5½ fl oz) corn syrup
1 teaspoon vanilla essence

1 Sift the flour into a bowl and rub in the butter with your fingertips until the mixture resembles fine breadcrumbs. Add the water and mix it in with a flat-bladed knife, using a cutting action, until the mixture comes together in beads. Gather the dough together, cover with plastic wrap and refrigerate for 20 minutes.
2 Transfer the dough to a sheet of baking paper and roll it out to a 3 mm (⅛ inch) thickness. It should be large enough to line a 23 cm (9 inch) pie dish, with some pastry left over to decorate the edge. Invert the pastry into the dish and remove the baking paper. Line the dish with the pastry, and remove the excess. Gather the dough scraps together and roll them out to a 3 mm (⅛ inch) thickness. Using small cutters, cut shapes from the pastry (if you are making leaves, score veins into the leaves with a small sharp knife). Brush the pastry rim with water, and attach the pastry shapes. Chill for 20 minutes. Preheat the oven to moderate 180°C (350°F/Gas 4).

3 Cover the decorative edge of the pastry with wide strips of foil to prevent burning. Line the pastry shell with a sheet of crumpled greaseproof paper and fill with baking beads or rice. Bake for 15 minutes, then remove the beads and paper and bake for 15 minutes more, until the base is lightly golden and dry. Remove the foil and set aside to cool before filling.
4 Place the pecans on the pastry base. Whisk together the eggs, butter, sugar, syrup, vanilla and a good pinch

of salt. Pour over the pecans. Place the pie dish on a baking tray, and bake for 45 minutes. Cool completely.

NUTRITION PER SERVE
Protein 10 g; Fat 50 g; Carbohydrate 50 g; Dietary Fibre 4 g; Cholesterol 160 mg; 2780 kJ (665 Cal)

NOTE: Use any decorative shape you like for the edge. Simple leaf shapes can be cut free-hand from the pastry, if you do not have small cutters.

Invert the pastry into the pie dish, then remove the baking paper.

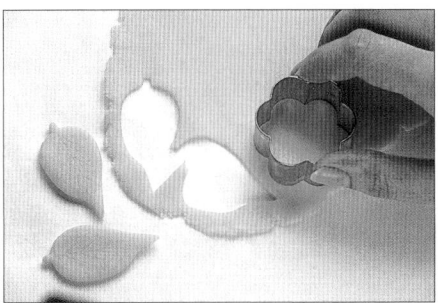
Use small cutters to make pastry shapes to decorate the pie edge.

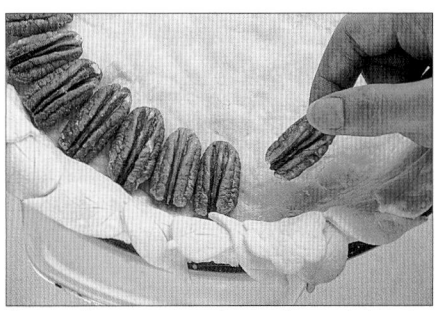
Arrange the pecans evenly over the cooled pastry base.

BERRIES IN CHAMPAGNE JELLY

**Preparation time: 10 minutes +
  refrigeration**
Total cooking time: 5 minutes
Serves 8

1 litre champagne or sparkling wine
1½ tablespoons gelatine
1 cup (250 g/8 oz) sugar
4 strips lemon rind
4 strips orange rind
1⅔ cups (250 g/8 oz) small
   strawberries, hulled
1⅔ cups (250 g/8 oz) blueberries

1 Pour 2 cups (500 ml/16 fl oz) champagne or sparkling white wine into a bowl and let the bubbles subside. Sprinkle the gelatine over the top in an even layer. Leave until the gelatine is spongy—do not stir. Place the remaining champagne in a large pan with the sugar, lemon and orange rind and heat gently, stirring, until all the sugar has dissolved.

2 Remove the pan from the heat, add the gelatine mixture and stir until thoroughly dissolved. Leave the jelly to cool completely, then remove the lemon and orange rind.

3 Divide the strawberries and blueberries among eight ½ cup (125 ml/4 fl oz) glasses or bowls and pour the jelly over them. Chill until the jelly has fully set. Remove from the fridge 15 minutes before serving.

NUTRITION PER SERVE
Protein 3 g; Fat 0 g; Carbohydrate 37 g;
Dietary Fibre 1.5 g; Cholesterol 0 mg;
965 kJ (230 cal)

Sprinkle the gelatine over the champagne in an even layer and leave until spongy.

Pour the jelly into the wine glasses or bowls, covering the berries.

BREAD AND BUTTER PUDDING

Preparation time: 15 minutes +
45 minutes standing
Total cooking time: 40 minutes
Serves 4

30 g (1 oz) butter
8 thick slices day-old bread
2 tablespoons sultanas
3 tablespoons caster sugar
1 teaspoon mixed spice

3 eggs, beaten
2 teaspoons vanilla essence
700 ml (23 fl oz) milk
½ cup (125 ml/4 fl oz) cream
1 tablespoon demerara sugar

1 Lightly grease a 22 x 18 x 8 cm (9 x 7 x 3 inch) ceramic ovenproof dish. Butter the bread and cut each slice in half on the diagonal. Layer the bread into the prepared dish, and sprinkle the combined sultanas, caster sugar and mixed spice over the top.

2 Whisk the eggs, vanilla, milk and cream and pour over the bread. Leave to stand for 45 minutes, then top with the demerara sugar. Preheat the oven to moderate 180°C (350°F/Gas 4).

3 Bake for about 35–40 minutes, or until the custard around the bread has set—check the very centre of the dish. Serve hot.

NUTRITION PER SERVE
Protein 15 g; Fat 30 g; Carbohydrate 50 g;
Dietary Fibre 1.5 g; Cholesterol 220 mg;
2300 kJ (550 Cal)

Cut the bread slices in half diagonally and layer them in the prepared dish.

Slowly pour the combined eggs, vanilla, milk and cream over the bread.

Leave to soak, then scatter the demerara sugar over the top.

VANILLA AND CARAMEL SWIRL ICE CREAM PIE

Preparation time: 1 hour + 6 hours
  freezing + 20 minutes refrigeration +
  cooling
Total cooking time: 20 minutes
Serves 6–8

250 g (8 oz) plain chocolate biscuits
150 g (5 oz) unsalted butter, melted
1 vanilla bean, split
1 cup (250 ml/8 fl oz) milk
2 cups (500 ml/16 fl oz) cream
⅔ cup (160 g/5½ oz) caster sugar
6 egg yolks

CARAMEL
½ cup (125 g/4 oz) caster sugar
¼ cup (60 ml/2 fl oz) cream
30 g (1 oz) unsalted butter

1 Lightly grease a 27 cm (11 inch) (top) 15.5 cm (6 inch) (base) 4.5 cm (1¾ inch) (deep) pie dish. Finely crush the biscuits in a food processor. Stir in the butter and mix until well combined. Spoon into the dish, pressing evenly and firmly over the base and side. Refrigerate.
2 Scrape the seeds from the vanilla bean into a saucepan. Add the pod, milk, cream and sugar and stir over medium heat until the sugar dissolves.
3 Whisk the egg yolks in a small bowl and slowly whisk in about ½ cup (125 ml/4 fl oz) of the warm cream mixture. Return this mixture to the saucepan and cook over low heat, stirring constantly, for 10 minutes, or until the custard thickens and coats the back of a spoon. Strain into a bowl and refrigerate for 20 minutes.
4 Pour the mixture into a shallow metal tray and freeze for 1½ hours until frozen around the edges. Transfer to a large bowl or food processor, beat until smooth, then pour back into the tray and return to the freezer. Repeat this three times. For the final freezing, pour the mixture into the pie dish and cover with baking paper.
5 To make the caramel, place the sugar and 1 tablespoon water in a small saucepan and stir over low heat until the sugar has dissolved, brushing down the side of the pan with a clean pastry brush dipped in water if any crystals appear. Increase the heat, bring to the boil and cook, without stirring, until pale caramel. Remove from the heat and gradually add the cream, butter and 1 tablespoon of water. Return to the heat and bring to the boil, stirring well. Remove and cool for 20 minutes. When slightly warm, spoon the caramel over the pie. Freeze until hard. Serve with any remaining caramel.

NUTRITION PER SERVE (8)
Protein 6.5 g; Fat 59 g; Carbohydrate 59.5 g; Dietary Fibre 0.5 g; Cholesterol 295 mg; 3255 kJ (780 Cal)

Stir the custard mixture until it thickens and coats the back of a spoon.

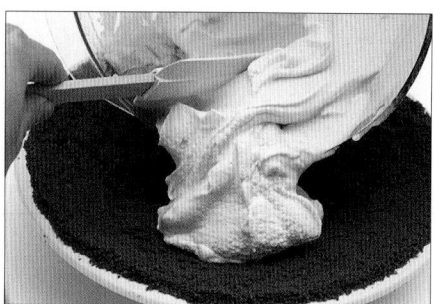
Spread the ice cream over the biscuit mixture in the pie dish.

APPLE CRUMBLE

Preparation time: 10 minutes
Total cooking time: 40 minutes
Serves 6

1 kg (2 lb) green apples, peeled,
   cored and thinly sliced
2 tablespoons caster sugar
¾ cup (90 g/3 oz) plain flour
1 teaspoon ground cinnamon
100 g (3½ oz) cold butter, chopped
½ cup (115 g/4 oz) firmly packed soft
   brown sugar
½ cup (50 g/1¾ oz) rolled oats

1 Preheat the oven to moderately hot 190°C (375°F/Gas 5). Brush a 1.25 litre shallow heatproof dish with melted butter. Put the apple in a large bowl and add the caster sugar and 3 tablespoons water. Mix to combine.
2 Sift the flour and cinnamon into a bowl. With your fingertips, rub in the butter until the mixture resembles coarse breadcrumbs. Add the brown sugar and rolled oats, and mix together well.
3 Spoon the apple into the prepared dish and sprinkle on the topping. Bake for 40 minutes, or until the apple is tender and the crumble topping is golden. Serve hot with custard or cream and a sprinkling of cinnamon.

NUTRITION PER SERVE
Protein 3 g; Fat 15 g; Carbohydrate 59 g;
Dietary Fibre 4.5 g; Cholesterol 45 mg;
1570 kJ (375 Cal)

Carefully peel and core the apples, then cut into thin slices.

Rub in the butter, then add the brown sugar and rolled oats.

Arrange the apple over the base of the dish and sprinkle on the topping.

WATERMELON AND VODKA GRANITA

**Preparation time: 10 minutes +
   5 hours freezing**
Total cooking time: Nil
Serves 6

1 kg (2 lb) piece of watermelon, rind
   removed (to leave 600 g/1¼ lb)
2 teaspoons lime juice
¼ cup (60 g/2 oz) caster sugar
¼ cup (60 ml/2 fl oz) citrus-flavoured
   vodka

1 Coarsely chop the watermelon, removing the seeds. Place the flesh in a food processor and add the lime juice and sugar. Process until smooth, then strain through a fine sieve. Stir in the vodka, then taste—if the watermelon is not very sweet, you may have to add a little more sugar.
2 Pour into a shallow 1.5 litre metal tin and freeze for about 1 hour, or until beginning to freeze around the edges. Scrape the frozen parts back into the mixture with a fork. Repeat every 30 minutes for about 4 hours, or until even ice crystals have formed.
3 Serve immediately or beat with a fork just before serving. To serve, scrape into dishes with a fork.

NUTRITION PER SERVE
Protein 0.5 g; Fat 0 g; Carbohydrate 18 g;
Dietary Fibre 1 g; Cholesterol 0 mg;
410 kJ (98 cal)

SERVING SUGGESTION: A scoop of the granita in a shot glass with vodka is great for summer cocktail parties.

VARIATION: A tablespoon of finely chopped mint may be stirred through the mixture after straining the liquid.

Coarsely chop the watermelon flesh, removing the seeds.

Scrape the frozen parts around the edge back into the mixture.

Scrape the frozen parts back into the mixture until even ice crystals form.

BANANA FRITTERS

Preparation time: 20 minutes +
** 30 minutes standing**
Total cooking time: 10 minutes
Serves 4

1 cup (125 g/4 oz) self-raising flour
1 tablespoon caster sugar
1 teaspoon ground cinnamon
oil, for deep-frying
4 bananas

1 Sift the flour and a pinch of salt into a bowl. Make a well in the centre, and gradually add 1 cup (250 ml/ 8 fl oz) water while gently whisking, drawing the flour in from the sides. Whisk until just combined. The batter will be slightly lumpy—overbeating the batter will make it tough. Stand for 30 minutes. Combine the sugar and cinnamon in a bowl, and set aside.
2 Fill a large deep pan one-third full of oil. Heat to 180°C (350°F), or until a cube of bread dropped into the oil browns in 15 seconds.
3 Cut the bananas in half crossways, slightly on the diagonal. Dip them into the batter. Quickly drain off any excess batter and deep-fry in the hot oil for 2 minutes, or until crisp and golden. The best way to do this is to use two pairs of tongs—one to dip the bananas in the batter and lift into the oil, and one to remove from the oil. Drain on crumpled paper towels. Repeat with the remaining bananas. Sprinkle with the cinnamon sugar and serve with ice cream or cream.

NUTRITION PER SERVE
Protein 3.5 g; Fat 15 g; Carbohydrate 35 g; Dietary Fibre 2 g; Cholesterol 0 mg; 1153 kJ (275 Cal)

Whisk the flour and water until the batter is just combined.

Heat the oil until a cube of bread dropped into the oil browns in 15 seconds.

Deep-fry the bananas until the batter is crisp and golden.

STICKY DATE PUDDING

**Preparation time: 25 minutes +
15 minutes standing
Total cooking time: 50 minutes
Serves 8**

1 cup (185 g/6 oz) pitted dates
1 teaspoon bicarbonate of soda
90 g (3 oz) butter, softened
½ cup (115 g/4 oz) firmly packed soft
    brown sugar
2 eggs, lightly beaten
1 teaspoon vanilla essence
1½ cups (185 g/6 oz) self-raising flour

SAUCE
1 cup (230 g/7½ oz) firmly packed
    soft brown sugar

1 cup (250 ml/8 fl oz) cream
90 g (3 oz) butter
½ teaspoon vanilla essence

1 Preheat the oven to moderate 180°C
(350°F/Gas 4). Brush a deep 18 cm
(7 inch) square cake tin with melted
butter and line the base with baking
paper. Put the chopped dates and
soda in a heatproof bowl and add
1 cup (250 ml/8 fl oz) boiling water.
Stir and leave for 15 minutes.
2 Using electric beaters, beat the
butter and brown sugar until light
and creamy. Beat in the eggs
gradually. Add the vanilla essence.
Fold in half of the sifted flour then
half of the date mixture. Stir in the
remaining flour and dates, mixing
well. Pour into the prepared tin and

cook for 50 minutes, or until cooked
when tested with a skewer. Leave
the pudding in the tin to cool for
10 minutes before turning out. Serve
warm with the hot sauce.
3 To make the sauce, put the sugar,
cream, butter and vanilla in a pan and
bring to the boil while stirring. Reduce
the heat and simmer for 5 minutes.

NUTRITION PER SERVE
Protein 5 g; Fat 33 g; Carbohydrate 75 g;
Dietary Fibre 3 g; Cholesterol 145 mg;
2530 kJ (605 Cal)

Using a sharp knife, chop the dates into small
pieces.

Pour boiling water over the dates and bicarbonate
of soda.

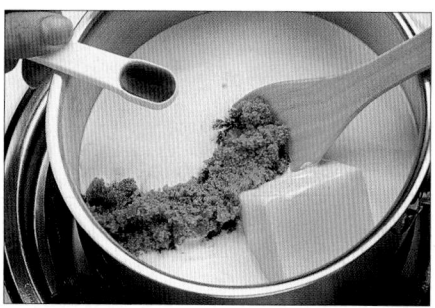

Put the brown sugar, cream, butter and vanilla
essence in a pan and simmer.

APPLE PIE

**Preparation time: 45 minutes +
  cooling time**
Total cooking time: 50 minutes
Serves 6

FILLING
6 large Granny Smith apples
2 tablespoons caster sugar
1 teaspoon finely grated lemon rind
pinch ground cloves

PASTRY
2 cups (250 g/8 oz) plain flour
3 tablespoons self-raising flour
150 g (5 oz) cold butter, chopped
2 tablespoons caster sugar
4–5 tablespoons iced water
2 tablespoons apricot jam
1 egg, lightly beaten
1 tablespoon sugar

1 Peel, core and cut the apples into wedges. Place in a heavy-based pan with the sugar, lemon rind, cloves and 2 tablespoons water. Cover and cook gently for 8 minutes, or until the apple is just tender, shaking the pan occasionally. Drain and allow to cool completely.
2 Sift the flours into a bowl and add the butter. Rub the butter into the flour using your fingertips until it resembles fine breadcrumbs. Add the sugar, mix well, and then make a well in the centre. Add the water and mix with a flat-bladed knife, using a cutting action, until the mixture comes together in beads. Gather the pastry together on a floured surface. Divide into two, making one half a little bigger. Cover with plastic wrap and refrigerate for 20 minutes.
3 Preheat the oven to moderately hot 200°C (400°F/Gas 6). Roll out the larger piece of pastry between two sheets of baking paper to line the base and side of a 23 cm (9 inch) pie plate. Peel off the top piece of paper and invert the pastry into the dish. Peel off the other baking sheet and trim off the excess pastry. Brush the jam over the base and spoon the apple filling into the shell. Roll out the remaining piece of pastry between the baking paper until large enough to cover the pie. Brush a little water around the rim, then place the top on, inverting the pastry off the baking paper. Trim off the excess pastry, pinch the edges together and cut a couple of steam slits in the top.
4 Bring together the excess pastry bits, gently re-roll and cut into leaves to decorate the top. Brush the top lightly with egg then sprinkle on the sugar. Bake for 20 minutes, then reduce the temperature to moderate 180°C (350°F/Gas 4) and bake for a further 15–20 minutes, or until golden.

NUTRITION PER SERVE
Protein 6.5 g; Fat 20 g; Carbohydrate 60 g;
Dietary Fibre 3.5 g; Cholesterol 95 mg;
1955 kJ (465 Cal)

Roll out the pastry between two sheets of baking paper.

Invert the pastry into the pie dish and peel off the baking paper.

Put the pastry lid on the pie and trim off any excess pastry.

SHAKER LEMON PIE

Preparation time: 20 minutes +
20 minutes refrigeration
Total cooking time: 50 minutes
Serves 6–8

2 lemons
½ cup (60 g/2 oz) plain flour
2 cups (500 g/1 lb) caster sugar
40 g (1¼ oz) unsalted butter, melted
4 eggs, lightly beaten
1 egg, extra, lightly beaten, to glaze

PASTRY
3 cups (375 g/12 oz) plain flour
185 g (6 oz) unsalted butter, chilled
   and cubed
2 tablespoons caster sugar
4–5 tablespoons iced water

1 Finely grate 1 lemon to give
2 teaspoons of rind. Place this in
a large bowl. Cut the pith off both
lemons and discard. Thinly slice the
lemon flesh, discarding the seeds.
2 Sift the flour into the bowl with the
rind, then stir in the sugar and
a pinch of salt. Add the butter and
egg and stir until smooth. Gently fold
in the lemon slices.
3 Preheat the oven to 200°C (400°F/
Gas 6) and heat a baking tray. Grease
a 20 cm (8 inch) pie dish.
4 To make the pastry, sift the flour
and ¼ teaspoon salt into a large bowl
and rub in the butter with your
fingertips until the mixture resembles
fine breadcrumbs. Mix in the sugar.
Make a well, add almost all the water
and mix with a flat-bladed knife,
using a cutting action, until the
mixture comes together in beads,
adding more water if necessary.
Gather together on a lightly floured
surface and press into a disc. Wrap in
plastic and refrigerate for 20 minutes.
5 Roll out two-thirds of the pastry
until large enough to fit the dish.
Spoon the filling into the pastry shell.
Roll out the remaining pastry until
large enough to cover the pie. Using
a sharp knife, cut out three small
triangles in a row across the centre of
the lid. Brush the rim of the pastry
base with beaten egg, then press the
lid in place. Trim off any excess.

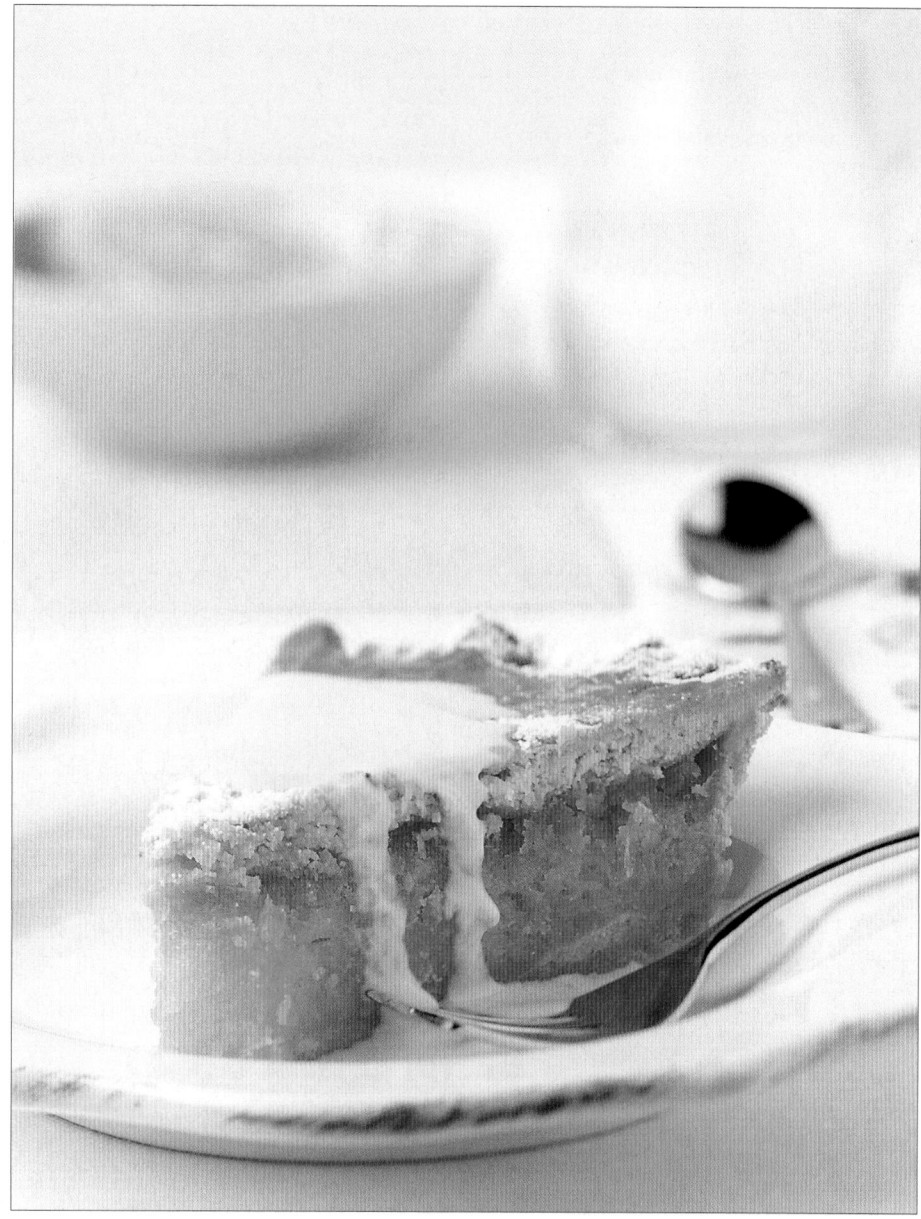

Scallop the edges with your fingers,
then go around the open scallops and
mark with the tines of a narrow fork.
Brush the top with egg glaze.
6 Bake on the hot tray for 20 minutes.
Reduce the temperature to 180°C
(350°F/Gas 4), cover the pie with foil
and bake for 30 minutes, or until the
filling is set and the pastry golden.

NUTRITION PER SERVE (8)
Protein 9 g; Fat 26 g; Carbohydrate 106 g;
Dietary Fibre 2.5 g; Cholesterol 161 mg;
2880 kJ (690 cal)

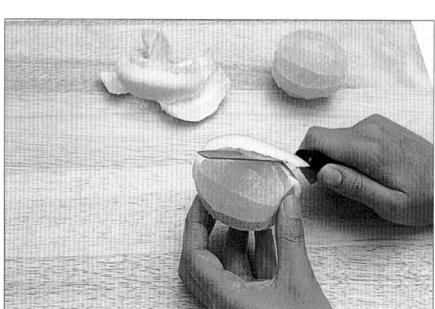

Use a small sharp knife to remove all of the skin
and pith from the lemons.

Gently fold the lemon slices into the butter and
egg mixture.

CREAMY CHOCOLATE MOUSSE

Preparation time: 5 minutes + overnight chilling
Total cooking time: 5 minutes
Serves 6

125 g (4 oz) dark chocolate, chopped
4 eggs, separated
¾ cup (185 ml/6 fl oz) cream, lightly
   whipped

1 Put the chocolate in a heatproof bowl. Bring a pan of water to a simmer, remove from the heat and place the bowl over the pan (don't let the base of the bowl touch the water). Stir the chocolate occasionally until melted. Remove from the heat and cool slightly. Lightly beat the egg yolks and stir into the chocolate mixture. Fold in the cream.
2 Using electric beaters, whisk the egg whites in a small dry bowl until soft peaks form. Fold one spoonful of the egg whites into the mousse with a metal spoon, then gently fold in the remainder, quickly and lightly.
3 Pour the mousse into six wine glasses or ¾ cup (185 ml/6 fl oz) ramekins. Cover with plastic wrap and refrigerate for 4 hours or overnight. Top with extra whipped cream and dust with cocoa powder, if desired.

NUTRITION PER SERVE
Protein 6 g; Fat 22 g; Carbohydrate 15 g;
Dietary Fibre 0 g; Cholesterol 160 mg;
1150 kJ (275 Cal)

Put the bowl of chocolate over a pan of simmering water and stir occasionally.

Gently fold the egg whites into the mousse with a metal spoon.

Pour the mousse into wine glasses or ramekins before covering and chilling.

SELF-SAUCING CHOCOLATE PUDDING

Preparation time: 10 minutes
Total cooking time: 40 minutes
Serves 6

1 cup (125 g/4 oz) self-raising flour
3 tablespoons cocoa powder
½ cup (125 g/4 oz) caster sugar
1 egg
½ cup (125 ml/4 fl oz) milk
60 g (2 oz) butter, melted
1 teaspoon vanilla essence
1 cup (185 g/6 oz) soft brown sugar

1 Preheat the oven to moderate 180°C (350°F/Gas 4). Brush a 2 litre heatproof dish with melted butter. Sift the flour and 1 tablespoon cocoa into a large bowl and add the sugar. Make a well in the mixture.

2 Beat the egg in a jug and add the milk, melted butter and vanilla essence. Pour the liquid into the dry ingredients and, using a wooden spoon, stir the batter until it is well combined and lump free. Pour into the prepared dish.

3 Combine the brown sugar and the remaining cocoa and sprinkle evenly over the batter. Pour 1½ cups (375 ml/ 12 fl oz) boiling water gently and evenly over the ingredients in the dish. Bake for 30–40 minutes, or until the pudding is cooked—a sauce will have formed underneath. Serve hot with whipped cream or ice cream.

NUTRITION PER SERVE
Protein 6 g; Fat 11 g; Carbohydrate 70 g; Dietary Fibre 1 g; Cholesterol 60 mg; 1640 kJ (390 Cal)

VARIATION: For a crunchy alternative, try adding ½ cup (60 g/2 oz) chopped walnuts to the pudding batter before baking.

Add the egg mixture to the dry ingredients and stir with a wooden spoon.

Sprinkle the combined sugar and cocoa over the batter.

Gently pour the boiling water evenly over the pudding.

TRIFLE

Preparation time: 15 minutes + chilling
Total cooking time: 10 minutes
Serves 6

½ cup (45 g/1½ oz) flaked almonds
250 g (8 oz) packet jam rollettes
    (mini jam swiss rolls)
⅓ cup (80 ml/2¾ fl oz) dry sherry
2 fresh mangoes or 2 fresh peaches,
    chopped
2½ cups (600 ml/20 fl oz) ready-made
    custard
300 ml (9½ fl oz) cream

1 Preheat the oven to moderate 180°C (350°F/Gas 4). Scatter the flaked almonds over a baking tray and cook in the oven for 6–8 minutes, or until golden. Cut the jam rollettes into 1 cm (½ inch) slices and place half on the base of a 2.5 litre glass serving bowl.

2 Sprinkle with half the sherry and half the mango or peach. Cover with half the custard. Repeat with the remaining ingredients, then refrigerate until cold.

3 Whisk the cream until stiff peaks form, then spread over the custard and scatter with the toasted almonds.

NUTRITION PER SERVE
Protein 9 g; Fat 27 g; Carbohydrate 45 g; Dietary Fibre 1.5 g; Cholesterol 130 mg; 1920 kJ (460 Cal)

NOTE: If possible, use fresh fruit. If you can't buy fresh, ripe fruit, use a 425 g (14 oz) can of drained peach or mango slices.

Scatter the almonds on a baking tray and cook until golden.

Sprinkle the sherry over the jam rollettes then add the fruit.

Whip the cream until stiff peaks form, then spread it over the custard.

CARAMEL BANANAS

Preparation time: 5 minutes
Total cooking time: 10 minutes
Serves 4

60 g (2 oz) butter
100 g (3½ oz) soft brown sugar
2 tablespoons lemon juice
1 tablespoon orange liqueur
4 firm, ripe bananas, sliced in half
   lengthways

1 Melt the butter in a large frying pan. Add the sugar and stir to combine, then simmer for 3 minutes, or until golden and bubbly.
2 Add the lemon juice and liqueur, and stir gently. Put the bananas in the sauce and simmer for 5 minutes, or until the sauce thickens. Occasionally spoon the sauce over the bananas to baste them. The caramel bananas are delicious served with good-quality vanilla ice cream or with waffles and whipped cream.

NUTRITION PER SERVE
Protein 0 g; Fat 10 g; Carbohydrate 28 g;
Dietary Fibre 0 g; Cholesterol 38 mg;
950 kJ (225 Cal)

VARIATION: This recipe also makes a delicious pancake filling if you chop the bananas instead of halving them. Try stacking the pancakes between layers of bananas and sauce. Sprinkle over demerara sugar and flash under a grill until toffee-like.

Add the brown sugar to the pan when the butter has melted.

Put the bananas in the pan when the caramel is golden and bubbly.

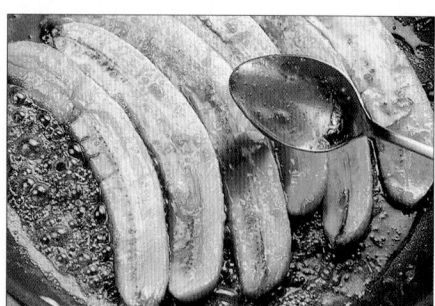

Spoon the caramel sauce over the bananas to baste them.

CREPES WITH HOT CHOCOLATE SAUCE

Preparation time: 5 minutes +
30 minutes standing
Total cooking time: 20 minutes
Makes 12 pancakes

2 cups (250 g/8 oz) plain flour
3 eggs, lightly beaten
1 cup (250 ml/8 fl oz) milk
60 g (2 oz) butter, melted

SAUCE
2 tablespoons butter
3 tablespoons sifted cocoa powder
1 cup (185 g/6 oz) soft brown sugar
300 ml (10 fl oz) cream

1 Sift the flour into a large bowl. Make a well in the centre and add the combined eggs, milk and ¾ cup (185 ml/6 fl oz) water. With a whisk gradually draw in the flour and whisk to a smooth batter. Stir in the melted butter. Pour into a jug and set aside for 30 minutes.

2 Heat a 20 cm (8 inch) crepe pan or non-stick frying pan and grease lightly with butter. When the pan is hot, pour in ¼ cup (60 ml/2 fl oz) of the mixture and tilt the pan to cover. Tip out any excess batter. When the edges begin to curl, gently turn the pancake over with a spatula. Cook until lightly browned on both sides, and slide onto a plate. If serving immediately, keep the crepes warm. Cook the remaining batter and stack the crepes on top of each other with a piece of greaseproof paper between each one.

3 To make the sauce, combine in a pan the butter, cocoa and sugar. Mix well, then add the cream and stir over low heat until it comes to the boil.

4 To serve, fold three crepes into quarters and put them on a plate. Pour a generous amount of sauce over the top and add some vanilla ice cream.

NUTRITION PER PANCAKE
Protein 6 g; Fat 20 g; Carbohydrate 33 g;
Dietary Fibre 1 g; Cholesterol 100 mg;
1395 kJ (335 Cal)

NOTE: This sauce will keep well in the refrigerator for up to a week.

Whisk together the flour, eggs, milk and water and stir in the melted butter.

Pour the mixture into the hot pan and tilt to cover the base.

When the edges begin to curl, gently turn the crepe over.

Cook the crepe until lightly browned on both sides.

Quick-mix puddings

Just saying the words "steamed pudding" conjures up a cosy fireside image. Everyone has their favourite flavour, be it traditional jam or the richness of banana caramel. Follow the recipe below and choose one of the flavourings from the opposite page. That's the hard part—choosing only one!

STEAMED PUDDING

1 Grease the base and side of a 1 litre pudding basin with melted butter. Place a round of baking paper in the bottom. Put the empty basin in a pan on an upturned saucer and pour in enough cold water to come halfway up the side of the basin. Remove the basin and put the water on to boil.
2 Sift 1¼ cups (155 g/5 oz) self-raising flour into a bowl. Add a pinch of salt, 120 g (4 oz) softened butter, ⅔ cup

(160 g/5½ oz) sugar and 3 eggs and beat together well. Pour into the basin.
3 Cover a sheet of foil with a sheet of baking paper, and make a large pleat in the middle. Grease the paper with melted butter. Place paper-side-down on top of the basin and tie with string securely around the rim of the basin and over the top to make a handle.
4 Lower the basin into the simmering water and cover with a tight-fitting lid. Cook for 1 hour 45 minutes.

Check the water level after an hour and top up to the original level with boiling water as needed. Try putting a coin in the base of the pan—it will stop rattling when the water is getting low.

NOTE: To reheat a steamed pudding after cooking, bring it back to room temperature and reboil for half the original cooking time. Alternatively, cut it into slices and reheat gently in the microwave individually.

TREACLE

Mix 2 tablespoons treacle into the pudding mixture and place **2** teaspoons treacle in the base of the pudding bowl. When you turn the pudding out, drizzle with a little golden syrup. Serve with custard and ice cream. Serves 4.

JAM

Place 2 tablespoons of strawberry jam in the base of the basin before adding the pudding mixture. Serves 4.

LEMON

Peel and remove the pith from a lemon. Slice and arrange the slices over the base and up the side of the basin. Sprinkle with 2 teaspoons sugar. Add 1 tablespoon grated lemon rind to the pudding mixture. Serves 4.

FRUIT MINCE

Sift ¼ teaspoon mixed spice with the flour, and stir ⅓ cup (60 g/2 oz) fruit mince into the pudding mixture. Serve with custard. Serves 4.

CHOCOLATE

Sift 2 tablespoons cocoa powder with the flour, and stir ½ cup (90 g/3 oz) milk choc bits into the pudding mixture. Serve with hot chocolate sauce. Serves 4.

BANANA CARAMEL

Pour 30 g (1 oz) melted butter into the pudding basin and sprinkle with 2 tablespoons soft brown sugar. Place slices of banana over the base and slightly up the side of the pudding basin. Add 1 mashed ripe banana to the pudding mixture and mix well. Serve with freshly whipped cream. Serves 4.

LEMON DELICIOUS

Preparation time: 10 minutes
Total cooking time: 40 minutes
Serves 4

30 g (1 oz) butter, softened
¾ cup (185 g/6 oz) caster sugar
1 teaspoon grated lemon rind
3 eggs, separated
¼ cup (30 g/1 oz) plain flour
½ cup (125 ml/4 fl oz) lemon juice
1½ cups (375 ml/12 fl oz) warm milk
icing sugar, to dust

1 Preheat the oven to moderate 180°C (350°F/Gas 4). Brush a 1.5 litre heatproof dish with melted butter. Place the butter, sugar, lemon rind and egg yolks in a bowl. Using electric beaters, beat until light and creamy.
2 Fold in the sifted flour in two batches, alternately with the lemon juice and milk. In a separate clean dry bowl, using electric beaters, whisk the egg whites until soft peaks form. Pour the lemon mixture down the inside of the bowl of beaten egg whites and fold the whites gently into the mixture.

3 Pour the combined mixture into the prepared dish and put the dish in a baking tin. Pour in enough warm water to come halfway up the side of the dish. Bake for 40 minutes, or until puffed and golden. Dust with icing sugar and serve with ice cream.

NUTRITION PER SERVE
Protein 9 g; Fat 15 g; Carbohydrate 60 g;
Dietary Fibre 0 g; Cholesterol 165 mg;
1630 kJ (390 Cal)

VARIATION: Try using limes or oranges for a new flavour.

Fold in the flour alternately with the lemon juice and milk.

Pour the lemon mixture down the inside of the bowl of beaten egg whites.

Gently fold the egg whites into the mixture with a spoon.

PLUM COBBLER

Preparation time: 25 minutes
Total cooking time: 35 minutes
Serves 6

750 g (1½ lb) plums
⅓ cup (90 g/3 oz) sugar
1 teaspoon vanilla essence

TOPPING
1 cup (125 g/4 oz) self-raising
    flour
60 g (2 oz) cold butter, chopped
¼ cup (55 g/2 oz) firmly packed
    soft brown sugar
¼ cup (60 ml/2 fl oz) milk
1 tablespoon caster sugar

1 Preheat the oven to moderately hot 200°C (400°F/Gas 6). Cut the plums into quarters and remove the stones. Put the plums, sugar and 2 tablespoons water into a pan and bring to the boil, stirring, until the sugar dissolves.
2 Reduce the heat, then cover and simmer for 5 minutes, or until the plums are tender. Remove the skins from the plums if desired. Add the vanilla essence and spoon the mixture into a 3 cup (750 ml/24 fl oz) ovenproof dish.
3 To make the topping, sift the flour into a large bowl and add the butter. Using your fingertips, rub the butter into the flour until it resembles fine breadcrumbs. Stir in the brown sugar and 2 tablespoons milk.

4 Stir with a knife to form a soft dough, adding more milk if necessary. Turn the mixture out onto a lightly floured surface and gather together to form a smooth dough. Roll out until the dough is 1 cm (½ inch) thick and cut into rounds using a 4 cm (1½ inch) cutter.
5 Overlap the rounds around the side of the dish over the filling. (The plums in the middle will not be covered.) Lightly brush with milk and sprinkle with sugar. Cook in the oven on a baking tray for 30 minutes, or until the topping is golden and cooked through.

NUTRITION PER SERVE
Protein 3 g; Fat 9 g; Carbohydrate 50 g;
Dietary Fibre 3.5 g; Cholesterol 25 mg;
1245 kJ (295 Cal)

Sift the flour into a bowl, then rub in the butter with your fingertips.

Stir with a flat-bladed knife to form a soft dough, adding more milk if necessary.

Roll out the dough to a thickness of 1 cm (1/2 inch), then cut into rounds.

CHOCOLATE TOFU CHEESECAKE

**Preparation time: 20 minutes +
  6 hours refrigeration**
Total cooking time: Nil
Serves 10

200 g (6½ oz) chocolate-flavoured
  biscuits
90 g (3 oz) butter, melted
1 tablespoon gelatine
600 g (1¼ lb) silken tofu, drained
250 g (8 oz) soy cream cheese
½ cup (125 g/4 oz) caster sugar
2 teaspoons vanilla essence
250 g (8 oz) dark chocolate, melted
  and cooled
2 tablespoons shaved chocolate
250 g (8 oz) strawberries, cut into
  quarters, to serve

1 Grease a 23 cm (9 inch) springform tin and line the base with non-stick baking paper.
2 Place the biscuits in a food processor and blend until finely crushed. Add the butter and process until combined. Spoon the biscuit mixture into the prepared tin and evenly smooth over the base with the back of a spoon. Refrigerate until required.
3 Meanwhile, sprinkle the gelatine evenly over ¼ cup (60 ml/2 fl oz) warm water in a small bowl. Leave until the gelatine is spongy—do not stir. Bring a small saucepan of water to the boil, remove from the heat and place the bowl in the pan. The water should come halfway up the side of the bowl. Stir the gelatine until clear and dissolved.
4 Place the tofu, soy cream cheese, sugar, essence, melted chocolate and

gelatine in a food processor and blend until smooth. Spoon the filling into the prepared tin and refrigerate for 6 hours, or until set.
5 Garnish with the shaved chocolate and serve with a generous pile of quartered strawberries.

NUTRITION PER SERVE
Protein 10 g; Fat 30 g; Carbohydrate 43 g;
Dietary Fibre 1.24 g; Cholesterol 50 mg;
1964 kJ (469 Cal)

Blend the butter and finely crushed biscuits until well combined.

Soak the gelatine in warm water until it becomes spongy.

Blend all the filling ingredients in a food processor until the mixture is smooth.

CHOCOLATE AND PEANUT BUTTER PIE

**Preparation time: 30 minutes +
4 hours refrigeration
Total cooking time: 5 minutes
Serves 12**

200 g (6½ oz) chocolate biscuits with
cream centre, crushed
60 g (2 oz) unsalted butter, melted
1 cup (250 g/8 oz) cream cheese
⅔ cup (90 g/3 oz) icing sugar, sifted
½ cup (125 g/4 oz) smooth peanut
butter
1 teaspoon vanilla essence
300 ml (10 fl oz) cream, whipped
¼ cup (60 ml/2 fl oz) cream, extra
3 teaspoons unsalted butter, extra
100 g (3½ oz) dark chocolate, grated
honey-roasted peanuts, to garnish

1 Mix the biscuit crumbs with the
melted butter until thoroughly coated.
Press the mixture into a deep 18 cm
(7 inch) pie dish and refrigerate for
15 minutes, or until firm.
2 Beat the cream cheese and icing
sugar with electric beaters until
smooth. Add the peanut butter and
vanilla and beat together well. Stir in
a little of the whipped cream until the
mixture is smooth, then very gently
fold in the remaining whipped cream.
3 Pour two-thirds of the filling into
the pie shell and smooth the top.
Refrigerate the pie and the remaining
filling for 2 hours, or until firm.
4 Put the extra cream and butter in a
small saucepan and stir over medium
heat until the butter is melted and the
cream just comes to a simmer. Remove
from the heat and add the grated
chocolate. Stir until smooth and silky.
Cool to room temperature, then pour
over the top of the pie, smoothing if
necessary with a spatula. Refrigerate for another 2 hours,
or until the topping is firm. Remove
the extra filling from the fridge about
30 minutes before you serve.
5 Fill a piping bag with the softened
filling and pipe rosettes or use two
small spoons to decorate the edges of
the pie. Top each rosette with a
honey-roasted peanut. Serve in thin
wedges as this pie is very rich.

NUTRITION PER SERVE
Protein 7 g; Fat 35 g; Carbohydrate 25 g;
Dietary Fibre 1.5 g; Cholesterol 76 mg;
1820 kJ (435 cal)

Gently fold the whipped cream into the loosened
peanut butter filling.

Pour the cooled chocolate over the top of the pie
and smooth with a spatula.

HOT CHOCOLATE SOUFFLE

Preparation time: 10 minutes
Total cooking time: 35 minutes
Serves 8

170 g (5½ oz) caster sugar
450 ml (14 fl oz) milk
70 g (2½ oz) plain flour
1 egg
4 eggs, separated
40 g (1¼ oz) butter, melted
¼ cup (30 g/1 oz) cocoa powder, sifted
1 tablespoon caster sugar, extra
icing sugar, to serve

1 Grease a 1.25 litre soufflé dish and preheat the oven to moderately hot 200°C (400°F/Gas 6).
2 Put the sugar and 1 cup (250 ml/8 fl oz) milk in a pan and stir over low heat until the sugar dissolves. Put the flour, egg and the remaining milk in a bowl and whisk to combine. Pour the hot milk mixture into the bowl and mix well with a whisk. When smooth, return the mixture to the pan and stir over low heat until it boils and thickens. Combine the egg yolks and butter with the cocoa and add to the pan, mixing well. Transfer to a bowl, cover the surface with plastic wrap and allow to cool completely.
3 In a large clean dry bowl, beat the egg whites until soft peaks form, then add the extra sugar. Continue beating until well combined and the egg whites are glossy. Carefully combine one spoonful of the egg whites with the chocolate mixture, then add the remaining egg white and fold in gently with a metal spoon.
4 Fill the soufflé dish to three-quarters full and place on an oven tray. Cook in a hot oven for 25–30 minutes, or until puffed up and firm to the touch. Dust with icing sugar before serving.

NUTRITION PER SERVE
Protein 7.5 g; Fat 10 g; Carbohydrate 35 g; Dietary Fibre 0.5 g; Cholesterol 135 mg; 1065 kJ (255 Cal)

Whisk or stir over low heat until the mixture thickens and comes to the boil.

Gently fold the egg whites into the chocolate mixture with a metal spoon.

Pour the mixture into the prepared dish to three-quarters full.

BAKED CUSTARD

Preparation time: 5 minutes
Total cooking time: 35 minutes
Serves 4

3 eggs
2 tablespoons caster sugar
1 teaspoon vanilla essence
2 cups (500 ml/16 fl oz) milk
½ cup (125 ml/4 oz) cream
ground nutmeg, to sprinkle

1 Preheat the oven to warm 160°C (315°F/Gas 2–3). Brush a 1.5 litre heatproof dish with melted butter. Put the eggs, sugar and vanilla essence in a bowl and whisk lightly to combine. (If you overwhisk you may have bubbles in your finished custard.) Heat the milk and cream together in a pan until just warm and stir into the eggs, mixing well.
2 Strain the mixture into the dish and sprinkle with nutmeg. Put the dish in a baking tin and pour enough hot water in the tin to come halfway up the side of the custard dish.
3 Bake for 35 minutes, or until the custard is set—it shouldn't wobble in the centre when shaken. Remove immediately from the baking tin and serve warm or at room temperature.

NUTRITION PER SERVE
Protein 9.5 g; Fat 22 g; Carbohydrate 17 g; Dietary Fibre 0 g; Cholesterol 195 mg; 1245 kJ (295 Cal)

VARIATIONS: To make a brandied raisin custard, soak 3 tablespoons of chopped raisins in 2 tablespoons of brandy for 30 minutes. Discard the brandy, and add the raisins to the custard mixture.
To make a vanilla bean custard, split a vanilla bean and add it to the milk and cream. When you heat the custard, remove the pod and scrape the seeds into the custard mix.

Strain the warm custard mixture into the prepared heatproof dish.

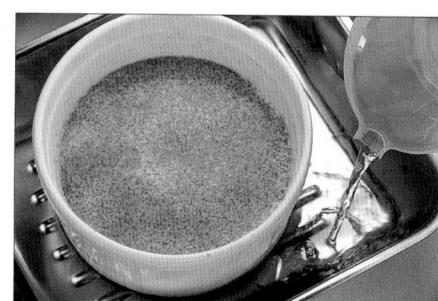
Pour hot water into the baking tin to come halfway up the side of the custard dish.

MANGO AND PASSIONFRUIT PIES

**Preparation time: 25 minutes +
  refrigeration**
Total cooking time: 25 minutes
Makes 6

750 g (1½ lb) sweet shortcrust pastry
3 ripe mangoes, peeled and sliced or
    chopped, or 400 g (13 oz) can
    mango slices, drained
¼ cup (60 g/2 oz) passionfruit pulp
1 tablespoon custard powder
⅓ cup (90 g/3 oz) caster sugar

1 egg, lightly beaten
icing sugar, to dust

1 Preheat the oven to 190°C (375°F/
Gas 5). Grease six 8 cm (3 inch) fluted
tart tins. Roll out two-thirds of the
pastry between two sheets of baking
paper until 3 mm (⅛ inch) thick. Cut
out six 13 cm (5 inch) circles. Line the
tins with the circles and trim the edges.
Refrigerate while you make the filling.
2 Mix together the mango, passionfruit, custard powder and sugar.
3 Roll out the remaining pastry
between two sheets of baking paper
to a thickness of 3 mm. Cut out six

11 cm (4½ inch) circles. Re-roll the
trimmings and cut out small shapes
for decorations.
4 Fill the pastry cases with the mango
mixture and brush the edges with egg.
Top with the pastry circles and press
the edges to seal. Trim the edges and
decorate with the shapes. Brush the
tops with beaten egg and dust with
icing sugar. Bake for 20–25 minutes,
or until the pastry is golden brown.

NUTRITION PER PIE
Protein 11 g; Fat 29 g; Carbohydrate 85 g;
Dietary Fibre 6 g; Cholesterol 114 mg;
2685 kJ (640 cal)

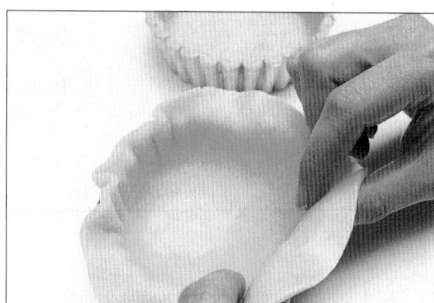

Line the tins with the pastry circles and trim away
the excess pastry.

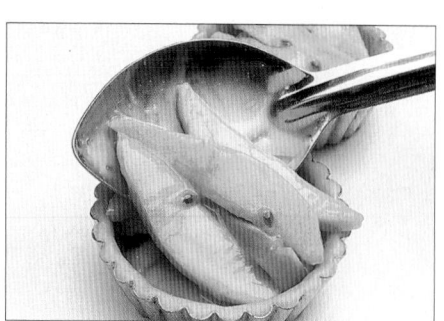

Spoon the mango and passionfruit filling into the
pastry cases.

Decorate the tops of the pies with shapes cut
from the pastry trimmings.

RICE PUDDING

Preparation time: 10 minutes
Total cooking time: 2 hours
Serves 4

¼ cup (55 g/2 oz) short-grain rice
1⅔ cups (410 ml/13 fl oz) milk
1½ tablespoons caster sugar
¾ cup (185 ml/6 fl oz) cream
¼ teaspoon vanilla essence
¼ teaspoon grated nutmeg
1 bay leaf

1 Preheat the oven to slow 150°C (300°F/Gas 2) and grease a 1 litre ovenproof dish. In a bowl, mix together the rice, milk, caster sugar, cream and vanilla essence, and pour into the greased dish. Dust the surface with the grated nutmeg and float the bay leaf on top.

2 Bake the rice pudding for 2 hours, by which time the rice should have absorbed most of the milk and will have become creamy in texture with a brown skin on top. Serve hot.

NUTRITION PER SERVE
Protein 5 g; Fat 24 g; Carbohydrate 25 g; Dietary Fibre 0 g; Cholesterol 77 mg; 1378 kJ (330 Cal)

VARIATION: Add grated lemon or orange rind to give a citrus flavour.

Mix together the rice, milk, caster sugar, cream and vanilla essence.

Pour the mixture into a greased ovenproof dish and dust with nutmeg.

Float the bay leaf on the top to allow its flavours to infuse.

RHUBARB AND PEAR CRUMBLE

Preparation time: 20 minutes
Total cooking time: 35 minutes
Serves 6

600 g (1¼ lb) rhubarb
2 strips lemon rind
1 tablespoon honey, or to taste
2 firm, ripe pears
½ cup (50 g/1¾ oz) rolled oats
⅓ cup (60 g/2 oz) soft brown sugar
¼ cup (35 g/1¼ oz) wholemeal plain flour
50 g (1¾ oz) butter

1 Trim the rhubarb, wash and cut into 3 cm (1¼ inch) pieces. Place in a medium pan with the lemon rind and 1 tablespoon water. Cook, covered, over low heat for 10 minutes, or until tender. Cool a little. Stir in the honey and remove the lemon rind.
2 Preheat the oven to moderate 180°C (350°F/Gas 4). Peel, core and cut the pears into 2 cm (¾ inch) cubes and combine with the rhubarb. Pour into a 1.25 litre dish and smooth the surface.
3 To make the topping, combine the oats, flour and brown sugar in a bowl. Rub in the butter with your fingertips until the mixture is crumbly. Spread over the fruit. Bake for 15 minutes, or until cooked and golden.

NUTRITION PER SERVE
Protein 3.5 g; Fat 8 g; Carbohydrate 30 g; Dietary Fibre 6 g; Cholesterol 0 mg; 885 kJ (210 cal)

Trim the rhubarb, wash thoroughly, then cut into short pieces.

Add the cubed pears to the cooked rhubarb and gently stir to combine.

Use your fingertips to rub the butter into the dry ingredients to make a crumble topping.

GRANDMOTHER'S PAVLOVA

Preparation time: 30 minutes
Total cooking time: 1 hour
Serves 6

4 egg whites
1 cup (250 g/8 oz) caster sugar
2 teaspoons cornflour
1 teaspoon white vinegar
2 cups (500 ml/16 fl oz) cream
3 passionfruit
strawberries, for decoration

1 Preheat the oven to warm 160°C (315°F/Gas 2–3). Line a 32 x 28 cm (13 x 11 inch) baking tray with a sheet of baking paper.
2 Place the egg whites and a pinch of salt in a small, dry bowl. Using electric beaters, beat until stiff peaks form. Add the sugar gradually, beating after each addition, until thick and glossy and all the sugar has dissolved.
3 Using a metal spoon, fold in the cornflour and vinegar. Spoon the mixture into a mound on the prepared tray. Flatten the top and smooth the sides. (The pavlova should be about 2.5 cm/1 inch high.) Bake for 1 hour, or until pale cream and crisp. Remove from the oven while warm and carefully turn upside down onto a plate. Allow to cool.
4 Lightly whip the cream until soft peaks form and spread over the soft centre. Decorate with pulp from the passionfruit and halved strawberries. Cut into wedges to serve.

NUTRITION PER SERVE
Protein 4 g; Fat 36 g; Carbohydrate 45 g;
Dietary Fibre 1.5 g; Cholesterol 113 mg;
2124 kJ (507 Cal)

Beat until the mixture is thick and glossy and all the sugar has dissolved.

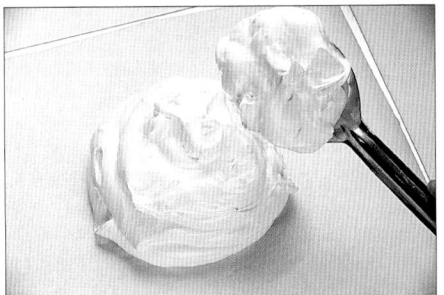

Spoon the mixture onto the baking tray with a metal spoon.

Smooth the top and sides to give the pavlova a cake shape.

GOLDEN SYRUP DUMPLINGS

Preparation time: 15 minutes
Total cooking time: 30 minutes
Serves 4

1 cup (125 g/4 oz) self-raising flour
40 g (1¼ oz) cold butter, chopped
1 egg
1 tablespoon milk
1 cup (250 g/8 oz) sugar
40 g butter, extra
2 tablespoons golden syrup
¼ cup (60 ml/2 fl oz) lemon juice

1 Sift the flour into a bowl and add a pinch of salt. Using your fingertips, rub the butter into the flour until the mixture resembles fine breadcrumbs, and make a well in the centre. Using a flat-bladed knife, stir the combined egg and milk into the flour mixture to form a soft dough.

2 To make the syrup, place 2 cups (500 ml/16 fl oz) water in a large pan with the sugar, butter, golden syrup and lemon juice. Stir over medium heat until combined and the sugar has dissolved.

3 Bring to the boil, then gently drop dessertspoons of the dough into the syrup. Reduce the heat to a simmer and cook, covered, for 20 minutes, or until a knife inserted into a dumpling comes out clean. Spoon onto serving plates, drizzle with syrup, and serve immediately with whipped cream.

NUTRITION PER SERVE
Protein 5 g; Fat 20 g; Carbohydrate 95 g;
Dietary Fibre 1 g; Cholesterol 97 mg;
2327 kJ (555 Cal)

Rub the butter into the flour until the mixture resembles breadcrumbs.

Stir the milk and egg into the flour mixture with a flat-bladed knife.

Carefully drop dessertspoons of dough into the boiling syrup.

CARAMELISED PINEAPPLE GRATIN

Preparation time: 15 minutes
Total cooking time: 15 minutes
Serves 4

800 g (1 lb 10 oz) ripe pineapple, cut into 1.5 cm (⅝ inch) cubes
¼ cup (60 ml/2 fl oz) dark rum
2 tablespoons unsalted butter
1 teaspoon vanilla essence
¼ cup (45 g/1½ oz) soft brown sugar
½ teaspoon ground ginger

300 g (10 oz) sour cream
¼ cup (60 ml/2 fl oz) cream
1 teaspoon finely grated lemon rind
½ cup (95 g/3 oz) soft brown sugar, to sprinkle, extra

1 Place the pineapple, rum, butter, vanilla, sugar and ginger in a saucepan and cook, stirring occasionally, for 8–10 minutes, or until caramelised. Remove from the heat.
2 Divide the pineapple among four individual gratin dishes and allow it to cool slightly.

3 Combine the sour cream, cream and lemon rind in a bowl, then spoon evenly over the pineapple. Sprinkle the extra brown sugar over each gratin.
4 Cook the gratins under a hot grill for 4–5 minutes, or until the sugar has melted and caramelised. Take care not to burn them. Serve immediately.

NUTRITION PER SERVE
Protein 4 g; Fat 44 g; Carbohydrate 53 g; Dietary Fibre 4 g; Cholesterol 142 mg; 2686 kJ (624 Cal)

Cook the pineapple cubes in a large saucepan until caramelised.

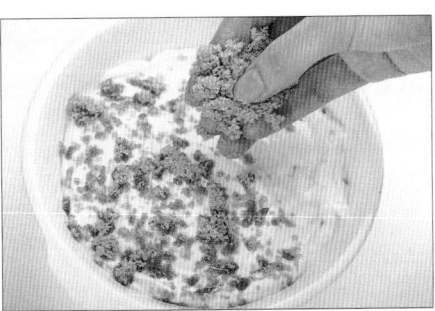

Evenly sprinkle the brown sugar over the top of each gratin.

Grill the gratins until the sugar has melted and caramelised.

POACHED PEARS IN SAFFRON CITRUS SYRUP

Preparation time: 10 minutes
Total cooking time: 30 minutes
Serves 4

1 vanilla bean, split lengthways
½ teaspoon firmly packed saffron
   threads
¾ cup (185 g/6 oz) caster sugar
2 teaspoons grated lemon rind
4 pears, peeled
biscotti, to serve (see NOTE)

1 Place the vanilla bean, saffron threads, sugar, lemon rind and 2 cups (500 ml/16 fl oz) water in a large saucepan and mix together well. Heat, stirring, over low heat until the sugar has dissolved. Bring to the boil, then reduce to a gentle simmer.
2 Add the pears and cook, covered, for 12–15 minutes, or until tender when tested with a metal skewer. Turn the pears over with a slotted spoon halfway through cooking. Once cooked, remove from the syrup with a slotted spoon.
3 Remove the lid and allow the saffron citrus syrup to come to the

boil. Cook for 8–10 minutes, or until the syrup has reduced by half and thickened slightly. Remove the vanilla bean and drizzle the syrup over the pears. Serve with biscotti.

NUTRITION PER SERVE
Protein 0.5 g; Fat 0 g; Carbohydrate 70 g; Dietary Fibre 4.5 g; Cholesterol 0 mg; 1155 kJ (276 cal)

NOTE: Biscotti are available in a wide variety of flavours. You can buy biscotti at gourmet food stores, delicatessens and supermarkets.

Stir the saffron citrus syrup until the sugar has completely dissolved.

Cook the pears until tender when tested with a metal skewer.

Bring the syrup to the boil and cook until it has slightly thickened.

LEMON GRASS AND GINGER INFUSED FRUIT SALAD

Preparation time: 20 minutes
Total cooking time: 10 minutes
Serves 4

¼ cup (60 g/2 oz) caster sugar
2.5 cm x 2.5 cm (1 inch x 1 inch piece fresh ginger, thinly sliced
1 stem lemon grass, bruised and halved
1 large passionfruit
1 Fiji red pawpaw (560 g/14 oz)
½ honeydew melon (800 g/1 lb 10 oz)
1 large mango (500 g/1 lb)
1 small fresh pineapple (1 kg/2 lb)
12 fresh lychees
3 tablespoons shredded fresh mint

1 Place the sugar, ginger and lemon grass in a small saucepan, add ½ cup (125 ml/4 fl oz) water and stir over low heat to dissolve the sugar. Boil for 5 minutes, or until reduced to ⅓ cup (80 ml/2¾ fl oz) and cool. Strain the syrup and add the passionfruit pulp.
2 Peel and seed the pawpaw and melon. Cut into 4 cm cubes. Peel the mango and cut the flesh into cubes, discarding the stone. Peel, halve and core the pineapple and cut into cubes. Peel the lychees, then make a slit in the flesh and remove the seed.
3 Place all the fruit in a large serving bowl. Pour on the syrup, or serve separately if preferred. Garnish with the shredded mint.

NUTRITION PER SERVE
Protein 7 g; Fat 2 g; Carbohydrate 80 g;
Dietary Fibre 13.5 g; Cholesterol 0 mg;
1485 kJ (355 Cal)

NOTE: If fresh lychees are not available, canned ones are fine.

Stir the passionfruit pulp into the strained ginger and lemon grass syrup.

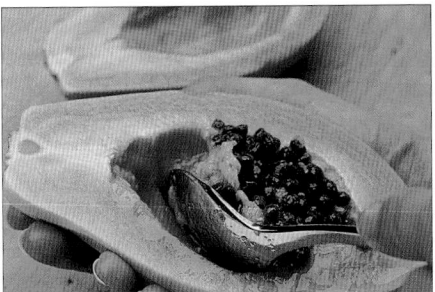

Peel the pawpaw, then remove the seeds with a spoon.

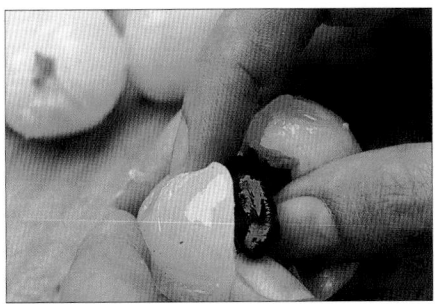

Peel the lychees, make a slit in the flesh and remove the seed.

Dessert sauces

Ice cream, pancakes, fresh fruit, waffles and puddings can all be elevated from the ordinary to the sublime in minutes with these mouth-watering sauces. From traditional favourites to exciting new flavour combinations, you'll be surprised how quickly the dessert bowls are scraped clean.

COFFEE SAUCE

Whisk 3 egg yolks, 2 tablespoons soft brown sugar and ½ teaspoon cornflour until thick. Heat ⅔ cup (170 ml/ 5½ fl oz) milk and 2 tablespoons ground coffee until almost boiling. Strain through a fine sieve. Gradually whisk into the egg mixture. Return the mixture to the pan and stir over low heat until it thickens and coats the back of a wooden spoon. Cool. Stir in ¼ cup (60 ml/2 fl oz) lightly whipped cream. For best results, serve on the day it is made. Makes 2 cups (500 ml/16 fl oz).

CHOCOLATE FUDGE SAUCE

Roughly chop 250 g (8 oz) dark chocolate. Place in a pan with ¾ cup (185 ml/6 fl oz) cream, 50 g (1¾ oz) butter and 1 tablespoon golden syrup. Stir over low heat until smooth and combined. Add a little more cream if the sauce is slightly grainy. Serve hot over ice cream, waffles, pancakes, poached fruit or puddings. Refrigerate in a sealed container for up to 1 month and gently reheat to serve. Makes 2 cups (500 ml/16 fl oz).

BRANDY BUTTER

In a food processor, process 125 g (4 oz) softened unsalted butter and ½ cup (60 g/2 oz) icing sugar until combined. Slowly add ¼ cup (60 ml/ 2 fl oz) brandy, beating well after each addition (do not overbeat or it will curdle). Brandy butter is traditionally served with Christmas pudding. Brandy butter will keep refrigerated for up to 1 month. Makes 2 cups (500 ml/16 fl oz).

BUTTERSCOTCH SAUCE

Place 125 g (4 oz) butter and ½ cup (95 g/3 oz) soft brown sugar in a pan and stir over low heat until the sugar has dissolved. Bring to the boil and add 2 tablespoons golden syrup and ½ cup (125 ml/4 fl oz) cream. Reduce the heat and simmer for 10 minutes, or until slightly thickened. Remove from the heat and add 1 teaspoon vanilla essence. Serve either hot or cold. Makes 1½ cups (375 ml/12 fl oz).

RASPBERRY SAUCE

In a small pan, stir to dissolve ½ cup (125 g/4 oz) sugar in ½ cup (125 ml/4 oz) water over low heat. Bring to the boil and cook for 10 minutes or until reduced and slightly thickened. Cool. In a food processor or blender, purée 300 g (10 oz) fresh or thawed frozen raspberries, the sugar syrup and 1 tablespoon lemon juice. Strain through a fine sieve. Store in a bottle or airtight container in the fridge for up to 1 week. Makes about 1½ cups (375 ml/12 fl oz).

VARIATION: Use strawberries, blueberries, blackberries or a combination of your favourite berries.

CHOCOLATE CHILLI SAUCE

Combine 1⅔ cups (250 g/8 oz) roughly chopped dark chocolate (not cooking chocolate), 1 cup (250 ml/8 fl oz) cream, 30 g (1 oz) butter and 1 teaspoon chilli powder in a pan. Cook over very low heat until all the chocolate is melted and the mixture is smooth. Can be refrigerated for up to 2 weeks and gently reheated when required. Serve warm or cold with fresh fruit; profiteroles, ice cream, cassata or waffles. Makes about 2 cups (500 ml/16 fl oz).

BLUEBERRY AND STAR ANISE SAUCE

In a small pan heat ½ cup (125 ml/4 fl oz) water and add ¼ cup (60 g/2 oz) caster sugar and stir until dissolved. Reduce the heat, add 2 star anise and simmer for 8–10 minutes, or until the mixture begins to thicken. Add 300 g (10 oz) fresh blueberries and cook for a further 8–10 minutes, or until the blueberries begin to break up. Remove from the heat and cool. Remove the star anise. Purée in a food processor or blender until smooth. Serve hot or cold. Can be kept in the refrigerator for up to 1 week. Makes about 1½ cups (375 ml/12 fl oz).

From left to right: Blueberry and star anise sauce; Coffee sauce; Chocolate chilli sauce; Butterscotch sauce; Brandy butter; Raspberry sauce; Chocolate fudge sauce.

PASSIONFRUIT MOUSSE

**Preparation time: 25 minutes +
    2 hours refrigeration
Total cooking time: 12 minutes
Serves 8**

5–6 passionfruit
6 eggs, separated
¾ cup (185 g/6 oz) caster sugar
½ teaspoon finely grated
    lemon rind
3 tablespoons lemon juice
1 tablespoon gelatine
1¼ cups (315 ml/10 fl oz) cream,
    lightly whipped
¾ cup (40 g/1¼ oz) flaked or shredded
    coconut, toasted

1 Cut the passionfruit in half and
scoop out the pulp. Strain, then
measure out 3 tablespoons of juice
and set aside. Add the seeds and pulp
to the remaining juice and set aside.
Put the egg yolks, ½ cup (125 g/4 oz)
of the sugar, lemon rind, lemon juice
and strained passionfruit juice in a
heatproof bowl. Place the bowl over
a pan of simmering water and, using
electric beaters, beat for 10 minutes,
or until thick and creamy. Remove
from the heat and transfer to a glass
bowl.
2 Sprinkle the gelatine over ½ cup
(125 ml/4 fl oz) water in a small bowl
and leave until spongy. Place the
bowl in a pan of just boiled water
(the water should come halfway up
the bowl) and stir until dissolved. Add

the gelatine to the mousse mixture
and mix well. Mix in the passionfruit
pulp and leave until cold, then gently
fold in the whipped cream.
3 Using electric beaters, whisk the
egg whites until soft peaks form
and gradually whisk in the remaining
sugar, beating until the sugar has
dissolved. Fold the egg whites into
the mousse mixture quickly and
lightly. Spoon into eight 1-cup (250 ml/
8 fl oz) ramekins or elegant stemmed
wine glasses, and refrigerate for
2 hours, or until set. Sprinkle with the
coconut just before serving.

NUTRITION PER SERVE
Protein 7 g; Fat 22 g; Carbohydrate 25 g;
Dietary Fibre 2.5 g; Cholesterol 185 mg;
1350 kJ (325 Cal)

Scoop the pulp out of the passionfruit and press
through a strainer.

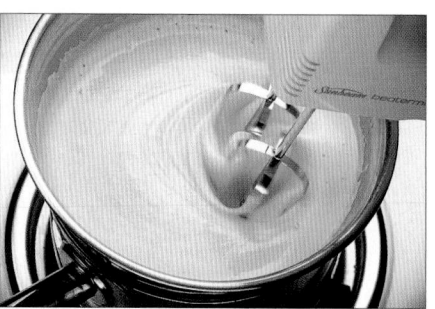

Beat the mixture over a pan of simmering water
until thick and creamy.

Lightly fold the whisked egg whites into the
mousse mixture.

PEAR AND ALMOND FLAN

**Preparation time: 15 minutes +
2 hours 30 minutes chilling**
Total cooking time: 1 hour 10 minutes
Serves 8

1¼ cups (155 g/5 oz) plain flour
90 g (3 oz) chilled butter, chopped
¼ cup (60 g/2 oz) caster sugar
2 egg yolks

FILLING
165 g (5½ oz) butter, softened
⅔ cup (160 g/5½ oz) caster sugar
3 eggs
1¼ cups (230 g/7½ oz) almond
    meal
1½ tablespoons plain flour
2 ripe pears

1 Grease a shallow 24 cm (9½ inch) round flan tin with a removable base. Place the flour, butter and sugar in a food processor and process until the mixture resembles breadcrumbs. Add the egg yolks and about 1 tablespoon of water until the mixture just comes together. Turn out onto a lightly floured surface and gather into a ball. Wrap in plastic wrap and refrigerate for 30 minutes. Preheat the oven to moderate 180°C (350°F/Gas 4).
2 Roll the pastry between baking paper dusted with flour until large enough to line the tin. Remove the baking paper, lift the pastry into the tin, and trim off any excess. Sparsely prick the bottom with a fork. Line with baking paper, fill with baking beads and bake for 10 minutes. Remove the beads and bake for 10 minutes.

3 To make the filling, mix the butter and sugar with electric beaters for 30 seconds (don't cream the mixture). Add the eggs one at a time, beating after each addition. Fold in the almond meal and flour and spread the filling smoothly over the cooled pastry base.
4 Peel and halve the pears lengthways and remove the cores. Cut the pears crossways into 3 mm (⅛ inch) slices. Separate the slices slightly, then place each half on top of the tart to form a cross. Bake for 50 minutes, or until the filling has set (the middle may still be a little soft). Cool in the tin, then chill for at least 2 hours before serving.

NUTRITION PER SERVE
Protein 7 g; Fat 30 g; Carbohydrate 48 g;
Dietary Fibre 2 g; Cholesterol 165 mg;
2085 kJ (500 Cal)

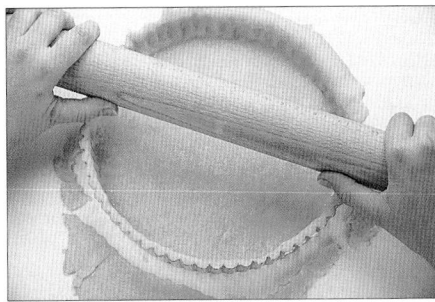

Trim off any excess pastry by rolling a rolling pin over the tin.

Fold in the almond meal and flour and mix until well combined.

Halve each pear lengthways and carefully remove the core.

GINGER AND LYCHEE JELLY

Preparation time: 10 minutes +
4 hours setting
Total cooking time: 5 minutes
Serves 6

565 g (1 lb 2 oz) can lychees
2 cups (500 ml/16 fl oz) clear apple
 juice (no added sugar)
⅓ cup (80 ml/2¾ fl oz) strained lime
 juice
2 tablespoons caster sugar
3 cm x 3 cm (1¼ inch x 1¼ inch) piece
 fresh ginger, peeled and thinly
 sliced
4 sheets gelatine (about 5 g/¼ oz)
fresh mint leaves, to garnish

1 Drain the syrup from the lychees
and reserve 1 cup (250 ml/8 fl oz)
of the syrup. Discard the remaining
syrup. Place the reserved syrup, apple
juice, lime juice, sugar and ginger in
a large saucepan. Bring to the boil,
then reduce the heat and simmer for
5 minutes. Strain into a heatproof
bowl.
2 Place the gelatine sheets in a large
bowl of cold water and soak for
2 minutes, or until they soften.
Squeeze out the excess water, then
add the gelatine to the syrup. Stir
until the gelatine has completely
dissolved. Allow to cool.
3 Pour 2 tablespoons of the jelly
mixture into each of six 150 ml
(5 fl oz) stemmed wine glasses, and
divide the lychees among the wine
glasses. Refrigerate the glasses until
the jelly has set. Spoon the remaining
jelly over the fruit and refrigerate
again until set. Before serving, garnish
with mint leaves.

NUTRITION PER SERVE
Protein 1 g; Fat 0 g; Carbohydrate 31 g;
Dietary Fibre 0.5 g; Cholesterol 0 mg;
530 kJ (125 Cal)

NOTE: Sprinkle 1 tablespoon slivered
almonds among the jelly, if desired.

After soaking, squeeze the sheets of gelatine to
remove any excess water.

Stir the gelatine sheets into the hot liquid until they
have dissolved.

Divide the lychees among the wine glasses,
gently dropping them into the jelly mixture.

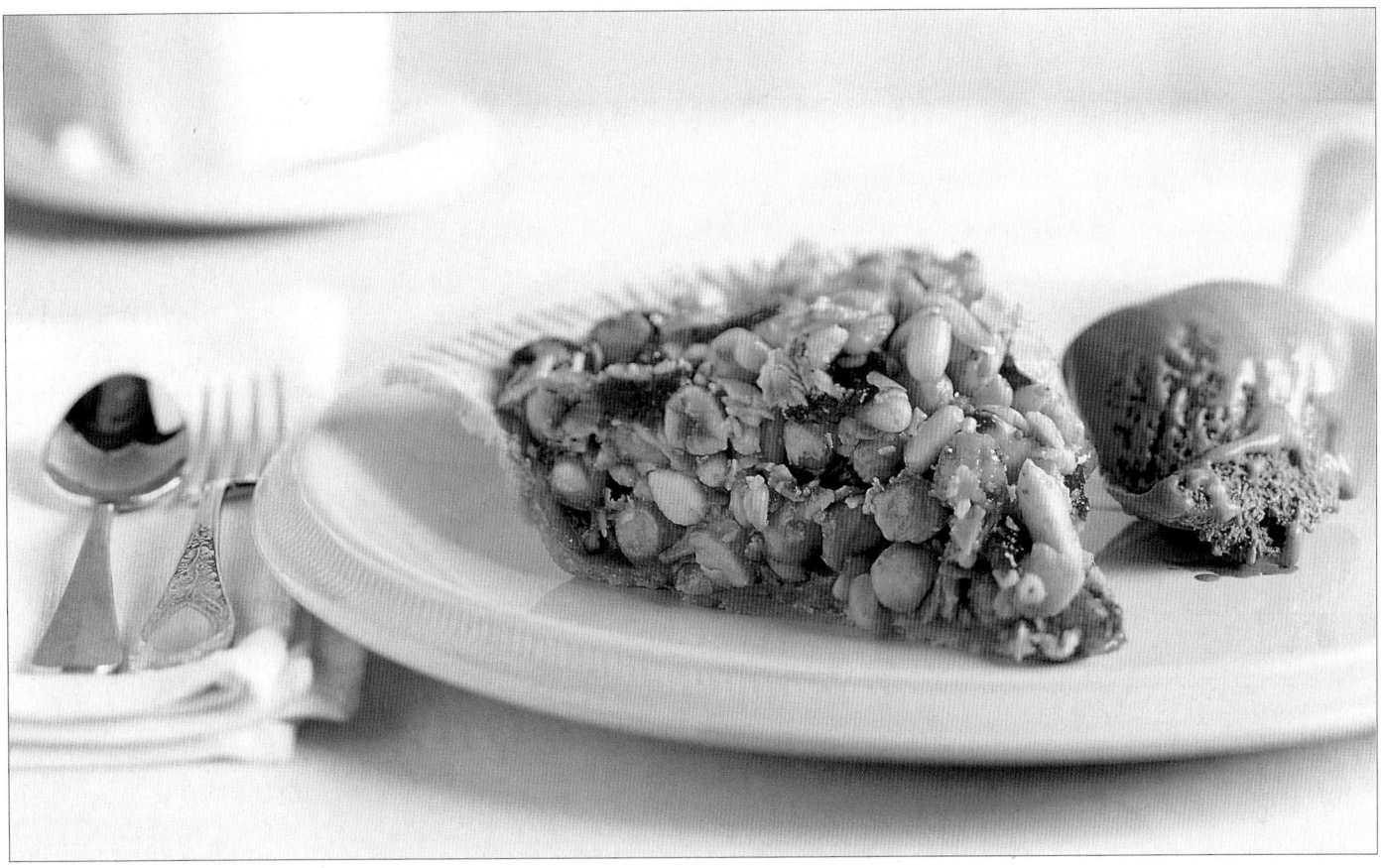

NUTTY FIG PIE

**Preparation time: 40 minutes +
 20 minutes refrigeration
Total cooking time: 1 hour
Serves 8**

375 g (12 oz) sweet shortcrust pastry
200 g (6½ oz) hazelnuts
100 g (3½ oz) pine nuts
100 g (3½ oz) flaked almonds
100 g (3½ oz) blanched almonds
150 ml (5 fl oz) cream
60 g (2 oz) unsalted butter
¼ cup (90 g/3 oz) honey
½ cup (90 g/3 oz) soft brown sugar
150 g (5 oz) dessert figs, quartered

1 Preheat the oven to 200°C (400°F/ Gas 6) and grease an 18 cm (7 inch) pie tin. Roll the pastry out between two sheets of baking paper until large enough to line the tin, trimming away the excess. Prick the base several times with a fork. Score the edge with a fork. Refrigerate for 20 minutes, then bake for 15 minutes, or until dry and lightly golden. Allow to cool.
2 Meanwhile, bake the hazelnuts on a baking tray for 8 minutes, or until the skins start to peel away. Tip into a tea towel and rub to remove the skins. Place the pine nuts, flaked almonds and blanched almonds on a baking tray and bake for 5–6 minutes, or until lightly golden.

3 Place the cream, butter, honey and brown sugar in a saucepan and stir over medium heat until the sugar dissolves and the butter melts. Remove from the heat and stir in the nuts and figs. Spoon into the pastry case and bake for 30 minutes. Remove and cool until firm before slicing.

NUTRITION PER SERVE
Protein 11 g; Fat 57 g; Carbohydrate 44 g; Dietary Fibre 5.5 g; Cholesterol 57 mg; 3030 kJ (725 cal)

Roll out the pastry until large enough to line the pie tin, letting the excess hang over the edge.

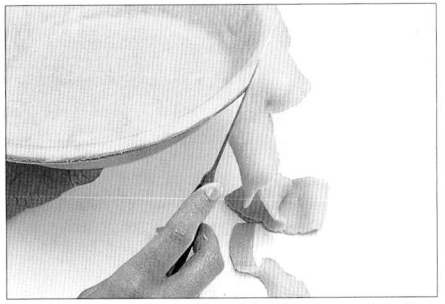

Use a small, sharp knife to trim the excess pastry from the edge of the dish.

Spoon the nut and fig filling into the pastry-lined pie tin.

CHOCOLATE FUDGE PECAN PIE

**Preparation time: 30 minutes +
40 minutes refrigeration + cooling
Total cooking time: 1 hour 20 minutes
Serves 6**

1¼ cups (150 g/5 oz) plain flour
2 tablespoons cocoa powder
2 tablespoons soft brown sugar
100 g (3½ oz) unsalted butter, chilled
and cubed
2–3 tablespoons iced water

FILLING
2 cups (200 g/6½ oz) pecans,
chopped
100 g (3½ oz) dark chocolate,
chopped
½ cup (90 g/3 oz) soft brown sugar
⅔ cup (170 ml/2¾ fl oz) corn
syrup
3 eggs, lightly beaten
2 teaspoons vanilla essence

1 Grease an 18 cm (7 inch) pie dish. Sift the flour, cocoa and sugar into a bowl and rub in the butter until the mixture resembles fine crumbs. Make a well, add the water and mix with a knife, adding more water if necessary.
2 Press the dough into a ball and refrigerate for 20 minutes. Roll out between two sheets of baking paper to fit the dish, trimming away the excess. Refrigerate for 20 minutes.
3 Preheat the oven to 180°C (350°F/Gas 4). Cover the pastry with baking paper and spread with a layer of baking beads or rice. Bake for 15 minutes. Remove the paper and beads and bake for 15–20 minutes, or until dry. Cool completely.
4 Put the dish on a tray. Spread the pecans and chocolate in the shell. Whisk the sugar, corn syrup, eggs and vanilla. Pour into the shell and bake for 45 minutes. Cool completely.

NUTRITION PER SERVE
Protein 11 g; Fat 45 g; Carbohydrate 82 g;
Dietary Fibre 4 g; Cholesterol 132 mg;
3240 kJ (775 cal)

Use a rolling pin to help line the pie dish with the chocolate pastry.

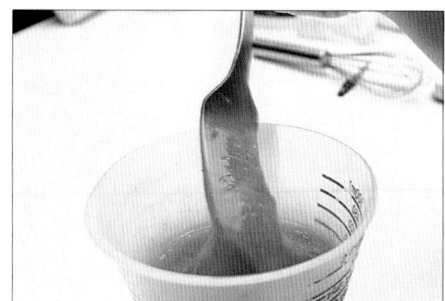
Whisk together the sugar, corn syrup, eggs and vanilla with a fork.

SPICED APPLE SPONGE

Preparation time: 15 minutes
Total cooking time: 45 minutes
Serves 4

850 g (1 lb 11 oz) Granny Smith
  apples
30 g (1 oz) butter
⅓ cup (40 g/1¼ oz) raisins
2 tablespoons lemon juice
4 cloves
1 cinnamon stick
pinch nutmeg
⅔ cup (160 g/5½ oz) caster sugar
2 eggs
finely grated zest of 1 lemon
¼ cup (30 g/1 oz) self-raising flour
¼ cup (30 g/1 oz) cornflour
sifted icing sugar, to serve

1 Preheat the oven to moderate 180°C (350°F/Gas 4). Peel, core and slice the apples into eighths. Melt the butter in a large frying pan, add the apple and cook, stirring occasionally, over high heat for 7 minutes, or until browned. Add the raisins, lemon juice, cloves, cinnamon, nutmeg, half the sugar and ½ cup (125 ml/4 fl oz) water. Bring to the boil, then lower the heat and simmer for 3 minutes, or until the apple is tender. Remove the cinnamon stick and cloves. Spoon the apple mixture into a deep 2 litre round ovenproof dish.
2 To make the sponge topping, beat the eggs, remaining sugar and lemon zest in a small bowl with electric beaters for 7–8 minutes, or until the mixture is light and creamy. Fold in the sifted flours with a metal spoon.

3 Spoon the sponge topping over the apples. Bake in the oven for 30 minutes, or until the sponge is well risen and golden. Dust with icing sugar before serving. Suggested accompaniments include ice cream, whipped cream, hot or cold custard, sweetened ricotta cheese, and spiced mascarpone.

NUTRITION PER SERVE
Protein 5.5 g; Fat 9 g; Carbohydrate 88 g; Dietary Fibre 5 g; Cholesterol 105 mg; 1833 kJ (438 Cal)

STORAGE TIME: The apple mixture can be prepared several hours ahead and reheated before spooning on the sponge topping. This dish is best eaten immediately.

Add the apple to the pan and cook until it is well browned.

Remove the cloves and cinnamon stick when the apple is tender.

Spread the sponge topping evenly over the apples before baking.

TIRAMISU

Preparation time: 20 minutes + overnight chilling
Total cooking time: Nil
Serves 8

1½ cups (375 ml/12 fl oz) strongly brewed espresso coffee
¾ cup (185 ml/6 fl oz) Kahlua or Tia Maria
500 g (1 lb) mascarpone
2 tablespoons caster sugar
½ cup (125 ml/4 fl oz) cream, lightly whipped
260 g (8 oz) thin sponge finger biscuits
¼ cup (30 g/1 oz) cocoa powder

1 Combine the coffee and ½ cup (125 ml/4 fl oz) of Kahlua or Tia Maria in a shallow dish.

2 Combine the mascarpone, sugar and remaining Kahlua or Tia Maria in a large bowl, then gently fold in the cream. Cover and refrigerate.

3 Quickly dip half the sponge finger biscuits in the coffee mixture (it is important to do this quickly so they do not go soggy), and place them in a single layer on the bottom of a 2 litre ceramic dish.

4 Spread half of the mascarpone mixture over the biscuits and dust liberally with half of the cocoa, using a fine sieve. Dunk the remaining biscuits in the coffee and lay them on top, then spread with the remaining mascarpone mixture. Dust with the remaining cocoa, then cover and refrigerate overnight to allow the flavours to combine and develop.

NUTRITION PER SERVE
Protein 9 g; Fat 26 g; Carbohydrate 64 g; Dietary Fibre 1 g; Cholesterol 82 mg; 2142 kJ (512 Cal)

NOTE: Tiramisu means 'pick-me-up' in Italian. Sometimes referred to as Italian trifle, tiramisu actually has a much lighter texture than trifle.

VARIATION: If you would prefer this as an alcohol-free dessert, you can omit the Kahlua or Tia Maria and use ¾ cup (185 ml/6 fl oz) more coffee to make up the loss of liquid.

Mix together the mascarpone, sugar and remaining Kahlua or Tia Maria.

Quickly dip half the biscuits in the coffee mixture and layer in the base of the dish.

Spoon half of the mascarpone mixture over the sponge finger biscuits.

Dust the top layer of the mascarpone mixture with finely sifted cocoa.

CHERRY PIE

**Preparation time: 30 minutes
+ refrigeration
Total cooking time: 1 hour
Serves 6**

500 g (1 lb) sweet shortcrust pastry
2 x 425 g (14 oz) cans seedless black
   cherries, drained well
⅓ cup (60 g/2 oz) soft brown sugar
1½ teaspoons ground cinnamon
1 teaspoon finely grated lemon rind
1 teaspoon finely grated orange rind
1–2 drops almond essence
¼ cup (25 g/¾ oz) ground almonds
1 egg, lightly beaten

1 Preheat the oven to moderately hot 190°C (375°F/Gas 5). Roll out two-thirds of the dough between two sheets of baking paper to form a circle large enough to fit a 22 cm (9 inch) (top) 20 cm (8 inch) (base) 2 cm (¾ inch) (deep) pie plate. Remove the top sheet of baking paper and invert the pastry into the pie plate. Cut away the excess pastry with a small sharp knife. Roll out the remaining pastry large enough to cover the pie. Refrigerate, covered in plastic wrap, for 20 minutes.
2 Place the cherries, sugar, cinnamon, rinds and almond essence in a bowl and mix to coat the cherries.
3 Line the pastry base with ground

almonds. Spoon in the filling, brush the pastry edges with beaten egg, and cover with the pastry lid. Use a fork to seal the edges of the pastry. Cut four slits in the top of the pie to allow steam to escape, then brush the pastry with beaten egg. Bake for 1 hour, or until the pastry is golden and the juices are bubbling through the slits in the pastry. Serve warm.

NUTRITION PER SERVE
Protein 7.5 g; Fat 24.5 g; Carbohydrate 61.5 g;
Dietary Fibre 4 g; Cholesterol 53.5 mg; 2055 kJ
(490 Cal)

Line the base of the pastry with a thin layer of ground almonds.

Spoon the cherry filling over the ground almonds in the pastry case.

Cover the pie with the lid, then use a fork to seal the edges.

BAKED APPLES

Preparation time: 30 minutes
Total cooking time: 50 minutes
Serves 4

4 Granny Smith apples
50 g (1¾ oz) dried apricots, finely
    chopped
50 g (1¾ oz) dates, finely chopped
1 tablespoon dry breadcrumbs
½ teaspoon ground cinnamon
1 tablespoon honey, warmed
2 teaspoons apricot jam, warmed
20 g (¾ oz) firm butter
ground nutmeg, to serve

1 Preheat the oven to moderate 180°C (350°F/Gas 4) and lightly grease an ovenproof dish.
2 Core the apples and, using a small sharp knife, run a small slit around the circumference of each apple (this will stop it splitting during baking).
3 Combine the dried apricots, dates, breadcrumbs, cinnamon, honey and jam in a bowl. Divide the mixture into four, and push it into the apples using two teaspoons or your fingers. Dot the top of each apple with the butter, and put the apples in the prepared dish.
4 Bake for about 45–50 minutes, or until the apples are tender all the way through—test with a skewer to be absolutely sure. Serve hot with cream or ice cream. Sprinkle some nutmeg over the top before serving.

NUTRITION PER SERVE
Protein 1 g; Fat 4 g; Carbohydrate 30 g;
Dietary Fibre 4 g; Cholesterol 13 mg;
685 kJ (165 Cal)

Carefully run a sharp knife around the circumference of each apple.

Push the mixture into each of the apples with teaspoons or your fingers.

APPLE SAGO PUDDING

Preparation time: 15 minutes
Total cooking time: 50 minutes
Serves 4

⅓ cup (90 g/3 oz) caster sugar
½ cup (100 g/3½ oz) sago
600 ml (20 fl oz) fat-reduced milk
⅓ cup (55 g/2 oz) sultanas
1 teaspoon vanilla essence
pinch ground nutmeg
¼ teaspoon ground cinnamon
2 eggs, lightly beaten

3 small ripe apples (about 250 g/8 oz),
    peeled, cored and very thinly sliced
1 tablespoon soft brown sugar

1 Preheat the oven to moderate
180°C (350°F/Gas 4). Grease a 1.5
litre ceramic soufflé dish. Place the
sugar, sago, milk, sultanas and ¼
teaspoon salt in a saucepan and heat,
stirring often. Bring to the boil, then
reduce the heat and simmer for 5
minutes.
2 Stir in the vanilla essence, nutmeg,
cinnamon, egg and the apple slices,
then pour into the prepared dish.

Sprinkle with the brown sugar and
bake for 45 minutes, or until set and
golden brown.

NUTRITION PER SERVE
Protein 9.5 g; Fat 5 g; Carbohydrate 70 g;
Dietary Fibre 2 g; Cholesterol 101 mg;
1495 kJ (355 Cal)

NOTE: If you prefer, you can use
skim milk instead of fat-reduced milk.

Bring the sugar, sago, milk, sultanas and salt to the boil, stirring frequently.

Stir the vanilla, ground spices, egg and apple slices into the milk mixture.

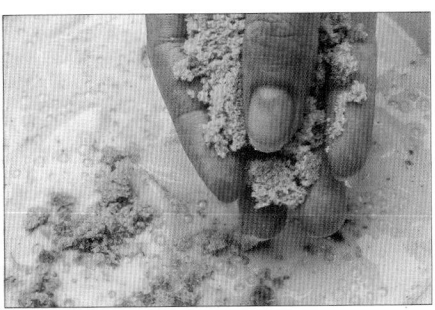

Sprinkle the surface of the pudding with the brown sugar.

BANANA CREAM PIE

**Preparation time: 25 minutes +
20 minutes refrigeration
Total cooking time: 30 minutes
Serves 6–8**

375 g (12 oz) shortcrust pastry
90 g (3 oz) dark chocolate chips
4 egg yolks
½ cup (125 g/4 oz) caster sugar
½ teaspoon vanilla essence
2 tablespoons custard powder
2 cups (500 ml/16 fl oz) milk
40 g (1¼ oz) unsalted butter, softened
1 teaspoon brandy or rum
3 large ripe bananas, thinly sliced
60 g (2 oz) dark chocolate, grated

1 Roll out the pastry between two sheets of baking paper to line an 18 cm (7 inch) pie tin, pressing it firmly into the side and trimming away the excess. Refrigerate for 20 minutes.
2 Preheat the oven to 190°C (375°F/ Gas 5). Line the pastry with baking paper and spread with baking beads or rice. Bake for 10 minutes, remove the paper and beads and bake for 10–12 minutes, until the pastry is dry and lightly golden.
3 While the pastry is still hot, place the chocolate chips in the base. Leave for 5 minutes to melt, then spread over the crust with the back of a spoon.
4 To make the filling, beat the egg yolks, sugar, vanilla and custard powder with electric beaters for 2–3 minutes, or until pale and thick. Bring the milk to boiling point in a small pan, then remove from the heat and gradually pour into the egg and sugar mixture, stirring well. Return to the pan and bring to the boil, stirring. Cook for 2 minutes, or until thickened. Remove from the heat and stir in the butter and brandy. Cool completely.
5 Arrange the banana over the chocolate, then pour the custard over the top. Refrigerate until ready to serve. Decorate with banana slices and the grated chocolate.

NUTRITION PER SERVE (8)
Protein 8 g; Fat 26 g; Carbohydrate 60 g;
Dietary Fibre 2 g; Cholesterol 124 mg;
2060 kJ (490 cal)

Beat the egg and sugar mixture until it is pale and thick.

Pour the custard into the pie shell over the banana slices.

CHERRY CLAFOUTIS (FRENCH BATTER PUDDING)

Preparation time: 15 minutes
Total cooking time: 40 minutes
Serves 6–8

500 g (1 lb) fresh cherries (see Hint)
¾ cup (90 g/3 oz) plain flour
2 eggs, lightly beaten
⅓ cup (90 g/3 oz) caster sugar
1 cup (250 ml/8 fl oz) milk
¼ cup (60 ml/2 fl oz) thick cream
50 g (1¾ oz) unsalted butter, melted
icing sugar, for dusting

1 Preheat the oven to moderate 180°C (350°F/Gas 4). Lightly brush a 1.5 litre ovenproof dish with melted butter.
2 Carefully pit the cherries, then spread into the dish in a single layer.
3 Sift the flour into a bowl, add the eggs and whisk until smooth. Add the sugar, milk, cream and butter, whisking until just combined, but being careful not to overbeat.
4 Pour the batter over the cherries and bake for 30–40 minutes, or until a skewer comes out clean when inserted into the centre. Remove from the oven and dust generously with icing sugar. Serve immediately.

NUTRITION PER SERVE (8)
Protein 4.5 g; Fat 11 g; Carbohydrate 23 g; Dietary Fibre 1.5 g; Cholesterol 75 mg; 855 kJ (204 Cal)

HINT: You can use a 720 g (1 lb 7 oz) jar of cherries. Make sure you thoroughly drain away the juice.

VARIATION: Blueberries, blackberries, raspberries, or small, well-flavoured strawberries can be used. A delicious version can be made using slices of poached pear.

Add the sugar, milk, cream and butter to the flour mixture and whisk well.

Carefully pour the batter into the dish over the single layer of cherries.

Cook until the batter is golden brown and nicely set. Test with a skewer.

PEAR AND PECAN PIE

Preparation time: 25 minutes +
  40 minutes refrigeration + cooling
Total cooking time: 50 minutes
Serves 6

PASTRY
1½ cups (185 g/6 oz) plain flour
75 g (2½ oz) unsalted butter, chilled
    and cubed
50 g (1½ oz) Copha (white vegetable
    shortening), chilled and cubed
1 teaspoon caster sugar
2–3 tablespoons iced water

40 g (1¼ oz) unsalted butter
½ cup (180 g/6 oz) golden syrup
2 tablespoons cornflour
¼ teaspoon ground ginger
½ teaspoon grated lemon rind
½ teaspoon mixed spice
4 pears, peeled, cored and thinly sliced
1 cup (100 g/3½ oz) pecans, chopped
1 tablespoon caster sugar
1 tablespoon ground pecans
1 tablespoon sugar
1 egg, lightly beaten

1 To make the pastry, sift the flour
and ¼ teaspoon salt into a large bowl
and rub in the butter and Copha with
your fingertips until the mixture
resembles fine breadcrumbs. Mix in
the sugar. Make a well, add almost all
the water and mix with a flat-bladed
knife, using a cutting action, until the
mixture comes together in beads,
adding more water if necessary.
2 Gather the dough together and lift
onto a lightly floured work surface.
Press into a ball and flatten slightly
into a disc. Cover in plastic wrap and
refrigerate for 20 minutes.

3 Preheat the oven to 200°C (400°F/
Gas 6) and heat a baking tray. Grease
an 18 cm (7 inch) pie dish. Roll out
two-thirds of the pastry between two
sheets of baking paper to line the
dish, trimming away the excess.
Cover and refrigerate for 20 minutes.
4 For the filling, heat the butter and
golden syrup in a saucepan over
medium heat for 2 minutes. Add the
cornflour, ginger, rind and mixed
spice and stir until smooth. Add the
pears, then stir in half the chopped
pecans and cook for 5 minutes, or
until the pear is tender. Cool
completely.
5 Combine the caster sugar and
remaining chopped pecans and
scatter over the pastry base. Add the
filling.
6 Combine the ground pecans and
sugar. Roll out the remaining pastry to
form a pie lid. Brush with beaten egg.
Cut long wide strips of paper and
arrange over the pie lid in straight
lines with wide gaps between. Scatter
the nut and sugar mixture over the
exposed pastry and roll lightly with
the rolling pin to embed them. Lift off
the paper strips, then position the lid
on the pie, pinching the edges down
to seal. Trim the rim.
7 Bake on the hot tray in the centre
of the oven for 20 minutes. Reduce
the oven to 180°C (350°F/Gas 4),
cover the top with foil and bake for
another 20 minutes. Cool in the tin.
Serve warm or cold.

NUTRITION PER SERVE
Protein 7 g; Fat 34 g; Carbohydrate 69 g;
Dietary Fibre 5 g; Cholesterol 62 mg;
2485 kJ (595 cal)

Peel the pears, remove the cores and cut them into thin slices.

Add the cornflour, ginger, lemon rind and mixed spice and stir until smooth.

Spoon the pear filling over the base of the pastry shell.

Scatter the nut and sugar mixture over the pastry top, so that it forms stripes.

Carefully remove the paper strips from the pastry top without dislodging the nut topping.

Position the deocorated lid on the pie and trim the edges neatly.

WALNUT PIE WITH CARAMEL SAUCE

Preparation time: 40 minutes + cooling
Total cooking time: 40 minutes
Serves 8

2 cups (250 g/8 oz) plain flour
180 g (6 oz) unsalted butter, chilled
    and cubed
⅓ cup (40 g/1¼ oz) icing sugar
1 egg yolk
3–4 tablespoons iced water
1 egg yolk, lightly beaten, to glaze
icing sugar and walnuts, to garnish

FILLING
2 eggs
210 g (7 oz) caster sugar
150 g (5 oz) walnuts, finely chopped

CARAMEL SAUCE
40 g (1¼ oz) unsalted butter
1¼ cups (230 g/7 oz) soft brown sugar
2 teaspoons vanilla essence
200 ml (6½ fl oz) cream

1 Sift the flour and ½ teaspoon salt into a large bowl and rub in the butter with your fingertips until the mixture resembles fine breadcrumbs. Mix in the icing sugar. Make a well, add the egg yolk and almost all the water and mix with a flat-bladed knife, using a cutting action, until the mixture comes together in beads.
2 Gather the dough together and lift onto a lightly floured work surface. Press together into a ball and flatten slightly into a disc. Wrap in plastic and refrigerate for 20 minutes.
3 Preheat the oven to 180°C (350°F/ Gas 4). Grease a fluted 36 x 11 cm (14 x 5 inch) pie tin. Beat the eggs and sugar with a spoon or whisk for 2 minutes. Stir in the walnuts.
4 Divide the dough into two portions, with one slightly larger than the other. Roll the larger portion out between two sheets of baking paper until large enough to line the base and sides of the pie tin. Refrigerate, covered in plastic wrap, while you roll out the remaining portion of pastry until it is large enough to cover the top of the tin.
5 Pour the walnut filling into the

pastry case, brush the rim with the egg yolk and position the lid in place, pressing the edges to seal. Trim the edge. Make a steam hole in the top. Brush with egg yolk and bake for 30–35 minutes. Leave to cool for at least 1 hour (do not refrigerate).
6 To make the caramel sauce, place the butter, sugar, vanilla and cream in a saucepan and cook, stirring, for

5 minutes, or until thick. Dust the pie with the icing sugar and sprinkle with walnuts. Drizzle with the caramel sauce to serve.

NUTRITION PER SERVE
Protein 9 g; Fat 50 g; Carbohydrate 84 g; Dietary Fibre 2.5 g; Cholesterol 193 mg; 3345 kJ (800 cal)

Pour the walnut filling into the pastry case and brush the rim with beaten egg yolk.

To make the caramel sauce, stir the butter, sugar, vanilla and cream over heat until thick.

BAKED CHEESECAKE

**Preparation time: 30 minutes + chilling +
overnight refrigeration**
Total cooking time: 1 hour
Serves 10

375 g (12 oz) plain sweet biscuits
180 g (6 oz) butter, melted

FILLING
500 g (1 lb) cream cheese
200 g (6½ oz) caster sugar
4 eggs
300 ml (10 fl oz) cream
2 tablespoons plain flour

1 teaspoon ground cinnamon
¼ teaspoon ground nutmeg
1 tablespoon lemon juice
2 teaspoons vanilla essence
ground nutmeg and cinnamon,
    to serve

1 Preheat the oven to moderate
180°C (350°F/Gas 4). Grease a 23 cm
(9 inch) shallow springform tin.
2 Put the biscuits in a food processor
and process until fine and crumbly.
Add the melted butter and process
for 10 seconds. Press into the base
and side of the tin, then refrigerate.
3 Beat the cream cheese and sugar
together until soft and creamy. Add

the eggs and cream and beat for
about 4 minutes. Fold in the flour,
cinnamon, nutmeg, juice and vanilla
essence. Pour the mixture into the
chilled crust. Bake for 1 hour, or until
firm. Let the cheesecake cool in the
oven, turned off with the door open
(to prevent sinking and cracking).
Refrigerate overnight. Sprinkle with
nutmeg and cinnamon. Delicious with
cream and strawberries.

NUTRITION PER SERVE
Protein 10 g; Fat 50 g; Carbohydrate 50 g;
Dietary Fibre 1 g; Cholesterol 215 mg;
2925 kJ (700 Cal)

Process the biscuits in a food processor until fine
and crumbly.

Press the biscuit mixture into the base and side
of the tin with a spoon.

Pour the mixture over the biscuit base and bake
for about an hour.

LEMON BERRY CHEESECAKE

Preparation time: 25 minutes + overnight refrigeration
Total cooking time: Nil
Serves 12

60 g (2 oz) plain biscuits, finely crushed
30 g (1 oz) butter, melted
300 g (10 oz) ricotta
2 tablespoons caster sugar
2 x 130 g (4¼ oz) tubs low-fat fromage frais or light vanilla Fruche
2 x 130 g (4½ oz) tubs low-fat lemon fromage frais or light lemon Fruche
2 teaspoons finely grated lemon rind
2 tablespoons fresh lemon juice
1 tablespoon gelatine
2 egg whites
250 g (8 oz) strawberries, halved

1 Lightly oil and line the base and sides of a 20 cm (8 inch) diameter springform tin with plastic wrap. Combine the biscuit crumbs and butter in a small bowl and press evenly over the base of the tin. Refrigerate while making the filling.
2 Combine the ricotta and sugar in a food processor until smooth. Add all the fromage frais, the lemon rind and juice and mix well. Put ¼ cup (60 ml/ 2 fl oz) water in a small bowl, sprinkle the gelatine in an even layer onto the surface and leave to go spongy. Bring a small pan of water to the boil, remove from the heat and put the gelatine bowl in the pan. The water should come halfway up the side of the bowl. Stir the gelatine until clear and dissolved, then cool slightly. Stir the gelatine mixture into the ricotta mixture, then transfer to a large bowl. Beat the egg whites until soft peaks form, then fold into the ricotta mixture.
3 Pour the mixture into the prepared tin and refrigerate for several hours or overnight, until set. Carefully remove from the tin by removing the side and gently easing the plastic from underneath. Decorate with the halved strawberries.

NUTRITION PER SERVE
Protein 5 g; Fat 6 g; Carbohydrate 8 g;
Dietary Fibre 1 g; Cholesterol 15 mg;
425 kJ (100 cal)

Combine the biscuit crumbs and butter, then press evenly over the base of the tin.

Gently fold the beaten egg white into the ricotta mixture with a large metal spoon.

FRUIT TARTS

Preparation time: 25 minutes +
  30 minutes refrigeration
Total cooking time: 20 minutes
Makes 8

1 cup (125 g/4 oz) plain flour
¼ cup (30 g/1 oz) custard powder
¼ cup (30 g/1 oz) icing sugar
40 g (1¼ oz) butter
2 tablespoons low-fat milk
2 x 130 g (4½ oz) tubs low-fat
   strawberry fromage frais or light
   strawberry Fruche
100 g (3½ oz) ricotta
strawberries, blueberries, kiwi fruit
2 tablespoons apricot jam

1 Grease eight 7 cm (2¾ inch) loose-based flan tins. Mix the flour, custard powder, icing sugar and butter in a food processor until fine crumbs form, then add enough of the milk to form a soft dough. Gather into a ball, wrap in plastic and chill for 30 minutes.
2 Preheat the oven to 200°C (400°F/ Gas 6). Divide the dough into eight portions and roll out to line the tins. Cover with paper and rice or dried beans. Bake for 10 minutes, remove the paper and rice and bake for another 10 minutes, or until golden. Cool and remove from the tins.
3 Mix the fromage frais and ricotta until smooth. Spread over the pastry bases and top with assorted fruit. Heat the jam until liquid, then brush over the fruit to glaze.

NUTRITION PER TART
Protein 3.5 g; Fat 8 g; Carbohydrate 20 g;
Dietary Fibre 1 g; Cholesterol 20 mg;
690 kJ (165 cal)

Add enough milk to the crumbly mixture to form a soft dough.

To blind bake, cover the pastry with baking paper and fill with uncooked rice or beans.

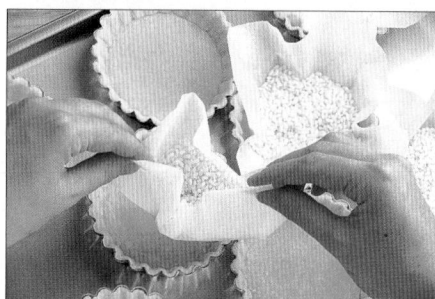

Remove the rice or beans and paper and return the pastry to the oven until golden.

PEARS POACHED IN DARK GRAPE JUICE

Preparation time: 15 minutes + overnight refrigeration
Total cooking time: 1 hour 20 minutes
Serves 6

6 beurre bosc (or any firm) pears
2 tablespoons lemon juice
2 cups (500 ml/8 fl oz) dark grape
   juice
2 cups (500 ml/8 fl oz) blackcurrant
   juice
2 tablespoons sweet sherry
4 cloves
350 g (11 oz) black grapes
1 cup (250 g/8 oz) low-fat natural
   yoghurt
½ teaspoon ground cinnamon
1 tablespoon honey

1 Core and peel the pears, leaving the stalks on. Place the pears, as you peel, in a bowl filled with cold water and the lemon juice, to prevent browning.
2 Put the grape and blackcurrant juices, sherry and cloves in a saucepan large enough to hold the pears. (The size of the saucepan will depend on the size of the pears.) Add the pears.
3 Bring the liquid to the boil, then reduce to a simmer. Cover and cook for 35–40 minutes, or until tender. Remove from the heat and leave the pears to cool in the syrup. Transfer the pears and syrup to a bowl and cover with plastic wrap. Refrigerate overnight.
4 To serve, strain the syrup into a pan, bring to the boil, then reduce to a simmer and cook for 40 minutes, or until reduced by about two-thirds.

Cool slightly, place a pear on each plate and pour syrup over the pears. Arrange the grapes next to the pears. Just before serving, mix the yoghurt, cinnamon and honey and spoon over the pears or serve on the side.

NUTRITION PER SERVE
Protein 4 g; Fat 0 g; Carbohydrate 95 g;
Dietary Fibre 4 g; Cholesterol 2 mg;
1630 kJ (390 cal)

Remove the core from the pears, then peel, leaving the stalks on.

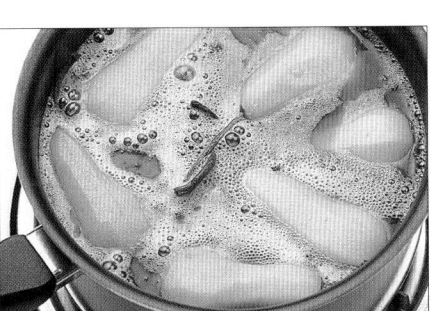

Bring the liquid to the boil, then reduce the heat and simmer until tender.

Mix together the yoghurt, cinnamon and honey just before serving the pears.

FIGS WITH ORANGE CREAM AND RAISINS

**Preparation time: 20 minutes +
  1 hour soaking**
Total cooking time: 12 minutes
Serves 4

1 cup (150 g/5 oz) raisins
75 ml (2½ fl oz) tawny port
1 tablespoon custard powder
1 cup (250 ml/8 fl oz) skim milk
1 tablespoon sugar
100 g (3½ oz) ricotta
200 g (6½ oz) low-fat fromage frais or
    light vanilla Fruche
rind strips and juice of 1 orange

1 teaspoon ground cinnamon
8 fresh figs

1 Soak the raisins in the tawny port for 1 hour, or until plumped up.
2 In a small saucepan, blend the custard powder with the skim milk, add the sugar and stir over low heat until dissolved. Increase the heat and stir until the custard boils and thickens. Remove from the heat immediately, pour into a small bowl and cover with plastic wrap. Cool completely. Transfer to an electric mixer, add the ricotta and fromage frais and beat until smooth.
3 Warm the raisin mixture with the orange rind, juice and cinnamon in a small pan. Cover and keep warm.
4 Starting from the top, cut the figs into quarters, slicing only two-thirds of the way down so they hold together. Transfer to ramekins or a serving dish or platter. Place 2 heaped tablespoons of the custard cream mixture into the centre of each fig, top with a spoonful of the warm raisin and orange mixture and serve at once.

NUTRITION PER SERVE
Protein 7 g; Fat 3.5 g; Carbohydrate 45 g;
Dietary Fibre 4.5 g; Cholesterol 15 mg;
1510 kJ (360 cal)

Stir the custard continuously until it boils and thickens, then remove from the heat.

When the custard has cooled, mix it with the ricotta and fromage frais.

Cut the figs into quarters, slicing only two-thirds of the way down.

CHOCOLATE TARTS

Preparation time: 30 minutes +
  20 minutes refrigeration
Total cooking time: 15 minutes
Makes 24

2 cups (250 g/8 oz) plain flour
2 tablespoons custard powder
125 g (4 oz) unsalted butter, chilled
    and cubed
1 egg yolk
2–3 tablespoons iced water

FILLING
250 g (8 oz) cream cheese, at room
    temperature
½ cup (125 g/4 oz) caster sugar
1 egg
125 g (4 oz) dark chocolate, melted
3 tablespoons ground almonds
100 g (3½ oz) white chocolate, melted

1 Preheat the oven to 180°C (350°F/ Gas 4). Lightly grease two 12-cup shallow patty tins. Mix the flour, custard powder and butter in a food processor for 30 seconds, or until fine and crumbly. Add the egg yolk and almost all of the water and process for 20 seconds or until the mixture just comes together, adding the rest of the water if necessary. Turn out onto a lightly floured surface and gather into a smooth ball. Wrap in plastic and refrigerate for 20 minutes.

2 Divide the dough in two; wrap one portion and set aside. Roll the other half between two sheets of baking paper until 3 mm (⅛ inch) thick. Cut rounds with a 7 cm (2¾ inch) fluted cutter to line the tins. Repeat with the other portion of pastry. Refrigerate the trays while preparing the filling.

3 Beat the cream cheese and sugar until light and creamy. Add the egg and cooled melted chocolate. Beat until no streaks are visible. Stir in the almonds. Spoon into the pastry cases. Bake for 15 minutes or until just beginning to firm (the filling will set on standing.) Cool on a rack. Drizzle with white chocolate and leave to set.

NUTRITION PER TART
Protein 3 g; Fat 12 g; Carbohydrate 20 g;
Dietary Fibre 1 g; Cholesterol 40 mg;
827 kJ (200 cal)

Process the mixture for 30 seconds, or until it is fine and crumbly.

Cut out pastry rounds with a fluted pastry cutter and use to line the patty tins.

Spoon the chocolate filling into the pastry bases and then bake until just firm.

FRUIT JELLIES

Preparation time: 20 minutes +
  refrigeration
Total cooking time: Nil
Serves 4

4 teaspoons gelatine
2 cups (500 ml/16 fl oz) cranberry and
  raspberry juice
330 g (11 oz) mixed berries, fresh or
  frozen

1 Sprinkle the gelatine in an even layer onto 3 tablespoons of the juice, in a small bowl, and leave to go spongy. Bring a small pan of water to the boil, remove from the heat and place the bowl in the pan. The water should come halfway up the side of the bowl. Stir the gelatine until clear and dissolved. Cool slightly and mix with the rest of the juice.

2 Rinse four ¾ cup (185 ml/6 fl oz) moulds with water (wet moulds make it easier when unmoulding) and pour 2 cm (¾ inch) of the juice into each. Refrigerate until set. Meanwhile, if the fruit is frozen, defrost it and add any liquid to the remaining juice. When the bottom layer of jelly has set, divide the fruit among the moulds (reserving a few berries to garnish) and divide the rest of the juice among the moulds, pouring it over the fruit. Refrigerate until set.

3 To turn out the jellies, hold each mould in a hot, damp tea towel and turn out onto a plate. Ease away the edge of the jelly with your finger to break the seal. (If you turn the jellies onto a damp plate you will be able to move them around, otherwise they will stick.) Garnish with berries.

NUTRITION PER SERVE
Protein 3 g; Fat 0 g; Carbohydrate 25 g;
Dietary Fibre 1.5 g; Cholesterol 0 mg;
420 kJ (100 cal)

Lower the gelatine bowl into the water and stir the gelatine until dissolved.

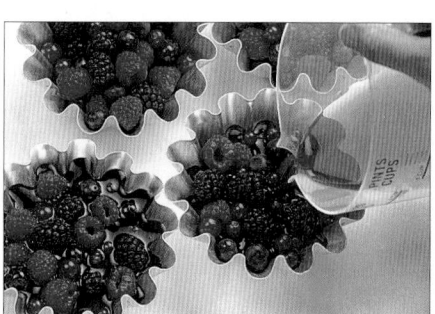

Divide the fruit among the moulds and pour in the rest of the juice.

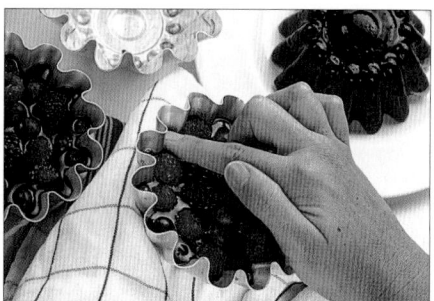

Use your finger to ease away the edge of the jelly to break the seal.

BRAMBLE PIE

**Preparation time: 30 minutes +
  30 minutes refrigeration
Total cooking time: 40 minutes
Serves 4–6**

1 cup (125 g/4 oz) self-raising flour
1 cup (125 g/4 oz) plain flour
125 g (4 oz) unsalted butter, chilled
    and cubed
2 tablespoons caster sugar
1 egg, lightly beaten
3–4 tablespoons milk

FILLING
2 tablespoons cornflour
2–4 tablespoons caster sugar, to taste
1 teaspoon grated orange rind
1 tablespoon orange juice
600 g (1¼ lb) brambles (see NOTE)
1 egg yolk, mixed with 1 teaspoon
    water, to glaze

1 Mix the flours, butter and sugar in a
food processor for 30 seconds or until
the mixture is fine and crumbly. Add
the egg and almost all the milk;
process for another 15 seconds or until
the mixture comes together, adding
more milk if needed. Turn onto a
lightly floured surface and gather into
a ball. Refrigerate for 30 minutes.
2 To make the filling, put the
cornflour, caster sugar, orange rind
and juice in a pan and mix well. Add
half the brambles and stir over low
heat for 5 minutes or until the mixture
boils and thickens. Leave to cool,
then add the remaining brambles.
Pour into a 750 ml (24 fl oz) pie dish.
3 Preheat the oven to 180°C (350°F/
Gas 4). Divide the pastry dough in
half and roll out one half until large
enough to cover the dish, trimming
away the excess. Roll out the other
half and, using heart-shaped pastry
cutters of various sizes, cut out
enough hearts to cover the pie top.
Brush the pie top with egg glaze.
Bake for 35 minutes or until golden
brown.

NUTRITION PER SERVE (6)
Protein 8 g; Fat 20 g; Carbohydrate 65 g;
Dietary Fibre 7 g; Cholesterol 115 mg;
1960 kJ (470 cal)

NOTE: Brambles include any creeping
stem berries, such as boysenberries,
blackberries, loganberries and
youngberries. Use just one variety or a
combination. You could use frozen or
canned berries if you drain them well.

When the mixture has thickened, add the
remaining brambles to the pan and stir.

Use small heart-shaped cutters to make shapes
to decorate the top of the pie.

STRAWBERRY AND BANANA ICE

Preparation time: 10 minutes + freezing
Total cooking time: Nil
Serves 4

300 g (10 oz) silken tofu, chopped
250 g (8 oz) strawberries, chopped
2 ripe bananas, chopped
¼ cup (60 g/2 oz) caster sugar

1 Blend the silken tofu, strawberries, banana and caster sugar in a blender or food processor, until smooth.
2 Pour the mixture into a shallow cake tin and freeze until almost frozen. Remove from the freezer and break up roughly with a fork or a spoon, then transfer to a large bowl and beat until it has a smooth texture. Pour the mixture evenly into a 15 x 25 cm (6 x 10 inch) loaf tin, cover and freeze again, until quite firm.
3 Alternatively, freeze the blended mixture in an ice cream machine until thick and creamy, then store in a covered container in the freezer.
4 Transfer to the refrigerator for about 30 minutes before serving to allow the ice to soften slightly.

NUTRITION PER SERVE
Protein 7 g; Fat 3 g; Carbohydrate 30 g;
Dietary Fibre 3 g; Cholesterol 0 mg;
710 kJ (170 cal)

Blend the tofu, strawberries, banana and caster sugar until smooth.

When partially frozen, use a fork or spoon to break up the mixture.

Transfer the chopped mixture to a bowl and beat until smooth.

PASSIONFRUIT BAVAROIS

Preparation time: 10 minutes
+ overnight refrigeration
Total cooking time: Nil
Serves 8

2 x 170 g (5½ oz) cans passionfruit in syrup
300 g (10 oz) silken tofu, chopped
600 ml (20 fl oz) buttermilk
2 tablespoons caster sugar
1 teaspoon vanilla essence
6 teaspoons gelatine
¾ cup (185 ml/6 fl oz) passionfruit pulp

1 Push the passionfruit in syrup through a sieve. Discard the seeds. Combine the strained syrup with the tofu, buttermilk, caster sugar and vanilla in a blender. Blend for 90 seconds on high, to mix thoroughly. Leave in the blender.
2 Put ⅓ cup (80 ml/2¾ fl oz) water in a small bowl and put the bowl in a slightly larger bowl of boiling water. Sprinkle the gelatine onto the water in the small bowl and stir until dissolved. Leave to cool.
3 Place eight 200 ml (6½ fl oz) dariole moulds in a baking dish. Add the gelatine to the blender and mix on high for 1 minute. Pour into the moulds, cover the dish with plastic wrap and refrigerate overnight.
4 When ready to serve, carefully run a spatula around the edge of each mould and dip the bases into hot water for 2 seconds to make removal easier. Place each on a plate and spoon the passionfruit pulp around the bases. Serve, topped with a few halved strawberries.

NUTRITION PER SERVE
Protein 8 g; Fat 2.5 g; Carbohydrate 10 g;
Dietary Fibre 10 g; Cholesterol 3 mg;
455 kJ (110 cal)

Blend the strained passionfruit syrup, tofu, buttermilk, sugar and vanilla.

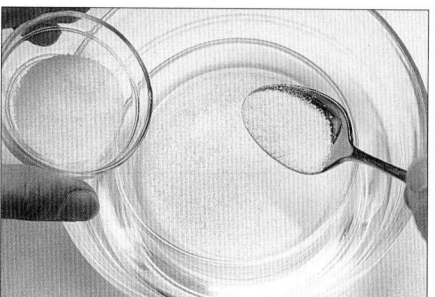

Sprinkle the gelatine over the surface of the water in the small bowl.

To remove, run a spatula around the edge and dip the base in hot water.

PASSIONFRUIT TART

Preparation time: 25 minutes +
  30 minutes refrigeration
Total cooking time: 1 hour
Serves 8

¾ cup (90 g/3 oz) plain flour
2 tablespoons icing sugar
2 tablespoons custard powder
30 g (1 oz) butter
3 tablespoons light evaporated milk

FILLING
½ cup (125 g/4 oz) ricotta
1 teaspoon vanilla essence
¼ cup (30 g/1 oz) icing sugar
2 eggs, lightly beaten
4 tablespoons passionfruit pulp
   (about 8 passionfruit)
¾ cup (185 ml/6 fl oz) light evaporated
   milk

1 Preheat the oven to 200°C (400°F/
Gas 6). Lightly spray a 22 cm (9 inch)
loose-based flan tin with oil. Sift the
flour, icing sugar and custard powder
into a bowl and rub in the butter until
crumbs form. Add enough evaporated
milk to form a soft dough. Bring
together on a floured surface until just
smooth. Gather into a ball, wrap in
plastic and chill for 15 minutes.
2 Roll the pastry out on a floured
surface to fit the tin, then refrigerate
for 15 minutes. Cover with baking
paper and fill with rice or dried
beans. Bake for 10 minutes, remove
the rice or beans and paper and bake
for another 5–8 minutes, or until
golden. Allow to cool. Reduce the
oven to warm 160°C (315°F/Gas 2–3).
3 Beat the ricotta with the vanilla
essence and icing sugar until smooth.
Add the eggs, passionfruit pulp

and milk, then beat well. Put the tin
with the pastry case on a baking tray
and pour in the filling. Bake for
40 minutes, or until set. Cool in the
tin. Dust with icing sugar to serve.

NUTRITION PER SERVE
Protein 8 g; Fat 6.5 g; Carbohydrate 25 g;
Dietary Fibre 3 g; Cholesterol 65 mg;
750 kJ (180 cal)

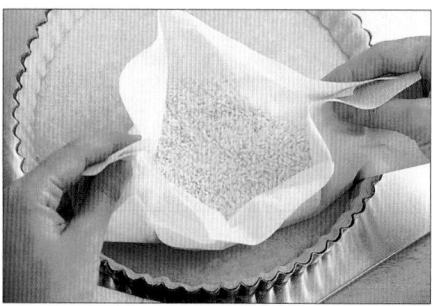

Remove the baking paper and rice or beans and
blind bake the pastry case again.

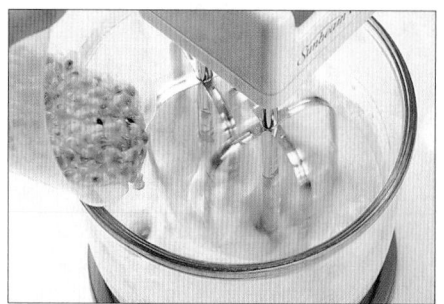

When the ricotta mixture is smooth, add the
eggs, passionfruit pulp and milk.

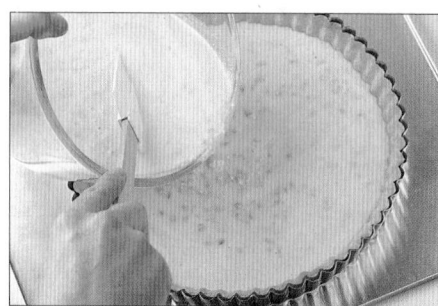

Put the tin on a baking tray to catch any drips
and gently pour in the filling.

922

LEMON GRANITA

Preparation time: 15 minutes + 2 hours
  freezing
Total cooking time: 5 minutes
Serves 6

1¼ cups (315 ml/10 fl oz) lemon juice
1 tablespoon lemon zest
200 g (6½ oz) caster sugar

1 Place the lemon juice, lemon zest and caster sugar in a small saucepan and stir over low heat for 5 minutes, or until the sugar is dissolved. Remove from the heat and leave to cool.
2 Add 2 cups (500 ml/16 fl oz) water to the juice mixture and mix together well. Pour the mixture into a shallow 30 x 20 cm (12 x 8 inch) metal container and place in the freezer until the mixture is beginning to freeze around the edges. Scrape the frozen sections back into the mixture with a fork. Repeat every 30 minutes until the mixture has even-size ice crystals. Beat the mixture with a fork just before serving. To serve, spoon the lemon granita into six chilled glasses.

NUTRITION PER SERVE
Protein 0 g; Fat 0 g; Carbohydrate 35 g;
Dietary Fibre 0 g; Cholesterol 0 mg;
592 kJ (140 cal)

Stir the juice, zest and sugar over low heat until the sugar has dissolved.

Scrape the frozen edges of the mixture back into the centre.

Beat the granita mixture with a fork just prior to serving to break up the crystals.

CREAMY LIME TART

**Preparation time: 30 minutes +
20 minutes refrigeration**
Total cooking time: 1 hour
Serves 12

1¼ cups (155 g/5 oz) plain flour
½ cup (95 g/3 oz) ground almonds
90 g (3 oz) butter, chopped

FILLING
6 egg yolks
½ cup (125 g/4 oz) caster sugar
100 g (3½ oz) butter, melted
⅓ cup (80 ml/2¾ fl oz) lime juice
2 teaspoons finely grated lime rind
2 teaspoons gelatine
½ cup (125 ml/4 fl oz) cream, whipped
½ cup (125 g/4 oz) sugar
rind of 4 limes, finely shredded

1 Preheat the oven to 180°C (350°F/ Gas 4). Sift the flour into a large bowl and add the almonds and butter. Rub in the butter until fine and crumbly. Add 1–2 tablespoons cold water and mix to a firm dough, adding more if necessary. Turn out onto a lightly floured surface and roll out to fit a 23 cm (9 inch) fluted flan tin. Trim the edge and refrigerate for 20 minutes.
2 Line with baking paper and beads or dried beans or rice and bake for 20 minutes. Remove the paper and beads and bake the pastry shell for a further 20 minutes, or until lightly golden. Cool completely.
3 To make the filling, put the egg yolks, sugar, butter, lime juice and rind in a heatproof bowl. Whisk together to dissolve the sugar. Place the bowl over a pan of simmering water and stir constantly for 15 minutes, or until thickened. Leave to cool slightly.

4 Put the gelatine and 1 tablespoon water in a small bowl. Leave until spongy, then stir until dissolved. Stir into the lime curd. Cool to room temperature, stirring occasionally.
5 Fold the cream through the lime curd and pour into the pastry case. Refrigerate for 2–3 hours until set, removing 15 minutes before serving. Put the sugar in a small pan with 3 tablespoons water. Stir without boiling until the sugar has completely dissolved. Bring to the boil, add the lime rind and simmer for 3 minutes. Remove the rind and dry on a rack then use to decorate the tart.

NUTRITION PER SERVE
Protein 4 g; Fat 21 g; Carbohydrate 32 g;
Dietary Fibre 1 g; Cholesterol 144 mg;
1391 kJ (332 cal)

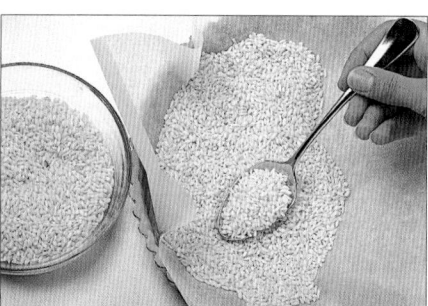
Blind bake the pastry case, filled with baking paper and baking beads or dried beans.

Mix the gelatine with the water and then stir into the lime curd.

To make the glazed lime rind, simmer the lime for 3 minutes in sugar syrup, then drain on a rack.

STRAWBERRY TRIFLE

**Preparation time: 20 minutes +
 4 hours refrigeration**
Total cooking time: Nil
Serves 8

2 x 85 g (3 oz) packets red jelly crystals
1 cup (250 ml/8 fl oz) brandy or rum
1 cup (250 ml/8 fl oz) milk
2 x 250 g (8 oz) packets thin sponge
  finger biscuits
500 g (1 lb) strawberries, sliced
750 ml (24 fl oz) carton custard

1¼ cups (315 ml/10 fl oz) cream,
  whipped

1 Mix the jelly crystals with 1¾ cups
(440 ml/14 fl oz) of boiling water and
stir to dissolve. Pour into a shallow
tin and refrigerate until the jelly has
just set but is not firm.
2 Combine the brandy and milk in a
dish. Dip half the biscuits in the
brandy mixture then place in a single
layer in a 3-litre glass or ceramic dish.
Spoon half the jelly over the biscuits.
Scatter with half the strawberries and
then half of the custard.

3 Dip the remaining sponge fingers
in the brandy mixture and place
evenly over the custard, followed by
the remaining jelly and custard.
Spread the whipped cream evenly
over the custard and top with the
remaining strawberries. Cover and
refrigerate for 4 hours before serving.

NUTRITION PER SERVE
Protein 13 g; Fat 24 g; Carbohydrate 75 g;
Dietary Fibre 2 g; Cholesterol 165 mg;
2570 kJ (615 cal)

Using a small sharp knife, hull the strawberries
and cut into slices.

Spoon half the jelly over the biscuits before
scattering on half the strawberries.

Dip the remaining biscuits in the brandy mixture
and layer evenly over the custard.

CHOCOLATE MOUSSE FLAN

Preparation time: 35 minutes
Total cooking time: 5 minutes
Serves 10

250 g (8 oz) plain chocolate biscuits,
    finely crushed
125 g (4 oz) butter, melted

FILLING
200 g (6½ oz) dark cooking chocolate,
    chopped
2 tablespoons cream
2 egg yolks
2 teaspoons gelatine
⅔ cup cream (170 ml/5½ fl oz), extra,
    whipped
2 egg whites

TOPPING
1½ teaspoons instant coffee
1 cup (250 ml/8 fl oz) cream
1 tablespoon caster sugar
cocoa powder, for dusting

1 Brush a 28 cm (11 inch) round fluted flan tin with melted butter or oil. Line the base with paper. Mix the biscuit crumbs and butter and press into the tin. Refrigerate until firm.
2 To make the filling, put the chocolate and cream in a small pan. Stir over low heat until smooth. Cool slightly, then stir in the yolks. Sprinkle the gelatine over 1 tablespoon water in a small bowl and leave until spongy, then stir. Cool slightly and stir into the filling. Fold in the whipped cream.
3 Beat the egg whites until soft peaks form. Fold into the filling and spread over the biscuit base. Refrigerate until set. Just before serving, remove from the tin and spread with the topping.
4 To make the topping, dissolve the coffee in 3 teaspoons water. Stir in the cream and sugar. Beat until soft peaks form, then spread over the flan. Dust with sifted cocoa powder to serve.

NUTRITION PER SERVE
Protein 6 g; Fat 37 g; Carbohydrate 32 g;
Dietary Fibre 1 g; Cholesterol 158 mg;
1983 kJ (474 cal)

Mix together the biscuit crumbs and melted butter and press into the tin.

Add the egg yolks to the cooled chocolate and cream mixture.

Beat the egg whites until soft peaks form and then fold into the filling.

Just before you are ready to serve, spread the topping over the flan.

COCONUT LIME ICE CREAM

**Preparation time: 10 minutes +
  30 minutes freezing
Total cooking time: Nil
Serves 4**

¼ cup (30 g/1 oz) desiccated coconut
1½ tablespoons grated lime rind
⅓ cup (80 ml/2¾ fl oz) lime
    juice
4 tablespoons coconut milk
    powder
1 litre good-quality vanilla ice cream,
    softened
coconut macaroon biscuits,
    to serve

1 Put the coconut, lime rind, lime juice and coconut milk powder in a bowl and mix together well.
2 Add to the ice cream and fold through with a large metal spoon until evenly incorporated. Work quickly so that the ice cream does not melt. Return the ice cream to the

freezer and freeze for 30 minutes to firm. Serve in glasses with coconut macaroons.

NUTRITION PER SERVE
Protein 5 g; Fat 19.5 g; Carbohydrate 19 g;
Dietary Fibre 1.5 g; Cholesterol 30 mg;
1230 kJ (293 cal)

Mix together the desiccated coconut, lime rind, lime juice and coconut milk powder.

Add the coconut mixture to the ice cream and fold in with a large metal spoon.

ALMOND AND PEAR POUCHES

Preparation time: 45 minutes +
10 minutes standing
Total cooking time: 40 minutes
Makes 4

4 beurre bosc (or any firm) pears
¼ cup (60 ml/2 fl oz) white wine
¼ cup (60 g/2 oz) caster sugar
1 cinnamon stick
2 cloves
1 vanilla bean
4 dates, roughly chopped
2 tablespoons sultanas
⅔ cup (85 g/3 oz) plain flour
1 egg, lightly beaten
1 cup (250 ml/8 fl oz) skim milk
2 tablespoons ground almonds
1 tablespoon soft brown sugar
½ teaspoon ground cinnamon
2 teaspoons flaked almonds
icing sugar, for dusting

STRAWBERRY SAUCE
125 g (4 oz) strawberries, chopped
1 teaspoon caster sugar
2 tablespoons orange juice

1 Remove the cores of the pears through the base using a melon baller, then peel. Combine 2 cups (500 ml/16 fl oz) water with the wine, sugar, cinnamon stick and cloves in a pan that is just large enough to fit the pears. Split the vanilla bean in half lengthways and scrape the seeds out. Add to the pan with the vanilla pod and stir over medium heat until the sugar has dissolved.
2 Add the pears to the pan and simmer, covered, for 20 minutes, or until just soft when tested with a skewer. Remove from the heat and allow to cool in the syrup. Drain and stand the pears on paper towels. Fill the base of each with the combined dates and sultanas.
3 To make the crepes, sift the flour into a bowl, gradually beat in the combined egg and milk, beating until smooth. Strain into a jug and set aside for 10 minutes.
4 Preheat the oven to moderately hot 200°C (400°F/Gas 6). Lightly oil a 24 cm (9½ inch) non-stick pan with oil spray, heat the pan and pour in a quarter of the batter, swirling to cover the base of the pan. Cook until lightly browned, turn and brown the other side. Remove and repeat with the remaining mixture.
5 Place the crepes on a work bench, place a quarter of the combined ground almonds, brown sugar and cinnamon in the centre of each and top with a pear. Gather the crepes around the pears and tie with string. Sprinkle with the flaked almonds. Bake on a lightly oiled baking tray for 5 minutes, or until the almonds and the edges of the crepes are golden and the pears just warm. Discard the string.
6 To make the strawberry sauce, blend the strawberries, sugar and orange juice in a blender until smooth and then strain.
7 Dust the pear pouches with a little icing sugar and serve with strawberry sauce. For a special effect, you can tie a piece of raffia or ribbon around each pouch before serving.

NUTRITION PER SERVE
Protein 9.5 g; Fat 7 g; Carbohydrate 80 g;
Dietary Fibre 7 g; Cholesterol 45 mg;
1740 kJ (415 cal)

Use a melon baller to remove the cores from the pears through the bases.

Split the vanilla bean lengthways, then scrape the seeds out with a knife.

Combine the dates and sultanas and fill the base of each pear.

Heat the pan and pour in a quarter of the batter, swirling to cover the base.

Put the ground almonds, sugar and cinnamon mix on the crepes.

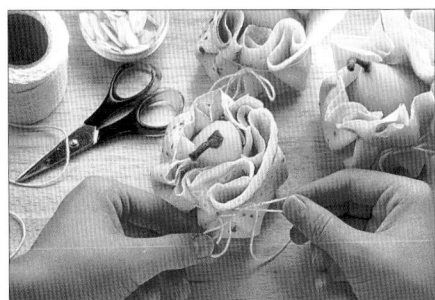

Gather the crepes around the pears and tie together with string.

CITRUS TART

Preparation time: 1 hour + 30 minutes refrigeration
Total cooking time: 1 hour 45 minutes
Serves 8

1 cup (125 g/4 oz) plain flour
75 g (2½ oz) unsalted butter, softened
1 egg yolk
2 tablespoons icing sugar, sifted

FILLING
3 eggs
2 egg yolks
¾ cup (185 g/6 oz) caster sugar
½ cup (125 ml/4 fl oz) cream
¾ cup (185 ml/6 fl oz) lemon juice
1½ tablespoons finely grated lemon rind
2 small lemons
⅔ cup (160 g/5½ oz) sugar

1 To make the pastry, sift the flour and a pinch of salt into a large bowl. Make a well in the centre and add the butter, egg yolk and icing sugar. Work together the butter, yolk and sugar with your fingertips, then slowly incorporate the flour. Bring together into a ball—you may need to add a few drops of iced water. Flatten the ball slightly, wrap in plastic and refrigerate for 20 minutes.
2 Preheat the oven to 200°C (400°F/ Gas 6). Lightly grease a shallow 21 cm (8 inch) loose-bottomed flan tin.
3 Roll the pastry out between two sheets of baking paper to about 3 mm (⅛ inch) thick to fit the tin. Trim away the excess pastry and refrigerate the tin for 10 minutes. Line the pastry with baking paper, spread with a layer of baking beads or rice and bake for 10 minutes, or until cooked.

Remove the paper and beads and bake for 6–8 minutes, or until the pastry is lightly golden and dry. Leave to cool.
4 Reduce the oven to 150°C (300°F/ Gas 2). Whisk the eggs, yolks and sugar together, add the cream and juice and mix well. Strain into a jug and add the rind. Place the tin on a baking sheet on the middle shelf of the oven and carefully pour in the filling. Bake for 40 minutes, or until just set—the filling will wobble in the middle when the tin is firmly tapped. Cool before removing from the tin.

5 Wash and scrub the lemons well. Slice very thinly. Combine the sugar and 200 ml (6½ fl oz) water in a small frying pan and stir over low heat until the sugar has dissolved. Add the lemon slices and simmer over low heat for 40 minutes, or until the peel is very tender and the pith looks transparent. Lift out of the syrup and drain on baking paper. Arrange over the top of the tart.

NUTRITION PER SERVE
Protein 6 g; Fat 18 g; Carbohydrate 60 g; Dietary Fibre 1 g; Cholesterol 180 mg; 1766 kJ (422 cal)

Work the butter, yolk and sugar together, then slowly incorporate the flour.

Bake the tart until the citrus filling is just set—it should still wobble when you tap the tin.

Simmer the lemon peel until it is very tender and the pith is transparent.

APPLE STRUDELS

Preparation time: 20 minutes
Total cooking time: 30 minutes
Serves 8

4 green cooking apples
30 g (1 oz) butter
2 tablespoons orange juice
1 tablespoon honey
3 tablespoons sugar
½ cup (90 g/3 oz) sultanas
2 sheets puff pastry
3 tablespoons ground almonds
1 egg, lightly beaten
2 tablespoons soft brown sugar
1 teaspoon ground cinnamon

1 Preheat the oven to 220°C (425°F/ Gas 7). Lightly grease two oven trays. Peel, core and thinly slice the apples. Heat the butter in a pan and cook the apples for 2 minutes until lightly golden. Add the orange juice, honey, sugar and sultanas and stir until the sugar dissolves and the apples are just tender. Leave to cool completely.
2 Place a sheet of pastry on a flat work surface. Fold in half and make small cuts in the folded edge of pastry at 2 cm (¾ inch) intervals. Open out and sprinkle with half of the ground almonds. Drain the apple and place half of the apple in the centre of the pastry. Brush the edges with egg and fold together, pressing firmly.

3 Place the strudel on the tray, seam-side down. Brush with egg and sprinkle with half of the combined sugar and cinnamon. Make another strudel with the other sheet of pastry and remaining apple filling. Bake for 20–25 minutes or until the pastry is golden and crisp.

NUTRITION PER SERVE
Protein 5 g; Fat 18 g; Carbohydrate 45 g; Dietary Fibre 4 g; Cholesterol 42 mg; 1412 kJ (337 cal)

VARIATION: Many types of fruit or canned fruit, such as pears, cherries or apricots, can be used for strudel.

Stir the fruit over heat until the sugar has dissolved and the apple is tender.

Make small cuts in the folded edge of the pastry at intervals.

Put the strudel on the oven tray and sprinkle with the combined sugar and cinnamon.

CREAMY RICE POTS

Preparation time: 15 minutes
Total cooking time: 1 hour
Serves 4

½ cup (110 g/3½ oz) short-grain rice
1 litre skim milk
¼ cup (60 g/2 oz) caster sugar
1 teaspoon grated orange rind
1 teaspoon grated lemon rind
1 teaspoon vanilla essence
20 g (¾ oz) hazelnuts
1 tablespoon soft brown sugar

1 Wash the rice in a sieve, then drain thoroughly. Combine the skim milk and caster sugar in a non-stick pan and stir over low heat until dissolved. Add the rice and rind and stir briefly. Bring to the boil and reduce the heat to as low as possible. Cook for 1 hour, stirring occasionally, until the rice is tender and the mixture thick and creamy. Stir in the vanilla essence.
2 While the rice is cooking, spread the hazelnuts on a baking tray and toast in a moderate 180°C (350°F/ Gas 4) oven for about 5 minutes. Rub the hot nuts in a tea towel to remove as much of the skin as possible. Cool and then grind in a food processor until coarsely chopped.

3 Spoon the rice into 4 heatproof ¾ cup (185 ml/6 fl oz) capacity ramekins. Combine the brown sugar and ground hazelnuts and sprinkle over the surface of the rice. Cook briefly under a very hot grill until the sugar melts and the nuts are lightly browned. Serve immediately.

NUTRITION PER SERVE
Protein 12 g; Fat 3.5 g; Carbohydrate 55 g;
Dietary Fibre 1 g; Cholesterol 7 mg;
1235 kJ (295 cal)

Cook the rice mixture over very low heat until thick and creamy.

Transfer the hot nuts to a tea towel and rub to remove as much skin as possible.

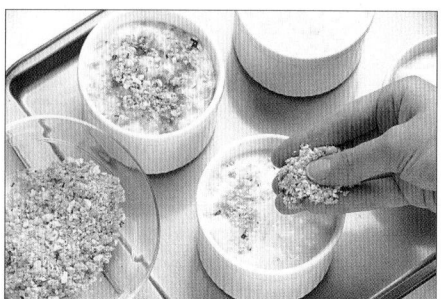

Sprinkle the combined sugar and ground hazelnuts over the top of the rice.

PUMPKIN PIE

Preparation time: 20 minutes +
40 minutes refrigeration + cooling
Total cooking time: 1 hour 30 minutes
Serves 6–8

1¼ cups (150 g/5 oz) plain flour
100 g (3½ oz) unsalted butter, chilled
    and cubed
2 teaspoons caster sugar
4 tablespoons iced water

FILLING
750 g (1½ lb) butternut pumpkin,
    cubed
2 eggs, lightly beaten
1 cup (185 g/6 oz) soft brown sugar
⅓ cup (80 ml/2¾ fl oz) cream
1 tablespoon sweet sherry or brandy
½ teaspoon ground ginger
½ teaspoon ground nutmeg
1 teaspoon ground cinnamon

1 Sift the flour into a large bowl and rub in the butter with your fingertips until the mixture resembles fine breadcrumbs. Mix in the caster sugar. Make a well in the centre, add almost all the water and mix with a flat-bladed knife, using a cutting action, until the mixture comes together in beads, adding more water if needed.
2 Gather the dough together and lift out onto a lightly floured work surface. Press into a disc. Wrap in plastic and refrigerate for 20 minutes.
3 Roll out the pastry between two sheets of baking paper until large enough to line an 18 cm (7 inch) pie dish. Line the dish with pastry, trim away the excess and crimp the edges with a fork. Cover with plastic wrap and refrigerate for 20 minutes.
4 Preheat the oven to 180°C (350°F/ Gas 4). Cook the pumpkin in boiling water until tender. Drain, mash, push through a sieve and leave to cool.
5 Line the pastry shell with baking paper and spread with a layer of baking beads or rice. Bake for 10 minutes, then remove the paper and beads and bake for 10 minutes, or until lightly golden. Set aside to cool.
6 Whisk the eggs and sugar together in a large bowl. Add the cooled pumpkin, cream, sherry and the spices and stir thoroughly. Pour into the pastry shell, smooth the surface and bake for 1 hour, or until set. If the pastry overbrowns, cover the edges with foil. Cool before serving.

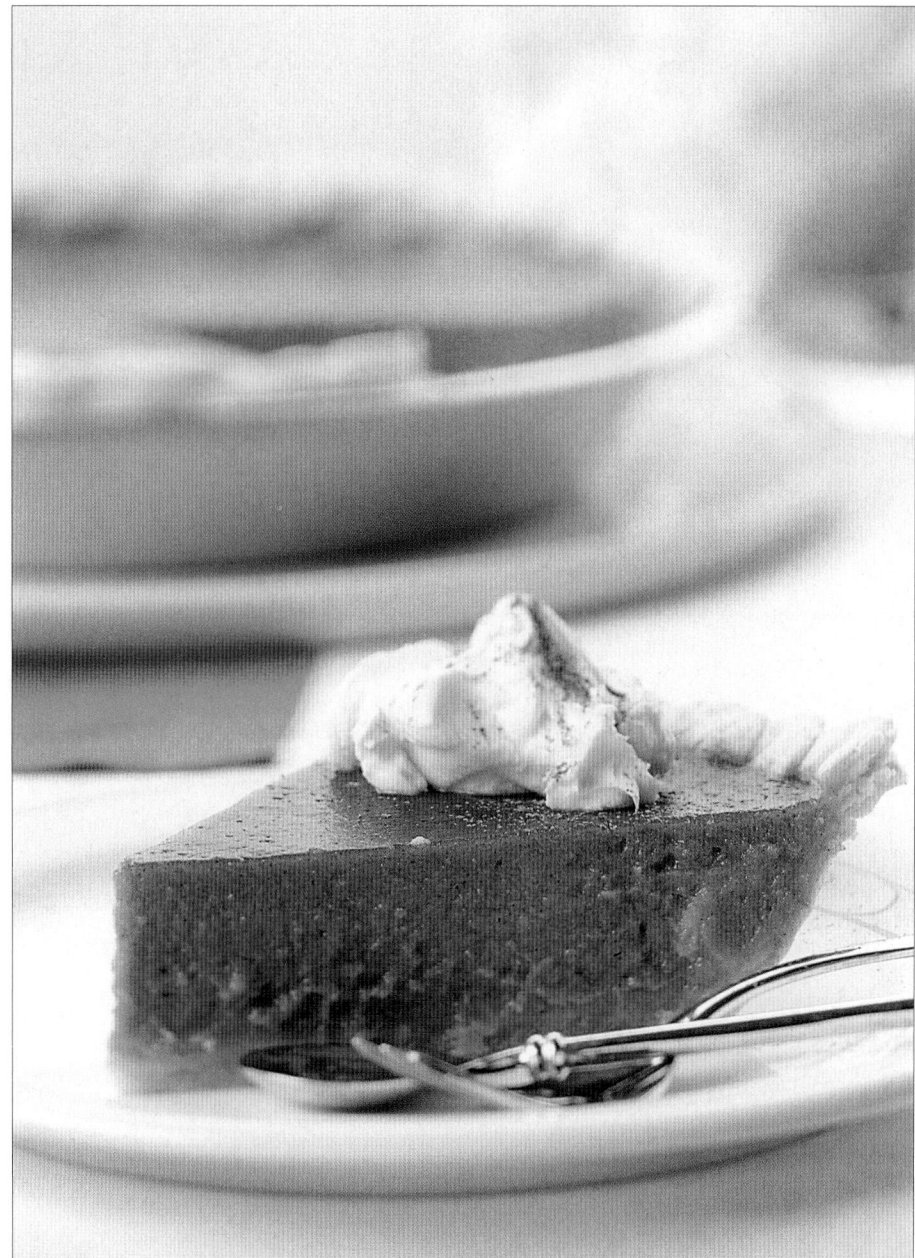

NUTRITION PER SERVE (8)
Protein 6 g; Fat 16.5 g; Carbohydrate 45 g; Dietary Fibre 2 g; Cholesterol 90 mg; 1470 kJ (350 cal)

Bake the pastry for 10 minutes, then remove the paper and beads and cook until golden.

Stir the pumpkin, cream, sherry and spices into the egg and sugar mixture.

CHOCOLATE MINT ICE CREAM

**Preparation time: 25 minutes +
   freezing
Total cooking time: 10 minutes
Serves 6**

1 cup (250 ml/8 fl oz) cream
3 tablespoons chopped fresh mint
100 g (3½ oz) dark chocolate, broken
60 g (2 oz) milk chocolate, broken
2 eggs, lightly beaten
1 tablespoon caster sugar

1 Place the cream and mint in a small pan. Stir over low heat until the cream is almost boiling. Cool slightly. Add the chocolate to the cream. Stir over low heat until the chocolate has melted and the mixture is smooth.
2 Whisk the eggs and sugar in a small bowl until creamy. Gradually add the warm chocolate mixture through a strainer. Discard the mint. Whisk until well combined and then cool.
3 Freeze the mixture in an ice-cream machine according to the manufacturer's instructions.

Alternatively, freeze in a metal container until just firm around the edges. Remove from the freezer and beat for 1 minute. Return to the freezer and freeze overnight.

NUTRITION PER SERVE
Protein 5 g; Fat 27 g; Carbohydrate 21 g;
Dietary Fibre 0 g; Cholesterol 118 mg;
1413 kJ (338 cal)

STORAGE: Ice cream can be stored in the freezer for up to 3 weeks.

Bring the cream to boiling point then allow to cool a little and add the chocolate.

Add the warm chocolate mixture slowly, through a strainer, discarding the mint.

If you don't have an ice-cream machine, freeze the mixture and then beat.

BANANA PANCAKES

Preparation time: 20 minutes + 1 hour
Total cooking time: 25 minutes
Makes 10

2 very ripe bananas, mashed
1 cup (150 g/5 oz) wholemeal flour
2 teaspoons baking powder
½ teaspoon ground cinnamon
pinch of ground nutmeg
1 cup (250 ml/8 fl oz) skim milk
1 tablespoon maple syrup
maple syrup and banana, for serving

1 Put the mashed banana in a large bowl. Sift the flour, baking powder, cinnamon and nutmeg onto the banana and return the husks to the bowl. Stir until the flour is moistened but not totally combined with the mashed banana.

2 Make a well in the centre, add the milk and syrup and stir constantly until smooth. Set aside for 1 hour.

3 Heat a large non-stick pan over medium heat and coat with cooking oil spray. Cook the pancakes in batches, using ¼ cup (60 ml/2 fl oz) of batter for each pancake. Cook for 3–4 minutes, or until small bubbles appear on the surface. Using a spatula, gently turn the pancakes over, loosening the edges first so they don't stick to the pan. Cook for another 3 minutes. Remove from the pan and keep warm. Spray the pan with a little oil after each batch and continue with the remaining mixture. Serve drizzled with maple syrup and a few slices of banana.

NUTRITION PER PANCAKE
Protein 3 g; Fat 0.5 g; Carbohydrate 17 g;
Dietary Fibre 2 g; Cholesterol 1 mg;
350 kJ (85 cal)

When you have sifted the wholemeal flour, return the husks to the bowl.

Stir the pancake mixture until smooth, then set aside for 1 hour.

Cook the pancakes over medium heat until small bubbles appear on the surface.

Custards & Creams

Cream, custard or ice cream are all ideal companions for sweet pies and tarts. If you want to be a little more adventurous, try one of these flavoured creams or custards.

LIQUEUR CUSTARD

Using a wire whisk, beat 3 egg yolks and 2 tablespoons of sugar in a bowl for about 3 minutes, or until very light and creamy. Heat 1½ cups (375 ml/ 12 fl oz) milk in a small pan until just boiling, then pour slowly onto the egg mixture, whisking constantly. Return to the pan and stir with a wooden spoon over very low heat for about 5 minutes, until the custard thickens enough to coat the spoon. Do not allow to boil or the custard will curdle. Stir in 1–2 tablespoons of your favourite liqueur to serve.
Serves 6–8

MASCARPONE BRANDY CREAM

Stir together 250 g (8 oz) mascarpone, ½ cup (125 ml/4 fl oz) cream and 1 tablespoon caster sugar until thoroughly combined. Beat 2 egg whites into firm peaks and fold through the mascarpone mixture with a metal spoon. Add brandy to taste (about 1–2 tablespoons) and stir to combine. Refrigerate for at least 1 hour before serving.
Serves 8

SABAYON

Place 4 egg yolks and 3 tablespoons caster sugar in a large heatproof bowl. Beat for 1 minute with electric beaters until the mixture is light and creamy. Stand the bowl over a pan of barely simmering water, add ½ cup (125 ml/ 4 fl oz) sweet white wine and continue beating for 5 minutes, until the mixture is thick, light and foamy. Serve immediately, as the sabayon will separate if left to stand.
Serves 8

YOGHURT CREAM

Whisk 1 cup (250 g/8 oz) plain yoghurt, ½ cup (125 g/4 oz) sour cream, 1 teaspoon of vanilla essence and 2 teaspoons of soft brown sugar together in a glass or ceramic bowl. Refrigerate for at least 8 hours before serving to let the cream thicken. Serves 6

ORANGE RICOTTA CREAM

Place 250 g (8 oz) ricotta cheese, ½ cup (125 ml/4 fl oz) cream, 1 teaspoon of finely grated orange rind and 2 tablespoons of caster sugar in a bowl. Beat with electric beaters for a minute until smooth. Add 2 tablespoons of Grand Marnier and beat until just mixed through. Refrigerate for 1 hour before serving. Serves 6–8

BERRY RICOTTA CREAM TARTLETS

Preparation time: 1 hour + 1 hour refrigeration
Total cooking time: 40 minutes
Serves 6

1½ cups (185 g/6 oz) plain flour
½ cup (90 g/3 oz) ground almonds
⅓ cup (40 g/1¼ oz) icing sugar
125 g (4 oz) unsalted butter, chilled
    and cubed
1 egg, lightly beaten

FILLING
200 g (6½ oz) ricotta
1 teaspoon vanilla essence
2 eggs
⅔ cup (160 g/5½ oz) caster sugar
½ cup (125 ml/4 fl oz) cream
½ cup (60 g/2 oz) raspberries
½ cup (80 g/2¾ oz) blueberries
icing sugar, to dust

1 Sift the flour into a large bowl, then add the almonds and icing sugar. Rub the butter into the flour with your fingertips until it resembles fine breadcrumbs. Make a well in the centre and add the egg and mix with a flat-bladed knife, using a cutting action, until the mixture comes together in beads. Turn out onto a lightly floured work surface and gather into a ball. Wrap in plastic and refrigerate for 30 minutes.
2 Grease six 8 cm (3 inch) loose-based tart tins. Roll out the pastry between two sheets of baking paper to fit the base and side of the tins, trimming away the excess. Prick the bases with a fork, then refrigerate for 30 minutes. Preheat the oven to 180°C (350°F/Gas 4).

3 Line the pastry bases with baking paper and spread with a layer of baking beads or rice. Bake for 8–10 minutes and then remove the paper and beads.
4 Mix the ricotta, vanilla essence, eggs, sugar and cream in a food processor until smooth.
5 Divide the berries and filling among the tarts and bake for 25–30 minutes, or until the filling is just set—the top should be soft but not too wobbly. Cool. Dust with icing sugar to serve.

NUTRITION PER SERVE
Protein 14 g; Fat 42 g; Carbohydrate 62 g; Dietary Fibre 3.5 g; Cholesterol 187 mg; 2780 kJ (665 cal)

Gently gather the dough together and press into a ball. Wrap in plastic and refrigerate.

Roll out the pastry between two sheets of baking paper to prevent sticking.

Divide the berries among the pastry cases and then pour in the filling over the top.

RASPBERRY MOUSSE

Preparation time: 30 minutes
  + refrigeration
Total cooking time: Nil
Serves 4

3 teaspoons gelatine
1 cup (250 g/8 oz) low-fat vanilla
  yoghurt
2 x 200 g (6½ oz) tubs low-fat fromage
  frais or light vanilla Fruche
4 egg whites
150 g (5 oz) raspberries, mashed
fresh raspberries and mint leaves, for
  serving

1 Sprinkle the gelatine in an even layer onto 1 tablespoon water in a small bowl and leave to go spongy. Bring a small pan of water to the boil, remove from the heat and place the bowl in the pan. Stir until clear.
2 In a large bowl, stir the vanilla yoghurt and fromage frais together, then add the gelatine and mix well.
3 Using electric beaters, beat the egg whites until stiff peaks form, then fold through the yoghurt mixture. Transfer half to a separate bowl and fold the mashed raspberries through.
4 Divide the raspberry mixture into the bases of 4 long glasses or serving bowls. Top with the vanilla mixture. Refrigerate for several hours, or until set. Decorate with fresh raspberries and mint leaves.

NUTRITION PER SERVE
Protein 9.5 g; Fat 2 g; Carbohydrate 10 g;
Dietary Fibre 2 g; Cholesterol 4 mg;
355 kJ (85 cal)

You can use fresh raspberries or frozen. Thaw frozen raspberries completely before mashing.

Stir the vanilla yoghurt and fromage frais together until combined.

Gently fold the mashed raspberries through half the yoghurt mixture.

TARTE TATIN

Preparation time: 15 minutes
Total cooking time: 1 hour 10 minutes
Serves 6

100 g (3½ oz) unsalted butter
¾ cup (185 g/6 oz) sugar
6 large pink lady or fuji apples, peeled, cored and quartered (see NOTE)
1 sheet puff pastry

1 Preheat the oven to 220°C (425°F/ Gas 7). Lightly grease a 23 cm (9 inch) shallow cake tin. Melt the butter in a frying pan, add the sugar and cook, stirring, over medium heat for 4–5 minutes, or until the sugar starts to caramelise and turn brown. Continue to cook, stirring, until the caramel turns golden brown.
2 Add the apple to the pan and cook over low heat for 20–25 minutes, or until it starts to turn golden brown. Carefully turn the apple over and cook the other side until evenly coloured. If much liquid comes out of the apple, increase the heat until it has evaporated—the caramel should be sticky rather than runny. Remove from the heat. Using tongs, arrange the hot apple in circles in the tin and pour the sauce over the top.
3 Place the pastry over the apple, tucking the edge down firmly with the end of a spoon. Bake for 30–35 minutes, or until the pastry is cooked. Leave for 15 minutes before inverting onto a serving plate. Remove the paper before serving.

NUTRITION PER SERVE
Protein 2 g; Fat 20 g; Carbohydrate 47 g; Dietary Fibre 1.5 g; Cholesterol 50 mg; 1544 kJ (370 cal)

NOTE: The moisture content of the different apples varies quite a lot, which affects the cooking time. Golden delicious, pink lady or fuji are good to use because they don't break down during cooking.

Cook the butter and sugar until the caramel is golden brown.

Remove the apple from the pan with tongs and arrange in circles in the tin.

Arrange the pastry over the top of the apple in the tin, to cover it completely, tucking down the edge.

MERINGUE BASKETS WITH FRUIT

Preparation time: 40 minutes + cooling
Total cooking time: 1 hour 30 minutes
Serves 6

2 egg whites
small pinch of cream of tartar
½ cup (125 g/4 oz) caster sugar
2 tablespoons custard powder
2 cups (500 ml/16 fl oz) skim milk
1 teaspoon vanilla essence
1 peach, cut into thin wedges
1 kiwi fruit, cut into thin wedges
2 strawberries, cut in half
2 tablespoons apricot jam

1 Preheat the oven to slow 150°C (300°F/Gas 2) and line a baking tray with baking paper. Beat the egg whites and cream of tartar with electric beaters until soft peaks form. Gradually add the sugar and beat until it is dissolved and the mixture is stiff and glossy.

2 Fit a piping bag with a medium star nozzle and pipe coiled spirals of the meringue (about 8 cm/3 inches) onto the tray. Pipe an extra ring around the top edge to make baskets. Bake for 30 minutes, then reduce the heat to very slow 120°C (250°F/Gas ½). Bake for 45 minutes, turn the oven off and cool with the oven door ajar.

3 Mix the custard powder with a little of the milk to form a smooth paste. Transfer to a pan with the remaining milk and the vanilla essence. Stir over medium heat until the mixture boils and thickens. Remove from the heat and place plastic wrap over the surface to stop a skin forming. Set aside and, when cool, stir until smooth. Spoon some of the cold custard into each basket. Top with fruit. Heat the jam until liquid, then brush over the fruit to glaze.

NUTRITION PER SERVE
Protein 5 g; Fat 0.5 g; Carbohydrate 30 g; Dietary Fibre 1 g; Cholesterol 3 mg; 590 kJ (140 cal)

Beat the egg whites and cream of tartar until soft peaks form.

Pipe an extra ring around the top edge of the coils to make baskets.

Lay a piece of plastic wrap directly onto the surface of the custard.

Cakes & Bakes

SACHER SQUARES

Preparation time: 1 hour
Total cooking time: 40 minutes
Makes 24

BASE
1 cup (125 g/4 oz) plain flour
60 g (2 oz) unsalted butter, chopped
¼ cup (60 g/2 oz) sugar
2 egg yolks, lightly beaten
2 teaspoons iced water

CAKE
1 cup (125 g/4 oz) plain flour
⅓ cup (40 g/1¼ oz) cocoa powder
1 cup (250 g/ 8 oz) caster sugar
100 g (3½ oz) unsalted butter
2 tablespoons apricot jam
4 eggs, separated
1 cup (315 g/10 oz) apricot jam, extra

TOPPING
250 g (8 oz) dark chocolate
¾ cup (185 ml/6 fl oz) cream

1 Preheat the oven to 180°C (350°F/ Gas 4). Cut an 18 x 28 cm (7 x 11 inch) rectangle of baking paper. To make the base, sift the flour into a bowl and add the butter. Using fingertips, rub butter into the flour until fine and crumbly. Stir in sugar. Add the yolks and almost all the water, and mix to a dough, adding more liquid if necessary. Knead for 30 seconds or until smooth. Roll out and cut to fit baking paper. Place on a baking tray. Bake for 10 minutes or until golden. Cool.

2 To make the cake, preheat the oven to 180°C (350°F/Gas 4). Lightly grease an 18 x 28 cm (7 x 11 inch) shallow rectangular tin and line with baking paper. Sift the flour and cocoa into a mixing bowl. Combine the sugar, butter and jam in a small pan. Stir over a low heat until butter has melted and sugar dissolved. Add the butter mixture to the dry ingredients. Stir until just combined. Add the egg yolks and mix well.

3 Place the egg whites in a clean, dry mixing bowl. Using electric beaters, beat until soft peaks form. Using a metal spoon, fold into the mixture. Pour into the prepared tin and bake for 30 minutes. Leave in the tin for 15 minutes before turning out onto a wire rack to cool completely.

4 Warm the extra jam over a saucepan of simmering water and push through a fine sieve. Brush the base with ¼ cup jam. Place cake on the base. Trim each side evenly, cutting 'crust' from cake and base. Using a sharp knife, cut into 24 squares. Brush with jam. Place on a wire rack, over baking paper, leaving 4 cm (1½ inch) between each.

5 To make the topping, break the chocolate into pieces and place in a small bowl. Place cream in a small saucepan and bring to the boil. Pour over chocolate and stir until melted. Cool slightly. Pour topping over each square and use a flat-bladed knife to cover completely. Scrape excess from the paper and spoon, with remaining topping, into a small paper piping bag. Pipe an 'S' onto each square.

FUDGE BROWNIES

Preparation time: 15 minutes
Total cooking time: 30 minutes
Makes 18 pieces

cooking oil spray
½ cup (60 g/2 oz) plain flour
½ cup (60 g/2 oz) self-raising flour
1 teaspoon bicarbonate of soda
¾ cup (90 g/3 oz) cocoa powder
2 eggs
1¼ cups (310 g/10 oz) caster sugar
2 teaspoons vanilla essence
2 tablespoons vegetable oil

200 g (6½ oz) low-fat fromage frais
140 ml (4½ fl oz) apple purée
icing sugar, for dusting

1 Preheat the oven to moderate 180°C (350°F/Gas 4). Spray a 30 x 20 cm (12 x 8 inch) shallow baking tin with oil and line the base of the tin with baking paper.
2 Sift the flours, bicarbonate of soda and cocoa powder into a large bowl. Mix the eggs, sugar, vanilla essence, oil, fromage frais and purée in a large bowl, stirring until well combined. Add to the flour and stir until combined. Spread into the prepared

tin and bake for about 30 minutes, or until a skewer inserted in the centre comes out clean.
3 The brownie will sink slightly in the centre as it cools. Leave in the pan for 5 minutes before turning onto a wire rack to cool. Dust with icing sugar before cutting into pieces to serve.

Stir together the eggs, sugar, vanilla essence, oil, fromage frais and apple purée.

Add the egg mixture to the flour and stir thoroughly until combined.

Test with a skewer. When the brownie is cooked, the skewer will come out clean.

CARROT CAKE

Preparation time: 20 minutes
Total cooking time: 1 hour 15 minutes
Makes 14 slices

2½ cups (310 g/10 oz) self-raising flour
1 teaspoon bicarbonate of soda
2 teaspoons ground cinnamon
1 teaspoon mixed spice
½ cup (95 g/3 oz) soft brown sugar
½ cup (60 g/2 oz) sultanas
2 eggs, lightly beaten
2 tablespoons vegetable oil
⅓ cup (80 ml/2¾ fl oz) low-fat milk
140 g (4½ oz) apple purée
300 g (10 oz) carrot, coarsely grated

RICOTTA TOPPING
125 g (4 oz) ricotta
¼ cup (30 g/1 oz) icing sugar
½ teaspoon grated lime rind

1 Grease a 10 x 18 cm (4 x 7 inch) loaf tin and line the base with baking paper. Preheat the oven to 180°C (350°F/Gas 4). Sift the flour, soda and spices into a large bowl. Stir in the sugar and sultanas.
2 Mix the eggs, oil, milk and apple purée and stir into the dry ingredients. Stir in the carrot. Spread into the tin and bake for 1¼ hours, or until a skewer comes out clean. Cool in the tin for 5 minutes, then on a wire rack.
3 To make the topping, beat the ingredients together until smooth. Spread over the cake.

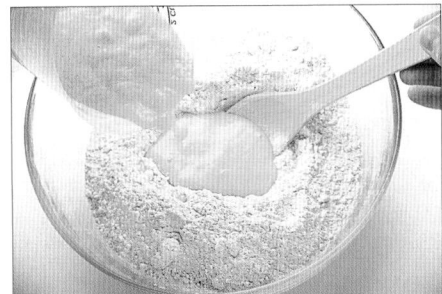

Stir the egg and apple mixture into the dry ingredients, then stir in the carrot.

A skewer inserted into the centre of the cake should come out clean when it is cooked.

Beat the topping ingredients together until smooth and spread over the cake.

BRAZIL NUT AND COFFEE BISCOTTI

Preparation time: 20 minutes
Total cooking time: 45 minutes
Makes 40 pieces

3 teaspoons instant coffee powder
1 tablespoon dark rum, warmed
2 eggs
½ cup (125 g/4 oz) caster sugar
1¼ cups (155 g/5 oz) plain flour
½ cup (60 g/2 oz) self-raising flour
1 teaspoon ground cinnamon
¾ cup (105 g/3½ oz) brazil nuts,
    roughly chopped
1 tablespoon caster sugar, extra

1 Preheat the oven to 180°C (350°F/ Gas 4). Dissolve the coffee in the rum. Beat the eggs and sugar until thick and creamy, then beat in the coffee. Sift the flours and cinnamon into a bowl, then stir in the nuts. Mix in the egg mixture.
2 Divide the mixture into two rolls, each about 28 cm (11 inches) long. Line a baking tray with baking paper, put the rolls on it and press lightly to flatten to about 6 cm (2½ inches) across. Brush lightly with water and sprinkle with the extra sugar. Bake for 25 minutes, or until firm and light brown. Cool until warm on the tray. Reduce the oven temperature to warm 160°C (315°F/Gas 2–3).
3 Cut into 1 cm (½ inch) thick diagonal slices. Bake in a single layer on the lined tray for 20 minutes, or until dry, turning once. Cool on a rack. When cold, store in an airtight container for 2–3 weeks.

Beat the coffee and rum mixture into the beaten eggs and sugar.

Put the rolls of dough on the lined baking tray and press lightly into shape.

Cut the cooked rolls into diagonal slices and bake until dry.

LEMON SEMOLINA CAKE

Preparation time: 15 minutes
Total cooking time: 45 minutes
Serves 8–10

6 eggs, separated
1¼ cups (310 g/10 oz) caster sugar
2 teaspoons finely grated lemon rind
⅓ cup (80 ml/2¾ fl oz) lemon juice
¾ cup (90 g/3 oz) semolina
½ cup (95 g/3 oz) ground almonds
2 tablespoons self-raising flour
thick cream, to serve

1 Preheat the oven to 170°C (325°F/ Gas 3). Grease a 24 cm (9½ inch) springform tin and line with baking paper. Using electric beaters, beat the yolks, 1 cup (250 g/8 oz) of the sugar, the rind and 2 tablespoons of the lemon juice in a mixing bowl for 8 minutes, or until thick and pale and the mixture leaves a trail when the beaters are lifted.

2 Beat the egg whites in a clean bowl with clean electric beaters until firm peaks form. Gently fold the whites with a metal spoon into the egg yolk mixture alternately with the combined semolina, ground almonds and flour. Take care not to overmix. Carefully pour the mixture into the prepared tin and smooth the surface. Bake for 35–40 minutes, or until a skewer comes out clean when inserted into the centre of the cake. Leave the cake in the tin for 5 minutes then turn out onto a wire rack to cool completely. Pierce a few holes in the cake with a skewer.

3 Place the remaining lemon juice and sugar in a small saucepan with ½ cup (125 ml/4 fl oz) water. Stir over low heat until the sugar has dissolved. Increase the heat and simmer for 3 minutes, or until thick and syrupy. Pour the hot syrup over the cooled cake. Serve with thick cream.

Use a metal spoon to fold the egg whites into the egg yolk mixture with minimal loss of volume.

Simmer the sugar mixture until it is thick and syrupy. Take care–it will be very hot.

GINGERBREAD PEOPLE

**Preparation time: 40 minutes +
 15 minutes refrigeration**
Total cooking time: 10 minutes
Makes 16

125 g (4 oz) unsalted butter, softened
⅓ cup (60 g/2 oz) lightly packed soft
    brown sugar
¼ cup (90 g/3 oz) golden syrup
1 egg, lightly beaten
2 cups (250 g/8 oz) plain flour
¼ cup (30 g/1 oz) self-raising flour
1 tablespoon ground ginger
1 teaspoon bicarbonate of soda
1 tablespoon currants

ICING
1 egg white
½ teaspoon lemon juice

1¼ cups (155 g/5 oz) icing sugar, sifted
assorted food colourings

1 Preheat the oven to 180°C (350°F/
Gas 4). Line two baking trays with
baking paper.
2 Using electric beaters, cream the
butter, sugar and golden syrup in a
large mixing bowl until light and
fluffy. Add the egg gradually, beating
well after each addition. Sift the dry
ingredients over the butter mixture
and mix with a knife until just
combined. Combine the dough with
your hands. Turn onto a well-floured
surface and knead for 1–2 minutes, or
until smooth. Roll out on a chopping
board, between two sheets of baking
paper, to 5 mm (¼ inch) thick. Chill
on the board for 15 minutes to firm.
3 Cut the dough into shapes with a
13 cm (5 inch) gingerbread person

cutter. Press the remaining dough
together and re-roll. Cut out shapes
and place the biscuits on the trays.
Place the currants as eyes and noses.
Bake for 10 minutes, or until lightly
browned. Cool on the trays.
4 To make the icing, beat the egg
white with electric beaters in a small,
clean, dry bowl until foamy. Gradually
add the lemon juice and icing sugar
and beat until thick. Divide the icing
among several bowls and add the food
colourings. Spoon into small paper
icing bags. Seal ends, snip the tips off
the bags and pipe on faces and
clothing.

STORAGE: These biscuits can be
stored in an airtight container for
up to 3 days.

Mix in the dry ingredients with a flat-bladed knife,
using a cutting action.

Use your favourite cutters to cut out the
gingerbread — a person shape is traditional.

Snip the tip off the icing bag to pipe features onto
the gingerbread people.

CHOCOLATE MUD CAKE

Preparation time: 30 minutes
Total cooking time: 2 hours
Serves 8

250 g (8 oz) unsalted butter
250 g (8 oz) dark chocolate, chopped
2 tablespoons instant coffee powder
150 g (5 oz) self-raising flour
150 g (5 oz) plain flour
½ teaspoon bicarbonate of soda
½ cup (60 g/2 oz) cocoa powder
2¼ cups (550 g/1 lb 2 oz) caster sugar
4 eggs, lightly beaten
2 tablespoons oil
½ cup (125 ml/4 fl oz) buttermilk

ICING
150 g (5 oz) unsalted butter, chopped
150 g (5 oz) dark chocolate, chopped

1 Preheat the oven to 160°C (315°F/Gas 2–3). Lightly grease a deep 22 cm (9 inch) round cake tin and line with baking paper, making sure the paper around the side extends at least 5 cm (2 inches) above the top edge.
2 Put the butter, chocolate and coffee in a saucepan with ¾ cup (185 ml/6 oz) hot water and stir over low heat until smooth. Remove from the heat.
3 Sift the flours, bicarbonate of soda and cocoa powder into a large mixing bowl. Stir in the sugar and make a well in the centre. Place the eggs, oil and buttermilk in a separate mixing bowl and mix until combined. Pour into the dry ingredients and mix together with a whisk. Gradually add the chocolate mixture, whisking well after each addition.
4 Pour the mixture (it will be quite wet) into the tin and bake for 1¾ hours. Test the centre with a skewer–the skewer may be slightly wetter than normal. Remove the cake from the oven. If the top looks raw, bake for another 5–10 minutes, then remove from oven. Leave in the tin until completely cold, then turn out and wrap in plastic wrap.
5 For the icing, combine the butter and chocolate in a saucepan and stir over low heat until the butter and chocolate are melted. Remove and cool slightly. Pour over the cake and allow it to run down the side.

Sift the flours and cocoa powder together into a large mixing bowl.

Stir the butter, oil, chocolate, sugar, coffee powder and water until melted and smooth.

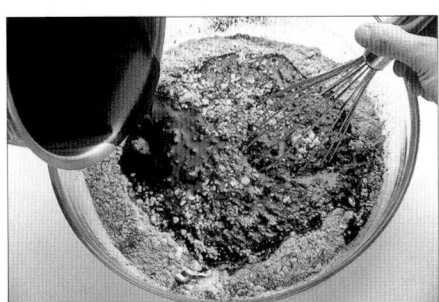
Whisk the chocolate mixture into the well in the dry ingredients.

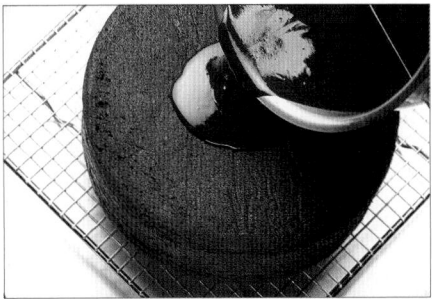
Pour the cooled chocolate topping over the upside-down cake.

SPICED APPLE SLICE

Preparation time: 25 minutes +
  30 minutes refrigeration
Total cooking time: 55 minutes
Serves 8

750 g (1½ lb) green apples
⅓ cup (90 g/3 oz) sugar
½ teaspoon ground cloves
2 tablespoons lemon juice
1 cup (125 g/4 oz) plain flour
1 cup (125 g/4 oz) self-raising flour
1 teaspoon ground cloves, extra
½ teaspoon ground cinnamon
150 g (5 oz) butter
½ cup (125 g/4 oz) caster sugar
1 teaspoon vanilla essence
1 egg, lightly beaten
1 tablespoon milk
1 tablespoon caster sugar, extra
1 teaspoon ground cinnamon, extra

1 Brush a 20 x 30 cm (8 x 12 inch) shallow tin with oil. Line the base with paper and grease the paper. Preheat the oven to 180°C (350°F/ Gas 4). Peel, core and slice the apples and put in a pan with the sugar, cloves and juice. Stir over heat to warm. Cover and simmer, stirring often, for 20 minutes or until soft. Remove from the heat, drain and cool.
2 Sift the flours with the extra cloves and cinnamon. Beat the butter and sugar until light and creamy. Add the vanilla and egg and beat thoroughly. Fold in the flour in batches, mixing after each addition. If the mixture is too dry, add a little milk. Knead gently on a lightly floured surface until smooth. Divide in half, cover with plastic wrap and chill for 30 minutes.
3 Roll out one portion of pastry to fit the tin base. Spread with apple filling. Place the second pastry sheet on top of the filling and press down gently.
4 Brush the top with milk and sprinkle with the extra sugar and cinnamon. Bake for 30 minutes or until golden brown. Leave for 15 minutes, then turn onto a wire rack to cool.

NUTRITION PER SERVE
Protein 5 g; Fat 17 g; Carbohydrate 64 g;
Dietary Fibre 3 g; Cholesterol 72 mg;
1772 kJ (423 cal)

Peel, core and slice the apples and put in a pan with the sugar, cloves and apple juice.

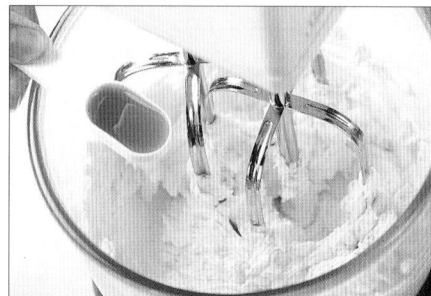

Beat the butter and sugar, then add the vanilla essence and egg.

Line the tray with one of the pastry sheets and spread the filling on top.

Brush the top of the slice with milk and then sprinkle with sugar and cinnamon.

SHORTBREAD STARS WITH LEMON GLAZE

Preparation time: 20 minutes
Total cooking time: 15 minutes
Makes 35

2 cups (250 g/8 oz) plain flour
2 tablespoons rice flour
200 g (6½ oz) unsalted butter
⅓ cup (40 g/1¼ oz) icing sugar
1 teaspoon finely grated
    lemon rind
2 tablespoons lemon juice
silver cachous, to decorate

LEMON GLAZE
1 cup (125 g/4 oz) pure icing sugar
2 tablespoons lemon juice, strained
yellow or orange food colouring

1 Preheat the oven to 180°C (350°F/ Gas 4). Line two baking trays with baking paper. Place the flours, butter and sugar in a food processor and process for 30 seconds or until the mixture is fine and crumbly. Add the lemon rind and juice and process for 20 seconds or until the mixture forms a soft dough.

2 Turn out onto a lightly floured surface and knead for 20 seconds or until smooth. Roll the dough out to 7 mm (¼ inch) thickness. Using a 6 cm (2½ inch) star cutter, cut out shapes. Bake for 15 minutes. Transfer to wire rack to cool.

3 To make the lemon glaze, place the icing sugar and lemon juice in a heatproof bowl over a pan of hot water. Stir until smooth. Dip the biscuits face down in glaze and drain any excess. Dip a skewer into food colouring and draw lines into icing before it sets. Decorate with a cachou.

STORAGE: Store for up to 5 days in an airtight container.

Add the lemon rind and juice to the mixture in the food processor.

Use a 6 cm (2¹/₂ inch) cutter to cut the star shapes out of the dough.

Use a skewer to carefully draw coloured lines into the icing before it sets.

SOUR CHERRY CAKE

Preparation time: 10 minutes
Total cooking time: 50 minutes
Serves 8–10

125 g (4 oz) unsalted butter, softened
¾ cup (185 g/6 oz) caster sugar
2 eggs, lightly beaten
½ cup (95 g/3 oz) ground almonds
1 cup (125 g/4 oz) self-raising flour
½ cup (60 g/2 oz) plain flour
½ cup (125 ml/4 fl oz) milk
680 g (1 lb 6 oz) jar pitted morello
    cherries, well drained
icing sugar, to dust

1 Preheat the oven to 180°C (350°F/
Gas 4). Grease and flour a 23 cm
(9 inch) fluted baba tin, shaking out
any excess flour. Beat the butter and
sugar with electric beaters until pale.
Add the beaten egg gradually, beating
well after each addition.
2 Stir in the ground almonds, then
fold in the sifted flours alternately
with the milk. Gently fold in the
cherries. Spoon the mixture into the
prepared tin and smooth the surface.

Bake for 50 minutes, or until a skewer
comes out clean when inserted into
the centre of the cake. Leave to cool
in the tin for 10 minutes before
turning out onto a wire rack to cool.
Dust with icing sugar before serving.

NOTE: This cake is best eaten on the
day it is made.

Beat the butter and sugar until the mixture is pale
in colour but not creamy.

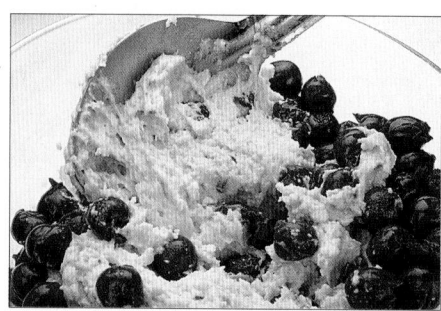

Gently fold in the cherries, taking care not to
break them up with the spoon.

SAND CAKE

Preparation time: 10 minutes
Total cooking time: 50 minutes
Serves 8–10

185 g (6 oz) unsalted butter,
   softened
2 teaspoons vanilla essence
1 cup (250 g/8 oz) caster sugar
3 eggs
1½ cups (185 g/6 oz) self-raising
   flour
⅓ cup (60 g/2 oz) rice flour
⅓ cup (80 ml/2¾ fl oz) milk

1 Preheat the oven to 180°C (350°F/
Gas 4). Lightly grease a 23 cm (9 inch)
square cake tin and line the base with
baking paper.
2 Beat the butter, vanilla essence,
sugar, eggs, flours and milk with
electric beaters at low speed until
combined, then beat at medium
speed for 3 minutes, or until the
mixture is thick and creamy.
3 Pour the mixture into the prepared
tin and smooth the surface. Bake for
50 minutes, or until a skewer comes
out clean when inserted into the
centre of the cake. Leave the cake for
10 minutes in the tin then turn out
onto a wire rack to cool completely.

Make sure the cake tin is lightly greased with
butter or oil before lining with baking paper.

The cake mixture must be thick and creamy
before you can stop beating.

Pour the mixture into the tin and smooth the
surface with a spoon.

Cake Toppings

Your favourite carrot cake just isn't the same without that delicious cream cheese icing, chocolate cake loses a little of its allure without its rich chocolate topping and a simple butter cake gains five-star standing when partnered with coffee buttercream. The icing on the cake can make all the difference.

GINGER AND LEMON GLACE ICING

Sift ⅓ cup (40 g/1¼ oz) icing sugar into a small heatproof bowl. Add ½ teaspoon ginger, 20 g (¾ oz) melted unsalted butter, 2 teaspoons milk and 1 teaspoon lemon juice and mix to form a paste. Place the bowl over a saucepan of simmering water, making sure the base does not touch the water, and stir until the icing is smooth and glossy. Remove the bowl from the heat. Drizzle the icing over the cake or spread with a knife dipped in hot water for even covering. Do not reheat.

LEMON CREAM CHEESE ICING

Place 60 g (2 oz) softened cream cheese and 30 g (1 oz) unsalted butter in a small mixing bowl. Using electric beaters, beat until combined. Add 1 tablespoon lemon juice and 1½ cups (185 g/6 oz) sifted icing sugar and beat until smooth.

BUTTERSCOTCH FROSTING

Chop 20 g (¾ oz) unsalted butter into small pieces and place in a saucepan with ½ cup (95 g/3 oz) lightly packed brown sugar. Stir constantly over low heat until mixture boils and the sugar dissolves. Simmer for 3 minutes. Remove from the heat, add ⅓ cup (90 g/3 oz) sour cream and stir. Leave to cool. Place 100 g (3½ oz) softened cream cheese in a mixing bowl and beat with electric beaters until light and creamy. Gradually add the cooled butterscotch mixture, beating well after each addition.

CHOCOLATE GANACHE

Combine ¼ cup (60 ml/2 fl oz) cream and 150 g (5 oz) dark chocolate in a small saucepan. Stir over low heat until the chocolate has melted and the mixture is smooth. Remove from the heat and allow to cool. Pour the ganache on to the cake, then smooth the top and around the side with a flat-bladed knife.

CARAMEL ICING

Place 1½ cups (185 g/6 oz) icing sugar, 1 tablespoon milk, 2 tablespoons golden syrup and 30 g (1 oz) softened unsalted butter in a bowl and beat with a wooden spoon until smooth. Spread over the cake with a flat-bladed knife.

COFFEE BUTTERCREAM

Dissolve 3 teaspoons instant coffee powder in 2 tablespoons boiling water. Place 125 g (4 oz) butter and 1½ cups (185 g/6 oz) icing sugar in a mixing bowl. Using electric beaters, beat until pale and creamy. Add ½ teaspoon vanilla, coffee mixture and 2 teaspoons milk and beat for 2 minutes, or until smooth and fluffy.

LIME ICING

Place 2 cups (250 g/8 oz) sifted icing sugar, 80 g (2¾ oz) softened unsalted butter and 2 tablespoons lime juice in a mixing bowl and beat with a wooden spoon until smooth, adding 1–2 tablespoons water, if necessary. Spread over the cake with a flat-bladed knife.

CHOCOLATE FUDGE ICING

Coarsely chop 150 g (5 oz) of dark chocolate and place in a small saucepan with 90 g (3 oz) unsalted butter and ½ cup (160 g/5½ oz) condensed milk. Stir over low heat until the chocolate and butter have melted and the mixture is smooth. Remove from the heat. Allow to cool until thick and spreadable.

ORANGE GLACE ICING

Sift 1 cup (125 g/4 oz) icing sugar into a heatproof bowl. Add 10 g (¼ oz) softened unsalted butter, 1 teaspoon grated orange rind and enough orange juice to make a soft pouring consistency. Place the bowl, making sure the base does not touch the water, over a saucepan of simmering water and stir until the icing is smooth and glossy. Remove from the heat. Drizzle over the cake and let it run down the sides.

VIENNESE FINGERS

Preparation time: 20 minutes
Total cooking time: 12 minutes
Makes 20

100 g (3½ oz) unsalted butter,
    softened
⅓ cup (40 g/1¼ oz) icing sugar
2 egg yolks
1½ teaspoons vanilla essence
1 cup (125 g/4 oz) plain flour
100 g (3½ oz) dark cooking chocolate,
    chopped
30 g (1 oz) unsalted butter, extra,
    for icing

1 Preheat the oven to 180°C (350°F/Gas 4). Line two baking trays with baking paper.
2 Using electric beaters, cream the butter and icing sugar in a small mixing bowl until light and fluffy. Gradually add the egg yolks and vanilla essence and beat thoroughly. Transfer the mixture to a large mixing bowl, then sift in the flour. Using a flat-bladed knife, mix until just combined and the mixture is smooth.
3 Spoon the mixture into a piping bag fitted with a fluted 1 cm (½ inch) piping nozzle and pipe the mixture into wavy 6 cm (2½ inch) lengths on the prepared trays.
4 Bake the cookies for 12 minutes, or until golden brown. Allow to cool slightly on the trays, then transfer to a wire rack to cool completely.
5 Place the chocolate and extra butter in a small heatproof bowl. Half-fill a saucepan with water and bring to the boil, then remove from the heat. Sit the bowl over the pan, making sure the base of the bowl does not sit in the water. Stir

occasionally until the chocolate and butter have melted together and the mixture is smooth. Dip half of each biscuit into the melted chocolate mixture and leave to set on greaseproof paper or foil.

STORAGE: Store in an airtight container for up to 2 days.
NOTE: To make piping easier, fold down the bag by 5 cm (2 inches) before adding the mixture, then unfold. The top will be clean and easy to twist, stopping any mixture from squirting out the top.

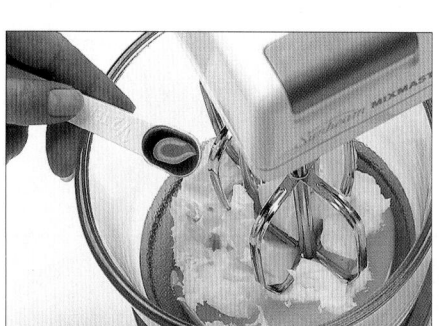

Beat the butter and icing sugar then add the egg yolks and vanilla essence.

Carefully pipe the mixture directly onto the prepared tray.

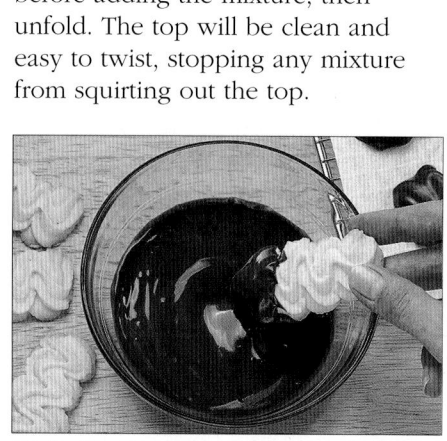

Dip the biscuits into the chocolate and butter mixture before leaving them to set.

TRIPLE-DECKER FUDGE SLICE

Preparation time: 25 minutes +
  refrigeration
Total cooking time: 50 minutes
Makes 20 pieces

½ cup (60 g/2 oz) plain flour
2 tablespoons cocoa powder
2 tablespoons caster sugar
60 g (2 oz) butter, melted
1 tablespoon milk
½ teaspoon vanilla essence

VANILLA TOPPING
250 g (8 oz) cream cheese, cubed
⅓ cup (90 g/3 oz) caster sugar
1 egg
1 teaspoon vanilla essence

CHOCOLATE TOPPING
125 g (4 oz) milk chocolate, chopped
125 g (4 oz) butter, chopped
2 eggs, lightly beaten
½ cup (125 g/4 oz) caster sugar
¼ cup (30 g/1 oz) plain flour
icing sugar, to dust

1 Lightly grease an 18 x 28 cm (7 x 11 inch) shallow tin and line with baking paper, overhanging two opposite sides.
2 Sift the flour, cocoa and sugar into a bowl. Add the butter, milk and vanilla and mix well to form a dough. Gently knead for 1 minute, adding more flour if sticky. Press into the prepared tin and refrigerate for 20 minutes. Preheat the oven to 190°C (375°F/Gas 5).
3 Cover the pastry with baking paper, fill with baking beads or rice and bake for 10–15 minutes. Remove the paper and rice and reduce the heat to 180°C (350°F/Gas 4). Bake for 5–10 minutes, then leave to cool.

4 To make the vanilla topping, beat the cream cheese in a mixing bowl until smooth. Gradually beat in the sugar, then the egg and vanilla essence. Beat well, pour over the base and refrigerate.
5 To make the chocolate topping, melt the chocolate and butter in a small saucepan, stirring over very low heat until smooth. Mix together the eggs and sugar. Stir in the chocolate mixture and flour until just combined.
6 Pour the chocolate topping over the cold vanilla topping and smooth with a spoon. Reduce the oven to 160°C (315°F/Gas 2–3) and bake for 35–40 minutes, or until just set. Leave to cool completely, then refrigerate for 2 hours, or until firm. Dust with icing sugar before cutting and serving.

Use your fingers to press the mixture into the lined tin, making sure it is evenly spread.

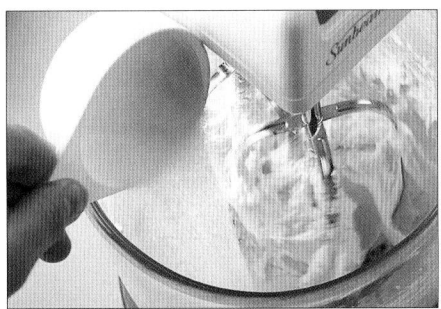

Gradually add the sugar to the cream cheese, beating well after each addition.

Smooth the chocolate topping over the vanilla topping with the back of a spoon.

SUGAR AND SPICE PALMIERS

**Preparation time: 20 minutes +
  15 minutes refrigeration**
Total cooking time: 20 minutes
Makes 32

1 sheet frozen butter puff pastry
2 tablespoons raw sugar
1 teaspoon mixed spice
1 teaspoon ground cinnamon
40 g (1¼ oz) butter, melted
icing sugar, to dust

1 Preheat the oven to 210°C (415°F/ Gas 6–7). Lightly grease two baking trays and line with baking paper. Thaw the pastry sheet as directed on the packet. Combine the sugar and spices in small mixing bowl. Cut the pastry sheet in half and brush with the melted butter. Sprinkle with the sugar mixture until the pastry sheet is well covered, reserving 2 teaspoons.
2 Fold the long edges of the pastry inwards, then fold again so that the edges almost meet in the centre. Fold once more, place the pastry on a baking tray and refrigerate for 15

minutes. Using a small, sharp knife, cut the pastry pieces into 32 slices.
3 Arrange the palmiers cut-side up onto the prepared trays, brush with butter and sprinkle lightly with the reserved sugar mixture. Bake for 20 minutes, or until golden. Transfer palmiers to a wire rack to cool completely. Dust lightly with icing sugar before serving.

STORAGE: Store for up to a day in an airtight container. Palmiers may be re-crisped in a 180°C (350°F/Gas 4) oven for 5 minutes before serving.

Generously sprinkle the sugar mixture over the sheet of puff pastry.

Fold the sides of the pastry inwards and then again so that they almost meet in the centre.

Using a pastry brush, lightly coat the palmiers with melted butter and sprinkle with sugar mixture.

CUSTARD BUTTER CAKE

Preparation time: 15 minutes
Total cooking time: 40 minutes
Serves 8–10

1 cup (125 g/4 oz) self-raising flour
⅔ cup (85 g/3 oz) custard powder
½ teaspoon bicarbonate of soda
125 g (4 oz) unsalted butter,
    chopped
¾ cup (185 g/6 oz) caster sugar
3 eggs, lightly beaten
¼ cup (60 ml/2 fl oz) buttermilk

ICING
100 g (3½ oz) white chocolate
¼ cup (60 ml/2 fl oz) cream
200 g (6½ oz) cream cheese, softened
⅓ cup (40 g/1¼ oz) icing sugar
silver cachous and crystallised violets,
    to decorate

1 Preheat the oven to 180°C (350°F/ Gas 4). Lightly grease a deep 20 cm (8 inch) square cake tin and line the base with baking paper. Sift the flour, custard powder and soda into a bowl and make a well in the centre.
2 Melt the butter and sugar in a small saucepan over low heat, stirring until the sugar has dissolved. Remove from the heat. Add the butter mixture and combined egg and buttermilk to the dry ingredients and stir until just combined. Spoon into the prepared tin. Bake for 35 minutes, or until a skewer comes out clean when inserted into the centre. Leave in the tin to cool.
3 To make the icing, melt the chocolate and cream in a saucepan over low heat. Cool and add to the cream cheese and icing sugar. Beat until smooth. Decorate with silver cachous and crystallised violets.

Make a well in the centre of the dry ingredients sifted into a large mixing bowl.

Spoon the mixture into the prepared tin and bake for 35 minutes.

959

PLAIN SCONES

Preparation time: 20 minutes
Total cooking time: 12 minutes
Makes 12

2 cups (250 g/8 oz) self-raising flour
pinch salt, optional (see NOTE)
30 g (1 oz) butter, cut into small pieces
½ cup (125 ml/4 fl oz) milk
⅓ cup (80 ml/2¾ fl oz) water
milk, extra, to glaze
jam and whipped cream, to serve

1 Preheat the oven to 210°C (415°F/ Gas 6–7). Lightly grease a baking tray. Sift the flour and salt, if using, into a large mixing bowl. Add the butter and rub in lightly using your fingertips.
2 Make a well in the centre of the flour. Add almost all of the combined milk and water. Mix with a flat-bladed knife to a soft dough, adding more liquid if necessary.
3 Turn the dough onto a lightly floured surface (use self-raising flour). Knead the dough briefly and lightly until smooth. Press or roll out the dough to form a round about 1–2 cm (½–¾ inch) thick.
4 Cut the dough into rounds using a floured round 5 cm (2 inch) cutter.

Place the rounds on the prepared tray and glaze with the milk. Bake for 10–12 minutes, or until golden brown. Serve with jam and whipped cream.

NOTE: Add a pinch of salt to your scones, even the sweet ones. Salt acts as a flavour enhancer and will not be tasted in the cooked product.

HONEY, DATE AND GINGER SCONES

Preparation time: 25 minutes
Total cooking time: 15 minutes
Makes 12

½ cup (90 g/3 oz) fresh dates
¼ cup (55 g/2 oz) glacé ginger
2 cups (250 g/8 oz) self-raising flour
½ teaspoon ground ginger
pinch salt
1 tablespoon honey
½ cup (125 ml/4 fl oz) milk
¼ cup (60 ml/2 fl oz) cream

HONEY GLAZE
1 tablespoon milk
1 teaspoon honey

1 Preheat the oven to 210°C (415°F/ Gas 6–7). Lightly grease a baking tray. Chop the dates and the glacé ginger into small chunks. Sift the flour, ground ginger and salt into a mixing bowl. Add the dates and glacé ginger. Stir to combine.
2 Combine the honey, milk and cream in a small saucepan and stir over low heat until combined. Add to the flour and mix lightly, with a flat-bladed knife, to form a soft dough, adding more milk if necessary. (The dough should have just lost its stickiness but not become dried or tough.)
3 Knead the dough briefly on a lightly floured surface until smooth and press out to 2 cm (¾ inch) thickness. Cut rounds with a floured plain 5 cm (2 inch) cutter. Place the rounds on the prepared tray and

brush with the honey glaze. Cook for 12–15 minutes, or until lightly golden.
4 To make the honey glaze, gently warm the milk and honey in a pan, stirring until well combined.

NOTE: Use self-raising flour on your hands and work surfaces.

Chop the dates and the glacé ginger to the desired size.

LEMON AND ALMOND SLICE

Preparation time: 25 minutes
Total cooking time: 35 minutes
Makes 15 pieces

½ cup (60 g/2 oz) plain flour
⅓ cup (40 g/1¼ oz) self-raising flour
2 tablespoons icing sugar
60 g (2 oz) butter, chopped
1 egg, lightly beaten
whipped cream, to serve
lemon zest, to garnish

ALMOND CREAM
3 eggs, at room temperature
½ cup (125 g/4 oz) caster sugar
2 teaspoons grated lemon rind
½ cup (125 ml/4 fl oz) lemon juice
⅔ cup (80 g/2¾ oz) ground almonds
1 cup (250 ml/8 fl oz) cream

1 Preheat the oven to 190°C (375°F/ Gas 5). Lightly grease a 23 cm (9 inch) square shallow tin.
2 Put the flours, sugar and butter in a food processor and process until the mixture resembles fine breadcrumbs. Add the egg and process briefly, until the dough just comes together, adding a small amount of water if necessary.
3 Press the dough into the base of the prepared tin and prick well with a fork. Bake for 10–12 minutes, or until pale. Allow to cool. Reduce the oven to 180°C (350°F/ Gas 4).
4 To make the almond cream, beat the eggs and sugar with a wooden spoon. Stir in the lemon rind, juice, almonds and cream. Pour over the pastry and bake for 20–25 minutes, or until lightly set. Leave to cool in the tin. Serve with whipped cream and garnish with zested lemon rind.

Put the flours, sugar and butter in a food processor and mix until crumbly.

Press the dough into the tin and prick all over with a fork before baking.

Beat the eggs and sugar, then stir in the rind, juice, almonds and cream.

HONEY AND COCONUT CAKE

Preparation time: 40 minutes
Total baking time: 30 minutes
Serves 18–20

125 g (4 oz) unsalted butter, softened
⅔ cup (140 g/4½ oz) raw sugar
2 large eggs, lightly beaten
1 teaspoon vanilla essence
¼ cup (90 g/3 oz) honey
½ cup (45 g/1½ oz) desiccated coconut
1¾ cups (220 g/7 oz) self-raising flour
1 teaspoon ground nutmeg
¼ teaspoon ground cinnamon
¼ teaspoon ground allspice
½ cup (125 ml/4 fl oz) milk
extra ground nutmeg, to decorate

HONEY AND CREAM CHEESE ICING
125 g (4 oz) cream cheese, softened
½ cup (60 g/2 oz) icing sugar
1 tablespoon honey

1 Preheat the oven to 180°C (350°F/ Gas 4). Lightly grease a 28 x 18 x 3 cm (11 x 7 x 1¼ inch) cake tin. Line with lightly greased baking paper. Using electric beaters, beat the butter and sugar in a small mixing bowl until light and creamy. Add the eggs gradually, beating thoroughly after each addition. Add the vanilla essence and honey. Beat until well combined.
2 Transfer the mixture to a large mixing bowl and add the desiccated coconut. Using a metal spoon, fold in sifted flour and spices alternating with milk. Stir until just combined and the mixture is almost smooth. Spoon into the prepared pan and smooth surface.
3 Bake for 30–35 minutes, or until the skewer comes out clean when inserted in the centre. Leave the cake in the tin for 10 minutes before turning out onto a wire rack to cool completely. Remove the baking paper from the cake. To make the icing, beat the softened cream cheese with electric beaters in a small mixing bowl until creamy. Add the sifted icing sugar and honey, beating for 3 minutes, or until the mixture is smooth and fluffy. Spread the icing evenly over the cake using a flat-bladed knife. Sprinkle the extra nutmeg over the top.

STORAGE: The cake can be stored for 4 days in an airtight container.

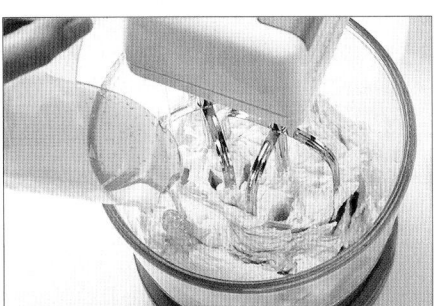

Add the honey and vanilla essence to the mixture while the electric beaters are still going.

Alternate folding in the milk with adding the sifted flour and spices.

Test to see if the cake is cooked by inserting a skewer into the centre.

PASSIONFRUIT SHORTBREAD

Preparation time: 45 minutes
Total cooking time: 20 minutes
Makes about 40

250 g (8 oz) butter
⅓ cup (90 g/3 oz) caster sugar
2¼ cups (280 g/9 oz) plain flour
¼ cup (45 g/1½ oz) rice flour
40 g (1¼ oz) white choc melts, melted

PASSIONFRUIT ICING
1¼ cups (155 g/5 oz) icing sugar, sifted
2 tablespoons passionfruit pulp
20 g (¾ oz) softened butter
1 tablespoon water

1 Preheat the oven to 160°C (315°F/ Gas 2–3). Line two baking trays with baking paper. Using electric beaters, beat the butter and sugar in a small mixing bowl until light and creamy. Fold in the sifted flours and mix until a soft dough forms. Turn out onto a lightly floured surface. Knead gently for 1 minute or until smooth.
2 Roll out the dough between two sheets of baking paper to 5 mm (¼ inch) thickness. Using a sharp knife, cut into 4 x 4 cm (1½ x 1½ inch)

diamonds. Place on the prepared trays, allowing room for spreading. Re-roll the pastry and cut out diamonds in the same way. Bake for 15 minutes, or until the biscuits are lightly brown. Stand for 5 minutes before transferring onto a wire rack to cool.
3 To make the passionfruit icing, combine the icing sugar, passionfruit pulp, butter and water in a bowl to form a smooth paste. Stand the bowl in pan of simmering water, stirring until the icing is smooth and glossy. Remove the pan from heat but leave the bowl of icing to stand in the warm water while icing the biscuits. Using a flat-bladed knife, spread each diamond with ½ teaspoon of icing.
4 Leave the biscuits to stand for 15 minutes to set, then drizzle or pipe a decorative pattern on top with the melted white chocolate.

STORAGE: These biscuits can be stored in an airtight container for up to 2 days.

NOTE: Overheating the icing will make it dull and grainy. Try to work as quickly as possible and dip the knife into hot water occasionally to give the icing a smooth finish. If fresh passionfruit is out of season, substitute canned pulp.

Use a large metal spoon to fold the flour into the butter mixture.

Use a ruler or other straight edge as a cutting guide to keep your lines straight.

After the biscuits have cooled, use a flat-bladed knife to spread the icing.

Drizzle the white chocolate over the biscuits in a decorative pattern and leave to set.

ANGEL FOOD CAKE WITH CHOCOLATE SAUCE

Preparation time: 15 minutes
Total cooking time: 45 minutes
Serves 8

1 cup (125 g/4 oz) plain flour
1 cup (250 g/8 oz) caster sugar
10 egg whites, at room temperature
1 teaspoon cream of tartar
½ teaspoon vanilla essence

CHOCOLATE SAUCE
250 g (8 oz) dark chocolate, chopped
¾ cup (185 ml/6 fl oz) cream
50 g (1¾ oz) unsalted butter, chopped
silver cachous, to decorate

1 Preheat the oven to 180°C (350°F/ Gas 4). Sift the flour and ½ cup (125 g/4 oz) of the sugar four times into a large mixing bowl. Set aside. Beat the egg whites, cream of tartar and ¼ teaspoon salt in a clean, dry large mixing bowl with electric beaters until soft peaks form. Gradually add the remaining sugar and beat until thick and glossy.
2 Add the vanilla essence. Sift half the flour and sugar mixture over the meringue mixture and gently fold in with a metal spoon. Repeat with the remaining flour and sugar. Spoon into an ungreased angel cake tin and bake for 45 minutes, or until a skewer comes out clean when inserted into the centre of the cake. Gently loosen around the side of the cake with a

spatula, then turn the cake out onto a wire rack to cool completely.
3 To make the sauce, place the chocolate, cream and butter in a saucepan. Stir over low heat until the chocolate has melted and the mixture is smooth. Drizzle over the cake and decorate with silver cachous. Serve.

NOTE: The tin must be very clean and not greased or the cake will not rise and will slip down the side of the tin.

Spoon the mixture into an ungreased tin then bake for 45 minutes.

Stir the chocolate, cream and butter over low heat until melted.

CHOC-MINT SWIRLS

Preparation time: 30 minutes
Total cooking time: 15 minutes
Makes 22

65 g (2¼ oz) unsalted butter
¼ cup (60 g/2 oz) caster sugar
½ cup (60 g/2 oz) plain flour
⅓ cup (40 g/1¼ oz) self-raising flour
2 tablespoons cocoa powder
1–2 tablespoons milk
22 choc bits

FILLING
100 g (3½ oz) unsalted butter, extra
1⅓ cups (165 g/5½ oz) icing sugar
few drops peppermint essence

1 Preheat the oven to 180°C (350°F/ Gas 4). Line two 32 x 28 cm (13 x 11 inch) baking trays with baking paper. Using electric beaters, beat the butter and sugar in a small mixing bowl until light and creamy. Add the sifted flours, cocoa and milk. Stir with a flat-bladed knife until the mixture forms a soft dough. Turn out onto a piece of baking paper and knead for 1 minute or until smooth.
2 Roll the dough out to 5 mm (¼ inch) thickness. Cut into rounds, using a 4 cm (1½ inch) plain biscuit cutter. Place on the prepared tray and bake for 15 minutes. Transfer to a wire rack to cool completely before decorating.
3 To make the filling, beat the butter with electric beaters until soft. Add

the icing sugar and beat until smooth, creamy and light. Add the peppermint essence and beat until combined. Using a piping bag fitted with a large fluted nozzle, carefully pipe a flower of peppermint cream onto each biscuit. Place a choc bit in the centre of each flower.

STORAGE: Store for up to 2 days in an airtight container

VARIATION: Dust the biscuits with one teaspoon each of icing sugar and cocoa powder, sifted together.

Sift the flours and cocoa powder into the mixture and combine with a flat-bladed knife.

Place the rounds at well spaced intervals on the baking tray to allow for spreading during baking.

Pipe the peppermint cream onto each biscuit and top with a choc bit.

COFFEE LIQUEUR GATEAU

Preparation time: 1 hour + 1 hour refrigeration
Total cooking time: 35–40 minutes
Serves 8–10

125 g (4 oz) brazil nuts
⅔ cup (100 g/3½ oz) blanched almonds
80 g (2¾ oz) hazelnuts
2 tablespoons plain flour
¾ cup (185 g/6 oz) caster sugar
7 egg whites
¼ cup (60 ml/2 fl oz) Tia Maria or Kahlúa
small chocolate buttons, to decorate (see NOTE)
sifted icing sugar, to dust

COFFEE CREAM
200 g (6½ oz) butter
1 cup (150 g/5 oz) dark chocolate, melted
2–3 teaspoons icing sugar
2 teaspoons warm water
3–4 teaspoons instant coffee powder

1 Preheat the oven to 180°C (350°F/Gas 4). Lightly grease a deep 20 cm (8 inch) round tin and line base and side with baking paper. Place the nuts on a baking tray and roast for 5–10 minutes, or until golden. Rub the nuts vigorously in a clean tea towel to remove hazelnut skins. Place in a food processor and process until finely ground.
2 Transfer the ground nuts to a large bowl. Add the flour and 125 g (4 oz) of the sugar and mix well. Using electric beaters, beat the egg whites in a large mixing bowl until soft peaks form. Gradually add the remaining sugar, beating until the mixture is thick and glossy and the sugar is dissolved. Using a metal spoon, fold the nut mixture into the egg mixture a third at a time. Spoon into the prepared tin and smooth the surface. Bake for 35–40 minutes, or until springy to the touch. Leave in the tin to cool.
3 To make the coffee cream, beat the butter in a small mixing bowl with electric beaters until light and creamy. Gradually pour in the melted chocolate, beating until well combined. Add the icing sugar and combined water and coffee. Beat until smooth.
4 To assemble the gateau, turn the cake onto a flat working surface. Using a sharp serrated knife, carefully cut the cake horizontally into three layers. (Use the top layer of cake as the base of gateau.) Brush the first layer with half the liqueur. Spread with one fifth of the coffee cream.
5 Place the second cake layer on top. Brush with the remaining liqueur and spread with a quarter of the remaining coffee cream. Place the remaining layer on top. Spread top and sides with the remaining coffee cream.
6 Decorate with the chocolate buttons and dust with the icing sugar. Refrigerate for 1 hour or until firm.

STORAGE: This cake can be prepared to 3 days in advance. Keep refrigerated in an airtight container.

NOTE: Make your own chocolate buttons with 150 g (5 oz) melted chocolate melts. Line two baking trays with baking paper. Place half the chocolate in a small paper icing bag. Seal the end of the bag, then snip off tip. Pipe small chocolate buttons onto trays. Tap trays lightly on bench to flatten buttons and leave to to set. Peel off paper and use to decorate.

To remove skins, rub the roasted nuts vigorously with a tea towel.

Fold the nut mixture, a third at a time, into the egg whites with a metal spoon.

Add the melted chocolate, while beating continuously, to the butter.

Use a serrated knife to slice the cake into three even layers.

Brush the cake layers with liqueur, then spread with the coffee cream.

Decorate the top of the cake with chocolate buttons and dust with icing sugar.

ORANGE POPPY SEED MUFFINS

Preparation time: 20 minutes
Total cooking time: 12 minutes
Makes 12

1¾ cups (215 g/7 oz) self-raising flour
1 tablespoon caster sugar
1 teaspoon baking powder
¼ teaspoon bicarbonate of soda
1 tablespoon poppyseeds
90 g (3 oz) butter
½ cup (160 g/5½ oz) orange
    marmalade
1 egg, lightly beaten
¾ cup (185 ml/6 fl oz) milk
icing sugar, to dust

1 Preheat the oven to 210°C (415°F/ Gas 6–7). Lightly grease a 12-hole muffin tin. Sift the flour, sugar, baking powder and soda into a mixing bowl. Add the poppy seeds and stir. Make a well in the centre.
2 Combine the butter and marmalade in a small saucepan and stir over low heat until marmalade becomes runny and butter has melted. Add the butter mixture and combined egg and milk to flour mixture; stir until just combined. (Do not overmix, the batter should be quite lumpy.)
3 Spoon the batter into the prepared tin and cook for 10–12 minutes or until golden. Loosen the muffins with a flat-bladed knife and transfer to a wire rack. Dust with the icing sugar.

TOPPING SUGGESTION: Beat 60 g (2 oz) soft butter, 2 tablespoons icing sugar and 1 teaspoon orange rind until light and creamy. Cut a small section from the top of the muffin, fill with mixture and replace the tops.

Make a small hole in the top of the muffin to accommodate the topping.

BLUEBERRY SHORTCAKE

Preparation time: 15 minutes
Total cooking time: 1 hour
Serves 8–10

¾ cup (100 g/4 oz) whole hazelnuts
2¼ cups (280 g/9 oz) self-raising flour
1½ teaspoons ground cinnamon
¾ cup (165 g/5½ oz) demerara sugar
150 g (5 oz) unsalted butter,
     chopped
2 eggs
½ cup (165 g/5½ oz) blueberry jam

1 tablespoon demarara sugar, extra
fresh blueberries, to serve
cream, to serve

1 Preheat the oven to 180°C (350°F/
Gas 4). Lightly grease a deep 20 cm
(8 inch) round cake tin and line the
base with baking paper. Spread the
hazelnuts on a baking tray and bake
for 5–10 minutes. Place in a clean tea
towel and rub together to remove the
skins, then roughly chop.
2 Process the flour, cinnamon, sugar,
butter and half the hazelnuts in a
food processor until finely chopped.

Add the eggs and process until
combined. Press half the mixture onto
the base of the prepared tin, then
spread the jam evenly over the
mixture.
3 Lightly knead the remaining
hazelnuts into the remaining dough,
then press evenly over the jam layer.
Sprinkle the extra sugar over the top
and bake for 50 minutes, or until a
skewer comes out clean when inserted
into the centre. Leave in the tin for
15 minutes before turning out onto a
wire rack to cool completely. Serve
with fresh blueberries and cream.

Roast the hazelnuts for 5–10 minutes, wrap in a
tea towel then rub together to remove the skins.

Process in a food processor until the mixture
resembles fine breadcrumbs.

Sprinkle the extra sugar over the top then bake
for 50 minutes.

GINGER DELIGHTS

Preparation time: 20 minutes + cooling
Total cooking time: 50 minutes
Makes 16 pieces

100 g (3½ oz) glacé ginger
1¾ cups (220 g/7 oz) plain flour
1 cup (220 g/7 oz) raw sugar
160 g (5½ oz) butter, melted
1 egg

GINGER ICING
80 g (2¾ oz) butter
1 tablespoon golden syrup
¾ cup (90 g/3 oz) icing sugar
1 teaspoon ground ginger
¼ cup (40 g/1¼ oz) chopped
    macadamia nuts, toasted

1 Preheat the oven to 180°C (350°F/
Gas 4). Lightly grease a 19 cm
(8 inch) square cake tin and line with
baking paper, overhanging two sides.
2 Toss the ginger in 1–2 tablespoons
of the flour, then chop finely. Put the
ginger in a mixing bowl with the
remaining flour, sugar, melted butter,
egg, pinch of salt and mix well.
3 Press the mixture into the prepared
tin and smooth the surface. Bake for
40–45 minutes, or until firm and
golden. Cool in the tin for 20 minutes
before lifting out.
4 To make the ginger icing, mix the
butter, syrup, icing sugar and ginger
in a pan over low heat. Stirring often,
bring just to the boil then remove
from the heat. Spread over the base
and sprinkle with macadamias. Leave
to cool before cutting.

Toss the ginger in a little flour to stop it sticking to
the knife when chopped.

Mix the ginger, flour, sugar, salt, egg and melted
butter in a bowl.

Stir the ginger icing until it comes to the boil, then
remove from the heat.

BRANDY ALEXANDER SLICE

Preparation time: 20 minutes + overnight refrigeration
Total cooking time: 5 minutes
Makes 12 bars

80 g (2¾ oz) unsalted butter, chopped
60 g (2 oz) dark cooking chocolate, chopped
250 g (8 oz) packet plain chocolate biscuits, crushed
300 g (10 oz) ricotta cheese
¼ cup (60 ml/2 fl oz) cream
⅓ cup (40 g/1¼ oz) icing sugar, sifted
½ cup grated milk chocolate
1 tablespoon brandy
1 tablespoon crème de cacao liqueur (see VARIATION)
½ teaspoon ground nutmeg
60 g (2 oz) dark chocolate melts

1 Lightly grease a shallow 30 x 20 cm (12 x 8 inch) rectangular tin and line with baking paper. Place the butter and chocolate in a small heatproof bowl. Stand over a pan of simmering water. Stir until the chocolate is melted and mixture is smooth. Remove from heat. Using a flat-bladed knife, mix chocolate mixture with the biscuit crumbs in a small mixing bowl.
2 Press the biscuit mixture evenly over the base of the prepared tin and set aside.
3 Using electric beaters, beat the cheese, cream and sugar in a small mixing bowl on medium speed for 3 minutes, or until mixture is light and creamy. Add the chocolate, brandy and liqueur and beat until combined.
4 Spread the cheese mixture over the prepared base and sprinkle with the nutmeg. Refrigerate for several hours or overnight. Cut into 12 bars before serving. Place the chocolate melts in a small heatproof bowl and stand over simmering water until melted. Place in a small piping bag and pipe the design on top of each bar.

STORAGE: Store in the refrigerator for up to 2 days.

VARIATION: Use Tia Maria in place of the crème de cacao.

To make the base, combine the melted chocolate and butter with the crushed biscuits.

Press the biscuit mixture firmly into the prepared baking tin, making sure it is evenly distributed.

Add the chocolate, brandy and liqueur to the light and creamy mixture.

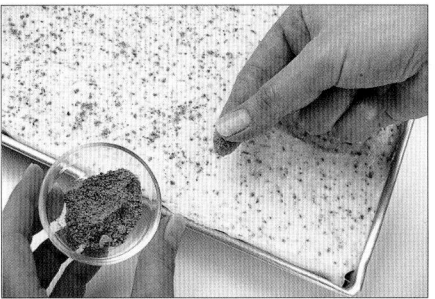

Spread the cheese mixture over the top, sprinkle with nutmeg and refrigerate until set.

AFGHANS

Preparation time: 20 minutes
Total cooking time: 20 minutes
Makes 25

150 g (5 oz) unsalted butter, softened
⅓ cup (60 g/2 oz) lightly packed soft
    brown sugar
1 egg, lightly beaten
1 teaspoon vanilla essence
1 cup (125 g/4 oz) plain flour
2 tablespoons cocoa powder
⅓ cup (30 g/1 oz) desiccated coconut

1½ cups (45 g/1½ oz) lightly crushed
    cornflakes
½ cup (90 g/3 oz) dark choc bits

1 Preheat the oven to 180°C (350°F/
Gas 4). Line two baking trays with
baking paper.
2 Using electic beaters, cream the
butter and sugar in a large mixing
bowl until light and fluffy. Add the
egg and vanilla essence and beat well.
3 Add the sifted flour and cocoa
powder to the bowl with the coconut
and cornflakes. Stir with a metal spoon
until the ingredients are just combined.

Put level tablespoons of mixture on
the prepared trays, allowing room for
spreading. Bake for 20 minutes, or
until lightly browned, then leave on
the tray to cool completely.
4 Place the choc bits in a small
heatproof bowl. Bring a saucepan of
water to the boil, then remove the
pan from the heat. Sit the bowl over
the pan, making sure the base of the
bowl does not sit in the water. Stir
until the chocolate has melted and the
mixture is smooth. Spread the top of
each biscuit thickly with the melted
chocolate and allow to set.

Add the dry ingredients to the mixture and gently
stir together with a metal spoon.

Drop tablespoons of the mixture onto the
prepared baking tray.

Spread the melted chocolate thickly across the
top of each biscuit.

PASSION MALLOW SLICE

**Preparation time: 25 minutes + overnight
 refrigeration**
Total cooking time: 30 minutes
Makes 20 pieces

150 g (5 oz) butter
¼ cup (60 g/2 oz) caster sugar
½ teaspoon vanilla essence
1 cup (125 g/4 oz) plain flour
½ cup (60 g/2 oz) self-raising flour

MARSHMALLOW TOPPING
½ cup (125 ml/4 fl oz) passionfruit pulp
    (or 5–6 passionfruit)
250 g (8 oz) white marshmallows
½ cup (125 ml/4 fl oz) milk
2 tablespoons caster sugar
2 teaspoons lemon juice
1¼ cups (315 ml/10 fl oz) cream,
    lightly whipped

1 Preheat the oven to 180°C (350°F/
Gas 4). Lightly grease an 18 x 28 cm
(7 x 11 inch) shallow tin and line with
baking paper, overhanging two
opposite sides.
2 Using electric beaters, beat the
butter and sugar in a mixing bowl
until light and creamy, and the sugar
has dissolved. Stir in the vanilla
essence. Sift the flours into a bowl,
then fold into the butter mixture and
mix to a soft dough. Knead gently to
bring together.
3 Press the dough into the prepared
tin and smooth with the back of a
spoon. Lightly prick the dough and
bake for 25 minutes, or until golden.
Remove from the oven and leave to
cool completely.
4 To make the topping, put the
passionfruit, marshmallows, milk and
sugar in a pan and stir over low heat
until the marshmallows have melted.
5 Stir in the lemon juice and transfer
to a bowl to cool. Refrigerate, stirring
occasionally, for 30 minutes, or until
slightly thickened. Quickly fold in the
cream so the marshmallow doesn't
set, then pour over the slice and
refrigerate overnight, or until set. Cut
into squares to serve.

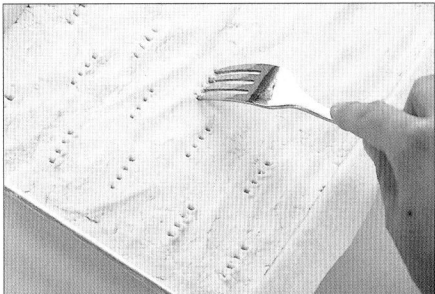
Press the dough into the tin, smooth the surface
and prick with a fork.

Fold the whipped cream into the mixture quickly,
so the marshmallow doesn't set.

FLOURLESS ORANGE AND ALMOND CAKE

Preparation time: 15 minutes
Total cooking time: 1 hour 30 minutes
Serves 8

2 oranges
1½ cups (280 g/9 oz) ground almonds
1 cup (250 g/8 oz) caster sugar
1 teaspoon baking powder
1 teaspoon vanilla essence
1 teaspoon Cointreau
6 eggs, lightly beaten
icing sugar, to dust

1 Wash the oranges well to remove any sprays or waxes. Place the whole oranges in a large saucepan, add enough water to cover them and place a small plate on top to keep the oranges submerged. Gradually bring the water to the boil, then reduce the heat and leave them to simmer for 40 minutes, or until the oranges are very soft. Preheat the oven to 180°C (350°F/ Gas 4). Place the cake tin on a sheet of baking paper and trace around the outside, then cut out the shape with a pair of scissors. Lightly grease the tin, then place the baking paper, pencil-side down, onto the base of the tin and smooth out any bubbles.
2 Cut each of the oranges into quarters and leave the pieces to cool. Remove any pips, then place the oranges in the bowl of a food processor and blend until they form a very smooth pulp. Add the ground almonds, caster sugar, baking powder, vanilla essence and Cointreau and, using the pulse button, process until all of the ingredients are combined. Add the egg and process again until just combined—take care not to over-process. Pour the orange mixture into the prepared tin and bake for 50 minutes, or until the cake is firm and leaves the side of the tin. Leave to cool completely in the tin. Dust with icing sugar to serve.

NOTES: This makes a great dessert cake served with fruit and cream. Try this cake with an orange syrup. Place 2 cups (500 ml/16 fl oz) of freshly squeezed and strained orange juice in a saucepan with ¾ cup (185 g/6½ oz) caster sugar and ¼ cup (60 ml/2 fl oz) Sauternes. Place the saucepan over a medium heat and stir until the sugar is dissolved. Reduce the heat and simmer for about 20 minutes, or until the liquid is reduced by half and has become slightly syrupy. Skim off any scum that forms on the surface as you go. The syrup will thicken further as it cools. Poke some random holes in the top of the cake to let the syrup absorb, or just drizzle the syrup over the cake before dusting with icing sugar and serving.

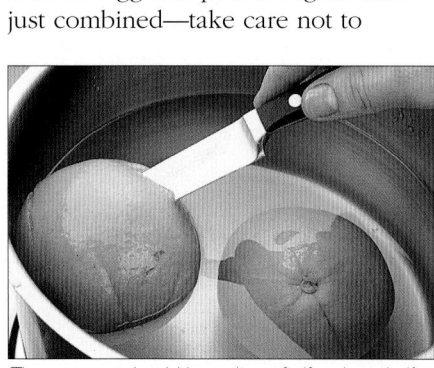
The oranges should be quite soft; if a sharp knife cuts into them easily, they are done.

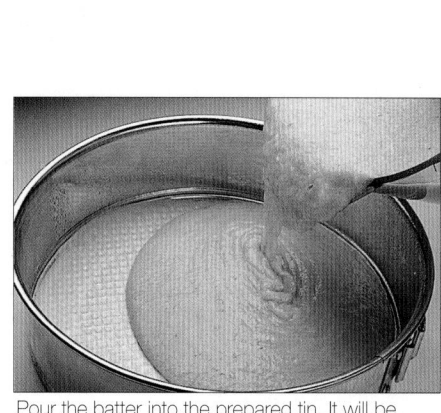
Pour the batter into the prepared tin. It will be quite thick and may look slightly lumpy

JAM AND CREAM SPONGE

Preparation time: 20 minutes
Total cooking time: 20 minutes
Makes one 20 cm round cake

½ cup (60 g/2 oz) plain flour
½ cup (60 g/2 oz) self-raising flour
4 eggs, separated
⅔ cup (160 g/5½ oz) caster sugar
4 tablespoons jam
½ cup (125 ml/4 fl oz) cream, whipped
icing sugar, to dust

1 Preheat the oven to 180°C (350°F/ Gas 4). Grease two shallow 20 cm (8 inch) sandwich tins. Sift the flours three times onto baking paper. Place the egg whites in a large mixing bowl. Using electric beaters, beat the egg whites until stiff peaks form. Add the sugar gradually, beating constantly until the sugar has dissolved and mixture is thick and glossy.
2 Add the egg yolks and beat for another 20 seconds. Using a metal spoon, fold in the flour quickly and lightly. Spread the mixture evenly into the prepared tins and smooth the surface. Bake for 20 minutes, until lightly golden and springy to the touch. Leave cakes in the tins for 5 minutes before turning onto wire racks to cool completely.
3 Spread the jam evenly onto one of the sponges. Spread whipped cream over the jam. Top with the second sponge and dust with sifted icing sugar before serving.

STORAGE: Unfilled sponges can be frozen for up to a month. Thaw cakes at room temperature for 20 minutes. Serve filled sponges immediately.

Using electric beaters, beat the mixture until it is thick and glossy.

Spread mixture into tins and smooth the surface with a flat-bladed knife.

Once you have put the sponge together, generously dust with icing sugar.

ZESTY OLIVE OIL CAKE

Preparation time: 10 minutes
Total cooking time: 45 minutes
Serves 8

2 eggs
⅔ cup (160 g/5½ oz) caster sugar
2 teaspoons finely grated orange rind
2 teaspoons finely grated lemon rind
½ cup (125 ml/4 fl oz) olive oil
1½ cups (185 g/6 oz) self-raising flour
¼ cup (60 ml/2 fl oz) milk
¼ cup (60 ml/2 fl oz) orange juice

1 Preheat the oven to 180°C (350°F/ Gas 4). Lightly grease a shallow 20 cm (8 inch) round cake tin and line the base with baking paper. Whisk the eggs and sugar in a large mixing bowl until well combined. Add the orange and lemon rind, then gradually stir in the olive oil.

2 Stir in the sifted flour alternately with the milk and orange juice. Stir the mixture gently for 30 seconds with a wooden spoon. Pour into the prepared tin. Bake for 45 minutes, or until a skewer comes out clean when inserted into the centre of the cake. Leave to cool in the tin for 5 minutes before turning out onto a wire rack.

NOTE: This cake can be dusted with icing sugar before serving, if desired.

Gradually add the olive oil to the cake mixture, making sure it is well combined.

Gently stir the mixture then pour into the prepared cake tin and bake for 45 minutes.

BEER CAKE

Preparation time: 15 minutes
Total cooking time: 1 hour 50 minutes
Serves 12

1 cup (125 g/4 oz) plain flour
½ teaspoon ground cinnamon
3 cups (750 g/1½ lb) caster sugar
275 g (9 oz) unsalted butter,
    chopped
3 eggs
4 cups (500 g/1 lb) self-raising flour
¾ cup (120 g/4 oz) sultanas
2 cups (500 ml/16 fl oz) beer

cream, to serve

1 Preheat the oven to 180°C (350°F/ Gas 4). Lightly grease a deep 25 cm (10 inch) round cake tin and line the base with baking paper. To make the topping, mix together the plain flour, cinnamon and 1 cup (250 g/8 oz) of the sugar. Place in a food processor with 125 g (4 oz) of the butter and process until combined.
2 Place the remaining butter in a large mixing bowl with the remaining sugar and beat with electric beaters until pale and creamy. Gradually add the eggs,

beating well after each addition. (The mixture may look curdled but once you add the flour, it will bring it back together.) Fold in the sifted self-raising flour, sultanas and beer.
3 Pour the mixture into the prepared tin and clump the topping together in your hands to form small balls, then sprinkle over the cake. Bake for 1 hour 50 minutes, or until a skewer comes out clean when inserted into the centre of the cake. Leave the cake to cool in the tin before turning out onto a wire rack. If desired, serve with cream.

To make the topping, process the flour, cinnamon, sugar and butter in a food processor.

Fold in the sifted flour, sultanas and beer into the cake mixture.

Mould the topping into small balls then crumble over the top of the cake.

CHOCOLATE CHERRY CAKE

Preparation time: 15 minutes
Total cooking time: 1 hour 10 minutes
Serves 8

200 g (6½ oz) dark chocolate, chopped
250 g (8 oz) unsalted butter, chopped
1 cup (230 g/7½ oz) firmly packed soft brown sugar
1 teaspoon vanilla essence
1¼ cups (155 g/5 oz) self-raising flour
½ cup (45 g/1½ oz) desiccated coconut
2 eggs

1 cup (180 g/6 oz) pitted sour cherries, drained
icing sugar, to dust
fresh cherries, to garnish

1 Preheat the oven to 160°C (315°F/ Gas 2–3). Lightly grease a 23 cm (9 inch) round cake tin and line the base with baking paper. Grease the paper. Place the chocolate, butter, sugar and vanilla essence in a heatproof bowl. Sit the bowl, making sure the base does not touch the water, over a saucepan of simmering water. Stir occasionally until the chocolate has melted and the mixture is smooth. Remove the saucepan from the heat and sit the bowl in a sink of cold water until cooled.

2 Combine the flour and coconut in a food processor. Add the chocolate mixture and eggs and process in short bursts until the mixture is just combined. Add the pitted sour cherries to the food processor and process until they are just chopped.

3 Pour the mixture into the prepared tin and bake for 1 hour 10 minutes, or until a skewer comes out clean when inserted into the centre of the cake. Leave the cake in the tin for 15 minutes before carefully turning out onto a wire rack to cool completely. If desired, dust with icing sugar and decorate with fresh cherries.

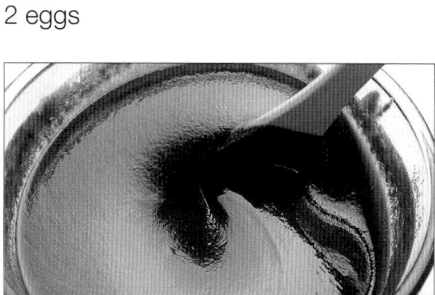

Stir the chocolate, butter, sugar and vanilla essence in a heatproof bowl.

Add the chocolate mixture and the eggs into a food processor with the flour and the coconut.

Leave the cake in the tin before turning out onto a wire rack to cool.

LAYERED PASSIONFRUIT TORTE

Preparation time: 45 minutes + chilling
Total cooking time: 25 minutes
Makes 1

6 eggs, separated
¾ cup (90 g/3 oz) icing sugar
½ cup (125 g/4 oz) sugar
½ teaspoon vanilla essence
½ cup (60 g/2 oz) cornflour
1½ teaspoons baking powder
¼ cup (30 g/1 oz) plain flour

FILLING
1 tablespoon lemon juice
1 tablespoon gelatine
pulp of 10 passionfruit
500 g (1 lb) cream cheese
1½ cups (185 g/6 oz) icing sugar,
    sifted
¾ cup (185 ml/6 fl oz) cream, lightly
    whipped
½ cup (125 ml/4 fl oz) cream, extra,
    whipped to stiff peaks
pulp of 2 passionfruit, extra
¼ cup (40 g/1¼ oz) roasted almonds or
    pistachios, chopped

1 Preheat the oven to 180°C (350°F/Gas 4). Lightly grease two shallow 23 cm (9 inch) round cake tins and line the bases with baking paper. Place the egg whites in a large dry mixing bowl. Beat with electric beaters until stiff peaks form. Add the sugar gradually, beating until all the sugar has dissolved and mixture is thick and glossy. Fold in the yolks and vanilla essence. Sift dry ingredients into the mixture and gently fold in until smooth. Spoon mixture evenly into the prepared tins. Bake for 20 minutes, or until the cakes shrink away from the sides of the tins. Leave the cakes in the tins for 5 minutes before turning out onto wire racks to cool completely.

2 To make the filling, combine the juice, gelatine and water in a small mixing bowl. Heat half the passionfruit pulp in a small saucepan until it boils. Add the gelatine mixture and stir over medium heat until dissolved. Strain the mixture through a sieve and add to remaining passionfruit pulp. Leave to cool slightly. Beat the cream cheese and sugar with electric beaters until the mixture is smooth and creamy. Add the passionfruit mixture. Fold in the lightly whipped cream.

3 To assemble the cake, cut each cake in half horizontally with a serrated knife. Place one layer on a serving plate and spread with one-fifth of filling. Continue layering, leaving enough filling to spread evenly over the top and side of the cake. Place extra whipped cream in a piping bag and pipe rosettes on top of the cake. Spread extra passionfruit pulp over top. Sprinkle the nuts over the rosettes. Refrigerate for several hours.

STORAGE: Assemble up to 3 days in advance but add the rosettes and pulp just before serving.

Using a metal spoon, gently fold the dry ingredients into the egg white mixture.

Heat half of the passionfruit pulp until nearly boiling then add the gelatine mixture.

Make sure you leave enough filling to cover the side and top of the cake.

BANANA MUFFINS

Preparation time: 15 minutes
Total cooking time: 15 minutes
Makes 12

2 cups (250 g/8 oz) self-raising flour
1 cup (75 g/2½ oz) oat bran
¾ cup (185 g/6 oz) caster sugar
60 g (2 oz) butter, melted
¾ cup (185 ml/6 fl oz) milk
2 eggs, lightly beaten
1 cup (240 g/7½ oz) mashed, ripe
    banana (2 medium bananas)

1 Preheat the oven to 210°C (415°F/ Gas 6–7). Lightly grease a 12-hole muffin tin. Sift the flour into a large bowl and add the oat bran and the sugar. Make a well in the centre of the dry ingredients.
2 Combine the butter, milk, eggs and banana in a separate mixing bowl and add to the flour mixture all at once. Using a wooden spoon, stir until just mixed. (Do not overbeat; the batter should remain lumpy.)
3 Spoon the mixture into the prepared tin. Bake for 15 minutes, or until puffed and brown. Transfer the muffins to a wire rack to cool completely.

TOPPING SUGGESTION: For muffins with a difference, beat 100 g (3½ oz) cream cheese, 2 tablespoons icing sugar and 2 teaspoons lemon juice with electric beaters until light and creamy. Spread over the muffins and top with dried banana slices.

Make a well in the centre of the dry ingredients and pour in the liquid ingredients.

INDIVIDUAL WHITE CHOCOLATE CHIP CAKES

Preparation time: 15 minutes
Total cooking time: 20 minutes
Makes 12

125 g (4 oz) unsalted butter,
   softened
¾ cup (185 g/6 oz) caster sugar
2 eggs, lightly beaten
1 teaspoon vanilla essence
2 cups (250 g/8 oz) self-raising flour,
   sifted
½ cup (125 ml/4 fl oz) buttermilk

1¼ cups (280 g/9 oz) white chocolate
   chips

1 Preheat the oven to 170°C (325°F/ Gas 3). Lightly grease a 12-hole ½-cup (125 ml/4 fl oz) muffin tin.
2 Place the butter and sugar in a large mixing bowl. Using electric beaters, beat until pale and creamy. Gradually add the beaten eggs, beating well after each addition. Add the vanilla essence and beat until well combined. Fold in the flour alternately with the buttermilk, then fold in the chocolate chips.
3 Fill each muffin hole three-quarters full with the mixture and bake for

20 minutes, or until a skewer comes out clean when inserted into the centre of each cake. Leave in the tin for 5 minutes before turning out onto a wire rack to cool completely. Use a flat-bladed knife to loosen around the edges of the cakes if they stick.

Prepare the muffin tin by lightly brushing with oil or melted butter.

Use a spoon to fold in the flour, buttermilk and chocolate chips.

Leave the cakes to sit in the tin for 5 minutes then turn out onto a wire rack.

BUTTERFLY CUPCAKES

Preparation time: 10 minutes
Total cooking time: 30 minutes
Makes 12

125 g (4 oz) unsalted butter, softened
⅔ cup (160 g/5½ oz) caster sugar
1½ cups (185 g/6 oz) self-raising flour
½ cup (125 ml/4 fl oz) milk
2 eggs
½ cup (125 ml/4 fl oz) thick cream
¼ cup (80 g/2¾ oz) strawberry jam
icing sugar, to dust

1 Preheat the oven to 180°C (350°F/ Gas 4). Line a flat-bottomed 12-hole cupcake tray with paper patty cases. Place the butter, sugar, flour, milk and eggs in a large mixing bowl. Using electric beaters, beat on low speed then increase the speed and beat until the mixture is smooth and pale. Divide the mixture evenly among the cases and bake for 30 minutes, or until cooked and golden. Transfer to a wire rack to cool.

2 Cut shallow rounds from the centre of each cake using the point of a sharp knife, then cut in half. Spoon 2 teaspoons cream into each cavity, top with 1 teaspoon jam and position two halves of the cake tops in the jam to resemble butterfly wings. Dust with icing sugar.

NOTE: If using foil patty cases instead of the standard paper cases as suggested, the size and number of butterfly cakes may vary.

Spoon the mixture into paper patty cases and bake until golden.

Cut a circle from the top of each cake then cut it in half to form the 'wings'.

RASPBERRY BUN SCONES

Preparation time: 20 minutes
Total cooking time: 12 minutes
Makes 8

2 cups (250 g/8 oz) self-raising
    flour
pinch salt
2 tablespoons caster sugar
½ cup (125 ml/4 fl oz) milk
30 g (1 oz) butter, melted
⅓ cup (80 ml/2¾ fl oz) water
1 tablespoon raspberry jam
1 tablespoon milk, extra
caster sugar, extra
butter, to serve

1 Preheat the oven to 210°C (415°F/ Gas 6–7). Lightly grease a baking tray. Sift the flour and salt into a large mixing bowl. Add the sugar and stir to combine.

2 Make a well in the centre of the flour. Place milk and melted butter in a separate bowl and combine. Add to the flour mixture all at once, reserving a teaspoonful for glazing. Add almost all of the water. Mix quickly, using a flat-bladed knife, to form a soft dough, adding more water if necessary.

3 Knead the dough briefly on a lightly floured surface until smooth. Cut the dough into 8 rounds using a floured 7 cm (2¾ inch) cutter. Turn each of scones over and make an indentation in the centre with your thumb. Place

½ teaspoon of jam in the indentation and fold over dough. Place the rounds, well apart, on the prepared tray and flatten tops. Brush with the milk and sprinkle with the extra caster sugar. Bake for 10–12 minutes, or until golden. Serve warm with butter.

Spoon the jam into the indentation, then fold the dough over.

BABY COFFEE AND WALNUT SOUR CREAM CAKES

Preparation time: 15 minutes
Total cooking time: 20 minutes
Makes 24

¾ cup (75 g/2½ oz) walnuts
⅔ cup (155 g/5 oz) firmly packed soft brown sugar
125 g (4 oz) unsalted butter, softened
2 eggs, lightly beaten
1 cup (125 g/4 oz) self-raising flour
⅓ cup (80 g/2¾ oz) sour cream
1 tablespoon coffee and chicory essence

1 Preheat the oven to 160°C (315°F/ Gas 2–3). Lightly grease two 12-hole ¼-cup (60 ml/2 fl oz) baby muffin tins. Process the walnuts and ¼ cup (45 g/1½ oz) of the brown sugar in a food processor until the walnuts are roughly chopped into small pieces. Transfer to a mixing bowl.
2 Cream the butter and remaining sugar together in the food processor until pale and creamy. With the motor running, gradually add the egg and process until smooth. Add the flour and blend until well mixed. Add the sour cream and essence and process until thoroughly mixed.
3 Spoon ½ teaspoon of the walnut and sugar mixture into the base of each muffin hole, followed by a teaspoon of the cake mixture. Sprinkle a little more walnut mixture over the top, a little more cake mixture and top with the remaining walnut mixture. Bake for 20 minutes, or until risen and springy to the touch. Leave in the tins for 5 minutes. Remove the cakes using a flat-bladed knife to loosen the side and base, then transfer to a wire rack to cool completely.

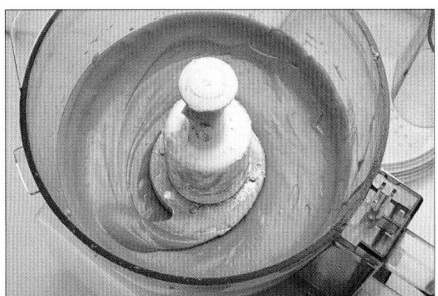

Process the walnuts and brown sugar in a food processor until walnuts are roughly chopped.

Process remaining ingredients until smooth and thoroughly combined.

Layer walnut and cake mixtures in the prepared tin, finishing with a layer of the walnut mixture.

CARAMEL PECAN SQUARES

Preparation time: 15 minutes +
  3 hours refrigeration
Total cooking time: 35 minutes
Makes 16 pieces

250 g (8 oz) plain chocolate biscuits
1 tablespoon drinking chocolate
1½ cups (150 g/5 oz) pecans
185 g (6 oz) butter, melted

CARAMEL TOPPING
½ cup (90 g/3 oz) lightly packed soft
    brown sugar
60 g (2 oz) butter
400 g (13 oz) can sweetened
    condensed milk
icing sugar, to dust
drinking chocolate, to dust

1 Preheat the oven to 180°C (350°F/ Gas 4). Lightly grease an 18 x 28 cm (7 x 11 inch) shallow tin and line with baking paper, overhanging two opposite sides.
2 Finely crush the biscuits, drinking chocolate and a third of the pecans in a food processor. Transfer to a mixing bowl and add the melted butter. Mix well and press firmly into the prepared tin. Press the rest of the pecans gently over the top.
3 To make the caramel topping, place the brown sugar and butter in a saucepan over low heat. Stir until the butter melts and the sugar dissolves. Remove from the heat, stir in the condensed milk, then pour over the biscuit base.
4 Bake for 25–30 minutes, or until the caramel is firm and golden–the edges will bubble and darken. Cool, then refrigerate for at least 3 hours.

5 Trim off the crusty edges and cut the slice into squares. Before serving, hold a piece of paper over one half of each piece and sprinkle the other half with icing sugar. Sprinkle the other side with drinking chocolate.

Arrange the rest of the pecans over the base, pressing them in gently.

Remove the butter and sugar from the heat and stir in the condensed milk.

Trim the crusty edges off the slice before cutting into squares to serve.

PLUM AND ALMOND SLICE

Preparation time: 30 minutes
Total cooking time: 1 hour 10 minutes
Makes 9 pieces

160 g (5½ oz) butter
⅔ cup (160 g/5½ oz) caster sugar
2 eggs
½ cup (60 g/2 oz) plain flour
⅓ cup (40 g/1¼ oz) cornflour
2 tablespoons rice flour

1½ tablespoons thinly sliced glacé ginger
825 g (1 lb 11 oz) can plums in syrup, drained and halved (see NOTE)
1 cup (100 g/3½ oz) flaked almonds
1 tablespoon warmed honey

1 Preheat the oven to 180°C (350°F/ Gas 4). Lightly grease a 20 cm (8 inch) square tin and line with baking paper, extending over the top edge of the tin on all sides.
2 Using electric beaters, beat the butter and sugar in a mixing bowl until light and creamy. Add the eggs one at a time, beating well. Fold the sifted flours into the mixture with the ginger. Spread into the tin. Arrange the plums on top, pressing them in. Scatter with the almonds, pressing in gently, then drizzle with the honey.
3 Bake for 1 hour 10 minutes, or until firm and golden (cover with foil if over-browning). Cool before cutting.

NOTE: If in season, use 7 ripe blood plums instead of canned. They may bleed more than the canned.

Drain the canned plums and cut in half, carefully removing the stones.

Arrange the plum halves on top, pressing gently into the filling mixture.

Scatter the flaked almonds over the top, then drizzle with the honey.

STREUSEL KUCHEN

Preparation time: 40 minutes +
2 hours standing
Total cooking time: 55 minutes
Serves 6–8

7 g (¼ oz) sachet dried yeast
2 tablespoons lukewarm water
½ cup (125 ml/4 fl oz) milk
¼ cup (60 g/2 oz) caster sugar
50 g (1¾ oz) butter
½ teaspoon salt
2¾ cups (340 g/11 oz) plain flour
1 egg, lightly beaten
½ cup (160 g/5½ oz) apricot jam
2 tablespoons water or lemon juice
2 x 410 g (13 oz) cans pie apple
    (see VARIATIONS)

CRUMBLE TOPPING
½ cup (95 g/3 oz) lightly packed soft
    brown sugar
⅓ cup (40 g/1¼ oz) plain flour
1 teaspoon cinnamon
60 g (2 oz) butter, cubed
1 cup (125 g/4 oz) walnuts, roughly
    chopped (see VARIATIONS)

1 Lightly grease a 30 x 25 cm (12 x 10 inch) Swiss roll tin. Dissolve the yeast in warm water and set aside for 5 minutes, or until frothy. Combine the milk, sugar and butter in a saucepan. Stir over medium heat until the butter has melted.

2 Sift 2½ cups (310 g/10 oz) of the flour and the salt into a large mixing bowl. Make a well in the centre and add the yeast, milk mixture and egg. Beat until well combined.

3 Add enough of the remaining flour to form a soft dough. Turn the dough onto a lightly floured surface and knead for 10 minutes, or until smooth and elastic. Place the dough in a lightly oiled bowl. Cover with lightly oiled plastic wrap and leave in a warm place for 1 hour or until dough is well risen. Knead the dough again for 1 minute.

4 Divide the dough in two, making one portion larger than the other. Roll out the larger portion to fit into the prepared tin. Place the dough in the tin, pressing up the sides of the tin.

5 Combine the jam and water in a small saucepan and stir over low heat until the jam is warm and slightly liquefied. Spread half of the warmed jam over the dough in the tin. Top with the pie apple and remaining jam. Roll out the remaining dough to make a lid and place on apple mixture. Scatter the crumble topping thickly over the dough. Cover and leave in a warm place for about 1 hour or until well risen. Preheat the oven to 210°C (415°F/Gas 6–7). Bake the dough for 5 minutes. Reduce the oven temperature to 180°C (350°F/Gas 4). Bake for another 40–50 minutes, or until the dough is cooked and the top is golden.

6 To make the crumble topping, combine the sugar, flour and cinnamon in small bowl. Using your fingertips, rub the butter in until the mixture resembles coarse breadcrumbs. Stir in the walnuts.

STORAGE: Store in an airtight container for up to 4 days. To freeze, wrap tightly in foil, place in a freezer bag and store for up to a month. Reheat in a 180°C (350°F/Gas 4) oven for 20 minutes.
VARIATIONS: Use an 825 g (1 lb 11 oz) can of apricot halves, making sure they are well drained, instead of pie apple. You can also replace the walnuts in the topping with shredded coconut.

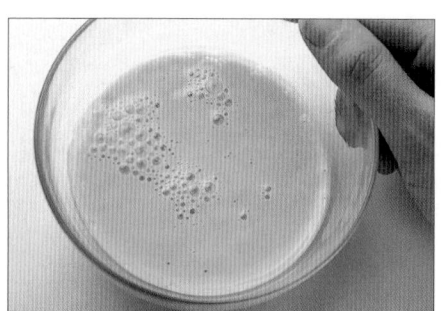

Dissolve the yeast in warm water and set aside for 5 minutes, or until frothy.

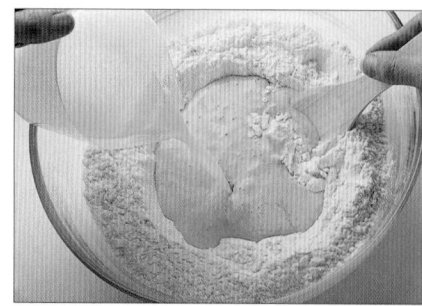

Make a well in the centre of the mixture and add yeast, milk mixture and egg.

Knead the dough on a lightly floured surface for 10 minutes, or until elastic.

Fit the dough into the Swiss roll tin, carefully moulding it so it reaches up the sides.

Spread the dough with half the liquefied jam, then top with the pie apple.

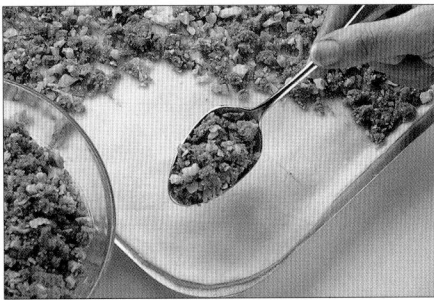

Place a thick layer of the crumble topping over the dough then set aside in a warm place.

WHITE CHOCOLATE AND MANGO SLICE

Preparation time: 25 minutes
Total cooking time: 45 minutes
Makes 10 pieces

100 g (3½ oz) butter
½ cup (125 g/4 oz) caster sugar
2 eggs, lightly beaten
1 teaspoon vanilla essence
1½ cups (185 g/6 oz) self-raising flour
½ cup (125 ml/4 fl oz) buttermilk
100 g (3½ oz) white chocolate, grated
2 x 425 g (14 oz) cans mango
    slices, drained, or 2 large fresh
    mangos, sliced
¼ cup (60 g/2 oz) caster sugar, extra

1 Preheat the oven to 180°C (350°F/ Gas 4). Lightly grease an 18 x 28 cm (7 x 11 inch) shallow tin and line with baking paper, overhanging two opposite sides.
2 Using electric beaters, beat the butter and sugar in a mixing bowl until light and creamy. Gradually add the egg and vanilla essence, beating until well combined.
3 Using a metal spoon, alternately fold the sifted flour and buttermilk into the mixture, stirring until just combined. Add grated chocolate. Pour into the prepared tin and smooth the surface. Arrange the mango over the top. Place the tin on an oven tray to catch any drips. Bake for 35–40 minutes, or until golden brown.
4 Put the extra sugar in a small saucepan with 1 tablespoon of water and stir over low heat until dissolved. Bring to the boil, then simmer for 1–2 minutes. Brush the syrup over the slice as soon as it comes out of the oven. Cut into pieces and serve hot.

Fold the flour and buttermilk into the mixture, then add the chocolate.

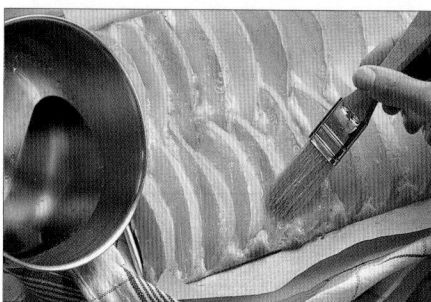

Brush the syrup over the slice as soon as it comes out of the oven.

RASPBERRY LINZER SLICE

Preparation time: 30 minutes
Total cooking time: 45 minutes
Makes 24 pieces

90 g (3 oz) butter
½ cup (125 g/4 oz) caster sugar
1 teaspoon vanilla essence
1 egg, lightly beaten
⅔ cup (85 g/3 oz) plain flour
⅓ cup (40 g/1¼ oz) self-raising flour
¾ cup (240 g/7½ oz) raspberry jam,
    warmed

HAZELNUT TOPPING
125 g (4 oz) butter

⅓ cup (90 g/3 oz) caster sugar
1 egg, lightly beaten
½ cup (60 g/2 oz) plain flour
1 tablespoon custard powder
1 teaspoon baking powder
1 cup (120 g/4 oz) firmly packed plain
    cake crumbs
½ cup (60 g/2 oz) ground hazelnuts
⅓ cup (80 ml/2¾ fl oz) milk

1 Preheat the oven to 180°C (350°F/ Gas 4). Lightly grease a 20 x 30 cm (8 x 12 inch) shallow tin and line with baking paper, overhanging two opposite sides.
2 Using electric beaters, beat the butter, sugar and vanilla essence in a mixing bowl until light and creamy.

Add the egg to the mixture gradually, beating well after each addition.
3 Sift the flours and fold into the mixture with a metal spoon. Spread into the tin and spread evenly with the raspberry jam.
4 To make the hazelnut topping, beat the butter and sugar with electric beaters until light and creamy. Add the egg gradually, beating well after each addition. Sift the flour, custard powder and baking powder and fold into the mixture with the cake crumbs and ground hazelnuts. Fold in the milk and spread over the base.
5 Bake for 45 minutes, or until firm and golden brown. Leave to cool in the tin before cutting to serve.

Spread the mixture evenly into the prepared tin, then spread with jam.

Fold in the flour, custard powder, baking powder, cake crumbs and hazelnuts.

Spread the mixture over the base and bake for 45 minutes.

APPLE CRUMBLE SLICE

Preparation time: 20 minutes
Total cooking time: 40 minutes
Makes 24 squares

¾ cup (90 g/3 oz) self-raising flour
¾ cup (90 g/3 oz) plain flour
1 cup (90 g/3 oz) desiccated coconut
250 g (8 oz) unsalted butter
¾ cup (140 g/4½ oz) lightly packed soft
    brown sugar
410 g (13 oz) can pie apple (see
    VARIATION)
⅓ cup (35 g/1¼ oz) rolled oats

¼ cup (35 g/1¼ oz) currants
¼ teaspoon ground cinnamon

1 Preheat the oven to 180°C (350°F/ Gas 4). Lightly grease an 18 x 27 cm (7 x 11 inch) shallow rectangular tin and line with baking paper, overhanging two opposite sides. Sift the flours into a large mixing bowl and add the coconut. Combine 200 g (6½ oz) of the butter and sugar in a small saucepan. Stir over low heat until the butter has melted and sugar has dissolved. Remove from heat and pour the butter mixture into the dry ingredients. Using a wooden spoon, stir until well combined.

2 Reserve one cup of mixture. Press the remaining mixture into the prepared tin. Bake for 15 minutes and leave to cool completely.
3 Spread the pie apple over the cooled base. Combine reserved mixture, remaining butter, oats and currants. Using fingertips, crumble mixture over the apple. Dust with the cinnamon. Bake for 35 minutes. Cool, lift from tin and cut into squares.

STORAGE: The slice can be stored for up to 2 days in an airtight container.
VARIATION: Pie apricots can be used instead of the apple.

Using a wooden spoon, stir melted butter and sugar into the sifted flours.

Place mixture into the prepared tin, pressing firmly with the back of a spoon.

After the base has cooled, spread the pie apple over the top and sprinkle crumble mixture over.

CHOCOLATE CARROT SLICE

Preparation time: 15 minutes
Total cooking time: 30 minutes
Makes 32

1 cup (125 g/4 oz) self-raising flour
1 teaspoon ground cinnamon
¾ cup (185 g/6 oz) caster sugar
½ cup finely grated carrot
1 cup (190 g/6½ oz) mixed dried fruit
½ cup (95 g/3 oz) choc bits
⅓ cup (30 g/1 oz) desiccated coconut
2 eggs, lightly beaten
90 g (3 oz) unsalted butter, melted
⅓ cup (40 g/1¼ oz) chopped walnuts

CREAM CHEESE FROSTING
125 g (4 oz) cream cheese
30 g (1 oz) unsalted butter
1½ cups (185 g/6 oz) icing sugar, sifted
1 teaspoon hot water

1 Preheat the oven to 180°C (350°F/ Gas 4). Lightly grease a 23 cm (9 inch) square shallow cake tin and line with baking paper, overhanging two opposite sides. Sift the flour and cinnamon into a large mixing bowl. Add the sugar, grated carrot, mixed fruit, choc bits and coconut and stir until just combined. Add the beaten eggs and butter. Stir until the mixture is just combined.
2 Spread the mixture evenly into the prepared tin and smooth the surface.

Bake for 30 minutes, or until golden. Leave to cool in tin and then turn out.
3 To make the cream cheese frosting, beat the cream cheese and butter with electric beaters in a small bowl until smooth. Add the icing sugar and beat for 2 minutes or until the mixture is light and fluffy. Add the water and beat until combined. Using a flat-bladed knife, spread the frosting on top of the slice and sprinkle with walnuts. Cut into 16 squares, then cut each square into triangles.

STORAGE: Slice may be stored for up to 2 days in an airtight container or up to 2 months in the freezer, without icing.
HINT: Sprinkle the frosting with grated chocolate if desired.

Combine the dry ingredients in a bowl before adding the eggs and melted butter.

Use a rubber spatula to spread the mixture evenly around the prepared tin.

After the slice has cooled, use a flat-bladed knife to spread the frosting over the top.

CHOC-NUT TRIANGLES

Preparation time: 25 minutes
Total cooking time: 20 minutes
Makes 16 pieces

1 cup (125 g/4 oz) self-raising flour
2 tablespoons cocoa powder
½ cup (125 g/4 oz) caster sugar
⅔ cup (60 g/2 oz) desiccated
    coconut
125 g (4 oz) butter, melted
1 teaspoon vanilla essence
1 cup (125 g/4 oz) chopped pecans
    or walnuts

CHOCOLATE ICING
1 cup (125 g/4 oz) icing sugar
1 tablespoon cocoa powder
15 g (½ oz) butter, melted
½–1 tablespoon milk
½ cup (60 g/2 oz) chopped walnuts or
    pecans

1 Preheat the oven to 180°C (350°F/ Gas 4). Lightly grease an 18 x 28 cm (7 x 11 inch) shallow tin and line with baking paper, overhanging two opposite sides.
2 Sift the flour and cocoa into a large mixing bowl. Stir in the sugar and coconut. Add the melted butter, vanilla essence and the nuts and stir until well combined. Press the mixture firmly and evenly into the prepared tin. Bake for 20 minutes, or until golden brown. Allow the slice to cool completely before removing from the tin.
3 To make the chocolate icing, sift the icing sugar and cocoa powder into a mixing bowl. Add the butter and enough milk to make a smooth, spreadable icing. Mix until well combined. Spread evenly over the cooled base, using a flat-bladed knife. Sprinkle with the nuts and leave to set for about 1 hour. Cut into triangles using a sharp knife.

Put the dry ingredients in a large bowl, then stir in the butter, vanilla and nuts.

Using your fingertips, press the mixture firmly and evenly into the slice tin.

Spread the chocolate icing over the base with a flat-bladed knife.

BERRY ALMOND SLICE

Preparation time: 25 minutes
Total cooking time: 1 hour 15 minutes
Makes 15 pieces

1 sheet puff pastry
150 g (5 oz) unsalted butter
¾ cup (185 g/6 oz) caster sugar
3 eggs, lightly beaten
2 tablespoons grated lemon rind
⅔ cup (125 g/4 oz) ground almonds
2 tablespoons plain flour
150 g (5 oz) raspberries
150 g (5 oz) blackberries
icing sugar, to dust

1 Preheat the oven to 200°C (400°F/ Gas 6). Lightly grease a 23 cm (9 inch) square shallow tin and line with baking paper, overhanging two opposite sides.
2 Place the pastry on a baking tray lined with baking paper. Prick all over with a fork and bake for 15 minutes, or until golden. Ease pastry into the tin, trimming the edges if necessary. Reduce the oven to 180°C (350°F/Gas 4).
3 Using electric beaters, beat the butter and sugar in a mixing bowl until light and fluffy. Gradually add the egg, beating after every addition, then the lemon rind. Fold in the almonds and flour. Spread over the pastry base.
4 Scatter the fruit on top and bake for 1 hour, or until lightly golden. Cool in the tin before lifting out to cut. Dust with icing sugar and serve.

Ease the cooked pastry into the lined tin, trimming the edges if necessary.

Fold the almonds and flour into the beaten mixture and spread over the base.

Frozen berries can be used instead, simply make sure they are thawed and drained.

CHOCOLATE PEPPERMINT SLICE

**Preparation time: 25 minutes +
    30 minutes refrigeration**
Total cooking time: 20 minutes
Makes 24 pieces

⅔ cup (85 g/3 oz) self-raising flour
¼ cup (30 g/1 oz) cocoa powder
½ cup (45 g/1½ oz) desiccated
    coconut
¼ cup (60 g/2 oz) sugar
140 g (4½ oz) unsalted butter, melted
1 egg, lightly beaten

PEPPERMINT FILLING
1½ cups (185 g/6 oz) icing sugar,
    sifted
30 g (1 oz) copha (white vegetable
    shortening), melted
2 tablespoons milk
½ teaspoon peppermint essence

CHOCOLATE TOPPING
185 g (6 oz) dark chocolate,
    chopped
30 g (1 oz) copha

1 Preheat the oven to 180°C (350°F/ Gas 4). Lightly grease a shallow tin measuring 18 x 28 cm (7 x 11 inches) and line with baking paper, leaving the paper hanging over on the two long sides. This makes it easy to lift the cooked slice out of the tin.
2 Sift the flour and cocoa into a bowl. Stir in the coconut and sugar, then add the butter and egg and mix well. Press the mixture firmly into the tin. Bake for 15 minutes, then press down with the back of a spoon and leave to cool.
3 For the peppermint filling, sift the icing sugar into a bowl. Stir in the

copha, milk and peppermint essence. Spread over the base and refrigerate for 5–10 minutes, or until firm.
4 For the chocolate topping, put the chocolate and copha in a heatproof bowl. Half fill a saucepan with water, bring to the boil, then remove from the heat. Sit the bowl over the saucepan, making sure the base of the bowl does not touch the water. Stir occasionally until the chocolate and copha have melted and combined. Spread evenly over the

filling. Refrigerate the slice for 20 minutes, or until the chocolate topping is firm. Carefully lift the slice from the tin, using the paper as handles. Cut into pieces with a warm knife to give clean edges. Store in an airtight container in the refrigerator.

Sift the dry ingredients into a bowl, then add the melted butter and egg.

Using a flat-bladed knife spread the peppermint filling evenly over the cooled base.

Stir the chocolate and copha in a heatproof bowl over simmering water.

CHOCOLATE CARAMEL SLICE

**Preparation time: 15 minutes +
  refrigeration**
Total cooking time: 20 minutes
Makes 24 triangles

125 g (4 oz) plain sweet biscuits,
  crushed
80 g (2¾ oz) unsalted butter,
  melted
2 tablespoons desiccated coconut
400 g (13 oz) can sweetened
  condensed milk
125 g (4 oz) butter
⅓ cup (90 g/3 oz) caster sugar
⅓ cup golden syrup
250 g (8 oz) milk chocolate melts
  (see VARIATION)
1 tablespoon vegetable oil

1 Lightly grease a shallow 30 x 20 cm (12 x 8 inch) rectangular cake tin and line with aluminium foil. Grease the foil. Combine the biscuits, melted butter and coconut together in a medium mixing bowl. Press the mixture evenly into the prepared tin and smooth the surface.
2 Combine the condensed milk, butter, sugar and syrup in a small pan. Stir over low heat for 15 minutes or until the sugar has dissolved and the mixture is smooth, thick and lightly browned. Remove from heat and leave to cool slightly. Pour over the biscuit base and smooth the surface.
3 Place the milk chocolate melts and oil in a small heatproof bowl. Stand over a pan of simmering water, stir until melted. Spread the chocolate mixture over caramel. Allow to partially set before marking into 24 triangles. Refrigerate until firm.

STORAGE: Slice may be stored in an airtight container for up to 2 days.
VARIATION: Use dark chocolate melts in place of milk chocolate.

Press the biscuit mixture firmly into the prepared tin, making sure it is evenly spread.

To make the caramel, heat the condensed milk, butter, sugar and syrup until thick.

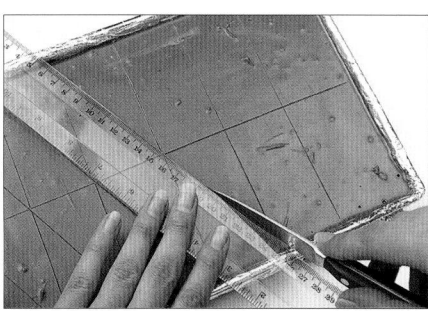

Using a sharp knife, mark out the 24 triangles before chilling and then cutting.

JAFFA FUDGE SLICE

**Preparation time: 20 minutes +
  40 minutes refrigeration**
Total cooking time: 3 minutes
Makes 32 pieces

200 g (6½ oz) plain sweet chocolate
  biscuits
1 cup (125 g/4 oz) chopped walnuts
125 g (4 oz) dark chocolate,
  chopped
½ cup (60 g/2 oz) icing sugar

125 g (4 oz) butter
1 tablespoon grated orange rind
125 g (4 oz) dark chocolate, extra,
  melted

1 Lightly grease an 18 x 28 cm (7 x 11 inch) shallow tin and line with baking paper or foil, overhanging two opposite sides.
2 Place the biscuits and walnuts in a food processor and process until the mixture resembles coarse bread-crumbs. Transfer to a large mixing bowl and make a well in the centre.

3 Put the chopped chocolate, sifted icing sugar and butter in a small saucepan and stir over low heat until melted and smooth. Remove from the heat, stir in the orange rind, then pour into the biscuit mixture and stir until well combined.
4 Press the mixture firmly into the prepared tin. Chill for 10 minutes. Spread the melted chocolate over and chill for 30 minutes to set.

STORAGE: Slice can be kept in an airtight container for up to a week.

Process the biscuits and chopped walnuts in a food processor until they are finely crushed.

Pour the chocolate mixture into the processed biscuits and walnuts.

Press firmly into the tin and then refrigerate for 10 minutes before covering with chocolate.

FUDGY COCONUT FINGERS

Preparation time: 20 minutes + cooling
Total cooking time: 25 minutes
Makes 20 pieces

1 cup (125 g/4 oz) plain flour
1 tablespoon cocoa powder
½ cup (125 g/4 oz) caster sugar
1 cup (90 g/3 oz) desiccated coconut
185 g (6 oz) butter, melted
1 teaspoon vanilla essence
125 g (4 oz) dark chocolate,
  chopped

2 tablespoons sour cream
½ cup (30 g/1 oz) flaked coconut,
  lightly toasted

1 Preheat the oven to 180°C (350°F/Gas 4). Lightly grease an 18 x 28 cm (7 x 11 inch) shallow tin and line with baking paper, overhanging two opposite sides.
2 Sift the flour and cocoa into a large mixing bowl. Add the sugar and desiccated coconut and mix until well combined. Add the butter and vanilla essence and mix until well combined. Press firmly into the prepared tin and bake for 20 minutes,

or until firm and golden brown. Leave to cool in the tin.
3 Stir the chocolate and sour cream in a heatproof bowl over a saucepan of simmering water until melted. Spread over the base and sprinkle with the coconut. Leave for 20 minutes before cutting into fingers.

STORAGE: Will keep in an airtight container for up to 4 days.

Sift the flour and cocoa powder together into a large mixing bowl.

Press the mixture firmly into the prepared tin, then bake for 20 minutes.

Stir the chocolate and sour cream in a heatproof bowl over simmering water.

Index

USEFUL INFORMATION

The recipes in this book were developed using a tablespoon measure of 20 ml. In some other countries the tablespoon is 15 ml. For most recipes this difference will not be noticeable but, for recipes using baking powder, gelatine, bicarbonate of soda, small amounts of flour and cornflour, we suggest that, if you are using the smaller tablespoon, you add an extra teaspoon for each tablespoon.

The recipes in this book are written using convenient cup measurements. You can buy special measuring cups in the supermarket or use an ordinary household cup: first you need to check it holds 250 ml (8 fl oz) by filling it with water and measuring the water (pour it into a measuring jug or a carton that you know holds 250 ml). This cup can then be used for both liquid and dry cup measurements.

LIQUID CUP MEASURES

¼ cup	60 ml	2 fluid oz
⅓ cup	80 ml	2¾ fluid oz
½ cup	125 ml	4 fluid oz
¾ cup	180 ml	6 fluid oz
1 cup	250 ml	8 fluid oz

SPOON MEASURES

¼ teaspoon	1.25 ml
½ teaspoon	2.5 ml
1 teaspoon	5 ml
1 tablespoon	20 ml

ALTERNATIVE NAMES (UK/US)

aubergine	—	eggplant
besan flour	—	chickpea flour
bicarbonate of soda	—	baking soda
bok choy	—	Napa cabbage
capsicum	—	red or green bell pepper
caster sugar	—	superfine sugar
chickpeas	—	garbanzo beans
coriander	—	cilantro
cornflour	—	cornstarch
courgette	—	zucchini
flat-leaf parsley	—	Italian parsley
grill	—	broil
hazelnut	—	filbert
icing sugar	—	confectioners' sugar
mangetout	—	snow pea
minced beef	—	ground beef
plain flour	—	all-purpose flour
polenta	—	cornmeal
prawn	—	shrimp
Roma tomato	—	plum or egg tomato
sambal oelek	—	chilli paste
single cream	—	cream
spring onion	—	scallion
thick cream	—	heavy cream
tomato purée	—	tomato paste
witloof	—	belgian endive

NUTRITIONAL INFORMATION

The nutritional information given for each recipe does not include any garnishes or accompaniments, such as rice or pasta, unless they are included in specific quantities in the ingredients list. The nutritional values are approximations and can be affected by biological and seasonal variations in foods, the unknown composition of some manufactured foods and uncertainty in the dietary database. Nutrient data given are derived primarily from the NUTTAB95 database produced by the Australian and New Zealand Food Authority.

OVEN TEMPERATURES

You may find cooking times vary depending on the oven you are using. For fan-forced ovens, as a general rule, set oven temperature to 20°C lower than indicated in the recipe.

WEIGHT

10 g	1/4 oz	220 g	7 oz	425 g	14 oz
30 g	1 oz	250 g	8 oz	475 g	15 oz
60 g	2 oz	275 g	9 oz	500 g	1 lb
90 g	3 oz	300 g	10 oz	600 g	11/4 lb
125 g	4 oz	330 g	11 oz	650 g	1 lb 5 oz
150 g	5 oz	375 g	12 oz	750 g	11/2 lb
185 g	6 oz	400 g	13 oz	1 kg	2 lb

NOTE: Those who might be at risk from the effects of salmonella food poisoning (the elderly, pregnant women, young children and those suffering from immune deficiency diseases) should consult their GP with any concerns about eating raw eggs.

Published by Bay Books an imprint of Murdoch Books Pty Limited.
Pier 8/9, 23 Hickson Rd, Millers Point NSW 2000, AUSTRALIA

ISBN 0 681 06828 4

Printed by Sun Fung Offset Binding Co Ltd. PRINTED IN CHINA. First printed 2005.